Handbook of Research on Information and Cyber Security in the Fourth Industrial Revolution

Ziska Fields
University of KwaZulu-Natal, South Africa

A volume in the Advances in Information Security, Privacy, and Ethics (AISPE) Book Series

Published in the United States of America by
    IGI Global
    Information Science Reference (an imprint of IGI Global)
    701 E. Chocolate Avenue
    Hershey PA, USA 17033
    Tel: 717-533-8845
    Fax: 717-533-8661
    E-mail: cust@igi-global.com
    Web site: http://www.igi-global.com

Library of Congress Cataloging-in-Publication Data

Names: Fields, Ziska, 1970- editor.
Title: Handbook of research on information and cyber security in the fourth
  industrial revolution / Ziska Fields, editor.
Description: Hershey, PA : Information Science Reference, [2018] | Includes
  bibliographical references.
Identifiers: LCCN 2017032400| ISBN 9781522547631 (hardcover) | ISBN
  9781522547648 (ebook)
Subjects: LCSH: Computer networks--Security measures. | Electronic
  information resources--Access control. | Computer crimes--Prevention. |
  Confidential communications--Protection.
Classification: LCC TK5105.59 .P744 2018 | DDC 658.4/78--dc23 LC record available at https://lccn.loc.gov/2017032400

This book is published in the IGI Global book series Advances in Information Security, Privacy, and Ethics (AISPE) (ISSN: 1948-9730; eISSN: 1948-9749)

British Cataloguing in Publication Data
A Cataloguing in Publication record for this book is available from the British Library.

All work contributed to this book is new, previously-unpublished material. The views expressed in this book are those of the authors, but not necessarily of the publisher.

For electronic access to this publication, please contact: eresources@igi-global.com.

Advances in Information Security, Privacy, and Ethics (AISPE) Book Series

Manish Gupta
State University of New York, USA

ISSN:1948-9730
EISSN:1948-9749

MISSION

As digital technologies become more pervasive in everyday life and the Internet is utilized in ever increasing ways by both private and public entities, concern over digital threats becomes more prevalent.

The **Advances in Information Security, Privacy, & Ethics (AISPE) Book Series** provides cutting-edge research on the protection and misuse of information and technology across various industries and settings. Comprised of scholarly research on topics such as identity management, cryptography, system security, authentication, and data protection, this book series is ideal for reference by IT professionals, academicians, and upper-level students.

COVERAGE

- Privacy-Enhancing Technologies
- Cookies
- Computer ethics
- Access Control
- Telecommunications Regulations
- Tracking Cookies
- Information Security Standards
- Risk Management
- Network Security Services
- Data Storage of Minors

IGI Global is currently accepting manuscripts for publication within this series. To submit a proposal for a volume in this series, please contact our Acquisition Editors at Acquisitions@igi-global.com or visit: http://www.igi-global.com/publish/.

Titles in this Series

For a list of additional titles in this series, please visit: www.igi-global.com/book-series

Handbook of Research on Network Forensics and Analysis Techniques
Gulshan Shrivastava (National Institute of Technology Patna, India) Prabhat Kumar (National Institute of Technology Patna, India) B. B. Gupta (National Institute of Technology Kurukshetra, India) Suman Bala (Orange Labs, France) and Nilanjan Dey (Techno India College of Technology, India)
Information Science Reference • copyright 2018 • 509pp • H/C (ISBN: 9781522541004) • US $335.00 (our price)

Cyber Harassment and Policy Reform in the Digital Age Emerging Research and Opportunities
Ramona S. McNeal (University of Northern Iowa, USA) Susan M. Kunkle (Kent State University, USA) and Mary Schmeida (Kent State University, USA)
Information Science Reference • copyright 2018 • 170pp • H/C (ISBN: 9781522552857) • US $145.00 (our price)

Security and Privacy Management, Techniques, and Protocols
Yassine Maleh (University Hassan I, Morocco)
Information Science Reference • copyright 2018 • 426pp • H/C (ISBN: 9781522555834) • US $205.00 (our price)

Multidisciplinary Perspectives on Human Capital and Information Technology Professionals
Vandana Ahuja (Jaypee Institute of Information Technology, India) and Shubhangini Rathore (IBS Gurgaon, India)
Information Science Reference • copyright 2018 • 400pp • H/C (ISBN: 9781522552970) • US $215.00 (our price)

Security, Privacy, and Anonymization in Social Networks Emerging Research and Opportunities
B. K. Tripathy (VIT University, India) and Kiran Baktha (VIT University, India)
Information Science Reference • copyright 2018 • 176pp • H/C (ISBN: 9781522551584) • US $155.00 (our price)

Critical Research on Scalability and Security Issues in Virtual Cloud Environments
Shadi Aljawarneh (Jordan University of Science and Technology, Jordan) and Manisha Malhotra (Chandigarh University, India)
Information Science Reference • copyright 2018 • 341pp • H/C (ISBN: 9781522530299) • US $225.00 (our price)

The Morality of Weapons Design and Development Emerging Research and Opportunities
John Forge (University of Sydney, Australia)
Information Science Reference • copyright 2018 • 216pp • H/C (ISBN: 9781522539841) • US $175.00 (our price)

Advanced Cloud Computing Security Techniques and Applications
Ihssan Alkadi (Independent Researcher, USA)
Information Science Reference • copyright 2018 • 350pp • H/C (ISBN: 9781522525066) • US $225.00 (our price)

701 East Chocolate Avenue, Hershey, PA 17033, USA
Tel: 717-533-8845 x100 • Fax: 717-533-8661
E-Mail: cust@igi-global.com • www.igi-global.com

Editorial Advisory Board

List of Contributors

Table of Contents

Detailed Table of Contents

Social engineering refers to the art of using deception and manipulating individuals to gain access to systems or information assets and subsequently compromising these systems and information assets. Information security must provide protection to the confidentiality, integrity, and availability of information. In order to mitigate information security's weakest link, it becomes necessary to understand the ways in which human behavior can be exploited via social engineering. This chapter will seek to analyze the role of social engineering in information security breaches and the factors that contribute to its success. A variety of social engineering attacks, impacts, and mitigations will be discussed. Human factors such as trust, obedience, and fear are easily exploited, thereby allowing social engineers to execute successful attacks. However, with effective countermeasures such as information security awareness training, education, and audit procedures, the impacts of social engineering can be decreased or eliminated altogether.

Chapter 2

Online human-to-human (and human-to-robot) hyper-personal relationships have evolved over the years, and their prevalence has broadened the available cyberattack surfaces. With the deployment of malicious socialbots on social media in the virtual and AI-informed embodied socialbots in the real, human interests in socializing have become more fraught and risky. Based on the research literature, abductive reasoning from in-world experiences, and analogical analysis to project into the Fourth Industrial Revolution, this work suggests the importance of greater awareness of the risks in interrelating in the virtual and the real and suggests that there are no safe distances.

"Ransomware" is a type of malware that tries to extort money from its victims by hijacking the victim's computer in some way and holding it to ransom. It renders the computer unusable until a ransom amount is paid to the extortionist. And it is very unfortunate that, in many cases, even after the ransom is paid, the victim's computer is not released. Ransomware, as we know it, is gaining popularity at an immense rate among the most notorious cyber-criminals of the world. It isn't just a virus, it's a damned good game plan to becoming a millionaire in a matter of months! This chapter details what ransomware is, how it originated, which families of attacks it falls under, how ransomware is classified, the impact of ransomware on a global scale, the life cycle of a typical ransomware attack, mitigation and containment strategies, trending strains of 2017, and future trends in ransomware attacks. In future, these attack types will dominate our industries and wreak havoc, destroying life and property, if left unchecked.

Cloud computing enables end users to make use of third party's resources to support their computing needs. The services offered by cloud computing make the technology very critical to the fourth industrial revolution. The benefits include cost minimization, scalability of services, speed, integration and higher data management, low innovation risk, and quicker response to organizational needs, among others. However, these benefits have been threatened by a number of security threats. This chapter seeks to curtail the effects of these threats by enlightening and educating users on the current ways to mitigate them. The chapter first defines cloud computing and highlights its relevance or benefits to businesses in the fourth industrial revolution. In addition, various security threats that are associated with cloud computing are brought to the fore. Thereafter, various measures that are used to mitigate the threats are discussed. The chapter concludes that with adequate enlightenment, the full benefits of cloud computing in industry 4.0 would be better enjoyed by users.

Chapter 5

The Fourth Industrial Revolution is seen as a digital one, extending the previous information revolution. This is exhibited by the pervasive connectivity of many smart devices, known as the internet of things (IoT). The data generated and access created by these devices provides opportunities in an information warfare context by providing new avenues of attack and abilities to enhance existing capabilities. Recent cyber-attacks have illustrated the relevance of IoT to cyber-operations. However, IoT can influence information warfare through the use of drones, the extent of network-centric operations, and other factors. The major impact of IoT is the increased attack surface and techniques available, and opportunities for data gathering.

A generic self-evolving multi-agent approach is proposed in this chapter. Most of the existing security approaches are custom designed for specific threats and attacks. However, the fusion of technologies and systems in the fourth industrial revolution and therefore the nature of its current cyber environment increasingly attracts multiple cyber threats in a single interface. In order to solve this problem, a generic self-evolving multi-agent approach is proposed. Multiple agents interact with each other in light of their reactions towards the environment and its inherent changes. Information from individual agents is collected and integrated to form the abstract compartment of the structure. The important aspects are analyzed including demonstrating how the abstract domain can be obtained from the custom interactions at the low-level domain of the proposed approach. The analysis explores the existing works in the area and how they have been advanced in the fourth industrial revolution.

This chapter discusses the importance of information security education for everyone, ranging from organizations to professionals and students, all the way through to individual users of information and communication systems. It discusses the different subject areas in information security and shows how instead of being intimidated by it, different categories of users can obtain varying depths of information security education based on their cyber-activities and need for knowledge. Information security professionals would require an in-depth knowledge in all aspects of information security, and information technology professionals and students would require an overall education in these areas, while most users of information and communication systems would only require a basic education to help protect their information assets in cyberspace.

Chapter 8

Bring your own device (BYOD) has infiltrated the work environment and businesses are enjoying the benefits coupled with the adoption of the trend. At the same time, the adoption of BYOD has introduced a number of security threats that businesses are failing to match. In the pursuit of addressing security threats that are introduced by the adoption of this technology trend, this chapter recommends a three-dimensional (3-D) security framework that can be used to mitigate the risks emanating from a BYOD enabled environment. Data was collected from the employees of two banks in Africa that supported BYOD trend to measure individual and organizational practices. This chapter investigates further on these practices in addressing implications of BYOD. Three categories of security threats are delineated in this chapter. A review of existing security frameworks is presented in this chapter. The chapter concludes by outlining a 3-D security framework as a potential solution to protect BYOD enabled business environment.

Security and reliability of information technologies have emerged as major concerns nowadays. Risk assessment, an estimation of negative impacts that might be imposed to a network by a series of potential sources, is one of the main tasks to ensure the security and is performed either statically or dynamically. Static risk assessment cannot satisfy the requirements of real-time and ubiquitous computing networks as it is pre-planned and does not consider upcoming changes such as the creation of new attack strategies. However, dynamic risk assessment (DRA) considers real-time evidences, being capable of diagnosing abnormal events in changing environments. Several DRA approaches have been proposed recently, but it is unclear which technique fits best into IT scenarios with different requirements. Thus, this chapter introduces recent trends in DRA, by analyzing 27 works and proposes a decision guide to help IT managers in choosing the most suitable DRA technique considering three illustrative scenarios – regular computer networks, internet of things, and industrial control systems.

Cautionary tales are structured stories that describe protagonists who are faced with critical decisions and often take wrong turns and suffer for it, sometimes irretrievably; these tales warn people of dangers. In cybersecurity communications, cautionary tales are an integral part of the strategic messaging. This chapter explores the uses of multimodal cautionary tales in strategic cybersecurity communications, in a convenience sampling of the following: mass-scale search terms, academic and mass media text sets, social imagery, related tags networks, and social video. This work identifies their strengths and weaknesses in suggesting methods for promoting personal cybersecurity safety. Some suggestions for higher efficacy in cybersecurity cautionary tales are suggested, in light of the advent of the Fourth Industrial Revolution.

This chapter examines and explains cyber resilience, internet of things, software-defined networking, fog computing, cloud computing, and related areas. Organizations develop these technologies in tandem with cyber resilience best practices, such as processes and standards. Cyber resilience is at the intersection of cyber security and business resilience. Its core capabilities encompass integrated strategic policies, processes, architectures, and frameworks. Governments and industries often align defensive and resilient capabilities, to address security and network vulnerability breaches through strategic management processes.

Chapter 12
Harold Patrick, University of KwaZulu-Natal, South Africa
Brett van Niekerk, University of KwaZulu-Natal, South Africa
Ziska Fields, University of KwaZulu-Natal, South Africa

The approach that the organization uses to manage its cyber-risk to its workforce, information, systems, and networks is paramount to ensure sustainability and continuity in the Fourth Industrial Revolution. Improving cyber-resiliency in the organization reduces the chance of future threats and attacks and builds better capability. Cyber resilience involves continuous operations, good governance, and diligence supported by the right security strategy of a computer security incident response team (CSIRT) that can protect government operations and control cyber-risks. CSIRT can build better resiliency at the decentralized provincial government level, and contribute to cyber awareness amongst the workforce, public, and other government departments. A CSIRT can further contribute to resilience to the organization by analyzing the threats and attacks, developing countermeasures for the future in protecting its systems and networks from threat actors.

Chapter 13
Thokozani Ian Nzimakwe, University of KwaZulu-Natal, South Africa

Cybersecurity is the practice of making the networks that constitute cyber space secure against intrusions. The aim is to maintain the confidentiality, the availability and integrity of information, by detecting interferences. Traditionally, cybersecurity has focused on preventing intrusions and monitoring ports. The evolving threat landscape, however, calls for a more dynamic approach. It is increasingly clear that total cybersecurity is impossible, unless government develops a cyber-security strategy. The aim of this chapter is to discuss government's dynamic approach to addressing challenges of cybersecurity. The chapter looks at the co-ordination of cyber-security activities so as to have a coordinated approach to cyber-crime. This chapter also highlights the idea of protecting sensitive data for the public good. It is generally accepted that technology has become indispensable in modern society. Government's cybersecurity presents a unique challenge simply because of the volume of threats that agencies working for government face on a daily basis.

Chapter 14
Harold Patrick, University of KwaZulu-Natal, South Africa
Brett van Niekerk, University of KwaZulu-Natal, South Africa
Ziska Fields, University of KwaZulu-Natal, South Africa

The frequency and sophistication of cyberthreats and attacks are increasing globally. All organizations including governments are at risk as more devices are connected to a growing network coverage. There is no doubt that the new technologies in the Fourth Industrial Revolution bring numerous opportunities for smarter and efficient ways of doing business. However, these new processes, technology, and people interacting increases the cyber-risks. Cyber-risks cause a threat to the reputation, operations, data, and assets of the organization. A holistic information security management plan is needed that will transform the organization's approach to mitigate the cyber-risks, protect its infrastructure, devices, and data. This approach will inevitably improve information technology governance and better accountability to the public.

Chapter 15

From curated "cyberwar" text sets (from government, mainstream journalism, academia, and social media), six-word stories are computationally induced (using word frequency counts, text searches, word network analysis, word clustering, and other means), supported by post-induction human writing. The resulting inducted six-word stories are used to (1) describe and summarize the underlying textual information (to enable a bridge to a complex topic); (2) produce insights about the underlying textual information and related in-world phenomena; and (3) answer particular research questions. These resulting six-word stories are analyzed along multiple dimensions: data sources (government, journalism, academia, and social media), expert calls-and-crowd responses, and by time periods (pre-cyberwar and cyberwar periods). The efficacy of this six-word story induction process is evaluated, and the extracted six-word stories are applied to cyberwar potentials during the Fourth Industrial Revolution (4IR).

Chapter 16

While a lot of studies focus on the contours of cybercrime and cyber terrorism as well as their effects in daily lives, less attention has been given to the use of ICT by terrorists. In fact, through the ebbs and flows of technology, the society of information seems to develop a particular vulnerability to the fear instilled by terrorism. This particularly reveals a paradox because the original technology, which was oriented to make of our lives safer, is used by terrorist cells to inspire a terror-driven atmosphere, which only nourishes intolerance and ethnocentrism. The authors, in this review chapter, discuss critically the cutting-edge role of technology in the struggle against terrorism.

Chapter 17

This chapter presents a case study of automated maritime container terminals (CTs). It has the aim of demonstrating that the risks derived from the use of technology associated with the Fourth Industrial Revolution (4IR) are both real and dangerous. The work explains the critical function of CTs in the global supply chain and outlines the economic and social consequences that could result if their operations were to be disrupted. The motivations of a range of threat-actors are presented, and it is established that there are feasible scenarios in which any one of the major threat-actor categories may wish to cause disruption at CTs. The vulnerabilities of yard cranes are investigated, and it is concluded that there are likely to be exploitable vulnerabilities in the industrial control system (ICS) networks used on these cranes. The chapter argues that many CT operations are likely to be exposed to significant cyber-based risks and that this exposure will increase with the roll-out of further 4IR technologies unless appropriate control measures are implemented.

Chapter 18

Paul Kariuki, University of KwaZulu Natal, South Africa

It is critical that cyber education curriculum considers the growing cyber technologies and which aspects of these technologies need to be aligned with the fourth industrial revolution. This chapter seeks to present a comprehensive analysis of the current level of cyber security education in South Africa. It will also track the current trends of cyber security education in the country as well as examining any challenges being experienced including any knowledge gaps. In the end, the chapter proposes recommendations for consideration in strengthening cybersecurity education in the country in to achieve advanced cyber security responses, capable of mitigating any cyber security threats. Offering quality cyber security education is important in preparing the next generation cyber security practitioners, who are highly competent and capable of developing innovative solutions in response to the growing global demand of cyber technologies. The chapter ends by proposing specific strategies that can guide towards this ideal in the context of the fourth industrial revolution.

Chapter 19

Thea Van der Westhuizen, University of KwaZulu Natal, South Africa
Thakur Singh, University of KwaZulu Natal, South Africa

Cybersecurity and security mechanisms of mobile device play an important part in product development, but are not often a top priority when customers select their favorite brand. A key factor that has been ignored as a result of the rapid pace of the market is that of youth brand loyalty. Brand loyalty remains one of the key factors in global markets that determine core consumers and security concerns feature became less important. This chapter aims to ascertain the key factors of brand loyalty and measure what consumers base their decision on whilst selecting a brand. The chapter will look at social value, emotional value, functional value, involvement, and perceived value of the consumer to the brand. Based on quantitative results, a conclusion will be drawn on what the key factors of brand loyalty are. Recommendations will be made on how mobile brand companies can use these KSFs when developing new products in order to procure more loyal consumers, as well as to increase awareness of the importance of the security features of the device when making a choice to purchase a brand.

Chapter 20

Bibi Zaheenah Chummun, University of KwaZulu-Natal, South Africa

A wide range of technologies impinges on all disciplines including financial services in this era of the Fourth Industrial Revolution. The deployment and security of mobile phones have considerably increased financial services access such as mobile money to the low-income households in developing African markets recently. The financial services that were once randomly accessible to those financially excluded have now become a potential pathway to enhance financial inclusion in allowing the low-income households to transact through mobile financial services in a more speedy, reliable, and secure manner. However, many security challenges remain to be addressed to promote a more inclusive mobile financial system. This chapter focuses on mobile devices security landscape and unprecedented security breaches by cyber criminals and how those threats can be mitigated in a view to promote financial inclusion in the mobile financial services sector of emerging African markets in the midst of the Fourth Industrial Revolution.

Foreword

Technology is affecting people on individual, business, governmental and societal levels and the disruptive development of new technology requires far greater security than ever before. Proper security has a broad range of possible attack vectors and vulnerabilities, and most of these are beyond a common user's awareness or full understanding. Information security and cybersecurity have become critical and important focus areas, which will become even more critical in the Fourth Industrial Revolution (4IR/ Industry 4.0) as they cause major technology disruption and affect lives in ways we never thought possible. In the Fourth Industrial Revolution cyber is broadened into people's bodies, cars, homes, the environment, social activities, and elsewhere.

The interconnectivity of, growing dependency on, and the disruptive and ongoing development of Information & Communication Technologies (ICT) creates a new and dangerous battlefield – *cyberspace*. Criminal elements target individuals daily as they use their personal devices such as smartphones, laptops, social media pages and their home security systems. Individuals are often unaware of the dangers and the privacy threats around them. Criminal elements inside and outside organizations gain access to information that can cause financial and reputational damage. Creative and innovative criminal minds plot to overthrow governments as they wage war using cyberspace. Information and cyber warfare are real and dangerous threats that can cause global chaos if not managed and secured properly.

Individuals, businesses and governments need to adapt to non-traditional, out-of-the-box, disruptive thinking to manage effectively the Fourth Industrial Revolution and the impact of technology on every facet of humans' lives. This revolution cannot be stopped in its tracks, but awareness, advanced knowledge and security can create a safer cyberspace.

This book, consisting of twenty chapters, contributes to creating awareness of the severity of the information threats on personal, business, governmental and societal levels; as well as what can be done to enhance security at these different levels.

The book starts by exploring a relative new concept called *social engineering* in information security breaches focusing on organizations specifically. Chapter 2 highlights cautionary tales in Strategic Cybersecurity Messaging Online to show some of the dangers in cyberspace. The so-called "Safe Distances" are then highlighted by looking at online and RL Hyper-Personal relationships as potential attack surfaces. Ransomware as the Cyber Extortionist is then explored, as well as the threats to Cloud Computing in the Fourth Industrial Revolution, and the impact of IoT on Information Warfare. The dangers of cyber-criminal activities are highlighted in these chapters and possible ways to overcome these security risks are offered. The book then explores how a 'Generic Self Evolving Multi-Agent Defense Approach' against cyber-attacks can be used, and the importance of Information Security Education to prepare and create more awareness in individuals of the potential risks and threats. The book then moves to Security Frameworks, Risk assessment and Cyber Resilience to mitigate risks. Information Security Management from a South African Public Sector perspective then follows to highlight the challenges and management of cyber-attacks. Six-Word Stories from curated text sets to anticipate Cyberwar and the connection of Terrorism and the Media in the Fourth Industrial Revolution are then discussed. In the last few chapters, information and cyber security risks are explored from a maritime, education, mobile device brand loyalty and mobile banking perspectives.

This book is an essential reference source offering further research opportunities, building on the available literature and expertise in the field of information technology, information security and the management of technology at various levels in society, focusing on information and cyber warfare, and information and cyber security specifically. The contemporary and future impact of technology and the Fourth Industrial Revolution in all facets of human activity, enhances the scholarly value of the publication. This book is suitable and beneficial to scholar-practitioners, educationalists, policy makers, government officials, students, researchers, entrepreneurs, executives in various business sectors, business leaders and managers, communities, and interested individuals.

This is a welcome contribution to the much needed literature in this field.

David Cropley
University of South Australia, Australia

Preface

The Fourth Industrial Revolution has been driven by unprecedented technological developments characterized by disruptive technologies that are connecting the physical, digital and biological worlds, impacting all disciplines, economies and industries (World Economic Forum, 2017). Previously, this unthinkable developments were only seen as Science Fiction, but this is no longer the case. It seems that the possibilities offered by new technologies are endless, and humans can only imagine what will come next, as their technological breakthroughs prove to be powerful enough to change the way humans perceive and interact with the world. This in itself pose unprecedented risks.

This book aims to highlight possible risks created by current and future technologies in an effort to create awareness and to encourage new thinking around information- and cybersecurity. In 2017, two large cybersecurity attacks occurred, highlighting the importance of new thinking around information and cybersecurity. North Korea launched the WannaCry in May 2017 and the NotPetya in June 2017, showing that the outcome of geopolitical conflicts will now depend on digital code as well and that political systems are and will be severely challenged in the Fourth Industrial Revolution (Davis Larsen, 2018). The negative consequences of security breaches and cyberwarfare extend far beyond personal and business data breaches, and can affect every system utilizing technology with direct and devastating consequences on people and the planet. The scary part is that there are not always immediate solutions to prevent or overcome well-designed attacks.

Klaus Schwab's book 'Shaping the Fourth Industrial Revolution' highlights "the urgent need for new action and thinking on the governance of emerging technologies" (World Economic Forum, 2018, p. 1). Dangers, known and unknown, need to be managed by ensuring relevant policies, norms, standards and incentives are developed and governments need to take the lead.

This book consists of twenty chapters.

Chapter 1, titled "Social Engineering in Information Security Breaches and the Factors That Explain Its Success: An Organizational Perspective," starts off by explaining that social engineering is the art of using deception in an effort to manipulate individuals to gain access to systems or information assets. In order to mitigate this problem, it is crucial to understand the ways in which human behaviour can be exploited via social engineering. This chapter analyses the role of social engineering in information security breaches and the factors that contribute to its success. A variety of social engineering attacks, impacts and mitigations are discussed. Human factors such as trust, obedience and fear are easily exploited, thereby allowing social engineers to execute successful attacks. However, with effective countermeasures, such as information security awareness training, education and audit procedures, the impacts of social engineering can be decreased or eliminated altogether.

Chapter 2, titled "Safe Distances: Online and RL Hyper-Personal Relationships as Potential Attack Surfaces," explores how online human-to-human (and human-to-robot) hyper-personal relationships have evolved over the years, and how these relationships broadened the available cyberattack surfaces. With the deployment of malicious socialbots on social media, human interests in socializing have become more fraught and risky. Abductive reasoning from in-world experiences, and analogical analysis to project into the Fourth Industrial Revolution, this chapter suggests the importance of greater awareness of the risks in interrelating in the virtual and the real worlds, and suggests that there are no safe distances.

Chapter 3, titled "Ransomware: The Cyber Extortionist," explains that 'Ransomware' is a type of malware that tries to extort money from its victims by hijacking the victim's computer in some way and holding it to ransom. It renders the computer unusable until a ransom amount is paid to the extortionist. And it is very unfortunate that, in many cases, even after the ransom is paid, the victim's computer is not released. Ransomware, as we know it, is gaining popularity at an immense rate among the most notorious cyber-criminals of the world. It isn't just a virus, it's a damn good game plan to becoming a millionaire in a matter of months. The chapter details what ransomware is, how it originated, which families of attacks it falls under, how ransomware is classified, the impact of ransomware on a global scale, the life cycle of a typical ransomware attack, mitigation and containment strategies, trending strains of 2017, and future trends in ransomware attacks. In future, these attack types will dominate our industries and wreak havoc, destroying life and property, if left unchecked.

Chapter 4, titled "Curtailing the Threats to Cloud Computing in the Fourth Industrial Revolution," describes how cloud computing enables end users to make use of third party's resources to support their computing needs and states that the services offered by Cloud computing make the technology very critical to the Fourth Industrial Revolution. The benefits are explained as well as how these benefits have been threatened by a number of security threats. This chapter seeks to curtail the effects of these threats by enlightening and educating users on the current ways to mitigate them. The chapter concludes that with adequate enlightenment, the full benefits of Cloud computing in industry 4.0 would be better enjoyed by users.

Chapter 5, titled "The Impact of IoT on Information Warfare," explores how the connectivity of many smart devices, known as the Internet of Things (IoT), generates large amounts of data and provides access by these devices. This connectivity provides opportunities in an information warfare context by providing new avenues of attack and abilities to enhance existing capabilities. Recent cyber-attacks illustrated the relevance of IoT to cyber-operations, however IoT can influence information warfare through the use of drones, the extent of network-centric operations, and other factors. The major impact of IoT is the increased attack surface and techniques available, and opportunities for data gathering.

Chapter 6, titled "A Generic Self-Evolving Multi-Agent Defense Approach Against Cyber Attacks," looks at a generic self-evolving multi-agent approach to overcome the threats of cyber-attacks. Most of the existing security approaches are custom designed for specific threats and attacks. However, the fusion of technologies and systems in the Fourth Industrial Revolution increasingly attracts multiple cyber threats in a single interface. In order to solve this problem, a generic self-evolving multi-agent approach is proposed in the chapter. Multiple agents interact with each other in light of their reactions towards the environment and its inherent changes. Information from individual agents is collected and integrated to form the abstract compartment of the structure. The important aspects are analyzed including demonstrating how the abstract domain can be obtained from the custom interactions at the low level domain of the proposed approach.

Chapter 7, titled "The Different Aspects of Information Security Education," highlights the importance of information security education for everyone, ranging from organizations to professionals and students, all the way through to individual users of information and communication systems. It discusses the different subject areas in information security and shows how instead of being intimidated by it, different categories of users can obtain varying depths of information security education based on their cyber-activities and need for knowledge. Information security professionals would require an in-depth knowledge in all aspects of information security, and information technology professionals and students would require an overall education in these areas, while most users of information and communication systems would only require basic education to help protect their information assets in cyberspace.

Chapter 8, titled "Optimized Three-Dimensional Security Framework to Mitigate Risks Arising From BYOD Enabled Business Environment," links to Chapter 5 in a way, as Bring Your Own Device (BYOD) has infiltrated the work environment and businesses are enjoying the benefits coupled with the adoption of the trend. At the same time, the adoption of BYOD has introduced a number of security threats that businesses are failing to match. In the pursuit of addressing security threats that are introduced by the adoption of this technology trend, this chapter recommends a three dimensional (3-D) security framework that can be used to mitigate the risks emanating from a BYOD enabled environment. Data was collected from the employees of two banks in Africa that supported BYOD trend to measure individual and organizational practices. This chapter investigates these practices in addressing implications of BYOD. Three categories of security threats are delineated in this chapter, as well as a review of existing security frameworks. The chapter concludes by outlining a 3-D security framework as a potential solution to protect BYOD enabled business environment.

Chapter 9, titled "Dynamic Risk Assessment in IT Environments: A Decision Guide," explains that security and reliability of information technologies have emerged as major concerns nowadays. Risk assessment, an estimation of negative impacts that might be imposed to a network by a series of potential sources, is one of the main tasks to ensure the security is performed, either statically or dynamically. Static risk assessment cannot satisfy the requirements of real-time and ubiquitous computing networks as it is pre-planned and does not consider upcoming changes such as the creation of new attack strategies. However, Dynamic Risk Assessment (DRA) considers real-time evidences, being capable of diagnosing abnormal events in changing environments. Several DRA approaches have been proposed recently, but it is unclear which technique fits best into IT scenarios with different requirements. Thus, this chapter introduces recent trends in DRA and proposes a decision guide to help IT managers in choosing the most suitable DRA technique, considering three illustrative scenarios – regular computer networks, Internet of Things and Industrial Control Systems.

Chapter 10, titled "Beware! A Multimodal Analysis of Cautionary Tales in Strategic Cybersecurity Messaging Online," explores how cautionary tales can be used to describe protagonists who are faced with critical decisions and often take wrong turns and suffer for it, sometimes irretrievably. These tales warn people of dangers. In cybersecurity communications, cautionary tales are an integral part of strategic messaging. This chapter explores the uses of multimodal cautionary tales in strategic cybersecurity communications, in a convenience sampling of the following: mass-scale search terms, academic and mass media text sets, social imagery, related tags networks, and social video. This chapter identifies their strengths and weaknesses in suggesting methods for promoting personal cybersecurity safety. Some suggestions for higher efficacy in cybersecurity cautionary tales are suggested, in light of the advent of the Fourth Industrial Revolution.

Chapter 11, titled "Cyber Resilience for the Internet of Things," examines and explains cyber resilience, internet of things, software-defined networking, fog computing, cloud computing and related areas. Organizations develop these technologies in tandem with cyber resilience best practices, such as processes and standards. Cyber resilience is at the intersection of cyber security and business resilience. Its core capabilities encompass integrated strategic policies, processes, architectures, and frameworks. Governments and industries often align defensive and resilient capabilities, to address security and network vulnerability breaches through strategic management processes.

Chapter 12, titled "Developing Cybersecurity Resilience in the Provincial Government," highlights that the approach that the organisation uses to manage its cyber-risk to its workforce, information, systems and networks are paramount to ensure sustainability and continuity in the Fourth Industrial Revolution. Improving cyber-resiliency in an organisation reduces the chance of future threats and attacks and builds better capability. Cyber resilience involves continuous operations, good governance and diligence supported by the right security strategy of a Computer Security Incident Response Team (CSIRT) that can protect government operations and control cyber-risks. CSIRT can build better resiliency at the decentralized provincial government level, and contribute to cyber awareness amongst the workforce, public and other government departments. A CSIRT can further contribute to resilience to the organisation by analyzing the threats and attacks, developing counter measures for the future in protecting its systems and networks from threat actors.

Chapter 13, titled "Government's Dynamic Approach to Addressing Challenges of Cybersecurity in South Africa," explains that it is increasingly clear that total cybersecurity is impossible, and that each government should develop a cyber-security strategy. The chapter focuses on South Africa's government's dynamic approach to addressing challenges of cybersecurity and the co-ordination of cyber-security activities to have a coordinated approach to cyber-crime. This chapter highlights the idea of protecting sensitive data for the public good especially and that Government's cybersecurity presents a unique challenge, simply because of the volume of threats that agencies working for government face on a daily basis.

Chapter 14, titled "Information Security Management a South African Public Sector Perspective," links to Chapters 12 and 13 and looks at the South African Public Sector and how the new technologies in the Fourth Industrial Revolution bring numerous opportunities for smarter and efficient ways of doing business and serving the public. However, these new processes, technology and people interaction increase cyber-risks. Cyber-risks cause a threat to the reputation, operations, data and assets of the public sector. The chapter states that a holistic information security management plan is needed to mitigate cyber-risks, protect infrastructure, devices and data. The authors believe that this approach will inevitably improve Information Technology governance and better accountability to the public.

Chapter 15, titled "Inducing Six-Word Stories From Curated Text Sets to Anticipate Cyberwar in 4IR," looks at curated "cyberwar" text sets (from government, mainstream journalism, academia, and social media), creates six-word stories are computationally induced (using word frequency counts, text searches, word network analysis, word clustering, and other means), and supported by post-induction human writing. The resulting inducted six-word stories are used to (1) describe and summarize the underlying textual information (to enable a bridge to a complex topic); (2) produce insights about the underlying textual information and related in-world phenomena; and (3) answer particular research questions. These resulting six-word stories are analyzed along multiple dimensions: data sources (government, journalism, academia, and social media), expert calls-and-crowd responses, and by time periods (pre-cyberwar and cyberwar periods). The efficacy of this six-word story induction process is evaluated, and the extracted six-word stories are applied to cyberwar potentials during the Fourth Industrial Revolution.

Chapter 16, titled "Terrorism in the Age of Information: Unpuzzling the Connection of Terrorism and the Media in the Fourth Industrial Revolution," explains that not a lot of attention has been given to the use of ICT by terrorists. In fact, through the ebbs and flows of technology, the society of information seems to develop a particular vulnerability to the fear instilled by terrorism. This particularly reveals a paradox, because the original technology, which was oriented to make of our lives safer, is used by terrorist cells to inspire a terror-driven atmosphere. This chapter critically discusses the role of technology in the struggle against terrorism in the Fourth Industrial Revolution.

Chapter 17, titled "Cybersecurity Risks and Automated Maritime Container Terminals in the Age of 4IR," presents a case study of automated maritime Container Terminals (CTs) to demonstrate that the risks derived from the use of technology associated with the Fourth Industrial Revolution (4IR) are both real and dangerous. The chapter explains the critical function of CTs in the global supply chain and outlines the economic and social consequences that could result if their operations were to be disrupted. The motivations of a range of threat-actors are presented and it is established that there are feasible scenarios in which any one of the major threat-actor categories may wish to cause disruption at CTs. The vulnerabilities of yard cranes are investigated and it is concluded that there are likely to be exploitable vulnerabilities in the Industrial Control System (ICS) networks used on these cranes. The chapter argues that many CT operations are likely to be exposed to significant cyber-based risks and that this exposure will increase with the roll-out of further 4IR technologies unless appropriate control measures are implemented.

Chapter 18, titled "Cyber Security Education in the Fourth Industrial Revolution: The Case of South Africa," links to Chapter 7 and seeks to present a comprehensive analysis of the current level of cyber security education in South Africa. It tracks the current trends of cyber security education in the country, as well as examining any challenges being experienced, including any knowledge gaps. The chapter proposes recommendations for consideration in strengthening cybersecurity education in the country to achieve advanced cyber security responses, capable of mitigating any cyber security threats. Offering quality cyber security education is important in preparing the next generation cyber security practitioners, who are and need to be highly competent and capable of developing innovative solutions in response to the growing global demand of cyber technologies. The chapter ends by proposing specific strategies that can guide towards this ideal in the context of the Fourth Industrial Revolution.

Chapter 19, titled "Mobile Device Brand Loyalty of Youth: Perceived Value vs. Cybersecurity Choices," aims to ascertain the key factors of brand loyalty and measure what consumers base their decision on whilst selecting a brand. The chapter looks at social value, emotional value, functional value, involvement and perceived value of the consumer to the brand; how mobile brand companies can use these when developing new products in order to procure more loyal consumers; and the importance of increasing awareness of the security features of the device when making a choice to purchase a brand.

Chapter 20, titled "Mobile Security in Low-Income Households' Businesses: A Measure of Financial Inclusion," explores the deployment and security of mobile phones and their use to increase financial services access on the low-income households in developing African markets. The financial services that were once randomly accessible to those financially excluded have now become a potential pathway to enhance financial inclusion in allowing the low-income households to transact through mobile financial services in a more speedy, reliably and secure manner. However, many security challenges remain to be addressed to promote a more inclusive mobile financial system. This chapter focuses on mobile devices security landscape and unprecedented security breaches by cyber criminals and how those threats can be mitigated in a view to promote financial inclusion in the mobile financial services sector of emerging African markets in the midst of the Fourth Industrial Revolution.

It is hoped that this book becomes an essential reference source in the field of information technology, information security and the management of technology in the constantly changing and growing cyberspace. The contemporary and future impact of the Fourth Industrial Revolution on all facets of human activity, makes a book like this important and beneficial to scholar-practitioners, educationalists, policy makers, government officials, students, researchers, entrepreneurs, executives in various business sectors, business leaders and managers, communities, and interested individuals.

Ziska Fields
University of KwaZulu-Natal, South Africa

REFERENCES

Davis, N., & Larsen, A. M. E. (2018). *5 ways the Fourth Industrial Revolution transformed 2017 (and 5 ways it did not)*. Retrieved from https://www.weforum.org/agenda/2018/01/5-ways-the-fourth-industrial-revolution-transformed-2017-and-5-ways-it-did-not

World Economic Forum. (2017). *Navigating the Fourth Industrial Revolution*. Retrieved from https://www.weforum.org/agenda/2017/08/fourth-industrial-revolution-990fcaa6-9298-471d-a45e-e6ed9238dde9/

World Economic Forum. (2018). *Fourth Industrial Revolution Book Calls for Urgent Upgrade to the Way We Govern Technology*. Retrieved from https://www.weforum.org/press/2018/01/fourth-industrial-revolution-book-calls-for-urgent-upgrade-to-the-way-we-govern-technology

Acknowledgment

A special thank you to all the authors and peer reviewers. Without your valued contributions, this publication would not have been possible.

Chapter 1
Social Engineering in Information Security Breaches and the Factors That Explain Its Success:
An Organizational Perspective

Jhaharha Lackram
University of KwaZulu-Natal, South Africa

Indira Padayachee
University of KwaZulu-Natal, South Africa

ABSTRACT

Social engineering refers to the art of using deception and manipulating individuals to gain access to systems or information assets and subsequently compromising these systems and information assets. Information security must provide protection to the confidentiality, integrity, and availability of information. In order to mitigate information security's weakest link, it becomes necessary to understand the ways in which human behavior can be exploited via social engineering. This chapter will seek to analyze the role of social engineering in information security breaches and the factors that contribute to its success. A variety of social engineering attacks, impacts, and mitigations will be discussed. Human factors such as trust, obedience, and fear are easily exploited, thereby allowing social engineers to execute successful attacks. However, with effective countermeasures such as information security awareness training, education, and audit procedures, the impacts of social engineering can be decreased or eliminated altogether.

DOI: 10.4018/978-1-5225-4763-1.ch001

INTRODUCTION

The fourth industrial revolution, or Industry 4.0 as it is commonly referred to, has been set in motion and will in due course have an impact on the way individuals and society functions as a whole. In Industry 4.0, all systems communicate with each other, as well as with humans thereby making data accessible via a medium such as the internet for operators and users alike (Chung and Kim, 2016). This element of human interaction and human accessibility poses a threat to information security which needs to be considered, since it is the human who poses the most risk in the information security chain (Workman, 2007; Pavkovic and Perkov, 2011).

A growing segment of research within the domains of information systems, information technology and computer science focuses on information security, which is a sub-discipline that centres on the protection of information assets from users with malicious intent (Pieters, 2011). In the event of an attack or security breach, it is imperative that the confidentiality, integrity and availability of information, commonly referred to as the CIA triad, must be protected via information security mechanisms and tools (Pieters, 2011).

The security of information systems is largely dependent on a myriad of both technical and non-technical aspects (Pavkovic and Perkov, 2011). The efficacy of technical-based attacks such as traditional hacking or malicious code attacks has decreased considerably due to the provision and adoption of technological security solutions by organizations (Janczewski and Fu, 2010). Due to the advent of advanced computer-based security or technical security, it has become common for attackers to instead rely on an alternative, non-technical means of gaining access to systems (Thompson, 2004). This phenomenon is referred to as social engineering, which refers to an attack that utilises the art of manipulating and using human interaction to execute an action or obtain valuable information. This ill-gotten information can be used to access or compromise the information systems of an organisation, thereby sabotaging the financial and economic health of the organisation (Jannson, 2011; Orgill et al, 2004; Kvedar, Nettis and Fulton, 2010).

As stated by Vidalis and Kazmi (2007), the human factor is a shared vulnerability of perceptions and decision making in the sense that it is human beings who interact with computers by typing in commands, automating processes and turning computers off should they think that it is not operating properly by misinterpreting its reactions.

A successful social engineering attack can result in the social engineer gaining control of an entire company's network servers (Manske, 2000). Social engineering leaves even the most technically secured computer systems extremely vulnerable, as it relies on the social engineers' social skills to compromise the information security of the organisation (Thompson, 2004). Most often, social engineering attacks are carried out with deception to the degree that the victim does not realize that (s)he has been manipulated, thereby making the identification of social engineering attacks extremely difficult (Gulati, 2003; Bezuidenhout, Mouton and Venter, 2010). Social engineering transpires at a psychological level with psychology being used to generate an authoritative atmosphere where the victim is persuaded into divulging information pertinent in the accessing of a system. Furthermore, these attacks also take place at a physical level, namely at the workplace where the victim feels secure via the medium of work telephone numbers or email (Orgill et al, 2004). More recently, the trend of Bring Your Own Device (BYOD) and cloud computing has given social engineers more opportunities to carry out attack vectors in the workplace (Kromholz et al, 2014; Hatwar & Chavan 2015).

Social engineers appeal to the emotions of possible victims, such as excitement and fear, in an endeavor to persuade victims to fulfill requests while other social engineers rely on creating a relationship, in order to allow the victim to feel a sense of trust or commitment towards the attacker (Workman, 2008; Kvedar, Nettis and Fulton, 2010). Many social engineering attacks are made possible via the help of insiders of the organization, which is commonly referred to as "the insider threat", (Orgill, et al, 2004). Part of the problem of generating awareness and countermeasures to combat social engineering lies in the fact that organisations are reluctant to admit (for example to a legal representative or to funding institutions) that a social engineering attack has transpired. Such a revelation would imply that the social engineering attack was successful only due to a lack of staff training or stringent information policy (Thompson, 2004).

With the advent of the fourth industrial revolution, organisations are becoming heavily reliant on information technology and it is due to this dependency that Bullée et al (2015) argue that social engineering poses the biggest threat to information systems exposure. This chapter's objectives are as follows: (1) To understand the phenomenon of social engineering from an organisational perspective in terms of social engineering attacks, the impact of social engineering attacks, and the mitigation techniques undertaken by organisations to prevent social engineering attacks (2) To determine the human factors that makes organisational employees vulnerable to social engineering attacks.

BACKGROUND

Social engineering, in its earliest and simplest form, first occurred in Greek mythology, when Odysseus used trickery to enable his men to gain access to Troy, thereby effectively illustrating that the human element is the most exploitable component of any information system (Thompson, 2004). Due to the low awareness of social engineering as a threat to information security, the phenomenon of social engineering has not been given much attention by researchers (Janczewski and Fu, 2010). This research aims to address this knowledge gap by examining the scope of social engineering attacks, its impacts thereof and resultant mitigation techniques.

Various studies that have explored the behaviour of individuals with regard to security have been undertaken to justify why individuals do not practice security considerations. These studies have unearthed situational barriers such as inadequate policies or inadequate implementation time for security professionals. However, none of the studies have shed light on personal factors that could explain the reasons behind why individuals fail to follow security policies. In addition, Workman (2008) states that human carelessness with regard to handling information is a major contributing factor to information security breaches. However, there has been a lack of empirical studies that have researched the behaviours of humans with regard to information carelessness and the ways in which this vulnerability is exploited by social engineers (Workman, 2008). Workman (2008) also states that existing literature is not theoretically grounded and studies that have been carried out do not focus primarily on social engineering threats or the reasons why individuals may or may not fall victim. This chapter attempts to bridge this gap by exploring the role of human factors in social engineering attacks.

SOCIAL ENGINEERING ATTACKS, IMPACTS AND MITIGATIONS

Kevin Mitnick, a notorious past hacker, who brought the social engineering concept into the mainstream, and who is now a current information security professional, has identified the stages of a social engineering attack to consist of research, establishing trust and rapport, exploiting trust, and thereafter using the information gained (Mitnick and Simon, 2002).

There exists a varied and established number of techniques that a social engineer can use in order to carry out a social engineering attack, largely due to the fact that social engineering relies predominantly on a variation of confidence trickery (Thompson, 2006). The extent of the attack vectors, as well as the scope of it depends upon the creativity of the social engineer to effectively respond to changing environments and people and other emerging situations (Manske, 2000; Jurišin and Ivanicka, 2010). Many social engineers who successfully execute attacks have become legendary in social engineering circles, and the details of their intrusions are often made available on websites for other current and future social engineers to attempt (Manske, 2000).

Social Engineering Attack Techniques

Peltier (2006) and Gulati (2003) suggest that social engineering attacks can be broadly classified into two categories namely technology-based attacks and human-based attacks. It is common for these two categories to overlap in the sense that technology-based attacks can be electronically propagated, but require a single trigger from a human for the attack to successfully execute (Kazim and Zhu, 2015). Orgill et al (2004), Sun, Yan and Feng (2012), Granger (2001) and Chitrey, Singh and Singh (2012) suggest that social engineering attacks transpire on two levels – namely that of the physical level and that of the psychological level. The physical setting for social engineering attacks includes the actual workplace, the telephone medium, dumpsters and the online environment, whereas persuasion takes place on the psychological level (Orgill et al, 2004; Granger, 2001).

Technology Based Attacks

Technology-based attacks are similar to traditional hacking techniques as they rely purely on manipulating and deceiving employees into confidently believing that they are interacting with genuine computer applications (Janczewski and Fu, 2010; Gulati, 2003). Technology-based attacks include malicious email attachments, phishing, pop-up windows and online social engineering (Janczewski and Fu, 2010). Despite the fact that technology based attacks are commonly perceived to be technical attacks, these attacks rely predominantly on carefully worded and strategically crafted messages to tempt victims into opening the attachments, which unbeknown to the victim, contain executables and programmes (Peltier, 2006). This element of trickery and deception in the messages relies upon human weakness for the attack to successfully transpire, despite the technical prowess required in the hacking component. When malicious links are clicked, the social engineer can gather sensitive and private information and credentials (Applegate, 2009). In some cases, the security of the victim's operating system can be compromised via the installation of malicious programs that allow the social engineer to gain full access to the victim's system (Applegate, 2009). Malware refers to malicious programs such as viruses and it is social engineering malware that has proliferated across the internet and subsequently infiltrated computers (Abraham and Chengalur-Smith, 2010).

Phishing, Spear-Phishing, Whaling, Pop-Up Windows, Denial of Service Attacks and Distributed Denial of Service Attacks

Phishing refers to the circulation of deceptive and camouflaged emails to entice users to fraudulent websites in order to elicit sensitive and confidential information (Vishwanath, Herath, Chen, Wang and Rao, 2011; Laribee, Barnes, Rowe and Martell, 2006). Such websites contain links, which will download malicious executables to the victim's computer once selected. Spear phishing takes place in an organisational setting and is a more evolved form of phishing in that the targeted victims are specific employees such as CEOs and other individuals with a high net worth (Vishwanath et al., 2011; Jurišin and Ivanicka, 2010). Krombholz et al (2014) refer to the prevalence of spear-phishing, with companies like The New York Times and RSA suffering the brunt of these attacks. Similar to spear phishing is whaling, which is an emerging social engineering threat that also refers to a targeted attack on corporate executives – "the big whales". In a whaling attack, public information pertaining to the organisation is gathered by the social engineer in an attempt to send emails to the corporate executives notifying them of high-priority issues that need to be addressed, such as a complaint from a business chamber about the organisation. Such emails contain malicious links and attachments which upon clicking by the executive leads to the installation of malware (Abraham and Chengular-Smith, 2010)

Pop-up windows manipulate the user into entering his/her username and password on a window that appears to be authentic, failing which the user would not be able to proceed with his/her current tasks online (Gulati, 2003).

Kazim and Zhu (2015) refer to the technical prowess needed in the hijacking of user accounts and services, which they classify as network attacks. Such network attacks take advantage of vulnerabilities in software, which subsequently lead to the hijacking of user accounts and/or services.

Similarly, a denial of service (DOS) attack and distributed DOS attack are effective attack vectors in that the malicious user originating the attack does so by taking advantage of network vulnerabilities. These attacks exhaust the cloud's resources and computing power, thereby causing a significant delay in services or sometimes making the cloud completely unresponsive (Kazim and Zhu, 2015).

Mobile Applications and the Age of BYOD

Social engineering is aggravated by the information age and the pervasiveness of BYOD whereby face-to-face interaction is greatly reduced as employees become more reliant on collaboration software such as Skype, Lync and LinkedIn (Krombholz et al, 2014). This information age signifies the transmission of huge amounts of information for daily work purposes and allows social engineers an opportunity to execute attack vectors. Increasingly mobile employees are more likely to use their own devices for the sake of convenience. In doing so they put their organisation at great risk when using personal devices to transmit sensitive data for work purposes. Smartphone applications commonly request sensitive user information, which present an opportunity for social engineers to either develop or hack such applications, thereby receiving this data as a starting point for an attack vector. (Krombholz et al, 2014).

Cloud Computing Attacks

Users connect to the cloud on a daily basis to fulfil their work responsibilities, but many remain unaware of the potential security threats available via this platform. Trojan horses, viruses and malware pose hazards to end user systems and cloud data centers alike. The cloud computing platform is exposed to the same threats as single machines but the fact that cloud infrastructure and its applications are hosted on a public network further increases susceptibility to social engineering attacks (Hatwar and Chavan, 2015). Such attacks include malicious individuals using botnets to spread malware and spam by invading public clouds; cross site scripting attacks whereby harmful script is inserted into the web; SQL injection attacks whereby harmful SQL code is inserted into a SQL query, which subsequently gives a social engineer unauthorised access to a database (Hatwar and Chavan, 2015).

Human Based Attacks

Human based attacks rely predominantly on persuasion and can be conducted personally or via telephonic means and include techniques such as impersonation, shoulder surfing, and reverse social engineering and direct requests (Thompson, 2006; Janczewski and Fu, 2010).

Impersonation

Impersonation is used by social engineers as a means to easily access a system by putting up a particular façade, either in person, or via telephonic means. It consists of two major tools, namely being familiar with particular terminology and vocabulary used at the organisation and having an in-depth knowledge of policies and personnel of the targeted organisation (Applegate, 2009; Tetri and Vuorinen, 2013; Thompson, 2006). This enables the social engineer to telephone or make personal contact with targeted victims under the false pretense of being from the information assurance department, another organisation, the media or a research institution such as a university (Applegate, 2009). In person, a social engineer can blend into their foreign surroundings by simply tailgating a user into the user's organization –once inside, the social engineer has unlimited access to equipment or sensitive documents within the organization which serves as a goldmine of information.

Shoulder Surfing

Shoulder surfing as its name suggests, refers to the social engineer simply looking over the shoulder of the targeted victim to observe their behaviour while operating programs or while typing in usernames and passwords (Peltier, 2006; Jurišin and Ivanicka, 2010). This is essentially spying on the victim. Not only will the social engineer gain a first-hand view of how to navigate his/her way around a system, but the social engineer will also be able to log into the system with the correct credentials after having observed the keystrokes being typed in by the victim.

Dumpster Diving

Dumpster diving, also known as trash trawling refers to social engineers physically going through the waste material of an organisation in the hope of finding sensitive information (Gulati, 2003; Jurišin and Ivanicka, 2010). This has become a common technique as organisations simply dispose of important information that they no longer deem necessary (Peltier, 2006). Mitnick and Simon (2001) have stated that dumpster diving is not an actual social engineering attack but rather a research instrument. Potential security leaks that are found in dumpsters include memos, company phone books, organizational charts, calendars containing important information, policy manuals pertaining to the respective organisation and hardcopies containing sensitive data such as usernames and passwords (Granger, 2001). Organisational charts provide a structure of the company's personnel, making the authority figures obvious, and phonebooks provide the numbers of all personnel within the company – if used together, they can provide a wealth of information for the social engineer to find and target (or impersonate) an employee of choice (Gulati, 2003; Granger, 2001). Policy manuals give the social engineer an idea of how well secured or not the company is and memos help create authenticity that the social engineer will use to convince his victim (Gulati, 2003; Granger, 2001). Company letterheads may be contained on certain papers, which the social engineer will use to create authentic looking, but falsified, correspondence and calendars may contain the dates of meetings, vacations and holidays that the social engineer can take care to mention in his execution of an attack (Gulati, 2003; Granger, 2001). Nyamsuren and Choi (2007) elaborate on digital dumpster diving, which distinguishes itself from traditional dumpster diving in the sense that digital dumpster diving aims to discover the disposal of digital devices. Due to the constantly changing landscape of technology and technological advancement, digital and mobile devices would be disposed of at a rapid rate, thereby allowing social engineers to gain a plethora of private information stored on such digital and mobile devices (Nyamsuren and Choi, 2007). Jurišin and Ivanicka (2010) also elaborate that once having gained access codes to the system in manuals that were disposed of, social engineers access the system and view the contents of the recycle bin on the victim's desktop.

Reverse Social Engineering

Reverse social engineering is a more complex and advanced attack vector that relies on the creation of a situation where the victim seeks out and depends on the social engineer for assistance thereby allowing a relationship of trust to be established from the victim's side (Kvedar, Nettis and Fulton, 2010; Jurišin and Ivanicka, 2010). Reverse social engineering provides the victim the opportunity to ask the social engineer questions and gain information from the social engineer – this attack vector has been said to be more successful for the social engineer in terms of gaining more valuable information (Gulati, 2003). Reverse social engineering eludes the attention of organisations and employees due to the fact that the victim willingly contacts the social engineer and is therefore at the mercy of the social engineer, thereby eliminating the possibility of a victim thinking they are being attacked (Kee, 2008).

Direct Requests

Even though some social engineering techniques are complex and rely on perfect planning, there are also some techniques that are simple yet still effective. One such technique is that of direct requests which refers to the social engineer eliciting information from the targeted victim by simply asking for it (Thompson, 2006).

Dimensions of Social Engineering Attacks

It is important to note that even though there are various social engineering attack vectors, in certain cases they can be similar. This has allowed Tetri and Vuorinen (2013) to propose three dimensions of social engineering attacks namely: persuasion, fabrication and data gathering.

Dimension of Persuasion

It is by human nature that individuals are predisposed to persuasion, thereby making resistance to this dimension unlikely (Bullée et al, 2015). Social engineering techniques that demonstrate the persuasion dimension include authority, being likeable, appealing to emotions, reciprocation, establishing rapport, subversion, and social validation. This dimension has the ultimate goal of encouraging the individual to fulfil inappropriate requests, which goes against conventional rule, for example, using authority to ask for the usernames and passwords (Tetri and Vuorinen, 2013). The use of subversion, threats or extortion also uses persuasion albeit in a stronger form (Tetri and Vuorinen, 2013). Interestingly enough, it has been found that psychological characteristics such as greed or laziness have been exploited by the persuasion dimension (Tetri and Vuorinen, 2013). Workman (2007) further found that psychological characteristics such as trust and fear can also be exploited in the case of persuasion tactics being employed by the social engineer. Persuasion has two attributes in that it must transpire during direct interaction (such as via a phone call, face-to-face meeting or email message) with the victim and that the social engineer has to actively engage the victim as well (Tetri and Vuorinen, 2013).

Dimension of Fabrication

The second dimension of social engineering as proposed by Tetri and Vuorinen (2013) is that of fabrication, which manifests itself via the portrayal of a particular role or via the fabrication of a particular event. This dimension includes social engineering techniques such as namedropping, impersonation, piggybacking, jargon and using false identification. Techniques such as using jargon and name dropping allow the victim to believe that the attacker is an insider who is familiar with and knows people inside the organisation and piggybacking provides the notion that the attacker forms an integral part of the organisation by belonging to the specific social circle or group (Tetri and Vuorinen, 2013). It therefore becomes necessary for the social engineer to have an in-depth knowledge of the terminology used at the organisation so as to prevent any suspicion from arising or raising alarm within the mind of the targeted victim when making a phone call or speaking face-to-face with the victim in question (Thompson, 2006). The social engineer needs to also be familiar with the organisational structure such that he/she can effectively pretend to be one of the authoritative leaders or to even claim to speak to one of the authoritative leaders (Thompson, 2006).

The fabrication dimension of social engineering can vary in its intensity with spoken words and messages constituting a weaker form of fabrication and utilising solid props such as printing fake business cards (Applegate, 2009) or utilising the correct uniforms or badges which enhance identification constituting a stronger form of fabrication (Tetri and Vuorinen, 2013).

The social engineer need not only impersonate an employee, as support staff such as janitors and repairmen can also be granted easy access into the organisation if wearing an appropriate handyman uniform (Gulati, 2003).

Dimension of Data Gathering

The final dimension of social engineering as proposed by Tetri and Vuorinen (2013) is that of data gathering which, unlike the previous two dimensions, ignores direct interaction and includes techniques such as shoulder surfing, dumpster diving, eavesdropping and phishing. Data gathering is essential since every attack requires background information on the intended targeted victim; however data gathering can also lead to the final goal in itself but often transpires in a separate phase altogether so as to minimize the risk of being caught while the attack is being executed (Tetri and Vuorinen, 2013). The dimensions of fabrication and persuasion can also be enhanced in the data gathering stages and this is obvious in the incident that Applegate (2009) recounts of a social engineer who wore a simple badge containing the universally known symbol for recycling, in order to get access from security guards to go through the dumpsters of the targeted organisation.

Impacts of Social Engineering Attacks

The impact of social engineering on an organisation can be long-lasting and extensive in nature, affecting the organisation on various levels (Manske, 2000). Information security breaches such as social engineering attacks have garnered unparalleled negative impacts on an organisation's reputation, customer confidence, profitability and general economic growth (Dlamini, Eloff and Eloff, 2009). These impacts are further heightened by pressure from regulatory parties and consumers and the growing political and economic uncertainty (Dlamini, Eloff and Eloff, 2009).

Impact on the CIA Triad

Janczewski and Fu (2010) submit that the impact of social engineering is twofold in the sense that there is a primary and a secondary impact. The confidentiality, integrity and availability (CIA triad) of information should be protected at all times and any risk of compromise could result in detrimental consequences for the organisation concerned. Hinson (2008) emphasizes the fact that the most common and direct impact of a social engineering attack is the loss of confidentiality, from an information security point of view. Janczewski and Fu (2010) and Hinson (2008) go on to elaborate that the information gathered by the social engineer will then be used to cause secondary impact and damage. Hinson (2008) further states that the loss of integrity impacted by social engineering is of a lesser degree, since the integrity of an organisation's security structures and measures can be investigated after a social engineering attack. Should a victim realize that they have been deceived, he/she may be more likely to question the integrity of future callers and subsequently reluctant to share confidential information (Hinson, 2008).

Impact on Computer Systems and Employee Productivity

In the aftermath of a social engineering attack, information technology costs escalate as it then becomes necessary to re-install backups and to investigate, repair and re-secure the compromised computers in order for them to operate efficiently again (Manske, 2000). The loss of systems availability or data availability may be another indirect impact of a social engineering attack should the attacker gain access to these resources (Hinson, 2008). Forensic analysis may have to be conducted by security professionals and consultants, as well as legal representatives, which implies that end users would not have access to such computing facilities or important data for extended periods of time. This implies that staff are largely unproductive in this period (Manske, 2000; Mataracioglu and Ozkan, 2011). There could also be backup failures thereby creating the need for data to be re-entered and re-processed which could be a timeous task and could negatively impact the staff responsible for executing these tasks (Manske, 2000).

Impact on Financial Health/Competitive Advantage of Organization

Social engineering attacks, from a commercial perspective, can negatively impact the financial health of an organisation as stolen data can cost companies tenfold (Herrmann, 2009). Due to the escalating financial costs associated with the impact of information security breaches such as social engineering, insurance companies have started covering losses that have resulted from breaches in security (Gulati, 2003). Hinson (2008) states that a competitor who gains access to proprietary information about confidential production processes could replicate the products or even sabotage the competitive advantage of that organisation. Organisations must therefore realize that their ability to create and sustain competitive advantage in predominantly uncertain and volatile markets is dependent on their capability to protect against security breaches by protecting their information assets and infrastructure (Dlamini, Eloff and Eloff, 2009).

Loss of Public Confidence

Public knowledge of security breaches in organisations such as financial institutions, where sensitive information (from a customer database, for example) was stolen, would result in irrevocable damage to that organisation's reputation. The subsequent loss of goodwill and reputation will discourage prospective clients from engaging in business with the organisation (Gulati, 2003). Manske (2000) adds that lawsuits could also result from public disclosure of the social engineering attack. Customers of the financial institution in question may lose confidence in the organisation and demand compensation by suing for damages. In addition to a tarnished image and the abovementioned direct losses, the organisation would also experience a loss of share price (Hinson, 2008; Janczewski and Fu, 2010).

HUMAN VULNERABILITY FACTORS IN SOCIAL ENGINEERING ATTACKS

One of the most widely stated principles of information security is that of the human being representing the weakest link in the security chain of information systems. As social engineering attacks constantly change and advance with countermeasures in turn also changing and evolving to defend against attacks, the human element remains unchanged. It is this human nature that will be explored, in terms of how human factors contribute towards making organizational employees vulnerable to a social engineering attack or even succumbing to such an attack.

Raman (2008) argues that an employee's vulnerability to social engineering attacks has its origins in the human brain where there is an interchange between emotion and reason. Human beings intrinsically struggle to separate emotion from reason and in cases where the two are in contradiction, emotion dominates over reason (Raman, 2008). It is this fact that has led social engineers to appeal to and manipulate the emotions of human beings in the various attack vectors they plan to execute.

It is suggested by early psychology that decision making by the individual follows an intricate path through interpretation rather than following a direct path provided by stimuli to response (Vishwanath et al., 2011). Social engineering attacks that use interpersonal deception rely on stimuli such as the verbal and nonverbal cues that the deceiver (social engineer) provides to the receiver (victim). The social engineer is at liberty to modify his behaviour as a result of and in response to the suspicion that may arise from the victim's part. However, the *interpersonal deception theory (IDT)* (Vishwanath et al., 2011), is limited in that it does not consider other levels of social engineering attacks.

Social engineers often make reference to the techniques used in marketing campaigns, which revolve around persuading an individual or gaining their cooperation and compliance (Workman, 2008). A theory that studies how information is processed or interpreted by the receiver is that of the *elaboration likelihood model (ELM),* posed by Petty and Cacioppo (1986), which was used as a tool for telemarketers to influence and persuade individuals to purchase specific products or services (Vishwanath et al., 2011; Workman, 2008). Despite the fact that social engineering does not sell products or services, it does have the goal of persuading individuals into providing sensitive information in a similar respect that advertising has in persuading individuals to succumb to advertisements to purchase a product or service (Workman, 2008). Thus, by using the theories of consumer behaviour, market research and persuasion, one can understand the reasons why victims succumb to social engineering threats and how they process deceptive information (Vishwanath et al., 2011).

Emotions Exploited via Persuasion

Peltier (2006) proposes that there are three aspects of psychology in social engineering, namely that of alternative routes to persuasion, beliefs and attitudes that in turn affect human interaction and techniques using influence and persuasion.

The two methods that the alternative routes to persuasion consist of are direct and then secondary routes. Direct routes make use of direct contact with the victim and exploit traits such as trust as the social engineer will be willing to invest the required time in order to build a pseudo relationship with the victim. The indirect route of persuasion relies on making the intended victim more vulnerable by making outright statements that invoke emotions such as fear or excitement (Peltier, 2006).

Hinson (2008) firmly states that the main reason why social engineering attacks succeed is due to the psychological traits possessed by the victim. The success of social engineering is largely attributed to the fact that human beings rely on the assumption that everyone else is essentially honest. Thompson (2006) further elaborates that social engineering works largely via the persuasion of humans by abusing trust and manipulating emotions. Raman (2008) puts forward that some of these emotions include fear, greed, sympathy and curiosity, which are universal in the sense that every human being will periodically experience such emotions.

Fear

Social engineering has recently applied the emergence of scareware, which has the sole purpose of creating fear in the mind of the user. Scareware manifests itself in the form of fake pop-up windows bearing news of fraud alerts or stating that disk corruption is imminent (Abraham and Chengular-Smith, 2010). Employees succumb to online social engineering attacks such as pop-up windows due to their fear of the unknown or due to their fear of losing the task they were currently working on and therefore comply with the instruction to enter in their username and password (Gulati, 2003). Furthermore, employees are afraid of being reprimanded and therefore comply with requests for information without thinking twice (Peltier, 2006). Social engineers who blackmail or threaten employees directly manipulate the victim's fear emotion (Raman, 2008).

Fear is also created in the mind of an employee via a phishing attack which contains attachments or messages declaring that further action needs to be taken to prevent repercussions by clicking on a certain malicious link unbeknown to the user (Applegate, 2009).

Greed

Hinson (2008) and Abraham and Chengular-Smith (2010) state that greed makes individuals susceptible to social engineering attacks. Social engineers that bribe victims manipulate the victim's greed (Raman, 2008). Nohlberg (2008) mentions a study that concluded that 64% of individuals would willingly reveal their computer passwords for a piece of chocolate. Similarly, social engineers when authoring phishing messages are aware of an individual's inherent weakness for free things (Abraham and Chengular-Smith, 2010). Phishing scams often contain links to competitions, which can be entered via filling in sensitive details. An employee's greed to win a specific prize could compromise the security of not only the employee (in terms of identity theft), but also the entire organization. Malware is present in many websites in the form of clickable links or pop-ups advertising prizes as trivial as free screensavers, coupons, movie tickets or more valuable prizes such as technological devices and cars. Social engineering attacks containing malware are common during seasonal holidays as individuals take advantage of offers to get free greeting cards or seasonal screensavers (Abraham and Chengular-Smith, 2010).

Curiosity

Curiosity as a psychological and human trait is also exploited in the event of opening email attachments from unknown senders (Gulati, 2003). Social engineers author emails that contain subject lines exploiting intrigue or curiosity in the mind of the recipient – this in turn captures the individual's attention and acts as bait to lure them into opening the attachments or links contained in the email (Abraham and Chengular-Smith, 2010).

Sympathy and Empathy

Sympathy and empathy are another two psychological traits of the victim that the social engineer takes advantage of and manipulates. This is illustrated in cases whereby the social engineer contacts the victim and paints a tragic picture of having lost information or pleads ignorance to the victim around issues that were supposed to have been known thus leading the victim to empathise with the social engineer and willingly provide him/her with the necessary information (Thompson, 2006).

Trust

Applegate (2009) elaborates that trust is one of the most common factors that make individuals prone to social engineering attacks. Trust is an especially important factor in an organizational environment and thus employees implicitly rely on trusting others who seemingly also appear to be trustworthy, credible or to portray likeability (Hinson, 2008). Social engineers therefore exude likeability and credibility in trying to establish a relationship with the victim (Applegate, 2009).

Employees automatically trust colleagues or insiders of the organisation to a greater extent than they would trust strangers, thereby allowing social engineers the opportunity to drop names of or even portray themselves to be such insiders (Hinson, 2008). The illusion of trust can be built in a myriad of ways such as via telephonic means, personal contact or even via wearing the correct uniform required by the organization to appear as a fellow employee (Hinson, 2008).

It has been argued that individuals like those whom they trust and trust those whom they like, therefore the victim is tricked into liking the social engineer such that a bond of trust can be established (Workman, 2008). Social engineers establish such relationships by taking advantage of a victim's loneliness or need for friendship and engaging with the victim to build similarity (Workman, 2008). This is akin to how online predators lure victims – by identifying that human beings will feel isolated at some point in time and subsequently offering friendship or support to ease loneliness. Workman (2008) echoes this sentiment in stating that online trust is necessary for the conducting of business transactions as well, but also contributes towards tactics employed by social engineers. This is evident in the fact that companies use familiar logos and icons on their e-commerce websites to establish trust with the consumer. Similarly, social engineers also use recognized images in the creation of fake websites to establish the same trust with the victim (Workman, 2008).

Obedience

Employees often comply with orders from authority mainly in an effort to avoid confrontation, therefore their fear and obedience leads to them willingly giving out information to social engineers (Applegate, 2009; Hinson, 2008). Workman (2008) stipulates that social engineers use authority in an attempt to provoke fear from the individual to comply with requests. An employee that demonstrates obedience is more vulnerable to being a social engineering victim as opposed to an employee that is skeptical and assertive (Workman, 2008). Hinson (2008) states that instilling too much of trust in authority figures becomes a problem in a hierarchical organization due to social engineers dropping names of such authority figures constantly in order to get information or tasks done. Hinson (2008) further states that junior employees are more vulnerable to having this psychological trait exploited by a social engineer due to the respective employee's naivety and low experience. Due to their ability to be easily influenced and their unawareness of repercussions of actions concerning the leakage of organizational information, Mataracioglu and Ozkan (2011) concur that employees at lower levels and new recruits of an organisation are mainly targeted by social engineers.

Interest in and Admiration for Famous Figures

Abraham and Chengular-Smith (2010) state that social engineering also takes advantage of an individual's rising interest in celebrities. Malware can infiltrate a computer system while the individual searches for online information about a specific celebrity. Malicious executables can also be attached to pictures of celebrities that individuals may download. Brad Pitt, a famous Hollywood actor, was ranked as the most dangerous celebrity to search for online until he was replaced by another Hollywood actress, Jessica Biel, in 2009 (Abraham and Chengular-Smith, 2010). Some social engineers go so far as to pretend to be a famous, likeable figure or enhance their physical appearance to build confidence in their interaction with the targeted victim, thereby allowing communication barriers to be broken down (Workman, 2008; Jurišin and Ivanicka, 2010).

Social engineers rely on the fact that humans are not islands in that humans constantly thrive on connecting with each other. This is evident in the growing number of social networking users. Social networks such as Twitter and Facebook are also used by famous celebrities to connect with their followers. Even during working hours, human beings seek out messages posted by these celebrities and social engineers have taken advantage of this fact by hacking into these accounts of celebrities and posting links to websites that contain malicious links and executables which results in the computer system of the individual being compromised (Abraham and Chengular-Smith, 2010). An individual's gullibility and faith or admiration in a celebrity lets them fall victim to such attacks. Additionally, an individual's inquisitiveness to ascertain the daily events in a public figure's life can also lead to the individual being a victim of social engineering attacks.

Tendency to Be Helpful

It is in a human being's nature to be helpful and helping generally tends to make one feel good about oneself. The social engineer exploits this factor of helpfulness by constantly appealing for help from the victim and the victim, thereby slips into an almost permanent role of being a helper, since the victim will find it difficult to suddenly stop their efforts of helping (Hinson, 2008). Thornburgh (2005) also states that because social engineering is largely cyclical in nature, social engineers can use an individual on numerous occasions to repeatedly gain access to systems for a variety of different goals and are thus unlikely to discard sources. Granger (2001) however, argues that social engineers are careful to not ask for too much of help all at once, or from the same person repeatedly as this may cause suspicion. Instead, social engineers target a myriad of employees and ask each employee for a small amount of information that may seem trivial at the time (Granger, 2001). After gaining information from the different sources, the information elicited, when put together, can constitute towards a very valuable bigger picture that the social engineer will use in subsequent attack vectors. Help-desks that form a part of any organisation and the subsequent help-desk employees are at particular risk of being targeted victims of a social engineering attack as their primary purpose is to help and assist in any query received (Granger, 2001). Employees who do not become suspicious of being asked for so much of help constantly are a prime target of social engineers. This is evident in the fact that help-desk employees are more vulnerable to social engineering attacks due to their poor security training and knowledge and the fact that they are instead trained to be friendly and share information, thereby leaving a security hole that can be easily penetrated by social engineers (Granger, 2001). Other corporate functions in the organisation such as public relations or sales and marketing also provide another source of vulnerability as employees belonging to these functions are tasked with regularly publishing and sharing information about the organisation (Hinson, 2008). Human resources personnel are also at particular risk of social engineering threats as it is the human resources department that is tasked with the storage of other employees' personal details (Jurišin and Ivanicka, 2010). Furthermore, receptionists, call-center employees and information technology administrators are at further risk since these employees are responsible for the handling of numerous calls and queries throughout the day, in addition to handling sensitive data thereby making them targets for social engineers (Jurišin and Ivanicka, 2010). In an organizational setting, management ensures that employees are well trained to be helpful such that customers can be satisfied with service delivery – it is this salesmen mentality of the client always being right that allows social engineers to manipulate employees (Peltier, 2006; Sandouka, Cullen and Mann, 2009). Furthermore, employees provide customers with needed information and assistance in order to obtain positive performance appraisals (Peltier, 2006). Organisations are responsible for developing the communication and assistance skills of employees, whilst social engineers, on the other hand are tasked with exploiting those characteristics (Hinson, 2008).

Appreciation and Gratitude

Kvedar, Nettis and Fulton (2010) state that in the event of a social engineer seemingly trying to help a victim, it is a natural human trait for the victim to feel indebted to the social engineer. The social engineering attack technique of reverse social engineering manipulates this human factor. This also links back to trust, however the victim additionally experiences a sense of obligation as a result of appreciation and gratitude to comply with further requests from the social engineer (Kvedar, Nettis and Fulton, 2010).

Laziness

Laziness is exploited due to the fact that individuals usually do not take the necessary time to verify information – they naturally assume that information is correct (Hinson, 2008). This holds true in the case of the identity of social engineers not being verified before they enter the physical organization, since it is automatically assumed that they are employees of the organization, if the correct uniform or an appropriate badge is worn. Employees are either too busy to verify the credentials and identity of visitors or are often hesitant to stop and ask visitors about their sole reason for visiting the organization (Hinson, 2008). Peltier (2006) argues that employees will not verify identification willingly due to negative reactions from superiors or should the case arise whereby an official may become offended. The trait of laziness in this case also overlaps with the trait of fear. Commonly an employee would prefer to open the door to a complete stranger instead of asking for a security pass or identity to be displayed (Hinson, 2008). Effective social engineers take comfort in this fact that their identity will never be questioned (Peltier, 2006).

Laziness is also manifested in the case of writing passwords on notes that are displayed for everyone to see, or displaying other sensitive information that should be restricted to certain users only (Peltier, 2006).

Carelessness

While carelessness is closely linked to laziness, it is mainly portrayed as individuals mindlessly discarding sensitive data that would allow a dumpster diver the opportunity to access that information and not taking care to examine one's surroundings when keying in usernames and passwords (Gulati, 2003; Hinson, 2008). Employees, out of carelessness or even laziness, do not think twice when leaving private information, however trivial (such as information pertaining to how every employee fits into the organizational structure) in public domains (such as the organisation's dumpsters or even website). Social engineers take advantage of this by gathering seemingly trivial pieces of information via a foot printing stage and then building up a holistic picture of the organisation and the targeted victims in order to successfully execute the attack. Employees are also guilty of leaving messages or automatic replies on their voicemail and email when they are out of the office. Such messages contain details such as the name and contact details of other employees who can attend to urgent queries. Such carelessness allows the social engineer to add to the organizational profile currently being built.

Social engineers are not discouraged that organisations have promoted security and user awareness as the number of social engineering malware threats have increased over the years. Organisations maintain that the Internet in itself remains an unsafe place to surf and encourage constant vigilance on the part of the user in terms of installing updates and patches as well as anti-virus software. The notion that the Internet is an unsafe place to surf has led social engineers to exploit such beliefs by presenting employees with fake pop-up windows advising them that their system has been infected with a virus and thus needs to be cleaned. Employees fall for this as the pop-up windows appear authentic as it comes from the organisation itself. In order to remove the virus, security patches or anti-virus software must be installed, and fake pop-up windows are used to direct users to a website containing malicious links and executables. An employee may also be afraid to not install the security solution as their computer may be compromised and important work may be lost. The psychological trait of obedience also stands out in such an event. Employees, now at the malicious website, are then encouraged to purchase the software solution by entering in sensitive data. At the very worst, the irony of the situation could result in a previously malware-free computer system now being infected by malware on this website (Abraham and Chengular-Smith, 2010).

SOLUTIONS AND RECOMMENDATIONS

Mitigating Measures

According to Manske (2000), social engineering attacks succeed because of three aspects, namely that of human weaknesses, a lack of information security awareness amongst employees and the failure to control company information. It, therefore, becomes necessary to address these problems and implement solutions for them in order to defend against social engineering. Kvedar, Nettis and Fulton (2010) stipulate that vulnerability to social engineering attacks arise from poor formal security management and poor education around the phenomenon, however due to the fact that a social engineering attack can be largely unpredictable, there are no definite solutions available.

Thornburgh (2005) describes that there is a myriad of tools and techniques available to solve the challenge of information insecurity, therefore motivating the need for a multi-faceted approach to be taken to secure an organisation against social engineering attacks. Mitnick and Simon (2001) have stated that there is no possible technology that can mitigate the risk of social engineering. The mere fact that social engineering targets the human element, implies that only a human solution can adequately mitigate the risk of a social engineering occurrence (Thompson, 2004). Technical solutions implement technology that provide security and include firewalls and anti-virus programs and even though these solutions may in their own right be effective, these solutions fail to realize that computers do not operate on a solely technical basis (Thompson, 2004). It is important to note that computers require extensive human interaction in order to carry out desired tasks, which has become more important in the fourth industrial revolution. It is this exact human interface that social engineers manipulate to gain access to computer systems and internal resources, thereby effectively illustrating that technical solutions are inadequate to prevent social engineering attacks as they only work by denying or granting access to authorised or unauthorised users respectively (Thompson, 2004). Due to the fact that the insider threat forms 70% of all security breaches (Applegate, 2009), this must be kept in mind whilst designing solutions to mitigate the social engineering risk. Twitchell (2006) states that the most common ways to defend against social engineering attacks include educating, training and making employees aware of the phenomenon and implementing policies supported by audits of its usage. Applegate (2009) concurs that education is the best defence against social engineering. Workman (2008) adds that some of these solutions include conducting risk mitigation and risk analyses. Thompson (2004) further elaborates that staff training and defensive information policies need to be established to give personnel the relevant details needed to prevent the occurrence of social engineering attacks.

Implementation of Information Security Policies and Information Security Management Strategies

Since organisations generally fail in their attempts to make employees aware of the concept of social engineering and how employees can be manipulated, as well as their defence against it, it becomes necessary for effective defensive information policies and an information security management strategy to be put in place to solve this problem (Thompson, 2004; Sun, Yan and Feng, 2012). Defensive information policies serve as a means to inform staff on the limits of assistance and information expected to be provided by them, thereby effectively ruling out the scenario of employees having to rely on their own judgement during a social engineering attack since they could refer to the policy instead (Thompson, 2004). Applegate (2009) recommends that some of the best defence strategies should include security awareness training, identification, as well as subsequent protection of important information, technical controls and security policies from an organisational perspective. Such countermeasures would invariably lead to the construction of a human firewall (Sandouka, Cullen, and Mann, 2009). In the case of BYOD, it is imperative that personal devices are security compliant and have the latest security software updates installed. Simply being aware of information security can greatly help users not fall prey to some obvious social engineering attacks such as phishing, if they took the precautions to double check email addresses and the validity of the fake websites. As a general rule of thumb, employees should take every care to use company-approved devices when transmitting, uploading or downloading sensitive information.

Ongoing Security Awareness Training

In the event that security awareness training is offered by organisations, it is usually only provided when a new employee begins employment at the organisation thus making it an isolated and irregular effort. This in itself causes failure in terms of protecting the organisation from a social engineering attack. The changing and evolving landscape of social engineering threats proves that security awareness training must be an ongoing effort and updated regularly to make provision for defending against new social engineering attack techniques. Knowledge bases and portals pertaining specifically to information security can be implemented in the form of a secure website where employees can go to if they ever required fixes, patches or information about persistent and new threats. Employees should be informed about such resources in order to fully utilise it to its maximum value. Tutorials (either physical or online self-tutorials) provide a convenient way for employees to educate themselves about social engineering and information security threats. This should be constantly updated to keep up with the latest technological trends and advances, especially BYOD policies and protocols. The type of training, either personal training or computer-based training should be dependent on the number of employees at the organisation. Cost is also a factor and thus computer-based training should be opted for if the organisation consists or a large number of employees. The information posted on knowledge bases and portals should be interesting and free of technical jargon to ensure that employees understand the concepts and continually log back into the website to check for updates (Abraham and Chengular-Smith, 2010)

Security Awareness Programs

Thornburgh (2005) identifies security awareness programs to be a vital tool in helping to mitigate against the risk of social engineering and recommends that posters, newsletters, websites, bulletins and awareness days to be implemented to help employees remember security considerations. Online social engineering attacks can be counteracted by simply being aware of misspelt words, badly phrased sentences or illegitimate pages (Kee, 2008). The best countermeasure is to ignore and delete such emails. Installing pop-up blockers and antivirus software can minimise the possibility of online social engineering attacks from occurring however it must be emphasised that the individual still be vigilant as cases can arise when software fails to detect illegitimate web pages (Kee, 2008).

Ongoing Education

Informing and making employees aware about something as basic as no one from the organisation would ask them for confidential and sensitive information such as their passwords would ensure that employees do not fall victim to a social engineering attack (Applegate, 2009). Education must be a constant feature in order for the policy to be effective (Gulati, 2003). There is no point in implementing organisation-wide policies if employees do not familiarise themselves with or abide by it. Organisations should explicitly require their employees to read policies regularly to ensure that they keep up to date with the revisions (Gulati, 2003). Employees should also be tested on their information security knowledge with regard to social engineering in an effort to gauge the success of the training programs. An employee's proficiency in security challenges must be measured and this can manifest in the form of questionnaires, surveys and security tests. Attendance at training programs should be taken and afterwards measured with relation to information security knowledge to deduce the effectiveness of the training programs (Abraham and Chengular-Smith, 2010).

Incidence Response Strategies

Incidence response strategies must be put in place to ensure that should the possibility of a security breach occurs, an employee will know exactly what steps to follow, even if under pressure (Allen, 2006). Sun, Yan and Feng (2012) further concur with establishing a security incident response team to implement strategies and solutions for the protection of information assets and to countermeasure social engineering attacks. Simulation tests and testing an employee's susceptibility to social engineering tests should be conducted by having members of the security team posing as social engineers and trying to elicit information from employees (Sun, Yan and Feng, 2012).

Audit Procedures

Audit procedures must be in place to ensure that policies are being complied with across the organisation and managers should review the access of employees and ensure that those who no longer need access do not have access (Gulati, 2003). This prevents disgruntled employees from sabotaging the organisation with the inside information that they already have to execute a social engineering attack.

Inspections

All too often, passwords are written on post-it notes to facilitate easier recall therefore it should be considered best practice for the organisation to implement a standard stipulating that passwords should never be divulged via telephonic, electronic or physical means (Peltier, 2006). Gulati (2003) suggests that random inspections of workspaces should be conducted to ensure that sensitive and confidential data is securely kept away and not on full display for unauthorised users to view.

Access Control

Protecting important information that ensures the successful and continual operation of the organisation can only be accomplished if that information is first identified (Applegate, 2009). Thereafter, it becomes necessary for a successful information systems architecture to be implemented and for information managers to have a thorough understanding and knowledge of it especially in terms of where that information is stored, as well as the ways in which it is transmitted (Peltier, 2006; Applegate, 2009). Managers must also be given the responsibility of promoting and maintaining a culture conducive towards information security within their respective supervising units and essentially the organisation as a whole (Abraham and Chengular-Smith, 2010). The key to protecting the CIA triad is to control who has access to that information by identifying the requestor of information, verifying the identity of the requestor and ensuring that the requestor has the necessary security clearance in order to view that information (Thornburgh, 2005). Cloud based service providers (such as Yahoo and Gmail) require a user to login with a valid username and matching password, which is susceptible to phishing and needs to be mitigated via identity and access management campaigns on the cloud service provider's behalf (Hatwar and Chavan, 2015). A common example of this is when a user gets locked out of their account and needs to answer personal preselected questions where current answers need to match historical answers previously stored.

Applegate (2009) also shares this view and suggests that access to critical information should be restricted to those who only have the need for it. Security clearance to access information is not an adequate means to protect information assets, therefore it is suggested that a two factor system should be implemented consisting of security clearance and the need to access the information. This will ensure that employees will not abuse their right to accessing information and by minimising access to information by restricting that access to a select few employees, it will be easier to investigate how the social engineering incident transpired and pinpoint the employee who was a victim of a social engineering attack (Applegate, 2009). Kazim and Zhu (2015) suggest that multi-factor authentication must be used with at least double credentials for remote access users. This can act as a deterrent for social engineers to guess the passwords since there can be almost infinite password combinations.

In addition to minimising access to information, minimising or restricting the release of information within the organisation and in the public domain, the type of information released should be overseen by security personnel (Applegate, 2009). This is particularly important since data gathering is utilised in social engineering attacks. Thus, well thought of and well documented policies revolving around the identification, protection and control of important information can greatly mitigate the risk of social engineering attacks occurring in that organisation (Applegate, 2009).

Due to the fact that many organisations do not require visitors to constantly wear a visitors' badge or for employees to wear photographic identification (employee badges instead just have the employee's name), social engineers are able to pose as established employees within the organisation (Peltier, 2006).

Thus, organisations need to rectify this and prevent against the social engineer using physical impersonation to enter the organisation under false pretences, by implementing photographic identification to be positive upon anyone entering the organisation to ensure that only those individuals who are authorised to be in the organisation are the ones who are actually granted access (Peltier, 2006, Jurišin and Ivanicka, 2010). Visitors should not be left to their own devices but should be instead escorted inside the building (Peltier, 2006). Employees should be trained to challenge strangers and employees in the reception area and should have adequate knowledge on how to verify employees (Peltier, 2006). Gulati (2003) suggests that physical technical solutions such as biometric readers should also be implemented to ensure that only the authorised employee gains access into the organisation. Access points thus need to be monitored to ensure that the policy around secured access is adhered to (Gulati, 2003).

Careful Handling of and Shredding of Paperwork

Jurišin and Ivanicka (2010) suggest that employees should immediately pick up printed information that has been printed at a shared printer to prevent sensitive information from falling into the hands of a social engineer. To prevent against dumpster diving, companies should invest in shredders. Papers containing critical information should be shredded to the point that it would not be able to be put together again – many social engineers take up the challenge of piecing together shredded bits of paper similar to how they would piece together a jigsaw puzzle. Should access to a shredder not be available at the time, confidential documents should be locked in a safe cabinet until shredding (Jurišin and Ivanicka, 2010).

Mitigating Phishing Attacks

Vishwanath et al., (2011) states that there are two approaches to protecting oneself from phishing attacks, namely those that emanate from computer science and the others from social science. Computer science solutions suggest the implementation of technological solutions that inherently detect phishing emails and subsequently prevent the email from entering the victim's inbox, or alternatively allow the email to enter the inbox but alert the victim with an advanced warning of the deception (Vishwanath et al., 2011). Thus, it is imperative for the behaviour of such malware during the spreading phase to be studied in order to create warning signs (Abraham and Chengular-Smith, 2010). The after-effects of malware can be significantly assuaged even if it is executed by an individual after circumventing the prevention stage, which means that the malware can be detected and subsequently blocked (Abraham and Chengular-Smith, 2010). However, this again comes back to the argument that technology alone is not adequate to successfully shield oneself from even a predominantly technological social engineering attack technique of phishing. Technological solutions, while having their merits, will ultimately eventually fail as phishers advance their attacks with evolved and matured technology and baiting techniques (Vishwanath et al., 2011). As a precaution, data should always be backed up to prevent complete loss in the event of a phishing attack having wiped out sensitive data. Protection of data is essential in maintaining the integrity and confidentiality of the CIA triad (Kazim and Zhu, 2015). Social science suggests studying the psychology of why the victim or potential victim responds to phishing attacks and then rectifying the mindset of the victim thereafter to prevent further responses to phishing emails from occurring (Vishwanath et al., 2011). Social engineering attack strategies must be identified by the organisation so as to develop and implement countermeasures as defensive techniques, which include the filtering of emails (Abraham and Chengular-Smith, 2010).

Adhering to Information Security Best Practices Outside the Work Environment

Security unawareness is exacerbated by the fact that the lines and boundaries between work life and home life is beginning to blur, as employees are merging the two together (Colwill, 2009). Orgnisations often tend to forget about the fact that their employees possess mobility and often take home incomplete work. Employees must thus be trained to continue following information security best practices in locations beyond the organisation itself. The security of employees' personal and residential computers is a commonly a neglected area within the organisational security domain. Work environments demand anytime, anywhere access to communication thereby forcing employees to access emails from a range of different devices in a range of different locations (Abraham and Chengular-Smith, 2010). Abraham and Chengular-Smith (2010) state that the results of a study conducted concluded that 50% of employees responded to using their personal computers for work-related purposes. Furthermore the study found that employees working from home are less aware of security considerations. Working from home brings in a new dimension to information security best practices and has to account for more factors than just those pertaining to an employee's knowledge of countermeasures to mitigate against the risk of social engineering. It must be kept in mind that a residential computer is usually used by more than one member of the family as employees may share the residential computer with members of the family who are not necessarily trained or aware of security considerations pertaining to social engineering. Additionally, personal computers may not be constantly monitored for malicious software thereby making it vulnerable to be compromised for an extended period of time without detection. Personal and residential computers must thus be installed with regular antivirus software to detect and filter out malicious emails and software. Organisations can help subsidize the cost of maintaining personal and residential computers by offering security tools at a discounted rate to employees. Employees should take it upon themselves to educate members of their family sharing their computer about information security best practices as social engineering poses a risk to any individual, not just employees. Social engineers may even use the vulnerability of family members to gain access to the employee's personal information and subsequently the information of the organisation (Abraham and Chengular-Smith, 2010).

FUTURE RESEARCH DIRECTIONS

Tetri and Vuorinen (2013) explain that what is lacking in terms of the current approach to social engineering is that the literature pertaining to grounded theory and empirical data regarding social engineering is generally limited. Existing literature on social engineering is often not specific and focused as it merely forms a small part of larger articles on general security concerns (Thompson, 2006). Flores et al (2013) state that one of the reasons for the limited research on human factors affecting social engineering revolves around the difficulty for information security researchers to gain access to the behaviour of individuals. In an organisational setting, this can be largely attributed to the reluctance of managers to let their employees participate in such studies measuring behaviour (Flores et al, 2013).

Empirical studies are limited in the field of social engineering due to the ethical considerations revolving around deceiving individuals without their prior consent or without being debriefed (Flores et al, 2013). These ethical considerations surrounding social engineering poses a difficulty in conducting research amongst organisational employees. Human behavior with respect to succumbing to social engineering attacks can be studied by executing the social engineering attacks on employees. This can provide an accurate depiction of an employee's vulnerability or invulnerability to social engineering. It can also yield results depicting the most successful social engineering attacks to which employees succumb. However, the element of deception would more than likely overpower studies and this would not be ethically sound. Social engineering in itself is a sensitive and limited area for researchers as employees or organisations may not be willing to divulge information pertaining to information security breaches caused by social engineering. The lack of available (and recent) research focused specifically on social engineering also poses a strong case for much needed future research to be done in the field. Future empirical studies should be conducted on incidences of a range of social engineering attack vectors in the private and public sectors, as well in small, medium and large organisations. It is also recommended that case study research be conducted on evaluating human factors that contribute to social engineering attacks in organisations, with a view to developing a conceptual model representing the role of non-technical factors in social engineering attacks.

CONCLUSION

The changing nature of social engineering has allowed social engineers to execute a myriad of attack strategies. Although some attack strategies are well known and commonly executed, there is nothing preventing social engineers from devising new attack strategies. Social engineering attacks are merely limited or constrained by the creativity of the social engineer in executing the attack vectors. Nevertheless, a comprehensive review of the various attack techniques was provided, highlighting the ways in which they are carried out by social engineers. The impact of such social engineering attack techniques on the organisation was thereafter provided and it can be deduced that the impacts were largely negative. The security of information systems, as well as the CIA triad remains the most devastating impact of such attacks, along with other secondary impacts that were explained. The impacts highlight the need for countermeasures to be taken to prevent such attacks. The importance of security awareness training and the implementation of policies can provide significant protection against social engineering attacks. However, such programs must be audited in order to ensure that it is regularly used by employees at all levels across the organisation. Employee vigilance and education must be highlighted such that employees can effectively identify social engineering attacks when they are being executed.

An analysis of the emotions and human factors that make employees vulnerable to social engineering attacks was also provided. Demonstrating high levels of fear, greed, sympathy, curiosity, sympathy, empathy, trust and obedience will inevitably lead to an employee being a prime target for a social engineering attack. Social engineers cleverly look for ways to manipulate these characteristics in human beings as such characteristics are universal in the sense that everyone will demonstrate them at some point or another. A human being's interest in and admiration for famous figures also allows social engineers to pose as these figures or to attach malicious codes and executables to stories or images containing these popular icons. An individual's false sense of security / illusion of personal invulnerability will be a source of vulnerability in succumbing to social engineers and social engineering attack techniques. This is due to the fact that these employees are less vigilant and aware of security considerations revolving around the social engineering phenomenon. The tendency to be helpful is exploited due to the fact that social engineers know that victims will experience a feel good factor in being able to offer assistance. Employees working in corporate functions such as sales and marketing, public relations, human resources and the help-desk are particularly susceptible to social engineering attacks due to the fact that they are especially trained to offer assistance to customers or clients in any way possible. The appreciation and gratitude of an employee is exploited as well and this comes across clearly in the attack technique of reverse social engineering where the victim will willingly give information to the social engineer as requested as a sign of appreciation and goodwill for having been "assisted" or "helped" by the social engineer before. Lastly, the laziness and careless of employees lead to social engineering attacks being effectively carried out simply due to negligence or indifference on the part of the employee by not exercising caution when discarding sensitive information or entering in passwords.

REFERENCES

Abraham, S., & Chengalur-Smith, I. (2010). An overview of social engineering malware: Trends, tactics, and implications. *Technology in Society*, *32*(3), 183–196. doi:10.1016/j.techsoc.2010.07.001

Allen, M. (2006). *Social engineering: A means to violate a computer system.* SANS Institute, InfoSec Reading Room. Retrieved from: http://www.sans.org/reading-room/whitepapers/engineering/social-engineering-means-

Applegate, S. D. (2009). Social Engineering: Hacking the Wetware! *Information Security Journal: A Global Perspective, 18*(1), 40-46.

Bezuidenhout, M., Mouton, F., & Venter, H. S. (2010). Social engineering attack detection model: SEADM. In Information Security for South Africa (ISSA), (pp. 1-8). IEEE.

Bullée, J. H., Montoya, L., Pieters, W., Junger, M., & Hartel, P. H. (2015). The persuasion and security awareness experiment: Reducing the success of social engineering attacks. *Journal of Experimental Criminology*, *11*(1), 97–115. doi:10.100711292-014-9222-7

Buller, D. B., & Burgoon, J. K. (1996). Interpersonal deception theory. *Communication Theory*, *6*(3), 203–242. doi:10.1111/j.1468-2885.1996.tb00127.x

Chitrey, A., Singh, D., & Singh, V. (2012). A Comprehensive Study of Social Engineering Based Attacks in India to Develop a Conceptual Model. *International Journal of Information and Network Security*, *1*(2), 45–53.

Chung, M., & Kim, J. (2016). The Internet Information and Technology Research Directions based on the Fourth Industrial Revolution. *Transactions on Internet and Information Systems (Seoul)*, *3*(10), 1311–1320.

Colwill, C. (2009). Human factors in information security: The insider threat–Who can you trust these days? *Information Security Technical Report*, *14*(4), 186–196. doi:10.1016/j.istr.2010.04.004

Dlamini, M. T., Eloff, J. H., & Eloff, M. M. (2009). Information security: The moving target. *Computers & Security*, *28*(3), 189–198. doi:10.1016/j.cose.2008.11.007

Flores, W. R., Holm, H., Svensson, G., & Ericsson, G. (2013). Using Phishing Experiments and Scenario-based Surveys to Understand Security Behaviours in Practice. *Proceedings of the European Information Security Multi-Conference.*

Granger, S. (2001). Social engineering fundamentals, part I: hacker tactics. *Security Focus*. Retrieved from: http://www.symantec.com/connect/articles/social-engineering-fundamentals-part-i-hacker-tactics

Gulati, R. (2003). *The Threat of Social Engineering and your defense against it*. SANS Institute, InfoSec Reading Room. Retrieved from: http://www.sans.org/reading-room/whitepapers/engineering/threat-social-engineering-defense-1232

Hatwar, V.S., & Chavan, H.K. (2015). Cloud Computing Security Aspects, Vulnerabilities and Countermeasures. *International Journal of Computer Applications, 119*(17), 46-53.

Herrmann, M. (2009). Security Strategy: From Soup to Nuts. *Information Security Journal: A Global Perspective, 18*(1), 26-32.

Hinson, G. (2008). Social engineering techniques, risks, and controls. *EDPAC: The EDP Audit, Control, and Security Newsletter, 37*(4-5), 32–46. doi:10.1080/07366980801907540

Janczewski, L. J., & Fu, L. (2010). Social engineering-based attacks: Model and new zealand perspective. *Computer Science and Information Technology (IMCSIT), Proceedings of the 2010 International Multiconference on Computer Science and Information Technology*, 847-853.

Jansson, K. (2011). *A model for cultivating resistance to social engineering attacks* (Doctoral dissertation). Retrieved from: http://dspace.nmmu.ac.za:8080/xmlui/handle/10948/1588

Jurišin, P., & Ivanička, K. (2010). Social engineering as a threat to it security in times of economic crisis. *6th International Scientific Conference, Vilnius, Lithuania. Business and management*, 836-841. 10.3846/bm.2010.111

Kazim, M., & Zhu, S. Y. (2015). A survey on top security threats in cloud computing. *(IJACSA). International Journal of Advanced Computer Science and Applications, 6*(3), 109–113. doi:10.14569/IJACSA.2015.060316

Kee, J. (2008). Social engineering: Manipulating the source. *GCIA Gold Certification*, 1-33. Retrieved from http://www.giac.org/paper/gcia/2968/social-engineering-manipulating-source/115738

Krombholz, K., Hobel, H., Huber, M., & Weippl, E. (2015). Advanced Social Engineering Attacks. SBA Research, Favoritenstrae 16, AT-1040 Vienna, Austria.

Kvedar, D., Nettis, M., & Fulton, S. P. (2010). The use of formal social engineering techniques to identify weaknesses during a computer vulnerability competition. *Journal of Computing Sciences in Colleges, 26*(2), 80–87.

Manske, K. (2000). An introduction to social engineering. *Information Systems Security, 9*(5), 1-7.

Mataracioglu, T., & Ozkan, S. (2011). *User Awareness Measurement through Social Engineering*. Academic Press.

Mitnick, K. D., & Simon, W. L. (2001). *The art of deception: Controlling the human element of security*. Indianapolis: Wiley.

Monk, T., Van Niekerk, J., & von Solms, R. (2009). Concealing the Medicine: Information Security Education through Game Play. ISSA, 467-478.

Nohlberg, M. (2008). *Securing information assets: understanding, measuring and protecting against social engineering attacks* (Doctoral dissertation).

Nyamsuren, E., & Choi, H. J. (2007). Preventing social engineering in ubiquitous environment. Future Generation Communication and Networking, 2, 573-577. doi:10.1109/FGCN.2007.185

Oosterloo, B. (2008). *Managing social engineering risk: making social engineering transparent.* Retrieved from: http://essay.utwente.nl/59233/1/scriptie_B_Oosterloo.pdf

Orgill, G. L., Romney, G. W., Bailey, M. G., & Orgill, P. M. (2004). The urgency for effective user privacy-education to counter social engineering attacks on secure computer systems. *Proceedings of the 5th conference on Information technology education*, 177-181. 10.1145/1029533.1029577

Pavkovic, N., & Perkov, L. (2011). Social Engineering Toolkit—A systematic approach to social engineering. *MIPRO, 2011 Proceedings of the 34th International Convention*, 1485-1489.

Peltier, T.R (2006). Social Engineering: Concepts and Solutions. *Information Systems Security, 15*(5), 13-21.

Petty, R.E., & Cacioppo, J.T. (1986). The elaboration likelihood model of persuasion. In *Communication and persuasion.* Springer.

Pieters, W. (2011). The (Social) Construction of Information Security, *The Information Society. International Journal (Toronto, Ont.), 27*(5), 326–335.

Raman, K. (2008). Ask and You Will receive. *Mcafee Security Journal,* 9-12.

Sandouka, H., Cullen, A. J., & Mann, I. (2009). Social Engineering Detection using Neural Networks. *CyberWorlds, 2009. CW'09. International Conference on CyberWorlds*, 273-278. 10.1109/CW.2009.59

Sun, S., Yan, C., & Feng, J. (2012). Analysis of Influence for Social Engineering in Information Security Grade Test. *Computer Science and Electronics Engineering (ICCSEE), 2012 International Conference on Computer Science and Electronics Engineering*, 2, 282-284. 10.1109/ICCSEE.2012.163

Tetri, P., & Vuorinen, J. (2013). Dissecting social engineering. *Behaviour & Information Technology,* 1–10.

Thompson, S. T. (2006). Helping the hacker? Library information, security, and social engineering. *Information Technology and Libraries, 25*(4), 222–225. doi:10.6017/ital.v25i4.3355

Thompson, S. T. C. (2004). Policies to Protect Information Systems. *Library & Archival Security, 19*(1), 1, 3–14. doi:10.1300/J114v19n01_02

Thornburgh, T. (2004). Social engineering: the dark art. *Proceedings of the 1st annual conference on Information security curriculum development*, 133-135. 10.1145/1059524.1059554

Twitchell, D. P. (2006). Social engineering in information assurance curricula. *Proceedings of the 3rd annual conference on Information security curriculum development*, 191-193. 10.1145/1231047.1231062

Vidalis, S., & Kazmi, Z. (2007). Security through deception. *Information Systems Security, 16*(1), 34–41. doi:10.1080/10658980601051458

Vishwanath, A., Herath, T., Chen, R., Wang, J., & Rao, H. R. (2011). Why do people get phished? Testing individual differences in phishing vulnerability within an integrated, information processing model. *Decision Support Systems, 51*(3), 576–586. doi:10.1016/j.dss.2011.03.002

Workman, M. (2007). Gaining access with social engineering: An empirical study of the threat. *Information Systems Security, 16*(6), 315–331. doi:10.1080/10658980701788165

Workman, M. (2008). Wisecrackers: A theory-grounded investigation of phishing and pretext social engineering threats to information security. *Journal of the American Society for Information Science and Technology, 59*(4), 662–674. doi:10.1002/asi.20779

Workman, M. (2008). A test of interventions for security threats from social engineering. *Information Management & Computer Security, 16*(5), 463–483. doi:10.1108/09685220810920549

KEY TERMS AND DEFINITIONS

CIA Triad: Common term used to refer to the confidentiality, integrity, and availability of information. It is this triad that information security mechanisms must seek to protect.

Human Vulnerability: Inherent human factors that social engineers manipulate and take advantage of when carrying out a social engineering attack.

Information Security: A sub-discipline within information systems and technology that focuses on providing protection to the confidentiality, integrity, and availability of information.

Phishing: A technology-based social engineering attack that relies on appealing to human vulnerability factors via the dissemination of deceptive emails which lead users to clicking on malicious links and/or sharing sensitive information on fraudulent websites.

Social Engineer: A malicious individual seeking unauthorized access to sensitive information to use for personal gain. A social engineer employees technological-based and non-technological-based methods or a combination of both in his attack strategy.

Social Engineering: An attack technique carried out by social engineers seeking unauthorized access to valuable information assets. This technique exploits human vulnerability in the interaction with humans by using deception and manipulation in order to bypass information security policy.

Chapter 2
Safe Distances:
Online and RL Hyper–Personal Relationships as Potential Attack Surfaces

Shalin Hai-Jew
Kansas State University, USA

ABSTRACT

Online human-to-human (and human-to-robot) hyper-personal relationships have evolved over the years, and their prevalence has broadened the available cyberattack surfaces. With the deployment of malicious socialbots on social media in the virtual and AI-informed embodied socialbots in the real, human interests in socializing have become more fraught and risky. Based on the research literature, abductive reasoning from in-world experiences, and analogical analysis to project into the Fourth Industrial Revolution, this work suggests the importance of greater awareness of the risks in interrelating in the virtual and the real and suggests that there are no safe distances.

INTRODUCTION

Only amateurs attack machines; professionals target people. And any solutions will have to target the people problem, not the math problem.
Bruce Schneier (Oct. 15, 2000, in "Semantic Attacks: The Third Wave of Network Attacks" on Schneier on Security blog)

Professional intelligence services hunting for prospective candidates for espionage now have Internet-enabled spotting, developing, and recruiting tools that work just as effectively for professional handlers seeking candidates to manipulate into espionage as they do for retailers seeking to target customers susceptible to advertising.
Dr. Ursula M. Wilder, in "Why Spy Now? The Psychology of Espionage and Leaking in the Digital Age" (2017)

DOI: 10.4018/978-1-5225-4763-1.ch002

It's always about sneaking up on people. It's always about getting there first, right? It's always about blocking the other side. And so, tactics don't change all that much. It's getting the jump on your enemy. It's not letting the enemy in your own ranks, whether it's cyber-wise or having a spy in there…Everybody had to worry about what your enemy was doing and whether they're going to infiltrate you. And that is true today because I don't care how many spy planes you have, how many satellites you have in the sky, how many computers you have running, in "humint" (human intelligence), it only takes one guy with the codes to screw up $20 billion worth of equipment…If you constantly rely on the technology to protect you, and you take your eye off the individual, it's somebody behind a curtain, it's the guy next to you wearing the old-school tie that you thought was so trustworthy, those are the people you have to keep your eye on because that's the Trojan Horse.
Col. (and Dr.) Rose Mary Sheldon, in "Ancient Espionage: The Greeks and the Great Game" (Oct. 20, 2017), when asked how ambush tactics described in her presentation apply to cyberwarfare

To use a technology-based concept, humans interface with the world around them, and they interface with each other. The drive for human connection is so powerful that people are willing to put at risk their sense of self-respect and their resources and their reputations in order to engage. On social media, they "friend" and "follow" socialbots at scale, with a majority not realizing that they are not interacting with humans on the other end but simple artificial intelligence (AI) or cyborg accounts (mixing script and human interactions). This challenge of how humans interact with both each other and with social robots only intensifies with the advent of the Fourth Industrial Revolution. Klaus Schwab, Founder and Executive Chairman of the World Economic Forum, writes:

The First Industrial Revolution used water and steam power to mechanize production. The Second used electric power to create mass production. The Third used electronics and information technology to automate production. Now a Fourth Industrial Revolution is building on the Third, the digital revolution that has been occurring since the middle of the last century. It is characterized by a fusion of technologies that is blurring the lines between the physical, digital, and biological spheres.

The world envisioned in this age involves humans augmented by heightened perceptions (like access to their own and others' thoughts based on electronic signals in their brains), empowered by exoskeletons to achieve speed and power not available otherwise, medical interventions that can prolong life and its enjoyment, and other seductive technologies. The melding of AI-informed human personalities into embodied socialbots is a capability that is already extant, and combined with human nature in its observed forms, the risks to humans are magnified. Before springing forward into the near-future, however, it may be helpful to explore what attempts at cyber-compromise may look like with current technologies. What follows are four non-fictional scenes of relation-based attempts to achieve cyber-compromise. In three of them, the author is the target. In one, a colleague is engaging in her own cyber-compromise and potentially that of her colleagues (including the author).

Real Scenes of Relational Risks

"Relational risks" are generally understood as those that emerge from people interacting with others, in both mediated and non-mediated ways.

Scene 1: Information Oversharing: The email arrives innocuously from an American security researcher. He wants to know about some data in a biosecurity database that he thinks is behind a data visualization that was used for an online training as a digital leave-behind. At first, I am not at all clear what he is asking for. I had not actually even remembered the visualization he mentioned until I had him send it to me. I do a quick Google Search, and there is one photo of him wearing sunglasses. It's all pretty thin stuff indicating a person. Memory refreshed, I let him know that I would not be able to send him anything and forwarded the email chain on to the owner of the project. Such stranger propositions are not altogether uncommon online, and in the real, they're not that uncommon either. People are on the make. This strikes me as a test to see how much I am willing to entertain a stranger's proposition. Would I share data? Would I spill people's names from the project? Or it's just another ask for something for nothing, a "gimme". There may be the idea in private industry that information handled in universities is out there for the taking, given open cultures. This approach is not a one-off. This approach straddles real-space and cyber together: after an international conference, one of the presenters sends an email and asks for university data for a collaborative research project. No-go.

Similar emails that are less complexly designed arrive daily. Many are spoofed emails from the school president and a department head. There are fake email elicitations from would-be employers on head-hunting efforts. There are faked emails from financial companies.

Scene 2: Narrowcasting Credentials and Passwords: I am working late. Most of the spaces in cubicle-land are empty. I walk by a colleague's cubicle, and there are two student employees there. They've logged on to her machine. When I ask them what they're looking at, they assure me that they're logged in with the owner's permission, and they are troubleshooting a work-related issue. They could have accessed what they needed from their own machines with their own credentials. One of the two people at her station is related to one of her family members. What my colleague has put at risk is a number of tech systems that she had access to, including those for which she had admin access. Later, when I asked her about the issue, she said she trusted that the student employees would abide by the contracts that they had signed, and that she wanted to show her trust of them. People do not often think about what they are giving away when they do a rule-bending common-sense-compromising "small favor" for trusted others. And it occurs to me that there are rules against nepotism for a reason.

Scene 3: Informal Threat Modeling and Limiting an Attack Surface: Based on professional curiosity, I had recently published an analysis of the Anonymous hacker collective and reverse-engineered a manifesto based on their actions and statements. Given their reputation for going after any whom they perceived as working against their interests, I thought it would be a good idea not to have much of an online profile in terms of email accounts, and I made sure to close one down (this was smart since the email system was hacked with all accounts compromised a few years later). Then, I made sure to have two-factor authentication on another email account. Since the publication of the work, there have been efforts at spear-phishing—friendly emails about topics of interest with links to click or files to download. There were some faked emails from administrators at my university that were clearly not from them (these show an awareness not only about my work context but the hierarchy). There was an indirect effort to capture my credentials with an individual using my email to open an image-sharing account. I only found out when the social media platform sent out an automated email to my account to ask for a validating click. There have been no direct critiques or expressions of unhappiness from the group. The various attempts at both phishing and spear-phishing may just be par for the course, with the target being the university systems or some other systems that I've touched. If nothing else, this does give the sense of how hard it is for a regular person to try to identify potential attackers…and even tougher, to try to build a sense of one's likely cybersecurity threats. [A more formal term may be "threat modeling," described as follows:

Threat modeling is a process by which potential threats can be identified, enumerated, and prioritized – all from a hypothetical attacker's point of view. The purpose of threat modeling is to provide defenders with a systematic analysis of the probable attacker's profile, the most likely attack vectors, and the assets most desired by an attacker. Threat modeling answers the questions "Where are the high-value assets?" "Where am I most vulnerable to attack?" "What are the most relevant threats?" "Is there an attack vector that might go unnoticed?" ("Threat model," Aug. 28, 2017).]

As with common users of online tools, I have never gone through a formal cyberthreat assessment. While there are more systematic ways to analyze and understand cyberthreats, even if one is not particularly active online and in the world, there are extant threats in the environment.

Scene 4: Let's Collaborate! The suggested game seems to be an exchange dynamic: something-for-something. The sender of the email has recently submitted a professional article to a publication related to a non-profit professional organization. After this has appeared in publication, he asks for a collaborative project with shared bylines. He wants introduction to other professionals in the field. He writes with an abundance of effusive warmth and over-friendliness; he clearly wants to parlay the initial interaction into something that might be money-making. This approach is similar to a number of other interactions—people who are working on non-paying projects who want to somehow monetize their participation. In more extreme cases, there are efforts at something-for-nothing: people trading cheap talk for costly signaling (professions of friendship for actual work, sob stories for access to one's professional contacts, using reputation as entre to others' social-professional circles).

The prior scenes are all factual. While these may read as "thin slicing" narrow windows of experience experienced by one individual, they are informative of some relational truisms (based on abductive reasoning): that people act in what they perceive as their own self-interests, at a minimum. People can do unto others and then split with alacrity. At the far end of malicious cyber activities, the anecdotes from news reports are many: people's lives are ruined for the lulz (the laughter or amusement of an individual or group at other's expense), and there have been high costs in finance, banking, government, corporations, and organizations (from direct losses from theft and fraud, systems recovery, and from direct costs for cybersecurity).

This work is built around the following related hypotheses:

Hypothesis 1: Hypersocial online relationships provide a broad attack surface for cyber compromise.
    Hypothesis 1a: The risks come from how people engage others in hypersocial online relationships.
    Hypothesis 1b: The risks come from the technology ecosystems, with new technological affordances.

Hypothesis 2: Human interactions and relations with AI-empowered socialbots in real-space, in the Fourth Industrial Revolution, stand to repeat the attack surface risks of human relating to other humans, robots, and cyborgs online.

Hypothesis 3: There are some practical ways to defend against some of the vulnerabilities identified in the study of hypersocial online relationships and embodied socialbot relationships in the real.

To generalize, people may have contact with others in any number of technologies: through VOIP (voice over Internet Protocols), social media, a virtual game, email, SMS (short message service), a shopping app, or some other way. They may have initiated the contact themselves, or they may have received the message. They can decide whether or not to begin a relationship or not. Each new interaction is a message to continue the tie. At each point, there is a choice to "go" or to "not go". While relationships apparently (and generally) cost little to maintain online, the costs may be far outsized if there are compromises in the other actors, the online platform, the online application, or any combination of the prior. This work explores the hypersocial human relationships online as a cyberattack surface through an exploration of the research literature and the application of abductive logic. In this work, automated social agents are seen as a risk because of their capabilities in emulating people and eliciting responses from real persons.

REVIEW OF THE LITERATURE

The original understructure that enables cyberspace was not initially conceptualized as "hypersocial" (intensely social, typified by friendly companionship and inter-relations, highly interactive). An "Internet relationship" is described as technology mediated interactions between persons:

An internet relationship is a relationship between people who have met online, and in many cases know each other only via the Internet. Online relationships are similar in many ways to pen pal relationships. This relationship can be romantic, platonic, or even based on business affairs. An internet relationship (or online relationship) is generally sustained for a certain amount of time before being titled a relationship, just as in-person relationships. The major difference here is that an internet relationship is sustained via computer or online service, and the individuals in the relationship may or may not ever meet each other in person. Otherwisde, the term is quite broad and can include relationships based upon text, video, audio, or even virtual character. ("Internet relationship," Sept. 1, 2017)

In the early days of the Web and Internet, the conceptualization of the technology was as a channel for efficient information exchange over various distances. In the early days of the Web, Web 1.0 was about static web pages that were shared for others' consumption. Web 2.0, the Read-Write Web and also the Social Web, focused much more on enriched interactivity between people and enriched collaborations. Web 3.0, the Semantic Web, is conceptualized as a space that both humans and computers trawl for data and services. For all the various iterations so far, the Web and Internet have been inherently social. In the current social age, these technologies enable a hyper-social—in which people are open to sharing a wide range of aspects of their lives, maintaining digital doppelgangers (sometimes multiple ones), taking on all comers, and engaging in the TMI ("too much information") and over-share.

Out-Of-This-World Potential

In the early heady days of the Internet and then the Web built on the Internet structure, there were popular narratives of cyberspace being alternate parallel universes, with massive potentials for identity exploration and new ways of being through digital avatars as extensions of the self. Here, people had magical powers. They could be alternate selves. They could experiment broadly, and what happened in cyberspace stayed in cyberspace, like ephemera. In early days, there was never the sense that what was done was likely permanent and left traces on any number of servers or that actions could be seen by any number of others. In a sense, the masses seemed to have experienced a simultaneous suspension of disbelief. There were ideas that the world's inequalities could be addressed via online connectivity, and the broad sharing of information in egalitarian ways. "Electronic democracy" would reign supreme.

Yet, even in those early days, there were some dark aspects—violent crimes against persons in virtual spaces, myth-making, dishonesty, and massive inequalities to access (Holeton, 1998). To head off misbehavior, people strove to define morality in virtual worlds, asserting that unless all participants sign informed consent and know "the nature of the environment in which they are participating, users have the same de facto duties towards each other when they interact within virtual spaces as they do when writing in print, talking over the telephone, or meeting in person" (Craft, 2007, p. 216). In virtual worlds, people are still moral agents. If only. What was the case that sparked the moral musings? "Members of the Guiding Hand spent a year infiltrating a rival organization before assassinating their leader and stealing in-game assets valued at 16,500 US dollars, effectively shattering the trust within the organization's social network setting its members back months of playing time" (Craft, 2007, p. 205).

If there is any question about the central role of the World Wide Web and Internet in people's lives today, all is required is a perusal of what human needs people go online to meet. For every level of Abraham Maslow's hierarchy of needs, there are online ways to meet those needs (assuming minimal financial means and savvy). Generally, on the Surface Web are licit information and services, and on the Deep Web (or Hidden Web) are dynamically available data, and on the Dark Web are illicit goods and services. These online nexuses may be seen in Figure 1, "Online Ways to Meet People's Hierarchy of Needs" (based on Maslow's 'Hierarchy of Needs')." Halfway up in this hierarchy is "love/belonging" or the achievement of friendships, intimacy, and family.

"Cyberspace" is a term that appeared first in Canadian novelist William Gibson's short story "Burning Chrome" (1982) and then later in his novel "Neuromancer: Cyberspace" (1984). [Norbert Wiener (1948) originated the term "cybernetics" in his description of "the scientific study of control and communication in the animal and the machine."] Cyberspace is a notional or conceptual space where people may intercommunicate and interact over computer networks. It is a space that resides in part in the human imagination, but its effects are wholly real.

Cyberspace is virtual but not imaginary. Like finance, it is a purely artificial domain that largely exists in the abstract and that has no intrinsic value beyond that which we place on it. Unlike finance, it is still very new, and therefore often only barely understood by both the public and policy makers alike. Despite having only a very recent history, cyberspace already plays an increasingly concrete role in everyday life for billions of people. For many of us, life without cyberspace, or its most visible manifestation in the global Internet, is simply difficult to envision anymore. Not only do we as individuals share and communicate information—data—in ways only dimly imagined some decades ago, so do our institutions of daily life: our governments, our businesses, our universities, our centers of research and

Figure 1. Online Ways to Meet People's Hierarchy of Needs (based on Maslow's "Hierarchy of Needs")

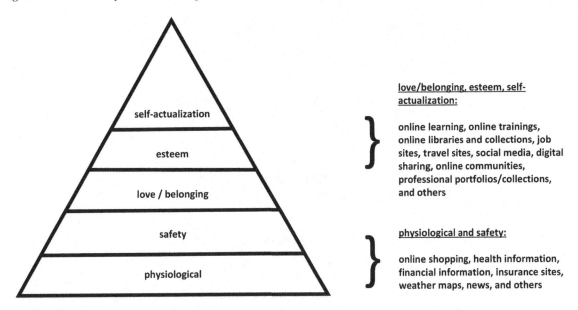

Online Ways to Meet People's Hierarchy of Needs
(based on Maslow's "Hierarchy of Needs")

worship. And not only do these institutions communicate in cyberspace, but our very possessions—from heavy machinery to cars to fridges and even toasters—are increasingly online. They are all wrapped in an ever increasing web that in its complexity and dimensions leaves it only dimly comprehensible. This exchange of data has become so integral to our daily life that some observers have gushed that 'data is the new money.' (Klimburg, 2017, p. 24)

The presence of cyberspace enablements is made even more present with the pervasive and continuous accesses to cyber spaces and applications via smart phones. Through mobile tools, cyberspace takes up a fair amount of people's attention and head space in what James E. Katz and Mark Aarkhus call "perpetual contact" (2002) and Kenneth J. Gergen calls "absent presence" (2002). What is virtual is further reified (or made real or concrete). Another conceptualization of cyberspace is as a four-layered upside-down pyramid (Figure 2). At the lowest level is the physical or hardware layer, then the logic (code) layer, then the data layer, and finally the social layer (people), which is the *raison d'être* for all the lower layers.

How People Relate Online

Said another way, on the social layer, people use computer-mediated communications to relate to each other over the Internet (Whitty & Gavin, 2001). People use computer-mediated communications (CMC) to express something of themselves—some mix of images, text, videos, and audio files—to share their personality and interests. People are the ones who animate a social site, and they are the ones who bring value to others on social media, because of what people inspire and spark in each other.

Figure 2. Cyberspace as an Upside-down Four-layered Pyramid (per Klimburg, 2017, pp. 28 – 29)

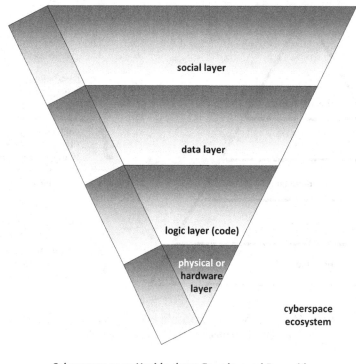

Cyberspace as an Upside-down Four-layered Pyramid
(per Klimburg, 2017, pp. 28 – 29)

According to the Privacy Trust Model, how much information people share of themselves and how willing they are to develop new relationships depend on various factors: their concern over Internet privacy, their trust in the respective social networking platforms, and their trust in the "other members of (the) social networking site" (Dwyer, Hiltz, & Passerini, 2007, p. 3). Trust in technologies is a critical factor in their use (Li, Hess, & Valacich, 2008). In terms of cyber-trust for e-commerce, this is based on both "socio-dynamics" and "tech-dynamics" and their interrelationships (Tsai, Lin, Chiu, & Joe, 2010, p. 1167); this suggests that socio-technical systems designs are critical for successful e-commerce.

How social systems are designed may affect how people interact with those systems and the types of socio-cultural practices engaged in there. In online social networks (OSNs), there are elicitations for plenty of personal information about "interests, hobbies, sexual preferences, religious beliefs and social attitudes" (Ledbetter, Mazer, DeGroot, Meyer, Mao, & Swafford, 2011, as cited in Taddei & Contena, 2013, p. 822). The other is that the "social proof" in others' sharing can encourage those who might be more reluctant. If users feel that their privacy will be protected and that they have "higher control," they are more likely to share more personal information (Taddei & Contena, 2013, p. 822).

How People Connect Online

People connect online around shared interests (Wellman & Gulia, 1997/1999). Online social relationships were initially seen as somewhat less valuable than offline ones and often used as stand-ins for missing offline social relationships (Cummings, Butler, & Kraut, July 2002). The authors write: "Claims regarding the Internet's usefulness for developing social relationships, however, remain controversial" (Cummings, Butler, & Kraut, July 2002, p. 103). One metric for psychological closeness in computer-mediated communications is the frequency of communications (Cummings, Butler, & Kraut, July 2002). They also form stronger social ties based on similarities, such as online friends with geographic closeness in residence and gender similarity (Mesch & Talmud, 2007, p. 455), which is suggestive of homophilous effects. In general, online relationships are thought of as less close than offline ones because of a lower level of joint activities and fewer topics of discussions (Mesch & Talmud, 2006, p. 1).

People also pursue interpersonal relationships online based on anticipated psychological rewards as they do in real spaces (Merkle & Richardson, Apr. 2000). Not only will there be relationships that started in-world that move online, but in networked societies, "mediated intimacies" and redefinitions of friendship are expected to emerge (Chamber 2013). Many adult users of the Internet form relationships with others because of positive and supportive interactions: "A path model revealed positive associations among the number of SNS friends, supportive interactions, affect, perceived social support, sense of community, and life satisfaction" (Oh, Ozkaya, & LaRose, 2014, p. 69). Some relationships start online but are reaffirmed and strengthened through physical in-world meeting (Xie, Sept. 2008); for example, students in large-scale massive open online course or "MOOCs" have gatherings around the world to meet each other and to socialize.

As such, expanded connectivity enable people to benefit from the cohesiveness of "weak ties" (Granovetter, 1973) and access information and resources that their own respective networks might not have access to otherwise. They benefit from "bridging capital" (Putnam, 2000) and opportunities for "latent ties" that would not be possible without mediating technologies (Haythornthwaite, 2005, as cited in Chamber, 2013, p. 15); after all, cyber extends people's reach beyond local physical place. Based on empirical data, researchers suggest salutary effects for high school students engaging in social networking sites to benefit from the connections and social resources of others in the gathering and to support relationship continuance when people move and have to mitigate distances (Ellison, Steinfield, & Lampe, July 2007).

People may form interdependencies in online relationships as well as in the real world. Those with communication apprehension tended to perceive "relational interdependence" in an online relationship, and those who were identified as introverted tended to be less likely to perceive relational interdependent in an online relationship (Mazur, Burns, & Emmers-Sommer, 2000, p. 397). The authors conclude: "…much-studied communication constructs in face-to-face relationships extend to relationships in the online environment" (p. 397).

Some suggest that people's going online to meet real-world needs is an incorrect pursuit. One researcher suggests that people pursuing "instantaneous, 24/7 connection and co-presence" are striving too hard to address an "existential lack" and a "radical sense of inadequacy and incompleteness as human beings" (Loy, 2007, p. 251). This prior author suggests that there are risks to using electronic means to fulfill spiritual needs.

In an early study of online relationships, while traditional values were desirable for relationship building, the online cues of such characteristics were not always present, in part because of limited communications bandwidth:

Sixty Internet users, ranging in age from 19–51 years, were interviewed about their online relationships. It was found that ideals that are important in traditional relationships, such as trust, honesty, and com-

mitment are just as important in online relationships; however, the cues that signify these ideals vary. (Whitty & Gavin, 2001, p. 623)

Based on Social Information Processing Theory, people develop online relationships develop and evolve through the exchange of social information (Sheldon, 2009, p. 2). Online relationships evolve from the impersonal to the personal along defined dimensions: "an increase in interdependence, breadth and depth of the interaction, a shared communicative code change (specialized ways of communicating), an interpersonal predictability and understanding, and a continued relationship into the future" (Parks & Floyd, 1996; Chung, 2003, as cited in Sheldon, 2009, p. 3). Relationships can deepen when there is a reduction in uncertainty through predictability (signaled by socialization, self-disclosure, and other online acts) (Sheldon, 2009, p. 11). A number of research studies have questioned how intimate Internet relationships can actually be, given the lack of nonverbal cues (Whitty, 2002, p. 343) or limited non-verbal cues. Non-verbal cues may be seen as including unintentional tells that may show some insight about the individual and so increase predictability and trust. In physical spaces, people can only hide so much of their "background and personality to produce a new identity, but such identity claims still cannot go beyond the limits set by embodiment" (Zhao, Grasmuck, & Martin, 2008, p. 1817). In other words, it may be much harder to age-bend, gender-bend, social-class-bend, in a physical context. In cyber contexts, though, it is much easier to fake self-attractiveness and likeability, and so encourage others' self-disclosure.

The purpose of this research was to test how social attraction on Facebook influences self-disclosure, predictability, and trust in another individual. Results of a survey of 243 students showed that we tell our personal secrets on Facebook to those that we like. Although many nonverbal cues are absent on Facebook, its users still perceive a high predictability of their Facebook friends' behavior. Facebook users have very little uncertainty about the behavior of the person to whom they intimately self-disclose to. Our findings support Uncertainty Reduction Theory – the more Facebook users talk, the less uncertainty they experience (Axiom 1) and are able to like each other more. The more certain they are about their behavior, the more they trust them, and the more they trust them, the more they disclose to them. (Sheldon, 2009, p. 1)

As technologies have become more complex and detail-rich, there are increased channels for self-expression of one's social presence—including verbal and nonverbal and paralinguistic cues. In other points-of-view, online relationships are more enriched than face-to-face or real-world ones because of "combinations of media attributes, social phenomena, and social-psychological processes" (Walter, 1996, p. 5). The author elaborates:

When is CMC hyperpersonal? When can users create impressions and manage relationships in ways more positively than they might be able to conduct FtF? When users experience commonality and are self-aware, physically separated, and communicating via a limited-cues channel that allows them to selectively self-present and edit; to construct and reciprocate representations of their partners and relations without the interference of environmental reality. Perhaps moreso when this communication is asynchronous and/or when the CMC link is the only link there is. (Walther, 1996, p. 32)

Some research suggests that trust may be less relevant in human relationships that are mediated by online communications means.

These results suggest that in online interaction, trust is not as necessary in the building of new relationships as it is in face to face encounters. They also show that in an online site, the existence of trust and the willingness to share information do not automatically translate into new social interaction. This study demonstrates online relationships can develop in sites where perceived trust and privacy safeguards are weak. (Dwyer, Hiltz, & Passerini, 2007, p. 1)

Research on multiple social networking sites found that "online relationships can develop in sites where perceived trust is low and protection of privacy is minimal" (Dwyer, Hiltz, & Passerini, 2007, p. 7). Online relationships can develop in spite of the lack of trust.

"Attachment relationships" are those built on bonds of affection, which endure over time and space (Ainsworth, Bichar, Waters, & Wall, 1978, as cited in Crittenden, Fall 1990, p. 261); these are ties that enhance people's survival function and so include parents, caregivers, extended family, and friends. "Dyads with an attachment relationship also may have other types of relationship, e.g., sexual, recreational" (Crittenden, Fall 1990, p. 261). There are non-attachment ways of connecting, which are conceptualized as "friendships, professional and business relationships" (Crittenden, Fall 1990, p. 273).

Human connectivity occurs across online system types. For example, early research found the creation of "strong friendships and emotional relationships" in massively multiplayer online role-playing games (MMORPGs) (Cole & Griffiths, 2007). These virtual spaces work as "arenas in which to explore new relationships, new places, and themselves" (Cole & Griffiths, 2007, p. 575), especially given that players can play singly from single computers (p. 576). As a matter of fact, quite a few MMORPG players were comfortable sharing sensitive issues with gaming buddies:

Two fifths of participants (39.3%) said they would discuss sensitive issues with their online gaming friends that they would not discuss with their real life friends. Females were more likely to do so, suggesting that online relationships provide an outlet to safely discuss serious matters that may be difficult to talk about with real life family and friends. One of the advantages of online friendships is anonymity, and while online, some people self-disclose or act out more frequently or intensely than they would in person. The appeal of discussing issues such as sexuality lies in the ease and anonymity with which online seekers can obtain advice and reassurance, particularly regarding sensitive topic.

Because of the age range of players, it is very easy to obtain advice from people who have more life experience. However, Suler25 notes that dissociative anonymity ("you don't know me") and invisibility ("you can't see me") will cause people to self-disclose more than they ordinarily would, which might explain why such a high proportion of players discuss sensitive issues online but not in real life. (Cole & Griffiths, 2007, p. 582)

A little under a third of research participants said that they experienced attraction to another player:

Another interesting finding was that 31.3% of participants had found themselves attracted to another player (26.2% males compared to 42.3% females). The presence of mutual attraction was just under 50%. This finding suggests that MMORPGs offer a safe environment for players to become emotion-

ally involved with others. Overall, 10.1% of players had developed a physical relationship with another player, again indicating that online gaming can be a highly sociable activity. Significant positive effects on relationships were found, especially with those gamers who played with close friends and partners. Two thirds of participants (67.4%) believed that MMORPGs had a positive effect on their relationships with those with whom they play the game. (Cole & Griffiths, 2007, p. 582)

Youth and Online Relationships

There may be generational issues with the uptake of social technologies, with younger generations being more entranced and amenable. In a national survey of adolescent Internet users, a number of online relationship types were identified:

Fourteen percent of the youths interviewed reported close online friendships during the past year, 7% reported face-to-face meetings with online friends, and 2% reported online romances. Two hundred forty-six youths provided details about one close online relationship. Most of these relationships were with same-age peers (70%) and crossed gender lines (71%). Many intersected with face-to-face social networks because they were initiated by introductions from friends or family (32%), involved people who lived in the vicinity (26%), were known to parents (74%), included offline contact by mail or telephone (70%), or involved face-to-face meetings (41%). Few youths reported bad experiences with online friends. (Wolak, Mitchell, & Finkelhor, Fall 2002, p. 441)

Some research involves the study of those who may be vulnerable to relational online exploitation, given that people "self-select" and "opt-in" to online relationships. A particular group of interest involves Western youth:

Girls who had high levels of conflict with parents or were highly troubled were more likely than other girls to have close online relationships, as were boys who had low levels of communication with parents or were highly troubled, compared to other boys. Age, race and aspects of Internet use were also related. We know little about the nature or quality of the close online relationships, but youth with these sorts of problems maybe more vulnerable to online exploitation and to other possible ill effects of online relationships. (Wolak, Mitchell, & Finkelhor, Fall 2003, p. 105)

As the authors clarify, they do not necessarily conclude that "young people with problems are drawn to the Internet"; rather, they suggest that cyberspace attracts youth who may be alienated from their peers and parents in ways that "well-adjusted youth" may not (Wolak, Mitchell, & Finkelhor, Fall 2003, p. 117). While stereotypes might suggest that those who are shy may be disproportionately involved in online relationships, research did not find that association; rather, those with higher levels of "computer confidence" were found to have "greater interpersonal competence initiation behavior" online (Ward & Tracey, 2004, p. 621).

Purposive Online Relationship Building

In the research literature, there are various purposes for the building of online relationships: online counseling (Trepal, Haberstroh, Duffey, & Evans, 2007); online teaching and learning, and others.

These findings presage some of the longer-term types of human bonds. Online sites have become an important part of the dating scene and "marriage markets." Similarly, "cyberaffairs" (or "extra-dyadic relationships") (Underwood & Findlay, 2004) have become a thing and have detrimental effects on of-fline partners and primary in-world relationships. "Cyberaffairs" are defined as follows:

...any romantic or sexual relationship initiated via online communication, predominantly electronic conversations that occur in virtual communities such as chat rooms, interactive games, or newsgroups (Young, 1999a). A Cyberaffair can either be a continuous relationship specific to one online user or a series of random erotic chat room encounters with multiple online users. Virtual adultery can look like Internet addiction as the increasing amounts of time utilizing the computer. Meanwhile, the person is addicted to the can online lover only to display compulsive behavior towards the utilization of the Internet as a means to meet and chat with a newfound love. (Young, Cooper, Griffiths-Shelley, O'Mara, & Buchanan, 2000, p. 59)

"Virtual adultery" has resulted in less time spent with "real people in their lives in exchange for soli-tary time in front of a computer" and resulting disruptions in real-world intimate relationships (Young, Cooper, Griffiths-Shelley, O'Mara, & Buchanan, 2000, p. 59). Online infidelities attract human attention and resources:

Whitty and her colleagues have argued that people construe acts such as cybersex, hotchatting, emotional self-disclosure, and falling in love online as relationship transgressions because partners view this as time and desire being taken away from oneself and given to another love object. Moreover, the very act of keeping one's sexual activities a secret can lead to understandings that online activities ought to be deemed as unfaithful. Of course, one's internet infidelities might initiate online and progress offline. Moreover, there are webpages that have been set up to hook up people looking for an offline affair. (Whitty, 2008, p. 13)

By 2009, "over 30 percent of Internet-enabled couples appear to have met through online dating" (Hogan, Li, & Dutton, Feb. 2011, p. ii).

It goes without saying that once people are in a relationship, they do not stop using the Internet. It is a technology that can be turned to many purposes. However, once people are in a relationship, they do not stop using the Internet for intimacy. Just as there are many shades of accessibility, from a comment on a blog to a full videoconference, there are many shades of intimacy from everyday chatting with an attractive person to cybersex and emotional attachments [Daneback et al., 2007, as cited in Hogan, Li, & Dutton, Feb. 2011, p. 28).

Paul Virilio, in a Q&A with Louise Wilson, suggested that virtuality would "destroy reality" by replac-ing the things of life with technical replacements: "The eye and the hand are replaced by the data glove, the body is replaced by a data suit, sex is replaced by cybersex" (1994, p. 5). Virilio said of cybersex:

Cybersex is similar: it is an accident of sexual reality, perhaps the most extraordinary accident, but still an accident I would be tempted to say; the accident is shifting. It no longer occurs in matter, but in light or in images. A Cyberspace is a light-show. Thus, the accident is in light, not in matter. The creation of a virtual image is a form of accident. This explains why virtual reality is a cosmic accident. It's the accident of the real." (as cited in Wilson, 1994, p. 3)

In the same way that people meet their intimate social relationship needs online, there is also engagement in "unfaithful Internet relationships." Research in these relationships found that "equal weighting (was) given to emotional and sexual betrayal" in Internet infidelity:

Unlike previous studies on offline infidelity (e.g., Shackelford & Buss, 1996) and in contrast to Whitty's (2003b) study on Internet infidelity, the participants in the current study did not consider sexual infidelity as having a more serious impact than emotional infidelity. Such a result suggests that cyberaffairs could create problems for an offline relationship for very different reasons than an offline affair might. This result has some important therapeutic implications and warrants more attention in future studies. (Whitty, 2005, p. 66)

Indeed, cyberaffairs not only arise from sites dedicated to find others who want to engage in stated affairs (such as Ashley Madison) but non-dedicated sites that are for other interests: gaming, socializing, and others. In the same way, people wittingly and unwittingly start relationships that proceed in directions of their own choosing or those of others'.

Researchers have worked on computational means to understand the "strength" of social ties on social media. One model, the "How strong?" one, is built on seven dimensions of tie strength: *Intensity, Intimacy, Duration, Reciprocal Services, Structural, Emotional Support* and *Social Distance"* (Gilbert & Karahalios, 2009, p. 3). Important predictors of closeness of relations on social media were as follows, in descending order: intimacy, intensity, duration, social distance, services, emotional support, and structural (Gilbert & Karahalios, 2009, p. 6).

Getting to know you better. Another cultural thread in online culture involves the elicitation from citizens of their surveillance capability to report to law enforcement authorities ("see something, say something"). Here, citizens are informally deputized to support law enforcement given their broad presence. This "lateral surveillance" spills over into online spaces, with self-appointed cyber sleuths working to solve crimes and prevent terrorism (Rossmiller, Apr. 21, 2011). Joshua Reeves (2017) suggests that there are risks in crowdsourcing policework and pushing liberal democracies that harness such citizen spying towards becoming more of a surveillance society, with citizens reporting intrusively on each other and resulting in more abuses of power, such as racial and ethnic stereotyping (p. 136). This author advocates resistance:

Rather, the silence we might seek is an affirmative quietude—in the words of Nick Dyer-Witheford and Greig de Peuter, 'a defection that is not just negative but a project of reconstruction'—that deprives liberal police power of its means of sustenance. If we are commanded to call the cops on our neighbors and family members, to send anonymous text messages that snitch on our fellow students, to scour our gated communities with little two-way radios, to rat out our parents for smoking pot, or to report every suspicious activity in sight, perhaps shutting up is the most radical and socially responsible course of action available to us. (Reeves, 2017, pp. 171 – 172)

Another option is to be more prosocial and selective in reportage to support the community vs. the state, by acting on behalf of people vs. government. Regardless of people's choices, there are individuals who go online to inter-relate, and in so doing, surveil others and to use information for various ends.

With hyperpersonal relationships coming to the fore on the Web and Internet, people who choose to engage need to understand their environment and how certain aspects of their thinking or behaviors or choices can raise their risk of being exploited by malicious actors. When people leak information or expose information networks or social networks, the losses are often irreversible, and the online environment can be unforgiving. While there is not in a practical sense "a safe distance," how people engage can increase their sense of safety online.

ON THE MAKE

Hypothesis 1 suggests that hypersocial online relationships provide a broad attack surface for cyber compromise, with risks coming from how people engage in hypersocial online relationships (1a) and from the technology ecosystems and new technological affordances (1b). Hypothesis 2 suggests that with the deployment of AI-powered embodied socialbots in real space, as part of the Fourth Industrial Revolution, humans will be vulnerable to this attack surface, too, in the same way they are vulnerable to other humans, robots, and cyborgs online. Hypothesis 3 proposes that there are some practical ways to defend against some of the vulnerabilities identified in the study of hypersocial online relationships and those with embodied socialbots in the real.

To explore these, it will help first to understand how online relationships may begin and unfold. While these hypotheses read as discrete elements, socio-technical spaces are better understood as ones where the human and technology factors are integrated. In that spirit, these hypotheses are investigated in an integrated way.

It may be helpful to map the trajectories of online relationships. It is likely in an initial interaction with another social entity (person, automated agent, or cyborg) or entities online that that person has limited information. There may be a reputation, shaped by the individual or others around the individual, and this reputation may be credible / non-credible. There may be an initial spark of emotional intensity, based on charisma and the phenomenon of "swift trust." Then, there are the initial shared experiences. By definition, initial contacts mean that the shared experiences are often minimal. These three factors, which may in turns be attractive or aversive or neutral (positive, negative, or neutral; +, -, or +/-), may be conceptualized as part of a trilemma—with usually one or two of the elements available, but not all three (Figure 3). A common combination may be an interaction with another based on their reputation and a light shared experience or two…but without any spark of emotional intensity. Or there may be a sense of emotional spark and a light shared experience but no knowledge of the other's reputation. Another way to think of the trilemma may be of each element as being attractive (drawing people closer), aversive (pushing people apart), or neutral (not moving people any closer or pushing them farther). An example may be that a person has a positive reputation, but an emotional intensity that is off-putting, and a shared experience that is neutral (in which case the directionality of the follow-on potential reputation may be in doubt). At the center of this conceptualized trilemma is an anticipated sense of the "future" of the relationship, future not with a capital "F", but the near-future, the mid-future, and the far long-term futures. All relationships require investments and effort to maintain, and they are not costless. Given this, do the individual respective parties in a potential relationship have a sense that there is a beneficial

Figure 3. Go or No Go? Cyber Relationship Trilemma

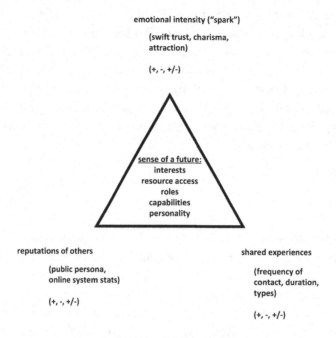

Go or No Go? Cyber Relationship Trilemma

future that they can work towards? If so, they will proceed with the communications and supporting actions. If not, they will devolve the initial contact back into mutual silences or make a clear hard break. Initial go/no-go decisions about online relations then are informed by little. How people make initial decisions to "go" or "no-go" in their online relationships depends on a variety of factors. The trilemma is different for every actor in a potential relationship.

After initial decisions, which tend to be low-cost, the participants decide whether or not to continue over time. While there may have been a high sense of potential and possibility initially, reality may set it and result in a gradual letting go. In the same way as not all in-world relationships are sustainable, so, too, with online relationships—even though these latter ones may be easier to maintain than in-world ones. This may be seen in Figure 04, the "Cyber-Relationship Continuance / Non-continuance Time-line." This visual suggests that commitments may be easy to break in online relationships. With inertia, a relationship may be broken just by stopping communications or not showing up in an online space. Some period of time of interaction may be needed to achieve hypersociality, but time alone is not sufficient to lead to relational depth.

In Figure 5, this decision tree shows a possibility of relationships going dormant but being picked up again by people. This gives the sense of relating as being part of a long-term engagement and a phenomenon pervasive and continuous in the environment.

Figures 4 and 5 may give a misleading sense of pre-set and deterministic path dependencies. Human connection building is often incremental. Relationships are original and unique in their own ways based on the individuals involved, and chemistries may be elusive. The ensuing relationships may vary in pacing, intensity, quality, tone, and exchanges, among other dimensions.

Figure 4. Cyber-Relationship Continuance / Non-continuance Timeline

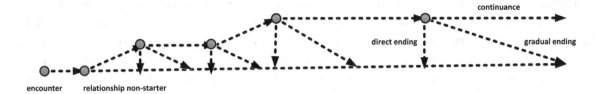

Cyber- Relationship Continuance / Non-continuance Timeline

Figure 5. A Go / No-Go Decision Tree for Online Connectivity and Relating over Time

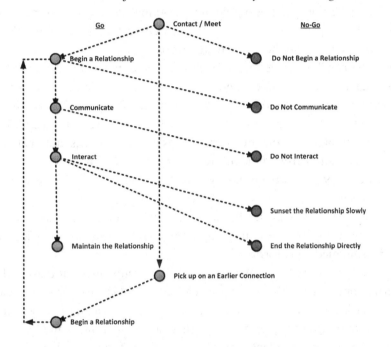

A Go / No-Go Decision Tree for Online Connectivity and Relating over Time

The same technologies that enable people to interact and relate with their respective persistent identities also enable, simultaneously, some potentially devastating long cons.

Virtual Affordances for Long Cons

Affordances of the online spaces for long cons, the ability to play long-term confidence ("con") games. If a con consists of six discrete steps, per Edward H. Smith's *Confessions of a Confidence Man: A Handbook for Suckers* (1923), then it may be helpful to conceptualize how online affordances may be brought to play in each step: foundation work, approach, build-up, pay-off or convincer, the hurrah, and the in-and-in. In the classic sense, a mark is identified, and something that he or she wants is offered by the con artist. The mark is rewarded with a small payoff "as a demonstration of the scheme's effectiveness". The "hurrah" refers to a "sudden crisis or change of events" that force the victim to act precipitously. The "in-and-in" refers to a co-conspirator in the con who affirms the (false) legitimacy of the endeavor, and in a successful con, the mark is taken for something of value ("Confidence_trick," Sept. 13, 2017). In online spaces, one type of cyber-based long con involves a faux love interest who makes a connection with a vulnerable lonely heart. The love interest experiences a setback and needs funds. Or the online love interest needs money to come to the mark. The money is exchanged, and the individual disappears…or has another excuse for needing money. In some cases, older people have lost life savings to such cons.

Online spaces provide technologies that support the short and long cons at each phase. For "foundation work," people may easily build backstories and identities. They can build legends and histories for their online characters ("sock puppets" or false identities online) by creating faux accounts on social media platforms. They can create profiles on social networking sites. They can create stories that others can find. They can build out personas as parts of the faux character's social networks. They can create photo albums for this character, and they can create videos.

In terms of an "approach," there are many social media spaces where people gather around shared interests. There are digital "watering holes" and hangouts where people in particular fields congregate. There are many opportunities to meet others for the bump (the designed first meeting). If a direct approach is not desired, it is easy enough to wrangle an introduction or to employ a middle-person to do the introduction. Apparent humans on social media platforms may be humans, automated scripts, or social cyborgs. People may maintain real-world identities that have nothing to do with their virtual identities (or avatars). Information may appear out of nowhere and be propagated artificially or naturally—and at viral spread and viral speeds.

The "build-up," "pay-off or convincer," the "hurrah," and the "in- and-in" are also fairly easily facilitated through online means. After all, digital impression management is not difficult to manage given the lax oversight of social media platforms.

Compromised social media accounts may be used for "man/woman-in-the-middle" attacks, with strangers taking on the appearances of known individuals, to compromise information and / or cause harm.

While there are some Deep Web sites that check people's identities against known backgrounds, many people with real identities may not pay attention to others using their own names. There are enough generic names that a swiped real-world identity may be taken for nefarious or abusive or confidence-game purposes. Nonymous (named) spaces enable the uses of self-assigned names, and they enable the uses of fake names; often, the highest level of verification is to a created email. On major social media platforms are a number of faked accounts. In 2012, a search found that 83 million Facebook social networking accounts were "fakes and dupes" (Kelly, Aug. 3, 2012). On the Twitter microblogging site, in 2017, some 48 million Twitter accounts were identified as not people (Newberg, Mar. 10, 2017). Artificial intelligence (AI) social robots (socialbots) are in virtual worlds and can maintain very credible oral and text conversations simultaneously, per the experiences of this chapter's author over eight years (2010 – 2017). People often cannot differentiate a scripted robot from actual other-humans, and their acting in response to 'bots puts themselves and their workplaces at risk (Shafahi, Kempers, & Afsarmanesh, 2016). On dating sites, users were consistently fooled by AI sexbots (Kushner, Feb. 1, 2016). Chatbots have come a long ways in the decades since they were first deployed, and artificial intelligence (AI) enhancements have made them credible beings as socialbots, particularly on social platforms that are limited in dimensionality (just-text interactions, for example). Many deployed AI bots have their own personalities based on psychology-research, and they can improvise with online news and imagery to carry on online conversations.

To contrast the affordances of such 'bots with people in the real, imagine how much effort it would take to materialize a person in role in real space to meet a human person. The harnessing of socialbots to collect information from people enables mass elicitations at a much lower cost-per-human response, and the data is already in digital format, which means heightened ease of analysis and exploitation. Robots can be set loose with strategic and tactical patience over long periods of time. From the perspective of those who deploy socialbots, if their cover is about to be blown, humans can step in as cyborgs in the social account and work on credible bona fides.

Seductive Technologies

The computer-mediated communications technologies themselves may affect how people approach online relationships. There is a solid body of literature about the online disinhibition effect, or the lowering of inhibitions when people are online, resulting in outside-norm self-disclosure, increased acting out (by frequency and / or intensity), and other behaviors. This disinhibition effect is based on six factors that interact with the individual's personality; they are: "dissociative anonymity, invisibility, asynchronicity, solipsistic introjection, dissociative imagination, and minimization of authority" (Suler, 2004, p. 321). When people are online, they feel anonymous and invisible. The asynchronicity of many of the interactions enable people to express themselves without an immediate response from others. The "solipsistic introjection" stems from the lack of face-to-face cues, which enables people to "feel that their mind has merged with the mind of the online companion. Reading another person's message might be experienced as a voice within one's head, as if that person's psychological presence and influence have been assimilated or introjected into one's psyche" (Suler, 2004, p. 323). The "dissociative imagination" refers to a mental splitting of "online fiction from offline fact" (Suler, 2004, p. 323). [This is a version of what happens in the virtual stays in the virtual, and vice versa, instead of realizing the effects of the "cyber-physical confluence." Cyber and physical influences mutually affect the other, and virtual effects manifest in real life (IRL).] Suler notes that online disinhibition can become toxic, manifesting as "rude language, harsh criticisms, anger, hatred, even threats. Or people visit the dark underworld of the Internet—places of pornography, crime, and violence—territory they would never explore in the real world" (Suler, 2004, p. 321).

In online spaces, many of the interactions—in virtual worlds, in immersive games—cater to the human imagination in play-acted roles. The in-world rules apply, not real-world street smarts. The distractions are many and multi-sensory-based. [Distractions lead to "vigilance decrement" (Casner, 2017, p. 27).] The feeling is that people may be risking their virtual selves, but that they have an infinite amount of do-overs, and somehow, what happens in the virtual is supposed to stay in the virtual. People are "captured" by the virtual. There are other examples of such capture. For example, people who are taking selfie images and videos have been so engaged in the pose that they have fallen off cliffs, buildings, rooftops, and ledges.

Faux Online Social Identities

Even those who are supposed to be trained to be paranoid and hyper-cautious can fall for illusory online "individuals." A cybersecurity researcher created Robin Sage, "a cyber femme fatale," in December 2009

Figure 6. A Human-Embodied Avatar in the Second Life Virtual World

and used this persona for a short two months to see what sort of response she would receive (Ryan, Oct. 9, 2011). Thomas Ryan, a cybersecurity researcher, achieved a lot of responses:

Almost all of them were working for the United States military, government or companies (amongst the only organizations that did not befriend Sage were the CIA and the FBI). Using these contacts, Ryan gained access to email addresses and bank accounts as well as learning the location of secret military units based on soldiers' Facebook photos and connections between different people and organizations. She was also given private documents for review and was offered to speak at several conferences. ("Robin Sage," Dec. 16, 2016)

What may seem like innocuous details can be information-bearing and used for compromise and harm. Also, the perceived attractiveness of the individual can be motivators for people to share (based on sexual competition and ego). This approach is not an unusual one in today's Web where it is much easier to create personas (even those built off of real people's information) and to backstop these personas with planted information in various findable social sites. Created identities have been cobbled off of others' images and biographical details. When identities are unconfirmed and so faceted and so selective, people consuming that information may have limited information on which to proceed and respond. Also, as people unwittingly interact with a created identity, they are unintentionally affirming the faux identity by being part of the social network.

The Parasocial and Immersive Parasocial

Another challenge with people is that they do not have to be in an actual relationship to feel like they are in one. Back in 1956, Donald Horton and R. Richard Wohl described how the then-new mass media ("radio, television, and the movies") could give viewers "the illusion of face-to-face relationship with the performer" (Horton & Wohl, 1956, p. 215); they called this "para-social relationship" a "bond of intimacy" (p. 217). They wrote:

Para-social relations may be governed by little or no sense of obligation, effort, or responsibility on the part of the spectator. He is free to withdraw at any moment. If he remains involved, these para-social relations provide a framework within which much may be added by fantasy. But these are differences of degree, not of kind, from what may be termed the ortho-social. The crucial difference in experience obviously lies in the lack of effective reciprocity, and this the audience cannot normally conceal from itself. To be sure, the audience is free to choose among the relationships offered, but it cannot create new ones. The interaction, characteristically, is one-sided, nondialectical, controlled by the performer, and not susceptible of mutual development. There are, of course, ways in which the spectators can make their feelings known to the performers and the technicians who design the programmes, but these lie outside the para-social interaction itself. Whoever finds the experience unsatisfying has only the option to withdraw. (Horton & Wohl, 1956, p. 215)

Updated to the present, persistent virtual immersive social spaces convey an even stronger sense of connection through the "immersive parasocial" given the multi-sensory cue-rich virtual environments (Hai-Jew, 2009). Parasocial relationships explain why "lurkers" interact passively in online communities (Ballantine & Martin, 2005, p. 197) because they are reacting emotionally to public figures as if they have a personal relationship after repeated exposures (Ballantine & Martin, 2005, p. 198).

Benign / Malign Human Agents

On social media platforms, people meet people of all kinds and engage in various types of relationships. In all relationships, there is a degree of unknowability about others, and people and the relationships themselves change over time, sometimes in highly unexpected and unpredictable ways. Shared interests may diverge over time.

Individuals who practice social engineering have a variety of ways to elicit information from people. They may use "mirror imaging" to gain another's trust (subconsciously or even unconsciously). They may use typical social norms of politeness to elicit information. They may offer favors in order to create a situation of social reciprocity. There are the direct elicitations (like the asking of questions) and then the indirect ones, such as the creation of silences and gaps, that may encourage others to fill the silence with information. These are generic approaches tailored to understandings of human nature. Of late, the understandings of human cognitive limits and behavioral science have also become part of cybersecurity or defense approaches (Pfleeger & Caputo, 2012). For example, human curiosity is a cyberrisk (Klimburg, 2017, p. 63) because it can lead to explorations of dangerous sites and software. The human factor is also an issue in con games, which "exploit characteristics of the human psyche, such as credulity, naïveté, compassion, vanity, irresponsibility, and greed" ("Confidence_trick," Sept. 13, 2017).

There are ways to "spear" target using even more sophisticated social engineering techniques. As a part of cyberattacker reconnaissance, the human target has usually been studied and remotely profiled as to their personality and interests and their life patterns (life schedules and habits). There is a saying that if one understands another's "religion" (worldview), one can manipulate them. What this means practically is that the more one reveals about one's thinking and feeling, one's social networks, one's values, and one's habits, the greater the attack surface one has created for others to potentially exploit. Each data point shows something about one's "religion" (meant in a secular sense). In personal information are the potential seeds to one's seduction and compromise. In one common analogy in cybersecurity, hacking is compared to lock-picking, with pin tumbler locks visualized; understanding another human being provides the proper settings of the pin tumblers to enable compromising the lock.

Higher up on the malicious spectrum are those who take on others' identities and actively deceive in order to capture personal data, personally identifiable information (PII), credentials including passwords, or other types of potentially compromising information, ultimately for more nefarious aims. Why human interrelationships are a special point of concern is that people tend to suspend critical judgment for those who are close to them. They are more suggestible towards those in their social network, particularly those with direct ties to them. Because of confirmation bias, people tend to "search for, interpret, focus on and remember information in a way that confirms one's preconceptions" ("List of cognitive biases," Oct. 2, 2017). Sharing information about one's tendencies may increase vulnerabilities, particularly with bad actors.

Intensifications of Online Relationships

Immersions in social spaces revealed a number of ways that online relationships may intensify. Some examples of observed progressions follow:

- On a website for informal commerce and adult interchanges, people may use email validated accounts to make proffers. To purchase anything, they merely have to contact the seller with a site-generated anonymized email. If there is interest, the seller may choose to reveal his / her private email. The two then exchange other contact information, their names, their locations, and maybe ultimately, personal checks or cash or cashiers' checks or whatever is being exchanged. The exchange relationship may be a one-off, or it may be a continuing one.
- On a social news site, people engage around a particular issue of interest. Some communicators hit it off. They decide to go "offline" from the site to talk. They may share their social networking circles. They may decide to meet in person.
- A number of people have downloaded a gaming app. The app enables an in-world game in the physical real, and people meet and socialize from there.
- A massive open online course (MOOC) is offered, and interested parties go online to study. They are randomly assigned to study groups. The professor travels the world, and he holds meetups in various coffee shops around the world. He announces those meetings about a week before the meeting, and he videotapes all participates who show up to share in the sense of broader sociality with those who cannot or do not physically attend.
- People meet online in any number of venues, and they intensify by becoming Facebook friends, and they share much more about themselves and their interests and their social circle (family, friends, and acquaintances).

- People microblog, and they start to find others with similar interests. Others who seem like-minded and / or are in physical proximity raise interest, and they connect via the microblogging platform. Later, they exchange emails. They share personally identifiable information (PII), and they are invited to each other's social networking circles.
- A work-based relationship starts with a query email, which escalates to a VOIP session. The discussions over work-related issues continues, and then, there are webinars during which the professional relationship is built. Finally, there meetups with company representatives who are in the area for conferences or demonstrations.
- Some relationships start in the physical and move to the cyber and the social media spaces.

How people interact with a humanoid socialbot imbued with human characteristics is not quite defined yet, but there are advancements in this field, and the uses of robots already as sexbots ("always ready to talk and play" according to one online ad). Fundamental assumptions of human love have and will continue to evolve with the phenomenon of "love and sex" with robots, particularly given personality matching with the human and other attractions (Cheok, Levy, & Karunanayaka, 2016). The authors describe "the formulation of love" with one such product:

The robot's intimacy software employs parameters derived and quantified from five of the most important reasons for falling in love [1]: proximity, repeated exposure, attachment, similarity and attraction. Intimacy in the robot is thereby related to those same factors that cause humans to fall in love. The robot utilizes audio and haptic channels in order to provide these different types of input which communicate the user's emotional state to the robot [8]. The audio channel carries data for five audio parameters that characterize emotional cues within a human voice. The haptic channel carries data relating to the user touching the robot – the area of contact between robot and human and the force of that touch. (Cheok, Levy, & Karunanayaka, 2016, p. 308)

If "pillow talk" (revealing private information after physical and emotional intimacies) is a risk with humans, it is particularly an issue with robots that can capture the information verbatim and elicit more. The potentials of *folie à deux* and *folie à trois* simply magnifies with the introduction of alluring AI, whether embodied or not. Resistance will require people to resist when all their senses tell them an experience is real; it will require people to resist when their survival instinct and training tell them something invisible (such as the self-interest or malice of agents) may be actually real. (In *Inception*, the spinning top served as the totem for a test of whether the human consciousness was in a dream world or in reality, and that analogy can apply here. The idea is that the seductive dream world cannot be so appealing that people do not care to be disillusioned and set straight.)

Discussion

To review, the hypotheses were as follows:

Hypothesis 1: Hypersocial online relationships provide a broad attack surface for cyber compromise.
    Hypothesis 1a: The risks come from how people engage others in hypersocial online relationships.
    Hypothesis 1b: The risks come from the technology ecosystems, with new technological affordances.

Hypothesis 2: Human interactions and relations with AI-empowered socialbots in real-space, in the Fourth Industrial Revolution, stand to repeat the attack surface risks of human relating to other humans, robots, and cyborgs online.

Hypothesis 3: There are some practical ways to defend against some of the vulnerabilities identified in the study of hypersocial online relationships and embodied socialbot relationships in the real.

Hypotheses 1, 1a, 1b, and 2 were borne out through the literature review, the abductive observations, and analogical reasoning. Hypothesis 3, the idea that these risks may be somewhat mitigated, also is supported. An explication of Hypothesis 3-based findings follows.

For the various attack vectors described above, each are strengthened if people approach others' communications with truth as a default assumption, which has some empirical support (Levine, 2014, p. 378). While there has been much prior research pointing to the human truth bias in assuming that others are "basically honest," Levine proposes that this presumption of honesty is adaptive for people themselves and the species (Levine, 2014, p. 378). This contribution to the deception and deception detection literature stands out because there are many findings that show that people are highly adept at deception (purposefully misleading others) as well as self-deception (unconsciously, subconsciously or consciously misleading oneself), and pretty poor at detecting others' deceptions at anywhere better than chance (50-50) in real time.

How to Be Vulnerable Not

Hypothesis 3 addresses ways that people may be strengthened against cyber compromise in hypersocial online relationships. To advance this, it helps to see how people become vulnerable in such relationships and how they can make themselves hardened targets. So what are some of the ways that people who engage in hypersocial relationships on cyber take on undue risks?

"Socio-Technical Technologies Are Transparent and Secure"

For many users of social platforms, there is a sense that people's general trust has been misplaced and that people themselves (their attention, their purchasing power, their social networks, and other aspects) have been the product being packaged and sold; worse yet, the consumers and citizens using such systems have to advocate on their own behalf because for many companies, their interests do not necessarily align with those of their users. Initial high minded rhetoric by tech company founders and leaders have not necessarily been borne out. One work described the benefit of the doubt offered by early users:

Almost from its inception, the World Wide Web produced public anxiety — your computer was joined to a network that was beyond your ken and could send worms, viruses and trackers your way — but we nonetheless were inclined to give these earnest innovators the benefit of the doubt. They were on our side in making the web safe and useful, and thus it became easy to interpret each misstep as an unfortunate accident on the path to digital utopia rather than as subterfuge meant to ensure world domination. (Cohen, Oct. 13, 2017).

In intervening years, with social media harnessed for foreign propaganda meant to hijack the U.S. electorate in the 2016 U.S. presidential election (Perlroth, Wines, & Rosenberg, Sept. 1, 2017), big data encroachments on people's privacy ("With Big Data Comes Big Responsibility," Nov. 2014), and a sense of corporate uncaring, public sentiment is starting to shift. Overtrust in technology systems may lead to oversharing and mis-use of such systems. For example, users do not set the parameters for their accounts to the correct level of private, semi-public, or public. They fail to account for the fact that most social media platforms have security vulnerabilities. They do not set their own account settings with the right levels of security to ensure against being compromised. They may or may not read the end user license agreements (EULAs), and they may not stay up-to-date with the changes in privacy and other policies on the social media platforms and socio-technical spaces. They may not understand how online spaces are designed to encourage addictive usage, and they may be sensitive to the design of the space to spill information that is not in their best interests. They may also not understand how data are collected and analyzed from the sites that they use. The types of analytics that can be applied to such data are many—and people may not realize what is discoverable in what they share. (Think social network analysis, sentiment analysis, time-to-event analysis, computational linguistic analysis, and other means.)

Anything that hackers can access—whether they are sensitive private images, copyrighted and published books—has been usurped and monetized in a broadscale way online. Stolen and leaked information is irreversibly and permanently gone and not able to be recouped, and there are no takebacks. Many openly share information that is "dual use" and can be abused for others' gain. People also often leak information without being aware of what they actually shared because all people have cognitive limits and varying degrees of self-control (or the lack thereof), which can lead to compromise. Until security improves, and this is not likely in the near-term because of people's uses of technology, uploading information is tantamount to leakage.

So while they may be having intense personal relationships with significant others, the materials are online for third-party compromise (and / or usage by the host of the online service). In other words, the moment a sexting image is shared…or secrets…or unique ID numbers…the information is out there in the cyber world for the exploitation. The local taboos do not apply, and the local protections are not assumed. What is shared for one limited purpose may be used for any number of others' purposes once systems are compromised. If one cannot reasonably exclude the possibility of data misuse, it should not be shared via unsecured or minimally secured systems.

Another technology challenge is that people may not be aware when they are dealing with automated robots or cyborgs. They may be interacting with automated entities, without any human being on the other side. Those who are aware never take an email at face value, and they will use the phone to validate a person's message because voices are much harder to fake. And even harder is the response of the individual in a live setting.

Some cautions may be expensive to undertake. For example, for those traveling to risky sites, they may do better with dedicated machines and have dedicated social accounts (unconnected to their daily ones) to explore. Such efforts are not low-cost, and the effort itself may be expensive.

And finally, it may be difficult to find out if one has been compromised unless the compromise is highly publicized or flagrant changes are made to a person's account.

"What Happens in Cyber Stays in Cyber"

As noted, many early uses of cyberspace used a magical thinking approach, with the idea that cyberspace provided access to an alternate universe with little spillover into the real. There was messaging of no consequences explorations, to wit that what is cyber stays in cyber. However, in the intervening years, it has become very clear that there are spillovers from the virtual to the real and vice versa, a large cyber-physical confluence. Some counter messaging in the real include the spillage of data from sensitive National Security Agency (NSA) databases, extra-marital dating sites, and other so-called hyper-private cyber spaces.

While the Web and Internet have now been around for decades, there are still "noobs" ["a person who is inexperienced in a particular sphere or activity, especially computing or the use of the Internet" (Google Dictionary)] coming online with each new generation, and newbies may be experiencing many of the same overwhelming feelings of excitement as earlier users. Even for long-term users of cyber, the being "carried away" hasn't gone away. People can still be (and are) dazzled by marquee names, celebrity culture, and "stardom"; new technologies and new apps; interactive games; new social media platforms, and new media releases. Each of these enthusiasms can mask risks. Those who are "captured" by their enamorment of cyber capabilities may be more vulnerable to cyberattacks than those who are informed and vigilant.

Cyber itself may seem somewhat lightweight and low-demand from a distance, but the relationships there still require real time, real mental focus, real emotions, real effort, and very real opportunity costs. There are real reputational risks as well.

"People Are Essentially Good and Generally Stay Good"

In the same way that people may be "captured" by the magic of technologies, they may also be intoxicated in their online intimacies. They may carry the understood roles from real-space to cyber: my (online) confidante, my (online) bestie, my (online) lover. In states of arousal ("hot states"), emotions can overwhelm rationality in actions. And in situations of sensory flooding, such as through high-sensory signals as in gaming sites and immersive virtual worlds, cognitive resources may be overwhelmed, leaving fewer faculties for decision-making and mindfulness.

How people build online relationships depends in part on their senses of themselves (their self-identities) and also their senses of others (from direct in-world experiences and the virtual). If the assumptions are that people are essentially good, that may suggest that the person begins with a sense of high trust and a suspension of disbelief, and they will not necessarily change their assumptions until some or many negative experiences. Combined with the speed of responses online, this swift initial trust can be dangerous, with over-sharing without being aware of how information may be used / misused. Thinking of interacting only within the confines of the relationship may block the awareness of third-party observers and the "alters" in others' social networks who may have access to semi-private shared information. (In social network analysis, even one or two degrees out from an ego neighborhood, there becomes a large crowd of people, many of them strangers to the target individual.)

A more careful assumption may be that people are essentially self-interested, and that has a different set of assumptions about what to share, how to interact, and how much vulnerability should be engaged. In many relationships, particularly in the absence of rich cues, people may be living interrelationships in their own mental spaces and with their own perceptions of what is going on relationally. With some healthy skepticism and caution, there may be some differentiating between "cheap talk" and "costly signaling." A more empirical approach may show that many relationships online are built on weak ties, and many do not last past either a one-off interaction or a few-off interaction. Even romances in social networking sites seem to average only a few years if they survive the initial first months (State, Feb. 12, 2014).

Without critical thinking, people are broadly friending socialbots, often without realizing that their "followers" and online "friends" are automated agents. In many documented cases, such agents have been used to share #fakenews, malicious software, foreign government propaganda, and other malicious contents.

Also, if people are not careful, they may expose their real and actual social networks of family, friends, and trusted colleagues to malicious individuals and automated agents. "Friend(s) of a friend" carry with them some implied trust—and the implied trust is transitive, or it moves among people through trust networks. An introduced other has the benefit of being "white-listed" into a network as a trusted entity. There are risks of illusory connections, illusory trust, and illusory passions, which may be intensified through social introductions (and the senses of social relations).

Friend of a friend (FOAF) social networks are highly popular in online social spaces and can result in shared social capital if exercised in the real, but with malicious individuals and digital agents in the mix, there can be larger compromises of people. Over-friending puts potential malicious agents one step out from real and important others. A "friend" has standing to make all sorts of requests, even those that can be high-cost, if people are not careful. Some researchers have observed that fraud is not just about financial motives but may be about thrill-seeking and getting away with something of value:

Offenders may simply enjoy sailing close to the wind, to see what they can get away with. Success in executing a complex fraud may be exhilarating. The sensation of power over another individual or individuals seems to be a powerful motivating force for some fraud offenders to the point that it becomes an end in itself. As one confidence man put it, "For myself, I love to make people do what I want them to, I love command. I love to rule people. That's why I'm a con artist" (quoted in Blum, 1972, p. 46). To quote another, "Half of being a con man is the challenge. When I score, I get more kick out of that than anything; to score is the biggest kick of my whole life" (quoted in Blum, 1972, p. 44, as cited in Grabosky & Walkley, 2007, p. 367).

Another mediating factor may be the carelessness of an organization or individual leading to "crimes of opportunity" (Grabosky & Walkley, 2007, p. 367).

Or people may be thought of as being capable of greed, malice, harm, selfishness, and violence. With each ratchet, higher levels of caution may have to be applied. These precautions do not preclude interacting but likely means that there will be reasonable hardening of the accounts, controls over the interactions, and awareness when making choices online. There may be improved defenses against information elicitations [Who is this person? (if knowable) What is the person asking for? (if knowable) Does he or she have a need-to-know? (if knowable) Does he or she have a formal standing to ask (or is this a pretense)? What can he or she do with this information as a stand-alone? In combination with other information? (if knowable)]. In the prior parentheses, the "if knowable" is an important point since there is a lot that cannot be validated with any real level of practical trust, given how easy it is to spoof so much online and to "front.".

"It Is Possible to Turn Back the Clock and Achieve Full Recovery After a Cyber Compromise"

There is no real putting a genie back into its bottle once private data are lost and distributed, once reputation has been harmed, once technology systems have been breached, and so on. Afterwards, there is only attempts at recovery and mitigation, and potential hardening against future attacks.

The four quoted assertions in this section identify inaccurate assumptions in approaching hypersocial online relationships that can lead to cyber compromise. The pursuit of online friending and relationships can bypass many of the cybersecurity tripwires and safeguards put into place to protect users from potential harm. While online relationships are critical to much of today's social and work lives, they should not be embarked on unthinkingly nor without due caution.

One weakness, as noted above, is that cyber compromises are still possible even if users are alert, attentive, aware, and cautious. In the cyber realm, the risks are many. Virtually most things digital can be spoofed. Cyberattacks are myriad, and they can be combined and stacked in highly complex ways that are difficult to recognize, defend against, and research for non-state-level defenders. The "physics" of cyberspace enable various compromises, and the making of hypersocial and hyperpersonal relationships is one such gap that can be hard to address and mitigate (and particularly not without compromising human free will and decision-making).

Also, there are four main areas of misconceptions that are fairly common in how common users interrelate on social media platforms (reverse-engineered from common cybersecurity compromises in the academic research literature and mass media reportage):

1. "Socio-technical technologies are transparent and secure."
2. "What happens in cyber stays in cyber."
3. "People are essentially good and generally stay good."
4. "It is possible to turn back the clock and achieve full recovery after a cyber compromise."

Addressing these assumptions can move people into a more secure position.

Hypothesis 2, the projection into the Fourth Industrial Revolution, posited risks to human relating with AI-informed physically-embodied robots. Those risks can only be answered initially and provisionally, almost as a thought experiment. The thinking goes like this: Humans engage their environment, and they engage with others as social creatures. With the AI-powered embodied social agents, humans will be attracted and seduced to interact and share, and they will be vulnerable to manipulation and compromise. (With the melding of the technological-artificial and the physical, cyber is no longer a light-show, but in-world, pervasive, and possibly undifferentiated. We may approach an android and ask, "Are you kin?"

These risks exist in "RL" or real-life as well. Based on the four areas of misconceptions listed prior, in this case, embodied socialbots are not necessarily transparent nor secure (1); what happens between a human and an embodied robot does not remain in cyber (2); people's essential natures will not necessarily change simply with the passage of time or the advent of new technologies(3); and damage from cyber compromises with a malicious embodied socialbot master (or a malicious embodied socialbot) will not likely be fully undone (simply because the rules of the physical universe are based in irrecoverable time) (4).

FUTURE RESEARCH DIRECTIONS

The observation that people may use digital spaces to create faux personas—whether fully human, fully automated, or cyborgian—is not novel. The uses of such entities, as individuals or as members of teams, to elicit information and to gain access to social networks and to access intellectual property (IP) are not new either. These risks have been addressed in news stories, academic research, and apocryphal tales shared in the cybersecurity community. What is novel is the synthesis of details and the update on complex cyber capabilities of malicious robots. Also, the idea of the uses of hyperpersonal relationships in composite threats, using a number of means, is fairly new.

In terms of future research, there would be value in documenting direct cases and mapping their evolution over time. Researchers may also explore ways to protect people against being used in their online interactions and hyperpersonal relationships, given slippery identity (in)validation and elusive awareness of compromise. What are ways to help make a population more resilient since people are the first point of contact and often the first line of cyberdefense? What are some ways to hone people's senses of danger to be more accurate to the threat? For those who are being groomed to compromise themselves or their colleagues or the organizations that they are parts of, are there ways to encourage people to disengage? Are there ways to encourage people to think about online propositions and to consider the following: "Who bears the actual costs? What is being given away? Who benefits? Who loses?"

In terms of an online culture of disregard in terms of the uses and exploitation of people—are there ways to discourage the negatives in social interrelating: cyberbullying, the trolling, flaming, misinformation, abuse, cyberstalking, the theft of intellectual property, the doxing, the data leaks, financial fraud, and other actions? Are there ways to reset so that Internet friendships can be mutually beneficial and positive?

CONCLUSION

And? So? Is the insight only that people online are on the make and that robots and cyborgs may be harnessed to those ends? A person advancing his / her interests are not uncommon, and they may engage in unethical or illegal ways to achieve their own ends, but they may not see themselves as malicious actors. It does not help to "other" those so much that they seem not quite human to people. In terms of "safe" distances, that is a purposefully unsuitable metaphor because distance and proximity are in many ways nullified by cyber means. Every interaction, while disembodied, is intimate and up-close, and the fighting is hand-to-hand (tech-to-tech). Human needs to socialize run deep and strong, and that transfers to virtual spaces. That said, these hyper-personal online relationships stand to benefit from greater awareness of potential cybersecurity compromises—through the online social systems themselves, social networks, the bad-acting members of those networks (whether human, automated, or cyborgian, or other combinations).

All points-of-contact online are potentially risky. All cyber systems have a concerning array of vulnerabilities, many likely as-yet undiscovered by the public. What people think, how they prepare and behave, and what they do will affect their well-being in this space. A beginning point in their cyber-preparedness is their orientation or how they see themselves and others in this space because this frames their perception (how what they see is interpreted). While a sense of self-preservation and defense is natural, the cybersecurity skill set is not intuited, but it is consciously built. Likewise, socializing is inherent to people and necessary for a common cyber defense; however, socializing online requires savvy and finesse to avoid being "pwned" ("player owned" or manipulated, compromised) by humans, technology systems, robots, or cyborgs.

How people live their digital identities and lives are fairly electronically permanent, and what is released in the wilds even on "private" channels have a way of being used in unintended secondary, tertiary, and other ways. A loose brag can be shared and retold in milliseconds. In a broad sense, the macro "public imaginary" affects what is possible (Dwight, Boler, & Sears, 2006) and also how well people prepare and how well they respond. The future of cyberspace does not only depend on individuals but on other players in this contested space. For example, strife over the future of cyberspace by nation-states and other entities using the Internet for their ambitions may lead to a "Darkening Web," a space that is much less usable and less trustworthy, according to one of the foremost thinkers in this space (Klimburg, 2017). By social practice and by evolving social norms, hyper-personal relationships are becoming the norm online, and this intensification changes up what strangers can ask of others, and how people respond to those asks (behaviorally, with intimacy, with resources, with connection). Human connections can be intensified through virtual means (through other people and through artificial socialbots). These changes in online interrelating have large-scale implications for social- and political- influence. Current virtual intimacies may serve as harbingers for newer ways of hyper-personal connection which may foundation-ally change who people are to each other and why, with a sense of both opportunity and threat.

This work does not suggest that people should not interact online for social or instrumental purposes. This work does not suggest that people should not go online to meet some parts of their hierarchy of needs. If the Fourth Industrial Revolution is actually upon as, given the "exponential" speed of change (Schwab, Jan. 14, 2016), the presence of AI-informed embodied socialbots may be one of the many seductive technologies on deck. People would do well to be both aware of themselves and the risks when they choose to engage and to disengage.

What this does suggest is that those who are online would benefit from knowing their relational vulnerabilities ("vulns"), some of the technological capabilities in the world, and how to navigate with some common sense (friending selectively, not oversharing, not live-casting, backing up files in smart ways, and so on). People would benefit from knowing their tendencies to leaven relationships with their imaginations and wishes, as in parasocial interactions—which can be abused by malicious others. It makes sense for people to hold information in reserve instead of spilling everything online; after all, a little discretion goes a long way. It makes sense to use good, sober, and informed judgments when engaging with others. (Humans are known as the "weak link" in most cybersecurity contexts because of their gullibility and lack of discipline in managing their accounts, exploring the Internet, sharing private information, and other behaviors.)

Stealth compromises occur continuously online, and those who think that they are immune and above it are misled. People's interests do not often align online, and people can and do use befriending as a strategy…because befriending another and using a surprise compromise is a strategic option. Also, for those who are comfortable deploying programs as social agents on social media platforms, they can amplify their malicious befriending to others' losses. This concept carries over to embodied AI-powered socialbots that exist in the real-world and engage with people. In this social-scape, such socialbots may be controlled by bad actors and malicious agents to their own ends. Even as the physical, digital, and biological co-evolve, human nature has not fundamentally changed. People are not necessarily of higher character than in history. They do not necessarily have greater empathy towards each other, and self-interest likely continues unabated as a core human survival instinct. If the socio-political experiments of the 20th century show anything, one major lesson is that people may accept a forced egalitarianism only in a state of fear and surveillance and coercion. Now, in the early 21st century, Francis Fukuyama's "end of history" has not actually arrived, and the "last man" has not been re-engineered for sufficient other-engagement so as to consider their needs above his or her own. In an ecosystem driven by human self-interest, human-human and human-socialbot (embodied and disembodied) relationships will always be somewhat fraught.

Mutual healthy and positive online relationships may be a rarity, in the future as now. These are human ties to aspire to, in cyber and in the real world. There is no avoiding risk in interacting with people, with their mix of motives, their self-concern, their charisma, and their capacities for any number of actions. Bad bargains are not hard to find: people trading away their well-being for ego, emotion, sentiment, and illusion; people confusing something shiny for something real, promises for actual delivery, something temporary for something permanent, something valuable for "15 seconds"; people triggered to unthinking and scripted actions by an image, a look, a word, a story; people going to rote politeness triggered by social engineers; and so on. As one security researcher said to me of vigilance, "You have to sleep sometime." Sometimes, all it takes to break an illusion is to ask the disconfirming question, to test the illusory shimmer of a connection (or non-connection).

There are no safe distances in the virtual…or in light of the Fourth Industrial Revolution, in the real. Maybe one approach is to fight close, as in jujitsu, to restrict the actions of an opponent. Ultimately, some level of comity is possible and necessary. After all, what would be a world without people? (Figure 7)

ACKNOWLEDGMENT

Thanks to the anonymous reviewers of the draft chapter for their insights.

This is for R. Max.

Figure 7. A World without People?

REFERENCES

Casner, S. (2017). *Careful: A User's Guide to our Injury-Prone Minds*. New York: Riverhead Books.

Chambers, D. (2013). *Social Media and Personal Relationships: Online Intimacies and Networked Friendship*. New York: Palgrave Macmillan. doi:10.1057/9781137314444

Cheok, A. D., Levy, D., & Karunanayaka, K. (2016). Lovotics: Love and sex with robots. In G.N. Yannakakis (Ed.), Emotion in Games. Springer.

Cohen, N. (2017, Oct. 13). Silicon Valley is not your Friend. Sunday Review. *The New York Times*. Retrieved from https://nyti.ms/2kLUnZP

Cole, H., & Griffiths, M. D. (2007). Social interactions in massively multiplayer online role-playing games. *Cyberpsychology & Behavior*, *10*(4), 575–583. doi:10.1089/cpb.2007.9988 PMID:17711367

Computer-mediated communication. (2017, Sept. 18). In *Wikipedia*. Retrieved from https://en.wikipedia.org/wiki/Computer-mediated_communication

Confidence trick. (2017, Sept. 13). In *Wikipedia*. Retrieved from https://en.wikipedia.org/wiki/Confidence_trick

Craft, A. J. (2007). Sin in cyber-eden: Understanding the metaphysics and morals of virtual worlds. *Ethics and Information Technology*, *9*(3), 205–217. doi:10.100710676-007-9144-4

Crittenden, P. M. (1990, Fall). Internal representational models of attachment relationships. *Infant Mental Health Journal*, *11*(3), 259–277. doi:10.1002/1097-0355(199023)11:3<259::AID-IMHJ22801103083.0.CO;2-J

Cummings, J. N., Butler, B., & Kraut, R. (2002, July). The quality of online social relationships. *Communications of the ACM*, *7*(45), 103–108. doi:10.1145/514236.514242

Dwight, J. S., Boler, M., & Sears, P. (2006). Reconstructing the Fables: Women on the Educational Cyberfrontier. In J. Weiss, . . . (Eds.), The International Handbook of Virtual Learning Environments: 1467 – 1494. Academic Press.

Dwyer, C., Hiltz, S. R., & Passerini, K. (2007). Trust and privacy concern within social networking sites: A comparison of Facebook and MySpace. *Proceedings of the Thirteenth Americas Conference on Information Systems*.

Ellison, N. B., Steinfield, C., & Lampe, C. (2007, July). The benefits of Facebook 'friends:' Social capital and college students' use of online social network sites. *Journal of Computer-Mediated Communication*, *12*(4), 1143–1168. doi:10.1111/j.1083-6101.2007.00367.x

Gilbert, E., & Karahalios, K. (2009). Predicting tie strength with social media. *Proceedings of the SIGCHI Conference on Human Factors in Computing Systems*, 211 – 220. Retrieved from https://dl.acm.org/citation.cfm?id=1518736

Grabosky, P., & Walkley, S. (2007). Computer Crime and White-Collar Crime. In H. N. Pontell & G. Geis (Eds.), *International Handbook of White-Collar and Corporate Crime*. Boston, MA: Springer. doi:10.1007/978-0-387-34111-8_17

Granovetter, M. S. (1973, May). The strength of weak ties. *American Journal of Sociology, 78*(6), 1360 – 1380. Retrieved from http://www.journals.uchicago.edu/doi/pdfplus/10.1086/225469

Hai-Jew, S. (2009). Exploring the immersive parasocial: Is it you or the thought of you? *MERLOT Journal of Online Learning and Teaching, 5*(3), 550 – 561. Retrieved from http://jolt.merlot.org/vol5no3/hai-jew_0909.pdf

Hogan, B. Li, N., & Dutton, W.H. (2011, Feb. 14). *A global shift in the social relationships of networked individuals: Meeting and dating online comes of age*. Me, My Spouse and the Internet Project. Oxford Internet Institute, University of Oxford.

Holeton, R. (1998). *Composing Cyberspace: Identity, Community, and Knowledge in the Electronic Age*. Boston: McGraw Hill.

Horton, D., & Wohl, R. R. (1956). Mass communication and para-social interaction: Observations on intimacy at a distance. *Psychiatry, 19*(3), 215–229. doi:10.1080/00332747.1956.11023049 PMID:13359569

Internet relationship. (2017, Sept. 1). In *Wikipedia*. Retrieved from https://en.wikipedia.org/wiki/Internet_relationship

Kelly, H. (2012, Aug. 3). 83 million Facebook accounts are fakes and dupes. *CNN*. Retrieved from http://www.cnn.com/2012/08/02/tech/social-media/facebook-fake-accounts/index.html

Klimburg, A. (2017). *The Darkening Web: The War for Cyberspace*. New York: Penguin Press.

Kushner, D. (2016, Feb. 1). Scammers and spammers: Inside online dating's sex bot con job. *Rolling Stone*. Retrieved from http://www.rollingstone.com/culture/features/scammers-and-spammers-inside-online-datings-sex-bot-con-job-20160201

Levine, T. R. (2014). Truth-Default Theory (TDT): A theory of human deception and deception detection. *Journal of Language and Social Psychology, 33*(4), 378–392. doi:10.1177/0261927X14535916

Li, X., Hess, T. J., & Valacich, J. S. (2008). Why do we trust new technology? A study of initial trust formation with organizational information systems. *The Journal of Strategic Information Systems, 17*(1), 39–71. doi:10.1016/j.jsis.2008.01.001

List of cognitive biases. (2017, Oct. 2). In *Wikipedia*. Retrieved from https://en.wikipedia.org/wiki/List_of_cognitive_biases

Loy, D. (2007). CyberBabel? *Ethics and Information Technology, 9*(4), 251–258. doi:10.100710676-007-9146-2

Mazur, M. A., Burns, R. J., & Emmers-Sommer, T. M. (2000). Perceptions of relational interdependence in online relationships: The effects of communication apprehension and introversion. *Communication Research Reports, 17*(4), 397–406. doi:10.1080/08824090009388788

Merkle, E. R., & Richardson, R. A. (2000, April). Digital dating and virtual relating: Conceptualizing computer mediated romantic relationships. *Family Relations*, *49*(2), 187–192. doi:10.1111/j.1741-3729.2000.00187.x

Mesch, G., & Talmud, I. (2006). The quality of online and offline relationships: The role of multiplexity and duration of social relationships. *The Information Society*, *22*(3), 1–25. doi:10.1080/01972240600677805

Mesch, G. S., & Talmud, I. (2007). Similarity and the quality of online and offline social relationships among adolescents in Israel. *Journal of Research on Adolescence*, *17*(2), 455–466. doi:10.1111/j.1532-7795.2007.00529.x

Newberg, M. (2017, Mar. 10). As many as 48 million Twitter accounts aren't people, says study. *CNBC*. Retrieved from https://www.cnbc.com/2017/03/10/nearly-48-million-twitter-accounts-could-be-bots-says-study.html

Oh, H. J., Ozkaya, E., & LaRose, R. (2014). How does online social networking enhance life satisfaction? The relationships among online supportive interaction, affect, perceived social support, sense of community, and life satisfaction. *Computers in Human Behavior*, *30*, 69–78. doi:10.1016/j.chb.2013.07.053

Perlroth, N., Wines, M., & Rosenberg, M. (2017, Sept. 1). Russian election hacking efforts, wider than previously known, draw little scrutiny. *The New York Times*. Retrieved from https://www.nytimes.com/2017/09/01/us/politics/russia-election-hacking.html

Pfleeger, S. L., & Caputo, D. D. (2012). Leveraging behavioral science to mitigate cyber security risk. *Computers & Security*, *31*(4), 597–611. doi:10.1016/j.cose.2011.12.010

Putnam, R. (2000). *Bowling Alone: Collapse and Revival of American Community*. New York: Simon & Schuster. doi:10.1145/358916.361990

Reeves, J. (2017). *Citizen Spies: The Long Rise of America's Surveillance Society*. New York: New York University Press.

Robin Sage. (2016, Dec. 16). In *Wikipedia*. Retrieved from https://en.wikipedia.org/wiki/Robin_Sage

Rossmiller, S. (2011, Apr. 21). Stalking terrorists online. International Spy Museum. *Spycast*. Retrieved from https://www.spymuseum.org/multimedia/spycast/episode/stalking-terrorists-online/

Ryan, T. (2011, Oct. 9). Identity, espionage, and social media. *Spycast*. *International Spy Museum*. Retrieved from https://www.spymuseum.org/multimedia/spycast/episode/identity-espionage-and-social-media/

Schneier, B. (2000, Oct. 15). Semantic Attacks: The Third Wave of Network Attacks. *Crypto-Gram*. *Schneier on Security*. Retrieved from https://www.schneier.com/crypto-gram/archives/2000/1015.html#1

Schwab, K. (2016, Jan. 14). *The Fourth Industrial Revolution: What it means, how to respond*. World Economic Forum.

Shafahi, M., Kempers, L., & Afsarmanesh, H. (2016). Phishing through social bots on Twitter. *Proceedings of the 2016 IEEE International Conference on Big Data (Big Data)*, 3703 – 3712.

Sheldon, P. (2009). "I'll poke you. You'll poke me!" Self-disclosure, social attraction, predictability and trust as important predictors of Facebook relationships. *Cyberpsychology (Brno)*, *3*(2), 1. Retrieved from https://cyberpsychology.eu/article/view/4225/3267

Sheldon, R. M. (2017, Oct. 20). Ancient Espionage: The Greeks and the Great Game. *Spycast. International Spy Museum*. Retrieved from https://www.youtube.com/watch?v=uVFJYCayeEs&ab_channel=IntlSpyMuseum

State, B. (2014, Feb. 12.) *Flings or lifetimes? The duration of Facebook relationships*. Retrieved from https://www.facebook.com/notes/facebook-data-science/flings-or-lifetimes-the-duration-of-facebook-relationships/10152060513428859/

Suler, J. (2004). The online disinhibition effect. *Cyberpsychology & Behavior*, *7*(3), 321–326. doi:10.1089/1094931041291295 PMID:15257832

Taddei, S., & Contena, B. (2013). Privacy, trust and control: Which relationships with online self-disclosure? *Computers in Human Behavior*, *29*(3), 821–826. doi:10.1016/j.chb.2012.11.022

Threat model. (2017, Aug. 28). In *Wikipedia*. Retrieved from https://en.wikipedia.org/wiki/Threat_model

Trepal, H., Haberstroh, S., Duffey, T., & Evans, M. (2007). Considerations and strategies for teaching online counseling skills: Establishing relationships in cyberspace. *Counselor Education and Supervision*, *46*(4), 266–278. doi:10.1002/j.1556-6978.2007.tb00031.x

Tsai, Y. H., Lin, C.-P., Chiu, C.-K., & Joe, S.-W. (2010). Learning cyber trust using a triadic functioning analysis: A qualitative approach. *Quality & Quantity Journal*, *44*(6), 1165–1174. doi:10.100711135-009-9273-4

Underwood, H., & Findlay, B. (2004). Internet relationships and their impact on primary relationships. *Behaviour Change*, *21*(2), 127–140. doi:10.1375/bech.21.2.127.55422

Walther, J. B. (1996). Computer-mediated communication: Impersonal, interpersonal, and hyperpersonal interaction. *Communication Research*, *23*(1), 3–43. doi:10.1177/009365096023001001

Ward, C. C., & Tracey, T. J. G. (2004). Relation of shyness with aspects of online relationship involvement. *Journal of Social and Personal Relationships*, *21*(5), 611–623. doi:10.1177/0265407504045890

Wellman, B., & Gulia, M. (1997/1999). Net surfers don't ride alone: Virtual communities as communities. In M. A. Smith & P. Kollock (Eds.), *Communities in cyberspace* (pp. 167–194). London: Routledge.

Whitty, M., & Gavin, J. (2001). Age/sex/location: Uncovering the social cues in the development of online relationships. *Cyberpsychology & Behavior*, *4*(5), 623–630. doi:10.1089/109493101753235223 PMID:11725656

Whitty, M. T. (2002). Liar, liar! An examination of how open, supportive and honest people are in chat rooms. *Computers in Human Behavior*, *18*(4), 343–352. doi:10.1016/S0747-5632(01)00059-0

Whitty, M. T. (2005). The realness of cybercheating: Men's and women's representations of unfaithful Internet relationships. *Social Science Computer Review*, *23*(1), 57–67. doi:10.1177/0894439304271536

Whitty, M. T. (2008). Liberating or debilitating? An examination of romantic relationships, sexual relationships and friendships on the Net. *Computers in Human Behavior*, *24*(5), 1837–1850. doi:10.1016/j.chb.2008.02.009

Wilder, U. M. (2017). Why Spy Now? The Psychology of Espionage and Leaking in the Digital Age. *Studies in Intelligence, 61*(2), 1 – 36. Retrieved from https://www.cia.gov/library/center-for-the-study-of-intelligence/csi-publications/csi-studies/studies/vol-61-no-2/pdfs/why-spy-why-leak.pdf

Wilson, L. (1994). Cyberwar, God and television: Interview with Paul Virilio. *Ctheory.net*. Retrieved from https://journals.uvic.ca/index.php/ctheory/article/view/14355

With big data comes big responsibility. (2014, Nov.) Harvard Business Review Staff. *Harvard Business Review*. Retrieved from https://hbr.org/2014/11/with-big-data-comes-big-responsibility

Wolak, J., Mitchell, K. J., & Finkelhor, D. (2002, Fall). Close online relationships in a national sample of adolescents. *Adolescence. Roslyn Heights*, *37*(147), 441–455. PMID:12458686

Wolak, J., Mitchell, K. J., & Finkelhor, D. (2003). Escaping or connecting? Characteristics of youth who form close online relationships. *Journal of Adolescence*, *26*(1), 105–119. doi:10.1016/S0140-1971(02)00114-8 PMID:12550824

Xie, B. (2008, September). The mutual shaping of online and offline social relationships. *IR Information Research*, *13*(3), 1–18.

Young, K. S., Cooper, A., Griffiths-Shelley, E., O'Mara, J., & Buchanan, J. (2000). Cybersex and infidelity online: Implications for evaluate and treatment. *Sexual Addiction & Compulsivity*, *7*(10), 59–74. doi:10.1080/10720160008400207

Zhao, S., Grasmuck, S., & Martin, J. (2008). Identity construction on Facebook: Digital empowerment in anchored relationships. *Computers in Human Behavior*, *24*(5), 1816–1836. doi:10.1016/j.chb.2008.02.012

ADDITIONAL READING

KEY TERMS AND DEFINITIONS

Abductive Logic: Reasoning that begins with in-world observations followed by the most-likely and simplest explanations; learning from the world.

Attack Surface: The totality of different attack vectors through which cyber compromises may occur.

Attack Vector: A point of vulnerability or possible cyber compromise; a means by which systems (or people) may be exploited; a possible path of exploitation.

Broadcast: The sharing of information to a broad and large-scale audience, in a one-to-many approach.

Cybersecurity: Information security (infosec) but broadly referring to technology and human systems that are built around the secure exchange, storage, and management of information.

Embodied Socialbot: A physical robot (or mannequin) imbued with artificial intelligence-informed personality, emotions, intellect, and communications capabilities (both verbal and non-verbal).

Hyperpersonal: Intimately related to an individual and his/her private or internal sense of self.

Hypersocial: Intensively engaged with others through intercommunications and interactions.

Mirror Imaging: The emulation of another person as an affirmation of that individual (may be consciously, subconsciously, or unconsciously done).

Narrowcast: The sharing of information to a defined and limited audience.

Parasocial Relationship: A one-directional non-reciprocated "relationship" of a person and often a public figure.

Performative: Related to purposeful expression and acting.

RL: Real life.

Social Engineering: The manipulation of another human being to reveal sensitive or private information (such as through deception), often used to commit fraud.

Social Network Analysis: The study of social networks and human interrelationships.

Spear Phishing: The targeting of particular individuals with tailored emails to get them to respond, click on links, or download attached files—in order to compromise the integrity of the individual, email, technology system, or organization.

Weak Link: The least dependable part of a group or organization.

Chapter 3
Ransomware:
The Cyber Extortionist

Rajashree Chaurasia
Government of NCT of Delhi, India

ABSTRACT

"Ransomware" is a type of malware that tries to extort money from its victims by hijacking the victim's computer in some way and holding it to ransom. It renders the computer unusable until a ransom amount is paid to the extortionist. And it is very unfortunate that, in many cases, even after the ransom is paid, the victim's computer is not released. Ransomware, as we know it, is gaining popularity at an immense rate among the most notorious cyber-criminals of the world. It isn't just a virus, it's a damned good game plan to becoming a millionaire in a matter of months! This chapter details what ransomware is, how it originated, which families of attacks it falls under, how ransomware is classified, the impact of ransomware on a global scale, the life cycle of a typical ransomware attack, mitigation and containment strategies, trending strains of 2017, and future trends in ransomware attacks. In future, these attack types will dominate our industries and wreak havoc, destroying life and property, if left unchecked.

INTRODUCTION

Technologically speaking, we are currently standing mid-way on a bridge connecting the Digital Revolution and the Fourth Industrial Revolution (4IR). We have had breakthroughs in many emerging fields of technology like artificial intelligence, machine learning and cognitive computing, quantum computing, the Internet of Things (IoT), smart-cities, nanotechnology, gene editing, the Analytics of Things (AoT), etc. Essentially, we are striving to make everything intelligent, be it inanimate objects like cars, watches, eyeglasses, etc. or living beings like bacteria and plants, that calls for an amalgamation of many evolving fields. We also wish to have everything connected to everything else to create a smarter world. However, there is still a long way to go before we can reach the other end of the bridge and truly enter a new age of Science. Furthermore, from the perspective of cyber security, these emergent technologies pose numerous security challenges that will have an impact much greater than financial loss or data loss – the loss of life.

DOI: 10.4018/978-1-5225-4763-1.ch003

Thus far, security and privacy issues pertaining to a few perspectives have been discussed in this book. Cybercrime, cyber threats as well as cyber warfare will be elucidated in detail in forthcoming chapters. However, this book will not be comprehensive enough without an exhaustive discussion on the topmost trending cybercriminal program – Ransomware. This infamous family of attacks warrants a separate chapter due to the extensive damage in terms of financial as well as data loss (and in extreme cases, loss of human life) that it has caused in recent years across the globe. In the decades to come, ransomware will take an even uglier form. For instance, hijacking of control systems in automated transportation may lead to loss of life on a large scale, the simplest being taking control of a self-driven car to extort money from the owner to prevent an impending accident at the hands of the hacker. Cyber criminals are always on the lookout for devices that can be compromised and with our growing dependency on smart devices, these bad guys are having the time of their lives. Ransomware programmers are evolving their strategies, keeping in step with technological advancements. Therefore, there is a need to address this issue whenever any new technology is put to practical use. So, let us begin with a modest characterization of this notorious cyber-thief…

'Ransomware' is a type of malware that tries to extort money from its victims by hijacking the victim's computer in some way and holding it to ransom. It renders the computer unusable until a ransom amount is paid to the extortionist. And it is very unfortunate that, in many cases, even after the ransom is paid, the victim's computer is not released.

Ransomware, as we know it isn't just a virus, it's a damn good game plan to becoming a millionaire in a matter of months! It is blackmail in its ugliest form – digital. But how did it develop into this intractable menace that it has grown into? Let us review the first known ransomware and the man who started it all…

RANSOMWARE: ORIGINS

A long time ago (in a galaxy far, far away…), before the world saw what the world wide web was, before the advent of email as we know it, before the Internet of Things, when people shared data and programs on meagre floppy disks through the postal service, a man invented a form of blackmail that would take the world by storm some three decades later. That man was Dr. Joseph Popp, an evolutionary biologist with a degree in anthropology from Harvard.

In the December of 1989, Dr. Popp mailed 5.25-inch floppy disks labelled 'AIDS Information - Introductory Diskette' to as many as 20,000 people in 90 countries through post (Jackson, 1990). At the time, he was a part-time consultant with the World Health Organisation (WHO) and was an active researcher in the study on the Acquired Immuno-Deficiency Syndrome i.e. AIDS (Mungo & Clough, 1992, pp. 141-169). The recipients of his disks were many, subscribers of PC Business World magazine, AIDS patients and attendees at a WHO International AIDS Conference to name a few. The disk contained a program to calculate the risk of contracting AIDS through a questionnaire and offered advice on reducing the risk of future infection. However, these diskettes were infected with a virus he wrote (which was later named the AIDS Trojan or PC Cyborg Trojan ("AIDS trojan disk", n.d.)) that entered any personal computer (PC) wherein the floppy was inserted, and observed the number of system boots. Once the boot count reached 90, it encrypted all filenames and concealed the directories. It then flashed a message on-screen in red (see Figure 1) that informed the victim that a so-called software lease from PC Cyborg Corporation (a phony company) had expired and the user needed to renew the license by paying $189 or $378, depending upon the type of lease chosen, to a post box number in Panama (Mungo & Clough,

1992, pp. 141-169). Until the fee was paid, the victim's PC was rendered unusable. This was the first ever extortion virus which is known as *Ransomware* in the present.

Dr. Popp was arrested and tried for his crimes but was soon let off due to the display of insanity, shortly after his arrest and during trial. Technical analysis of the virus by Jim Bates (1990) revealed that the encryption mechanism used by Popp was a very crude one and that it could be cracked easily, thereby restoring the system. AIDSOUT and CLEARAID were successful programs developed by Bates (1990) to remove the virus and decrypt the system.

Adam Young and Moti Yung (1996) showed how public-key cryptography (against the breakable symmetric-key cryptography used by Dr. Popp) could be used to effectively develop crypto-viruses that were potentially impossible to decrypt by tractable means. Their work gave motivation and direction to the cyber-attackers of modern society on developing these crypto-viruses and using them to extort money from unsuspecting users.

RANSOMWARE: LA FAMILIA

A variety of attack families have been discussed in earlier chapters of this book. Many of these families intersect in the sense that attack types in the current digital era cannot be distinguished as solely belonging to a particular class of attacks. For the same reasons, Ransomware falls under the umbrella of many of these families with good reason. Let us take a brief tour of the clans ransomware belongs to.

Ransomware may be considered under all the following families of attack and possibly more:

1. **Malware Attack:** Malicious software or malware refers to all forms of intrusive and hostile (Moir, 2003) programs which includes viruses, worms, spyware, adware, ransomware, Trojans, etc. Ransomware is both an intrusive as well as a hostile program that renders the user's PC unusable. Ransomware has spread through a variety of means – Trojans, worms, adware, hostile web links, etc. For example, WannaCry is a ransomware worm that can spread quickly across the network

Figure 1. The AIDS Ransom Note (Popp, 1989)

```
Dear Customer:

It is time to pay for your software lease from PC Cyborg Corporation.
Complete the INVOICE and attach payment for the lease option of your choice.
If you don't use the printed INVOICE, then be sure to refer to the important
reference numbers below in all correspondence. In return you will receive:

- a renewal software package with easy-to-follow, complete instructions;
- an automatic, self-installing diskette that anyone can apply in minutes.

Important reference numbers: A5599796-2695577-

The price of 365 user applications is US$189. The price of a lease for the
lifetime of your hard disk is US$378. You must enclose a bankers draft,
cashier's check or international money order payable to PC CYBORG CORPORATION
for the full amount of $189 or $378 with your order. Include your name,
company, address, city, state, country, zip or postal code. Mail your order
to PC Cyborg Corporation, P.O. Box 87-17-11, Panama 7, Panama.

               Press ENTER to continue
```

without user intervention. Trojan: W32/Ransom is another ransomware that spreads using many tactics like software and email bundling.

2. **Social Engineering Attack:** These attacks involve some sort of psychological manipulation to coerce people into submission by playing on their emotions like trust, fright, urgency of action, curiosity, empathy, hate, etc. Many a times people are tricked into downloading ransomware by luring them with freebies. In May 2016 ("Why Ransomware Works", 2016), many thousands of Amazon.com users were tricked into downloading the Locky ransomware using the baiting technique of social engineering. The Amazon customers got an email from a legitimate Amazon email address stating that their order had been dispatched. The attachment that claimed to contain the order information was actually a file carrying Locky as payload.

3. **Impersonation Attack:** Many cybercriminals use impersonation as a means to scare their victims into compromising their data. Impersonation attacks are popular as they feed the most powerful beliefs in human nature, trust and fear. This type of ransomware encrypts all data on the victim's drives and displays a message on the screen posing to be from a legitimate organization like the police department, an investigation agency like the Federal Bureau of Investigation (FBI), a court, etc. inducing panic in the victim. For example, Reveton is a ransomware that locks the computer and the message it displays claims to be from the police department stating that some child pornographic content has been found on the user's drives and thus, the user must pay up a fine for viewing pornography. A large number of users actually pay up due to embarrassment and fear of arrest and/or legal action.

4. **Financial Attack:** The financial service industry has been a major target of cyberattacks causing large scale security breaches and financial loss. For example, in 2015, ransomware attacked the computers of a small law firm based in Rhode Island which was able to unlock its data by paying a $25,000 ransom. However, the attack resulted in a three-month interruption in the company's work-flow and caused a $700,000 revenue loss (Weiss, 2017). With small and big businesses as targets, the idea is not only to extract money, but also to steal sensitive data and intellectual property, thereby damaging the reputation of the company and crippling business. Ransomware has all these capabilities and more. Some ransomware not only lock and encrypt all the important files on the drive, but also threaten to publicize sensitive data found. Further, they may even sell the stolen information to rival companies. This is a serious form of blackmail and as technologies advance, it could become a real threat to the survival of an industry and give rise to cyberwarfare, if left unchecked.

5. **Sophisticated Attack:** Ransomware of today uses the same high-level encryption algorithms that are being used by legitimate security software. With innovative programming and sophisticated algorithms being used for extortion, organizations that are at the receiving end of such attacks must learn to maintain high-level security on their network. Unsupported and non-secure systems become vulnerable to cyberattacks that encourages criminal organizations to invest in creating more and more advanced assault products.

6. **Data Breach Attack:** Not all ransomware attacks are data breach attacks. If ransomware copies user data to its servers and that data contains any kind of sensitive information such as customer information, financial data, healthcare information, biogeographical information, social security numbers, etc., then it is known as a data breach. Loss of control of sensitive information establishes a data breach. In such cases, the company must inform all its customers that a data breach has occurred and notify concerned authorities. However, it is often difficult to identify whether a

data breach has or has not occurred as the victim might not be able to find out if the ransomware has actually made copies of his sensitive data over the network. Thus, the best practice is then to regain control of the data as soon as possible. Trying to understand the behaviour of the ransomware program is another method, but, it is often impossible to gauge this behaviour if you are not an expert in security and programming or the attack strain is new.

7. **Vulnerable Software Attack:** Ransomware programmers have been known to exploit vulnerabilities in operating system code. For example, WannaCry caused mayhem as it spread to over 150 countries targeting banks, hospitals and government agencies by exploiting known security holes in older Microsoft operating systems ("WannaCry ransomware attack", n.d.). From time to time, operating system manufacturers bring out security patches and security updates to close the identified security holes or bugs in the operating system code. Users must install these updates in order to reduce the risk of an infection that exploits such vulnerabilities.

8. **Covert Attack:** In many ransomware attacks, covert channels are used to evade detection in the nascent stages of infection. These channels are protocol based tunnels like ICMP (Internet Control Message Protocol), HTTP (Hyper-Text Transmission Protocol), Domain Name Service (DNS) tunnelling. It is very difficult to detect these covert channels and blocking data traffic across the tunnels is even more complex. Such channels are also used to copy sensitive data out of the victim's computer.

9. **Drive-by Download and Advertising:** Many ransomware strains transfer to the victim's computer through drive-by downloads and ad-clicks. Hostile websites, websites displaying pornographic content, torrent clients, etc. contain a large amount of illegal, pirated and explicit content together with malicious links, advertisements and defective pop-up windows that are meant to transmit ransomware payload to the victim's computer. The only way to effectively prevent such an attack is to refrain from visiting such websites. Users must be made aware of the dangers of downloading illegal content, opening email attachments and emails from untrusted sources and clicking on superfluous links.

RANSOMWARE: CLASSIFICATION

Now that we have discussed the attributes of ransomware, let us elaborate upon their broad categorization depending upon different criteria.

Criteria: Target Platform

Ransomware may be classified into five categories based on the current target platforms that are most popular viz. PC Ransomware, Mobile Ransomware, Ransomware for Cloud, Servers and Smart TV, that are discussed in the following subsections. In times to come, we may see novel ransomware strains that will target more advanced smart technologies.

PC Ransomware

A large section of ransomware targets the personal computer and laptop platforms. The most common operating system that is targeted is the Microsoft Windows Operating System (OS) due to its abundance in the market. The current market trends show a whopping 89% market share for Windows based OS, followed by MacOS X and other operating systems and Linux platforms ("Net Market Share", 2017). Of the many flavours of Windows OS available, Windows 7 has the most share in the current market scenario, followed by Windows 10 ("Net Market Share", 2017). Since ransomware cybercriminals gain profits by extorting money, it is understood that personal computers and laptops running the most popular operating systems will be targeted the most i.e. Microsoft Windows variants.

It is also worth noting that using older versions of Windows or any other OS, for which support from the makers has ceased, is another window open for such malware to creep in and cause havoc. Support from the company means important security updates and software patches are released from time to time to do away with any vulnerabilities that may have been discovered after release.

The Windows 10 Creators Fall Update has a new feature, the Windows Defender Exploit Guard, that comes with a rich set of intrusion rules and policies to protect organizations from advanced threats like ransomware. The latest build aims at curbing the encryption of users' files by switching on the Controlled Folder Access option in Windows Defender (Figure 2). Controlled folder access monitors change that an application makes to files in certain protected folders and additional locations added by the user. If any change to these files is made, the application is blacklisted, and the user gets a notification.

Ransomware needs to be specifically personalized for each different operating system. This is because many times, ransomware code uses API (Application Programming Interface) functionality that is embedded in the operating system, like in-built encryption libraries, to decrypt themselves as well as

Figure 2. Controlled Folder Access in Windows Defender Security Center

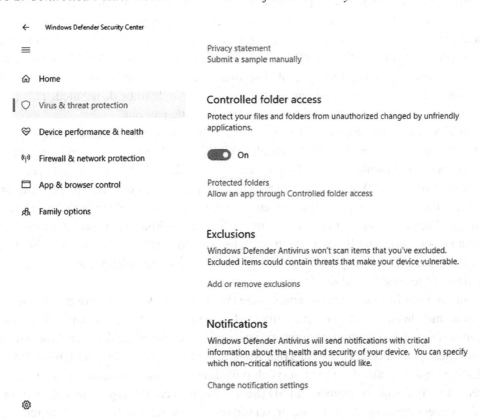

encrypt all the user data. Instead of writing their own encryption algorithms, cybercriminals exploit the already bundled encryption procedures the operating system uses. They also use hooking techniques to generate fake API call outputs in order to remain concealed.

It is easy to target PC and laptop users as most people don't patch and update their systems regularly. This leaves security holes open for exploitation by malware. Most users do not have a backup of their data to recover from a catastrophic situation such as ransomware. Also, many users do not have enough knowledge of cyber threats and how they spread. Thus, they may only have rudimentary security protection like basic antivirus programs that are largely ineffective in dealing with modern ransomware.

Not all ransomware is created exclusively for Windows-based devices. KillDisk attacks not only Windows based desktops and laptops, but also Linux systems. Figure 3 shows a sample ransom message from a KillDisk affected Linux machine. It renders the PC unbootable with permanent destruction of data and asks for $250,000 in bitcoin ("Destructive KillDisk", 2017). KeRanger ("KeRanger", 2016) is another non-Windows ransomware that affects Mac OS platforms. It spreads via the BitTorrent client, Transmission, and has a valid Mac application development certificate to bypass Apple's Gatekeeper security. It encrypts important user files and demands $400 in bitcoin.

Mobile Ransomware

Mobile devices like smartphones, tablets and phablets are the next major target platforms for ransomware. Devices running Android have more than 65% market share followed by iOS with 32% share ("Net Market Share", 2017). Every person owning a desktop or laptop also carries a smartphone or tablet which is used more extensively than PCs or laptops. But between Android and iOS, the former offers much greater prospects in terms of profit by extortion. This is because Android lets you install third party software applications from external sources or even untrusted sources, making it easier for malware to gain access to such devices using malicious APK (android application package) files. Thus, ransomware for iOS platforms are fewer. To break the Apple iOS security even on a rooted device, ransomware carrier applications must have a valid signature and certificate from Apple to be distributed. This process poses risks of cancellation of certificates and blacklisting, with little pay-out.

According to a Kaspersky blog (Snow, 2016), the largest mobile ransomware attack family was Fusob and was responsible for 56% of Android device attacks in 2016. Fusob infiltrates a device when a user visits certain porn sites and downloads a media player for porn videos. It then blocks all access to the device and demands $100 to $200 in iTunes gift cards to unblock. It does not encrypt anything on the device. It only locks the user out by preventing access to other apps and settings and from uninstalling the ransomware (see Figure 4). Another example is the Android.Lockdroid.E (Sundar, n.d.) variant that came bundled with a porn video application which could be downloaded from an adult website. It was a Trojan impersonating the FBI and displayed a warning, demanding a fine of $500 for accessing forbidden pornographic websites and locked the device.

Mobile ransomware is still in its developmental stage. We are yet to see a massive explosion of ransomware attacks on mobile devices as we have witnessed in the case of PC ransomware. One reason is that Android and other mobile operating systems offer the option for automatic data synchronization via cloud storage or other applications. This means that when the network data speed is high, or a Wi-Fi is connected to, the device automatically initiates a synchronization procedure to backup any changes made to the file system of both, the phone storage and SD (Secure Digital) card storage. Thus, important data like photos, videos, messages, contacts, etc. are preserved outside the device, to be used for recovery in

Figure 3. KillDisk Ransom Note on Linux ("Destructive KillDisk", 2017)

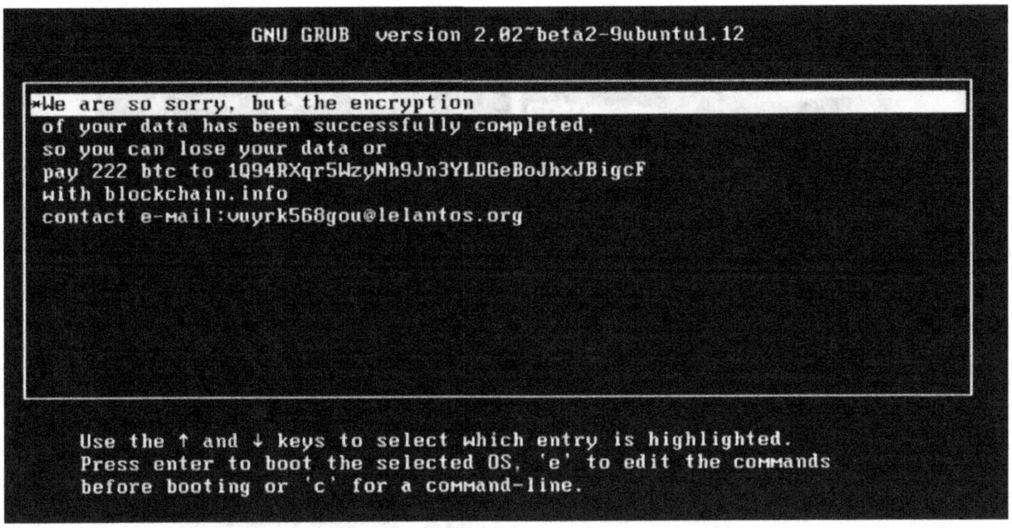

```
        GNU GRUB   version 2.02~beta2-9ubuntu1.12

*We are so sorry, but the encryption
of your data has been successfully completed,
so you can lose your data or
pay 222 btc to 1Q94RXqr5WzyNh9Jn3YLDGeBoJhxJBigcF
with blockchain.info
contact e-mail:vuyrk568gou@lelantos.org




        Use the ↑ and ↓ keys to select which entry is highlighted.
        Press enter to boot the selected OS, 'e' to edit the commands
        before booting or 'c' for a command-line.
```

case of a failure. In the event of a ransomware attack that encrypts all data files, the user can get these back without paying the ransom using the synchronization feature. This makes the attack less profitable causing cybercriminals to focus their attention on desktop and laptop computer variants. Another reason for discouragement for cybercriminals may be that desktops and laptops contain more sensitive data as well as a greater amount of it as compared to mobile devices. Also, enterprises, healthcare, government organizations, businesses, educational institutions all carry their important data on desktops and laptops. This prompts victims to pay up ransom if attacked, as retrieving the locked or encrypted information as soon as possible is a major concern of such institutions. However, with increasing mobile computing power and storage miniaturization, smartphones and tablets may become comparable to desktop and laptop computing, thereby encouraging cybercriminals to shift their focus to mobile ransomware development on a wide scale.

Ransomware for Servers

Servers are central repositories for documents, source code, financial records, financial transactions, user databases, and trade secrets, making them high-value potential targets for cybercriminals (Savage, Coogan, & Lau, 2015). Servers usually have integrated backup and restore facilities to protect data and business loss due to criticality of sensitive data. They even employ data mirroring on backup servers for business continuity. Despite this, hijacking a critical server even for a short time could be incredibly upsetting and detrimental to company reputation.

Cyber-attackers blackmail businesses by unleashing an unanticipated, distributed denial-of-service (DDoS) attack against an establishment's servers and then follow up with a ransom demand. However, with DDoS mitigation services in place, ransomware creators need to look elsewhere to cause trouble. Some groups do this by infiltrating the target server and patching the software to encrypt all stored data along with all backup files (Savage, Coogan, & Lau, 2015). Further, the cybercriminals remove the decryption key and then make their ransom demands, which could be pretty high.

Figure 4. Fusob Ransom Message for Android (Olenick, 2016)

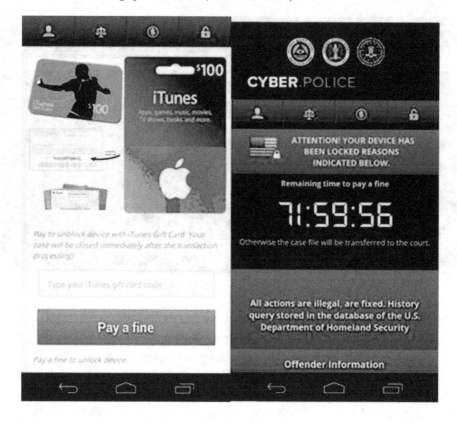

For example, the WannaCry ransomware, took control of servers by exploiting a Microsoft Windows Service Message Block (SMB) protocol vulnerability in May 2017 ("WannaCry ransomware attack", n.d.). In South Korea, in June 2017, 153 Linux servers of a web-hosting company were compromised by the Erebus ransomware, which resulted in loss of critical data for more than 3400 businesses that used the company's services ("Erebus Linux Ransomware", 2017).

Ransomware for Cloud

Cloud storage has gained immense popularity since its inception. It is cost-effective and easy to access. It is also one of the safest data storage options. According to a report by Right Scale (*State of the Cloud,* 2017), more than 80% of all companies are already using multi-cloud storage for their business data storage. This trend is going to increase in future as small and medium businesses and institutions become inherently dependent on cloud storage strategies. Cybercriminals are more interested in targeting bigger organizations that are data intensive and therefore, they have started developing ransomware to target cloud services for disrupting business.

According to a report by Netskope (*Netskope Cloud Report*, 2016), 43.7% of cloud malware contains ransomware payload with 56% of these files shared publicly. The most common types include JavaScript droppers, Microsoft Office macros, PDF exploits, Linux malware and backdoor programs.

Attacking cloud service providers is extremely profitable to cybercriminals. A single ransomware attack can affect every user using the cloud service compromised. The cloud can also be utilized as a vehicle for distributing ransomware payload through automatic synchronization and sharing of malware infected files. Since the cloud storage is always in sync with local storage, any changes cause the automatic sync feature to replicate the changes back to the cloud. During a ransomware attack, the local files are encrypted which changes their state on the device, thereby inducing automatic synchronization to write the encrypted files back to the cloud storage. Versioning is a technique that can reduce the impact a ransomware attack causes. In this strategy, every new change to a file is recorded as a new version on the cloud. However, it is not a fool proof method of dealing with these attacks as many cloud service providers do not have this as an option or it is simply turned off by default.

The Virlock ransomware variant attacks specifically cloud storage, collaborative and social networking platforms for distribution and extortion (Vamshi, 2016). It spreads very quickly to all users in that network, jeopardizing all enterprise data. Cerber is another ransomware that targets Microsoft Office 365 users through the use of corrupt email attachments laced with malware carrying macros in spam mail ("Ransomware", n.d.).

Cloud servers have become one of the most common ways of spreading malware with 1 in 10 companies carrying malware in their cloud storage facility (Johnson, 2016). It is therefore necessary that these companies employ automated daily backups and daily cloud application auditing in order to detect and recover from such attacks.

Ransomware for Smart TV

A majority of Smart TVs run the Android operating system. Today's Smart TVs have plenty of features that allow the user to download apps as on mobile devices and browse the internet using the built-in browser bundled into the smart TV firmware. Being Android, third party apps can also be installed on certain brands and models.

Ransomware on Smart TV is still uncommon but several research groups from security solution providers have tested ransomware on Smart TVs and found them difficult to get rid of. FLocker is a common type to infect Smart TVs. In Dec 2015 (Constantine, 2017), a family got the worst Christmas surprise when a relative accidently infected the TV with FLocker after downloading a movie app and playing a movie. Half-way through the movie, their TV screen suddenly displayed a ransom message posing to be from the FBI asking for a fine of $500 which wouldn't go away. It was very difficult to remove even for LG Electronics Ltd. which was the TV supplier. In the end, a factory reset of the TV had to be done to get rid of the ransomware.

Criteria: Intimidation Strategy

Based on the methodology used to intimidate users, Ransomware may be classified as: Encrypting and Non-encrypting ransomware, Leak-ware and browser locker and website locker ransomware.

Encrypting Ransomware

We have already learnt in a previous section, how the idea of ransomware was conceived with the advent of the AIDS Trojan ransomware back in 1989. The design flaws of the first ransomware were pointed out by Jim Bates in his technical analysis report (1990) who also wrote two programs to remove the threat and unscramble the files to recover content. Further, Adam Young and Moti Yung pointed out in their 1996 paper (Young & Yung, 1996) that strong public key cryptography could be used as a means for extortion and data hijack. They called their encrypting malware a '*cryptovirus*'. Though they also discussed countermeasures and mitigation strategies to cope with such attacks, they more or less triggered the full-blown development of these difficult-to-crack malware strains. This was a time when the world was oblivious to such a form of cybercrime and their research was not taken as seriously as it should have been until we saw a surge in crypto-viruses that used these techniques starting 2005.

Crypto viruses use both symmetric as well as asymmetric key cryptography. Symmetric encryption algorithms like AES (Advanced Encryption Standard) employ a small (usually 256-bit) single key to encrypt and decrypt data. On the contrary, asymmetric means of encryption like RSA (Rivest, Shamir and Adleman) use separate keys, a public key to encrypt data and a private key to decrypt the encrypted data. Knowing the encryption key in symmetric key cryptography, one can easily decrypt the encrypted data as the same key is being used for both purposes. Therefore, ransomware programmers must protect the symmetric key until encryption is complete and thereafter delete the key and all its references from the infected system before being discovered. However, the advantage of quick encryption that this technique offers, as compared to asymmetric methods, works to their benefit. In contrast, the public key need not be given as much protection when using asymmetric means as a separate private key (which is held by the cybercriminals alone) is needed to decrypt information. However, asymmetric methods are slower, and ransomware must take precautions to remain concealed for at least as long as the program takes to find important files to encrypt and thereafter, encode them using the public key. Encryption is also used to secure the communication between the ransomware and its command and control server (C&C), which holds the private key or know how to recover it. One advantage of public key algorithms is that no matter how large the number of affected victims, the cybercriminals need only to protect a single private key.

Older ransomware like AIDS Trojan used only symmetric key algorithms. With time, Trojan such as Cryzip, Gpcode began using the asymmetric algorithms like RSA with larger and larger keys.

Modern crypto viruses use dual encryption methods i.e. symmetric algorithms for encrypting the victim's files and asymmetric key cryptography to encrypt the symmetric key used in the first step. For example, CryptoLocker uses AES for user file encryption and RSA for AES key encryption.

With advances in the field of cryptography, the next generation encryption algorithms like ECC (Elliptic Curve Cryptography) and hashed algorithms may make ransomware even more challenging to crack. These algorithms create smaller keys and provide greater efficiency in terms of speed and strength of encryption, and may therefore become the algorithms of choice for cybercriminals to wreck more businesses and cause even greater damage.

Non-Encrypting Ransomware

This is a lesser known strain of ransomware and also the less effective kind in generating revenue for the bad guys. Rather than encrypting the user's important files, this type of malware simply blocks access to them and displays ransom messages to unblock them. Some threaten their victims with legal action if the ransom is not paid within a stipulated time frame. They are also known as lockers as they freeze the user screen on the ransom message disallowing the user to access any service of the operating system by displaying the ransom note on an infinite loop. These ransomware strains use API functionality of the underlying operating system to perform their tasks. Most of them impersonate a certain police organization or an authentic investigation agency to scare their victims into paying up the ransom. They also use geospatial targeting techniques like geographical IP (here IP stands for Internet Protocol) lookups, traffic routing services, email targeting, etc. to display location-specific ransom messages.

Earlier ransomware, like the screen lockers of 2009 which were Russia-based (see Figure 5), claimed to be from Microsoft and stated that the computer was locked and in order to be activated, the user needed to enter a specific code that could be obtained by sending an SMS to a premium rate number (O'Gorman & McDonald, 2012). Then during 2009 and 2010, a new type emerged which displayed a pornographic image on the screen that wouldn't go away until the victim paid $10 by sending a premium rate SMS to receive an unlock code (O'Gorman & McDonald, 2012). In 2010, ten people responsible for Winlock were arrested in Moscow. However, they had made $16 million from this SMS scheme within a year! Most people paid up as this ransomware played on human emotions such as embarrassment and fear.

In 2011, a ransomware that imitated the Windows Product Activation notice came about. It stated that the system's Windows installation had to be re-activated due to being pirated. The Trojan eventually asked the victim to call an international number (claiming to be toll-free) to input a code. This call was then channelled to a rogue operator in a country with high international calling rates who placed the call on hold, causing the user to suffer huge international long-distance call charges.

Figure 5. A Russian-based ransomware screen locker posing as a Microsoft warning (O'Gorman & McDonald, 2012)

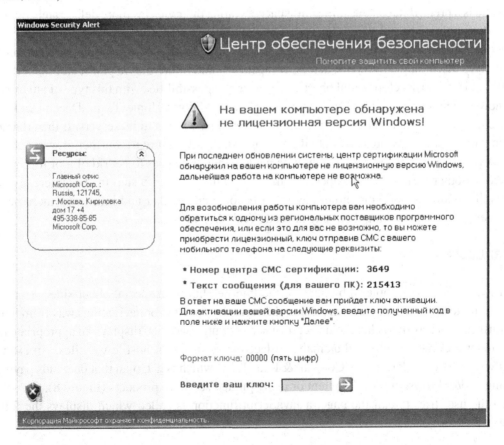

Screen lockers were not as popular as their encrypting cousins because it was not too difficult to get rid of the annoying ransom messages without paying. Most of the time, it was only a matter of reinstalling the operating system and restoring data from a previous back up. There was also an option to get rid of the virus in the very short intervals in which the message could be closed, but this approach didn't always work, especially for non-technical users who did not know much about operating systems, API calls, etc.

Leakware

Leakware threatens to go public with the private information it has gathered from the victim rather than denying the user access to them, unless a ransom is paid. It is a type of blackmail to keep a company's or a user's secrets from the public. It often targets private email messages or word documents, private images, videos or contacts.

Leakware is also known as Doxware. Doxing is a term that refers to the public release of private data. Leakware can be more effective in terms of generating profit revenues for cybercriminals who develop and distribute them as people are still okay with losing all their data rather than the leaking of their private information on the web. This is truer for businesses and government institutions, civic bodies, law enforcement agencies, education institutions, etc. No company wants its confidential information to be released for the public eye. They would rather lose all their data to encrypting ransomware than to be blackmailed in this fashion. There would be no choice but to pay the ransom demanded to keep their secrets with them. No number of backups or decrypting programs can save them from such a situation where the criminal gangs have got hold of precious information.

Doxware is a premeditated attack, meaning hackers target their victims more deliberately, giving corporate leaders, politicians, celebrities, and other public figures cause for concern. In 2014 (Ensey, 2017), Sony Pictures suffered an email phishing attack that released private conversations between producers and executives discussing employees, actors, competitors, and future movie plans, etc.

Leakware is still in developmental phases. However, the possibilities with this type of attack are endless. A new variant discovered by Malware Hunter Team (MalwareHunterTeam, December 12, 2016) not only encrypts user data, but also copies all discovered passwords to its servers. It then threatens to go public with all the passwords and data if a ransom isn't paid (Figure 6). Further, it warns the victim that all his files will be deleted, and data will be made public if he tries to get rid of it or tries rebooting the device. Another variant called Popcorn Time (see Figure 7) goes a step further in creativity. This one gives the victim an option to either pay up or become an attacker and infect two more people by sending them a link and making them pay instead. Yeah, horrid!

Browser Locker

Browser lockers are like simple web pages on the Internet, but with special client-side scripting code like JavaScript to prevent the user from closing the currently open tab or navigating away from it to other tabs. It further uses geo-IP tracking to detect the user's country and then displays an appropriate ransom note. Browser lockers are delivered as malware-laced advertising on hostile websites. An example of such malware is Browlock (Savage, Coogan, & Lau, 2015) which is a Trojan that demands payment for possessing and/or browsing illegal content or using pirated software products (Figure 8).

When the user tries to exit the page, a JavaScript function is called which displays the following warning to the user:

Figure 6. Leakware ransom message (Source: MalwareHunterTeam, December 12, 2016)

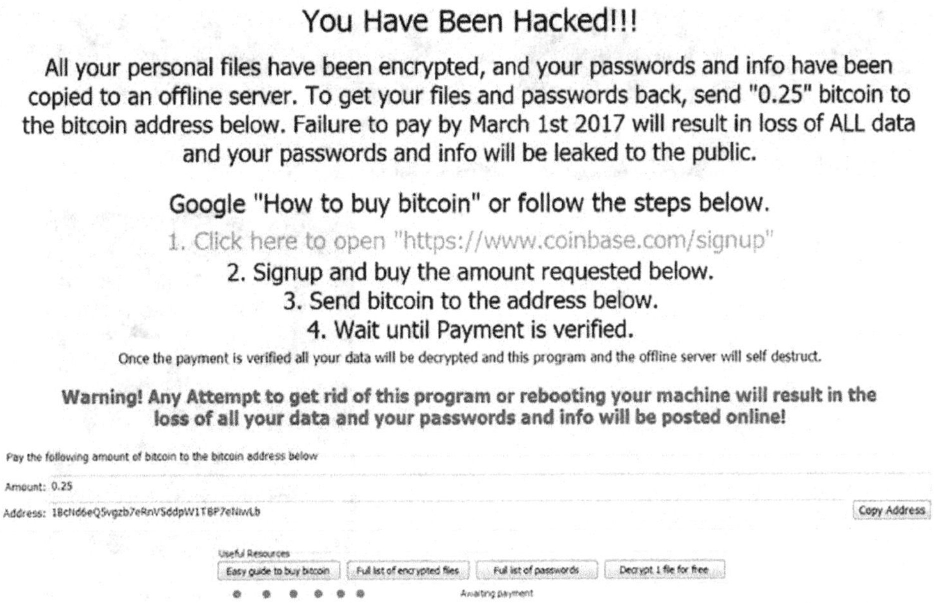

You Have Been Hacked!!!

All your personal files have been encrypted, and your passwords and info have been copied to an offline server. To get your files and passwords back, send "0.25" bitcoin to the bitcoin address below. Failure to pay by March 1st 2017 will result in loss of ALL data and your passwords and info will be leaked to the public.

Google "How to buy bitcoin" or follow the steps below.

1. Click here to open "https://www.coinbase.com/signup"
2. Signup and buy the amount requested below.
3. Send bitcoin to the address below.
4. Wait until Payment is verified.

Once the payment is verified all your data will be decrypted and this program and the offline server will self destruct.

Warning! Any Attempt to get rid of this program or rebooting your machine will result in the loss of all your data and your passwords and info will be posted online!

Pay the following amount of bitcoin to the bitcoin address below

Amount: 0.25

Address: 18cNd6eQ5vgzb7eRnVSddpW1T8P7eNiwLb   [Copy Address]

Useful Resources
[Easy guide to buy bitcoin] [Full list of encrypted files] [Full list of passwords] [Decrypt 1 file for free]

● ● ● ● ● ●   Awaiting payment

Figure 7. Popcorn Time (Source: MalwareHunterTeam December 7, 2016)

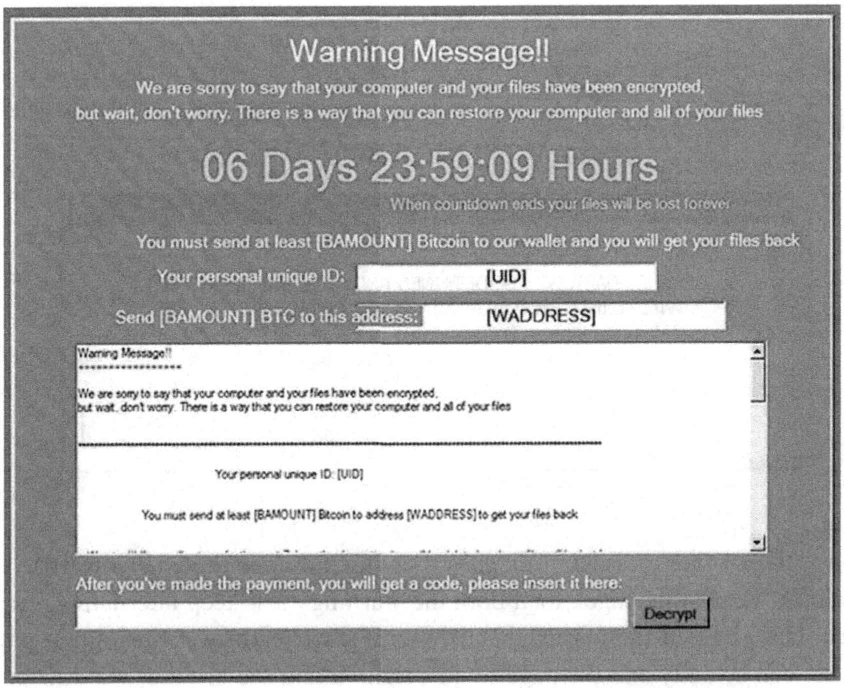

Warning Message!!

We are sorry to say that your computer and your files have been encrypted, but wait, don't worry. There is a way that you can restore your computer and all of your files

06 Days 23:59:09 Hours

When countdown ends your files will be lost forever

You must send at least [BAMOUNT] Bitcoin to our wallet and you will get your files back

Your personal unique ID: [UID]

Send [BAMOUNT] BTC to this address: [WADDRESS]

Warning Message!!
****
We are sorry to say that your computer and your files have been encrypted,
but wait, don't worry. There is a way that you can restore your computer and all of your files

Your personal unique ID: [UID]

You must send at least [BAMOUNT] Bitcoin to address [WADDRESS] to get your files back

After you've made the payment, you will get a code, please insert it here:

[   ] [Decrypt]

Figure 8. Browlock ransom message (Savage, Coogan, & Lau, 2015)

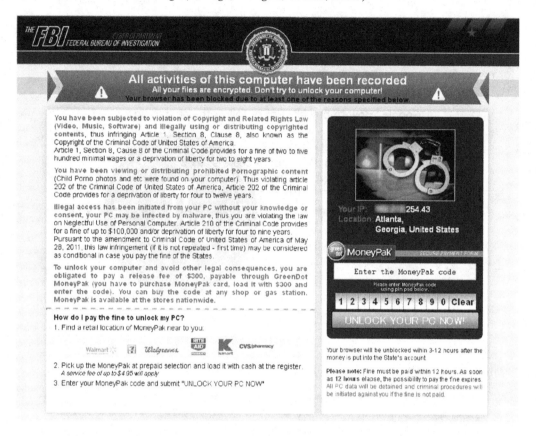

Figure 9. Browlock Warning#1 (Savage, Coogan, & Lau, 2015)

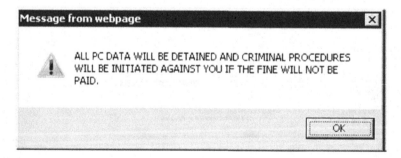

After clicking OK, another message is displayed saying the same thing (Figure 10).

If the user clicks 'Leave this page', then both the warnings just keep alternating, creating a never-ending sequence. This gives the impression that the user is stuck on the website until he pays the ransom. However, the user can actually exit the page by just terminating the browser window process through Task Manager.

Browser lockers are not effective enough as they can be disabled without payment. However, their development doesn't take much effort and they also offer the advantage of being cross-platform. They

Figure 10. Browlock Warning#2 (Savage, Coogan, & Lau, 2015)

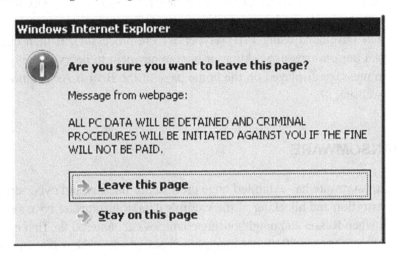

can be used on any browser or any operating system without being specifically designed for each. That's why they are still around and constitute as a side profit for bad guys.

Website Locker

This type of ransomware targets entire websites and locks them out by displaying ransom message on their home page. They generally target outdated content management websites with vulnerabilities like Wordpress.com.

Figure 11. CTB-Locker affects a website (Saxena, 2016)

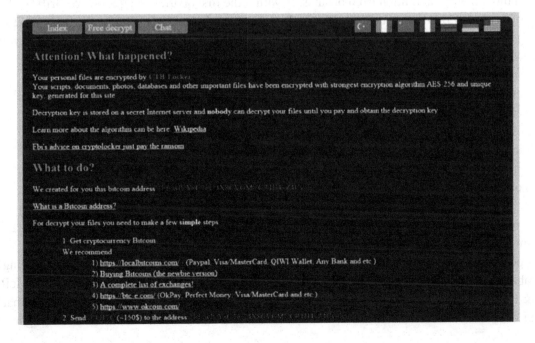

A notable example is the Curve-Tor-Bitcoin-Locker or CTB-Locker that targets and infiltrates a web server and once installed, it replaces the website's home page with its own ransom page. CTB-Locker is written for websites developed using PHP (Hypertext Pre-processor). It then encrypts the entire website and displays a ransom message asking for bitcoin payment to decrypt it. Figure 11 shows the CTB-Locker ransom message displayed on the home page of the British Association for Counselling and Psychotherapy website.

IMPACT OF RANSOMWARE

Since its inception, ransomware has exhibited huge promise for hackers and cyber-criminal gangs as a very subtle way of extortion and hijacking of the victim's data. Ransomware have seen an exponential increase since 2009, when Russia and neighbouring countries encountered the first extortionist screen-lockers. During much of 2009 and 2010, pornographic ransom-lock variants became commonplace.

Starting 2011, ransomware spread to many parts of Europe and from there into the Unites States and other countries across the globe. From individual cyber criminals, programmers and hackers, this money-raking business spread to form cyber-criminal gangs that operate exclusively to develop and distribute this notorious malware.

Ransomware has evolved from targeting individual users to targeting businesses, government agencies, healthcare and educational institutions, leading to financial loss and data breach. The payment methods have also improved from SMS and phone-based payment to prepaid electronic payment such as Ukash, MoneyPak and PaySafe, with the latest trend being digital currencies like Bitcoin. However, this approach has certainly increased the revenues for these criminals as these organizations often pay up the ransom amount in the hopes of reducing downtime and getting their sensitive data back as fast as possible. Hospitals seem to be the worst hit since it can become a matter of life and death for patients if critically important services are unavailable. In April of 2016, the FBI warned that cybercriminals had extorted more than $209 million from businesses within the first quarter (Fitzpatrick & Griffin, 2016)! The profits go way overboard the costs incurred by these gangs in advertising, buying exploit kits, recruiting developers, etc. So, it is definitely very profitable for them to continue doing this in the future.

Ransomware leads to many undesirable consequences, some of which are:

- Temporary or permanent loss of sensitive or copyright information,
- Leakage of company secrets and personal data to the public,
- Disruption to regular business operations,
- Financial losses incurred to restore systems and files,
- Damage to an organization's reputation, and
- Loss of life due to extreme circumstances or non-availability of critical services.

According to a quarterly threat summary review by Proofpoint (*Quarterly Threat Summary*, 2016), ransomware accounts for 70% of all malware attacks (Figure 12)!

As per the report, the number of ransomware variants increased by a factor of 30x, Locky being the most abundant strain among them. However, a recent study sponsored by Google (Invernizzi, McRoberts, & Bursztein, 2017) has revealed that the ransomware extortion industry is a fast-changing market. From Locky in 2016, the most abundant ransomware variant has shifted to Cerber in 2017 (Figure 13).

Figure 12. Malware distribution (Based on Proofpoint's Quarterly Threat Summary, 2016)

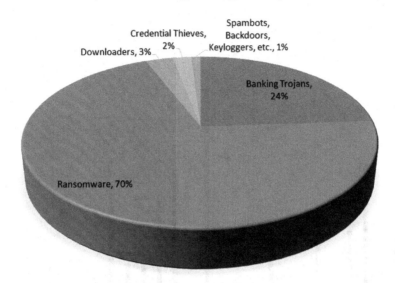

Not only are newer strains taking over older ones with each passing year, the ransom demands also fluctuate as much. Figure 14 shows that the average ransom demand has increased in 2017 to $1077 according to a report by Symantec (*Internet Security Threat Report*, 2017). Each year we see many new strains of the malware that are becoming harder and harder to crack. Trend Micro's 2016 report (*The reign of ransomware*, 2016) showed an increase in strains from 29 in 2015 to 79 new families of ransomware by the end of 2016. It is therefore inevitable that a global crisis is just around the corner waiting to pounce.

Ransomware results in similar consequences for both, home users as well as organizations. The only difference is that, in the case of the latter, the attack is large-scale and may be specialized to target a particular organization for achieving a predetermined goal. The impact of ransomware on individuals and businesses is discussed in the following subsections.

Impact on Individual Users

Home users are easy targets for a ransomware attack due to a number of reasons:

- Most users are unaware of what it is, how it spreads and what it is capable of doing,
- Home users are prone to opening hostile links, clicking on ads, opening untrusted email attachments, etc.,
- They are prone to trust everyone and therefore will click on anything lucrative,
- A large number of them access adult sites, porn sites, etc.,
- Almost all home users have at some point downloaded illegal software, pirated movies and music, torrents containing illegal content, etc.,
- Layman users tend to panic when given a scare by any ransomware posing as a police agency or threatened by legal action or arrest,
- Most do not patch and update their operating system regularly leaving them at risk of attacks exploiting such vulnerable machines,

Figure 13. Quarterly market share of notable strains 2016-2017 (Based on data from Invernizzi, McRoberts, & Bursztein, 2017)

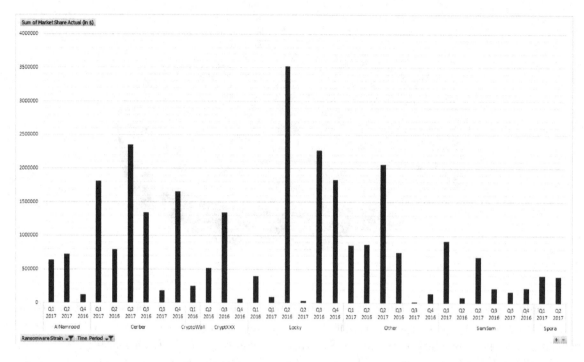

Figure 14. Average ransom demand trends (Based on data from Internet Security Threat Report, 2017)

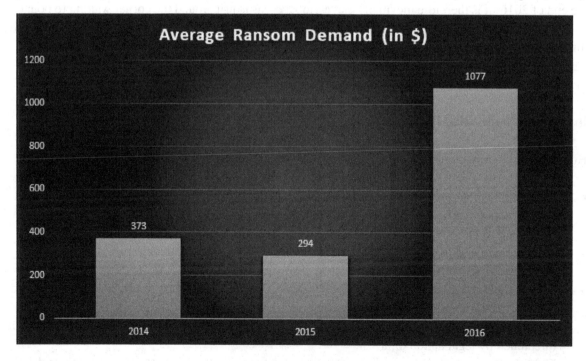

- Some ransomware strains can be evaded without paying, but users do not educate themselves and therefore fall victim to paying up,
- Home users do not have enough security awareness and tend to install only the most basic cyber protection software like a basic antivirus that cannot deal with new ransomware,
- They do not have data backups to recover in the event of a sudden data hijack.

Thousands of users have shared their personal experiences with different variants of ransomware across blogsites and social media on the Internet. Many of them accepted that they fell prey to the attackers and paid up. In one case, the victim was asked to pay ransom in bitcoin within a week after which her ransom would be doubled. Since she was unaware of how bitcoin worked, she failed to pay and requested the attacker to let her have some more time. The bargain worked, and she ended up paying only the $500. Well… she still paid. In another case, a research student lost 2 years of thesis work as he had no backup. And the timing was awful as his thesis was due shortly. No one knows whether he paid up and submitted that thesis in time, but it did teach him a lesson for life. According to a Kaspersky 2016 report (Ivanov, Emm, Sinitsyn, & Pontiroli, 2016), an individual was attacked every 10 seconds by the third quarter of that year!

In an extreme case of murder and suicide due to ransomware, in 2014 (Ghosh, 2014), a 36-year-old Romanian man, Marcel Datcu, murdered his 4-year-old son and then hanged himself after he received a fake warning from the police stating that his computer was found to possess illegal pornographic content and that he visited illegal adult websites. The ransom note asked him for a hefty fine of around $22,000 or go to jail for 11 years. The forensic examiner believed him to be suffering from a personality disorder and presented this as a reason for his thinking the threat was real. To add to that, Marcel had actually been surfing porn when his computer was infected with ransomware.

In another case, in January 2015 (Pleasance, 2015), a seventeen-year-old boy named Joseph Edwards, who suffered from Autism spectrum disorder committed suicide by hanging himself in his Windsor, Berkshire home because he took a ransom email message (claiming to be from the local police) seriously. The message claimed that he had been visiting illegal websites and demanded he pay a £100 fine or face legal action.

Impact on Businesses

Attacking businesses has been very lucrative due to the following reasons:

- Businesses suffer downtimes and losses in terms of data as well as revenue and therefore often pay up more readily than others as a quick solution to an immediate problem,
- Along with computers and other devices, attackers can cause greater damage by accessing the cloud based services and server systems used by businesses,
- Many businesses do not admit to having been attacked or having paid ransom in order to protect their reputation as a secure system,
- Small businesses often do not invest a lot into cyber security leaving them vulnerable to attacks,
- Cybercriminals also get the opportunity to steal sensitive data and company secrets to sell them to rival businesses and blackmail the victim company on the side.

The 2016 State of Ransomware report conducted by Osterman Research and sponsored by Malwarebytes (Zamora, 2016) shows that at least 40% of businesses were hit by ransomware. The highest number of attacks were recorded in the United Kingdom, followed by the United States (see Figure 15-Figure 17).

The global impact of ransomware on industries is massive and still growing. According to the 2016 report by Kaspersky Labs (Ivanov, Emm, Sinitsyn, & Pontiroli, 2016), attacks on businesses has increased three-fold in September 2016 from what it was in January, and this is in a span of half a year alone! They also reported that only a fifth of the small and medium businesses (SMBs) actually got their data back after paying the ransom. Figure 18 shows some of the alarming statistics from that report.

Table 1 shows the various industrial sectors and their corresponding percentage of ransomware attacks. The education industry seems worst hit in 2016 followed by the Information Technology (IT) and Telecom sectors. This may be because students in educational institutions click on anything and everything that attracts them. They also lack cyber security awareness and indulge in bad Internet surfing practices. In addition, computers in such institutions have weaker protection and most often remain unpatched and unsupported. The attackers then infect all systems connected to the institutional network and hijack student records, teaching material, registration files, mark sheets, certificates, etc. to halt processes. Similarly, IT and Telecom sector employees introduce the entire network to ransomware, thereby corrupting servers, computer systems, websites, etc. to bring down and stall projects.

The deadliest impact of ransomware has been observed in the healthcare sector. These attacks result in numerous consequences, some of which can deem fatal to the lives of patients. Encrypting healthcare data means patient's medical history becomes inaccessible that may cause significant delays in treatment. Further, lab reports are stalled as they cannot be transmitted by a hijacked computer. Certain medical

Figure 15. Statistics on ransomware for businesses (Based on data from Zamora, 2016)

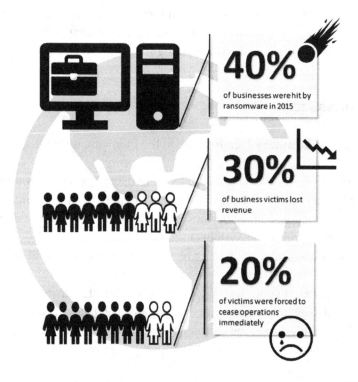

Figure 16. Country wise attack percentages (Based on data from Zamora, 2016)

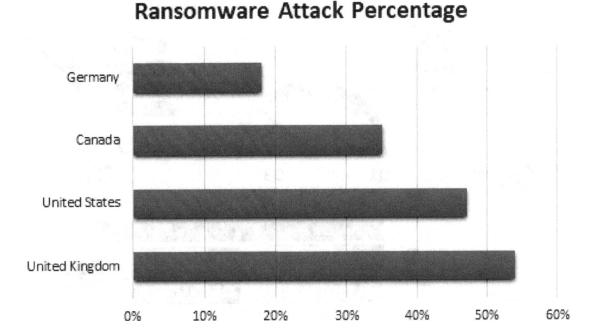

Figure 17. Ransom demands from businesses (Based on data from Zamora, 2016)

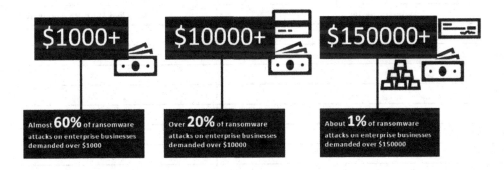

devices become inoperable that rely on computers to run, like MRI (Magnetic Resonance Imaging), ultrasound, etc., delaying treatment and putting lives at stake.

In May 2017 ("WannaCry ransomware attack", n.d.), the world shook when a ransomware crypto worm known as WannaCry infected more than 300,000 Windows PCs in over 150 countries in a single day! The UK's National Health Service (NHS) was worst affected. In many hospitals across the UK, employees were forced to revert to manual recording of information or using alternative means like mobiles and tablets. Many surgical appointments had to be cancelled and patients had to be turned away. Besides the NHS, a large number of corporations were affected in several countries including FedEx, Hitachi, Honda, hospitals in Indonesia and Slovakia, government organizations in India and Russia, universities in Italy, Indonesia, Canada and Greece and many more.

Figure 18. Global statistics on ransomware (Based on the data from Ivanov, Emm, Sinitsyn, & Pontiroli, 2016)

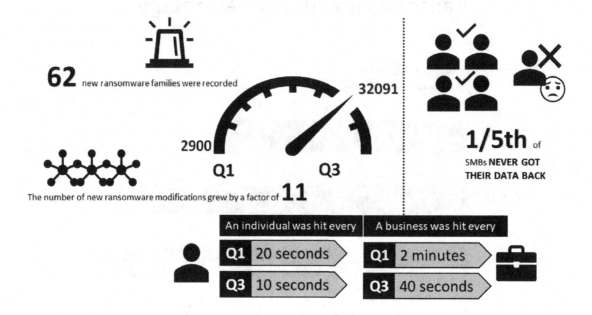

Table 1. Industry sectors and their risk of attack in 2016 (Based on data from Ivanov, Emm, Sinitsyn, & Pontiroli, 2016)

Industry Sector	% Attacked With Ransomware
Education	23
IT/Telecoms	22
Entertainment/Media	21
Financial Services	21
Construction	19
Government/ Public Sector/Defence	18
Manufacturing	18
Transport	17
Healthcare	16
Retail/wholesale/leisure	16

LAUNCHING RANSOMWARE: LIFE CYCLE

Given below are the stages of a typical ransomware attack (see Figure 19).

- **Stage I:** Dissemination of Infection
- **Stage II:** Installation and Contamination
- **Stage III:** Payload Staging

Figure 19. Life cycle of a typical ransomware

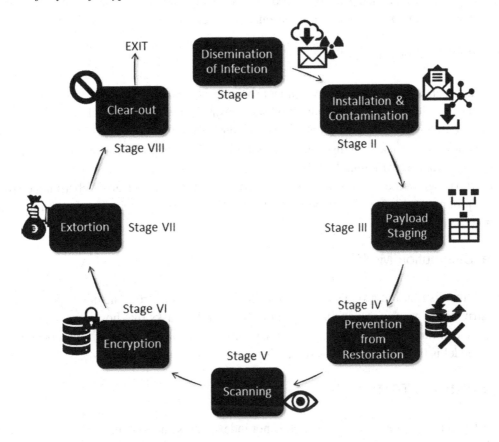

- **Stage IV:** Prevention from Restoration
- **Stage V:** Scanning
- **Stage VI:** Cryptographic Encryption
- **Stage VII:** Extortion
- **Stage VIII:** Clear-out

Stage I: Dissemination of Infection

Cybercriminals use various techniques like social engineering, phishing, advertisements, etc. to distribute their ransomware. Since ransomware has become a huge enterprise in itself, several business models are in place that disseminate it over the network effectively. Let us discuss some of the prevalent models.

Vertical Distribution Model

In this business model, the cybercriminal gang is responsible for all activities starting from the programming of ransomware, hosting it and its droppers to managing all distribution channels as well as collection of ransom via blockchain, altchain or other means (*The anatomy of a ransomware attack*, 2016). Figure 20 illustrates the vertical distribution model.

This strategy offers the advantage of 100% profit retention by the gang. On the downside, they need to involve expert hackers and programmers, professional managers and other gifted individuals for all tasks.

Outsourced Distribution Model

In this model, the ransomware code development, hosting and ransom collection is still done by the cybercriminal gang. However, the distribution of ransomware created by them is handled by third party distribution groups (Figure 21). This model is preferred over the vertical model in many cases as distribution is a painstaking task. The distribution group generally gets 50 – 75% of the ransom collected (*The anatomy of a ransomware attack*, 2016).

Hackers who program the ransomware create an affiliate market on the Dark Web asking distribution specialists to join in (see Figure 22). Sometimes, these affiliate networks may even ask for a special fee as a one-time membership fee.

Horizontal Distribution Model

In this model, the distribution group purchases ransomware programs from the developers for a licence fee. The distribution group is responsible thereafter for all other tasks like hosting, dissemination and therefore, they can rake in 100% of the profit for themselves (*The anatomy of a ransomware attack*, 2016). This model is the inverse of the vertical distribution model (Figure 23).

The Dark Web and TOR

The dark web is a part of the deep web (which is not indexed by search engines) or an overlay network that uses the Internet but requires specific software or authorization to gain access into. Popular dark

Figure 20. Vertical Distribution Scheme (Model based on The anatomy of a ransomware attack, 2016)

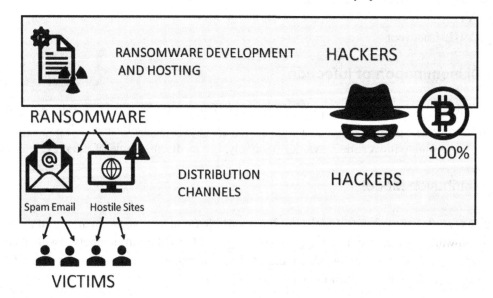

Figure 21. Outsourced Distribution Model (Model based on The anatomy of a ransomware attack, 2016)

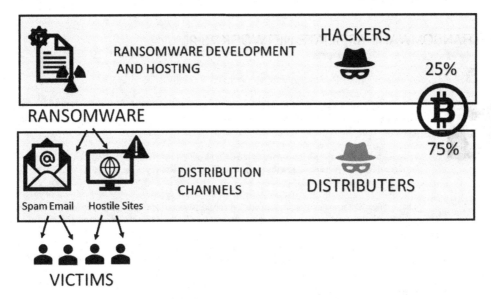

networks are Tor, Freenet and I2P (Invisible Internet Project). Tor is also called 'onionland' due to the use of onion routing for anonymity. Tor is the most popular dark web browser and can be identified by the domain '.onion'. The dark web is being used for a large number of illicit undertakings like child pornography, illegal pornography, human trafficking, black marketing, drug trafficking, bitcoin services, hacking activities, scamming, phishing, crowdfunding of assassinations, hoaxes, illegal arms deals, software exploits, fraud services, terrorism, whistleblowing, etc. Communication between dark net users is highly encrypted allowing users to talk, blog, and share files confidentially. In order to gain access to a dark web network, the user must first obtain a VPN (Virtual Private Network) software to encrypt all network traffic that provides fake IP addresses from another country so that authorities cannot trace any activity back to the dark net user. Next, the user needs to download and install the Tor Browser from their website and then open the Tor browser to visit any dark market website.

RaaS (Ransomware-as-a-Service) Model

RaaS is a booming business on the dark web or Tor sites and is similar to the affiliate networks discussed previously. However, the way they function is different from these affiliates. RaaS developers host their ransomware on a portal from where interested parties can deploy them. The portal dashboard contains additional options to configure or customize the ransom demands depending upon timeframes and even view estimates of profit before signing on. The sites also assist affiliates in making their dropper or distribution models like macros, CHM (Compiled HTML) installers, drive-by downloads, JavaScript code, etc. which will be used by the RaaS to distribute the ransomware via spam emails, hostile links, advertisements, word documents, etc. Some even have the option for multi-language support that allows hackers to generate ransom messages in many languages to be used to target victims geographically.

Figure 22. A ransomware affiliate network on the dark web (The anatomy of a ransomware attack, 2016)

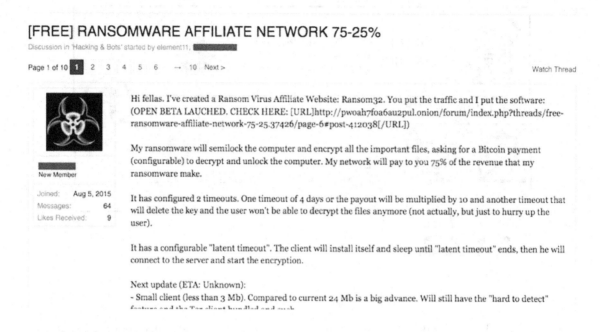

Figure 23. Horizontal Distribution Model (Model based on The anatomy of a ransomware attack, 2016)

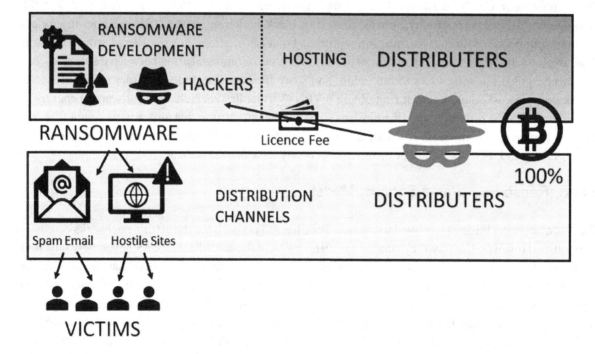

Some RaaS developers offer their code for free with a profit-sharing model making it a win-win for both parties. Examples of such RaaS ransomware packages have already been seen such as Satan (Figure 24), Cerber, Flux, Hostman, etc.

Stage II: Installation and Contamination

There are many paths that may lead to a ransomware infection such as exploit kits, botnet infections, social engineering attacks, spam email attachments, etc. (Figure 25). These are known as droppers or infection vectors - they initiate the attack. Some that are most prevalent contamination methods are discussed in the following subsections.

Email Droppers

Spam email attachments are the most common infection vectors that contaminate devices. Email droppers pose to come from banks or companies which lure the user into opening the attachments that are malware-laced. These are generally word documents with malicious macros. When opened, they force users to enable macros in order for them to view the document correctly. Another type of attachment is an executable .exe file posing as a pdf file. Since Windows does not display the file extensions by default, the actual file extension remains hidden. For example, a user gets an email from Amazon.com

Figure 24. Satan's RaaS dashboard (Osborne, 2017)

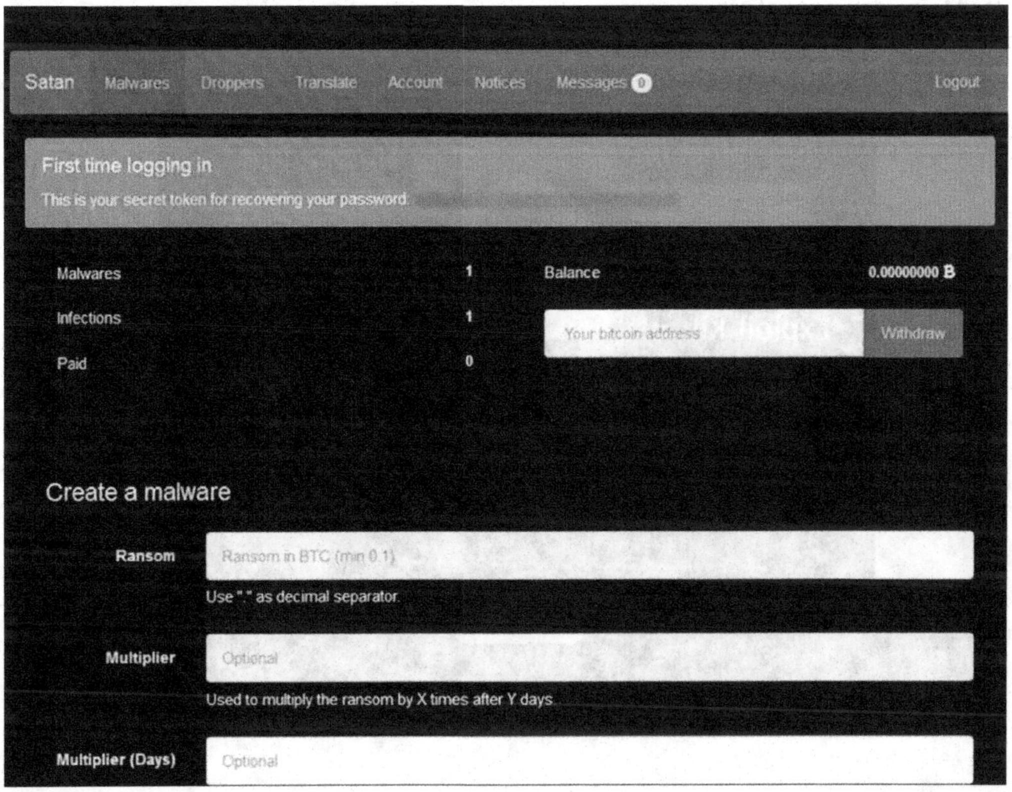

that appears legitimate and carries an order invoice as an attachment (that has the Adobe Reader icon) and is named invoice.pdf. The unsuspecting user opens the harmless looking pdf only to discover that it is actually an executable malware invoice.pdf.exe!

Exploit Kits

Exploit Kits are software programs that are designed to identify software vulnerabilities in clients connected to web servers that they infiltrate, with the intent of dropping ransomware on the client machines. A large pool of machines is unpatched and unsupported which gives an opportunity to these kits to drop malware to them. Further, exploit kits gain access to legitimate web servers via covert channels evading detection form server managers and clients.

Once an exploit kit infects a web server, it silently watches all the client machines connected to the web server and reports vulnerable applications, type of vulnerabilities, success rate of infection by certain strains of malware that abuse the said weaknesses, to the attackers. The attacker can then download ransomware to the victim's computer which is executed automatically by the exploit kits.

These toolkits are extremely easy to use and the attackers or hackers employing an exploit kit need not understand how they work. They come with a sophisticated user interface application that runs on the attacker's device and monitors potential victims. These toolkits generally attack applications like Adobe Flash Player, Java Runtime Environment and web browsers. Examples of latest kits are Angler and Blackhole.

Figure 25. Major droppers of ransomware

Botnet Infection Vector

Botnets are networks of infected devices that can be used to spread the infection farther. These infected machines run bots that perform automated tasks on the Internet. So basically, a network of web robots to do your dirty work for you! The owner of the botnet controls the entire network remotely using command and control (C&C) software. The server that runs this software is often known as the command and control server. Bringing down this server sometimes brings down the entire botnet to foil their malicious intents. However, these botnets generally engage many such servers that are strategically placed in different countries to make it difficult to identify and bring them down all at once.

In 2016, the Dridex botnet owners started spreading the Locky ransomware using spam campaigns and corrupt macros in attachments. The Dridex sent out around 4 million spam messages accounting for 18% of the total spam detected at the time ("Dridex botnet", 2016).

Other routes such as maladvertisements, social engineering attacks, drive-by downloads, data breach attacks, etc. have already been discussed briefly in previous sections of this chapter and as a part of other chapters of this book. These methods are used in conjunction with others to make sure the success rates of contamination remain high. After, contamination, the ransomware is installed through the dropper by copying the executables to a local directory like %APPDATA% or %TEMP% in the user's profile. This information can be used for early detection by monitoring such folders and preventing the actual launch of the infection.

Stage III: Payload Staging

Certain vulnerable situations (like common buffer overflow vulnerabilities) identified by exploit kits and other dropper techniques have constrains on the number of bytes that can be downloaded into a contiguous block of memory. Therefore, ransomware payloads may be divided into two parts: stager and stages. The stager is responsible for setting up a secure connection between the attacker and victim, downloading a larger payload called the stage into memory and passing execution to it. The attacker makes stagers as small as possible so that it can be used with many exploits. After the stager starts executing, the dropper is terminated and removed from the host machine.

Staging is also beneficial in evasion from anti-virus software as it does nothing more than get another payload from the attacker. If the stager passes the antivirus program successfully (which it usually does!), the stages are also likely to pass through too. The stages constitute the actual ransomware code.

Stage IV: Prevention from Restoration

Once the payload (ransomware) execution begins, it performs essential maintenance operations before doing any harm:

- The ransomware might move to another folder,
- It also disables the Task Manager in order to prevent the victim from terminating its process,
- It might add or modify certain registry entries in Windows Registry pertaining to software vulnerabilities like Internet Explorer,
- It then checks the local user configuration and registry entries looking for rights and permissions it can utilize,

- It checks proxy settings, user privileges, accessibility options, and other information it might need,
- It then adds certain persistence mechanisms so that the ransomware can pick up where it left off even between boots and run in safe mode or recovery mode too. The common persistence method for ransomware is to create Run and RunOnce registry keys or copy the malware into the %UserProfile%/Start Menu\Programs\Startup folder.
- It also disables recovery mode so that the victim cannot use the built-in recovery disk to restore the system,
- Some ransomware programs restrict the number of websites the victim can access, especially the security websites like Symantec, Kaspersky, etc., so that user cannot do any research on it and educate himself to mitigate its effects.

Within a few seconds of its execution, ransomware has performed all its housekeeping tasks. It then targets any backup files and folders on the system and deletes them in order to prevent any restoration attempts. In Windows, the vssadmin.exe tool is used by ransomware code to remove all the volume shadow copies from the machine. The user can change the extension of this file or rename it in order to save it from being deleted by the malware. This is a good preventive practice to recover without payment in the event of a sudden attack.

Ransomware now prepares to communicate with its command and control server over an encrypted covert channel and execute a carefully crafted handshaking protocol. Each victim is identified by a unique identifier to differentiate between keys generated for each victim. The C&C server then sends two cryptographic keys: a public and a private key generated using a strong encryption algorithm. The public key is transmitted to the victim machine and the private key is kept at the hacker's servers. Communication with these servers can be monitored to prevent the attack. However, some ransomware strains do not use the C&C server for this purpose. Such advanced strains do all the encryption locally.

Stage V: Scanning

The ransomware now scans the entire local system as well as other file systems that can be reached through the network, such as file systems shared over the network, cloud storage systems connected to the network, etc. Each encrypting ransomware has a predetermined list of file extensions to look for. Local file scanning generally takes only a few seconds. However, scanning the entire network and attached device file systems, determining which can be encrypted by checking read-write permissions, may take anywhere between minutes to hours (Figure 26).

Stage VI: Cryptographic Encryption

When ransomware has discovered all the files and folders that it can lock down, it begins the actual encryption phase which may take a long time depending on the amount of data that needs to be encrypted. Each file is locally encrypted using the public key gained from the rendezvous with the C&C server, the encrypted contents are written to the original folder, and the original file is deleted permanently. For every file, auto generated ransom notes are created in multiple formats like html, text, etc.

Figure 26. Scanning Stage (Based on The anatomy of a ransomware attack, 2016)

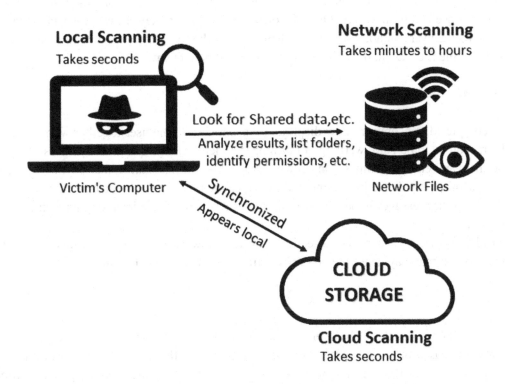

Figure 27. Encryption process (Based on The anatomy of a ransomware attack, 2016)

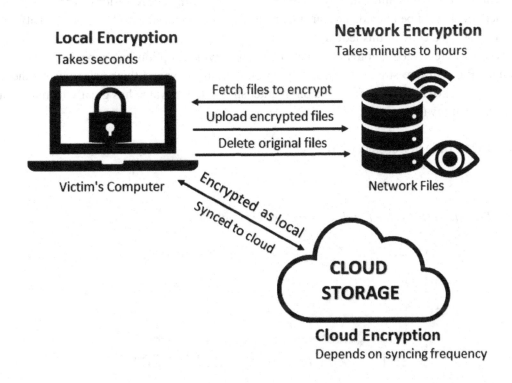

Once the encryption process finishes, the ransomware will erase the session key from its memory, making sure no trace is left anywhere. Only the owner of the private key, which was generated and is stored only on the malware author's server, is able to decrypt the session key from within the encrypted files and decrypt the files again, once the victims have paid the ransom.

Stage VII: Extortion

Encryption completed, ransomware now displays a ransom note to the user together with instructions on how the ransom is to be paid, warnings informing the victim of the dire consequences of trying to remove the malware, etc. Sometimes, ransomware displays warnings stating that payment of ransom must be done within a stipulated time frame, failing which the ransom will be increased, or files will be deleted forever. Some messages impersonate police agencies to create panic among its victims causing them to pay up.

We have already discussed in previous sections how ransomware intimates its victims. Let us briefly look at the most common payment method current strains are using – the bitcoin.

Bitcoin

Bitcoin is a digital currency that is built on the blockchain technology. Further, it is a cryptocurrency and its creation is based on open source cryptographic protocols that are independent of any central authority. Transactions in Bitcoin take place directly i.e., without an intermediate party, verified by network nodes and recorded in blockchain (a public distributed ledger). Every transaction that has ever taken place is recorded in groups called blocks and these blocks form a chain that gives a high level of security to bitcoin. To manipulate any transaction in a block, the entire series of blocks succeeding the modified block must be altered. This arrangement makes it impossible to break its security as each network node keeps a copy of this ledger.

This type of unregulated, anonymous, instantaneous payment option has appealed greatly to cybercriminals. Ransomware strains are now relying on bitcoin to expand their notorious business. All this has surely worked to the benefit of bitcoin market shares and its value has greatly increased due to cybercriminal activity (Figure 28).

1 BTC ≈ \$15746 USD in December 2017!

Figure 28. Bitcoin market value trends (Source: www.google.com)

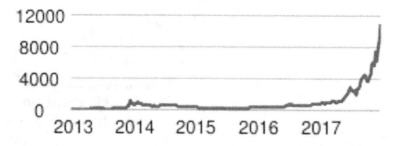

The payment transaction through bitcoin works as illustrated in Figure 29 (Sarah, 2017). When the victim decides to pay ransom after being infected with ransomware, he must first purchase required number of bitcoins from a bitcoin exchange online. Then the victim needs to transfer the bitcoin ransom amount to the hacker's bitcoin wallet. The hackers then use a bitcoin mixer service which exchanges bitcoin for other bitcoins of the same value but takes a small fee from the bitcoin value as commission. This helps to cover any tracks leading to the attackers. The cyber gang then may use the converted bitcoins to trade them for other currencies.

Stage VIII: Clear out

After the ransom is paid by the victim, the attackers may provide them with a link that they can use to download their decryption key or a decryption program. But this happens only a fifth of the times someone is attacked. Therefore, it is advised that the victim not pay the fine at all.

The ransomware then terminates and deletes itself from the user's system without leaving any forensic traces that can be tracked to the attackers or be investigated to prevent further attacks of the strain.

To Pay or Not to Pay: That Is the Question!

It is often difficult to make this choice and no amount of advice helps! Every situation is unique, and no one should be judged about the choices they make. However, federal agencies do advise users to refrain from paying ransom and encouraging the criminals. They offer guidelines to restore the systems and prevent future attacks, some of which are outlined in this chapter as well. Nevertheless, emergency situations do arise that sometimes coerce organizations to pay up and get rid of that nagging headache.

Figure 29. How ransom payment methods work through bitcoin (Based on Sarah, 2017)

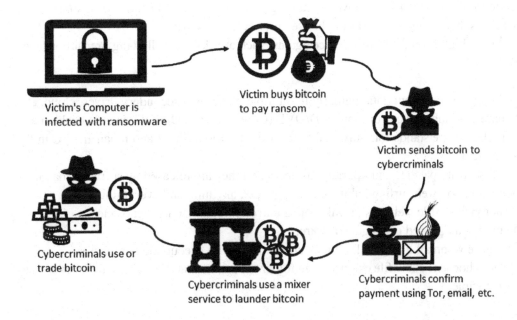

In many cases, the ransom is less than the amount needed to try to reinstate infected systems and remove the malware. There is no thumb-rule to deciding. In short - to each his own!

MITIGATION AND CONTAINMENT SOLUTIONS

Ransomware commonly uses social engineering techniques like phishing to gain access to a victim's files. Preventing these attacks therefore warrants proper education, training and awareness programs for users of systems holding data important to businesses, healthcare, educational institutions and the like. There is a growing need for an Incident Response Plan (IRP) (Brewer, 2016) among organizations to check the spread of these attacks and therefore discourage the involved criminal gangs from improvising and investing in this type of blackmail.

A sample plan of action is presented in this chapter as an exemplary model for mitigation and containment of such attacks in future:

- **Stage I:** Guidelines for Prevention from a ransomware attack
- **Stage II:** Mitigation Guidelines
- **Stage III:** Detection and Containment
- **Stage IV:** Elimination and Restoration

Stage I: Guidelines for Prevention

Operating system vendors, software companies whose product vulnerabilities have been exploited by ransomware thus far, antivirus manufacturers, etc. are working hard to patch weaknesses and provide better solutions for tackling ransomware attacks. However, attackers keep evolving their strategies and invent new methods to extort money.

Corporate companies must educate their staff about the dangers of unscrupulous web surfing practices. Sensitization programmes for employees detailing what ransomware is and how it spreads and infects machines, must be included as part of cyber security awareness drive.

To ensure a high level first line defence against such attacks, the following precautions can be kept in mind:

- Backup your important data regularly in multiple places like secondary drives, cloud, etc.,
- Prepare a bootable rescue disk on a CD/DVD (Compact Disk/ Digital Versatile Disk) or a bootable-USB (USB here stands for Universal Serial Bus) to troubleshoot and repair the PC in the advent of an attack,
- Install security patches and upgrades as and when they are released by software manufacturers,
- Inculcate good web surfing habits and do not click anything and everything,
- Do not visit hostile websites or links, open untrusted email attachments, etc.,
- Do not install pirated or illegal software,
- Configure webmail like gmail to block attachments with executables or macros,
- Always choose to show file extensions in folder options so that the real extension of any suspicious file is visible,

- Always keep your firewall running and enhance security by setting up the firewall appropriately,
- Disable Windows PowerShell if it is not necessary as it contains weaknesses,
- Deactivate AutoPlay on plug and play USB sticks,
- Disable file sharing on the network and remote services if not absolutely necessary,
- Immediately switch off the internet connection in the event of suspicious activity,
- Disable vssadmin.exe or rename it so that shadow copies are not deleted by ransomware,
- Install ad blockers, antimalware software and an additional firewall with good features, etc.

Stage II: Mitigation Guidelines

In the event of an attack, there are many things that can be done to reduce the impact of the infection especially when the target is a corporation or institution. Before the Encryption stage of ransomware's life cycle is reached, we can get a window of opportunity to stall the infection. When ransomware starts encrypting files, the real damage is done and very little can be done to stop it.

Some mitigation guidelines for organizations are enumerated below:

- Fragment the organization's network into subnetworks as this will reduce the spread of ransomware to a great extent,
- Ensure that important databases and storage systems are accessed only by authenticated users and only authorized devices connect to the subnetwork,
- Deploy good network access control authentication by setting up proper rules so that the security of the network can be managed easily,
- Use multi-factor authentication schemes to authenticate users with important roles,
- Develop a backup and restore plan and identify critical data sources that need regular backup,
- Maintain secure images of the current state of important systems like operating system and software installed along with their settings and configurations,
- Implement an Incident Response (IR) plan to outline procedures in the event of an attack,
- Deploy latest anti-virus and spam filter protection on email gateways, desktops and servers,
- Configure anti-virus software to automatically execute an in-depth malware scan of removable media when plugged in,
- Use application whitelisting to ensure that only trusted and approved programs are allowed to run,
- Restrict administrative privileges to the operating system and applications on the basis of user roles,
- Disable popups, macros, plugins and auto run feature for mounted drives,
- Conduct cyber security awareness programs across the organization.

Stage III: Detection and Containment

Detecting ransomware attacks in its nascent stages can save the victim from losing data. Ransomware needs some time before it can cause havoc on the system.

Ransomware detection includes the monitoring of known ransomware extensions. Additionally, machine learning, behavioural modelling and change rate monitoring can improve detection probabilities.

Some early detection guidelines are given below:

- Monitoring folders like %APPDATA%, %TEMP%, etc. where ransomware executables are known to copy themselves upon arrival,
- Monitoring the backup and shadow copy deletion commands of the operating system like vssadmin.exe of Windows OS is another method to detect ransomware before encryption,
- Network administrative software should contain network protocols to check executable files arriving on the network before they are delivered to the attached machines,
- Network administrators should monitor an increase in suspicious file rename activity like file name extensions being changed to .crypt, .encryptRSA, .encryptedAES, etc. before a ransom note is generated,
- Deploy enhanced security software with features for detecting and preventing ransomware rendezvous with C&C servers,
- Static detection techniques involving signature scanners for known ransomware signatures may be deployed for early detection.

In addition to static techniques, dynamic detection methods can be employed to detect ransomware whose signatures are not known or haven't been identified yet as they are relatively new. Behavioural detection is one of the most prevalent dynamic methods in place. Ransomware strains have some specific behavioural traits like addition of persistence mechanisms, modification of registry entries, deleting backup copies, stealth techniques to evade detection, etc. Ransomware also checks its surroundings to gauge the user profile such as selected language, country, file system architecture, security settings, permissions, attached network files systems, etc. It further checks to see whether it is executing on a real machine or in a virtual environment. By analysing the setup behaviour of unknown executable files, we can ensure early detection.

Another dynamic approach is supervised machine-learning based detection. This process involves training a decision-making algorithm to recognize behavioural traits of executing files to determine whether they are malicious ransomware or not. This training requires a training dataset containing samples of known ransomware and benign executables, quantification of behavioural traits and a classification scheme. This performance intensive method involves high levels of expertise in data mining, neural networks and data preparation and analysis.

It is often difficult to discover ransomware attacks in early stages as it takes only a few seconds on typical computers to start its encryption phase. The behavioural based methods cannot be used by normal users. They are employed by security solution providers and research engineers. Therefore, the next step is to contain the situation in the event of advancement of ransomware execution beyond the scanning stage. Some containment guidelines are listed below:

- Disconnect the infected systems from the network as fast as possible to prevent ransomware from spreading,
- Try to identify the ransomware strain that infected these systems and find solutions to recover from and remove it,
- Review the impact of the strain and weaknesses that were exploited by it so that future attacks of this kind can be prevented.

Stage IV: Elimination and Restoration

It is often difficult to remove ransomware infection from computer systems, especially if a part of an organization is under attack. This may be because ransomware code multiplies and hides in many locations of the system and just sits there as a benign executable, ready to pounce again after restoration. Therefore, it is most often advised to format the entire system. However, it is not so easy to do if there are servers, mailboxes or shared storage system infected. Then, the next best strategy is remove all traces of ransomware and continue monitoring the system for ransomware signatures or behavioural traits after restoration.

If the antivirus software is unable to remove the ransomware, the user can search the web for any known decryption tools available for the ransomware variant that infected the system. Many developers put up removal and decryption tools for different ransomware strains, on their blogs or other forums for users to download free of cost. If there are no decryption tools available, the victim may perform the following steps to eliminate and recover from the infection:

- Try to enter Safe Mode with Networking on the computer. If it doesn't work, try to enter into Safe mode with command prompt.
- Logon to the user account that infected the system with ransomware and download a good anti-ransomware protection software.
- Scan the entire system for malware and delete the threats found by the anti-ransomware application.
- If this doesn't work, try to restore the computer to a previous checkpoint. On the command prompt type: cd restore after entering safe mode with command prompt. Next type rstui.exe for Windows systems. The System Restore screen shows up from where the user may restore his computer to an automatic restore point. After restoration, download anti-ransomware for removal of residual encrypted ransomware files.
- If all else fails and user cannot enter safe mode at all, try booting from a rescue disk or a bootable backup and restore CD, if available.

TRENDING STRAINS

The year 2017 has been reported as the year of the ransomware as it became a global epidemic (Morrison, 2017). Each day, some or other ransomware variant makes headlines across the Internet for its notoriety. In the following subsections, we discuss briefly the most hazardous strains that have wreaked havoc in 2017.

WannaCry 2.0

In May 2017 ("WannaCry ransomware attack", n.d.), WannaCry initiated its first attack somewhere in Asia and spread rapidly across the globe affecting thousands of computers in at least 150 countries (Figure 30). It has a number of aliases WanaCryptor, WannaDecryptor, etc.

A large number of organizations were affected with UK's National Health Service (NHS) worst hit. WannaCry is a ransomware crypto worm that propagates automatically without human intervention. It targets Windows systems and demands ransom in bitcoin (Figure 31).

WannaCry exploits the Windows SMB (Server Message Block) protocol known as EternalBlue (believed to be developed by the United States National Security Agency or the U.S. NSA) to gain access to a vulnerable system and then uses the DoublePulsar backdoor implant toolkit (also developed by the NSA) to install and execute it. EternalBlue mishandles specially crafted packets from remote attackers, allowing them to execute arbitrary code on the target computer ("Vulnerability CVE-2017-0144", 2017).

The U.S. NSA came under the scanner as it is widely believed now that NSA knew about the vulnerability but chose to refrain from reporting it to Microsoft for its own hacking tasks. Microsoft took emergency steps and quickly released patches for all versions of Windows – supported and unsupported and prompted users to install them, thereby reducing the rate of new attacks within a few days.

Following the global attack, a web security researcher from England discovered a 'kill switch' in WannaCry's code (by reverse engineering its program), which slowed the infection immensely. However, the cybercriminals responsible for WannaCry also evolved their attack strategy and new attacks no longer had the kill switch. But, due to patches and updates from Microsoft, the risk of WannaCry outbreak has greatly reduced.

NotPetya

In June 2017, a new version of Petya known as NotPetya or Nyetna began spreading quickly, with initial attack sites in Ukraine, to Germany, Russia, India, UK, USA, Australia and many others ("Petya (malware)", n.d.). However, the bulk of the attacks - more than 80%, was in Ukraine. NotPetya encrypts the Master file table and forces the PC to restart. Then it displays a ransom message to pay $300 in bitcoin to decrypt the PC.

Like WannaCry, NotPetya also spreads without human intervention. The initial infection vector used by this notorious ransomware is a backdoor program implanted in M.E. Doc, an accounting software used by most companies in Ukraine ("Petya (malware)", n.d.). After initial infection, it spreads via the EternalBlue and EternalRomance exploits in Windows SMB protocol to computers attached to the network infected. NotPetya encrypts everything on the hard drive including operating system files and file allocation tables, wrecking hard drives beyond repair, even after paying up. No kill switch has been identified yet to stop it in its tracks.

Bad Rabbit

On October 24, 2017, a new ransomware called Bad Rabbit attacked users in Russia and Ukraine ("Ransomware", n.d.). This version is similar to NotPetya as it also encrypts the file tables to damage hard drives beyond repair. It was believed to be distributed a drive-by download, a fake Adobe Flash Player update. It also used the EternalRomance exploit to spread to other countries like Turkey, Germany, Poland, Japan, South Korea and USA ("Ransomware", n.d.). It seems that the cybercriminal gang responsible for Bad Rabbit are great fans of the popular Game of Thrones (GoT) series (Ivanov, Mamedov, & Sinitsyn, 2017), as the code contains references to the three dragons – Viserion, Drogon and Rhaegal (Figure 32) and Gray Worm (the leader of the Unsullied) (Figure 33).

Kaspersky Labs discovered that Bad Rabbit does not delete the victim's shadow copies. Thus, it is possible to restore from them if, under rare circumstances, the file encryption stage was thwarted midway.

Figure 30. Countries affected on initial attack ("WannaCry ransomware attack", n.d.)

Figure 31. WannaCry ransom message ("WannaCry ransomware attack", n.d.)

Figure 32. References to GoT dragons in Bad Rabbit (Ivanov, Mamedov, & Sinitsyn, 2017)

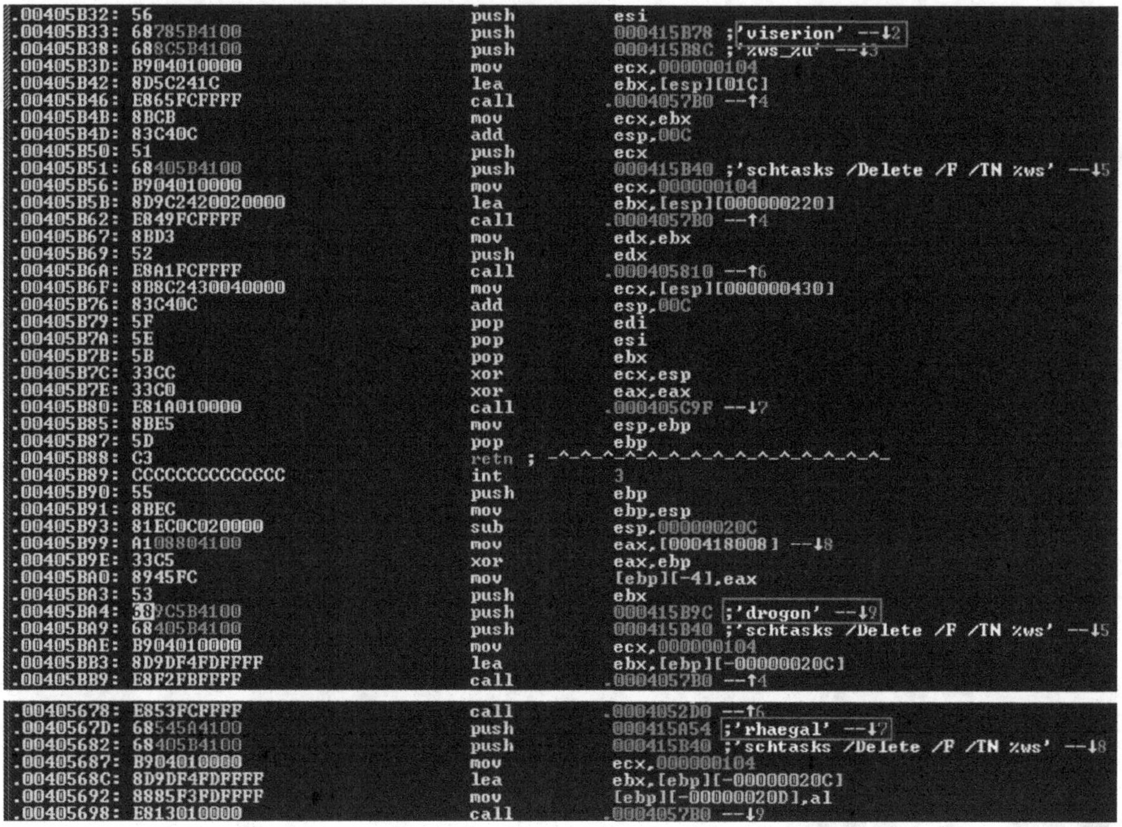

Figure 33. References to GoT characters in Bad Rabbit (Based on Ivanov, Mamedov, & Sinitsyn, 2017)

```
BLOCK "StringFileInfo"
{
    BLOCK "000904b0"
    {
        VALUE "FileDescription", "Microsoft Display Class Installer"
        VALUE "FileVersion", "1.1.846.118"
        VALUE "Legal Copyright", "http://diskcryptor.net/"
        VALUE "OriginalFilename", "dispci.exe"
        VALUE "ProductName", "GrayWorm"
        VALUE "ProductVersion", "1.1"
    }
}
```

FUTURE TRENDS

Ransomware has begun to mutate to strains that are using advanced encryption systems and untraceable crypto currencies. They are becoming deadlier in their encryption strategies that makes every bit on the victim's PC inaccessible and non-recoverable. New ransomware strains are using newer intimidation techniques to force the victim to pay. An example being, Doxware that extorts money by threatening the victim to publicize captured sensitive data. A new Star-Trek themed strain, Kirk, demands ransom in Monero, another blockchain based cryptocurrency that was created in 2014. It focusses on privacy, security and is untraceable. Monero is a step ahead of bitcoin in the sense that it hides the identity of the sender as well as the amount of every transaction that has ever taken place.

Ransomware-as-a-service has already arrived for hire, which can be used by any person or organization for hijacking and spreading cyber terrorism. With the advent of the fourth industrial revolution, we will be seeing a lot of the things that were only perceived in science fiction movies. Industries and factories will be using automated robots on a large scale, where little or no human intervention is required. Even today, many industries are using automated robotics to aid production and manufacturing. According to a recent report from Trend Micro (Maggi, Quarta, Pogliani, & Polino, 2017), the current status of these robots in terms of cybersecurity is rather questionable. The team demonstrated how these robots can be compromised over the network as the software running them is mostly outdated with weak authentication systems in place. Future ransomware attacks on such robots may introduce small defects in the production chain and then demand ransom from the company for revealing which lot was affected and which was not (Maggi, Quarta, Pogliani, & Polino, 2017). If the ransom demanded is found to be lesser than the cost of identifying and removing the faulty product units from the supply chain, the manufacturer will most probably think of paying up. Another attack strategy could look for sensitive data to steal, like robotic calibration parameters, that are trade secrets of the manufacturing company. The attacker can then demand ransom to prevent this data from being sold to competitors or being made public. In another, and more dangerous hypothetical situation, the attackers may take total control of the robot, threatening to cause damage to life and property in certain circumstances, if a ransom demand is not immediately met. This is similar to cyberterrorism and cyber-hijacking. Already, robotics is being put to use in the healthcare industry to assist in complex surgeries. Ransomware can wreak havoc in these scenarios! For example, hijacking a robot assisting in a surgery of an important person and demanding ransom to release control of it to prevent fatalities. Not only robots, but lifesaving medical devices like pacemakers and infusion pumps are also prone to such attacks ("Advisory ICSA-15-125-01B", 2015; "Cybersecurity Vulnerabilities", 2017). Pacemakers are embedded medical devices that regulate abnormal heart rhythms, while infusion pumps, generally used intravenously, are used to administer medication, fluids, etc. into the body in a controlled manner. Thankfully, no attack has ever been reported for these kinds of devices to date. However, the future is not promised, and we may see ransom being demanded to prevent one's own death after cybercriminals gain control of such medical devices. The window for ransom payment in such attacks will be very small, like a time bomb ticking away that goes off at the press of a button. The same theme of attacks can be applied to other implantable or wearable devices of the future. In forthcoming decades, artificial intelligence and robots with cognitive abilities will form the backbone of our industries, replacing human effort for most tasks that do not involve critical thinking. It is therefore, the responsibility of our industries and robot manufacturing companies to seriously consider security issues so that future catastrophes can be prevented. Vulnerabilities need to be identified and addressed as soon as is possible, strong security options must be available to prevent unauthorized access to these machines, monitoring of attempted unauthorized changes in real time must be done to avert cyberattacks.

In the age of the fourth industrial revolution, everything we have will be intelligent and connected – from the clothes we wear to the cars we drive, from our homes to the cities we live in. In the age of self-driven transportation systems, ransomware will open new horizons for terrorist organizations, intelligence agencies, organized criminal gangs, assassins, governments, etc. The attack models that can be imagined are endless, but they all lead to something that is irreversible – the loss of life. Terrorists can employ RaaS agencies over the dark web to crash automated public transportation carrying hundreds of innocent citizens.

Smart homes with smart furniture, smart kitchens, smart security systems, and the like, a ransomware attack on a small scale might mean demanding money to not set fire to the house while the owner is out of town. For the automated car that drives us in the future, a ransomware attack may mean demanding ransom under a short window to prevent crashing the car along with its passengers. The possibilities are limitless. The solutions are limited. Right now, we just don't have the expertise needed to deal with such situations. But we must learn to deal with them before we are tested on them.

CONCLUSION

In this chapter, the author has discussed a very serious form of cybercrime that is gaining ground among the cybercriminals of the present, due to its success and impact on the world. Ransomware originated as a very humble program whose damage could be reversed without submitting to the whims of the attacker. However, it has learnt to cause irreversible harm, in many ways, in recent years. Submitting to it has become the only way for many due to circumstances best known to them. Ransomware now comes in a large variety of strains, each one more complex and damaging than its predecessor. The author has discussed the various family of attacks ransomware belongs to, its classification and life-cycle pertaining to the present-day scenario. Possible solutions and mitigation strategies have also been detailed in the chapter. However, it won't be long before these highly sophisticated attack schemes take the world by storm forcing businesses to shut down, causing huge monetary losses and data leaks, putting lives at risk. Cyber-warfare, cyber-terrorism, ransomware disguised as artificial intelligence, cyber-hijacking, etc. will become a reality. Ransomware will leave other cyberattacks behind to become the most abundant and damaging if we do not strengthen our security. There is a lesson to be learnt from each outbreak in the history of ransomware attacks and we must strive to be a step ahead, each time.

REFERENCES

Advisory ICSA-15-125-01B: Hospira LifeCare PCA Infusion System Vulnerabilities (Update B). (2015, June 10). Industrial Control Systems Cyber Emergency Response Team (ICS-CERT). Retrieved from: https://ics-cert.us-cert.gov/advisories/ICSA-15-125-01B

AIDS trojan disk. (n.d.). Retrieved from the Virus Information wiki: http://virus.wikia.com/wiki/AIDS_trojan_disk

Bates, J. (1990, January). Trojan Horse: AIDS Information Introductory Diskette Version 2.0. *Virus Bulletin*, 3-6.

Brewer, R. (2016). Ransomware attacks: Detection. Prevention and cure. *Network Security, 2016*(9), 5–9. doi:10.1016/S1353-4858(16)30086-1

Constantine, L. (2017, January 3). Ransomware on smart TVs is here and removing it can be a pain. *PC World*. Retrieved from: https://www.pcworld.com/article/3154226/security/ransomware-on-smart-tvs-is-here-and-removing-it-can-be-a-pain.html

Cybersecurity Vulnerabilities Identified in St. Jude Medical's Implantable Cardiac Devices and Merlin@ homeTransmitter: FDA Safety Communication. (2017, January 9). Retrieved from: http://www.fda.gov/MedicalDevices/Safety/AlertsandNotices/ucm535843.htm

Destructive KillDisk malware encrypts Linux machines, ESET researchers discover. (2017, January 5). Retrieved from: https://www.eset.com/us/about/newsroom/press-releases/destructive-killdisk-malware-encrypts-linux-machines-eset-reseachers-discover/

Dridex botnet spreading Locky Ransomware. (2016, March 10). Retrieved from: http://www.security-week.com/dridex-botnet-spreading-locky-ransomware-javascript-attachments

Ensey, C. (2017, January 4). *Ransomware Has Evolved, And Its Name Is Doxware*. Retrieved from: https://www.darkreading.com/attacks-breaches/ransomware-has-evolved-and-its-name-is-doxware/a/d-id/1327767

Erebus Linux Ransomware: Impact to Servers and Countermeasures. (2017, June 15). Retrieved from: https://www.trendmicro.com/vinfo/us/security/news/cyber-attacks/erebus-linux-ransomware-impact-to-servers-and-countermeasures

Fitzpatrick, D., & Griffin, D. (2016, April 15). Cyber-extortion losses skyrocket, warns FBI. *CNN Tech*. Retrieved from: http://money.cnn.com/2016/04/15/technology/ransomware-cyber-security/

Ghosh, M. (2014, August 4). *Computer Ransomware Leads a Man to Kill Himself & Son*. Retrieved from: http://trak.in/tags/business/2014/03/14/computer-ransomware-threat/

Internet Security Threat Report. (2017, April). Symantec Corporation. Retrieved from: https://www.symantec.com/content/dam/symantec/docs/reports/istr-22-2017-en.pdf

Invernizzi, L., McRoberts, K., & Bursztein, E. (2017). *Tracking desktop ransomware payments* [Google Slides]. Presented at the Black Hat USA 2017 Conference. Retrieved from: https://www.elie.net/talk/tracking-desktop-ransomware-payments-end-to-end

Ivanov, A., Emm, D., Sinitsyn, F., & Pontiroli, S. (2016, December). Story of the year: The Ransomware revolution. *Kaspersky Security Bulletin 2016*. Retrieved from: https://securelist.com/kaspersky-security-bulletin-2016-story-of-the-year/76757/

Ivanov, A., Mamedov, O., & Sinitsyn, F. (2017, October 24). *Bad Rabbit ransomware*. Retrieved from: https://securelist.com/bad-rabbit-ransomware/82851/

Jackson, K. (1990). *Electronic computer conferencing and the AIDS disk. In Virus Bulletin* (p. 7). Oxon, UK: Virus Bulletin Ltd.

Johnson, K. (2016, November 28). Ransomware Attacks the Cloud! *Posted to the cloud Cybersecurity blog*. Retrieved from: https://spinbackup.com/blog/ransomware-attacks-cloud/

KeRanger: First Ransomware to Target Mac Users Found in BitTorrent Client. (2016, March 7). Retrieved from: https://www.trendmicro.com/vinfo/us/security/news/cybercrime-and-digital-threats/keranger-ransomware-target-mac-users-bittorrent-client/

Maggi, F., Quarta, D., Pogliani, M., & Polino, M. (2017, May 3). *Rogue Robots: Testing the limits of an industrial robot's security*. A TrendLabs Research Paper. Retrieved from: https://www.trendmicro.com/vinfo/us/security/news/internet-of-things/rogue-robots-testing-industrial-robot-security

MalwareHunterTeam. (2016, December 12). *Someone is continuously working on a new ransomware in the past days.* Retrieved from https://twitter.com/malwrhunterteam/status/808280549802418181

MalwareHunterTeam. (2016, December 7). *Next ransomware on the table: Popcorn Time*. Retrieved from https://twitter.com/malwrhunterteam/status/806595092177965058

Market Share Statistics for Internet Technologies. (2017). *Net Market Share*. Retrieved from: https://www.netmarketshare.com/

Moir, R. (2003). *Defining Malware: FAQ*. Retrieved from: https://technet.microsoft.com/en-us/library/dd632948.aspx

Morrison, J. (2017, March 29). *2017: The Year of Ransomware. Posted to plixer cyber-attack blog.* Retrieved from: https://www.plixer.com/blog/cyber-attack-2/ransomware-attacks-2017/

Mungo, P., & Clough, B. (1992). *Approaching zero: The extraordinary underworld of hackers, phreakers, virus writers, and keyboard criminals*. New York, NY: Random House.

Netskope Cloud Report. (2016, September). Retrieved from: http://go.netskope.com/rs/665-KFP-612/images/september-2016-worldwide-cloud-report.pdf

O'Gorman, G., & MacDonald, G. (2012). *Ransomware: A growing menace*. Symantec Security Response. Retrieved from: http://www.symantec.com/content/en/us/enterprise/media/security_response/whitepapers/ransomware-a-growing-menace.pdf

Olenick, D. (2016, June 13). *FLocker ransomware now targeting Smart TVs*. Retrieved from: https://www.scmagazine.com/flocker-ransomware-now-targeting-smart-tvs/article/529419/

Osborne, C. (2017, January 20), *Satan RaaS starts trading in the Dark Web*. Retrieved from: http://www.zdnet.com/article/satan-ransomware-as-a-service-starts-trading-in-the-dark-web/

Petya (malware). (n.d.). Retrieved from Wikipedia wiki: https://en.wikipedia.org/wiki/Petya_(malware)

Pleasance, C. (2015, January 22). *Autistic A-level student, 17, hanged himself after being sent a fake police email claiming he was being investigated for having indecent images and demanding £100*. Retrieved from: http://www.dailymail.co.uk/news/article-2921979/Autistic-level-student-17-hanged-sent-fake-police-email-claiming-investigated-having-indecent-images.html

Popp, J. (1989). *Part of AIDS DOS trojan horse payload* [Image: PNG]. Retrieved from Wikipedia wiki: https://commons.wikimedia.org/wiki/File:AIDS_DOS_Trojan.png

Quarterly Threat Summary: Q4 2016 & Year in Review. (2016, December). Proofpoint Report. Retrieved from: https://www.proofpoint.com/sites/default/files/proofpoint_q4_threat_report-final-cm.pdf

Ransomware. (n.d.). Retrieved from Wikipedia wiki: https://en.wikipedia.org/wiki/Ransomware

Sarah. (2017, August 15). *Ransomware payment methods. Posted to Emsisoft blog.* Retrieved from: https://blog.emsisoft.com/2017/08/15/ransomware-payment-methods/

Savage, K., Coogan, P., & Lau, H. (2015). *The evolution of ransomware.* Symantec Security Response. Retrieved from: www.symantec.com/content/en/us/enterprise/media/security_response/whitepapers/the-evolution-of-ransomware.pdf

Saxena, H. (2016, February 14). *CTB-Locker Ransomware hijacks the entire BACP website.* Retrieved from: http://news.thewindowsclub.com/ctb-locker-ransomware-website-82130/

Snow, J. (2016, June 29). *Ransomware on mobile devices: knock-knock-block.* Posted to Kaspersky Lab Daily. Retrieved from: https://www.kaspersky.com/blog/mobile-ransomware-2016/12491/

State of the Cloud. (2017). *Right Scale Report.* Retrieved from: https://www.rightscale.com/lp/state-of-the-cloud

Sundar, R. (n.d.). *Android.Lockdroid.E.* Symantec Security Response. Retrieved from: https://www.symantec.com/security_response/writeup.jsp?docid=2014-103005-2209-99&tabid=2

The anatomy of a ransomware attack. (2016). Exabeam Threat Research Report. Retrieved from: https://www.exabeam.com/library/anatomy-ransomware-attack/

The reign of ransomware. (2016). TrendLabs 2016 1H Security Roundup. Retrieved from: www.trend-micro.com/cloud-content/us/pdfs/security-intelligence/reports/rpt-the-reign-of-ransomware.pdf

Vamshi, A. (2016, September 27). *Cloud Malware Fan-out with Virlock Ransomware.* Posted to Cloud Security Blog – Netskope. Retrieved from: https://www.netskope.com/blog/cloud-malware-fan-virlock-ransomware/

Vulnerability CVE-2017-0144. (2017). *Common Vulnerabilities and Exposures.* Retrieved from: https://www.cve.mitre.org/cgi-bin/cvename.cgi?name=CVE-2017-0144

WannaCry ransomware attack. (n.d.). Retrieved from Wikipedia wiki: https://en.wikipedia.org/wiki/WannaCry_ransomware_attack

Weiss, D. (2017, May 2). *Victimized by ransomware, law firm sues insurer for $700K in lost billings.* Retrieved from: http://www.abajournal.com/news/article/victimized_by_ransomware_law_firm_sues_insurer_for_700k_in_lost_billings

Why Ransomware Works: The Psychology and Methods Used to Distribute, Infect and Extort. (2016, June 16). Retrieved from: https://www.trendmicro.com/vinfo/us/security/news/cybercrime-and-digital-threats/why-ransomware-works-psychology-and-methods-to-distribute-infect-and-extort

Young, A., & Yung, M. (1996). Cryptovirology: Extortion based security threats and countermeasures. In *Proceedings of the IEEE Symposium on Security and Privacy*. Oakland, CA: IEEE. 10.1109/SEC-PRI.1996.502676

Zamora, W. (2016, October 19). *The global impact of ransomware*. Posted to Malwarebytes Labs blog. Retrieved from: https://blog.malwarebytes.com/101/2016/10/the-global-impact-of-ransomware/

ADDITIONAL READING

Bates, J. (1990). *High Level-Programs & the AIDS Trojan. Virus Bulletin* (pp. 8–10). Oxon, England: Virus Bulletin Ltd.

Kharaz, A., Arshad, S., Mulliner, C., Robertson, W., & Kirda, E. (2016). UNVEIL: A Large-Scale, Automated Approach to Detecting Ransomware. *In the Proceedings of the 25th USENIX Security Symposium*, Austin, Texas: USENIX.

Kolodenker, E., Koch, W., Stringhini, G., & Egele, M. (2017). PayBreak: Defence Against Cryptographic Ransomware. *In Proceedings of the 2017 ACM on Asia Conference on Computer Communications Security*, Abu Dhabi, UAE, 599-611. doi: 10.1145/3052973.3053035

Mungo, P., & Clough, B. (1992). *Approaching zero: The extraordinary underworld of hackers, phreakers, virus writers, and keyboard criminals*. New York, NY: Random House.

Nieuwenhuizen, D. (2017). *A behavioural-based approach to ransomware detection*. MWR Labs Whitepaper. Retrieved from: labs.mwrinfosecurity.com

Scaife, N., Carter, H., Traynor, P., & Butler, K. (2016). CryptoLock (and Drop It): Stopping Ransomware Attacks on User Data. *IEEE 36th International Conference on Distributed Computing Systems*, Nara, Japan: IEEE. doi: 10.1109/ICDCS.2016.46

Schwab, K. (2016). *The Fourth Industrial Revolution*. Geneva, Switzerland: World Economic Forum.

Young, A., & Yung, M. (2004). *Malicious Cryptography – Exposing Cryptovirology*. Indianapolis, Indiana: Wiley Publishing Inc.

Young, A., & Yung, M. (2017). Cryptovirology: The Birth, Neglect, and Explosion of Ransomware. *Communications of the ACM, 60*(7), 24–26. doi:10.1145/3097347

KEY TERMS AND DEFINITIONS

Cryptovirus: A term used by Adam Young and Moti Yung to describe malware that encrypts the victim's important data before demanding ransom to decrypt it.

Digital Revolution: Also called the third industrial revolution, it is the era of digital electronic equipment that started around the 1980s and is still continuing.

Fourth Industrial Revolution: It is the ensuing era of computing, with the amalgamation of emergent technologies like cognitive and machine learning, artificial intelligence, internet of things, wearable technology, biotechnology, 3D printing, smart cities, etc., to create a smart world where everything communicates with everything else intelligently, with the purpose of achieving the unthinkable.

Ransomware: A type of malware that tries to extort money from its victims by hijacking the victim's computer in some way and holding it to ransom.

Screenlocker: A type of ransomware that only locks the user out of his/her data without encrypting the actual files and directories.

Trojan: A type of malware that impersonates legitimate content to gain entry into a victim's system. It gets its name from a Greek myth involving a wooden horse in the Battle of Troy.

Worm: A malware that spreads quickly over the network without the need of user intervention by exploiting vulnerabilities in software.

Chapter 4
Curtailing the Threats to Cloud Computing in the Fourth Industrial Revolution

John Gyang Chaka
University of Kwazulu-Natal, South Africa

Mudaray Marimuthu
University of Kwazulu-Natal, South Africa

ABSTRACT

Cloud computing enables end users to make use of third party's resources to support their computing needs. The services offered by cloud computing make the technology very critical to the fourth industrial revolution. The benefits include cost minimization, scalability of services, speed, integration and higher data management, low innovation risk, and quicker response to organizational needs, among others. However, these benefits have been threatened by a number of security threats. This chapter seeks to curtail the effects of these threats by enlightening and educating users on the current ways to mitigate them. The chapter first defines cloud computing and highlights its relevance or benefits to businesses in the fourth industrial revolution. In addition, various security threats that are associated with cloud computing are brought to the fore. Thereafter, various measures that are used to mitigate the threats are discussed. The chapter concludes that with adequate enlightenment, the full benefits of cloud computing in industry 4.0 would be better enjoyed by users.

INTRODUCTION

The fourth industrial revolution, also known as Industry 4.0 has been viewed as an era where technology will play a major role like never before in the way that people live and relate to one another (Schwab, 2015). This era builds on the third industrial revolution, which had electronics and information technology at its centre. It combines information technology (dealing with business process and office automations) with operational technology (dealing with industrial process and factory automations). Since the fourth industrial revolution, which integrates various computational systems including sensor networks, Internet

DOI: 10.4018/978-1-5225-4763-1.ch004

communication infrastructure, intelligent real-time processing management, automated management of systems, and advanced robotics, will involve Big Data it requires a scalable data processing, which single individuals or organizations may not be able to handle in isolation. Thus, the Internet serves as the core in this era (Bloem et al., 2014). In other words, the fourth industrial revolution is expected to further tilt the world into a digitized entity – cyberspace, where human activities are more driven or dependent on centralized use of information and mechanical systems.

The Internet, the core of the fourth industrial revolution, serves as the converging point and superhighway on which every operation depends. It is estimated that Industry 4.0 will consist of about 50 billion connected devices. By implication, interdependence and shareability of resources among organizations are the top features of the fourth industrial revolution. This makes cloud computing a critical component of the fourth industrial revolution since the backbone of this era, which is the Internet, will mainly function by utilizing cloud computing services (Moavenzadeh, 2015). No wonder Alcorta (2017), the director, Policy, Research and Statistics, United Nations Industrial Development Organization (UNIDO), mentions cloud computing as one of the technological breakthroughs that will play a vital role in transforming manufacturing in the Industry 4.0 era.

However, while it is obvious that cloud computing will play a vital role in the fourth industrial revolution, as more resources will tend to be interconnected and shared, one major concern is the security of cyberspace (Alcorta, 2017; Bigger, 2015). Cyberspace, specifically cloud computing is witnessing some security challenges, or different forms of attacks, which seem to threaten the efficacy of the fourth industrial era if mitigating measures are not taken. Therefore, as part of measures to ensure a safer use of cyberspace and promote the success of the fourth industrial revolution, this chapter highlights some cyber threats that are detrimental to cloud computing and more importantly educates the audience on various ways by which the threats can be curtailed or mitigated.

BACKGROUND

Cloud computing signifies or represents a deviation from the traditional storage and management of computing resources which are limited by factors such as size, space and cost among others. Cloud computing describes an environment where computing resources can be accessed on a larger scale by users through the Internet and the Web (Chappell, 2011; Stair & Reynolds, 2016). It is simply a way of maximizing the use of resources while minimising cost. Perhaps a clearer description of cloud computing is provided by Rao, Leelaran, and Kumar (2013, p. 3390) who simply see cloud computing as "using the Internet to access someone else's software running on someone else's hardware in someone else's datacenter". Among resources that can be shared in a cloud are hardware, data storage and data management facilities, applications, and many other services (Hatwar & Chavan, 2015). These resources are not only shared simultaneously by multiple users but can be used in turns by re-allocation to users in different time zones. This way, less demand is made on the environment since less power, air conditioning and space would be required for the same services. Typical examples of cloud services include iCloud, Google drive, and Dropbox. Other services include those provided by social networking sites such as Facebook and LinkedIn (Kazim & Zhu, 2015). The most common example of cloud services that is used by most people is the electronic mail (e-mail) service provided by Google, Yahoo and other providers (Chou, 2013).

Origin of Cloud Computing, Cloud Services and Deployment Models

Origin of Cloud Computing

There seems to be no agreement on the origin of cloud computing. For instance while some authors (Bartholomew, 2009; Bogatin, 2006) believe that cloud computing was first coined by Eric Schmidt – chief executive officer of Google™ in 2006, Kaufman (2006) attributes the origin of cloud computing to use of virtual private networks (VPN) by telecommunications networks in the 1990s. In another dimension, the origin of cloud computing has been linked to the application of large-scale mainframe computers in academia and corporations in the 1950s. In the academia and corporations, client or terminal computers which were known as "dumb terminals" were used to connect to the mainframes, which had the sole computational or processing capability. The concept of cloud computing became clearer and defined in 2007. Amazon.com played a key role in advancing the technology through the modernization of its data centre, which provided access to their Web services (Rao et al., 2013). Since then, many organizations including Google, IBM, and universities have found cloud computing very beneficial in view of its scalability, ability to manage large sets of data and the fact that it reduces operational costs among others (Hatwar & Chavan, 2015). Cloud computing can be provided or deployed in the form of services. The three main services include Infrastructure as a Service (IaaS), Platform as a Service (PaaS), and Software as a Service (SaaS) (Bhadauria & Sanyal, 2012; Chou, 2013).

Cloud Computing Services

Infrastructure as Service (IaaS) refers to the provision or deployment of computing facilities, specifically hardware, by a third party. IaaS provides facilities such as servers, data processing and storage supports, networks and other vital infrastructure for the use of a consumer or user through the Internet by someone else (Rao et al., 2013). In this case, the user neither has control of the resources that he is using nor does he know their exact location. In fact, in most cases, the different cloud infrastructures being used by a user might be provided or controlled by different individuals or groups (IBM, 2009). Subsets of IaaS are applicable to different industries. For example, Communication as a Service (CaaS) is more peculiar to IP telephony services. Some examples of infrastructural services in the cloud include Google's Compute Engine, Amazon's Elastic Compute Cloud, Dropbox, and Microsoft Windows Azure storage (Dekker, Livery, & Lakka, 2013).

Platform as a Service (PaaS) is a service that provides an environment for applications to be developed or run (Chappell, 2011). The service provides tools and libraries that are essential for the development and running of applications. This service relieves users of the cost of buying tools that are needed to develop applications as well as configuration settings (Chou, 2013). Platforms that can be provided as a service could include Web servers, database servers, and applications servers (Bhadauria & Sanyal, 2012). Examples of Platform services include Amazon Web Services (AWS), Microsoft Azure, and SalesForce among others (Oredo & Njihia, 2014).

Software as a Service (SaaS) enables users to run complete applications which are hosted on the Internet (Cloud) through a sort of renting arrangement. Computer applications are not only expensive to purchase, but they are often updated regularly. This service relieves users of the burden of buying, installing, and maintaining in their local computers any application that they require to use. In order to achieve this goal, two servers – Main Consistence and Domain Consistence Servers are deployed. The security of the Main Consistence Server (MCS) is crucial as any damage to it amounts to a loss in control to the cloud environment (Bhadauria & Sanyal, 2012). The Web or online versions of Microsoft office applications and GoogleApps are typical examples of SaaS.

Deployment Models

A number of deployment models for cloud computing exist. The four common deployment models are private, public, hybrid, and community clouds (Backe & Lindén, 2015; Rao et al., 2013; Stair & Reynolds, 2016).

Private cloud deployment refers to a situation where the sharing of resources is restricted to individuals within the confine of a private network. Resources in a private cloud can be managed either internally by the user organization or by a third party. Furthermore, the resources can be hosted either internally or externally. A typical example is an organizational data centre which houses resources such as database servers, mail servers and other resources that are centrally used by all individuals within an organization.

Public cloud deployment refers to a deployment method in which the sharing of resources is open to the general public. Resources on public cloud may be freely shared and the users of resources can be individuals or companies. In terms of architecture, the difference between private and public clouds is very slim. However, substantial differences may exist in terms of security. An example of public cloud providers is the Amazon Web Services (AWS).

Hybrid cloud deployment is a deployment method which allows businesses to combine the services of two or more cloud models. The different clouds maintain their distinct individual identities but are bound together through the offering of benefits of the different models to the same client. Simply put, hybrid cloud deployment crosses isolation and provider boundaries such that it is not simply identified as falling into any specific deployment model. An example is a situation where an organization stores its sensitive data in its private network but interconnects the application using this data locally to another application (such as a business intelligence application) that is provided in a public cloud and runs as software service (Moore, 2014).

Community clouds allow several businesses to form a specific community with common concerns to share cloud computing resources. The needs or concerns of the community may be in relation to security, compliance, jurisdiction or any other issue. Community clouds can be managed internally or by a third party. They can also be hosted internally or externally to the user community.

Benefits of Cloud Computing to Industry 4.0

Considering the various services that can be provided in the cloud as already discussed, and the emerging trends in the application of new technologies, the benefits of cloud computing to industry 4.0 are numerous (Saint-Marc, 2014). Macias and Thomas (2011) see the benefits of cloud computing as comparable to the use of common public utilities in place of individual ones. For example, the use of public power in place of a personal generator, or the choice of using a public transport system instead of personal cars by people are relevant scenarios. Although this is not the main focus of the chapter, a brief discussion on some of the benefits of cloud computing is considered vital in providing a good background to the chapter. On this basis, a few of the benefits, which span across different businesses or industries are briefly highlighted below.

Cost Minimisation

As already mentioned, cloud computing enables businesses to minimise their expenditure. It saves businesses the cost of buying and maintaining infrastructure such as networking and storage facilities; application development platforms such as servers and operating system; and relevant application software. In other words, businesses are liberated from worrying about purchases of new computing facilities, revaluation of existing facilities, or the monthly review of the level of utilization of facilities. One important cost benefit of cloud computing is found in business start-ups. Cloud computing can be very beneficial in the starting up of businesses through the provision of access to facilities that may be very expensive to acquire. This is particularly important for small businesses that may not be able to afford facilities that can support advanced processes. Another way in which cloud computing minimises cost is through labour optimisation. Since most of the organization's services are virtual, their labour requirements are drastically reduced to only mission critical activities (Macias & Thomas, 2011). Furthermore, most cloud providers operate on a pay-as-you-go basis, thus users are charged only for services that they use (Chappell, 2011). By implication, the expenditures of most business is reduced to mainly operational expenditures as they are relieved of the heavier burdens of capital expenditure (Saint-Marc, 2014).

Choice and Scalability

With cloud computing, businesses are offered the benefit of making choices that are based on their needs and operational budgets at any particular time. This suggests that cloud computing provides the opportunity for every business to operate within the confines of their operational budgets (Saint-Marc, 2014). Another implication is that businesses in the fourth industrial revolution have the choice and opportunity of expanding easily to any level depending on their needs (Chou, 2013). Businesses can simply scale up their services by exploring the services of a cloud provider that are appropriate for their needs (Chappell, 2011).

Speed and Faster Rollout Capability

Cloud computing offers businesses the fastest means to rollout new capabilities and innovations. This is because organizations sometimes take a lot of time to finalize arrangements towards deploying IT infrastructure internally. This situation in most cases results in huge losses of revenue to the organizations (Chappell, 2011). Additionally, advertisements and information about products can be accessed by unlimited numbers of people irrespective of location and distance (Saint-Marc, 2014). Therefore, with cloud computing, businesses have the opportunities to cope with the expected market demands of Industry 4.0.

Integration and Big Data Management

Being host to several databases and applications which are properly organized, cloud computing serves as a good means of integrating various data components. In other words, cloud computing has opened the doors for effective generation and management of Big data (Chou, 2013; Saint-Marc, 2014). In this regard, Saint-Marc (2014) states that the cloud has the ability to provide countless application program interfaces (APIs) to be used by third party services; coordinate access to various database components

(OData, JSON, JSONP, XML) by APIs; and also ensure flexible and easier access to traditional databases including SQL and NoSQL databases.

Low Innovation Risk

Every business tries to stay ahead of others by way of rolling out regular innovations. However, each innovation has a risk of failure associated with it. Chappell (2011) states that the extent of the risk that is attached to an innovation is proportional to the financial obligation associated with the innovation. He maintains that the benefit of cloud computing to businesses is that it makes innovations less expensive and thus less risky. No doubt, this is a good motivation for businesses in the fourth industrial revolution as businesses are sure of rolling out more innovations with fewer risks.

Flexibility

Cloud computing makes room for high flexibility in terms of the use of resources. Organizations are not tied to the use of resources for life. Businesses can withdraw from the use of resources at any time when they no longer require such resources. Since these resources can be reallocated to other users, wastages due to redundant resources are minimised.

Business Continuity Planning and Centralizing Volatility of Businesses

This point serves as one of the major benefits of cloud computing. Business continuity planning or management refers to an organizational approach or approaches towards preventing or responding to situations that may affect the organizational assets negatively. It involves the implementation of measures that provide quick response to contingencies or crises of different origins so that at least vital business processes continue to run. Business continuity planning considers events such as malfunctioning of equipment, contingencies and crises. Traditionally, business continuity and disaster recovery techniques require the purchase and maintenance of a complete set of hardware that can mirror an enterprise's critical systems. For example, sufficient storage systems may be required to back up the complete set of a company's data. The maintenance fee and cost of regular replication of data on the mirror systems can be very high. Added to this cost is the cost of ensuring that the application software in use synchronizes all data locations. Cloud computing provide opportunities for companies to ensure the continuity of their businesses through adequate and cost effective disaster planning and recovery management. In the event of a disaster, business continuity planning is not hampered through the application of disaster recovery measures including cold or hot backups, high-redundancy, and data duplication backups among others, which are provided by different cloud service providers (Saint-Marc, 2014). Most cloud providers invest heavily towards ensuring the safety and resilience of their infrastructure to attacks. The Microsoft Cloud platform – Azure for example is ISO 27001 certified thus, it provides disaster recovery as a service. The implication is that in the unlikely event of any data loss, data recovery is guaranteed (Petrowisch, 2017). Therefore cloud computing assures organizations in Industry 4 of business continuity as they are relieved of the burdens and complexities associated with disaster planning and recovery.

Improved Agility and Adaptability

Two important potentials that cannot be detached from the fourth industrial revolution are effectiveness and efficiency in relation to organizational operations or business agility. Cloud computing promotes these potentials in organizations through the deployment of IT resources such as applications that support user requirements in real time (Oredo & Njihia, 2014). Most resources in the cloud are virtual, suggesting that cloud computing is built with mobile productivity in mind (Bigger, 2015). Thus, employees of organisations, especially ICT experts, are provided with better opportunities to quickly respond to the needs of their jobs using a variety of personal devices irrespective of their locations (Macias & Thomas, 2011). In other words, as long as Internet connection is available, job performance of employees or the services that organizations render to customers, are not limited to any time zone or geographic location (Apostu, Puican, Ularu, Suciu, & Todoran, 2014). Furthermore, the efficiency of organizations' IT departments is enhanced since their operations will no longer be limited by on-site infrastructure. Additionally, the IT departments are no longer concern about software upgrades and other major issues of the organization except minor ones that may pop up occasionally (Bigger, 2015).

Drawbacks or Challenges Associated With Cloud Computing and Implications for Industry 4.0

Although the benefits of cloud computing in relation to Industry 4.0 are enormous, a number of challenges have been identified which may be acting against the successful deployment and use of cloud computing services. Some of these challenges are presented below.

Technical Issues/Availability

Although a major benefit of cloud computing is that it promotes business agility, there must be moments when systems fail. In other words, no technology can be perfect. Apostu et al. (2014) state that even the best cloud service providers experience outages from time to time. Since organizations that utilize cloud services may not have control over the resources that they use, the organizations are helpless and their operations are truncated when cloud services become unavailable perhaps due to technical faults in the cloud. This suggests that businesses or organizations must embrace industry 4.0 with some caution and vigilance.

Security Issues

Security has been identified as one of the greatest concerns in cloud computing (Chou, 2013; CSA, 2016; Liu, Sun, Ryoo, Rizvi, & Vasilakos, 2015). Organizations or individuals that use cloud computing services surrender sensitive data to the cloud service providers which are mostly third parties (Oredo & Njihia, 2014). Information that is hosted in the cloud is subjected to different forms of external attacks which places organization that utilize cloud services in some form of danger. Without critically weighing all options before choosing cloud service providers by businesses, the benefits of cloud computing may be undermined (Apostu et al., 2014). This puts the success of Industry 4.0 on shaky ground.

Cost

As was discussed earlier, cost is considered to be one of the benefits of cloud based on the reasoning that organizations incur costs for only services that they use. However, it has been observed that the situation may not always be the same across all service providers. In some cases, cloud service providers present a predetermined suite of services to clients as a single contract irrespective of usage (Apostu et al., 2014). Indirectly, clients still pay for services that they do not use.

Inflexibility/Vendor Lock

Using cloud computing services makes business operations sort of inflexible. The choice of a cloud computing vendor by an organization is as good as restricting the operations of the organisation to the proprietary applications or formats of the cloud computing vendor (Oredo & Njihia, 2014). Apostu et al. (2014) cite the difficulty or restriction in inserting a document that has been created in a different application into a Google Docs spreadsheet as a typical example.

Inadequate Support

Poor support in terms of lack of prompt response to the needs of customers has been viewed as a challenge in cloud computing. For most businesses, a halt or a little delay in operations can result in significant losses. Therefore poor support emanating from long delays in responding to customers on the part of cloud service providers surely have negative consequences for businesses (Campbell, 2010). These consequences could have negative implications for Industry 4.0.

Cultural Resistance

In line with Isaac Newton's law of motion, people always develop some form of resistance when changes occur. Shifting from traditional computing to cloud computing may result in a change in the roles of members of an organization especially the IT department. In addition, uncertainties and inadequate preparations towards the changes may result in high resistance to the adoption of cloud computing.

Limited Scope for Customisation

The joy of most users or organizations is to use applications that fit adequately into their operations. Most cloud solutions are generic. This means that they may not completely satisfy the yearnings of users in terms of fitting tightly into their specific business (Oredo & Njihia, 2014).

Lack of Investment on Infrastructure/Big Data Management

The success of cloud computing and by extension, Industry 4.0 depends on accessibility to high quality, reliable, and ubiquitous broadband connectivity to infrastructure. Following Cisco's projection that Internet traffic may reach a monthly estimate of 14.1 zettabytes in 2020, investments in vital infrastructure such as broadband connectivity, data storage facilities that will ensure uninterrupted Internet access to all businesses information, remain a big challenge (Access_Partnership, 2017). This explosive growth in data traffic no doubt places a higher demand on already strained existing infrastructure. Thus, unless a corresponding response in terms of large investments on appropriate infrastructure is ensured, the success of the fourth industrial revolution may be limited. New technologies and platforms which may offer better services are emerging. Some of the new technologies include "5G mobile systems, new satellite broadband networks, TV White Space radios" among others (Access_Partnership, 2017, p. 7). However, the ability to handle or manage the amount of data that may be generated through emerging technologies remains a challenging task.

Lack of Appropriate Incentives for Adoption/Regulatory and Compliance Restrictions

The full benefits or positive impact of cloud computing on businesses and by implication Industry 4.0 can only be felt in the presence of policies that enable users to leverage its capabilities. However, policies that for example ensure respect for privacy rights which are considered critical components of trust in the digital economy have either not been properly put in place or need to be addressed. Further compounding the situation are laws which seek to restrict international transfer of data (Access_Partnership, 2017). A number of countries particularly European countries have regulations in place that seek to serve as bottle necks in the international transfer of personal information (Oredo & Njihia, 2014). Such regulations prohibit personal information and any sensitive data from being physically located outside their States or countries. Although the intention behind such rules may be 'good', the regulations pose a challenge to the deployment of cloud computing services. Cloud services providers have to consider setting up data centres exclusively for such countries in order to comply with such regulations. This development negates the cost benefits of cloud computing which in turn impacts negatively on Industry 4.0 to a large extent.

Inadequate Workforce Skills

Cloud computing and by extension Industry 4.0 place more demands on individuals and organizations in terms of IT skills. Access Partnership (2017) reports that cloud computing and Industry 4.0 will require a shift in workforce skills to areas such as digital literacy and perhaps data science, which have been reported to have a massive skills gap.

TOP SECURITY THREATS ASSOCIATED WITH CLOUD COMPUTING

Hatwar and Chavan (2015) classified the top security threats that are associated with cloud computing to include those identified by Cloud Security Alliance, those inherited from networking perspectives, and other additional security threats.

The main threats that were identified by Cloud Security Alliance (CSA, 2016) include but are not limited to abuse and nefarious use of cloud computing, insecure interfaces and application program interfaces (APIs), malicious insiders, shared technology issues, data loss or leakages, account or service hijacking, and unknown risk profiles. Some other threats are not peculiar to cloud computing alone, but occur due to shared resources used in the cloud. Examples of these include cross sites scripting (XSS) attacks, sniffer attacks, SQL injection attacks, denial of service (DoS) attacks, man-in-the-middle attacks, distributed denial of service (DDoS) attacks, re-used IP addresses, hypervisor related security issues, google hacking, cookie poisoning, and cracking CAPTCHA (Arif & Shakeel, 2015; Dunn, 2009; Liu et al., 2015; Lua & Yow, 2011). These threats have become a great concern to most users of the technology as they appear to have downgraded the benefits of the technology (Stair & Reynolds, 2016). To ease understanding, a brief discussion on the top security threats to cloud computing and by extension, Industry 4.0 is presented in three categories – data security threats, network security threats, and cloud environment security threats.

Data Security Threats

Data Breaches

A data breach is a situation where vital information belonging to an individual or organization is leaked to an unauthorised individual or group (Bhadauria & Sanyal, 2012; Kazim & Zhu, 2015; Racuciu & Eftimie, 2015). A data breach may occur as a result of a deliberate attack on the target or due to human error, application vulnerability and/or improper security practices (CSA, 2016; Hatwar & Chavan, 2015). Depending on the value of such information to the interested party (attacker), a data breach in the cloud has no limit to the kind of information that it affects. It can involve different kinds of information including personal, financial, trade secret and intellectual property. The most worrisome data breach is that which originates from unauthorized insiders who may not be detected easily. Hence, data breaches are rated among the top security threats in organizations' clouds (CSA, 2016). The main sources of data breaches are cloud provider personnel and their devices as well as third party partners of the cloud providers.

The impact of data breaches on organizations will vary depending on the sensitivity of the data involved. The impact may include large fines incurred by companies, lawsuits or litigations, cost for investigations, and perhaps criminal charges. Damage to reputation which may result in loss of business opportunities is another dimension to the impact of data breaches. Industry 4.0 is based on the principles of cloud computing. Data breaches will serve as a set-back to the fourth industrial revolution because most organizations are still not confident in moving to the cloud (Bhadauria & Sanyal, 2012).

A practical example of a data breach as reported by CSA (2016) is the case of an antivirus firm – Bit-Defender which had the usernames and passwords of some of its customers stolen in 2015 as a result of a security vulnerability in its public cloud application that was hosted by Amazon Web Services (AWS).

Data Loss

Apart from malicious attacks and data breaches, there are other actions or events that can result in permanent loss of data in organizations or clouds. Some of these actions or events include accidental deletion of data by a service provider or a physical disaster like fire or earthquake, data corruption, loss of encryption keys, and perhaps faults in storage equipment (CSA, 2016; Kazim & Zhu, 2015). As already mentioned, data remains the most valuable asset to organizations, hence its permanent loss can be terrifying. Kazim and Zhu (2015) state that 44% of cloud service providers faced challenges due to brute force attacks which led to data loss and leakages in 2013. The attack on Sony, which resulted in the leaking of confidential information such as email exchanges in November, 2014; the hacking of Code Spaces (an online hosting and code publishing provider) in June, 2014, which led to the compromise and complete destruction of most customers' data are practical examples of attacks that have resulted in huge data losses (CSA, 2016). In view of this development, threats that result in data loss are considered as top threats.

System Vulnerability

System vulnerabilities result from bugs in programs which are exploited by attackers to infiltrate computer systems. The aim of an attacker may be to steal the organizations data, take entire control of the system or disrupt the services of the organization. Data is the most valuable asset of organizations, thus, system vulnerabilities can cost organizations a lot. With networks and cloud computing, the risk associated with system vulnerability is extended to remote attacks (CSA, 2016). In industry 4.0, more data is expected to be generated, systems and resources are expected to be shared by more organizations, and thus the impact of system vulnerability may be higher if not mitigated.

Network Security Threats

Account Hijacking

Account or service hijacking involves methods that are used to steal the credentials of users with the aim of gaining access to their accounts or other computing services. Attack methods include phishing, fraud, cross site scripting and exploiting of software vulnerabilities (CSA, 2016; Kazim & Zhu, 2015). Account or service hijacking results in access to critical cloud computing services thereby compromising the confidentiality, integrity, and availability of these services and the data to which the services relate. Account hijacking can also result in damaging the reputations of organizations as well as their clients. A practical example is the hijacking of credentials from the Amazon site in 2010 due to a cross-site scripting (XSS) bug. A more recent example is the compromise in Code Space's account with Amazon AWS in June, 2014 which saw the failure of the system to shield the administrative console with multifactor authentication. This attack is reported to have put the company out of business as virtually all their assets were destroyed (CSA, 2016).

Denial of Service Attacks (DoS)

DoS attacks are forms of attacks that deny legitimate users access to services that they should ideally have access to. These services could include the users' data, applications, storage facilities, cloud network and other services (CSA, 2016; Kazim & Zhu, 2015). Denial of service attacks tend to consume excessive amounts of critical system resources, for example processor power, memory, and bandwidth thereby causing unnecessary slowdown in terms of the system response to the needs of legitimate users (Racuciu & Eftimie, 2015). In Distributed Denial of Service (DDoS) attacks, which are more common in cloud environments, the attacker sends a large number of requests from multiple sources in the network. These requests consume critical resources which should provide services to users. The result is that requests from legitimate users either do not get access to these system resources or are responded to very slowly or inappropriately. Some types of attacks that relate to DDoS include DNS amplification attacks, malformed UDP and TCP packets, and asymmetric application-level attacks among others (CSA, 2016; Racuciu & Eftimie, 2015, p. 106). These attack mostly exploit vulnerabilities in Web-based services (Kazim & Zhu, 2015). The impact of DoS attacks has been compared with being in a rush-hour traffic gridlock with no way forward or backwards (CSA, 2016).

Shared Technology Vulnerabilities

As discussed earlier, cloud services are delivered to customers through the sharing of resources (infrastructure, platforms and applications). These services are sometimes deployed using off-the-shelf hardware and/or software (for instance CPUs and GPUs) which do not meet the security requirements for cloud computing environments. For example, the components that are used to deploy various services may not have been designed with isolation properties which can enable multiple clients to share infrastructure or platforms securely. This situation exposes the cloud providers to newer threats resulting from the vulnerabilities of shared technologies (Kazim & Zhu, 2015; Racuciu & Eftimie, 2015). The impact of shared technology vulnerability can be high because it extends to the entire cloud environment. For instance, any attack on the hypervisor – a computer software that runs virtual machines specifically in the cloud - will expose the entire cloud environment to risk. The CSA 2016 (p.33) mentions the "construction of an access-driven side-channel attack by which a malicious virtual machine (VM) extracts fine-grained information from a victim VM running on the same physical computer" as a typical example.

Malicious Insiders

The malicious insider threat is a threat that emanates from someone who may have vital information relating to an organization. It is a threat that is associated with current or former employees of organizations, contractors or other business partners who may have access to vital resources (network, system, data) of the organization and decide to misuse privileges in a manner that affects the organization negatively (CSA, 2016; Kazim & Zhu, 2015). The impact of a malicious insider can be high. For example, an insider such as a system administrator or cloud administrator could have access to critical systems of organizations. The risks can be higher in clouds since they provide services to several organizations. A hobbyist hacker is another type of malicious insider. The intention of a hobbyist hacker is to have access to sensitive information just for fun (Kazim & Zhu, 2015). By implication, malicious insiders constitute a big threat to Industry 4.0 where virtually all aspects of organizations are expected to be driven by centralized machines. CSA (2016) reports that the insider threat is not always related to malicious activities. The negative action(s) of the insider could just be accidental. For example, uploading a customer's data into a public database (CSA, 2016).

Advanced Persistent Threats (APTs)

An APT is a kind of parasitical threat which usually infiltrates a system in order to establish a sort of base in targeted organizations' computing infrastructure. The attackers then use the foothold or base that they have established to smuggle or steal data and intellectual property from such organizations (CSA, 2016). Advanced persistent threats operate in an environment for an extended period of time in order to study and adapt to various security measures that have been set against them. Attack techniques and common points of entry for APTs include "spear phishing, direct hacking systems, delivering attack code through USB devices, penetration through partner networks and use of unsecured or third party networks" (CSA, 2016, p. 22). They achieve this objective by blending with normal traffic in organisations or cloud networks. CSA (2016) reports that typical examples of APTs are the 'Carbanak' gang which targets banks, and Chinese Cyber-Espionage which has stolen data amounting to hundreds of terabytes from several organisations since 2006.

Cloud Environment Security Threats

Insufficient Identity, Credential and Access Management

Another top security concern in cloud computing emanates from the lack of a scalable identity access management system, lack of multifactor authentication techniques, use of weak passwords, and the lack of ongoing automated rotation of cryptographic keys, among other issues (Hatwar & Chavan, 2015). CSA (2016) reports that these threats can be responsible for numerous forms of attacks such as the data breach that was discussed previously. Embedding of credentials and cryptographic keys in source code or their distribution in repositories such as GitHub, which are accessible by the public constitute a big threat to information in the cloud since such keys can be discovered and misused.

Insufficient identity, credential and access management may provide the opportunity for malicious actors to masquerade as legitimate users to modify and/or delete data, assume control of management functions; snoop on data or inject malicious software that appears to be coming from a genuine source (CSA, 2016). In other words, insufficient identity, credential and access management makes room for unauthorised access to data resulting in a huge damage to organizations and end users. The fourth industrial revolution involves an unprecedented number of users and interconnected and shared resources. Therefore, the impact of insufficient identity, credential and access management may be catastrophic.

A practical example of an attack that results from insufficient identity, credential and access management is the cloud-based Password Cracking Service launched by Paetorian – a Texas-based information security solutions provider. CSA (2016) reports that the service leverages the computing power of Amazon Web Services in order to crack passwords.

Insecure Interfaces and Application Program Interfaces (APIs)

Users interact with cloud services via software known as User Interfaces or Application Program Interfaces (APIs) which are provided by the cloud service providers. Since cloud providers manage their services through these interfaces, it implies that the security and availability of the various services that are provided in the cloud depends on the security of these interfaces (CSA, 2016; Racuciu & Eftimie, 2015). Organizations and third parties also make use of these interfaces by building on them in order to provide services to their own customers. Thus the new APIs that have been introduced result in increased risk since the organizations that are involved may be required to disclose their credentials to the third party in order to ensure smooth interoperability. Weak APIs have been associated with a number of risks which concern confidentiality, integrity, availability and accountability of organizations' data (CSA, 2016; Racuciu & Eftimie, 2015). A typical example is the exposure of about 300,000 records of the US internal revenue service via unsecured APIs in 2015 (CSA, 2016).

Insufficient Due Diligence

Due diligence refers to deliberate attempts or efforts by individuals or organizations to have a complete understanding in terms of what is needed to assess risks that may be associated with the use of certain business services prior to using such services (Kazim & Zhu, 2015). For example, an organization's attempt to understand all aspects of cloud computing and the risks that are associated with its services before adopting any of the services can be described as due diligence (Racuciu & Eftimie, 2015). On the other hand, an organization which rushes into adopting cloud services without a prior in-depth assessment of such services (insufficient due diligence) may be exposing itself to a myriad of risks such as financial, commercial, technical and compliance risks (CSA, 2016). Risks associated with insufficient due diligence are capable of jeopardizing the entire success of an organisation, hence they are considered among the top security risks in cloud computing. A practical example is the challenge that was experienced in 2013 by Nirvanix – a company which provided cloud services to IBM, Dell, and other services. The challenge led to Nirvanix operations being shuttered and clients were given a two week period to relocate their data to other services. This development had the potentials of leading to situations such as data losses, operational disruptions, security breaches and issues of non-compliance especially for clients that had not envisaged such challenges (CSA, 2016).

Abuse and Nefarious Use of Cloud Services

This threat relates to the inappropriate delivery of cloud services to consumers and/or the misuse of cloud services by consumers through illegal or unethical behaviours in the cloud. Activities that can be associated with the abuse and nefarious use of cloud services include deployment of poorly secured cloud services, free cloud service trials, and fraudulent account sign-ups (CSA, 2016), and using cloud network addresses for spam by malicious users (Kazim & Zhu, 2015). These actions provide room for malicious users (attackers) to leverage cloud computing resources to target individual customers, organizations, and even other cloud service providers. Examples of attacks that are associated with misuse of cloud resources include "distributed denial of service attacks (DDoS); email spam and phishing campaigns; 'mining' for digital currency; large-scale automatic click fraud; brute-force compute attacks of stolen credential databases; and hosting of malicious or pirated content" (CSA, 2016, p. 29; Kazim & Zhu, 2015). One major impact of abuse and nefarious use of cloud services is inefficiency on the part of the cloud service provider. In other words, it results in a drastic reduction in available capacity to respond to legitimate customers that the cloud service provider is hosting. A typical example is the attack on Amazon's Elastic cloud computing division in July, 2014, where the attackers created an easily accessible backdoor into the organization's "massive bank of available processing power" (CSA, 2016, p. 30).

SECURITY MEASURES FOR CLOUD COMPUTING

As already highlighted previously, the Internet is the main platform that allows for data communication and application accessibility in a cloud computing environment. Hence, the Internet can be subjected to many types of attacks. It is therefore vital that various security measures are implemented to protect data and applications over the Internet (Jose & Sajeev, 2011; Musa & Sani, 2016; Patidar & Bhardwaj, 2011). The measures are presented in three broad categories as discussed below.

Data Security

Data Encryption

Data encryption using secure socket layer (SSL) and transport layer security (TLS) is one measure that can be used to encrypt data as they flow over the Internet (Dua, 2013). SSL which was developed by

Netscape allows for secured communications between a web browser and a web server. It allows a web browser to authenticate a web server. The secured hypertext transfer protocol (HTTPS) allows encrypted information to flow between devices on the Internet. This is done using a RSA algorithm which is a public key for encryption and decryption of data (Dua, 2013). To establish whether devices on the Internet are interacting with trusted devices, SSL and TLS make use of Certificate Authorities that issue certificates to communicating devices. These authorities then verify the authentic identify of devices in the cloud (Dua, 2013).

To keep the data secure during the communication, TLS/SSL uses cryptographic techniques. Confidentiality, integrity, authentication and non-repudiation are amongst the four aims of cryptography. Three (confidentiality, integrity, and authentication) of these four aims are successfully implemented in TLS/SSL protocols in two steps. The first step uses asymmetric cryptography and X509 digital certificates (Dua, 2013). These certificates use the internationally accepted X.509 public key infrastructure (PKI) standard that ensures that the public key belongs to the device identity contained within the certificate. This step allows for entities involved in data exchange to be authenticated. The second step guarantees confidentiality through the use of message authentication code (MAC) and symmetric encryption. Packets transmitted are also verified in this step to assure confidentiality (Dua, 2013).

However, some drawbacks have been associated with encrypting data for storage in the cloud. One such is that it is difficult to disseminate decryption keys to authorised users, thus efficient key management techniques are required (Wan, Liu, & Deng, 2012). Remote key management service helps with this drawback by allowing clients to maintain the key management systems (KMS) solution on-premises. In this scenario, clients own, maintain and support their own KMS, thereby leaving hosting and processing to the cloud providers and ownership and control of KMS to the customer (CSA, 2012). Another drawback to encryption is that, as the number of legitimate users becomes greater, the solution becomes inefficient since it lacks scalability and flexibility. If a valid user needs to be withdrawn, re-encryption of related data needs to occur and all existing valid users must be supplied with new keys again. For this process to successfully occur, all data owners must encrypt or re-encrypt data and new keys supplied to authorised users.

Internet Protocol Security (IPSec) is a transmission protocol that also can be utilised to secure data over a cloud network. It works by ensuring that each and every packet in the communication session is encrypted and authenticated. IPsec's can act as data protectors between host pairs and also between security gateway pairs. They can additionally provide data protection between a host and a security gateway. IPSec also has a replay protection function that avoids hackers making changes to a packet as it travels between source and destination (Alhumrani & Kar, 2016). Hence, IPSec supports data confidentiality, data integrity, data origin authentication and anti-play capability.

Encryption and authentication discussed above can be used to secure data in transit and at rest. Apart from these, stored data can be protected by users' ensuring that data is stored on backup drives and verified that key words in files remain unchanged. Before upload into servers, the hash of the file is calculated to guarantee that the data is not altered (Raoa & Selvamanib, 2015). Data stored in the cloud can also be filtered before storing. Since large amount of data that is stored consists of important and unimportant data and it is difficult to encrypt all the data, data therefore needs to be filtered to determine the important data that needs to be encrypted and then stored (Matloob & Siddiqui, 2017). "Content address storage can be used instead of physical storage like physical drives etc., because the physical device consists of a physical address which can be copied whereas content address storage stores the information with a unique identity which is unique to the stored information and cannot be copied" (Matloob & Siddiqui,

2017, p. 1493). It is also vital that private and sensitive data not be stored in the public cloud but stored by the client in private clouds thus making is more difficult to be accessed by unauthorised individuals.

Robust Access Control

Access control is another measure that can be used to protect data in the cloud. Access control can be defined as an action that denies, restricts or disallows users' entry to a system. It can also record and monitor all attempts that are made to gain entry to a system, as well as identify unauthorized users who are attempting to access a system. It is a very useful protection mechanism in computer security. There are numerous access control models that are in use including Discretionary and Mandatory Access Control, Role Based Access Control (RBAC) and Attribute Based Access Model (ABAC), to name a few. These models are identity based access control models since users (subjects) and resources (objects) are identified using unique names. The identification can be done directly or via roles assigned to the subjects. These types of access control methods work best in distributed systems that do not change and where the users and services are known (Khan, 2012).

An Identification Based Access Control (IBAC) model allows users into the system by verifying their user's identity. However, as the number of networks and users increases IBAC becomes limited in scalability and problematic for distributed systems. To overcome the limitation of this model, the Role Based Access Control (RBAC) model was introduced. This model allowed users to access the system based on their roles. RBAC uses the minimum amount of permissions required to complete their tasks. However, this model has proved to be difficult when trying to determine user roles across administrative domains (Khan, 2012). To address this difficulty, Varsha and Patil (2015) propose trust models that enable roles of individuals to be determined by data owners and users using cryptographic role-based access control (RBAC) schemes. The model guarantees that data is accessible only by those documented in access policies. This development improves the security of data stored in the cloud and removing the weaknesses of other RBAC models.

Attribute based access control is considered to be better. It was developed to address the problems of some RBAC models. In this model the user is granted access based on attributes that can be proved. An example of such attributes is identity number or date of birth (Khan, 2012). Most of the access controls that implement attribute-set-based encryption (ASBE) are inflexible in implementing access controls that have complex policies. To have access controls that have scalability, flexibility and fine-grained access control so as to provide a high level of privacy, a hierarchical attribute set based encryption (HASBE) is suggested. This measure is achieved by "extending ciphertext-policy attribute-set-based encryption (ASBE) with a hierarchical structure of users" Wan et al. (2012, p. 743). This model combines the flexibility and fine-gained access control that is part of ASBE with a hierarchical structure of users, achieving scalability, flexibility and fine-gained access control. It also deals more efficiently with user revocation by having access expiration time assigned in numerous value assignments.

Cloud computing is used to host data and applications from multiple customers, known as tenants. Hence, in order to protect data and applications from being accessible by other tenants, it is important to separate this data and applications into different compartments for each tenant. Therefore this security ability must be supported by the cloud. This is achieved using the Multi-tenancy based control model (MTACM) which implements the security duty separation principle by incorporating a two granule level access control mechanism. One granule is to compartmentalize different customers and the other granule is for client applications so that clients can control access to their own applications only. Li,

Shi, Guo, and Ma (2011) revealed that the implementation of MTACM show a good performance and is technically and practically feasible.

Intrusion Detection Systems

In cloud computing it is important to distinguish between authorised and unauthorised users. Intrusion detection systems (IDS) incorporate behaviour based and knowledge based techniques in the detection of unauthorised users (Pathak, 2015). For these techniques to be effective, an Intrusion Detection System Agent component is needed that will gather information about users, and all activities of the users are tracked and forwarded to the IDS system for further analysis (Narwane & Vaikol, 2012).

Behaviour based analysis involves analysing previous behaviour patterns of users in the cloud with the current behaviour. This method automatically or manually builds a profile of users that describes normal activity which will serve as a baseline profile. When a deviation to this baseline profile occurs the system administrator is informed of possible suspicious activity (Narwane & Vaikol, 2012).

Knowledge based techniques make use of information accumulated from previous attacks and system vulnerabilities. When an intrusion occurs that meets the profile of previous attacks, an alarm is activated and the system administrator is informed (Narwane & Vaikol, 2012).

Protection Against Data Loss

The ways in which data, information and applications are stored have changed tremendously since the introduction of cloud computing. This development allows users to access their applications, information and documents, anytime and anywhere using different types of devices (Wu, Ping, Ge, Wang, & Fu, 2010).

Availability and reliability are some of the benefits offered by cloud storage. Cloud providers continually backup data, ensuring reliability of data (Kamara & Lauter, 2010; Kazim & Zhu, 2015). Data is also duplicated across multiple physical machines to ensure that information and data stored within the cloud is protected from accidental deletion and hardware crashes. By so doing, the cloud is operational regardless if one or more machines are offline since the data is duplicated on other machines within the cloud (Kamara & Lauter, 2010). Nate (2016) states that in cloud environments, daily backup and off-site storage of data is critical to protect against data loss.

Isolation of Virtual Machines

Cloud computing is made possible through virtualization. Virtualization is the simulation of a device or resource to one or more client devices. A virtual machine (VM) is an operating system or a software program that portrays the behaviour of a computer and also is able to run applications and programs like a separate computer.

VMs provide cost effective security, since virtualization utilizes one physical machine to the fullest by running multiple VMs on it. This measure allows only for perimeter security mechanisms to be implemented on one physical server rather than multiple servers, thereby reducing the cost of security (Randell, 2006).

Despite this advantage VM poses some security risks such as attack on hypervisor, virtual library checkout, migration attack and encryption attack (Zheng & Jain, 2011).

Isolation of virtual machines is a resilient defence characteristic of virtualization. Basically, each virtual machine can run without knowing any information about other virtual machines. This process makes it complicated for a malicious attacker to access other virtual machines from a compromised virtual machine since only the hypervisor knows about the existence of other virtual machines (Zheng & Jain, 2011).

Cloud service providers aim to uphold a high level of isolation between virtual machine (VM) instances, including isolation between inter user processes. A robust isolation between virtual machines could be able to restrict an attacker from integrating malicious code in a neighbouring virtual machine. Isolation of virtual machines is helpful in alleviating metadata spoofing attacks and backdoor channel attacks (Modi, Patel, Borisaniya, Patel, & Rajarajan, 2013).

Network Security

Preventing Account and Service Hijacking

The stealing or hijacking of a user's account or service is referred to as account or service hijacking. For this to be successfully executed, perpetrators need to obtain personal and confidential information. Exploitation of software vulnerabilities, phishing, spoofed emails, social engineering, and guessing of passwords are some of the techniques that criminal hackers use to obtain this personal and confidential information. When illegal access to network resources is successfully gained, the integrity, availability and confidentiality of services are compromised. To reduce account hijacking, two-factor authentication approaches can be used (Racuciu & Eftimie, 2015). The process uses the user name and password as one factor of authentication and a personal piece of information that only the user knows as the second factor (Racuciu & Eftimie, 2015). To make authentication more reliable for its cloud applications, multi-factor authentication is implemented in Microsoft's Windows Azure Active Directory. Three authentication factors are used. These are one-time password, an automated phone call, and a text message (SMS) (Dasgupta, Roy, & Nag, 2016). To reduce the dependency on passwords, Fast Identity Online (FIDO) alliance developed a framework for online authentication that uses biometric authentication and PIN-codes. This framework supports multi-factor authentication without the use of conventional passwords (Dasgupta et al., 2016).

Other techniques that can be used to prevent account hijacking are encryption management systems, prohibiting the sharing of account credentials between users and services, and employing an identification management system to detect unauthorised activity (Christina, 2015; Racuciu & Eftimie, 2015). In addition, non-technical techniques also need to be used to prevent service hijacking. According to Pereira et al. (2016), the user also needs to play a role to prevent hackers from obtaining the credentials to hijack services. Therefore users need to be aware of social engineering and phishing attacks that hackers use to obtain information.

Protection Against Denial of Service Attacks

Stopping of cloud services by flooding the server with illegitimate requests leading to damage of hardware or data is caused by a denial of service (DoS) attack and a distributed denial of service attack (DDoS). A DoS attack is carried out by a single device whereas a DDoS attack can be carried out by multiple devices. Bakshi and Yogesh (2010) propose a method for securing cloud services from attacks using DDoS and an Intrusion Detection System (IDS). "In this method, a Snort based Network Intrusion Detection System (NIDS) tool is connected on a virtual machine to detect if any untrusted activity is occurring. If such activity happens, the IP address of that activity is determined and all data from that IP address is blocked. If a DDoS attack is established, the service running on the attacked virtual machine is moved to another virtual machine.

Sullivan (2014) mentions that a DDoS attack can also be prevented by measures such as deep data checking and using hardware situated on the network to examine data. Khalil, Khreishah, and Azeem (2014) observed that the most dangerous attacks in cloud computing are accounted for by denial of service attacks (DoS) especially HTTP, XML or Representational State Transfer (REST) based DoS attacks. These attacks, according to Khalil et al. (2014) start off with the attacker initiating requests in XML which are sent through the HTTP protocol. Attackers construct the system interface using REST protocols such as those used in Microsoft Azure and Amazon EC2. In view of the vulnerability of the system-interface, it is difficult for cloud security experts to overcome these forms of denial of service attacks. Denial of service attacks caused by XML or HTTP are the hardest to overcome (compared to traditional attacks) because there are no measures put in place to avoid them from occurring. Implementing security over these protocols is therefore important in cloud computing in order to ensure the secured development of the cloud. As a way forward Karnwal, Sivakumar, and Aghila (2012) propose a five staged framework called "cloud defender" that attempts to countermeasure denial of service attacks. The first four stages of the framework detect HTTP-based DoS attacks whereas the fifth stage detects XML-based DoS attacks. REST-based attacks are not catered for in this framework as they are mainly an attack on the user interface which varies for different users and systems.

The solutions proposed by the framework of Karnwal et al. (2012) are as follows:

1. **Sensor:** Detects the incoming requests and if it identifies an increase in the number of requests from the same user it flags a warning where it marks the user as suspicious.
2. **HOP Counter Filter:** Counts the number of hops (the number of nodes the request went through) and compares this to the pre-defined hop count. The request is marked as suspicious if there is a difference between these values as it may indicate that the header of the message was altered by the attack's system
3. **IP Frequency Divergence:** Marks a request message suspicious if it detects the same frequency of IP messages.
4. **Puzzle Solver:** It helps in identifying a legitimate request by determining the ability of the requester to solve a puzzle.
5. **Double Signature:** Doubles the number of XML signatures such that if there is an attack, both XML signatures need to be validated.

Puzzle Solver involves the solving of complex puzzles where the solution of the puzzle is inserted into the header of a Simple Object Access Protocol such that if the cloud suspects a possible attack, it will send the puzzle to the IP from which it received the messages. If the solved puzzle is sent back to the cloud, then the user is identified as not a threat, otherwise the message is identified as a HTTP DoS attack (Khalil et al., 2014). An example of puzzle solver is Graphical Turing Tests, which distinguish between human users and robots. CAPTCHA (Completely Automated Public Turing Tests to Tell Computers and Humans Apart) is used for a Graphical Turing Test. Furthermore, Yadav and Sujata (2013) recommend a Two-Tier CAPTCHA. The method is described as Two-Tier CAPTCHA in the sense that a cloud attack defence system known as a CLAD node needs to generate two things – first an alphanumeric CAPTCHA code and second a query related to that CAPTCHA code. In this method, a human can provide input according to a query that is not easy for software bots.

Another form of preventive mechanism against DDoS is to guard web services right at the application level (Vissers, Somasundaram, Pieters, Govindarajan, & Hellinckx, 2014). The suggested method is aimed at guarding against Oversized XML, Oversized Encryption, HTTP flooding and so on, through the use of a reverse proxy which serves as a sieve to interrupt all service requirements.

The most severe denial of service attacks on cloud computing are XML based Denial of Service (X-DoS) and HTTP-based Denial of Service (H-DoS). Using countermeasures such as firewalls, updates to patches and intrusion detection systems is inefficient in preventing these attacks (Alotaibi, 2015). On this note, a neural network to find and remove X-DoS and H-DoS attacks was proposed (Chonka, 2011). The system discovers attacks immediately using Cloud TraceBack (CTB) and identifies and removes these attacks using Cloud Protector. Furthermore, Sarhadi (2013) developed a cloud defender system known as Cloud Service Queuing Defender (CSQD) which increases the effectiveness and efficiency in the detection and elimination of XML weaknesses in web services. It is also capable of determining the source of an attack and prevents future attacks by self-learning from previous attacks.

Protecting Against Shared Technology Vulnerabilities

According to Ashktorab and Taghizadeh (2012), various steps can be taken to confront this threat. The first step is to implement security best practices during the installation and configuration of hardware and software components. The environment should also be monitored for unauthorised changes and activities. Strong authentication and access control must be promoted for administrative access and operations. Service level agreements should also be enforced with cloud vendors that will create agreements for patching and vulnerability remediation and to perform regular vulnerability testing and configuration audits (Ashktorab & Taghizadeh, 2012).

The hypervisor plays a crucial role in the cloud architecture since it is responsible for facilitating interactions between virtual machines and the physical hardware. Hence to allow for optimal functioning of all virtualization components, the hypervisor must be secured and isolation between VMs must be implemented (Kazim & Zhu, 2015). It is important to develop and implement a strategy to prevent shared technology threats for all the service models that includes infrastructure, platform, software and user security. When creating the strategy, it is suggested that all cloud components must have baseline requirements established and these requirements must be used in the design of the cloud architecture (Kazim & Zhu, 2015).

Protecting Against Advanced Persistent Threats (APTs)

Security awareness training is important in preventing advanced persistent threats. This will assist in combating social engineering techniques like spear-phishing emails (Musa & Sani, 2016). In addition, organizations can deploy traditional defence mechanisms measures such as patch management, anti-virus software, firewalls, and intrusion detection systems among others (Chandra, Challa, & Hussain, 2014; Hudson, 2014). Advanced malware detection using sandboxing execution can assist with the identification of advanced unknown malware (Hudson, 2014). Anomaly detection methods can be utilized to detect suspicious network traffic and system activities. Confidential data while in use, in motion and at rest can be monitored and blocked by using a Data Loss Prevention system that detects and prevents possible data breach (Chen, Desmet, & Huygens, 2014). Chen et al. (2014, p. 8) further state that "since APT actors typically launch repeated attacks against the target, defenders can create an intelligence feedback loop, which allows them to identify patterns of previous intrusion attempts, understand the adversaries' techniques, and then implement countermeasures to reduce the risk of subsequent intrusions".

Cloud Environment Security

APIs

Clients use application program interfaces (APIs) to access services on the cloud. The API of a cloud is responsible for observing and managing the various services offered by a cloud so it is therefore important to validate the details of the user. As such, unprotected APIs constitute a major security risk to the cloud environment (Gonzalez et al., 2012). One way of mitigating this threat is to restrict access to the cloud environment by ensuring that APIs are provided with robust authentication, encryption, as well as reliable activity monitoring mechanisms (Hatwar & Chavan, 2015; Modi et al., 2013). According to Gunjan, Tiwari, and Sahoo (2013), the most common way of securing APIs is by having passwords to check if the identity of the user attempting to access the cloud application is valid. For this measure to be more successful, it is required that clients and service providers must work in collaboration with one another (Shaikh & Haider, 2011). Thus, the *Confidentiality*, *Integrity*, and *Availability* (CIA) of data in the cloud environment can be guaranteed. In this case, the cloud service provider must offer security features that include tested encryption of schema which ensures that all data on the shared environment is guarded; stringent access controls that will help prevent unauthorized users from gaining access to the data; scheduled data backup and ensuring safe storage of backed-up data (Kaufman, 2009).

Musa and Sani (2016), suggest that security-focused code reviews and penetration testing during application development are also reliable countermeasures to this type of attack.

Preventing Abuse of the Cloud

A number of measures can be adopted to negate or prevent the risk of abuse of cloud computing. The first prevention method relates to cloud service providers obscuring the internal structure of the cloud to complicate any abusive attempts on the cloud. Secondly, the use of blinding techniques will reduce the data or information that can be retrieved by external or unethical sources. This requires that all side-channels should be recorded and be blinded (Ristenpart, Tromer, Shacham, & Savage, 2009). These decisions are believed to be the best ways to prevent the abuse of the cloud (Ristenpart et al., 2009).

Furthermore, various technical and non-technical measures can be implemented to prevent abuse in the cloud environment. The technical measures include measures such as intrusion prevention systems (IPS), network traffic filtering and logging. The non-technical measures on the other hand include measures such as acceptable use policies, account verifications and financial incentivisation (Lindemann, 2015). Service level agreement between user and service provider can incorporate policies to protect critical assets of organizations. From these policies users can be aware of the legal recourse organization can pursue if they violate this agreement (Kazim & Zhu, 2015).

IPS is an extension of intrusion detection systems (IDS). However, similar to IDS, IPS may generate false reports which, if acted upon, may result in incorrect clients being removed from the cloud.

This situation can result in disruptions of the clients' operations which may expose the cloud vendor to litigation due to a breach in service level agreement. Acceptable use policies between client and vendor can also assist to deter abuse. Although this measure may not completely protect against abuse, it will make users aware that certain types of use will not be tolerated. The measure is especially important since previously, cloud users were allowed trial use of cloud services without proper verification thereby increasing the possibility of abuse. Account verification by requesting users' phone numbers and sending a verification code to them via SMS can also help to verify the trustworthiness of users. Another useful measure is financial incentivisation which allows clients to make a deposit (Bit coin) and if a client commits any form of abuse in the cloud, the deposit is forfeited (Lindemann, 2015).

Malicious Insiders

According to Kandias, Virvilis, and Gritzalis (2011) two types of insiders pose a threat to the cloud. The first is an insider that works for the cloud service and can cause large amounts of damage to the user as well as service provider. The second is an insider that is part of the organization that decides to outsource the cloud service (Kandias et al., 2011).

Some countermeasures that can be used to address the threat of malicious insiders include; Cloud Service Provider and Client Identity, Access Management, Multi factor authentication, Log analysis and auditing, IDS/IPS and Insider prediction/detection models (Kandias et al., 2011). Another measure is to implement a strict supply chain management which conveys a complete supplier assessment (Hatwar & Chavan, 2015). cloud providers can supply information to clients on how their data and services are secured by providing them information on security and management practices as well as enlightening them on security breaches (Claycomb & Nicoll, 2012). Other security measures that can be taken to protect clouds against insiders that are looking to take advantage of cloud services' flaws include implementing basic security controls such as data loss prevention, separation of duties, limiting access based on job role and consistent auditing just to mention a few (Claycomb & Nicoll, 2012; Rashid, 2016). Attacks on local and external resources by employees can also be prevented by limiting employee's access to external resources or by using host based controls such as firewalls and proxies (Claycomb & Nicoll, 2012).

Overcoming Insufficient Due Diligence

It is critical that the risks associated with cloud implementation be fully understood by organization before shifting their business and critical assets like data to the cloud (Kazim & Zhu, 2015). Furthermore, the type of cloud services that organizations will be using together with their risk tolerance levels must be determined (Mahajan & Giri, 2014). "Data security measures combined with risk transfer in the form of insurance coverage and the acceptance of taking risk from the cloud service providers is the major solution to this problem" (Kumar & Padmapriya, 2014, p. 624).

cloud providers must disclose to customers the infrastructure such as firewall, or methods such as encryption, that will be used to protect data (CSA, 2017). Also, cloud vendors should use industry standards when implementing cloud applications and services. Both quantitative and qualitative risk assessments need to be periodically conducted to examine the storage, flow and processing of data (Kazim & Zhu, 2015). Organizations can also follow the record of self-assessed security practices maintained by the Cloud Security Alliance (Mahajan & Giri, 2014).

DISCUSSION

The fourth industrial revolution represents a paradigm shift from the traditional way of processing and storing data. This shift is masterminded by the principles of cloud computing technology which allows individuals or organisations to share resources (infrastructure and software) over the Internet. This provides room for greater availability of IT resources and decrease costs.

However, while laudable, cloud computing is perceived to entail a high degree of risk owing to new security threats that are being launched on cyberspace regularly. No doubt, the consequences of these threats, if unchecked, can be grievous in view of the multitenancy nature of cloud computing. In this case, it will not be out of place to state that the success of cloud computing is dependent on the implementation of proper security measures as the success of the fourth industrial revolution depends on cloud computing. Therefore, user enlightenment on mitigating the various security threats, which forms the basis of this chapter, remains critical to the success of the fourth industrial revolution.

The chapter has brought to the fore benefits of cloud computing services, security threats and security measures that are currently used to mitigate these threats. As already mentioned, creating awareness of the various measures that can be used to curtail the security threats to cloud computing is considered imperative. This is because the fourth industrial revolution is centred on the principles of cloud computing thus, threats to cloud computing imply threats to the fourth industrial revolution. For example, threats to data such as data breaches, data losses and system vulnerabilities may result in loss of confidence on cloud service providers. This implies that industries would rather be sceptical towards the integration and use of shared resources which industry 4.0 leans on. Similarly, the Internet constitutes a superhighway for the transmission and sharing of resources. This makes its role vital in the fourth industrial revolution, especially in the coordination of inter-organizational operations. Despite the importance of this infrastructure, threats such as account hijacking, denial of service attacks, shared technologies vulnerabilities, malicious insiders and advanced persistent threats appear to be acting against its efficacy. However, with the appropriate security measures put in place as already discussed, the impact of most of the threats on the fourth industrial revolution can be minimised. Furthermore, the cloud environment itself results in some security threats. Most of the cloud environment threats are associated with inappropriate decisions and/or improper use of various cloud services. Some of the cloud environment threats which have been discussed include insufficient identity, credentials and access management; insecure interfaces and application program interfaces; insufficient due diligence; and abuse and nefarious use of cloud services.

The measures that have been discussed cannot be said to be perfect. For example, during encryption, the storing of these certificates on the vendor sever can result in a problem because the data of various clients can be compromised if the certificates are stolen. Although remote key management is suggested as another way of handling this situation, the best security measure will be to prevent any attempt from occurring in the first place. This is achievable using intrusion detection systems. However, as earlier highlighted, one of the main disadvantages of intrusion detection systems is false alarms. For instance if the response to all alarms results in the automatic removal of a client from the cloud and a client is removed as a result of a false alarm, then the cloud vendor may breach the service level agreement. An important consideration in this situation is to determine the nature of an alarm before any action is taken. This must be done within a reasonable timeframe, otherwise delaying may allow time for malicious hackers to gain entry into the cloud.

Furthermore, due to the multitenancy of the cloud, any infiltration of the cloud network will result in many clients being affected. Therefore the isolation of virtual machines is considered key to reducing the impact of malicious hackers since it will hide the identity of other virtual machines in the cloud.

Apart from looking for technical vulnerabilities such as open ports on a network, hackers also try to hijack the accounts and services of users by using various social engineering techniques. Therefore, the awareness of clients about the different ways in which they can be scammed becomes vital. While the two key authentication techniques that have been discussed can be effective against preventing access to the network, including the verification code sent via SMS, the possibility that the codes can be hijacked may not be ruled out. Therefore, it is important that clients be aware of social engineering techniques that are continuously being devised by hackers. In addition, the multifactor method of authentication as implemented in Microsoft's Windows Azure Active Directory combined with biometrics may also go a long way in mitigating the threats of account hijacking.

In another dimension, Puzzle Solvers make use of Graphical Turing Tests such as Two-Tier CAPTCHA to help to distinguish between machines and humans that are trying to access the network. The Solvers rely on human intelligence to distinguish between numeric characters and alpha characters. However, with rapid advancements in artificial intelligence, methods that use human intelligence to distinguish humans from machines are under threat since robots will have the intelligence of humans and will be able to make similar decisions as humans. Fortunately, advances in biometric authentication methods can help to distinguish between humans and machines.

CONCLUSION

This chapter has highlighted the potential threats to cloud computing and the potential measures that can be implemented to counter these threats. From the discussion above, it is clear that there are however inherent weaknesses in some of the current measures. As yet there is no silver bullet to securing the cloud computing infrastructure from malicious hackers and insiders. Therefore, in order for cloud computing to be secure a variety of measures must be implemented. It is therefore vital for businesses, cloud designers and implementers to be aware of the array of measures available and how to use these measures to secure the cloud.

REFERENCES

Access_Partnership. (2017). *Delivering the fourth industrial revolution: The role of government*. Retrieved from Washington, DC: Author.

Alcorta, L. (2017). *Manufacturing the Future: the 4th Industrial Revolution and the 2030 Development Agenda*. Retrieved from http://unctad.org/meetings/es/Presentation/cstd2016_p23_Alcorta_en.pdf

Alhumrani, S. A., & Kar, J. (2016). Cryptographic Protocols for Secure Cloud Computing. *International Journal of Security and Its Applications*, *10*(2), 301–310. doi:10.14257/ijsia.2016.10.2.27

Alotaibi, K. H. (2015). Threat in Cloud- Denial of Service (DoS) and Distributed Denial of Service (DDoS) Attack, and Security Measures. *Journal of Emerging Trends in Computing and Information Sciences*, *6*(5), 241–244.

Apostu, A., Puican, F., Ularu, G., Suciu, G., & Todoran, G. (2014). New Classes of Applications in the Cloud. Evaluating Advantages and Disadvantages of Cloud Computing for Telemetry Applications. *Database System Journal*, *5*(1), 3–14.

Arif, M., & Shakeel, H. (2015). Virtualization Security: Analysis and Open Challenges. *International Journal of Hybrid Information Technology*, *8*(2), 237–246. doi:10.14257/ijhit.2015.8.2.22

Ashktorab, V., & Taghizadeh, S. R. (2012). Security Threats and Countermeasures in Cloud Computing. *International Journal of Application or Innovation in Engineering & Management*, *1*(2), 234–245.

Backe, A., & Lindén, H. (2015). *Cloud computing security: A systematic review*. Uppsala University.

Bakshi, A., & Yogesh, B. (2010). Securing cloud from DDOS Attacks using Intrusion Detection System in virtual machine. *ICCSN '10 Proceedings of the 2010 Second International Conference on Communication Software and Networks*, 260-264.

Bartholomew, D. (2009). *Cloud rains opportunities for software developers*. Retrieved from http://career-resources.dice.com/articles/content/entry/cloud_rains_opportunities_for_software

Bhadauria, R., & Sanyal, S. (2012). Survey on Security Issues in Cloud Computing and Associated Mitigation Techniques. *International Journal of Computers and Applications*, *47*(18), 47–66. doi:10.5120/7292-0578

Bigger, J. (2015). *5 Benefits of Cloud Computing for the Financial Services Industry*. Retrieved from https://blog.marconet.com/blog/5-benefits-of-cloud-computing-for-the-financial-services-industry

Bloem, J., Doorn, M., Duivestein, S., Excoffier, D., Maas, R., & Ommeren, E. (2014). *The Fourth Industrial Revolution: Things to tighten the link between IT and OT*. Retrieved from Online: https://www.fr.sogeti.com/globalassets/global/downloads/reports/vint-research-3-the-fourth-industrial-revolution

Bogatin, D. (2006). *Google CEO's new paradigm: Cloud computing and advertising go hand-in-hand*. Retrieved from http://www.zdnet.com/blog/micro-markets/google-ceos-new-paradigmcloud-computing-and-advertising-go-hand-inhand/369

Campbell, A. (2010). *These issues need to be resolved before Cloud computing becomes ubiquitous*. Retrieved from https://www.openforum.com/articles/these-issues-need-to-be-resolvedbefore-cloud-computing-becomesubiquitous-1

Chandra, J. V., Challa, N., & Hussain, M. A. (2014). Data and Information Storage Security from Advanced Persistent Attack in Cloud Computing. *International Journal of Applied Engineering Research*, *9*(2), 7755–7768.

Chappell, D. (2011). *The Benefits and Risks of Cloud Platforms - A Guide for Business Leaders*. Retrieved from http://www.storm.ie/PublishingImages/Documents/Azure%20for%20Business%20Leaders.pdf

Chen, P., Desmet, L., & Huygens, C. (2014). Lecture Notes in Computer Science: Vol. 8735. *A Study on Advanced Persistent Threats*. Berlin: Springer.

Chonka, A. X. Y., Zhou, W., & Bonti, A. (2011). Cloud security defence to protect cloud computing against HTTP-DoS and XML-DoS attacks. Elsevier.

Chou, T. (2013). Security threats on cloud computing vulnerabilities. *International Journal of Computer Science & Information Technology*, 5(3), 79–88. doi:10.5121/ijcsit.2013.5306

Christina, A. A. (2015). Proactive Measures on Account Hijacking in Cloud Computing Network. *Asian Journal of Computer Science and Technology*, 4(2), 31–34.

Claycomb, W. R., & Nicoll, A. (2012). *Insider threats to cloud computing: Directions for new research challenges*. Paper presented at the Computer Software and Applications Conference (COMPSAC), 2012 IEEE 36th Annual. 10.1109/COMPSAC.2012.113

CSA. (2012). *SecaaS Implementation Guidance, Category 8: Encryption*. CSA.

CSA. (2016). *The Treacherous 12: Cloud Computing Top Threats in 2016*. CSA.

CSA. (2017). *Security Guidance - For Critical Areas in Cloud Computing v4.0*. CSA.

Dasgupta, D., Roy, A., & Nag, A. (2016). Toward the design of adaptive selection strategies for multi-factor authentication. *Computers & Security, 63*, 85-116.

Dekker, M., Livery, D., & Lakka, M. (2013). *Cloud security incident reporting*. Academic Press.

Dua, I. V. (2013). Data Security in Cloud Oriented Application Using SSL/TLS Protocol. *International Journal of Application or Innovation in Engineering & Management*, 2(12), 79–85.

Dunn, J. E. (2009). *Spammers break Hotmail's CAPTCHA yet again*. Retrieved from NetworkWorld website: http://www.networkworld.com/article/2262871/lan-wan/spammers-break-hotmail-s-captcha-yet-again.html

Gonzalez, N., Miers, C., Redigolo, F., Simplicio, M., Carvalho, T., Näslund, M., & Pourzandi, M. (2012). A quantitative analysis of current security concerns and solutions for cloud computing. *Journal of Cloud Computing: Advances. Systems and Applications*, 1(11), 1–18.

Gunjan, K., Tiwari, R. K., & Sahoo, G. (2013). Towards Securing APIs in Cloud Computing. *International Journal of Computer Engineering & Applications, 2*(2), 27-34.

Hatwar, S. V., & Chavan, R. K. (2015). Cloud Computing Security Aspects, Vulnerabilities and Counter-measures. *International Journal of Computers and Applications, 119*(17), 46–53. doi:10.5120/21163-4218

Hudson, B. (2014). *Advanced Persistent Threats: Detection, Protection and Prevention*. Retrieved from http://resources.idgenterprise.com/original/AST-0112935_sophos-advanced-persistent-threats-detection-protectionprevention.pdf

Jose, G. J. A., & Sajeev, C. (2011). Implementation of Data Security in Cloud Computing. *International Journal of P2P Network Trends and Technology*, 18-22.

Kamara, S., & Lauter, K. (2010). *Cryptographic Cloud Storage*. Paper presented at the Financial Cryptography and Data Security, Tenerife, Canary Islands, Spain. 10.1007/978-3-642-14992-4_13

Kandias, M., Virvilis, N., & Gritzalis, D. (2011). *The insider threat in cloud computing*. Paper presented at the International Workshop on Critical Information Infrastructures Security.

Karnwal, T., Sivakumar, T., & Aghila, G. (2012). *A Comber Approach to Protect Cloud Computing against XML DDoS and HTTP DDoS attack*. Paper presented at the 2012 IEEE Students' Conference on Electrical, Electronics and Computer Science, Bhopal, India.

Kaufman, L. M. (2006). Data security in the world of cloud computing. *IEEE Security and Privacy*, 61–64.

Kazim, M., & Zhu, S. Y. (2015). A survey on top security threats in cloud computing. *International Journal of Advanced Computer Science and Applications*, *6*(3), 109–113. doi:10.14569/IJACSA.2015.060316

Khalil, I. M., Khreishah, A., & Azeem, M. (2014). Cloud Computing Security: A Survey. *Computers*, *3*(4), 1–35. doi:10.3390/computers3010001

Khan, A. R. (2012). Access control in cloud computing environment. *Journal of Engineering and Applied Sciences (Asian Research Publishing Network)*, *7*(5), 613–615.

Kumar, S. V. K., & Padmapriya, S. (2014). A Survey on Cloud Computing Security Threats and Vulnerabilities. *International Journal of Innovative Research in Electrical, Electronics, Instrumentation and Control Engineering*, *2*(1), 622–625.

Li, X.-Y., Shi, Y., Guo, Y., & Ma, W. (2011). *Multi-Tenancy Based Access Control in Cloud*. Paper presented at the Computational Intelligence and Software Engineering (CiSE).

Lindemann, L. (2015). *Towards Abuse Detection and Prevention in IaaS Cloud Computing*. Paper presented at the Availability, Reliability and Security (ARES), 10th International Conference on. 10.1109/ARES.2015.72

Liu, Y., Sun, Y., Ryoo, J., Rizvi, S., & Vasilakos, A. V. (2015). A Survey of Security and Privacy Challenges in Cloud Computing: Solutions and Future Directions. *Journal of Computing Science and Engineering: JCSE*, *9*(3), 119–133. doi:10.5626/JCSE.2015.9.3.119

Lua, R., & Yow, K. (2011). Mitigating DDoS attacks with transparent and intelligent fast-flux swarm network. *IEEE Network*, *25*(4), 28–33. doi:10.1109/MNET.2011.5958005

Macias, F., & Thomas, G. (2011). *Cloud Computing Advantages in the Public Sector*. Retrieved from http://www.cisco.com/c/dam/en_us/solutions/industries/docs/c11-687784_cloud_omputing_wp.pdf

Mahajan, H., & Giri, N. (2014). Threats to Cloud Computing Security. *International Journal of Application or Innovation in Engineering & Management*.

Matloob, G., & Siddiqui, F. (2017). Data at rest and it's security solutions-A survey. *International Journal of Advanced Research in Computer Science*, *8*(5), 1491–1493.

Moavenzadeh, J. (2015). *The 4th Industrial Revolution: Reshaping the Future of Production*. Paper presented at the DHL Global Engineering & Manufacturing Summit, Amsterdam.

Modi, C., Patel, D., Borisaniya, B., Patel, A., & Rajarajan, M. (2013). A Survey on Security Issues and Solutions at Different Layers of Cloud Computing. *The Journal of Supercomputing*, *63*(2), 561–592. doi:10.100711227-012-0831-5

Moore, J. (2014). *Business tntelligence takes to Cloud for small businesses*. Retrieved from https://www.cio.com/article/2375744/business-intelligence/business-intelligence-takes-to-cloud-for-small-businesses.html

Musa, F. A., & Sani, S. M. (2016). Security Threats and Countermeasures In Cloud Computing. *International Research Journal of Electronics & Computer Engineering*, *2*(4), 22–27.

Narwane, S. V., & Vaikol, S. L. (2012). *Intrusion Detection System in Cloud Computing Environment*. Paper presented at the International Conference on Advances in Communication and Computing Technologies (ICACACT).

Nate, L. (2016). *Data Security Experts Reveal The #1 Information Security Issue Most Companies Face with Cloud Computing & Storage*. Retrieved from https://digitalguardian.com/blog/27-data-security-experts-reveal-1-information-security-issue-most-companies-face-cloud

Oredo, J. O., & Njihia, J. (2014). Challenges of Cloud computing in business: Towards new organizational competencies. *International Journal of Business and Social Science*, *5*(3), 150–160.

Pathak, P. K. (2015). Integrated Intrusion Detection System in Cloud Computing Environment. *International Journal of Innovations & Advancement in Computer Science*, *4*, 206–210.

Patidar, P., & Bhardwaj, A. (2011). Network Security through SSL in Cloud Computing Environment. *International Journal of Computer Science and Information Technologies*, *2*(6), 2800–2803.

Pereira, N., Elvitigala, V., Athukorala, M., Fernando, P., Ehelepola, D., Sameera, K., & Dhammearatchi, D. (2016). Secure User Data in Cloud Computing through Prevention of Service Traffic Hijacking and Using Encryption Algorithms. *International Journal of Scientific and Research Publications*, *6*(4), 350–355.

Petrowisch, J. (2017). *The benefits of cloud computing in the manufacturing industry*. Retrieved from http://www.techpageone.co.uk/industries-uk-en/benefits-cloud-computing-manufacturing-industry/

Racuciu, C., & Eftimie, S. (2015). Security threats and risks in Cloud computing. *Mircea cel Batran. Naval Academy Scientific Bulletin*, *18*, 105–108.

Randell, R. (2006). *Virtualization Security and Best Practices*. Retrieved from http://www.cpd.iit.edu/netsecure08/ROBERT_RANDELL.pdf

Rao, C., Leelaran, M., & Kumar, Y. R. (2013). Cloud: Computing Services And Deployment Models. *International Journal Of Engineering And Computer Science*, *2*(12), 3389–3392.

Raoa, R. V., & Selvamanib, K. (2015). Data Security Challenges and Its Solutions in Cloud Computing. *Procedia Computer Science*, *48*, 204–209. doi:10.1016/j.procs.2015.04.171

Rashid, F. Y. (2016). *The dirty dozen: 12 cloud security threats*. Retrieved from http://www.infoworld.com/article/3041078/security/the-dirtydozen-12-cloud-security-threats.html

Ristenpart, T., Tromer, E., Shacham, H., & Savage, S. (2009). Hey, you, get off of my cloud: exploring information leakage in third-party compute clouds. *Proceedings of the 16th ACM conference on Computer and communications security.* 10.1145/1653662.1653687

Saint-Marc, E. (2014). *7 benefits of cloud from an enterprise architect point of view.* Retrieved from IBM Cloud Computing News website: https://www.ibm.com/blogs/cloud-computing/2014/03/seven-benefits-of-cloud-from-an-enterprise-architect-point-of-view/

Schwab, K. (2015). *The Fourth Industrial Revolution: What It Means and How to Respond.* Retrieved from http://www.vassp.org.au/webpages/Documents2016/PDevents/The%20Fourth%20Industrial%20Revolution%20by%20Klaus%20Schwab.pdf

Shaikh, F. B., & Haider, S. (2011). *Security Threats in Cloud Computing.* Paper presented at the 6th International Conference on Internet Technology and Secured Transactions, Abu Dhabi, UAE.

Stair, R. M., & Reynolds, G. W. (2016). *Principles of information systems* (12th ed.). Boston: Cengage Learning.

Sullivan, D. (2014). *Protecting cloud networks against DDoS and DoS attacks* Retrieved from http://searchcloudcomputing.techtarget.com/answer/Protecting-cloud-networks-against-DDoS-and-DoS-attacks

Varsha, M., & Patil, P. (2015). A Survey on Authentication and Access Control for Cloud Computing using RBDAC Mechanism. *International Journal of Innovative Research in Computer and Communication Engineering, 3*(12), 12125–12129.

Wan, Z., Liu, J., & Deng, R. H. (2012). HASBE: A hierarchical attribute-based solution for flexible and scalable access control in cloud computing. *IEEE Transactions on Information Forensics and Security, 7*(2), 743–754. doi:10.1109/TIFS.2011.2172209

Wu, J., Ping, L., Ge, X., Wang, Y., & Fu, J. (2010). *Cloud Storage as the Infrastructure of Cloud Computing.* Paper presented at the 2010 International Conference on Intelligent Computing and Cognitive Informatics. 10.1109/ICICCI.2010.119

Yadav, P., & Sujata. (2013). Security Issues in Cloud Computing Solution of DDOS and Introducing Two-Tier CAPTCHA. [*International Journal on Cloud Computing: Services and Architecture, 3*(3), 25–40.

Zheng, M., & Jain, R. (2011). *Virtualization security in data centers and clouds.* Retrieved from http://www.cse.wustl.edu/~jain/cse571-11/ftp/virtual.pdf

Chapter 5
The Impact of IoT on Information Warfare

Brett van Niekerk
University of KwaZulu-Natal, South Africa

Barend H. Pretorius
University of KwaZulu-Natal, South Africa

Trishana Ramluckan
University of KwaZulu-Natal, South Africa

Harold Patrick
University of KwaZulu-Natal, South Africa

ABSTRACT

The Fourth Industrial Revolution is seen as a digital one, extending the previous information revolution. This is exhibited by the pervasive connectivity of many smart devices, known as the internet of things (IoT). The data generated and access created by these devices provides opportunities in an information warfare context by providing new avenues of attack and abilities to enhance existing capabilities. Recent cyber-attacks have illustrated the relevance of IoT to cyber-operations. However, IoT can influence information warfare through the use of drones, the extent of network-centric operations, and other factors. The major impact of IoT is the increased attack surface and techniques available, and opportunities for data gathering.

INTRODUCTION

The Fourth Industrial Revolution is seen as a digital one, extending the previous information revolution. "It is characterized by a fusion of technologies that is blurring the lines between the physical, digital, and biological spheres" (Schwab, 2015). This is exhibited by the pervasive connectivity of many smart devices, known as the Internet of Things (IoT). These systems can generate more data than before, and provide remote access and control over basic daily tasks to more complex industrial processes. This may provide opportunities in an information warfare (IW) environment to enhance operations and capabili-

DOI: 10.4018/978-1-5225-4763-1.ch005

ties or provide new avenues for attack. As IoT has the potential to complicate the already complex IW operational concept, it is important to investigate the implications thereof in order to begin the discussion of identifying new threats and mitigating these.

The IoT concept usually refers to network-capable 'smart' devices, and is sometimes called the Internet of Trouble (Kenny, 2017), ominously referring to the possible security issues. They usually comprise of sensors, and transmit the data over some form of network, and some are able to perform functions or control physical processes (Government Accountability Office, 2017). For an IoT architecture, there are commonly three layers: the sensors, the network layer, and the applications layer with which humans will interact (Kumar & Patel, 2014). While the IoT concept appears recent, in practice the forerunners have been part of everyday life for years and are often missed when IoT is discussed. Examples include office multi-function devices (printer, fax, and scanner) and some industrial systems that have had remote connections. The Industrial Internet of Things (IIoT) differ from IoT. Henning (2015) defines the IIoT as machines, input / output devices and controllers that manufacture the IoT devices such as smart TVs, toasters, and smart wearables. Consumers use IoT whereas engineers and manufactures use IIoT. Technologies behind IIoT have existed for many years, these include remote access, and cloud and are an evolution as the underlying data are now being accessed. The technologies behind IoT is a revolution as consumers are being exposed to it for the first time. Bowne (2015) list some differences:

- IIoT is an evolution versus commercial IoT being a revolution;
- IIoT can leverage off existing devices and standards versus IoT including new devices and requiring additional standards;
- IIoT can often be mission critical versus IoT being at most important;
- IIoT has more structured connectivity versus IoT's ad-hoc connectivity.

A similar concept which expands IoT to the Internet of Everything, which also includes non-physical entities (Simmons, 2015). In addition to the advantages to industry (hence the term Fourth Industrial Revolution), IoT has advantages for city management and service delivery to citizens, known as "smart cities" (Clarke, 2013). Due to the pervasive connectedness of devices and the data they generate, IoT can be seen as closely connected with other technological trends, such as big data analysis, cloud computing, social media and mobile computing (Clarke, 2013). A challenge becomes when there are devices that are connected, which can be considered unnecessary, such as toasters, particularly if they have security vulnerabilities (Vaughn-Nichols, 2017). Due to the possible over-connectedness, there are opportunities to leverage or abuse IoT for IW purposes that is scalable to impact an individual to a city, or possibly wider.

Information warfare and information operations (IO) began to gain prominence in the 1990s, however in many cases there tended to be a preference for information operations (Ventre, 2016). The two concepts are sometimes used interchangeably, however information operations can be considered broader and applicable during both peacetime and war, whereas IW is limited to times of conflict. Different nations and organizations have different perspectives on IW and IO, therefore the definitions and composition of activities vary (van Niekerk, 2011). These activities can be conducted in the physical (including the electro-magnetic spectrum), the virtual or cyber, and the cognitive of psychological domains (Brazzoli, 2007; Cronin & Crawford, 1999). The primary goal if IW and IO is to ultimately gain information superiority of an adversary (Brazzoli, 2007; Hutchinson & Warren, 2001; Waltz, 1998). For the purposes of this chapter, the following will be considered as components of IW and IO:

- **Cyber-Operations (or Computer Network Operations):** Operations to attack, defend and exploit the use of computer networks and information systems.
- **Critical Infrastructure Protection:** The protection of infrastructure crucial for social cohesion and national functioning.
- **Network-Centric Operations or Information Infrastructure Warfare:** Usage of networking and information technologies for enable operations.
- **Command and Control Warfare:** Attacks against, and defense of, the decision making function.
- **Electronic Warfare:** Attacks against and protection of activities in the electro-magnetic spectrum.
- **Intelligence-Based Operations**: The acquisition and exploitation of information about an adversary, and the protection of one's own information from adversary intelligence gathering attempts.
- **Psychological Operations (PSYOP):** Targeting the human mind to induce uncertainty or behavior conducive to one's needs (Brazzoli, 2007; Hutchinson & Warren, 2001; Waltz, 1998).
- **Strategic Communication:** "Governments efforts in understanding and engaging key audiences in the creation, strengthening and/, or preservation of conditions favourable for the advancement of a governments interests, policies, and objectives using coordinated programs, plans, themes, messages, and products synchronized with the actions of all instruments of national power" (Joint Chiefs of Staff, 2016: 226).

Figure 1 illustrates a conceptual hierarchy of IW concepts. The six concepts are traditionally represented as six 'pillars' of IW, however they are represented as three layers for clarity. The bottom three functions are grouped together as they are the activities which create an effect on the other layers. The middle layer enables the decision making process by providing the technology and information. The top layer, command and control, is ultimately where the core decision making function resides. Even though these are predominantly military-related concepts, there is strong application to personal and corporate settings, as discussed by Cronin and Crawford (1999) and Hutchinson and Warren (2001). As

Figure 1. Conceptual structure of IW concepts

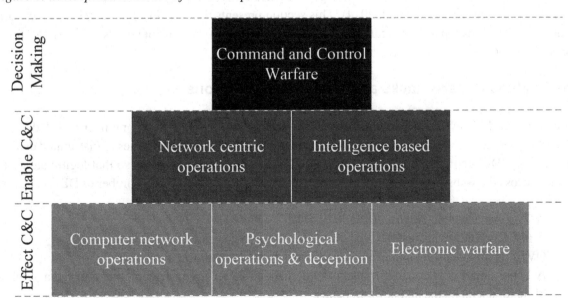

organizations increase their digital footprint and introduce more IoT technologies, the relevance of these concepts will increase. As technology evolves, there is convergence amongst the various areas of IW, for example social media allows for cyber-based psychological operations, and the prevalence of wireless and mobile devices provides a complimentary alignment between electronic warfare and computer-network operations (van Niekerk, 2015). While there is ongoing discussion regarding the convergence, particularly related to cyber and electronic warfare, it can be considered that operations in the areas can converge, even if the domains remain separate (van Niekerk, 2015). As with previous technological growth, the progression of IoT can impact IW and increase the convergence and complementary nature of the various IW activities. Therefore the relationship between IW and IoT can be considered in the following ways: IoT is an enabler of IW; IoT is a target of IoT; and IoT affects the relationship amongst the IW functional areas.

The topic of IW and IoT is a large one, with many facets. Therefore the scope of the chapter is limited to the possible use of IoT in an IW environment and its impact on IW as an operational concept will be considered. Other facets, such as the ethical and legal dimensions, will be covered in future research. This chapter begins with the enablement of cyber-attacks through the use of IoT in terms of distributed denial-of-service attacks (DDoS), network penetration, cyber-espionage, and Internet-based psychological attacks. Thereafter unmanned vehicle are discussed, followed by networked or smart vehicles and the networked soldier under the term of network-centric operations. Other considerations, such as the use improvised devices as IoT are then discussed. From these, a discussion and conclusion on the impact of IoT on IW is presented. The concepts in this chapter are discussed using reports of incidents or events to illustrate the legitimacy and potential impacts of IoT, in addition to theoretical academic research.

IOT-ENABLED CYBER-OPERATIONS

As IoT are ultimately connected devices, they have a role to play in Internet-based attacks. These devices themselves can store information, the data is communicated through the network, and then the application layer processes the data, providing three points where confidentiality or integrity of the information could be impacted (Kumar & Patel, 2014). This section presents their use in cyber-attacks and network penetrations, to deliver psychological attacks, or for espionage and profiling of targets. Some suggestions for securing networked IoT devices are then provided.

IoT-Enabled Cyber-Attacks and Network Penetrations

Compromised IoT devices can be used to conduct attacks over the Internet. A number of IoT devices under the malicious control of the attackers (known as a botnet) conducted a series of distributed denial-of service (DDoS) attacks, which flood the target with traffic and/or requests so that legitimate users cannot access the website or service. The Mirai Botnet was used to conduct a number of DDoS attacks:

- A 280Gbps attack in August 2016;
- A 665 Gbps attack against the blog of a cyber-security journalist;
- OVH, a French hosting company, was targeted by a 1Tbps attack;
- A 1Tbps attack in October 2016 against a domain name service provider, Dyn, affected a number of major social media and news websites;

- An attack which effectively blocked Liberia from the Internet (Kan, 2016; Ogundeji, 2016; Verizon, 2017; Woolf, 2016).

It appeared that this large attack compromised of 100 000 devices; reports indicate infected devices span across 164 countries, most of the devices being CCTV cameras and digital video recorders (Kan, 2016; Woolf, 2016). To place the magnitude of the attacks in perspective, Kan (2016) indicates that most large corporations would not be able to withstand a DDoS attack of 100Gbps; this attack was the largest recorded attack, almost double the previous largest (Woolf, 2016). The fact that CCTV cameras were strongly involved illustrates the risk that everyday devices that one might not include into IoT present in terms of cyber-security. If vulnerable devices are forgotten or missed by security reviews, they could provide an entry point or pivot point in the enterprise network, or be used to participate in other attacks. Another example of misused equipment is to be found in the healthcare industry. Certain medical devices were show to be vulnerable to possible cyber-attack; these included x-ray machines, heart monitors and insulin pumps. Subsequently, it has been confirmed that compromised medical equipment contributed to the theft of personal medical information (Higgins, 2015). Other common 'smart' household and business devices have been compromised and contributed to attacks or the distribution of spam: a fridge, smart TVs, multimedia centres, electronic billboards, and routers (Chen, 2016; Kovacs, 2014; Starr, 2014). As more devices become connected, the risks of vulnerable or insecurely configured devices increases; organizations will therefore become more susceptible to online-attacks such as ransomware (which encrypts data and requests payment for the key to decrypt the data), a number of hospitals have been affected by such attacks resulting in disruptions (Bryce, 2017).

With IoT, it may be possible for an organization to attack itself; an example of this is a university reportedly suffering a DDoS attack due to its smart devices being compromised by an IoT botnet. When a device was compromised, the default password was changed, it conducted brute-force attacks to gain access to other devices, and then flooded the institution's domain name server resulting in legitimate requests dropping (Cimpanu, 2017). Traditionally with a DDoS attack, the malicious traffic is coming from external to the organization, therefore perimeter security devices can be used to protect the organization. When the IoT devices internal to the organization are used to conduct the attack, the perimeter security may be limited in mitigating the impact. To make matters worse, as the passwords of the devices were changed, the administrators would not be able to log in and recover them; all devices would need to be taken off the network before being reset. As it was the default password that was reportedly changed, the lesson is always to change the default password on networked devices.

Another IoT botnet, Hajime, appears to have used some Mirai botnet code after the author made the code available online. This botnet is more stealthy, gains access to IoT devices using Linux by leveraging off unsecure Telnet connections, and then uses peer-to-peer protocols to communicate and transfer data (Edwards and Profetis, 2016). However, the purpose of the botnet appears unclear, but it is possible that this is someone attempting to secure vulnerable devices (Bisson, 2017). The techniques used by this botnet again illustrates that default passwords and logins should be changed, but also that unused ports should be blocked. The concept used here, called a Nematode, is highly controversial in that it uses malware to remove or block other malware; it is usually not advised due to the uncontrolled nature of the worm (Spam Laws, 2017; The Virus Encyclopedia, n.d.), or it can be re-used for more malicious purposes. Ronen, O'Flynn, Shamir and Weingarten (c. 2017) investigated the possibility of an IoT-worm propagating over ZigBee wireless connection, with smart lamps as the target devices. As the worm propagated over the ZigBee connection, no Internet connection was needed, and a drone can be used to deliver the equipment to perform the initial infections (Ronen et al, c. 2017). Drones will be discussed later in this chapter, however the ability of worms to propagate over non-IP networks is concerning.

Use of Micro Computing to Conduct Attacks

Polish trams were derailed by a teenager who managed to rig electronic devices to manipulate the switching gear remotely (Leyden, 2008). Devices to capture key strokes were used to gain access to the systems in the port of Antwerp, allowing smugglers to track the containers with their contraband (Dunn, 2013). These examples illustrate the impact small devices introduced into the network can have. However, with microcomputers such as the Raspberry Pi and Arduino, far more advanced hacking capability can be introduced and hidden in an enterprise for malicious purposes.

A hacker and developer, Samy Kamkar, has taken a $5 IoT device and turned it into a device that can hack a PC in 30 seconds, including those that are password protected (Anshul, 2017). This device is called PoisonTap and works off a Raspberry Pi Zero. This can also work with a normal Raspberry PI. The Raspberry PI's run an operating system called Raspbian and is based on Linux (Raspberry Pi Foundation, n.d.). There are off the shell commercial IoT devices available like the USB Rubber Ducky, Lan Turtle, Wi-Fi pineapple and Bash Bunny that have a similar capability, but comes at a price (Hak5, n.d.). PoisonTap only requires an open web browser in the background to install a backdoor which could give an attacker remote access to the PC. Similar devices can also be used to install a backdoor into a network to gain physical access. All that is required is a Raspberry Pi with a mobile / 3G expansion to provide remote access to a network. Creating this remote connection is fairly easy (Giess, 2015).

Another use of a Raspberry Pi is to build a portable hacking device using Kali Linux, an operating system build specifically network penetration testing. Once Kali Linux is installed on a SD card, the Raspberry Pi can be turned into a device that that crack or hack wireless networks, create fake access points or networks, and snoop another device's traffic (Klosowski, 2015). This is a light portable device that can be easily deployed. Having a Raspberry Pi connected to the network with a 3G connection will circumvent most perimeter security mechanisms like firewalls and air gapped networks.

Possible Implications for Critical Infrastructure (IIOT)

The first major attack on critical infrastructure occurred in 2000, when a disgruntled employee of supplier with access to equipment and an understanding of the system implementation modified systems to release sewerage into public waterways in Australia (Abrams & Weiss, 2008; Wyld, 2004). This illustrates the vulnerability to threats internal to, or with knowledge of internal structures. The Stuxnet incident of 2010 illustrated the vulnerability of connected industrial controls devices to malware, and it was the first attack of its type which resulted in a physical impact (Kushner, 2013). Subsequently there has been the Havex malware which targeted industrial systems (Walker, 2014), and the Sednit espionage malware has been known to transverse across air gaps (ESET, 2016). This indicates that even network segments that are logically and physically separate can be compromised. The use of IoT can aid in breaching air gaps and affecting critical industrial systems; IoT devices can in essence act as an insider threat. IoT therefore increases the complexity regarding critical infrastructure protection.

IoT-Enabled Psychological Attacks

Cyber-terrorism means more than just a virtual attack on a government or individual, it has a psychological impact on the public, by elevating fear and anxiety (Viva Sarah Press, 2015). Compromised IoT devices can be used to deliver attacks such attacks. With reference to Newman (2017), hackers interfered with sirens and emergency communications used for tornado warnings in Dallas. In 2017, a radio frequency trigger hack resulted in a larger number of emergency sirens to sound concurrently for over an hour, causing widespread confusion (Patterson, 2017). The incident reflects the fast-growing concern that cyber-attacks could be used against a country's infrastructure for the sole purpose of making a statement. As the Dallas emergency warning system only used radio communication without an internet connection, it illustrates the insecurity in such a system. However, it also meant that the hacker had sufficient knowledge on radio frequencies. The hacking of TV, Radio, cell phones and even road signs is an inevitable occurrence as they become connected to networks. In 2015 the French television network TV5Monde was supposedly taken down by ISIS militants, and its website and Facebook page was hijacked by the militants. The attack is significant as it highlighted the risk involved with broadcasters moving from analogue to digital, as well as for online operations and the growing shift to more destructive attacks (Ashford, 2015). A radio station in the US was hacked through their Internet connection, and the attackers repeatedly plays anti-Trump music in early 2017 (Veix, 2017). These incidents illustrate that traditional broadcast systems can be compromised and misused to distribute political messages or threats by terrorists, activists, and nation-states to effect perceptions.

Other devices have also been compromised to display political messages. An example of the hacking and controlling of electronic road signs occurred in Dallas where it began on May 31, 2016, with the message "DONALD TRUMP IS A SHAPE SHIFTING LIZZARD" followed by "BERNIE FOR PRESIDENT" and "WORK IS CANCELLED- GO BACK HOME" (Mettler, 2016). The electronic road signs were meant for commuters as a mechanism to update traffic information. The psychological impact of these messages meant to reflect the viewpoints of the hacker in an attempt to influence the ultimate result of the US National election in November 2016. However, more malicious groups could use there insecure devices as a platform to distribute hate speech or fear. It is possible that fake information is presented on the road signs to magnify the impact of an ongoing terrorist incident.

People have become accustomed to push notifications, on which they often become dependent on for any new feeds of information, usually related to social media on mobile phones. This provides another platform for malicious distribution of messages. In 2008 and 2009 it was reported Israeli military forces compromised mobile phone networks in Gaza to message the general population with warnings and reward offers for information (StrategyPage.com, 2008; 2009). Within the IoTs, push messages can be transmitted directly to smart TVs, streaming devices, mobile phones, 'smart' appliances with displays, and any networked system capable of receiving them. Secondary information (outside the original source), magnifies the impact of any incident or occurrence, and may amplify a crisis or disaster, for example, the recent increase as what's been termed "fake news", for example that Pope Francis had endorsed Donald Trump as the President prior to the elections (Ritchie, 2016). People using wearable devices may be more susceptible to these psychological attacks as they can receive notifications where ever they are, no matter what they are doing. Aside from the obvious cyber-terrorism use for these attacks, they can be leverage by governments for internal strategic communications, or by external nation states to influence a population to pressure their government into behavior desired by the attacker. These attacks illustrate a convergence of PSYOP and strategic communication with cyber-operations in that devices are compromised through the cyber-attack, however the payload is ultimately a message targeting the psychology of the victims.

Profiling and Espionage Through IoT

The data collected from IoT sensors can give a wealth of insight which can be used for espionage and profiling. Rehman, Liew, Wah, Shuja and Daghighi (2015) discuss the data mining of personal information from wearable devices and mobile phones. Motti and Caine (2015) indicate that users are concerned regarding the privacy around this; particularly when there is social media connectivity. The risk with these devices is that when enabled with GPS and time stamps, it is very easy to profile movements of individuals. Storm (2017) indicated that hackers can exploit smart watches and fitness trackers to access ATM pins, with researchers running multiple tests resulting the conclusion that there are "serious security breaches in wearable devices within the context of divulging secret information e.g. key entries." Whilst user concerns is focused on cell phone and wearable devices, other IoT technology can also be used for profiling.

Connected entertainment devices which allow for voice or camera input could potentially be used for spying if compromised or due to insecure third-party data usage (Lomas, 2015). There have been cases of compromised video conferencing systems, where large amount of data was infiltrated from the organization. If the video and audio of the system was compromised, the attackers could access to a wealth of sensitive corporate information that has the potential to impact its competitive advantage (Darktrace, 2016). Documents stored in printer memories could potentially reveal information, and compromised CCTV cameras and web cameras can be used for remote surveillance and espionage. Reports of a compromised biometric access management system indicates that it is possible to allow unauthorized access, or steal biometric information for attacking another system or facility (Darktrace, 2016). Therefore compromising the security of IoT devices are useful in espionage activities, where there is the potential to steal sensitive information, or gain illegitimate physical access.

Usage patterns for Internet access, smart entertainment services, and other smart devices such as fridges may be used to profile user movements, and changes in behavior can then indicate the user is not home. From an espionage and counter-intelligence perspective, changes in user behavior (such as erratic behavior) may indicate that a source is taking psychological strain; agents may be able to use this information to indicate that a source or asset is about to burn the agent (Brown, 2011). IoT devices, as indicated above, can be used as reprogrammable spy kits: add-on cameras, microphones and communication modules could allow small devices to be placed in an organization to infiltrate information.

Securing Organizations for IOT Deployments

Dooley (2017) considers the Fourth Industrial Revolution as having increased the potency of attacks. Given this potential for increased attacks and risks that IoT can introduce from a computer network operations perspective, it is important to provide security to address the new attack vector. Chen (2016) indicates that should the predictions of hyper-connectivity be realized, that the IoT devices will result in a much larger attack surface than traditional cyber-security; Fortinet (2017) estimates that 25% of cyber-attacks will target IoT devices. It is key that all devices with network connectivity of any kind are considered in risk assessments, and that the IoT deployments fall within the organizational risk appetite. IoT devices should be separated from the main network as far as possible, using a separate VLAN, IoT gateways, firewalls, or a combination of these. All unused ports should be blocked both at the external and internal gateways and firewalls. This will mitigate the likelihood of any compromised IoT devices from providing an entry point into the primary organizational network. As is illustrated with the above examples, default login credentials need to be changed. As malware can jump air-gaps, and IoT can be used to bridge these gaps, it is important that reliance is not placed on this to provide security. Detection and monitoring can play an important role in detecting unusual activity on the network; correctly employed detective techniques can help identify rogue IoT devices on the network.

UNMANNED VEHICLES

Unmanned systems are becoming more commonplace as they can enter geographic areas too hazardous for humans. Their uses include remote sensing to take measurements by carrying sensors, general aerial surveillance, tracking of livestock and wildlife, and search and rescue (Marcella & Terwilliger, 2017; Schlag, 2013). This makes them ideal for IW-related activity with the benefit that humans are not placed at risk. Commonly people refer to the surveillance and attack drones used by the military as unmanned aerial vehicles (UAVs), however these are just one component of an unmanned aerial system (UAS) which includes the UAV, the controller, and the communication linking the two (UAV Insider, 2013). This section will discuss both military and commercial or hobbyist unmanned systems, and technology to counter these systems.

Military Unmanned Vehicles

Military applications for drones have primarily been for reconnaissance and bomb disposal (Schlag, 2013; Allison, 2016). Whilst bomb disposal drones have been in existence for 40 years, they have evolved to be controlled by wireless communications and have technology to detect and disarm explosive devices (Allison, 2016). For surveillance, the Global Hawk and Predators are often thought of first. These however have been upgraded to include attack variants.

In addition to traditional military drone activity, drones appear to be taking on electronic warfare capability. There is a history of UAVs with electronic warfare capability: the US deployed these in the Vietnam War and Israel demonstrated their potential in the 1982 Lebanese Bekaa Valley operation, where they were used in conjunction with electronic warfare and ground attack aircraft to destroy air defense systems (Kunkel, 2008; Schlag, 2013). Modern UAS are far more network-oriented, and therefore can be considered as part of the IoT concept. Since the 1982 operation, there have been report of Israeli drones being used to disrupt broadcasts and cellular phone communications in (Shachtman, 2008). A number of nations were reported to be developing electronic warfare payloads for UAVs in 2008, including Israel, France, USA, UK, South Africa, Germany, Italy and China (Kunkel, 2008). The US Marine Corps electronic warfare strategy includes the use of UAS, with funding to develop an electronic warfare payload beginning in FY18 (Pomerleau, 2017). The Canadian navy is experimenting using remote-controlled units for electronic warfare, with a particular focus on protecting warships from anti-ship missiles (Israeli Homeland Security, 2017a). It is reported that Russia is developing UAVs with electronic warfare capability specifically to jam cellular phone communications and deliver fake messages to the devices (Israeli Homeland Security, 2017b). This concept will allow electronic warfare payloads to be delivered closer to the intended target, or to track the target, while minimizing the risk to pilots of traditional fixed-wing aircraft with electronic warfare capability. This makes the drones dispensable to a certain degree, similar to the Canadian navy's drones acting as possible decoys to misdirect incoming missiles (Israeli Homeland Security, 2017a). The Russian example raises the possibility of UAVs with an integrated electronic warfare and cyber warfare capability, where signals can be hijacked, and cyber-espionage or cyber-attack tools can then be delivered into the system. Ronen et al. (c. 2017) suggest drones being controlled by and delivering malware, and Yokogawa raises concerns of drones being used to affect industrial systems (Larson, 2016), which again illustrates the possible use for electronic warfare and cyber-attacks. By extension, drones using a directed energy payload could disrupt targeted electronic systems, potentially including radar, enterprise computers and industrial systems. A more destructive concept is a drone armed with an electro-magnetic pulse weapon, which could potentially have a wider effect.

Commercial and Hobbyist Drones

One of the key concerns around drones is privacy: there are a number of complaints about drones hovering around sunbathers (Kaminski, 2016). Subsequently a number of laws across the US have been implemented to protect people's privacy from drones; some of these also restricted the use by law enforcement for surveillance (Fifield, 2016). The initial privacy concerns and investigations into regulations in the US began in 2012 and 2013 (Schlag, 2013), however similar measures in the EU stalled (Bolton, 2015). These privacy concerns raises the aspect that individuals, criminal groups or terrorists can easily acquire near-military capability through the purchase of a drone, which will help them conduct surveillance and possibly plan their operations.

Drones have been used to smuggle banned goods into prisons (Dillow, 2016) and across national borders (Berger, 2015), and a model remote-controlled aircraft has been used to make drops in espionage operations (Brown, 2011). This concept illustrates a potential for the use of drones in intelligence-based operations. A small flash drive or data card, containing gigabytes worth of data, can be transferred in plain sight by taping it to a drone, and flying it to the drop point. This will make the exact source difficult to trace.

Drones have been crashed, accidentally or on purpose, into sensitive areas such as the White House or public areas, such as the stands at the U.S Open (Dillow, 2016). Pilots have also reported seeing drones from the cockpit (Dillow, 2016), and a landing aircraft was damaged in Mozambique after a drone collided with it (Jones, 2017), and it appeared that there was a collision between an aircraft and a drone in the UK (Hume & Greene, 2016).

The extremist group Islamic State weaponized commercial drones with improvised explosive devices (IEDs) to target Iraqi forces in Mosul; the Iraqi troops used UAVs to drop grenades on Islamic State positions. However, the effectiveness of these improvised solutions is uncertain (Mawhinney, 2017). There are general concerns of terrorist attacks using carrying explosive devices to attack aircraft on landing or take-off (Bolton, 2015). Similar methods could be used to disrupt the power grid or key components for a national information infrastructure, such as the landing point for undersea cables; this provides both kinetic attack options using drones in addition to the electronic payloads described by Larson (2016). Where the drones have proven very effective for Islamic State is to provide an intelligence view of the surrounding areas for armoured suicide car-bombs waiting to ambush Iraqi forces; they can use these to locate the target and guide the drivers to them, and video the attack for propaganda purposes (Mawhinney, 2017). In addition to filming attacks, drones could be used to deliver pamphlets or other material for propaganda purposes. An example is a drone carrying a pro-Albanian flag onto the pitch of an Albania-Serbia Euro 2017 qualifier in Belgrade, which resulted in fights erupting and the match being abandoned (Bolton, 2017).

Anti-Drone Technology and the Hacking of Drones

With the increasing concerns over commercial and hobbyist drones being used for terrorist attacks or espionage, a number of anti-drone technologies are being developed. A number are physical in nature, such as a launcher which fires a net up to 100m to capture the drone (Reynolds, 2016) or trained birds of prey to catch drones in flight (Hackett, 2016). Some systems only provide monitoring, using acoustic or specialty radar to detect approaching drones, whereas others are more aggressive and shut down the drone's autopilot by using malware (Reagan, 2015).

A 'ray-gun' with a longer range than the net (2km) uses signal jamming to disrupt the communication link to the controller and force the drone to land, and is also reported to jam positioning systems (Burgess, 2017). Another system provides detection and tracking through multiple methods including radar and signal tracking, which can be used for direction finding to locate the controller; if necessary the targeted drone can be hijacked and landed (Dillow, 2016). These methods are equivalent to electronic warfare, where the wireless communication signals for the control and positioning is degraded or denied.

There are vulnerability in military UASs: in 2009 it was reported that fighters in Iraq and Afghanistan had managed to intercept the video feeds from the US UAVs, aided by commercially available software, which gave them early warning of possible strikes (Shachtman, 2009b; 2009c). In 2011 the US drones were again compromised, this time by malware on the control systems which took weeks to clear (Roberts, 2011; Shachtman, 2011). These vulnerabilities indicates that where there is a connection, it is possible to at least intercept information; and it is not far-fetched to possibly crash or hijack military UAVs. The ability to hack and gain control of a make of hobby drone was demonstrated by Kamkar in 2013: this method uses commonly available code to force the target drone's wireless connection with the controller to drop, then then reconnect to the hijacking controller (Fisher, 2013). In 2017 it was shown that a number of other drone systems were vulnerable and could be hacked (Brook, 2017). As mentioned above, there are reported anti-drone systems that use malware to crash the drones (Reagan, 2017). Researchers go further to suggest a botnet of compromised drones which could be used to conduct DDoS attacks or being used to infect corporate networks (Brook, 2017; Ronen et al., c. 2017). Therefore drone assets could become an internal propagation vector whereby it is infected, and then all devices that connect to it are then compromised. This echoes the concern by Yokogawa that drones could enable attacks against industrial facilities (Larson, 2016).

NETWORK-CENTRIC OPERATIONS

Network-centric operations attempts to improve agility in command and control and sense making in the battlefield. Through information sharing amongst various platforms and sensors, a more complete picture of the battlefield and friendly forces (Alberts and Hayes, 2003). The commercial equivalent to this is now emerging as the Fourth Industrial Revolution. This section considers both the concepts of smart vehicles and networked soldiers.

Networked and Smart Vehicles

Connected military platforms allow for coordinated targeting, communications and command and control. Combined with the IoT concept of sensors, this allows a variety of information about the 'smart' vehicles to be collected and collated to gain an improved understanding of the status of the equipment. In a commercial sense, this can provide the status for fleets of ships, trucks, trains and aircraft to assess performance and maintenance. However, vehicles have been shown to be vulnerable to hacking: vulnerabilities in Jeeps have been demonstrated (Chen, 2016), with concerns over aircraft (Zetter, 2015). Malware has affected an operating oil rig (this was apparently downloaded via a mobile phone) and warships, and it has been demonstrated that spoofing GPS can be used to hijack yachts; a number of other maritime systems on vessels are also vulnerable (Israeli Homeland Security, 2013; Kirk, 2009; Swanbeck, 2015; van Niekerk, 2017). This hyper-connectivity presents an ideal situation for IoT related attacks.

When considering a fleet of vehicles, from tanks to commercial aircraft to ships, there is a likelihood that there are multiple units of any one variant. Each one of these individual vehicles can therefore be expected to have the same vulnerabilities. Given that ships and oil rigs have been shown to be susceptible to malware and IoT worms have been demonstrated to spread over non-traditional networking protocols, it is therefore conceivable that malware can spread from vehicle to vehicle. The IoT concept in vehicles are unusually the weak-point for entry for the hackers who have demonstrated these vulnerabilities. Therefore IoT can be seen to result in a mass vulnerability across all similar vehicles, thereby increasing the attack surface for the commercial fleet or military group.

Enhanced Soldiers

The power of connectivity through mobile devices and social media in a number of protests from Arab Spring to student protests in South Africa. This connectivity allowed the sharing of ideas, coordination, and awareness. The connectedness had a noticeable impact on protests, and provided for global visibility of local events (Ramluckan, Ally, & van Niekerk, 2017). Such coordination can potentially be extended to terrorist attacks, where reports indicate that the attackers in Paris were being directed by mobile phone form outside the country (Rubin, 2015). With micro computing devices, it is possible that attackers can create non-traditional communication and coordination systems. Similar concepts have existed in the military context.

The concept of networked soldiers has existed since the 1990s (Gourley, 2013), when the US military began developing a system to provide soldiers with more information about the battlefield; the most well-known of the iterations is Land Warrior. Soldiers were provided with an eyepiece attached to the helmet to view the information. The soldiers were networked together, and images from digital and thermal cameras, and target designation from a laser rangefinder, could be shared across the network (Coburn, 2007). However, the system does not fully deliver: there are time lags with the locations on the maps, initial designs were too heavy, and after being reworked using commercial components they became manageable. However, soldiers are still supposed to carry a battery, communications gear, GPS units, and a processor (which is outdated) to operate the equipment (Shachtman, 2009a). Subsequent attempts by the US include commercial smart phones and tablet devices. A number of other nations are attempting to build similar systems, some are also based around tablets (Gourley, 2013).

Modern IoT: Can It Resurrect the Networked Soldier?

Given the reported challenges that the Land Warrior system experienced, one can look at modern mobile phones and their accessories for similar capability. A smart phone or tablet can contain some or all of the following: GPS, camera, multiple communications (GSM, 3G, LTE, Wi-Fi, Bluetooth, or Near Field Communications (NFC)) with the ability to create Wi-Fi hotspots, accelerometers, biometrics, applications to control hobby drones, and apps to connect to wearable fitness/health trackers. The CAT S60 even has thermal imaging camera capabilities, and is ruggedized (CAT, 2017). Most devices have the processing power, memory and storage equivalent to PCs. With lightweight power banks and small solar chargers, it is possible to keep devise powered for extended periods. In the future it might be possible to use NFC technology as an additional safety for smart weapons, to mitigate the likelihood of unauthorized use. The solution to the networked soldier may therefore lie in modern commercial smart mobile devices and their accessories. Micro computing devices such as the Raspberry Pi can also provide a basis, or component, of the networked soldier systems; they have numerous expansions which can allow for displays and networking.

ADDITIONAL CONSIDERATIONS FOR IOT IN IW

Some additional considerations, which do not fit into the previous sections, are covered here. These include the use of improvised explosive devices, software defined radios, and audit challenges.

Improvised Explosive Devices as IoT

Often IEDs make use mobile phones or remote controls as the detonation trigger (Eshel, 2007). As these are making use of networks, we can consider them as IoT, or an extension of IoT. Electronic warfare systems can be used to jam the signal, preventing the detonation, or in some cases electronic warfare aircraft have been used to transmit signals in an attempt to prematurely detonated devices along a convoy route (Eshel, 2007). It is feasible that cheap micro computing devices can be used as the detonator. With the expansion modules available, various networking types can be employed: GSM, Wi-Fi, and Bluetooth. This will add a degree of resiliency to the detonator as all frequencies and forms of communications will need to be jammed to prevent detonation, but at the same time its vulnerability increases due to a larger attack surface. Electronic warfare solutions will then have more options to trigger premature detonations.

Software Defined Radios: Plug and Play Electronic Warfare

Software defined radios can be programmed to communicate with a variety of communication protocols, depending on the limitations of the device. These devices are ideal to combine electronic warfare and cyber-attacks (du Plessis, 2014). The software defined radio can be programmed to connect the wireless communication, and then a cyber-based attack can be injected. The software defined radio also provides the ability to intercept a variety of wireless communications using a laptop, and possible broadcast to interfere with signals. This provides a cheap and easily accessible form of electronic warfare capability to general population with the relevant skills (or ability to learn them), although the solutions may not be as powerful as traditional military electronic warfare systems.

Audit and Forensics

Auditing and forensics with IoT has numerous challenges, particularly when it comes to penetration testing. Apart from the fact that devices can be plugged in and out of the network at any point in time and might not come up on a network scan, security testing is a challenge. Francis (2017), mentions although there are similarities in testing IoT devices and normal network devices, analyzing firmware and communication is the challenge. Different IoT devices have different operating systems, mainly based on Linux and each one has its own vulnerabilities. The communication between IoT devices can use non-standard protocols such as Zigbee, which differs from traditional protocols like Wi-Fi and TCP/IP making assessing and governing these IoT devices more difficult. Traditionally, computers and laptops were seized by forensic investigators for imaging and analysis. With IoT, forensic investigators need a smart forensic approach as the data from sensors (fixed and moving) and communication devices needs to be collected from different locations throughout buildings (Salama, 2017). This requires an extended toolkit and specialized techniques to allow forensic investigators keep pace with the new industry trends (Bollo, 2017). The size of some smart devices, such as X-ray machines and smart fridges, present a huge challenge whether to seize the devices and appliances. In such cases, the forensic investigators would need to remove the microchips and flash memory from the relevant devices and at the same time download the data (Jin, 2017); therefore they can image the microchips and flash memory for further analysis.

Zawoad and Hasan (2015) highlight that investigator needs to collect the data from the local memory of the IoT device (device level forensics) as well as the network and cloud forensics. The challenge becomes that there are huge amounts of data to be collected and analyzed: because of the numerous devices connected throughout the networks it difficult to obtain the evidence from all the suspicious devices, and the forensic investigator needs to identify any attacks from log analysis of the different networks segments. In addition, additional techniques are needed to filter and identify the data that was deleted or modified (Hegarty, Lamb, & Attwood, 2014). Due to possible IoT data stored in the cloud and privacy regulations, there may be challenges legally obtaining and accessing the data from the different environments (Zawoad and Hasan, 2015). Additionally, there will challenges locating the data in the cloud or data centre and the location of the storage. Storage devices used by investigators may not be able to hold the quantity of data from the data centre, therefore preserving the data may be a challenge (Hegarty et al., 2014). With the rapid growth of IoT and new devices, it is difficult to ascertain what standard should be maintained for forensics (Boddington, 2015).

DISCUSSION: THE EFFECT OF IOT ON IW

The examples presented in this chapter have illustrated the IoT use in cyber-attacks, espionage, psychological attacks, and to enable networked operations and command and control. Figure 2 summarizes these points with reference to an IW hierarchy.

The key impacts of IoT on IW is the increased attack surface, and the ability to leverage off data gathering and sharing. Insecurely configured or vulnerable IoT devices can be used as an entry point to the network. Once the device is compromised, it can then be leveraged off of to conduct other activities, ranging from intelligence gathering to participating in cyber-attacks. Providing security, audits and foren-

Figure 2. A summary of IoT relationships to IW concepts

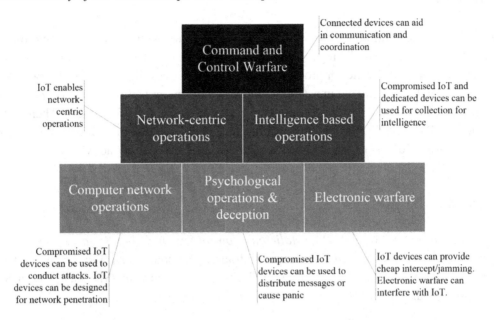

sics to protect against IoT attacks and investigate incidents can prove to be challenging. Not only do all devices need to be securely configured, there needs to be proper architecting and monitoring of the IoT environment. In some cases, the ad-hoc nature of IoT may allow malicious devices to escape detection by network scans and audits, and can be removed from the network to complicate forensic investigations.

The benefits of IoT in an IW context revolve around data acquisition. Sensors across vehicles and soldiers can provide detailed status updates to allow for a holistic view of units and the battlefield. In particular, remotely controlled vehicles can be used for reconnaissance and surveillance without placing humans at risk; this extends to other functions such as bomb disposal. The video feeds from these drones and the sensors embedded on other platforms and soldiers will gather large quantities of data; therefore the concept of big data will be relevant. Challenges may therefore be experienced in the storage and processing of such large quantities of information, particularly when needing to distill it to provide the most pertinent intelligence to commanders. It is possible that advances with commercial mobile phone technology and micro computing devices may result provide impetus to the networked soldier initiatives, however improvised equivalents may be developed by non-state actors in conflict areas.

Another impact is that IoT contributes towards the convergence of the IW activities. This can be seen in that cyber-attack techniques are required to compromise IoT devices, which can then be leveraged to conduct intelligence gathering and psychological operations. Devices such as software defined radios can provide for combined electronic warfare and cyber-attacks. Whilst drones are useful for conducting surveillance, physical attacks, or delivering psychological messages, they are in-turn vulnerable and can be targeted by either cyber or electronic warfare techniques to disable them. In van Niekerk (2015) it is illustrated how social media and mobile technologies aid in this convergence; IoT devices provide another mechanism for the natural convergence of IW activities.

CONCLUSION

The Fourth Industrial Revolution exhibits the pervasive connectivity of many 'smart' and micro computing devices, known as the Internet of Things. These systems provide opportunities in an IW environment to enhance operations and capabilities or provide new avenues for attack. Such devices can be leveraged to improve visibility and sensing to aid in network-centric operations and command and control. However, examples illustrate the numerous ways IoT can be compromised and used for attacks. Therefore the key impacts of IoT on IW is the increased attack surface and exposure, and the ability to leverage off data gathering and sharing. IoT also contributes towards the convergence of IW activities.

REFERENCES

Abrams, M., & Weiss, J. (2008, July 23). *Malicious Control System Cyber Security Attack Case Study - Maroochy Water Services, Australia*. National Institute of Standards and Technology. Retrieved 30 December 2010 from http://csrc.nist.gov/groups/SMA/fisma/ics/documents/Maroochy-Water-Services-Case-Study_report.pdf

Alberts, D. S., & Hayes, R. E. (2003). *Power to the Edge: Command and Control in the Information Age*. CCRP. Retrieved 18 June 2017 from http://www.dodccrp.org/files/Alberts_Power.pdf

Allison, P. R. (2016, July 15). What does a bomb disposal robot actually do? *BBC*. Retrieved 7 June 2017 from http://www.bbc.com/future/story/20160714-what-does-a-bomb-disposal-robot-actually-do

Anshul. (2017, June 14). This $5 Device Can Hack Password-Protected Computers In Just 30 Seconds. *Hacking-News & Tutorials*. Retrieved 13 June 2017 from http://hackingnewstutorials.com/this-5-device-can-hack-password/

Ashford, W. (2015, April 10). French TV5Monde network cyber-attack the latest in destructive trend in system intrusions. *Computer Weekly*. Retrieved 15 June 2017 from http://www.computerweekly.com/news/4500244107/French-TV5Monde-network-cyber-attack-the-latest-in-destructive-trend-in-system-intrusions

Berger, S. (2015, 13 August). Mexico Drug Trafficking: Drone Carries 28 Pounds of Heroin across Border to US. *International Business Times*. Retrieved 6 June 2017 from http://www.ibtimes.com/mexico-drug-trafficking-drone-carries-28-pounds-heroin-across-border-us-2051941

Bisson, D. (2017, April 19). The Hajime IoT worm fights the Mirai botnet for control of your devices. *Graham Cluley*. Retrieved 20 April 2017 from https://www.grahamcluley.com/hajime-iot-worm-fights-mirai-botnet-control-devices/

Boddington, R. (2015, March 17). *The Challenges of digital forensics*. Retrieved 22 June 2017from https://phys.org/news/2015-03-digital-forensics.html

Bollo, J. (2017). *Mobile Forensics Must Keep Up with the Times*. Retrieved 22 June 2017 from https://www.forensicmag.com/article/2017/06/mobile-forensics-must-keep-times

Bolton, D. (2015, December 6). Terrorists could use Drones to Attack Planes and Spread Propaganda. *The Independent*. Retrieved 7 May 2017 from http://www.independent.co.uk/life-style/gadgets-and-tech/news/drone-terrorist-attack-isis-propaganda-colin-smith-a6762411.html

Bowne, M. (2015, August 18). IOT VS. IIOT. *Profinet.com*. Retrieved 13 June 2017 from http://us.profinet.com/iot-vs-iiot/

Brazzoli, M. S. (2007). Future Prospects of Information Warfare and Particularly Psychological Operations. In L. le Roux (Ed.), South African Army Vision 2020 (pp. 217-232). Pretoria: Institute for Security Studies.

Brook, C. (2017, May 4). Many Commercial Drones 'Insecure by Design'. *ThreatPost*. Retrieved 8 May 2017 from https://threatpost.com/many-commercial-drones-insecure-by-design/125420/

Brown, A. (2011). *The Grey Line: Modern Corporate Espionage and Counterintelligence*. Amur Strategic Research Group.

Bryce, H. (2017, May 18). *The Internet of Things Will Be Even More Vulnerable to Cyber Attacks*. London: Chatham House. Retrieved 13 June 2017 from https://www.chathamhouse.org/expert/comment/internet-things-will-be-even-more-vulnerable-cyber-attacks

Burgess, M. (2017, January 23). This ridiculous drone gun can shoot down UAVs from 2km away. *Wired*. Retrieved 6 June 2017 from http://www.wired.co.uk/article/droneshield-dronegun-shoot-drone-uav-sky

CAT. (2017). *CAT® S60 Smartphone*. Retrieved 14 June 2017 from http://www.catphones.com/en-gb/phones/s60-smartphone

Chen, P. (2016, July 12). Why security in the Internet of Things is different from cybersecurity. *EDN-Europe*. Retrieved 12 July 2016 from http://www.edn-europe.com/blog/why-security-internet-things-different-cybersecurity

Cimpanu, C. (2017, February 14). University DDoSed by Its Own IoT Devices. *Bleeping Computer*. Retrieved 20 February 2017 from https://www.bleepingcomputer.com/news/security/university-ddosed-by-its-own-iot-devices/

Clarke, R. Y. (2013, October). Smart Cities and the Internet of Everything: The Foundation for Delivering Next-Generation Citizen Services. *IDC Government Insights*. Retrieved 7 June 2017 from http://119.15.167.84:8080/share/proxy/alfresco-noauth/api/internal/shared/node/q9Ij_C2XQhS0ElSMmjJnA/content/GI243955.pdf

Coburn, D. (2007, May 30). Land Warrior System: Inside the Pentagon's New High-Tech Gear. *Popular Mechanics*. Retrieved 18 June 2017 from http://www.popularmechanics.com/military/a1591/4215725/

Cronin, B., & Crawford, H. (1999). Information Warfare: Its Application in Military and Civilian Contexts. *The Information Society*, *15*(4), 257–263. doi:10.1080/019722499128420

Darktrace. (2016). *Darktrace Discoveries: Global Threat Case Studies 2016*. Accessed 14 June 2017 from http://www.informationweek.com/whitepaper/cybersecurity/security/darktrace-discoveries-global-threat-case-studies-2016/383043

Dillow, C. (2016, February 12). This Counter-Drone System Will Safely Hijack and Capture Rogue Drones. *Fortune*. Retrieved 19 February 2016 from http://fortune.com/2016/02/12/falcon-shield-counter-drone-system/

Dooley, R. (2017, June 15). Cyber security at the heart of the Fourth Industrial Revolution. *UK Construction Online*. Retrieved 15 June 2017 from https://www.ukconstructionmedia.co.uk/features/cyber-security-industrial-revolution/

du Plessis, W. (2014). Software-Defined Radio (SDR) as a Mechanism for Exploring Cyber-Electronic Warfare (EW) Collaboration. *6th Workshop on ICT uses in Warfare and the Safeguarding of Peace, Proceedings of the 2014 Information Security for South Africa Conference*. Retrieved 14 June 2017 from http://icsa.cs.up.ac.za/issa/2014/Proceedings/Workshop/15_Final_Document.pdf

Dunn, J. E. (2013, October 16). Hackers planted remote devices to smuggle drugs through Antwerp port, Europol reveals. *Techworld*. Retrieved from http://news.techworld.com/security/3474018/hackers-planted-remote-devices-to-smuggle-drugs-through-antwerp-port-europol-reveals/

Edwards, S., & Profetis, I. (2016, October 16). Hajime: Analysis of a decentralized internet worm for IoT devices. *Rapidity Networks*. Retrieved 20 April 2017 from https://security.rapiditynetworks.com/publications/2016-10-16/hajime.pdf

ESET. (2016, October). En Route with Sednit, Part 3: A Mysterious Downloader. *We Live Security*. Retrieved 12 June 2017 from https://www.welivesecurity.com/wp-content/uploads/2016/10/eset-sednit-part3.pdf

Eshel, D. (2007). Defeating IEDs. *Journal of Electronic Defense*, *30*(12), 38–42.

Fifield, J. (2016, July 1). How drones raised privacy concerns across cyberspace. *Stateline*. Retrieved 6 June 2017 from http://www.pbs.org/newshour/rundown/how-drones-raised-privacy-concerns-across-cyberspace/

Fisher, D. (2013, December 3). How to Skyjack a Drone in an Hour for Less Than $400. *ThreatPost*. Retrieved 5 December 2013 from http://threatpost.com/how-to-skyjack-drones-in-an-hour-for-less-than-400/103086

Fortinet. (2017, February 9). *Understanding the IoT Explosion and its Impact on Enterprise Security*. Retrieved 13 August 2016 from https://www.fortinet.com/demand/gated/WP-Understanding-The-IoT-Explosion-And-Its-Impact-On-Enterprise-Security.html

Francis, R. (2017, May 25). How to conduct an IoT pen test. *Network World*. Retrieved 15 June 2017 from http://www.networkworld.com/article/3198495/internet-of-things/how-to-conduct-an-iot-pen-test.html

Giess, M. (2015, June 18). How to fit a Raspberry Pi with mobile M2M connectivity. *EMnify*. Retrieved 15 June 2017 from https://www.emnify.com/2015/06/18/how-to-fit-a-raspberry-pi-with-mobile-connectivity/

Gourley, S. R. (2013, June 25). The Rise of the Soldier System. *Defense Media Network*. Retrieved 18 June 2017 from http://www.defensemedianetwork.com/stories/the-rise-of-the-soldier-system/

Government Accountability Office. (2017, May). *Internet of Things: Status and implications of an increasingly connected world*. Report to Congressional Requesters, Technology Assessment GAO-17-75.

Hak5. (n.d.). Hakshop. *Hakshop.com.org*. Retrieved 15 June 2017 from https://hakshop.com/

Hackett, R. (2016, February 2). Drones Stand No Chance Against Trained Assassin Eagles. *Fortune*. Retrieved 6 June 2017 from http://fortune.com/2016/02/02/drone-eagle-take-down-video/

Hegarty, R. C., Lamb, D. J., & Attwood, A. (2014). Digital Evidence Challenges in the Internet of Things. *Proceedings of the Tenth International Network Conference*, 163-172.

Henning, C. (2015, March 3). IOT is not IIOT. *Profinet.com*. Retrieved 13 June 2017 from http://us.profinet.com/iiot-is-not-iot/

Higgins, K. J. (2015, June 10). Hospital Medical Devices Used as Weapons in Cyberattacks. *Dark Reading*. Retrieved 10 June 2015 from http://www.darkreading.com/vulnerabilities---threats/hospital-medical-devices-used-as-weapons-in-cyberattacks/d/d-id/1320751

Hume, T., & Greene, R. A. (2016, April 18). Investigations launched after suspected drone strikes passenger jet in London. *CNN*. Retrieved 6 June 2017 from http://edition.cnn.com/2016/04/17/europe/london-heathrow-drone-strikes-plane/index.html

Hutchinson, W., & Warren, M. (2001). *Information Warfare: Corporate Attacks and Defence in a Digital World*. Oxford, UK: Butterworth Heinemann.

Insider, U. A. V. (2013). *What is the difference between a Drone, a UAV and a UAS?* Retrieved 5 June 2017 from http://www.uavinsider.com/what-is-the-difference-between-a-drone-a-uav-and-a-uas/

Israeli Homeland Security. (2013, August 7). *$80 million yacht hijacked by students spoofing GPS signals*. Retrieved from http://i-hls.com/2013/08/80-million-yacht-hijacked-by-students-spoofing-gps-signals/

Israeli Homeland Security. (2017a). *Unmanned Surface Drones Supply Naval Electronic Jamming*. Retrieved 13 April 2017 from http://i-hls.com/archives/75887

Israeli Homeland Security. (2017b, April 12). *Drone-Based EW System Will Hijack Phones*. Retrieved 20 April 2017 from http://i-hls.com/archives/76008

Jin, S. (2017). *IoT Devices Forensic Research*. Retrieved 22 June 2017 from https://www.troopers.de/downloads/troopers17/TR17_What_happened_to_your_home.pdf

Joint Chiefs of Staff (2016, February 15). *Joint Publication 1-02: Department of Defense Dictionary of Military and Associated Terms*. US Department of Defense.

Jones, S. (2017, January 6). Drone crashes into Boeing 737 jet plane coming into land at Mozambique airport. *The Mirror*. Retrieved 6 June 2017 from http://www.mirror.co.uk/news/world-news/drone-crashes-boeing-737-jet-9574073

Kaminski, M. E. (2016, May 17). Enough With the "Sunbathing Teenager" Gambit. *Slate*. Retrieved 6 June 2017 from http://www.slate.com/articles/technology/future_tense/2016/05/drone_privacy_is_about_much_more_than_sunbathing_teenage_daughters.html

Kan, M. (2016, October 26). DDoS attack on Dyn came from 100,000 infected devices. *Computer World*. Retrieved 31 October 2016 from http://www.computerworld.com/article/3135434/security/ddos-attack-on-dyn-came-from-100000-infected-devices.html

Kenny, L. (2017, April 12). IoT: The Internet of Trouble. *Security Intelligence*. Retrieved 7 June 2017 from https://securityintelligence.com/iot-the-internet-of-trouble/

Kirk, J. (2009, January 19). Virus attacks Ministry of Defence. *CIO.co.uk*. Retrieved from http://www.cio.co.uk/news/3460/virus-attacks-ministry-of-defence/

Klosowski, T. (2015, October 29). How to build a portable hacking station with a Raspberry Pi and Kali Linux. *Lifehacker.com*. Retrieved 19 June 2017 from http://lifehacker.com/how-to-build-a-portable-hacking-station-with-a-raspberr-1739297918

Kovacs, E. (2014, June 6). Default password exposes digital highway signs to hacker attacks. *Security Week*. Retrieved from http://www.securityweek.com/default-password-exposes-digital-highway-signs-hacker-attacks

Kumar, J. S., & Patel, D. R. (2014). A Survey on Internet of Things: Security and Privacy Issues. *International Journal of Computers and Applications*, *90*(11), 20–26. doi:10.5120/15764-4454

Kunkel, M. (2008a). EA/SIGINT Payloads for UAVs. *Journal of Electronic Defense*, *31*(6), 32–40.

Kushner, D. (2013, February 26). The Real Story of Stuxnet. *IEEE Spectrum*. Retrieved 12 June 2017 from http://spectrum.ieee.org/telecom/security/the-real-story-of-stuxnet

Larson, K. (2016, October 4). Drones open new cyber-physical attack vector. *Control Global*. Retrieved 17 October 2016 from http://www.controlglobal.com/articles/2016/drones-open-new-cyber-physical-attack-vector/

Leyden, J. (2008, January 11). Polish teen derails tram after hacking train network. *The Register*. Retrieved from http://www.theregister.co.uk/2008/01/11/tram_hack/

Lomas, N. (2015, February 10). Samsung Edits Orwellian Clause Out Of TV Privacy Policy. *Tech Crunch*. Retrieved 12 June 2017 from https://techcrunch.com/2015/02/10/smarttv-privacy/

Marcella, A. J., & Terwilliger, B. A. (2017). *Rise of the Drones: Is Your Enterprise Prepared?* Rolling Meadows, IL: ISACA.

Mawhinney, M. (2017, April 4). Islamic State using hobby drones with deadly effect. *Sky News*. Retrieved 7 May 2017 from http://news.sky.com/story/islamic-state-using-hobby-drones-with-deadly-effect-10823505

Mettler, K. (2016, June 6). Somebody keeps hacking these Dallas road signs with messages about Donald Trump, Bernie Sanders and Harambe the gorilla. *Washington Post*. Retrieved 15 June 2017 from https://www.washingtonpost.com/news/morning-mix/wp/2016/06/06/somebody-keeps-hacking-these-dallas-road-signs-with-messages-about-donald-trump-bernie-sanders-and-harambe-the-gorilla/

Motti, V. G., & Caine, K. (2015). Users' Privacy Concerns about Wearables: impact of form factor, sensors and type of data collected. *19th International Conference Financial Cryptography and Data Security 2015*. Retrieved 12 June 2017 from http://fc15.ifca.ai/preproceedings/wearable/paper_2.pdf

Newman, L. H. (2017, April 4). That Dallas siren hack wasn't novel- it was just really loud. *Wired*. Retrieved 17 June 2017 from https://www.wired.com/2017/04/dallas-siren-hack-wasnt-novel-just-really-loud/

Ogundeji, O. (2016, November 4). Mirai malware aims DDoS attacks on Liberia. *ITWeb Africa*. Retrieved 10 February 2017 from http://www.itwebafrica.com/security/808-liberia/237027-mirai-malware-aims-ddos-attacks-on-liberia

Patterson, D. (2017). Cyberweapons are now in play: From US sabotage of a North Korean missile test to hacked emergency sirens in Dallas. *Tech Republic*. Retrieved 17 June 2017 from http://www.techrepublic.com/article/cyberweapons-are-now-in-play-from-us-sabotage-of-a-north-korean-missile-test-to-hacked-emergency/

Pomerleau, M. (2017, April 7). Drones 'a critical component' for Marine electronic warfare tactics. *C4ISR Net*. Retrieved 13 April 2017 from http://www.c4isrnet.com/articles/drones-a-critical-component-for-marines-electronic-warfare-tactics

Ramluckan, T., Ally, S. E., & van Niekerk, B. (2017). Twitter Use in Student Protests: The Case of South Africa's #FeesMustFall Campaign. In M. Korstanje (Ed.), *Threat Mitigation and Detection of Cyber Warfare and Terrorism Activities* (pp. 220–253). Hershey, PA: IGI Global. doi:10.4018/978-1-5225-1938-6.ch010

Raspberry Pi Foundation. (n.d.). *Raspbian*. Retrieved 15 June 2017 from https://www.raspberrypi.org/downloads/raspbian/

Reagan, J. (2015, June 4). 5 Anti-Drone Solutions That Could Change the Game. *dronelife*. Retrieved 6 June 2017 from http://dronelife.com/2015/06/04/5-anti-drone-solutions-that-could-change-the-game/

Rehman, M. H., Liew, C. S., Wah, T. Y., Shuja, J., & Daghighi, B. (2015). Mining Personal Data Using Smartphones and Wearable Devices: A Survey. *Sensors (Basel)*, *15*(1), 4430–4469. doi:10.3390150204430 PMID:25688592

Reynolds, M. (2016, March 4). Anti-drone net launcher can down quadcopters from 100 metres. *Wired*. Retrieved 6 June 2017 from http://www.wired.co.uk/article/anti-drone-net-launcher-downs-quadcopters

Ritchie, H. (2016, December 30). The biggest fake news stories of 2016. *CNBC*. Retrieved 17 June 2017 from http://CNBC.Com /2016/12/30/read-all-about-it-the-biggest-fake-news-stories-of-2016

Roberts, P. (2011, October 12). Air Force struggled for weeks with malware in drone fighter systems. *ThreatPost*. Retrieved from http://threatpost.com/en_us/blogs/report-air-force-struggled-weeks-malware-drone-fighter-systems-101211

Ronen, E., O'Flynn, C., Shamir, A., & Weingarten, A. (2017). *IoT Goes Nuclear: Creating a ZigBee Chain Reaction*. Retrieved 5 June 2017 from http://iotworm.eyalro.net/iotworm.pdf

Rubin, A. J. (2015, December 30). Cellphone Contacts in Paris Attacks Suggest Foreign Coordination. *The New York Times*. Retrieved 19 June 2017 from https://www.nytimes.com/2015/12/31/world/europe/cellphone-contacts-in-paris-attacks-suggest-foreign-coordination.html

Salama, U. (2017, March 22). *Smart Forensics for the Internet of Things (IoT)*. Retrieved 22 June 2017 from https://securityintelligence.com/smart-forensics-for-the-internet-of-things-iot/

Schlag, C. (2013). The New Privacy Battle: How the Expanding Use of Drones Continues to Erode Our Concept of Privacy and Privacy Rights. *Journal of Technology Law & Policy, 13*. Retrieved 6 June 2017 from http://tlp.law.pitt.edu

Schwab, K. (2015, December 2). The Fourth Industrial Revolution: what it means, how to respond. *Foreign Affairs*. Retrieved 2 June 2017 from https://www.foreignaffairs.com/articles/2015-12-12/fourth-industrial-revolution

Shachtman, N. (2008, March 4). Isreali Drones Jamming Phones in Gaza? *Wired*. Retrieved 12 August 2009 from http://www.wired.com/dangerroom/2008/03/israel-drones-j/

Shachtman, N. (2009a, October 30). The Army's New Land Warrior Gear: Why Soldiers Don't Like It. *Popular Mechanics*. Retrieved 18 June 2017 http://www.popularmechanics.com/military/a1590/4215715/

Shachtman, N. (2009b, December 17). Insurgents Intercept Drone Video in King-Size Security Breach (Updated, with Video). *Wired*. Retrieved 18 December 2009 from http://www.wired.com/danger-room/2009/12/insurgents-intercept-drone-video-in-king-sized-security-breach/

Shachtman, N. (2009c, December 21). Report: Drone Feeds Gave Insurgents 'Early Warning' (Updated). *Wired*. Retrieved 22 December 2009 from http://www.wired.com/dangerroom/2009/12/drone-feds-gave-insurgents-early-warning-report/

Shachtman, N. (2011, October 8). Computer virus hits US Predator and Reaper drone fleet. *ARS Technica*. Retrieved from http://arstechnica.com/business/news/2011/10/exclusive-computer-virus-hits-drone-fleet

Simmons, L. (2015, October 14). What is the difference between the Internet of Everything and The Internet of Things. *Cloud Rail Blog*. Retrieved 7 June 2017 from https://blog.cloudrail.com/internet-of-everything-vs-internet-of-things/

Spam Laws. (2017). *Good Computer Viruses: The Future?* Retrieved 12 June 2017 from http://www.spamlaws.com/good-computer-viruses.html

Starr, M. (2014, January 19). Fridge caught sending spam emails in botnet attack. *CNET*. Accessed 10 March 2015 from http://www.cnet.com/news/fridge-caught-sending-spam-emails-in-botnet-attack/

Storm, D. (2017). Hackers can exploit smartwatches, fitness trackers to steal your ATM PIN. *Computer World IDG*. Retrieved from http://www.computerworld.com/article/3092407/security/hackers-can-exploit-smartwatches-fitness-trackers-to-steal-your-atm-pin.html

StrategyPage.com. (2008, December 3). *Israeli Telephone Commandos Strike Again*. Retrieved April 7, 2010, from StrategyPage.com: http://www.strategypage.com/htmw/htiw/20081203.aspx

StrategyPage.com. (2009, January 2). *Gaza Cell Phones Targeted*. Retrieved July 27, 2009, from StrategyPage.com: http://www.strategypage.com/htmw/htiw/articles/20090102.aspx

Swanbeck, S. (2015, June 22). Coast Guard Commandant Addresses Cybersecurity Vulnerabilities on Offshore Oil Rigs. *CSIS-Tech.org*. Retrieved from http://www.csis-tech.org/blog/2015/6/22/coastguard-commandant-addresses-cybersecurity-vulnerabilities-in-offshore-oil-rigs

The Virus Encyclopedia. (n.d.). *Nematode*. Retrieved 12 June 2017 from http://virus.wikidot.com/nematode

van Niekerk, B. (2011). *Vulnerability Assessment of Modern ICT Infrastructures from an Information Warfare Perspective* (Doctoral Thesis). Durban, South Africa: University of KwaZulu-Natal.

van Niekerk, B. (2015). Convergence of functional areas in information operations. *South African Journal of Information Management, 17*(1). doi:10.4102ajim.v17i1.605

van Niekerk, B. (2017). Analysis of Cyber-Attacks against the Transportation Sector. In M. Korstanje (Ed.), *Threat Mitigation and Detection of Cyber Warfare and Terrorism Activities* (pp. 68–91). Hershey, PA: IGI Global. doi:10.4018/978-1-5225-1938-6.ch004

Vaughn-Nichols, S. (2017, May 3). The Internet of messy things. *Computer World*. Retrieved 8 May 2017 from http://www.computerworld.com/article/3193941/internet-of-things/the-internet-of-messy-things.html

Veix, J. (2017, February 3). Hackers Hijack Radio Stations to Play YG's Anti-Trump Anthem 'FDT'. *Newsweek*. Retrieved 19 June 2017 from http://www.newsweek.com/hackers-hijack-radio-stations-play-ygs-anti-trump-anthem-fdt-552003

Ventre, D. (2016). *Information Warfare* (2nd ed.). London, UK: Wiley. doi:10.1002/9781119004721

Verizon. (2017). *2017 Data Breach Investigations Report* (10th ed.). Author.

Viva Sarah Press. (2015, April 5). Cyber terrorism triggers psychological and physical stress. *ISREAL 21c*. Retrieved 17 June 2017 from https://www.israel21c.org/cyber-terrorism-exposure-triggers-psychological-and-physical-stress/

Walker, D. (2014, June 25). 'Havex' malware strikes industrial sector via watering hole attacks. *SC Magazine*. Retrieved 27 July 2014 from http://www.scmagazine.com/havex-malware-strikes-industrial-sector-via-watering-hole-attacks/article/357875/

Waltz, E. (1998). *Information Warfare: Principles and Operations*. Boston: Artech House.

Woolf, N. (2016, October 26). DDoS attack that disrupted internet was largest of its kind in history, experts say. *The Guardian*. Retrieved 9 June 2016 from https://www.theguardian.com/technology/2016/oct/26/ddos-attack-dyn-mirai-botnet

Wyld, B. (2004, July 17). The Fear Factor. *The Age*. Retrieved 31 July 2009 from http://www.theage.com.au/articles/2004/07/16/1089694549469.html

Zawoad, S., & Hasan, R. (2015). FAIoT: Towards Building a Forensics Aware Eco System for the Internet of Things. *2015 IEEE International Conference on Services Computing (SCC)*, 279-284. 10.1109/SCC.2015.46

Zetter, K. (2015, May 15). Feds say that banned researcher commandeered plane. *Wired*. Retrieved from http://www.wired.com/2015/05/feds-say-banned-researcher-commandeered-plane/

KEY TERMS AND DEFINITIONS

Critical Infrastructure Protection: The protection of infrastructure critical to national or social cohesion from cyber and physical threats.

Cyber-Attack: Attacks conducted in cyber-space primarily aimed at disrupting information services or operations, steal information, or making political statements.

Cyber-Security: Protecting information, systems, and networks from cyber-threats.

Electronic Warfare: Denying adversary use of the electromagnetic spectrum while protecting one's own activities in the spectrum.

Drones: Vehicles or systems that are remotely controlled or piloted over networked or radio communications.

Industrial Internet of Things: An evolution of industrial control systems along the lines of the internet of things.

Internet of Things: The proliferation of "smart" connected devices.

Microcomputer: Small computing device that provides basic processing, with expansions for various input/output and communication options.

Psychological Operations: Information-based operations targeting the psyche of the audience to influence decision making or behavior.

Strategic Communication: Engaging audiences to shape conditions favorable to the communicator's objectives.

Chapter 6
A Generic Self–Evolving Multi–Agent Defense Approach Against Cyber Attacks

Stephen Mugisha Akandwanaho
University of KwaZulu-Natal, South Africa

Irene Govender
University of KwaZulu-Natal, South Africa

ABSTRACT

A generic self-evolving multi-agent approach is proposed in this chapter. Most of the existing security approaches are custom designed for specific threats and attacks. However, the fusion of technologies and systems in the fourth industrial revolution and therefore the nature of its current cyber environment increasingly attracts multiple cyber threats in a single interface. In order to solve this problem, a generic self-evolving multi-agent approach is proposed. Multiple agents interact with each other in light of their reactions towards the environment and its inherent changes. Information from individual agents is collected and integrated to form the abstract compartment of the structure. The important aspects are analyzed including demonstrating how the abstract domain can be obtained from the custom interactions at the low-level domain of the proposed approach. The analysis explores the existing works in the area and how they have been advanced in the fourth industrial revolution.

INTRODUCTION

Cyber-security in the fourth industrial revolution has increasingly become a high-priority area of research due to its significant importance. Moreover, cyber-security is not only about the safety of cyberspace information (Igor, 2007), but encompasses networks and systems operating in the cyber world as well. It is also one of the three strands of the fourth industrial revolution aside from biological and physical realms that form the *industry 4.0* or what is commonly known as the *fourth industrial revolution*. In this revolution there is a massive convergence and confluence of technologies and systems which create a new digital world with immense benefits but also enormous challenges (Piggin, 2016; Prisecaru, 2016).

DOI: 10.4018/978-1-5225-4763-1.ch006

One of the intrinsic challenges of this revolution include cyber-attacks which are as complicated and evolving as these hyper-inter-connected systems. The magnitude of the risks posed by these attacks require intelligent and agile mechanisms that can adapt and evolve their capabilities to outmatch the strengths and complexities of today's cyber threats. The convergence of different technologies and networked systems create a new level of sophistication in cyber-attacks. This convergence should therefore be considered when developing cyber defense mechanisms. One of the reasons behind this sophistication is that more advanced tools and techniques are being used to breach into networks and systems. This is aggravated by not only the ubiquitous nature of the attacks but the ability of these attacks to circumvent detection and cause enormous harm to people and systems. Given the adoption of mobile devices and proliferation of various devices in the cyber space, new levels of threats have sprang up due to this unprecedented convergence of disparate technologies and systems (Grobler, vanVuuren, & Jannie, 2013). The reality of globalization has dramatically changed under the fourth industrial revolution due to the unmitigated dependence on cyber systems by people and organizations. Hence, the risks have grown in large proportions as the severity of attacks increases in today's hyper-globalization. Even though the advent of globalization brought about a host of benefits such as improved communication and a multitude of opportunities (Herzog, 2011), the ever increasing and evolving cyber security threats and vulnerabilities have increasingly detracted from the benefits and increased anxiety. The existing strategies are not keeping up with the rapidly evolving and complicated cyber threats of this time adequately. Towards this end, multi-layered intelligent techniques are needed to give robust protection to systems and information on many fronts within the same interface. The bespoke protection methods cause runaway attacks when the specific category of the attack is not covered by the protective approach employed since the protective approach can only protect a specific category of cyber-attacks.

In order to combat these threats a multifaceted approach that is reactive, proactive and self-evaluating is required. Firstly, the reactive aspect should encompass both static and dynamic protection controls in neutralizing and fending off attacks. The second aspect which is proactive should be a key component of any security measure in the fourth industrial revolution. The current cyber threats are difficult to track due to their dynamic and adaptive nature (Walters, 2017; Ganapathy, Yogesh, & Kannan, 2012). Hence the combative defense mechanisms should be prescient with the ability not only to detect but also counteract cyber-attacks in a rapidly changing cyber environment. The third component is self-evaluation of the intelligent defense mechanisms. This aspect involves evaluating the mechanism's capabilities against the threat being posed. The evaluation entails a self- evolving capacity to ensure that the optimality and applicability of the defense system in mitigating the risks are dynamically strong as the threats continue to evolve diversely in cyber space.

An effective cyber security defense mechanism should also be multi-layered so that protection is provided on multiple security fronts (Igor, 2005; Igor & Alexander, 2005). The threats in the fourth industrial revolution have increasingly become nested and evolving as systems converge into a single interface. The majority of traditional methods have always been based on niche designs where for example some of them focus on prevention, detection, intrusion detection, and others (Igor, 2010). The current attack patterns require integrated solution systems in cyber space that can collect data, analyze patterns, trace threats, avert attacks and other capabilities integrated into a single interface. The required mechanisms should demonstrate intelligent ability to interact and cooperate with systems so as to learn behaviors and provide robust protection on many fronts in the cyber realm.

One of the objectives of this chapter is to explore the current trends of cyber-attacks in the fourth industrial revolution. In particular a premium is placed on exploring the vulnerabilities brought about by the convergence and confluence of technologies and systems in cyber space. Sequel to the assessment of these trends, an appropriate measure is introduced based on artificial intelligence. The measure is a generic self-evolving intelligent defense framework that is reactive, proactive and self-evaluating as explained in this section. While an intelligent system exhibits some sort of intelligence that is created by training the system with data, but not explicitly using programming, an artificial intelligent system is a branch of study on how to make such systems using fields such as probability, psychology, linguistics, mathematics and cognitive sciences.

In the proposed framework, the intelligent agents in a multi-agent approach, are split into self-evolving attack and defense agents. The defense agents keep changing their defense system according to the threat posed. In addition, they are not bespoke to a specific threat since the inherent capabilities are threat-independent and this helps to mitigate a wide range of cyber-attacks. The proposed approach leverages the cooperation and collaboration of intelligent agents to form a robust counteraction mechanism against a wide range of attacks.

BACKGROUND

Security systems based on multi-agent technology are preferred increasingly by experts in cyber security (Hedin & Moradian, 2015) due to their strong adaptability and collaborative nature. Essentially, a multi-agent system is a computerized system that consists of intelligent agents that interact with each other to share information as they interact with the environment. These software agents could equally be robots, human or human teams. As multi-agents cooperate, they model system behavior and try to adapt to all the various dynamic changes of the system. This helps eventually to create strong techniques that can keep up with the complexity of today's cyber-attacks in the fourth industrial revolution. In order to give robust protection to the system, it's important for the technique to have full system knowledge so that internal vulnerabilities can be discovered and handled effectively by the deployed security mechanism (Hedin & Moradian, 2015). Agent-based programming of security mechanisms is a new approach relative to other existing paradigms. It is intrinsically based on artificial intelligence and operates in a distributed fashion with multiple agents representing different scenarios. This helps to model a complex environment and make necessary behavior predictions as well.

This area of research has attracted enormous interest from researchers because of the frequent breaches in cyber-security systems and a high proliferation of cyber-attacks (Bendovschi, 2015). Many organizations and individuals are scrambling to find solutions about how to safeguard their data and systems against these sophisticated cyber-attacks that are prevalent in the fourth industrial revolution. Cyber-attacks were ranked in the top 10 global security risks in the 2016 global risk report (World Economic Forum Report, 2016). The report highlights risks that are likely to have the greatest global impact over a period of ten years. Experts in security are being increasingly staggered and overwhelmed by a variety of vectors used in the attacks that are being launched as well as the sophistication of tools that are used to aid cyber-attacks. As a corollary artificial intelligence tools are considered more effective in addressing these unprecedented cyber-attacks in the fourth industrial revolution (Nadine & Hadas, 2017).

Anitha, Girish and Savera (2016) presented a cyber defense system using artificial intelligence. The system focuses on detection of security attacks in wireless networks. The key aspect of this mechanism is its on-the-fly authentication process. The system generates passwords for users using artificial intelligence as they access resources in cyber space. This is similar to the work by Livadas, Walsh, Lapsley, et al. (2006) where machine learning techniques are used to identify botnet traffic. A machine learning classification model is used to identify hosts that are compromised especially from the internet relay chat traffic (Livadas, Walsh, Lapsley, et al., 2006).

Numerous techniques have been suggested to monitor traffic in cyber space and especially packet assessment where harmful packets are separated out from innocuous packets (Moore & Zuev, 2005; Roughan, Sen, Spatscheck, et al., 2004; Sen, Spatscheck, & Wang, 2004). The techniques that are used here focus on reading packet syntax to study their inherent characteristics and these techniques range from Bayesian classification to statistical mechanisms. These type of intelligent mechanisms have been widely used for example, Hooper(2008) created an intelligent model with the ability to predict, monitor and measure security of the network protocol. The prediction is based on good interpretation of traffic patterns and behaviors of different technologies and protocol interactions. Similar concepts are proposed by Nagpal, Kumar and Vij (2016) to mitigate the security challenges that have continued to beset the internet of things. Artificial intelligence is used to model the behavior of interactions between the system and the user as well as provide collaboration between different techniques. This kind of artificial intelligence was also applied by Idris and Shanmugam (2005) to intrusion detection where network intuitions are captured by the technique so as to know the patterns of protocol behaviors and interactions. This information is then used to fend off attacks. Tyugu (2011) observes that the defense of cyber space in today's times cannot be left to the traditional applications and processes that have already failed to cope with the rapidly evolving attacks and the magnitude of the risks they pose. This calls for mechanisms that are considerably automated and self-evolving that can counteract the powerful attacks in cyber space.

Bowen, Segal, Shanbhag, et al. (2000) developed an intelligent approach largely for detecting threats but with the ability to trace and isolate them. The approach leverages patterns observed over the course of several events and different behaviors of the system. An important function of this model is the interception of packets and then analyzing them with a view to isolate untoward packets that could potentially cause harm. In order to achieve good behavioral and pattern learning, (Servin & Kudenko, 2008) created a reinforcement learning mechanism using intelligent sensor agents in a network. The agents then make various observations and report them to a central agent. In case of intrusions, the signal is sent to the central agent which then triggers the alarm. This is similar to the mechanism proposed by Nian, Sunjun, Rui, et al.(2009) where multi-agents are used to detect intrusions. The agents are adaptable and diverse with a memory component. The multi-agents interact in different directions and at different levels to strengthen its self-learning mechanism. The system distribution allows other nodes not to be disrupted by the attack on a single node in the network.

Most of the existing research focus on methods that are tailored to specific threats in cyber space. This implies that if a tailored method is being used to safeguard a resource against a specific threat, due to the convergence of systems in the fourth industrial revolution, then a different threat that emerges may not be protected adequately against an attack. The current industrial revolution requires techniques with a wide variety of capabilities due to the inherent integration of technologies in cyber space. In this chapter a generic self-evolving multi agent defense mechanism that can counteract a multiplicity of cyber-attacks based on artificial intelligence is presented.

MAIN FOCUS OF THE CHAPTER

This chapter focuses on exploring the artificial intelligence techniques that can strengthen cyber security in the fourth industrial revolution. Artificial intelligence techniques intelligently model cyber systems behavior in relation to the environment in which the systems operate. Due to the increasing complexity of today's cyber-attacks, intelligent agents have been increasingly adopted because they can adapt and evolve to keep up with the changing threats in the cyber space (Such, Criado, Vercouter, Rehak, 2016). Intelligence agents are self-adaptive and sensitive to the environmental behaviors and changeability. In order for them to guard against sophisticated and non-sophisticated attacks alike, they have to study and learn the environment so that they can readily respond intelligently to the unforeseen changes. Learning also involves drawing from the experiences from past attacks and responses to these attacks. This knowledge helps to equip the intelligent agents with the ability to decisively deal with various threats and prevent the onslaught of cyber-attacks.

Intelligent agents can be categorized to rule-based and goal-based approaches because of how they operate. The rule based category is where adaptability and responsiveness to changes conform to the rules that define how agents behave towards and interpret the environmental dynamic conditions. In the goal-based approach all information obtained is compared with the set goals and action must be in keeping with the standard goals that have been set. In addition, the defined goals help in the quality evaluation and assessment of efficiency by determining if the intended goals were achieved (Ganapathy, Yogesh, & Kannan, 2012). The cyber security battle in the fourth industrial revolution is a moving target that can be tackled by intelligent and intrinsically dynamic techniques. To this end, our focus rests on intelligent agents in artificial intelligence by examining the collaboration and cooperation that largely define their interactive behavior. The intelligent agents always want to be steeped in the environment so that they can easily sense the changes and make necessary adjustments to adapt to the changes. This process is important in cyber security where the changes are rapid and attacks are unpredictable. The deployed security technique is able to avert threats and counter attacks through adaptability and close collaboration with the environment. The adaptability component ensures that the deployed technique evolves as the threats change to keep up with their sophistication and capability requirements, to match the complexity of these cyber threats and attacks.

The agents use sensors and effectors to gather information from the environment and then take the necessary action thereby making agents reactive (Potiron, El Fallah, Taillibert, 2013). Intelligent agents can also take pro-active steps in anticipation to the environment changes based on its goals. They are configured with the goals and agents take initiatives to ensure that these goals are met. The third component as shown in Figure 1, is the interaction and collaboration exhibited by the agents, demonstrating the ability to socialize so as to collectively achieve their goals. These behaviors give the agents the ability to deal with today's multi-faceted and evolving cyber threats and attacks.

The fourth industrial revolution has affected not only the complexity of the attacks in the cyber space but the scale of attacks. Due to the integration of systems in the fourth industrial revolution, the scale of attacks can no longer be limited by the peculiarity and size of systems and networks (Hegazy, Al-Arif, Fayed, et al., 2003). The convergence of technologies and systems bring an additional layer to cyber security that makes threats extremely difficult to control given a deeply diverse technological environment and the large scale damage inflicted by sophisticated attacks. The fourth industrial revolution has also resulted in the emergence of tools that cause enormous destruction (Espen & Anja, 2015). Information has hitherto been weaponized due to its democratization in the fourth industrial revolution. Moreover, fusing of technologies and merging disparate systems unexpectedly spawn threats based on unpredictable patterns which make them challenging and difficult to prevent with the traditional methods in the current cyber space. In order to deal with these threats, new intelligent approaches that are more adaptive with the ability to track unpredictable patterns and mitigate the threats posed by the challenging dynamics of the current cyber security, must be developed.

Issues, Controversies, Problems

The explosive growth of the fourth industrial revolution continue to confound experts in many different ways. Firstly, there are extraordinary benefits of the fourth industrial revolution (Adeniran & Adetayo, 2016). The synergies of these technologies bring about extraordinary opportunities in every aspect of life. Organizations leverage them to enhance productivity and increase output. In addition, there are myriad breakthroughs in innovations and research, for example in medicine, manufacturing, Technology and a host of others which have been aided by the synergies of these technologies and given that the explosive growth of this revolution is not limited by boundaries, this global phenomenon is steadily spreading across boundaries and creating a global impact. The controversy generated by the advent of this phenomenon plus the wave of technologies that is rapidly sweeping the world is whether this growth is matched by the readiness to provide necessary adequate cyber security against a multiplicity of sophisticated attacks in the current global merge of technologies and systems.

The desire to infuse different technologies in all that we do has created an imbalance between the growth of technological advancements and security systems that ensure safety of data and systems from more and more cyber-attacks. The existential threats continue to pose great challenges due to, in part being overwhelmed by attacks but also inadequate response and existing counter-attack approaches that match the precision and robustness of attacks (Adeniran & Adetayo, 2016)..

Cyber security risks should be identified and strategies deployed before the fourth industrial revolution technologies are implemented (Rene, Tyler Lewis, & Carton, 2017). The technologies should be inherently risk-free by subsuming intelligent mechanisms that automatically detect risks, predict and forestall attacks.

As billions of Internet of Things devices get deployed by 2020, manufacturers should incorporate stronger countermeasures and security strategies that address the myriad security risks that are presented by these devices in the fourth industrial revolution. Consumers of technology have effectively failed to implement the available protection practices - even simple tasks such as, updating software, changing passwords and applying security techniques and countermeasures. The cyber security risks that emerge from the integration of technologies and systems need to be considered during manufacturing so that more secure systems can be developed and deployed. However the current threats increasingly evolve and change which requires equally strong and evolving countermeasures. This implies that even when countermeasures are subsumed in the systems at the manufacturing stage, security cannot be guaranteed due to the current landscape of cyber threats. The threats are evolving and become more complicated as environment changes. In addition, with limited human intervention, they spread across devices and technologies thus making it challenging for the existing approaches to track and prevent attacks.

In the context of hyper connectivity and ever changing complex nature of cyber-attacks in the fourth industrial revolution, the collaborative aspect of security strategies is very important especially when there is interaction and collaboration between security techniques against existential threats (Rene, Tyler Lewis, & Carton, 2017). The fourth industrial revolution should not only embody fusion of technologies and systems but also fusion and collaboration of different cyber counter attacks so as to produce a strong force against complex and evolving attacks in the current cyber space.

In today's age of amalgamation of technologies and systems, organizations that opt to use insecure systems for whatever reasons, create a huge risk for other systems in the network because insecure systems are always soft targets for cyber criminals and hackers. Once attacks are successful on the vulnerable systems, it means that a door is opened which potentially puts the rest of the systems at risk (Gorodetski, 2012). One of the major controversies for organizations is a choice to tradeoff providing online services through unsecured channels and steering clear of threats by allowing customers without encryptions and security restrictions (Martin, 2016). It is important that mechanisms be established to impel companies to secure their cyber services and systems. Moreover organizations may lack the necessary expertise and resources to have the robust security systems that the fourth industrial revolution cyber space requires. These controversies are fueling the need for strategies and mechanisms that can create cyber resilience for systems and help organizations to withstand the security hazards of the fourth industrial revolution. The proliferation of mobile devices plugged in today's cyber space creates another layer of security for concern and complexity. These devices are increasingly targeted given that most people may plug their devices in cyber space without much protection thus putting information and systems at risk.

The integration of technologies and systems has also recently resulted in a massive cyber-attack by ransomware which affected more than 150 countries (Mark & Jethro, 2017) including USA, UK, Spain, Russia and South Africa. Ransomware is a dangerous malware that holds devices to hostage until a certain amount of money is paid. The malware has hitherto spread rapidly across networks and systems causing significant damage including millions of people losing their files. The attack was enabled by outdated systems including those that are bespoke and incompatible to modern platforms. The systems in the current industrial revolution are always vulnerable to cyber-attacks due to the risk associated with fusion of systems and technologies. The would-be attackers continue to take advantage of the weak cyber security systems because of the custom nature of these systems. This implies that the vulnerability in any system in cyber space potentially puts all the other systems at great risk because of the interconnectedness and interdependence of these cyber systems in the fourth industrial revolution. The interconnectedness involves different cyber systems linking to each other in order to collectively gather a full spectrum of data where as interdependence is premised on the notion that shared platforms enhance efficiency through collaboration to yield desired results. Cyber systems in the fourth industrial revolution not only co-exist but are interdependent which adds another layer of security risk because a risk in a single system creates a window of vulnerability in interconnected and dependent systems.

SOLUTIONS AND RECOMMENDATIONS

Agents are important in solving problems that are interdependent with sub-problems that relate to each other (Gorodetski, 2012). The interaction amongst agents is beneficial in terms of learning the environment and being steeped in its security needs in order to produce a multifaceted security framework. The agents are autonomous and interact with each other in the same environment. They also have exterior interactions to expand their knowledge and area of influence (Grzonka, Jakobik, Kolodziej, et al.1999). The objective of the proposed approach is to have a generic multi-agent system that is able to evolve and adapt to new environments so that it can respond to a wide range of attacks. This is shown in Figure 2 where autonomous individual agents interact with each other to share information. This information from individual agents is then distilled into collective information to provide the approach with the ability to be applied to a wide array of security situations. The generic aspect at the abstraction level ensures that the information gathered from disparate agents is not bespoke or customized to any specific security context so that it can effectively be applied to a broad spectrum of problems. One of the significant benefits of this model is that the approach easily adapts to new environmental changes and landscape with regard to cyber security due to its generic component, which is a key inherent feature of intelligent agents (Yamaguchi & Watanabe, 2000). It's not limited by the capacity of an individual agent due to leveraging of information and abilities resulting from multiple agents and their inherent interactions.

Agents are known to possess memory which helps them to store information over the course of their learning (Xiao-Feng & Jiming, 2009).The interactions are not only between internal agents but also with agents that are external to the environment so as to expand their orbit of social interactivity. In addition, they react to events and changes both immediately during the attack and proactively to prevent an attack. This kind of flexibility is important for agents to respond appropriately to changes in the environment and the unpredictability of security attacks in the cyber space. The experiences gathered by these agents are also shaped by being steeped in cultural and social knowledge which is accumulated over the course of behavioral adaptability and inherent interactions and responsiveness to the vicissitudes of the environment. Agents have got an inherent capability to break down problems into sub-tasks which helps them to tackle even very complex problems (Knorn, Chen, & Middletone, 2016).Agents are also well known for their unpredictability. They operate well in situations that are both predictable and unpredictable.

In this work, agents are created with sensors to perceive and intelligently interact with the environment. The knowledge obtained from learning the environment is used to guide the decision making process of agents and eventually to effectively tackle changing and complex threats. Also, the agents' interactions allow tackling difficult problems that would be impossible to solve by a single agent. The created environment has regions and events that trigger the interactions of agents in the environment. Agents interact first with their immediate neighbors through sensors which help them to perceive the inherent changes in the environment so that they can suitably adjust and react accordingly. This coordination of agents is largely symmetric so that one agent is not favored over the other during the coordination process. The cooperation between agents is controlled by the constraints to ensure that all the desired aspects of the interactions are achieved. The constraints also eliminate errors to ensure the mechanism zero in on essential information to be drawn from the mutual sharing and interactions. An agent can also perform multiple tasks and react to multiple events as defined by the constraints.

In this work, emphasis is placed on neighbor interactions or agents that are close to each other in the sample space. There are constant updates in the iterations as agents receive feedback from each other so as to self-adapt to the environment changes. This approach is inspired by the multi-agent model that is based on biological control algorithm (Chih-Han, 2010). The guiding concept for agents can be mathematically formulated as follows:

$$x_i\left(t+1\right) = x_i\left(t\right) + \alpha \sum_{a_{j \in N_i}} f_j\left(.\right), \tag{1}$$

where $x_i(t)$ is the agent's state at time (t), N_i denotes neighbors for the agent a_i, and $f_j(.)$ denotes the feedback function attached to the neighbor agent, a_j. In order to guide the agents and control the interactions, three constraints are introduced (Chih-Han, 2010) as follows:

$$g\left(\theta_i,\theta_j\right) - \theta_{i,j}^* = 0 \leftrightarrow \theta_j - \theta_i = \theta_{i,j}^* \tag{2}$$

$$sign\left(x_j(t) - x_i - \Delta_{i,j}^*\right) = sign\left(g\left(\theta_i,\theta_j\right) - \theta_{i,j}^*\right) \tag{3}$$

$$g\left(-\theta_i,-\theta_j\right) = -g(\theta_i,\theta_j) \tag{4}$$

In order to confirm that the intended agent's objectives are achieved, constraint (2) is applied. Constraint (3) points the agent's sensors to the right direction in order to satisfy constraints defined between the agent and its neighbors. The last constraint defines the nature of the interaction between agents, for example asymmetric for the expression in equation (4). The key component of this approach is to aggregate the information obtained from interactions between agents so as to create information that is not bespoke and representative of the nature of environment as a whole instead of specific aspects of the environment as shown in equation (5).

$$X\left(t+1\right) = A\left(t\right).X\left(t\right) + \bar{b} \text{ (t) Let } X\left(t\right) = \left(x_1(t), x_2(t), \dots, x_n(t)\right)' \tag{5}$$

A(t) denotes the matrix that captures interactions between different agents in relation with time, nxn (Seneta, 1981) and $\bar{b}$ (t) is the vector for the timely activities performed by the agents to form part of the collective information.

Figures 3, 4 and 5 demonstrate agents' behavior in Matlab, sharing of information in the sample space and collecting disparate information from individual agents.

Figure 1 illustrates the interaction between the agent and the environment

The agents exist in a dynamic environment which constantly changes. Figure 1 captures the interactions and reactions at both the abstraction and individual level of the agents. The input process takes place as the specific agent tries to perceive the environment and provide their reactions during the interactions. The output is modeled as a multi-agent mix of reactions towards the non-stationary environment.

Figure 2 illustrates the interaction between agents at the low level and the generic information at the abstract level

The intelligent agents share individual information before the information is integrated at the abstract level of the proposed framework in Figure 2. The abstract mature allows the cyber system security to be independent of threats. The framework is equipped with a multiplicity of information that enables it to be widely applicable and provide protection against an array of attacks. The sample space was created in Matlab with different agents with similar settings. The sample agents are created in Figure 3 and interactions with the environment are captured in Figure 4. After interactions, all information is encapsulated

Figure 1. Agents' reactions to the environment

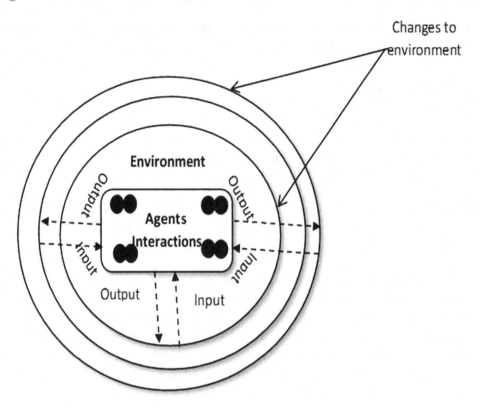

Figure 2. Low level and abstract domains in the proposed framework

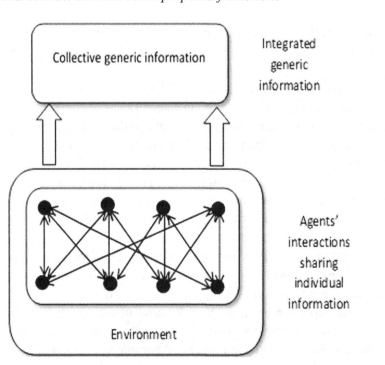

Figure 3. Sharing of agents information in the sample space

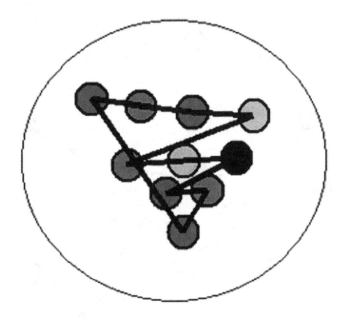

Figure 4.Agents and the environment

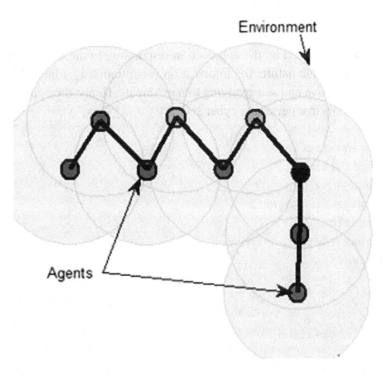

Figure 5.Collection of agents' information

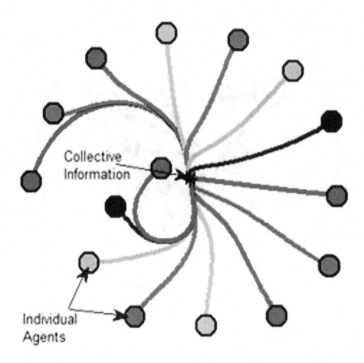

into a collective structure to be used by the approach in responding to the environment changes at the abstract level. Due to its dynamic nature, the information is continuously adjusted as the environment changes so as to remain adaptive and self-evolving to new threats. Hence the approach can then be applied to a variety of problems that pertain to cyber security.

```
Procedure Agents' interaction
Initialize P(a) arbitrarily
Send a message to agent2
    Receive a message from agent2
      Store information
If there are changes to the environment
      Update information
End if
End Procedure


Procedure Generic information
  loop
Initialize P(a) arbitrarily
Agents' interactions
      Store information
If there are changes to the environment
      Update information
```

```
End if
Collect generic information
End Procedure


Procedure Apply information
  loop
   Initialize P(a) arbitrarily, set of agents
   Initialize P(s), set of problems
     Agents' interactions
      Store information
  If there are changes to the environment
Update information
  End if
     Sift out custom information
   Collect generic information
Combine problems
     Apply
     Generate solutions
  If there are changes to the environment
     Update information
     Improve solutions as environment changes
  End if
 End Procedure
```

The procedure for agents' interaction starts by initializing a set of agents which acts as a population sample. The agents in the sample communicate to each other through sending messages whenever there is a change in the environment. Information is stored in memory and constantly updates as different reactions are obtained from agents. The updated information is used to improve solutions so as to make them better suited to solve current problems.

FUTURE RESEARCH DIRECTIONS

This area holds great prospects for interesting research that builds on the foundation that has been laid. One of directions would be implementing the proposed approach against multiple cyber security threats at a time. In a similar vein, another research direction is the creation of diverse self-evolving tasks that can be solved by the approach in the cyber space. In addition, exploring the dynamic landscape would be a significant step further for this research. Research can be directed to moving optima in cyber space and how it can be tracked using self-evolving multi-agents.

It would also be worthwhile to explore the role of distributed sensors and how they affect the effectiveness of agents in the cyber realm. The additional component would be studying the rules that agents apply in handling multiple tasks and various threats in the environment. This can be strengthened by exploring the coordination techniques of agents, better ways of their interactions and how they effectively use the information at their disposal to predict future threats and cyber space changes in the fourth industrial revolution.

CONCLUSION

A self-evolving multi-agent approach has been presented in this work. The theoretical components of the approach have been analyzed. These include, agents' interaction to the environment, sharing of information and creation of the abstraction layer of the proposed framework. One of the problems that this approach addresses is niche-based cyber security which implies having a single security system that is customized to safeguard the systems against a single threat in the cyber space. As has been stressed in the work, the fourth industrial revolution attracts myriad threats due to the fusion of systems and technologies. Therefore a customized system for a single threat cannot give adequate protection to systems and data. To this end, a generic approach that is able to tackle multiple threats in one interface is very important for safeguarding systems in the fourth industrial revolution. The presented approach employs self-evolving multi-agents that can adapt to the constant changes in the rugged environment. The multi-agents use sensors to study the environment and perceive the changes so as to react accordingly.

In the proposed structure, a set of individual agents is defined. The agents interact with each to share information giving their sensory feedback to each other on the environment changes and their respective tasks. The relevant information is gathered and collectively used to form a generic phase of the structure where it is applied to solve wide ranging problems without any niche or custom limitations. The information from the custom level is sifted to remove the individualized aspects so that only aspects that are generic can be allowed into the abstract level of the structure. As explained in the work, this approach will result in robust security applications that are multifaceted and resilient to an array of threats in the fourth industrial revolution. This is in part enabled by the fast convergence due to less custom environment that adapts quickly to the changes in the environment.

REFERENCES

Aderiran, & Adetayo, O. (2016). Impacts of the fourth industrial revolution on the transportation in the development nations. *International Educational Scientific Research Journal*, 56-60.

Anitha, A., Girish, P., & Savera, K. (2016). Cyber defense using artificial intelligence. *International Journal of Pharmacy and Technology*, 25352-25357.

Bendovschi, A. (2015). Cyber-Attacks – Trends, Patterns and Security Countermeasures. *Procedia Economics and Finance*, 28, 24–31. doi:10.1016/S2212-5671(15)01077-1

Bowen, T., Segal, M., Shanbhag, T., & Uppuluri, P. (2000). Building survivable systems: an integrated approach based on intrusion detection and damage containment. *Proceedings of the DARPA Information Survivability Conference and Exposition*, 84-99.

Chih-Han, Y. (2010). *Bilogically-Inspired Control for Self-Adaptive Multiagent Systems* (PhD Thesis). Harvard University.

Ernst & Young. (2014). *Cyber threat intelligence - how to get ahead of cybercrime.* Author.

Espen, B. E., & Anja, K. (2015). *The dark side of the Fourth Industrial Revolution – and how to avoid it.* Retrieved from World Economic Forum: https://www.weforum.org/agenda/2015/11/the-dark-side-of-the-digital-revolution-and-how-to-avoid-it/

Ganapathy, S., Yogesh, P., & Kannan, A. (2012). Intelligent Agent-Based Intrusion Detection System Using Enhanced Multiclass SVM. *Computational Intelligence and Neuroscience, 2012,* 1–10. doi:10.1155/2012/850259 PMID:23056036

Gorodetski, V. I. (2012). Self-organization and multiagent systems: I. Models of multiagent self-organization. *Journal of Computer and Systems Sciences International, 51*(2), 256–281. doi:10.1134/S106423071201008X

Grobler, M., vanVuuren, J. J., & Jannie, Z. (2013). Preparing South Africa for Cyber Crime and Cyber Defense. *Systemics, Cybernetics and Informatics,* 32-41.

Grzonka, D., Jakobik, A., Kolodziej, J., & Pllana, S. (2017). *Using a multi-agent system and artificial intelligence for monitoring and improving the cloud performance and security. In Future Generation Computer Systems.* Elsevier.

Hedin, Y., & Moradian, E. (2015). Security in Multi-Agent Systems. *Procedia Computer Science, 60,* 1604–1612. doi:10.1016/j.procs.2015.08.270

Hegazy, I. M., Al-Arif, T., Fayed, Z. T., & Faheem, H. M. (2003). A multi-agent based system for intrusion detection. *IEEE Potentials, 22*(4), 28–31. doi:10.1109/MP.2003.1238690

Herzog, S. (2011). Revisiting the Estonian Cyber. *Journal of Strategic Security,* 49-60.

Hooper, E. (2008). Intelligent Techniques for Effective Network Protocol Security Monitoring, Measurement and Prediction. *Internal Journal of Security and its Applications,* 1-10.

Idris, N. B., & Shanmugam, B. (2005). Artificial Intelligence Techniques Applied to Intrusion Detection. *INDICON 2005 Annual IEEE Conference,* 52-55.

Igor, K. (2005). Agent-Based Modeling and Simulation of Cyber-Warfare between Malefactors and Security Agents in Internet. *Proceedings of 19th European Simulation Multiconference on Simulation in wider Europe,* 1-25.

Igor, K. (2007). Multi-agent Modelling and Simulation of Cyber-Attacks and Cyber-Defense for Homeland Security. *IEEE International Workshop on Intelligent Data Acquisition and Advanced Computing Systems: Technology and Applications,* 614-619.

Igor, K. (2010). Agent-based modelling and simulation of network cyber-attacks and cooperative mechanisms. *Discrete Event Simulations,* 1-25.

Igor, K., & Alexander, U. (2005). Agent-based simulation of DDOS attacks and defence mechanisms. *Journal of Computers,* 1–10.

Knorn, S., Chen, Z., & Middleton, R. H. (2016). Overview: Collective Control of Multi agent Systems. *Proceedings of the IEEE Transactions on Control of Network Systems,* 334-347.

Livadas, C., Walsh, R., Lapsley, D., & Strayer, W. T. (2006). Using Machine Learning Technliques to Identify Botnet Traffic. *Proceedings of the 31st IEEE Conference on Local Computer Networks*, 967-974.

Mark, T., & Jethro, M. (2017, May 14). *CNN tech*. Retrieved from CNN Money Website: http://money.cnn.com/2017/05/14/technology/ransomware-attack-threat-escalating/

Martin, W. (2016, February 17). *Security: are we overlooking the most critical aspect of the fourth industrial revolution?* Retrieved from Memeburn: https://memeburn.com/2016/02/security-are-we-overlooking-the-most-critical-aspect-of-the-fourth-industrial-revolution/

Moore, A. W., & Zuev, D. (2005). Internet traffic classification using bayesian analysis techniques. *Proceedings of the 2005 ACM SIGMETRICS international conference*, 50-60. 10.1145/1064212.1064220

Munir, A. M. (2014). An Integrated Approach to Enterprise Risk. *ISACA Journal*, 1-10.

Nadine, W., & Hadas, K. (2017). Artificial Intelligence in Cybersecurity. *Cyber, Intelligence, and Security*, 103-119.

Nagpal, B., Kumar, M., & Vij, S. (2016). Internet of Things: Effective Security View through Artificial Intelligence. *International Journal of Science Technology & Engineering*, 1-10.

Nian, L., Sunjun, L., Rui, L., & Yong, L. (2009). A Network Intrusion Detection Model Based on Immune Multi-Agent. *International Journal of Communications, Network and System Sciences*, 569-574.

Piggin, R. (2016). *Risk in the Fourth Industrial Revolution*. Academic Press.

Potiron, K., El Fallah, S., & Taillibert, P. (2013). *From Fault Classification to Fault Tolerance for Multiagent systems*. Springer-Verlag. doi:10.1007/978-1-4471-5046-6

Prisecaru, P. (2016). Challenges of the Fourth Industrial Revolution. *Knowledge Horizons - Economics*, 57-62.

Rene, W., Tyler Lewis, R. H., & Carton, R. (2017, March 21). *Managing risk in an age of connected production*. Retrieved from Deloite University Press: https://dupress.deloitte.com/dup-us-en/focus/industry-4-0/cybersecurity-managing-risk-in-age-of-connected-production.html

Roughan, M., Sen, S., Spatscheck, O., & Duffield, N. (2004). Class-of-service mapping for qos: a statistical signature-based approach to ip traffic classification. *Proceedings of the 4th ACM SIGCOMM conference on Internet measurement*, 135-148. 10.1145/1028788.1028805

Sen, S., Spatscheck, O., & Wang, D. (2004). Accurate, scalable innetwork identification of p2p traffic using application signatures. *Proceedings of the 13th international conference on World Wide Web*, 512-521.

Seneta, E. (1981). *Non-negative Matrices and Markov Chains*. Springer Verlag. doi:10.1007/0-387-32792-4

Servin, A., & Kudenko, D. (2008). Multi-Agent Reinforcement Learning for Intrusion Detection: A Case Study and Evaluation. *Proceedings of the German Conference on Multiagent System Technologies*, 159-170. 10.1007/978-3-540-87805-6_15

Such, J. M., Criado, N., Vercouter, L., & Rehak, M. (2016). Intelligent Cybersecurity Agents. *IEEE Intelligent Systems*, *31*(5), 2–7. doi:10.1109/MIS.2016.79

Tyugu, E. (2011). Artificial Intelligence in Cyber Defense. *Proceedings of the 3rd International Conference on Cyber Conflict*, 1-11.

Walters, R. (2017). US Federal Cyber Breaches in 2012 Analysis. *Eurasiareview*. Retrieved December 2017 from http://www.eurasiareview.com/08012018-us-federal-cyber-breaches-in-2017-analysis/

World Economic Forum Report. (2016). *The Global Risks Report 2016.* Author.

Xiao-Feng, X., & Jiming, L. (2009). Multiagent Optimization System for Solving the Traveling Salesman Problem (TSP). *IEEE Transactions on Systems, Man, and Cybernetics. Part B, Cybernetics*, *39*(2), 489–502. doi:10.1109/TSMCB.2008.2006910 PMID:19095545

Yamaguchi, L., & Watanabe, R. (2000). Interactive self-self-reflection based multiagent reinforcement learning for coordination. *The Third Asia-Pacific Conference on Simulated Evolution And Learning*, 2885-2890. 10.1109/IECON.2000.972456

Chapter 7
The Different Aspects of Information Security Education

Suchinthi Fernando
Rutgers University, USA

ABSTRACT

This chapter discusses the importance of information security education for everyone, ranging from organizations to professionals and students, all the way through to individual users of information and communication systems. It discusses the different subject areas in information security and shows how instead of being intimidated by it, different categories of users can obtain varying depths of information security education based on their cyber-activities and need for knowledge. Information security professionals would require an in-depth knowledge in all aspects of information security, and information technology professionals and students would require an overall education in these areas, while most users of information and communication systems would only require a basic education to help protect their information assets in cyberspace.

INTRODUCTION

Information is power. All important decisions, whether personal or corporate decisions, short-term or strategic long-term decisions, are made based on information available at a given time. The importance of acquiring and managing up-to-the-minute and accurate information has become more and more important in this digital era leading up to the fourth industrial revolution, where information technology prevails over all other types of technology. Managing information entails not only maintaining the integrity of the information, but also preserving its confidentiality to gain that much required edge over competitors, or ensuring that the privacy of any groups or individuals is not violated. As important as it is to obtain the latest information in order to gain that competitive advantage, it is even more important to ensure that that information does not fall into the wrong hands, since the damage caused by an information security breach, both financially as well as to the reputation of an organisation or any individual, could be phenomenal. As the race for acquiring information gets heated leading to all out cyber warfare, the difficulty of managing information also increases exponentially.

DOI: 10.4018/978-1-5225-4763-1.ch007

Cyber-security has become a focal point of most organisations, where they strive to provide information security and assurance by creating more resilient structures and systems to keep the never-ending, ever-increasing threats and attacks at bay. Where they previously used to focus only on other aspects of information technology, such as faster networks with higher bandwidths, higher processing speed and power, timely and cost effective software delivery, etc., information technology now revolves around information security, where secure networks, stronger encryption protocols, stronger and more robust systems, secure software development, etc. have taken the centre stage. The software and information industry has finally come to the realization that information security is not something that can be plugged in at the end, but is, in fact, an integral component of information technology that needs to be considered and planned for from the start, incorporated into the design of systems and software, and where the implementation of software systems should be carried out around the established information security standards and procedures. Thus, information security is now finally acknowledged as a journey and not simply as an end destination. Almost all corporations now incorporate information security at all levels and in all branches of business by setting up the required perimeter, hardware and software security systems in place and laying out information security policies and procedures.

The weakest link in all these security measures, however, is the users of these information systems. No matter how strong the technological security measures are, or how well conceived the security policies, procedures and protocols are, if these policies, procedures and protocols are not properly administered or followed, therein lies the biggest vulnerability of any system. The human aspect of information security is the leading cause of information security breaches, and is the component that is most commonly and easily exploited, whether it is in the form of intrusions from the outside or insider threats. This stands true whether it is a corporation, a government, or an individual – the weakest component in an information system is its users. The only way to guard against this is to ensure that information users are properly educated and made aware in the ways of securing information, and thereby, securing their lives.

Living in this digitized age, using all kinds of communication devices which allow people to access and share information in a multitude of ways, without at least a basic awareness of information security is analogous to being in the driver's seat in a car on a busy highway without knowing how to drive. This does not mean that one must shy away from all technology and not be socially active in this digital world. As extensive as the subject of information security is, the fear of not being able to acquire all that knowledge should not deter people from using the technology available to them. Instead, they should gear themselves up by learning what they need to learn about information security, so they may be ready to function in this digital era without having to face major threats.

Information security covers a vast range of subject areas, but not each user needs to be thoroughly educated in each of these different areas. Based on what their job entails and the level of engagement they have with the information, and the criticality of the information they deal with, their information security education can be catered to suit each user role accordingly. Some users might require in-depth knowledge of certain areas, while needing only a basic understanding in others, whereas other users might need only basic awareness overall, and others need an all-round detailed understanding. Regardless of a user's job within a certain organisation, all individual users of information and communication systems should also be cognizant in information security so they may know how to protect their privacy and not put their lives at risk. The mission of this chapter is to discuss the importance of information security education, the different aspects of such an education, and the varying depths and levels of information security education and awareness required by different types of users based on their user roles within an information system. This chapter aims to provide information users with a basic education on information security, and list best practices to help them stay protected in cyberspace.

BACKGROUND

Information security is an essential and timely component in information technology (IT) education, especially in the present digital era of the fourth industrial revolution. Yet, even though the teaching of basic IT skills such as basic programming, database and web development, etc. has become an integral part of education regardless of whether or not the students major in computer or information sciences, information security is most often overlooked and left out (Senanayake & Fernando, 2017). This is quite an unfortunate situation as information security has much broader scope than IT, and is, in fact, an integral part of any information and communication system which stores information and allows its users to access and share that information. According to Harris and Maymi (2016), today's fast-paced growth of the IT industry, which does not allow sufficient time for educating people on how to properly maintain and safeguard their information, leaves less time for information security professionals to discover new security practices and procedures, while, unfortunately, giving more time for adversaries to learn how to circumvent the security mechanisms in place (Harris & Maymi, 2016). Information systems should enable proper and secure access to and communication of information to authorized users through authorized channels instead of simply allowing access to anyone. Thus, users of information systems should receive sufficient education in information security to enable them to properly utilize the system, while ensuring their privacy, as well as the confidentiality and integrity of the information. Education in information security, therefore, is required not only by students and professionals, but also by any and all users of information and communication systems.

When it comes to possible information security vulnerabilities and threats, ignorance is not bliss. Unfortunately, risk and uncertainty are difficult concepts for people to evaluate (West, 2008), as the human brain perceives security somewhat differently from its reality (Schneier, 2008). While the reality of security is mathematical, based on the probability of different risks and the effectiveness of different countermeasures, the feeling of security is based on the individual person's psychological reactions to these (Schneier, 2008). This divergence between the reality and the brain's perception of security leads to gaps between the required and implemented security countermeasures, where if the threat is perceived to be greater than what it actually is, one can feel paranoid even when they are secure, resulting in expensive, unnecessary security mechanisms, whereas when they fail to comprehend the real intensity of the risk they may become complacent and undermine it, thereby increasing their vulnerability to attacks. Gains in security involve trade-offs in terms of money, time, convenience, capabilities or liberties, and humans make these trade-offs intuitively, exaggerating some risks or costs, while downplaying others (Schneier, 2008). When aspects of trade-off such as the severity of risk, probability of risk, magnitude of the costs, effectiveness of countermeasures at mitigating the risk, and comparison of disparate risks and costs are evaluated incorrectly, perceived trade-offs also diverge from the actual trade-offs. Schneier (2008) categorizes behavioural heuristics as risk, probability, cost, and decision heuristics, where risk heuristics also include Prospect Theory by Kahneman and Tversky (1979), where people accept small sure gains rather than risking or chancing a larger gain, whereas they risk larger losses rather than accepting smaller sure losses (Kahneman & Tversky, 1979), among others. West (2008) further states that some of the predictable and exploitable characteristics in the human decision-making process are their belief of being less at risk, risk homeostasis or maintaining an acceptable degree of risk in their minds and thus increasing risky behaviour to suit increased security measures (for e.g.: driving faster to compensate for wearing a seatbelt, etc.), and cognitive miserliness (i.e.: having only a limited capacity for information processing and multitasking). These lead to feeling less motivated by abstract concepts such as security, and to making quick, uninformed decisions based on learned rules and heuristics instead. Hence, security only becomes a priority when people start to have problems with it (West, 2008). Therefore, an important part of information security education is teaching users that anyone could fall victim to an information security attack at any time. It is important to perceive risk accurately, in order to implement necessary countermeasures to avert that risk. As tighter security mechanisms help to keep vulnerabilities and attacks at bay, and thereby, keep risk below the 'accident zone', periodic risk perception renewals are also required in order to maintain risk perception in the human mind at an acceptable level, so that people will maintain security mechanisms above an acceptable threshold (Gonzalez & Sawicka, 2002).

When the concept of information security was first developed, it focused mainly around technological aspects such as network security and cryptography, etc. (Bishop, 2003), but as the realization that the users of the system were the weakest link and that human errors played the biggest role in information security breaches was dawned, so was the importance of the human aspect pertaining to security recognized (Fernando, 2014). As the focus of information security thus shifted from being technology-oriented to management-oriented (Lacey, 2009), international standards such as ISO/IEC 270001 (2005) etc. also emphasized the need to take human resource security into consideration when managing information security. As explained by Vroom and von Solms (2003), effective information security requires not only physical and technical controls, but also operational controls, which concern the behaviour and actions of users with regards to information security and are listed under security policies, procedures and guidelines. They further state that even though these policies, etc. are audited to ensure their effectiveness, instead of also auditing the performance of users, their adherence to these policies, procedures and guidelines are simply assumed (Vroom & von Solms, 2003). This is inadequate as people often find ways to work around such established policies, etc. instead of actually following them. In order to succeed in business in today's world, ensuring that access to information is strictly limited to the personnel who need to know it in order to perform their assigned tasks is mandatory (Schweitzer, 1996), leading to the implementation of the latest and strongest security mechanisms to limit unauthorized access to information by most organisations. In such cases, tricking people to reveal confidential information is much easier than penetrating the myriad of layers of technological security mechanisms that are put in place. In fact, most information security attacks such as social engineering, spear phishing, or willing or unwilling, knowing or unknowing collusion from an insider, etc. require a human element in order to succeed (Williams, 2011).

Another interesting observation is that 60%-70% of attacks originate, not from intrusions from the outside, but from 'trusted folk' already inside the system (Lynch, 2006). This number increases further when including users with non-malicious intent wittingly or unwittingly involved in attacks (Grimes, 2010). An intrusion is an activity violating system's security policy (Ning, Jajodia & Wang, 2003), while an insider threat is when trusted users with legitimate access abuse system privileges (Liu, Martin, Hetherington & Matzner, 2005), or when individuals possessing substantial internal access to system enact intentionally disruptive, unethical or illegal behaviour (Mills, Grimaila, Peterson & Butts, 2011), Thus, expensive and sophisticated intrusion detection systems are rendered worthless against these insider attacks, which are nearly to completely indistinguishable from normal actions as inside attackers already have authorization to use and access the system, and these actions are not too different from the normal operation of applications and processes (Liu, et al., 2005). Thus, malicious insider activities such as exploitation, extraction, manipulation, reconnaissance, entrenchment, etc. could easily pass off as normal activities such as database administration, word processing, web browsing, command-prompt interaction, etc. Therefore, it is advised to design security systems by accepting that the adversaries are already inside the system (Sabett, 2011). According to Foley (2011), the components required for a proactive and sustainable security program include preventive, detective, corrective and feedback mechanisms, from credentialing users and restricting their access through authorization of identity, time and place, to auditing, reviewing, monitoring, increasing security awareness and deterring inappropriate activity, to updating credentials, restricting or removing access based on the user's contribution to the compromise, severity of the compromise, and the risk of incident being repeated, to dynamic, reactive and planned feedback to create solutions (Foley, 2011).

In today's world where nearly everyone is digitally interconnected with each other, and where the Internet of Things (IoT) plays a very important role in the day to day life of people as they utilize the Internet for most of their activities including shopping, banking, managing their health, ordering their meals, etc. (Kim & Solomon, 2016), companies and organisation dealing with vast amounts of data and information are not the only subjects at risk of information security breaches, but any person connected to a network through a communication device of any sorts could be a victim of information security attacks (Senanayake & Fernando, 2017). Hence, it is of the utmost importance for any person using information systems for any purpose, whether professional or personal, to be cognizant in information security and be aware of threats and vulnerabilities they could be faced with, and thus, to acquire at least the basic knowledge on countermeasures against these threats and vulnerabilities. ISO/IEC 270001 (2005) emphasizes the importance of training, awareness and competence of users of an information security management system; while Peltier (2002) states that the user's level of awareness should be taken into consideration when developing security awareness programs (Peltier, 2002). This chapter intends to show that different users can obtain varying levels of education in different areas of information security education based on their job tasks and user roles and aims to bridge the gaps currently existing in most information systems and organisations by encouraging information system users to obtain the required education or awareness in order to minimize the risk of falling victim to cybercrimes.

DIFFERENT ASPECTS OF INFORMATION SECURITY

Information Security Subject Areas

The Certified Information Systems Security Professional (CISSP) certification defines eight CISSP domains as Security and Risk Management, Asset Security, Security Engineering, Communication and Network Security, Identity and Access Management, Security Assessment and Testing, Security Operations, and Software Development Security (Harris & Maymi, 2016).

The author identifies the basic subject areas of an overall information security education as listed below.

Subject Areas of an Information Security Education

- **Risk Assessment and Management:** Assessing potential risk factors to determine the appropriate level of security.

- Proper identification of all assets (including facility, hardware, software, data, human assets, knowledge, etc.).
- Valuation of assets (determine the value of assets based on the cost of acquiring new assets to replace assets if lost/damaged, cost of developing/getting the assets back to original state, cost of maintaining assets, cost of lost productivity when assets are unavailable, cost of replacing corrupt/lost data, value to owners and users, value to adversaries, value of intellectual property, price others are willing to pay for it, liability issues if assets are compromised, usefulness of assets, etc.).
- Identify threats to assets, their exposure rates and probabilities of risk.
  - Major risk categories include physical damage (for e.g.: fire, water, vandalism, power loss, natural disasters, etc.), human errors (i.e.: accidental/intentional action or inaction that disrupts productivity), equipment malfunction (i.e.: failure of systems and peripheral devices), inside and outside attacks (i.e.: hacking, cracking, attacking), misuse of data (for e.g.: sharing trade secrets, fraud, espionage, theft, etc.), loss of data (intentional/unintentional through destructive means), and application errors (for e.g.: computation, input, buffer overflows, etc.) (Harris & Maymi, 2016).
- Classify threats by category and calculate actual magnitude of potential loss in order to rank severity of identified vulnerabilities and prioritize potential risks.
- Identify possible security countermeasures to reduce identified risks to an acceptable level.
- Establish required level of security by implementing the suited security countermeasures selected through cost/benefit comparison (comparing security budget with the required protection; i.e.: the safeguard should only be implemented if the cost of loss of assets is greater than the cost of the safeguard).

- **Security Architecture and Models:** How the security model is determined based on security requirements and priorities of the organisation.
  - Classify data/information based on their criticality (i.e.: level of secrecy, value to the organisation, value to outside sources, the loss/damage that would occur should the data/information be disclosed/compromised, etc.).
  - Establish the role of trust, process activity, device maintenance, etc. within the organisation, and operating states, kernel functions, memory mapping, etc. of the systems used within the organisation.
  - Establish different user roles within the organisation.
  - Determine the security clearance levels of personnel based on their job descriptions (tasks needed to perform), need-to-know, department, occupation, level within the organisational hierarchy, and the least privileges required by them.
  - Determine the Security Model to be adapted by the organisation based on which factors/ objectives of information security (i.e.: main factors such as confidentiality, integrity, availability, and other factors such as accountability and non-repudiation) matter the most to the organisation (Harris & Maymi, 2016).
    - The most basic security model for when confidentiality is prioritized over other aspects is the Bell-laPadula model, which ensures no read-up and no write-down.
    - If integrity is the priority, the Biba model ensures no read-down and no write-up.

- Other security models include Clark-Wilson model, Information Flow model, Non-interference model, Brewer and Nash (Chinese Wall) model, Graham-Denning model, and Harrison-Ruzzo-Ullman model, etc.
  ○ Implement the organisation's security model based on security clearance levels of users and classification levels of data/information objects.
- **Security Management Practices:** How the organisation's security system is established and managed.
  ○ Evaluate business objectives, security risks, user productivity, functionality requirements and objectives of the organisation.
  ○ Establish security policies, procedures, standards, baselines, and best practices stating what to do and how to do it in order to ensure organisation's security.
  ○ Establish guidelines on how to act in unforeseen, unanticipated circumstances.
  ○ Determine the security consciousness and awareness levels of users; categorize users based on their level of understanding and observance of security principles, policies, procedures, guidelines and best practices, and conduct personnel security training and awareness.
    - Conduct periodic risk perception renewals to ensure that risk perception and security consciousness of users remain within an acceptable level.
- **Access Control Systems and Methodology:** Controlling access to information based on privileges assigned to a specific user or user role.
  ○ Authentication to verify user's identity/credentials to ensure they are who they claim to be.
    - Something the user knows (for e.g.: signature, password, personal identification number/PIN, passcode, key phrase, etc.).
    - Something the user has (for e.g.: key, swipe card, token, etc.).
    - Something the user is (biometrics, for e.g.: fingerprint, facial scan, voice print, iris scan, retina scan, palm scan, hand geometry, hand topology, signature dynamics, keyboard dynamics, etc.). Biometric authentication systems require proper calibration to reduce false negatives and false positives.
  ○ Verifying user's authorization to access the requested information.
    - Verify if the user has the need-to-know and authorization to access that information/data object based on the organisation's security model, by comparing the user's security clearance level with the information/data object's classification level.
    - Verify the methods or modes through which the user is allowed to access that information (for e.g.: through a graphical user interface, command line interface, direct access to the back-end database, etc.).
    - Validate what actions the user is allowed to perform on the information (i.e.: enter/input/create new information, view/read, update, or delete existing information).
    - Best method is to default to 'no access' and to allow access only to those users that have been explicitly authorized access rather than to first allow access to anyone who meets the criteria and then deny access to blacklisted users.
  ○ Proper identification and authentication of user and verification of authorization ensures accountability of users to their actions.
  ○ Single Sign-On (SSO) systems such as Kerberos allow users to access many interconnected systems during the session by signing on once.

- ◦ Access control models include Discretionary Access Control (DAC), Mandatory Access Control (MAC), and Role-Based Access Control (RBAC).
- ◦ Access control should happen at different levels and layers of the security system through physical, technical and administrative controls, starting with access to the facility at the security perimeter, access to the building, access to the user's computer, access to the system and network limited by access control lists (ACLs) implemented on firewalls, constrained user interfaces which limit access only to data/information objects a user is authorized to access, etc.
- ◦ Penetration testing should be conducted on the system periodically to ensure that access control mechanisms are solid and not easily penetrable.

- **Telecommunications and Network Security:** How network structures and communication systems are designed and implemented to ensure secure communication of information.
  - ◦ Network structure includes the architecture and design of the network and the material used for constructing it (Kim & Solomon, 2016).
    - ▪ Type of network (i.e.: wide area network/WAN, local area network/LAN, metropolitan area network/MAN, etc.), topology of the network (for e.g.: ring, bus, mesh, star topology, etc.), access technologies (for e.g.: Ethernet, token ring, Carrier-sense multiple access/CSMA with collision detection or collision avoidance, etc.), and wireless technologies (for e.g.: frequency hopping or direct sequence spread spectrum, etc.).
    - ▪ Wireless medium or cabling (for e.g.: coaxial or twisted pair copper cables, fibre optics, etc.) optimized for different parts of the network to ensure the least noise, attenuation, crosstalk, etc., while staying within a reasonable budget based on distance/length of cabling needed, fire rating of cabling material, network structure, type of transmission (whether analog or digital, asynchronous or synchronous, broadband or baseband), etc.
    - ▪ Intranets, Extranets, Network Address Translation (NAT), Internet Protocol (IP) addressing formats (i.e.: version 4 – Ipv4 or version 6 – Ipv6), subnets and subnet masks.
    - ▪ Firewall types (i.e.: Packet Filtering, Stateful Inspection, Application Proxy, etc.).
    - ▪ Firewall architectures for segregation and isolation of different network domains based on who has access to information in each domain and criticality of information (for e.g.: Bastion host, Screened host, Screened subnet with a demilitarized zone/DMZ between the public and private network portions, etc.).
    - ▪ Type of encryption, i.e. Link encryption (encrypt all data including headers, routing data, addresses, etc., along a communication path, requiring decryption at each hop, but providing extra protection against packet sniffers) or End-to-End encryption (where headers, addresses, routing data, etc. are not encrypted, thus eliminating the need for decryption at each hop).
  - ◦ Establish the devices (for e.g.: hubs, switches, routers, repeaters, bridges, gateways, etc.) to be used at different layers/levels of the network.
    - ▪ The International Standards Organisation's Open Systems Interconnected (ISO/OSI) 7-layered reference model consists of physical layer, data-link layer, network layer, transport layer, session layer, presentation layer, and application layer.
    - ▪ The Transmission Control Protocol / Internet Protocol (TCP/IP) 4-layered network model consists of network interface layer, internet layer, transport layer, and application layer.

○ Implement networking protocols best suited for the level of security needed based on who accesses information through the system, ways in which information is accessed, and how critical the information is.

- Networking protocols at transport layer include Transmission Control Protocol (TCP) and User Datagram Protocol (UDP), while protocols at the internet or network layer include Internet Protocol (IP), etc.

- Other protocols include Dynamic Host Configuration Protocol (DHCP), Internet Control Message Protocol (ICMP), Internet Message Access Protocol (IMAP), Simple Mail Transfer Protocol (SMTP), Post Office Protocol (POP), Simple Network Management Protocol (SNMP), Point to Point Protocol (PPP), Layer 2 Tunnelling Protocol (L2TP), Internet Protocol Security (IPSec), Transport Layer Security (TLS), Secure Socket Layer (SSL), Wireless Access Protocol (WAP), File Transfer Protocol (FTP), FTP over TLS/SSL (FTPS), Secure FTP (SFTP), Hypertext Transfer Protocol (HTTP), HTTP over TLS/SSL (HTTPS), etc.

○ Establish the ports for certain protocols and services as best suited for the organisation.

- Common ports include ports 20 and 21 for FTP, 25 for SMTP, 80 for HTTP, 110 for POP, 143 for IMAP, etc.

- Close all ports which are not being utilized, so as to not allow adversaries the chance to attack through those ports.

○ Establish network connection methods.

- Dedicated Links, Switching (i.e.: Packet Switching or Circuit Switching), Frame Relay, and Virtual Circuits.

- Remote Access, Virtual Private Network (VPN) and Tunnelling.

○ Establish policies on network usage.

- Times at which network access is allowed to ensure that no untimely access is possible, and to identify attempts to access the network at unusual times.

- Locations/terminals through which network access is allowed, remote access policies, etc. to limit access to the network from specified terminals/locations, and to identify attempts to access the network from unspecified remote locations, etc.

- Amount of network access allowed in one session, and number of sessions allowed per day, etc., so that access can be limited as needed, and excessive access or changes in access patterns could be identified.

- **Cryptography:** The art and science of disguising data.

  ○ Being Greek for 'hidden secret', cryptography is the way of storing and transmitting data in a form that can only be read and processed by its intended users/recipients.

  ○ Information can be protected by encoding/encrypting/enciphering it into an unreadable format, so as to hide it from unauthorized users.

  ○ The authorized users or intended recipients of the transmitted coded message can decode/decrypt/decipher it with the proper key.

  ○ The roots of cryptography run as far back as Egyptian hieroglyphics. Cryptography later evolved into a mechanism to securely pass messages through hostile environments (Harris & Maymi, 2016).

  - Used during wars by Spartans (i.e.: Scytale cipher, a papyrus sheet which can be read only if wrapped around a staff of the proper diameter), Greeks (for e.g.: messages tattooed on carrier's shaved head and covered by the growing hair, etc.), Mary, Queen of Scott's, and Benedict Arnold, all the way through to the Enigma machine used by the Germans during World War II (the cracking of which by the Turing machine is said to have shortened the war by two years).

- Early ciphers included 'Atbash Cipher' (a Hebrew cryptographic method which flips the alphabet over), and 'Caesar Cipher' (where Julius Caesar shifted the alphabet to the right by three positions).

○ Types of ciphers include substitution ciphers (where letters of the plaintext are substituted with different characters to create the cipher-text), transposition ciphers (where letters of the plaintext are scrambled to create the cipher-text), running key cipher (where the key may be hidden in the physical world and could for e.g. refer to a certain letter in a certain word in a certain line on a certain page of a certain book, etc.), and concealment cipher (where a certain agreed upon key, such as every third letter of the message, is used).

- Atbash Cipher, Caesar cipher, Vigenere Cipher, One Time Pad, etc. are examples of substitution ciphers.

○ Steganography is the method of hiding data in another media such as in an image, audio or video file.

○ Current encryption algorithms apply complex mathematical formulae in a specific sequence to plaintext in order to encrypt it.

○ The strength of the cryptosystem depends on the encryption algorithm (the more complex the algorithm, the more difficult it is to crack, and the higher the security), secrecy and length of the key (the longer it is, the more difficult it is for an adversary to guess it), and initializing vectors for key generation, etc.

- The stronger the cryptosystem, the more effort is needed to break it.
- A cryptosystem is considered strong if it is still secure when the encryption algorithm is made public and only the key is kept secret.

○ Stream ciphers perform mathematical functions on individual bits in a stream (where a key determines which functions are applied in what order), whereas block ciphers divide the plaintext message into blocks of bits and perform substitution, transposition, and other mathematical functions to it (where the algorithm dictates the functions to be used and the key dictates the order in which they should be used).

○ Cryptosystem can use symmetric keys (same key for decrypting as for encrypting) and asymmetric keys (different, but related key for decrypting than for encrypting).

- Symmetric keys are faster than asymmetric keys.
- By having a private key and public key combination (where the private key is secret and known only to its owner, and the public key is known by other users) asymmetric keys are much more secure, but carry significant overhead and are slower compared to symmetric keys.
- In addition to added security (by not sharing the private key), asymmetric keys also enable verification of sender's identity as the sender's private key acts as the sender's signature. In order to both ensure security and verify sender's identity, the message will have to be encrypted twice (once using the sender's private key, and once using the receiver's public key) and also decrypted twice (using the receiver's private key, and the sender's public key). Double encryption and double decryption adds further overhead

to the performance of asymmetric keys, but also verify the identities of both parties in secure communication.

- Symmetric cryptographic systems include Data Encryption Standard (DES), Triple-DES (3DES), etc., while asymmetric encryption algorithms include RSA (named after its inventors Rivest, Shamir, and Adleman), El Gamal, Elliptic Curve Cryptosystems (ECCs), etc.
- Hybrid methods utilize both symmetric and asymmetric keys to get the best of both worlds, by encrypting a symmetric session key using secure asymmetric keys, and then using the faster, symmetric session key for both encrypting and decrypting messages communicated within that session (thereby making the communication faster and more efficient due to lack of extra overhead), and then destroying that session key at the end of the communication session (to ensure further security).

- Public Key Infrastructure (PKI) uses the services of a Certificate Authority (CA) to vouch for the trustworthiness of parties (especially servers) included in communication (especially in client-server communications), by issuing a certificate verifying their identity. The CA is a third party trusted by both communicating parties.

- Hashing is a form of one-way encryption (where decryption is not possible, but message integrity can be verified by comparing against the original hash/message digest).
  - Password files should be stored in either encrypted or hashed form. It is best to hash the passwords and store the hash instead of the password itself. Then, each time the user enters their username and password combination, the entered password will be hashed and this hash will be compared against the stored hash corresponding to the entered username. If it is exactly the same, then the entered password is correct (as the smallest change to the plaintext will make a significant change in the hash) and the user is authenticated.
  - A hash value encrypted with the sender's private key creates their digital signature.
  - Hashing algorithms include MD5, Secure Hashing Algorithm (SHA) and HAVAL, etc.

- Cryptanalysis is the science of studying and breaking the secrecy of encryption algorithms.
  - Frequency analysis is comparing the most frequently used letters and words in the cipher-text to those in the alphabet of the plaintext, to figure out patterns and thereby figure out the key and break the cipher.

- Key management is important to ensure the trust on which cryptography is based.
  - Keys need to be securely distributed (protected during transmission, etc.) to the correct entities and continuously updated.
  - Key Escrows help by maintaining back-up keys in case they need to be recovered.
  - Multiparty control of emergency key reduces potential for abuse.

- Message and e-mail encryption standards include Multipurpose Internet Mail Extension (MIME), Privacy-Enhanced Mail (PEM), Message Security Protocol (MSP), Pretty Good Privacy (PGP), etc.

- **Physical Security:** The physical elements contributing to information security.
  - Information security begins with securing the perimeter and restricting access to secure areas within the facility.
    - Closed Circuit Television (CCTV), motion detectors, sensors, alarms, security guards, fences, walls, etc. help enforce perimeter security and physical access control.

- Monitoring activities, examining devices taken inside and outside of the facility, signing out material, etc. help to reduce and deter theft of physical items.
- Intrusion detection systems (for e.g.: proximity detection, photoelectric/photometric detection, wave pattern detection, passive infrared/IR, acoustical-seismic detection, electromechanical detection, vibration detection, etc.) and intrusion prevention systems help to detect and deter intruders. Alarms should notify law enforcement officials of intrusions.
  - Authorization methods and controls such as biometrics, individual access badges, magnetic swipe cards, wireless proximity readers (recognizing presence of approaching object), and tokens, etc., locked cases on individual computers, placing the most sensitive assets in guarded controlled zones, etc. add extra layers of security, and thereby multiple barriers that need to be circumvented in order to access resources.
  - Proper facility construction, protection from fire and water damage, proper heating, ventilation and air-conditioning (HVAC) controls, antitheft mechanisms, etc. are required to protect all assets of the organisation including human assets.
  - Main threats to physical security include theft, interruption of services, physical damage, compromised system integrity, unauthorized information disclosure, etc. (Harris & Maymi, 2016).
    - Location, visibility and accessibility of facility (i.e.: natural camouflage or attracting intruders), likelihood of natural disasters, construction material (fire protection/combustibility levels), load borne by walls, beams and columns, reinforcement for secured areas, implementation of physical controls such as fences, gates, locks, lighting, etc. should be considered before building the facility.
    - Placement of doors, windows, secure hinges, fire rating, resistance to forcible entry, directional opening (opening out from the facility), electric locks reverting to disabled state for safe evacuation in power outages (if a 'safety first' approach is followed), bulletproof/shatterproof glass, etc.
    - Load and weight bearing floors and ceilings, non-conducting surfaces and anti-static flooring, etc. Eliminate drop ceilings so intruders cannot lift ceiling panel and climb over partitioning walls.
    - Back-up and alternate electrical power supplies, back-up procedures in cases of power loss (as disabled IDS makes intrusion easier), clean and steady power source (without interference/line noise, fluctuation, electromagnetic interference/EMI, radio frequency interference/RFI, or transient noise.), proper placement of distribution panels and circuit breakers to allow easy access.
    - Surge protectors, orderly shutting down of devices, power line monitors, regulators, grounded connections, shielded lines (magnetic induction), three-prong connections and adapters. Avoid fluorescent lights (to eliminate RFI). Avoid plugging outlet strips and extension cords to each other.
    - Proper placement of water and gas lines, shut-off valves, positive flow (where material flows out of and not into the building).
    - Positive air pressure in HVAC systems, protected intake vents, dedicated power lines, emergency shut-off valves and switches, proper placement, etc.

- Fire detection and suppression through proper placement of the best suited type of sensors and detectors (i.e.: smoke activated, heat activated, or flame activated) and sprinklers (for e.g.: wet pipe, dry pipe, pre-action, deluge, etc.). Alternatives to sprinklers are to shut down air circulation, use carbon dioxide (CO_2), and alert fire station.
        - Illuminated and visible exit signs and unblocked fire exit doors to ensure safe evacuation in emergencies.
        - Regular monitoring of HVAC controls, climate controlled atmosphere, and reduced contaminants (corrosion, blockage, hazardous gases, etc.).
    - Location of facility components is important.
        - Data centres should not be located in top floors (in case of fire) or in basements (in case of floods), but at the core of the building (easy access to emergency crews).
        - Secure assets located in semi-secluded areas with limited accessibility.
        - Computer and equipment rooms located near wiring distribution centres, and having only a single access door (impossible to access through public areas).
    - Cipher (programmable) locks such as door delays (alarms triggered if held open too long), key-override (special key combination for emergencies overrides normal procedure), master-keying (supervisory personnel can change access codes), and hostage alarm (key combination alerting guards/police when under duress), etc., increase security.
    - Device locks for hardware include switch controls (covering on/off switches), slot locks (mounted bracket and steel cable securing system to stationary component), port controls (blocking access to drives/unused serial and parallel ports), peripheral switch controls (on/off switch between unit and slot), and cable traps (prevent removal of input and output devices by passing cables through lockable unit), etc.
    - Stationary, revolving doors and turnstiles for mantraps (small room with two doors, both needing authentication, but having entered through the first, the person is locked inside while guards verify their identity and unlock the second).
    - Weight detectors to prevent piggybacking (entering through a door that was opened for another person).
    - Physical access needs to be audited (date and time of access attempt, entry point, user identification, unsuccessful attempts, attempts at unauthorized times, etc.).
- **Applications and Systems Development Security:** Secure software development.
    - Integrate information security into the software development life cycle beginning with the requirements gathering phase (identify required level of security), moving on to the analysis and design phase (incorporate suitable security measures in the software design), through to the implementation phase (develop the designed security features), testing and debugging phases (also test security mechanisms for accuracy and correctness), deployment phase (configure security mechanisms properly), all the way through to the maintenance phase (constantly test, assess and update security mechanisms to suit current security needs).
    - Multiple layers of software security starting with the front-end user interface (validate user input to filter out invalid input or malicious code), through to the back-end database (screen and parse data before inserting it into the database).
    - Proper separation of user roles through the software system's user interface by only enabling and making visible the options for functionality that particular user/user role is authorized for.

- Not seeing other possible functionality available only to other users is an extra layer of security as not knowing about their existence helps limit users only to functionality that is allowed to them.
  - Options for users to select input from (i.e.: radio buttons, check boxes, drop-down menus, etc.) whenever applicable to reduce possible input errors.
  - Adopt best practices for programming/software development to ensure no room has been left for unforeseen security breaches.
    - Close back-doors/maintenance hooks (i.e.: alternate channels created by programmers to enable easy testing of the module instead of navigating through the proper access path each time) and other covert paths, which, if remained opened, would also allow unauthorized users access to the system.
    - Check for other programming loopholes which could lead to information security problems/breaches (for e.g.: buffer overflows, which can be exploited to enter lengthy inputs which overflow the buffer's boundaries and overwrite other memory locations adjacent to it, etc.).
- **Operations Security:** Ensure smooth operation of routine activities to allow the system to run in a secure manner.
  - Continually assess personnel and job functions, and provide training.
  - Monitor and audit activity, and ensure resource protection.
  - Security mechanisms can be categorized as preventive (to prevent an intrusion from happening), detective (to detect an intrusion once it has happened), deterrent (to deter or discourage intruders from attempting intrusion), corrective (to correct presently problematic mechanisms), and recovery (mechanisms such as data back-ups to help recover from attacks/intrusions).
  - Ensure standards compliance and due care.
  - Administrative management of personnel.
    - Enforce separation of duties (by breaking up high risk activities into multiple separate components to be carried out by different personnel) to ensure that a single user alone cannot compromise the organisation's security.
    - Job rotation to ensure that another person would be knowledgeable and experienced in handling the tasks of any person who is unavailable, and would thereby be able to step in.
    - Enforce 'least privilege' and 'need-to-know' principles to ensure users only have access to information and system resources they need to perform their tasks.
    - Mandatory vacations to allow the organisation time to find and correct any fraudulent activities should any have happened.
  - Change management to ensure smooth transition when required.
  - Back-up and recovery systems.
- **Business Continuity Planning and Disaster Recovery Planning:** How business impact analysis is performed to help recover from disasters and continue business.
  - Development, implementation and maintenance of a short term disaster recovery plan to deal with the disaster and its ramifications while still in emergency mode right after the disaster has struck.

- Minimize effects of a disaster by creating contingency plans to ensure that resources, personnel and processes can resume operation in a timely manner.
  - Longer term business continuity plan for continuing critical business operations in a different mode, through alternate channels, possibly at a different location, until regular conditions are available again.
  - Crisis management to deal with customers, suppliers, shareholders, and other stakeholders, in order to restore the organisation's reputation and regain the trust of these third parties.
  - Different back-up and recovery alternatives.
    - Concurrent/simultaneous soft back-ups such as to a Redundant Array of Inexpensive Disks (RAID), allow quick recovery to the latest data/information.
    - Frequent back-ups to storage media kept in a different location (within the facility) from the servers and other system resources allow somewhat fast recovery to recent data/information.
    - Less frequent, periodic hard back-ups where storage media is moved to a different location outside the facility, allow recovery (albeit not to the most recent data/information) from disasters which destroy the facility.
  - Proper, easy to reach, easily comprehensible documentation clearly detailing out the steps in recovery and restoration of assets.
  - Determine whether the organisation will adopt a 'safety first' approach (where human lives will be prioritized over the security of other assets) or a 'security first' approach (where the highly critical nature of data/information requires the prioritization of their security).
    - A safety first approach is preferable, allowing people to evacuate from the facility, even though the security of other assets could be compromised.
    - At high security organisations such as military organisations which deal with high risk data, unfortunately the facility would revert to complete lock-down to ensure that the security of its information assets cannot be compromised, even though that could also mean that personnel would also be trapped inside the facility during the disaster.
  - Periodic testing and drills to ensure people know how to respond in emergencies (based on emergency evacuation procedures, etc.) without panicking.
- **Security Laws, Investigations and Ethics:** The different components of Cyber-law.
  - Enforce software licensing and privacy to ensure that intellectual property rights are not violated.
  - Educate users on security laws, regulations and ethics which they should abide by, liability and ramifications of actions, etc.
  - Surveillance, search, seizure, and intrusion of privacy.
    - Constant surveillance or monitoring of user activity may intrude on user's privacy, but might be required at times though not very ethical.
  - Different types of digital evidence and their admissibility in court.
  - Incident handling practices to conduct forensic investigations with the least disruption to productivity and business operations (Volonino & Anzaldua, 2008).
  - Identification and prosecution of perpetrators, and protection of assets.
  - Software crimes and conducting digital forensic investigations without compromising the evidence, and while maintaining chain of custody, etc.

- **Information Security Attacks:** Methods and forms of attacks and possible countermeasures.
  - ○ Eavesdropping, network sniffing, wiretapping, intercepting/capturing data passing over the network, etc., are passive attacks, where the attacker is not affecting protocol, algorithm, key, message, or encryption system.
    - ▪ Passive attacks are hard to detect, thus should be prevented rather than detected.
    - ▪ Passive attacks are usually for reconnaissance before an active attack
  - ○ Altering messages, modifying system files, masquerading/spoofing, etc., are active attacks, where the attacker does something with the gathered data instead of simply reading it.
  - ○ Tools such as protocol analysers, port scanners, operating system (OS) fingerprint scanners, vulnerability scanners, exploit software, war-diallers, password crackers, keystroke loggers, etc., and malicious software such as viruses, worms, Trojan horses, rootkits, spyware, etc. could be used in information security attacks.
  - ○ Access control monitoring helps to keep track of attempts to log in (especially unsuccessful attempts), and thereby help identify any intrusion attempts.
  - ○ Honey pots are open (not locked-down) computers with their services enabled, but with no real company information, used to entice would-be attackers.
    - ▪ Enticement does not induce an attacker to commit the crime and is thus, legal. Entrapment, however, is inducing to committing a crime, and is thereby unethical and illegal.

Table 1 describes some of the more complex information security attacks and the security components they compromise.

Varying Depths and Areas of Information Security Education for Different Users

The information security subject areas listed in the previous section may seem daunting and intimidating, but not all users need to acquire knowledge about all these areas. While information security professionals require an in-depth knowledge in these to enable them to perform risk analysis, identify countermeasures, and implement solid security practices to help protect the facility, network, system, and information, by efficiently and predictably balancing risk with service (Harris & Maymi, 2016), software engineers, other IT professionals and students of computer and information sciences, etc. would require an overall understanding in information security, along with further exploration of certain identified domains. Even though each user of an information and communication system needs to be educated in information security in today's digitally interconnected world, for most users, a basic education on how to protect oneself and one's information assets in cyberspace would suffice.

Figure 1 depicts the varying depths of information security education in different subject areas required for different user roles based on their tasks in cyberspace.

Table 1. Complex information security attacks

Name	Description	Security Aspects Compromised
Man-in-the-middle	• Attack on asynchronous keys. • Man-in-the-middle intercepts the 1st user's public key before it reaches the 2nd user, replaces it with their public key and sends to the 2nd user, and masquerades as the 1st user to the 2nd user. • He then does the same with the 2nd user's public key, and masquerades as the 2nd user to the 1st user. • The users believe they are communicating with each other, but they are both communicating with the man-in-the-middle instead. • Can be averted by using a certificate signed by a trusted third party such as a CA.	Compromises confidentiality, integrity, and availability of the system.
Dictionary attack	• Attack on user authentication. • Run commonly-used passwords (or known words existing in a dictionary) through the encryption system to compare with passwords in the password file to find passwords.	Compromises the password and the authentication mechanism.
Brute-force attack	• Attack on user authentication. • Continually try different combinations of input until the correct password is uncovered. • Once part of the password is revealed through dictionary attack, it is easier to figure out the rest of the password through brute-force as there are fewer combinations required.	Compromises the password and the authentication mechanism.
Birthday attack	• Attack on the cryptographic system. • Mathematically exploiting the probability of finding a collision in the hash function by repeatedly evaluating the function through brute-force to compromise the hashed password files.	Compromises the hash algorithm, the passwords and the authentication mechanism.
Denial of Service (DoS) and Distributed Denial of Service (DDoS)	• Attack on network resources. • Flooding the network with unnecessary requests and occupying system resources by unnecessary tasks so as to deny service to legitimate users. • If all or most attacks originate from the same IP address, the system can track down and block requests from that IP address. • DDoS attack is when the requests originate from multiple different distributed locations and spoofed IP addresses so as to avoid detection.	Compromises the availability of system resources such as network, etc.
Phishing and Spear Phishing	• Attack on private information. • Trick users into providing private information such as credit card information, passwords, etc. via e-mails or instant messages, where the message appears to come from a legitimate source. • The obtained information is then used for identity theft. • Can be avoided by validating credentials before communicating, and by refraining from clicking on unknown links, etc. • Spear Phishing targets a specific organisation to gain unauthorized access into the system.	Compromises confidentiality of data and the authentication mechanism.
Pharming	• Attack on private information and DNS. • Poison the DNS to spoof IP addresses and thereby redirect users to a fake/bogus website where they would unknowingly provide their private information to the fake server/attacker. • Targets large groups of users simultaneously.	Compromises integrity of the DNS, and confidentiality of personal data.
Session Hijacking	• Attack on communication session. • Monitor connection to determine sequence numbers used by the two users, and generate traffic as if coming from one party. • Overload a legitimate user with excess packets to make them drop out of the session and steal the session from that user, and thereby take control of an existing communication between two users.	Compromises network and system availability.
Replay attack	• Attack on data transmission. • Capture data in transit and replay it later. • Can be prevented by enforcing time stamps, provided that the clocks of both parties in communication are synchronized.	Compromises network availability and the authorization mechanism.
Social Engineering	• Attack on human sociability and trust. • Trick people into unintentionally and unknowingly revealing confidential information.	Compromises data confidentiality.
Phreaking	• Attack on the telephone system. • Exploit bugs and glitches existing in the telephone system to gain unauthorized access to the system.	Compromises the authorization mechanism.
War-dialling	• Attack on the telephone system. • Insert a long list of phone numbers into a war-dialling program to find a modem that can be exploited to gain unauthorized access to.	Compromises the authorization mechanism.
Emanations capturing	• Attack on physical security of the facility. • Capturing electrical waves emanated into the surrounding environment to intercept transmitted information.	Compromises data confidentiality.
Asynchronous attack	• Attack on system booting. • Replace the boot-up instruction file with a malicious file during the time difference between when the system checks for the file and when it executes those instructions.	Compromises system availability and integrity.
Keystroke monitoring	• Attack on user authentication. • Review and record keystrokes entered by the user during an active session to figure out the user's authentication credentials.	Compromises the password and the authentication mechanism.
Shoulder surfing	• Attack on user authentication. • Look over the user's shoulder while the user is keying in their password/PIN to figure out the user's authentication credentials.	Compromises the password and the authentication mechanism.

Source: Compiled by the author with data obtained from Harris and Maymi (2016) and Kim and Solomon (2016)

Figure 1. Varying depths and areas of information security education for different users
Source: Compiled by the author

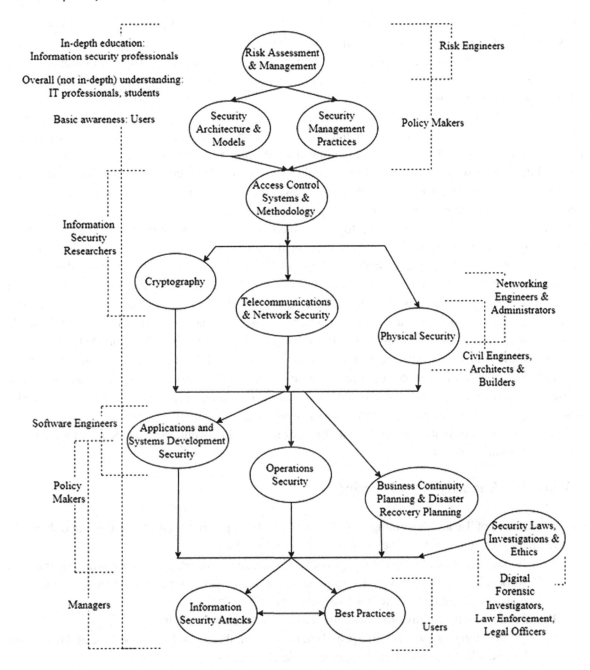

SOLUTIONS AND RECOMMENDATIONS

As a solution to the problem of being intimidated by the vast subject that entails information security, users can identify the aspects and depth of information security education they need based on their cyber-activities, as shown in Figure 1 in the previous section. Thus, information security professionals would need to study each of the subject areas shown in Figure 1 in-depth in order to understand the theoretical concepts behind information security, be able to identify information security risks, evaluate available information security tools, select the best tools and countermeasures for averting identified risks, gain experience and develop skills in using such tools in order to best configure and utilize them to suit the necessity and to constantly keep up with the information security of the organisation and information system. Information security policy makers should focus more on the areas of risk assessment and management, security architecture and models, security management practices, operations security, disaster recovery and business continuity planning, etc., while cryptologists and other such information security researchers will be focusing on new cryptographic methods, access control methodologies, and so on. Networking engineers and administrators will focus on the telecommunications and networking concepts, tools, architecture, models, etc., in order to figure out how best to design and implement the network of the system, whereas civil engineers, architects and builders will be focusing on how best to design and build the facility in the safest and most secure manner. Software engineers and software architects should study about secure software development and incorporate these practices in their work, while forensic experts and investigators, as well as law enforcement officials, should be knowledgeable about the security laws and other legal aspects of information security. While IT professionals and students of computer and information sciences require an overall understanding about each of these subject areas, all users of information systems should receive at least a basic awareness in information security in order to allow them to protect their information assets in cyberspace.

In addition, the information security best practices listed below would help users in further protecting their information assets.

Information Security Best Practices

- **Separation of Tasks:** Separating work-related tasks from personal tasks to ensure that only work-related cyber behaviour will be monitored (Fernando, 2014).
  - Avoiding personal web browsing, personal e-mails or instant messaging while engaged in work-related activities would help preserve the user's privacy better as their personal information will not be travelling across public networks, etc.
- **Password Security Behaviour:** Best practices for managing password security.
  - Adopt strong passwords with special characters, numbers, and both uppercase and lowercase letters, which are not obvious, and are difficult to guess.
  - Change password frequently, as the chances of a password being intercepted grow higher the longer a password is in use.
    - Avoid reusing former passwords.

- Avoid saving, writing down, or storing passwords in places easily accessible by others.
  - Use an algorithm that is meaningful in some sense to generate passwords that are not easily forgotten.
  - Avoid incorporating name, date of birth, address, etc. and other such personal information that can be easily found by others within one's password.
- Avoid sharing the same password across different applications.
- Avoid sharing passwords with others.
- **Data Back-Up Behaviour:** Frequently and periodically perform data back-ups (both work and personal data) in multiple forms and in multiple storage media to enable recovery of data should it be needed.
- **Data Sanitization Behaviour:** Ensure that unnecessary copies (both hard and soft copies) of data are destroyed (Bishop, Bhumiratana, Crawford, & Levitt, 2004).
  - Regularly sanitize external storage media.
  - Control access by others to personal storage media.
  - Minimize using storage media belonging to others, and when used ensure that they are scanned before use and sanitized after use before returning them.
  - Periodically delete temporary files, cookies, browsing history, saved passwords, etc.
- **Network Security Behaviour:** Best practices concerning network security.
  - Ensure that firewalls are enabled.
    - If firewalls were disabled or relaxed to allow different applications access to the system, and if privileges were escalated to allow installation of software, etc., reset escalated privileges and re-enable firewalls after installation of programs.
  - Periodically update antivirus software and scan computer disks and drives.
  - Check for authenticity of websites (requesting certificates by trusted CAs), e-mail attachments, etc. before clicking on links or opening attachments.
  - Validate credentials of the other party before correspondence.
- **Physical Security Behaviour:** Best practices concerning physical security (Fernando, 2014).
  - Be aware of the surrounding (whether other people are around, whether one's computer monitor is visible to others, etc.).
  - Lock computers when leaving the desk.
  - Lock cupboards, desks, office, home, vehicle, etc.
  - Ensure that confidential or personal items (documents, computers, storage media, password hints, etc.) are not left unattended.
  - Avoid sharing personal items with others whenever possible (for e.g.: lending or borrowing keys, etc.), and exercise caution should such a need arise.
  - Avoid using unknown items without validation.

FUTURE RESEARCH DIRECTIONS

Information security has always been and will continue to be a game between the good and evil doers. As one strives to strengthen their security system by patching up holes, eliminating vulnerabilities, improving the strength and efficiency in encryption algorithms, networking protocols, etc., another would find a way to circumvent that new security mechanism. Unfortunately, in most cases, the tools used for ethical hacking and penetration testing by organisations to test the strength of their security systems are themselves used by adversaries to intrude into those systems. Yet, in order to ensure the protection of people and their information assets in cyberspace, new research concerning cryptography (such as lattice encryption, etc.), network security, data sanitization, digital forensics, access control, and other areas of information security should and will continue to emerge.

CONCLUSION

Even though there are many facets to information security, and acquiring an education in information security is not a simple task, it is mandatory to be cognizant in information security in order to protect oneself and one's information assets in cyberspace. Being intimidated by the vast subject range of information security is no reason to stay away from today's heavily interconnected cyber-world. Instead, one can obtain an awareness and basic education in information security that would suffice to help stay protected in cyberspace. As the depth and areas of information security education required by different users vary based on their user roles and cyber-activities, those users who require in-depth education in certain areas of information security can obtain such in-depth education, while other users can obtain only a basic awareness and understanding as deemed appropriate.

REFERENCES

Bishop, M. (2003). *Computer Security – Art and Science*. Boston, MA: Pearson Education.

Bishop, M., Bhumiratana, B., Crawford, R., & Levitt, K. (2004). How to sanitize data. *Proceedings of the 13th IEEE International Workshops on Enabling Technologies: Infrastructure for Collaborative Enterprises*.

Fernando, S. (2014). *Internal Control of Secure Information and Communication Practices through Detection of User Behavioural Patterns*. Niigata, Japan: Nagaoka University of Technology.

Foley, K. (2011). Maintaining a proactive and sustainable security program while hosting and processing personally identifiable information. *Information Systems Security Association Journal, 9*(5), 25–32.

Gonzalez, J. J., & Sawicka, A. (2002). A framework for human factors in information security. *Proceedings of 2002 World Scientific and Engineering Academic Society International Conference on Information Security*.

Grimes, R. A. (2010). How to thwart employee cybercrime. *Insider Threat Deep Drive – Combating the Enemy Within, InfoWorld – Special Report*, 2-7. Retrieved August 5, 2012, from http://resources.idgenterprise.com/original/AST-0001528_insiderthreat_2_v1.pdf

Harris, S., & Maymi, F. (2016). *CISSP All-in-One Exam Guide* (7th ed.). New York, NY: McGraw-Hill Education.

ISO/IEC 270001. (2005). *Information technology – Security techniques – Information security management systems – Requirements*. Geneva, Switzerland: ISO.

Kahneman, D., & Tversky, A. (1979). Prospect theory: An analysis of decision under risk. *Economoetrica, 47*(2), 263–291. doi:10.2307/1914185

Kim, D., & Solomon, M. G. (2016). *Fundamentals of Information Systems Security* (3rd ed.). Burlington, MA: Jones & Bartlett Learning.

Lacey, D. (2009). *Managing the Human Factor in Information Security: How to win over staff and influence business.* West Sussex, England: Wiley.

Liu, A., Martin, C., Hetherington, T., & Matzner, S. (2005). A comparison of system call feature representations for insider threat detection. In *Proceedings of the 2005 IEEE Workshop on Information Assurance.* West Point, NY: United States Military Academy. 10.1109/IAW.2005.1495972

Lynch, D. M. (2006). Securing against insider attacks. *Information Security and Risk Management,* 39-47. Retrieved August 5, 2012, from http://www.csb.uncw.edu/people/ivancevichd/classes/MSA%20516/Supplemental%20Readings/Supplemental%20Reading%20for%20Wed,%2011-5/Insider%20Attacks.pdf

Mills, R. F., Grimaila, M. R., Peterson, G. L., & Butts, J. W. (2011). A scenario-based approach to mitigating the insider threat. *Information Systems Security Association Journal, 9*(5), 12–19.

Ning, P., Jajodia, S., & Wang, X. S. (2003). *Intrusion Detection in Distributed Systems – An Abstraction-Based Approach.* Norwell, MA: Kluwer Academic Publishers.

Peltier, T. R. (2002). *Information Security Policies, Procedures and Standards: Guidelines for Effective Information Security Management.* Boca Raton, FL: Auerback Publications.

Sabett, R. V. (2011). Have you seen the latest and greatest "security game changer"? *Journal of Information Systems Security Association, 9*(5), 5.

Schneier, B. (2008). *The psychology of security.* Retrieved August 5, 2012, from http://www.schneier.com/essay-155.html

Schweitzer, J. A. (1996). *Protecting Business Information.* Newton, MA: Butterworth-Heinemann.

Senanayake, T., & Fernando, S. (2017). Information Security Education: Watching your steps in cyberspace. *Proceedings of the International Science and Technology Conference 2017.*

Volonino, L., & Anzaldua, R. (2008). *Computer Forensics for Dummies.* Indianapolis, IN: Wiley Publishing.

Vroom, C., & von Solms, R. (2003). Information security: Auditing the behaviour of the employee. *IFIP TC11 18th International Conference on Information Security (SEC2003).*

West, R. (2008). The psychology of security. *Communications of the ACM, 51*(4), 34–41. doi:10.1145/1330311.1330320

Williams, B. R. (2011). Do it differently. *Journal of Information Systems Security Association, 9*(5), 6.

KEY TERMS AND DEFINITIONS

Authentication: Validating the identity of a subject. Proving that a subject is actually who they claim to be.

Authorization: Granting privileges and allowing access to objects for specified subjects.

Availability: The ability to use services and resources when requested.

Cipher-Text: Data that is encoded into an unreadable format.

Confidentiality: The ability to ensure secrecy and prevent unauthorized disclosure of information.

Countermeasure: A safeguard to mitigate potential risk by eliminating the vulnerability.

Identity: The name by which a subject can be uniquely identified.

Integrity: The correctness and accuracy of data or information.

Plaintext: Un-coded data that is human- or machine-readable.

Chapter 8
Optimized Three–Dimensional Security Framework to Mitigate Risks Arising From BYOD–Enabled Business Environment

Lizzy Oluwatoyin Ofusori
University of KwaZulu-Natal, South Africa

Ncamiso Nkululeko Jahalenkhosi Dlamini
University of KwaZulu-Natal, South Africa

Prabhakar Rontala Subramaniam
University of KwaZulu-Natal, South Africa

ABSTRACT

Bring your own device (BYOD) has infiltrated the work environment and businesses are enjoying the benefits coupled with the adoption of the trend. At the same time, the adoption of BYOD has introduced a number of security threats that businesses are failing to match. In the pursuit of addressing security threats that are introduced by the adoption of this technology trend, this chapter recommends a three-dimensional (3-D) security framework that can be used to mitigate the risks emanating from a BYOD enabled environment. Data was collected from the employees of two banks in Africa that supported BYOD trend to measure individual and organizational practices. This chapter investigates further on these practices in addressing implications of BYOD. Three categories of security threats are delineated in this chapter. A review of existing security frameworks is presented in this chapter. The chapter concludes by outlining a 3-D security framework as a potential solution to protect BYOD enabled business environment.

DOI: 10.4018/978-1-5225-4763-1.ch008

INTRODUCTION AND BACKGROUND

Mobile technologies are increasingly becoming a preferred way of communication as a result of the evolution of the fourth Industrial revolution (Niesen, Houy, Fettke, & Loos, 2016). Most manufacturing organizations continuously evolve into smart and interconnected production systems. As mobile devices are becoming more dependable, they are also becoming prevalent in workplaces (Astani, Ready, & Tessema, 2013). This pervasiveness has enabled Bring Your Own Device (BYOD) in most organizations. BYOD is a growing trend that allows individuals of an organization to bring their own devices such as smartphones, laptops and tablets to work. This interconnectivity of smart devices has resulted in massive amounts of data from individuals, organizations and society (Niesen et al., 2016). Hence, the likelihoods of millions of people connected by mobile devices, with unprecedented storage capacity, processing power and access to knowledge, are unlimited. This data from individuals results in lack of privacy, data from organizations leads to lack of integrity while data from society leads to security issues. Presently, the number of mobile devices connected to the internet is more than the population of the world. This margin will keep expanding and thus create an avenue for cyber-attack in large scale.

The effect of allowing individuals to access any network with their mobile devices has impacts on network access, network control, helpdesk resources and even information ownership (Astani et al., 2013). Similarly, protection of organizational data becomes a challenge because these personal gadgets are mobile, hence employee are able to carry company data wherever they go. Some other security challenges such as keeping the network malware-free, understanding who and what is on the network, lack of control over the amount of information that should be stored at the endpoint on a BYOD device and giving the appropriate access policies to enforce compliance and audit requirements were identified by Astani et al. (2013). As technological development continues to grow, the threat to individual, organizations and society also increases (Lee, 2015). The major concern is how the connectivity can be harnessed for productive use without affecting privacy, security and integrity.

This chapter provides an overview of the BYOD trend and some key attributes that led to BYOD becoming a business standard. This chapter further presents the security threats and legal issues that confront organizations together with current practices that have been adopted to cushion against these threats. A framework is proposed to illustrate the distinction amongst threats that continuously affect businesses and the society at large through embracing the BYOD trend. A discussion explaining the difference between threats emanating from BYOD adoption and the Cyberspace is provided. Thus, the chapter proposes a 3-D BYOD security framework that can be used to prioritize awareness in order to ensure data integrity is maintained by all means.

In order to measure the BYOD security threats, some data were collected from the banking sectors in the African continent: Nigeria and Swaziland. These two countries are considered from two different extremes: Nigeria is one of the countries where the use of technology is accepted and is being used by the population at large. There are policies and a regulatory framework that have been incorporated to support the use of technology (Umar, 2015). On the other hand, Swaziland is one of the economically under developed countries in the continent. At present, there are no policies that have been implemented that specifically regulate the use of personal gadgets in the work environment. Swaziland has inadequate policy and regulatory frameworks; consequently, the integration of information and communication technologies (ICT) is currently uncoordinated and uncontrollable regardless of the current initiatives (Madzima, Dube, & Mashwama, 2013). As a result, there is lack of adequate planning, technical support and inadequate infrastructure which affects the introduction and adoption of ICT in the country (Madzima et al., 2013).

LITERATURE REVIEW

Evolution of BYOD

The infiltration of personally owned mobile devices like smartphones gave birth to the Bring Your Own Device (BYOD) phenomenon, where personal gadgets started entering the workspace. According to Copeland and Crespi (2012), the technological world witnessed a new paradigm shift in consumerization, where individuals were not just bringing personal devices but started using web applications for work tasks. Zahadat, Blessner, Blackburn, and Olson (2015) define BYOD as a movement that has been around for some time, characterized by individuals bringing their own personal gadgets to the workplace and installing preferred programs to accomplish tasks assigned to them. Broomhead (2013) redefined this movement using statement like "the rise of mobility and marginalization of the PC" and "move-and–do culture".

Efforts were made to stop the infiltration. For example, IT departments were disabling USB ports on company PCs and they used central software based on policy controls to monitor desired workstations to extents that were deemed necessary (Zahadat et al., 2015). Organizations' efforts to stop these privately-owned devices from entering their environments were not successful but they had no option but to acknowledge that employees would always want to use their mobile devices in their working area. Employees would always make a case and argue that consumer apps were cheaper (Harris, Ives, & Junglas, 2012). This resulted in mobile devices owned by employees, and the organizations provided financial and technical support for these devices (Vignesh & Asha, 2015). IT departments had to adjust their budgets and increase security measures to accommodate personal devices entering the work environment. Gartner (2012) considers the use of mobile devices in the workplace to be among the ten most important strategic trends. Broomhead (2013) echoes Gartner by mentioning that BYOD has become disruptive in the sense that employees always want to bring personal devices to the organization and want to connect to everything. Consequently, these connections are without proper accountability or oversight.

Moavenzadeh (2016) a member of the Management Committee of the World Economic Forum and head of mobility industries, raised the following concerns about the fourth industrial revolution. Firstly, the agility and fast pace in technology innovation has led to there not being a clear cut meaning of privacy and security as a result of real time availability of information. Secondly, how will the technology world collaborate to build regulatory frameworks and standards that promote growth and adoption of new technologies? According to Schwab (2016), the fourth industrial revolution profoundly affects the nature of security in businesses. Thus, the recommended framework in this chapter can be the first step in dealing with regulatory mandates that have strict security measures in order to promote compliance in businesses. Basically, the framework can help in data management since the fourth industrial revolution has shifted the focus to develop cyber-physical systems to monitor and control physical processes (Stancioiu, 2017). Understanding the security domains covered in this chapter can also serve as a decision framework or tool that can help businesses comprehend and prioritize the needs of employees and goals of the organization at large.

Benefits of BYOD in the Fourth Industrial Revolution

As mobile technologies are increasingly becoming a preferred way of communication in the fourth industrial revolution (Niesen et al., 2016), the possibilities of billions of people connected by mobile devices, with unprecedented storage capacity, processing power, and access to knowledge, are unlimited. These possibilities are increased by the emerging trend of BYOD in most organizations. Copeland and Crespi (2012), outline different steps that most of the organizations took in adopting BYOD. Firstly, companies started encouraging personal devices and connecting them to corporate internet servers. Secondly, companies started connecting personal devices to corporate applications. Finally, the companies stopped providing phones and laptops to employees thereby adopting the option of BYOD strategy. According to Bello, Armarego, and Murray (2015), BYOD became a compelling trend because organizations embraced the following benefits: lower costs, increased productivity and less technical training to employees. Lebek, Degirmenci, and Breitner (2013) mentioned that by adopting BYOD, organizations realized that there was greater freedom and flexibility, increased motivation and easier adoption of the technology. Another benefit identified by Baldassari and Roux (2017) is smart connectivity. Through smart connectivity, mobile devices and company systems can now interact to deliver greater efficiencies and capabilities, hence, there is optimized software, hardware and people (Baldassari & Roux, 2017). Understanding and realizing the benefits of the BYOD trend and the recommended framework delineated in this chapter can contribute to coming up with initiatives that can improve all business dimensions.

Individual Practices

The sudden rise in the usage of mobile devices has significantly increased the figure of interconnected devices to 12.5 billion while the population of the world is at 6.8 billion as at 2010 (Cisco, 2013). As a result of the high rate of growth of personal mobile devices connecting to corporate networks, it is unsurprising that the number of security incidents is also expected to grow. According to Company85 Briefing (2012), most of the personally owned devices connect to many unregulated networks such as restaurants, cafes and bars. Another study conducted by Cisco (2013) also revealed that 69 per cent of mobile device users had unapproved applications installed on their mobile device. However prior to the installation of these apps, mobile device users sometimes grant access requests to device resources as part of terms and conditions to install (Disterer & Kleiner, 2013). This leads to privacy invasion as users' private information can now be used without their knowledge. Also some of these downloaded applications are malicious and thus pave the way for hackers to penetrate and hack into the system(Pratt Jr & Jones, 2013). A recent study by Uz, (2014) points out that the adoption of cloud storage services as a concern for security of corporate data. Most employees are now using cloud services (e.g. iCloud, Drop box and Google drive) because of the insufficient memory on their mobile devices. These cloud storage services enable employees to copy files into the cloud for later retrieval but corporate information residing in such services may pose a security risk since they no longer reside in the protected corporate boundaries (Uz, 2014). The various mobile devices brought to work by employees make it challenging for the IT department to track the applications running on these devices. Similarly, most employees devices are not configured by the organization and thus pose a security threat (Disterer & Kleiner, 2013). The individual practices would have been stopped but most organizations have adopted this practice because of the profound benefits they derived from it and this has gradually led to the practice in organizations.

Organization's Practices

The organization's principles, policies and values define the practices of employees within the organizations. Some organizations carry out training to ensure employees' compliance to laid down principles and security policies governing the sector. This helps to avoid any form of security threats that may arise in the course of employees discharging their duties. However, Osterman Research (2012) points out that allowing personal devices to be used within the BYOD environment implies catering for the risks that it can bring into the organization. Tu and Yuan (2015) add that by allowing the use of personal devices, information security becomes exposed to new risks. One of the alarming concerns is the protection of valuable assets of organizations. Valuable assets refer to the information that is recorded, processed or stored and which the organization holds the ownership of (Bello et al., 2015). Protection of organizational data becomes a challenge because these personal gadgets are mobile; hence employees are able to carry company data wherever they go. According to report by Dimensional Research (2014), among organizations that allow personal devices to connect to corporate networks 93 per cent face challenges adopting BYOD policies, 94 per cent raise a concern over lost or stolen device, 66 per cent admit higher security risk for careless employees than cybercriminals. Another survey by Aruba Network (2013) pointed out that 75 per cent of IT managers have expressed concern about BYOD devices. Since BYOD enables employees to access corporate data any place, any time, it is important to ensure the security of corporate information and assets.

It is essential to protect confidentiality of corporate data on devices used within a BYOD environment. Furthermore, it is not only essential to protect confidentiality of corporate data, but also important to monitor and reject unauthorized and illegal access of corporate data. Unauthorized access comes from insiders (employees) when they are not supposed to access corporate data. Illegal access comes from outsiders when they want to recover corporate data stored on a device, e.g. malicious users try to steal data from a lost device. Once data is downloaded to a device, it is easy to make copies and transfer files from the device to other media. Thus, unauthorized and illegal data access on personal devices should be monitored and rejected.

Legal Issues in BYOD

Allowing employees to use their mobile devices for work purposes has raised a number of legal concerns. In a BYOD context, legal concerns emphasize properly addressing the existing policies, regulations and legislations between employers and employees (Lebek et al., 2013). The BYOD philosophy causes violations of working hour regulations (Lebek et al., 2013) because employees are forever connected to jobs even after working hours. Employees are able to access work material on weekends even on vacations. Consequently, this can lead to employees demanding compensation for the expanded working hours (Lebek et al., 2013). In addition to that, there is an assumption that employees are concerned about being liable when corporate information gets lost and when employees lose or damage their devices.

Implications of BYOD

In recent years, companies have enjoyed the compelling advantages of BYOD (Bello et al., 2015). Firstly, there is the low corporate cost whereby the acquisition and maintenance of these devices is solely the responsibility of the employee. Secondly, simplicity of use and the availability of content is another factor that has prompted the adoption of the BYOD (Dunnett, 2012). There is less technical training required for employees due to employees using mobile devices they are familiar with (Bello et al., 2015). Thirdly, BYOD has proved to increase employee productivity and efficiency as employees are no longer confined to do work only when they are on the organizational premises. They can now carry corporate data wherever they are (Garba, Armarego, Murray, & Kenworthy, 2015). Bello et al. (2015) concur that BYOD has become common in the corporate place and it is re-organizing ownership and control of organizational information systems and resources. BYOD has infiltrated a number of companies, there has been one major drawback: making end users or employees aware of the different threats introduced by using personally owned mobile devices for work purposes.

The issue of privacy has been one of the major concerns since BYOD has made the line between work and private become less distinct. Mora et.al. (2015), assert that different studies reveal that it becomes a challenge to distinguish between personal and organizational data once employees use their personal devices in an organizational context. From a business point of view, it raises the question of data integrity as company data is moved from corporate network to a personal device which the company has no control over. In a BYOD aspect, the privacy aspect focuses on employees' concern that their personal information (e.g. photos, emails, GPS data) becomes at the employer's disposal (Lebek et al., 2013). There is privacy invasion once an employer wants access to an employee's personal device hence such actions can lead to litigation if the subject of privacy is not properly addressed. Securing personally owned devices has become a nightmare for ICT departments because each new device brought into the company leaves the company with less control over what is transmitted and most importantly how it is transmitted (Twinomurinzi & Mawela, 2014). This difficulty emanates from the fact that personal devices are not locked down or configured to corporate standards to determine the amount of access that can be given to each personal device. BYODs are extensions of enterprise networks (Wang, Wei, & Vangury, 2014). However, it is difficult to ensure compliance with enterprise security policies for BYODs (Wang et al., 2014). Although there are some BYOD security measures, they all have limitations when applied on a BYOD environment. Furthermore, BYODs are personal devices which are mostly adopted for business use. It is practically not possible to manually review an employee's personal device due to the large number of devices and also the ownership. Alternative automatic options should be explored to enforce enterprise security policies on a BYOD (Xu, Saïdi, & Anderson, 2012)

BYOD SECURITY THREATS AND CYBER THREATS

A cyber threat is any malicious act that attempts to gain access to a control system and/or computer network without permission or authorization from the owners (Olasanmi, 2010). Today, cyberspace is witnessing the advent of a complete range of mobile devices and applications that have made organizations susceptible to security threats from all types of miscreants. Cybercriminals take advantage of the fact that almost everyone uses a mobile device and as such make it easy to spread threats through the pervasive technology (Wada & Odulaja, 2012). A typical example is the recent security threat called "wannacry ransomware" that has affected about 74 countries (Ehrenfeld, 2017). This security threat must have started from an individual, then organizations, before affecting the society which involves about 74 countries. As BYOD evolves, cyber criminals have now targeted mobile devices. The main difference between BYOD security threats and cyber threats is found in what the literature describes as concerns (Brodin, 2016). For BYOD there is an extra factor which creates even more concern; risk of mixing the organization's and the employee's personal data, software licensing issues, shared use of devices with non-employees and when the employee leaves the organization. There is a high risk that the organization's data is mixed with private data, and in the end, it will be difficult to distinguish who owns what. Similarly, when an employee leaves the organization, the person keeps the device where the data is stored. The responsibility for protecting BYODs has always been the users' responsibility. However, the move of organizational control of the device to private individuals raises security concerns and increases the demand on the user for security awareness (Brodin, 2016).

Security Threats Resulting From BYOD

While organizations in an effort to boost productivity and increase service delivery use ICT, they are confronted with inherent security threats frustrating the advancement of its progress (Ehimen & Bola, 2010). However, these threats can be categorized under technical, mobility and social threats. Figure 1, shows the categories security threats.

Visual Perspective of the Risk Levels

Figure 2 provides a visual perspective of how the three categories of the security threats are interwoven and constitute a security risk to any organization. Low risk (LR) represents those threats that are specific to the each domain. The threats contributing to the intersection of two domains represents medium risk (MR). While the threats contributing to the intersections of three domains in the 'Venn diagram' represent high risk (HR); which is invisible to the current security measures (refer Figure 2)

HR constitutes those threats that cut across the technical, social and mobility domains. They can be very harmful to the banking sector as they bring down the three domains at the same time. MR are security threats that are harmful but not to the same extent as the HR and are more harmful than the LR. These threats are only related to two domains and can bring down the two domains if the right security measures are not put in place. Meanwhile, LR are security threats that are harmful but not to the same scale as the other two risks (HR and MR). These security threats are only related to a particular domain; it does not affect more than one domain. The following sections identify the threats under each domain and classify them within the appropriate category. Although the MR is the intersection of two domains, they are categorized under a particular domain based on their characteristics.

Figure 1. Categories of security threats (Author's own)

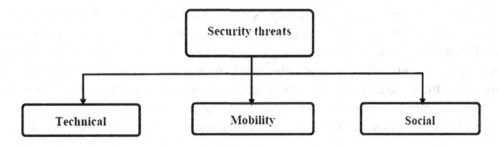

Figure 2. Classification of the risk levels (Author's own)

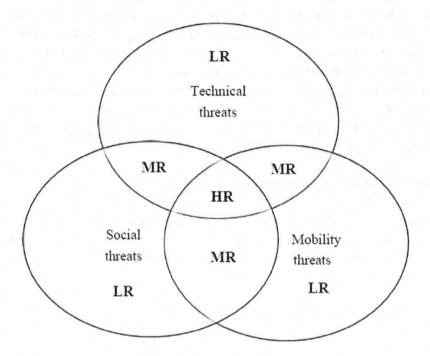

Technical Threats

In the context of this chapter, the technical threats represent threats emanating from the technical knowledge in the use of mobile device. It is important to identify these threats because by their very nature, they are complex to detect yet harmful to mobile device users and organizations to the extent they expose them to other threats that require a separate security management. The following section presents some of the key technical threats related to mobile device users in any organizations.

Phishing

One of the major concern is the issue of phishing, where hackers are using any means to gain access, and intercept personal and company sensitive data. This is not just any attack, but a selective attack known as spear phishing where specific personnel and their company are being targeted once the attacker has specific knowledge about the company and the individual (Ngoqo & Flowerday, 2015). A hacker may send an email to management asking them to respond to an attached survey on how the company executes performance management. The managers may fall for this phish and download the survey, which automatically installs malware to the company network. Phishing can take many forms; attackers have shifted from using emails to instant messaging, social networking sites and short message service (SMS). According to Hong (2012), spear phishing attacks have victimized big entities like the Australian Prime Minister's Office and the Canadian government between the year 2010 and 2011. Thus, the study highlights the importance of awareness mainly because phishing is not just a technical issue but also a social issue. Phishing is capable of infiltrating any organization regardless of the powerful firewalls, proxy servers and encryptions the company may have. The main points of entry into an organization are individuals not the systems put in place. What it takes is to deceive a person and that person innocently gives information to the wrong person. It is imperative for employees and employers to be educated on such issues to prevent them from falling for a phish. Thus, phishing can be regarded as LR as it requires the consent of a targeted person or organization to respond or download an attached email.

Malware

Malware is a well-known threat to mobile devices and is speedily increasing as a result of BYOD implementation (Felt, Finifter, Chin, Hanna, & Wagner, 2011). Malware is often disguised as a patch, game, utility, or third-party software application that can be installed, which may include viruses, spyware and Trojans (Gharibi, 2012). As soon as it is installed on mobile devices, it can cause massive attacks (Pratt Jr & Jones, 2013). The malicious application can function in numerous ways such as accessing sensitive information, accessing location information, activating the device's camera or microphone in order to record information, initiating phone calls or gaining access to user's browsing history (Felt et al., 2011). For example, Wannacry is a type of malware that gets into the computer or mobile device through email attachments or WhatsApp messages, and automatically encrypts every file (Ehrenfeld, 2017). Malware can also be regarded as LR because it requires the cooperation of the targeted individual or organization to comply by installing disguised software or opening an attachment. This can be prevented if the user is aware of what constitutes a potential threat.

Keystroke Logging

This is when an attacker monitors and archives keystrokes in order to access sensitive information (Boyles, Smith, & Madden, 2012). Key loggers' common practice is that they transmit information gathered to a cybercriminal's website or email address (Boyles et al., 2012). Thus the study emphasizes employee awareness and education on security threats in order for employees to understand the consequences of their mobile device activities. Keystroke logging, also known as key logging, is used to record typed characters on mobile devices in order to capture valuable or sensitive information such as user's ID, password and credit card numbers (Ladakis, Koromilas, Vasiliadis, Polychronakis, & Ioannidis, 2013). The captured information is usually transferred to a cyber-criminal email address or website (Pratt Jr & Jones, 2013). Keystroke logging can be considered LR because it only records typed characters on mobile devices, however, if employees are well informed, it can be avoided.

Rogue Device

A rogue device can be defined as an unauthorized connection of mobile devices to the network which pose a security threat to the organization (Golde, Redon, & Borgaonkar, 2012). It is used to breach the key areas of security for mobile subscribers such as intercepting communication, impersonating traffic, and tracking phones (Chen, Chen, Lin, & Sun, 2014; Golde et al., 2012). Rogue device can be considered LR because it can easily be detected if the organization puts the right security measures in place.

Data Interception

Data interception refers to the obstruction of data transmission to and from the device, and remotely altering the messages (Evripidis, 2008). This can be a major threat to wireless networks used by BYOD devices (Bello et al., 2015). If information is sent over the internet by a mobile user and it is intercepted, it becomes a serious concern, because of the risk that the data can be accessed, edited, or destroyed. Data such as personal information, chats, emails and passwords are being intercepted using a tool called packet sniffer or packet analyzer (Wu, 2009). Mobile devices such as smartphones, tablets and laptops are easily commjacked. This is when an attacker spies on data exchanges being transmitted to a mobile device (Evripidis, 2008). Public Wi-Fi has been good medium exploited by attackers. Attackers will capture and alter data packets between devices when mobile devices connect to unsecure Wi-Fi networks; this is referred to as a man-in-the-middle attack (Bello et al., 2015). Thus data interception can be regarded as MR because it remotely intercepts and alters messages sent to and from devices. In some instances, the user may not be aware that the message has been altered.

Network Exploit

Mobile systems that operate on cellular or local (e.g. Wi-Fi or Bluetooth) networks often experience software flaws (Pratt Jr & Jones, 2013). Network exploits take advantage of such flaws to propagate malware and in most cases they succeed without user interference. Attackers make use of special tools to find users on a Wi-Fi network and hijack the users' information which is then used to impersonate a user online (NEEDHAM & Lampson, 2008). Furthermore, there is a possible attack known as bluesnarfing which gives attackers access to sensitive information (e.g. credit card details) by exploiting a software flaw in a Bluetooth-enabled device (Pratt Jr & Jones, 2013). Thus network exploit can be considered MR because it takes the advantage of software flaws to propagate malware and in most cases they succeed without user interference.

Mobility Threats

Mobility threats refer to those threats associated with employees' traveling with their mobile devices that contain work documents. These devices are connected to secure and unsecure networks where the security policies differ.

Lost/Stolen Device

Studies have shown that in every year there are million cases of data breaches as a result of lost or stolen mobile devices (Juniper Network, 2011; Karen, 2015). However, many mobile device users do not realize these security loopholes. While the portability of these mobile devices allows continuous access to work related functions and personal information from any location, valuable information can easily fall into the wrong hands, and may be used for fraudulent and other illegal purposes when stolen or lost (Juniper Network, 2011). Thus, the implication of such lost or stolen mobile devices is that sensitive information can be compromised by a malicious hacker.

Organizations are most worried about the loss of data when employees are allowed to access corporate networks using personal devices. This is due to devices getting lost or stolen. According to Alfreds (2013) the escalating number of mobile devices users lost has led to criminals targeting the mass market of mobile devices with the intention of stealing personal information like banking details. According to Leavitt (2013), passwords can be intercepted by hackers with the intention of stealing credentials, collecting sensitive corporate data and installing malware that can take over devices. Information leaks to unauthorized users because organizations have difficulty to detect the leakage before it happens. As a result IT departments hardly have an opportunity of taking preventive measures to minimize the impact which is usually possible at the early stage of diagnosis (Pillay et al., 2013). This problem is propelled by the challenge of not being able to wipe out company sensitive information when the devices get lost hence such devices are not configured or locked down by the IT department. Thus lost/stolen devices can be regarded as LR because the individual or organization has the ability to wipe out personal or confidential information once the right security measures are put in place.

Wi-Fi Eavesdropping

Accessing the Internet on Wi-Fi networks at any locations such as airports, shops, street is not secure (Du & Zhang, 2006). Hackers take advantage of such wireless networks to eavesdrop on conversations and remotely modify messages from the mobile device. The hackers (cyber attacker) often create a hotspot with a device and such device is used to compromise a legitimate WiFi network in order to steal the user's information and in turn commit online fraud or hack into the bank's database (Balachandran, Voelker, & Bahl, 2005). Wi-Fi eavesdropping can be considered LR because if mobile device users do not access free Wi-Fi at any location it can easily be prevented.

Unauthorized Location Tracking

Location tracking enables the position of registered mobile devices to be recognized and tracked. While it is used openly for legitimate purposes in the banking sector, it can also be used under wraps (Enck et al., 2014). A legitimate software application or malware installed on the user's mobile device can be used to obtain the location data (Pratt Jr & Jones, 2013). Current smartphones are endowed with various sensors that can be used to deduce the user's whereabouts (Nguyen et al., 2013). Unauthorized location tracking can be considered MR because it is used under wraps to deduce a user's location without the knowledge of the user.

Social Threats

In the context of this chapter, social threats represent users' attitudes and awareness levels in using mobile devices. Whilst these threats are normally not well addressed because of their invisibility compared to other forms of threats, it is important that organizations recognize their influence on their security system. Otherwise if they are unchecked they have the potential to expose organizations to other security threats due to their association with people. The following section briefly discusses some of the main social threats that pose a risk to any organization.

Malicious Insider Threats

Malicious insider threats occur when individuals in a position of trust abuse the trust for personal benefits (Bowen, Salem, Hershkop, Keromytis, & Stolfo, 2009). Malicious insiders can be a current employee, a former employee, contractor, consultant or a trusted partner taking advantage of the special access privileges and knowledge to commit security breaches (Mathew, Upadhyaya, Ha, & Ngo, 2008). BYOD employees who are malicious insiders have the likelihood of performing phishing, malware attacks, spoofing and data interception. Similarly theft of mobile devices can easily occur without notice in the organizations. Most employees ignorantly share sensitive information which can be hijacked by a malicious insider before getting to the intended user (Mathew et al., 2008). Malicious insiders can be considered LR because the threat can be avoided if the working conditions from employers accommodate employees' demands which are associated with BYOD.

User Policy Violations

BYOD devices are easily exposed to vulnerabilities due to user policy violation. Carelessness and ignorance such as disabling firewall and antivirus applications to increase performance and speed, downloading and accessing unsecured websites that might contain malware, can expose BYOD devices to vulnerabilities and threats. Most organizations are constantly facing challenges of ensuring their employees adhere with user policies (Vance, Siponen, & Pahnila, 2012). Bello et al. (2015) noted that *"no matter how well developed and structured organizational policies are, they are rendered useless if not used adequately by employees"*. A recent study has pointed out a breach that exposed over 5000 customers' data as a result of employees using a peer-to-peer (P2P) file sharing application from a BYOD laptop device on the network (Bello et al., 2015). According to Dimensional Research (2013) only 38 per cent of organizations actually enforce their policies by blocking these file-sharing applications on the corporate network, while 28 per cent admit that some employees don't follow the policy. Thus user policy violations can be regarded as LR because they can only occur as a result of users' ignorance or carelessness which inadvertently exposes the device to security threats.

Data Ownership Violation

A recent study has pointed out the adoption of file-sharing sites such as iCloud, Drop box and Google drive, as a concern for security of corporate data (Uz, 2014). These file sharing services enable employees to copy files into the cloud for later retrieval but corporate information residing in such services may pose a security risk since they no longer reside in the protected corporate boundaries. According to Dimensional_Research (2013) only 38 per cent actually enforce their policies by blocking these file-sharing sites on the corporate network, while 28 per cent admit that some employees don't follow the policy. Data ownership violation can be considered as MR because any data stored outside the protected boundary of an organization is susceptible to attack.

Data Privacy Violation

Most employees of banks use social media such as Facebook, Twitter, Instagram, WhatsApp and LinkedIn as a platform to interact with other colleagues or other users (Aula, 2010; Chanda & Zaorski,

2013). Unfortunately some of the personal and company's information that is made available on the social media is being hijacked by knowledgeable hackers who buy and sell the personal and company's information in order to commit security breaches (Aula, 2010). Thus data privacy violation can also be regarded as MR because once confidential or personal information is made available on social media; it is no longer within the users' control.

Mitigating all these risks is impossible due to lack of awareness. Lack of awareness is capable of infiltrating all the risk domains regardless of the powerful firewalls, proxy servers and encryption the organization may have (Kathleen, 2015). Astani et al. (2013) have also argued that the security awareness of BYOD devices is so poor leaving businesses vulnerable to security threats. Thus, lack of awareness is major security threat associated with HR domain. Organization needs to be aware of this and acknowledge that employees can be "weakest link" in the security environment because they fail to perform specified security behavior due to insufficient awareness.

PROMINENT EXISTING SECURITY MEASURES FOR BYOD

There are various types of security measures available to address BYOD security threats and many more are being developed. According to Shazmeen and Prasad (2012) the on-going development is as a result of new measures to attack existing technologies which are also being developed at a similar rate. Thus, the existing security measures are not sufficient as mobile devices often create different sets of threats that require additional or special control. However, it is necessary to review some of the existing technologies available and their effectiveness.

Password Authentication

To increase mobile device security through authentication, the concept of user name and password has been a fundamental way of protecting sensitive and confidential information (González, Tapiador, & Garnacho, 2008; Sree, 2008). Although, there are different tools used to verify the identities electronically, the most common authentication method is the use of user ID and passwords. According to González et al. (2008) a properly designed and implemented multifactor authentication method (e.g. password) is more reliable and stronger against any fraud attempt. A study by Bilal and Sankar (2011) reveals a more effective alternative method which is to use digital signatures together with supplementary devices such as smart cards. However, such methods by themselves have significant weaknesses in practice and are dependent upon strict enforcement of password security (Gui-Hong, Hua, & Gui-Zhi, 2010).

Anti-Malware

Anti-malware software is used as a signature-based detection on mobile devices to identify, prevent and take action to remove malicious software programs, such as malware, viruses and worms (Friedman & Hoffman, 2008). There is an auto-update feature in most antivirus programs that enables the program to download profiles of new viruses. The anti-virus program is known to scan several files on a user's system to identify matches between each file's code and those in the signature database. Such identified matches are flagged as malware. According to Srinivasan (2007) documents must always be authenticated by antivirus software before downloading. More importantly, they must be checked to be certain they originated from a trusted and reliable source and cannot be altered and thus good antivirus software is essential to protect the devices from viruses. However, Friedman and Hoffman (2008) have identified some problems associated with signature-based malware detection: first it can only detect known malware. This implies that unknown malware cannot be detected. Second, the authors of malware create self-modifying malware that alters its own signature every time. Third, encryption can disguise the signature of a malware program. Thus, signature based detection is a must but not a completely reliable form of protection.

Anti-Phishing

According to James and Philip (2012), anti-phishing can be defined as an application integrated into the browser as an extra plug-in. Presently, many anti-phishing solutions have been proposed and some approaches have attempted to solve the phishing problem at the e-mail level (Gharibi, 2012). Such techniques are closely related to anti-spam research, although anti-spam techniques have proved to be very effective in also intercepting phishing e-mails (James & Philip, 2012). However the effectiveness of anti-spam techniques mostly depends on many critical factors such as regular filter training and the availability of anti-spam tools that are currently not used by the majority of Internet users (Gharibi, 2012).

Firewall

A firewall is a software program or piece of hardware that is used to protect corporate resources from outside intruders (e.g. hackers, viruses, and worms) that try to reach the mobile devices over the internet. According to Clark (2013) a firewall can be referred to as a security system that controls access to a protected network, such as a corporate network. It examines all messages entering or leaving the internet and blocks those that do not meet the specified security requirement. Friedman and Hoffman (2008) have also identified an important role of firewall on mobile devices which is to block the use of Wi-Fi, Bluetooth and phone communication. This explains the reason why firewall is not mostly use in mobile devices but is used in computer systems. However, while firewalls can play an important role in detecting malware, they can be compromised by an unauthorized intruder (Kahate, 2013).

Encryption

Data encryption at rest and in motion helps to prevent data loss in case of stolen/lost devices (Gharibi, 2012). Sensitive data such as passwords, login information and accounts must by no means travel unencrypted over a wireless system because wireless systems can be easily sniffed and thus compromised (Gui-Hong et al., 2010). This is to protect the device from hackers breaking into the personal device.

Intrusion Detection System (IDS)

Intrusion Detection System (IDS) technology is used to detect both pre-mortem and or post-mortem security threat (Amer & Hamilton, 2010). In IDS a monitoring component is included to specifically arrest network packets moving to and from the IDS. This also helps to determine any malicious usage or activity by automatically sending a malicious detection signal (Scheidell, 2009). This prompt signal can include barricading the network transmission coming from the attacker's internet protocol and also the transmission of an electronic mail message to a system administrator

Mobile Device Management

A Mobile Device Management (MDM) is basically used for the management of a mobile device (e.g. bring your own technology (BYOD) and also to enforce some specific security policies on those devices (Wang et al., 2014). A few examples of MDM are: Zenprise MobileManager, FiberLink Maas360, Air Watch MDM, and Mobile Iron. However, there are several limitations and drawbacks to this approach. First, MDM does not separate corporate and personal space on a mobile device. Additionally, due to lack of space isolation, the security policies administered by MDM are on the entire device (Wang et al., 2014). Thus if MDM is used, employees might lose the flexibilities associated with the personal space

Training on Acceptable Use of ICT Policy

Employees are being trained on acceptable use of ICT policy in the banking sector and access to the bank's information must be carried out within the specified acceptable boundaries (Broughton, Higgins, Hicks, & Cox, 2009). Similarly employees are given a copy of the ICT policy and it is the responsibility of the employee to get familiar with the terms of policy. Unfortunately not all employees get acquainted with this policy (Mulligan & Gordon, 2002)

Enforcement of Security Policies

Most banks enforce security policy on the employee to avoid any form of security breaches. Employees are forced to comply with the terms of the policy and where it is confirmed that an employee has violated the policy, such employee is disciplined or reprimanded (Herath & Rao, 2009). However despite the policy enforcement there are still recurring social security threats such as insider attack, social media attack and file sharing attack (Bulgurcu, Cavusoglu, & Benbasat, 2010). Thus the social security measures are incapable of completely mitigating these security threats.

EXISTING SECURITY FRAMEWORKS

Security frameworks refer to series of documented processes that are used to define procedures and policies around the ongoing and implementation of information security controls in an organization (Granneman, 2013). These frameworks come in various degrees of complexity and are used to build an information security program to reduce vulnerabilities and manage risks.

ISO/IEC 27000 Series

The International Standards Organization established the ISO 27000 series of standards. The main focus of ISO 27000 series is on information security issues. It provides an extensive information security framework that can be adopted by any organization (Granneman, 2013). However for the purpose of this research, the strengths and weaknesses of ISO 27001 and ISO 27005 will be explored in line with the prevailing demands for successful and robust security frameworks.

1. **ISO/IEC 27001:** The specification for an Information Security Management System (ISMS) is the ISO 27001 standard. The standard states the requirements for establishing, implementing, operating, monitoring, reviewing, maintaining, and improving an Information Security Management System within an organization for overall business risks (ISO, 2005). This will ensure the selection of ample and commensurate security controls to safeguard information assets. The standard introduces a model called the "Plan-Do-Check-Act" (PDCA) which helps in establishing, implementing, monitoring and improving the effectiveness of an organization's ISMS. However, some organizations basically adopt ISO 27001 in order to pursue an effective means for operational information security risk management but ignore the fact that the standard was not designed to be used at operational level but at the high level as an ISMS framework. The ISO 27000 series also consists of ISO 27002 which is considered as an extension to ISO 27001 (Barlette & Fomin, 2010). It provides recommended controls that an organization can adopt to address information security risks.

2. **ISO/IEC 27005:** The existing gaps in terms of information security risk management in ISO 27001 and ISO 27002 were closed by the introduction of ISO 27005 standard. The standard was used to elaborate and build up on the core that was introduced in ISO27001 by means of identifying inputs, actions, guidelines for implementation and outputs for every single statement. However, studies have shown that the adoption of this standard as a means for information security risk management is minimal (Dobson & Hietala, 2011), because it is not intended to be used as an information security risk assessment methodology (ISO, 2005).

While ISO/IEC 27000 series framework is helpful in establishing, implementing, monitoring and improving the effectiveness of an organization's ISMS, its adoption for security management is minimal (Dobson & Hietala, 2011). Al-Ahmad and Mohammad (2012) have also argued that the implementation is minimal because it was not designed to be used as methodology for information security risk assessment. Sequel to the arguments by Al-Ahmad and Mohammad (2013), this framework is completely inadequate to protect the banking sector from security threats arising from the use of mobile devices.

PCI DSS

Payment Card Industry Data Security Standard (PCI DSS) assists to protect cardholder data, maintain a vulnerability management program, build and maintain a secure network and assist to implement solid access control measures (Council Payment Card Industry, 2010). Every user that transmits or stores debit or credit card data is mandated to comply with PCI requirements (Al-Ahmad & Mohammad, 2012). This helps organizations to reduce losses resulting from fraud, manage information security risks and safeguard consumer data (Council Payment Card Industry, 2010). However, studies have shown that PCI DSS is not designed to be used as an information security framework or assessment framework (Al-Ahmad & Mohammad, 2013; Council Payment Card Industry, 2010) and therefore does not fit into the objectives of this study.

COBIT

One of the most increasingly adopted information technology frameworks for IT Governance is COBIT (Control Objectives for Information and related Technology) developed by the Information Systems Audit &Control Association (ISACA, 2011). The focus of COBIT is to define IT control objectives and develop the controls to meet the objectives. It comprises thirty four (34) processes that manage and control information and the technology (Brand & Boonen, 2007). A study has shown that COBIT can be used to create the IT governance framework, create the needed alignment between business and IT, establish the IT risk management organization and improve IT processes (Tambotoh & Latuperissa, 2014). Some studies have also shown that COBIT can be used to meet the organization's requirements, compliance needs and to create IT policies and procedures (Al-Ahmad & Mohammad, 2013; Barlette & Fomin, 2010). In a similar view, Parvizi, Oghbaei, and Khayami (2013) reveal that COBIT is used as a means to conduct audit, standardize IT processes and increase organization effectiveness and maturity levels. Security threats can be minimized with proper IT governance, however, some studies have argued that COBIT only establishes the foundation for having a solid IT organization in an organization but does not provide a methodology to conduct information security risk assessments (Al-Ahmad & Mohammad, 2012; ISACA, 2011). Similarly, the framework work did not emphasize user awareness as a means to avoid or reduce these security threats. This makes the COBIT framework inadequate in mitigating these security threats.

NIST SP 800 Series

The National Institute of Standards and Technology (NIST) Special Publication 800 series is one of the frameworks used to properly address information security (NIST, 2012). It was published in 1990 and has grown to provide an extensive variety of risk factors needed to determine information security risk. Its major activities include the following; assess the security controls using appropriate methods and procedures; categorize information systems and the information within those systems; authorize information systems operation based on a determination of the risk to organizational operations and assets; implement security controls in the systems; monitor and assess selected security controls in information systems on a continuous basis (Al-Ahmad & Mohammad, 2012). For ease of use, ideal assessment scales, tables and templates for common risk factors were included. This enables maximum flexibility in the design of risk assessments based on the organization's established scope, purpose, assumptions and constraints (Ross, 2011). However, to ensure that ultimate value is provided by security assessments, analysis must be conducted which implies that organizations must address the technical weaknesses as well as weaknesses in organizational process and procedure (Stouffer, Falco, & Scarfone, 2008). This technical weakness as well as organizational process and procedure weakness is one of the major issues why this framework is inadequate to address security. Similarly, user awareness on these security threats was not fully addressed.

CISCO SCF (Security Control Framework)

Cisco security control framework is made up of a model, control structure/set and methodology basically designed to assist in assessing the technical risk in infrastructure architecture. The 'model' explains the security objectives and security actions as a means to address the underlying principles and to organize individual controls. The control structure elucidates the individual controls and control sets in an organization and its relationship with the Cisco SCF model and methodology. The methodology outlines the requirements needed to perform an assessment on the security architecture using the Cisco SCF. However, Cisco SCF is designed based on the definition and use of appropriate control sets for specific business environments and assessment objectives. Thus it only consists of a set of rules used to assess architecture in an orderly manner.

IBM Security Framework

IBM has created a bridge to help with security challenges that addresses communication gaps between the technical and business perspectives. The IBM security framework addresses security challenges in the following domains: data and information, people and identity, application and process, physical infrastructure, network, server and endpoint, security governance, risk management and compliance. However, according to Buecker, Borrett, Lorenz, and Powers (2010), IBM security framework, only focuses on the 'what' not the 'how' and can only help to interpret users requirements into coarse-grained business solutions, not into specific IT solutions or IT components

Following the review of these frameworks, the limitations identified are a deterrent to the fourth industrial revolution. With the fourth industrial revolution, the possibilities of billions of people connected by mobile devices, with unprecedented storage capacity, processing power, and access to knowledge, are unlimited. These possibilities will be multiplied by emerging trends such as BYOIoT. However, all of these existing frameworks have their shortcomings and do not adequately address the significant impact of the fourth industrial revolution to accommodate the security threat to domains (Figure 1). Hence, a security framework is required to address these domains in the fourth industrial revolution.

DISCUSSION

Two similar studies were conducted in the banking sector of Nigeria and Swaziland to find out the implication of a BYOD enabled environment. Due to the type of transactions and sensitive information processed within the banking system, risk management is a critical aspect that must be addressed when developing a security framework (Wang et al., 2014).This study intended to contribute towards developing a security framework for BYOD environment. The findings from a study conducted in Nigerian banks shows that despite the security measures put in place, security threats are still on the increase. Furthermore, BYOD security awareness is not provided for the employees. Likewise those that provide security awareness training do not ensure employees' compliance to these security policies. Supporting these findings, Elwess (2015) states that as much as organizations may have knowledge on the subject of BYOD, research findings show that individuals are either still not aware of the potential threats or decide to ignore them. The data on individual practices (employees' practises) reveals that 77 per cent of mobile device users configured their mobile device to automatically connect to wireless network and 78.8 per cent click on links, images, advertisement, videos and games respectively on social media. This implies that organization data residing on employees' personal devices becomes exposed to all these unprotected environments. Mora et.al. (2015), assert that it has become a challenge to distinguish between private and organizational data once employees use their privately owned devices in an organizational context. The study further reveals that 83 per cent of Nigerian bank employees backup work documents on internal memory and cloud services of their mobile device as against the stipulated policy to back up on the bank's server.

Similarly, data collected from Swazi Bank in Swaziland revealed that a significant number of employees (93%) still connect to public Wi-Fi which makes mobile devices vulnerable to cyber-attacks. In addition to that, a majority of employees (92%) save company data on cloud based sharing services. Such findings show lack of awareness and comprehension amongst employees on the severity and vulnerability of using mobile devices in a work context. Thus, it is important for any organization to have a measure of awareness. This means management need to acknowledge that employees can be the weakest link in the security environment because they fail to perform specified security behaviours due to insufficient awareness (Johnston, Warkentin, McBride, & Carter, 2016).

Similarly as outlined in Figure 2, HR domains are security threats that can be very harmful to the organization as they affect the three threats domains (technical, mobility and social) at the same time. While MR domains are security threats that are pertaining to two threats domains and can bring down the two domains, and LR domains are security threats that are pertaining to a particular domain: it does not affect more than one domain. It is very important for an organization to be aware of these risk domains particularly the HR domain which is invisible to the current security measures. However, there is no suitable security measure to overcome lack of awareness. Thus this chapter proposes a 3-D security framework that will assess individual, organization and third party knowledge on BYOD threat. This chapter recommends that awareness is viewed holistically in three different levels: individual; organization; and third party.

Individual Perspective

The studies conducted in Nigeria and Swaziland revealed user perception as a common factor that influences technology. User perception can be explained by perceived severity of security threats, perceived vulnerability of mobile devices to security threats, security measure efficacy and self-efficacy in executing security policies. Perceived severity of security threats focuses on employees' perception of the magnitude or seriousness of possible threats that they are exposed to when using their mobile devices in the workplace. Perceived Vulnerability on the other hand looks at assessing how employees understand the chances of falling victim to security threats. Security Measure Efficacy focuses on how an individual feels or perceives that security measures put in place can effectively protect the company and the user. Self-efficacy looks at if individuals feel comfortable executing security policies required for mobile devices in the workplace.

The results show that a significant number of employees agreed that the organization would be prone to security threats if they did not adhere to security controls. Therefore, the greater the exposure the greater they perceived the vulnerability of mobile devices to security threats. The results indicate that a significant number of employees believed that existing policies could protect them. The results show differences in the way employees think of the effectiveness of security measures. This suggests that it is imperative for organizations to be cautious when aligning training programs and policies to promote compliance in the organization. Moreover, results highlighted that employees felt comfortable executing security policies required for mobile devices in the workplace. Thus, the framework emphasizes that organizations must have policies that employees can easily comprehend and execute. This is to ensure that employees can be able to follow security policies even with minimum assistance. The findings support Alexandrou's (2016) argument that an individual will be successful in adopting security controls on a mobile device only if there is high confidence in applying the security controls.

Studies also highlighted that attitude had a significant influence on employees 'awareness. The determining factors in attitude toward security response cost, regulatory concern and reaction to security policies. When looking at the security response cost of using mobile devices results revealed that employees are mostly concerned about time, convenience, and comprehension, which can be barriers when adopting security measures for their mobile devices. Employees feel such barriers may result in frustration and reduce motivation to comply with security policies. Results suggest that there are higher chances for employees not to follow policies that are too restrictive which may result in low employee job satisfaction. This further shows that employees are looking for simplicity; they need something they can easily comprehend and implement.

Organizational Perspective

The recommended framework postulates that organizations need to invest in educating and training the workforce. Creating awareness on the subject of organizational assets is key. Organizational assets include Corporate Intellectually property, Classified Information, Financial Assets, Device and service availability and functionality and Political reputation. Failing to do so means employees cannot comprehend the importance of data or information to the organization. The organization cannot achieve employee commitment in securing company information. As a result, employees can hardly understand what exactly will be at stake if information is compromised. Consequently, this can lead to regulatory fines, damage to company reputation and loss of intellectual property. For example, both studies revealed that there were no sufficient efforts done in addressing the subject of organizational assets; hence, some employees could not fully comprehend the consequences of non-compliance.

A point to bear in mind is that learning is a continuum; it begins with awareness, builds to training and leads to education (Wilson & Hash, 2003).Organizations may have all the necessary resources to protect and improve the security of corporate information assets but employees still remain one of the threats that need to be dealt with. According to Freedman (2015)), information systems managers are more interested on technical issues and solutions such as intrusion, routers and firewalls and pay less attention to soft issues caused by users' lack of security awareness. Rose (2013) states that it has been demonstrated that employees who do not adhere to company security policies are the main hazard for company security. This implies that organizations need to engage employees through training and awareness programs to enlighten them on how to protect company data. As employees are increasingly accessing privileged corporate information and applications, it is vital for organizations to understand and address the implications caused by unknown devices entering the organizational environment (Twinomurinzi & Mawela, 2014). Awareness programs are designed to allow employees the flexibility to use their personal devices and at the same time mitigate the security and concerns of the ICT department (Twinomurinzi & Mawela, 2014).

Third Party

The framework further recommends that the third party (e.g. Internet service provider, device manufacturer etc) needs to ensure that organizations comply with stipulated control system. It may be common knowledge that requirements for secure integration of mobile devices can be derived from standards such as COBiT or ISO 2700 (Disterer & Kleiner, 2013). The fact remains that users first need to buy into the idea of information security. This control system is meant to validate data integrity and keep the organizations in check. Cross data validation helps to assess the organization for non-compliance.

CONCLUSION AND RECOMMENDATIONS

The benefits of BYOD to most organizations include increased productivity, flexibility and efficiency. In spite of these benefits, privacy invasion, security and data integrity have been a major concern for individuals, society and organizations that adopt BYOD. Securing personally owned devices has become a nightmare for ICT departments because each new device brought into the company leaves the company with less control over what is transmitted and most importantly how it is transmitted (Twinomurinzi & Mawela, 2014). Miller, Voas, and Hurlburt (2012), distinguish two main threats to corporate information security that can be introduced by the BYOD philosophy. The first one is malware intrusion (worms, viruses, trojans) as privately owned devices are integrated into corporate network facilities (Miller et al., 2012). Exchanging personal and professional information in personal devices will enable the user to navigate inside social networks which can result in important organizational data being leaked in the event of a security incident (Mora et.al, 2015). The second threat is the increase in the possibility of data loss and theft (Miller et al., 2012). Corporate information may fall into the wrong hands when an employee misplaces or loses his or her personal device.

The validity and integrity of data is lost through data contamination. This is due to personal information and confidential business information sharing the same storage space on personally owned mobile devices. According to Romer (2014), contamination happens when personal files accidentally end up on corporate file servers, even worse, personal files containing malware spread to business files from the mobile device to corporate internal file servers. Data is no longer under control once information migrates to a device that is not controlled by the company (Miller et al., 2012).

The adoption of BYOD resulted in IT departments having the challenge of how to secure data and prevent information systems from being misused or compromised. The departments confronted the question of how to secure sensitive information and how to address privacy concerns when personal devices enter work space (Alexandrou, 2016, p. 1). Furthermore, with the advent of the fourth industrial revolution, there is an acceleration in innovation and an influx of mobile device entering the work space. Thus productivity has been improved (Schwab, 2016). However, the rapid pace of change in innovation has led to adverse effects in legislation and regulations (Schwab, 2016). This implies that regulators have to adapt to the fast changing environment, thus no single framework is sufficient to address the drawbacks of the fourth industrial revolution. Matinde (2015) points out that the magnitude of BYOD challenges will always intensify as long as business models continuously evolve to increase mobility especially when there is evident growth in the mix of users and geographically diverse business offices. Elwess (2015) states that as much as organizations may have knowledge on the subject of BYOD, research findings show that individuals are either still not aware of the potential threats or decide to ignore them. Similarly, some of the organization's management who are involved in decision making are also employees who are lacking in awareness. Thus there is an urgent need for a 'unified single point of context aware' security framework outlined in Figure 3 to help curb these security threats.

Figure 3. 3-D BYOD security framework (Author's own)

Dimensions	Motivating factors	Role	Response
Individual	End user perception	Learn	Attitude
Organization	Security assurance	Train	Control disruptive behaviour.
Third party	Compliance to device and service	Device usage control	Data integrity support

As employees are increasingly accessing privileged corporate information and applications, it is vital for organizations to understand and address the implications caused by unknown devices entering the organizational environment (Twinomurinzi & Mawela, 2014). Awareness programs are designed to allow employees the flexibility to use their personal devices and at the same time mitigate the security and concerns of the ICT department (Twinomurinzi & Mawela, 2014).

The end process in the model is to conduct an evaluation, where employees are expected to show full commitment (prescriptive commitment) in adhering to company security policies when using mobile devices in the work place. Sipponen (2000) laments that companies are still struggling to reach a point where the workforce would internalize and follow given guidelines. As a result you find that employees are still unaware of policies or they fail to apply them. Prescriptive commitment can take different forms like having employees who will avoid installing unnecessary applications, avoid sharing company sensitive data especially over unprotected networks, avoid jail-breaking, have good physical control of mobile devices. On the part of the organization, the objective should be enforcing security policy and awareness compliance, while the third party is expected to carryout data cross validation to ensure data integrity.

Looking to the future Mark (2014) has predicted that by 2020, BYOD will evolve into BYOIoT (Bring Your Own Internet of Things), where we have so many inter-connected devices. According to Mark (2014), BYOIoT elements are now working their way into the office environment because they do have the potential to make businesses even more efficient in day-to-day operations. It is however easy to see the potential benefits along with the possible pitfalls. While BYOIoT has the potential to make businesses even more efficient in day-to-day operations, they pose more security threats to the organizations by the huge amount of data coming from the smart devices that is not controlled or checked by the organizations. However, the fourth industrial revolution has proved to have effects on national and international security whereby there have been conflicts involving different states (cyberwar) which have become increasingly "hybrid" in nature. It is worth mentioning that the developed framework does not address fourth industrial revolution issues relating to conflicts between two states, which requires further research.

REFERENCES

Al-Ahmad, W., & Mohammad, B. (2012). Can A Single Security Framework Address Information Security Risks Adequately? *International Journal of Digital Information and Wireless Communications*, 2(3), 222–230.

Al-Ahmad, W., & Mohammad, B. (2013). Addressing information security risks by adopting standards. *International Journal of Information Security Science*, 2(2), 28–43.

Alexandrou, A. (2016). *A security risk perception model for the adoption of mobile devices in the healthcare industry*. Pace University.

Alfreds, D. (2013). *News 24. BYOD security threats to SA firms*. Retrieved April 2, 2016, from http://www.news24.com

Amer & Hamilton. (2010). Intrusion detection systems (IDS) taxonomy-a short review. *Defense Cyber Security, 13*(2).

Aruba Network. (2013). *Conquering today's bring your own device challenges: A framework for successful BYOD initiatives*. Aruba White Paper.

Astani, M., Ready, K., & Tessema, M. (2013). BYOD Issues and strategies in organizations. *Issues in Information Systems, 14*(2).

Aula, P. (2010). Social media, reputation risk and ambient publicity management. *Strategy and Leadership, 38*(6), 43–49. doi:10.1108/10878571011088069

Balachandran, A., Voelker, G. M., & Bahl, P. (2005). Wireless hotspots: Current challenges and future directions. *Mobile Networks and Applications, 10*(3), 265–274. doi:10.100711036-005-6421-5

Baldassari, P., & Roux, J. (2017). Industry 4.0: Preparing for the Future of Work. *People & Strategy, 40*(3), 20–23.

Barlette & Fomin. (2010). The Adoption of Information Security Management Standards. *Information Resources Management: Concepts, Methodologies, Tools and Applications: Concepts, Methodologies, Tools and Applications*, 69.

Bello, A., Armarego, J., & Murray, D. (2015). Bring your own device organizational information security and privacy. *Journal of Engineering and Applied Sciences (Asian Research Publishing Network), 10*(3), 1279–1287.

Bilal, M., & Sankar, G. (2011). Trust & Security issues in Mobile banking and its effect on Customers. *School of Computing. Blekinge Institute of Technology, SE-371*, 79.

Bowen, B. M., Salem, M. B., Hershkop, S., Keromytis, A. D., & Stolfo, S. (2009). Designing host and network sensors to mitigate the insider threat. *IEEE Security and Privacy, 7*(6), 22–29. doi:10.1109/MSP.2009.109

Boyles, Smith, & Madden. (2012). Privacy and data management on mobile devices. *Pew Internet & American Life Project, 4*.

Brand, K., & Boonen, H. (2007). *IT Governance based on CobiT® 4.1-A Management Guide*. Van Haren.

Brodin, M. (2016). *BYOD vs. CYOD: What is the difference?* Paper presented at the 9th IADIS International Conference Information Systems 2016.

Broomhead, S. (2013). *Gartner says BYOD is disruptive*. Retrieved February 23, 2016, from http://www.ehna.acfee.org/read/art-54e605c41el4a

Broughton, A., Higgins, T., Hicks, B., & Cox, A. (2009). Workplaces and social networking-The implications for employment relations. Institute for Employment Studies, Brighton.

Buecker, A., Borrett, M., Lorenz, C., & Powers, C. (2010). *Introducing the ibm security framework and ibm security blueprint to realize business-driven security*. International Technical Support Organization.

Bulgurcu, B., Cavusoglu, H., & Benbasat, I. (2010). Information security policy compliance: An empirical study of rationality-based beliefs and information security awareness. *Management Information Systems Quarterly*, *34*(3), 523–548. doi:10.2307/25750690

Chanda, R. A. J. I. B., & Zaorski, S. T. E. V. E. (2013). Social media usage in the financial services industry: Toward a business-driven compliance approach. *Journal of Taxation and Regulation of Financial Institutions*, *26*(5), 5–20.

Chen, C.-M., Chen, Y.-H., Lin, Y.-H., & Sun, H.-M. (2014). Eliminating rouge femtocells based on distance bounding protocol and geographic information. *Expert Systems with Applications*, *41*(2), 426–433. doi:10.1016/j.eswa.2013.07.068

Cisco. (2013). *BYOD Smart Solution*. Retrieved 7 January, 2015, from http://www.cisco.com/web/solutions/trends/byod_smart_solutions/index.html

Clark, P. G. (2013). *Firewall policy diagram: Novel data structures and algorithms for modeling, analysis, and comprehension of network firewalls*. Academic Press.

Company85 Briefing. (2012). *BYOD and the security implications of consumerization*. Retrieved May 5, 2016, from http://safebridge.pt/Whitepapers/BYOD/Company85%20BYOD%20and%20the%20security%20implications%20of%20consumerisation.pdf

Copeland, R., & Crespi, N. (2012). *Analyzing consumerization-Should enterprise business context determine session policy?* Paper presented at the Intelligence in Next Generation Networks (ICIN), 2012 16th International Conference on. 10.1109/ICIN.2012.6376024

Council Payment Card Industry. (2010). *PCI DSS 2.0*. PCI Council Publication/United States.

Device, Y. O. (n.d.). Retrieved March 10, 2015, from http://www.bringyourownit.com/2012/06/25/byod-bring-your-own-device/

Dimensional Research. (2013). *The impact of mobile devices on information security: A survey of professionals*. Retrieved 30 December, 2014, from http://www.dimensionalresearch.com

Dimensional_Research. (2013). *The impact of mobile devices on information security: A survey of professionals*. Retrieved 30 December, 2014, from http://www.dimensionalresearch.com

Disterer, G., & Kleiner, C. (2013). *BYOD Bring Your Own Device*. Retrieved 19 December, 2014, from http://www.dx.doi.org/10.1016/j.protcy

Dobson, I., & Hietala, J. (2011). *Risk Management: The Open Group Guide*. Van Haren Pub.

Du & Zhang. (2006). *Risks and Risk Control of Wi-Fi Network Systems*. Academic Press.

Dunnett, R. (2012). *Information Security, Mobile Security and Internet of Things*. BYOD- Bring.

Ehimen & Bola. (2010, January). Cybercrime in Nigeria. *Business Intelligence Journal*, 93-98.

Ehrenfeld, J. M. (2017). WannaCry, Cybersecurity and Health Information Technology: A Time to Act. *Journal of Medical Systems*, *41*(7), 104. doi:10.100710916-017-0752-1 PMID:28540616

Elwess, T. (2015). *Bring your own device* (Doctoral dissertation). Utica College.

Enck, W., Gilbert, P., Han, S., Tendulkar, V., Chun, B.-G., Cox, L. P., ... Sheth, A. N. (2014). TaintDroid: An information-flow tracking system for realtime privacy monitoring on smartphones. *ACM Transactions on Computer Systems*, *32*(2), 5. doi:10.1145/2619091

Evripidis, R. (2008). *Lawful Interception and Countermeasures: In the era of Internet Telephony*. Academic Press.

Felt, A. P., Finifter, M., Chin, E., Hanna, S., & Wagner, D. (2011). A survey of mobile malware in the wild. *Proceedings of the 1st ACM workshop on Security and privacy in smartphones and mobile devices*. 10.1145/2046614.2046618

Freedman, A. (2015). Managing personal device use in the workplace: How to avoid data security issues and to dig yourself out of your failed BYOD policy. *Suffolk J. Trial & App. Adv.*, *20*, 284–361.

Friedman, J., & Hoffman, D. V. (2008). Protecting data on mobile devices: A taxonomy of security threats to mobile computing and review of applicable defenses. *Information, Knowledge, Systems Management*, *7*(1-2), 159–180.

Garba, Armarego, Murray, & Kenworthy. (2015). Review of the information security and privacy challenges in Bring Your Own Device (BYOD) environments. *Journal of Information Privacy and Security*, *11*(1), 38-54.

Gartner. (2012). *Creating a Bring Your Own Device (BYOD) Policy*. Retrieved April 4, 2016, from https://www.gartner.com/doc/1983515/creating-bring-device-byod-policy

Gharibi, W. (2012). *Some Recommended Protection Technologies for Cyber Crime Based on Social Engineering Techniques--Phishing*. arXiv preprint arXiv:1201.0949

Golde, N., Redon, K., & Borgaonkar, R. (2012). *Weaponizing Femtocells: The Effect of Rogue Devices on Mobile Telecommunications*. Paper presented at the NDSS.

González, Tapiador, Estévez, & Garnacho. (2008). *Content authentication and access control in pure peer-to-peer networks*. Universidad Carlos Iii De Madrid.

Granneman, J. (2013). IT security frameworks and standards: Choosing the right one. *TechTarget Network*. Available: http://searchsecuri ty. tech target. comlti p/IT-securi ty frameworks-and-standards-Choosing-the-right-one

Gui-Hong, L., Hua, Z., & Gui-Zhi, L. (2010). *Building a Secure Web Server Based on OpenSSL and Apache*. Paper presented at the 2010 International Conference on E-Business and E-Government. 10.1109/ICEE.2010.334

Harris, J., Ives, B., & Junglas, I. (2012). IT Consumerization: When Gadgets Turn Into Enterprise IT Tools. *MIS Quarterly Executive*, *11*(3).

Herath, T., & Rao, H. R. (2009). Protection motivation and deterrence: A framework for security policy compliance in organisations. *European Journal of Information Systems*, *18*(2), 106–125. doi:10.1057/ejis.2009.6

Hong, J. (2012). The state of phishing attacks. *Communications of the ACM*, *55*(1), 74–81. doi:10.1145/2063176.2063197

ISACA. (2011). *COBIT 4.1*. Retrieved 24 May, 2016, from www.isaca.org

ISO. (2005). *Information technology–Security techniques–Information security management systems–Requirements*. ISO.

James, D., & Philip, M. (2012). *A novel anti phishing framework based on visual cryptography*. Paper presented at the Power, Signals, Controls and Computation (EPSCICON), 2012 International Conference on. 10.1109/EPSCICON.2012.6175228

Johnston, A. C., Warkentin, M., McBride, M., & Carter, L. (2016). Dispositional and situational factors: Influences on information security policy violations. *European Journal of Information Systems*, *25*(3), 231–251. doi:10.1057/ejis.2015.15

Pratt Jr. & Jones. (2013). Mobile device management in the DoD enterprise network. *Practice*, *44*(3), 179-196.

Juniper Network. (2011). *Mobile Device Security- Emerging threats, Essentials Strategies*. Retrieved 29 December, 2015, from www.google.co.uk/url?sa=t&rct=j&q=&esrc=s&source=web&cd=1&ved=0ahUKEwj60-6g5oDKAhWMWBoKHWjtASwQFggyMAA&url=http%3A%2F%2Fwww.bytes.co.uk%2Fdownload_file%2Fview%2F943%2F537%2F&usg=AFQjCNGVmC_t7GmVQqdw36AgYt-v9orttwg

Kahate, A. (2013). *Cryptography and network security*. Tata McGraw-Hill Education.

Karen, T. (2015). *Device Debacles – Lost, Stolen, and Neglected Data Risks*. Retrieved from https://www.allclearid.com/blog/device-debacles-lost-stolen-and-neglected-data-risks

Kathleen, R. (2015). *Lack of cybersecurity awareness linked to CIOs*. Retrieved from www.searchsecurity.techtarget.com/opinion/Lack-of-cybersecurity-awareness-linked-to-CIOs

Ladakis, E., Koromilas, L., Vasiliadis, G., Polychronakis, M., & Ioannidis, S. (2013). You can type, but you can't hide: A stealthy GPU-based keylogger. *Proceedings of the 6th European Workshop on System Security (EuroSec)*.

Leavitt, N. (2013). Today's mobile security requires a new approach. *Computer*, *46*(11), 16–19. doi:10.1109/MC.2013.400

Lebek, Degirmenci, & Breitner. (2013). *Investigating the Influence of Security, Privacy, and Legal Concerns on Employees' Intention to Use BYOD Mobile Devices*. Academic Press.

Lee, N. (2015). *Cyber attacks, prevention, and countermeasures. In Counterterrorism and Cybersecurity* (pp. 249–286). Springer.

Madzima, K., Dube, E.L., & Mashwama, P.M. (2013). *ICT Education in Swaziland Secondary Schools: Opportunities and Challenges*. Academic Press.

Mark, O. (2014). *Bring your own internet of things*. Retrieved 01 January, 2015, from http://www.bringyourowninternetofthingscomingtobusinessin2015/

Mathew, S., Upadhyaya, S., Ha, D., & Ngo, H. Q. (2008). *Insider abuse comprehension through capability acquisition graphs*. Paper presented at the Information Fusion, 2008 11th International Conference on.

Matinde, V. (2015). *The rise of BYOD and corporate data threats*. Academic Press.

Miller, Voas, & Hurlburt. (2012). BYOD: Security and privacy considerations. *IT Professional, 14*(5), 0053-0055.

Moavenzadeh, J. (2016). *The fourth industrial revolution: Reshaping the future of production*. Retrieved 20 November, 2017, from www.eiseverywhere.com/file_uploads/fe238270f05e2dbf187e2a60cbcdd68e_2_Keynote_John_Moavenzadeh_World

Mulligan, P., & Gordon, S. R. (2002). The impact of information technology on customer and supplier relationships in the financial services. *International Journal of Service Industry Management, 13*(1), 29–46. doi:10.1108/09564230210421146

Needham & Lampson. (2008). *Network Attack and Defense*. White Paper.

Ngoqo, B., & Flowerday, S. V. (2015). Information Security Behaviour Profiling Framework (ISBPF) for student mobile phone users. *Computers & Security, 53*, 132–142. doi:10.1016/j.cose.2015.05.011

Nguyen, Tian, Cho, Kwak, Parab, Kim, Yuseung, . . . Zhang. (2013). *UnLocIn: Unauthorized location inference on smartphones without being caught*. Paper presented at the Privacy and Security in Mobile Systems (PRISMS), 2013 International Conference on.

Niesen, T., Houy, C., Fettke, P., & Loos, P. (2016). *Towards an integrative big data analysis framework for data-driven risk management in industry 4.0*. Paper presented at the System Sciences (HICSS), 2016 49th Hawaii International Conference on.

NIST. (2012). *NIST Special Publication 800-30, Revision 1, "Guide for Conducting Risk Assessments"*. Retrieved 8 June, 2016, from www.nist.org

Olasanmi, O. O. (2010). Computer crimes and counter measures in the Nigerian banking sector. *Journal of Internet Banking and Commerce, 15*(1), 1.

Osterman Research. (2012). *The Byod (Bring Your Own Device) Trend- Putting IT in control of BYOD*. Retrieved May 13, 2017, from http://www.hyperoffice.com/byod-whitepaper/

Parvizi, R., Oghbaei, F., & Khayami, S. R. (2013). *Using COBIT and ITIL frameworks to establish the alignment of business and IT organizations as one of the critical success factors in ERP implementation.* Paper presented at the Information and Knowledge Technology (IKT), 2013 5th Conference on. 10.1109/IKT.2013.6620078

Pillay, Nham, Tan, Diaki, Senanayake, & Deshpande. (2013). *Does BYOD increase risks or drive benefits?* Academic Press.

Romer, H. (2014). Best practices for BYOD security. *Computer Fraud & Security, 2014*(1), 13–15. doi:10.1016/S1361-3723(14)70007-7

Rose, C. (2013). BYOD: An examination of bring your own device in business. *The Review of Business Information Systems (Online), 17*(2), 65. doi:10.19030/rbis.v17i2.7846

Ross, R. S. (2011). Guide for conducting risk assessments. *NIST Special Publication*, 800-830.

Scheidell, M. (2009). *Intrusion detection system*. Google Patents.

Schwab, K. (2016). Navigating the fourth industrial revolution. *BIZNEWS*. Retrieved from http//www. biznews.com/wef/davos-2016/01/20/Klaus-schwab-navigating-the-fourth-industrial-revolution/

Shazmeen & Prasad. (2012). A Practical Approach for Secure Internet Banking based on Cryptography. *International Journal of Scientific and Research Publications, 2*(12), 1-6.

Sree. (2008). Exploring a novel approach for providing software security using soft computing systems. *International Journal of Security and Its Applications, 2*, 51-58.

Srinivasan, R. (2007). *Protecting anti-virus software under viral attacks*. Citeseer.

Stancioiu, A. (2017). The fourth industrial revolution "industry 4.0". *Fiability & Durability/Fiabilitate si Durabilitate,* (1).

Stouffer, K., Falco, J., & Scarfone, K. (2008). NIST SP 800-115: Technical Guide to Information Security Testing and Assessment. National Institute of Standards and Technology.

Tambotoh & Latuperissa. (2014). *The Application for Measuring the Maturity Level of Information Technology Governance on Indonesian Government Agencies Using COBIT 4.1 Framework.* Intelligent Information Management.

Tu & Yuan. (2015). *Coping with BYOD Security Threat: From Management Perspective.* Academic Press.

Twinomurinzi, H., & Mawela, T. (2014). Employee perceptions of BYOD in South Africa: Employers are turning a blind eye? *Proceedings of the Southern African Institute for Computer Scientist and Information Technologists Annual Conference 2014 on SAICSIT 2014 Empowered by Technology.* 10.1145/2664591.2664607

Umar. (2015). Financial Regulations and the Nigeria's Banking Sector. *Journal of Research in Business and Management, 3*(11),05-13.

Uz, Ali. (2014). *The Effectiveness of Remote Wipe as a Valid Defense for Enterprises Implementing a BYOD Policy.* Academic Press.

Vance, A., Siponen, M., & Pahnila, S. (2012). Motivating IS security compliance: Insights from habit and protection motivation theory. *Information & Management, 49*(3), 190–198. doi:10.1016/j.im.2012.04.002

Vignesh, U., & Asha, S. (2015). Modifying security policies towards BYOD. *Procedia Computer Science, 50*, 511–516. doi:10.1016/j.procs.2015.04.023

Wada, F., & Odulaja, G.O. (2012). *Electronic Banking and Cyber Crime In Nigeria-A Theoretical Policy Perspective on Causation.* Academic Press.

Wang, Y., Wei, J., & Vangury, K. (2014). *Bring your own device security issues and challenges.* Paper presented at the Consumer Communications and Networking Conference (CCNC), 2014 IEEE 11th. 10.1109/CCNC.2014.6866552

Wilson & Hash. (2003). Building an information technology security awareness and training program. *NIST Special Publication, 800*(50), 1-39.

Wu, X. (2009). *SIP on an Overlay Network.* Academic Press.

Xu, R., Saïdi, H., & Anderson, R. J. (2012). *Aurasium: practical policy enforcement for android applications.* Paper presented at the USENIX Security Symposium.

Zahadat, N., Blessner, P., Blackburn, T., & Olson, B. A. (2015). BYOD security engineering: A framework and its analysis. *Computers & Security, 55*, 81–99. doi:10.1016/j.cose.2015.06.011

KEY TERMS AND DEFINITIONS

BYOD: A trend that allows employees to bring their personal mobile devices to the workplace. They have the freedom to use mobile devices (such as laptops, tablets, or smartphones) for work-related purpose.

BYOIoT: A trend where we have so many inter-connected devices. These devices are sometimes connected to corporate network and they communicate with each other.

Rogue Device: An unauthorized connection of mobile devices to the network which pose a security threat to the organization.

Data Interception: Refers to the obstruction of data transmission to and from the device, and remotely altering the messages.

Eavesdropping: An unauthorized real-time interception of a private communication, such as instant message, a phone call, or videoconference.

Intrusion Detection System (IDS): A technology used to detect both pre-mortem and or post-mortem security threats.

Keystroke Logger: This is also known as key logging is used to record typed characters on mobile devices in order to capture valuable or sensitive information such as user's ID, password, and credit card numbers.

Mobile Device Management (MDM): Used for the management of mobile device and also to enforce some specific security policies on those devices.

WiFi: Facility that allows computers, smartphones, or other devices to connect to the internet or communicate with one another wirelessly within a particular area.

Chapter 9
Dynamic Risk Assessment in IT Environments:
A Decision Guide

Omid Mirzaei
Universidad Carlos III de Madrid (UC3M), Spain

José Maria de Fuentes
Universidad Carlos III de Madrid (UC3M), Spain

Lorena González Manzano
Universidad Carlos III de Madrid (UC3M), Spain

ABSTRACT

Security and reliability of information technologies have emerged as major concerns nowadays. Risk assessment, an estimation of negative impacts that might be imposed to a network by a series of potential sources, is one of the main tasks to ensure the security and is performed either statically or dynamically. Static risk assessment cannot satisfy the requirements of real-time and ubiquitous computing networks as it is pre-planned and does not consider upcoming changes such as the creation of new attack strategies. However, dynamic risk assessment (DRA) considers real-time evidences, being capable of diagnosing abnormal events in changing environments. Several DRA approaches have been proposed recently, but it is unclear which technique fits best into IT scenarios with different requirements. Thus, this chapter introduces recent trends in DRA, by analyzing 27 works and proposes a decision guide to help IT managers in choosing the most suitable DRA technique considering three illustrative scenarios – regular computer networks, internet of things, and industrial control systems.

DOI: 10.4018/978-1-5225-4763-1.ch009

INTRODUCTION

Information Technology (IT) deals with the use of computers to store, manipulate and retrieve any kind of data, ranging from business to personal, and in most cases, sensitive data. This field is receiving more attention in recent years due to the emergence of computer networks, wireless networks, and interconnected smart devices also known as the Internet of Things (IoT). In particular, Industrial IoT (IIoT), known as 4th Industrial Revolution (4IR), has received significant attention. In 4IR, real and virtual capabilities are merged into Cyber-Physical Production Systems (CPPS) through extensive usage of cloud services and applications, and, also, big data analytics (Sadeghi, Wachsmann, & Waidner, 2015).

In order to make sure that 4IR helps in achieving both economic and social improvements, authorities must anticipate and cover all involved security risks. Particularly, security of information needs to be addressed in order to provide a satisfying degree of reliability, confidentiality, integrity, and availability (Gehling & Stankard, 2005). It must be noted that numerous threats may affect these four factors. Thus, passive attacks (e.g. eavesdropping) or active ones (e.g. packet injection) may harm this environment (Deka, Kalita, Bhattacharya, & Kalita, 2015), (Nadeem & Howarth, 2013).

Regardless the type of threat or attack, they impose a magnitude of unreliability to information which is commonly known as "risk". Speaking more precisely, the term "risk" is an estimation of the degree of exposure to a threat that may occur on one or more assets causing damage to an organization (Awan, Burnap, & Rana, 2016). In a computer network scenario, an asset may be any of its components (e.g. hardware devices or their software) as well as other related elements such as the network users.

Managing risks is critical to ensure the overall corporate security. For this reason, information security governance is already assumed to be an integral part of the corporate IT governance (Von Solms, 2005). In particular, Wilkin et al. highlight that risk management forms this process along with other corporate aspects such as strategic alignment, value delivery, resource management and performance measurement (Figure 1) (Wilkin & Chenhall, 2010). Thanks to risk management, it is possible to properly handle risks as it serves to identify, assess, prioritize, mitigate and track them (Garvey, 2008). Among these steps, risk assessment deserves special attention since it involves measuring an intangible factor – the degree of risk posed by an action (S. Fu & Zhou, 2011), (Benini & Sicari, 2008). This complex task is essential for responding to the threat (Shoemaker & Conklin, 2011).

Currently, there are two major risk assessment approaches, namely static and dynamic ones (Alireza Shameli-Sendi, Naser Ezzati-jivan, Masoume Jabbarifar, & Michel Dagenais, 2012). In a static system, risks are evaluated based on static values of factors related to risks, including assets, threats, and vulnerabilities. Today, with the dynamicity of threats, there is an urgent need for Dynamic Risk Assessment (DRA) processes. Particularly, choosing an appropriate risk assessment method in IIoT systems is challenging since they provide different attack surfaces at multiple abstraction layers ranging from electronic devices (e.g. processors and memories to process data and sensors and actuators to control physical processes) to software (e.g. operating systems and applications), humans, and, last but not least, network connections (e.g. WiFi). In such a context, adapting classic static risk assessment methods is not straightforward, and, thus, requires another method, at an additional cost, which allows systems to update the risk level at real-time, as well as dealing with the changing nature of security threats (Holgado, Perez, Perez, & Villagra, 2015) and various abstraction layers which are usually involved.

Due to the importance of risk assessment process, several surveys have been published dealing specifically with security risks in information systems and computer networks. For instance, information security risk assessment concepts are presented in (Zhiwei & Zhongyuan, 2012), (Behnia, Rashid, &

Figure 1. Risk assessment process as part of IT Governance areas

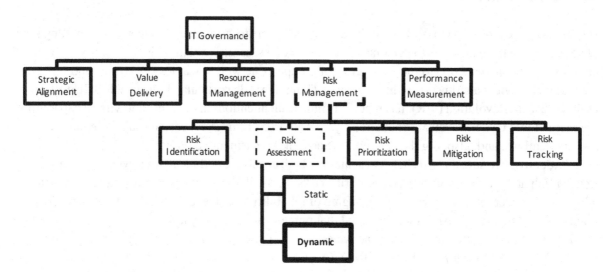

Chaudhry, 2012), and, moreover, various risk evaluation methodologies for information systems are analyzed based on the structures of these systems. A recent work also proposes a method to assess risks in such an environment (de Gusmão, e Silva, Silva, Poleto, & Costa, 2016).

Beside these, analyzing risks in Cyber-Physical Systems (CPS) (Lee, 2008), (Poovendran, 2010), like smart cities and smart grids, is discussed in (Kurosu, 2013), (Zhou & Chen, 2012). However, as a result of current incline of research community to DRAs, another work (López, Pastor, & Villalba, 2013) discusses dynamic risk management concepts for computer networks, and a short literature review of DRA approaches is presented therein.

Despite the abundance of DRA approaches in recent years, IT managers face the challenge of implementing DRA in very assorted scenarios. For the sake of illustration, we identify three representative settings – regular computer networks, Internet of Things (IoT) environments and Industrial Control Systems (ICS). These three settings are typically found in the underlying IIoT systems resulting from 4IR. Thus, ICSs usually govern computers and IoT devices to automatize the production process. These settings differ significantly in the degree of centralization and the resources of their nodes. Thus, regular computer networks are formed by potentially unconstrained devices which can be managed from a single manager system. On the contrary, IoT devices are resource-limited elements which usually operate in a decentralized manner. In-between these two, ICSs are formed by sensors with limited capacity, which are managed by regional devices with enough computational resources. Since each factory of the 4IR can be formed, to different extents, from these settings, we analyze them separately. This makes the analysis be suitable for any IIoT settings, as well as for any general IT environments in which these systems come into play.

In order to assist IT managers in choosing the most suitable DRA technique for their particular setting, in this paper we analyze 27 DRA works and provide an overview of how they deal with the three main issues in a DRA mechanism – assets, threats and risk calculations. Furthermore, we also study how these mechanisms have been applied into the aforementioned IT settings. Thus, our main contribution is a decision guide that is intended to provide IT managers (of IIoT systems, but not only) with enough background on DRA and the suitability of existing techniques for their concrete scenario.

The remainder of this paper is organized as follows: Section 2 provides a background on security and risk management in computer networks. Risk assessment is presented in Section 3. The analysis on dynamic risk assessment models and approaches is presented in Section 4. Section 5 points out open research directions and, finally, Section 6 concludes the paper.

BACKGROUND

In this Section, the main notions of IT security governance, and risk management are introduced. These issues form the context in which risk assessment is placed.

IT Security Governance

Due to extraordinary extension of computer networks and the Internet, there is an ever increasing need for security. Therefore, IT security governance is gaining attention from both academia and industry to improve the reliability of computer networks.

Several standards have addressed this issue. On the one hand, generic IT governance standards such as COBIT (De Haes, Van Grembergen, & Debreceny, 2013) and ITIL (Clinch, 2009) have covered security aspects as one of the areas in which controls have to be included. On the other hand, ISO 27001 (Calder & Watkins, 2010) specifically focuses on security management. Among the different steps involved in this process, ISO 27001 provides with a guideline for risk assessment and management.

Risk Management

Risk management is a general process which consists of some important sub-processes. It usually includes risk identification, risk assessment, risk prioritization, risk mitigation and risk tracking (recall Figure 1) (Garvey, 2008). These procedures are not independent from each other, but related as shown on Figure 2.

According to the description by Garvey, risk identification (No. 1 in Figure 2) is the first step in the risk management process (Garvey, 2008). Its objective is the early identification of risks that can impact on the system's assets in particular, and on system's performance in general. In the second step (No. 2 in Figure 2), an assessment is made based on the impact that each risk event could have on the assets of system. Hardware devices such as routers, software applications, information, people, and also procedures can all be considered as critical assets.

After risk identification and assessment, security risks are assigned different priorities (No. 3 in Figure 2). A major purpose for prioritizing risks is to form a basis (link 3 → 5 in Figure 2) for allocating critical resources, including additional personnel or funding to resolve those risks (Garvey, 2008). Different risk mitigation plans (No. 4 in Figure 2) are designed to manage, eliminate, or reduce risks to an acceptable level (Garvey, 2008), (Chołda & Jaglarz, 2016). Apart from the previous sequential tasks, risk tracking (No. 5 in Figure 2) is also considered as a supervisory procedure (Garvey, 2008). The main goal of risk tracking is the exact monitoring of risk assessment (link 5 → 2 in Figure 2) and mitigation (link 5 → 4 in Figure 2) strategies based on the priorities of risks.

Figure 2. A general view of a risk management system

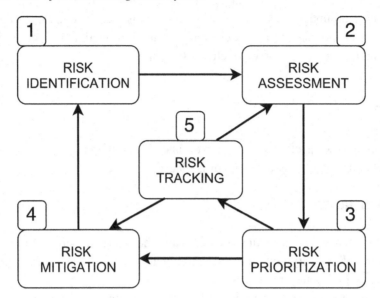

RISK ASSESSMENT

Among the risk management tasks described in Section 2.2, risk assessment is receiving attention for its relevance to determine the impact of risks (Dongmei, Changguang, & Jianfeng, 2007). For this purpose, several methodologies have been proposed (Ionita, Hartel, Pieters, & Wieringa, 2013). CRAMM (Yazar, 2002), OCTAVE (Caralli, Stevens, Young, & Wilson, 2007), NIST SP800-30 (Blank & Gallagher, 2012), and MAGERIT (Crespo, Amutio-Gómez, Candau, & Mañas, 2006) are among the most popular ones (Ionita et al., 2013), (Shedden, Scheepers, Smith, & Ahmad, 2011). All of these methods have three identifiable steps in common, namely (1) asset identification and analysis; (2) threat and vulnerability identification, and (3) countermeasure selection. In the first step, all the assets of an organization are specified. In the second step, vulnerabilities and threats are identified, and, finally, numerous security strategies and plans are set in the third step to mitigate or eliminate the risk posed by identified threats.

It is worth emphasizing that assets, vulnerabilities, and threats are considered as key factors in most risk assessment models. However, vulnerabilities are usually considered implicitly along with security threats since there would not exist any threat until there are some vulnerabilities within the system. For the sake of simplicity and without loss of generality, in what follows the process of risk assessment and its underlying concepts are explained taking MAGERIT methodology as the basis.

Basic Steps

Risk assessment involves some important steps and concepts which are shown in Figure 3 (Crespo et al., 2006). They are summarized as follows.

1. Determining the essential assets, their inter-relationships, and their importance (value) for the organization.
2. Determining the threats to which those assets are exposed.

3. Estimating the impact, defined as the damage to the asset arising from the appearance of the threat.
4. Estimating the risk degradation level, i.e. the level (the amount) of damage which is produced by threats.
5. Estimating the occurrence probability (frequency or likelihood) of degradations which is caused by threats.
6. Estimating the risk using the calculated probability and the impact from the aforementioned steps.

The assets of an organization have some values. These values are not initially limited to numeric magnitudes, but they can be observed from the "need to protect assets" perspective-- the more valuable an asset is, the higher protection it will need. In assigning values to assets, several dimensions, namely confidentiality, integrity, availability, authenticity, and accountability should be considered (Crespo et al., 2006).

Once it has been determined which security dimensions are of interest in each asset, they must be valued. Valuation is in fact the determination of the loss of value caused by an incident. For example, the integrity of data may have higher importance in contrast with other factors. Therefore, it should be assigned a higher weight in determining the value of this asset. After the valuation process, some administrators may consider priorities for their organization's assets according to their values (Boyer, Dain, & Cunningham, 2005). For instance, software assets could probably have more priority than physical assets since disruption of one or two devices would lead to fewer losses in comparison to a software incident. However, this is totally dependent to the application context and priorities that are considered by administrators.

When assets are the victims of threats, not all of their dimensions are affected and not all to the same degree (Crespo et al., 2006). As an example, the integrity of information in the software database might be the target of attackers. Therefore, the exposure of assets must be estimated considering the degradation and the likelihood of threats. Degradation is the amount of damage which is produced by threats and will be imposed to the assets, and likelihood is the frequency or probability of threats' occurrences. Likelihood can be modeled either numerically (e.g., number of occurrences in a period) or descriptively (e.g., from "very frequent" to "rare"). Sometimes, likelihood of attacks can be expressed by numerical values, and, sometimes, it cannot be performed in that way and should be modeled by nominal scales.

By knowing the values of assets (in their different dimensions) and the degradation caused by attacks, the impacts of assets can be determined directly using Equation 1. Here, D .is the amount of degradation caused by a particular threat, and V .is the overall value of a particular asset. Thus, as it is clear, impact (I . is a function of threats' degradations and assets' values (Equation 1). Thus, the higher the degradation of threats and the higher the value of assets is, the more impact of threats.

$$I = f\left(D, V\right).$$

(1)

By knowing the impact of threats to assets, the risk can be derived directly taking into account the likelihood of threats' occurrences. Thus, the total risk of an IT environment formed by assets is calculated following Equation 2 (Kaplan & Garrick, 1981) similar to another formulation which has been proposed for Supervisory Control and Data Acquisition (SCADA) systems (Cherdantseva et al., 2016).

Figure 3. Main elements of a risk assessment system

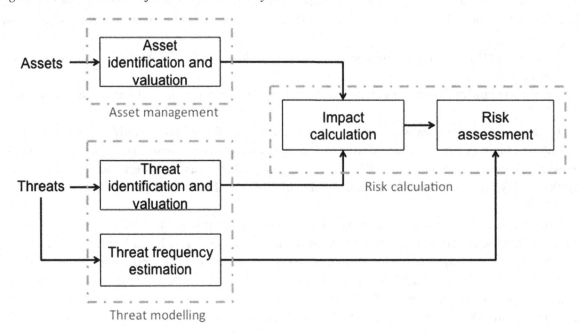

$$R_{Total}\left(t\right) = f\left(R_{ij}\left(t\right)\right) = f\left(P_{ij}\left(t\right), I_{ij}\left(t\right)\right), \quad i = 1,2,\dots,M, \ j = 1,2,\dots,N \ . \tag{2}$$

Thus, the total risk is indeed a function of individual risks caused by various threats (i .in Equation 2) on each asset (j .in Equation 2), and an individual risk on each asset j .is a function of all threats' probabilities (P_{ij} .in Equation 2) and their impacts (I_{ij} .in Equation 2). As it is obvious from Equation 2, all these magnitudes may change over time

Types of Risk Assessment

Risk assessment can be discussed considering two criteria - first, how risk values are calculated and presented; second, how frequent they are evaluated and actually updated.

Regarding the first criterion, risk assessment methods can be implemented by following either a quantitative or a qualitative approach (Zhang, Jiang, Cui, Zhang, & Xia, 2010). Quantitative risk assessment systems use formulas and mathematical expressions to produce numeric estimates for risks. On the other hand, qualitative risk assessment methods estimate risks descriptively by using terms, such as "low", "medium", and "high". The latter approach is preferred for areas in which risk can hardly be estimated as an explicit value or in occasions where all the threats cannot be identified and registered technically.

Considering the second criterion, risk assessment systems can follow either a static or dynamic approach. Recalling Figure 3, in dynamic settings, several things may change over time. Initially, threats may be variable in three main areas (Holgado et al., 2015), (Crespo et al., 2006). First of all, new attack methods might devise in future (dynamicity of type), and, more importantly, the assessment of threats' capabilities would become inappropriate (Crespo et al., 2006). Secondly, the frequency of attacks (dynamicity of frequency) may also change over time, i.e. the probabilities of threats' occurrences are considered to be variable in dynamic risk assessment systems (López et al., 2013). Thirdly, the severity of threats (dynamicity of severity) may also change from time to time. Apart from threats, different aspects of assets may also change. This change would be the addition, modification, or suppression of assets within an organization, or even a change in their valuation (López et al., 2013). Finally, vulnerabilities of assets to attacks could also be variable at different points of time (Holgado et al., 2015).

Considering all these issues, static methodologies for risk assessment lack practical sense in changing scenarios, since they evaluate risks at discrete time intervals, thus being unable to adapt to new threats or changes in assets. On the contrary, Dynamic Risk Assessment (DRA) systems should be capable of estimating risks continuously considering the dynamic nature of environment.

DYNAMIC RISK ASSESSMENT

Once the basic concepts of risk assessment have been introduced, this Section focuses on the core of this paper – Dynamic Risk Assessment (DRA) techniques. For this purpose, each of the three main elements of a DRA mechanism (asset management, threat modeling and risk calculation, recall Figure 3) is described separately based on the information gathered in Table 3. The purpose of this Section is to illustrate the different DRA approaches taken in literature. Based on these alternatives, a decision guide will be presented in the following section to help the reader decide which ones best fit to his current environment.

Assets Management

Assets management deals with three main issues, including types of the assets which need to be considered, their behavior, and, also, their valuation. Regarding the types of assets, (Haslum, Abraham, & Knapskog, 2007) assumes that they can be both hardware and software, while (Haslum & Årnes, 2006) and (Årnes et al., 2005) have a more general view since the assets are considered to be within a computer network; however, they do not discuss exactly which components of a computer network have been considered as assets. Beside these, (Qi, Liu, Zhang, & Yuan, 2010) takes some extra options into account, including fame, reputation, public trust, and employees' confidence. Regarding the behavior of assets, (Holgado et al., 2015), (Qi et al., 2010), (W. Li & Guo, 2009), (G. Chen, 2010), and (Årnes, Valeur, Vigna, & Kemmerer, 2006) consider the change in assets although they do not discuss the aspects through which assets might change.

Speaking about the valuation of assets, several works such as (Haslum & Årnes, 2006), (Årnes et al., 2005), (Årnes et al., 2006), (Ma, Li, & Zhang, 2009), (Yu-Ting, Hai-Peng, & Xi-Long, 2014), (Liao, Li, & Song, 2010), (Poolsappasit, Dewri, & Ray, 2012), (Wu & Zhao, 2014), and (Cheng, Xu, Jia, & Zou, 2008) consider confidentiality, integrity, and availability dimensions in order to valuate assets, while (Wrona & Hallingstad, 2010) has a special focus on the availability. (Haslum et al., 2007) and (Haslum, Abraham, & Knapskog, 2008) concentrate on other factors, namely cost, criticality, sensitivity, and recovery, while (Qi et al., 2010) assumes that assets are valuated manually. Ultimately, a few number of works (Boyer et al., 2005), (W. Li & Guo, 2009) propose the dynamicity of assets' priorities. Within these models, assets are assigned different priorities that can change at various moments according to any modifications in the administrator's policies.

Threat Modeling

This section focuses on the threats' assumptions, and, also, the threat modeling technique adopted in different DRA works. Concerning threats, most of the systems consider Distributed Denial of Service (DDoS) attacks (W. Li & Guo, 2009), (Årnes et al., 2006), (Ma et al., 2009), (Wu & Zhao, 2014), (Wrona & Hallingstad, 2010), (Haslum, Abraham, et al., 2008), (Ahmed, Al-Shaer, Taibah, & Khan, 2011), (Rezvani, Ignjatovic, Bertino, & Jha, 2014). However, (Liao et al., 2010) and (Phillips & Swiler, 1998) have developed a program to simulate the behavior of an intruder. Several models also focus on the dynamicity of threats in different aspects. Security threats may change in type (i.e. new threats might emerge) (Ahmed et al., 2011), (Phillips & Swiler, 1998); the frequency of threats can be variable (Poolsappasit et al., 2012), (Wrona & Hallingstad, 2010), (Phillips & Swiler, 1998), (Volftrub & Polikarpov, 2007), (Hu, Ding, & Huang, 2008); and, also, their severity may change over time (Qi et al., 2010), (W. Li & Guo, 2009), (Haslum, Abraham, et al., 2008). From the analyzed collection, some works exist (Holgado et al., 2015), (Wu & Zhao, 2014), (Cheng et al., 2008) which do not have any assumptions on the changes of threats.

To model threats, researchers have used a variety of tools, including Hidden Markov Models (HMMs), attack graphs and threat clustering, to name a few. According to our observations, HMMs (taken in 10 works) and graph-based data structures (suggested in 7 works) are the most frequent techniques used for threat modeling. Threat modeling becomes critical as they influence how the likelihood (probability) of threats and their impacts on assets are measured. Therefore, each of these techniques is described in what follows.

Hidden Markov Models (HMMs)

HMMs are statistical models, mainly based on state transitions (e.g. security states of assets), that are triggered by events (or threats) which happen randomly according to a probability distribution (Haslum, Moe, & Knapskog, 2008). Moreover, it can be used to predict future unobserved events based on previous records and witnesses (Gao, Sun, & We, 2003). Hidden Markov models have been used in a variety of works (Holgado et al., 2015), (Haslum et al., 2007), (Haslum & Årnes, 2006), (Årnes et al., 2005), (W. Li & Guo, 2009), (G. Chen, 2010), (Årnes et al., 2006), (Ma et al., 2009), (Yu-Ting et al., 2014), (Haslum, Abraham, et al., 2008) to model security threats.

In an HMM, the assets of interest are assumed to have different security states s_i .which are defined and set by administrators and are demonstrated in Figure 4. For instance, three security states, including "Safe", "Under Attack", and "Compromised" may be considered for each asset.

HMM includes a triple to model the state of the system (W. Li & Guo, 2009). These are "Initial Matrix", "Observation (Probability of Observation) Matrix" and "Transition Matrix" (I, P and T in Figure 4, respectively). Initial matrix demonstrates the initial security state of an asset. Observation matrix is our observation (O_i .in Figure 4) about the probability of an attack (p_i .in Figure 4) when an asset is in a particular state. Ultimately, Transition matrix includes the probabilities of transitions between the states of an asset (t_{ij} .in Figure 4). Transitions are due to different types of attacks over time. One of the key aspects of HMMs is the definition of these matrices. Thus, some approaches have applied techniques such as genetic algorithms to optimize the values of these matrices (W. Li & Guo, 2009).

Figure 4. A general view of a Hidden Markov Model (HMM)

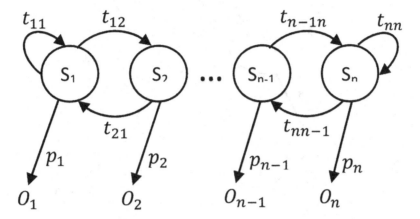

$$HMM = (T, P, I)$$

Several HMMs can also be combined together for modeling threats. For instance, within the system proposed in (Haslum, Abraham, et al., 2008), the information of HMMs is combined to extract the probability of an attack, and, next, this parameter is mixed with other factors such as probability of threat success and its severity using fuzzy logic (explained later in this Section).

Graph-Based Modeling Techniques (GMs)

Graphs are also applied to several models of dynamic risk assessment. There is a slight difference between various graphs used here and HMM. Within these graph structures, nodes show the attacker states whereas in HMM nodes represent security states of assets and the probability of an attack to be exercised in each state. Thus, HMM can be considered as an asset-centric threat modeling technique while graph-based modeling techniques are attack-centric showing different attack steps an attacker can pass to reach the desired target. Three graph structures are used for this purpose, namely Attack Graphs (AGs), Bayesian Networks (BNs) and Petri nets (PT Nets) which are introduced briefly in what follows.

An attack graph demonstrates possible multi-step attacks (attack paths) by representing the causal relationships among different vulnerabilities (J. H. Li & Levy, 2010). In particular, an AG model our knowledge about how multiple vulnerabilities may be combined for an attack. Here, nodes represent attack states while edges show exploits. Also, nodes can be assigned a numerical value reflecting the likelihood of an exploit in a particular state or the expected impact. This technique is adopted in works such as (Phillips & Swiler, 1998) and (Alhomidi & Reed, 2013) in combination with quantitative metrics.

A small sample of an attack graph is illustrated in Figure 5 to provide a general imagination of this modeling technique. According to this figure, "vertex 8" shows the target of any possible attacker which depends upon some combination of the other vertices. Ellipse vertices, called "AND" (e.g. vertex 5), can be exploited only if both pre-conditions (vertices 1 and 3) are satisfied, while diamond vertices, called "OR" (e.g. vertex 8) can be exploited by either or both of the pre-conditions (e.g. vertices 6 and

Figure 5. A simple Attack Graph (AG)

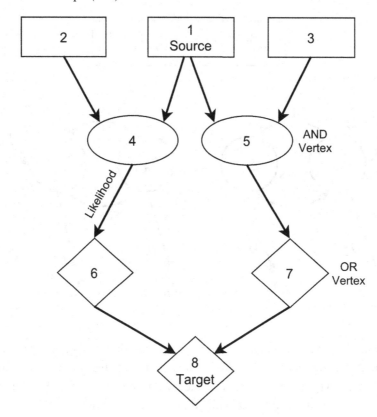

7). Lastly, vertices 1, 2, and 3 are called "leaf" vertices representing either a network configuration (e.g. an open port) or an existing vulnerability.

A critical problem regarding attack graphs is that the attackers' plans are not always completely known. In other words, there exists a degree of uncertainty in attackers' behavior (J. H. Li & Levy, 2010), and, for this reason, the logical causality modeled by a deterministic attack graph is not sufficient to identify all security threats. Moreover, AGs cannot handle situations where the exploitation of a vulnerability affects the likelihood of exploiting another vulnerability. Thus, BNs are proposed in some papers (Poolsappasit et al., 2012), (Wu & Zhao, 2014), (Wrona & Hallingstad, 2010), (Dantu, Kolan, & Cangussu, 2009) as an alternative although their construction from an attack graph is not a trivial task (J. H. Li & Levy, 2010).

There are some differences between BNs and AGs in terms of modeling. In BNs, nodes represent random variables (e.g. attack state, hypotheses) while edges show conditional dependencies which do exist between these variables. BNs make use of a Conditional Probability Table (CPT) to demonstrate the probability of a single variable (node) with respect to other nodes (its parents). Using this modeling technique resolves some issues which arise in AG modeling for instance when the order in which vulnerabilities are exploited is important. This technique determines quantitative values representing the overall system security by considering the combined effect of all known vulnerabilities. Another major difference which exists between BNs and AGs is in the risk calculation process which will be discussed later. One important application of BNs is to represent the uncertainty of an unavailable period – it may be due to misconfiguration or the result of a DoS attack.

As a third graph-based structure, PT Nets (Place-Transition Nets) are appropriate to model discrete event systems and represent dynamic processes, specifically when few events may occur concurrently (Tabak & Levis, 1985). Therefore, in what comes to security threats, they can provide a model for estimating risks continuously (Liao et al., 2010). As shown in Figure 6, a basic PT Net is a directed bigraph with two disjoint set of nodes such that no two graph vertices from the same set are adjacent. The first set of nodes are Places (i.e. conditions, represented by cycles), and the second set of nodes are Transitions (i.e. events that may occur, represented by bars). The directed arcs describe which places are preconditions and/or post-conditions for which transitions (signified by arrows). The other advantage of using PT Nets is that they are well described by an algebraic formalism as a quadruple which include the set of Places (P .in Figure 6), Transitions (T .in Figure 6), Pre-(and Post-) conditions (Pre and Post in Figure 6) as shown in Figure 6.

Another variant of graph-based modeling can be observed in the work by Alhomidi and Reed (Alhomidi & Reed, 2013). They propose an epidemiological-based technique which base on the very behavior of the nature while addressing infections (Alhomidi & Reed, 2013). Within this model, a set of cells are considered that can send "danger" or "alarm" signals to some aggregators. These aggregators can further inform other group of cells, which decide whether the signals are enough to declare infection. In such a case, a set of countermeasures (e.g. killer cells) are deployed. By using such signals and communications and by imitating the immune response system of human body, this system is capable of modeling security threats in an efficient way.

Hierarchical Modeling Techniques (HMs)

Hierarchical threat models assume that any system can be structured in such a way that several hierarchical levels can be identified within it. Components can belong to different levels, and a higher component can include others of lower hierarchical level. They can also be united into sub-systems in a specific

Figure 6. A basic PT Net

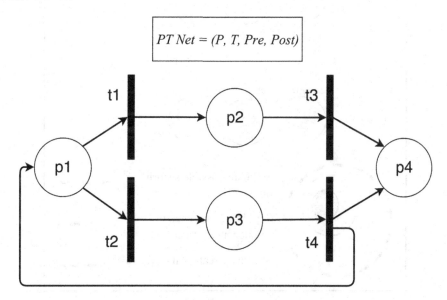

hierarchical level (Volftrub & Polikarpov, 2007). Each of these components are assumed to be vulnerable to a sub-set of threats from the set of all possible security threats which may appear. Also, not all of the threats would be of interest, but only those which may have negative impacts on the components and may lead to risk events.

Additionally, particular sets of threats can be determined for each sub-system (Volftrub & Polikarpov, 2007). These threats are not related to any object included in a sub-system, but only to the sub-system as a whole. Sub-systems can also be united into larger groups for which the same rule exists. This process is continued until the level of the whole system is reached (Figure 7).

Threats Clustering (TC)

Clustering of security threats is another modeling technique presented in a number of works (Liu, Chen, Dai, Wang, & Cai, 2005), (Y. Chen, Jensen, Gray, Cahill, & Seigneur, 2003). Within this model, each interaction (of mobile and autonomous entities in a ubiquitous computing environment as in (Y. Chen, Jensen, Gray, Cahill, & Seigneur, 2003)) with the environment is considered as a feature vector which consists of some elements that specify the context of the interaction, the participants, and other relevant historical or current information.

Figure 7. The hierarchical threat modeling technique in (Volftrub & Polikarpov, 2007)

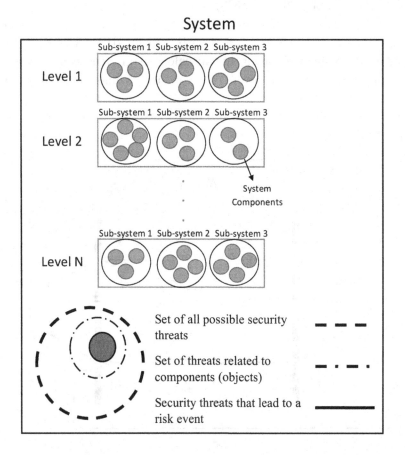

A clustering procedure is used to group different feature vectors which have been derived from the historical data. When clusters are produced and confirmed, the number of unexpected points in clusters are easy to collect for historical data, from which the risk value is easy to calculate. More details for the process of risk calculation are presented in Risk Calculation section.

Fuzzy Logic (FL)

Fuzzy logic is another threat modeling technique proposed in (Michalopoulos, Mavridis, & Jankovic, 2014) due to the complexity and uncertainty which exist in ubiquitous computing environments (Liu et al., 2005). Fuzzy logic has become increasingly popular in addressing imprecision, uncertainty and vagueness (Liu et al., 2005). A fuzzy logic system can be defined as the nonlinear mapping of an input data to a scalar output data (Mendel, 1995). It consists of four main parts, namely fuzzifier, rules, inference engine, and defuzzifier (Rutkowski & Cpalka, 2003) (Figure 8).

In this modeling technique, initial numerical (or scalar) values of threats (and their impacts) are first converted to fuzzy sets using fuzzy membership functions. Fuzzy sets usually carry names that conform to adjectives we usually use in our daily linguistic usage such as "low", "medium" and "high" which may demonstrate the severity of threats and help in dealing with uncertainties. This process is known as fuzzification. In the second step, an inference is made based on a set of rules (also known as fuzzy IF-THEN rules) which is important in the process of risk calculation and will be discussed later. Finally, membership degrees of the fuzzy sets are interpreted into a real value of risk through deffuzification process.

Other Models

Other works are not based on any of the discussed models (Boyer et al., 2005), (Qi et al., 2010), (Ahmed et al., 2011), (Rezvani et al., 2014), (C. Fu, Ye, Zhang, Zhang, & LanSheng, 2010). For instance, (Boyer et al., 2005) models and security threats by a set of rules written in Security Assessment Declarative Language (SADL). This language can combine knowledge of the IT environment, including critical

Figure 8. A general view of a fuzzy logic system

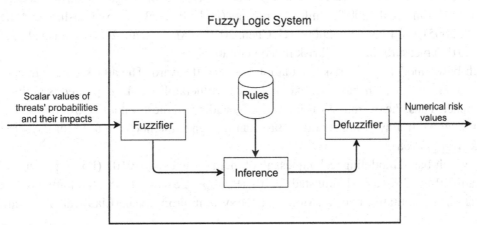

assets and vulnerabilities. Additionally, it separates information about the local network configuration from information about common attack patterns.

Risk Calculation

Once security threats are modeled, risk can be estimated considering the probability (frequency) and the impact of all possible threats as demonstrated earlier in Figure 3. In what follows, risk calculation will be discussed separately for each of the threat modeling techniques presented in Threat Modeling section. Before entering into this discussion, two dimensions need to be considered precisely regarding the risk calculation process. First, it must be analyzed whether risks are evaluated using quantitative or qualitative metrics (recall Section 3.2). In considered works, quantitative metrics are adopted in the majority of contributions (24 works). The second issue to consider is whether DRA approaches re-estimate and update risk values continuously or by intervals, due to the changes that may occur at different periods of time. Approaches which capture risk values continuously (11 works) can provide with a real-time evaluation of risks. Nevertheless, it comes at a cost of using a flexible threat modeling technique capable of timely adapting to these changes. On the other side, models which capture risk values at short intervals (suggested in 7 works) are less complex as they are based on simpler threat modeling techniques. However, they are prone to miss new security threats which might happen between these intervals.

In HMM modeling, the risk at each security state can be estimated by having the probability of threats (in Figure 4), and the impact of those threats on asset in a specific security state (recall Eq. 3). Finally, the overall risk is calculated by adding up these risks as the asset moves from one state to the other.

Among models proposed based on HMMs, 6 systems (Haslum et al., 2007), (W. Li & Guo, 2009), (Årnes et al., 2006), (Ma et al., 2009), (Yu-Ting et al., 2014), (Haslum, Abraham, et al., 2008) re-estimate risk values in considerably short time intervals using Discrete Time HMM (DTHMMs) in order not to miss any new changes in the environment, and 4 models (Holgado et al., 2015), (Haslum & Årnes, 2006), (Årnes et al., 2005), (G. Chen, 2010) evaluate risks using Continuous Time HMM (CTHMMs). In DTHMM, observations are updated at specific and regular points of time, while in CTHMM, observations are made at irregular (continuous) time points as the security states of assets evolve in continuous time (Elliott, Aggoun, & Moore, 2008). Transition probabilities in CTHMMs are a function of time and of transition intensities (Elliott et al., 2008). Briefly speaking, another matrix is also constructed in this type of HMM except the three aforementioned ones called "Transition Rate/Intensity Matrix".

Qualitative risk assessment based on HMMs measures risks using linguistic terms such as low, medium, or high (Haslum et al., 2007), while other works (Holgado et al., 2015), (Haslum & Årnes, 2006), (Årnes et al., 2005), (W. Li & Guo, 2009), (G. Chen, 2010), (Årnes et al., 2006), (Ma et al., 2009), (Yu-Ting et al., 2014) measure the overall risk in a quantitative way.

In graph-based modeling, the risk calculation is straightforward. The attack path is traced from the root to the target, and, at each state, the likelihood of a vulnerability to be exploited is multiplied by its negative impact. Thus, the overall risk is measured by adding all these values at different states from the source to the target. In Bayesian networks, Bayesian inference methods are used for the same purpose (Frigault & Wang, 2008).

Among graph-based modeling techniques, all of them (Liao et al., 2010), (Poolsappasit et al., 2012), (Wu & Zhao, 2014), (Wrona & Hallingstad, 2010), (Phillips & Swiler, 1998), (Alhomidi & Reed, 2013) evaluate risks in a quantitative manner. Moreover, the systems proposed in (Liao et al., 2010) and (Wrona

& Hallingstad, 2010) update risk values continuously, while other systems are not clear in terms of how frequent they update risk values.

In epidemiological-based models, risk is calculated similar to graph-based modeling techniques. In particular, different cells percept security threats from the environment and send appropriate alarms to some aggregators based on the frequencies and the impacts of threats. Then, these aggregators sum up the total risk values received from all the cells and can also trigger other cells if this value exceeds a predefined threshold. Systems that are based on this model (Alhomidi & Reed, 2013) can estimate risk values continuously or in real-time.

Models based on clustering divide security threats into different groups or clusters based on some features. When clusters are produced, risk probabilities of all inner feature vectors are calculated typically using a parameter called Average Loss Rate (ALR). ALR is actually a proportion which shows the number of unexpected interactions (between mobile and autonomous entities in a ubiquitous computing environment as in (Y. Chen, Jensen, Gray, Cahill, & Seigneur, 2003)) to the total number of interactions. An intuitive idea is to see how each feature vector is close to the average vector within any clusters. Therefore, the risk probability associated with each feature vector depends on its similarity to the average vector and the ALR.

When the framework or architecture is trained using the historical data, it can be used to have a prediction of risks in future by following a similar process. In particular, a new vector is produced by extracting all features from the current information. Then, the clustering procedure is applied to this new vector after which it should belong to one of the previous constructed clusters. Finally, the risk value of this feature vector is calculated through multiplying its similarity rate to the average vector by the ALR parameter. It must be noted that history information usually involves a significant amount of risk-related information. Thus, some methods are suggested in (C. Fu et al., 2010) to reduce the data dimension.

Both of the works that use clustering for modeling security threats (Liu et al., 2005), (Y. Chen et al., 2003) evaluate risks quantitatively. Furthermore, regarding how frequent they update risk magnitudes, (Y. Chen et al., 2003) uses a continuous mechanism, while (Liu et al., 2005) does not present any information about this criterion.

In a fuzzy based model, a fuzzy set is constructed based on several linguistic input parameters (such as threats and their corresponding impact). Then, a system is used to make an inference using some predefined (if-then) rules (e.g. "*if the threat has a high probability and its impact is very high, then the risk value is very high*"). Finally, the resulting fuzzy output is mapped to a crisp value (numerical value) using the membership functions (through the defuzzification process). This output represents the risk according to the input values. As an example, the work by Michalopoulos et al. measures risks qualitatively using this modeling technique and re-estimates (updates) risk values continuously (Michalopoulos et al., 2014).

Other methods calculate risk values in a different way and are not based on any of the aforementioned threat modeling techniques. The framework introduced in (Ahmed et al., 2011) quantifies objectively the most significant security factors, which include existing vulnerabilities, historical trend of vulnerabilities of the remotely accessible services, prediction of potential vulnerabilities for these services and their estimated severity, unused address space, and, finally, propagation of attacks. The first five factors are used to calculate the threats likelihood, while the last parameter, propagation of attacks, is used to estimate the impact of threats on the assets. Doing so, the overall risk is evaluated considering the likelihood of threats and their impacts on assets. The framework proposed here is in fact based on this hypothesis that if a service has a highly vulnerability prone history, then there is higher probability that the service will become vulnerable again in the near future. However, as mentioned earlier, history information usually includes an extra amount of risk-related information. Thus, (C. Fu et al., 2010) proposes a method to reduce the data dimension. Different from (Ahmed et al., 2011), economical loss derived from security risks is taken into account in (Qi et al., 2010).

Finally, in another model (Rezvani et al., 2014), the risks for both hosts (as an asset) and information flows are assessed, different from other systems that only rely on the risks of flows. The mentioned system is based on this idea that the risk score of a flow influences that of its source and destination hosts, and also the risk score of a host is evaluated by taking into account the scores of flows initiated by or terminated at the host.

From these contributions, all of them evaluate risks quantitatively. Furthermore, (Boyer et al., 2005) and (Ahmed et al., 2011) update risk values continuously different from (Rezvani et al., 2014) that re-estimates risk magnitudes at short time intervals. Other works (Qi et al., 2010), (C. Fu et al., 2010) do not include any information regarding this criterion.

DECISION GUIDE ON DRA FOR DIFFERENT SETTINGS

After a brief introduction of DRA main elements, including assets management, threat modeling, and risk calculation, an appropriate decision guide is presented in this section for three important application contexts related to the 4IR and its underlying IIoT -- Computer Networks (CNs), the Internet of Things (IoT) and Industrial Control Systems (ICSs). In particular, we do address three main issues in what follows. First, how to select the best threat modeling technique based on the identified assets and threats and the characteristics of the application context. Second, what specific architecture to adopt in calculating risk values of a DRA process for each context. Finally, what type of risk calculation to choose based on the assets and threats.

An efficient and reliable DRA is challenging without having a precise modeling of threats. Identifying the type and amount of critical assets, the behavior of threats, and, also, specific characteristics of the application context to which DRA is going to be applied are all some crucial factors which need to be considered in threat modeling. Table 1 shows the suitability of threat modeling techniques based on different assumptions for assets and threats. DRA is particularly useful when threats do change over time (Figure 9). So, once threats are known to be variable, critical assets need to be identified and valued. Then, if threats are found to be categorizable as well, hierarchical modeling techniques can be applied to model threats. Here, a threat on one component in a specific level of system hierarchy would not have the same impact as another threat on a different component in the higher level. If variable threats are not categorizable, the amount of assets and the uncertainty in threats should be considered in adopting other modeling techniques. Therefore, when the amount of assets is big and a high uncertainty exists in threats, using graph structures to model threats (GMs), fuzzy logic (FL) or threats clustering (TC) are the most appropriate techniques. However, when the amount of assets is limited and a high uncertainty exists in threats, HMM modeling is applied. This technique is particularly useful when assets of interest have different security states. Moreover, when assorted types of threats are expected, any modeling techniques can be used except the hierarchical ones in the case we are sure threats are not categorizable.

Due to the uncertain nature of threats appearing in CNs and IoT, HMMs and GM are widely used to model security threats in these application contexts. However, as mentioned earlier, HMMs are suitable when the amount of assets is limited. Furthermore, both of these modeling techniques do not scale well when the number of assets grows excessively. On the other hand, due to the limited number of assets which usually exist in an ICS, HMMs and GM have been used widely to model security threats. Nevertheless, other threat modeling techniques can also be applied as there is less uncertainty in the upcoming threats in this context. Risk assessment systems proposed for ICSs may need to be complemented with some additional considerations that do not exist when doing the same process for traditional IT systems since the impact of threats in an ICS may include both physical and digital effects. As for the goal of this study, decision guides proposed for DRA systems are focused on the risks which are related to information not physical devices.

Risk calculation architecture is the second import issue in DRA which have to be chosen based on the key characteristics of CNs, IoT and ICSs. Some of these characteristics include but not limited to scale, geographical distribution, constraints in power, the Internet usage, need for human interaction, and, finally, the possibility of facing physical impacts as a result of threats.

CNs are the first important area in which security threats may appear, and, thus, the reliability of information needs to be addressed accurately as organizations and enterprises usually own a local network of interconnected computers. However, the scale of computer networks is not limited to small business corporations, and, in most cases, it expands to a vast area. For this reason, computer networks are commonly highly distributed in terms of geographical position. In such a context, computers have direct interactions with users, and, commonly, are not constrained in resources (e.g. processing units and memory). Moreover, they have access to the Internet which may pose considerable amount of potential threats. Last but not least, most of the threats in computer networks may not impose direct physical impacts.

IoT is the second emerging area in which security and privacy is of great concern. It involves a huge amount of connected devices highly distributed in different geographical positions and ranging from smart objects to physical devices, buildings, and also vehicles to name a few. Suitable IoT frameworks should allow the interaction between all these devices and help in the development of distributed applications. These devices do have continuous interactions with users regularly and are commonly resource-constrained. Furthermore, they may not connect to the Internet constantly. Security threats in IoT context would impose both physical and non-physical impacts. Here, threats do appear with uncertainty as well. Also, they may have different levels. So, any of threat modeling techniques capable of dealing with uncertainty such as HMMs, GM, HM or FL are applicable. Nevertheless, HMMs and GM scalability issues should not be neglected.

ICSs are the third area in which security has turned to be a major global concern in recent years. Therefore, ensuring the security of information in such context is critically important. In particular, threats that may lead to loss of information or service in other environments may result in real and

Table 1. Suitability of threat modeling techniques based on assets and threats

Threat Modeling Technique	Assets	Threats
HMMs	• Limited to average number of assets • Assets with different security states	• Threats with uncertainty
GM	• Limited to average number of assets	• Threats with uncertainty
HM	• Large number of assets	• Threats with different levels
TC	• Large number of assets	• Limited known threats
FL	• Large number of assets	• Threats with uncertainty

physical impacts on connected network of industrial control systems. As an example, the Stuxnet worm was mainly developed to target Programmable Logic Controllers (PLCs) that lay at the heart of the centrifuges used by the Iranian government (Campbell, 2016). Another important issue is that ICSs may include devices or components which may or may not be resource-constrained with the ability to be connected to the Internet continuously. They have less human interaction comparing with computer networks and IoT devices. Finally, they are not highly distributed geographically in contrast with IoT devices and computer networks.

Risk assessment systems for computer networks tend to calculate the associated risk of each computer separately and in a centralized manner as it will show the degree of exposure of each of these devices to security threats. Nevertheless, a decentralized risk assessment system would also work for such an application context. Centralized models (proposed in 21 works) assess the risk using a single platform, i.e. they collect the information of different security threats (i.e. their likelihood and impact) in one place in order to evaluate the overall risk of a computer network. On the other side, decentralized models (proposed in 5 works) consider a distributed or a multi-agent framework for this purpose. A decentralized architecture can decrease the computational burden by breaking the task of risk assessment between distributed agents. Furthermore, it provides mechanisms for agents' communications, and, as a result, can lead to better dynamic risk estimation. However, the agents need to be implemented very simple; otherwise, a decentralized model would have a low performance in large complicated networks.

In an IoT context, risk assessment systems need to be designed based on a distributed (decentralized) architecture in order to address the reliability of information in an efficient way. One important aspect is that decentralization involves having several data sources. This issue is beneficial for learning mechanisms such as HMMs, which are well-prepared to combine and mix information elements with different degrees of certainty. However, decentralization needs an additional infrastructure to gather data from different sources (Figure 9). Thus, given a system with a set of agents (in (Haslum et al., 2007), each one being a sensor), each one is equipped with an HMM. In an IoT context, these agents can be assigned to different devices (assets) which are involved. Agents are usually lightweight in order to avoid battery drain in IoT devices (Figure 9). Based on the received information, the goal is to model and predict the next step of attackers considering all the threats and the calculated risks. 4 works (Holgado et al., 2015), (Haslum et al., 2007), (Haslum & Årnes, 2006), (Haslum, Abraham, et al., 2008) present a decentralized architecture for risk assessment based on HMM threat modeling technique (Table 3).

Another decentralized system which can be applied to IoT context is the Epidemiological-based threat modeling technique (Alhomidi & Reed, 2013). Here, a number of cells are employed and assigned to assets, with the capability of communicating with each other through sending and receiving signals. Doing so, the overall risk can be calculated by integrating all the estimations from different cells. More importantly, these signals impose a low computational burden as they do not carry huge amount of information. Thus, this approach has the potential to be applied to large IoT environments for the evaluation of risks due to the constraints in resources.

A dynamic risk assessment system for ICSs may either hold a centralized architecture when it is designed for one particular component (or a number of components), or a decentralized architecture when it is intended to break down the risk assessment process into several agents assigned to the components of an industrial control system. From centralized architectures, (Boyer et al., 2005), (Ahmed et al., 2011), (Rezvani et al., 2014), (Qi et al., 2010), (C. Fu et al., 2010), and, also, all the systems investigated in (Cherdantseva et al., 2016) can be applied to ICS application context. From decentralized architectures,

Figure 9. An overall decision guide for threat modeling, and risk calculation architecture and risk calculation type

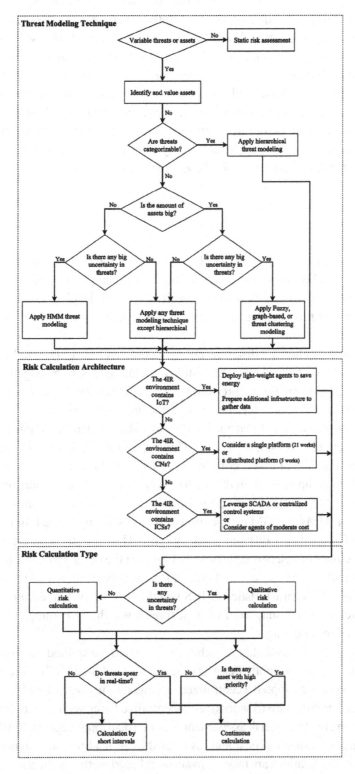

DRA systems proposed for IoT can be adopted for ICSs as well; however, those proposed for ICSs cannot be applied to IoT necessarily as they are constrained in terms of resources.

Finally, risk calculation type (i.e. quantitative/qualitative and continuous/by short intervals) is the third critical issue in DRA which is commonly chosen based on the identified assets and expected appearing threats. Qualitative risk calculation is usually applied when there is an uncertainty in the upcoming threats. As neither the probability of threats nor their impact is known, human linguistic terms are used to help modeling the uncertain threats and measure risk values. Moreover, continuous risk calculation is used when either assets have a high priority (i.e. a minor impact on any of them would impose a huge amount of risk to the overall system) or threats are expected to appear in real-time. In cases where threats do not appear in real-time, risk values are calculated by short intervals though there is always a concern of missing some threats which may appear in these intervals.

CONCLUSION

Security and reliability of information need to be addressed taking into account the current threats in IT environments. This task becomes a challenge taking into account that networks, systems and attacks evolve rapidly over time. In order to achieve the desired security level, it is critical to assess the risk level in a suitable way. For this purpose, different Dynamic Risk Assessment (DRA) approaches have been proposed in the past.

In this work, we have studied 27 different DRA systems and have analyzed them based on three important building blocks of risk assessment systems, including assets management, threat modeling technique, and risk calculation method. Moreover, we have summarized key characteristics of three main application areas which are of great concern nowadays and have suggested decision guides to the security experts in order to choose the best threat modeling and risk calculation techniques for their contexts which are Computer Networks (CNs), Internet of Things (IoT) and Industrial Control Systems (ICSs).

CNs and IoT do contain lots of assets both from hardware and software, and, thus, are considerably larger in terms of scale in comparison with ICSs. Moreover, threats are quite more uncertain and variable in the two former contexts than the latter. Therefore, due to the uncertain nature of threats appearing in computer networks, HMMs and GM can be used to model security threats. In particular, HMMs are suitable when assets of interest have different security states. However, these modeling techniques do not scale well when the number of assets is significantly high. On the other hand, due to the limited number of assets which exists in ICSs and the assorted type of threats appearing, any of the modeling techniques are applicable here. Specific characteristics of ICS should also be considered. For instance, due to the limited human interaction which may exist in ICS, threats which are coming from these interactions should not be neglected in modeling.

There are commonly two risk calculation architectures which are applied based on the characteristics of the application context. In CNs, both architectures can be used potentially. However, the majority of works studied (21 works) have adopted a centralized architecture in contrast with a few ones which have adopted a decentralized architecture (5 works). A decentralized architecture can decrease the computational burden by breaking the task of risk assessment between distributed agents. Furthermore, it provides mechanisms for agents' communications, and, as a result, can lead to better dynamic risk estimation. However, some extra considerations are taken into account based on the application area. For instance, in an IoT context, lightweight agents are assigned to different IoT devices to save energy and avoid battery drain, and, in an ICS context, agents are expected to be of moderate cost. Furthermore, there is always a need to an additional infrastructure to gather data in a distributed architecture.

Rather than considering an architecture for risk calculation process, two main decisions have to be made regarding the type of risk calculation. First, it must be clarified whether risks should be evaluated using quantitative or qualitative metrics. Commonly, qualitative methods are used when there is an uncertainty in the upcoming threats. In considered works, quantitative metrics are adopted in the majority of contributions (24 works). The second issue is to decide whether DRA approaches need to re-estimate and update risk values continuously or by intervals, due to the changes that may occur at different periods of time. Approaches which capture risk values continuously (11 works) can provide with a real-time evaluation of risks. Nevertheless, it comes at a cost of using a flexible threat modeling technique capable of timely adapting to these changes. On the other side, models which capture risk values at short intervals (suggested in 7 works) are less complex as they are based on simpler threat modeling techniques. However, they are prone to miss new security threats which might happen between these intervals.

ACKNOWLEDGMENT

This work has been partially supported by MINECO grants TIN2016-79095-C2-2-R (SMOG-DEV), TIN2013-46469-R (SPINY: Security and Privacy in the Internet of You) and CAM grant S2013/ICE-3095 (CIBERDINE), co-funded with European FEDER funds.

REFERENCES

Ahmed, M. S., Al-Shaer, E., Taibah, M., & Khan, L. (2011). Objective risk evaluation for automated security management. *Journal of Network and Systems Management, 19*(3), 343–366. doi:10.100710922-010-9177-6

Alhomidi, M., & Reed, M. (2013). Risk assessment and analysis through population-based attack graph modelling. In *Internet Security (WorldCIS), 2013 World Congress on* (pp. 19–24). Academic Press. 10.1109/WorldCIS.2013.6751011

Årnes, A., Sallhammar, K., Haslum, K., Brekne, T., Moe, M. E. G., & Knapskog, S. J. (2005). Real-time risk assessment with network sensors and intrusion detection systems. In *International Conference on Computational and Information Science* (pp. 388–397). Academic Press.

Årnes, A., Valeur, F., Vigna, G., & Kemmerer, R. (2006). Using Hidden Markov Models to Evaluate the Risks of Intrusions. *Recent Advances in Intrusion Detection*, 145–164. 10.1007/11856214_8

Awan, M. S. K., Burnap, P., & Rana, O. (2016). Identifying cyber risk hotspots: A framework for measuring temporal variance in computer network risk. *Computers & Security, 57*, 31–46. doi:10.1016/j.cose.2015.11.003

Behnia, A., Rashid, R. A., & Chaudhry, J. A. (2012). A survey of information security risk analysis methods. *SmartCR, 2*(1), 79–94.

Benini, M., & Sicari, S. (2008). Risk assessment in practice: A real case study. *Computer Communications*, *31*(15), 3691–3699. doi:10.1016/j.comcom.2008.07.001

Blank, R. M., & Gallagher, P. D. (2012). *Guide for Conducting Risk Assessments*. NIST Special Publication.

Boyer, S., Dain, O., & Cunningham, R. (2005). Stellar: A fusion system for scenario construction and security risk assessment. In *Information Assurance, 2005. Proceedings. Third IEEE International Workshop on* (pp. 105–116). IEEE. 10.1109/IWIA.2005.16

Calder, A., & Watkins, S. G. (2010). *Information Security Risk Management for ISO27001/ISO27002*. Retrieved from https://books.google.com/books?hl=es&lr=&id=8Ffa1dOFgO4C&pgis=1

Campbell, T. (2016). Information Security Implementation. In *Practical Information Security Management* (pp. 63–70). Springer. doi:10.1007/978-1-4842-1685-9_5

Caralli, R. A., Stevens, J. F., Young, L. R., & Wilson, W. R. (2007). *Introducing octave allegro: Improving the information security risk assessment process*. Academic Press.

Chen, G. (2010). Research on network security real-time risk assessment model. In *Electronics and Information Engineering (ICEIE), 2010 International Conference On* (Vol. 2, pp. V2--548). ICEIE. 10.1109/ICEIE.2010.5559746

Chen, Y., Jensen, C. D., Gray, E., Cahill, V., & Seigneur, J.-M. (2003). *A general risk assessment of security in pervasive computing*. Retrieved from Https://www. Cs. Tcd. Ie/publications/techreports/reports, 3

Cheng, W., Xu, X., Jia, Y., & Zou, P. (2008). Network Dynamic Risk Assessment Based on the Threat Stream Analysis. In *The Ninth International Conference on Web-Age Information Management* (pp. 532–538). IEEE. 10.1109/WAIM.2008.65

Cherdantseva, Y., Burnap, P., Blyth, A., Eden, P., Jones, K., Soulsby, H., & Stoddart, K. (2016). A review of cyber security risk assessment methods for SCADA systems. *Computers & Security*, *56*, 1–27. doi:10.1016/j.cose.2015.09.009

Chołda, P., & Jaglarz, P. (2016). Optimization/simulation-based risk mitigation in resilient green communication networks. *Journal of Network and Computer Applications*, *59*, 134–157. doi:10.1016/j.jnca.2015.07.009

Clinch, J. (2009, May). ITIL v3 and information security. *Clinch Consulting White Paper*, 1–40.

Crespo, F. L., Amutio-Gómez, M. A., Candau, J., & Mañas, J. A. (2006). Methodology for Information Systems Risk Analysis and Management (MAGERIT version 2). In Book II-Catalogue of Elements. Madrid: Ministerio de Administraciones Públicas.

Dantu, R., Kolan, P., & Cangussu, J. (2009). Network risk management using attacker profiling. *Security and Communication Networks*, *2*(1), 83–96. doi:10.1002ec.58

de Gusmão, A. P. H., Silva, L. C., Silva, M. M., Poleto, T., & Costa, A. P. C. S. (2016). Information security risk analysis model using fuzzy decision theory. *International Journal of Information Management*, *36*(1), 25–34. doi:10.1016/j.ijinfomgt.2015.09.003

De Haes, S., Van Grembergen, W., & Debreceny, R. S. (2013). COBIT 5 and Enterprise Governance of Information Technology: Building Blocks and Research Opportunities. *Journal of Information Systems*, *27*(1), 307–324. doi:10.2308/isys-50422

Deka, R. K., Kalita, K. P., Bhattacharya, D. K., & Kalita, J. K. (2015). Network defense: Approaches, methods and techniques. *Journal of Network and Computer Applications*, *57*, 71–84. doi:10.1016/j.jnca.2015.07.011

Dongmei, Z., Changguang, W., & Jianfeng, M. (2007). A risk assessment method of the wireless network security. *Journal of Electronics (China)*, *24*(3), 428–432. doi:10.100711767-006-0247-6

Elliott, R. J., Aggoun, L., & Moore, J. B. (2008). *Hidden Markov models: estimation and control* (Vol. 29). Springer Science & Business Media.

Frigault, M., & Wang, L. (2008). *Measuring network security using bayesian network-based attack graphs*. IEEE. doi:10.1109/COMPSAC.2008.88

Fu, C., Ye, J., Zhang, L., Zhang, Y., & LanSheng, H. (2010). A Dynamic Risk Assessment Framework Using Principle Component Analysis with Projection Pursuit in Ad Hoc Networks. *Ubiquitous Intelligence & Computing and 7th International Conference on Autonomic & Trusted Computing (UIC/ATC), 2010 7th International Conference on*, 154–159. 10.1109/UIC-ATC.2010.42

Fu, S., & Zhou, H. (2011). The information security risk assessment based on AHP and fuzzy comprehensive evaluation. In *2011 IEEE 3rd International Conference on Communication Software and Networks* (pp. 124–128). IEEE. 10.1109/ICCSN.2011.6014018

Gao, F., Sun, J., & We, Z. (2003). The prediction role of hidden Markov model in intrusion detection. *CCECE 2003 - Canadian Conference on Electrical and Computer Engineering. Toward a Caring and Humane Technology (Cat. No.03CH37436)*, *2*, 893–896. 10.1109/CCECE.2003.1226038

Garvey, P. R. (2008). *Analytical methods for risk management: A systems engineering perspective*. CRC Press. doi:10.1201/9781420011395

Gehling, B., & Stankard, D. (2005). eCommerce security. In *Proceedings of the 2nd annual conference on Information security curriculum development - InfoSecCD '05* (p. 32). New York: ACM Press. 10.1145/1107622.1107631

Haslum, K., Abraham, A., & Knapskog, S. (2007). DIPS: A Framework for Distributed Intrusion Prediction and Prevention Using Hidden Markov Models and Online Fuzzy Risk Assessment. In *Third International Symposium on Information Assurance and Security* (pp. 183–190). IEEE. 10.1109/IAS.2007.67

Haslum, K., Abraham, A., & Knapskog, S. (2008). Fuzzy online risk assessment for distributed intrusion prediction and prevention systems. *Proceedings - UKSim 10th International Conference on Computer Modelling and Simulation, EUROSIM/UKSim2008*, 216–223. 10.1109/UKSIM.2008.30

Haslum, K., & Årnes, A. (2006). Multisensor real-time risk assessment using continuous-time hidden markov models. In *International Conference on Computational and Information Science* (pp. 694–703). Academic Press. 10.1109/ICCIAS.2006.295318

Haslum, K., Moe, M. E. G., & Knapskog, S. J. (2008). Real-time intrusion prevention and security analysis of networks using HMMs. *2008 33rd IEEE Conference on Local Computer Networks (LCN)*, 927–934. 10.1109/LCN.2008.4664305

Holgado, P., Perez, M. G., Perez, G. M., & Villagra, V. A. (n.d.). Evolving from a static toward a proactive and dynamic risk-based defense strategy. Jornadas Nacionales de Investigacion en Ciberseguridad (JNIC 2015).

Hu, Z.-H., Ding, Y.-S., & Huang, J.-W. (2008). Knowledge-based framework for real-time risk assessment of information security inspired by danger model. In *Intelligent Information Technology Application Workshops, 2008. IITAW'08. International Symposium on* (pp. 1053–1056). Academic Press.

Ionita, D., Hartel, P. H., Pieters, W., & Wieringa, R. J. (2013). *Current established risk assessment methodologies and tools*. Technical Report TR-CTIT-14-04, Centre for Telematics and Information Technology, University of Twente, Enschede. Retrieved from http://eprints.eemcs.utwente.nl/24541/01/%5Btech_report%5D_D_Ionita_-_Current_Established_Risk_Assessment_Methodologies_and_Tools.pdf

Kaplan, S., & Garrick, B. J. (1981). On the quantitative definition of risk. *Risk Analysis*, *1*(1), 11–27. doi:10.1111/j.1539-6924.1981.tb01350.x PMID:11798118

Kurosu, M. (2013). Human-Computer Interaction: Towards Intelligent and Implicit Interaction. In *15th International Conference, HCI International 2013 Proceedings* (Vol. 8008). Springer.

Lee, E. A. (2008). Cyber Physical Systems: Design Challenges. *2008 11th IEEE International Symposium on Object and Component-Oriented Real-Time Distributed Computing (ISORC)*, 363–369. 10.1109/ISORC.2008.25

Li, J. H., & Levy, R. (2010). Using Bayesian networks for cyber security analysis. *2010 IEEE/IFIP International Conference on Dependable Systems & Networks (DSN)*, 211–220. 10.1109/DSN.2010.5544924

Li, W., & Guo, Z. (2009). Hidden Markov Model Based Real Time Network Security Quantification Method. *2009 International Conference on Networks Security, Wireless Communications and Trusted Computing*, 94–100. 10.1109/NSWCTC.2009.375

Liao, N., Li, F., & Song, Y. (2010). Research on real-time network security risk assessment and forecast. In *Intelligent Computation Technology and Automation (ICICTA), 2010 International Conference on* (Vol. 3, pp. 84–87). Academic Press. 10.1109/ICICTA.2010.273

Liu, F., Chen, Y., Dai, K., Wang, Z., & Cai, Z. (2005). *Research on Risk Probability Estimating Using Fuzzy Clustering for Dynamic Security*. Academic Press.

López, D., Pastor, O., & Villalba, L. J. G. (2013). Dynamic risk assessment in information systems: State-of-the-art. *Proceedings of the 6th International Conference on Information Technology*, 8–10. Retrieved from http://sce.zuj.edu.jo/icit13/images/Camera Ready/Sorftware Engineering/772.pdf

Ma, J., Li, Z., & Zhang, H. (2009). A fusion model for network threat identification and risk assessment. In *Artificial Intelligence and Computational Intelligence, 2009. AICI'09. International Conference on* (Vol. 1, pp. 314–318). Academic Press. doi:10.1109/AICI.2009.487

Mendel, J. M. (1995). Fuzzy logic systems for engineering: A tutorial. *Proceedings of the IEEE, 83*(3), 345–377. doi:10.1109/5.364485

Michalopoulos, D., Mavridis, I., & Jankovic, M. (2014). GARS: Real-time system for identification, assessment and control of cyber grooming attacks. *Computers & Security, 42*, 177–190. doi:10.1016/j.cose.2013.12.004

Nadeem, A., & Howarth, M. P. (2013). A survey of manet intrusion detection & prevention approaches for network layer attacks. *IEEE Communications Surveys and Tutorials, 15*(4), 2027–2045. doi:10.1109/SURV.2013.030713.00201

Phillips, C., & Swiler, L. P. (1998). A graph-based system for network-vulnerability analysis. In *Proceedings of the 1998 workshop on New security paradigms* (pp. 71–79). Academic Press. 10.1145/310889.310919

Poolsappasit, N., Dewri, R., & Ray, I. (2012). Dynamic security risk management using bayesian attack graphs. *IEEE Transactions on Dependable and Secure Computing, 9*(1), 61–74. doi:10.1109/TDSC.2011.34

Poovendran, R. (2010). Cyber-physical systems: Close encounters between two parallel worlds. *Proceedings of the IEEE, 98*(8), 1363–1366. doi:10.1109/JPROC.2010.2050377

Qi, W., Liu, X., Zhang, J., & Yuan, W. (2010). *Dynamic Assessment and VaR-Based Quantification of Information Security Risk. In 2010 2nd International Conference on E-business and Information System Security* (pp. 1–4). IEEE; doi:10.1109/EBISS.2010.5473537.

Rezvani, M., Ignjatovic, A., Bertino, E., & Jha, S. (2014). Provenance-aware security risk analysis for hosts and network flows. In Network Operations and Management Symposium (NOMS), 2014 IEEE (pp. 1–8). IEEE. doi:10.1109/NOMS.2014.6838250

Rutkowski, L., & Cpalka, K. (2003). Flexible neuro-fuzzy systems. *IEEE Transactions on Neural Networks, 14*(3), 554–574. doi:10.1109/TNN.2003.811698 PubMed

Sadeghi, A.-R., Wachsmann, C., & Waidner, M. (2015). Security and privacy challenges in industrial internet of things. In *Proceedings of the 52nd Annual Design Automation Conference on - DAC '15* (pp. 1–6). New York: ACM Press. 10.1145/2744769.2747942

Shameli-Sendi, A., Ezzati-jivan, N., Jabbarifar, M., & Dagenais, M. (2012). Intrusion Response Systems : Survey and Taxonomy. *International Journal of Computer Science and Network Security, 12*(1), 1–14. Retrieved from http://paper.ijcsns.org/07_book/201201/20120101.pdf

Shedden, P., Scheepers, R., Smith, W., & Ahmad, A. (2011). Incorporating a knowledge perspective into security risk assessments. *Vine, 41*(2), 152–166. doi:10.1108/03055721111134790

Shoemaker, D., & Conklin, W. A. (2011). *Cybersecurity: The Essential Body Of Knowledge*. Cengage Learning. Retrieved from https://books.google.com/books?id=TUUKAAAAQBAJ&pgis=1

Tabak, D., & Levis, A. H. (1985). Petri net representation of decision models. *IEEE Transactions on Systems, Man, and Cybernetics. SMC, 15*(6), 812–818. doi:10.1109/TSMC.1985.6313468

Volftrub, A. B., & Polikarpov, A. K. (2007). Methods of multifactor damage risk management in automated information systems. *Automatic Documentation and Mathematical Linguistics*, *41*(1), 46–52. doi:10.3103/S0005105507010074

Von Solms, S. H. (2005). Information Security Governance - Compliance management vs operational management. *Computers & Security*, *24*(6), 443–447. doi:10.1016/j.cose.2005.07.003

Wilkin, C. L., & Chenhall, R. H. (2010). A Review of IT Governance: A Taxonomy to Inform Accounting Information Systems. *Journal of Information Systems*, *24*(2), 107–146. doi:10.2308/jis.2010.24.2.107

Wrona, K., & Hallingstad, G. (2010). Real-time automated risk assessment in protected core networking. *Telecommunication Systems*, *45*(January), 205–214. doi:10.100711235-009-9242-1

Wu, T., & Zhao, G. (2014). A novel risk assessment model for privacy security in Internet of Things. *Wuhan University Journal of Natural Sciences*, *19*(5), 398–404. doi:10.100711859-014-1031-3

Yazar, Z. (2002). *A qualitative risk analysis and management tool--CRAMM.* SANS InfoSec Reading Room White Paper.

Yu-Ting, D., Hai-Peng, Q., & Xi-Long, T. (2014). Real-time risk assessment based on hidden Markov model and security configuration. In *2014 International Conference on Information Science, Electronics and Electrical Engineering* (Vol. 3, pp. 1600–1603). IEEE. 10.1109/InfoSEEE.2014.6946191

Zhang, Y., Jiang, S., Cui, Y., Zhang, B., & Xia, H. (2010). A qualitative and quantitative risk assessment method in software security. In *2010 3rd International Conference on Advanced Computer Theory and Engineering(ICACTE)* (Vol. 1, pp. V1-534-V1-539). IEEE. 10.1109/ICACTE.2010.5578960

Zhiwei, Y., & Zhongyuan, J. (2012). A survey on the evolution of risk evaluation for information systems security. *Energy Procedia*, *17*, 1288–1294. doi:10.1016/j.egypro.2012.02.240

Zhou, L., & Chen, S. (2012). A survey of research on smart grid security. In *Network Computing and Information Security* (pp. 395–405). Springer. doi:10.1007/978-3-642-35211-9_52

KEY TERMS AND DEFINITIONS

Assets Management: It deals with three main issues, including types of the assets which need to be considered, their behavior, and, also their valuation.

Risk: An estimation of the degree of exposure to a threat that may occur on one or more assets causing damage to an organization.

Risk Assessment: An assessment which is made based on the impact that each risk event could have on the assets of system.

Risk Identification: Early identification of risks that can impact on the system's assets in particular, and on system's performance in general.

Risk Management: A general process to handle risks as it serves to identify, assess, prioritize, mitigate, and track them.

Risk Mitigation: Plans which are designed to manage, eliminate, or reduce risks to an acceptable level.

Risk Prioritization: A major purpose for prioritizing risks is to form a basis for allocating critical resources, including additional personnel or funding to resolve those risks.

Risk Tracking: The main goal of risk tracking is the exact monitoring of risk assessment and mitigation strategies based on the priorities of risks.

Threat Modeling: It models security threats which may impose risks to assets of interest.

APPENDIX

Table 2. Dynamic Risk Assessment Models in IT environments

DRA Approach	Assets		Threats		Threat Modeling Technique						Risk Calculation				Setting		
	Type	Valuation	Type	Evolution	HMMs	GM	HM	TC	FL	Others	Quantitative	Qualitative	Continuously	In Short Intervals	CN	IoT	ICS
(Holgado et al., 2015)	NA	NA	NA	Dynamic	×						×			×		×	
(Haslum et al., 2007)	Data, Devices	Cost, Criticality, Sensitivity, Recovery	NA	NA	×						×		×			×	
(Haslum & Årnes, 2006)	Computer Network	Confidentiality, Integrity, Availability	NA	NA	×							×		×		×	
(Årnes et al., 2005)	Computer Network	Confidentiality, Integrity, Availability	NA	NA	×						×	×			×		
(W. Li & Guo, 2009)	NA	NA	Multi-step DDoS	Dynamic	×						×	×			×		
(G. Chen, 2010)	NA	NA	NA	NA	×						×			×	×		
(Årnes et al., 2006)	NA	Confidentiality, Integrity, Availability	DDoS	NA	×						×	×			×		
(Ma et al., 2009)	NA	Confidentiality, Integrity, Availability	Multi-step DDoS	Dynamic	×						×			×	×		
(Yu-Ting et al., 2014)	NA	Confidentiality, Integrity, Availability	Attacks that destruct confidentiality, integrity and availability	NA	×						×			×	×		

DRA Approach	Assets		Threats		Threat Modeling Technique						Risk Calculation				Setting		
	Type	Valuation	Type	Evolution	HMMs	GM	HM	TC	FL	Others	Quantitative	Qualitative	Continuously	In Short Intervals	CN	IoT	ICS
(Haslum, Abraham, et al., 2008)	NA	Cost, Criticality, Sensitivity, Recovery	DoS, User to Root, Remote to Local, Probing	Dynamic	×							×		×		×	
(Phillips & Swiler, 1998)	NA	NA	Simulated attacks	Dynamic		×					×				×		
(Alhomidi & Reed, 2013)	NA	NA	NA	NA		×					×					×	
(Poolsappasit et al., 2012)	NA	Confidentiality, Integrity, Availability	NA	Dynamic		×					×				×		
(Wu & Zhao, 2014)	NA	Confidentiality, Integrity, Availability	Various kinds of attacks including DoS	Dynamic		×					×				×		
(Wrona & Hallingstad, 2010)	NA	Main focus on Availability	DoS	Dynamic		×					×		×		×		
(Dantu et al., 2009)	NA	NA	NA	NA		×					×				×		
(Liao et al., 2010)	NA	Confidentiality, Integrity, Availability	A simulated intruder	NA		×					×		×		×		
(Hu et al., 2008)	NA	NA	NA	Dynamic		×					×		×		×		
(Volftrub & Polikarpov, 2007)	NA	NA	NA	Dynamic			×				×				×		
(Liu et al., 2005)	NA	NA	NA	NA					×		×				×		
(Y. Chen et al., 2003)	NA	NA	NA	NA					×		×		×		×		
(Michalopoulos et al., 2014)	NA	NA	Grooming attacks	NA					×			×	×		×		

continued on following page

Table 2. Continued

DRA Approach	Assets		Threats		Threat Modeling Technique						Risk Calculation				Setting		
	Type	Valuation	Type	Evolution	HMMs	GM	HM	TC	FL	Others	Quantitative	Qualitative	Continuously	In Short Intervals	CN	IoT	ICS
(Boyer et al., 2005)	NA	NA	NA	NA						×	×		×				×
(Qi et al., 2010)	Software, Hardware, Data, Fame, Reputation, Public trust, Employees' confidence	Assets are recognized and assigned a value manually	NA	Dynamic						×	×						×
(Ahmed et al., 2011)	NA	NA	DDoS	Dynamic						×	×		×				×
(Rezvani et al., 2014)	NA	NA	DDoS	NA						×	×			×			×
(C. Fu et al., 2010)	NA	NA	NA	NA						×	×						×

HMMs: Hidden Markov Models
GM: Graph-based Modeling
HM: Hierarchical Modeling
TC: Threats Clustering
FL: Fuzzy Logic
CN: Computer Networks
IoT: Internet of Things
ICS: Industrial Control Systems

Chapter 10

Beware!
A Multimodal Analysis of Cautionary Tales in Strategic Cybersecurity Messaging Online

Shalin Hai-Jew
Kansas State University, USA

ABSTRACT

Cautionary tales are structured stories that describe protagonists who are faced with critical decisions and often take wrong turns and suffer for it, sometimes irretrievably; these tales warn people of dangers. In cybersecurity communications, cautionary tales are an integral part of the strategic messaging. This chapter explores the uses of multimodal cautionary tales in strategic cybersecurity communications, in a convenience sampling of the following: mass-scale search terms, academic and mass media text sets, social imagery, related tags networks, and social video. This work identifies their strengths and weaknesses in suggesting methods for promoting personal cybersecurity safety. Some suggestions for higher efficacy in cybersecurity cautionary tales are suggested, in light of the advent of the Fourth Industrial Revolution.

INTRODUCTION

A basic definition of cyber reads: "relating to or characteristic of the culture of computers, information technology, and virtual reality" in Google's built-in dictionary to Google Search. For common users of cyber tools, "cyber" may evoke social spaces, distal connectivity, information-sharing, convenience for everyday life activities, entertainment, and even some bit of magic. While users may be aware of risks in cyberspace, these perils may be relegated to ephemera, the great unreal.

Whether people directly access cyberspace or not, they are vulnerable to cyber risks because of the heavy reliance on cyber for virtually every aspect of modern life (at least in the West). "Cybersecurity" refers to a wide range of efforts to try to shore up these technologies and systems to not only preserve the systems and their contents, but also their functionalities and what these provide for people's lives:

DOI: 10.4018/978-1-5225-4763-1.ch010

Cybersecurity is the body of technologies, processes and practices designed to protect networks, computers, programs and data from attack, damage or unauthorized access" and includes "application security, information security, network security, disaster recovery / business continuity planning, operational security (and) end-user education ("cybersecurity," Nov. 2016).

Those who are tasked with cybersecurity—in public and private sectors—have a range of tools to protect both the human populations and "cyberspace". Theirs is a mixed role because they have to maintain user confidence by not scaring users (their "installed base") unduly or else risk mass defections while encouraging proper behaviors that promote both cybersecurity and cyber safety.

Law enforcement (government) also has to make cyber a governed space, where rule-of-law applies. They have a range of tools (legal, technological, and others) to actualize this.

In the area of "end-user education," strategic messaging plays an important role. One of the strategic messaging tools that has evolved over the years is the "cautionary tale," a holdover from folklore with its oral traditions. The purpose of these stories was to warn hearers of risks, so they could avoid punishing outcomes. Most cautionary tales of old are comprised of three parts:

First, a taboo or prohibition is stated: some act, location, or thing is said to be dangerous. Then, the narrative itself is told: someone disregarded the warning and performed the forbidden act. Finally, the violator comes to an unpleasant fate, which is frequently related in expansive and grisly detail. ("Cautionary tale," May 31, 2017)

They have appeared in many forms of oral storytelling and also have been with humanity in writing as well, initially in religious texts, and then secular ones, fables, and children's stories. The core dynamic is the caution of what not to do to serve as an inoculant against poor decision-making. Cautionary tales are a popular part of pop culture; they have appeared in memes; they have appeared as exaggerated "urban legends," which could be true…but are not. Cautionary tales have even spawned "legend tripping" ("in which a cautionary tale is turned into the basis of a dare that invites the hearer to test the taboo by breaking it") ("Cautionary tale," May 31, 2017).

Some common cybersecurity taboos or prohibitions in the current age (for common users) are that thou shalt *not*…

- …share personally identifiable information (PII) in public forums
- …leak data through mishandling hardware, improperly vetting shared information, de-identifying information, or other steps
- …overshare, drunk tweet, get caught or start a tweet storm, start a feud, troll others, or misuse social media
- …take insane risks like buildering or sexting to grab attention in selfie-taking and selfie-sharing
- …respond to phishing or spear-phishing emails by giving away credentials or downloading key-loggers or malware to the local machine
- …share or download copyrighted contents online
- …install malware and spyware on a computer advertently or inadvertently
- …allow one's computers to be used as part of a botnet
- …avoid updating operating systems, software, and other dated systems
- …friend 'bots while unaware that they are 'bots

- …get fooled by robots used to spread inaccurate information as news
- …install insecure devices into their homes in the timely Internet of Things (IoT)
- …get pwned or p0wned ("player owned" or exploited) in any way, shape, or form in cyberspace
- …get rid of hardware without clean wipes of all the contents and / or physical destruction of the devices
- …mishandle devices and memory drives
- …without information about cybersecurity compromises if sharing the information will help others not be similarly compromised
- …consider leaking sensitive data that one does not legally have any right to and risk national security
- …fall for 'bot girlfriends, Nigerian prince boyfriends, or other common frauds and hoaxes
- …carry fully loaded laptops and mobile devices with sensitive information while traveling abroad
- …loan computer devices to others along with their own personal credentials
- …confuse the fake with the real, the illusory parasocial with the social, the virtual with the analog, *ad infinitum*
- …go down the dark alleyways of the Dark Web, and so on …

From even the partial list above, it is clear that those who would exercise proper cybersecurity handling have a broad range of possible attack vectors and vulnerabilities, and most of these are beyond a common user's purview. This is especially true in the Fourth Industrial Revolution (4IR), which broadens cyber into people's bodies (for health, for augmentations, for pleasure, and others), cars (for self-driving, for driver awareness, for entertainment, and others), homes (for convenience, environmental controls, entertainment, security, and others), environment, and elsewhere.

Cautionary tales in cybersecurity are not necessarily so formulaic, particularly in terms of any lock-step chronological sequence, but many are set up to warn people of risks in order to change their behaviors. In many cases, the taboo or prohibition is not directly stated. The narrative may begin with a character in a context, a decision point, a decision, and then impacts. It is only after a close reading and parsing out details and maybe bringing in some knowledge about cybersecurity that the lessons become clearer. In terms of general stories, narrations from of old, the typical story arc builds up tension to a climax, and then a denouement or resolution follows. Certainly, stories are a familiar form of conveying knowledge, and they are in the realm of the deeply familiar. As such, they are fairly effective as part of an overall communications strategy for cybersecurity warnings, assuming several things are achieved:

- The story hearer (reader) has to care sufficiently to consume the cautionary tale.
- The story recipient has to understand the information.
- The person has to trust the information (and the source of that information).
- The person has to be sufficiently invested to follow the suggestions for a safer and more secure use of cyber.

The crux of harnessed cybersecurity cautionary tales is to raise awareness and to change behaviors. Behavior change communication (from healthcare) suggests that a person goes through the following stages: "Unaware > Aware > Concerned > Knowledgeable > Motivated to change > Practicing trial behavior change > Sustained behavior change" ("Behavior change communication," July 17, 2017), and such changes are hard and require long-term engagement.

The different instantiations of cautionary tales in cybersecurity is positive because many audience members would be turned-off by didactic lessons masquerading as stories. One accusation is that some cautionary tales are set up in a "ham-fisted" way ("Cautionary tale," May 31, 2017). As a form, cautionary tales are somewhat questionable because they are used by those "whose job it is to enforce conformity" ("Cautionary tale," May 31, 2017). Those tasked to enforce conformity sound suspiciously like law enforcement, sufficiently to spark some social resistance. These cautionary tales take different forms based on digital modalities. For example, the lessons may be much clearer and more direct in some forms (text, cartoons, digital posters, social videos, and others) than others (mass-scale search data, social imagery, related tags networks, and others). Still, cautionary storytelling is a central part of cybersecurity outreaches on the Web and Internet.

This sounds simple enough. Capture attention. Convey information with clarity (and control for misunderstandings). Be credible by being trustworthy and accurate. And encourage people's senses of efficacy and commitment. Done. Not quite. Where are some main challenges?

1. **Cyber and Cybersecurity are Fast-Evolving Fields:** The threats that are being identified are evolving. They can come from any combination of technologies, hardware and software. They can evolve the compromises of people, such as through social engineering. They can involve compromises of systems. Recognizing threats is a rare art form. What is true in one context—yes, install an optimization tool that cleans off digital garbage from a PC—may not be true in another (Constantin, Sept. 21, 2017). Put any software system into a Google Search, and the auto-fill will often include "hacked" after the software name. Cybersecurity involves a high level of intrinsic cognitive load based on essential complexities. Even if a person took all cyber-precautions, there is still a range of areas of potential compromises—of data, personal credentials, finances, and peace-of-mind. It is hard to fault people for user fatigue. It is also easy to understand why there is a focus on recoverability and resilience—to get past some of the almost inevitable network and / or data compromises.

2. **Reaching Humans is Hard Because They are Complex and Diverse:** They approach the topic of cybersecurity with differing levels of knowledge and differing attitudes. Should the amount of emotional intensity in a cautionary tale be dialed up or down for a particular learner? What will that learner respond to vs. what other learners respond to? And how can people be reached when they select their own sources of news? After all, recent research suggests that 62% of U.S. adults "get news from social media, and 18% do so often" (Gottfried & Shearer, May 26, 2016). Even when people are broadly exposed to a wide range of news sources, they may well tune out or be cognitively biased against what they do not already yet believe given human hard wiring. As noted in the main body of the chapter, cautionary tales in cybersecurity may not necessarily be fully specified. There may or may not be behavioral suggestions to the story. How different people respond to a particular tale may vary, and besides, the news consumption of individuals may also vary greatly (there is now no longer a homogeneous audience which consumes a few sources of convergent media). Still, there may be some sense of somewhat desirable responses: improved awareness, empowerment to act effectively, informed decision-making, and so on.

3. **There are Limits to the Respective Digital Modalities:** What can be told through a social image is different than what can be told through a video or an academic article or a folk tag network. Where the "medium is the message," the mediums can affect the messaging.

Two main hypotheses are explored in this work. They are focused on both the harnessing of cautionary tales as strategic communications in cybersecurity and various strategic strengths / weaknesses of this form as practiced in selected cybersecurity messaging on the Web and Internet. They are the following:

Hypothesis 1: Cautionary tales re: cybersecurity (in multimodal digital formats) are strategic messages to convey ways for individuals and populations to avoid cyber compromises.

> **Hypothesis 1a:** Cautionary tales re: cybersecurity are structured messages that have aspects that enhance their strategic messaging role to mainstream users of cyber.

> **Hypothesis 1b:** The counter assertion is also true: cautionary tales regarding cybersecurity will have aspects that detract from their strategic messaging role to mainstream users of cyber.

Hypothesis 2: There are strategic ways to improve the uses of cautionary tales re: cybersecurity to enhance their effectiveness for receivers of those messages (in terms of non-expert individuals and populations).

To test the hypotheses, various sources of cybersecurity-based information designed for a mass and public audience were explored: mass-scale search terms, academic and mass media text sets, social imagery, related tags networks, and social video. This is not a comprehensive capturing of digital and multimodal data sources online, but these are a start. And while these are convenience samples, in many cases, they are not insubstantial. When "cyber security" was placed in the general Google Search, there were 4,450,000 results; when it was put into Google Scholar, in quotation marks, 108,000 results were surfaced. There are a number of resources related to cyber security online. To address a very live topic in academic writing, it is sometimes necessary to access online sources and more gray literature. Also, a number of technologies were used for the research and creation of this chapter: Google Correlate, Google Search, Google Translate, Flickr, Flickr Downloadr, NVivo 11 Plus, Microsoft Excel, Network Overview, Discovery and Exploration for Excel (NodeXL), Adobe Photoshop, Microsoft Visio, and others. (The author does not have any formal tie to the software makers, and this mention does not indicate endorsement.)

REVIEW OF THE LITERATURE

Cybersecurity is a core concern of governments, industry, and general populations. For governments, there is a range of concerns, which involve ensuring that the government can function effectively in all its responsibilities: national security, public safety, administration of law and justice, free and fair elections, taxation, diplomacy, and so on. In a cyber sense, these responsibilities include the following:

- Setting up a credible defense and offense against cyber warfare
- Ensuring cyber capabilities for law enforcement
- Protecting infrastructures from cyber attack
- Protecting government systems from cyber espionage
- Providing government services even in context
- Protecting elections from foreign manipulation, and others.

There is the sense that what is valued in the U.S. is at risk through cyber means:

Things we value—personal wealth, national economic prosperity, intellectual property, national secu-rity secrets—are all targets. More and more, these treasures reside in or depend upon cyberspace—the new battleground or, in Pentagon parlance, the "warfighting domain where adversaries are already operating." Ability to keep pace with the cyber evolutionary curve, or perhaps to stay a step ahead of those who wish to do harm, depends on the ability to visualize how to fight in this new domain, just as strategists from earlier eras had to imagine how operating in the air, or with nuclear weapons, changed military affairs. (Goldman & Arquilla, 2014, p. 1)

A common analogy used to rally policymakers, the general public, and those on the front lines in cybersecurity has been the historical event of Pearl Harbor (when the Imperial Japanese Navy Air Service attacked the U.S. naval base at Pearl Harbor on Dec. 7, 1941, resulting in 2,400 deaths of U.S. sailors and 1,200 wounded, and the damage or destruction of 19 ships and damage to over 159 aircraft and the destruction of 169 airplanes ("Remembering Pearl Harbor: A Pearl Harbor Fact Sheet," n.d.) As an analogical cautionary tale, a "cyber Pearl Harbor" suggests that the U.S. should not be caught off guard by another nation-state again in a catastrophic infrastructure attack and that it should be prepared with a proper defense. This idea of a potential mega-scale attack through cyber means (in part or in whole) dates back to 1991 (Lawson, Dec. 7, 2016). The concept of a potential cyber Pearl Harbor has been critiqued as not directly applicable and hyperbolic. This analogy is inappropriate because it overplays the power of tactical surprise:

Although operational or tactical surprise in war is universally endorsed as a force multiplier, relying on surprise as a "war winning" initiative at the outset of hostilities is an extraordinarily risky gamble. It is attractive to the weaker party in a potential conflict because of its military inferiority vis-à-vis the stronger party. One of the most common misconceptions surrounding surprise attack is that it occurs because the weaker party launching the attack overestimates its military prowess; in fact, both the weaker and the stronger party, for that matter, generally possess an accurate picture of the military balance. Because the weaker party recognizes its military inferiority, it seeks to develop various stratagems to circumvent a stronger opponent's military might in order to achieve some fait accompli or to alter the incentives of the stronger. (Wirtz, 2014, p. 7)

One instantiation of a cyber Pearl Harbor may be the taking out of the U.S. power grid, which has been a not-uncommon conceptualization in fiction as well as in non-fictional scenario building. In such a case, after a cyber attack on the U.S. national power grid, there are a number of follow-on effects: law and order breaks down, food stores run out, sanitation becomes a major problem, and mass numbers of people are in dire need of help. These scenarios cannot be conceptualized independent of tensions in international relations. News accounts have suggested that "logic bombs" have been found emplaced in various parts of the U.S. power grid that could be activated in cases of active hostilities. In a recently published book, in a chapter titled "Warfare 2.0," one author begins a nonfiction work with a doomsday scenario… profound darkness following the shut-down of a city when its electricity has been turned off from a cyberattack, and what happens?

There are emergency preparedness plans in place for earthquakes and hurricanes, heat waves and ice storms. There are plans for power outages of a few days, affecting as many as several million people. But if a highly populated area was without electricity for a period of months or even weeks, there is no master plan for the civilian population (Koppel, 2015, n.p.).

Much thought has also gone into how best a cyber defense may be set up. For example, there have been public debates about whether those tasked with military-grade cyberdefense should have predelegation powers in the same way as in the prior nuclear war era to enable faster and more effective responses (Feaver & Geers, 2014, p. 33), or whether more strategic patience may carry the day against a hostile cyberattack. Two authors share some of the thinking:

In stark contrast to a nuclear attack, most cyber attacks can be stopped—at least in a tactical sense—with purely defensive measures. There is no immediate need to know who the perpetrators are, where they are located, or their true intentions. The urgency stems from a need to locate, isolate, and neutralize malicious code as fast as possible. Furthermore, blocking malicious data is far easier than shooting down a ballistic missile. In this light, cyber predelegation may not even be necessary, because system administrators already have the authority and capability to protect their networks from what has become an incessant barrage of malware. (Feaver & Geers, 2014, p. 41)

Others have brought in "just war" doctrines and the ideas of proportionality in cyber response to a cyberattack. One work explored the ethics of cyber defenses through theoretical "worked cases" on four dimensions: "scope of effects, degree of cooperation, types of effects, and degree of automation" (Denning & Strawser, 2014, p. 64). "Active defenses," defined as "direct actions taken against specific threats" are contrasted with passive defenses, such as protection of cyber assets (Denning & Strawser, 2014, p. 66); currently, passive defenses are the publicly accepted *status quo*, with the reasoning that active defense might be provocative and should actually not be practiced by non-pros with legal cover and high-level skills and tools. Active defenses also fall into the realm of cybercrime in the U.S. when practiced by private companies (Denning & Strawser, 2014, p. 69). Government itself cannot engage in active defense without the proper legal authorities. An "active defense" could include actions like "hack backs" and the non-cooperative cyber defense (without the permission of the user or network owner) may involve taking down of botnets (Denning & Strawser, 2014, p. 66 and 69). The authors offer another case, which they analyze analogically:

Again using the air defense analogy, the steps taken to block the exfiltration of files from compromised computers to the drop servers could be likened to jamming the transmission of sensitive data acquired with a stolen reconnaissance plane to the thieves' drop center (Denning & Strawser, 2014, p. 67).

One reason why active defensive measures have to be, well, measured, is that the computers used to launch cyberattacks may themselves have been taken over by a malicious bad actor (a botnet master, for example). There have to be considerations for secondary effects of active defenses to noncombatants (Denning & Strawser, 2014, p. 70). The actions taken have to be proportionate to the potential harm, and they have to also be ethically and morally justifiable. Tactically, defensive and offensive actions should not raise antagonisms where they are not needed, or these risk making a situation worse.

A hard problem that has been in the works for years is that of attribution—to understand who the bad actors are on cyberspace. For individuals and corporations, attribution may be highly difficult, if not possible. For nation-states, with access to all-source intelligence, attribution can be achieved to the level of legal standards and surety. (Nye, Winter 2016 / 2017, p. 51)

With cyber as its own domain in warfare (under "information"), along with the classic four domains air, land, sea, space, much more attention has been paid to vulnerabilities in this area. The sense of national-scale vulnerabilities is dire. In 2007 dollars, one study suggested that "thirty hackers with a budget of $10 million" could be devastating, with attacks on power grids, emergency systems, the floodgates of dams, and other critical parts of the U.S. infrastructure (Dynes, Goetz, & Freeman, 2007, 15 – 27). Another issue is how much automation should be applied to cyber defense sequences. The analogy here in warfare would be automated robots that have capabilities of taking human life without human oversight. Having a (hu)man-in-the-loop has long been a required aspect of critical decision-making, but automated sequences have been parts of a national security response *in extremis*. The speed of potential cyberattacks, though, has made it necessary to consider taking humans out of the loop in some potential high-stakes scenarios.

Cyber world is also a world of rapidity. The speed at which events can happen in the cyber domain makes real world events seem lugubrious; not only does the cyber domain span the globe, but it does so in a near instantaneous fashion. There is no kinetic analog for this phenomenon—even the most global-spanning weapons, like missiles, take thirty-three minutes to reach their distant targets. (Rosenzweig, 2012, p. 393)

Given international dependence on the Internet for economic health and free trade, nation-level defenses require inter-country cooperation and coordination, a shared defense, as well as private-public partnerships (Hathaway, Summer-Fall 2016, p. 57):

The cross-border flow of goods, services, people, technology, ideas and information is being limited by those who would exploit these channels to commit crime and provoke conflict. Nations need to recognize that while the goals of these disruptive forces may vary (exploitation of children, propagation of extremist messages to recruit terrorists, or electronic crime for example) the means being used are the same. Moreover, these activities are being carried out using the public infrastructure, distributing "goods" such malware or botnet and services like extortion, espionage, money raising, message distribution, and mobilization with broad anonymity. (Hathaway, Summer-Fall 2016, p. 58)

For industry, the private sector is expected to lose some $2 trillion annually to cybercrimes by 2019 (Morgan, Jan. 17, 2016). The losses are understood at mass scale:

The effects of cyberattacks are being felt across the globe in multiple sectors and industries. The damages incurred include direct financial damages as well as reputation issues, the loss of business, the inability to provide the expected services, opportunity costs, and the loss of trust. According to the Center for Strategic and International Studies (2014), the world economy sustained 445 billion dollars in losses from cyberattacks in 2014. The United States suffered a loss of 100 billion dollars, Germany lost 60 billion dollars, China lost 45 billion dollars, and the United Kingdom re- ported a loss of 11.4 billion dollars due to cybersecurity lapses. The think tank also presented an analysis that indicated that of the

2 trillion dollars–3 trillion dollars generated by the Internet annually, about 15%–20% is extracted by cybercrime. Adversaries in the cyber realm include spies from nation-states who seek our secrets and intellectual property; organized criminals who want to steal our identities and money; terrorists who aspire to attack our power grid, water supply, or other infrastructure; and hacktivist groups who are trying to make a political or social statement (Deloitte, 2014). (Nagurney & Shukla, Dec. 2016, p. 588)

In the same way that nation-states benefit from coordinated and collaborative work, private industry could also benefit (Nagurney & Shukla, Dec. 2016, p. 599).

Industry tools involve a mix of cybersecurity tools, capabilities, and training. It is common practice to dissect malware, test malware on virtual machines, set up honey pot traps to attract attacks, set up bug bounties to identify vulnerabilities, and shore up the creation of secure software.

For common citizens, they stand to lose valuables: money, reputation, data, and other elements. In their defense, they have access to off-the-shelf tools, technologies, and methodologies. (In many cases, the general public seems to be part of a "test plot," and their compromises and infections inform both government and private industry. The public is generally very hard to protect without their cooperation. Even with user cooperation, there is no absolutely failsafe way to guard against every potential harm. This is a vulnerable population "in the wild.")

To give a sense of what a cautionary tale in cybersecurity may look like, in extended form, a meta-level one is offered. The narrative here suggests that there is a tension between government and business interests and those of common citizens. The threat here is that there is an impending surveillance state, which will limit citizens' rights.

A Meta-Cautionary Tale in Cybersecurity: Going to a Surveillance State

One common cautionary tale in cybersecurity goes like this. People are going about their daily lives and are focusing on the things that matter to them. They share personal details about their lives with their online friends. They sometimes drunk-tweet and overshare. They treat their mobile phones like personal companions and have them close-at-hand at every moment 24/7. When they receive a message, they respond quickly because that's the culture. They share a lot of selfies that show themselves in their best light—as friendly and funny and approachable. When they buy mobile devices, they care a lot about the design, the convenience, and the features; security is not even a real consideration for them because that is someone else's worry. (In their trilemma, they can have two of the features but not all three per Figure 1.) If their credit card gets compromised, they'll just close one account and open another. If their computer systems get corrupted at work, they can just get IT (information technology) on it and maybe even get a new laptop.

While people are merrily living their day-to-day, governments are increasing their haul in terms of personal data, which enables them to profile individuals at will and locate them to a particular space on Earth. With the Edward Snowden revelations, there is a heightened sense of mistrust of government in some circles. This mistrust has been a continuing theme, from the disastrous National Security Agency (NSA) proposal of a universal backdoor to encryption dubbed the Clipper Chip, which rallied the cybersecurity community against government overreach (Rotenberg, 2015, pp. 1 – 18). There is the sense that even though government security agencies "are overwhelmed by the sheer volume of information available to them" (Dover, 2016, p. 103), they still want more.

Figure 1. A Common Cybersecurity Trilemma with Devices and Online Services

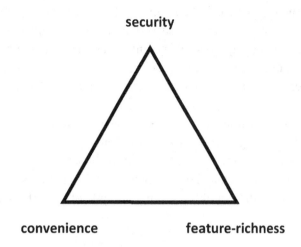

**A Common Cybersecurity Trilemma with
Devices and Online Services**

Electronic communications are not particularly private, and it's not only "The Man" (popular lingo for the government). Private companies provide free services in exchange for people's information, with one cybersecurity expert warning: "The bargain you make, again and again, with various companies is surveillance in exchange for free service" (Schneier, Data and…, 2015, p. 4). This public apathy is not affected even as both make deeper incursions into citizens' lives, closing off their options for balancing government and corporate power. Citizens justify increasing government power to fight crimes and disorder based on ancient brain responses (Schneier, 2015, Fear and…, pp. 200 - 203). Meanwhile, "government surveillance piggybacks on existing corporate capabilities" (Schneier, Fear and…, 2015, p. 202), and the major flows of digital data from people are being harvested to inform decisions and planning in the meat-space analog world (McKelvey, Tiessen, & Simcoe, 2015, p. 578). People's online interactions have become datafied into "simulations" of tomorrow:

If digital technologies and the Internet have become generators of digitally inflected simulations, how can these simulations be understood? By simulation, we do not mean a reproduction or representation of reality 'as it is out there', nor do we mean simply a Baudrillardian 'hyperreal' wherein signs of the real substitute for or parody the real itself (Baudrillard, 2001). Rather, we refer to a digital reality that generates analogue 'realities' not by creatively constructing false narratives or representations but by manufacturing the realities of tomorrow by data-mining and diagnosing the desires of today. So while Baudrillard (1995) once suggested that we falsely 'believe we exist in the original' (p. 97), these days the simulation we are living in is in fact (an) original, that is, a digitally generated original that simulates and iterates the logics of the digital. This real digitally modulated reality gets created as our algorithmically driven machines churn through and (data-)mine the events, dispositions and desires of today in order to produce the seemingly inevitable events of tomorrow. (McKelvey, Tiessen, & Simcoe, 2015, p. 579)

The World Wide Web (WWW) and Internet have become "a giant global experiment or honeypot" (McKelvey, Tiessen, & Simcoe, 2015, p. 539), a trap which forecloses on people's potential tomorrows. Here, there is only an electronic panopticon, a surveillance state in which people have ever-lessening privacy. Even when being assiduously aware of potential data leakage and being assiduously careful, data compromises are inevitable (Schneier, Data and…, 2015). People live in a surveillance state based on technologies, their emergent behaviors, and the perceived needs and responsibilities of government and industry.

And the fallout? People are constrained in their life choices, their friends, their communications, and they will live lesser lives. If people gather to strike or to express dissatisfaction with their governments, they can be tracked locationally, suppressed, and harmed. Information from the past may be brought up again and held against a person. Data may be used predictively to anticipate criminal actions, and law enforcement may pre-empt what they think may happen. Some of the cybersecurity risks may be seen in Figure 2.

Figure 2. Cybersecurity Risks for Users over Time and Projected Impact

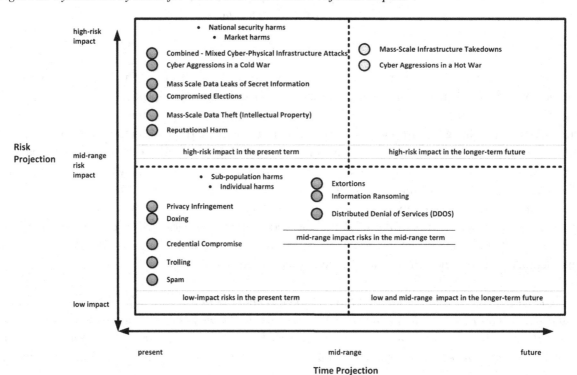

Cybersecurity Risks for Users over Time and Projected Impact

AN ANALYSIS OF CAUTIONARY TALES IN THE CYBERSECURITY SPACE

Cautionary Tales in Cybersecurity From Mass-Scale Google Search and Google Correlate

At a macro scale, it is possible to explore search terms used in Google Search from 2004 – present and to find co-associated search terms over extended time (some 13 years) with the same time-based frequency patterns (based on normalized representations based on z-scores). The thinking is that such highly associated correlations in search may reflect mass-mind associations. To see what shared searches may correlate with "cyber security," this query was run across the 50 countries represented in the Google Correlate tool (https://www.google.com/trends/correlate/) to capture the top 20 correlates. (The run together form "cybersecurity" does not result in any findings, so the two word setup was used) The resulting search terms came from a number of different languages based on the UTF-8 character set. A few were mixed-language phrases, within the search term itself. The non-English languages included (in alphabetical order, and in this partial list): Arabic, Chinese (simplified), Chinese (traditional), French, Hebrew, Japanese, Korean, Serbian, Spanish, Thai, and others. The non-English terms were copied into Google Translate, and the automated language-identification feature was used for the translations. Once all terms were clearly rendered, the general sorts of associations with the "cyber security" search term were noted. The data may be seen in Table 1.

Interestingly, some of the "cyber security"-associated search terms referenced vaccines, particularly for influenza, in some regions. Others focused on entertainment, technology, technology jobs, and a mix of references. No direct relation was seen in these searches between the search term and any sense of a cautionary tale in a cyber context. (If there were, one would expect to see some mentions of the disambiguated names of various named cyber-threats or cyber attacks or cyber attackers. Of course, the speed of change for named cyber attacks is fast, so this may be harder to see over extended time.) In Figure 3, there is a "cyber security" and "bmw x1" association over extended time in France.

In Figure 4, a related scatter plot follows that shows the high level of correlation.

CAUTIONARY TALES IN CYBERSECURITY FROM ACADEMIC TEXTS

In academic texts, cautionary tales tend to be ones that are either fact-based or imagination-based. These tend to include more technological depth, theoretical implications, historical information, and analytics. For example, in one work, there is a theme that people are getting left behind in terms of cybersecurity, supported by a litany of cautionary tales from the headlines (Bodenheimer, 2012). The main purposes of the included cautionary tales seem to be to support the analytics and not necessarily to encourage behavior change in readers. If root causes of cybersecurity compromises are included anywhere, it would generally be in an academic research context.

Another form of a cautionary tale include counter assertions such as un-caution. Cybersecurity expert Schneier shares one at the beginning of his book *Liars & Outliers* (2012):

Just today, a stranger came to my door claiming he was here to unclog a bathroom drain. I let him into my house without verifying his identity, and not only did he repair the drain, he also took off his shoes so he wouldn't track mud on my floors. When he was done, I gave him a piece of paper that asked my

Table 1. Top Google Search Correlates of Search Terms with "Cyber Security" in 50 Countries over Extended Time (2004 – 2017) in Google Correlate

Country	Search Correlate Themes (in descending order, all in lower case per Google Correlate)	General
Argentina	mi vida en grecia, the tv show, alcoholexia, Naruto shippuden 130, shippuden 130, a pradise, el arte de la elegancia, naruto shippuden 131, shippuden 131, naruto shippuden capitulo 131, eckerdt, casino de rosario, alcoohorexia, sacate la ropa, wrong turn 3, turn 3, estadio libertadores de america, estadio libertadores, casino rosario, los sabados secretos	anime show, entertainment
Australia	medical abbreviation, hubspot, vic rego, clyde north, dahua, npm, flexbox, flower wall, data science, myhealth, 中文, o365, nourished, pixabay, da trakcer, meaning, voltex, influencer, through meaning, sibo	mixed
Austria	sterillium, who did, oltás, vakcina, squatting, b12, literally, happens, schnuller, simptome, serialy, belirtileri, oder nicht, ausmalbild, yan etkileri, vitamin b12, bmw x1, which, wochenende, did	mixed
Belgium	(no results)	N/A
Brazil	valorização dos idosos, valorização do idoso, hospital tabajara ramos, trailer, valorizacao do idoso, valorização do idoso, distrito 9 filme, balloon boy, metro bus, valorizaçao do idoso, tatiane guedes, 0fan 150 2009, homer dos simpsons, filme distrito, distrito nove, unilever produtos, distrito 9, filme distrito 9, bifidobacterium animalis, seis caminhos da dor	film
Bulgaria	(no results)	N/A
Canada	barre, skyn condoms, misguided, design thinking, vaccine cost, copenhagen wintergreen, lbs in kg, medical abbreviation, sertraline, calming, in asl, duration, kjv, wrha, inch to mm, rqhr, meaning, hubspot, lifelabs, therapy dog	mixed
Chile	(no results)	N/A
China	groovy, implement, descriptor, trace, pending, file size, web app, terminated, gen8, incompatible, configuration, goto, utc, expand, get file, document, already, ssl, gcc, branch	technology
Colombia	lorena perez, naruto shippuden 130, shippuden 130, naruto shippuden 131, shippuden 131, amor para dos, naruto shippuden capitulo 131, amar a morir, resultados pruebas icfes 2009, resultados icfes 2009, muñeca de la mafia, munecas de la mafia, naruto shippuden capitulo 130, las munecas de la mafia, resultados del icfes 2009, your universe, pruebas icfes 2009, icfes 2009, design your universe, la muñeca de la mafia	entertainment
Croatia	the character, for which, peter murphy, kmetija, the tv, marko lončar, which of these, mekki, talent show, this is it, pro evolution soccer 2010, mekki torabi, modul 2, which movie, soccer 2010, torabi, jurisa, vitamin d3, gripa simptomi, polarna noć	entertainment, sports
Czech Republic	bazar zbrani, ranu, microsoft store, redtu, office 365, prekladač, fordító, anglicky, sbazar, meziplyn, kaufland jarov, mockup, equa bank, woocommerce, detska, wedos mail, equa, kitchenette, на английском, trello	technology
Denmark	(no results)	N/A
Egypt	جاهز رجب, رداب مكلهم, سن الحسن واو, تس خاسنق, اونا عاون المحايل, تالات, حالات, اساسيات غنيه ابابا ابين ,الجلامل, سن الحسن تس ,فيلدنم لودج ,بوستان, port ghalib, 1205, g530, login error, الغلا الجنلانية غنيه, ابابا ابين ,فيليدنم تس الحسن, زوجاه, بلومي احلى فزع ,مفه	entertainment
Finland	(no results)	N/A
France	bmw x1, mise à jour windows 7, boulettes, dessert paris, x1, latest episode, cereal lion, elle se fait masser, 50 ans, solidaire, agorassas, ruban, x1 bmw, qui dessert, tier 10, forever aloe vera, en ingles, rice and fish, wannonce., bforbank	mixed
Germany	agile, angolul, перевод на, доброе утро, αγγλικα, спряжение, po angielsku, angielsku, značenje, schönen abend, two characters, niemiecku, po niemiecku, on premise, bol u, iskustva, jelentése, németül, prijevod, öffnungszeiten dr	mixed
Greece	195/65r15, καθεται, αγκαλιες harmanis, what character, dark x, 205/55r16, σαλαμινα καιρος, what movie, αγγλικα, ρουλης, ταμπα, αστικο κτελ ηρακλειου, meaning in, blue air, νιουζ, γυναικεια, λιντλ, pharmasept, στα αγγλικα	mixed

continued on following page

Table 1. Continued

Country	Search Correlate Themes (in descending order, all in lower case per Google Correlate)	General
Hungary	the character, which of, for which, is it, who plays, lead singer, euro noliker, hollós korvin lajos, deck, universe wallpaper, coffee machine, most tv, ket, aldi győr, kézfertőtlenítő, which movie, 0napiszar., fine dining, árfolyam portfolio, papír 200	mixed
India	आप, if, before, dermatologist, kg, care, hone, check, pronounce, should, to check, benefit of, months, to kg, study chair, spelling, change gmail, carousel, boutique, to stop	mixed
Indonesia	mata di, bo kep, download lagu tiada guna lagi, chord cinta pertama dan terakhir, mantan mp3, jika ada yang bilang ku tak setia, sahabat menjadi cinta, mantan lirik, tomat buah, jogja kota, cicak, truno, lagu sahabat jadi cinta, by which, kerja keras, diawan, zigat, smx, lirik lagu sahabat jadi cinta, download lagu zigaz sahabat jadi cinta	mixed, love songs
Ireland	Docker, turmeric, google sheets, spc, core portal, npm, shopify, prevoditelj, iot, 3 top, Eventbrite, canva, hikvision, escitalopram, navigate to, memes about, birthday meme, data science, microbiome, spring boot	technology
Israel	github, 365, mockup, js, רחשה תוכרב, crunchbase, rest api, git, bitbucket, webstorm, ושאר םויל םיליהת, to usd, office 365, aws, רחשה תכרב, trello, wetransfer, redis,, rdo (with leading comma--author note), טפשמה טנ	technology
Italy	(no results)	N/A
Japan	meaning, ハローズ チラシ, 50 代, あります 英語, ホット スナック, パック おすすめ, các, artinya, 40 代, là, イラスト ac, 売れる もの, qq 邮箱, khoai, が あります 英語, freecad, twitter まとめ, meaning in, カード ローン 返済, アクセント クロス	mixed
Malaysia	cyber security malaysia, akpk, pptx, endpoint, laptop, pinjaman koperasi, cimb islamic, 谷 歌, rock kapak, jkns, cube, mamy poko, alphard, cititel express, virtualbox, 狗 狗, xlsx, symantec endpoint, savetube, endpoint protection	technology
Mexico	teresa forcades, forcades, aldo raine, on the tv, naruto shippuden 131 sub español, the tv show, albornoz, sector 9, naruto shippuden capitulo 131, valentina de albornoz, karla de jeans, naruto shippuden 131, shippuden 131, sector 9 pelicula, naruto shippuden 130, shippuden 130, karla jeans, pelicula sector 9, nubes extrañas, naruto shippuden 130 sub español	anime
Morocco	resultat quatro, base quinte, freepik, قشع قصق, machine learning, smadav, 128gb, quatro, zone turf, صباح درولا, dessin facile, سور, صباح حلا,, telecharger tub, rufus, mahakim, sorec, quatro maroc, tub mat, جمعة طيبة	technology
Netherlands	synonym, in r, en ingles, ted talk, github, sap hana, cvrm, blouse, youtube mp4, git, why how, fijne avond, mailchimp, logo png, why how what, to json, how what, markdown, qgis, dental clinics	technology
New Zealand	tick, copy and paste, copy and, meaning, salary nz, out meaning, usd to nzd, usd to, gateau house, usd, phone holder, days from, meaning in, turmeric, synonym, aws, 영어 로, trello, convert usd to nzd, azure	mixed
Norway	november 2009, bivirkninger vaksine, alle skal få, szczepionka, nils georg, dj hero, tamiflu, bloons tower defence 4, vaksine, pandemrix, vaksinering, impfung, vaccin, vakcina, svineinfluensa vaksine, nefes, saw 6, svineinfluensa symptomer, vaccine, vaksine bivirkninger	vaccine
Peru	(no results)	N/A
Philippines	(no results)	N/A
Poland	galeria sandecja sklepy, akcje pge, yas, pge akcje, 195, katarzyna popowska, tomboys, pila 6, 7 avenue, dr house s06e06, popowska mam talent, my shining star, 198, kasia popowska mam talent, forflex, chylinska agnieszka, piła vi, not it, what film, dr house sezon 6 odcinek 6	entertainment
Portugal	is it, orphan, tomar vacina, da boca, dona beija, boca, which of these, vacina, decathlon castelo branco, benuron, js, vodafone power, bebê, i sell, joaquim chaves, in english, absorvit, ben u, ben u ron, bmw 5 series	mixed

continued on following page

Table 1. Continued

Country	Search Correlate Themes (in descending order, all in lower case per Google Correlate)	General
Romania	voila, this it, this is it, the rebound, radio killer voila, rebound, idila cu dadaca, muñoz, spread subtitrare, is it, jackson this is it, michael jackson this is it, dragoste fara preaviz, number 9, deoparte, windows 7 retail, idila cu dadaca mea, cronica de familie, the keeper, bulibasa	entertainment
Russian Federation	поликлиника 12, рецепт подливы, см клиник, малиновый цвет, поликлиника 14, расписание работы врачей, микрофинансовые организации, поликлиника 17, на приём, мир квартир, поликлиника 15, куриные сердечки, м 6, хеликс, поликлиника 25, доктор плюс, творожная запеканка, филорга, поликлинику, прием врачей	healthcare, mixed
Saudi Arabia	الهلال يا كوروب, بروك يا, كوروب يا ,we transfer, الهلال يا, meaning, wetransfer, synonym, check, bootstrap, in english, office 365, كارهيم, صحالةي, وكيز, mockup, kwd, meaning in english, ksa, turmeric, in cm	mixed, technology
Singapore	google form, meaning in tamil, tableau, data analytics, meaning in, meaning in chinese, google forms, redmart, skyscanner, meaning in malay, sengkang health, npm, horme, meaning in hindi, airbnb, rest api, share price, logo png, quora, node js,	technology
Spain	grana padano, padano, its magic, is it, realidad, which movie, 63, watch phone, cruda, which of these, on the tv, the tv show, someday my prince will come, basilio cantante, gocce, which tv, after trailer, 7275, bmw x1, x1	entertainment
Sweden	biverkningar influensavaccin, rokote, vaccinera, vaccinera sig, kent röd, vaccin, لقاح, barn vaccin, pandemrix, biverkningar vaccin, vaccin uppsala, vakcina, vaccinet, ullared tv, vaccinera barn, vaccin svininfluensa, svenska sesam, vaccine, länsvaccinationer uppsala, wave 4	vaccine
Switzerland	coop restaurant, trello, angular, office 365, niemiecku, 365, niemiecku, jelentése, in inglese, meaning, mister auto, png, outlook 365, buchstaben, gazeta express, python, translate english, coworking, buonanotte, rest api	technology
Taiwan	家 樂 福 楠 梓, search 中文, 最新 電視劇, hole 中文, 感傷 的 (in total--note by the author)	mixed
Thailand	ขม, เกาหลี ซับ ไทย, กรมธรรม์ ไทย ประกันชีวิต, หนัง ไม, แม่ สอน, ฝัน ถึง, กิน ข้าว คน เดียว, เย็น แม่, จิ บิ, ไม่มี สัญญาณ. คำ คม ความ สำ เร็ จ, with me แปล วา, การ บ้าน อาบ, psn store, workup, เกาหลี ภาษา, การ บ้าน อาบ อบ นวด, mql4, arduino, จำ นำ รถ	mixed
Turkey	(no results)	N/A
Ukraine	google disk, ворк юа, рст, райффайзен онлайн, лінкедин, вито 639, єдрср, лун юа, pull request, роутер тп линк, eway, ворк, ueuk lbcr, тп линк, 1node js, гугл диск, купить ваз 2106, бразерс, жк софия, sweetness	technology, mixed
United Kingdom	cyber security jobs, αγγλικα, hubspot, aws, μεταφραση, python 3, png, brunch places, glassdoor, me to work, trustpilot, coffee shops near, azure sql, influencers, logo png, onenote online, who called, medical abbreviation, aws ec2, who called me	technology, mixed
United States	what is cyber security, in english, in cm, hub., assist synonym, scientist salary, friendly synonym, en anglais, ensure synonym, relaxing music, health provider, asthma icd, job meaning, qhs medical, cyber security jobs, data analyst, wue, anxiety and depression, in list, nature throid	technology jobs, mixed
Venezuela	(no results)	N/A
Viet Nam	(no results	N/A

bank to give him some money. He accepted it without a second glance. At no point did he attempt to take my possessions, and at no point did I attempt the same of him. In fact, neither of us worried that the other would. My wife was also home, but it never occurred to me that he was a sexual rival and I should therefore kill him. (Schneier, 2012, p. 1)

He goes on to point to the evolutionarily arrived-at depth of human cooperation as a plank on which to build continuing trust in society and as a balance against paranoia that might suggest threats everywhere

Figure 3. A Linegraph of Correlation between "cyber security" and "bmw x1" in France over Extended Time (Google Correlate)

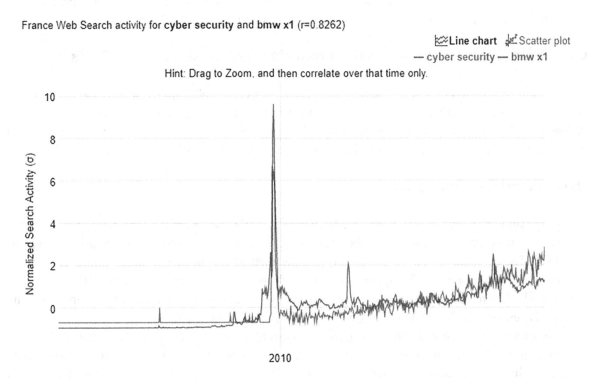

Figure 4. A Scatterplot of Correlation between "cyber security" and "bmw x1" in France over Extended Time (Google Correlate)

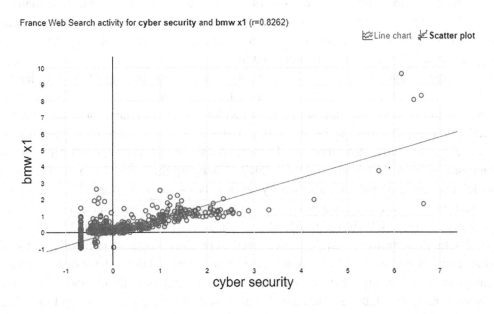

(and the concomitant expenditures for nonexistent risks). Another cautionary tale dealt generically with expertise and advisement, suggesting that receivers of expert advice should be careful that the advice is thoughtful and from that expert's area of expertise (Dillon & Carlson, 2017).

Cautionary Tales in Cybersecurity From Mainstream Mass Media Texts

Mass media seemed to contain the highest number of cautionary tales related to cybersecurity. These stories are also the most complete in terms of including context, character(s), warning(s), choice(s)/action(s), and often implied outcomes and implied lessons. In the mass media texts, the focus seems to be on attitude and behavior change, which goes to the agenda-setting role of mass media.

User-Based Cautionary Tales

For users, cautionary tales are about revealed cyber risks…and also about incorrect uses of cyber tools.

One common cautionary message is the high risk of using cyber weapons and malware tools created by others. The example is of a guy who used hacking methods to break into hotel rooms and how he ended up incarcerated albeit still bragging about his exploits (Greenberg, Feng, & Chin, 2017). Ironically, in this work, the protagonist is still dreaming big dreams about aligning with famous hackers, whom he apparently respected. (He would be looking for a job on his release.)

In another work, a Canadian physiologist's wise warning is peripherally related to cyber but has cautionary impact. Dr. Gordon Geisbrecht of the University of Manitoba is credited with advising people in cars sinking in water to not automatically reach for their cell phones. "Time is critical. If you touch your cell phone you're probably going to die," Geisbrecht said (Galvin, 2013). Rather, the idea is to get out of the car and swim to safety first before trying to call for help. The warning: Cell phones do not have magical powers to bring help in time-critical moments.

Another warning is about how incorrectly setting up wifi can result in more trouble than one might have expected. An innocent man who did not set up his wireless router correctly (with password protection) had another person freeride his connection to access child pornography (Thompson, Apr. 24, 2011), and he was falsely accused and took a reputational hit.

Then, too, mass media are replete with stories of the social oversharing (TMI!), which turns into compromising detail in an unanticipated future. In light-hearted cases, the response to an overshare may be the collective online "Ewwww!" and some online needling. In environments of designed personas and the artificial, glimpses of the real can be off-putting. There are the politicians who slip up and overshare on a hot mic, with the results released online. There are politicians who accidentally "like" a porn video on his microblogging account (Diaz, Sept. 13, 2017). There are the "tells" from the friends on social media, which can reveal an individual's identity (even if he or she is hidden). There is an innocuous message on a 1990s bulletin board that connects a person's pseudonym with his real identity and reveals him as a kingpin on the Dark Web (and results in years in prison) (Greenberg, Oct. 2, 2013). Sometimes, one clue is all it takes to unravel carefully crafted layers of pseudonymous identities. Then, too, there are the warning stories of stalkers who have connected with an individual through his or her online messaging and imagines a relationship where none existed. Cyberstalking is a "thing" and a risky one at that. These may seem apocryphal, but all are factual. The lesson: Strategic ambiguity and in-definition are preferable in order not to turn off followers, colleagues, friends, family, and allies.

Post the 2016 national presidential election, in the U.S., there were warnings for U.S. voters and citizens to not be being fooled by social bots propagating false news. This was also a theme during the German elections in a German presidential election in 2017 (Neudert, 2017).

Work-Based Cautionary Tales

There are workplace-based cautionary tales. There are nightmare scenarios of lost information, insider attacks, and individual compromises through which the "deep pockets" of the corporation may be accessed. One cautionary tale reads like this:

Outside a typical American middle school, papers were blowing around in the wind beside a garbage container. A student, seeing the papers, grabbed some and read about the special needs assessment for a seventh-grader named Kevin, including his IQ score, psychological assessment data, behavioral information, and family history. Some time later, the prying student and his friends were passing Kevin's private information around the school. It doesn't take a career educator to guess what happened next: Over the next few weeks, students relentlessly taunted Kevin, calling him "stupid," "dumb," and "retarded." They might just as well have applied the first of those adjectives to their school. In one careless stroke, the school's poor data security practices had led to the direct harm of one of its students.

Unfortunately, this cautionary tale isn't apocryphal. Part of a very real case out of Minnesota, it not only points out the ethical need to secure student data, but highlights the legal implications of failing to do so. Kevin's family sued the school district, and at the trial court, the jury returned a verdict that found the district liable for $60,000 in past damages and $80,000 in future damages--and also awarded more than $45,000 in legal fees to the family (although the legal fees were later reduced on appeal). (Bathon, Nov. 5, 2013)

Another explains the importance of regularly spring-cleaning off digital files that can be sources of compromise (Newman, May 28, 2017).

There is the highly publicized story of contractor Edward Snowden who exfiltrated massive amounts of sensitive and secret government data from the NSA and shared these broadly to journalists and the larger public. The lesson here is about insider threats and the need to have proper surveillance and counter-intelligence to mitigate such potential losses.

A common message is about various vulnerabilities that have come to light. One example described a "watering hole" cyberattack in which popular niche sites with certain human crowds are targeted in order to compromise those individuals. This type of attack is "inspired by predators in the natural world who lurk near watering holes, looking for opportunities to attack desired prey" ("watering hole attack," 2017). For example, an online Chinese takeout menu was used to access the servers of an oil company (the actual high-value target) ("Cyber Security Understanding the Cyber World," Mar. 8, 2017).

Cautionary Tales in Cybersecurity-Tagged Social Imagery (Flickr)

On the Flickr social image-sharing site, it is possible to capture a number of images with the cybersecurity tag. Using the Flickr Downloadr app on Google Chrome, a set of over 2,000 unique images was captured from the site. (Figure 05)

Figure 5. "Cybersecurity" Social Imagery from Flickr through the Flickr Downloadr Add-on to Google Chrome

A majority of these images showed various aspects of cybersecurity-based conferences from various locales from around the world (1970); a few were decorative graphics (in the vein of shadowy hackers lit by reflective computer screens) (114), and very few were informational graphics such as data tables and geographical maps (26) (Figure 6).

While a range of images suggested that there were efforts and preparations against extant and impending threats, most extractable stories from the social images did not offer full story arcs or full articulations. In general, the cautionary tales are addressed in two ways: (1) a third-person point-of-view (see what's happened or going to happen to this character, or (2) direct address (see what's going to happen to you if you're not careful).

In some cases, the imagery went straight to the warning. One image read: "he who sacrifices online freedom for cybersecurity deserves neither" (alongside a photo of a painting of Benjamin Franklin, in reference to his historical quote: "Those who would give up essential Liberty, to purchase a little temporary Safety, deserve neither Liberty nor Safety.") In other words, citizens should not give up their privacy to a government that is accessing online information in order (ostensibly) to provide citizen security. Another text-only message shows a word cloud with related terms (in rough descending size order): hacker attack, terrorism, crime, target, hacker attack, theft, international, warfare, criminal, mail, pornography, and others. The associations of "cybersecurity" contrasted against negative words are clear. The warning: There are threats out there in cyberspace.

Another direct warning: A stern-faced Uncle Sam in a giant hat and the words, "I want you to stop clicking." This is evocative of Uncle Sam warning posters from wartime ("I want you for U.S. Army" and "I'm counting on you!") and from voting campaigns: "I want you—vote!" and others. It is not that Uncle Sam wants people to literally stop clicking…but to do so mindfully. Another image (from a dif-

Figure 6. "Cybersecurity" Social Imagery on Flickr (2000+ Image Set)

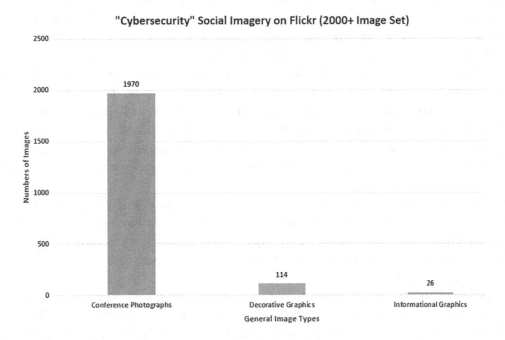

ferent poster) includes the advice: "Stop Think Connect." [As an aside, many of the conference images show a clear government interest and presence. Some participants are high profile government officials. Some participants and presenters are in military uniform. One of the images in the social image set shows the FBI warning common at the beginning of recorded audiovisual media.]

A more common image than a direct warning was that of a lurking hacker, suggesting the ever presence of threat while online. One image shows a man with two hands on a computer keyboard. His left hand shows him wearing a dress shirt and a watch; the right hand is wearing a black leather glove. Both "good" and "evil" are sharing the same cyberspace. Another abstract sense of threat involved a drawing showing a computer screen with a padlock on it and a lot of floating human eyes around it. If the computer is not protected, there are many out there in the world willing to take advantage.

Another image showed a young woman engaging happily on the Internet through a laptop while a shadowy hacker wearing a hoodie was leaning in to look from behind her. His presence suggests malice, doxing, lulz, and trolling. (One of the images was a recruitment poster with a shark swimming in a tunnel of 0s and 1s.) In another image of human cluelessness, two figures are standing back-to-back and typing feverishly into their mobile devices—one an Apple device, and the other Android, and neither seems to be aware of anything going on around them. The warning: You should be aware of the threats online.

In an illustration, a thief—replete with face mask and striped shirt—reached through a computer screen to hand a bouquet of flowers to a beaming woman. Cyber-aided romance is an attack surface. The warning: You don't know who you're dealing with online.

Another social image tagged with "cybersecurity" showed a 2D map with pins and highlights of two locations from which threats emanate (as expressed with red concentric circles from two locations). The map conveys that the cyber threat is real, and it is simultaneous, and it is in the real world (not some other space).

One image was evocative of a backstory, a real-world cautionary tale. This showed a computer screen with a message from a health organization: "We are making good progress with restoring our clinical and non-clinical IT and telephone systems that have been affected by the problems we began to experience over the weekend…Things may take longer than normal, so thank you for your patience and understanding during this time." (A sentence with identifying information was removed where the ellipses are.) The warning: Healthcare is at risk from cyber means, and people's lives are on the line. For real.

Another visual-based cautionary tale shows a man wearing black, including a face mask. Overlaid on this is a message from the individual who has promised that the readers' "pictures, documents, etc." have been encrypted with his ransomware. At the bottom of this narrative overlay, "So User do you want to play a game?" The warning: Know the rules before you engage in cyber, or else you are putting a lot of valuables at risk.

In this social image set, there two images of a poster for "The Interview" along with a receipt of the image-taker, as proof that he had seen this movie, which is known for having so enraged a leader of a foreign country that he had approved a hack of Sony Pictures, in order to try to disrupt the film's release. This image tells a counter cautionary tale. This is a message of defiance those who might try to squelch free speech American-style.

Another way to use data from Flickr is by mapping the related tags networks. Folk tags are the words that people who are single or batch-uploading imagery may apply to their image sets. These tags are called "folk" ones because they are tags by amateurs (non-professionals). Tags are related or associated if they co-occur or are used together to describe the uploaded objects. Initially, "cybersecurity" and "cyber security" were tried as seeding tags for a Flickr related tags network, but neither had sufficient related tags to register. "Hacker" was sufficiently related to a number of other tags. Network Overview, Discovery and Exploration for Excel (NodeXL) was used to extract related tags networks from the Flickr API. In a one-degree network, the "hacker" tag has direct links to 51 vertices (other tags). Figure 07 shows a one-degree network of direct ties to the "hacker" tag. This network was drawn using the Harel-Koren Fast Multiscale Layout Format.

A 1.5-degree network of the "hacker" tag shows direct ties to 51 vertices, with 374 edges. This means that there is a fairly high degree of node-based transitivity or heightened associations between the one-degree tags in the "hacker" related tags network.

Graphs from Table 2 follow in Figures 8 and 9. A 1.5 degree related tags network of "hacker" on Flickr results in four clusters or groups of related tags, based on the Clauset-Newman-Moore algorithm. Broadly speaking, the four clusters may be human-summarized based on the tags (from the left and clockwise):

- **Group 1:** Known hacker events
- **Group 2:** Technology related tags
- **Group 3:** A Yahoo-sponsored event in Sunnyvale, California
- **Group 4:** Las Vegas hacker events.

The treemap layout is used to represent this data in Figure 8.

Another version of Figure 9 follows, this time with thumbnail imagery representing the respective Flickr tags.

Finally, a two-degree related tags network is the most diffuse but may be evocative in a different way, by showing more distant interrelationships between tags for social imagery on Flickr.

Figure 7. Related Tags Network for "Hacker" on Flickr (1 deg.)

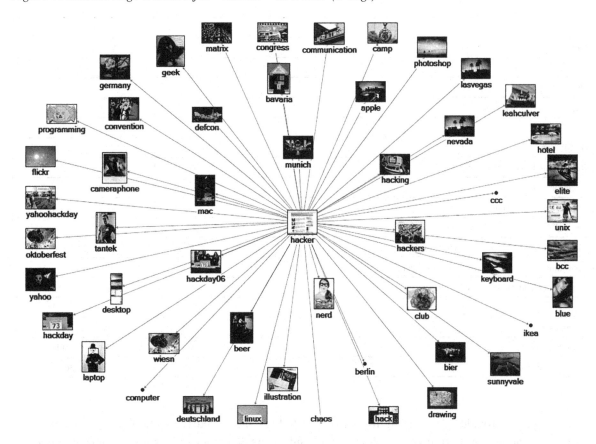

At two degrees, the "hacker" ego network was wired for transitive connectivity, and then each of those "alters" had their one-degree networks mapped. This two-degree network may be seen in Figure 10, with its 11 groups in a treemap visualization. These groups are also suggestive of grouped tag meanings. The thumbnail images related to the respective tags were not included in the figure because these would occlude the tag names and make the visualization harder to read.

Cautionary Tales in Cybersecurity-Labeled Social Videos (From YouTube)

Socially shared videos around issues of cybersecurity seem to be from some basic sources:

- Professional conferences sponsored by professional groups, governments, industry, and other stakeholder groups;
- Mass media organizations;
- Individual self-identified cybersecurity experts (and hackers);
- Institutions of higher education (and related degree programs and professional organizations);
- Businesses (selling technology products and services, head hunters for cybersecurity talent);
- Podcasters, and so on.

Table 2. Graph Metrics for the Related Tags Network for "Hacker" on Flickr (1.5 deg.)

Graph Metric	Value
Graph Type	Directed
Vertices	52
Unique Edges	374
Edges With Duplicates	0
Total Edges	374
Self-Loops	0
Reciprocated Vertex Pair Ratio	0.26779661
Reciprocated Edge Ratio	0.422459893
Connected Components	1
Single-Vertex Connected Components	0
Maximum Vertices in a Connected Component	52
Maximum Edges in a Connected Component	374
Maximum Geodesic Distance (Diameter)	2
Average Geodesic Distance	1.743343
Graph Density	0.141025641
Modularity	Not Applicable
NodeXL Version	1.0.1.336

The content providers are sharing for self-interested reasons—to drive an audience, to attract business, to sell advertising, to increase followership, and others. The viewers also have their own reasons for accessing these videos: professional skills development, curiosity, career enhancement, entertainment, and others.

From the days of physicist Clifford Stoll's *The Cuckoo's Egg: Tracking a Spy through the Maze of Computer Espionage* (1989), there has been a "gotcha" sensibility in cybersecurity. His book described the setting up of one of the (or "the") earliest publicized cyber honey pots as traps for would-be intruders in a network. In the intervening years, the technologies have become that much more complex and capable.

From this video set, several dozen videos were viewed. A majority of these were from the white hat hacker / white hat cybersecurity point-of-view showing how easily people were faked out by social engineering, technology systems were tricked to misbehave, or computer languages were harnessed for unintended compromises. The message: Be vigilant because all systems (human, technological, cyber, and others) can be compromised and turned to malicious use. Another subtext is that there is a wide gulf that separates the truly skilled cybersecurity individuals from the aspirants (derisively called "script kiddies"). These latter individuals are known for borrowing others' cyber tools for hacking and applying them at their own risks. A step up from those who apply others' tools are those who have learned a trick or two that they want to share; these are individuals who are on their way to expertise. If history is any indication, though, the elite who are able to find (or create) zero days are few. (Expert hackers have to know systems in depth, down to the last byte, and to be able to understand interaction effects between complex systems, and how to design tools to those realities.) Those who are truly serious about cyber security tend to assiduously work in the shadows. In obscurity, their secrets are safe, and they will not

Figure 8. Related Tags Network for "Hacker" on Flickr (1.5 deg.)

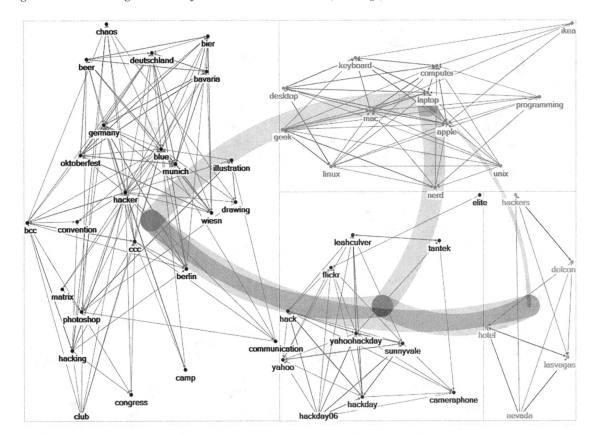

be accidentally leaking capabilities and skills. For them, even in "cheap talk," they realize they may be leaking "costly signaling." Cybersecurity experts are part of an insular tribe, and the cultural tendency is towards "not tell" vs. "tell"; they do not tend to give away advantage for the fool's gold of attention. One of the core rules is not to be lured by the dull dazzle of bright shiny objects that have no substantive inherent value. A certain type of cybersecurity professional courts the spotlight, and a few of these are the super achievers in their fields.

From a 13,000-word set from the titles of the YouTube videos, a word cloud was extracted. Figure 11 shows some of the more common terms listed in the video titles and related descriptive text offered by the sharers of the videos.

A related word tree follows in Figure 13; within the software tool (NVivo 11 Plus), the word tree is interactive. Each branch may be clicked on to take the user to the specific underlying message from the text set for a larger view of the textual context. This partial image of a complete word tree shows some of the textual contents surrounding "cybersecurity" in the textual references in the YouTube video collection. Both Figures 11 and 12, as summary data visualizations, were from a 12,000+ word text set based on the YouTube video titles and descriptions.

***

Figure 9. Related Tags Network for "Hacker" on Flickr (1.5 deg.), with Thumbnail Tag Imagery

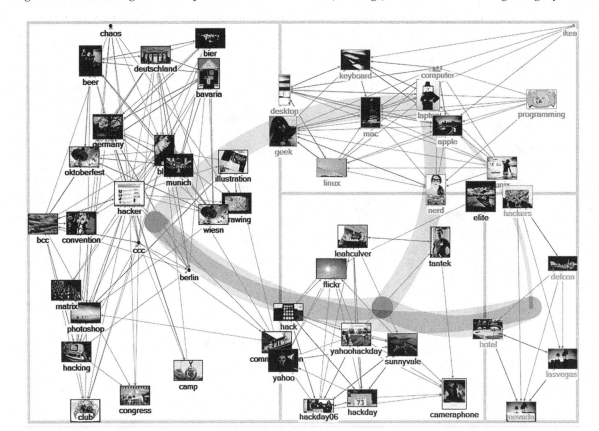

A Real-World Cautionary Tale in Cybersecurity (#1): "Let's Talk Securely About Your Money!"

One of my colleagues who works in information technology (IT) was working late, as usual, and he received an email from his bank. The email suggested that he should log into his bank account in order to securely provide a response to a message that he had received. He had been in discussions with his local bank about some issues, so he logged in, provided his message, and logged back off. He went on with his work, rested, and next the morning, woke in a panic when he realized that he had never been reached out to via email by his bank. He logged on to his account, and he saw that $3,000 was missing. He called his bank first thing the next morning at opening and let them know about the compromise. Ultimately, the bank made him whole and replaced the missing money. Meanwhile, they were hard at work to track down the electronic funds.

- **The Lessons:** Be present and mindful when engaging online. Never share personal credentials when responding to an email from an unknown sender (or even an apparently known sender).

Table 3. Graph Metrics for the Related Tags Network for "Hacker" on Flickr (2 deg.)

Graph Metric	Value
Graph Type	Directed
Vertices	1089
Unique Edges	3008
Edges With Duplicates	0
Total Edges	3008
Self-Loops	0
Reciprocated Vertex Pair Ratio	0.026971663
Reciprocated Edge Ratio	0.052526596
Connected Components	1
Single-Vertex Connected Components	0
Maximum Vertices in a Connected Component	1089
Maximum Edges in a Connected Component	3008
Maximum Geodesic Distance (Diameter)	4
Average Geodesic Distance	3.489124
Graph Density	0.002538757
Modularity	Not Applicable
NodeXL Version	1.0.1.336

A Real-World Cautionary Tale in Cybersecurity (#2): "About That Loan...or Whatever You Want to Talk About"

Usually, shortly after news of another large data breach has emerged, the phone calls to a private and highly protected phone line start to ring. There are numerous calls—dozens a day—from unknown numbers. Occasionally, a message will be left on the line. When the calls are answered, the person starts to insist that he or she had received a call from one's phone number. Or they will start in a friendly tone saying that the loan (or in one case, a mortgage) is going through...but some more information is needed.

- **The Lessons:** Sometimes, to fully exploit personal information that a person may have captured or purchased, he or she or they may need more information. Reaching out by phone with sham messages of loans-in-process are one way to try to capture that information.

A Real-World Cautionary Tale in Cybersecurity (#3): "Here's a Link / Paper / Photo / Video for You, and Let's Trade Info!"

For many people, receiving an email with the promise of an insightful research paper may be a non-starter. However, the point of spear-phishing is to micro-target messages to individuals or thin slices of the population because there is a chance that they may respond to the particular message. In an email system, there are any number of promissory emails: Here is a job for you! Here is romance! Here is a publishing opportunity! Here is an opportunity to earn some money by sharing expertise!

Figure 10. Related Tags Network for "Hacker" on Flickr (2 deg.)

Figure 11. A Word Cloud Summary of Cybersecurity YouTube Video Titles

Figure 12. A Word Cloud of Titles and Descriptions of Cybersecurity Videos from YouTube (12,000 Words)

Figure 13. A Word Tree of Cybersecurity YouTube Video Titles

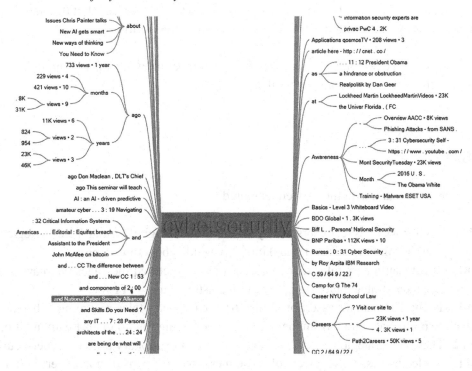

The idea is never to click on a link or download a file from an email from an unknown sender (or that of a person one supposedly knows but whose identity has been swiped to create the faux email). It is a good idea to report any such (spear)phishing emails through the email system (or in any of the ways that the organization's cybersecurity team suggests).

- **The Lessons:** It helps to be aware of the messages that might sway oneself and to be aware of one's own vulnerabilities, so as not to get taken—no matter how the elicitation arrives.

A Real-World Cautionary Tale in Cybersecurity (#4): "Authenticating Multiple Ways: It's Me! It's Me!"

Sometimes, for whatever reason, a spear-phishing attempt gets a little more ornate. There are several ways one can become aware of this. One is a notification from a social media platform that a request has been made for a new password. Does one want one? And if not, click here to let the social media service know.

Another one goes like this. A person sets up an account on a social media site using one's name. An email arrives asking whether one will authenticate that account. That suggests a purposeful attempt to possibly usurp one's account.

Another one is a notification that a person has maxed out tries to get into one's email account.

A common basic defense against misuse of one's emails is to set up two-factor authentication. Here, not only are passwords required, but there is also a necessary dynamically generated code that one also has to input (or a biometric verification). This way, a dynamically generated code can be sent to one's telephone, and that adds a deeper layer of protection against cyber vulnerability.

Of course, if one has to contact a firm, one does not do so through a link…but through direct access to the verified company's site with the protections of an https connection.

- **The Lessons:** Every person is "ground zero" for a number of cyberattacks, and they should treat themselves that way…with constant vigilance and care.

***

DISCUSSION

In this early work, two main hypotheses were explored:

Hypothesis 1: Cautionary tales re: cybersecurity (in multimodal digital formats) are strategic messages to convey ways for individuals and populations to avoid cyber compromises.

  Hypothesis 1a: Cautionary tales re: cybersecurity are structured messages that have aspects that enhance their strategic messaging role to mainstream users of cyber.

  Hypothesis 1b: The counter assertion is also true: cautionary tales regarding cybersecurity will have aspects that detract from their strategic messaging role to mainstream users of cyber.

Hypothesis 2: There are strategic ways to improve the uses of cautionary tales re: cybersecurity to enhance their effectiveness for receivers of those messages (in terms of non-expert individuals and populations).

In the cybersecurity-based convenience samples—including mass-scale search terms, academic texts, mass media texts, social imagery, related tags networks, and social video—various elements of and whole cautionary tales were identified. Whether (1) based on facts and describing real-world events or (2) based on the imagination and describing potential present or future worlds, cautionary tales can be highly effective in conveying a sense of cyber threat and potentially motivating behavioral change. In terms of the types of cybersecurity cautionary tales told in the respective digital source types, they seem to vary. Table 4 contains a basic summary of what the general cybersecurity cautionary tales look like in the respective digital content source types based on the author-defined five elements of a cybersecurity cautionary tale.

As regards Hypothesis 1, cautionary tales are harnessed as strategic messages for people to avoid cyber compromises (whether or not the original communicators were aware that this "cautionary tale" construct was a part of their messaging). As to 1a and 1b, there are aspects of cautionary tales that seem more effective than others in communicating cyberthreats effectively. For example, more abstract instantiations of cyberthreats seem less effective than more clearly defined ones. Stories of individuals who experienced the cyber compromises are more emotionally compelling than cool facts of tens of millions of people having their health information stolen. Real-world events are more compelling than scenarios, which may seem elusive, apocryphal, and maybe the product of overheated malign imaginations. There is plenty of research about what attracts human attention: messages of threat (that go to survival and risk), conflict (that go to wars, feuds, and struggles), sex (that go to attraction), emotion (that go to people's emotional needs), identity (that speak to people's professional and other senses of self), and so on. The related research may be used to improve cybersecurity cautionary tales and other strategic messaging. As to Hypothesis 2, as with all types of messaging, there is room for enhancements and improvements to improve the message. The idea, though, is to build on this initial work by setting up lab experiments, in-world experiments, surveys, and other forms of research, to find out what is actually effective.

One interesting angle for future research may be to look at how effectively a cautionary tale impacts the story consumer's emotions. For example, the late psychologist Robert Plutchik created a Wheel of Emotions (1980) that identifies eight primary emotions, which exist in oppositional balance in the following ways: joy vs. sadness, trust vs. disgust, fear vs. anger, and anticipation vs. surprise. He communicated his ideas visually, with one version depicted by Machine Elf 1735 (2011) and available in the public domain. This annotated image may be seen in Figure 14. In this wheel, the emotional response leading to vigilance in cybersecurity may be to emotionally tune the communications towards both "aggressiveness" and "optimism" to evoke "vigilance," "anticipation," and "interest". Further, fear and surprise may create a sense of alarm, whereas trust and surprise to lead to curiosity ("Motivation and emotion/book/2014/Plutchik's wheel of emotions," Sept. 23, 2017). The hard work will be to identify elements of cautionary tale communications that lead to particular emotional responses and to tune these factors to be the most effective.

It may be helpful to see if digital modalities make a difference. In this initial work, how cautionary tales instantiate in different media does vary. The current variety across modalities may be optimal since people are so selective in their mass media consumption; however, if these can be designed and developed to be more effective in encouraging healthy cybersecurity behaviors, that would be positive.

Table 4. A Summary of Digital Modalities in Terms of Cautionary Tale Contents, Non-fictional or Fictional, and Role of Message Recipient

Presence of Five Elements of Cybersecurity Cautionary Tales by Digital Source Types						
Five elements of cautionary tales in cybersecurity (as defined in this chapter)	**Mass-scale search terms**	**Academic text set**	**Mass media text set**	**Social imagery**	**Related tags networks**	**Social video**
context	inferred, if present; often not present	specified	specified	inferred, if present	inferred by associated words in networks and groups / clusters	specified in some cases, inferred in others
character(s)	implied "you"	defined as either general users or by name	defined as either general users or by name	general person, implied "you"	general	general person, implied "you"
warning(s)	"threat out there"	range of specific and wide spectrum	range of specific and wide spectrum	"threat out there"	"threat out there"	range of specific and wide spectrum
character choice(s)/ action(s)	diffuse	defined	defined	diffuse	diffuse	defined
outcomes / lessons (including implied ones)	general damage or harm	specified harm from minor to catastrophic	specified harm from minor to catastrophic	general damage or harm	general damage or harm	specified or general damage or harm
Predominantly Nonfictional or Fictional / Imaginary						
	mass-scale search terms	**academic text set**	**mass media text set**	**social imagery**	**related tags networks**	**social video**
predominantly nonfictional or fictional (imaginary, projective scenario)	unclear	non-fictional and fictional (such as counterfactuals, anticipatory threat scenarios, and others)	non-fictional	unclear	unclear	non-fictional
Role of Targeted Message Recipient						
	mass-scale search terms	**academic text set**	**mass media text set**	**social imagery**	**related tags networks**	**social video**
apparent behavioral role (in descending rank order): (1) awareness, (2) specific actions, (3) general values	awareness, general values, specific actions	analytics, methods*	specific actions, awareness, general values	awareness, general values, specific actions	awareness, general values, specific actions	specific actions, awareness, general values

* In terms of the message receiver role in academic text sets, those seemed to fall outside the initial conceptualization of message recipient roles—namely, that academic cautionary tales seem to be more about analytics and methods. In some ways, it may be assumed that the consumers of academic writing may be assumed to have the requisite cybersecurity awareness, specific actions, and general values that are minimal to successful functioning in cyber environments.

Figure 14. Aiming for "Vigilance" in Cybersecurity (from "Optimism" and "Aggressiveness" on Robert Plutchik's "Wheel of Emotions")

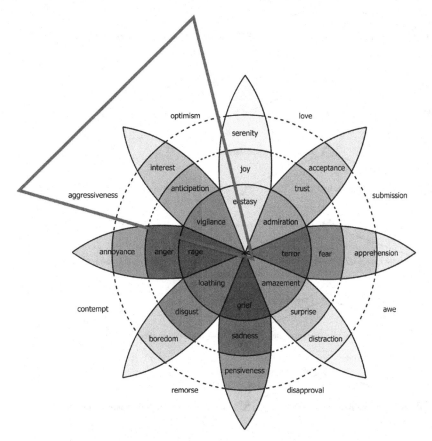

Aiming for "Vigilance" in Cybersecurity
(from "Optimism" and "Aggressiveness" on Robert Plutchik's "Wheel of Emotions")

Another angle may be to test if particular cybersecurity cautionary tales travel well in retellings. Do they hold their accuracy robustly across tellers? Across spaces? How so, and how not?

Also, this work did not include any measuring of effects. It would be critical to be able to objectively test user outcomes after exposure to cautionary tales in cybersecurity. Figure 15 refers to some possible constructive and non-constructive responses. Having people reject the warning, miss the points, show incuriousness as a response, or go to passivity, would all be negatives. People are not consuming cautionary tales in a vacuum; after all, there are constantly a stream of competing narratives around cybersecurity, and this is a hotly contested space.

The behavioral responses for those who consume these tales are in three basic categories: (1) awareness, (2) specific actions, and (3) general values. The awareness (1) refers to the consciousness of risks, attack vectors, attack methods, and signs of compromise. The specific actions (2) refers to steps they need to take to heighten security, prevent compromise, recover from exposure, and prepare appropriately for different cyber contexts. The general values (3) refer to the larger-scale competitions between values and ideals held in mutual tension: personal privacy, security, surveillance, governance, free speech, law,

Figure 15. Possible Constructive/Nonconstructive Responses to the Cybersecurity-based Cautionary Tale

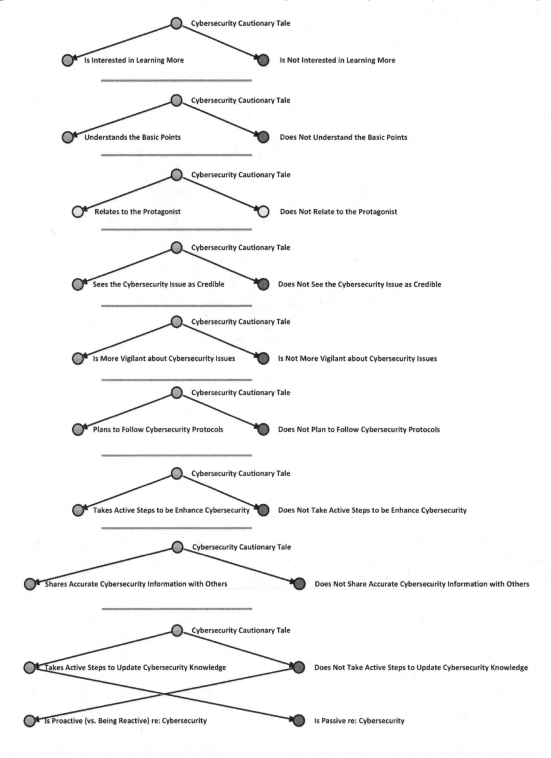

Possible Constructive / Nonconstructive Responses to the Cybersecurity-based Cautionary Tale

ethics, encryption/decryption, and other aspects. These refer to meta-narratives. In many cases, cautionary tales may fit in one of these three categories; in other cases, two of them or even all three. In some cases, as in the academic text set, the reader response is outside of the three response categories…into the realm of analytical and methodological analysis. [In at least one research work, researchers found that a narrative-based training approach to small teams resulted in more insightful analytical outcomes representing more real-world complexity in a cyber situational awareness context than either a training focused on tools or a combined tools/narrative-based approach (Stevens-Adams, Carbajal, Silva, Nauer, Anderson, Reed, & Forsythe, 2013).] In terms of reading for relevance, these three areas are the most critical. As to how hackers or security professionals look, how they dress, how they talk, that's all the irrelevant "shiny" that captures mainstream attention, but the hope is to lead them to deeper understandings. In Figure 16, the two hypotheses are expressed as a visual, and there is a small section that offers some early theorizing on methods to improve the efficacy of cautionary tales told to general users for cybersecurity responsiveness.

While this work focused on "cautionary tales" as a strategic communications form in cybersecurity, this is not to suggest that this is the core structure; it is merely one of many strategies. Also, how such tales instantiate in various information sources differs. In mass-scale search sets over extended time, such tales show up as co-occurring word associations. In both academic and mass media text sets, these are fact-based recounted stories or imagination-based scenarios. In social imagery, cautionary tales instantiate as either single-panel images or multi-panel ones (such as comics; diptychs, triptychs, etc.). In imagery, these may contain all basic elements: context, character(s), warning(s), choice(s)/action(s), and often implied outcomes and implied lessons. The morals of the story may be a little more elusive and

Figure 16. Early Theorizing on Ways to Raise Efficacy of Cautionary Tales told for Cybersecurity…

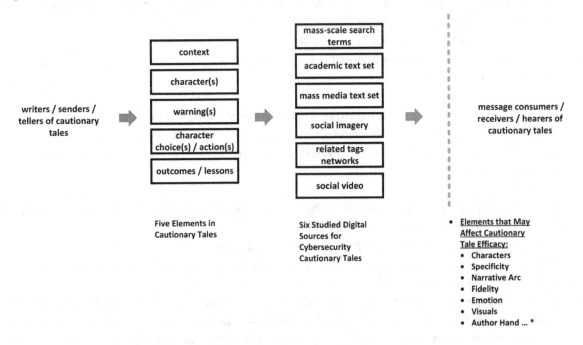

Early Theorizing on Ways to Raise Efficacy of Cautionary Tales told for Cybersecurity
(Hypotheses 1, 1a, 1b, and 2, as Researched, with * Theorizing)

abstract in imagery. In related tags networks, the instantiation of cautionary tales is similar to those in mass-scale search terms, with associated and co-associated terms appearing in the same set or network. In the graphs, they may be communicated in a more abstract way. In such cases, coherence has to be applied to the collection of co-appearing words in close relational proximity. In social videos, these often contain the full elements of a cautionary tale although the stories told in oral form may generally only hit highlights. In cases where presenters offer closer-in details with visuals, that is where the technological depth and sophistication may occur.

Cybersecurity "Cautionary Tales" for the Fourth Industrial Revolution

In the Fourth Industrial Revolution (4IR), with ever tighter integrations between the "physical, digital, and biological spheres" (Schwab, Jan. 14, 2016), cautionary tales regarding cyber will continue to be important even if the warnings differ and the way stories are told is in a multimodal way. What are some anticipated "Thou shalt nots…" in the Fourth Industrial Revolution? Thou shalt not…

- …augment one's body with cyber tools and enhancements that are from untrusted companies
- …augment one's body with enhancements that have not been tested or which have "vulns" to hackers
- …enter into competitions of showing off having the most augmentations of anyone in the world
- …add cyber tools to one's home that can be turned against the homeowner
- …engage in "pillow talk" with embodied sexbots
- …fall for the allure of embodied AI agents
- …trading away one's locational and informational privacy for free services
- …put one's own reputation and others' reputations at risk by poor behavior, which can be observed along any number of digital channels
- …compromise physical health with poorly designed embeds
- …immerse into the full-sensory delights of cyber-augmented spaces and entertainments, and neglect the real and physical

Early signs signal how the Fourth Industrial Revolution may unfold with salutary benefits to human health and health interventions, environmental benefits, smart cities, enhanced work-life balances, and evocative full-sensory entertainments. However, the advancements also come with very human risks.

There are some other extant questions:

- How do you keep anything private when there are sensors in everything and the human mind can be read electronically (and report on the self)?
- How do you protect and air gap if everything is virtually connected?
- How can one protect against monopolies of power when only a few corporations and governments hold power and jealously guard it?
- How can people compete for romance and human affections in competition with AI-informed embodied sexbots (or sexpots?) that are programmed with awareness of how people turn on and turn off and can be custom-programmed to fit perfectly to a particular person? How hard is it to turn away from the artificial to the real (with all of its challenges and some nasty surprises)?

People certainly have power in their solidarity as humans and in their ability to co-create the world that is and the one that is fast approaching, informed by advancements in the various sciences but also by their values and empathic care for each other.

FUTURE RESEARCH DIRECTIONS

This work provided an initial look at the uses of cautionary tales in strategic cybersecurity messaging and has suggested some ways to improve the design and telling. No formal taxonomy of cautionary tales in cybersecurity was offered, but this could be helpful for future research. Early movements have been to look at digital modalities as a way to lead to type. Initial impressions suggest some value in dimensions like non-fiction vs. fiction, point-of-view (omniscient narrator, limited narrator; first, second, or third-person, and others), defined "prohibitions of the story" vs. undefined "prohibitions," high / medium / low levels of detail, fast or slow pacing, emotional tone, technical depth vs. shallowness, and so on.

While this work suggests some possible desirable behavioral outcomes to the messaging, based on theory and reasoning, there is plenty of room to explore the emotional impacts of the cautionary tales, possible digital modality effects on learners, and how respondents think and behave differently in the aftermath of different designed cautionary tales (in the short-term, mid-term, and long-term. This follow-on work may be done with empirical research, user surveys, and other methods. Closing the loop with actual data will be important. Behavior change is a difficult proposition, and while a naïve view might suggest that a story or two or three or ten may make a big difference, the more likely finding is that behavior change in cybersecurity itself is challenging and will require multiple, strategic, concerted, and continuing efforts.

Also, this work did not achieve anywhere near a comprehensive compendium of cautionary tales related to cybersecurity. This limitation has impacts on the observable features these communications. There is also the challenge of "survivorship bias," that only those cautionary tales told in public through certain data sources are studied while those which are shared in analog (paper) form, in live talks, in private settings, are currently unavailable and do not contribute to current understandings. These limitations should be understood to properly contextualize this work.

Other potential sources for data come easily to mind. There are multimodal social messaging datasets that may be explored, blogging sites, formal audio podcasts, social slideshows, and others. In mainstream films, fictional suspense thrillers, and other works, these, too, also contain cautionary tales related to cybersecurity. Often, these are echoic of disastrous scenarios visualized by defense experts who share their ideas through various public venues as well. Also, there may be more in-depth analytical methods applied to the sources already studied.

It is important to note that at the time of this chapter's creation, the mainstream media was dealing with "reverse cautionary tales," counter narratives of non-hacking that were apparently designed for particular political effect. There is a value to studying these counterfactuals and denialism of cyberthreat.

CONCLUSION

To summarize, in cybersecurity communications, cautionary tales are a form of purposive storytelling, "object lessons" for how to engage cyber securely. Their appropriation makes a positive fit with the behavioral messaging for end-users of cyber tools. They were identified in a number of different types of online sources and in different modalities. Certain features were identified as more effective than others in terms of inspiring human awareness, behaviors, and values. This work offered some early ideas about how to improve the uses of cautionary tales in cybersecurity communications to users.

As strategic communications, cybersecurity cautionary tales address multiple audiences simultaneously, and they convey different messages to each. As such, these are seldom ends to themselves: they are used to attract ad funds; bring in or retain customers; burnish a reputation; maybe, secondarily, they are to educate. Technically, people play an important role in their own cybersecurity to protect their own peace-of-mind, finances, privacy, and reputation. To capture and maintain proper attention from the various stakeholders, cautionary tales in cybersecurity have to be well designed; otherwise, they will end up in the collection of texts in the Great Unread or in image sets and video sets that are the Great Unviewed.

However, in the larger scheme of things, the actual defenders are those who engage cybersecurity in corporations and in government. Most systems are locked down by their makers to limit potential compromises by users. In larger-scale defenses, there are moves to automation, with humans taken out of the loop because of the speeds of potential cyber attacks.

Those forward-looking professionals in the field suggest that the abuses that may be wrought are going to be much worse than has been experienced so far (Segal, July 31, 2017). In such cases, of course, it should be all hands on deck, users looped-in and included.

ACKNOWLEDGMENT

This is for R. Max.

REFERENCES

Bathon, J. (2013, Nov. 5). How little data breaches cause big problems for schools. *Legal Issues in IT*, 1–5.

Behavior change communication. (2017, July 17). In *Wikipedia*. Retrieved from https://en.wikipedia.org/wiki/Behavior_change_communication#cite_note-:0-5

Bodenheimer, D. Z. (2012). Cyberwarfare in the Stuxnet age: Can cannonball law keep pace with the digital battlefield? *The SciTech Lawyer*, *8*(3), 1–4.

Cautionary tale. (2017, May 31). In *Wikipedia*. Retrieved from https://en.wikipedia.org/wiki/Cautionary_tale

Constantin, L. (2017, Sept. 21). Researchers link CCleaner hack to cyberespionage group. *Motherboard*. Retrieved from https://motherboard.vice.com/en_us/article/7xkxba/researchers-link-ccleaner-hack-to-cyberespionage-group

Cyber Security Understanding the Cyber World. (2017, Mar. 8). The Sage Group.

cybersecurity. (2016, Nov.). Retrieved from http://whatis.techtarget.com/definition/cybersecurity

Denning, D. E., & Strawser, B. J. (2014). Active cyber defense: Applying air defense to the cyber domain. In *Cyber Analogies*. Calhoun: The National Postgraduate School (NPS) Institutional Archive. Retrieved Sept. 19, 2017, from http://hdl.handle.net/10945/40037

Diaz, D. (2017, Sept. 13). Cruz blames 'staffing issue' for porn video 'liked' on his Twitter account. *CNN Politics*. Retrieved from http://www.cnn.com/2017/09/12/politics/ted-cruz-twitter/index.html

Dillon, R. L., & Carlson, K. (2017). *Seeking advice from experts: A cautionary tale.* IEEE.

Dover, R. (2016, Summer-Fall). Regulation by revelation: The opportunities and challenges of information control in an intelligence era. *SAIS Review (Paul H. Nitze School of Advanced International Studies)*, *36*(2), 103–111.

Dynes, S., Goetz, E., & Freeman, M. (2007). Cyber security: Are economic incentives adequate? *International Conference on Critical Infrastructure Protection*, 15 – 27. https://link.springer.com/chapter/10.1007/978-0-387-75462-8_2

Elf, M. (2011, Feb. 12). Robert Plutchik's Wheel of Emotions (1980). In *Wikipedia*. Retrieved from https://commons.wikimedia.org/wiki/File:Plutchik-wheel.svg

Galvin, J. (2013, May 24). How to escape a submerged car. *Popular Mechanics*. Retrieved Sept. 24, 2017, from http://www.popularmechanics.com/adventure/outdoors/tips/a11919/how-to-escape-a-submerged-car-15510924/

Goldman, E. O., & Arquilla, J. (2014, Feb. 28). *Cyber Analogies*. Calhoun: The National Postgraduate School (NPS) Institutional Archive. Retrieved Sept. 19, 2017, from http://hdl.handle.net/10945/40037

Gottfried, J., & Shearer, E. (2016, May 26). *News use across social media platforms 2016*. Pew Research Center. Received Sept. 22, 2017, from http://www.journalism.org/2016/05/26/news-use-across-social-media-platforms-2016/

Greenberg, A. (2013, Oct. 2). End of the Silk Road: FBI says it's busted the Web's biggest anonymous drug black market. *Forbes*. Retrieved from https://www.forbes.com/sites/andygreenberg/2013/10/02/end-of-the-silk-road-fbi-busts-the-webs-biggest-anonymous-drug-black-market/#4039e6275b4f

Greenberg, A., Feng, L., & Chin, C. (2017). The hotel room hacker. *Wired Magazine*. Retrieved Sept. 18, 2017, from https://www.wired.com/2017/08/the-hotel-hacker/

Hathaway, M. E. (2016, Summer-Fall). Toward a closer digital alliance. *SAIS Review (Paul H. Nitze School of Advanced International Studies)*, *36*(2), 57–67.

Koppel, E. J. (2015). *Lights Out: A cyberattack, a nation unprepared, surviving the aftermath.* New York: Crown Publishers.

Lawson, S. (2016, Dec. 7). Does 2016 mark the end of Cyber Pearl Harbor hysteria? Tech. *Forbes Magazine*. Retrieved from https://www.forbes.com/sites/seanlawson/2016/12/07/does-2016-mark-the-end-of-cyber-pearl-harbor-hysteria/#346ddd3d22c2

McKelvey, F., Tiessen, M., & Simcoe, L. (2015). A consensual hallucination no more? The Internet as simulation machine. *European Journal of Cultural Studies*, *18*(4-5), 577–594. doi:10.1177/1367549415584856

Morgan, S. (2016, Jan. 17). Cyber crime costs projected to reach $2 trillion by 2019. *Forbes Magazine.* Retrieved from https://www.forbes.com/sites/stevemorgan/2016/01/17/cyber-crime-costs-projected-to-reach-2-trillion-by-2019/#95c83ba3a913

Motivation and emotion / Book/ 2014 / Plutchik's wheel of emotions. (2017, Sept. 23). In *Wikiversity.* Retrieved from https://en.wikiversity.org/wiki/Motivation_and_emotion/Book/2014/Plutchik%27s_wheel_of_emotions#Plutchik.27s_wheel_of_emotions

Nagurney, A. & Shukla, S. (2016, Dec.) Multifirm models of cybersecurity investment competition vs. cooperation and network vulnerability. *European Journal of Operational Research, 260*(2017), 588–600.

Neudert, L.-M. N. (2017). *Computational propaganda in Germany: A cautionary tale.* Working Paper No. 2017.7. University of Oxford. Computational Propaganda Research Project. Retrieved from http://comprop.oii.ox.ac.uk/2017/06/19/computational-propaganda-in-germany-a-cautionary-tale/

Newman, L. H. (2017, May 28). How to spring clean your digital clutter to protect yourself. *Wired Magazine.* Retrieved Sept. 18, 2017, from https://www.wired.com/2017/05/spring-clean-digital-clutter-protect/

Nye, J. S. Jr. (2016/2017, Winter). Deterrence and dissuasion in cyberspace. *International Security, 41*(3), 44–71. doi:10.1162/ISEC_a_00266

Remembering Pearl Harbor. A Pearl Harbor Fact Sheet. (n.d.). National WWII Museum. U.S. Census Bureau. Retrieved Sept. 24, 2017, from https://www.census.gov/history/pdf/pearl-harbor-fact-sheet-1.pdf

Rosenzweig, P. (2012). Making good cybersecurity law and policy: How can we get tasty sausage? *I/S: A Journal of Law and Policy for the Information Society,* 388 – 407.

Rotenberg, M. (2015). EPIC: The first twenty years. In *Privacy in the Modern Age: The Search for Solutions* (pp. 1–18). New York: The New Press.

Schneier, B. (2012). *Liars and Outliers: Enabling the Trust that Society Needs to Thrive.* Indianapolis, IN: John Wiley & Sons, Inc.

Schneier, B. (2015). *Data and Goliath: The Hidden Battles to Collect your Data and Control your World.* New York: W.W. Norton & Company.

Schneier, B. (2015). Fear and convenience. In *Privacy in the Modern Age: The Search for Solutions* (pp. 200–203). New York: The New Press.

Schwab, K. (2016, Jan. 14). *The Fourth Industrial Revolution: What it means, how to respond.* World Economic Forum. Retrieved from https://www.weforum.org/agenda/2016/01/the-fourth-industrial-revolution-what-it-means-and-how-to-respond

Segal, A. (2017, July 31). The hacking wars are going to get much worse. *The New York Times.* Retrieved Sept. 18, 2017, from https://nyti.ms/2ub9j36

Stevens-Adams, S., Carbajal, A., Silva, A., Nauer, K., Anderson, B., Reed, T., & Forsythe, C. (2013). Enhanced training for cyber situational awareness. In D.D. Schmorrow & C.M. Fidopiastis (Eds.), AC/HCII 2013, LNAI 8027 (pp. 90 – 99). Spriger. doi:10.1007/978-3-642-39454-6_10

Stoll, C. (1989). *The Cuckoo's Egg: Tracking a Spy through the Maze of Computer Espionage*. New York: Doubleday, Random House.

Thompson, C. (2011, Apr. 24). Innocent man accused of child pornography after neighbor pirates his wifi. *HuffPost Tech*, 1 – 4.

Watering hole attack. (2017). Retrieved from http://searchsecurity.techtarget.com/definition/watering-hole-attack

Wirtz, J. J. (2014, Feb. 28). The cyber Pearl Harbor. In *Cyber Analogies*. Calhoun: The National Postgraduate School (NPS) Institutional Archive. Retrieved Sept. 19, 2017, from http://hdl.handle.net/10945/40037

ADDITIONAL READING

Clarke, R. A., & Knake, R. K. (2010). *Cyber War: The Next Threat to National Security & What to Do About It*. New York: HarperCollins Publishers.

Stoll, C. (1989). *1990). The Cuckoo's Egg: Tracking a Spy through the Maze of Computer Espionage*. New York: Doubleday, Random House.

KEY TERMS AND DEFINITIONS

Algorithmic Surveillance: The uses of computer programs to identify data of interest from a population.

Cautionary Tale: A form of story to warn people against certain risky choices (based on an oral folklore tradition).

Cyber: Relating to information technology (IT), computers, and computer networks, as well as virtuality.

Cyber Safety: Freedom from danger and harm when engaging with cyber technologies.

Cybersecurity: Protection against criminal access to one's data and information and against criminal manipulation of computer networks/data/systems.

Data Leakage: The advertent or inadvertent sharing of private and/or confidential information.

Dossier: A file with documents about an individual.

Folk Tagging: The amateur labeling of digital media.

Mass-Scale Search Data: Summary data indicating how people use web-based search engines.

Multimodal: Involving multiple modes/modalities of digital communications.

Panopticon: A term referring to a circular prison in which the prisoners can be viewed at all terms (and a term coined by Jeremy Bentham in the late eighteenth century).

Related Tags Network: A relational graph of co-occurring tags (in various degrees, such as 1, 1.5, and 2.0).

Social Imagery: Original imagery shared through social media.

Social Video: Original videos shared through social media.

Chapter 11
Cyber Resilience for the Internet of Things

Marcus Tanque
Independent Researcher, USA

Harry J. Foxwell
George Mason University, USA

ABSTRACT

This chapter examines and explains cyber resilience, internet of things, software-defined networking, fog computing, cloud computing, and related areas. Organizations develop these technologies in tandem with cyber resilience best practices, such as processes and standards. Cyber resilience is at the intersection of cyber security and business resilience. Its core capabilities encompass integrated strategic policies, processes, architectures, and frameworks. Governments and industries often align defensive and resilient capabilities, to address security and network vulnerability breaches through strategic management processes.

INTRODUCTION

Cyber resilience architectures and frameworks involve security models, procedures and practices. Industry develops solutions architecture and methods with greater capabilities to measure, evaluate, withstand, resist, mitigate, monitor, recover and protect critical infrastructure systems from cyber-attacks. These perspectives comprise (operational security, defensive and reactive functions) focused on deterring cyber-attacks or disruptive events (NIST, 2014). Besides this chapter lays emphasis on cyber resilience, the future direction of cyber resilience capabilities and Internet of Things (IoT) solutions. Additionally, the authors analyze how global organizations may benefit and learn from past and recent technology problems, to enhance the advance of IoT infrastructure data-sharing and provisioning (EU, 2011). This study also emphasizes technological solutions, progressions and capabilities; specifically, speed, volume, security and user's privacy for sustaining consumers and organizations' commonplace requirements (Cyber Resilience, 2016).

DOI: 10.4018/978-1-5225-4763-1.ch011

On global organizations' critical infrastructures cyber-attackers have steadily increased over the course of years (Cyber Resilience, 2016). As such, governments and high-tech companies continue to develop cyber resilience solutions, policies, methods, trials and standards, to satisfy business and management practices (EU, 2011). Human occurrences and natural tragedies generally originate deliberate cyber-attacks—this includes both intended/inadvertent events. Every perspective being presented in this article further exemplifies authors' useful, sound and real-world expertise. Similarly, the authors put emphasis on specific areas involving cyber resilience and IoT capabilities. To further explain, the background section delivers decades of empirical technology knowledge base. This includes domains supplementing cyber resilience capabilities, and how bad actors 'adversaries' may maximize every opportunity presented to indiscriminately launch cyber-attacks against planned or target of opportunities within the infrastructure. The contextual section also evaluates events, methods and concerts for progressing an organization's all-inclusive business objectives.

BACKGROUND

In the present decade, cyber resilience solutions have played a vital role in protecting organization's infrastructures. This includes spanning organization's ability to in tandem deliver predictable results aimed at decreasing adversative, circumstantial and consequential cyber activities—merging policy and security capabilities, such as information security, business continuity operations and structural resilience. Thus, the advent of cyber resilience capabilities has evolved extending from significant technology and security elements, to contemporary business processes. Such cyber activities can be viewed as security components that span availability, integrity and confidentiality (AIC).

Today AIC triad serves as an epitome for supporting an organization's organizational policies. Similarly, these security elements continue to play a considerable role in the global enterprise's environment. These processes are designed to support IT systems, data and services as well as ensuring IoT systems are capable of withstanding active or future threats. The next section discusses the evolution, impact and future trends affecting cyber resilience, IoT systems and relatively other infrastructure areas.

EVOLUTION, IMPACT AND FUTURE TRENDS

For many years, organizations have advanced from implementing cyber resilience capabilities. For instance, opponents could take advantage of avantgarde and custom-tailored solutions, to launch cyber-attacks, which may often be successful (McCarthy, Collard, & Johnson, 2017). The advent of modern-day distributed computing solutions comprises (Cyber Resilience, 2016): mobile access, cloud computing and IoT systems (EY, 2015). Often cyber-attacks are deliberate or planned—strategic cyber-attacks typically occur when security analysts or specialists, fail to update software or conduct network vulnerability scanning on system(s). The authors describe cybersecurity a method comprising procedures, measures and technologies. These services are developed to provide continuing protection of organization's security capabilities. Similarly, these methods stem from protecting businesses' IoT infrastructure resources; core systems, networks and technologies. Yet, cyber resilience covers (policy, processes, procedures and infrastructure). These mechanisms include cyber security and business resilience among others (McCarthy et al, 2017).

This chapter also situates and amplifies on the transformations pointed to cyber-resiliency architectures, engineering and business processes. These methods and practices point out cyber agility, cyber assessment frameworks, cyber risks, cyber threats and resilience management (WEF, n.d.). Cyber resilience components aim to support distributed and wanton Internet environments (WEF, 2015). Governments and technology industries develop standards and guidelines for cyber risks and threats as well as involved areas of significance. The authors predict that the next generation of IoT computer system hardware infrastructure will involve: advanced autonomous devices, Internet connected, residential appliances and driverless vehicle interoperability. The authors also have concluded that these standards, along with guiding principles are designed to support global cyber resilience and critical infrastructure assets as well as distributed IoT systems. The following sections are tailored to cyber resilience key strategies essential to sustain organization's business and technical areas; explicitly methods required for applying these solutions (EU, 2011). These technology domains also provide relevant details on IoT services and related specifics, such as standards and guidelines. This segment also points out to vital techniques attackers/hackers may apply in the cyber universe to disrupt organizations/friendly forces infrastructure capabilities. Additionally, this segment aims to strengthen on procedures and practices for assessing and averting present or future cyber-attacks. To further illustrate, this chapter highlights modern-day and future resilience architectures or methods.

The following list of Secure Development Lifecycle contains step-by-step procedures for mobile devices, intelligent sensors, processors and actuators (WEF, 2015; WEF, n.d.):

- End default and weak passwords;
- Securely update software, operating systems, and firmware;
- Design privacy mechanisms and policies to discuss security concerns;
- Develop robust secure communication and authentication methods and techniques; and
- Review security incident response processes, procedures, and methods.

National Institute of Standards and Technology defines Resilience as;

The ability to prepare for and/or adapt to shifting conditions, such as the ability to withstand and recover rapidly from disruptive attacks. In addition, resilience is the capability to prepare, find, protect, detect, respond, and recover from deliberate cyber-attacks, such as accidents, or naturally occurring risks, threats, and incidents. (NIST, 2014; Cyber Resilience, 2016)

IoT devices pose significant risks and threats on small, medium to large-scale organizations IT infrastructures (WEF, 2015; WEF, n.d.). Enabling entry points to the Internet infrastructure may pose larger security and technical challenges to customers and IT resources. Thus, Kane recommends the following resilience practices (NIST, 2014):

- Adopt cyber resilience and security frameworks following the NIST standards;
- Elevate cyber and IoT issues to the Chief Executive Officer decision level;
- Educate customers and stakeholders on the importance of data security;
- Extend beyond the four walls of the company to better assess physical and cyber risks and threats; and
- Ensure that security practices are priority to the development of IoT products.

McCarthy et al (2017) outlines resilience "the ability of a system to withstand changes in its environment and still function." While cyber resilience is developed to support an organization's infrastructure capacity and delivers unified security/policy capabilities, to forestall cyber threats and protect these IT infrastructures from adversarial attacks. Despite any failures, which may affect an organization both IT and security capabilities, cyber resilience services are deployed beyond an organization's on-premises perimeters for reinstating infrastructure normal functions and business continuity and planning. These events include, but are not circumscribed to system backups and disaster recovery planning that every organization may require for running without further disruption/high infrastructure latency (McCarthy et al, 2017).

How cyber analysts, defenders and managers may assess risks and threats is based on modeling and simulating current or future security and network data breaches (WEF, 2015; WEF, n.d.). These gaps also entail physical, network, security vulnerabilities and data discoveries. To mitigate such security risks and threats, hi-tech companies, should develop and implement security solutions, for safeguarding critical infrastructure assets (NPPD, 2015). These security practices stem from resilient business continuity of operations programs. In cyber resilience environment, the "Designing for Failure" is a sheer process designed to diagnosing complex systems or millions of variables. Many enterprises frequently adopt defensive and resilient capabilities, to screen and report physical, network security breaches as well as vulnerabilities gaps. These procedures are intended to offering organizations advanced resilience solution capabilities to stay operational in the event of any cyber-attacks.

Organizations use these forward-looking security and technological solutions, to measure and protect their business and IT infrastructures. While best practices are developed to support organizations' everyday business activities and IT solutions. The rapidly evolving distribution of Internet-connected sensors, processors and actuators has resulted in continuous technological opportunities--this occurs over system failures or through malicious exploitation. This section puts emphasis on the resilience concerns associated with identified technical issues, for instance those affecting IoT technologies (NIST, 2014). Cyber threat management is one of the key domains being discussed in this chapter. How organizations manage IoT technologies is vital to quality of services, productivity, and business growth.

Cyber Threat Management

Cyber Threat Management focuses on protecting critical infrastructure resources. Quite the reverse, cyber attackers rely on adaptive-predictive security methods, such as strategies, processes and techniques, to launch attacks and degrading organizations IT capabilities (USCERT, 2017). Such approach stems from cyber-attackers engaging in computer data thefts. To indorsing these activities, cyber attackers often employ adaptive-proactive measures and modern secure services to disrupting organizations' defensive and offensive capabilities. Mostly, these solutions are encrypted software solutions focused on masquerade fingerprints from an attacked system. Besides, cyber-attackers engage in disorderly or irregularly cybernetic attacks (IBM, n.d.).

Cyber Risk and Resilience Management

Cyber risks and threats continue to pose prevalent security challenges on governments and public-private sector infrastructures (Contos, 2015; IBM, n.d.; Li, Jin, & Hannon, 2016; Sikula, Mancillas, &

Linkov, 2015). Many organizations are paying more attention on how to effectively manage solutions for implementing and modernizing business and technological assets (Goldman et al, 2011; Li et al, 2016).

Cyber Threat Intelligence

This intelligence process aims to offer security capabilities for protecting large-scale IT infrastructure systems (WEF, 2015; WEF, n.d.). Thus, cyber-attacks are changing how organizations used to develop strategies for protecting their critical infrastructure assets (Goldman et al, 2011; IBM, n.d.; IDG, 2016). Nonetheless, the cyber threat intelligence framework spans unified methods and processes an organization would need for delivering, mitigating, protecting and withstanding from active/future risks or threats. These security methods vary from developing cyber threat intelligence capabilities, to amassing action-able cyber intelligence data, and evaluating/distributing acceptable IT resources. Using other materials stored in cyber intelligence event reports, to determining risks and threats is a vital role for decision makers (McCarthy et al, 2017). Figure 1 displays an orderly cyber threat intelligence framework and its consecutive procedures.

For many decades, businesses have benefited from components in the above CTI framework. This includes assessing and hardening infrastructure capabilities. In some way, CTI methods and standards are critical in gathering raw data entries, to parse, mitigate and forecast on emerging risks/threats.

Cyber Resilience Architectures and Frameworks

Cyber resilience architectures and frameworks are essential for the functionality, sustainability and resilience of IoT environments (Oteafy & Hassanein, 2017). These security architectures are germane to the adoption of assorted IoT technologies (Goldman et al, 2011). Such architectures and frameworks involve security models, procedures and techniques regarding cyber resilience architectures and frameworks. Consistent with the authors, solutions architecture and methods may be advanced with enhanced capabilities aiming to evaluate, protect, withstand, resist, mitigate, monitor and recover from any cyber-attacks. Moreover, these authors describe cyber risk framework a systematic concept for supporting organizational resilience solutions: security toolset, processes, procedures and techniques to find, evaluate and mitigate IT dependencies affecting business and IT infrastructure. Strengthening cyber risk management solutions is key for protecting IT systems (Contos, 2015; Goldman et al, 2011). Strategic policy and security experts develop standards for governments, public-private sector organizations.

Figure 1. Cyber threat intelligence framework

Elected standards focus on supporting the security of critical infrastructure assets, business and IT capabilities. Such procedures cover operational security, defensive and reactive measures for deterring cyber-attacks or disruptive events (USCERT, 2017). These methods use distributed and mobile computing for on-premise/off-premise, cloud-based solutions, wired-wireless networks, integrated, to smart sensors, processors and actuators. Managing policy solutions and security-based architectures and frameworks is an integral role that decision makers often plan for within their organization. Resilience design and engineered principles are fundamental components of IoT infrastructure performance. Critical cyber resilience is also outlined in the NIST special publication series. This chapter also addresses the adverse and survivability elements, that is hazards, distractions, and threats. It also highlights techniques, technologies, unified concepts and practices (WEF, 2015).

Resilience Design and Engineered Principles

Resilience Design and Engineered Principles ranges from applicability, to systematic and architectural IT domains. These principles include the following four characteristics: capacity, flexibility, tolerance, and cohesion (Jackson & Ferris, 2012). Thus, resilience design and engineered principles are a cataloging of technologically advanced methods and principles supporting a system's functions. These processes or procedures take into consideration the following upmost areas: capability, flexibility, tolerance and cohesion. Each of these integral methods can be preserved by a vertical list of technology subgroups and/or corresponding areas. Accordingly, Table 1 represents a revised catalogue of resilience design & engineered systems and/or matching attributes (Goldman et al, 2011).

The following categories provide a unique/chronological style, including every feature listed in the above table. Each of these items are complemented by wide-ranging definitions and sub-classes singly (Cyber Resilience, 2016; Jackson & Ferris, 2012):

- **Capacity:** The ability of the system to survive, withstand and resist any threats
  - ○ Absorption; physical redundancy; functional redundancy; layered defense

Table 1. Resilience design and engineered system nomenclature

Resilience of Engineered Systems			
Capacity	**Flexibility**	**Tolerance**	**Cohesion**
Absorption	Reorganization	Localized capacity	Inter-node interactions
Physical redundancy	Human-in-the-loop	Drift correction	Reduce hidden interactions
Functional redundancy	Reduce complexity	Neutral state	
Layered defense	Repairability		
	Loose coupling		

Source: Jackson and Ferris (2012)

- **Flexibility:** The ability of the system to adapt to active or future threats
  - ○ Reorganization; Human-in-the-loop; reduce complexity; reparability; loose coupling
- **Tolerance:** The ability of the system to degrade gracefully if any threat arises
  - ○ Localized capacity; drift correction; and neutral state
- **Cohesion:** The ability of the system to act as a unified entity in the face of any threat
  - ○ Inter-node interactions; and reduce hidden interactions

Many organizations have modernized their resilience of engineered systems, to adapt with modern-day cyber resilience capabilities. Along with Cisco, cyber resilience initiatives incorporate seven key capabilities (Cyber Resilience, 2016; Jackson & Ferris, 2012):

- **Identification**
  - ○ Finding critical and valuable organizational assets to decrease risks and threats
- **Protection**
  - ○ Defining robust cyber resilience policies and processes for safeguarding system integrity
- **Detection**
  - ○ Defining policies and processes for gathering, analyzing, influencing and verifying system integrity
- **Recovery**
  - ○ Articulates policies & processes for restoring business and IT systems, to original state of integrity
- **Visibility**
  - ○ Consents for continuous awareness of system integrity components
- **Analytics**
  - ○ Delivers effective analytical toolset for monitoring and calling for system integrity
- **Forensics**
  - ○ Functioning investigative tools for exploring and evaluating event warning

While resilience principles can be managed and refined for large critical systems, hence, major network failures may occur, as a result of lacking multiple resilience implementation principles (Jackson & Ferris, 2012). Jackson and Ferris allude to several historical and contemporary examples, for example the New York Shirtwaist Triangle Fire (Absorption Principle), Nimrod Aircraft Failure and Layered-Defense Principle. However, Table 2 lists a revised list of resilience principles and meanings. This list has originated from relevant peer-review research materials, expressly resilience principles and meanings and corresponding subclasses. Items in the below table were cautiously bespoke to align with their germane meanings (Jackson & Ferris, 2012).

Resilience principles and meanings can be advanced and managed for large critical systems. Conceivably major network failures often occur, due to lack of implementation of single or multiple resilience principles (Jackson & Ferris, 2012). Organizations need integrated-adaptive cyber threat defense solutions to measure, protect and deter active/future threats (Cyber Resilience, 2016).

Table 2. Resilience principles and meanings

Principle	Meaning
Absorption Physical Redundancy Functional Redundancy Layered Defense "Human in the Loop"	Capability of "absorbing the size of the disruption" Reducing the probability of failure through independent or redundancy components Offering more than one way to perform critical tasks Applying multiple resilience principles to single points of vulnerability within the network Ensuring human intervention when critical decision-making process can be made
Reduce Complexity Reorganization	Design no more complexity than needed Designing systems that can self-reconfigure when facing threats
Reparability	Ensuring the ability to restore the system to partial or full operation
Localized Capacity	Distributing functionality amid multiple nodes, to ensure continuous operation if a node or network failures
Loose Coupling Drift Correction Neural State	Limits the propagation of failures among system components Limiting deterioration of components through neglect or persistent threat Delaying action until adequate, relevant, and correct information is available
Internode Interaction Reduce Hidden Interactions	All nodes should be able to communicate, cooperate and share data with other systems—harmful interactions among nodes should be reduced

Source: Jackson and Ferris

Integrated-Adaptive Cyber Threat Defense

Integrated Adaptive-Cyber Threat Defense (IA-CTD) is an evolving area that requires organizations' continuous attention (Contos, 2015). Critical infrastructure cyber experts are developing adaptive and cohesive security solutions, to protect IoT systems. These methods incorporate strategic policies, procedures, processes and techniques. Selected solutions ensure that cyber defenders and analysts have the security capabilities for adapting, identifying, preventing, predict, deter and mitigating known/unknown cyber threats. IA-CTD solutions focus on protecting consumers and organizations from random cyber-attacks (Contos, 2015).

Use Case

Implementing security tools and best practices may offer customers the ability to becoming accustomed with novel techniques, approaches and procedures. In addition, these capabilities incorporate utmost practices for balancing an organization's security measures. Cyber resilience capabilities ensure that public-private sector customers have the tools for identifying, mitigating, deterring, predicting and preventing cyber-attacks. An effective implementation of security capabilities may give an organization, the ability to quickly engage and recover from active cyber-attacks. These events range from adapting, measuring, restraining, reacting and preventing cyber threats (Contos, 2015; IDG, 2016).

Cyber Risk Management

Cyber Risk Management (CRM) involves key strategic policies and management framework. These policy and framework emphasize the cyber resilience processes, procedures, and techniques. CRM features the following fundamentals: protects valuable data, improves cyber intelligence, reports, acts and monitors all cyber risks. CRM further ensures that managers and analysts have an overarching insight of an organization's cyber perimeter (IDG, 2016).

Cyber Resilience Architectures

Cyber resilience is a method involving reliable architectures and processes, to withstand, respond and recover from any physical, cyber-crime or cyber-attacks (Contos, 2015; IDG, 2016). Such process provides senior leaders or decision makers with security capabilities for making informed decisions (Kim, Kolesnikov & Thottan, 2012).

Cyber Agility

Describes reliability, uniformity, speed and reaction involving cybersecurity or resilience events. The method also aims to evaluate, identify, address, monitor, mitigate, sustain, disrupt and protect IoT infrastructure (Kim et al, 2012). Hence, tech industries and governments develop policies, best practices and methods for protecting cyber resilience systems (WEF, 2015). Essentially, critical infrastructure assets and IT solutions span financial institutions/industries, such as defense, aerospace, banking, automobile, telecom, retail, supply chain and others (Contos, 2015).

Cyber Resilience Assessment Framework

In essence organizations should adapt to industry-based cyber resilience specifications—hence cyber capabilities offer executive managers key insights specifically expertise and practical standards for developing new IT solutions/policies to protect critical infrastructure assets. Yet, legislators encourage organizations to implement cyber resilience policies, architectures, procedures and frameworks to withstand daily security threats/practices (Contos, 2015). These standards also deliver security capabilities for protecting IT infrastructures. Developing effective cyber resilience practices give decision makers the tools for evaluating and protecting critical infrastructure asserts. Cyber resilience framework, consist of:

- **Identify:** Advances an enterprise's perceptiveness and direction necessary to evaluate any cyber risks or threats affecting IT infrastructures, information, or services. These chief functional areas include;
    - **Managing Information and Communications Technology Resources:** Human capital, systems, and infrastructures;
    - Governments are responsible for ensuring that assigned and trusted data among subordinate agencies are handled properly. This also ensures that these standards are following federal directives and regulatory specifications;
    - Selected entities have the responsibility to evaluate cyber risks associated with known or imminent security vulnerabilities affecting internal controls; a proper care that should be considered. This includes monitoring active and future cyber threats affecting the global network infrastructure. Such standards also guarantee that IT managers have both ethical and legal rights, to selected policy areas for supporting organizational infrastructure IT capabilities; and

- ○ Governments are responsible for articulating, defending and ensuring that proper management strategies are communicated to right customers and stakeholders.
- **Protect:** Discusses applicable organizational activities for developing/warranting that proper safety measures are wisely elected for critical infrastructure assets—these procedures include:
  - ○ Monitoring and managing routine access to Information and Communications Technology resources or organization's facilities;
  - ○ **Implementing Adequate Technological Solutions:** Computer system hardware and applications software solutions to safeguard IoT infrastructures and the entire organization's data;
  - ○ Motivating and training organization's employees: decision makers, human capital personnel and selected stakeholders;
  - ○ Basic security specifications specifically confidentiality, integrity and availability be preserved with higher urgency and efficacy
  - ○ To guarantee that continuous and healthy operational IoT environment poses a genuine concept for computer and software component deployment;
  - ○ Organizations should be expected to treat and safeguard data with higher level of integrity. Data integrity is a premier area executives and decision makers, first examine, when preparing for a cyber resilience assessment; and
  - ○ Access control systems should be kept for restoring business continuity and operation postures. This includes ensuring organizations are suitably equipped to with safe measures for protecting their IoT infrastructures.
- **Detect:** Essential toolkit for finding and evaluating cyber security activities and solutions. Suspicious activities should be treated with higher integrity, mitigated, and confirmed with high degree of urgency. Introducing best practices and toolkit to support the monitorization of IoT infrastructure includes: hardware and software components. Often these solutions are required to sustain continuity of operations. Organizations should have suitable tools or solutions to evaluate, detect and mitigate network vulnerabilities, and patch reported gaps. This includes remediating functioning and physical security issues affecting the institution's business continuity operation
- **Respond:** Security analysts, cyber defenders and managers should be prepared to deal with risks or threats affecting organizational IT infrastructure resources. This include, detecting cybersecurity activities and deciding on actionable measures for addressing or discussing current/future risks or threats
- **Recover:** A method for developing right security strategy to withstand or survive from any cyber security events is indispensable.

Use Case

Early cyber resilience and IoT capabilities presented limited functions. Such disadvantage ranges from leveraging/modernizing legacy systems, to meeting customers' business and technology requirements. Essentially, the technology deployment timeframe was untenable and thus, did not satisfy business demands. Vendors have begun modernizing IT solutions to satisfy client's requirements. Upgrading legacy technological systems, to fulfilling organization's continuous business requirements has been the core for such infrastructure/technology transformation. Hence, cyber attackers' objective is to disrupt the global network, based on detailed operational knowledge: prior, continuous, or random collection of reports these systems generate, once connected to the network (Buyya, Caheiros & Son, n.d.).

While devices are being monitored, cyber attackers may exploit susceptible network systems. These events give attacker(s) a leverage to launch malicious activities on varied sensors, processors, and actuators, while adapting on disruptive/selective threat methods and techniques (Buyya et al, n.d.). Section 3 discusses specifics of the general IoT domain, focused on devices and interfaces (Coyne, 2016). This ranges from supporting infrastructure that Software-defined Networking (SDN) provides. The next section underlines three key domains: IoT, SDN and fog computing (Buyya et al, n.d.). It also discusses the differences between FC, SDN, and IoT, and how these technologies interact. The next section discusses both the internet of things and software-defined networking solutions, along with other relevant areas of significance.

INTERNET OF THINGS AND SOFTWARE-DEFINED NETWORKING

IoT technology offers dynamic technology capabilities to monitor energy consumption for residential and commercial facilities, doctor's appointments/schedules or medical diagnosis. Many organizations use IoT solutions to influence industrial-based activities: manufacturing, cyber resilience, healthcare, IT management, Internet, research & development, defense, social media, cyber security, big data analytics, agriculture, artificial intelligence, airborne, marketing, sports, automotive, wearable, supply chain, telecommunications, machine learning, research, academia, robotic solutions among others. Enhanced digital solutions, offer many institutions the capability for increasing productivity and growth. Organization decision makers are responsible for making informed decisions that increase to growth and redefine technology advances. More work is yet to be done in the business and technology sectors comprising IoT infrastructure. In contrast, these economic and development opportunities are significant in cyber resilience and IoT environments (WEF, 2012).

Industry develops hardware and software components e.g., security toolkit to assess, defend, deter, resist and mitigate customers or stakeholders' critical infrastructures (Cyber Resilience, 2016). While governments and hi-tech industries remain at the front-line of developing best practices to mitigate cyber risks (MacIntosh et al, 2011; USDHS, 2013). Yet, the authors agree that private-public sector customers, should use permitted or recommended cyber resilience reference material to evaluate, manage, mitigate and reduce global cyber risks or threats on the IT infrastructure. High-tech industries (Amazon, Cisco, Apple, Google, Facebook, Microsoft, IBM and others) continue to develop Information Technology (IT) perimeter-oriented security solutions to support customers. These vendors are equipped with advanced security solutions, such as defensive capabilities for addressing emergent cyber-attacks affecting customers' IT infrastructures (Grieco, 2017). Understanding how cyber attackers/hackers function in the cyber universe may decrease and prevent both active and future cyber-attacks (EY, 2015).

IoT capabilities are being applied in diverse industry environments (Cyber Resilience, 2016). The following institutions or entities have benefited from sensors and actuators' advances and technical capabilities involving these industries: healthcare, aviation, manufacturing, retail, defense, maritime, law enforcement, surveillance, research, academia, construction, real estate, telecommunications, social media, broadcasting and television (Cyber Resilience, 2016). These devices can be mounted on other systems as add-on kits, to generate motion and regulate performance. The systems also lay emphasis on dynamic wireless sensors network methods, practices, and techniques. This section also discusses relevant cyber resilience domains, explicitly cloud computing, IoT and Software-defined Networking

'SDN.' Such domains support cyber resilience, risk/threat management. Hence, disruptive cyber-attacks pose major risks & threats to business and IT infrastructures.

IoT is a broad-based industry concept that was developed to support the adoption of intelligent sensors, processors, actuators, specifically Closed-Circuit Television (CCTV) and wired-wireless devices. These systems are installed in many residential and commercial buildings. Yet, some of these autonomous and independent devices or systems can be deployed as smart cities application components (Coyne, 2016; Internet Society, 2015). The next sub-section emphasizes the smart cities applications and drives.

Smart Cities Applications and Drives

Smart cities applications frequently are adopted in business and technology and other industry domains: transportation, communication, electronic systems, water and waste systems (Vertical Market, n.d.; Wind River, 2015). The term "smart city" refers to autonomous and technology transformation solutions, such as sensors, processors, actuators. Such systems include traffic lighting, robotic systems and monitoring devices mostly CCTV and video surveillance systems (Vertical Market, n.d.; Wind River, 2015). These IoT solutions technology consist of autonomous and independent, which can be installed on dispersed devices/systems through the IoT infrastructure (Caragliu, Del Bo & Nijkamp, 2009; Musa, n.d.; Nicos, 2013).

Internet of Things Devices

IoT systems are becoming more crucial to many organizations. In part, continuous growth in this domain is due to massive global deployment of IoT devices and systems (Geer, 2014; Kane, n.d.). In general, IoT systems are equipped with the latest hardware and software solutions offering customers robust connectivity and system operability (Geer, 2014). Such IoT solutions comprise: sensors, processors and actuators. When deployed on IoT infrastructure, these objects are equipped with embedded connectivity features to strengthen system performance (Wind River, 2015). These features range from data sharing and device's functionality (Marsan, 2015; NSTAC, n.d.). Although IoT devices continue to be vulnerable to cyber and physical attack, Many IoT hardware and software components are devised to assess, protect and deter cyber-attacks (Smart Things, 2015; Kane, n.d.). The next section articulates Byzantine Fault Tolerance (BFT) for cyber resilience.

BYZANTINE FAULT TOLERANCE FOR CYBER RESILIENCE

IoT solutions are built with advanced features for degrading cyber threat and safeguarding IoT infrastructure. This method also warrants that IoT devices are properly configured to provide continuous system operability (Marsan, 2015). Vendors often introduce security measures for guarding IoT infrastructure solutions from cyber risks/threats. The next section discusses byzantine fault tolerance and its specifics related to cyber resilience domain. Byzantine Fault Tolerance (BFT) is a method that plays a significant role in cyber resilience capabilities (Olstik, 2014; Schneier, n.d.). This solution stems from security issues: vulnerabilities, methods and techniques applicable to IoT global-scale. The next section aims at byzantine fault tolerance and how this technology may apply to cyber resilience. Besides, BFT is also a process aiming to protect IoT objects against Byzantine's General (BG) attacks. Distributed systems are complex, autonomous and independently deployed to IoT infrastructure (Geer, 2014; Wind River, 2015). This includes IoT autonomous devices and intelligent systems, which do not interact with each other. Nevertheless, autonomous objects are self-governed and are designed to interact with other IoT devices. Such devices and systems may also lead to accidental malfunctions. Any device or system failures and remediation can be exhibited using the classic BG issues. BG methods form consents for coordinating many actions. These activities may be difficult to implement, if only connected as autonomous and independent systems. Such lack of interoperability may be due to limited technical specifications. (Geer, 2014). BFT attacks may be launched asynchronously or via distributed IoT computing environments. In BFT environment, both 'hybrid and practical methods' continue to pose key security challenges. In addition, BFT security issues are based on consensus voting algorithms. The authors conclude that, BFT affects the resilience of IoT security devices. Having the ability to degrade any system redundancy and introduce random hardware or application failures on IoT infrastructure may be one of the BFT challenges affecting organizations.

Lacking best practices and advanced security solutions to protect and mitigate infrastructure security vulnerabilities, would further pose many challenges on the network. The following sections discuss DDoS attacks (Cyber Resilience, 2016). These are methods and techniques that attackers use to send malicious codes, to single/multiple devices or systems (Kim et al, 2012).

Use Case

Decentralized IoT environments are subject to consensus building based on the vulnerability for the BG problems. These activities also cyber-attackers' opportunities for launching random attacks on IoT systems (Kim et al, 2012). These events may be initiated through Wireless Fidelity platforms (Wi-Fi) or dedicated network solutions. Using these devices hackers may be able to attack single/multiple systems (Cyber Resilience, 2016). For example, attackers can indiscriminately modify password characters (Kim et al, 2012). Through this process attackers are often able to crack passwords by randomly generating/sending out encrypted packets, which would flood the entire network (*Geer, 2014*). After gaining complete access, the attackers may erase/adjust computer logs and thus, exploiting consensus building. Besides, any attacks against single or multiple targeted computers can be launched via a DoS or DDoS (Kim et al, 2012; UDOSA, 2013).

Denial of Service

DoS attacks are a type of cyber-attack making a system unreachable. Attackers select and send malicious software to flood systems over the network with excessive/limited processing. These malicious activities are mostly intended to disrupt services or systems connected to the Internet (UDOSA, 2013).

Distributed Denial of Service

DDoS attacks are distributed or decentralized—hence, in DDoS the attacks generally enlist a number of distributed systems to flood single or multiple systems. As such, cybercriminals are able to launch, disrupt, and degrade IT systems or networks that lack resilience physical capabilities. These forms of computer-generated attacks may be directed to single or multiple targets by using the following methods (UDOSA, 2013): DDoS, massive attacks, spyware, firmware, cyber warfare operations, ransomware, honeypots, malicious software, samba vulnerability and others. In contrast, attackers may use User Datagram Protocol (UDP) to launch, degrade or disrupt IoT systems: grid computing or distributed systems. Similarly, the attacker(s) may also spoof Internet Protocol (IP) addresses embedded in the UDP packets. Attackers may also opt for using Transmission Control Protocol, to launch single or multiple occurrences to target systems or nodes. In part, IoT devices and systems are becoming more omnipresent. This range from everyday activities regarding IoT interconnected and automated world. The next sections accentuate the importance of wireless sensors, processors, and actuators networks when deployed on IoT environments.

Wireless Sensor and Actuator Networks

Individual sensors interacting with actuators, may pose similar network concerns. Such activities often occur when actuators are powered through sensory devices, despite performance that could a challenge, due to the lack of resilience capabilities (Geer, 2014). Wireless Sensor Networks (WSNs) are also known as Wireless Sensor and Actuator Networks (WSANs). Overall, these devices which are physically decentralized or distributed to various infrastructure-based locations (Kim et al, 2012). Thereby these devices are assembled and deployed for screening several activities: collect, share, and process data in real-time (Cyber Resilience, 2016). These smart objects often can be adopted to collect, share, screen, process and regulate residential or commercial building temperature and sound as well as vehicle weights. In this instance, collected data can be shared via the standalone or the Internet (WEF, 2012; Kim et al, 2012). While modern WSANs devices may send and receive signals bidirectionally. This method further ensures that sensors, processors, or actuators have ability to autonomously screen, control and process any events, with limited intervention.

Use Case

This use case describes WSANs as autonomous, computerized or programmable systems (Cyber Resilience, 2016). These processes/activities develop from implementing basic tasks, to regulating residential or office building temperatures or performing surgical operations; gathering and controlling automated defense ordnance systems. Likewise, these systems may be used on space, geospatial, maritime and terrestrial satellite ground systems, to delivering imagery and data collection (Cyber Resilience, 2016). In addition, IoT sensors, processors and actuators are used to screen, assess, collect data, prevent and direct other activities as directed (WEF, 2012).

Dynamic Wireless Sensor Network Architectures

Dynamic Wireless Sensor Network (DWSN) abstraction and architectures continue to support the IoT environment. Decoupling each of these wireless communication devices from their core operational functions often can be advantageous or challenging task for IoT organizations. There are three independent abstractions in every IoT node. These abstractions consist of: wireless communications, device functionality and hardware components (Oteafy and Hassanein, 2017). Given that all nodes are interconnected, software updates can be carried out dynamically. The authors also see the confluence of these nodes, within IoT environment, as a dynamically distributed process. Essentially, DWSN aims to support the absolutely functioning of IoT devices/systems. Oteafy and Hassanein (2017) allude to DWSN solutions as segmented sensors dynamically interconnected with the IoT infrastructure (Cyber

Resilience, 2016). The use of nearby smart phones and individual sensory systems is one of the core examples of these functions.

Smart phones are not part of the DWSN environment, though this wireless technology relies on neighboring/decentralized cell towners/mobile phones to establish communication with the DWSN's IoT sensors. Additionally, IoT systems may be adopted or deployed using Commercial-Off-The-Shelf (COTS) products such as (hardware and software components). Moreover, COTS solutions offer customers, the ability to select specific hardware and software components as well as deciding on suitable deployment methods and practices (Cyber Resilience, 2016). Hence, each node is equipped with matching wireless capabilities/functionalities or parity hardware settings. Aimlessly technical glitches may occur or affect the overall IoT infrastructure's operability. Mostly, these issues can be mitigated and troubleshot by using a unit of IoT nodes focused on resilience and increased system performance (Cyber Resilience, 2016). The following segment underlines solutions for both interoperability and standards, its developing security trends, capabilities and best practices.

INTEROPERABILITY AND STANDARDS

In 2014 the National Security Telecommunications Advisory Committee authored a report on interoperability, best practices, and standards (NSTAC, n.d.). Such report also serves as a guiding principle for adopting IoT best practices and solutions. It also amplifies on delivering methods for assessing various threat levels and decrease risks (Vertical Market, n.d.). Organizations' failures to develop robust security solutions may result in crises affecting the entire IoT infrastructure. The report places more emphasis on the following technical and non-technical recommendations (Vertical Market, n.d.):

- Develop a working group, to assess IoT technical definition or best practices;
- Direct delegated government agency(ies), to assess all federal IoT capabilities;
- Develop contingency plans focused on setting up an inter-agency task force to gather relevant requirements e.g., find security gaps; develop security awareness programs, and offering the academic community motivation to investigate IoT security challenges; and
- Direct the highest government office, as delegated, to review existing IoT capabilities and making recommendation for areas requiring immediate research & development funding.

These standards and procedures underline IoT non-technical conditions, nevertheless these IoT technologies may still be in their early stages. The authors believe that this chapter will contribute to continuing adoption of IoT technology. Hence, the development of new IoT technology could pose greater impact on an organization's everyday operations (Vertical Market, n.d.). Many technology experts estimate that by 2020, tens of billions of IoT devices will be connected to the Internet. Same security experts predict that a better control of data provisioning and evidence flow is key to securing the Internet. Governments and tech industries continue to develop architectures, such as policy and regulatory standards, to support IoT organizational solutions/capabilities. Hence, the below section discusses IoT security concerns and limitations (NSTAC, n.d.).

Internet of Things-Security Concerns

In general, IoT solutions pose greater security concerns to many organizations. Often cyber attackers or cybercriminals have exploited many vulnerabilities, which may lead to network incidents. Arbitrarily, cyber adversaries use mixed computer system hardware and applications software assets, to launch cyber-attacks at technical and non-technical forces. These risks include: granting illegal access and embezzlement of user's information; aiding in cyber operatives to penetrate onto the network without prior authorization; and posing antithetical risks to users' safety. Organizations are encouraged to adopt these best practices when safeguarding IT infrastructure assets (Antonio & Forti, 2017).

- Employ a privacy and security risk assessment;
- Minimize and monitor data provisioned on the network; and
- Test and ensure security measures are compatible to assigned device and features.

Tech industry builds IoT hardware components and application solutions, to support practical security measures for protecting customers and stakeholders' IT infrastructure (Guinard, Trifa, & Mattern, 2011). These practical security events or best practices, vary from device-to-device and machine-to-machine. Data confidentiality and how security vulnerabilities may be assessed, mitigated, or patched often play a key role in the IT infrastructure security. How this data is converged or processed often may pose security concerns (Guinard et al, 2011).

Consumer and Socio-Economic Impact

Growing socio-economic problems have shifted the digital information technology landscape. While continuous collaboration among organizations and consumers may allow for better data sharing the holistic process is yet to thrive (Havlin, Kenett, & Ben-Jacob, 2012;): freight, logistics, rail, retail, airborne, aviation, maritime, automobile, health care, engineering, IT, marketing, business and others. Consumers and organizations benefit from a mixture of services IoT technology may offer. The convergence of mobile systems, embedded sensors, processors, actuators, CCTV or video surveillance monitoring devices often deliver technology capabilities, the ability for connecting, interacting and provisioning data in real-time (WEF, 2012).

Vertical and Horizontal Market Systems

In the recent decade, IoT technology has increased its vertical and horizontal global market footprints (Antonio & Forti, 2017). Thus, vertical market system is a type of marketplace that merchants have the ability to deliver commodities and services, aiming to specific businesses, trade and vocation or customers, whose specific requirements are predefined. While horizontal market system is focused on goods or services aiming to certain goals. This includes a large number of consumers across different sectors of an economy. The confluence of these economic, business, and technologies results in gains for consumers and organizations. Vertical market system integrates driverless vehicles, electrical grid, individual and collective health needs. These industry perspectives are aligned with a variety of horizontal business solutions instituted to support both consumers and organizations marketing paradigms along with business processes and future trends (WEF, 2012).

Security, Privacy and Trust

Tech industry develops responsive IoT systems with end-to-end encryption protocols. Today's cyber challengers aim to exploit network vulnerabilities through DDoS attacks. Reducing colossal cyber-attacks, industry designs security solutions to prevent disorderly malicious attacks on organizations' IT infrastructures is vital to data security, privacy and trust (Funk, Zarzhitsky & Carrol, n.d.). Governments, regulates and drafts security policies, procedures; develops processes, and techniques to assess, defend, deter, mitigate, and disrupt any physical or cyber-attacks (Funk et al, n.d.). These resilience capabilities offer organizations improved solution convergence and interoperability.

SOFTWARE-DEFINED NETWORKING

Early SDN technology adoption consisted of larger computing platforms capable of supporting other infrastructure functions. For such reason, vendors must develop proven capabilities to support resilience solutions for software-defined networking (Haleplidis, Pentikousis, & Denazis, 2015). Autonomous IT systems and networks solutions have played a crucial role in the resilience for future Internet paradigm. DDoS attacks on the Internet will increase. This increase may affect the convergence of hardware components and application solutions. Security and privacy deterrents affecting the system mobility and scalability of devices on the Internet pose time-critical and high-bandwidth application degradation over an extended period of time. The rising of Cloud Computing (CC) technology allows for more flexible and scalable infrastructure performance. Thus, virtual services increase the vulnerability of SDN devices and systems. This poses exclusive resilience challenges for IoT devices and systems.

In light of these technological advances, SDN plays an essential role in IoT environments (WEF, 2012). SDN is a computer networking method for defining and monitoring the network services and functions. This technique, is supported via a lower-level functionality abstraction on the network (Haleplidis et al, 2015). When starting a section network administrators routinely monitor any behavior on the network and manage features or functions embedded on the network in real-time through open interfaces (Buyya et al, n.d.; Haleplidis et al, 2015). These traditional architecture & static networks cannot support the following features: dynamic, computing scalability, and storage capabilities.

Use Case

Many industry publications suggest that vendors design contemporary mobile devices, data centers, campus network infrastructures capable of supporting organizations and customers' needs (Buyya, Caheiros & Son, n.d.). These classic technology shifts include: changing traffic patterns, the IT consumerization, the increase of cloud services, the introduction of big data analytics solutions to increase bandwidth for scalable data provisioning and abstraction.

TECHNOLOGY EVOLUTION AND TRENDS

In 2003 Robert Burke and Zac Carman were contributory in leading the progress of Content Delivery Control Network (CDCN). CDCN patent application is a product that earlier gained industry attention ranging from the telecommunications and traditional IT domains (Haleplidis et al, 2015). The scientific assumption in support of this revelation, concludes that these SDN findings underline the corroboration embedded network collection methods and procedures. These procedures were earlier projected to control the operation of network elements: "content servers, routers, switches, and gateways (Buyya et al, n.d.). The authors suggest that this technical development's goal should protect data from being compromised. In the Telecom industry modernization process has transformed the way enterprises used the global mobile sector. In the most recent decade, the conversion of smartphone devices and content, server virtualization. This includes a myriad of service offerings accessible via the cloud technology. SDN is equipped with advanced and real-time capabilities capable of autonomously reconfigure distributed networks in the public domain (Haleplidis et al, 2015). Figure 2 explains a holistic SDN architecture, relevant applications, and controls (Haleplidis et al, 2015).

Use Case

Two decades ago, Ericsson began research on the SDN solutions. In the same year, Ericsson's soft switch development ended. Decommissioning this research program may be due to a commercially SDN soft switch Research & Development efforts the company embarked on afterward. SDN network technology was developed to reconfigure IP networks in real-time. This reconfiguration includes optimizing quality of service, applications software, network management, and system resilience augmentation. SDN is adopted on smart grid communication and system resilience environment, to prevent malicious attacks and accidental failures. Future adoption of SDN solutions will offer grid operators, the ability to power, deter, mitigate, and protect IT infrastructures cyber-attacks. The following is a list of SDN's architectural components (Buyya et al, n.d.):

Figure 2. Software-defined networking architecture

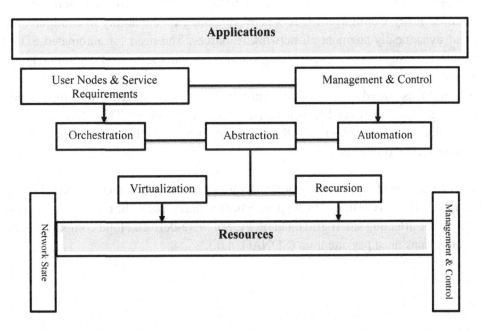

- SDN Application; SDN Controller; SDN Datapath;
- SDN Control to Data-Plane Interface also known as CDPI; and
- SDN Northbound Interfaces or NBI.

In the SDN environment, automated management function is a critical component of IoT infrastructures. This function is imperceptible to manual configuration, monitoring, and updating of myriad devices located on extensive networks (Havlin et al, 2012). Integrating solutions through SDN control plane is crucial to the overall network operations. The logical control implementation of SDN solutions within the network may pose scalability constraints, when the network size and dynamic forces surge (Buyya et al, n.d.).

Resilience Solutions for Software-Defined Networking

In SDN ecosystem, network traffic monitors, processes, controls and manages the flow level of the complete network performance (SDNAO, n.d.). This process focuses on augmenting, changing, and ensuring that the network has embedded synchronous response time and updated functions, to support the users and/or network applications requirements (Haleplidis et al, 2015). These solutions underline the degree of separation arranged between control and data plane. The architectural framework of SDN has the following properties (SDNAO, n.d.):

- **Directly Programmable:** A direct technique such as programmable network control. This process is based on separation-based advancing functions taking place on SDN technologies;
- **Agile:** Abstraction of control spanning functions offering network administrators the ability to dynamically configure network-wide traffic flow to fulfill the behavioral requirements;
- **Centrally Managed:** Encompasses network intelligence centralization. In centrally managed environment, software-based and SDN solutions support the utter view of the network. This process includes applications and policy-based engine functions offered as a single and logical switch;
- **Programmatically Configured:** Offers network managers, the ability to configure, manage, secure, and dynamically augment all network resources. The need for automated SDN programs allows selected programs to self-governing activities within the network without relying on exclusive software performance; and
- **Open Standards-Based and Vendor-Neutral:** When these practical features are adopted, the SDN's design and operational lifecycle activities can be simplified. This consents for programmable instructions to be carried on by SDN controllers instead of relying on multiple vendor-specific network devices or protocols.

In the SDN environment, decoupling offer controllers the ability to manage services on the network (Buyya et al, n.d.). SDN was designed to support cyber resilience capabilities. To date, SDN is regarded a vital security topic affecting smart grid technology. Software-defined cloud computing is another key area that organizations must pay attention (SDNAO, n.d.).

Software-Defined Cloud Computing

Industry develops cloud network solutions to support consumers, organizations, and individual citizen's day-to-day requirements. Software-defined Cloud Computing; better known as Software-defined Clouds (SDC) is a virtual networking platform which regulates computer processes. SDC offers to its users the best capability necessary for performing cloud configuration through the virtualization process in support of data center network resources e.g., computer system hardware resources and applications software solutions. This process focuses on reconfiguring and adaptation of computer hardware assets that are deployed in the cloud infrastructure. The process aims to support the Quality of Service (QoS) requirements by means of an application software deployed to orchestrate and manage all cloud activities in the infrastructure (Cyber Resilience, 2016). Hence, SDC incorporates bandwidth-aware, QoS-aware bandwidth, and energy-resourceful simulated machine deployment (Antonio & Forti, 2017). The following components define the SDC environment in greater detail (Venkatraman, 2013): system virtualization, cloud computing, mobile cloud computing, software-defined networks, software-defined middlebox networking, and network virtualization. The technology industries consider several technology evolution and trends when developing or adopting IoT solutions. All classifications and practices are discussed in the software-defined storage section.

Software-Defined Storage

Software-defined Storage (SDS) focuses on the following classifications and practices: computer data storage, storage virtualization, data deduplication, thin-provisioning, backups, and mirroring, file system, and storage asset management (Rouse, 2013; Robinson, 2013). These services include: "data deduplication, replication, thin provisioning snapshots, and backup solutions." (Buyya et al, n.d.; Haleplidis et al, 2015). SDS computer system hardware solutions have limited concept or "abstraction," data-sharing and computerized software capabilities. SDS components include: In a resilience-based environment, SDS offers unified computational capabilities, along with "policy-focused provisioning and data management or autonomous storage solutions. This comprises storage virtualization, which separates hardware components from managing application solutions. Below are examples illustrating this a process (Robinson, 2013):

- Abstraction; Storage virtualization; virtual volumes or vVols; parallel NFS or pNFS; and
- OpenStack, Ceph or Cinder APIs; and automation and policy-based storage provisioning: SLAs, SMI-S; Commodity hardware along with storage logic abstraction.

If employed as software solution, along with "commodity servers" embedded with built in disks, this may well be theorized as simulated or universal file scheme. VMware coined similar term Software-defined Data Center (SDDC). SDDC integrates "virtual storage systems, security resources, servers and networking" assets (Buyya et al, n.d.). Coraid is a nonoperational commercial firm adopted the term SDS. As illustrated in the below section, fog computing continues to play a fundamental role in IoT environments and cyber resilience domains (SNIA, 2014). Fog computing section is incorporated, to complement all prior domains being discussed in this chapter.

FOG COMPUTING

Fog Computing (FC) is a multi-layered system architecture where the majority of the processing is distributed and close to the users. Having computation close to the users is edge computing. Conceptually, FC relies on a distributed architecture that scales horizontally, which contributes to its reliability (Grieco, 2017). Adding or removing nodes is easy since the horizontal layers are extended or contracted. FC technology plays a key role in SmartGrid and SmartLocalGrid (SLG) domains; OpenFog, 2017). SLG incorporates: sensory systems, machines, network applications, and built-in capability solutions (Bar-Magen, 2013). Cisco invented FC stretch CC solutions beyond an enterprise's system boundaries (Arkian & Pourkhalili, 2017; Bar-Magen, 2013). These edges are called "edge computing or simply fogging." (NSH, n.d.; Stojmenovic & Sheng, 2014).

Use Case

Cisco designed FC to ease the workload burden, while simplifying compute operations to between computer system hardware and applications software. The confluence of these systems and applications includes: D2D, and data center-to-data center. Cisco developed a subgroup of FC better known as Mist Computing (MC). MC is a lightweight computing platform deployed between the core of the enterprise and adjacent edges (Stojmenovic & Sheng, 2014). The MC infrastructure includes devices, for instance microcomputers and microcontrollers (*Cisco, n.d.*). These devices can be deployed in the cloud environment to crossing point with the FC systems.

IoT infrastructure devices and systems are interconnected to provide better functionality. How these nodes can be custom-tailored is far-reaching to the continuance network performance. These solutions should be hardened with agile and responsive security capabilities. The nature of these solutions prevents attackers from using cyber resilience capabilities. FC is a technology method spanning cloud systems and big data analytics. The limited capabilities that FC offers to cloud systems and big data is illustrated by precise content delivery. FC consist of the following components: data plane and control plane.

Technology Challenges

Cyber resilience challenges include, preparing and planning for active or future threats; reacting, and recovering from disruptive incidents and adjusting to emerging risks or threats. These cyber resilience domains pose unique challenges. A report from IDG on the State of Resilience has five technology management areas with the resulting subcategories (IDG, 2016):

- Migration Challenges; High Availability and Disaster Recovery; and
- Data Sharing; Cloud Technology; Professional Services/Outsourcing.

In cyber resilience, technical barriers can be overcome collaboratively. This includes constructive collaboration among organizations; for instance, managing data centers, computer system hardware and applications software solutions. Most of computer systems rely on legacy schemes to perform daily operations, even with greater risks these systems may meet, defective or corrupted data and downtime. Various technology companies surveyed that these conclusions include a partnership between IBM and

Ponemon Institute research. The adoption of cyber resilience solutions consists of: (Ponemon Institute, 2016)

- Planning and readiness;
- Technology complexity and business procedures; and
- Event responsive strategies.

The Ponemon report indicates, corporate decision makers have not changed perception on cyber resilience challenges. These challenges may affect productivity, profit margins, and brand reputation. In the cyber resilience environment, botnets are high profile malicious software solutions used for cyber-attacks. Any cyber-attacks launched on IoT devices (sensors, actuators and CCTV systems) may disrupt continuous operations of major computer systems. This includes outages affecting hardware components and applications software (Ponemon Institute, 2016). Figure 3 illustrates the fog computing architecture and its network nodes/edge devices.

In the FC environment, the data plane powers computer services. These services can be arrayed to edge networks rather than to the server infrastructure or the data center. FC supports end-users and on-premise operations activities or capabilities. This includes the delivery of physical asset sharing, latency decreased systems—for instance, network resource savings offering agile and enhanced QoS capabilities. This method incorporates power analytics or rivulet data mining for higher user-practice or redundancy if system experience some level of degradation or failure. FC solutions interact with IoT devices: driverless vehicles, augmented reality equipment, for example Google glasses. FC also plays a vital role in the applications software solutions. This entails the automotive industry, transportation, supply chain, and sensory networks (Cisco, n.d.).

Figure 3. Fog computing architecture

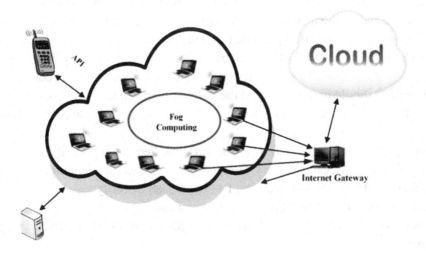

Use Case

In the recent decade, fog solutions have been applied in the electrical grid, intelligent meters, smart traffic lights, CCTV, or video surveillance systems, emergency vehicles specifically ambulances, police cars; sensory highway lights, tolls, autonomous bridge functioning, wireless systems, wearable devices, actuators, and smart building control system (Krebbs, 2016).

IoT deployments require resilient back-end infrastructure collaboration to sustain the connectivity and data transmission requirements. Devices/systems' flexibility, elasticity, and scalability objects require enough bandwidth to perform diverse activities. Fog solutions sustain cloud computing service and deployment models when deployed to IoT environments. Cloud computing is an integral area, which supports everyday functionality of cloud solutions. The next section discusses cloud computing, evolution, methods and trends as well as its architectural solutions.

CLOUD COMPUTING

Industry develops innovative security and technological solutions, to protect governments and public-private sector's IT infrastructures from cyber-attacks (Winkler, 2011). Organizations should be vigilant and insightful in finding, evaluating, investigating, deterring, or preventing emerging cyber-attacks. Exploring cyber actors' behavior is critical for planning, executing, and implementing novel security or technological solutions, strategic policies, procedures, and techniques. The evolution and deployment of private, public, and hybrid cloud architectures is essential, such as supporting IoT implementation (CSA, n.d.; Winkler, 2011).

Cloud Architectures

Cloud architectures are vital to an organization's business continuity and IT operational postures. Massive scale of cloud service and deployment models prompted Amazon and Google to have a comprehensive understanding on how to design and implement IT architectural processes and practices.

These methods aim to protect and offer resilience to the global technology infrastructure in case of a hardware and software failures. To efficiently implement these procedures, cyber defenders, security architects, and analysts should perform each of the tasks by using checklists: Cloud Security Alliance's and cloud controls metrics. These proposed security specifications comprise (Cyber Resilience, 2016):

- Policy, standards, and guidelines; Transparency; Legal; Personnel Security;
- Third Party Providers; Legal; Business Continuity; Resources Provisioning; Software Assurance; Network Security; Host and VM Security; PaaS and SaaS Security;
- Identity and Access Management; Key Management and Cryptography; and
- Data Center Physical Security; Data Center Asset Management; Operational Practices; Incident Management.

These provisions present unique challenges to IoT implementation policies. These policies support access and management of IoT devices and cryptology key solutions (Perrig, Canetti, & Tygar, 2002). Cyber resilience is an essential component of a comprehensive cyber defense strategy, cyber security, and information security domains. Approaches to these components should be coherently and carefully well-defined. This encompasses continuing adoption of IoT solutions. Aside from these underlying advances, drawbacks and challenges, there is more work in cyber resilience domain. Exploiting these operational and economic advantages requires all entities' participation, collaboration, and transparency (Poelker, 2014).

Device-to-Device and Device-to-Cloud Communication

Improved cyber resilience defense and/or threat capabilities, should be deployed to support Device-to-Device (D2D) and Device-to-Cloud (D2C) global communication infrastructure. D2D communication is a type of radio technology or system for delivering digitized communications. Technology experts describe D2D platforms as devices functioning for many hours with reduced energy consumption (Cyber Resilience, 2016). These devices have embedded features offering improved data rates in areas, where parity communication frequency is desirable. Hence, these interfaces offer voice, video and data communication capabilities.

An attacker can take a full control of a system by sending out broadcast packets on the network. Communication devices have built-in and resilient security features to secure, monitor, mitigate, and deter any physical or security vulnerabilities. To protect these devices from active and future cyber resilience risks and threats, the communications infrastructure can assess, react, withstand, survive, resist, and mitigate any adversarial cyber-attacks. The design of D2D systems incorporates several technology specifications: discovering, researching, planning, testing, executing, implementing, deploying, and supporting. key advantages of D2D communication architecture include (Cyber Resilience, 2016):

- **Capacity Gains:** Distributes spectrum data between mobile and device users through smart phones, computers and iPads is crucial;
- **User Data Rate Gains:** Achieves high peak rates or D2D transactions as well as propagating signals through this media is key to an equitable and sustainable level of service; and
- **Latency Gains:** End-to-end platform latency through reduced communication pattern, while allowing these devices to reconcile or exchange data by a direct link.

D2D solutions are essential technology assets to many organizations. Technology experts describe D2D platforms as capable to functioning for many hours with lessened energy consumption. These devices are equipped with embedded features offering improved data rates in areas, where parity communication frequency is desirable. Designing D2D systems may contain several technology specifications: discovering, researching, planning, testing, executing, implementing, deploying, and supporting. Figure 4 illustrates an improved D2D communication architecture (Cyber Resilience, 2016). The below figure discusses D2D architecture and its pertinent subcategories.

Major weaknesses in devices are due to the lack of physical security. Constrained devices offer limited physical security capabilities. Attrition rates can be accepted, due to a low expense. Instead, this concept sustains constrained systems. D2C communication comprises single or multiple IoT systems synchronously connected to the global network through an Internet-based cloud application service. In

Figure 4. D2D communication architecture

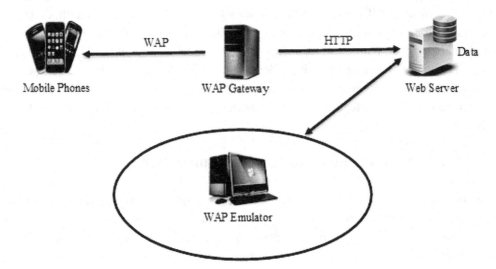

D2C environment, systems can be interconnected via the Application Service Provider, Internet Service Providers, or Managed Service Providers enabled services. Once connected, the devices provision, share, manage, and route information to single or multiple nodes' destinations. Control Message Traffic (CMT) solutions have played a crucial role in D2C network infrastructure (Cyber Resilience, 2016).

CMT emphasizes the delivery of "traditional wired Ethernet" or Wi-Fi computer solutions connected by cloud infrastructure services. Every connection between a device and the cloud is started by an IP network. The IP network serves as a gateway between one or multiple devices and the cloud infrastructure. This type of D2C solutions can be adopted by many consumers and customers, whose devices are connected to IoT infrastructure (Cyber Resilience, 2016).

Device-to-Gateway/Device-to-Application Layer and Back-End Data-Sharing Model

The Device-to-Gateway (D2G) or Device-to-Application-Layer Gateway (D2ALG) model was developed to interact with systems which are deployed on IoT infrastructure. These IoT systems are capable of interacting with other devices connected to the cloud-based infrastructure. All local gateways or endpoints are equipped with embedded application software solutions. These solutions are gateway or interfaces between IoT systems and the cloud. Once configured the interface displays encrypted functions including data and protocol translation.

Mobile devices are often deployed as interfaces between IoT environment and cloud service. The interface serves as medium for relaying information between IoT devices and cloud service. In residential and commercially owned properties D2G devices are interfaces for residents and tenants, whose devices are connected to IoT infrastructure. both *Z-Wave* and *ZigBee* solutions may be deployed in the enterprise offering interoperability functions to other devices. For users who are connected to SmartThings cloud service, D2G devices may deliver data-provisioning and accessibility of solutions, via mobile devices or embedded applications to the Internet (Cyber Resilience, 2016).

Back-End Data-Sharing Model (BDSM) is a communication system allowing users to analyze and transfer data installed in smart object via cloud service and information sharing capability. These provisions entail technology resources that can be accessible from, or via decentralized/distributed nodes on the network. The BDSM stems from the "Single Device-to-Cloud Communication Model. This is a legacy concept for managing information silos in IoT environments. An adapted back-end sharing architecture process was coined to ensure that the information was collected from single or multiple devices.

When adopted IoT solutions may be combined and examined for processing. Cloud Service Providers recommend that users consider the federated cloud service approach, when deploying solutions using the back-end data-sharing. These services include using Application Programming Interfaces, viewed as preferred solutions for delivering interoperable solutions for smart device data hosted. The back-end data-sharing architecture is applied in many business case scenarios. In this scenario, IoT sensors are deployed in standalone environment. Today, businesses can retrieve and examine data being produced by cloud service or by a single or multiple IoT devices in real-time. The authors envisage that businesses can predict future operation requirements that may enhance productivity level and help reduce operational and capital expenditures. Today machine-to-machine communication plays a principal role in the marketplace (Cyber Resilience, 2016).

Machine-to-Machine Communication

Machine-to-Machine (M2M) communication covers methods, protocols, algorithms, and systems for conveying information. These machines range from monolithic systems to sensor networks. The impact of resilience for M2M communication ranges from communication and network viability. Key resilient solutions keep trusted systems functional whether in the times of crises; particularly when network nodes have compromised keys. Network capabilities range from basic network functionality and operational infrastructure postures. To offer continuous protection on organizational assets, industry should develop customized or light-weight security solutions. These solutions can be specified to offer IT infrastructures a supportable level of performance, security, scalability, and reliability. These capabilities can be built with embedded End-to-End security features enhance privacy practices and overall protection of the network. Resilient security capabilities deliver enhanced security functions. Ensuring that networks are designed to withstand, resist, react against risks or threats. These services can readily be available, even when nodes' keys are unguarded or lack security.

The key exposure resilience concept is essential given that sensors are simply physically captured. On large networks, if sensors' keys are compromised, some of the security features may be revealed to attackers. This may include single or multiple sensors' security functions for a large-scale re-keying. Such incident(s) may result in the denial of specified sensor's functions. In the resilience ecosystem, key exposure is critical for effective and efficient sensory networks. Assigned security features may be clustered in pairs; giving the network better performance and resilience capabilities. On symmetric crypto systems processing data with public keys is very expensive. Consequently, group key infrastructures consist of: adding or removing sensors is very expensive. The next segment provides a summary of the overall chapter and its respective domains (Cyber Resilience, 2016).

FUTURE INTERNET RESILENCE

Many organizations explore reasonable and agile methods for improving data sharing and provisioning. This concept specifies technological solutions, processes and capabilities (speed, volume and security) to include user's privacy for satisfying day-to-day consumers and organizations' requirements (Wu, Manton, & Moran, 2013). The number of cyber-attacks on the nations' critical infrastructures and global network system are on the rise. Vendors develop leading-edge strategic policy and security solutions to deter, protect, prevent, and mitigate cyber-attacks launched by cyber actors or operatives. Vendors advance resilient system models to protect and increase performance on network operations). This allows for unified interoperability amid natural disaster preparedness and emergency management. The process focuses on conducting all-year-around-exercise in support of hurricanes, earthquakes, storms; man-made or natural disasters. These annual exercises are vital in deciding about the landscape and resilience of the future, for instance, Internet operability, performance, and sustainability.

The future direction of cyber resilience for the IoT systems is pervasive. Hence, industry and governments should continue to collaborate on innumerable technology research areas. This will allow for continuous dissemination of technology knowledge base coupled with technology capabilities when necessary. This approach aims to strengthen unified/collaborative efforts among decision makers and related contributing stakeholders. Governments and high-tech companies, should cooperatively research, develop, and deliver forward-thinking technology capabilities to support customer and business' requirements. Additional debates on cyber resilience/IoT technology have been incorporated in the 'discussion and conclusion' section. Thus, the 'future internet resilience' section intends to provide organizations with a technology roadmap to help improving data-sharing and provisioning capabilities (Sterbenz & Kulkarni, 2013). This includes developing ground-breaking technological solutions: processes, solutions, agility, responsiveness, volume, security, user's privacy capabilities among others. The next section concludes with empirical discussions and conclusions relevant to this article.

DISCUSSION AND CONCLUSION

Vendors' understanding of technology opportunities, such as trends and impacts may help redefine or readdress practical knowledge-based constraints. How industry articulates, studies, develops, forecasts, and adopts IT solutions to better serve consumers and organizations' requirements is paramount to organizations growth. The methods, however, includes but is not limited to the ability to develop and grasp technology requirements: IoT and M2M specifications as well as align these solutions with both vertical and horizontal clientele's capabilities to maximize immediate and long-term productivity growth. Vendors develop and deliver IoT capabilities and business methods to satisfy the consumer and organization's requirements. Security, privacy, and trust continue to pose major challenges in IoT environments (Antonio & Forti, 2017).

The authors' final analysis spans in-depth concepts with emphasis on expert perspectives on IoT and cyber resilience its threat and defense strategies. Selected audiences for this chapter include technical and non-technical readers wishing to deepen their knowledge in the selected policy-based strategic domains: cyber resilience, cyber risk & threat management, cloud computing, cloud architectures, software-defined networking and IoT technologies. This investigation also targets technical and non-technical readers; mostly students in higher education and/or tertiary level of education, alongside those pursuing specialized information security and other technology research studies. This research also aims to deliver circumstantial and valuable details to support technologists, consultants and practitioners' present and future cyber resilience for IoT requirements. To further accentuate, the authors have provided a painstaking analysis of the cyber resilience trends, for instance, the evolution and complementary objective areas, aiming to enhance the future of IoT infrastructure capabilities. The overall content in this chapter is bespoken by the main topic of this book. In conclusion, the authors have taken into consideration all suitable and logical assessments and rationalities regarding cyber resilience and IoT systems. These concepts might valuable to vendors, when developing new best practices. In essence, greater policies, processes, methods and services should be developed to enhance or mature cyber resilience and IoT functioning capabilities.

REFERENCES

A Survey on Centralised and Distributed Clustering Routing Algorithms for WSNs. (2015). In *IEEE 81st Vehicular Technology Conference*. Glasgow, UK: IEEE. doi:10.1109/VTCSpring.2015.7145650

Antonio, B., & Forti, S. (2017). QoS-aware Deployment of IoT Applications Through the Fog. *IEEE Internet of Things Journal*. doi:10.1109/JIOT.2017.2701408

Arkian, H. R., Diyanat, A., & Pourkhalili, A. (2017). MIST: Fog-based data analytics scheme with cost-efficient resource provisioning for IoT crowdsensing applications. *Journal of Network and Computer Applications*, *82*, 152–165. doi:10.1016/j.jnca.2017.01.012

Bar-Magen, N. J. (2013). *XMPP Distributed Topology as a Potential Solution for Fog Computing*. MESH 2013 The Sixth International Conference on Advances in Mesh Networks.

Buyya, R., Caheiros, R. N., & Son, J. (n.d.). *Software-Defined Cloud Computing: Architectural Elements and Open Challenges*. Department of Computing and Information Systems, The University of Melbourne, Australia. Retrieved from http://www.cloudbus.org/papers/SDCC-Keynote2014.pdf

Cisco RFP-2013-078. (n.d.). *Fog Computing, Ecosystem, Architecture, and Applications*. Cisco.

Cloud Endure. (2017). *Five Experts Predict Cloud Computing Trends for 2017*. Retrieved from https://www.cloudendure.com/blog/5-cloud-experts-predict-cloud-computing-trends-2017/

Cloud Security Alliance. (n.d.). *Cloud Controls Matrix Version 3.0.1*. Retrieved from https://cloudsecurityalliance.org/group/cloud-controls-matrix/#_overview

Contos, B. (2015). *Cyber Security Culture is A Collective Effort*. Retrieved from http://www.csoonline.com/article/2977014/security-awareness/cyber-security-culture-is-a-collective-effort.html

Coyne, E. M. (2016). Huawei Exec: SDN's Become a Completely Meaningless Term. *Light Reading*. Retrieved from http://www.lightreading.com/carrier-sdn/sdn-architectures/huawei-exec-sdns-become-a-completely-meaningless-term/d/d-id/726364

Cyber Resilience. (2016). *Safeguarding the Digital Organization*. Retrieved from https://www.cybrary.it/channelcontent/cyber-resilience-safeguarding-digital-organization-white-paper/

Ernst and Young. (2015). *Cybersecurity and the Internet of Things*. Retrieved from http://www.ey.com/Publication/vwLUAssets/EY-cybersecurity-and-the-internet-of-things/$FILE/EY-cybersecurity-and-the-internet-of-things.pdf

European Union Agency for Network and Information Security. (2011). *Measurement Frameworks and Metrics for Resilient Networks and Services. Challenges and Recommendations*. Retrieved from https://www.enisa.europa.eu/publications/metrics-tech-report/at_download/fullReport

Funk, G., Zarzhitsky, D., & Carrol, T. (n.d.). *Security and Privacy Challenges for the Internet of Things*. Retrieved from cybersecurity.pnnl.gov/documents/security_and_privacy.pdf

Geer, D. (2014). *The Internet of Things: Top Five Threats to IoT Devices*. Retrieved from http://www.csoonline.com/article/2134265/network-security/the-internet-of-things--top-five-threats-to-iot-devices.html?page=2

Goldman, H., McQuaid, R., & Picciotto, J. (2011). Cyber resilience for mission assurance. In *Technologies for Homeland Security (HST), 2011 IEEE International Conference on* (pp. 236-241). IEEE. 10.1109/THS.2011.6107877

Grieco, A. (2017). *Demanding a Plan for Cyber Resilience in the IoT*. Retrieved from https://blogs.cisco.com/security/demanding-a-plan-for-cyber-resilience-in-the-iot

Guinard, D., Trifa, V., & Mattern, F. (2011). *From the Internet of Things to the Web of Things: Resource Oriented Architecture and Best Practices*. Springer.

Haleplidis, E., Pentikousis, K., & Denazis, S. (2015). *Software-defined Networking (SDN): Layers and Architecture Terminology*. RFC 7426, IETF. Retrieved from https://www.rfc-editor.org/info/rfc7426

Havlin, S., Kenett, D. Y., Ben-Jacob, E., Bunde, A., Cohen, R., Hermann, H., ... Solomon, S. (2012). Challenges in network science: Applications to infrastructures, climate, social systems, and economics. *The European Physical Journal. Special Topics*, *214*(1), 273–293. doi:10.1140/epjst/e2012-01695-x

How It Works. SmartThings. (2015). Retrieved from http://www.smartthings.com/how-it-works

International Business Machines. (n.d.). *Cyber Resilience in the Age of IoT: Ask Bruce*. Retrieved from https://www.resilientsystems.com/cyber-resilience-knowledge-center/cyber-resilience-age-iot-ask-bruce/

International Data Group. (2016). *State of Resilience*. Retrieved from http://resources.idgenterprise.com/original/AST-0175041_2016-State-of-Resilience-Report.pdf

Internet of Things Council. (n.d.). *The Internet of Things*. Retrieved from http://www.theinternetofthings.eu/what-is-the-internet-of-things

Jackson, S., & Ferris, T. (2012). *Resilience Principles for Engineered Systems*. Wiley. DOI 10.1002ys.21228

Kane, G. (n.d.). *The internet of things: An argument for cyber resilience.* Retrieved from https://www.zurich.com/_/media/dbe/corporate/knowledge/docs/zna-iot-an-argument-for-cyber-resilience.pdf

Kim, Y. J., Kolesnikov, V., & Thottan, M. (2012). Resilient end-to-end message protection for large-scale cyber-physical system communications. *2012 IEEE Third International Conference on Smart Grid Communications (SmartGridComm)*, 193-198. 10.1109/SmartGridComm.2012.6485982

Krebbs, B. (2016). *Hacked Cameras, DVRs Powered Today's Massive Internet Outage.* Retrieved from https://krebsonsecurity.com/2016/10/hacked-cameras-dvrs-powered-todays-massive-internet-outage/

Li, Z., Jin, D., & Hannon, C. (2016). Assessing and mitigating cybersecurity risks of traffic light systems in smart cities. *IET Cyber-Physical Systems: Theory & Applications*, *1*(1), 60–69.

MacIntosh, J. P., Reid, J., & Tyler, L. R. (2011). *Cyber Doctrine: Towards A Coherent Evolutionary Framework for Learning Resilience.* Institute for Security and Resilience Studies, UCL. Retrieved from https://www.ucl.ac.uk/isrs/publications/CyberDoctrine

Marsan, D. C. (2015). IAB Releases Guidelines for Internet-of-Things Developers. *IETF Journal, 11*(1), 6-8. Retrieved from https://www.internetsociety.org/sites/default/files/Journal_11.1.pdf

McCarthy, I. P., Collard, M., & Johnson, M. (2017). Adaptive organizational resilience: An evolutionary perspective. *Current Opinion in Environmental Sustainability*, *28*, 33–40. doi:10.1016/j.cosust.2017.07.005

Musa, S. (n.d.). *Smart City Roadmap.* Retrieved from http://www.academia.edu/21181336/Smart_City_Roadmap

National Institute of Standards and Technology. (2014). *Framework for Improving Critical Infrastructure Cybersecurity.* Retrieved from http://www.nist.gov/cyberframework/upload/cybersecurity-framework-021214.pdf

National Institute of Standards and Technology. (2017). *The National Initiative for Cybersecurity Education (NICE) National Initiative for Cybersecurity Education.* Retrieved from http://csrc.nist.gov/nice/about/index.html

National Institute of Standards and Technology. (n.d.). *Cybersecurity Framework Draft Version 1.1.* Retrieved from https://www.nist.gov/cyberframework/draft-version-11

National Institute of Standards and Technology. (n.d.). *Cybersecurity Framework Draft Version 1.1.* Retrieved from https://www.nist.gov/cyberframework/draft-version-11

National Institute of Standards and Technology. (n.d.). *Special Publication 800-160: Systems Security Engineering.* Retrieved from http: http://www.nist.gov

National Protection and Programs Directorate - Office of Cyber and Infrastructure Analysis. (2015). (n.d.). The future of smart cities: Cyber-physical infrastructure risk, U.S. *Department of Homeland Security New Solutions on the Horizon.*

National Security Telecommunications Advisory Committee. (n.d.). *STAC, NSTAC Report to the President on the Internet of Things.* Retrieved from https%3A%2F%2Fwww.dhs.gov%2Fsites%2Fdefault%2Ffiles%2Fpublications%2FIoT%2520Final%2520Draft%2520Report%252011-2014.pdf

Nicos, K. (2013). What makes cities intelligent? In *Smart Cities: Governing, Modelling and Analyzing the Transition* (p. 77). Taylor and Francis.

Olstik, J. (2014). *The Internet of Things: A CISO and Network Security Perspective*. Enterprise Strategy Group. Retrieved from http://www.cisco.com/c/dam/en_us/solutions/industries/docs/energy/network-security-perspective.pdf

OpenFog. (2017). *OpenFog Reference Architecture for Fog Computing*. Produced by the OpenFog Consortium Architecture Working Group. Retrieved from https://www.openfogconsortium.org

Oteafy, S. M. A., & Hassanein, H. S. (2017). Resilient IoT Architectures Over Dynamic Sensor Networks with Adaptive Components. *IEEE Internet of Things Journal*, *4*(2), 474–483. doi:10.1109/JIOT.2016.2621998

Poelker, C. (2014). *The foundation of clouds: Intelligent abstraction*. Academic Press.

Ponemon Institute. (2016). *The Second Annual Study on the Cyber Resilience Organization*. Retrieved from http://info.resilientsystems.com/hubfs/IBM_Resilient_Branded_Content/White_Papers/2016

Robinson, S. (2013). Software-defined Storage: The reality beneath the hype. *Computer Weekly*.

Roger, R., Apeh, E., & Richardson, C. J. (2016). Resilience of the Internet of Things (IoT) from an Information Assurance (IA) Perspective. *10th International Conference on Software, Knowledge, Information Management & Applications (SKIMA)*. 10.1109/SKIMA.2016.7916206

Rouse, M. (2013). *Definition: software-defined storage*. Tech Target.

Schneier, B. (n.d.). *Click Here to Kill Everyone*. Retrieved from http://nymag.com/selectall/2017/01/the-internet-of-things-dangerous-future-bruce-schneier.html

Schneier, B. (n.d.). *The internet era of fun and games is over*. Retrieved from https://www.dailydot.com/layer8/bruce-schneier-internet-of-things/

Sikula, N. R., Mancillas, J. W., Linkov, I., & McDonagh, J. A. (2015). Risk management is not enough: A conceptual model for resilience and adaptation-based vulnerability assessments. *Environment Systems & Decisions*, *35*(2), 219–228. doi:10.100710669-015-9552-7

Software-Defined Networking. (n.d.). *Definition*. Retrieved from https://www.opennetworking.org/sdn-resources/sdn-definition

Software-Defined Networking Architecture Overview. (n.d.). Retrieved from https://www.opennetworking.org/images/stories/downloads/sdn-resources/technical-reports/SDN-architecture-overview-1.0.pdf

Sterbenz, P. G., & Kulkarni, P. (2013). *22nd International Conference on Computer Communication and Networks (ICCN)*. Doi: : 2013.661412510.1109/ICCCN

Stojmenovic, I., & Sheng, W. (2014). The fog computing paradigm: Scenarios and security issues. In *Computer Science and Information Systems (FedCSIS), 2014 Federated Conference on*. IEEE 10.15439/2014F503

Storage Networking Industry Associates. (2014). *Technical Whitepaper: Software Defined Storage*. Author.

The Internet Society. (2015). *The Internet of things: An overview*. Retrieved from https://www.internet-society.org/sites/default/files/ISOC-IoT-Overview-20151014_0.pdf

Understanding Denial-of-Service Attacks. (2013). *United States Computer Emergency Readiness Team*. Retrieved from https://www.us-cert.gov/ncas/tips/ST04-015

United States Computer Emergency Readiness Team. (2017). *Assessments: Cyber Resilience Review (CRR)*. Retrieved from https://www.us-cert.gov/ccubedvp/assessments

U.S. Department of Homeland Security. (2013). *NIPP 2013: Partnering for Critical Infrastructure Security and Resilience*. Retrieved from https://www.dhs.gov/sites/default/files/publications/NIPP-Fact-Sheet-508.pdf

U.S. Department of Homeland Security. (n.d.). *Cybersecurity & Privacy*. Retrieved from https://www.dhs.gov/sites/default/files/publications/privacy_cyber_0.pdf

Venkatraman, A. (2013). *Software-defined datacenters demystified*. TechTarget.

Vertical Market. (n.d.). Retrieved from http://www.investorwords.com/5242/vertical_market.html

Wind River. (2015). *Security in the Internet of Things: Lessons from the Past for the Connected Future*. Retrieved from http://www.windriver.com/whitepapers/security-in-the-internet-of-things/wr_security-in-the-internet-of-things.pdf

Winkler, V. (2011). *Securing the Cloud*. Elsevier Inc.

World Economic Forum. (2012). *Global Risk Report, Davos, Switzerland*. Retrieved from http://www3.weforum.org/docs/WEF_GlobalRisks_Report_2012.pdf

World Economic Forum. (2015). *Advancing Cyber Resilience: Project Scoping Workshop*. Retrieved from http://www3.weforum.org/docs/IP/2015/ICT/19Nov_CyberResilience_PreRead.pdf

Chapter 12
Developing Cybersecurity Resilience in the Provincial Government

Harold Patrick
University of KwaZulu-Natal, South Africa

Brett van Niekerk
University of KwaZulu-Natal, South Africa

Ziska Fields
University of KwaZulu-Natal, South Africa

ABSTRACT

The approach that the organization uses to manage its cyber-risk to its workforce, information, systems, and networks is paramount to ensure sustainability and continuity in the Fourth Industrial Revolution. Improving cyber-resiliency in the organization reduces the chance of future threats and attacks and builds better capability. Cyber resilience involves continuous operations, good governance, and diligence supported by the right security strategy of a computer security incident response team (CSIRT) that can protect government operations and control cyber-risks. CSIRT can build better resiliency at the decentralized provincial government level, and contribute to cyber awareness amongst the workforce, public, and other government departments. A CSIRT can further contribute to resilience to the organization by analyzing the threats and attacks, developing countermeasures for the future in protecting its systems and networks from threat actors.

INTRODUCTION

Government services are the backbone to service delivery and social upliftment (Education, health and energy). Minimal disruptions in this infrastructure are crucial to ensure reliable information, resilience and secure services and networks (Hoffman, 2015, p. 2). An organisation can reorganize its efforts and save costs by prioritizing irregular and suspicious cybersecurity events, thereby allowing cybersecurity

DOI: 10.4018/978-1-5225-4763-1.ch012

response persons to focus on the actual security threat or breach (Symantec, 2017, p.1). Government departments need to build resilience capabilities to ensure that they can improve on cybersecurity preparedness and response capabilities. Data (such as cybersecurity statistics and intelligence) provides the department with reliable information that can be used improve to decision-making (Hoffman, 2015, p.2) and thereby reducing the impact of disruption of government services. The government department can monitor cybersecurity incidents which it is aware of before the impact of the attack or breach increases. This speedy response allows the provincial department to isolate the cybersecurity incident so the government networks are not maliciously further targeted. With the introduction of the Fourth Industrial Revolution, government needs a radical shift to better design and build technologies that will meet their technological progress or economic productivity. Strong government leadership is needed to improve government capabilities and proactively manage cyber-risks.

In the Fourth Industrial Revolution, imminent encounters between organisations and countries will be fought through the cyberspace environment (Cole, 2017, p. 1). Organisations, government and threat actors would use the target network and systems to deliver cyber incidents like social engineering, malware, spear phishing and denial of service to disrupt the organisation or government operations and services. This chapter will discuss cyber resilience, South African government initiatives, cybersecurity incident management mainly on CSIRT as a resilient approach to managing cybersecurity risks in the Fourth Industrial Revolution.

BACKGROUND

South African Government Structure and Spheres

There are three spheres in the South African government namely: (1) National, (2) Provincial; and (3) Local government. National government (National departments') mandate are developing for policies and developing national standards, norms, and regulations. Provincial government (Provincial departments) are responsible for provincial planning, health, school education, and social grants (Department of Public Service and Administration, 2003, pp. 15 & 17). Provincial departments do not receive any monies for services rendered therefore they are dependent on National department for revenue. Hence, they receive the largest budget allocation from National Department (Department of Public Service and Administration, 2003, p. 30). Local government (Municipalities) functions are to care for providing municipal roads, local amenities, electricity, water, housing and local amenities (Parks and gardens)

Cyber-Resilience

Cyber-resilience is the ability of the organisation to prepare, withstand and recover from a cybersecurity incident, threat and attack (Department of Homeland Security, 2017, p. 1). Cyber resilience provides a strategic direction for the management of cybersecurity incidents, which includes: (1) Recognizing, (2) Managing (which can include business continuity, disaster recovery and CSIRT); and (3) Responding to the threat or adversary. The CSIRT as a main approach to management of cybersecurity incidents will be discussed later and will provide the incident response. The importance of cyber-resilience in government is to develop and support a cybersecurity culture and build a solid base to deal with cyber-risks (The

Scottish Government, 2015, p. 5). A cyber-resilience approach can also lower data breaches because of a quicker incident response by a CSIRT (Ponemon Institute, 2016, pp. 11 & 24).

The impact of cyber-resilience to an organisation are:

- The perception of what important assets that need protection,
- The budget available to create cyber-resilience; and
- Expectations of future threats and attacks and how to minimise operational and financial risk (Goche & Gouveia, 2014, p. 3).

Senior management assurance for cyber-resilience is the most important driver in the organisation to implement the appropriate solution to build cyber-resilience (Business Continuity Institute, 2017, p. 15). The components to build a cyber-resiliency in an information technology environment to respond to cyber-attacks and cyber-threats include: (1) Cybersecurity strategy, (2) Governance, (3) Cybersecurity incident management (4) Cybersecurity awareness; and (5) Cybersecurity infrastructure and technology (Hewlett Packard Enterprise, FireEye & Companies, 2016, pp. 3-8). This chapter would discuss the key component cybersecurity incident management with the clear functioning of CSIRT in this role.

SOUTH AFRICAN GOVERNMENT RESPONSE TO THE CYBER-RESILIENCE NEED

Electronic Communication Security: Computer Security Incident Response Team (ECS-CSIRT)

The ECS-CSIRT is a South African response team that is positioned within the State Security Agency. In April 2012, the ECS-CSIRT began publishing awareness newsletters (ECS-CSIRT, 2012, p. 1). Security incident information pertaining recent security updates and threats are also published in the newsletter. The CSIRT role reflected on their website is silent (State Security Agency, 2016, p. 1). In addition, it was established that there is no mechanism for the government departments to request assistance, neither is there a mechanism for them to report cybersecurity incidents. The newsletter further highlights security-incidents and threats in other countries. (ECS-CSIRT, 2012, p. 13) A further review of the ECS-CSIRT indicate an online link for the user (i.e., government official, and private individual and private organisation) to measure and report on their level of ECS-CSIRT awareness. Original analysis and trends of cybersecurity incidents in SA are not indicated for awareness (Patrick, 2016, pp. 6-7). Tamarkin (2014) notes that the ECS-CSIRT offers very limited assistance and support in assisting government entities in responding to cybersecurity incidents and concerns (p. 1).

Cybersecurity Hub

The Minister of Department Telecommunications and Postal Services, Cele, in October 2015, launched the national Cybersecurity Hub for South Africa (SA). ECS-CSIRT formed a partnership with the Council for Scientific and Industrial Research to establish the Hub. The Hub would also be collaborating with other stakeholders to respond cybersecurity incidents in SA and manage cyber-crime (African News

Agency, 2015, p. 1). The cybersecurity Hub roles and responsibilities are mandated by the National Cybersecurity Policy Framework (Department of Telecommunications & Postal Services, 2016b, p. 1).

The Cybersecurity Hub would be a centralized point for cooperation amongst stakeholders and government departments. Organisations and private persons would be able to directly contact the Hub and report a cyber-incident for investigation (Von Solms, 2015). The Hub will also support cyberawareness in SA. The Cybersecurity Hub will promote best practice in relation to international standards and develop security policies for all sectors in SA (Ngubeni, 2014, p. 1). The Hub would also be responsible for providing protection to SA network infrastructure from possible attacks and threats (Cwele, 2014, p. 1). The Cybersecurity functions would include (Cwele, 2015, p. 1):

- Receiving incident reports and institute the procedure for incident management,
- Publish threat intelligence information to all stakeholders,
- Documenting all security incidents which would provide a better knowledge of security incidents; and
- Chairing meeting with all stakeholders to report on security incidents and attacks.

The Cybersecurity Hub will not analyse and find the resolution for the cybersecurity incidents. The Cybersecurity Hub will assist in identifying which government or organisation representative should respond to the cybersecurity incident and will follow up with them (Department of Telecommunications & Postal Services, 2016a, p. 1). The Cybersecurity hub also aims to encourage cyber citizens, departments and organisations to engage responsibility while undertaking online actions (Ajam, 2015, p. 1)

The major disadvantage of the Hub is that they only operate within normal working hours being 8:00 am to 16:30 pm and not on public holidays (Department of Telecommunications & Postal Services, 2016a, p. 1). Cybersecurity incidents or attacks have no specific time or timeframe to occur and disrupt or cause damage to an organisation's system and networks. This suggests that if the provincial government needs to report the cybersecurity incident or threat to the hub for assistance and awareness, the provincial government officials would need to wait to do this during the office hours. This waiting to report might cause greater disruptions to the provincial department's networks and system.

Draft Cybercrime and Cybersecurity Bill

The Bill features additional new offences included: (1) Hacking (when a person or persons illegally attempt to gain access to individuals or organisation's computer or network. A key logger tool could be deployed to retrieve access passwords), (2) Ransomware (this is a malware that limits access to an individual or organisation's networks until the victim or organisation makes a payment in exchange to regain access to the computer or network); and (3) Unlawful interference of data (which could imply altering the original state of the data, in order to use this information to one's advantage either for selling to make a profit) (Michalsons, 2017, p. 3). This proposed bill strives to put processes in place that will assist SA to proactively and effectively manage cyber-crime. The Bill aims to:

- Recommend the applicable penalties for violations relating to cybercrime,
- Legalise powers for admission and seizure of items and devices arising from cyber-crime,
- Regulate collection of evidence, and

- Legalize international cooperation with other countries and stakeholders to investigate cyber-crime (2015).

Chapter 10 (Section 54) in the Bill, states that the government minister accountable for state security must launch the CSIRT team for government and maintain capacity to give effect to the cybersecurity. The minister of Police must ensure that there are sufficient human and operational capacity to detect and investigate cyber-crime effectively and in a timely manner. The Minister responsible for Telecommunications and Postal Services must maintain the Cybersecurity Hub, which must deal with the private sector and other nodal points (Department of Justice and Constitutional Development, 2017, p. 36). In addition, if a nodal point or private sector fails to establish a CSIRT, the Minister of Telecommunications and Postal Services will create that response team and that particular sector will be liable for the cost of establishment. The nodal points will be responsible to:

- Distribute information about cybersecurity incidents,
- Receive new information of cybersecurity incidents, and
- Receive cybersecurity incidents from the Cybersecurity Hub and report it to the Cybersecurity Hub (Department of Justice and Constitutional Development, 2017, p. 37).

Bernstein, Ebrahim, and Cibane (2015) state that offences relating from cyber-crime would be codified (p. 1). However, they add that a definition of example electronic communication service provider is too broad and requires additional clarity. In addition, clause 16(5)(b) also states that "any person who unlawfully and intentionally, (1) Possesses, (2) Communicates, (3) Receives data which is the possession of the state and which is classified as confidential, is guilty of an offence" is identical to the Protection of State Information Bill of 2008. Fripp (2015) notes that the Bill encroaches on Constitutional rights in that a citizen's privacy might be breached in search and seizure of devices (p. 1).

CYBERSECURITY INCIDENT MANAGEMENT

The Centre for Cyber Security (Cyber Security Coalition, 2015, p. 6) defines cybersecurity incident management as the procedures for reporting, detecting, assessing and responding to a cybersecurity incident and learning from these incidents. Cybersecurity incident management is a holistic approach that identifies critical information, assets, vulnerabilities, and threats in the event of cyber security incident or attack (Centre for the Protection of National Infrastructure & National Technical Authority for Information Assurance, 2015, p. 7). While organizations tend to allocate resources to proactively preventing threats and attacks, they should be investing more resources in cyber-incident management that would assist an understanding of the scope of the detected cybersecurity incidents and threats (ObserveIT, 2014, p. 4).

With a cybersecurity incident management procedure in place, an organisation can better manage its cybersecurity incidents and threats and thereby determine an effective process for cybersecurity incident assessment. The organisation can use the assessment information to develop better defensive strategies (ID Experts, 2014, p. 1). When an organisation analyses cybersecurity event data to detect unusual and suspicious activities, it can easily identify potential indicators of compromise (Prelert, 2015, pp. 3-4) that were previously unknown. Thus, a cybersecurity incident response infrastructure development is crucial to responding to cybersecurity incidents (Greene, 2015, p. 51) and quickly detect potential attacks, contain the damage, eliminates the potential attack and reinstates the network and systems. Cybersecurity incident management also deals with exposing potential vulnerabilities and designing the corrective controls to minimize the impact on the organisation (ISACA, 2013, p. 218).

All government systems must undergo a cyber-risk assessment to assess if the government department is capable of managing cybersecurity incidents and whether a cybersecurity incident management measure is needed (National Cryptologic Centre, 2017, pp. 8 & 10). The phases in cybersecurity incident management will be discussed next.

Cyber Incident Response Plan

The rapid respond of an organisation in responding to a cybersecurity incident or attack and the data it can gather may decide whether the potential attack or threat is eventually successful in breaching the organization's networks and systems (Lee, 2014, p. 1). A response plan is a necessity for an organisation, which would define what action for example when cybersecurity incident is detected should be taken (Symantec, 2014a, p. 5).

The preparedness of the organisation and cybersecurity incident response plan can also influence a cybersecurity incident, threat and breach (IBM, 2014, p. 1). Moreover, without a response plan the organization's resources and significant downtime of the response team will affect the reaction time in trying to assess and analyze the potential attack and threat. This lack of resources and time wastage can lead to reputation damage to the organisation. The IBM (2014) report additional states that two constituents, specifically, (1) Thoroughness; and (2) Usability should be drafted into the cybersecurity incident response plan (p. 1).

A cybersecurity incident response plan is a fundamental element of an organization's cybersecurity incident management (AppliedTrust, 2008, pp. 1-2). A cybersecurity response plan also dictates the organization's effectiveness in deploying the correct response when the cybersecurity occurs (Govloop, 2014, p. 20). The supplementary knowledge the organisation has, the better informed its cybersecurity incident response plan is to improve its cybersecurity strategy (Ashford, 2012, p. 1). Communication in an organisation is imperative to enhance efficiency and innovation, thus ensuring that the organisation functions successfully (Jones & George, 2009, p. 569). It is also essential that all stakeholders involved be kept informed through regular formal and well-organized communication mechanisms. The organisation must designate a person or persons responsible for external communication to ensure that timely updates are provided to all stakeholders. Organizations should update their cybersecurity incident response plan at least twice a year (IBM, 2014, p. 4). An organisation that has a well-designed cybersecurity response plan is better placed to respond to threats and breaches (Wright & Schaetzel, 2015, p. 7).

The cybersecurity incident response plan should include the following elements:

- Technical know-how of protection (for example how to manage and protect access to the systems and networks);
- Whose responsibility is to take control of the cyber-incident (this would include classifying the cybersecurity incident and assigning to the incident handler);
- Communication mechanisms of the cyber incident (for example whether the cybersecurity would be published in the internal print medium or intranet);
- Identifying the categories of cyber incidents (this would include classifying the priority of the cybersecurity incident);

- At what point will external cyber experts be consulted (management of the CSIRT would decide this based on the required skills need to investigate and contain the cybersecurity incident);
- Structure and duties of the cyber incident response team (this would normally be allocated by the management of the CSIRT); and
- What data, assets and infrastructure need protection (the CSIRT can provide assistance to management in identifying vulnerable areas) (Cyber Security Coalition, 2015, p. 8).

Cybersecurity Incident Reporting Mechanism

Identifying and responding to unversed cybersecurity events in real time is not an easy task, and a cybersecurity incident reporting mechanism would enable the organisation to gather the before and after data of incidents (Hewlett-Packard, 2014, p. 46). This will enable the organisation to detect attacks and threats earlier so that further damage is minimized to the organisation networks and system.

It is a reality that most organizations do not know their particular security position and neither do they have adequate knowledge of the potential threats and attacks, which could ultimately affect their capability to protect the organisation and its employees (RSA, 2012, p. 2). It is vital that organizations understand and recognize the cybersecurity attacks and threats they face and their position countering such threats (RSA, 2012, p. 4). The report highlights two important examples: (1) If the organisation does not have latest data it will not recognize and respond to the newest attack techniques; and (2) A database of cybersecurity incidents is important to identify the trends of malicious activity. A cybersecurity incident reporting mechanism provides a plan detailing how an incident is managed in the organisation (Sritapan, Stewart, Zhu, & Rohm Jr, 2014, p. 58). Cybersecurity incident reporting provides an internal analysis of the security landscape of the organisation (Sritapan et al., 2014, p. 56).

The organisation requires the current data relating to cybersecurity incidents so that it can determine what cyber-risks are relevant and make real-time decisions so that the appropriate action can be taken (RSA, 2012, p. 2). Most organizations are unwilling to report a cybersecurity incident or breach because of the relaxed and broadly drafted laws on reporting such incidents (Holtfreter & Harrington, 2014, p. 56). In addition, management might not want to report these incidents because it might be reflective of their management culture. Employees need to know how, what and to whom they need to report a suspicious cybersecurity incident (MS-ISAC, 2013, p. 7). A cybersecurity incident can be reported by means of: (1) In person, (2) Online tools, (3) E-mail; and (4) Phone (Department of Homeland Security, 2014, p. 1). It is also important for employees to be aware of type of cybersecurity (for example suspected incidents, hacking and network intrusions) that warrants reporting in the organisation. The cybersecurity manual reporting form or online design should consider the following: (1) Details of occurrence, (2) Details of detection, (3) Threat path, (4) Location of system or device; and (5) Contact details including anonymity (US-CERT, 2015, p. 1). Countries and organizations are reliant on their political will and governance culture in deciding on cybersecurity reporting structure. For example, in the New York State Department, Computer Incident Response Team (CIRT) coordinates incident reporting and all cybersecurity incidents must be reported to CIRT or the National Information Sharing and Analysis Center (Miller, 2015, p. 1). In South Africa, the organizations and the general public can report a cybersecurity incident by using the Cyber Security Hub managed by the Department of Telecommunications and Postal Services. The government departments can report a cybersecurity incident by contacting the State Security CSIRT.

Computer Security Incident Response Team

Every organisation should have a CSIRT (Ross, 2013, p. 5) to respond to cybersecurity incidents, attacks and breaches. A CSIRT is an important component of a cybersecurity incident management (ECS-CSIRT, 2012, p. 1) since the CSIRT needs to take the lead and be the respondent to respond swiftly to cybersecurity incidents, attacks and threats (Rainys, 2006, p. 73). The CSIRT supports the organisation to take rapid and operative actions (Ross, 2013, p. 5) should there be a potential or suspicious cybersecurity incident.

The development of a CSIRT can speed up the organization's capabilities of responding to malicious threats (Stewart, 2014, p. 2). The quick response can ensure minimal disruption of public services to other government departments and the citizens. Organizations need to be prepared and constantly informed of new cybersecurity incidents, trends because the insider threats from employees are becoming bolder, and hackers are continually becoming more sophisticated. Hence, the organisation cybersecurity response must be able to respond to the incidents and attacks at short notice (Computer Sciences Corporation, 2014, p. 1). The quicker the CSIRT concludes the cybersecurity investigation; they can limit the time hackers have to disseminate and sell off the intellectual property. Every step of the cybersecurity investigation needs be documented to ensure no further disruptions before connecting networks and systems to operations (Govloop, 2014, p. 20).

Gagnon and Mickahail (2014) claim if government departments are to evaluate and effectively respond to cybersecurity challenges, it is essential that they develop and support a diverse security team which might comprise: (1) Incident handlers who will take responsibility for the cybersecurity incident, (2) Information technology and physical security to prevent any further intrusion and not contaminate the digital evidence; and (3) Forensic experts who will digitally images of the incidents and save original information prior to the intrusion (p. 3). This is imperative that organizations have the skills of security expertise (ISACA, 2013: 216-217) and knowledge to respond to potential or confirmed cybersecurity incidents.

Oltsik (2013) states that security operations and cybersecurity incident response teams in organizations are understaffed (p. 6). This is concerning and suggests that the organizations will not have the capacity to rapidly respond to and succeed in managing cybersecurity incidents. Cyber Threat Defense Report for 2014 also notes that, one in four organizations do not have the resources to investigate the source and impact of cybersecurity incidents and attacks (CyberEdge Group, 2014, p. 5). Von Solms, notes that SA has a shortage of skills of CSIRT to respond and manage cyber-crime (cited in Jones, 2014, p. 1) and (Doyle, 2017, p. 1) notes that SA has a severe skills crisis when it comes to cybersecurity skills. An organisation needs personal skills like integrity to respond and maintain confidentiality and in addition technical skills like incident handling is also needed. Without these skills, the organisation will not adequately respond to cybersecurity incidents, execute the analysis and communicate the mechanics and update of the cybersecurity within the organisation and with their staff (ISACA, 2013, p. 217).

National Institute of Standards and Technology Roles and Responsibilities for a Computer Incident Response Team

The National Institute of Standards and Technology (NIST) (2012) is a non-regulatory agency in the United States that encourages innovation and continually tries to ensure applicable standards to enhance security and improve the quality of life for citizens and organizations (TechTarget, 2015). Although there are various cybersecurity incident management frameworks internationally, the NIST standards are an excellent (Greene, 2015, p. 51) (Ross, 2015, p. 4) basis of guidance. Thompson (2015, p. 1) notes that the NIST guidance documents are an excellent basis for designing enhanced practices for managing networks and systems. The NIST 800-61 determines how to successfully respond to a cybersecurity incident (Granneman, 2014, p. 1) and if further provides a complete methodology, which provides structured procedures for a cybersecurity incident.

The SP 800-61 provides the best guidance and current practices for organizations to mitigate the IT security risks. The guideline contains an effective cybersecurity incident response methodology (National Institute of Standards and Technology, 2012, p. 4). The NIST recommends four phases in incident management, specifically, (1) Preparation, (2) Analysis, (3) Containment & recovery; and (4) Post incident activity (National Institute of Standards and Technology, 2012, p. 21). The different actions in the phase will be highlighted below.

Preparation

Cybersecurity incidents are inevitable; and organizations must implement an improved security position in order to be better prepared for cybersecurity incidents. Cybersecurity teams need to be adequately prepared to deal with cybersecurity incidents and 'table top exercises' would provide good expertise in responding and investigating different cybersecurity incidents (Guidance Software, 2013). Cybersecurity incident preparation and response require a thorough understanding of the information risks and threats the organisation might face. The improved responses can provide guidance to cybersecurity teams through the incident response steps. They assist the organisation to react swiftly and successfully to the revealed cybersecurity incident without added confusion or loss of operational time (Whitman & Mattord, 2011, p. 276). In this phase, obtaining the cybersecurity intelligence information is vital in gaining an understanding the current threat landscape and preparing for the possible threat or attack. This information will also provide valuable assistance to the CSIRT in envisaging future attacks and threats (Symantec, 2014a, p. 2) and are important in preventing cybersecurity incidents and attacks (National Institute of Standards and Technology, 2012, p. 21).

Analysis

In this phase, the organisation needs to quickly identify the category of attack and threat, and evaluate the internal network and systems affected. Methods for detecting cybersecurity incidents; (1) The organization's workforce, (2) Deployment of technology, (3) Endpoint protection, (4) Detection tools (for example intrusion detection systems) (Cyber Security Coalition, 2015, p. 20). In addition, the source of cyber-incidents need to be identified to establish if it is a precursor of occurring in the future or indicator that the cybersecurity incident happened or is going to happen (National Cryptologic Centre, 2017, p. 14). Continuous monitoring is initiated to identify any further indicators of attacks and threats. This phase is utmost in containing attacks and threats, and concluding and closing out cybersecurity incidents (Symantec, 2014a, p. 5). All indicators like false positives from intrusion detection and the server being unavailable have to be investigated in order to establish the validity of the sign (National Institute of Standards and Technology, 2012, p. 28). The NIST emphasizes (2012, p. 28) that this phase is the most demanding in cybersecurity incident management since all indicators do not show the identical symptoms.

Containment and Recovery

Containing the cybersecurity incident is limiting the destruction and the attack (Cyber Security Coalition, 2015, p. 22). This is crucial to prevent the attack from re-engineering itself and further attacking the organization's system and network. Containment is critical before a cybersecurity incident can override the networks and system and increase disruption. Once the cybersecurity incident is confined, the incident response team has a period to develop an approach to handle the cybersecurity incident (National Institute of Standards and Technology, 2012, p. 35). A sandbox is used to redirect the threat actor to this containment intervention. This intervention also allows the incident team to evaluate networks and systems for further cybersecurity incidents and attacks. The malware contained in the sandbox allows for its lifecycle to be observed and understood in relation to its capabilities (Guidance Software, 2013). Documenting the cybersecurity and the evidence in phase is also important. The cybersecurity incident team must also undertake an original system snapshot, which would assist in the investigation phase. All evidence collected must be recorded in a comprehensive (National Institute of Standards and Technology, 2012, p. 37). After containing the cybersecurity incident, all related components must be eradicated for example: (1) Alleviating exploited vulnerabilities; and (2) Deleting breached user accounts.

While undertaking the analysis and investigation of the cybersecurity incident it is crucial that the evidence is persevered in pursuit of possible prosecution. The incident response team should adhere to the procedures in the response plan and should be mindful of not instantly shutting down the server and cutting off the server from the internet. Also, the team should not restore the backup system if they are uncertain if the backup system is infected. The team should also not re-install the same server without a forensic copy (Cyber Security Coalition, 2015, p. 23). A thorough recording of the evidence should be maintained and such information is: (1) Identification and location of host name and internet protocol address, (2) The details of the person collecting the evidence, (3) The date and time when the evidence was processed, and (4) Location details where the evidence is stored (National Cryptologic Centre, 2017, p. 22).

The type of cybersecurity incident, will also dictate the extent of recovery phase, which ultimately affects the time, cost and data loss (Cyber Security Coalition, 2015, p. 25). Next, a recovery phase must be in operation so that infected artefacts can be cleaned out. Remedial action should be taken to patch any vulnerabilities and passwords should be changed immediately. Afterwards the system must be restored after the initial backup was done preceding to the cybersecurity incident. The networks should then be continuously monitored during the recovery period (National Institute of Standards and Technology, 2012, p. 37). Recovery phase is vital in developing and employing applicable IT internal systems controls in order to reinstate network services in the organisation (Symantec, 2014a, p. 6). The organization's cybersecurity strategy must include disaster recovery and business continuity plans, which would guide the organization's actions to recover from a cybersecurity, attack and threat (Symantec, 2014a, p. 6).

Post Incident Activity

This phase should not be overlooked (National Institute of Standards and Technology, 2012, p. 39). Reflecting on the cybersecurity incident and potential fresh, sophisticated attacks and threats is important to learn valuable lessons are enhancing current information technology security actions. The post cybersecurity information can be used to provide future training of cybersecurity incident response teams and for employee awareness. It is imperative that cybersecurity incidents are officially reviewed after the intervention to identify if further prevention is needed as well (Cyber Security Coalition, 2015, p. 30).

The Cyber Security Coalition identify further actions that should be taken in this phase:

- Confirm compliance with the cyber security management plans;
- Check the recovery to the normal operation and whether this was inhibited;
- Establish if any precursors that should be further monitored;
- Confirm if all information about the cybersecurity incident obtained and communicated; and
- Establish if the response team need additional resources (Cyber Security Coalition, 2015, p. 30).

A post mortem should be done in order to establish the nature of the cybersecurity incident, if the current IT controls failed, what approach worked and what needs improvement (Guidance Software, 2013, p. 7). The evidence collected should be preserved for the stipulated time in the organization's cybersecurity incident management strategy (National Institute of Standards and Technology, 2012, p. 41). In this phase, it is important to share cybersecurity incident information with other authorized third parties. Because they could be experiencing the same incident or threat. This will assist them in preparing to respond to the suspicious incident or threat. This sharing of information is also benefiting to the targeted organisation in that, a future threat or attack might require a specific forensic software or tool and the third party has that capability (National Cryptologic Centre, 2017, p. 24). Based on mutual trust assistance can be obtained to deal with cybersecurity incidents.

CYBER RESILIENCY IN THE FOURTH INDUSTRIAL REVOLUTION

The Impact to Government

The Fourth Industrial Revolution drives technology into a fast pace therefore connecting different organizations, digital connectivity, more knowledge and information from various sources and ecosystems. All these changes and adaptation transform the organisation operations with innovation and efficiency. Even though these changes are positive and driving change, huge pressure is placed on the organization's information technology cybersecurity ecosystem in that cyber-risks have not been enhanced or considered with the new operations, technology and information. Information technology cyber-risk needs to accompany with these new developments. So that a significant benefit and opportunities can be realized for the Fourth Industrial Revolution. If an organisation does not reassess their cyber-risks, the security and reliability of technology will decrease impacting on the organization's operations (Scarlett, 2016, p. 2).

Also, information will be reduced and thereby exposing the organisation to cyber-attacks and threats. Reducing cyber-risks is important to transform the organisation. If cyber-risks and cyber-resiliency are not considered, the government and organizations will not be agile to the technology changes and disruptions of the networks and systems will occur. The gap between the cyber-risk and technology will increase (Sutcliffe, 2017, pp. 1-3). It is crucial that government understand these cyber-risks and cyber-resiliency and offer more protection to networks and systems.

With the introduction of new technologies, the government aims to decrease costs and improve performance in its operation. This rise of digitization and technologies place added pressure on the government to protect its networks and systems from attacks and minimizing vulnerabilities. Minimizing these attacks and vulnerabilities is high so that critical infrastructure is secure. A resilient plan is needed that would provide oversight of the cybersecurity incidents and ensure the protection of cyber-risks from the new technologies which increase automation of systems (Sutton, 2016, p. 1).

New threats and unknown attacks will rise as a result of the technology and connectivity. It is imperative that government strengthens their resilience to support its operations (Global Forum on Cyber Expertise, 2016, p. 1). Cyber-resiliency will be effected if the government does not face the technological transformation it is currently going through. Cyber-resiliency needs to be an approach that the government needs to ensure efficiency, sustainability and better IT governance and overcome the challenges of the Fourth Industrial Revolution (Sutcliffee, 2017, pp. 4-5).

The government networks and systems are impossible to protect and secure. A defensive approach to the introduction of encryption, firewalls and password authentication alone cannot eliminate the threats, attacks and breaches (Wright & Schaetzel, 2015, pp. 2-3). The challenge is to adopt a fresh approach to cyber resilience to limit the sophisticated and innovated cyber criminals. Cyber-attacks and vulnerabilities are evolving, and threat actors are continuously trying to outmaneuver organizations' measures. Many of the attacks and threats are difficult to mitigate (Haraoka, 2017, p. 45). The organisation also needs better visibility over its systems, networks and new technologies (Symantec, 2014b, p. 7). The emphasis is on a systematic approach such a CSIRT as a mechanism to detect, respond accordingly and recover to limit cyber risk in the organization's operations.

Cyber-attacks from different actors will continue to increase; increasingly the confidentiality, integrity and availability of data will also be targeted. Also cyberterrorism is on the increase. This is when certain individuals or groups or countries are using the internet and technology to launch attacks to other countries information, systems and networks with the intention of causing severe disruptions to their information, systems and networks (Langley, 2017, p. 2). These attacks will continuously be problematic to government. As a country or organisation cannot be complacent to cyber-attacks, cyber-threats and cyber-defenses need to enhance cyber resilience, a CSIRT can embed a better security position and cyber-culture for government by being proactive and respond quickly to cyber-attacks and cyber-threats (Kganyago, 2016, pp. 2-3). The government thereby also need to ensure their critical infrastructure is protected (European Cybersecurity Forum, 2016, p. 5). An organisation continually needs improvement to build the resilience to adapt and take action against cyber risks (World Economic Forum, 2017, p. 28). As such, the CSIRT will foster a partnership within the organisation and outside to provide valuable insights of cyber risks affecting the current landscape.

According to the Deputy Minister of the Department of Telecommunications & Postal Services, South Africa needs to strengthen cyber resilience to withstand threats, attacks and create cyber awareness (Ndabeni-Abrahams, 2017, p. 1). A CSIRT presence can assist my making an organisation a less likely target by threat actors because they are aware that a CSIRT will be a resilient force in defending the systems and networks (Symantec, 2014b, p. 8). A CSIRT will be able to provide analysis of the attacks, breaches and vulnerabilities experienced by the provincial government department encourage new research into new cyber security design (Piggin, 2016, p. 1). The speed of the CSIRT in responding to cyber incidents, the real time data and threat intelligence provided by the CSIRT will drive and improve government's resilience to threats and attacks (Wright & Schaetzel, 2015, p. 7).

Without cyber resilience in the organisation, it will be problematic for the organisation to safeguard the networks and systems and thereby take advantage of the Fourth Industrial Revolution. The organisation needs to the tools and mechanisms to increase their capabilities against cyber risk and create a secure cyber environment within the organisation (Dobrygowski, 2017, p. 1).

Government departments are continuously trying to provide online services to its citizens to ensure better access to government services. This online service also reduces operational cost to ensure efficient and quick service. Citizens need confidence whilst interacting digitally online that their information with government is protected and secured. At the same time, government needs to ensure that the new technologies introduced are not vulnerable to hostile threats and attacks. By so doing also protecting its reputation as a safe government department. Government departments will always be vulnerable to threats and attacks from other government departments, individuals, or specific interest groups with the intention of stealing intellectual property and gaining competitive advantage (The Scottish Government, 2015, pp. 1-2).

The Fourth Industrial Revolution brings a host of asymmetry of cyber-risks for government departments, which underpins the importance of cyber resilience to ensure strong harmonization between national, provincial and local government level. Thus, the political action can be given to a CSIRT and the management of cyber security incidents. The Fourth Industrial Revolution is also influencing government to move from a current centralized model of technologies to a decentralized role-model because the new technology is making this shift possible (Schwab, 2016, p. 1). Based on an approach it is crucial that provincial government embrace this approach to create better efficiency and create competitiveness, which would lead to better government services to the public. Cyber-resilience by the provincial government can catapult their approach to map and manage the cybersecurity incidents to protect networks and systems from future threats and attacks (Cole, 2017, p. 2). Provincial departments need their own centrally located Provincial CSIRT to protect its national assets and build defensive resiliency to outpace potential threats and attacks. This CSIRT capability ensures continuation of government digital systems thereby allowing essential services.

It is important that government have a well-structured approach to protecting its networks and systems and privileged information. Being prepared can deliver superior results being ready for any threat or attack. A CSIRT can be a seen as an advantage to support government is the Fourth Industrial Revolution strategy (Matsubara, 2016, p. 1). A CSIRT can be the responsibility of ensuring that the government network and system are safe from vulnerabilities and cyber-attacks and ensure government critical infrastructure and information is safe. An internal CSIRT can respond swiftly to incidents as opposed to external contracted teams (Krehel & Bloom, 2016, p. 1). A CSIRT is an important initiative that enhances resiliency and which can inevitably enhance confidence in the approach to managing cybersecurity incidents and attacks (European Cybersecurity Forum, 2016, p. 2). The CSIRT would enhance the technical capabilities of government and encourage robust information sharing and coordination amongst stakeholders. A CSIRT will be able to analyze the logs of networks and systems. Identify whether the cybersecurity incident is true positive or false positive. This will assist in responding and managing future cyber threats and attacks (Zaidi, 2016, p. 1).

Provincial Government Status About Cybersecurity Incident Management

Provincial departments only report cybersecurity incidents, threats and breaches to the Provincial Treasury (Provincial department level) when they require intervention and assistance in responding and investigating the cybersecurity incident (Patrick, 2016, pp. 6-7). If the Provincial Treasury cannot assist, it escalates the problem to the National Treasury (National Department). Presently, each department or institution can communicate directly with the South African Police Services when reporting a cybersecurity incident, threat and breach. It is not compulsory for the reporting of the cybersecurity to the National Treasury or other National Department. National Treasury or other National Departments do not need cybersecurity incidents, attacks and breaches to be reported to them.

A study of security information flow was undertaken in the public sector to assess the current cybersecurity incident management position, initiatives, challenges (Patrick, 2016, pp. 166-167). The study indicated that employees in the provincial government prefer having a Provincial CSIRT at a Provincial level, which is decentralized and locally situated. The study further highlighted that there is very limited management of cyber security incidents. The study also showed that a majority of employees were not sure whether their department has a cybersecurity incident reporting mechanism. In addition, 10.5% of employees stated that there was no cyber security incident reporting mechanism. In response to an incident response plan, 40.7% of the government employees were not certain if their department had a cybersecurity incident plan (Patrick, 2016, pp. 182-184). Also 34.5% of government employees indicated they were unsure of the provincial CSIRT and 18.2% confirmed that there was no CSIRT (Patrick, 2016, pp. 182-184).

While the provincial government departments have IT teams, they do not have security incident response teams. Without a CSIRT, the department would do well in managing cybersecurity incidents, attacks and threats thereby causing minimal disruptions to their services and operations. A CSIRT would provide support and assist the departments in managing cybersecurity incidents and threats, and offer valuable training to encourage awareness. It would also enable sharing of cybersecurity information within the departments and between other Provincial Departments.

One of the important functions of a CSIRT is to render cybersecurity awareness training to the employees so that they are better prepared to identify potential cybersecurity incidents; therefore, if a CSIRT does not exist there will be limited cybersecurity awareness and training. This finding also implies that there is no management support for a cybersecurity incident reporting mechanism and for the establishment of a CSIRT to investigate cybersecurity incidents, attacks and threats. There is a strong provision in the literature for a CSIRT. The development of a CSIRT can increase the quickness with which the organisation is able to respond to malicious cybersecurity and threats (Stewart, 2014, p. 2). It is critical to respond to cybersecurity incidents in the speediest time possible in order to avoid disruption of the delivery of public services.

SOLUTIONS AND RECOMMENDATIONS

Cybersecurity Incident Management

The need for cybersecurity incident management is supported by the Department of Public Service and Administration guidelines that the department must limit the security incidents or other weaknesses that limit the government operations (Department of Public Service and Administration, 2017, p. 15). The head of the department must also demonstrate support and commitment to the cybersecurity incident management to ensure monitoring and assessment of the efficiency of the cybersecurity incident management (Department of Public Service and Administration, 2017, pp. 6-7). King IV also emphasizes that the organisation needs to make provision for business resilience and proactively monitor threat intelligence to respond to the cybersecurity incidents, threats and attacks (Institute of Directors South Africa, 2016, p. 62)

Cybersecurity incident management execution and procedures need to be simultaneously introduced within with the organizational change. The changes that need to be introduced are (1) Modification of reporting structures, (2) Re-engineering of business processes; and (3) IT controls enhancement (Kolkowska & Dhillon, 2013, p. 1). Zhou et al. (2010, p. 1), emphasizes that organizations need to co-operate with each order to support sharing of cybersecurity threat information and thereby support each other in the execution of complex tasks.

Organisation support for cybersecurity incident management is crucial because this initiative can swiftly investigate potential cybersecurity incidents and thereby lowering security costs. Cybersecurity incident management elements namely: (1) Reporting mechanism for internal and external person relating to potential and suspicious cybersecurity incidents and attacks and; (2) the creation of a CSIRT. A formal process must be approved that summarizes when to respond, analyze and recover from cybersecurity incidents, attacks and threats. Minimal disruptions of the organization's operation is critical and a response and a CSIRT can assist the organisation to lower the impact of cybersecurity incident. A CSIRT would promote cybersecurity incident training and awareness, which would tremendously assist the departments in managing cybersecurity incidents. It would also enable cybersecurity information and adversaries to be shared in the department's section and between other Provincial departments.

The literature provides a strong support for the development of a provincial CSIRT. It is suggested that CSIRT be a shared role amongst the Provincial Departments. The Office of the Premier will be the centralized organizational structure department in the province that would be responsible for coordinating with the entire departments. The development of a provincial CSIRT will have minimal implications on each department because the departments would be sharing in the establishment costs, cybersecurity incident program costs and human resources expenditure. Subsequently, the department's CSIRT will respond by investigating the cybersecurity incidents. Lastly, the CSIRT will manage the established cybersecurity incident and quarantine it in order to avert additional compromise of the department's network and system. The proposed high-level structure for the departments will be discussed further on to manage cybersecurity incidents, attack and threats.

Computer Security Incident Response Team Outcomes in the Fourth Industrial Revolution

With the introduction of the Protection of Personal Information Act 4 of 2013 in SA, provincial government also needs to introduce measures to safeguard confidential and privileged information from cyber threats and attacks. A CSIRT would be able on a local level to protect the infrastructure and manage the security incidents. One of the roles of a CSIRT is to promote and provide cybersecurity awareness training, if a CSIRT does not exist then there will be limited training and the employees would not be prepared to recognize potential cybersecurity incidents and threats. There is an agreement in the literature for a CSIRT. The development of a CSIRT can increase the rapidity to which the organisation is able to respond to cybersecurity incidents, attacks and malicious threats (Stewart, 2014, p. 2). It is vital to respond to cybersecurity incidents and investigate the incidents swiftly to stop disruption of the provision of public services.

The key function of a CSIRT would play a reactive role in which it responds to cybersecurity incidents and threats that affect the organization's technology, processes and people. Another key function of the CSIRT would be to manage the cybersecurity incidents so that the organisation can recover to normal operations without minimal disruptions to the organization's networks and systems.

The CSIRT's other responsibilities would include:

- Responding to cybersecurity incidents and threats;
- Prioritizing alerts and responsibilities;
- Cyber forensics into the security incidents and threats;
- Developing communication strategy for the workforce, management and outside organizations; and
- Maintaining a cybersecurity incident and threat log for future interventions and measures (Andre, 2017, p. 3).

The CSIRT can publish and disseminate robust cyber-trend and information awareness to its employees and to other collaborated partners being the national, provincial and local government. The trend information will assist government decision makers and academia to understand the threats, attacks and develop better cyber-response capabilities. The provincial government skill level of cybersecurity accountabilities and capabilities of their CSIRT will be better developed from the real-time training. The capacity training will better prepare the CSIRT to be able to protect the critical infrastructure better. The CSIRT can actively join international CSIRT's and participate in dialogue and cybersecurity initiatives, which positively will augment cyber-expertise.

Challenges for the CSIRT in the Fourth Industrial Revolution

The technology is constantly evolving with new technologies being introduced and connecting different devices and organizations and countries. This technological pace and trend are so complex. Coupled with this exponential growth and innovation is the new generation threats and which are equally getting complex and causing severe disruptions to organizations networks and systems. Ensuring the CSIRT has the required skill level is of the utmost importance to ensure they can respond and manage the cybersecurity incidents. If there are not upskilling their self with new technology and threats they will not be relevant in the Fourth Industrial Revolution and will not ensure the organization's network, and systems are adequately protected and secure. This would affect the organization's cyber-resiliency and would not encourage and empower the organisation to accept new business operations and minimize their information technology risks. This unpreparedness would make the organization's information technology networks, and systems vulnerable to breaches. A further challenge could be not having the latest technology and tool to respond to the cybersecurity incident and manage the cybersecurity incident or threat. This lack of skills and technology could affect the response time to a cybersecurity and threat. If the response is not swift, the organization's networks, system and information could be compromised and further disrupting the operations affecting the processes, technology and people.

Proposed CSIRT for Provincial Government

The National Cybersecurity Framework ensures that cybersecurity actions and initiatives need to be centralized. The framework does stipulate that the departments that must strength intelligence of threat and attack information, foster good cooperation amongst government, citizens and organizations (State Security Agency, 2015, p. 18). This framework also encourages other CSIRT sector formation. The provincial CSIRT can make a strong contribution to the cybersecurity knowledge and swift detection and investigation of the threats and attacks.

In terms of the draft Cybercrime and Cybersecurity Bill, Government Departments are now mandatory to have sector CSIRTs. Also, the bill requires that an organisation must have a mechanism for persons to report cyber security incidents and cybercrime (Gill & Bokhari, 2016, p. 7). The proposed high-level organizational structure would ensure compliance with the Bill once it is propagated. A dedicate local CSIRT is better placed locally, to respond to cyber incidents and contain attacks and breaches swiftly. Because they have the insight into the local networks and systems and will have a stronger connection with the workforce and other departments (Krehel & Bloom, 2016, p. 1).

The draft Policy for Cyber-crime makes for exclusive operations of a centralized model, however the provincial government want a local centralized CSIRT to respond to cybersecurity incidents and share threat information. This signals a move to a more decentralized model. The study highlighted that the interview participants felt that the Provincial Department they preferred a provincial CSIRT structure, which would ensure that cybersecurity information is communicated (Patrick, 2016, p. 165). In addition, it was noted that interview participants showed a strong need for the development of a provincial CSIRT to manage cybersecurity incidents, attacks and threats at a local provincial level.

The Provincial government needs to upgrade their network tools and capability. After that, the Provincial government can hold joint sessions and training to observe and manage the different scenarios of cyber risk, incidents and attacks. In addition, the Provincial government need to automate the management of the cyber incident and attacks so that response rate is much improved and potential cyber-risks are mitigated effectively.

Decision makers in Provincial and National government need to engage in cooperation for the establishment and regulation of the Provincial CSIRT's. That Central government and National government together with provincial departments consider amending the draft policy to also cater for decentralized provincial government CSIRT constituency. If this recommendation is not considered, then the provincial departments do have recourse to establish a CSIRT under the other 'nodal point' (section 55) within the Department of Telecommunication and Postal Services (Department of Justice and Constitutional Development, 2017, p. 32).

Establishment

Government departments have severe pressure to deliver good and efficient services to the public within a restricted budget. A big portion of provincial government budget would be allocated to the basic services to address SA social-economic imbalances. Based on this argument it is too prudent to have cost cutting measures in place; by this, the Provincial CSIRT will be formed with sub groups cybersecurity incident response teams which multidisciplinary groups within the other provincial departments. Combining budgets eliminates the burden on one provincial department to be responsible for the financial operations costs.

The CSIRT will fall under the Office of the Premier and assist the other provincial departments by providing an adequate and rapid assessment of cybersecurity incidents. The Provincial Legislature would mandate the Office of the Premier to be the central point of contact in the Province for the coordination. If the need arises for third party service providers to assist managing cybersecurity incidents, the Office of the Premier should be mandated to obtain such services. The Office of the Premier would support the provincial departments, including Health, Education, Agriculture, Environmental Affairs and Rural Development, Human Settlements and Public Works and Economic Development.

Scope

The provincial CSIRT target communities would be the other provincial departments' cybersecurity incident response teams, National CSIRT, Cybersecurity Hub, Sector CSIRT, State Information Technology Agency, and State Security. The authority model will be a shared authority in the Provincial Departments.

The services that the Provincial CSIRT will be responsible for are the Proactive services (Monitoring services, alert and report). Research and development (cyber security audits, forensic analysis), reactive services (cyber security incident management). Other services, (training, awareness, business continuity). The Provincial CSIRT would offer basic services (cybersecurity incident management, monitoring, vulnerability response alerts) after 1-2 year the organisation operations can be reassessed to determine the maturity level and whether the operations can adhere to the intermediate or advanced services offered by the Provincial CSIRT. Accompanying this maturity assessment should be the timeline of the Provincial CSIRT to achieve enhanced maturity.

The other provincial departments would report the detected cybersecurity incidents and threats to them. The need for the provincial CSIRT is that this primary function will assist in response and recovery to the cybersecurity incidents and events. The CSIRT analyze the trends and directs the departmental approach to improve the cyber risk controls (Department of Public Service and Administration, 2017, p. 16). Figure 1 is a proposed CSIRT Structure for Provincial Department, which was designed from the literature review and discussed with interviewees (key decision makers) who communicated strong support for such an organisation structure (Patrick, 2016, pp. 166-167).

Policy and Procedures

It would be important for the provincial departments to draft common policies and procedures for them. The policy drafting should include the following: (1) Cybersecurity incident response, (2) Communication policy, (3) Segregation of duties, (4) Training policy; and (5) Co-operation policy.

Service level agreements between the provincial departments must be completed to outline the expectations and actions.

Organizational Structure

The suggested high-level structure for the Provincial department proposes a shared organizational structure pertaining explicitly to cybersecurity. The Office of the Premier will be the centralized coordinating department. This is in line with its executive authority in the Province. The Director General will represent the Office of the Premier who would have executive oversight. The organizational structure supports a specialized post for the Chief Information Security Officer (CISO) for the province. The State Security Agency and State Information Technology Agency will have a central point of contact with the CISO. The CISO will also have the equivalent status as the Chief Information Officer (CIO) and/ or Chief Government Information Technology Officer (CGITO). The CIO and CISO will provide support to each other's roles in executing cybersecurity responsibilities in the province. The CSM function will have a manager or deputy manager reporting directly to the CISO. A cybersecurity incident investigation analyst and a liaison analyst will report directly to the manager or deputy manager in the cybersecurity incident management portfolio. The provincial departments each have their own CIO. A manager or deputy manager will report directly to the department CIO. A cybersecurity incident investigation analyst and a liaison analyst will report directly to the manager or deputy manager. The incident investigation analyst will investigate security incidents, threats and attacks to the government system and network. The liaison analyst will be responsible for liaising with the other departments in the province and contractors.

This suggested organizational structure encourages interns from a University of other higher learning institutions to be attached to the incident investigation analysts. Undergraduate students in University would receive real-life job experience and afterwards their period of service; the department would have highly skilled people to recruit on a permanent basis. The interns would further be in cybersecurity and prepare them for the next generation of cyber warriors. The CSIRT would be responsible for internal and external communication and deal with other organizations, share the alert information, vulnerability intelligence, cybersecurity information via the government intranet network to create a better response and awareness in the departments.

The structure of a CSIRT needs to be designed and implemented by the national and provincial government, and they need to draft policies for the provincial level so cybersecurity incidents can be predicted before they occur. Also, security experience and technical skills and expertise are a need for persons who will be involved in the government CSIRT this, in turn, will build a better knowledge hub. The government also needs to endorse mandates with Universities, Further Education Training Colleges and other higher education training institutions to train and mentor the next generation security experts to ensure a strong talent pool for the Fourth Industrial Revolution.

A provincial CSIRT can have their interprovincial network. This network can be established as an 'Information hub' for information sharing on threat information and initiatives. The information hub can also act as a repository for knowledge and expertise, which would assist the provincial government with the expertise to build an effective cyber-resilience (Oliver Wyman, 2017, p. 14). The CSIRT as a hub can also improve preparedness to responding to cyber incidents (Hoffman, 2015, p. 2).

Challenges for the Proposed Provincial CSIRT

Each provincial department operates as a separate entity with its autonomy, to obtain buy-in from management for funding and information sharing and create an environment of trust between the provincial departments. Obtaining political support and management support of the various provincial departments and buy-in for the provincial CSIRT to eliminate any problematic perceptions may also be a challenge. Another challenge is management support to commit to research development and sustainability of the provincial CSIRT.

Attracting the right specialized cybersecurity skills and maintaining the personnel is going to be a challenge because of the demand for this specialized skill. It is also important to attract the appropriate personnel that can make decisions under pressure within the political and government landscape. It is important which provincial government department is going to take the responsibility of updating the policies and procedures for the CSIRT so that CSIRT operations will always be operating in formal and legal frameworks.

A major challenge is getting the different provincial departments to streamline their information technology and cyber security operations. Therefore, that will accomplish consistency and allow for clear and smooth operations and interaction with the Provincial CSIRT. It will be important to obtain

Figure 1. Proposed CSIRT Structure for a Provincial Department

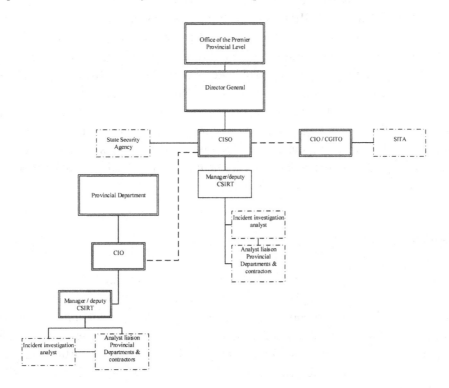

cooperation for the CSIRT information technology tools and information. Also a provincial executive decision needs to be taken to establish which provincial department will be responsible for buying the latest technology and tools and ensuring the data is also safe and updated.

RECOMMENDATIONS

The CSIRT would be functioning within an organization's cybersecurity incident management. The main purpose of the CSIRT is to reduce and control cyber incidents across the organisation (Andre, 2017, p. 3). Government as a matter of urgency create the CSIRT organisation structure at a Provincial level. Develop inter-operability regulations and policies between the department and the organizations to share threat intelligence data so that the Protection of Personal Information Act compliance and privacy rights are still adhered to. Develop the workflow and procedures for a cyber-incident reporting mechanism for government workforce and civilian reporting. All future software and new technology implementation are procured and developed with cybersecurity measures. Develop a cybersecurity education for the workforce for a broader understanding of cyber-risks.

A cybersecurity maturity assessment is crucial so that the cybersecurity roadmap can be developed which can also identify capacity and resources needed that to be phased in the department to an acceptable maturity level. There is a need for CSIRT legal and regulatory framework development in cybersecurity governance to ensure better harmonization so that the provincial department, Office of the Premier and national government will better understand their roles and responsibilities. The existing governance and organizational structures needs to be further researched to establish how best these structures could adapt to CSIRT establishment. Building CSIRT and Law Enforcement skills and capacity building which will ensure those Provincial departments and the Law Enforcement persons have the specialized skills to investigate cybersecurity incidents. Virtual CSIRT training opportunities for the provincial government response teams this would ensure that teams are better prepared to response to cybersecurity incidents and validates technical capability skills. A need exists for CSIRT automation processes to enhance swifter response to cyber-risks and threats. This process will save time in receiving the cybersecurity incidents and ensuring response time to investigate the cybersecurity incident and isolate the threat or attack. This automation process will also reduce the cost of the government's defense expenditure. A CSIRT role in the cyber physical systems so that cyber risks are managed and contained that provincial can resume government operation with minimum future interruptions.

CONCLUSION

Achieving cyber-resiliency is going to be challenging in that the government would need the right skill, technology and tools to manage the cybersecurity incidents and threats. SA is regarded as a developing economy, a country that has socio-economic challenges like a high rate of unemployment, basic services like water and sanitation for its citizens. If it does not get a balance between these socio-economic issues and new technology and innovation, SA will not enjoy the benefits of the Fourth Industrial Revolution because, as a country, its immediate priority is social services, SA needs to consider new initiatives like a CSIRT should not be overlooked in that it can assist the government departments to respond and protect its networks and systems.

The primary challenge to the proposed CSIRT for the provincial government is going to be the lack of the specialized cybersecurity skills for responding to cybersecurity incidents, attacks and threats and management of these incidents. Getting the right cybersecurity professionals and retaining their skills will be crucial. In addition, contribution to a central budget for the provincial CSIRT would also be a challenge, in that some departments have bigger budgets and other provincial departments and might not be able to contribute an agreed monthly amount for the maintenance of the CSIRT personnel function and hardware and software maintenance. The challenge would ensure that provincial departments commit to coordinating and sharing cyber-attack information amongst themselves through the CSIRT.

The key function of the CSIRT in the cyber-resiliency to ensure that CSIRT response to cybersecurity incidents, threats, manages these cybersecurity incidents so that the organisation recover swiftly from the incidents and threats back to normal operations. If government departments co-operate and commit to information sharing, they will not ensure that new threats and attacks are quickly responded to and managed. This can immensely affect the function of the CSIRT in a Fourth Industrial Revolution.

A CSIRT can build trust and confidence in provincial government, national and at an international level. It would also provide a transparent snapshot of the cyber processes, threats and attacks. A CSIRT can be the heart of the cybersecurity incident management, which will be a potent mechanism that can manage and mitigate cyber-threats and attacks in the Fourth Industrial Revolution. A CSIRT can also ensure that provincial government can take responsible actions to ensure sustainability during the Fourth Industrial Revolution.

REFERENCES

African News Agency. (2015). New cybersecurity hub to protect SA. *Independent Media*. Retrieved from http://www.iol.co.za/news/politics/new-cybersecurity-hub-to-protect-sa-1.1938479

Ajam, K. (2015). Cybersecurity Hub launched at CSIR. *Independent Media*. Retrieved from http://www.iol.co.za/saturday-star/cybersecurity-hub-launched-at-csir-1938670

Andre, J. (2017). *What is the Difference between a SOC and a CSIRT?* Retrieved from https://blog.komand.com/difference-between-a-soc-and-a-csirt

AppliedTrust. (2008). *Every company needs to have a security program*. Retrieved from https://www.appliedtrust.com/resources/security/every-company-needs-to-have-a-security-program

Ashford, W. (2012). *UK to expand cyber info-sharing hub after initial success*. Retrieved from ComputerWeekly.com website: http://www.computerweekly.com/news/2240149725/UK-to-expand-cyber-info-sharing-hub-after-initial-success-says-minister

Bernstein, D., Ebrahim, W., & Cibane, S. (2015). *SA's cybersecurity bill raises big concerns*. Retrieved from http://www.techcentral.co.za/sas-cybersecurity-bill-raises-big-concerns/60695/

Business Continuity Institute. (2017). *BCI Cyber Resilience Report*. Berkshire, UK: Author.

BusinessDictionary. (2017). *Definition of system*. Retrieved from http://www.businessdictionary.com/definition/information-system.html

Centre for the Protection of National Infrastructure, & National Technical Authority for Information Assurance. (2015). *Security Incident Management*. Retrieved from https://www.ncsc.gov.uk/content/files/guidance_files/Security%20Incident%20Management%20%28Good%20Practice%20Guide%20 24%29_1.2_0.pdf

Cole, J. (2017). *Why Cyber Resilience is the UK's first line of Defence*. Retrieved from https://www.publictechnology.net/articles/opinion/why-cyber-resilience-uks-first-line-defence

Computer Sciences Corporation. (2014). *Is Your Organisation Prepared to Respond to a Cyber-Attack*. Retrieved from http://www.csc.com/cybersecurity/offerings/107161/103293-cybersecurity_incident_response

Cwele, S. (2014). *Minister Cwele Budget Vote Speech 2014*. Retrieved from http://www.dtps.gov.za/mediaroom/minister-s-speeches-mr-yunus-carrim/348-minister-cwele-budget-vote-speech-2014.html

CweleS. (2015). *Launch of Cybersecurity Hub*. Retrieved from http://www.gov.za/speeches/minister-siyabonga-cwele-launch-cybersecurity-hub-30-oct-2015-0000

Cyber Security Coalition. (2015). *Cyber Security Incident Management Guide*. Retrieved from Belgium: https://www.cybersecuritycoalition.be/content/uploads/cybersecurity-incident-management-guide-EN.pdf

CyberEdge Group. (2014). *Cyberthreat Defense Report*. Retrieved from USA: http://www.brightcloud.com/pdf/CyberEdge-2014-CDR.pdf

Department of Homeland Security. (2014). *Law Enforcement Cyber Incident Reporting*. Author.

Department of Homeland Security. (2017). *What is Security and Resilience?* Retrieved from https://www.dhs.gov/what-security-and-resilience

Department of Justice and Constitutional Development. (2015). *Justice publishes draft Cybercrimes and Cybersecurity Bill for public* [Press release]. Retrieved from http://www.gov.za/speeches/justice-publishes-cybercrimes-and-cybersecurity-bill-public-comments-28-aug-2015-0000

Department of Justice and Constitutional Development. (2017). *Cybercrimes and Cybersecurity Bill*. Pretoria: Author.

Department of Public Service and Administration. (2003). *The Machinery of Government*. Pretoria: Department of Public Service and Administration, Retrieved from http://www.dpsa.gov.za/dpsa2g/documents/lkm/mog.pdf

Department of Public Service and Administration. (2017). *Information and Communication Technology Security Guideline*. Pretoria: Author.

Department of Telecommunications & Postal Services. (2016a). *Incident Management Process*. Retrieved from https://www.cybersecurityhub.gov.za/incident-management-process

Department of Telecommunications & Postal Services. (2016b). *The National Cybersecurity Hub*. Retrieved from https://www.cybersecurityhub.gov.za/

Dobrygowski, D. (2017). *Why being a responsible leader means cyber resilient*. Retrieved from https://www.weforum.org/agenda/2017/01/why-being-a-responsible-leader-means-being-cyber-resilient/

Doyle, K. (2017). *SA lacks cyber security skills*. Retrieved from http://www.itweb.co.za/index.php?option=com_content&view=article&id=160813

ECS-CSIRT. (2012). *CSIRT Newsletter*. Pretoria: State Security Agency.

European Cybersecurity Forum. (2016). *CYBERSEC 2016 Recommendations*. Retrieved from Krakow: https://azor.app.box.com/v/CYBERSEC2016Recommendations

Experts, I. D. (2014). *The CISO's Secret Weapon for Reducing Enterprise Risk*. Retrieved from http://forms.madisonlogic.com/FormConfirmation.aspx?pub=18&pgr=259&src=2318&cmp=13434&ast=41617&frm=446&pd=3147146-19-7-57-336-0

Fripp, C. (2015). *Why the draft cybercrimes bill should concern South Africans*. Retrieved from http://www.htxt.co.za/2015/09/14/why-the-draft-cybercrimes-bill-should-concern-south-africans/

Gagnon, B., & Mickahail, A. (2014). *Building top-notch information security teams*. Retrieved from http://fcw.com/articles/2014/10/31/building-top-notch-information-security-teams.aspx

Gill, S., & Bokhari, B. (2016). *Technology and Sourcing Alert*. Retrieved from Johannesburg https://www.cliffedekkerhofmeyr.com/export/sites/cdh/en/news/publications/2016/Technology/downloads/Technology-and-Sourcing-Alert-11-May-2016.pdf

Global Forum on Cyber Expertise. (2016). *Outcomes High-Level Meeting Cyber Security*. Retrieved from file:///C:/Users/patrick/Downloads/OutcomeReport+FINAL%20(1).pdf

Goche, M., & Gouveia, W. (2014). *Why Cyber Security Is Not Enough: You Need Cyber Resilience*. Retrieved from US: https://www.forbes.com/sites/sungardas/2014/01/15/why-cybersecurity-is-not-enough-you-need-cyber-resilience/#5c4f237c1bc4

Govloop. (2014). *Your Cybersecurity Crash Course*. Retrieved from http://img.en25.com/Web/GovDeliveryInc/%7B85bade5e-e97f-49d4-8c74-3aacea547259%7D_Your-Cybersecurity-Crash-Course2.pdf?elq=~~eloqua.type--emailfield.syntax--recipientid~~&elqCampaignId=~~eloqua.type--campaign.campaignid--0.fieldname--id~~

Granneman, J. (2014). *Basing incident response management on NIST SP 800-61*. Retrieved from http://searchsecurity.techtarget.com/tip/Basing-incident-response-management-on-NIST-SP-800-61

Greene, F. (2015). Cybersecurity Detective Controls Monitoring to Identify and Respond to Threats. *ISACA, 5,* 51–53.

Guidance Software. (2013). *Incident Response: Six Steps for Managing Cyber Breaches*. Author.

Haraoka, N. (2017, March). Cybersecurity: A Challenge to Business in the Era of the Fourth Industrial Revolution. *Japan Spotlight,* 1-45.

Hewlett-Packard Enterprise. (2014). *Cyber risk report 2013*. Hewlett-Packard Enterprise.

Hewlett Packard Enterprise, FireEye, & Companies, M. M. (2016). Cyber resiliency in the Fourth Industrial Revolution. Author.

Hoffman, P. A. (2015). *National Critical Infrastructure Security and Resilience Month: Improving the Security and Resilience of the Nation's Grid*. Retrieved from https://energy.gov/articles/national-critical-infrastructure-security-and-resilience-month-improving-security-and

Holtfreter, R. E., & Harrington, A. (2014). Towards a Model for Data Breaches: An Universal Problem for the Public. *International Journal of Public Information Systems, 10*(1).

IBM. (2014). *Building a security incident response plan that works*. Retrieved from USA: http://www-01.ibm.com/common/ssi/cgi-bin/ssialias?infotype=PM&subtype=XB&htmlfid=SEE03005USEN&attachment=SEE03005USEN.PDF#loaded

Institute of Directors South Africa. (2016). *KING IV*. Johannesburg: Author.

ISACA. (2013). *CISM Review Manual 2013*. .

Jones, G. (2014). *South Africa neglects alarming effect of cybercrime*. Retrieved from http://www.bdlive.co.za/business/2014/01/14/south-africa-neglects-alarming-effect-of-cybercrime

Jones, G. R., & George, J. M. (2009). *Contemporary Management* (6th ed.). McGraw-Hill/Irwin.

Kganyago, L. (2016). *Collaboration for building cyber resilience* [Press release]. Retrieved from http://www.bis.org/review/r160825b.pdf

Kolkowska, E., & Dhillon, G. (2013). Organisational power and information security rule compliance. *Computers & Security*, *33*(0), 3–11. doi:10.1016/j.cose.2012.07.001

Krehel, O., & Bloom, E. (2016). *Data breach readiness*. Retrieved from http://www.securitysa.com/8655a

Langley, S. (2017). *What is your Understanding of Cyberterrorism?* Retrieved from https://tcsfs.org/2017/01/12what-is-your-understanding-of-cyber-terrorism/

Lee, M. (2014). *IT security is not an optional extra*. Retrieved from ZDNet website: http://www.zdnet.com/it-security-is-not-an-optional-extra-7000025991/

Matsubara, M. (2016). *Cybersecurity is Not a Cost - Leverage the Fourth Revolution for Economic Growth*. Retrieved from https://researchcenter.paloaonetworks.com/2016/06/cso-cybersecurity-is-not-a-cost-leverage-the-fourth-industrial-revolution-for-economic-growth/

Merriam-Webster. (2017). *Definition of resilience*. Retrieved from https://www.merriam-webster.com/dictionary/resilience

Michalsons. (2017). *Cybersecurity Bill - Overview of the Cyber Bill*. Retrieved from https://www.michalsons.com/blog/cybercrimes-and-cybersecurity-bill-the-cac-bill/16344

Miller, M. (2015). *New York State Cyber Incident Reporting Procedures*. New York: New York State.

MS-ISAC. (2013). *Cyber Security Getting Started: A Non Technical Guide*. Retrieved from http://msisac.cisecurity.org/resources/guides

National Cryptologic Centre. (2017). *National Security Framework Cyber-Incident Management*. Retrieved from Spain: https://www.ccn-cert.cni.es/pdf/2025-ccn-stic-817-national-security-framework-cyber-incident-management/file.html

National Institute of Standards and Technology. (2012). *Computer Security Incident Handling Guide*. Author.

Ndabeni-Abrahams, S. (2017). *4th Industrial Revolution and the continued pursuit of inclusive economic growth through ICTs: Investing in the Youth*. Cape Town: Department of Telecommunications & Postal Services. Retrieved from https://www.dtps.gov.za/index.php?option=com_content&view=article&id=710:address-by-ms-stella-ndabeni-abrahams,-the-deputy-minister-of-telecommunications-postal-services-parliament,-cape-town&catid=10:deputy-minister-s-speeches&Itemid=137

Ngubeni, T. (2014). *Govt working on 'cyber security hub'*. Retrieved from http://www.itweb.co.za/index.php?option=com_content&view=article&id=136238:Govt-working-on-cybersecurity-hub-&catid=234

Observe, I. T. (2014). *Your Critical Missing Security Vantage Point*. Author.

Oliver Wyman. (2017). *Cyber risk in Asia-Pacific*. Retrieved from http://www.oliverwyman.com/content/dam/oliver-wyman/v2/publications/2017/may/Cyber_Risk_In_Asia-Pacific_The_Case_For_Greater_Transparency.pdf

Oltsik, J. (2013). *The Big Data Security Analytics Era Is Here*. Retrieved from http://southafrica.emc.com/collateral/analyst-reports/security-analytics-esg-ar.pdf?isPublic=false

Oxford Dictionaries. (2017). *Definition of cyberattack*. Retrieved from https://en.oxforddictionaries.com/definition/cyberattack

Patrick, H. (2016). *Security Information Flow in the Public Sector: KZN Health & Education* (Unpublished doctoral dissertation). University of KwaZulu-Natal.

Piggin, R. (2016). *Is Europe ready to defend critical infrastructure?* Retrieved from http://www.atkins-global.com/en-gb/angles/all-angles/is-europe-ready-to-defend-critical-infrastructure

Ponemon Institute. (2016). *The Cyber Resilient Organisation in the United Kingdom: Learning to Thrive against Threats*. Author.

Prelert. (2015). *Anomaly Detective for IT Security*. Author.

Rainys, R. (2006). Network and Information Security. Assessments and Incidents Handling. *Electronics and Electrical Engineering*, *6*(70), 69–74.

Ross, S. (2013). Barbarians at the Ramparts. *ISACA*, *3*, 4–5.

Ross, S. (2015). Frameworkers of the World, Unite 2. *ISACA*, *3*, 4–6.

RSA. (2012). *Getting ahead of advanced threats: Achieving Intelligence-Driven Information Security*. Retrieved from http://www.emc.com/collateral/industry-overview/ciso-rpt-2.pdf

Scarlett, L. (2016). *Energy Evolves as Fourth Industrial Revolution Looks to Nature*. Retrieved from https://www.livescience.com/53555-energy-and-technology-will-drive-fourth-industrial-revolution.html

Schwab, K. (2016). *The Fourth Industrial Revolution: what it means, how to respond*. Retrieved from https://www.weforum.org/agenda/2016/01/the-fourth-industrial-revolution-what-it-means-and-how-to-respond/

Security Agency. (2016). *Computer Security Incident Response Team (CSIRT)*. Retrieved from http://www.ssa.gov.za/CSIRT.aspx

Sritapan, V., Stewart, W., Zhu, J., & Rohm, C. Jr. (2014). Developing a Metrics Framework for the Federal Government in Computer Security Incident Response. *Communications of the IIMA*, *11*(3), 5.

State Security Agency. (2015). *The National Cybersecurity Policy Framework (NCPF)*. Pretoria: Author.

Stewart, J. (2014). *Rethinking cyber security in an interconnected world*. Retrieved from http://www.scmagazine.com/rethinking-cybersecurity-in-an-interconnected-world/article/358555/

Sutcliffe, H. (2017). *The 4th Industrial Revolution or the 1st Empowerment Revolution?* Retrieved from http://societyinside.com/4th-industrial-revolution-or-1st-empowerment-revolution

Sutcliffee, H. R. (2017). *The 4th Industrial Revolution or the 1st Empowerment Revolution*. Retrieved from http://societyinside.com/4th-industrial-revolution-or-1st-empowerment-revolution

Sutton, D. (2016). *Cybersecurity at the heart of the Fourth Industrial Revolution*. Retrieved from http://www. smartbuildingsmagazine.com/features/cybersecurity-at-the-heart-of-the-fourth-industrial-revolution

Symantec. (2014a). *The Cyber Resilience Blueprint: A New Perspective on Security*. Author.

Symantec. (2014b). *A Manifesto for Cyber Resilience*. Author.

Tamarkin, E. (2014). *South Africa must pay attention to cybercrime*. Retrieved from http://www.issafrica. org/crimehub/news/south-africa-must-pay-more-attention-to-cybercrime

TechTarget. (2015). *NIST definition*. Retrieved from http://searchsoftwarequality.techtarget.com/definition/NIST

The Scottish Government. (2015). *Safe, Secure and Properous: A Cyber Resilience Strategy for Scotland*. Author.

Thompson, K. (2015). *The Best Guides for Information Security Management*. Retrieved from http:// www.crypt.gen.nz/papers/infosec_guides.html

US-CERT. (2015). *US-CERT Federal Incident Notification Guidelines*. Author.

Von Solms, B. (2015). What South Africa is doing to make a dent in cybercrime. *The Conversation*. Retrieved 8 December 2015, from The Conversation Africa, Inc http://theconversation.com/what-south-africa-is-doing-to-make-a-dent-in-cyber-crime-49470?utm_medium=email&utm_campaign=Latest+from+The+Conversation+for+November+4+2015+-+3749&utm_content=Latest+from+The+Conversation+for+November+4+2015+-+3749+CID_575028a66d3378263b9e824989e78ed8&utm_source=campaign_monitor_africa&utm_term=What%20South%20Africa%20is%20doing%20to%20make%20a%20dent%20in%20cyber%20crime

West-Brown, M. J., Stikvoort, D., Kossakowski, K., Killcrece, G., Ruefle, R., & Zajicek, M. (2003). *Handbook for Computer Security Incident Response Teams (CSIRTs)*. Carnegie Mellon Software Engineering Institute. doi:10.21236/ADA413778

Whitman, M., & Mattord, H. (2011). *Roadmap to Information Security For IT and Infosec Managers*. Course Technology, Cengage Learning.

World Economic Forum. (2017). *Advancing Cyber Resilience*. Geneva: Author.

Wright, G. A., & Schaetzel, T. N. (2015). *Cyber Security: Designing and Maintaining Resilience*. Retrieved from http://www.globalsciencecollaboration.org/public/site/PDFS/cyber/Cyber%20Security%20white%20paper%20final.pdf

Zaidi, K. (2016). *Finding the Right Balance in Cyber Security Operations*. Retrieved from https://www. cybrary.it/0p3n/finding-right-balance-cybersecurity-operations/

Zhou, B., Arabo, A., Drew, O., Llewellyn-Jones, D., Merabti, M., Shi, Q., Yau, A. K. L. (2010). *Data flow security analysis for system of systems in public security incident*. Academic Press.

KEY TERMS AND DEFINITIONS

Containment: The act of limiting a process or thing from expanding.

Detection: The process of determining the true extend of the fact.

Networks: Interconnection of devices and technology that allows the user or the organization to share information.

Chapter 13

Government's Dynamic Approach to Addressing Challenges of Cybersecurity in South Africa

Thokozani Ian Nzimakwe
University of KwaZulu-Natal, South Africa

ABSTRACT

Cybersecurity is the practice of making the networks that constitute cyber space secure against intrusions. The aim is to maintain the confidentiality, the availability and integrity of information, by detecting interferences. Traditionally, cybersecurity has focused on preventing intrusions and monitoring ports. The evolving threat landscape, however, calls for a more dynamic approach. It is increasingly clear that total cybersecurity is impossible, unless government develops a cyber-security strategy. The aim of this chapter is to discuss government's dynamic approach to addressing challenges of cybersecurity. The chapter looks at the co-ordination of cyber-security activities so as to have a coordinated approach to cyber-crime. This chapter also highlights the idea of protecting sensitive data for the public good. It is generally accepted that technology has become indispensable in modern society. Government's cyber-security presents a unique challenge simply because of the volume of threats that agencies working for government face on a daily basis.

INTRODUCTION

Information and Communications Technologies (ICTs) are indispensable in modern society. The interconnectivity of computer networks contributes significantly to economic growth, education, citizens' participation in social media and many other aspects. This new electronic environment is commonly known as cyber space. The dependence of the daily functioning of society on information communication technology solutions has led to a concomitant need for the development of adequate security measures. This is because the danger that cybersecurity threats pose is real. The numerous cyber-attacks launched in

DOI: 10.4018/978-1-5225-4763-1.ch013

recent years against advanced information societies aimed at undermining the functioning of public and private sector information systems have placed the abuse of cyber space high on the list of international and also local security threats. Given the seriousness of cyber threats and of the interests at stake, it is therefore imperative that the comprehensive use of information communication technology solutions be supported by a high level of security measures and be embedded in a broad and sophisticated cyber-security culture. This chapter discusses the concepts of cyberspace and cyber security, the influence of information-related technology, initiatives in relation to preventing cybersecurity, an understanding of the threat of cybercrimes, the closing of the cyber skills gap and understanding the government's approach in addressing cybersecurity challenges. The chapter also discusses cyber-security awareness and an education framework for South Africa that could assist in creating a cyber-secure culture in South Africa as one of the many users of the internet. The chapter further discusses the link between cybersecurity and the Fourth Industrial Revolution. Finally, the chapter proposes solutions and future research directions in terms of cyber threats.

BACKGROUND

Cybersecurity is complex and multi-faceted. There are current means to create cyber security awareness designed to make an impact. The fragmented and uncoordinated nature thereof, has, however, the potential to create its own dynamics for the Fourth Industrial Revolution. The increase in mobile use (mobile phones with web connectivity) is, unfortunately, opening the door for cyber criminals to exploit mobile users with little or no cyber-safety knowledge. Reliance on information systems (IS) has increased and now places government operations at higher security risk. Nowadays, the cyber threat is one of the newest and most challenging threats to security, being able to jeopardise not only the safety of a state entity, but also the functioning of international organisations and economic and financial companies (Dinicu, 2014).

Cyberattacks involving ransomware, in which criminals use malicious software to encrypt a user's data and then extort money to unencrypt it, increased 50% in 2016, according to a report from Verizon (Kahn, 2017). Despite technology and electronic devices and media being used more regularly in easing everyday activities, these technological advances are also used in sophisticated criminal activities. The current information age comes with an aggressive technological growth to which there is no foreseeable end. One of the challenges associated with the technological revolution is that cyberspace is full of complex and dynamic technological innovations that outwit any lagging administrative and legal system.

According to Kortjan and Von Solms (2014), the Internet is becoming increasingly interwoven in the daily lives of many more individuals, organisations and nations. It has, to a large extent, had a positive effect on the way people communicate. It has also introduced new avenues for business, and it has offered nations an opportunity to govern online. However, although cyberspace offers an endless list of services and opportunities, it is also accompanied by many risks, of which many Internet users are not aware. As such, various countries have developed and implemented cyber-security awareness and education measures to counter the perceived ignorance of the Internet users. There is a view that people are currently living in an age where the use of the Internet has become second nature to millions of people (Kortjan and Von Solms, 2014).

INFLUENCE OF INFORMATION-RELATED TECHNOLOGY

Cybersecurity is the practice of making the networks that constitute cyber space secure against intrusions, thus maintaining confidentiality, availability and integrity of information, detecting intrusions and incidents that do occur, and responding to and recovering from them (National Cybersecurity Policy Framework for South Africa, 2015).

Information sharing via the electronic web or through cyber space has revolutionised the world and the way in which people interact with one another. It has brought exciting opportunities in developing economies, improving health care, education, agricultural production, and the provision of services. Electronic computing and communication does, however, bring with it some of the most complex challenges the world has ever faced. They range from protecting the confidentiality and integrity of transmitted information to deterring any compromise which could have devastating consequences for individuals, companies and governments (Mahlobo, 2017).

At the individual level, untold suffering is experienced as a result of cyber bullying, phishing, defamation of character and others. Corporates have not been spared either, with billions being lost through cyber-crime and cyber espionage. More often than not, the net effect of such incidents is largely not being communicated for a variety of reasons which could range from potential reputational damage to loss in share value. In the year 2016 alone, a number of critical government data bases throughout the world, which were holding millions of personal records and sensitive information were subjected to hacking. The argument by Mahlobo (2017) is that such attacks, if successful, can bring untold catastrophe to governments around the world.

Technological advances have changed the manner in which ordinary citizens conduct their daily activities. Many of these activities are carried out over the Internet. These include filling in tax returns, online banking, job searching and general socialising. Increased bandwidth and proliferation of mobile phones with access to the internet in South Africa imply increased access to the internet by the South African population. Such a massive increase in access to the internet increases vulnerability to cybercrime and attacks and threatens the national security (Dlamini and Modise, 2012).

Cyberspace and Cybersecurity

Cyberspace had humble beginnings, according to Kortjan and Von Solms (2014). Over time, it has progressed immensely, providing individuals with endless opportunities. Embedded in these opportunities, however, are risks that compromise the safety and security of the individuals that participate in cyberspace. It would seem, however, that people are largely unaware of these risks and so they put themselves, as well as businesses and governmental assets and infrastructure, at risk. In recognition of this, South Africa wishes to promote a culture of cybersecurity among its citizens. Cybersecurity awareness and education together play a major role in cultivating such a culture. Accordingly, this chapter discusses a cybersecurity awareness and education framework that could assist South Africa in promoting its envisaged cybersecurity culture.

Many users lack awareness and knowledge; consequently, they are ignorant of the need to protect their personal and confidential information. Moreover, users' unsecured online behaviour makes them easy targets for exploitation. The lack of cyber-security awareness amongst adults also negatively impacts on their role of protecting the children in their care.

E-GOVERNMENT SERVICES IN THE 21ST CENTURY

Information technology, the internet and the development of e-government all contribute to innovative ways of providing services, sharing data, communicating, and completing the tasks and work of government. The South African government is aware of the important role that information technology can play in transforming government, and providing information and public services to citizens. Technology has developed quickly over the past decades, having been initially embraced by the private sector to encourage innovation. The public sector can also benefit by making use of information technology to improve innovation and productivity, reduce costs and create new ways of providing public services (Van Jaarsveldt 2010).

E-Government and E-Governance

E-government can be described as the use of digital technology to enable taxpayers, citizens and visitors to access information and services from government. It is a commitment by government to provide services by electronic means that is cost-effective, enhanced and efficient. E-government can be defined as an IT-led configuration that includes knowledge, power, skills and purpose (Holtzhausen in Draai, 2016). E-governance goes beyond the scope of e-government as it is focused on more than just processes and structures that must be in place to provide information and services. Holtzhausen (in Draai, 2016) states that e-governance allows government to interact more broadly with the networking economy and creates a mechanism whereby citizens can use digital technologies within existing structures to build more efficient policy solutions and legitimacy.

The benefit of e-government for service delivery is that the digital divide is narrowed. If government information and services are delivered digitally, greater digital access needs to be created for citizens. These services include the use of mobile phones to access services and public service forms being available online. There are already a number of e-government services available to citizens in South Africa. Examples include e-procurement which allows the procurement processes to be conducted online, and the online tax-filing services offered by the South African Revenue Services. While there are benefits in offering government services online, this benefit has its own dangers and challenges in terms of cyber-attacks.

Grobler, Van Vuuren and Zaaiman (2013) contend that the current increase in broadband access throughout the African continent may potentially increase cyber-related vulnerability drastically. As a result, a compromise of the integrity, confidentiality, authenticity or availability of the technological systems can have dramatic consequences, regardless of whether it is a temporary interruption of connectivity, or a longer-term disruption caused by a cyber-attack.

CYBER-ATTACKS ON ELECTRONIC BUSINESS SERVICES

Cyber-attacks involving ransomware in which criminals use malicious software to encrypt a user's data and then extort money to unencrypt it, have increased. According to Kahn (2017), criminals have increasingly shifted from going after individual consumers to attacking vulnerable organisations and businesses. Government organisations have been the most frequent target of ransomware attacks, followed by health-care businesses and financial services. While elements of cybercrime have been delivered through infected websites, increasingly, criminals have been turning to phishing, using fraudulent e-mails designed to get a user to download attachments or click on links to websites that are infected, in order to carry out attacks.

Yahoo indicated in December 2013 that thieves stole information from 500 million customer accounts, from e-mail addresses to scrambled account passwords. Kahn (2017) states that such a data cache may allow criminals to go after more sensitive personal information elsewhere online. In the past most ransomware simply encrypted the data on the device where it was first opened, however, criminals are now increasingly using more sophisticated hacking techniques, seeking out business-critical systems and encrypting entire data servers. There is increased sophisticated surveillance and targeting of organisations to maximise profit.

Economic and financial companies and individuals could also be the targets of cyber-attacks if one takes into consideration the growing digitisation of payments and services and greater use of the internet for communication purposes. According to Dinicu (2014), cyber security embraces both the public and the private sector and spans a broad range of issues related to national security, whether through terrorism, crime or industrial espionage.

INITIATIVES IN RELATION TO CYBERSECURITY

Rowe, Reeves, Wood and Braun (2010) paint a frightening picture about the level of cyber security threats on the African continent as a whole. They argue that "about 80 percent of PCs on the African continent are already infected with viruses and other malicious software". They voice their concern in this way: "The worrying news for cyber security experts is that broadband services are opening on the continent, which means more users will be able to access the web, translating into more viruses and spam from online". The worst part of it all perhaps is that many of these users, sadly, have no idea of how to protect themselves and their personal information against the cyber-attacks directed at their gadgets (Rowe, Reeves, Wood and Braun, 2010).

Initiatives in relation to cybersecurity have been influenced by cyber trends and effects. These trends and their impact are discussed in the following subsections.

Data-Driven World

Both businesses and individuals are largely dependent on data. This dependence relates not only to the physical data, but also to the means of getting access to the data at any time, i.e. interconnectedness via smart devices. According to Grobler and Dlamini (2012), user-generated content such as digital pictures, tweets and emails are fast tracking the data-driven world. Everywhere the quantity of data and the visual representation of information are multiplying at an alarming rate. With the strong digital component that forms part of modern-day businesses, the multiplicity of cyber security is becoming more prominent.

The threat coming from cyber space is implemented through various methods such as socially engineered Trojans and network-travelling worms, phishing attacks, compromising confidential information by physical theft or loss, rogueware, spam, targeted attacks, identity theft, information leakage, search engine manipulation, or fake digital certificates. This type of threat/attack is becoming more and more "sophisticated" because it requires a special skill set. The actual costs concerning the undertaking of a cyber-attack are not large attacks; only require highly-trained performers, able to identify security breaches of the network or system based on sophisticated technology. These methods, alone and through their continuous improvement, are those which determine not only the mark of sophistication of this type of attack, but also its novelty (Dinicu, 2014).

Bandwidth and Internet Penetration

The rate of bandwidth consumption or utilisation in South Africa increases daily. Since South Africa is ranked quite high on the African continent, internet penetration as an upward trend has a prominent impact on South Africa's global positioning. With regard to bandwidth and internet penetration, South Africa has a major role to play in terms of ensuring the safety of online users to the entire continent (Grobler and Dlamini, 2012).

Social Aspects

The concern regarding social interaction in the cyber domain is that people often forget that they are in the public global domain. Grobler and Dlamini (2012) contend that, especially with day-to-day human computer interaction, people tend to forget that it is not just a document being typed on a faceless computer, but rather text that is posted on a public forum, to be read by anyone that has the time and understands the language. According to Microsoft, traditional cybercrimes are evolving towards social networking. Phishers are moving away from targeting financial sites and are now focusing more on social networking sites. All of these cyber trends show that people in general are becoming more comfortable with using technology (Microsoft, 2011).

It is the responsibility of the state to ensure that the users are educated in terms of behaviour on social sites or internet use in general. This will not only assist the user to mind their behaviour while online but will further safeguard the communication infrastructures of the nation.

Some Major Cybersecurity Challenges in Africa

Kritzinger and Von Solms (2012) state that there are four different types of cybersecurity challenges that need to be highlighted in order to address the worrying question of cybercrime in the African continent:

- **Lack of Focused Research Into Cybersecurity:** Focused research in Africa is required to create new cybersecurity solutions for the continent;
- **Lack of a Proper Integrated Framework on Legal and Policy Aspects:** Some African countries have no legal regulations in place to stop or prosecute online crime, thus providing a safe haven for cyber criminals;
- **Lack of Cybersecurity Awareness and Regulation:** There is still a large percent of the population in Africa that lacks basic knowledge of computers. Internet cafes in some regions, though widespread, are unable to afford anti-virus software and botnet operators; and
- **Lack of Technical Security Measure:** Some cyber users in Africa do not have up-to-date technical security measures such as anti-virus packages, and some of the operating systems used are not regularly patched.

Proposed Cybersecurity Solutions for Africa

The following are the proposed solutions to address cyber-security challenges being experienced in Africa (Kritzinger and Von Solms, 2012):

- **Lack of Focused Research in Cyber Security:** An African Cyber Security Centre for cyber prevention is proposed. The Centre must be the central place and contact point in Africa where all aspects related to critical information infrastructure protection (CIIP) and cyber security are co-ordinated and where expertise and skills in these areas can be found. The main focal point of this solution is the collaboration of all stakeholders to establish a Centre that will prevent cybercrime throughout Africa.
- **Lack of a Proper Integrated Framework on Legal and Policy Aspects:** There is a need for different role players that will involve law enforcement, legislators, anti-crime commissions and researchers. The main focus of this approach is identifying different stakeholders involved in an attempt to decrease cybercrime in Africa, and identifying different legislative and policy frameworks to support cyber safety.
- **Lack of Cyber-Security Awareness and Regulation:** The main focus of this approach is to ensure that all cyber users are exposed to information-security awareness tools to assist them to use the most secure route to connect to the web.
- **Lack of Technical Security Measures:** The main focus of this approach is to incorporate the assistance of Internet Service Providers (ISPs) to assist in the responsibilities home-users have in securing themselves and their information.

Cybersecurity has proven to be daunting because the nature of the threat is constantly evolving. Each major technological development, i.e. mobile, social, cloud computing, brings a host of new risks. Typically, in the early stages, innovators focus less on security than on creating a minimum viable product. Cyber criminals, on the other hand, aim to exploit new technologies before developers discover their weaknesses.

UNDERSTANDING THE THREAT OF CYBERCRIMES AND CLOSING THE CYBER SKILLS GAP

South Africa is not immune to cybercrimes and the government has made strides in protecting its information infrastructure. Information technology has improved economies and strengthened service delivery, but also poses a risk in the form of ransomware. This has hit various countries, crippling, among other things, railway and health-care services, and hitting major economies globally (The Mercury, 17 May 2017). The threat of cybercrime has increased significantly, partly because of the increasingly complex nature of organisations and cyber space, and the ease with which software can be used to commit cyber-attacks and information can be obtained. Booysen (2017) argues that to date, businesses have based their controls on the assumption that they will be successful in their attempts to prevent cybercrime but believes that this approach needs to change to one where businesses should assume they will fail.

As already stated, attacks on any of the networks can potentially have disastrous consequences for individuals and for society. This was witnessed in 2017 in the recent ransomware attack in more than 100 countries and which affected thousands of organisations worldwide. South Africa is one of the targets for cybercrime and research shows small companies and ordinary citizens, especially unsuspecting children, are being targeted more and more by cyber criminals, state actors and 'hacktivists'. Ransomware, identity theft, cyber bullying, internet banking fraud, misuse of social networks and many other types of attack are prevalent. According to Booysen (2017), although businesses across the world are recognising the need for cyber-security strategies to combat cybercrime, the most vulnerable are still at risk of attack. Grant Thornton advisory services states that research has shown that businesses in certain developing economies are more adept at taking extra precautions to protect their most valuable data from cyber criminals than those in developed Western economies.

South Africa has legislation currently before Parliament in the form of the Cybercrime and Cyber Security Bill that will bolster efforts to protect the country's infrastructure against hackers. The Bill deals with threats to the territorial integrity and sovereignty of states, damage to the economy, the use of technology to recruit people for terrorist activities, criminals using computer data to commit offences, and the use of social media to violate public order or ignite hatred and discrimination (Nair, 2017).

Cybercrimes in South Africa

The cybercrimes that remain at the top of the list of South Africa's major cyberattacks and threats include phishing attacks, identity theft and monetary fraudulent activity at all levels of national society. Other cybercrimes and security threats that have been experienced in South Africa include adware, botnet, cyber bullying, cyber stalking, data theft, hacking, hoax e-mails, key logging, malware, social engineering, spam spyware and trojan virus (IST-Africa, 2011).

Cybersecurity Awareness

Cybersecurity awareness is the security training that is used to inspire, stimulate, establish and rebuild cyber-security skills and expected security practice from a specific audience. Dlamini and Modise (2012) contend that it is used to promote and encourage Internet users to practise safety precautions, and train them on online defence methods. Furthermore, it equips these users with cyber-security skills on all the aspects of cyber security so that not only national network infrastructure is kept resilient to cyberattacks and threats, but also keeps the users well informed.

Cyber security awareness and education should be included as high-level, cyber security objectives in the national cyber-security policies, according to Kortjan and Von Solms (2014). For example, in the United States, the goal of cyber-security awareness and education is to raise the level of awareness in the nation of the risks of cyber space, and how to circumvent these risks. In the United Kingdom, the goal is to support individuals and businesses by informing and educating them on the issue of cyber security. In Australia and Canada, the ultimate goal is a cyber-security culture that can be fostered through awareness and education. In these countries, it is evident that documented cyber-security awareness and the education goal is assigned to one or more departments or organisations to carry out. This allocation of responsibilities promotes accountability and, furthermore, it establishes a focal point, thus, there should be a dedicated administration that should serve as a focal point for cyber-security awareness and the implementation of educational initiatives.

Australia has taken a significant lead in working across government and the private sector to shore up collective defences. The Australian Cyber Security Centre (ACSC) plays many roles by raising awareness of cyber security, reporting on the nature and extent of cyber threats, encouraging the reporting of incidents, analysing and investigating specific threats, coordinating national security operations and heading up the Australian government's response to hacking incidents. At its core, it is a hub for information exchange: private companies, state and territorial governments, and international partners all share discoveries at the Australian Cyber Security Centre (Eggers 2016). The Australian approach begins with good network hygiene: blocking unknown executable files, automatically installing software updates and security patches on all computers and restricting administrative privileges. The programme then aims to assess adversaries, combining threat data from multiple entities to strengthen collective intelligence. The system uploads results of intrusion attempts to the cloud, giving analysts from multiple agencies a larger pool of attack data to scan for patterns (Eggers 2016).

Based on the national cyber-security awareness and educational initiatives by the above-mentioned countries, a number of deductions can be made. *Firstly*, the focus of the cyber-security awareness and education campaigns and programmes should be prevalent in every grouping of society. *Secondly*, each target audience should be presented with topics that are relevant to them. This suggests that research has to be done to identify the individual awareness and educational needs. *Thirdly*, the medium of communication used to deliver cyber-security awareness and education should be well suited to the particular target audience. *Fourthly*, the environment should be taken into consideration when developing cyber-security awareness and education campaigns and programmes because this may influence the approach and/or tools to be used by the campaign or programme. Finally, within the analysed cyber-security awareness and education initiatives, there are definite role-players. It is clear that cyber-security awareness is a shared responsibility and everyone enjoying the cyberspace has a role to play (Kortjan and Von Solms, 2014).

Peltier (2005), quoted by Dlamini and Modise (2012) believes that in order for the cybersecurity awareness programme to be successful, there are five key factors that need to considered and ensured. These include:

- A clear process to take the message to the users or targeted audience in order to reinforce cyber-security as a significant concept;
- Identification of the individuals who are responsible for the implementation of cybersecurity awareness programme;
- Determination and evaluation of the sensitivity of information and the criticality of cyber security infrastructure, applications and systems;
- The reasons for the implementation of cybersecurity concepts and awareness programmes in convincing the audience of the significance of cyber-security awareness programmes that must be implemented; and
- Ensuring that the related government department or the related management supports the goals and objectives of the cybersecurity awareness programme for the community.

There should be some sort of monitoring and evaluation of the progress made in these cybersecurity awareness and education efforts. Cybersecurity awareness and education is indeed a cross-cutting matter that warrants diligent handling. The government should take the lead in this regard, and, accordingly, establish national and international partnerships that would encourage all users of cyber space to play their part (Kortjan and Von Solms, 2014).

Eggers (2016) argues that a cyber-security strategy means nothing without the skills and talent needed to execute it. Technology companies and banks with world-class cyber security capabilities owe much of their success to top-flight technical staff. While the defence and intelligence sectors generally can attract high-calibre talent, government and other state agencies find it difficult to compete with the private sector. Governments, therefore, must cast a wider net for cybersecurity professionals. Experts agree that cyber security requires different skill sets than other IT work, and in particular, a talent for understanding systems and getting into challengers' heads. It can therefore be argued that any cyber security awareness initiative should have a plan, clearly defined goals and objectives, expected results, delivery methods, risks and methods to evaluate the initiative.

ADDRESSING CYBERCRIME AND CYBERSECURITY CHALLENGES

In terms of addressing cyber security concerns, the public sector challenges run deeper. Government stores far more data than the private sector and often keeps it on older, more vulnerable systems. Agencies are regularly targeted not just by opportunistic hackers but by teams funded and trained by other nations and cyber attackers. Governments may want to try and protect themselves against hostile intruders, but on the other hand, employees and citizens alike want their data conveniently available anytime, anywhere. Government cybersecurity presents a unique problem simply due to the huge volume of threats that agencies face on a daily basis, and the scale of the potential consequences if the threats are not foiled. A blanket approach is not good enough and businesses often end up spending more money by employing sophisticated systems to protect data that is not overly sensitive, while sometimes neglecting the information that is crucial to a business's survival and longevity (Booysen, 2017).

Threats are growing in volume, intensity and sophistication, and they are not going away, ever. Recent failures call into question the effectiveness of the billions already sunk into cyber security. Traditionally, cyber security has focused on preventing intrusions, defending firewalls, monitoring ports, and the like. The evolving threat landscape, however, calls for a more dynamic approach. New thinking in this arena involves three fundamental capabilities built around being secure, vigilant and resilient. These three principles reflect the fact that defence mechanisms must evolve. Government agencies cannot rely on perimeter security alone. They should also build strong capabilities for detection, response, inspection, and recovery (Eggers 2016). Prevention is ideal, but detection is a must, and effective recovery plans are important when there has been a cyber-attack.

In South Africa, cybersecurity awareness initiatives are delivered through a variety of independent, uncoordinated mechanisms. According to Dlamini and Modise (2012), various entities are engaged in cybersecurity awareness training, each with their specific objectives and focus areas. Cyber security is complex and multi-dimensional. An effective approach is that which accommodates and integrates all the dimensions, therefore, the effectiveness of the current initiatives regarding the delivery of cybersecurity awareness initiatives that are relevant needs to be evaluated.

Current approaches to cybersecurity are more focused on saving money or developing elegant technical solutions than on working and protecting lives and property. They largely lack the scientific or engineering rigour needed for a trustworthy system to defend the security of networked computers in three dimensions at the same time: mandatory access control (MAC) policy, protection against subversion, and verifiability; what Schell (2016) calls a defence triad. According to Schell (2016), all three defence triad components are critical for defence of both confidentiality and integrity of information, whether the sensitive information is personally identifiable information, financial transactions (for example, credit cards), industrial control systems in the critical infrastructure, or something else that matters. All three are practically necessary although not sufficient for perfect security. These dimensions can be thought of as three strong "legs of a stool".

Security for cyber systems built without a trustworthy operating system (OS) is simply a scientific impossibility. Proven scientific principles of the "Reference Monitor" model enable engineering a verifiably-secure operating system on which one can build secure cyber systems. For Reference Monitor implementation to work, it must ensure three fundamental properties: Firstly, it must validate enforcement of the security policy for every reference to information. Secondly, it must be tamper-proof, that is, it cannot be subverted. Lastly, it must be verifiable, so that one has high assurance that it always works correctly. These three fundamental properties are directly reflected in the cyber defence triad (Schell, 2016).

Most government hacks are elusive, targeting state and city agencies, stealing social security numbers or tax returns. Eggers (2016) states that whatever the motive, it is clear that governments are the highest-value targets for hackers today; thus, it is critical that agencies invest in strong cyber defences; stronger, if anything, than those found in the private sector. At the state and local levels in particular, however, most agencies simply are devoting too little manpower and funding to the problem. Most of the government chief information security officers say governments are not spending enough on cybersecurity, and are not attracting and retaining the right talent. This continues to be difficult due to low government salaries, a lack of clear career paths and complex hiring processes.

Government agencies need to examine and understand all aspects of their operations in cyberspace. Agencies must therefore review their data to determine levels of sensitivity. Eggers (2016) contends that managers often do not understand how cybersecurity works. Another core security principle is to rethink network security. All too often, leaders think of it as a wall. Governments thus need to deploy their advantages and strengths against their opponents' disadvantages and weaknesses. The important test lies in how government officials anticipate and counter moves by an ever-shifting cast of criminal rivals. Digital governments will need speed, skill, and adaptability to succeed on this new battlefield.

PROTECTING SENSITIVE DATA FOR THE PUBLIC GOOD

The nature of the attacks which happened in 2017 targeting several countries should serve as a lesson to all organisations, including those responsible for national infrastructures such as dams and energy sites. Having knowledge of their systems, and differentiating the information within it, are crucial to providing effective protection against cyber-attacks. Cybersecurity threat stems from the rapidly changing nature of the internet, which was not designed with security in mind, and this involves protecting systems from intrusions (Gray, 2015; Tien, 2012).

Efforts by South Africa in Combatting Cyber Attacks

Judging by recent activities of cyber-attacks, Grobler, Van Vuuren and Zaaiman (2013) affirm that it is clear that both the South African Government, the defence environment and industry are becoming increasingly aware of the threats posed by, and implications, of using the cyber environment. It is also clear that the threats are becoming more sophisticated and advanced when used as an element of cyber warfare and cybercrime, especially since cyber defence often needs to address an unseen threat. Cyber terrorists have the capacity to shut down South Africa's power, disrupt financial transactions and commit crimes to finance their physical operations. Organised crime is also increasingly making use of the internet as a means of communication and financial gain. South Africa therefore needs a national cyber defence system with which everybody should comply.

Since the mid-1990s, South Africa has taken the first steps to protect its information. It passed legislation, such as the Constitution of the Republic of South Africa of 1996, to protect privacy. In 2000, however, the *Promotion of Access to Information Act (No 2 of 2000)* was passed to reaffirm citizens' right of access to information enshrined in Section 32 of the South African Constitution, subject to justifiable limitations (PAIA Act 2000). These limitations are aimed at the reasonable protection of privacy, commercial confidentiality and good governance in a manner that balances the right of access to information with any other rights, including the rights in the Bill of Rights in Chapter 2 of the South African Constitution (SA Constitution 1996). Linked to this Act is the Promotion of Access to Information Regulations regarding the promotion of information of access to information (Grobler et al, 2013). The regulations outline the manner of access and grounds on which access may be denied (Dassah, 2014 in Thorhnill, Van Dijk and Ile, 2014).

The *Electronic Communications and Transactions Act (No 25 of 2002)* was promulgated to facilitate and regulate electronic communications and transactions (ECT 2002). Also in 2002, the *Regulation of Interception of Communications and Provision of Communication-related Information Act (No 70 of 2002)* was passed to regulate the interception of certain communications, the monitoring of certain signals and radio frequency spectrums and the provision of certain communication-related information. This Act also regulates the making of applications for, and the issuing of, directions authorising the interception of communications and the provision of communication-related information under certain circumstances (RIC Act 2002).

South Africa also adopted the Council of Europe Cyber Crime Treaty in Budapest in 2001. The treaty contains important provisions to assist law enforcement in their fight against trans-border cybercrime. It is therefore imperative that South Africa ratifies the cybercrime treaty to avoid becoming an easy target for international cybercrime. The ratification will hopefully be done soon, although the South African government seems to be presently focused on basic service delivery and more traditional crimes given the current local crime situation. In combination with this treaty, all the South African bills and acts play an important role in the potential future collaboration of South Africa with other nations in the domain of cyber defence.

A group of cybersecurity specialists and diplomats, representing 15 countries (including South Africa) has agreed on a set of recommendations to the United Nations' Secretary General for negotiations on an international computer security treaty. In recent years, an explosion in cybercrime has been accompanied by an arms race in cyber weapons, as dozens of nations have begun to view computer networks as arenas for espionage and warfare. The recommendations to the United Nations from the specialists and diplomats reflect an effort to find ways to address the dangers of the anonymous nature of the Internet, as in the case of the object of a cyber-attack misconstruing the identity of the attacker (Grobler et al, 2013).

From a legal perspective, a number of concerns can be identified, such as:

- Lack of collaboration between industry and the defence environment;
- Capacity of the legal fraternity to comprehend the complexity of the cyber environment and to deliver a verdict based on a thorough understanding of the facts;
- Collaboration between countries and the agreements on protocols;

- Lack of collaboration between governments on cyber warfare and cybercrime;
- Lack of collaboration between municipalities, districts, regions and provinces; and
- Lack of collaboration between urban and tribal authorities (Grobler et al, 2013).

According to Eggers (2016) the public sector's difficulties in defending itself against these attacks are well known, therefore there is a need for cyber experts with deep intelligence regarding hacker networks. By understanding their methods, governments can better anticipate and recognise future risks thus thwarting hacks before they start.

CYBERSECURITY AND THE FOURTH INDUSTRIAL REVOLUTION

The proliferation of cyber threats has prompted asset owners in industrial environments to search for security solutions that can protect their assets and prevent potentially significant monetary loss and brand erosion. While some industries, such as financial services, have made progress in minimising the risk of cyber-attacks, the barriers to improving cybersecurity remain high. More open and collaborative networks have made systems more vulnerable to attack (Dooley, 2017). Furthermore, end user awareness and appreciation of the level of risk is inadequate across most industries outside critical infrastructure environments.

Uncertainty in the regulatory landscape also remains a significant restraint. With the increased use of commercial off-the-shelf IT solutions in industrial environments, control system availability is vulnerable to malware targeted at commercial systems. However, inadequate expertise in industrial IT networks is a sector-wide challenge. Against this backdrop, organisations need to partner with a solutions provider who understands the unique characteristics and challenges of the industrial environment and is committed to security.

The fourth industrial revolution brings with it a new operational risk for connected, smart manufacturers and digital supply networks, namely cyber. The interconnected nature of Industry 4.0–driven operations and the pace of digital transformation mean that cyberattacks can have far more extensive effects than ever before, and manufacturers and their supply networks may not be prepared for the risks. For cyber risk to be adequately addressed in the age of Industry 4.0, cybersecurity strategies should be secure, vigilant, and resilient, as well as fully integrated into organisational and information technology strategy from the start (Waslo, Lewis, Hajj, and Carton, 2017).

The fourth industrial revolution is both enabling vast business innovation and also creating sizable cybersecurity risks. This involves the readiness to mitigate business cyber risks for the connected community (Mussomeli, Gish and Laaper, 2017). The fourth industrial revolution, the age of the Internet of Things, machine learning, cognitive computing and artificial intelligence increases the security risks exponentially. If not secured from the beginning, the consequences may be measured in lives lost, not just money lost. According to KPMG's 2016 Global CEO Outlook, the world's leading CEOs are beginning to learn the lessons from the third industrial revolution and, going forward, they recognise the risks of the new wave of technologies. The argument is that when organisations went through the third industrial revolution, they failed to secure the Internet effectively, but have learnt their lessons (KPMG International, 2016). To be able to thrive in the fourth industrial revolution, companies need mainstream cyber capabilities, i.e. people in all parts of the organisation who understand cyber issues. Each major decision needs to be looked at through the cybersecurity lens.

RECOMMENDATIONS

Training in the area of information security awareness is imperative, and appears to be a worldwide problem for the public sector. Research conducted by PriceWaterhouseCoopers (2012) shows that there has been degradation in employee security awareness training and disaster recovery planning and information security management strategies in the public sector. Kyobe, Matengu, Walter and Shongwe (2012) strongly recommend that government departments and other stakeholders engage in initiatives to create awareness of the cyber risks. While the government continues to invest in technology and related mechanisms for detection and prevention, it is equally important to develop a culture of sharing information on cybercrime and development of skills in accounting and management of cyber risks.

Research indicates that lack of clear guidance on how to calculate losses, a lack of understanding of the legislation and knowledge of how it may assist in limiting cybercrime, lack of training and creation of awareness of cybercrime, and lack of knowledge and capability to assess risks regularly are major factors inhibiting private sector and public institutions from recognising and reporting losses from cyber-attacks. There is a need for the co-ordination of cybersecurity activities so as to have a harmonised approach to cybercrime, especially for the Fourth Industrial Revolution.

FUTURE RESEARCH DIRECTIONS

There have been several measures taken by the government and researchers to address cybercrime challenges. For example, in South Africa recently, the Department of Communications published the draft Cyber Security Policy of South Africa. Furthermore, there are many factors that influence recognition and reporting of losses from cyber-attacks on government institutions. Those examined include human behaviour (i.e. attitude of managers toward information security), lack of understanding of the regulations governing the use of electronic media, and lack of accounting skills and methods required to prepare for losses. A conceptual model can be developed and the relationships between the elements of the model can be studied further and analysed. Kyobe et al (2012) propose that human behaviour (e.g. attitude of top management and staff members towards information security), understanding of the information technology regulations that deal with cybercrime, and possession of relevant accounting skills and methods influence the ability to recognise and prepare loss estimates arising from cybercrime in government institutions.

The internet is a new environment with its own rules and its own dangers. In the past two decades, people have connected the economy and society via the internet, a platform designed primarily for sharing information, not protecting it (Eggers, 2016). This connectivity has driven innovation and high performance in the public and private sectors alike, yet as connectivity reshapes government in positive ways, it presents business opportunities for criminals with cyber talents. As institutions extend their capabilities through cloud computing, IT outsourcing, and partnerships, they increasingly rely on complex infrastructure not fully within their control. Similarly, government efforts to engage citizens and employees through social media introduce gaps and opportunities attackers will doubtless try to exploit.

Figure 1. Factors influencing recognition and reporting of losses from cyber attacks
Source: Adapted from Kyobe, Matengu, Walter and Shongwe (2012)

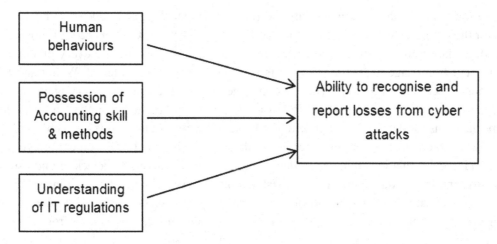

CONCLUSION

This chapter indicated that an analysis shows that the current initiatives are effective and have been able to address cybersecurity issues despite being on a small scale and despite the fact that South Africa is yet to develop a cybersecurity policy. Presently, universities are at the forefront of the initiatives but with limited participation from the government. The business sector, on the other hand seems to be engaging in cybersecurity awareness activities, though separately. A savvy cybersecurity-aware nation requires that all levels of society be serviced. The internet has changed almost all aspects of human life, including the nature of warfare. Every political and military conflict, every public sector entity, business in its broadest sense and now the general public has a cyber dimension, whose size and impact are difficult to predict and quantify.

The chapter highlighted the view that it is clear that cybercrime is a reality that unfortunately often targets the individuals least able to identify cyber fraud or how to keep their computers protected. It is critical for every organisation to change the kinds of conversations they are having about cyber risk, and to institute some variation in a secure, vigilant and resilient approach. The reality is that cyber risk is not something that can always be avoided, however, it must be managed. By understanding what data is most important, management can then determine what investments in security controls might be needed to protect an organisation's critical assets.

REFERENCES

Booysen, J. (2017, May 19). Most vulnerable remain at risk of cyber-attack. *Business Report*, p. 4.

Dassah, M. (2014). Role of Technology in the functioning of the State. In C. Thorhnill, G. Van Dijk, & I. Ile (Eds.), *Public Administration and Management in South Africa: A Developmental Perspective* (pp. 338–372). Cape Town: Oxford University Press.

Dinicu, A. (2014). Cyber threats to national security, specific features and actors involved. *Buletin Stiintific, 2*(38), 109–113.

Dlamini, Z., & Modise, M. (2012). Cyber Security Awareness in South Africa: A Synergy Approach. *7th International Conference on Information Warfare and Security: ICIW 2012.*

Dooley, R. (2017). *Cyber security at the heart of the Fourth Industrial Revolution.* Retrieved 09 October 2017, from https://instrumentsignpost.wordpress.com/2017/02/08/cybersecurity-at-the-heart-of-the-fourth-industrial-revolution-schneiderelec-pauto-industrie40/

Eggers, W. D. (2016). Government's cyber challenge: Protecting sensitive data for the public good. *Deloitte Review, 19*, 138–155.

Gray, A. (2015). A new generation of cyber risks: Is NZ ready for what's coming? *NZ Business+Management,* 8-12.

Grobler, M., & Dlamini, Z. (2012). Global Cyber Trends: A South African Reality. *IST-Africa 2012 Conference Proceedings.*

Grobler, M., Van Vuuren, J. J., & Zaaiman, J. (2013). Preparing South Africa for Cyber Crime and Cyber Defense. *Sytematics. Cybernetics and Informatics, 11*(7), 32–41.

Holtzhausen, N. (2016). Ethical public information services. In E. Draai (Ed.), *A practical introduction to Public Management* (pp. 91–115). Cape Town: Oxford University Press.

IST-Africa. (2011). Conference & Exhibition in Botswana. Gaborone: Author.

Kahn, J. (2017, May 03). Cyber extortion on the rise: Government organisations targeted. *Network,* 8.

Kortjan, N., & Von Solms, R. (2014). A conceptual framework for cyber-security awareness and education in SA. *South African Computer Journal, 52*, 29–41. doi:10.18489acj.v52i0.201

KPMG International. (2016). *Cybersecurity for the fourth industrial revolution.* Author.

Kritzinger, E., & Von Solms, S.H. (2012). A Framework for Cyber Security in Africa. *Journal of Information Assurance & Cybersecurity.* DOI:10.5171/2012.322399

Kyobe, M., Matengu, S., Walter, P., & Shongwe, M. (2012). Factors inhibiting recognition and reporting of losses from cyber-attacks: The case of government departments in the Western Cape province of South Africa. In *Proceedings of the European Conference on Information Management and Evaluation.* Academic Conferences Ltd.

Mahlobo, D. (2017, March 27). Time to protect confidentiality of information. *Business Report,* p. 14.

Microsoft. (2011). *Microsoft Security Intelligence Report* (Vol. 11). Microsoft Corporation.

Mussomeli, A., Gish, D., & Laaper, S. (2017). *The rise of the digital supply network Industry 4.0 enables the digital transformation of supply chains.* Deloitte University Press. Retrieved 11 October 2017, from https://dupress.deloitte.com/content/dupress/dup-us-en/focus/industry-4-0/digital-transformation-in-supply-chain.html

Nair, Y. (2017, May 17). Cybercrimes a threat to SA, warns minister. *The Mercury,* p. 6.

PricewaterhouseCoopers LLP. (2012). *Eye of the Storm: Key findings from 2012 Global State of Information Security Survey.* Retrieved May 13, 2017, from: http://www.pwc.se/sv_SE/se/riskhantering/assets/2012-global-state-ofinformation-security-survey.pdf

Republic of South Africa. (1996). *Constitution of the Republic of South Africa of 1996.* Pretoria: Government Printer.

Republic of South Africa. (2002). *Promotion of Access to Information Act No 2 of 2002.* Pretoria: Government Printer.

Republic of South Africa. (2002). *Electronic Communications and Transactions Act No 25 of 2002.* Pretoria: Government Printer.

Republic of South Africa. (2002). *Regulation of Interception of Communications and Provision of Communication-related Information Act No 70 of 2002.* Pretoria: Government Printer.

Republic of South Africa. (2015). National Cybersecurity Policy Framework for South Africa. No 39475. Government Gazette, 4 December 2015. Pretoria: Government Printer.

Rowe, B., Reeves, D., Wood, D., & Braun, F. (2010). *Estimating the market for Internet service provider-based cyber security solutions.* Retrieved June 15, 2017, from: https://www.ihssnc.org/portals/0/2010%20IHSS%20Research%20Summit_Rowe.pdf

Schell, R. R. (2016, November). Privacy and Security: Cyber Defense Triad for where Security Matters. *Communications of the ACM, 59*(11), 20–23. doi:10.1145/3000606

Tien, J. M. (2012). The next industrial revolution: Integrated services and goods. *Journal of Systems Science and Systems Engineering, 21*(3), 257–296. doi:10.100711518-012-5194-1

Van Jaarsveldt, L. C. (2010). Information technology skills for the South African Public Service. *Administratio Publica, 18*(4), 174–192.

Waslo, R., Lewis, T., Hajj, R., & Carton, R. (2017). *Industry 4.0 and cybersecurity: Managing risk in an age of connected production.* Deloitte University Press. Retrieved 11 October 2017, from: https://dupress.deloitte.com/dup-us-en/focus/industry-4-0/cybersecurity-managing-risk-in-age-of-connected-production.html

KEY TERMS AND DEFINITIONS

Cyber Threat: Is a threat to information technologies (i.e., technologies that allow the access, exchange, and the transaction of information).

Cyberattack: Is a deliberate exploitation of computer systems, technology systems, and networks. Cyberattacks use malicious code to alter computer code, logic or data, resulting in disruptive results that can compromise data. It is an illegal attempt to harm someone's computer system or the information on it, using the internet.

Cybercrime: Is all illegal acts, the commission of which involves the use of information and communication technologies. It is generally thought of as any criminal activity involving a computer system.

Cybersecurity: Is defined as the collection of tools, policies, security concepts, security safeguards, guidelines, risk management approaches, actions, training, best practices, assurance and technologies that can be used to protect the cyber environment, organization, and user assets.

Cyberspace: Refers to a physical and non-physical terrain created by and/or composed of some or all of the following: computers, computer systems, networks, and their computer programs, computer data, content data, traffic data, and users.

E-Governance: Is the application of Information Technology to the process of government functioning in order to bring about simple, moral, accountable, responsive, and transparent (SMART) governance.

Information and Communication Technologies (ICT): Refers to technologies that provide access to information through telecommunications. It is similar to information technology (IT), but focuses primarily on communication technologies. This includes the Internet, wireless networks, cell phones, and other communication mediums.

Ransomware: Is the use of malicious software to encrypt a user's data and then extort money to unencrypt it.

Chapter 14
Information Security Management:
A South African Public Sector Perspective

Harold Patrick
University of KwaZulu-Natal, South Africa

Brett van Niekerk
University of KwaZulu-Natal, South Africa

Ziska Fields
University of KwaZulu-Natal, South Africa

ABSTRACT

The frequency and sophistication of cyberthreats and attacks are increasing globally. All organizations including governments are at risk as more devices are connected to a growing network coverage. There is no doubt that the new technologies in the Fourth Industrial Revolution bring numerous opportunities for smarter and efficient ways of doing business. However, these new processes, technology, and people interacting increases the cyber-risks. Cyber-risks cause a threat to the reputation, operations, data, and assets of the organization. A holistic information security management plan is needed that will transform the organization's approach to mitigate the cyber-risks, protect its infrastructure, devices, and data. This approach will inevitably improve information technology governance and better accountability to the public.

INTRODUCTION

South African Government departments are not sharing information security incidents, and they are not communicating threat information and breaches within their various sections in the department and amongst other Provincial or National departments. In the United States of America (US), four out of 10 security incidents and breaches go undetected (Deltek Solutions, 2014, p. 4). Although increased reliance on the Internet offers numerous benefits and advantages, it also offers countless opportunities for

DOI: 10.4018/978-1-5225-4763-1.ch014

criminals to exploit South Africa's cybersecurity vulnerabilities. Tamarkin (2014) notes that cyber-crime is on the rise and thus has become a very significant concern in South Africa (SA) (p. 1). South Africa should consider the following: (1) Defining roles and responsibilities for government departments, (2) Collaborating with and other government departments and sharing of security incidents and threat data (Tamarkin, 2014, p. 1).

If the government have the political will, resources and skills, their challenges to digital transformation would be better improved. The government would effect and shift a better security position in the Fourth Industrial Revolution. Embedding information security management would lead to the deployment of new technologies, which would lead to improve accountability in government and lead to improved service delivery to its citizens. This is a necessity to grow the digital maturity of the government departments. This chapter will present the global perspective of information security initiatives and the current information security management landscape in government. South African laws about information security will be discussed. Finally, solutions for managing the information security management in the Fourth Industrial Revolution will be discussed.

BACKGROUND

Cyber-attacks are an international and local reality, therefore, it is essential that management accept that threat actors are moving towards espionage, crime and intentional disruptions of their networks and systems. Management and government leaders must acknowledge this reality and institute measures to curb threats and attacks (Ross, 2014, p. 4). As new technology is introduced universally, timely, and easy access to government networks and services will be essential to ensure good quality and complete information. Technology in the digital age will continue to drive organisations, creating information security concerns for management and the designated information technology staff (TraceSecurity, 2012, p. 1). Government departments are under excessive strain to protect their networks and systems from cyber-threats a result of new modernizing technology to render better services to the public (Govloop, 2014, p. 10). An insider or external threat or attack can disrupt government services and critical infrastructure operations. Therefore, government departments need to be resilient against these potential threats and attacks. Also, government departments are already part of the interconnected world of technologies and other organisations and will continue to be vulnerable to threats and attacks by cyber-criminals (Ixia, 2014, p. 4).

Information Security will continue to be an organisation and global problem that will involve different elements, including people, government and organisations. Government departments' efforts to deliver faster, transparent and better services will be hampered by the intricacy of information security, lack of information security capacity skills among the workforce will inevitably place enormous burdens on their networks and systems (Australian Signals Directorate, 2014, p. iii), thus creating new opportunities for adversaries. Optimizing the existing Information technology infrastructure and implementing new information technology developments and applications, (e.g. online services) have become a critical intervention in successfully managing the demands and pressure on the government to ensure quicker connectivity to organisations' own networks and systems as well as those of other organisations. Government's failure to implement new technologies and system applications can severely compromise delivery of government services (EMC Corporation, 2014, p. 10). It is vital that designated Chief Information Officers and infrastructure architects create and maintain a suitable infrastructure that will achieve the organisation's strategic objectives and considers information security and the relationship of other service departments' role into consideration (Rainys, 2006, p. 73).

Technological leap and influence in government operations will continually affect the deliverance of key critical public services like education and health because these technology developments are surpassing government's capability to respond (Kirkpatrick, 2014, p. 1). New application programs and systems will influence government services and dictate government approach to ensure uninterrupted delivery of services to the public and to other Provincial governments and municipalities.

New York, Maryland and Ohio government websites were hacked by an Islamic State of Iraq and Syria group called Team System Dz, which was in retaliation for the US military role in Muslim countries (Barth, 2017, p. 1). The Australian departments of Astride and Defence Science Technology Group networks and systems were hacked and infiltrated. Confidential information of Australia's project details and plans were stolen. The Australian government claims these attacks were state sponsored by Beijing (Besser, Sturmer, & Sveen, 2016, p. 1). The British Houses of Parliament networks and systems were attacked, in which email accounts of the members of parliament and staff were breached. It was found that 9000 email accounts were compromised. The government response was that this was suspected to be stated sponsored attack (MacAskill & Syal, 2017, p. 1). The government of Kenya's networks and systems were hacked. It is estimated that losses suffered from the vulnerabilities and attack are estimated to be USD146 million for a year. These attacks are increasing because of Kenya's increased web-connected of government devices (IT-Online, 2016, p. 1). The Swedish transport department database was breached in which military information and private information of its citizens leaked by contractors employed (eNews Channel Africa, 2017b, p. 1).

Organisations and governments are also now victims of ransomware, which is delivered through spear phishing and by threat actors using a remote desktop protocol. Once accessed and installed the victim's computer is locked and the organisation or government networks are locked. The organisation will thus have to pay ransom in exchange for the information and access to be unlocked. In 2016, the losses because of ransomware were estimated to be $2, 4 million (Masters, 2017, p. 1). The WannaCry ransomware is thus far making the biggest impact, as a malware to have affected organisations in exchange for unlocking the victim organisation had to pay in the Bitcoin currency (Fin24, 2017, p. 1).

An upsurge of attacks in Ukraine's bank, Russian company Rosneft and Britain's WPP advertising company and France's Saint-Gobain have seen there is a new ransomware called 'Petrwrap.' This ransomware is similar to the WannaCry ransomware (eNews Channel Africa, 2017a, p. 1). AP Moller-Maersk in India's Jawaharlal Nehru Port shipping system was attacked thereby affecting the loading and unloading at the port (Kotoky, 2017, p.1). Globally 391.7 million records from government organisations were stolen in attacks. This shows a dramatic increase of 27.3% compared to 2015 (Gemalto, 2017, p. 10). In the South African government context, the attacks on their websites and networks increased by 10% from the 50% in 2015 to 2016 (IT News Africa, 2017, p. 1).

Distributed denial of service (DDOS) attacks are growing in stealth and is regarded as one of the most common cyber-attacks. In this cyber-attack, the attacker will spread malicious software, which eventually takes control of the organisation's networks and systems and further spreads to other computers and email accounts. This in turn creates a network of infected devices called a botnet. The attacker thus will instruct the botnet and organisations' networks will eventually slow down (Palo Alto Networks, 2017, p. 1). In the Fourth Industrial Revolution, more technology and devices are connected to each other. A DDOS attack will cause serious disruption to devices that are unsecured. A Mira which is regarded an internet of thing botnet infected the Deutsche Telekom in Germany. Unsecured devices such as the digital video recorders and internet protocol cameras were infected, and Mira (Mercer, 2017, p. 2) shut down the websites.

INFORMATION SECURITY

Every organisation depends on the Internet, technology and information technology systems that include people, networks and processes. This dependence is to conduct business whether private or public and deliver and/or render a service (BMC, 2017, p. 1). The technology and information technology systems enable these services and must be protected from risks, threats and attacks. Threats to information can come in different forms for example (1) Malware, (2) Identity theft, (3) Ransomware; and (4) Phishing attacks (Teravainen, 2016, p. 1). It is important to note that any information asset can be competitive and thus needs safeguarding from cyber-criminals, other predator organisations or other countries seeking an added advantage. Information security management integrated into the organisation's daily operations, and policymaking leads to a better security culture that makes solid initiatives to mitigate threats and the occurrence of security incidents. Thus, information security management can be viewed as a mandatory methodology for organisations (Beaver, 2015, 1).

The objectives of information security are:

- To ensure the availability of information when required and the ability of the organisation technology, systems and networks to resist threats and recover from an attack;
- That only authorised persons have access to confidential information;
- The integrity of the information is protected; and
- Exchange of information between departments and other organisations is authentic and acceptable (BMC, 2017, p. 1).

The elements of information security management include: (1) Security persons responsible for information security; (2) Risk assessment; (3) Policies and procedures; (4) Security awareness; (5) Compliance with industry standards; (6) Information technology security audits; and response and recovery result from a security incident (AppliedTrust, 2008, pp. 1-3).

In all organisations the internal processes and systems change when new technology is introduced in the pursuit of profit, services and other advance likewise information security needs to adapt to these changing environment so as to be an effective approach to protecting the organisation's information and assets (Perry Johnson Registrars, 2017, p. 1). Information security management can be perceived as a strategic driver to the organisation and management to achieve their strategy and goals and thereby manage information technology and information risk (Evans, 2015, p. 1).

Global Government Initiatives to Manage Information Security

The Singapore Government in 2015 established a cyber-crime command within the Singapore Police and in 2016; they launched the National Cyber-crime Action Plan (Cybersecurity Agency of Singapore, 2016, p. 7). In Brazil, the government created a centre for Cyber-defense, which is managed by the Brazilian army. The army now controls and investigates all threats to the state infrastructure (Muggah, Diniz, & Glenny, 2014, p. 1).

The Russian government launched the development of a cyber-military unit, and it would be operational in 2017. This unit would strengthen the country's cyber defences (Tripwire, 2014, p. 1). In Kenya, the government boosted its cybersecurity initiatives with investing Kshs. 13 Billion in cybersecurity (Wainaina, 2016). In addition, Kenya opened a Cyber Coordination Centre in 2016, and the Computer and Cyber-crime Bill was approved in 2016 (Rwakenya, 2017, p. 1). The government of India introduced a privacy and encryption policies to manage the growing cybersecurity risks. An added measure is the development of a framework for cybersecurity architecture, which will provide a useful resource for organisations (Kumar, 2016, p. 1).

The United Kingdom (UK) government announced that it would allocate £1.9 billion to fund the development of the cybersecurity automated cyber defence to protect and safeguard its citizens and businesses in the UK from potential cyber threats and attacks (Flinders, 2016, p. 1). The Scottish government will over the next three years invest £36 million in its digital strategy to prepare this citizens and employees to learn from cyber-attacks and recover from these cyber-incidents (UK Construction Online, 2017, p. 1).

INFORMATION SECURITY IN SOUTH AFRICA

In 2013, the cost of phishing attacks in SA amounted to approximately $320 million (Fripp, 2014, p. 1). The country accounts for 5% of global phishing attacks. SA was ranked 11th of 50 top countries that reported the most Internet-related queries (Federal Bureau of Investigation, 2013, p. 21) which further showed that 534 complaints originated SA. In SA data breaches were reported as at 2016 to have cost organisations R28.6 million (TechFinancials, 2016, p. 1). SA is one of the countries that has the highest likelihood of a breach occurring in the subsequent 24 months (Ponemon Institute, 2017, p. 5).

Almost all organisations need and depend on the internet technology. Organisations and researchers rely on national and international cyber-crime data, however; the real dimensions of security incidents and breaches are not reflected. In South African Police Service's Directorate of Priority Crime, (the Hawks) has identified cyber-crime an important crime in South Africa (Hubeschle, 2011). Therefore the Hawks are putting more resources to investigate these crimes. Cyber-criminals are more organised and have sophisticated technology, which is also much prepared to launch an attack at any given time; hence, organisations in SA and the South African government should not think that they are exempt from hacking attacks. Thus, these organisations must be aware of an imminent threat or attack from those cyber-criminals operating locally and internationally.

Lyra and Simoes (2015) notes that, daily, the government collects information and stores enormous data deals with the vast amount of data (p. 48). Some of the information pertains to the public and must be treated with confidentially and protected. Government departments must urgently address and improve their Information technology governance to ensure transparency and accountability while providing better services for example health to citizens (PricewaterhouseCoopers, 2013, p. 28). Government departments must consider formulating information security policies and processes so that they can reduce the impact of information security risks to the organisation's information, systems and networks from theft and manipulation. Government departments especially service-oriented departments must ensure that the confidentiality, integrity and availability (CIA) of information of patient health records, social security details and bank account information. CIA components must be met for the security of information (Teravainen, 2016, p. 1). The former South African Finance Minister Gordhan indicated that SA information, communication and technology expenditure in 2017 would exceed R287 million to prioritise e-services in health, education and agriculture (Venktess, 2017, p. 1).

The Scalability of Information Security Incidents in South Africa

Some of the more prevalent information security incidents and breaches that occurred in South Africa include:

- In 2011, South Africa was ranked third in the most attacked nation with high attack volumes (Moorad, 2011).
- Between January 2012 and March 2012, 3 million attacks were experienced by South Africans (Alfreds, 2012).
- A keystroke logging device was used to covertly steal login details in the Department of Minerals and Energy's Basic Accounting System (financial system). As a result, R15 million was illegally transferred from the department's bank account (Tengimfene, 2013, p. 3).
- A syndicated gained access to the South African Revenue Service's system and fraudulently amended the bank account details of citizens expecting tax refunds. By doing this R77 million of refunds were channelled to the bank account belonging to the syndicates (Tengimfene, 2013, p. 3).
- Cybercrime losses were estimated to be R5.8 billion in 2014 (Booysen, 2015, p. 1).
- South Africa is one of the top targets for cyber-crime. The South African Banking Risk Information Centre highlight that R1billion is lost to cybercrime. This statistic increased by 30% since 2013 (Naidoo, 2016, p. 1).
- The South African Broadcast Corporation's website was hacked by the group called 'Anonymous'. The radio websites of SA-FM and 5-FM (eNews Channel Africa, 2016, p. 1).
- The group called 'World Hacker Team' breached the South African Department of Water Affairs networks and systems. Confidential data of emails, the identity number of the government employees were leaked (Cimpanu, 2016, p. 1).
- The Government Communication and Information System website and database was hacked. Details of employees such as identity numbers, phone numbers and e-mail addresses were exposed (Mokati, 2016, p. 1).
- The South African owned arms vendor Armscor's website was hacked by the hacktivist group called 'Operation Africa'. Armscor supplier and Armscor, customer details of Denel and Airbus were exposed (Techcentral, 2016, p. 1).
- Department of Basic Education website was hacked by the group called 'Team System DZ' who executed this attack in the name of Islamic State. This attack was in response to the actions taken against Muslim people (The Huffington Post, 2017, p. 1).

South African Legal Frameworks Relating to Information Security

Laws and regulations are important for countries to safeguard their national assets, information, services and critical infrastructure from real risks of being hacked or stolen. This measure is further needed to prevent some cyber-crime threats and attacks (Qasaymeh, 2015, p. 4). SA does have applicable legal frameworks to address Information Security (Wolfpack, 2013, p. 8). Some of the related laws are: (1) Minimum Information Security Standards, (2) Electronic Communications and Transactions Act 25 of

2002, (3) Protection of Information Bill of 2008, (4) Protection of Personal Information Act No. 4 of 2013, (5) National Critical Information Protection Bill, (6) Draft Cybercrimes and Cybersecurity Bill; and (7) King IV.

Electronic Communications and Transactions Act 25 of 2002

This Act regulates electronic communications and transactions in SA to prevent the misuse of the organisation's information systems by unauthorised persons (Department of Communication, 2002, p. 2). Section 86 (1) outlines the unlawful nature of unauthorised access to data. Section 86 (2) highlights the unauthorised modifying of data and section 86 (3) and (4) addresses the hacking of secure data and disabling security processes. Section 86 (5) deals with the intrusion of the organisation's information system and networks (Department of Communication, 2002: 72).

Protection of Personal Information Act No. 4 of 2013

The Act No. 4 of 2013 outlines the requirements for the lawful handling of personal information that includes (Department of Communications, 2013, pp. 22-36): (1) The organisation must demonstrate accountability and what measures they have in place, (2) The treating of personal information should be handled with minimum intrusion on privacy of the data subject. The data subject must consent to the processing of the information, (3) The organisation must take steps to ensure that the personal information is complete, true, not distorted and updated, (4) The data subject must be aware that information is being collected and what the intention is to use the information, (5) The integrity and confidentially measures are needed to protect the personal information, (6) The data subject can request the organisation to change or remove the personal information.

In summary, organisations must demonstrate how they will gather, use, issue and store data belonging to persons or organisations. Organisations must undertake a risk analysis of their systems and networks to establish the current measure and what measures need to be implemented to safeguard personal information. Also, if the organisations do not comply they then will be liable for a fine (Finnigan, 2017, p. 1). In the Protection of Personal Information Act no. 4 of 2013, section 22 the responsible parties must notify the regulator and affected parties when they believe that data information (for example suppliers and employees) had been illegally accessed or attained by an unauthorised individual or individuals. Failure to notify all the parties could result in penalties (Blom, 2017, p. 1). Protection of Personal Information Act does not provide a clear guide for the reporting of security incidents (Jump, 2015, p. 3). Therefore, security incident management in an organisation is essential.

Minimum Information Security Standards

The Minimum Information Security Standards defines information security as a process that creates and maintains the establishment and application of an organisation of documents, personnel, and physical, computer and security measures to safeguard sensitive data (State Security Agency, 1996, p. 8). The Minimum Information Security Standards outlines the duties of departments and their head of the institution (McKinley, 2003). The head of the institution must accept the accountability for the provision and upkeep of security. They must design effective an information security management system, which suits the organisation's operations. The head of security (physical security) in the department must firstly, increase security, secondly, co-ordinate and liaise with the governing organisations and thirdly, report all security incidents or alleged breaches to the correct departments or organisations.

It is the responsibility of the head of the department to ensure that employees that use computers for work operations have the essential security training and that they receive regular awareness training. The Head of Department or his/her nominee must introduce the following procedures: (1) Backup of department systems and information, (2) Physical security measures, (3) Roles and responsibilities about computer security; and (4) Passwords are allocated to employees. Chapter 9 states that all security incidents must be reported to the Head of Department of the organisation for action.

Protection of Information Bill, 2008

The Bill applies to all government departments, juristic bodies and the public (State Security Agency, 2010, pp. 8-9). The purpose of the Act is to (1) Regulate how state information is protected, (2) Encourage transparency and promote governance; and (3) establish guidelines how the state information may be controlled and secured. The principles of the bill are: (1) Information is accessible and transparent, (2) To allow that information is shared in order to promote openness and good governance; and (3) Promote security and safety.

The minister must ensure applicable criteria for the protection of information against alteration and destruction of information so that information security processes are adhered to and complied with. The further outlines of the National Intelligence Agency duties are to (1) Monitor the information policies and programs accepted by the government, (2) Provide direction and expert advice to government departments; and (3) Report to the minister on work executed. Information security is defined in the bill as a means of protection of information, but is not restricted to: (1) Information and communication technology security measures, (2) Continuity planning, (3) Reporting security incidents; and (4) Investigating security incidents.

Draft National Critical Infrastructure Protection Bill

The proposed bill aims to: (1) Protect the critical infrastructure within government, (2) Create procedures for the determination of critical infrastructure, and (3) Ensure that the department is accountable for the security of the Critical infrastructure. The Bill ensures the protection of strategic information that could prejudice the security of the country, prejudice the essential services like health and disrupt the country economy (Gill & Bokhari, 2016, p. 9). Mbhele emphasises that this bill in its current context is worrying in that; (1) the details of critical infrastructure sites will be classified, (2) the criteria outlining what a strategic critical information infrastructure is unclear, and (3) parliament has excluded itself as an oversight body from this Bill (Petterson, 2016, p. 1). This bill gives the minister of police the power to decide the sites of critical infrastructure (Right2Know, 2016, p. 1).

The draft bill does not sufficiently deal with the concerns of transparency and openness, for instance, national key points would not be made public, and this of national key points could be subjectively compiled and deliberately kept from the public (Right2Know, 2016, p. 1). This approach would be open to abuse by the officials in charge of key points.

King IV

The King code is for good governance which organisations in South Africa should adhere to to create a culture of governance. King IV introduce this governance code approach as apply and explain (Myburgh & De Costa, 2017, p. 1). King IV (Institute of Directors South Africa, 2016, p. 22) aims to promote governance:

- Creating an ethical culture, ensure good organisation performance, tangible control and validity;
- Ensure easy implementation across all organisations;
- Reinforce a holistic governance approach;
- Support transparent reporting to all stakeholders;
- Promote ethical awareness and proper conduct in the organisation.

The King IV principle 12 improves technology and information governance (1) the organisation must accept responsibility for technology and information and policies that support this principle; (2) ensure oversight of technology and information in respect of people, technology and information and integration of risks in people and processes into organisation risk management; (3) management of information in respect of security information and information architecture supporting confidentiality, integrity and availability of information (Institute of Directors South Africa, 2016, pp. 62-63).

The King IV places emphasis on information technology governance and further states that policies must develop and be transparent (Giles, 2016, p. 1). Giles (2016, p. 1) further highlights that the King IV should have the term 'Information communication and technology' as opposed to the universal term information technology governance. Also, the cybersecurity risk is excluded, with reference only being made to information security risk.

King IV is developed for applying and easy adaption to all types of organisations being public, private and non-governmental organisations. It is the organisation's duty to ensure protection and management of security risks (Harduth & Sampson, 2017, pp. 7-10). King IV emphasise the importance of protecting the organisation's information and assets which aides and supports POPI compliance and requirements (Clamp, 2017, p. 4).

Cybercrime and Cybersecurity Bill

The proposed bill ensures to build a safer cyber-space for the citizens, business and government. The bill is also an important element in the fight against cyber-crime (Jeffery, 2017, p. 1). This planned legislation seeks to put processes in place that will allow SA to address cyber-crime and manage it successfully. The Department of Justice and Constitutional Development (Department of Justice and Constitutional Development, 2017, p. 2) specifies that the Bill intentions are to:

- Prescribe offences and penalties to cybercrime,
- Regulate the applicable jurisdiction,
- Regulate rules for admission and seizure of items and devices used in cybercrime,
- Regulate evidence gathering, and
- Regulate cooperation within the government and other countries to investigate cybercrime.

In chapter six (section 53) of the bill the State Security ministry must establish multiple government security incident response teams (Department of Justice and Correctional Services, 2015, pp. 82-86) and that a memorandum of agreements must be concluded with the various Heads of Departments.

Bernstein, Ebrahim, and Cibane (2015) state that the Bill will classify offences involving cybercrime. However, clarity is needed on some aspects of the Bill. The electronic communications service provider term is too general, and this might be challenging when applying its requirements. Additionally, clause 16(5) (b) states that "any person who unlawfully and intentionally, (1) Possesses, (2) Communicates, (3) Receives data which is the possession of the state and which is classified as confidential, is guilty of an offence" is comparable to the Protection of State Information Bill, 2008. Fripp (2015), emphasises that the Bill encroaches on constitutional independence (p. 1).

The bill affects the digital rights and freedom of the citizens and puts more power over to the State Security Department (Duncan, 2015, p. 1). The bill states that organisations or persons other than the person suspected of the crime are obligated to provide the data or information or assistance in the investigation of the crime (Gill & Bokhari, 2016, p. 3). The Bill also introduces hacking as an offence. State Security Agency and South Africa Police Service have now the powers to search, access and seize computers and network information (Van Zyl, 2016:p.1). The bill also ensures that data must be seized and preserved to be presented as part of the crime in the South African court (Jeffery, 2017, p. 2). The bill ensures the creation of the cyber response committee and a 24/7 contact point to deal with cybersecurity incidents. However, the cyber hub mandate and brief on the Postal services website, explicitly states that the cyber hub operation hours are 8 am to 4 pm, which is normal working hours only. This mandate is in clear conflict with the bill (Pillay, 2017, p. 3).

Industry-specific nodes are to be created. South African law enforcement agencies have jurisdiction to investigate any South African citizen or organisation who operate in South Africa. The failure to protect and safeguard personal information will lead to a fine of a minimum of R50,000 (Finnigan, 2017, p. 1) for the organisation. The Bill now states that two structures namely 24/7 Point of Contact and Cyber Response Committee for managing cyber-crime whereas eight government structures were initially proposed (Crawford, 2017, p. 1).

The literature notes that SA have the laws and regulations that require organisations to abide by minimum-security requirement and initiatives. These measures are necessary for government and organisations to create a culture of security and information technology governance so that they can leap into the Fourth Industrial Revolution with confidence knowing that they have the information technology controls in place, thereby enjoying the introduction of new technology.

Auditor General: South Africa's Assessment of Information Security

The Auditor General South Africa is viewed as the highest audit body that ensures oversight, governance and accountability in the public sector (namely National government, the provincial government, local government and State-owned entities) (Auditor General South Africa, 2015). An organisation that demonstrates an appreciation for information technology governance, auditing of security and information technology risks promotes a culture of information security. This further will imply compliance with information security regulatory standards (Broderick, 2006, p. 31). The audits for information technology and governance are important in that business processes are flagged when there is non-compliance and recommends the corrective measures. AGSA audit reports for the government departments highlight important findings relating to information technology risk, security and information technology governance. A summary of the pertinent findings will be discussed in the paragraph below.

A summary of the findings by the Auditor General South Africa consolidated reports for the financial years 2012-2013, 2013-2014, 2014-2015. The Auditor General South Africa has consistently reported significant findings for the audit focus areas for information technology controls, information technology governance, and security management. The reports for the financial years stated that the government departments were not performing well in the audit focus areas, which noted material findings and in most incidents information technology controls needed to be designed. The Auditor General South Africa also reported that some of the government departments needed intervention in designing controls. They also lacked acceptable governance frameworks, security policies and procedures. It is noted that the findings are common for the financial years, which implies that the government departments are not doing well in managing information security (Auditor General South Africa, 2013, p. 47, 2014, p. 80, 2017, pp. 70-71). The Auditor General South Africa audit outcome reports also highlighted serious findings of the shortage of skilled information technology resources and the increased levels of information technology risk in government. This suggests that National departments and Provincial departments are not managing Information technology risk and information technology governance well (Patrick, 2016, pp. 39-40).

IMPORTANCE OF INFORMATION SECURITY MANAGEMENT FOR THE FOURTH INDUSTRIAL REVOLUTION

New technologies are driving the Fourth Industrial Revolution, which are disintegrating country precincts between government, people, organisations, the physical world and the internet (Montresor, 2016, p. 1). With the advent of the Fourth Industrial Revolution, new ways are needed to approach information technology governance (Davis, 2016, p. 1). It is argued that this revolution will emphasise three core areas namely security, identity and inequality (Davis, 2016, p. 1). New and emerging technologies combined with the digital domain creates more security risks and inevitably make information technology governance more challenging (Davis, 2016, p. 1). Also, governments can become increasingly more vulnerable and accessible to other countries and non-state actors who seek to exploit risks and vulnerabilities in persuit of the cyber space dominance (Davis, 2016, p. 1). The Fourth Industrial Revolution is essentially changing the way governments interact and work with each other because of the unclear cyber-space boundaries (Schwab, 2016a, p. 1).

To shift into Fourth Industrial Revolution mode and navigate the emerging technologies, the elementary and pertinent security questions of infrastructure and current systems of the organisation, needs to be solved (Schwab, 2016a, p. 1). Importantly the Government departments must reflect whether the current systems designed and implemented can serve their efforts to better information technology governance and improve organisations' accountability and progress to its citizens (Schwab, 2016a, p. 1). The deficiencies in security risks must be overcome to advance into the opportunities of the Fourth Industrial Revolution (Coleman, 2016, p. 1). If governments fail to mitigate the disrupting effects of the new technology, the task for the government will then become too great to rectify and lead to the potential collapse of services (Lye, 2017, p. 1). Governments need a planned approach in handling the impact of the evolution to the new technologies that would include the management of cybersecurity risks. (Lye, 2017, p. 1).

The introduction of interdependences and new technology leads to better efficiency and easy access to government services for example health (Prisecaru, 2016, pp. 59-60). It is crucial for governments to understand that with new technologies and digital transformation, their entire systems of governance and management are intertwined (Meads, 2017, p. 1). The Government Departments that support the new technologies and implements cybersecurity will boost the economic growth of the country and enable innovation and new models for service delivery (Meads, 2017, p. 2). They thus must take responsibility, prioritise their response to cyber-risks, and offer a better delivery of government services.

The impact of the Fourth Industrial Revolution is creating new improved ways of serving current needs and be able to introduce better speed, and quality of service thereby maximising the benefits of the Fourth Industrial Revolution (Thomas, 2017, p. 1). The challenge is for governments to protect its infrastructure and systems find solutions and apply active information security procedures and programs (Ha, 2017, p. 1).

Government and organisations will seek to capitalise on the benefits of the new opportunities; they are not resistant to the new threats, a strong and approachable information security position (which includes policies, roadmap and program) is critical to protecting its infrastructure and systems (Vaid & Holme, 2016, p. 1). The government needs to be more security sensitive to secure its assets and ultimately prosper in this digital revolution (Kudelski, 2016, p. 1). Governments will continuously be confronted by the pressure of adapting the existing systems and policies to the Fourth Industrial Revolution to improve efficiency and transparency. They must endure these changes and innovations to be competitive (Schwab, 2016b, p. 1).

An important driver of the Fourth Industrial Revolution is the ability of the government or organisations to change the existing ways of work and create new processes and systems and roles (Lowman, 2016, p. 1). The Fourth Industrial Revolution imposes on government and organisations to shorten their response time to public queries, delivery of services and to reduce additional cost of services without compromising on the quality of services to the public (British Broadcasting Corporation, 2017, p. 3).

RESEARCH METHODOLOGY

Research Method

A quantitative and qualitative research method was employed for this study. The quantitative method targeted the employees in the provincial government, and the senior management was targeted for the qualitative semi-structured interviews to identify information security status, challenges and initiatives. A total number of 258 respondents were obtained. Five senior management participated out of the identified eight participants.

Results

Two hundred and fifty-eight respondents formed the final sample for this mixed method study. The respondents were presented with a set of 21 online information security questions to be answered. The participants were also presented with 13 questions particularly relating to the organisation's initiatives to managing information security. Table 1 below presents the online findings from the respondents. Table 2 indicates the participant's response to the interview question 'Organisation initiatives to manage

Table 1. Online interview question and response (Patrick, 2016, pp. 131-133-136)

Online Interview Question	Interview Response
The level of management support of information security initiatives in your organisation is high.	The responses indicated that 29.5% agreed and 3.9% strongly agreed with this statement. Also, the responses show that 17.8% disagreed and 8.1% strongly disagreed, and 27.1% were neutral. Also, some respondents (13.6%) did not reply to this statement.
Approved information security management program	The majority of the respondents (53.1%) were not certain if their organisation had an Information security management program, although 20.5% responded in the positive and 17.1% did not respond to this question.
An information security management program is a vital tool in improving the information technology security position.	The response to this statement showed that respondents strongly agreed (22.5%) and 45.7% were in agreement with this statement. There was an overwhelming agreement (68.2%) with this statement to be true.

information security.' The participants indicated that their organisation is not doing enough to manage information security. This implies that more initiatives should be adopted.

The respondents (25.9%) indicated that they disagreed that management support of information security initiatives is high. Of concern is that 27.1% of the respondents remained neutral on this issue and only 33.4% agreed with the statement. This suggests that management support for information security initiatives in the Government department is inadequate. The literature highlights that management support for information security in these departments is of concern; there are no formal information security management program and policy.

The majority of the respondents (53.1%) were unsure if their department had an approved Information security management program. This could suggest that either there is no approved Information security management program or that the program is not adequately communicated throughout the departments. Every organisation needs some dimension to assess how secure its networks and systems are from security incidents, threats and attacks. The Thawte Report (2014), highlights building an information security program is the best approach that would provide senior management with a complete assessment of the organisation's practices (p. 6). With this comprehensive understanding, the organisation would be better placed to ascertain the appropriate information security strategy including systems that would deliver higher maturity levels of protection that are required. The approved information security program outlining the appropriate security strategy can prevent, detect, and mitigate potential security incidents and threats.

Many of the respondents (68.2%) agreed that an Information security management program is vital in enhancing the department's Information technology security position. It is noted in the literature that Information security management is critical in protecting an organisation's networks, systems and information resources and assists in managing its risk exposure in information technology domain. An organisation that has implemented an information security management program will be able to reduce the control weaknesses of Information technology and in addition, prevent security incidents and breaches (Ahmad, Maynard, & Park, 2014, p. 357) and avoid reputational risk and lawsuits from individuals or other organisations (ISACA, 2013, pp. 141-143).

Table 2. Interview question and response (Patrick, 2016, p. 163)

Interview Question	Interview Participant number	Interview Response
Organisation initiatives to manage information security	1	"No."
	2	"Do not know."
	3	"No."
	4	"I am not aware of any initiatives currently underway."
	5	"I don't think the organisation is doing well. We could still invest more on managing information security."

DISCUSSION OF RESULTS

Of concern is the low level of management support for Information security, which resulted in a lack of a formal Information Security management program. The study also found that government employees had a very limited awareness of the Information Security management program in their departments. Based on the literature review and results there is a strong acknowledgement that an Information Security management program would advance the government department's security levels.

Regarding King IV, it is essential that the organisation takes prudent steps to address information security in its systems, networks and procedures so that the CIA of information is protected (Institute of Directors South Africa, 2016, p. 63). By drafting an applicable security policy, the department will ensure compliance with King IV. The draft security provided to all role players in the departments for consultation before being officially adopted. Awareness of the information security policy should be publicised internally and externally in the department to gain support.

Government departments must make in-depth preparations to endure and improve from unexpected security events and attacks from accidental or deliberate acts (Sommer & Brown, 2011, p. 5). Government departments need to be better prepared and take responsibility for ensuring information security culture that would assist in curtailing the increasing occurrences of compromised government networks and systems. The non-existence of sharing and co-ordination amongst government departments has hindered the management of security incidents, threats and attacks. Government departments must take responsibility for developing their management preparedness for information security Government Departments because they are the "iron in the fire" and can make an immediate difference (ICSPA, 2012, p. 1). A PWC report (2013, p. 12) stated that government departments must break down the silo walls between themselves so they can be part of the connected networks of organisations and government. Senior management in a government department and political leaders must overcome political hindrances and co-operate amongst themselves to build a better environment of good governance. Information sharing of a security incident and threat intelligence and collaboration amongst the different government structures being national, provincial and local government can streamline the workflows to in decreasing security incidents, thereby ensuring swifter response to security incidents and ensuring least disruption of government operations (Lyons, 2013, p. 1).

Bailey, Kaplan and Rezek (2014) claim that operational and administrative issues confound the process of employing information security management particularly risk assessment which can proactively identify security risks and mitigate IT controls preventing potential security incidents, threats and attacks

(p. 1). This chapter focuses on the Information security management to identify issues and initiatives that can develop an enhanced security position for the public sector.

Bailey et al. (2014), identify some initiatives that organisations can consider to improve the security management in the organisation (p. 1):

- Engage in decision-making to limit the disruption of operations;
- Consider the implications of information security priorities;
- Ensure communication of security so that employees are better prepared to understand information security risks;
- Ensuring a better information technology governance culture which includes a reporting mechanism which the organisation can use to communicate security initiatives and milestones. Information security initiatives also empower the employees to protect their selves and the organisation's networks' and systems potential threats and attacks (Centrify, 2013, p. 5).

Information Security for the Public and the Fourth Industrial Revolution

The South African government wants all services to be online by 2030 in line with the National development plan (African National Congress, 2017, p. 17). However, given the current context, infrastructure challenges still have not been resolved. One can only hope that the proposed establishment of the Fourth Industrial Revolution Commission in SA will provide status and direction to meet the challenges of the revolution (African National Congress, 2017, p. 17).

It is clear that the South African government is still focused on the impact of the revolution about social and economic systems and what this shift would do (African National Congress, 2017, p. 2). This approach will affect and put added pressure on the South African government to keep pace with the Fourth Industrial Revolution. A further challenge is that SA is only now recommending new stakeholder involvement amongst all role players (which includes; academic sector, private, public and nonprofit) to develop a comprehensive framework to take South Africa forward with a view to discuss and resolve digital skills, innovation and research (African National Congress, 2017, p. 12). In SA, government and organisations are delayed by their general averseness to invest in new technologies with the view of saving costs first approach (Deloitte, 2017, p. 15). IT security management is immediately needed to improve operational security against potential threats and attack (Deloitte, 2017, p. 28). The South African government will develop a National Cybersecurity Strategy, which would deal with emerging threats (African National Congress, 2017, p. 4).

The South African government needs a fundamental shift in cybersecurity by prioritising cybersecurity management of their infrastructure, data and assets. The South African government also need to start prioritising cybersecurity risk assessment and consider adopting an automated process. Also, they need to develop and enforce cybersecurity policy so that anticipation of future incidents can be managed. This will ensure convergence and integration of existing systems and processes, cybersecurity and new information technology to benefit from the Fourth Industrial Revolution. In this approach, the cybersecurity risks can be identified and the different processes and systems. Also, the government needs to protect the confidential information they store and hold of citizens, organisations and other government departments. Highly sensitive and confidential information should be encrypted thus allowing only authorised government officials access to the information during the performance of their work. Contractors and other third-party partners should also be included in the information security program to ensure only appropriate access across platforms and applications and protect unauthorised access and manipulation of information.

The South African government needs to invest in future research and establish partnerships with academia and other research organisation. This would assist in cybersecurity innovations, technology transfer, norms and policy enhancement. The Minister of State Security further stated that partnerships with the higher learning institution would assist in building capacity for government to respond to cyber threats and attacks (Mahlobo, 2017, p. 4).

A situational analysis of the cybersecurity policies and procedures are needed to ensure better cybersecurity hygiene, so that best practice and approach for information security can be adopted. South Africa also needs the government to invest in organisation structure for information security skills set and ensure capacity building. Political leadership is needed to invest in new technologies and not allow these new technologies to be also a barrier to prosperity. One of the other effective ways of mitigating cybersecurity risks and vulnerabilities is for government to invest more in cybersecurity education and training of its employees. Young (cited in Ashford, 2017, p. 32) states that human and machine interaction can be more effective. This provides an informed trend and development of training interventions. Some of the other initiatives the government departments can take:

- All sensitive government information and citizen information are encrypted, thereby ensuring only authorised users have access to the information;
- Government employees are given new devices to undertake work, and some employee devices are subsidised by the government, since more devices are being connected to the government networks and system. The security policy needs to be enhanced so that only legitimate and authorised devices can connect to government networks and systems (Organisation of American States & Symantec, 2014, p. 32);
- Educate the end-users about cybersecurity and how to interact responsibly with government devices connected to the networks and systems;
- Government departments need to ensure that there are regularly backing up sensitive information of its operations and citizen information.
- South African government while already in partnerships with other countries, need to actively engage with leading countries e.g. the US, UK, the Netherlands and Singapore and learn from their cybersecurity experience.

Future Research Directions

The South African government urgently needs to do a cyber-risk assessment of their current infrastructure in the departments. This assessment will outline whether the infrastructure meets essential cybersecurity checks and is capable of supporting new technologies. A skills audit is needed to assess the current work skills and what level capacity building and technology transfer should take place.

These future research opportunities are needed so that the South African government can enjoy the benefits of new technologies and economically prosper as a country. Which will benefit government's economic and social interventions?

CONCLUSION

Governments need to learn from their vulnerabilities and information technology risks and implement improved approaches to diffuse potential threats and contribute to the future of the Fourth Industrial Revolution (Davis, 2016, p. 1). The government needs to engage actively with all role-players (private, public) including other governments in understanding IT governance issues and complexities to lead the revolution and provide confidence to its citizens (Schwab, 2016a, p. 1). Government and organisations need to pay urgent attention to real threats they face and make the capital investment information security (Ha, 2017, p. 1). The South African government needs a visionary approach to unlock the enormous economic benefits of the Fourth Industrial Revolution.

A government role is a regulator. However, the government holds the authority to produce and shape a better favourable landscape to manage cyber-risks (Oliver Wyman, 2017, p. 13). Information security management can transform the government's strategy and goals in the Fourth Industrial Revolution thereby ensure an innovated and excellent public service to its citizens.

REFERENCES

African National Congress. (2017). *5th National Policy Conference*. Johannesburg: African National Congress.

Ahmad, A., Maynard, S., & Park, S. (2014). Information security strategies: Towards an organizational multi-strategy perspective. *Journal of Intelligent Manufacturing*, *25*(2), 357–370. doi:10.100710845-012-0683-0

Alfreds, D. (2012). *Hackers hit SA web users*. Retrieved from http://www.news24.com/SciTech/News/Hackers-hit-SA-web-users-20120702

AppliedTrust. (2008). *Every company needs to have a security program*. Retrieved from https://www.appliedtrust.com/sites/default/files/assets/resources/every-company-needs-a-security-program.pdf

Ashford, W. (2017). *Human-machine teaming key to cyber defence, says Intel Security*. Retrieved from http://www.computerweekly.com/ehandbook/Focus-Securing-for-the-future

Auditor, G. S. A. (2013). *PFMA 2012-2013 Consolidated General Report*. Pretoria: Auditor General South Africa.

Auditor, G. S. A. (2014). *PFMA 2013-2014 Consolidated General Report*. Pretoria: Auditor General South Africa.

Auditor, G. S. A. (2015). *About Us*. Retrieved January 29, 2015, from http://www.agsa.co.za/Home.aspx

Auditor, G. S. A. (2017). *Consolidated general report on the national and provincial audit outcomes 2015-16*. Pretoria: Auditor General South Africa.

Australian Signals Directorate. (2015). *Australian Government Information Security Manual*. Australian Signals Directorate. Retrieved from http://www.asd.gov.au/publications/Information_Security_Manual_2015_Exec_Companion.pdf

Bailey, T., Kaplan, J., & Rezek, C. (2014). *Why senior leaders are the front line against cyberattacks*. Retrieved from http://www.mckinsey.com/insights/business_technology/why_senior_leaders_are_the_front_line_against_cyberattacks

Barth, B. (2017). *Pro-ISIS hacker group defaces state, local government websites*. Retrieved from https://www.scmagazine.com/pro-isis-hacker-group-defaces-state-local-government-websites/article/671041/

British Broadcasting Corporation. (2017). *Rebooting industry for the digital age*. Retrieved from http://www.bbc.com/future/bespoke/specials/connected-world/industry-4-0.html

Beaver, K. (2015). *The Importance of a Security Culture Across the Organization*. Retrieved from https://securityintelligence.com/the-importance-of-a-security-culture-across-the-organization/

Bernstein, D., Ebrahim, W., & Cibane, S. (2015). *SA's cybersecurity bill raises big concerns*. Retrieved from http://www.techcentral.co.za/sas-cybersecurity-bill-raises-big-concerns/60695/

Besser, L., Sturmer, J., & Sveen, B. (2016). *Government computer networks breached in cyber attacks as experts warn of espionage threat*. Retrieved from http://www.abc.net.au/news/2016-08-29/chinese-hackers-behind-defence-austrade-security-breaches/7790166

Blom, K. (2017). *FinTech - new opportunities (and risks)*. Retrieved from http://www.itweb.co.za/index.php?option=com_content&view=article&id=162426

BMC. (2017). *ITIL Information Security Management*. Retrieved from http://www.bmcsoftware.co.za/guides/itil-information-security-management.html

Booysen, J. (2015). *Cybercrime cost SA R5bn in 2014*. Retrieved from IOL Business website: http://www.iol.co.za/business/news/cybercrime-cost-sa-r5bn-in-2014-1.1810007

Broderick, J. S. (2006). ISMS, security standards and security regulations. *Information Security Technical Report, 11*(1), 26–31. doi:10.1016/j.istr.2005.12.001

Centrify. (2013). *TOP 3 Reasons to Give Insiders a Unified Identity*. Retrieved from http://www.centrify.com/downloads/public/centrify-top-three-reasons-to-give-insiders-a-unified-identity.pdf

Cimpanu, C. (2016). *Anonymous hacks and leaks South African Dept of Water Affairs data*. Retrieved from https://www.databreaches.net/anonymous-hacks-and-leaks-south-african-dept-of-water-affairs-data/

Clamp, C. (2017). *King III vs King IV What you really need to know*. Retrieved June 22, 2017, Johannesburg: https://www.grantthornton.co.za/globalassets/1.-member-firms/south-africa/pdfs/kingiv_feb17.pdf

Coleman, G. (2016). *How Africa can lead the way in the Fourth Industrial Revolution*. Retrieved from https://www.weforum.org/agenda/2016/05/how-africa-can-lead-the-way-in-the-fourth-industrial-revolution/

Crawford, K. (2017). *Cybercrimes and Cybesecurity Bill to be tabled in Parliament*. Retrieved from https://www.fanews.co.za/article/legal-affairs/10/general/1120/cybercrimes-and-cybersecurity-bill-to-be-tabled-in-parliament/21678

Cybersecurity Agency of Singapore. (2016). *Singapore's Cybersecurity Strategy*. Singapore: Author.

Davis, N. (2016). *What is the fourth industrial revolution?* Retrieved from https://www.weforum.org/agenda/2016/01/what-is-the-fourth-industrial-revolution/

Deloitte. (2017). *Industry 4.0 Is Africa ready for digital transformation.* Johannesburg: Author.

Deltek Solutions. (2014). *Guide to Data Security.* Retrieved from http://www.informationweek.com/whitepaper/Security/Attacks-Breaches/guide-to-data-security-wp1412021175?articleID=200000757&download=true&popup=true&_=1415718908717&thankyou=true

Department of Communication. (2002). *Electronic Communications and Transactions Act 2002 (23708).* Pretoria: Author.

Department of Communications. (2013). *Protection of Personal Information Act 2013 (4).* Pretoria: Author.

Department of Justice and Correctional Services. (2015). *Cybercrimes and Cybersecurity Bill.* Pretoria: Author.

Department of Justice and Constitutional Development. (2017). *Cybercrimes and Cybersecurity Bill.* Pretoria: Author.

Duncan, J. (2015). *Inside SA's cyber-insecurity problem.* Retrieved from https://mg.co.za/article/2015-10-15-inside-sas-cyber-insecurity-problem

Corporation, E. M. C. (2014). *ECM as a Service in Government.* Retrieved from http://www.emc.com/collateral/white-papers/h12586-ecm-as-a-service.pdf

eNews Channel Africa. (2016). *Hackers shut down SABC websites.* Retrieved from www.enca.com/south-africa/hackers-shut-down-sabc-websites

eNews Channel Africa. (2017a). *New Wave of cyber attacks spreads from Russia across the globe.* Retrieved from http://www.enca.com/technology/new-wave-of-cyber-attacks-spreads-from-russia-across-globe

eNews Channel Africa. (2017b). *Sweden rattled by massive confidential data leak.* Retrieved from http://www.enca.com/technology/sweden-rattled-by-massive-confidential-data-leak

Evans, B. (2015). *The Importance of Building an Information Security Strategic Plan.* Retrieved from https://securityintelligence.com/the-importance-of-building-an-information-security-strategic-plan/

Federal Bureau of Investigation. (2013). *Internet Crime Report.* Author.

Fin24. (2017). *Alert: Massive cyber attack hits several companies.* Retrieved from http://www.fin24.com/Tech/News/alert-massive-cyber-attack-hits-several-companies-20170627

Finnigan, J. (2017). *Cybercrimes and Cybersecurity Bill introduced in Parliament.* Retrieved from http://www.wylie.co.za/articles/cybercrimes-and-cybersecurity-bill-introduced-in-parliament/

Flinders, K. (2016). *UK government re-announces £1.9bn cybersecurity spend.* Retrieved from http://www.computerweekly.com/news/450402098/UK-government-re-announces-19bn-cybersecurity-spend

Fripp, C. (2014). *South Africa is second most targeted for Phishing Attacks.* Retrieved from IT News Africa website: http://www.itnewsafrica.com/2014/04/south-africa-is-second-most-targeted-for-phishing-attacks/

Fripp, C. (2015). *Why the draft cybercrimes bill should concern South Africans*. Retrieved from http://www.htxt.co.za/2015/09/14/why-the-draft-cybercrimes-bill-should-concern-south-africans/

Gemalto. (2017). *Breach Level Index Report 2016*. US: Author.

Giles, J. (2016). *King IV Code and IT Governance*. Retrieved from https://www.michalsons.com/blog/king-iv-code-and-it-governance/18691

Gill, S., & Bokhari, B. (2016). *Technology and Sourcing Alert*. Retrieved from https://www.cliffe-dekkerhofmeyr.com/export/sites/cdh/en/news/publications/2016/Technology/downloads/Technology-and-Sourcing-Alert-11-May-2016.pdf

Govloop. (2014). *Your Cybersecurity Crash Course*. Retrieved from http://img.en25.com/Web/GovDeliveryInc/%7B85bade5e-e97f-49d4-8c74-3aacea547259%7D_Your-Cybersecurity-Crash-Course2.pdf?elq=~~eloqua.type--emailfield.syntax--recipientid~~&elqCampaignId=~~eloqua.type--campaign.campaignid--0.fieldname--id~~

Ha, T. (2017). *Ensuring Information Security in 4th Industrial Revolution*. Retrieved from https://www.vietnambreakingnews.com/2017/04/ensuring-information-security-in-4th-industrial-revolution/

Harduth, N., & Sampson, L. (2017). *A Review of the King IV Report on Corporate Governance*. Retrieved from http://www.werksmans.com/assets/pdf/061741%20WERKSMANS%20king%20iv%20booklet.pdf

Hubeschle, A. (2011). *The Dark Side of the Internet: Cybercrime*. Retrieved from http://www.issafrica.org/iss-today/the-dark-side-of-the-internet-cybercrime

ICSPA. (2012). *Government needs to address cybersecurity at top level*. Retrieved from https://www.icspa.org/media/icspa-news/icspa-news-publications/p/6/article/government-needs-to-address-cybersecurity-at-top-level-23/abp/7/

Institute of Directors South Africa. (2016). *KING IV*. Johannesburg: Author.

International Organization for Standardization. (2017). *ISO/IEC 27000 family - Information security management systems*. Retrieved from https://www.iso.org/isoiec-27001-information-security.html

ISACA. (2013). *CISM Review Manual 2013*. Author.

IT-Online. (2016). *Kenya cyber attacks growing in sophistication*. Retrieved from http://it-online.co.za/2016/12/07/kenya-cyber-attacks-growing-in-sophistication/

IT News Africa. (2017). *2016 Breach Level Index Shows 86% Rise in Data Breaches*. Retrieved from http://www.itnewsafrica.com/2017/03/2016-breach-level-index-shows-86-rise-in-data-breaches/

Ixia. (2014). *Cyber Range: Improving Network Defense and Security Readiness*. Retrieved from http://info.ixiacom.com/rs/ixiacom/images/915-6729-01-Cyber-Range.pdf

Jeffery, J. (2017). *Media briefing on Cybercrimes and Cybersecurity Bill*. Retrieved from http://www.gov.za/speeches/cybercrimes-and-cybersecurity-bill-19-jan-2017-0000%20

Jump, S. (2015). *Keeping your Organisation Safe wherever you are*. Paper presented at the National Science and Technology, South Africa: National Science and Technology Forum.

Kirkpatrick, D. (2014). *Can Government Get a Better Grip on Tech?* Retrieved from Techonomy website: http://techonomy.com/2014/11/can-government-get-better-grip-tech/

Kotoky, A. (2017). *Cyberattack reaches Asia as new targets hit by ransomware.* Retrieved from http://www.fin24.com/Tech/News/cyberattack-reaches-asia-as-new-targets-hit-by-ransomware-20170628

Kudelski, A. (2016). *The dark side of the Fourth Industrial Revolution.* Retrieved from https://www.weforum.org/agenda/2016/01/the-dark-side-of-the-fourth-industrial-revolution/

Kumar, A. (2016). *As India Gears Up for Cybersecurity Challenges, Threats Are Multiplying.* Retrieved from https://securityintelligence.com/as-india-gears-up-for-cybersecurity-challenges-threats-are-multiplying/

Lowman, S. (2016). *WEF 2016: 4th Industrial Revolution. 5mn jobs, women in the firing line.* Retrieved from http://www.biznews.com/wef/davos-2016/2016/01/18/wef-2016-4th-industrial-revolution-5mn-jobs-women-in-the-firing-line/

Lye, D. (2017). *The Fourth Industrial Revolution and Challenges for Government.* Retrieved from http://www.gereports.com/fourth-industrial-revolution-challenges-government/

Lyons, J. (2013). *How can Governments be motivated to collaborate internationally to mitigate cybercrime effectively?* Retrieved from https://www.icspa.org/uploads/media/John_Lyons_Chief_Executive_ICSPA_GES_Kiel_2013_Challenge.pdf

Lyra, M., & Simoes, J. (2015). Checking the Maturity of Security Policies for Information and Communication. *ISACA, 2,* 48–53.

MacAskill, E., & Syal, R. (2017). *Cyber-attack on UK parliament: Russia is suspected culprit.* Retrieved from https://www.theguardian.com/politics/2017/jun/25/cyber-attack-on-uk-parliament-russia-is-suspected-culprit

Mahlobo, D. (2017). *State Security Agency Budget Vote 2017/18.* Pretoria: State Security Agency.

Masters, G. (2017). *Loss from cybercrime exceeded $1.3B in 2016.* Retrieved from https://www.scmagazine.com/loss-from-cybercrime-exceeded-13b-in-2016-fbi-report/article/671047/

McKinley, D. (2003). *The State of Access to Information in South Africa.* Retrieved from http://www.ritecodev.co.za/csvrorig/docs/trc/stateofaccess.pdf

Meads, D. (2017). *Here's how Africa can take advantage of 4th Industrial Revolution.* Retrieved from http://ewn.co.za/2017/05/02/here-s-how-africa-can-take-advantage-of-the-fourth-industrial-revolution#

Mercer, C. (2017). *What is a DDoS attack? What happens during a DDoS attack.* Retrieved from http://www.techworld.com/security/how-does-ddos-attack-work-3659197/

Mokati, N. (2016). *Panic hits as Anonymous hack SA sites.* Retrieved from http://www.iol.co.za/news/politics/panic-hits-as-anonymous-hack-sa-sites-1984103

Montresor, F. (2016). *The 7 technologies changing your world.* Retrieved from https://www.weforum.org/agenda/2016/01/a-brief-guide-to-the-technologies-changing-world/

Moorad, Z. (2011). *Local business 'underinsured against hacking'.* Retrieved from http://mg.co.za/article/2011-06-21-local-business-underinsured-against-hacking

Muggah, R., Diniz, G., & Glenny, M. (2014). *Brazil doubles down on cybersecurity.* Retrieved from https://www.opendemocracy.net/robert-muggah-gustavo-diniz-misha-glenny/brazil-doubles-down-on-cybersecurity

Myburgh, F., & De Costa, A. (2017). *The key differences between King III and King IV.* Retrieved from http://www.polity.org.za/article/the-key-differences-between-king-iii-and-king-iv-2017-01-11

Naidoo, S. (2016). *SA losing billions each year to cyber-crime.* Retrieved from http://www.sabc.co.za/news/a/d2825f804c7c4a338a38db3b0fa74342/SA-losing-billions-each-year-to-cyber-crime-20160421

National Institute of Standards and Technology. (2012). *Computer Security Incident Handling Guide.* US: Author.

Oliver Wyman. (2017). *Cyber-risk in Asia-Pacific.* Retrieved from http://www.oliverwyman.com/content/dam/oliver-wyman/v2/publications/2017/may/Cyber_Risk_In_Asia-Pacific_The_Case_For_Greater_Transparency.pdf

Organization of American States, & Symantec. (2014). *Latin American + Caribbean Cybersecurity Trends.* Retrieved from https://www.thegfce.com/initiatives/c/cybersecurity-initiative-in-oas-member-states

Palo Alto Networks. (2017). *What is a Denial of Service Attack DoS?* Retrieved from https://www.paloaltonetworks.com/cyberpedia/what-is-a-denial-of-service-attack-dos

Patrick, H. (2016). *Security Information Flow in the Public Sector: KZN Health & Education* (Unpublished doctoral dissertation). School of Management Information Technology & Governance, South Africa.

Perry Johnson Registrars. (2017). *What is an Information Security Management System?* Retrieved from http://www.pjr.com/standards/iso-27001/information-security-management-system

Petterson, D. (2016). *Critical Infrastructure Protection Bill under fire.* Retrieved from http://www.infrastructurene.ws/2016/07/06/critical-infrastructure-protection-bill-under-fire/

Pillay, K. (2017). *Cybercrime and Cybersecurity Bill.* Retrieved from http://www.polity.org.za/article/cybercrime-and-cybersecurity-bill-2017-04-06

Ponemon Institute. (2017). *Cost of Data Breach Study.* Author.

PricewaterhouseCoopers. (2013). *Future of Government.* Author.

Prisecaru, P. (2016). Challenges of the Fourth Industrial Revolution. *Knowledge Horizons - Economics, 8*(1), 57-62.

Qasaymeh, K. (2015). *The Effectiveness of South Africa's Legislative Framework Governing Cybersecurity in Nuclear Facilities.* Paper presented at the National Science and Technology Forum, Gauteng, South Africa.

Rainys, R. (2006). Network and Information Security. Assessments and Incidents Handling. *Electronics and Electrical Engineering, 6*(70), 69–74.

Right2Know. (2016). *R2K briefing: the draft Critical Infrastructure Protection Bill*. Retrieved from http://www.r2k.org.za/2016/06/14/briefing-draft-critical-infrastructure-protection-bill/

Ross. (2014). Cyber Recovery Preparation. *Journal of ISACA, 3*, 3-5.

Rwakenya, E. (2017). *Kenya set to pass cyber-crime bill as east Africa seeks legal harmony*. Retrieved from https://www.scmagazineuk.com/kenya-set-to-pass-cyber-crime-bill-as-east-africa-seeks-legal-harmony/article/652047/

Schwab, K. (2016a). *Four leadership principles for the Fourth Industrial Revolution*. Retrieved from https://www.weforum.org/agenda/2016/10/four-leadership-principles-for-the-fourth-industrial-revolution/

Schwab, K. (2016b). *The Fourth Industrial Revolution: what it means, how to respond*. Retrieved from https://www.weforum.org/agenda/2016/01/the-fourth-industrial-revolution-what-it-means-and-how-to-respond/

Security Breach. (2015) In *BusinessDictionary online*. Retrieved from http://www.businessdictionary.com/definition/security-breach.html

Sommer, P., & Brown, I. (2011). Reducing Systemic Cybersecurity Risk (IFP/WKP/FGS(2011)3). OECD.

State Security Agency. (1996). *Minimum Information Security Standards*. Pretoria: Author.

State Security Agency. (2010). *The Protection of Information Bill Pretoria*. Department of Communication.

Tamarkin, E. (2014). *South Africa must pay attention to cybercrime*. Retrieved from http://www.issafrica.org/crimehub/news/south-africa-must-pay-more-attention-to-cybercrime

Techcentral. (2016). *Hacktivists breach Armscor website*. Retrieved from https://techcentral.co.za/hacktivists-breach-armscor-website/66835/

TechFinancials. (2016). *Data breaches cost South Africa R28,6 million*. Retrieved from https://techfinancials.co.za/2016/07/26/data-breaches-cost-south-africa-r286-million/

Tengimfene, N. (2013). *Media Statement on Progress made by the Justice, Crime Preventation & Security Cluster in the Fight Against Corruption*. Pretoria: Government Communications and Information System.

Teravainen, T. (2016). *Information security (infosec)*. Retrieved from http://searchsecurity.techtarget.com/definition/information-security-infosec

Thawte. (2014). *Top 10 Website Security Security Myths Revealed*. Author.

The Huffington Post. (2017). *Department of Basic Education Website Hacked*. Retrieved from http://www.huffingtonpost.co.za/2017/06/29/department-of-basic-education-website-hacked_a_23007370/?utm_hp_ref=za-news

Thomas, G. (2017). *Industrial Revolution and the potential challenges and opportunities for Wales*. Retrieved from https://assemblyinbrief.wordpress.com/2017/03/31/march-of-the-robots-the-fourth-industrial-revolution-and-the-potential-challenges-and-opportunities-for-wales/

TraceSecurity. (2012). *Five Critical Components for a Strategic and Risk-Based Information Security Program for SMBs*. Author.

Tripwire. (2014). *Russia Announces Development of Cyber Military Unit*. Retrieved from Portland: https://www.tripwire.com/state-of-security/latest-security-news/russia-announces-development-cyber-war-military-unit/

UK Construction Online. (2017). *Scottish government outlines new digital strategy*. Retrieved from https://www.ukconstructionmedia.co.uk/news/scotland-outline-new-digital-strategy/

Vaid, S., & Holme, G. (2016). *Fourth industrial revolution poses new security challenges*. Retrieved from http://www.channelwise.co.za/fourth-industrial-revolution-poses-new-security-challenges/

Van Zyl. (2016). *Controversial cybersecurity bill gets Cabinet approval*. Retrieved from http://www.fin24.com/Tech/News/controversial-cybersecurity-bill-gets-cabinet-approval-20161212

Venktess, K. (2017). *SA ICT spend to exceed R287m*. Retrieved from http://www.fin24.com/Budget/sa-ict-spend-to-exceed-r287m-20170222

Wainaina, E. (2016). *Kenya Government to boost Cybersecurity efforts with Kshs. 13 Billion Investment*. Retrieved from http://www.techweez.com/2016/01/28/cybersecurity-in-kenya/

Wolfpack. (2013). *The South African Cyber Threat 2012/3 Barometer*. Author.

KEY TERMS AND DEFINITIONS

Digital: Is the introduction of electronic technology.
Mitigation: Is a process that reduces the exposure of a risk.

Chapter 15
Inducing Six-Word Stories From Curated Text Sets to Anticipate Cyberwar in 4IR

Shalin Hai-Jew
Kansas State University, USA

ABSTRACT

From curated "cyberwar" text sets (from government, mainstream journalism, academia, and social media), six-word stories are computationally induced (using word frequency counts, text searches, word network analysis, word clustering, and other means), supported by post-induction human writing. The resulting inducted six-word stories are used to (1) describe and summarize the underlying textual information (to enable a bridge to a complex topic); (2) produce insights about the underlying textual information and related in-world phenomena; and (3) answer particular research questions. These resulting six-word stories are analyzed along multiple dimensions: data sources (government, journalism, academia, and social media), expert calls-and-crowd responses, and by time periods (pre-cyberwar and cyberwar periods). The efficacy of this six-word story induction process is evaluated, and the extracted six-word stories are applied to cyberwar potentials during the Fourth Industrial Revolution (4IR).

INTRODUCTION

A cyberwar collection of six-word stories follows:

- Cyberwar rules ≠ defined clear explicit
- **Cyberwar:** Milliseconds are of the essence
- **Cyberwar:** Stealth weapons to exploit weaknesses
- **Cyberwar:** Stealthy devastating fast, mysterious complex
- **Cyberwar Salvo:** Damage done b4 uknowit
- **4IR Cyberwar:** Humans in the loop
- **All-Seasons Cyberwar:** Running "hot" and "cold"

DOI: 10.4018/978-1-5225-4763-1.ch015

- **Cyberwar:** On/off toggle, high-low dial, no-switch

- **Cyberwar:**
  - Hand-to-hand,
  - Team-to-team,
  - Techno-to-techno,
  - System-to-system,
  - Nation-State-To-Nation-State

- **Cyberwar Cyber-Physical Confluence:** Code to boom!
- **Cyberwar:** ID who & return address
- **Cyberwar Source:** Fingerprinted seeable legally-responsible
- **Cyberwar Collateral Damage:** You and me
- **Cyberwarriors:** Professionally paranoid, *sub rosa,* attentive
- **Cyberweapons Design:** Compartmented, precise, tested *ad nauseam*
- **Cyberweapons Design:** Working with industry occasionally
- **Cyberweapons**: Getting ahead of response curve
- **#Cyberwar:** Exploring "dog that doesn't bark."
- Stuxnet $\geq$ hard-power violence and mayhem
- **Stuxnet:** Hit || on nuclear ambitions
- **Stuxnet:** Cyberwar Rubicon crossed…with style

- **Realpolitik Cyberthreat Modeling:** Advanced persistent threats
- States militaries corporations media = hard targets;
- You and me = just a means-to-an-end

The above six-word stories about cyberwar and the harnessing of cyber capabilities for higher-intensity human conflicts between nation-states were drafted after a close human reading of hundreds of documents, research articles, journalistic articles, student research works, and social media accounts about cyberwar, and they focus on particular facets of cyberwar. These pithy stories were manually created as a back-of-the-napkin exercise to partially represent the objectives of this chapter, namely, the creation of partially computer-induced six-word stories from curated "cyberwar" text sets. More formally, cyberwar refers to the following:

…conducting, and preparing to conduct, military operations according to information-related principles. It means disrupting if not destroying the information and communications systems, broadly defined to include even military culture, on which an adversary relies to "know" itself: who it is, where it is, what it can do when, why it is fighting, which threats to counter first, etc. It means trying to know all about an adversary while keeping it from knowing much about oneself. It means turning the "balance of information and knowledge" in one's favor, especially if the balance of forces is not. It means using knowledge so that less capital and labor may have to be expended. (Arquilla & Ronfeldt, Spring 1993, p. 30)

Ultimately, the idea is to extract six-word stories that may be sufficiently insightful, abstract, and general, to transfer into the future: namely, how cyberwar may manifest in the Fourth Industrial Revolution (4IR). Six-word stories are stories comprised of six words, somewhat mediated by punctuation and symbols. As stories, they are suggestive of narrative tensions, dramas, problems to be addressed, states of the world, ironies, emotional intensities, and other very human observations. People write stories for people. While such brief stories are often personal, they have been applied to truisms of the human condition. While brief, six-word stories may be applied to complex and serious topics at more global levels. It is in that spirit that they are applied to cyberwar. In some cases, the meanings may be superficial, light and insubstantial. They may aim for wit. They may aim for a laugh. Six-word stories should be read a little like small puzzles, with readers having to do a little work to understand the references and to know something about the topic to see (hear) the reverberations. Their brevity ensures over-focus on particular single elements, so these have to be referential and have to evoke information from outside of the story.

In this context, the aim is not to particularly predict how technologies will evolve nor how humans will express their conflict and extreme competition with each other, within the constraints and enablements of technologies, cultures, laws, and other factors. These six-word stories are explored to see how well technological methods may be used to identify dynamics and terms-of-interest in cyberwar and how well the methods of such six-word story writing may be harnessed for the expressive and analytic purpose.

***

Klaus Schwab, founder and executive chairman of the World Economic Forum, observed the advent of the Fourth Industrial Revolution in 2016 and envisioned this age as defined by emerging technologies in "artificial intelligence (AI), robotics, the internet of things (IoT), autonomous vehicles, 3D printing, nanotechnology, biotechnology, materials science, energy storage and quantum computing, to name a few" (Schwab, 2016, p. 1). At this moment, several years into the concept and reality of the Fourth Industrial Revolution (4IR), the bare outlines of the future are not yet clear and may not come into clarity for many years. A generic explanation describes "a range of new technologies that are fusing the physical, digital and biological worlds, and impacting all disciplines, economies and industries" ("Fourth Industrial Revolution," Oct. 16, 2017). These technological advancements are expected to affect mass-scale economies and work lives, human health and longevity, human lifestyles, and how people make meaning. Figure 1, "A Summary View of the Four Industrial Revolutions," offers a sense of these macro changes over time.

Figure 1. A Summary View of the Four Industrial Revolutions

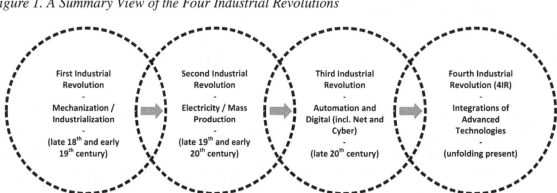

A Summary View of the Four Industrial Revolutions

In terms of understanding what the future may hold, there are initial efforts by projecting technologies linearly into space-time and making assumptions about human responses. There are analogical arguments to understand what the future may portend, and there are shaping efforts using the levers of laws, public debate and opinion, funding, education, development of expertise, and leadership. The insights are piecemeal and in general, doubt because there are so much dynamism and so many players in this space. There are many "known unknowns" and plenty of "unknown unknowns." To ask what "cyberwar" may look like in this near-future space is challenging because "cyber" will manifest in a range of different ways as likely will "war." Warfighting from ancient times has always involved the manipulation of information and the deployment of spies. In recent years, targeting computers for warfighting aims has been a constant part of this space. What is the difference is the deployment of cyber in so many aspects of modern life and the critical dependencies on cyber, which has resulted in the focus on cyber as its own "domain" for military attention?

Treating cyberspace as an operational domain is an excellent idea, but doing so quickly reveals differences between internet conflict and warfare on land, sea, in the air, or in space. Deterring or even defending against cyberattack may prove difficult, as others have argued, but it will prove much harder still for an attacker to figure out how to benefit from internet aggression unless cyberattacks occur in conjunction with attacks in other domains. (Gartzke, Fall 2013, p. 44)

CYBERWAR IN 4IR

A typical brainstorm list of questions—without regard for their practical answerability—might include the following ones about cyberwar in 4IR:

Cyberwar and How It May Manifest

- What will cyberwar look like in 4IR? Why?
- What will winning a cyberwar look like? What will losing a cyberwar look like? What will a truce in a cyberwar look like? How enforceable would such truces be?
- What does cyberwar look like when used as "soft" power? When used as "hard" power? What will cyberwar look like in the cyber-physical confluence and cyber-physical and cyber-human and cyber-animal and cyber-environment systems?
- What are technological advancements of special concern for cyberwar in 4IR?
- What are ways to prepare the coming (current) battlespace?

Understanding Others and the Self

- What are likely acceptable ways for adversaries to employ cyberwar based on their culture, thinking, leaders, and other relevant factors? What are known capabilities? What are cyberweapons stockpiles? What are capability gaps? What would targets of interest be for various potential adversaries in a cyberwar? Why?
- What are likely acceptable ways for one's own country to employ cyberwar based on culture, civilian and military thinking, leadership, and other relevant factors?

- What would targets of interest be, and why?
- How would accurate attributions be made to understand the originating attacker(s)? What are levels of confidence needed before attribution is made? Why?
- If attacked via cyberwar, how would likely adversaries respond? Not respond? Why?
- If one is attacked via cyberwar, how would one likely respond? Not respond? Why?
- Who are likely adversaries, and what threats do they pose? What will likely paths they take to achieve their aims? What are ways to defend against such approaches?

Cyberweapons

- What will cyberweapons look like in 4IR? What will their capabilities be? How will these be deployed? How will these be deployed in various combinations with other weapons and efforts (for different effects)? Why?
- What are ways that cyber can be employed in a "cold war"? A "hot war"?
- What sorts of cyberweapons should be "stockpiled"? For how long? What sorts of technological capabilities should a society develop? What sorts of human talent should be cultivated and developed?
- How can the various Internet of Things (IoT) systems, transportation systems, automotive systems, health systems, electronic grid systems, and others…be compromised? How can various cyber systems be compromised in the context of cyberwar?

Awareness

- What will cyber forensics techniques look like in 4IR? What will cyber defence tools look like? How will they be deployed? How will these deployed in various combinations (for different effects)? Why?
- Where will you look for indicators of a cyberattack? How will you lay tripwires and sensors to acquire early warning of cyberattacks? How will you continue monitoring evolving cyberattacks and their effects?
- What are ways to assess how far potential adversaries are in their cyberwar toolkit? Thinking?

Cyberwarrior Skills

- What skills will cyberwarriors need in 4IR? What are tendencies that will hurt cyberwarriors in 4IR? Why? What are tendencies that will help cyberwarriors in 4IR? Why?
- What are some ways (diplomatic and others) to de-escalate tensions between peoples to head off cyberwar possibly? Mitigate cyberwar?
- What are the various levels of intensities in cyberwarfare? Why? What do escalations look like? De-escalations?
- Are there ways to pull back a cyberattack once started? How so? How not?

Security Postures

- What are ways to create a credible defence against 4IR cyberattack and cyberwar?

- What are ways to create resilience against cyberwar in 4IR?
- What are ways to harden important infrastructure against cyberwar in 4IR?

Attack Postures

- What are effective attack postures for cyberwar in 4IR?
- What are ways to finesse this to harness political leadership and diplomacy as well?

Cyberwar Frameworks?

- What are important ethical frameworks to apply to the starting, maintaining, and ending of cyberwar?
- What are some important legal frameworks to apply to the starting, maintaining, and ending of cyberwar?
- What are important strategic frameworks to apply to the starting, maintaining, and ending of cyberwar? What are related tactical frameworks?
- What are important technological frameworks to apply to the starting, maintaining, and ending of cyberwar?

And others…

If there are risks to reasoning linearly…and too granularly…and in any restrictive future predictive way, is it possible to take what is known now about "cyberwar" (from some of the best minds thinking today on the topic in an open and public space) and extract foundational insights in abstract six-word stories to expand into 4IR? Also, is it possible to computational and manually induce usable six-word stories from four curated text sets from (1) government, (2) mainstream journalism, (3) academia, and (4) social media, using word frequency counts, text searches, word network analysis, word clustering, and other computational means) and apply post-induction human writing for edited six-word stories? Can these stories then be to used to…

1. Describe and summarize the underlying textual information (to enable a bridge to a complex topic);
2. Produce insights about the underlying textual information and related in-world phenomena; and
3. Answer particular research questions.

Can the resulting six-word stories be analyzed based on data sources (government, journalism, academia, and social media), expert calls-and-crowd responses, and by time periods (pre-cyberwar and post-cyberwar periods)? How efficacious is this process, using contemporaneous technologies? How well can the extracted six-word stories be applied to cyberwar potentials during the Fourth Industrial Revolution?

Framed as hypotheses, the main explorations are as follows:

Hypothesis 1: Six-word stories may be computationally and manually induced from curated text sets about cyberwar (sourced from the government, mainstream journalism, academia, and social media).

    Hypothesis 1a: The six-word stories may describe and summarize the underlying textual information to succinctly bridge readers to a complex topic.

Hypothesis 1b: The six-word stories may produce insights about the underlying textual information and related in-world phenomena.

Hypothesis 1c: The six-word stories may be used to answer particularly focused research questions.

Hypothesis 2: Six-word stories may be induced about cyberwar expert "calls" (through government, mainstream journalism, and academic text sets) and non-expert "responses" (through social media text sets) to analyze the communications cycle.

Hypothesis 3: Six-word stories may be induced about human thinking about cyberwar in the pre-cyberwar period (1987 – 2006) and the current cyberwar period (2007 – present).

Hypothesis 4: Induced six-word stories about cyberwar may inform some truisms to carry forward to the Fourth Industrial Revolution (4IR) space.

Next, a review of the literature follows. Then, the induction of six-word stories based on four source types ensues. Six-word stories are induced from the pre-cyberwar period (1987 – 2006) and the current cyberwar period (2007 onwards). Then, some induced six-word stories are analyzed for their potential use in projecting what cyberwar may look like in 4IR.

To summarize, this work explores the process of inducing six-word stories about a topic using both computational text analysis means and follow-on human editing means. To get a sense of how brief six-word stories are, some samples are available in the "Sidebar: What do six-word stories about cybersecurity look like?"

***

What Do Six-Word Stories About Cybersecurity Look Like?

ILoveYou * Titan Rain * Heartbleed * OPM * Stuxnet/DuQu/Gauss/Flame

@socialmedia: "Sell you, sell me,…naturally" (to the tune of Lionel Richie's "Say You, Say Me")

cyberfraud: 0s and 1s to 0s

cyber-overshare: everything but the Soc Number

"I" in #selfie: "the tell" to "tell-all."

2016 U.S. Presidential Election: Vote Russian

cybermemory $\infty \neq$ memorable nor relevant

hostile cyber-takeovers: from botnets to human-nets

singularity: woke humans and woke machines

inattention and unthinkingness: the road to cybercompromise?

airgapping…but air still a medium

in place and ready: insider cyberthreat

"trust but…": friendlies a cyberattack surface

Head? Heart? Cyberromance is dead, hotstuff

Surface Web / Deep Web / Dark Web

Social engineering: friend me click here

***

Some Delimitations

This work shows a first-run at the induction of six-word stories by a combined computational text analysis and human writer approach. How well this works for a topic as serious as cyberwar is unknown, and this approach is not considered a replacement for other analytical methods—but rather something that may complement and augment known current techniques and as a way to broaden the human imagination, particularly when applying concepts into the near-future and the far-future. There are many factors that can affect outcomes: how texts are curated, how social media datasets are extracted from the data providers, how texts are cleaned, how resulting data visualizations are interpreted, the analytical software used, and the author hand in creating the six-word stories. While the resulting induced six-word stories are minimalistic, the process of arriving at these are non-trivial. The sizes of the text sets are fairly large, and the computational processing is demanding on regular workplace laptops and desktop machines.

Besides the difficulty of actualizing this work, it may be difficult to validate/invalidate the six-word stories. Both "cyberwar" and "Fourth Industrial Revolution" (4IR) are lightly defined currently, and definitions and understandings for both phenomena are evolving.

The computational text analyses are reproducible; however, the author hand in the stringing together of the excerpted words may be highly original and less reproducible, less repeatable. What is missed in this approach will be insights available from close-in analysis and maybe novel ideas (unless the human reader is careful in checking the long tail of a word frequency curve for what is discussed in the margins). A critical assumption is that whoever uses this process has to have read the literature in depth-first because the background informs the writing of the six-word stories. To write with extreme brevity requires some expertise. Ultimately, this approach is about collecting summary insights based on large curated text sets for meaning-making. Where nonsensical words emerge from computational text analysis processes, those are positive because they may expand human thinking and imagination about the topic.

REVIEW OF THE LITERATURE

"Cyber" has been around longer than many think. The first word transmitted on an electronic communications network was "Lo" in 1969, by a scientist in the University of California, Los Angeles, (UCLA) trying to connect to a receiving computer at Stanford University. The message was supposed to be "log" except for the receiving computer's crash (Singer & Friedman, 2014, pp. 16 – 17). The U.S. Advanced Research Projects Agency Network (ARPANET) started work on the Internet in 1983 when it adopted TCP/IP protocols to connect network devices to the nascent Internet. "Cyberspace" was first mentioned in a short story "Burning Chrome" (1982) by Canadian science fiction author William Gibson, who is thought to have created his term from Norbert Wiener's concept of "cybernetics" from his 1948 text (Rid, 2016). The World Wide Web (built on the Internet) was first conceptualized in 1991 by Tim Berners-Lee, and the first web page went live in 2014 ("History of the World Wide Web," Nov. 8, 2017). Security was not a core feature of the Internet or the Web. Early software had abysmal security features. There were so many underlying vulnerabilities in the "physics" of the Internet and Web and the monoculture in the adoption of ubiquitous software (Lucas, 2015, pp. 173 – 188), and in human susceptibilities to social engineering, that it would be hard to imagine that people would not take advantage of this situation.

About cyberwar. "Cyberwar" ("cyber warfare" or "cyber war") has been debated for decades but without a consensus definition. An early work ranked "forms of harm" in cyberspace on a harm continuum: from probes, computer network exploitation (CNE), "implants in advance of attacks," costs in "small $ amounts," costs in clean-up, costs in "large $ amounts", the creation of casualties, affecting military operations, and interfering with nuclear systems (in that general order) along a "spectrum of seriousness (Libicki, 2009, p. 181).

For many, cyberwar is an escalation of a cyberattack to a higher level of seriousness. A cyber-escalation ladder reads (in ascending order):

- **Rung One:** Cyber vandalism and 'hacktivism'
- **Rung Two:** Cyber crime
- **Rung Three:** Cyber espionage
- **Rung Four:** Cyber terrorism
- **Rung Five:** Cyberwar (Cavelty, 2010, p. 1)

The author describes the fifth rung: "Refers to the use of computers to disrupt the activities of an enemy country, especially deliberate attacks on communication systems. In military terms, such activities are known as Computer Network Attack (CNA), a concept that is part of the official information operations doctrine. Two types need to be distinguished: CNA as a tactical-operational means in the context of an overall operation or CNA as a strategic stand-alone tool" (Cavelty, 2010, p. 1). Cyberwar is thought to factor in middle-range conflicts (MRCs) and high-intensity conflicts (HICs) and nation-state actors. Another suggests that cyberwar involves "aggressive operations in cyberspace, against military targets, against a State or its society: (Ventre, 2011, p. ix). There has been a range of definitions of cyber war based on different authors and their respective disciplines and evolutions over time (Hughes & Colarik, 2017).

In the larger context of warfare, cyberwar is nowhere near the top of human escalation: "Cyberwar does not sit on top of the escalation ladder, or even close to the top. Thus, it is not necessarily the last word between states" (Libicki, Spring 2011, p. 134). Cyber capabilities challenge adversaries to tighten up their information systems under threat of having them compromised during heated hostilities: "Building up our offensive capabilities is a confidence game. It says to those who would compete in our league: are you confident enough in your cyberwar skills that you can build your military to rely on information systems and the machines that take their orders?" (Libicki, Spring 2011, p. 145)

Fitting offensive cyber into an overall strategy is part of the challenge. One approach is to harness cyber for espionage for leverage (Gartzke, Fall 2013, p. 46). There are signs that cyber weapons are being pre-placed pre-emptively in order to shape the battlespace, such as with the placement of so-called "logic bombs" on electronic network grids to cause failures in case of escalations in nation-state tensions, and even direct intrusions and "hands-on access to power grid operations" (Greenberg, Sept. 6, 2017). Cyber may also be deployed in hybrid ways, mixing cyber with other forms of attacks:

If the ultimate weapons of mass destruction, nuclear weapons, and the supreme weapons of soft power, information warfare, are commingled during a crisis, the product of the two may be an entirely unforeseen and unwelcome hybrid. Crises by definition are exceptional events. No Cold War crisis took place between states armed with advanced information weapons and with nuclear weapons. But given the durability of the two trends—interest in infowar and nuclear weapons—the potential for overlap and its implications for nuclear crisis management deserve further study and policy consideration. The discussion below proceeds toward that end, by looking at relevant concepts and examples including information warfare, crisis management, the link between cyberwar and nuclear crisis management, and its implications. (Cimbala, Spring 2011, p. 117)

"Netwar" refers to "societal-level ideational conflicts waged in part through internetted (sic) modes of communication" and includes "nations or societies" and does not generally include military (Arquilla & Ronfeldt, Spring 1993, pp. 27 - 28) or state actors (Gartzke, Fall 2013, p. 46) in the conflict. There is also a general split between "soft" cyberpower as in information-based public diplomacy and "hard" cyberpower as in cyber weapons that may destroy physical infrastructures (Bronk, 2013, p. 13). While "netwars" are not generally thought to include violence, they might on occasion in "the worst of cases" and result in "low-intensity conflict scenarios" (Arquilla & Ronfeldt, Spring 1993, p. 29). A major policy challenge is how to address "cyberwar" as an "act of war" and how to engage in proper measure and for the proper desired outcomes. One current definition reads:

Cyber warfare involves the actions by a nation-state or international organization to attack and attempt to damage another nation's computers or information networks through, for example, computer viruses or denial-of-service attacks. ("Cyber Warfare," 2017)

A nation-state requires what political scientist Dwight Waldo's five factors or the five "pillars of any society and government" for it to function: legitimacy (legitimized government and ability to deliver "good society"), authority ("the ability to implement policy"), knowledge management (proper handling and utilizing knowledge "within the bureaucracy"), control ("the ability to control what we want to control in the bureaucracy"), and confidence ("trust people have that government delivers the expected benefits and the removal of fear for the future" (Kallberg, Thuraisingham, & Lakomaa, 2013, p. 213). Societal cyberwar theory suggests that in nation-state targeting that various aspects of governance will be undermined. In their targeting matrix, examples of targets are connected to the factors: legitimacy ("legislature, welfare benefits, classified information"), authority ("law enforcement, local government"), knowledge management ("cadastral data, tax collection"), control ("air-traffic control, railways"), and confidence ("energy providers, retirement funds, public financial support transfers") (Kallberg, Thuraisingham, & Lakomaa, 2013, p. 215). If a society has weaknesses in any of the five pillars, those will be targeted, according to societal cyberwar theory (Kallberg, Thuraisingham, & Lakomaa, 2013, p. 214). In part, this is why having a prepared society and government is so important. Also, leaders of nation-states need to avoid over-reaction to others' provocations and actions—so as not to magnify other nation-states' advantages.

Just the presence of nation-states engaging in cyber for advantage does not mean an aggressive action is an "act of war," which has legal and escalatory implications. For example, cyber has long been used by the main cyber-capable nation-states for espionage, but while the rhetoric about this practice may become heated, this practice is generally accepted as a matter-of-course and not as a reason to escalate into hard power conflict. Cyberattacks and exploitations may be conceptualized on a continuum of escalation, and at some theoretical point, cyber exploits may cross a line to "use of force." There is "no consensus as to when a cyberattack becomes cyberwar" (Feil, 2012, p. 516). Also, calling an act on "cyber" an "act of war" has implications: "The characterization of cyber warfare as an act of war triggers far-reaching consequences as it leads to restrictions on the waging of war" (Döge, Dec. 2010, p. 487).

Cyberwar may challenge the existing domestic regulatory regime for war-making based on the power of the U.S. President by the Constitution, the Supreme Court, and Congress, argue others. This phenomenon may raise questions of foreign relations law, so there are both internal and external legal concerns (Abebe, 2016, p. 1). Because of the potential for misunderstandings in nation-state behavior and some ambiguities in attribution for respective cyberattacks, policymakers have long called for a "digital Geneva Convention" (Tworek, May 9, 2017), so that there may be understood norms for nation-state behaviors (and to inform cost-benefit considerations of taking offensive steps). Internally, there are debates, too, about whether doctrines have to be changed. Some suggest the sufficiency of the law of armed conflict to address cyberwar (Dunlap, Spring 2011), and others argue differently. At present, there are differing rules of engagement by different nations with cyberoffense capabilities (Brose, 2015).

One suggests using the "legal framework for unmanned aerial vehicles (UAVs)" to guide a framework for cyberwar (Feil, 2012, p. 517). Overseeing the military, of course, are duly elected civilians. The decision of how to wage war does fall to civilian decision-makers in the democratic West, and the calculation is generally how to prevail at an acceptable cost.

Based on offense-defense theory, "how state decision makers *perceive* the offense-defense balance plays an important role in determining state behavior, and a contributing role in outcomes" (Huntley, 2016, p. 5589); this is whether their perceptions are accurate and linked to reality or not. M.C. Libicki (2009) suggests that nation-states may end up in a cyberwar either "through deliberate provocation or escalation" (Libicki, 2009, p. 118). Their considerations cannot be a simple one-off with the assumption of first-mover advantage because there are follow-on events, first, second, third, and other orders of effects, and potential (likely) unintended effects.

Deliberate engagement involves a cost-benefit calculus in which engaging results in desirable outcomes for a nation-state; escalation and counter-escalation cycles may result in cyberwar where deterrence fails (and this latter one suggests some degree of accidental miscalculation). Cyberdeterrence measures themselves are seen as not particularly effective at deterring engagement in cyberwar. Given the incentive environment, as seen through a game theory lens, strategic nation-states would do well to engage in cyber to their advantage, undeterred.

Teaching someone a lesson that cyberviolence does not pay by hitting them back harder calls for more aggression; inducing them to reduce their aggression by showing forbearance calls for a calibrated reduction in aggression. One objective that cyberwar cannot have is to disarm, much less destroy, the enemy. In the absence of physical combat, cyberwar cannot lead to the occupation of territory. It is almost inconceivable that a sufficiently vigorous cyberwar can overthrow the adversary's government and replace it with a more pliable one. Ultimately, because cyberwar cannot disarm cyberwarriors, the contest becomes, as the Duke of Wellington is reported as saying, a matter of "who can pound the longest" and takes it better. Perhaps neither can pound long enough or hard enough to do anything more than annoy the other. (Libicki, 2009, p. 119)

For countries with much of its infrastructure and resources connected to cyber, it is incumbent on them to harden or securitize their systems—anything connected to the Web and Internet, and anything digital. After all: "If a cyberwar ensues, it can only be against a state with a good set of targets" (Libicki, 2009, p. 120) or a large "attack surface." The amount of heft the threat of a cyberattack carries also depends on a number of factors (Libicki, 2013). Countries are constantly working to strengthen their defenses (Feil, 2012, p. 513) and identifying weaknesses in others.

R.A. Clarke and R.K. Knake (2010) highlight U.S. vulnerabilities, given their first-in and widespread adoption of cyber, which leaves a wide potential attack surface. They point to the possibility of coming up short even though American scientists were some of the earliest contributors to what would become the Internet and Web:

A nation that has invented the new technology, and the tactics to use it, may not be the victor, if its military is mired in the ways of the past, overcome by inertia, overconfident in the weapons they have grown to love and consider supreme. The originator of the new offensive weaponry may be the loser unless it has also figured out who to defend against the weapon it has shown to the rest of the world. (p. xi)

A number of cybersecurity experts have evoked an "Electronic Pearl Harbor" with the idea that a surprise attack on the then-neutral U.S. during W.W.II was devastating and hugely costly, bringing the U.S. into the Second World War. As a cautionary tale, the concept of a Cyber Pearl Harbor is meant to discourage those in national defence against any lack of vigilance and any failure of the imagination in the cyber realm.

In another perspective, the U.S. is an empire with global reach, and cyberwar is one of the tools it uses to maintain its hegemonic reach:

To sum up America's rise to world power over the past 120 years, imagine three distinct phases precipitated by those endless wars: first, following the Spanish-American War, a brief yet transformative experience with colonial rule in the Caribbean and the Pacific from 1898 to 1935; next, a sudden ascent to global dominion in the decades after World War II; and, finally, a bid to extend that hegemony deep into the twenty-first century through a fusion of cyberwar, space warfare, trade pacts, and military alliances. In the century from the Spanish-American War to the end of the Cold War, Washington had developed a distinctive form of global governance that incorporated aspects of antecedent empires, ancient and modern. This unique US imperium was Athenian in its ability to forge coalitions among allies; Roman in its reliance on legions that occupied military bases across most of the known world; and British in its aspiration to merge culture, commerce, and alliances into a comprehensive system that covered the globe. (McCoy, 2017, p. 21)

Through cyber, a US agency was able to "monitor the entire globe by penetrating just 190 data hubs—an extraordinary economy of energy for both political surveillance and cyberwarfare" (McCoy, 2017, p. 122). Cyberwarfare, of course, is about both defence and offence. Tools created for the one can be used for the other. And defense against cyber involves analogue as well: Can the military still function if some or all advanced technologies are taken out—from cyber and other attacks? Can they conduct the basics of their craft? Can they continue with their logistics? Can they revert to older technologies and methods if the newer ones are taken out?

The risk of cyberattacks has to do with how interconnected, so many elements of modern life are, and cyber is an attack surface that enables broad penetrative reach. Based on imbalances in interests and in vulnerabilities, long-term competitor nations may go to cyber to compete and to take measure of each other's methods (Kozlowski, 2015).

Those who find the drumbeat of threat excessive suggest that some are exaggerating risks for their own ends. The counterpoint? "Cassandras," those who see prophetically but are disbelieved, may be the ones who are seeing a dire situation accurately and should be heard (Clarke & Knake, 2010, pp. 135 – 137). While many of the more dire risks predicted—"in which the lights go out, banking locks up, planes fall from the sky and general mayhem ensues"—other incidences have shown cybersecurity vulnerabilities (Bronk, 2013, pp. 9, 12).

Those who dislike usage of the term "cyberwar" have different reasons. One is that cyberwar is an "empty threat" and not able to wreak the destruction possible through other "kinetic" weapons. Others have argued that cyber is just another tool in the area of information warfare and electronic warfare, and that it shouldn't be treated as something other. Some suggest that cyberwar is how WWIII and / or "future war" will manifest. If cyber can be deployed in a cost-benefit-risk consideration, then cyberwar becomes more of a possibility; however, if considering the context, that cannot be done, that cyberwar becomes much less likely:

A cyberattack, of any of these types, can happen if and only if the attacker can gain more than it loses, even in the face of a kinetic response. This, in turn, reduces the questions to enemy capability, the potential for serious damage from a cyberattack, and the risk of retaliation. In other words, things aren't quite that bad. Really damaging attacks aren't that easy; perpetrating one at a large scale requires many trained people and a fair amount of luck. Small differences in configuration make a very big difference in how an attack must be launched; the attacker needs really good intelligence and weapons customized for each target. (Bellovin, May/June 2013)

"Cyberwar" sounds like hyperbole for some (Blunden, 2010). Some suggest that this phenomenon is promoted to create commercial demands for security products and to attract research funding for cybersecurity. One writes:

There is a significant fault, however, in the theme of the impending cyber apocalypse: it is far from clear that conflict over the internet can actually function as war. Predictions about the nature or significance of cyberwar generally commit a common fallacy in arguing from opportunity to outcome, rather than considering whether something that could happen is at all likely, given the motives of those who can act. Cyber pessimism rests heavily on capabilities (means), with little thought to a companion logic of consequences (ends). Much that could happen in the world fails to occur, largely because those who can act discern no meaningful benefit from initiating a given act. Put another way; advocates have yet to work out how cyberwar enables aggressors to accomplish tasks typically associated with terrestrial military violence. Absent this logic of consequences, cyberwar is unlikely to prove as pivotal in world affairs, and for developed nations, in particular, as many observers seem to believe. (Gartzke, Fall 2013, p. 42)

From most indicators, "cyberwar" is a "growth market," with commercial interests in this concept (Bendrath, 2001). Indeed, in 2015, "the global cybersecurity market of firms offering a smattering of security solutions had surpassed $75 billion, swelling at double-digit rates" (Rid, 2016, p. x).

One author suggests that the 2007 Estonian cyberwar was the touchstone in "western security discourse" that catapulted the awareness of cyberwar threat to the forefront of the public imagination and has shaped how national cybersecurity is enacted:

We argue that an event that occurred in 2007 catalyzed cyberwar's actualization as a new policy object, and has continued to affect the discursive practices materializing cyberwar since 2007.

After a brief genealogy of cyberwar imaginings before 2007, the article interrogates how the 2007 events catalyzed cyberwar's materialization, and the discursive practices that have worked performatively to stabilize and institutionalize a knowledge-power assemblage named cyberwar as a new policy object. In particular, it traces the ways in which the site and situation of cyberwar's birth have affected the emerging apparatuses of cybersecurity, how the event enabled Estonian cybersecurity specialists and political and military elites as "catalyzing agents and shimmering points" in the emerging cyberwar resonance machine, while Tallinn became elevated as a cybersecurity center of calculation, and finally how the events of 2007 have served as a precautionary baseline for the anticipatory actions through which future cyberwars are made present. (Kaiser, 2015, p. 11)

Cyberwar has since "become institutionalized" and material (Kaiser, 2015, pp. 18 - 19) and has informed people's senses of the world, their discussions, their cybersecurity actions, and funding, and the author calls for a critical analysis of "cyberwar" as a "newly ascendant policy object" (Kaiser, 2015, pp. 18 - 19).

There may be positives to using cyberattacks to achieve particular aims, especially if soft power can be used in lieu of violent hard power. Another argument is that cyberattacks may reduce the need for some violence in a hot war:

If cyberattacks reduce the amount of violence inherent in conflict, and if they often take the form of sabotage or espionage, then many officials and commentators who have been warning about the dawn of cyberwar have been ringing false alarms. Digital violence does have implications for ethics and national security strategy, however. Weaponized code, or cyberattacks more generally, can achieve goals that used to require conventional force. The most sophisticated cyberattacks are highly targeted, and cyber-weapons are unlikely to cause collateral damage in the same way conventional weapons do. Therefore, in many situations, the use of computers would be ethically preferable to the use of conventional weapons: a cyberattack might be less violent, less traumatizing, and more limited (Rid, Nov. / Dec. 2013, p. 85)

Interestingly, the idea of "cyberwar" has been around longer than the standing up of cyberspace because of the roles of fictional books and movies. One author cites the following: "Shockwave Rider in 1975 (Lesk 2007: 77), to War Games (1983) and Terminator (1984), capping the period off with the 2007 blockbuster Live Free or Die Hard, which was playing in theaters in Tallinn during the summer of the cyberattacks" (Kaiser, 2015, p. 12). Political and military think tanks also had started exploring cyberwar "in the early 1990s" (Kaiser, 2015, p. 12). Anticipating and planning for risks benefits first movers. J. Arquilla and D. Ronfeldt (1993) coined "cyberwar" in the nonfiction space as an "emergent mode of conflict" (p. 141).

If the "you know it when you see it" approach is sufficient to identify cyberwar, that not only requires "cyberwar" events to have happened in world, to be observed and interpreted by experts, to be publicized through mass media channels, and to be more widely understood as "cyberwar." Based on this simple measure, the first event is thought to have happened in 2007 – 2008, when Russian individuals (of unclear origin—whether "military electronic warriors, patriotic hackers, cyber-crooks" (Hollis, Jan. 6, 2011, p. 2) apparently launched cyberattacks against Estonia in response to their relocating of a Soviet WWII memorial; the cyberattack leveraged distributed denial of service (DDOS) technologies that unplugged Estonia from the Internet for a time (Krebs, 2014, p. 11). This event was mentioned as "what may be the first war in cyberspace" in *The New York Times* (Landler & Markoff, 2007, as cited in Stohl, 2014, p. 91).

In the same year as the Estonian cyberwar, Israeli pilots bombed a nuclear facility being built by North Koreans in Syria in an endeavor labeled Operation Orchard; in this attack, Syrian air defences were blinded through cyber means (Clarke & Knake, 2010, pp. 1 – 11). This latter event combined cyber with air power:

The 2007 Israeli air strike attack on an alleged Syrian nuclear facility illustrates another kind of manipulation. The strike was reportedly accompanied by cyberattack in which the Israelis, perhaps using a mobile platform, manipulated Syrian defence radars to show the situation as normal.4 Instead of a noisy jamming attack that would have alerted the Syrians, air defense radar screens showed the airspace as empty and peaceful, preserving the element of surprise. Astute attackers will use cybertechniques to not only better understand opponents but also degrade the warning and response. (Lewis, Sept. / Oct. 2011, p. 26)

In 2008, Russian entities used cyberweapons to take down military and government networks in Georgia as well as many related to communications and finance (Hollis, Jan. 6, 2011, p. 2). Other "cyberwars" often mentioned include the uses of cyber between Israelis and Palestinians, the U.S. and Israel vs Iran (particularly their nuclear program), Russia and the U.S. and a number of European countries (over various government election meddling), and others. More recently, cyber has been harnessed by nation states—"North Korea, China, the United States, Russia and Israel"—for various actions to promote state interests (Stohl, 2014, p. 92); these include hacking and releasing an international corporation's private data; accessing corporate and military secrets for espionage purposes; destroying information on private company servers; laying the groundwork for future sabotage; deceptively influencing democratic elections (through robot-based impression management and "gaslighting"), and others.

While some see cyber as resulting in a "revolution in military affairs" (RMA), others suggest something closer to a transition and a sense of limits to the destructive capabilities of cyberweapons:

…unlike previous transitions in warfare, cyber is unlikely to immediately multiply the level of destructive power in ways that previous technological innovations did. Because of its reliance on indirect effects, cyber's effects will have a less long-term destructive impact. That is, attacks that change GPS codes or shut down the energy greed would be quite devastating. But they would be nowhere near the destruction visited by explosive-filled bombs and incendiaries upon Dresden or the permanent irradiation of Hiroshima (Singer & Friedman, 2014, p. 132).

No matter how cyber is deployed, there is the sense that "…the weapons and operations in cyberwar will be far less predictable than traditional means" (Singer & Friedman, 2014, p. 132). The formal entry of nation-states into the cyber exploitation realm is thought to change the game because of the number of resources that can be brought to bear on the issue (Kallberg & Thuraisingham, May/June 2013). And further, there is the sense that cyberwar "is becoming increasingly real, urgent, and crucial for national and human security by the day" (Eun & Abmann, 2016, p. 353). This lack of certainty about how warfare in the cyber realm may manifest and the crucial impetus to avoid surprise has meant that various researchers with both scientific knowledge and "malign" imaginations have been at work trying to project how cyberwar may shape out. Unconventional thinking is *de rigueur*. The assumption is that anything connected to cyber is activate-able: humans, technological systems (attached to data centers, communications systems, dams, electrical grids, health implants, GPS, satellites, space stations, and well, pretty much everything). It is telling that de-linking something from the Internet has its terminology, "airgapping," because the default assumption is to go connected and cyber. The approaches have to consider offence-in-depth because various capabilities may be used in combination, including with non-cyber means, to achieve malign effects. Various thinkers are collating insights for cyberwar playbooks (Tinnel, Saydjari, & Farrell, 2002).

Cyber-weapons have evolved over the years. In early days, people apparently wrote simple snippets of code often to cause an effect and to add to the code writer's renown. There was pranksterism, with students wiping each other's work (Bowden, 2011, p. 5). Early weapons were about script kiddies harnessing others' tools and deploying them for the "lulz" or self-amusement and showing off. Then, "zero days" (unknown unpatched vulnerabilities in software) were much more common given the general lack of attention to security in software creators and software companies. As time passed, other types of code were written to break into the system to steal information and money. Early cyber weapons were created for mass effects and were often sold on the Dark Web.

Initially, some nation-states rallied so-called patriotic hackers to send messages to adversaries and to take on other efforts on behalf of state interests, with some level of official deniability. These early efforts involved website defacements and distributed denial of service (DDOS) attacks (Allen & Demehak, March – April 2003, p. 54). Such efforts date back to the late 1990s and early 2000, with Israeli teenage hackers engaging Palestinian and other organizations responding with so-called e-Jihad (Allen & Demehak, March – April 2003, p. 52). Some of these early hacker wars include "Israeli vs Arab/Muslim (Sept 2000), India vs Pakistan, US vs China (April-May 2001), Russian vs Estonia (April-May 2007), etc…)" for state interests (Hollis, Jan. 6, 2011, pp. 2 - 3). Using cyber for political aims was considered especially beneficial for those unable to directly wield hard power; in this case, cyber-enabled some nation-states to engage in asymmetric warfare (Trendle, Apr. 2002), especially given the relative low-cost of attacks balanced against the high-cost of defending networks and recovering from losses (which can range in the billions, such as from "reduced productivity and business downtime" (Jenik, April, 2009, p. 4). For example, the ILOVEYOU virus in 2000 cost $5.5 billion (Bowden, 2011, p. 77).

Initially, a core feature of cyberattacks was its stealth and invisibility—often without identifiable indicators for common users. This sense of invisibility also applies to cyberwar (Flowers & Zeadally, Fall 2014) because there are ways to try to mask the identities of various actors on cyber. In early days, attribution of cyber actors was considered a "hard problem," but this has been apparently solved in many instances sufficient for nation-states to call out bad actors and to pursue legal means to hold those accountable for their actions.

In the U.S., state investment in cyberwar "started around 2006. Today, several intelligence studies claim that more than 140 countries have a cyber weapon development programme" (Kelson, Paganini, Gittins, & Pace, June 25, 2012). In terms of defences, the earliest U.S. military exercise to test network operations was from 1997 and named "Eligible Receiver" (Singer & Friedman, 2014, p. 127). In this effort, NSA Red Team staffers took on the roles of N. Korean and Iranian hackers to attack U.S. critical infrastructures and its communications networks, and the result: the U.S. as "unprepared and defenceless for a cyber attack" (Kaplan, Mar. 7, 2016). There is a need to "play to the edge" in this space by taking "advantage of the entire playing field right up to the sideline markers and endlines" (Hayden, 2016, p. xiv).

Then, newer versions of cyber weapons emerged aimed at surveillance and espionage, and the focus was on stealth and invisibility and unfindability. Another advancement harnessed supervisory control and data acquisition (SCADA) systems to access industrial systems. For example, Stuxnet is regarded as the first real cyberweapon of cyberwar given its finesse in using a reported four zero days and exacting skills to create a weapon that could have stayed hidden and wreaked quiet havoc where it not for somehow making its way outside of a custom context and being identified by multiple cybersecurity researchers. (Stuxnet was apparently designed to sabotage Iranian nuclear centrifuges to hinder—for some months— this illegal weapons program. This non-violent measure was used in lieu of military intervention.)

A more recent cyberweapon was ransomware (a cryptoworm) dubbed WannaCry which "affected more than 230,000 computers in over 150 countries" in 2017 (Nakashima, Dec. 19, 2017). This malware affected computers running the Microsoft Windows operating system ("WannaCry ransomware attack," Dec. 19, 2017) affected hospital systems as well as those of other businesses and prevented access to critical data, which was locked cryptographically until a ransom was paid in Bitcoin cryptocurrency (and often did not release the data even after ransoms were paid). This weapon was attributed to North Korea by the U.S. government's intelligence agencies.

These were bespoke and customized cyber-weapons requiring complex skill sets, testing on expensive and complex testbeds, and likely requiring some cooperation with commercial companies. As weapons, cyber ones have some unusual characteristics, namely "perishability" (becoming "ineffective after a single use") and "obsolescence" (becoming "ineffective without being used at all")…because such weapons are only efficacious as long as systems are unpatched (Huntley, 2016, pp. 5592 - 5593).

Nation-states, in their cyber units, have an interest in identifying vulnerabilities in systems and developing cyber-weapons to attack systems in silence, sparking contemporaneous cyber arms races (Huntley, 2016, pp. 5593) and cyberweapon stockpiling. One of the most nuanced and fabled cyberweapons is the military-grade Stuxnet (revealed in 2010 and followed by Duqu and Flame, written to specification to slow the Iranian nuclear program by destroying that country's nuclear centrifuges. Cyber-weapons may be used as one-offs and as stand-alone attacks, but often, they are used in combination with other forms of warfare to amplify kinetic attacks (Eun & Abmann, 2016). Lucas (2015) describes how cyber may be employed to destabilize an adversary:

In the event of war—or as a means of intimidation—digital weapons offer useful capabilities. Attacks on computers and networks could cripple the adversary's financial system, close down critical infrastructure, induce public panic, paralyse (sic) communications, and ultimately break the will of the political leadership. The saboteurs will necessarily reveal their hand when they use their tools, so they want to stay secret as long as possible. (p. 133)

There is not a public compendium of cyber-weapons. Over the years, a number have been described in the mainstream press but usually by functions alone. For example, a recent news source described global positioning system (GPS) spoofing affecting locational and time data (Darwish, Nov. 3, 2017). Many cyber capabilities for offence and defence are unnamed in the public space. Some are simple tools whose functionalities are harnessed for mayhem, such as website load-testing tools used for DDOS attacks.

A survey suggested that the general public perceives of cyberwar in specific contexts: "virus applied to nuclear reactors," "blackout, then attack," "simultaneous attacks." The respondents were split on whether "nonfatal nuclear hacking" would be cyberwar. What they did not consider "cyberwar," generally speaking, include "stolen information," "Chinese backdoor trap," "data for sale," or "patriotic attacks" (Carr, 2011, as cited in Eun & Abmann, 2016, p. 348). In a sense, respondents were voting based on active harm but also on linkability to a nation-state. Interestingly, some of what they identify in the non-cyberwar category can easily be harnessed for hotwar aggressions. For example, placing and using backdoors can provide paths forward for nation-states to compromise those systems and do worse—in case hotwar aggressions break out. Another way to understand "cyberwar" is through descriptors applied to it: "real...happens at the speed of light...global...skips the battlefield (bypasses traditional national geographic and other defences)...has begun" (Clarke & Knake, 2010, pp. 30 – 31). With the escalatory potential of cyberwar, researchers have admonished nation-states to think before deploying, with the restraints of *jus in bello* (laws of war) and *jus ad bellam* (laws before the war) (Feil, 2012, p. 523). In terms of defences, those are closely held, but one story released to the public is that the U.S. has a switch that can disconnect U.S. networks from connections from around the world, to protect cyber resources and enablements from attacks from without. Certainly, cyberattacks may be launched from within as well; insider attacks have been and continue to be a constant worry given vulnerabilities and given empirical research that shows high levels of insider threat.

About Six-Word Stories and Their Supposed Origin

Six-word stories were first mentioned in playwright John deGroot's play "Papa" (1984), about Ernest Hemingway. Supposedly cobbled from various "events as described by Ernest Hemingway or those who knew him well" (Holden, May 6, 1996), the play includes a scene in which Hemingway apparently challenges the audience to a bet:

Bet you I can write a complete short story using only six words.
Any takers?
No?"
GRINS.
"Okay, then.
A short story in 6 words:
'For sale.
Baby shoes.
Never worn.'"
GRINS, PLEASED WITH HIMSELF. (Wright, Apr. 2014, p. 328)

When asked if he was using "dramatic license" by including the above scene, deGroot claimed that this information was gleaned from one of the Hemingway biographies, but thorough searches have failed to locate this information. One researcher explains:

The story surrounding the six-word text doesn't seem to appear until after de Groot's play was performed in the 1980s. Even though Hemingway died in 1961, the story about the six-word text doesn't seem to circulate until the 1980s, indeed not really catching on until the 2000s. Among the Hemingway materials are numerous anecdotes and examples of Hemingway's sense of competition with other writers such as when he describes metaphorically boxing with Leo Tolstoy (Baker 673) or explains that "Faulkner gives me the creeps" (Baker 862); yet, no mention exists of the baby shoes text and the bet surrounding it. Its earliest appearance in print appears to be in 1988 in an essay by Arthur C. Clarke called "The Power of Compression..." (Wright, Apr. 2014, p. 329)

Finally, playwright John deGroot was known for "literary hoaxes" (Wright, Apr. 2014, p. 329). Could the story have come from other sources? Historians have pored through the documentary evidence from Hemingway's life to see if they can corroborate that the prior incident was fact-based but have been stymied. A Snopes exploration suggests that the assertion that "Ernest Hemingway once won a bet by crafting a six-word short story" is FALSE. The researchers at Snopes have offered several alternate explanations of the origin of this from either the playwright or a newspaper classified ad ("Ernest Hemingway—Baby Shoes," Oct. 29, 2008). While the link to Hemingway is doubtful, this apocryphal story has captured the public imagination.

Six-word stories have been used for research (using six-word stories as elicitations), for students at a law school to share their experiences (Dunnewold, May 2000), for individuals at a workplace to describe their work ("Burlington Associates Share their Six-Word Stories," Jan. 12, 2016), and interacting on social media (microblogging sites, subreddits, Facebook pages, and others). This form was used for personal memoirs in 2006 in the "Six-Word Memoirs" project (Roncero-Menendez, S., May 16, 2014). This form has been harnessed for various online storytelling magazines. The brevity of the six-word stories format enables "repeated close readings" (Botzakis, Oct. 2013, p. 162).

How six-word stories manifest in the world varies. On Google Search, "six-word stories" (without the quotation marks) results in 116 million results, and 238,000 links with the quotation marks. The auto-complete feature in this web search engine shows differentiations of such stories based on sources (tumblr, imgur, reddit) and emotional features (funny, sad, heartbreaking, scary, happy) and topics (love, lesson plan) and rank orders (best, famous). This information is at the summary level. On the bing web search engine, "six-word stories" without the quotation marks results in 47,600,000 results, and with the quotation marks, 51,300,000 results. The auto-complete feature in bing results in company-based stories (Burlington), rankings (best), emotional features (creepy, happy), and quality (good). A perusal of some of the available six-word stories online show some personal stories, lessons, observations, puzzles, jokes, and memes.

In terms of effective six-word stories, they should offer some insight. The words may be colloquial and conversational. The personal has to have relevance for the general public. Wordplays are de rigueur. Style matters. Humor matters. Six-word stories have to be able to both stand-alone meaningfully and to be read in a larger context meaningfully. They have to function like grafs in news articles to ground the story in a context. While six-word stories offer a context, they also need to contribute a new insight or two.

The core elements required for a six-word story are just the six words, with no other elements defined per se. There may be a need for a beginning, a middle, and an end (in terms of basic requirements for a story) or a narrative trajectory with a starting point, a build-up in tension, a climax, and a denouement (in terms of basic requirements for a narrative). Six-word stories, in their brevity, are often referential and point to other elements well beyond the six words. For example, one six-word story shared on social media read "Two dead birds, one less (sic) stone" as a play on the proverb of "kill two birds with one stone." Others are brief jokes: "I leave. Dog panics. Furniture shopping" (by "Reed) and "Alzheimer's Advantage: new friends every day!" ("Six Word Stories," 2013). Appendix 1, "More about Six-word Stories on the Social Web," offers some more findings about how these stories are used on several different social media platforms.

INDUCING SIX-WORD STORIES FROM CURATED TOPIC-BASED TEXT SETS

In terms of cyber risk, the general public is thought to think more about mundane issues of fraud and identity theft and "other sorts of personal fears" regarding cyber than cyberwar (Clark, Winter 2011, p. 63). Cyber is so integrated into people's lives that cyber itself may be invisible:

Indeed, we are so surrounded by computers that we don't even think of them as 'computers' anymore. We are woken by computerized clocks, take showers in water heated by a computer, drink coffee brewed in a computer, eat oatmeal heated up in a computer, then drive to work in a car controlled by hundreds of computers, while sneaking peeks at the last night's sports scores on a computer. And then at work, we spend most of our day pushing buttons on a computer... (Singer & Friedman, 2014, pp. 1 – 2)

There are some online sources of information for trying to understand how much public awareness there is of cyberwar. If search results are anything to go by, "cyberwar" is something that is present in online spaces and the public imagination. On Google Search, <cyberwar> has 1,590,000 results (in 0.65 seconds) and 13,200,000 on the bing web search engine; within quotation marks, "cyberwar" has 1.6 million results on Google for "cyberwar" and 5.1 million results on bing web search engine.

The Google Books Ngram Viewer enables a non-consumptive way to access the texts of published works over time from the 1500s to the present. The English text set shows frequency linegraphs of "cyberwar," "cyber war," "cybersecurity," and "cyber security" from 1960 – 2000. Figure 2 shows 1975 as a pivotal year when "cybersecurity" and "cyberwar" both sparked in published books. At present, "cyberwar" is trending among the four terms as the most common referent followed by "cyber security," "cyber war," and "cybersecurity." (A case insensitive search results in the same general frequency dynamics over time.) The non-consumptiveness in this tool refers to the fact that the underlying texts are not directly accessible by users of the research tool, so the underlying texts are not "consumable." This restriction is because of copyright concerns.

Another "big data" way to approach understanding how far the concept of "cyberwar" has penetrated is to see how many Google Search correlations there are between "cyberwar" and "cyber war" (treated different) in all the available countries in Google Correlate. The correlations are listed in Table 1. For many of the countries, there are no month-to-month correlations of either "cyberwar" or "cyber war" to any other search terms over extended time (2004 – present). It is possible to query by week-to-week, in a more granular-time search. Some countries have intermittently blocked the use of Google, so that may be a reason for some of the "No results." The extended series of dots for the U.S. correlations are a little confusing. Are these to be interpreted as extended ellipses? For a few countries, there are some correlations that bring up terms related to "cyberwar." The related words are underlined in the table. One other note: the search terms are in various languages, enabled by UTF-8. There are terms in Japanese, Chinese, Dutch (such as "spoorlaan oss" or "track us"), Turkish, Spanish, and others.

The month-over-month search term correlations in Indonesia, for example, result in some search terms that evoke "cyber," "hacking," "DDOS" (distributed denial of service), and "anonymous. (Figure 3)

For a closer-in view of the Google Correlate data in the U.S., it is possible to look at differences in large-scale Google Search term selections by state in a choropleth map. Correlations between search terms may be seen in side-by-side U.S. maps (Figure 4). "Cyberwar" looks to be a popular search term in the following locales: Washington, D.C.; Virginia; Maryland; South Dakota, and Washington state.

Figure 2. "Cyberwar," "Cyber war," "Cybersecurity" and "Cyber security" on Google Books Ngram Viewer (1960 – 2000)

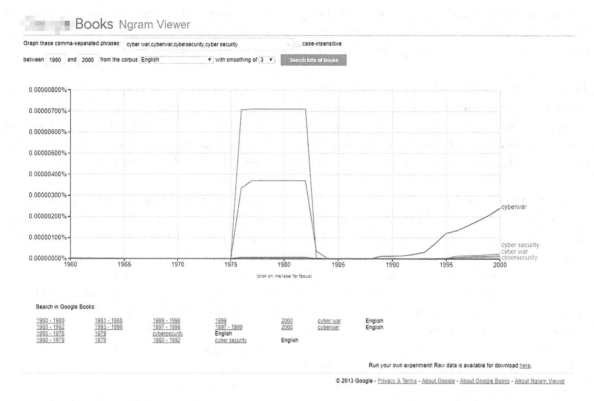

The earlier explorations of "cyberwar" in the contemporary moment does seem to show awareness of this phenomena broadly speaking if not so much in specific details.

THE SIX-WORD STORY INDUCTION PROCESS

In this particular case of inducing six-word stories through computational text analysis means combined with human story-writing from the captured words, the process may be described in eight steps (Figure 5). The Steps to the Six-Word Story Induction Process include the following:

1. Conceptualize the work.
2. Collect topic- and source-based text sets.
3. Read the texts.
4. Clean the text sets.
5. Run word frequency counts, text searches, computational text analyses.
6. Create data visualizations.
7. Induce six-word stories.
8. Validate or invalidate the stories.

Table 1. "Cyberwar" Correlations on Google Search over Extended Time (2004 – 2017) through Google Correlate

Countries	"cyberwar" Correlations based on Monthly Time Series	"cyber war" Correlations based on Monthly Time Series
Argentina	No results	No results
Australia	1s, telstra shop near me, s console, jess and rory, jess gilmore girls, kmart north lakes, gen 7, steep, logan gilmore girls, ben hall movie, 逃避, murray river organics, jess gilmore, petrol stations near me, pokemon cards kmart, logan gilmore, emily gilmore, grimer, sun and moon, 2g network	travelex canberra, lymph nodes cancer, what is scarlet, darlington point nsw, emerald to rockhampton, hotline phone, kimpton hotel, food deliver, 粘液, screenshots on windows, pc mode, compress pdf file, holden port melbourne, affordable tyres, party top, borked, the anonymous, fire boat, next level racing, moon transit
Austria	öyle bir gecer zaman ki, just the way you are songtext, zaman ki, öyle bir gecer zaman, laura jansen, esra erol evlen, esra erol evlen benimle, just the way you are chords, the way you are chords, castle 4, evlen benimle, sofitel vienna stephansdom, nba jam, evlen, live hub, öyle bir, öyle bir geçer, freiwilligkeit, 5742g, farmeramania	No results
Belgium	No results	No results
Brazil	marcos gois, pringo, 2 belas caipiras, luiza barros, tv macho, samba gamboa, carla maffioletti, matheusinho, o jogo da cobrinha, personal rh manaus, app twitter, alexandra rodrigues, quem e essa mulher, tipos de risadas, cante as escrituras, porto de mucuripe, vokes, www.sermilweb.eb.mil.br, o que é tumblr, cantora amanda	google e facebook, meijer, speed dating brasil, sherlock holmes 1, another 3, quando nascemos fomos programados, filme sherlock holmes 1, cruzeiro do sul empregos sorocaba, jornal cruzeiro do sul empregos sorocaba, ataque de pitbull em curitiba, impress.js, assistir diarios de um vampiro online, vitoria almeida, qual seu nome?, 140s, gmail port, financiamento imoveis banco do brazil, www detran rj vistoria, resumo do filme era uma vez, cofermeta ferramentas bh
Bulgaria	No results	No results
Canada	smackdown live, wwe smackdown live, saiki, 1060, cubone, auriel, kusuo, avalor, guild calgary, saiki kusuo, vulprix, grimer, lcbo delivery, sweet like candy, la bicicleta, go facebook, wishers, not nice, higher or lower, raichu	cyber warfare, skope, drear, find market, boy characters, detail., dylan blowin in the wind, trivento, buster baxter, bob dylan blowin in the wind, I was about to, black deer, ge profile gas range, so too, picture profile, glittered, profile pictures, hpv symptoms in men, shore club ottawa, loacker
Chile	No results	No results
China	No results	No results
Colombia	No results	No results
Croatia	No results	No results
Czech Republic	No results	No results
Denmark	No results	No results
Egypt	No results	No results
Finland	No results	No results
France	monster curve, livret a sup, b 500, crayon publicitaire, sos cuisine, hormone de croissance pour grandir, lycee emilie du chatelet, livret a sup cic, 相亲, conrad lille, blouson starter, freiman, cyberguerre, socolofi, action s, blue bay grand esmeralda, blue bay grand, musique parrain, 47 rue berger, linea di	No results
Germany	cyber war, asus x72j, x72j, hd iPhone, navigation controller, you are chords, rules.com, 15800, airbag test, alex marte, doodle, vapiano karlsruhe, räuchermischung, monster remix, alignment tool, novation ultranova, college rules.com, 16 - 18, private mansion, tamron sp 70-300mm	cyberwar, college rules.com, they sleep, airbag test, alex marte, rep, rules.com, vapiano karlsruhe, tamron sp 70-300mm, schwarzkopf perfect mousse, perfect mousse, ikea berlin lichtenberg, ich töte dich, the cosmopolitan, asus x72j, vpcea3s1e, private mansion, onkel otto sindelfingen, x72j, hilton pattaya
Greece	No results	No results
Hungary	No results	No results
India	ankur saxena, sprinkled, what is jojoba, rouf dance, あなた, pictures baby, hotel seychelles, fast train videos, faciam, international taekwondo, maltese dogs, neeraj tiwari, youtube group, oil heat, aut viam inveniam aut faciam, viam inveniam aut faciam, flip game, samanyu, so wrong, sports park	incentive program, folder attributes, notepad virus, bay girl, rameswaram hotels, hematopoeictic stem cells, zoom control, badminton techniques, tamil monica, millionaire in india, sanctuary map, free photo recovery, icici bank credit card reward points, pondicherry beaches, buyya, central staffing scheme, how to calculate home loan, mumbai to neral, vamsoft, mahindra xylo e8

continued on following page

Table 1. Continued

Countries	"cyberwar" Correlations based on Monthly Time Series	"cyber war" Correlations based on Monthly Time Series
Indonesia	cyber war, perang cyber, sendy mamahit, perang cyber indonesia, cyber indonesia, anonymous indonesia, berita hacker, ddos online, edit foto menjadi karikatur, 1001 fakta, film that winter the wind blows, pengertian ddos, download karikatur, edit foto sketsa, jonas dan asmirandah, stm lodaya, hacker indonesia yang terkenal, edit foto karikatur online, download ddos, fire imdb	perang cyber, cyberwar, lagu that winter the wind blows, perang cyber indonesia, film that winter the wind blows, 1001 fakta, cyber indonesia, download lagu ost that winter the wind blows, ddos online, belajar ddos, cara menggunakan ddos, berita hacker, edit foto karikatur online, download ddos, pemain that winter the wind blows, the winter, hacker indonesia yang terkenal, keluarga asmirandah, jay rodriguez, anonymous indonesia
Ireland	No results	No results
Israel	No results	No results
Italy	No results	No results
Japan	No results	No results
Malaysia	No results	No results
Mexico	No results	No results
Morocco	No results	No results
Netherlands	cees van vliet, beneath the surface, move controller, 4 seizoenen banden, kenwood cooking chef, kenwood cooking, spoorlaan oss, entrances, apprecieer, the eye of the storm, jan terlouw boeken, herziene statenvertaling, kjc, cyber war, rotterdam outlet, herziene, davidoff champion, o ring, long jacket, kulas	cyberwar, lions international, all-weather, spoorlaan oss, me and julio down
New Zealand	No results	No results
Norway	No results	No results
Peru	No results	No results
Philippines	No results	No results
Poland	No results	No results
Portugal	No results	No results
Romania	No results	No results
Russian Federation	No results	No results
Saudi Arabia	No results	No results
Singapore	No results	No results
Spain	No results	No results
Sweden	No results	No results
Switzerland	8043, seltene erden, oui mais, mais non, easy a, endlessly, nano touch, move games, ps3 move, alpha and omega, 3 move, ps3 jailbreak, ipod nano touch, barbie modezauber in paris, barbie modezauber, mords, takers, wii party, modezauber in paris, take one	No results
Taiwan	No results	No results
Thailand	No results	No results
Turkey	No results	siber savaş, ahaa, soğan sarımsak, kandirdim akor, whiskey glass, qan, faka muzeyyen, muse parfüm, yüz kurdu, vik ecem, phytocyane, sozlesmeli askerlik, ponçik tarifi, kil kurtlari, osmanlıca küfür, lswt, modern muse parfüm, şemsiyeli adam, fakat muzeyyen bu derin bir tutku, rus rublesi dolar
Ukraine	No results	No results
The United Kingdom	lorelai gilmore, pneumonia recovery, rory gilmore, kelly bishop, kinect adapter, claas xerion, makuhita, h45, e5 price, gilmore girls rory, s-a, pokemon xbox, stars hollow, how to get lyrics, pokemon clothing, slowpoke evolve, pokemon t, font facebook, southern rail, swarovski uk	c3 battery, the kings head teddington, kings head teddington, cyber warfare, mic for iphone, cqc dental, aylesbury waterside, dagelijkse kost, cote highgate, tobar an dualchais, chris haughton, i joke, equality act, zoom r24, maplewood chinese, global dividend fund, savoy american bar, cote ealing, equality act 2010, sms tyres

continued on following page

Table 1. Continued

Countries	"cyberwar" Correlations based on Monthly Time Series	"cyber war" Correlations based on Monthly Time Series
United States	full hd,, el ruedo, ruedo, damn good time, font on facebook, ..., cafe24, ..., ..., gülümse, me entere lyrics, gucci mane clothing, ..., nunca me olvides, ..., reporte de puentes en vivo, 3 deluxe, suzuki van van, miranda la, party animal	cyber warfare, rainbow unicorn, nisei lounge, boot iphone, special rice, holiday inn mumbai, costco omega, medal meaning, zdf mediathek, what does he want, e translate, hobo 2, showgirl movie, happily ever, did wiki, happily ever after, pil pil, mediathek, kush, menton boston
Venezuela	No results	No results
Viet Nam	No results	No results

Figure 3. "cyberwar" – "cyber war" Correlations by Month in Indonesia for Extended Time (2004 – 2017) on Google Correlate

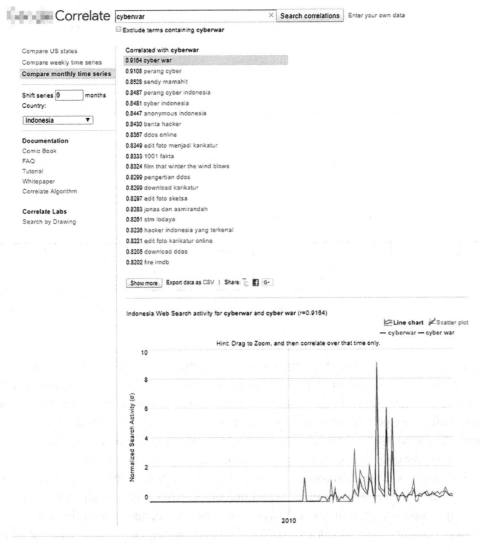

Figure 4. "cyberwar" Search Correlations by U.S. States

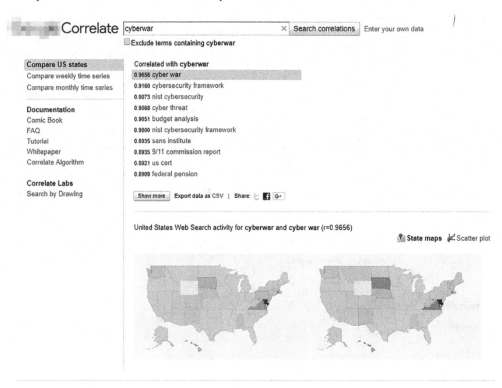

Figure 5. The Six-Word Story Induction Process

1. Conceptualize the Work	2. Collect Topic- and Source-based Text Sets	3. Read the Texts	4. Clean the Text Sets	5. Run Word Frequency Counts, Text Searches, Computational Text Analyses	6. Create Data Visualizations	7. Induce Six-Word Stories	8. Validate or Invalidate the Stories

The Six-Word Story Induction Process

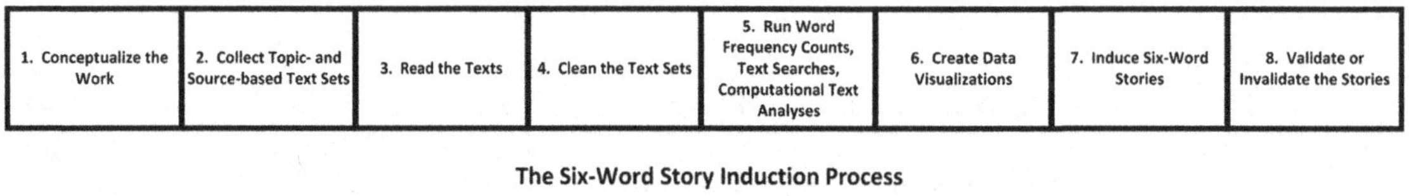

Inducing a six-word story from text sets then involves selecting and limiting data. In word frequency counts, these involve selecting the most frequent words for salience. (The least frequent words in the long tail may also be relevant.) In a text search with a resulting word tree, induction may result in the identification of all the respective sentence contexts in which the particular word or phrase or alpha-numeric sequence is used; these limit the data and enable riffing off of existing verbatim texts (albeit without contravening the copyright of the original work). The target terms or other occurring terms may be used as fulcrums around which six-word stories may be built. Variations in the parameter settings of computational text analyses may result in variant outcomes. Also, there are a number of autocoding methods (like topic modeling, sentiment analysis -> topic modeling, and others) that can result in the induction of word sets for six-word stories. Also, human coding may be coupled with autocoding for various effects. Finally, if people want to closely read the target literature, they can skip computer-based induction and go right to the six-word stories—but they would do so without the benefit of computer-based insights. This method is based more on bottom-up coding and grounded theory approaches instead of any theoretical framework. The method involves both quantitative and qualitative methods, and the resulting six-word stories are built off empirical data, reproducible computation-based text induction methods, and unreproducible human writing of the stories (with the seeded texts). This process is about creating six-word stories (pseudo-narratives) from patterns in text data.

In the actual work, Step 7 benefits from some non-restrictive guidelines.

Words to Include

- Practically speaking, words extracted computationally can be used in different grammatical formats. Synonyms may be brought into play. If needed, a word in its various forms may be used multiple times in the story.
- If an added word not found in the original set from the computational induction could be useful to make a coherent six-word story that is usable.
- Proper nouns may be used to represent both the specific and symbolically a general category or thing.

Expressing Relationships Between Entities and Elements

- With such sparsity, six-word stories may benefit from efficiencies in expressing relationships. Syntax words, coordinate conjunctions, subordinate conjunctions, mathematical operators, punctuation, and symbols can be added to represent relationships. (The punctuation marks do not count as part of the six words, but the mathematical operators and symbols do.)
  - Common coordinate conjunctions may be brought into play: for, and, nor, but, or, yet, and so.
  - Subordinate conjunctions may be engaged: because, since, although, unless, etc.
  - Mathematical operators may include any of the following and others: $=$ equal; $\neq$ not equal to; $\approx$ almost equal / almost similar; $\equiv$ identical to; $\leq$ less than or equal to; $\geq$ greater than or equal to, and others.
  - There may be logic-based constructions, like "if-then," and "if and only if," etc.
- Relationships may include any of the following and more:
  - Time-based sequentiality (one issue came before another)
  - Spatial-based
  - Location-based
  - Geography-based
  - Associative
  - Comparative
  - Contrastive
  - Similarity (such as being listed of a type)
  - Dissimilarity
  - A positive correlation
  - A negative correlation
  - Causation
  - Negation

- ◦ Transitivity
- ◦ Example
- ◦ Non-example, and others

Social Web and Social Media Colloquialisms

- The lingo of the Social Web (word mash-ups, abbreviations, hyphenated word sequences) and social media (#hashtags, emoticons) may be harnessed to shorten terms by erasing white spaces and enabling more combinatorial complexities than stand-alone words.

Multiple Languages

- Multiple languages may be used, in the spirit of the Web and Internet, and the world.

Not Truth but Truth and Not Truthiness

- The six-word stories are not representing Truth but should not veer towards truthiness (falsehoods disguised as pseudo-truth) either.

Word Play and Variations in Thinking

- Some six-word stories will be readable forwards and backwards (such as lists).
- In the spirit of word play, there may be puns, rhymes, partial rhymes, word repetitions, purposeful misspellings for effect, and other linguistic engagements. There may be code-switching.
- Six-word stories that make assertions should also be expressed as their counterfactual as well as a range of alternate realities—to test for appropriateness and understanding. The idea is to help the six-word story authors be mentally limber.
- In this case, six-word stories are for brainstorming and for riffing off a topic; they should not be over-thought. (Thumb-typing six-word stories about something as serious as cyberwar was purposefully approached to contrast a light-hearted wordplay method with something overwhelming and complex.)
- Six-word stories, by nature, will be polysemic and interpretable.
- Six-word stories are not necessarily an end in themselves but may lead to other ideas.
- Six-word stories may be used in a variety of ways to understand a non-fiction topic: descriptively, prescriptively, analytically, and in other ways.

Originating Text Sets

- Six-word stories may be inspired by / partially derived from zoomed-out macro-level extracted words from text sets, or they may be zoomed-in micro-level extracted words from word trees (albeit not as verbatim representations).
  - ◦ The data visualizations that inspire the stories are not to be taken in a wooden or literal sense. They should be inspirational bases for the stories.
- Six-word stories should not contravene any copyright; they should be original works.

Process

- Six-word stories may begin in a rough-cut way, but they have to be revised and edited to a level of readability and meaning.
- Six-word stories often have a fair amount of referents beyond the sentence itself, for meaning-making.

Appeals of Six-Word Stories

- The six-word stories may appeal to human readers in various senses: intellect, emotion, knowledge, aesthetics, humor, and others.

Typography of Six-Word Stories

- Six-word stories may be laid out in a vertical way, not just in a linear horizontal way.
- Text colors, ALL CAPS, boldfacing, italicizing, and other typographical approaches may be applied for communications purposes.

In the next section, cyberwar text sets collated by categories of sources are computationally analyzed to induce text sets...to be used as seeds for six-word stories. The four sources are government (1), mainstream journalism (2), academia (3), and social media (4). Some of the created six-word stories created from these respective text sets will be shared at the end of the next section.

PART I: COMPARING CYBERWAR TEXT SETS BY SOURCES

The extracted data visualizations from the respective text sets show differences in focus, emphasis, contemporaneity, and knowledge.

Government Sources Text Set (1)

Ideally, the government sources text set would contain information from all three branches of government: the executive, legislative, and judicial. In this case, the reports are congressional reports only. (In terms of governance, additional texts may be those from the military and specifically the National Security Agency or "NSA" in terms of leaked documents. In this case, though, only legally acquired documents were used.)

In Figure 6, auto-coding was applied to the set of congressional documents related to cyberwar, and these were coded at sentence level. This linegraph shows the top-level topics based on the seven documents used and what each contributes to a particular topic. The topics are listed in alphabetical order on the x-axis: adversary, attack, capabilities, computer, computer systems, electromagnetic, energy, information, infrastructure, network, operations, policy, power, security, systems, and warfare. From these top-level topics, it is clear that the report sets engage issues related to cyberwar and policy, the protection of critical infrastructure, and the facing of nation-state adversaries. Running an auto-coding by topic approach on separate documents enables differentiation among the documents as their own sub-sets of texts.

Figure 6. Auto-Topic Modeling of Set of Congressional Documents Related to Cyberwar (as a Linegraph)

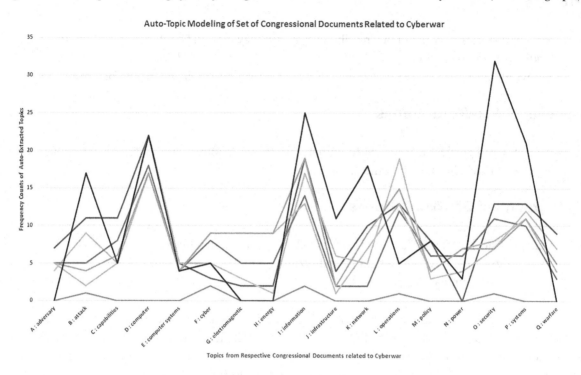

A summary view of the topics may be seen in Figure 7 in the treemap diagram. In descending order, the summary topics are a computer, systems, information, operations, security, and so on, starting with the left side of the treemap.

Mainstream Journalism Sources Text Set (2)

The mainstream journalism text set contains 82 articles from a number of journalistic sources. A word frequency count of these texts found a focus on the current year, cyberwar, and locales of interest like Russia (as a "bad actor" in cyber) and Ukraine (as a place where cyberattacks have been practised), and so on. These works are time-based. (Figure 8)

Autocoding by topic-modelling was applied to this text set, and the results may be seen in a treemap diagram in Figure 9. Main focuses—in one-grams or unigrams—are cyber, security, attack, hackers, systems, networks, military, and so on. Close readings of the respective works show common patterns: evidence of cyberattacks and comments on responses, the seriousness of cyberwar, various international actors and their roles in hostile cyber actions, and so on.

Placing the data in a Pareto chart helps clarity the actual frequency counts of these auto-extracted topics (Figure 10).

Academic Sources Text Set (3)

In terms of academic sourcing, there were two main text sets: (1) academic publications in peer-reviewed publications, and (2) theses and dissertations by graduate students. Both sets were vetted by professionals

Figure 7. Auto-Topic Modeling of Set of Congressional Documents Related to Cyberwar as an Integrated Treemap

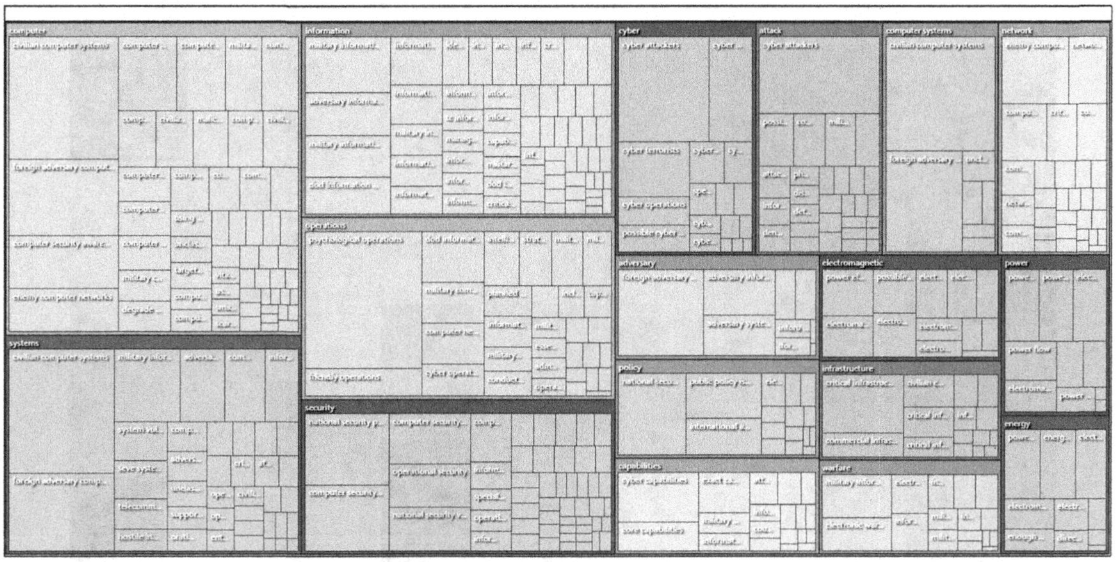

Figure 8. Mainstream Journalistic Articles about Cyberwar Expressed in a Word Cloud

Figure 9. Mainstream Journalistic Articles about Cyberwar (Auto-coded Themes as a Treemap Diagram)

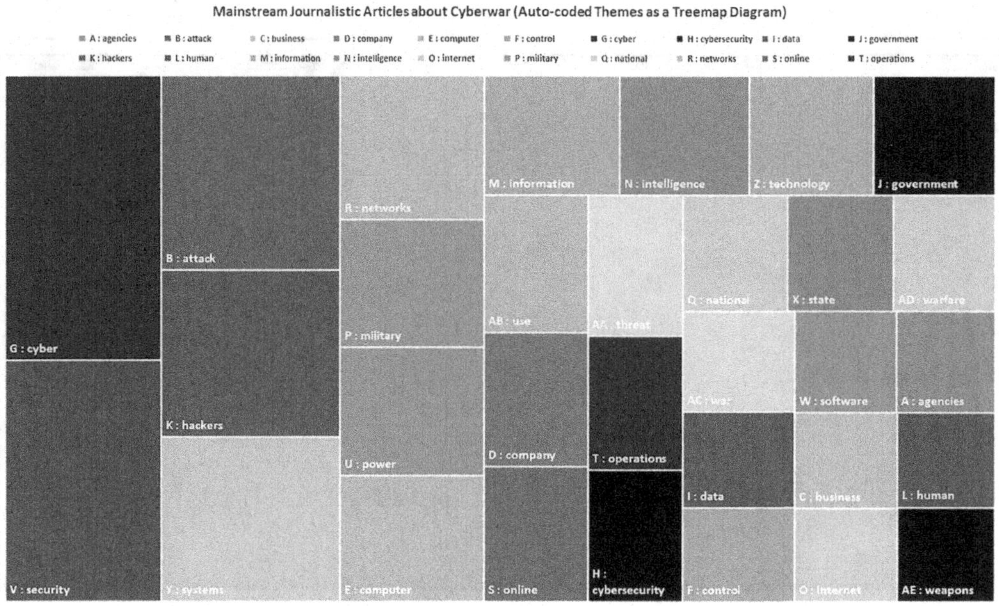

Figure 10. Auto-coded Themes from the Mainstream Journalistic Article Text Set around Cyberwar

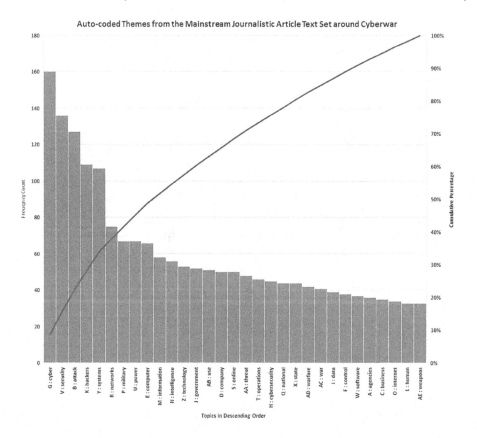

in the field, but the first set is considered more professional and formal, and the second set is considered more non-professional and amateur (by professionals-in-the-making). The first set consists of some 500 pp. of academic works on cyberwar; the latter consists of 20,000 pp. The ratio is approximately 9:36, which makes these sets not directly comparable. Also, the latter set's size was so large that auto-coding could not be applied to it even on some pretty robust machines.

So, first, the academic text set: in this, the main focuses are cyber, security, military, government, forces, and so on (Figure 11). A lot of the research is focused on topics of threats and addressing them. A visual perusal of the treemap diagram gives a sense of the interested parties behind the academic research—as funders—such as government entities and the military.

A word frequency count of the academic text set highlights focuses on the research as well but with more detailed nuance (Figure 12).

Some highlights: "Cyber security" is the main focus. There are named actors: Russia, China, and locales, such as Georgia. One of the main publishers appears—the Journal of Conflict and Security Law (JCSL). There is clear work on technologies, policy, strategy, and others. The years cited span 2007 to 2017, with stops in between.

Finally, from the word frequency count, a cluster analysis was created to find words which co-occurred in proximity (Figure 13). On this figure, red circles have been drawn around some of the related clusters. In one of the larger red-circled word sets, there are a range of potentials from the available words: Air, Force, Operations, Capabilities, System, First, Two, Intelligence, Networks, Control, Command, Military, Weapons, Forces, Warfare, and Networks. Another set reads Infrastructure, Security, International, Internet, Global, National, Example, Information, System, Government, Public, Defense, Policy, Threat, Strategic, Strategy, Intelligence, Many, However, World, and Power. There are smaller clusters: United States, Nuclear. (This might portend some very serious discussions of serious risks.) Another small cluster contains "Red" and "Stuxnet." These sets contain semantic terms, with promise for various six-story words.

Figure 11. Top-level Auto-coded Themes from the Academic Text Set

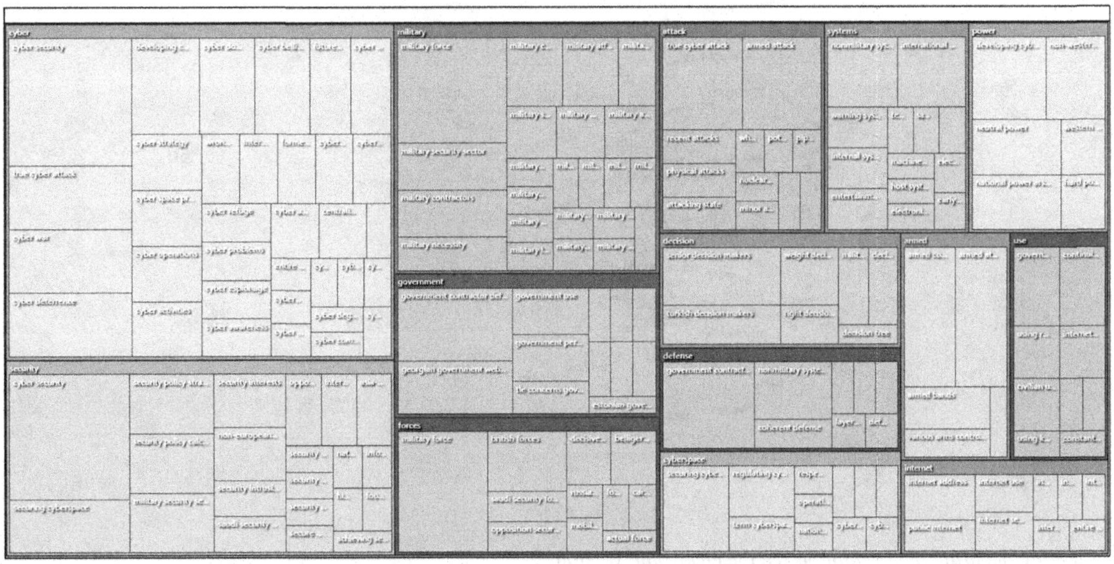

Figure 12. A Word Frequency Word Cloud of the Academic Text Set

Figure 13. 2D Cluster Analysis from Cyberwar Academic Articles Set

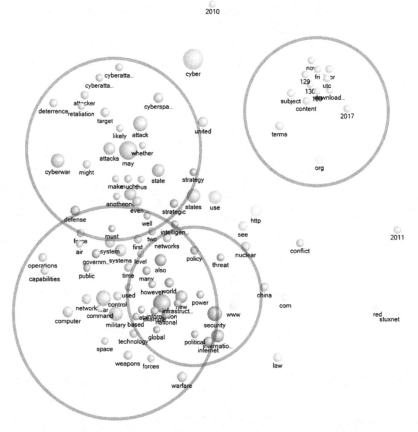

For a more accurate representation see the electronic version.

In academia, there are also works by professionals-in-the-making. Next, in the graduate student thesis/dissertation text set around "cyberwar," a word-frequency word cloud was created (Figure 14).

In Figure 15, the relations between the words in the cyberwar thesis/dissertation text set may be seen as a diagram.

As mentioned earlier, the long tail is relevant as well as the most frequent words. Figure 16 shows some of the elements in the long tail on the x-axis. Some of the interesting words with single appearances in the text set? They include the following: hybrid, regime, Hawaii, deputies, apathetic, hebb1980, jailbroken, fractiousness, icloud, oshlyansky, infected0996, anjard, microsoftunveils, macewan, and others—all interesting for various reasons.

Figures 17, 18, and 19 show word trees created from target terms in the thesis/dissertation text set: cyberwar, revolution, and weapon. These text search-based trees enable close-in readings of the data and more granular inspirations for the six-word stories. In a sense, some of these may be "found" six-word stories and may be used if they are properly cited (so as not to contravene copyright). One example of a "found" six-word story is a snippet from a text": "(cyber)worm drifts in like a mote" (Bowden, 2011, p. 53) or Sun Tzu's erudite observation about the "art of war" as "life and death; safety or ruin" (Sun Tzu, 5th century BC). This references the ability of digital worms to hide invisibly in network operations unless network administrators are sufficiently attentive and have the technologies to identify these infections.

Figure 20 shows a branch of the word tree highlighted. Inside NVivo 11 Plus, this word tree is interactive, and double-clicking on the branch will take the researcher to the actual raw data from which the word tree was induced (from a verbatim text search). [It is possible to extract words from a "fuzzy" search as well, by using stems, synonyms, specializations, and generalizations of the target term.]

Figure 21 shows a 3D cluster diagram of the "cyberwar" thesis / dissertation text set. \

Figure 14. A Word-Frequency Word Cloud from 132-Item "Cyberwar" Thesis / Dissertation Text Set

Figure 15. A 2D Related Word-Cluster Diagram from 132-Item "Cyberwar" Thesis/Dissertation Text Set

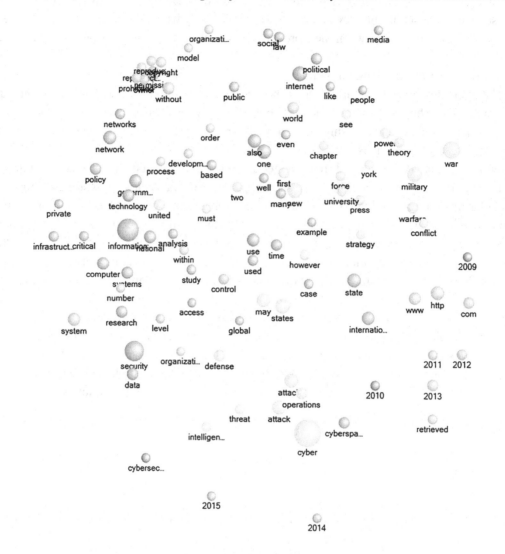

Social Media Sources Text Set (4)

If the government, mainstream journalistic, and academic works are "calls," then the "responses" are those postings from the masses, the general non-experts. Certainly, cyberwar is a topic of discussion on the social web.

On Facebook Social Networking Site

The @cyberwarbooks account on Facebook (https://www.facebook.com/cyberwarbooks/) apparently brings together aficionados of the named books. From this account, 2,848 posts and 16 comments were exported, using NCapture of NVivo 11 Plus. Some common topics, in descending order, are the following: product, product prices, picture, whole, the whole picture, online, buy, use, features, information,

Figure 16. Exploring the Long Tail from a 132-Item "Cyberwar" Thesis / Dissertation Text Set

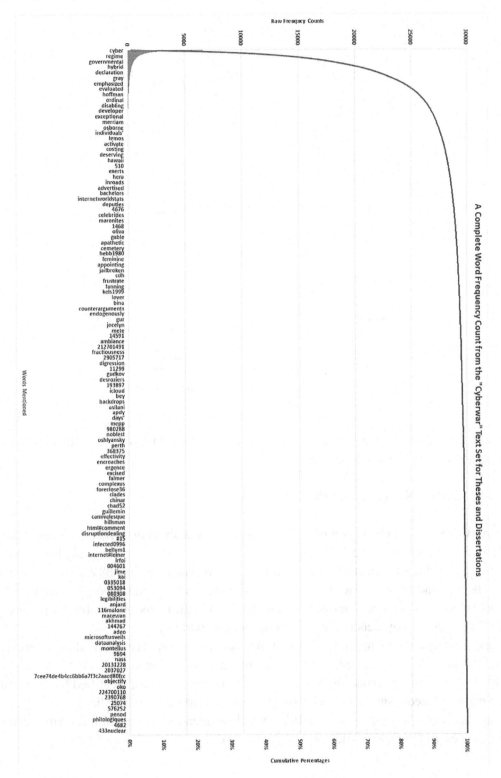

Figure 17. A "Cyberwar" Word Tree from 132-Item "Cyberwar" Thesis / Dissertation Text Set

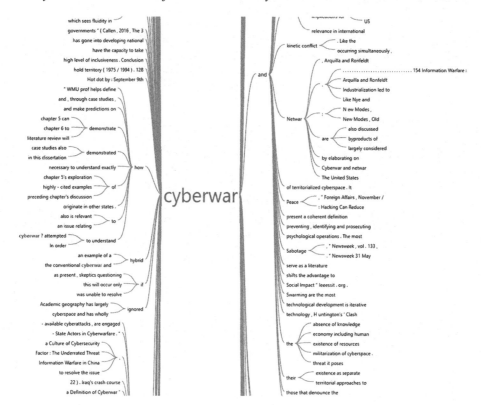

availability, availability…, others, security, pilot, and others. An auto extraction of themes shows basic commercial interests in Figures 22, 23, and 24.

On Reddit Social News Sharing Site

There were two sub-reddit discussion boards used to seed an analysis of "cyberwar" discussions from Reddit. The CyberWarfare subreddit (https://www.reddit.com/r/CyberWarfare/) only had 47 messages, and the freshest posting was apparently from a year ago. This board only had 68 readers and was moderated by "billcube" and "mon0." The other one, TechWar (https://www.reddit.com/r/TechWar/) featured 3.945 readers and 995 available messages (spanning from eight hours old to about three years ago). "TechWar" is moderated by webdoodle, kalden31, and LtCmdrData.

For the word frequency count (Figure 25), common occurring words typical in a thread were removed, including "submitted," "save," "share," "report," "comment," "years," "months," "com," "year," "month," and so on. The word cloud seems somewhat dominated by personalities, identified by their handles… and some names of media sites, along with some key words ripped from headlines.

An auto extraction of topics in Figure 26 shows close attention to technological advancements, in hacks, in policies, and in technologies (such as quantum).

Figure 18. A "Revolution" Word Tree from 132-Item "Cyberwar" Thesis / Dissertation Text Set

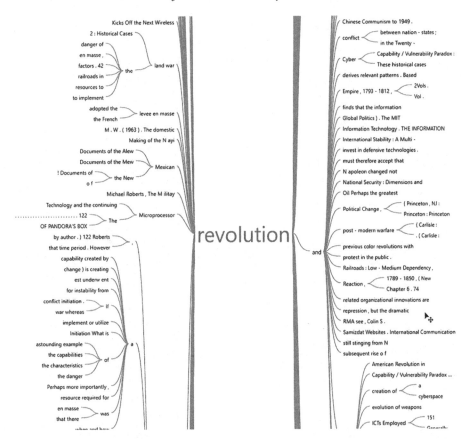

On the Twitter Microblogging Site

Groups on Twitter that set their accounts to public enable a kind of digital eavesdropping. For example, #hashtag networks may be created to show who is discussing a particular #hashtagged topic at any one time…going back about a week. It is also possible to map @accounts to capture some members of their network and maybe some of the messages exchanged. The Twitter API enables access to a small amount of data, nothing near an N = all. (Full data sets are available from a commercial provider.) A keyword search for "cyberwar" resulted in the mapped networks and groups in Figure 27. Account names can be used for six-word stories…assuming the author goes into sufficient research to be able to make solid assertions. This particular network is comprised of seven groups based on the Clauset-Newman-Moore grouping algorithm.

The graph metrics may also be captured as in Table 2. This gives the size of the network and its structural characteristics, which may be used to understand the power and social dynamics, based on positionality and interactions.

The data extraction includes the capture of the messaging between the entities as well. Those graphics are not included here. It is also possible to capture #hashtag networks based on labeled discussions. In this case, the discussions around #cyberwar were captured on Twitter. Twenty-five groups were identified in this latter graph. (Figure 28)

Figure 19. A "Weapon" Word Tree from 132-Item Curated "Cyberwar" Thesis / Dissertation Text Set

Table 3 contains the graph metrics for the #cyberwar hashtag network.

It is possible to extract the top URLs from the Tweets, the top domains, the top hashtags, the top words, the sentiment, the top word pairs, the top replied-to social accounts, the top mentioned accounts, and the top Tweeters in the graph (Table 4). The top terms in the discussions may provide seeding terms for six-word stories.

Another approach involves capturing linked article-article networks on Wikipedia, an edited and crowd-sourced online encyclopedia by the Wikimedia Foundation. This work is built on the MediaWiki platform and enables the capture of article linkages. Figure 29 shows how complex cyberwarfare is and also how much publicly available information is out there. The article graph captures a number of semantic-laden keywords that may be explored for six-word stories.

Induced Six-Word Stories From Respective Text Sets

So based on the various extracted text sets, induced six-word stores about cyberwar are possible. Some examples follow.

Figure 20. A "Cyberweapon" Word Tree from 132-Item Curated "Cyberwar" Thesis/Dissertation Text Set

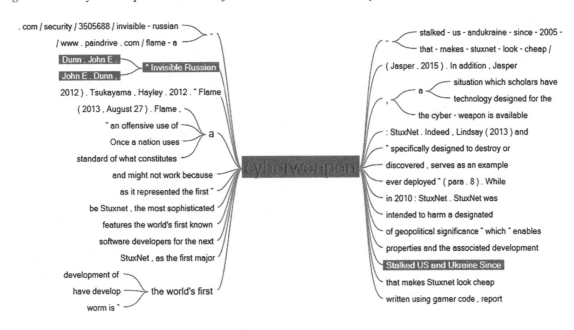

Figure 21. A 3D Cluster Diagram of the "Cyberwar" Thesis / Dissertation Text Set

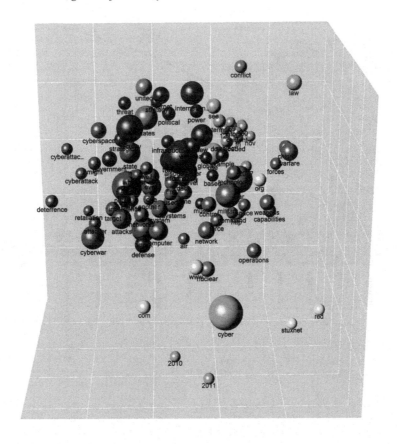

Figure 22. @cyberwarbooks on Facebook posts (2,848 posts and 16 comments)

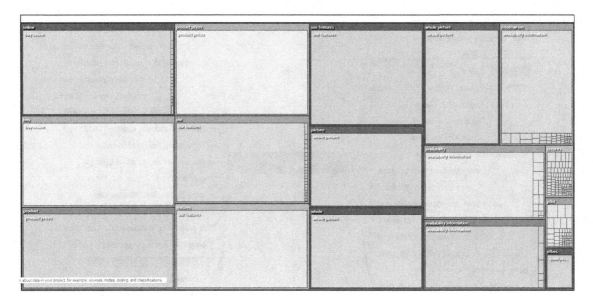

Figure 23. Auto-extracted Themes in the @cyberwarbooks on Facebook (in a pareto chart)

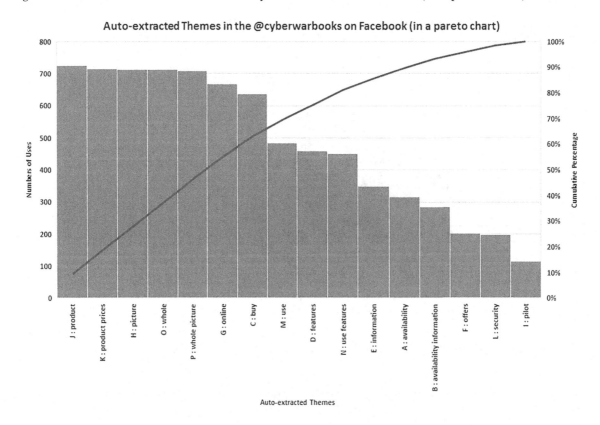

Figure 24. "Security" Topic and Related Subtopics @cyberwarbooks on Facebook posts (2,848 posts and 16 comments)

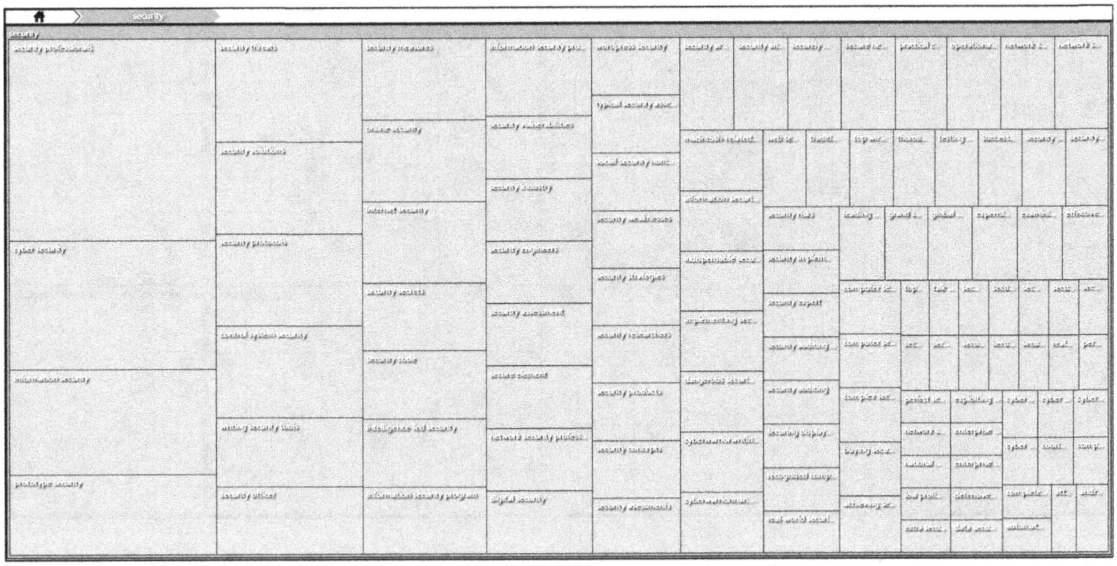

Figure 25. A Word Frequency Word Cloud from Collected Titles from Two Subreddit Lists: CyberWar and TechWar

- **Cyberwar:** Cyberweapons coded with whose program?
- **Cyberweaponry:** Geopolitical significance of tech capabilities
- **Inducted into Drone Cyberarmy:** Unpatched machines
- **Stuxnet:** Most sophisticated cyberweapon ever deployed

Figure 26. Autocoded Themes from the Two Subreddits on CyberWar and TechWar

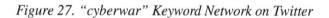

Figure 27. "cyberwar" Keyword Network on Twitter

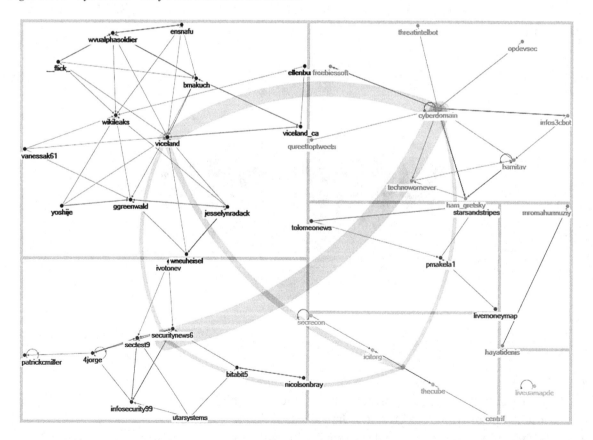

Table 2. "cyberwar" Keyword Network on the Twitter Microblogging Platform

Graph Type	Directed
Vertices	42
Unique Edges	96
Edges With Duplicates	74
Total Edges	170
Self-Loops	44
Reciprocated Vertex Pair Ratio	0.247058824
Reciprocated Edge Ratio	0.396226415
Connected Components	4
Single-Vertex Connected Components	1
Maximum Vertices in a Connected Component	35
Maximum Edges in a Connected Component	162
Maximum Geodesic Distance (Diameter)	5
Average Geodesic Distance	2.285714
Graph Density	0.06155633
Modularity	Not Applicable
NodeXL Version	1.0.1.336

- Once a nation uses a cyberweapon…
- **Elite Cyber Club:** Nation-states haves have-nots
- **Future Cyberweaponry:** Antipersonnel, physical damage, chaos
- **IoT Cyberweaponry:** Activate anything at will
- Swarming nano in space & matter
- Cyber in UAVs, balloons, 'bots, human
- Invisible Russian cyberweapon stalked US Ukraine
- **About NSA Hacker(S)/Leaker(s):** Don't know 5Ws1H!
- World power must wield strategic cyber
- World power must wield intelligent cyber
- **Shadowbrokers:** TAO crown jewels – send bids
- Light fever chills call digital epidemiologists
- **Trojan:** A gift from near / far
- **Fighting Malware:** Patching a small start
- **Cyberwar Weaponry:** Cleverer than brute force
- **Getting Cyberwar Right:** Truth and consequences
- Conficker worm world's first global cyberweapon

- From here:
  - Black-hats
  - Gray-hats
  - White-hats
  - No-hats

Figure 28. #cyberwar Hashtag Network on Twitter

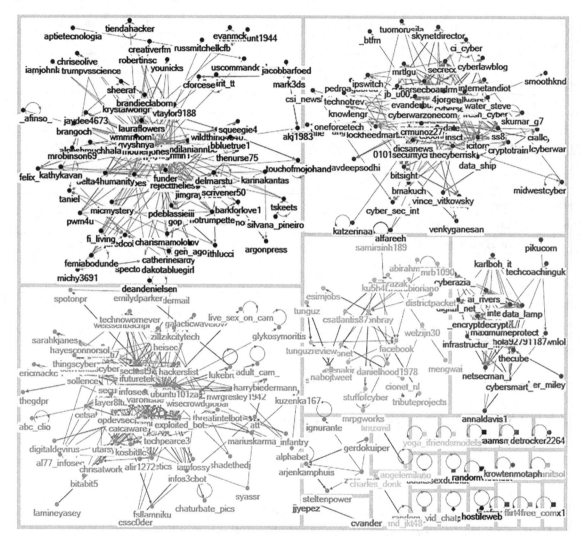

- **Considering Cyberwar:** First-order, second-order third-order effects
- Perfect memory to profile ID hacker
- **From Emergence to End:** Hacker signature
- **4IR Cyberweapons:** malware by AI machines
- **Cyber Hidden Hand:** Messages roil humanity
- **Avatar Cosplay Online:** Real for you?
- Tabletop exercises to take down systems
- **Cyberwar:** Human ingenuity harnessed for advantage
- **Cyberwar Manoeuvres:** Schumpeter's creative destruction. Full stop.
- Cyberwar no replacement for actual hard-power
- **Cyberwar:** Code multiuse & binary: good/evil

Table 3. Graph Metrics for the #cyberwar Hashtag Network on the Twitter Microblogging Platform

Graph Type	Directed
Vertices	255
Unique Edges	1305
Edges With Duplicates	308
Total Edges	1613
Self-Loops	100
Reciprocated Vertex Pair Ratio	0.195208518
Reciprocated Edge Ratio	0.326651819
Connected Components	19
Single-Vertex Connected Components	16
Maximum Vertices in a Connected Component	235
Maximum Edges in a Connected Component	1592
Maximum Geodesic Distance (Diameter)	6
Average Geodesic Distance	2.603414
Graph Density	0.020796665
Modularity	Not Applicable
NodeXL Version	1.0.1.336

Table 4. Extracted Notable Information from #cyberwar Hashtag Network on Twitter

Top URLs in Tweet in Entire Graph	Entire Graph Count
https://www.hackread.com/silence-malware-steals-your-cash-silently/	12
http://amp.irishexaminer.com/business/saving-mobile-from-cyber-attack-462301.html	11
https://economictimes.indiatimes.com/tech/internet/no-one-is-safe-how-internet-has-become-a-playground-for-cyber-criminals/articleshow/61418856.cms?utm_content=buffer892fb&utm_medium=social&utm_source=twitter.com&utm_campaign=buffer	11
https://www.engadget.com/2017/11/02/russian-hackers-hundreds-of-us-targets/	9
http://nymag.com/daily/intelligencer/2017/11/the-russian-hacking-scandal-is-way-bigger-than-donald-trump.html	8
https://paper.li/zillz/1461792715?edition_id=33829410-c24f-11e7-9048-0cc47a0d164b	8
http://www.kosbit.net/top-10-easy-steps-protect-organisation-cyberspace/	7
https://www.darkreading.com/vulnerabilities---threats/how-to-make-a-ransomware-payment---fast/d/d-id/1330255	7
https://www.theguardian.com/technology/2017/sep/22/major-cyber-attack-happen-soon-warns-uks-online-security-boss?utm_content=buffer2f740&utm_medium=social&utm_source=twitter.com&utm_campaign=buffer	5
https://www.helpnetsecurity.com/2017/11/03/estonia-id-certificates-blocked/	5
Top Domains in Tweet in Entire Graph	**Entire Graph Count**
cyberwarzone.com	55
twitter.com	47
hackread.com	15
indiatimes.com	14

continued on following page

Table 4. Continued

theguardian.com	11
irishexaminer.com	11
darkreading.com	11
webcamreports.com	10
paper.li	10
engadget.com	9
Top Hashtags in Tweet in Entire Graph	**Entire Graph Count**
cyberwar	373
cybersecurity	162
infosec	95
security	71
cyberattack	65
hacking	61
oldpost	42
hacker	40
retweet	38
cyberarmy	31
Top Words in Tweet in Entire Graph	**Entire Graph Count**
Words in Sentiment List#1: Positive	92
Words in Sentiment List#2: Negative	177
Words in Sentiment List#3: (Add your own word list)	0
Non-categorized Words	5169
Total Words	5438
cyberwar	398
rt	270
cybersecurity	162
cyber	103
infosec	95
Top Word Pairs in Tweet in Entire Graph	**Entire Graph Count**
rt,cyberwarzonecom	55
cyberattack,cyberwar	45
cybersecurity,cyberattack	42
infosec,security	41
security,cybersecurity	41
oldpost,retweet	38
cyberwar,hacker	37
rt,bamitav	36
cyberarmy,cyberwar	30
cyberwar,cybersecurity	29

continued on following page

Table 4. Continued

Top Replied-To in Entire Graph	Entire Graph Count
jaredcohen	3
akj1983	1
funder	1
cforcese	1
taniel	1
robertinsc	1
charismamolotov	1
michy3691	1
ninamorton	1
Top Mentioned in Entire Graph	**Entire Graph Count**
cyberwarzonecom	55
bamitav	36
gvyshnya	24
thecube	23
icitorg	22
centrif	22
wisecrowdglobal	13
cybersecboardrm	8
zillz	7
kosbitllc	6
Top Tweeters in Entire Graph	**Entire Graph Count**
myemoji	767414
sectest9	711738
cyberdomain	650039
gen_ago	416834
pdeblassieiii	413429
securitynews6	378138
infosecurity99	332585
evanderburg	305061
nytimes	298157
staronline	243516

- **Cyberwar Skirmishes:** Offense-defense, connections-disconnections, human-machine-cyborg, surveillance-sampling-awareness
- Online security bubbles; honeypots; traps; elicitations

In regard to Hypothesis 1 and the related sub-hypotheses: This first section shows that six-word stories may be induced computationally and written manually from curated "cyberwar" text sets (sourced from

Figure 29. A "cyberwarfare" article network on Wikipedia (1 deg.)

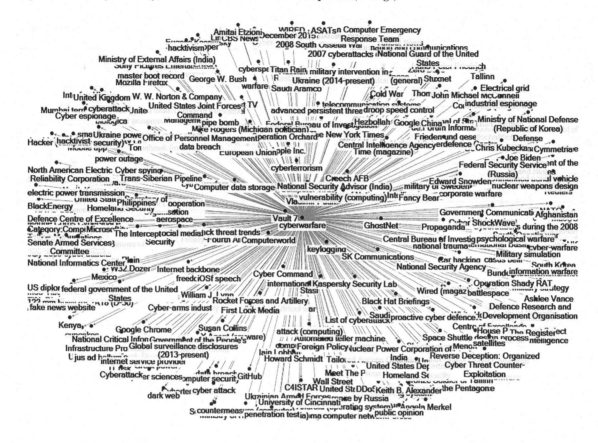

the government, mainstream journalism, academia, and social media). These hyper-brief stories can be descriptive and evocative. Based on how the texts are curated, this approach may be used to answer basic research questions, such as how cyberwar may be conceptualized broadly or some of the more cutting-edge issues in cyberwar research (in the long tail of frequency count text sets and zoomed-in views of word trees).

PART II: CALLS AND RESPONSES ABOUT CYBERWAR

From the extracted text sets, it is possible to conceptualize the government, mainstream journalistic articles, and academic research around cyberwar as "calls" and the social media data sets as "responses." A call is originated from the subject matter experts (SMEs) in the field, and a response comes from the general public. Calls tend to be broadcast from a specific source to many receivers. Responses tend to be more narrowcast among smaller groups.

The response is reflective of the expert works—and they entail a behavioral response. For example, they go to a social networking site and socialize around cyberwar books on Facebook. Or, on a social news sharing site, people "read" articles about cyberwar, engage about it, vote commentary up or down, and specify that they "read it" ("reddit"). Or they go on a microblogging site and share online resources through URLs and discuss breaking news and research. Their responses are derivative of original information that is sourced from elsewhere. (This is not to say that the general public does not have SMEs because many SMEs engage on social media, too. Many interact under the auspices of their web logs, podcasts, websites, and social media accounts. Their social interactions are framed as those of experts.)

As regards Hypothesis 2, six-word stories can be induced from cyberwar expert "calls" (through government, mainstream journalism, and academic text sets) and non-expert "responses" (through social media text sets). In terms of six-word stories from the "call" and "response" data sets do not necessarily seem that different. Hypothesis 2 shows some promise, but it needs to be explored in more depth for any definitive conclusion.

PART III: CYBERWAR BY TIME PERIOD [THE PRE-CYBERWAR PERIOD (1987 – 2006); CYBERWAR PERIOD (2007 – PRESENT)]

To explore whether there are differences in six-word stories from articles written in the pre-cyberwar period (1987 – 2006) and the current cyberwar period (2007 – present), a popular database was used to extract academic "cyberwar" articles from the two periods (based on filtering tools in the federated subscription database). For "cyberwar" articles before 2007, there were 407 results found, and those included full-texts, there were 337. For "cyberwar" articles appearing after 2006, there were 1,502 identified, and with the "full text" pre-requisite, 1,395. To keep the sets somewhat comparable, just slightly over 100 articles were downloaded from each time period, in descending order of relevance. The text sets were combined into one large document (417 pp. for the pre-cyberwar set, and 515 pp. for the current cyberwar period set).

In Figure 30, the pre-cyberwar set reads as much more tentative and concerned with processes while the latter one focuses more on in-world events and actual operations and direct worked cybersecurity problems.

Figure 30. Pre-Cyberwar and Cyberwar Period Side-by-Side Word Clouds

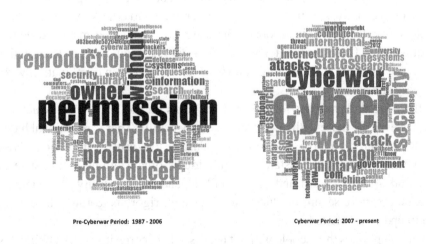

Pre-Cyberwar Period: 1987 - 2006   Cyberwar Period: 2007 - present

Pre-Cyberwar Period vs. Cyberwar Period Word Clouds by Frequency Counts

In the comparative treemap diagrams of auto-extracted themes (based on a sentence level) in Figure 31, the pre-cyberwar period focuses on many of the same issues of cybersecurity as in the current cyberwar period, but the latter contains more instantiated data, such as of botnet attacks.

A direct comparison of themes from a combined run of the two text sets shows the 1987 – 2006 articles triggering more frequently across most categories of the auto-extracted themes but with the 2007 – present set showing fewer frequency references. This is likely because the earlier literature had more references to the frequency topics, which reveals as dominance in the linegraph of the older set (Figure 32). The newer data focuses on more minutiae of cyberattacks, skirmishes, technologies, and those would appear more on a long tail than a top-level machine-extracted topic modeling visualization.

From these visualizations, it is clear that there are some major differences in a pre- and a current-age analysis of academic research articles about cyberwar. In a way, actualized events focus human attention and provide sources of information and paths forward to newer understandings.

So in regards to Hypothesis 3, there is support for the assertion: "Six-word stories may be induced about human thinking about cyberwar in the pre-cyberwar period (1987 – 2006) and the current cyberwar period (2007 – present)."

PART IV: CYBERWAR IN 4IR

As for Hypothesis 4, do the induced six-word stories about cyberwar inform some truisms to carry forward to the Fourth Industrial Revolution (4IR) space? 4IR involves an exponential rise in cyberattack surfaces, and if these are not secured, there is potential for very costly destruction and disruption.

If past is prologue… In the literature, there are some suggestive signs and speculations. Smart/cell phones, child monitors, laptop and computer cameras and microphones, have all been used as spying devices with malware used to activate these systems. Social media postings have been used to stalk people, to determine when to rob a home or workplace, and others. Cybersecurity specialists have pointed to the lack of protection for heart implants and other medical devices that may be hijacked and disrupted, putting human well-being and their very lives at risk. (One company offered to inject chips into their employees to enable their security access to company resources.) Smart homes have been a space for the Internet of Things (IoT), with devices that can control many aspects of that living environment: digitally displayed artwork, sound, security, temperature, and others. Autonomous cars have been hacked and made to stop from 60-0 in seconds. There are fears that cyber may be used to release water from dams in catastrophic floods or to interrupt food product or to interrupt or destroy the electric grid or to sabotage industrial sites. The literature shows the uses of cyber in combination with other means to carry off military attacks.

At present, there are dark markets for cyber attack tools on the Dark Web, which enables malign harnessing of cyber even for those with low-level or no cyber skills. There are national hideouts for cyber criminals protected by their respective governments against the long arm of international law enforcement. The payload of cyberattacks can be devastating for individuals, organizations, nation-states, and societies.

How people work to build smart and secure will depend on the ability of societies to train their workforces to engineer more secure products (smart design, rigorous testing, close engagement with customers) and to update as needed.

The working assumption is that people will not necessarily become less self-seeking, less advantage-seeking, less competitive, nor less conflictual. They will not suddenly lack criminal intent. Insider threat

Figure 31. Auto-coded Themes from the Pre-Cyberwar and Cyberwar Period

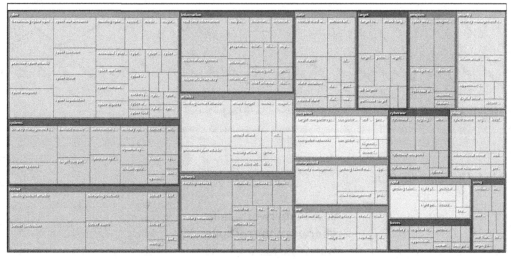

Pre-Cyberwar Period: 1987 - 2006

Cyberwar Period: 2007 - present

Auto-coded Themes from Pre-Cyberwar Period vs. Cyberwar Period (in Treemaps)

will not suddenly disappear in future time. Data leaks will not suddenly become non-existent. The forces of stability and those of anarchic impulses will not suddenly disappear. Nation-states' interests will have moments of convergence and divergence, and their reads on history will be typified by consensus and dissensus.

In general, understanding cyberwar in 4IR will depend on having more than the few induced six-word stories included here and on how the future shapes out. Do people assigned to security and defence have to be taught and re-taught about how to be careful? How to combat other human beings, in their full capabilities? The ever-changing complexities of technologies? Maybe not. However, for those new to a field, would six-word stories be somewhat informative? Maybe. (Figure 33)

Figure 32. Auto-coded Themes re Pre-Cyberwar (1987 – 2006) vs Cyberwar Period (2007 – present)

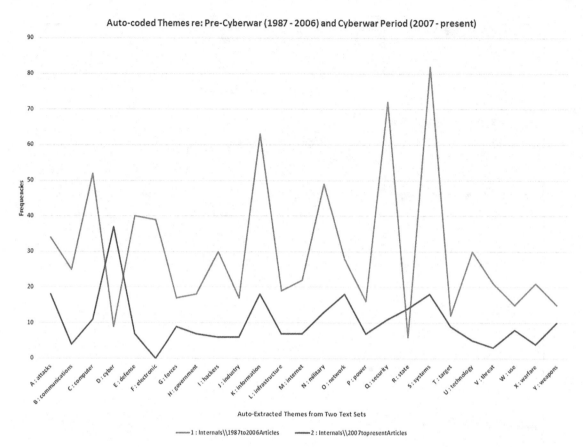

Figure 33. A Threat in the Data

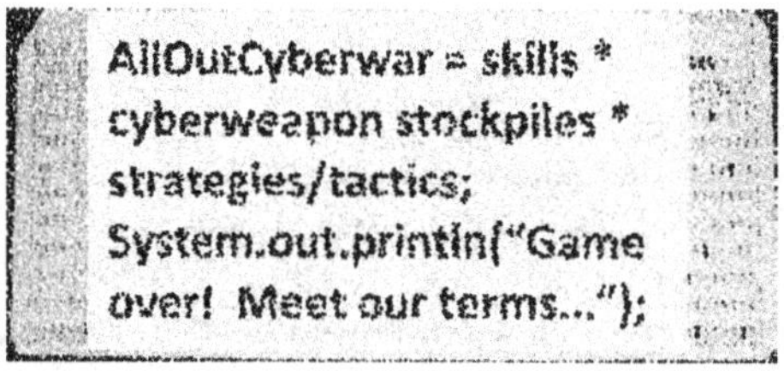

```
AllOutCyberwar = skills *
cyberweapon stockpiles *
strategies/tactics;
System.out.printin("Game
over! Meet our terms...");
```

DISCUSSION

Computationally-induced and human-written six-word stories have application in the following contexts, to...

1. Describe and summarize the underlying textual information (to enable a bridge to a complex topic);
2. Produce insights about the underlying textual information and related in-world phenomena; and
3. Answer particular research questions.

The four hypotheses in this work include the following:

Hypothesis 1: Six-word stories may be computationally and manually induced from curated text sets about cyberwar (sourced from the government, mainstream journalism, academia, and social media).
> **Hypothesis 1a:** The six-word stories may describe and summarize the underlying textual information to succinctly bridge readers to a complex topic.
> **Hypothesis 1b:** The six-word stories may produce insights about the underlying textual information and related in-world phenomena.
> **Hypothesis 1c:** The six-word stories may be used to answer particularly focused research questions.

Hypothesis 2: Six-word stories may be induced about cyberwar expert "calls" (through government, mainstream journalism, and academic text sets) and non-expert "responses" (through social media text sets) to analyze the communications cycle.

Hypothesis 3: Six-word stories may be induced about human thinking about cyberwar in the pre-cyberwar period (1987 – 2006) and the current cyberwar period (2007 – present).

Hypothesis 4: Induced six-word stories about cyberwar may inform some truisms to carry forward to the Fourth Industrial Revolution (4IR) space.

To reiterate then, there is some support for all four hypotheses, but Hypothesis 2 especially will require more work for a more confident conclusion, as will Hypothesis 4. So what are some linguistic features of the induced six-word stories around cyberwar?

Text Analysis of Six-Word Stories Around "Cyberwar"

When the collected six-word stories were run in the LIWC tool, the texts were found to be highly Analytic (95.68) or "formal, logical, and hierarchical thinking"; of medium Clout (55.63) (ranging between "high expertise" and confidence vs. "a more tentative, humble, even anxious style"; low in authenticity (8.51), indicating "distanced form of discourse), and low in emotional tone (1.00), or a lack of emotionality; the quoted explanations of the scores were from the "Linguistic Inquiry and Word Count: LIWC2015 Operator's Manual" (Pennebaker, Booth, Boyd, & Francis, 2015, pp. 21 - 22). In terms of sentiment, these six-word stories trend negative over positive (6.38 negemo to 0.00 posemo). In terms of time focus, they rank as follows: focuspast (1.42), focuspres (1.42), and focusfuture (0.71), suggesting that these brief short stories are focused more on the past and present, and less on the future, as on the linguistic qualities of the language used.

FUTURE RESEARCH DIRECTIONS

So what are some possible next steps in the study of "cyberwar" using induced six-word stories? Certainly, there are a number of other text sets that have not been explored: those in non-private holdings, those in non-English languages, and so on. There are image sets that may be tapped that may be manually coded or auto-coded and studied. This topic may be studied in terms of social networks in other geographical locales on social media. Also, video sets, audio sets, multimedia, and mixed media may all be harnessed for this work.

With the lack of popularity of reading, six-word stories are eminently consumable. They may be used to help bridge non-readers into more complex understandings of the world, given that the underlying texts of this issue may well remain in the Great Unread in terms of the mass public. Sometimes, epiphanies may be found in the telltale small details. Beyond bridging a complex issue to the broader public, how else may six-word stories be used?

Then, too, there can be further formal studies of six-word stories, beyond the computational text analysis of the extracted stories from this work. What are the strengths and weaknesses of this extreme and radical brevity? (Six words are somewhat arbitrary, and if there are benefits in raising the count, that may be a constructive way forward.) For example, in this work, some six-word stories have been clustered to illuminate a phenomenon, and that may be a variation...to have "collections" of six-word stories. In another sense, the six-word stories are not "the point" of the exercise, but wrangling with the ideas is. This is about training the reader to see insights through this eight-step process.

Also, there are other computational text analysis methods that can reduce text sets and result in different identified words and phrases—such as in text network analysis.

If the Estonia event was Cyberwar 1.0 and Stuxnet was Cyberwar 2.0, by the time this work is published, readers may well find humanity in Cyberwar 3.0, and beyond. Certainly, the scope of understanding this phenomenon of cyberwar will remain relevant into the future.

Technologies employed. The technologies used in this work include the following: NVivo 11 Plus; NCapture; Linguistic Inquiry and Word Count (LIWC); Network Overview, Discovery and Exploration for Excel (NodeXL); Google Books Ngram Viewer; Google Correlate; Google Translate; Adobe Photoshop; Microsoft Visio; Microsoft Excel; Gadwin Printscreen, and others. This listing does not indicate endorsement of the technologies. The author does not have any formal ties to any of the software makers.

CONCLUSION

The novelty in this work is several-fold. One involves the use of computational text analysis methods to reduce large-scale data into brief word sets, which can then be turned into six-word stories by human analysts. This induction of six-word stories is original. It adds a layer of analysis and radical simplification to the results of selected computational text analyses. This approach enables access to meaning-making from large-scale data. While this process assumes a well-read "author" for the six-word stories, this may be applied to contexts in which the "authors" are engaging with the topic "blind" to see what insights are possible from computational analyses; in this case, those who curate the text sets and run the analyses may be one part of a team, and the analysts a separate team without access to the initial process but only the resulting data visualizations. A degree of non-sensical and inchoate in the resulting induced text sets is beneficial because this may open up the imagination and thinking space and prompt new insights. This process also assumes "readers" who are somewhat prepared for the topic because of the need for some referential fluency. In an age of extreme brevity from microblogging, six-word stories have come of age, and they can be harnessed for more serious ends than memoirs, jokes, and witticisms.

How cyberwar manifests in 4IR depends on many factors: how humans organize, what their group (nation-state) ambitions may be, the natures of cyber, and what captures the attention of decision-makers and their constituents. Large-scale competitions between nation-states, in the 20th century, have been dark and destructive, with uses of weapons of mass destruction (nuclear, chemical, and biological). The weapons have been deployed in defense of lands, of ideas, of national pride, of self-governance, and any number of other rationales and mixes of rationales. Into the 21st century, human strife will continue to manifest but in unpredictable ways. If cyber can be harnessed to national ends, it will be. If history has been written based on human adventurism, miscalculations, and testing of limits, this will be so in new centuries and new industrial revolutions. And if leadership is about strategy and vision and capabilities, so too, here.

Cyberwar may be one of those statecraft phenomena that occur in the shadows, without public attention except episodically. Cyberattacks are represented episodically and maybe as one-offs, but these are likely continuous and stealth. In the public sphere, phenomena become a "thing" only if there are interests promoting it, and in many cases, the main stakeholders may not have any reason to broadcast widely. (At present, the most common communicators of cyberattacks are companies that have security products and services to market.)

Writing six-word stories from complex information can be quite challenging. It is easy to fall into sloganeering and hard to acquire fresh insights. Structuring such short works requires being highly selective of the words and the symbols, and it requires playing some of the spaces between and beyond the words.

Cyberwar prep for that inevitable day…

Note: There are six-word stories about cyberwar from an initial scraped social imagery set in Appendix 2. This may provide a way forward for integrating imagery about a topic for the inducing of six-word stories about a topic.

ACKNOWLEDGMENT

This is for R. Max.

REFERENCES

Abebe, D. (2016). Cyberwar, international politics, and institutional design. *The University of Chicago Law Review. University of Chicago. Law School, 83*(1), 1–22.

Allen, P. D., & Demehak, C. C. (2003, March – April). The Palestinian –Israeli cyberwar. *Military Review*, 52–59.

Arquilla, J., & Ronfeldt, D. (1993, Spring). Cyberwar Is Coming! *Comparative Strategy, 12*(2), 141–165. doi:10.1080/01495939308402915

Bellovin, S. M. (2013, May/June). Military cybersomethings. *IEEE Security and Privacy, 11*(3), 88. doi:10.1109/MSP.2013.63

Bendrath, R. (2001). The cyberwar debate: Perception and politics in the U.S. critical infrastructure protection. *Information & Security, 7*, 80–103.

Blunden, B. (2010). Manufactured consent and cyberwar. In *Proceedings of Lockdown 2010*. University of Wisconsin-Madison. Retrieved from http://www.belowgotham.com/LD-2010-WP.pdf

Botzakis, S. (2013). Reviewed works: Six word memoirs. *Journal of Adolescent & Adult Literacy, 57*(2), 162 – 163.

Bowden, M. (2011). *Worm: The First Digital World War*. New York: Atlantic Monthly Press.

Bronk, C. (2013). Between War & Peace: Considering the Statecraft of Cyberspace. In J. Krüger, B. Nickolay, & S. Gaycken (Eds.), *The Secure Information Society*. London: Springer. doi:10.1007/978-1-4471-4763-3_1

Brose, R. (2015). Cyberwar, netwar, and the future of cyberdefense. *Proceedings of the 2015 7th International Conference on Cyber Conflict: Architectures in Cyberspace*. Retrieved from https://www.youtube.com/watch?v=0vWG62o_XaA&ab_channel=CareersatBurlington

Cavelty, M. D. (2010). Cyberwar concept, status quo, and limitations. *CSS Analysis in Security Policy*, *71*, 1–3.

Cavelty, M. D. (2010). The reality and future of cyberwar. *CSS Analysis in Security Policy*. Retrieved from https://pdfs.semanticscholar.org/bbba/7d388cb67e0d2b2ca7d7b2ed60ca2de65b1c.pdf

Cimbala, S.J. (2011). Nuclear crisis management and 'cyberwar.' *Strategic Studies Quarterly*, 117 – 131.

Clark, D. D. (2011). Protecting the Internet as a public commons. *Bulletin - American Academy of Arts and Sciences. American Academy of Arts and Sciences*, *64*(2), 62–63.

Clarke, R. A., & Knake, R. K. (2010). *Cyber War: The Next Threat to National Security and What to Do about It*. New York: HarperCollins Publishers.

Cyber Warfare. (2017). RAND Corporation. Retrieved from https://www.rand.org/topics/cyber-warfare.html

Darwish, M. (2017, Nov. 3). Did Russia make this ship disappear? *Cable News Network (CNN)*. Retrieved from http://money.cnn.com/2017/11/03/technology/gps-spoofing-russia/index.html

Döge, J. (2010). Cyber warfare: Challenges for the applicability of the traditional laws of war regime. *Archiv des Völkerrechts*, *48*(4), 486–501. doi:10.1628/000389210794439416

Dunlap, C.J. (2011). Perspectives for cyber strategists on law for cyberwar. *Strategic Studies Quarterly*, 81 – 99.

Dunnewold, M. (2000). Why am I here? Six-word stories about the first month of law school. *Journal of Legal Education*, *59*(4), 653–656. Retrieved from https://jle.aals.org/cgi/viewcontent.cgi?referer=https://www.google.com/&httpsredir=1&article=1285&context=home

Ernest Hemingway – Baby Shoes. (2008). *Snopes*. Retrieved from https://www.snopes.com/language/literary/-babyshoes.asp

Eun, Y.-S., & Abmann, J. S. (2016). Cyberwar: Taking stock of security and warfare in the digital age. *International Studies Perspectives*, *17*, 343–360.

Feil, J. A. (2012). Cyberwar and unmanned aerial vehicles: Using new technologies, from espionage to action. *Case Western Reserve Journal of International Law*, *45*, 513–544.

Flowers, A., & Zeadally, S. (2014). Cyberwar: The what, when, why, and how. *IEEE Technology and Society Magazine*, 14–21.

Fourth Industrial Revolution. (2017). In *Wikipedia*. Retrieved from https://en.wikipedia.org/wiki/-Fourth_Industrial_Revolution

Gartzke, E. (2013). The myth of cyberwar: Bringing war in cyberspace back down to earth. *International Security, 38*(2), 41–73. doi:10.1162/ISEC_a_00136

Greenberg, A. (2017, Sept. 6). Hackers gain direct access to U.S. power grid controls. *Wired Magazine*. Retrieved from https://www.wired.com/story/hackers-gain-switch-flipping-access-to-us-power-systems/

Hayden, M. V. (2016). *Playing to the Edge: American Intelligence in the Age of Terror*. New York: Penguin Press.

History of the World Wide Web. (2017). In *Wikipedia*. Retrieved from https://en.wikipedia.org/wiki/History_of_the_-World_Wide_Web

Holden, S. (1996). Theater Review: Hemingway, two years before the end. *The New York Times*. Retrieved from http://www.nytimes.com/1996/05/06/theater/theater-review-hemingway-two-years-before-the-end.html

Hollis, D.M. (2011). Cyberwar case study: Georgia 2008. *Small Wars Journal,* 1 – 10.

Hughes, D., & Colarik, A. (2017). The hierarchy of cyber war definitions. In G. A. Wang & ... (Eds.), *PAISI 2017. 15 – 33*. doi:10.1007/978-3-319-57463-9_2

Huntley, W. L. (2016). Strategic implications of offense and defense in cyberwar. *2016 49th Hawaii International Conference on System Sciences*, 5588 – 5595. 10.1109/HICSS.2016.691

Jenik, A. (2009). Cyberwar in Estonia and the Middle East. *Network Security*, 4–6.

Kaiser, R. (2015). The birth of cyberwar. *Political Geography, 46*, 11–20. doi:10.1016/j.polgeo.2014.10.001

Kallberg, J. & Thuraisingham, B. (2013, May/June). State actors' offensive cyberoperations: The disruptive power of systematic cyberattacks. IT Pro. *IEEE Computer Society*, 32 – 35.

Kallberg, J., Thuraisingham, B., & Lakomaa, E. (2013). Societal Cyberwar Theory applied: The disruptive power of state actor aggression for public sector information security. *2013 European Intelligence and Security Informatics Conference (EISIC)*, 212 – 215. 10.1109/EISIC.2013.47

Kaplan, F. (2016). Inside 'Eligible Receiver': The NSA's disturbingly successful hack of the American military. *Slate*. Retrieved from http://www.slate.com/articles/technology/future_tense/2016/03/inside_the_nsa_s_-shockingly_successful_simulated_hack_of_the_u_s_military.html

Kelson, R., Paganini, P., Gittins, B., & Pace, D. (2012). The 'cyber war' era began long ago. *Security Affairs*. Retrieved from http://securityaffairs.co/wordpress/6776/security/the-cyber-war-era-began-long-ago.html

Kozlowski, A. (2015). *The 'cyber weapons gap.' The assessment of China's cyber warfare capabilities and its consequences for potential conflict over Taiwan*. University of Lodz Repository

Krebs, B. (2014). *Spam Nation: The Inside Story of Organized Cybercrime—from Global Epidemic to your Front Door*. Naperville: Sourcebooks, Inc.

Lewis, J. A. (2011, September). Oct.) Cyberwar thresholds and effects. *IEEE Security and Privacy*, *9*(5), 23–29. doi:10.1109/MSP.2011.25

Libicki, M. C. (2009). *Cyberdeterrence and cyberwar. Project Airforce*. RAND Corporation.

Libicki, M.C. (2011). Cyberwar as a confidence game. *Strategic Studies Quarterly,* 132 – 146.

Libicki, M. C. (2013). Brandishing cyberattack in a nuclear confrontation. In *Brandishing Cyberattack Capabilities*. RAND Corporation.

Lucas, E. (2015). *Cyberphobia: Identity, Trust, Security and the Internet*. New York: Bloomsbury.

McCoy, A. W. (2017). *In the Shadows of the American Century: The Rise and Decline of US Global Power*. Chicago, IL: Haymarket Books.

Nakashima, E. (2017). U.S. declares North Korea carried out massive WannaCry cyberattack. National Security. *The Washington Post*. Retrieved from https://www.washingtonpost.com/world/national-security/us-set-to-declare-north-korea-carried-out-massive-wannacry-cyber-attack/2017/12/18/509deb1c-e446-11e7-a65d-1ac0fd7f097e_story.html?utm_term=.0d8c6361a841

Pennebaker, J. W., Booth, R. J., Boyd, R. L., & Francis, M. E. (2015). *Linguistic Inquiry and Word Count: LIWC2015 Operator's Manual*. Austin, TX: Pennebaker Conglomerates. Retrieved from www.LIWC.nethttps://s3-us-west-2.amazonaws.com/downloads.liwc.net/LIWC2015_OperatorManual.pdf

Rid, T. (2013). Cyberwar and peace: Hacking can reduce real-world violence. *Foreign Affairs*, *92*(6), 77–87.

Rid, T. (2016). *Rise of the Machines: A Cybernetic History*. New York: W.W. Norton & Company.

Roncero-Menendez, S. (2014). In six words, these writers tell you an entire story. *Huffington Post*.

Schwab, K. (2016). *The Fourth Industrial Revolution*. Geneva: World Economic Forum.

Singer, P. W., & Friedman, A. (2014). *Cybersecurity and Cyberwar: What Everyone Needs to Know*. Oxford, UK: Oxford University Press.

Six Word Stories. (2013). Retrieved from http://www.sixwordstories.net/category/subject/funny/

Stohl, M. (2014). Dr. Strangeweb: Or how they stopped worrying and learned to love cyber war. Ch. 5. In Cyberterrorism (pp. 85 – 102). New York: Springer.

Sun Tzu. (5th century B.C.). *The Art of War* (L. Giles, Trans.). Retrieved from http://classics.mit.edu/Tzu/artwar.html

Tinnel, L. S., Saydjari, O. S., & Farrell, D. (2002). Cyberwar strategy and tactics: An analysis of cyber goals, strategies, tactics, and techniques. *Proceedings of the 2002 IEEE Workshop on Information Assurance*, 228 – 234.

Trendle, G. (2002). Cyberwar. *The World Today*, *58*(4), 7–8.

Tworek, H. (2017, May 9). Microsoft is right: We need a digital Geneva Convention. *Wired Magazine*. Retrieved from https://www.wired.com/2017/05/microsoft-right-need-digital-geneva-convention/

Ventre, D. (2011). *Cyberware and information warfare*. London: Wiley. doi:10.1002/9781118603482

WannaCry ransomware attack. (2017). In *Wikipedia*. Retrieved from https://en.wikipedia.org/wiki/WannaCry-_ransomware_attack

Wright, F. A. (2012). 2014). The short story just got shorter: Hemingway, narrative, and the six-word urban legend. *Journal of Popular Culture*, *47*(2), 327–340.

ADDITIONAL READING

Clarke, R. A., & Eddy, R. P. (2017). *Warnings: Finding Cassandras to Stop Catastrophes*. New York: HarperCollins.

Clarke, R. A., & Knake, R. K. (2010). *Cyber War: The Next Threat to National Security and What to Do About It*. New York: HarperCollins.

Hayden, M. W. (2016). *Playing to the Edge: American Intelligence in the Age of Terror*. New York: Penguin Books.

Kaplan, F. (2016). *Dark Territory: The Secret History of Cyber War*. New York: Simon & Schuster.

Koppel, T. (2015). *Lights Out: A Cyberattack, a Nation Unprepared, Surviving the Aftermath*. New York: Crown Publishers.

Singer, P. W., & Friedman, A. (2014). *Cybersecurity and Cyberwar: What Everyone Needs to Know*. New York: Oxford University Press.

KEY TERMS AND DEFINITIONS

Cold War: A state of heightened antagonism between nation-states that is expressed as suppressed and somewhat-restrained hostilities; stops short of open warfare.

Cyber Hard Power: The use of cyber to cause physical damage, injuries, and death (as in an escalatory war situation).

Cyber Soft Power: The use of cyber to convey information in a strategic way.

Cybersecurity: Freedom from potential compromise and potential harm stemming from unauthorized access to computers and computer networks.

Cyberwar: The uses of computer technology to advance nation-state interests against an adversary.

"Found" Six-Word Stories: Fragments of sentences or full sentences comprised of six words that may be read insightfully as authored/designed six-word stories.

Fourth Industrial Revolution (4IR): A label of the current and near-future of impending changes and disruptions due to advancements in cyber and biological and other technologies; a concept by Klaus Schwab.

Great Unread: A notional and practical collection of texts which do not attract human attention for reading.

Hack: Use of a computer (or social engineering or other deceptive methods) to gain access to system data.

Hard Cyber Power: Uses of cyberweapons to destroy physical infrastructure.

Hot War: Human conflict with destructive attacks on physical infrastructure and peoples; open warfare.

Induction: Extraction of text sets from computational means.

Infrastructure: Physical facilities needed for the maintenance of society.

Internet of Things (IoT): Internet-based connections between computing devices ("things"), such as those in cars, homes, commercial spaces, bodies (health devices), smart phones, and others.

Machine Reading: Uses of computers to create meaning from text sets, also referred to as auto-coding in some contexts.

Narrative: A story about connected events.

Netwar: Information warfare among non-state actors, including citizens and social activists.

Six-Word Story: A brief literary form of six-word "narratives" that originated in the 1980s.

Sociograph: A visualization of nodes (entities) and links (relationships) showing interrelationships (such as between individuals/groups on a social media platform).

Soft Cyber Power: Information warfare, public diplomacy, propaganda.

Stealth: Something hidden or invisible (often based on design and deployment); surreptitious.

APPENDIX 1

More About Six-Word Stories on the Social Web

On different social media platforms, six-word stories manifest in different ways. This is based on several likely factors. One involves the types of individuals attracted to particular platforms and the cultures that evolve around particular sites (based on leadership and on participants as well as the socio-technological enablements).

A Month of Posts on the Sixwordstories Subreddit

The social news-sharing site reddit has a subreddit for six-word stories: https://www.reddit.com/r/six-wordstories/. Participants may vote particular stories up or down. A set of posting titles (which are the whole six-word stories) comprised of 15,344 words in 120 pp. were collected, and a word frequency count was created from this set to capture a sense of some of the main topics (Figure 34). A close read of a more recent text set shows observations about life, with themes of lost love and sexually transmitted diseases (STDs), disses, politics, humor ("What's her blood type? French Roast."), philosophy, and others.

It is possible to query the same information from the subreddit six-word stories using auto-coded topic-modeling (Figure 35).

On Twitter

Microblogging enables people to share short texts, images, and video snippets in a one-to-many way (broadcasting) and a one-to-few way (narrowcasting), and in a many-to-many way (broadcasting). Sev-

Figure 34. A Word Frequency Cloud of "sixwordstories" from the Sub-reddit

Figure 35. An Auto-coded Topic-Modeling Sense of "sixwordstories" from the Sub-reddit

eral sites on the Twitter microblogging platform were built around six-word stories. Some of them are examined here.

One account [@sixwordshort at https://twitter.com/sixwordshort] was launched in May 2014. It had 25,255 Tweets, 128 following, 1,002,348 followers, and 4 likes on the day data about this account was extracted through the Twitter application programming interface (API). A total of 3,235 messages were collected, with retweets included. In the profile, the description reads: "quiet people have the loudest mind," and its top-level images are all words. The topics seem to be about daily life issues (Figure 36), based on a word frequency count.

There are ways to auto-code themes through topic-modeling of each of the cells of data; the most common topics are shown in a treemap diagram (Figure 37). In descending order, the most frequent topics include the following: people, happiness, nights, hearts, thoughts, gave happiness, empty, everyone, things, time, everything, friends, 2am thoughts, tears, promises, slow burn, left unsaid, trusted people, granting factory, perfect ones, rainy nights, sick animal, story, mighty oaks, broken people, comforting company, different plans, familiar voice, filled cracks, right person, road trip, saying goodbye, people mistake, much anger, words, wrong number, wrong time, etc.

It is possible to extract the lead-up words and lead-away words to a target phrase or word, to engage in close-in reading of the concepts and to understand the context of the word use (Figure 38).

In terms of its network of those it is following, and interacting with, a few seem to be commercial accounts, and others seem to promote particular political stances, among other interests (Figure 39). The sociography is a directional one albeit with only outward-point arrows, showing following relationships (based on *ad hoc* interactivity, not declared following relationships).

In terms of geographical locale for this social network, most of the recently active members seem clustered around Chicago (Figure 40).

Figure 36. Messaging @sixwordshort on Twitter Microblogging Platform (Word Frequency Count)

Figure 37. Most Frequent Auto-coded Themes in @sixwordshort on Twitter Microblogging Platform

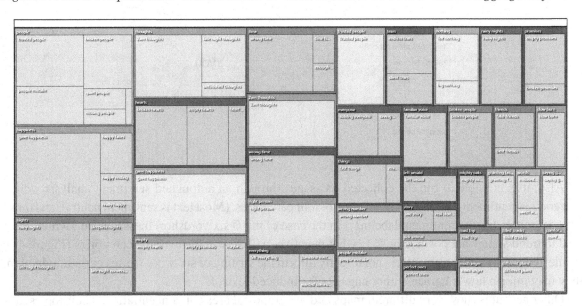

Figure 38. "Love" in all its Senses in @sixwordshort on Twitter Microblogging Platform

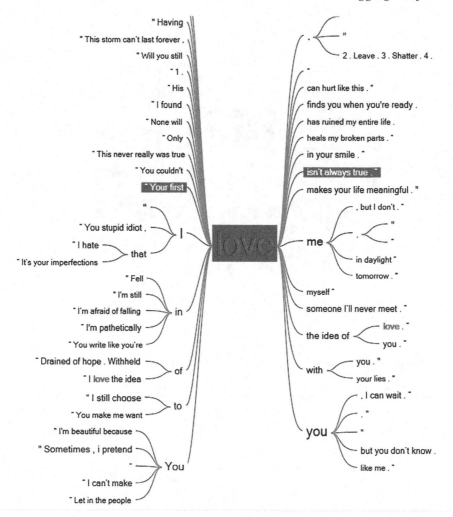

Also, it is possible to run the collected messages through an automated sentiment analysis, which categorizes sentiment-bearing terms into one of four categories. (Most text is sentiment neutral, and those are not included in the sentiment labeling.) In the case of the @sixwordshort messages on Twitter, most tend to trend somewhat positive or somewhat negative, with few in the extreme categories (Figure 41). While geography and sentiments do not directly inform the writing of six-word stories or their induction, they may inform how a human author engages the induced texts.

Other accounts show very different maps and geographical areas of concentration. Their topics also vary.

The @itssixwordstory (https://twitter.com/itssixwordstory) joined Twitter in August 2010 and had 29,513 Tweets, 542 following, 833,537 followers, 902 likes, and two lists when its data was captured. Only 3,225 messages were in the captured dataset, including retweets. This network is mostly located around Mauritania and the American Northeast (particularly New York). (Figure 42)

The topics discussed on the more recent messaging are shown in Figure 43.

Figure 39. @sixwordshort following network on Twitter as a directional sociography

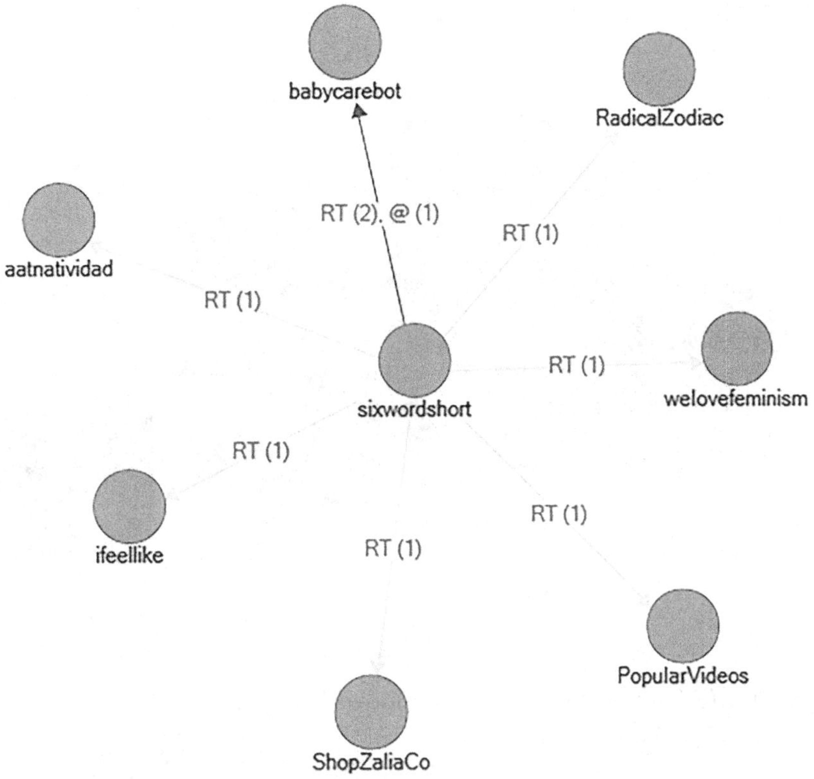

Figure 40. A Geographical Map of @sixwordshort Social Network on Twitter

Figure 41. A Sentiment Analysis of @sixwordshort Social Network Messaging

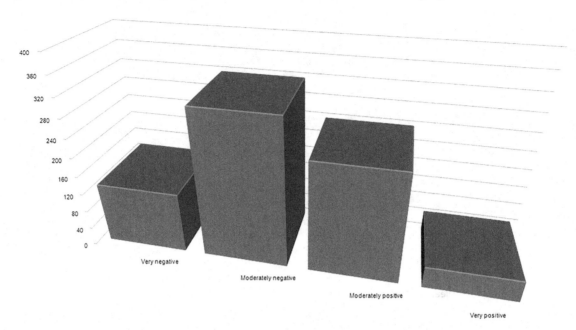

Figure 42. Geographical Map of @itssixwordstory Social Network on Twitter

Yet another account, @sixwordstories (https://twitter.com/sixwordstories?lang=en) had 1,776 Tweets, 15 following, 15,932 followers, and 3 likes at the moment of the data capture. All 1776 messages were collected. The most recent one seems to have been from 2014. The account was created back in December 2008, about two years after Twitter was founded. This account messaging shows interest in assassins. (Figure 45)

Figure 43. Messaging @itssixwordstory on Twitter Microblogging Platform (Word Frequency Count)

Figure 44. Most Frequent Auto-coded Themes in @itssixwordstory on Twitter Microblogging Platform

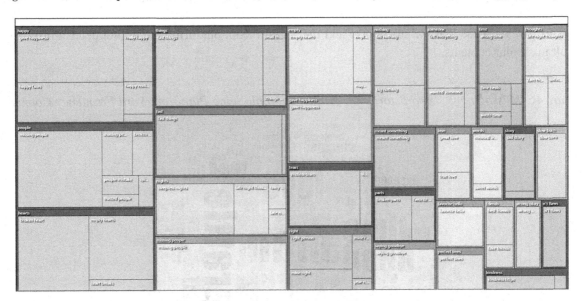

Figure 45. Most Frequent Auto-coded Themes in @sixwordstories on Twitter Microblogging Platform

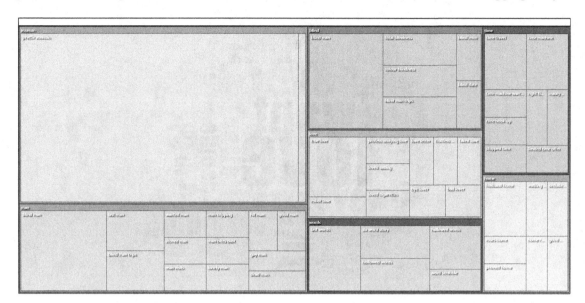

The focus on preferred topics may also be seen in a word cloud derived from a word frequency count (Figure 46).

This gives a sense that the story form and the social media platform type do not deterministically result in similar contents.

Figure 46. Messaging @sixwordstories on Twitter Microblogging Platform (Word Frequency Count)

APPENDIX 2

Six-Word Stories About Cyberwar From an Initial Social Imagery Set

Harnessing multimodal data enables access to learning not only through the traditional text datasets. In that spirit, six-word stories may also be induced from "cyberwar" image sets scraped from Web 2.0 or the Social Web. The size of the image set use was 626 images. These were scraped from a search of Google Images, and the images were collected using the Picture Downloader Professional (add-on to Google Chrome). A screenshot of some images in this set follows in Figure 47.

A few additional details of this image set may be helpful. In a manual coding of the image types, while trying to capture some aspects of the "long tail," the images were of the following mixed types (Figure 48).

The same data in Figure 48 is offered in Figure 49, albeit in descending order as a Pareto chart.

Most common as the following, in descending order: events and presenters; website / mobile screens, heads of state; public demonstration / march; photo illustration; poster; customized illustration; stock imagery / decorative; book cover; map; selfies, and so on.

Also, only about 1% (7/626) of the images were informational (data visualizations, legible posters, and data tables). The rest are generally informative but not in the way data visualizations are in a granular sense. To generalize, the images show people working to shore up cybersecurity, print and digital media about cyberwar, toys set up presentationally to show combat, and others. Some messaging was clearly to make political statements, such as one event with marchers around the Anonymous hacker collective. Others celebrate those who work in cybersecurity, such as some people wearing decorated "gas masks" with cyber elements.

Figure 47. A Screenshot of the Cyberwar Image Set Imagery as Thumbnails

Figure 48. Categories of Imagery in the Cyberwar Image Set (alphabetized bar chart)

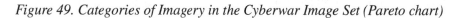

Figure 49. Categories of Imagery in the Cyberwar Image Set (Pareto chart)

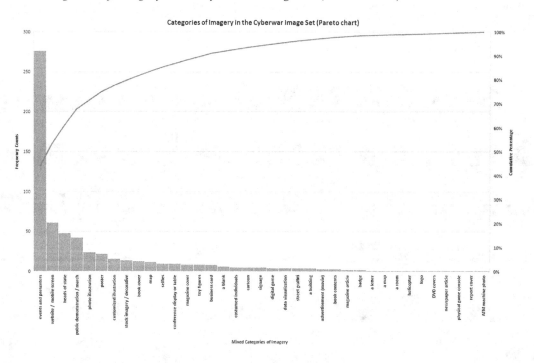

So riffing from the imagery, what are some possible six-word stories about cyberwar? A few follow:

- **Cyberwar Fronts:** Governance, law, technology, public
- **Prep 4 Cyberwar:** #Gocreative #gobig #gofun
- **Cyberwar Prep:** Share among trusted parties
- **Cyberwar Prep:** Understanding systems codes people

Slideshows based on "cyberwar" were also extracted from SlideShare, but many of these are fairly derivative of mass media reports on cyberwar and some research in this field. An early analysis of these were not fruitful in terms of information.

Chapter 16
Terrorism in the Age of Information:
Unpuzzling the Connection of Terrorism and the Media in the Fourth Industrial Revolution

Maximiliano Emanuel Korstanje
University of Palermo, Argentina

Adrian Scribano
University of Buenos Aires, Argentina

Freddy Alex Timmermann
Catholic University Silva Henriquez, Chile

ABSTRACT

While a lot of studies focus on the contours of cybercrime and cyber terrorism as well as their effects in daily lives, less attention has been given to the use of ICT by terrorists. In fact, through the ebbs and flows of technology, the society of information seems to develop a particular vulnerability to the fear instilled by terrorism. This particularly reveals a paradox because the original technology, which was oriented to make of our lives safer, is used by terrorist cells to inspire a terror-driven atmosphere, which only nourishes intolerance and ethnocentrism. The authors, in this review chapter, discuss critically the cutting-edge role of technology in the struggle against terrorism.

INTRODUCTION

Ethnocentrism should be defined as the act of judging others cultures under the lens of cultural values alone. No matter the time or the background, cultures have tended to develop an ethnocentric viewpoint of the alterity, which was widely theorized by ethnology and anthropology. Over years, the global empires have developed socio-centric explanations about their so-called superiority that were culturally

DOI: 10.4018/978-1-5225-4763-1.ch016

internalized by the peripheral nations. This symbolic center-periphery dependency not only paved the ways for the multiplications of discovery-related travels but also situated as the precondition for globalization (Martell, 2010). Any Empire combines the military stronghold with economic solvency and the monopoly of technological information. This opens the doors to what Baudrillard named as "the principle of reversibility", which means that the foundations of a system are daily eroded while it is in expansion. As historians agree, this explains the rise and rapid declines of Empires worldwide, but what is most important, the role of technology in increasing the vulnerability of the Empire (Coulter, 2012). To set a recent example, the attacks to New York in 2001 were possible since terrorists weaponized civilian airplanes against important symbolic targets. While the blow hits the exemplary center – not the periphery – of capitalist culture, nations of the four continents reacted energetically expressing their solidarities with the US. Paradoxically, the same technology which made our life safer was used to create terror. In this process, the mass media played a crucial role not only packaging but also disseminating the terror-related news towards a global audience. This chapter explores the effects of terrorism, oddly closing the borderlands or neglecting hospitality to aliens, while it interrogates on the revolution of technology and information as one of the veins terrorism fills. For the sake of clarity, capitalism evolved through the articulation of different stages, which were defined as "revolutions". The first revolution, which occurred during the 18th and 19th centuries, appealed to a mechanization of labor disciplining the bodies into standardized forms of production. The first industrial nations experienced a rapid migration to the cities, which were rapidly and densely populated in question of years. Instead the second revolution – during the 20th century – applied on the standardization of scale production stimulating not only a further specialization but also innovating extensively in the transport means. The third revolution alluded to a process of decentralization that was suddenly prompted by the Arab-Israeli War which derived in an Oil embargo that placed the western sources of energy in jeopardy. The Fourth Revolution consists of the use of robots and robotization not only for yielding the war abroad, but also to domesticate the workforce internally. This broader movement involves not only the media informational system but also the usage of technology to perform routine tasks. For some reasons, some voices have alerted that the rise of unemployment or economic instability are fertile grounds for the rise of terrorism globally, but especially in the Third World. Samuel Huntington said that the process of securitization, which the Fourth Industrial Revolution (4IR) needs, leads to an inevitable clash between civilizations in which case the failures of capitalism to undermine poverty in under-developed nations increases the risks of a much deeper radicalization or anti-American sentiment. As a result of this, Huntington adds, the US should not only scrutinize migration but also promotes free trade to better the local economies of non-western nations (Huntington 1993; 1997; 2000). The climate of violence, where terrorism operates, needs from a previous state of resentment which is the combination of failed states, inefficient economic policies and political instability (Barro, 1991; Pollins, 1989; Phillips, 2008). This chapter not only confronts with such a belief but also it holds the thesis that Western ethnocentrism impedes the reconciliation with the alterity reinforcing the obsession for terror consumption in the publics. In the society of information, terrorism not only serves as a catalyst to produce a state of panic, which is conducive to the status quo, but also accelerates economic programs that otherwise would be rejected by citizenry. This review chapter explores the ethical dilemmas of media in a hyper-technologized world as well as how international terrorism uses technologies to instill its message of fear. Sociologically speaking, more than a century ago, Lebon and Tarde demonstrated that contagion took a collective dynamic of mimicry which merited attention by the side of scholarship. In the same way, terrorism exploits the emotional basis of contagion to impose a message of extortion and violence (Ahnf. 2011; Chmiel et al., 2011; Schweitzer & Garcia, 2010). Contagion showed to guide the collective and individual behaviour (Kramer, Guilroy & Hancock, 2014; Marenko, 2010; Von Solms & Van Niekerk, 2013).

PRELIMINARY DISCUSSION

The American political scientist, Samuel Huntington (1993; 1997) sets forward an intriguing and provocative thesis when he affirms that terrorism should be considered as the immediate consequence of the clash of civilizatory projects. Some years earlier than 9/11 he traced back to the historical encounters between Islam and Christianity as the main reasons that explain terrorism today. These two civilizations, because of cultural incompatibilities are irreducibly forced to collide. In Huntington´s account, some nations are not culturally programmed to welcome democracy. Though he toys with the belief that these cultural differences should lead inevitably to conflict, he received much criticism to overlook the fact that Muslims and Christians share a common Abrahamic Tradition (Said, 2001; Karim & Eid, 2012; Fuller, 2010). In his seminal book *The Clash of Barbarism,* Gilbert Achcar (2015) calls the attention to the "narcissist commission" as an ideological discourse aimed at subordinating the periphery towards a temporal empathy with the center. As he brilliantly observed, traumatic events like 9/11 reinforced a sentiment of solidarity given in view of the victims, while other similarly-minded events were glossed over. In this vein, terrorism revitalizes the frustrations of relegated citizens who feel the same that privileged citizens feel. Years of oppression and direct interventions of US are blurred into the culture of horror and fear, which places the Muslim other as the main threat of democracy. This process of demonization, adjoined to the need to take part of the chosen peoples, seems to be the ideological core of terrorism. Rather, J. B Revel (2003) focuses on the sentiment of Anti-Americanism" as the proof of French cynicism that situates Europe as the axis of Venus (as great pacifists) while the US fulfill the role of Mars (which reflects the investment of millions of dollars in the security budget). The same point was widely explored by Robert Kagan (2004) who found that America and Europe went through different paths. While Europe cultivated a climate of prosperity and peace, which was based in the liberal trade the United States conducted led-invasions to the Middle East. In this token, Robert Reich (2005) and Jacob Weisberg (2005 lamented the rise of a long-dormant class of politicians, radical conservatives (radcons) which took preferred positions and seats in Bush`s administrations. Though radcons were not in direct responsibility of 9/11 as the conspiracy theories preclude, they overreacted adopting the "preemptive platform", which was adjoined to the preventive attack doctrine as the key international policy.

Against this backdrop, *radcons* set a bipolar cosmology of foes and friends that ushered the world into a climate of fear and mistrust. Here two assumptions should be made. On the one hand, the Bush administration received the unconditional and unilateral support of those countries such as Spain and Great Britain which underwent similar situations in the past. On the other hand (Muslim) terrorism became the threat of the West at the turn of the century (Robertson, 2002). This raises the question: to what extent the *war on terror* and *the doctrine of preventive attack* are effective actions in the society of information.

MEDIA, TERROR AND THE FOURTH INDUSTRIAL REVOLUTION

As explained in the introduction, society went through different stages of production. The fourth industrial revolution consists of a different wave, where intelligent robots are leading a dramatic change in daily life. One of the authoritative voices in this theme, Klaus Schwab (2017) acknowledges that others revolutions glossed over the power of animals in view of more efficient machines which contributed to the progress of mankind, but the new emergent fourth revolution disposes of digital technologies that blurs the contours between the physical and virtual world. Those governments, organizations and nations which fail in achieving an adaptation to this new facet of extreme competition will perish. In this respect, John Naisbitt (1993) alerts he global paradoxes technologies engender. While the bigger the economies returns, the more influential are the small players. This creates a new, more global but decentralized order where uncertainness and anxiety prevails (Naisbitt, 1993). Henry Giroux (2016) brilliantly showed, the central modalities of this new capitalism signals to oppressive forms of consumerism that are highly individualized. The surface of a new media is based on the possibilities to impose shared apocalyptic fears instead of coordinated forms of liabilities. The spectacle of terrorism, he adds, nation-state appeals to a culture of fear to calibrate its security functions. David Altheide (2017) has fleshed out an interesting model to understand the importance of terrorism and media screens. He addresses the visual and verbal discourses promoted by media to cover daily news. Illustrating the symbolic attachment of citizens to security, the American social imaginary has been historically bombarded to form a culture of fear in which case, an individual logic of survival and exploitations remained. Far from what journalism precludes, the current climate of fear has not created by terrorism, it has long dormant roots in the American Culture. At the same time terrorism was used as a political discourse to discipline citizens, further risks of racialized and radicalized forms of living politics emerge. Without the politics of fear, Donald Trump would never have been elected president of the US. To wit, Brigitte Nacos (2016) sheds light on the intersection of terror and publicity. Historically, though terrorists searched for publicity, the world remained disconnected, limiting the mouth-to-mouth advertising. However, in this hyper-connected society, where people are embedded with networking and consuming networks, the propaganda of terrorism fueled the veins of hyper-communication. As a drama where heroes defeat villains, media recreates a simulated landscape which fits with the goals of retaining audiences. In a seminal book, entitled *Global Terrorism and New Media,* Seib and Janbek (2010) explore the opportunities of new media as expanding the message of terrorism as well as the counter-responses of society. Regional attacks or even blows planned by few people resonate in a globalized public as never before creating not only misconceptions around the issue but also a constant display of disconnected images that obscure more than clarify. Marc Augé (2002) wrote that the problem of media alludes to the multiplication of dispersed images where the connections between the events are blurred. Lay-people not only misunderstand the reasons of terrorism but also are receptive to externally-designed explanations which alienate them from reality.

Lastly, Zygmunt Bauman and David Lyon (2013) paid their attention to the term adiaforization which means the banality of what is ethically incorrect. On behalf of security and to struggle against terrorism, the US and UK invested considerable efforts and resources to use technology at the battlefront. Per the discourse, technology not only would save lives but also would curb the costs of war. Disturbed by the degree of indifference army forces show respect to the victims, authors explain that the next wars will be fought by drones and military personnel trained to kill thousands operating a machine from its desk. Still, further, capitalism concentrated loads of resources in a few hands, making from competence the mainstream cultural value. Paradoxically, the fourth industrial revolution is introducing technology to mediate between humans, to make more predictive relationships, but it runs a serious risk, the lack of interest for the other. This point will be précised when we deal with the concept of Thana Capitalism in the ending sections. The climate of terror derives not only from the acts of terrorists but also by the lack of confidence in the other. Since each citizen over-valorizes its own possibilities to defeat its neighbor in the Darwinist capitalism, instrumentality and technology cement a bubble of narcissism where the other`s pain has transformed in the main exchangeable commodity. This creates a circular dependency because viewers are shocked by terror-related news but can`t stop to consume them.

THE CLASH OF VISIONS

Nowadays, in the fields of terrorism two contrasting understandings converge. While some scholars call the attention on undemocratic forms of governments as a fertile ground to nourish an anti-western discourse, which is rechanneled by potential radical groups (Fukuyama, 1989; Huntington, 1993; 1997; Kristol and Kagan, 1996; Vargas-Llosa, 2002; Rashid, 2002; Kepel, 2002; Keohane & Zeckhauser, 2003; Sunstein, 2005; Pojman, 2006), others are certainly worried about the advances of authoritarian practices which take terrorism as an ethical justification (Altheide, 2006; 2009; Sontag, 2002; Said, 2001; Holloway & Pelaez, 2002; Bernstein, 2006; Baudrillard, 1995a; 1995b; 2006; Gray, 2007; Smaw, 2008; Corey, 2009; Wolin, 2010).

In her book *Disciplining Terror,* Lisa Stampnitzky (2013) outlines an all-encompassing model to understand the role of expertise in terrorist-related studies. As she observed, the invention of terrorism as dialectic social issue involves not only terrorists but also experts who theorize on the importance of a nation-state to anticipate next attacks. While some Marxist scholars mistakenly preclude that analysts are prone to the status quo, other liberal writers understand that terrorism signals to the rise and evolution of a new type of violence that was articulated as a counter-response to poverty and grievance but as Stampnitzky puts it, neither the economy nor the center-periphery dependency suffices to explain the origin of terrorism in Western civilization. She describes how experts rarely have a genuine connection with authorities, whereas in other cases, the "war on terror" threatens to be a self-perpetuating discourse to justify one-sided decisions which often confronts with the already existent jurisprudence. Her main thesis is that at the time terrorism applied research advanced consolidating the epistemological borders towards the maturation of discipline, further moral connotations emerged. Originally aimed at disciplining conflict to gain further legitimacy internally but supporting the doctrine of national security within the sphere of international law, the government conducted the first *war on terror* to form a new conceptual framework, wherein their irrationality terrorists are situated as the mean threat of the West. For current literature, terrorists are seen as irrational agents, evildoers, maniacs or even worse bloodthirsty demons who thwart the well-functioning of democracy in Occident.

The moral of terrorism remains unchecked in the specialized literature, in part because, terrorists are seen as maniacs, filled-hatred killers who had sold their soul to the devil; in other contexts, there is a serious misunderstanding on what terrorism is. One might speculate that terrorism was defined as "an illegal form of violence", which operates from the clandestinely to pose a message of extortion to state. This definition leads to moral conceptions that obscure the epistemology of the object. While experts are pressed by the government to reveal ethnographical information or fieldworks which would be helpful to prevent the next attack, no less true is that Television is filled with pseudo-experts whose diagnoses are based on mere speculations. The stagnancy of terrorism applied research denotes the proliferation of pseudo-experts who are more interested in their personal advertisement than in deepening in the understanding of the issue. At some extent, the rigorous research in terrorism should escape to speculations focusing only in its effects in the modern-day culture (Silke, 2001; Young & Findley, 2011; Howie, 2012; Sageman, 2014). One of the most authoritative voices in the study of media and terrorism, David Altheide (2009) suggests that the recently-adopted policies against terrorism are aimed at vulnerating the rights of rank and file workers through the articulation of neoliberal programs and the precaritization of working conditions. Geoffrey Skoll argues convincingly that the US expanded militarily and economically thanks to the imposition of a culture of fear, which demonizes others to protect the interests of the elite. While governing through terror facilitates the executive branch to overcome the check and balances forces; Skoll adheres, it results in a culture of mistrust where the other is seen as an enemy (Skoll 2011; 2016; Skoll & Korstanje, 2013; Korstanje, 2015a; 2015b; 2016). This point of entry in the discussion sounds vital to our argumentation because it explains the role of technology in the process of securitization. As Skoll puts it, the use of high-technology aims to make of this world a more stable and safer place, but paradoxically, it contributes to a climate of mistrust where the other is a complete stranger. With the benefits of hindsight, Luke Howie discusses critically the political discourses revolving around terrorism in the English-speaking nations. He found that the interest of media for terrorism reproduces the semiotics of terror, which emulates the world of celebrities, where the other's gaze is more important than self-consciousness. While terrorists captivate the audience attention through the cruelty of their acts, media reproduces such a logic packaging and disseminating news to keep citizens entertained. Through the logic of witnessing, Howie said, terrorism became a form of entertainment (2009; 2011a; 2011b; 2012). Last but not least, Howie's concerns are validated by Mahmoud Eid (2014) who envisaged an intersection of media and terrorism. Terrorists draw the attention of Western leaders by the use of illegal violence whereas journalists are fascinated to cover these types of news, given the amassed profits. This reproduces paradoxically a vicious circle, in which case, journalism facilitates terrorism with the oxygen to survive, since media corporations gain further sponsors.

TERRORISM IN INFORMATION SOCIETY

It is tempting to say that the information society evolves as a creation, where the use of information is conducive to enhance production and cultural activity. While the distribution requires from legal jurisprudence to protect the ownership of produced knowledge, information society needs from plenty of channels or drivers which ensure a digital communication. Digital citizens appear to be the emerging class, which is formed by lay-people who are familiar in the ways this technology should be employed (Webster 2002; Hilbert, 2012; Ramluckan & Van Niekerk, 2009). Jacques Ellul (1964) lamented that the main problem of the information society was associated with the excess of rationality, which leads towards human depersonalization. Per his viewpoint,

The rationality given to irreversibly to the technique constructs a mechanical form of organization, which divorces culture from the environment and natural life. At the time society produces standardized commodities, efficiently-organized by knowledge and technology, further risks of creating an artificial system upsurges. As a result of this, the natural world not only is subordinated to capitalism, but may be substituted or eliminated if the necessaries arise (Ellul, 1964; 1965).

As Carl Mitcham, one of the most prominent Ellul`s experts stressed that ethics should be introduced in the discussion of the information society to escape to the commoditization of culture. The question whether technology is subordinated to the goals of capitalism, which rests on the achievement of goals no matter the costs, nature will be placed in jeopardy (Mitcham 1997). The dissociation of humankind from nature can be possible by the introduction of a second element, which was widely explored by Ellul, *propaganda*. Far from popular parlance defines as propaganda, Ellul understands the term as *a range of techniques* that conform a communicative process typically-integrated to technology-centered society. Since the society are in quest of incorporating the major number of individuals as possible, to impose standardized lifestyles and behaviour, propaganda not only serves as obtrusive forms of communication, which sets an alien form of subordination, but it enlarges a psychological dissonance between the individual cosmology of society developed biographically by each citizen and a one-sided argument fabricated by elite. In Ellul`s terms, though he never shed the light on this, propaganda seems to be conceptually in consonance with ideology (Winner, 2013). With the benefits of hindsight, Ellul illustrated the generations to come that the dissemination of knowledge and propaganda imposed a distorted sense of truth. T. Druckrey (1996) exerts an interesting criticism of virtual culture. Lest digital technologies would be ethically reconsidered, there are serious risks that economies enter in the exchange of abstract signs, which would usher mankind into the dark side of virtual reality. The dilemma of capitalism has been given by the juxtaposition between production and representation, where over the recent decades the rise of an electronic grammar jeopardizes to overwrite the past.

The fundamental event of the modern age, writes Heidegger, is the conquest of the world as a picture. Enveloped by a concept of the world understood already structured as an image, the dynamic shifts in the making of art in the past decade make more sense. Characterized by deconstruction, encoding, and reconceptualization, the sphere of the image has assumed greater and greater effect, despite mounting doubts concerning the stability of the image as information (Druckrey, 1996: p 25)

Beyond the monopoly of ocular-centrism, which means a cultural tendency to valorize the gaze over other sensorial forms, Paul Virilio (2010) exerts a radical criticism over how information is produced, as well as the role played by science and university in disseminating information in global postmodern societies.

The camera is a lot more than a recording device. It is a medium through which messages reach us from another world, trilled Orson Wells, that the world is no longer eccentric. It has become hypercentric, since its telescopy brings us face to face with the greatest object in history: this objectum that is nothing less than our life-giving star (Virilio, 2010: p. 68)

As the previous backdrop, Virilio alerts that *Science* is more interested in protecting the profits and interests of pharmaceutical laboratories as well as large corporations than in finding path-breaking outcome that marks altruistically the pace towards well-being. As a result of this, the risk has been specially posed as a spectacle, which engages the media, this is the example of the thousands of tourists who daily visit dark sites, battlefront or war-related zones at once army forces are fighting. Instead of tackling of the causes of risk, like climate change or deforestation which is wreaking havoc in local agrarian economies, Science encouraged by modern capitalism appeals to a spectacle of disaster, which acts as cultural entertainment for bored masses (Virilio 2010).

Undoubtedly, Jean Baudrillard eloquently hits the nail on the head when he says the concept of reality, as we know to date, was replaced by *pseudo-reality*. Originally obsessed by the role of cinema in the configuration of the modern mind, Baudrillard contends that cinema not only exhibits a reflection of reality but the way the self-engages with an ever-increasing technocratic conception of the picture. To put this in other terms, the power of image as capitalism imposed it does not rest in what it overtly shows, but in its efficacy in subtracting us from the real world. To set a clear example, readers should remind the definition of hyperreal he introduces in his analysis of minority report, a Spielberg`s film framed in a near future, where *precogs (medium-like persons who supported by high-tech predicts the future)* defy the classic jurisprudence anticipating to crimes before they take place. In fact, although Police was successful in stopping murderers by forecasting crimes before being committed, something turns wrong when Captain John Anderton, who developed drug-addiction after losing his family, is accused to be the murder of man whose name is Leo Crow, in approximately a couple of days. Though the rest of story is well known, Baudrillard uses this plot to trace an analogy with the world in the global capitalism, where risks are elaborated from the future to rule the present life (Baudrillard 1995a; 1995b; 2006).

Douglas Kellner (2003), one of the exegetes of Baudrillard, writes that to what extent Baudrillard theorized in the right direction can be debated, but what is most important, he unveils the intersection of reality and fictionality, from where terrorism feeds. Within Marxist tradition, Hans Enzenberger (1996) differentiates the radical positions of Virilio and Baudrillard from the benefits of technology in the years to come. He insists that not only technology reproduces a more egalitarian democracy but also many of the stereotypes and prejudices that formed the critical turn comes from a long-dormant discourse, which is enrooted in the European Bourgeoise.

TERRORISM SURFING THROUGH THE HYPER-CONNECTED SOCIETY

The use of digital technology or ICT escapes to the classic literature which emphasizes the clash of civilization, or an ever-increasing anti-American sentiment. This turns a situation very hard to grasp. Many native Americans perpetrate cyber-attacks or cyber-crimes against financial targets as international banks or agencies of security, while many terrorists as *John Jihadi* uploads their executions to youtube for being consumed by western audience on-line. This point defies the old paradigms formulated by Frankfurt School which focused on the hypodermic needle theory (Lim 2005; Farwell 2014). Following the conceptual pillars of this theory, people were passive actors who receive and digest information in a one-sided way. Those agents who lack a rational logic not only is unfit to manipulate these types of technologies but live alienated from the real world. The clue we want to pursue in this book chapter is that the intriguing horizons of digital technology are disposed of by the state to tighten the surveillance in borderlands (Bauman & Lyon, 2013; Lyon, 2010) but also are used for terrorists to amplify the effects of fear (Korstanje 2016b). Interesting studies have widely discussed to what extent the use of websites by lone-wolves determines or triggers their hostility against their hosting societies (Simon, 2013). The irreversible process of globalization shortened the geographical distances but at the same time the psychological, ethical barriers between what ought or not to do. For some specialists, the resentment nourished by some ethnic minorities, which daily suffers practices of discrimination or xenophobia as Muslims in France, augments the probabilities to be radicalized (McCauley & Moskalenko, 2008). Equally important, globalization seems to trigger a paradoxical situation because once the available means of transport connect distant cities in hours, shortening the ethnical difference among cultures, no less evident is that some counter-reactions as xenophobia and discrimination are triplicated in the most important global cities.

Doubtless, globalization generated a faster homogenization of cultures, which rested on the monopoly of rationality and technology as two pillars of Western capitalism. The specialized literature emphasizes terrorism as the direct consequence of political instability and poverty. For these scholars, because it operates from clandestinity, the dialogue with state seems to be breached or temporarily suspended (Connolly, 1993). The violence fulfils the gap between dissidents and the nation-state. The crimes perpetrated by terrorism not only brings with a political message, but they are defined as evil acts (Schmid, 2004). Calibrating their techniques to more sophisticated forms, terrorists over the last years have used the already-existing technology, which was the bulwark of Occident against civilian targets (Kepel, 2002). This suggests that technology and terrorism are inextricably intertwined. As Mahmoud Eid (2015) puts it, we are educated to imagine terrorism as a criminal act while media are a positive phenomenon. Both sides are being helped by each other, simply because the treatment of media facilitates the terrorist to achieve their goals, while the perpetration of attacks gives substantial content and debate to journalism. Understanding terrorism as a means of communicating a violent message, this project exerts a considerable criticism to free-value media. The medialization of terrorism corresponds with a tactic further beneficial for terrorists than governments. In this vein, Eid (2015) overtly writes that

Meanwhile, for both to survive, terrorists seek to garner public attention and the media seek to find top-stories to sell. In a sense, both parties target wide-ranging audiences (although for different purposes); hence, they interact in a highly toxic relationship that involves a process of exchange necessary for their survival. The exchanging process contributes to the survival of each party; acts of terrorism provide media stories that result in more broadcasting airwaves, press texts, and digital data bytes, while the media coverage brings public attention to terrorists—the oxygen necessary for their existence (Eid, 2015: 24).

Sociologically speaking, terrorism historically moved towards three different meanings, which will be discussed in the following sections, *a) terrorism as an illegal form of violence, b) terrorism as a disciplinary instrument towards a climate of fear, c) terrorism as a form of extortion.*

Each family of theories deserves wider attention, but because of time and space issues, we synthesize its main salient ideas as follows:

Terrorism as an illegal form of violence forms a set of theories that start from the Hobbesian doctrine of Leviathan, which suggests that in a climate of insecurity, tyranny or violence, the probabilities that terrorism prospers are higher than democracies (Hallsworth & Lea 2011; Feldman 1991; Piazza 2007; 2011). While in some cases, terrorism derives from failed-states or unconsolidated democracies (Piazza 2011) it is important not to lose sight of when a group is pressed to work in the shadows of democratic system violence surges as an alternative (Bejarano, 1983; Palacios, 2003; Timmermann, 2014). This is the type of terrorism that not only whipped Latin America in the 70s decade but also the classic cells as IRA or ETA in Europe.

Terrorism as a disciplinary instrument lumps some divergent theories together under the auspices of the fear not only as the touchstone of terrorism but the excuses of government. While the theory signals to the needs of terrorism to instill panic for their claims to be heard, with the time, states employ a discourse of fear to discipline their workers internally (Altheide 2009). One might ask whom terrorism serves instead of what terrorism is.

Finally, terrorism as-a-form of extortion exhibits the most interesting aspect of the discussion. Through the globe, the arrival of hi-tech caused a double effect in culture. While active rank-and-file workers experienced a serious reduction in their opportunities to get further jobs, they are pressed to tribute state supporting an ever-increasing number of pensioners. The expansion of life expectancies adjoined to the different advances in health, resulted in serious changes for the social security system (Taylor-Gooby, 2004). Globalization and modernity needs from creative destruction to survive, which calls to the needs of adopting the maxims of social Darwinism. The logic of extortion which acts as the key factor of terrorism does not come from Islam nor Muslims, it is enrooted in the heart of capitalism. For these scholars, terrorists not only are educated in the best Western universities, dotted with their abilities to negotiate like capital owners, but they are educated in the principal instrumentality that paves the paths for the appearance of extortion (Korstanje, 2015; 2016a; 2016b; 2017).

The Future of Terrorism in the Society of Information

As discussed, the spectacle of disaster promoted by terrorism, which entertains daily global audiences worldwide, creates a vicious circle. On the one hand, it affects the sensibility of the audience, but paradoxically, it affirms the ego of first-world citizens. In earlier works, we have discussed the term *Thana Capitalism* to describe the uncanny dependency between terrorists and media. Capitalism has abandoned the risk-stage to a new facet of production, where the consumption of disasters, mass death, and even terrorism played a leading position.

The Old society of risk, technically, starts with the nuclear accident in Chernobyl, Ukraine. This event reorganized the already-existent hierarchal order into a new reflective logic. In decline, the classic institutions created by the welfare state were unable to protect citizens any longer. In the society of risks, the process of knowledge production leads to a state of complexity that creates a paradoxical situation. The same technology originally designed to make safer the life of people, if unregulated it can result in real disaster. The old World of classes where the first Marxists exerted their radical critique has set the pace to a new one. The classic division between riches and poor, or have and have-nots has gone forever. Now, all citizens seem to be equal to risk. The stage of globalization that accelerated the transport orchestrated a closed-system which is very well market-oriented to mass-consumption. For exegetes of Thana Capitalism, who echo social Darwinist, economic inequalities among class can be compared to the conception of life. If millions of spermatozoids compete for the fecundation of an ovule, this suggests that only one will be the winner.

The epicenter of Thana-Capitalism stems from 9/11, which at the turn of the century, acted as a founding event. For the popular parlance, this shocking blow represented a turning point where Islam radicalism showed not only the weaknesses of the West but also how the means of transport which were the badge of US, were employed as mortal weapons directed towards civil targets. Educated and trained in the best western universities, jihadists showed the dark side of the society of mass consumption. The Darwinist allegory of the survival of the strongest can be found as the main culture value of Thana-Capitalism in a way that is captivated by cultural entertainment industries and cinema. Films as Hunger Games portray an apocalyptic future where the elite govern with iron rule different colonies. A wealthy capital which is geographically situated in Rocky Mountain serves as an exemplary center, a hot-spot of consumption and hedonism where the spectacle prevails. The oppressed colonies are rushed to send their warriors who will struggle with others to death, in a bloody game that keeps people exciting. Although all participants work hard to enhance their skills, only one will reach the glory. The same can be observed in realities such as Big Brother, where participants neglect the probabilities to fail simply because they over-valorize their own strongholds. This exactly seems to be what engages citizens to compete with others to survive, to show "they are worth of surviving." In sum, the *sentiment of exceptionality* triggered by these types of ideological spectacles disorganizes the social trust.

The cultural entertainment, in the society of Thana-Capitalism, disseminates death as a form of mediating with others. Thousands of tourists leave their homes to visit spaces of mass-death, destruction or even hit by mega-disasters while news on terrorist bombings or crimes enjoy the audience 24 hours per day. Still furthermore, TV channels and programs dedicated to the biography of serial killers as *Investigation discovery, Criminal Minds or* plots as Zodiac, *Hannibal, Hostel, Texas Chainsaw Massacre* or *Natural Born Killers* feature the figure of killers as strong and engaged with their aims. In a secularized society, where Gods have died, death not only is negated, but it remains as synonymous of weakness.

Thana-Capitalism theatralizes death (among others) as a Spectacle to not only revitalize the daily frustrations but enhances a harmed ego. Visiting spaces of disasters during holidays, or watching the news on terrorist attacks at home, all represent part of the same issue: *the advent of new class death seekers.* This uncanny fascination for consuming the others´ death explains through the novel *Hunger Games,* where an exemplary center oppresses different colonies known as *districts* which send their warriors who will struggle with others to death, in a bloody game that keeps people excited. Although all participants work hard to enhance their skills, only one will reach the glory. The same can be observed in realities as Big Brother, where participants neglect the probabilities to fail simply because they over-valorize their own strongholds. This exactly seems to be what engages citizens to compete with others to survive, to show "they are worth of surviving". In sum, the *sentiment of exceptionality* triggered by these types of ideological spectacles disorganizes the social trust. Therefore, observing closer how the patterns of holiday-makers as well as leisure practices evolved is a valid lens to understand much deeper social changes. Detractors of industrialism, as Hofstadter, ignite the discussion around social Darwinism. We are playing a game, which has fewer probabilities of success. In Thana-Capitalism we fall happy for the Others´ failure. The competition fostered by the ideology of capitalism offers the salvation for few ones, at the expense of the rest. To realize the dream of joining the "selected people", we accept the rules. Whenever one of our direct competitors fails, we feel an insane happiness. We finally argue that a similar mechanism is activated during our visit to dark tourism sites: we do not strive to understand, we are just happy because we escaped death and have more chances to win the game of life.

To cut a long story short, Thana-Capitalism alludes to what Baudrillard names "The Spectacle of Disaster", as the main criterion of attraction. Disasters provide Thana-Capitalism with the commodity to disorganize the social ties among workers to introduce an atmosphere of social Darwinism where all compete with all to survive. Since the death of others exhibits a new opportunity to be still in the trace, modern spectorship, in the society of information, is subject to a paradoxical situation. While media provides the necessary oxygen that terrorism needs (citing Mahmoud Eid, 2014), terrorism produces counter-factual effects, giving back to Thana-Capitalism the necessary background to work. This poses a serious dilemma for policy makers, officials and experts who devote their effort to prevent the advance of terrorism in globalized urban cities. One of the examples that describe better how terrorism evolves in Thana-capitalism days is the recent attacks perpetrated in Nice, France. Instead of stopping the driver, people in the celebration were attempting to take pictures with their mobile phone while terrorists were running over pedestrians. This cruel scene validates the rise of a new class which Luke Howie (2012) dubbed as "witnesses to terror" in Korstanje´s works (2016) as "death-seekers".

CONCLUSION

To date, terrorism appears to be one of the threats today jeopardizing Western civilization. The rise of a radicalized Islam that presses for contaminating the ethical borders of democracy and Western civilization seems to be the homogenized discourse of politicians when they are asked on thinking about this slippery matter. Quite aside from this, a much deeper look suggests precisely the opposite. Neither is there a clash of civilization, which is previously supported by the contrast of some cultural values between Muslims and Christians, nor undemocratic cultures looming at the doors of heaven. As we have discussed in this chapter, terrorism is culturally enrooted in the core of capitalism, to be more precise in the process of industrialization that accelerated the expansion of mobility and tourism as main industries, but equally important, in a world where digital technology paved the ways for a hyper-connected society where information flourishes elsewhere or connects in second distant geographical points. Coming across this society of information terrorism found a fertile ground to mushroom affecting our individual behavior as well as our collective hopes and expectancies. In the times of Thana-Capitalism, which was described as a new launch to a decentralized facet of capitalism, where death plays as a conduit for citizens in engaging to the social institutions.

REFERENCES

Achcar, G. (2015). *Clash of Barbarisms: The Making of the New World Disorder*. Abingdon, UK: Routledge.

Ahnf, J. (2011). Cyberemotions – Collective Emotions in Cyberspace. *Procedia Computer Science*. DOI: 10.1016/j.procs.2011.09.076

Altheide, D. (2006). *Terrorist and the Politics of Fear*. Oxford, UK: Altamira Press.

Altheide, D. (2009). Moral Panic, from sociological concept to public discourse. *Crime, Media, Culture*, 5(1), 79–99. doi:10.1177/1741659008102063

Altheide, D. (2017). *The Politics of Terrorism*. New York: Rowman and Littlefield.

Augé, M. (2002). *Diario de Guerra: el mundo después del 11 de Septiembre*. Barcelona: Gedisa.

Barro, R. (1991). Economic Growth in a cross section countries. *The Quarterly Journal of Economics*, 106(2), 407–443. doi:10.2307/2937943

Baudrillard, J. (1995a). *The systems of the objects*. Siglo XXI.

Baudrillard, J. (1995b). *The Gulf War Did Not Take Place*. Sydney: Power Publications.

Baudrillard, J. (2006). Virtuality and Events: the hell of power. *Baudrillard Studies, 3*(2). Available at http://www.ubishops.ca/BaudrillardStudies/

Bauman, Z., & Lyon, D. (2013). *Liquid surveillance: A conversation*. New York: John Wiley & Sons.

Bejarano, J. A. (1983). Campesinado, luchas agrarias e historia social: Notas para un balance historiográfico. *Anuario Colombiano de Historia Social y de la Cultura*, (11): 251–304.

Chmiel A, Sienkiewicz J, Thelwall M, Paltoglou G, Buckley K, et al. (2011). Collective Emotions Online and Their Influence on Community Life. *PLoS ONE, 6*(7). doi:10.1371/journal.pone.0022207

Connolly, W. (1993). *The Terms of Political Discourse*. Princeton, NJ: Princeton University Press.

Corey, R. (2009). *Fear, the history of Political Ideas*. Fondo de Cultura Económica.

Coulter, G. (2012). *Jean Baudrillard: from the ocean to the desert or the poetics of radicality*. Intertheory Press.

Druckrey, T. (1996). *Electronic Culture: technology and visual representation*. New York: Aperture.

Eid, M. (Ed.). (2015). *Exchanging Terrorism Oxygen for Media Airwaves: The Age of Terroredia: The Age of Terroredia*. Hershey, PA: IGI Global.

Ellul, J. (1964). *The Technological society*. New York: Vintage books.

Ellul, J. (1965). *Propaganda*. New York: Knopf.

Enzenberger, H. (1996). Constituents of a theory of media. In T. Druckrey (Ed.), *Electronic culture: technology and visual representation* (pp. 62–85). New York: Aperture.

Farwell, J. P. (2014). The media strategy of ISIS. *Survival, 56*(6), 49–55. doi:10.1080/00396338.2014.985436

Feldman, A. (1991). *Formation of Violence: the narrative of the body and the political terror in Northern Ireland*. Chicago: University of Chicago Press. doi:10.7208/chicago/9780226240800.001.0001

Fukuyama, F. (1989). The End of History. *National Interest, 16*(Summer), 4–18.

Fuller, G. E. (2010). *A world without Islam*. New York: Little Brown.

Giroux, H. (2016). *Beyond the Spectacle of Terrorism. Global Uncertainty and the challenges of a new media*. Abingdon, UK: Routledge.

Gray, C. S. (2007). *The Implications of Preemptive and Preventive war Doctrines: Reconsideration*. Department of the Army, Department of Defense, US Government. Available at http://www.strategic-studiesinstitute.army.mil/Pubs/display.cfm?pubid=789

Hallsworth, S., & Lea, J. (2011). Reconstructing Leviathan: Emerging contours of the security state. *Theoretical Criminology, 15*(2), 141–157. doi:10.1177/1362480610383451

Hilbert, M. (2012). How much information is there in the "information society"? *Significance, 9*(4), 8–12. doi:10.1111/j.1740-9713.2012.00584.x

Holloway, J., & Paláez, E. (2002). La guerra de todos los estados contra toda la gente. In *Guerra Infinita: hegemonía y terror mundial* (pp. 159–166). Buenos Aires: CLACSO.

Howie, L. (2009). A Role for Business in the War on Terror. *Disaster Prevention and Management, 18*(2), 100–107. doi:10.1108/09653560910953180

Howie, L. (2011a). *Terror on the Screen: Witnesses and the Re-animation of 9/11 as Image-event, Popular Culture*. Washington, DC: New Academia Publishing, LLC.

Howie, L. (2011b). They were created by Man and they have a plan: Subjective and objective violence in BattleStar Galactica and the war on terror. *International Journal of Zizek Studies*, *5*(2), 1–23.

Howie, L. (2012). *Witnesses to terror: Understanding the meanings and consequences of terrorism.* Basingstoke, UK: Pallagrave-Macmillan.

Hungtinton, S. P. (1997). *The Clash of Civilizations: Remaking of World Order*. New York: Touchstone Book.

Huntington, S. P. (1993). *The Third Wave. Democratization in the Late Twentieth Century*. Oklahoma University Press.

Huntington, S. P. (2000). The Clash of Civilizations? In Culture and Politics (pp. 99-118). Palgrave Macmillan US.

Kagan, R. (2004). *Of Paradise and Power: America and Europe in the new World Order*. New York: Vintage books.

Karim, K. H., & Eid, M. (2012). Clash of ignorance. Global Media Journal—Canadian Edition, 5(1), 7-27.

Kellner, D. (2003). Jean Baudrillard. In The Blackwell companion to major contemporary social theorists. Oxford, UK: Blackwell Publishing.

Keohane, N., & Zeckhauser, R. (2003). The ecology of Terror defense. *Journal of Risk and Uncertainty*, *26*(2-3), 201–229. doi:10.1023/A:1024167124083

Kepel, G. (2002). Los Hechos del 11 de Septiembre de 2001. In El Mundo Después del 11 de Septiembre de 2001. Barcelona: Editorial Península.

Korstanje, M. E. (2013a). Preemption and Terrorism. When the Future Governs. *Cultura*, *10*(1), 167–184. doi:10.5840/cultura20131019

Korstanje, M. E. (2013b). Del Patrimonio al Terrorismo. Regular el Turismo en una Época de Incertidumbre. *Rosa Dos Ventos*, *5*(4), 655–658.

Korstanje, M. E. (2015a). *A Difficult World: examining the roots of capitalism*. New York: Nova Science Publishers.

Korstanje, M. E. (2015b). *The Anthropology of dark Tourism, exploring the contradictions of Capitalism*. Centre for Ethnicity and Racism Studies, CERS. School of Sociology and Social Policy, University of Leeds UK. Working Paper #22.

Korstanje, M. E. (2016a). *The rise of Thana Capitalism and Tourism*. Abingdon, UK: Routledge.

Korstanje, M. E. (2016b). *Threat Mitigation and Detection of Cyber Warfare and Terrorism Activities*. Hershey, PA: IGI Global.

Kramer, A. D. I., & Guillory, J. E., & Hancock, J. T. (2014). Experimental evidence of massive-scale emotional contagion through social networks. *Proceedings of the National Academy of Sciences of the United States of America*, (24): 17. PMID:24889601

Kristol, W., & Kagan, R. (1996). Toward a Neo-Reaganite Foreign Policy. *Foreign Affairs*.

Lim, M. (2005). Islamic radicalism and anti-Americanism in Indonesia: The role of the Internet. *Policy Studies*, (18).

Lyon, D. (2010). Liquid surveillance: The contribution of Zygmunt Bauman to surveillance studies. *International Political Sociology*, *4*(4), 325–338. doi:10.1111/j.1749-5687.2010.00109.x

Marenko, B. (2010). Contagious Affectivity. The Management of Emotions in Late Capitalist Design. *"Negotiating Futures – Design Fiction"*. *Proceedings from the 6th Swiss Design Network Conference*, 134-149.

Martell, L. (2010). *The sociology of globalization*. Cambridge, UK: Polity Press.

McCauley, C., & Moskalenko, S. (2008). Mechanisms of political radicalization: Pathways toward terrorism. *Terrorism and Political Violence*, *20*(3), 415–433. doi:10.1080/09546550802073367

Mitcham, C. (1997). Thinking Ethics in Technology. Golden, Division of liberal arts and international Studies. Colorado School of Mines.

Nacos, B. (2016). *Mass-mediated terrorism: Mainstream and digital media in terrorism and counterterrorism*. New York: Rowman & Littlefield.

Naisbitt, J. (1993). *Global Paradox: The Bigger the World Economy, the More Powerful Its Smallest Players*. New York: William Morrow & Co., Inc.

Palacios, M. (2003). *Entre la legitimidad y la violencia: Colombia 1875-1994*. Bogotá: Editorial Norma.

Phillips, D. E. (2008). Terrorism and Security in the Caribbean Before and After 9/11. *Conflict Management, Peace Economics and Development.*, *7*, 97–138. doi:10.1016/S1572-8323(08)07007-0

Piazza, J. A. (2011). Poverty, minority economic discrimination, and domestic terrorism. *Journal of Peace Research*, *48*(3), 339–353. doi:10.1177/0022343310397404

Pojman, L. (2006). *Terrorism, Human Rights and the case for World Government*. Lanham: Rowman and Littlefield.

Pollins, B. M. (1989). Does trade still follow the flag? *The American Political Science Review*, *83*(2), 465–480. doi:10.2307/1962400

Ramluckan, T., & Van Niekerk, B. (2009). The Terrorism/Mass Media Symbiosiys. *Journal of Informatfion Warfare*, *8*(2), 1–12.

Rashid, A. (2002). Los Hechos del 11 de Septiembre de 2001. In El Mundo Después del 11 de Septiembre de 2001. Barcelona: Editorial Península.

Reich, R. B. (2005). *Reason: why liberals will win the battle for America*. New York: Vintage Books.

Revel, J. F. (2003). *Anti-americanism*. San Francisco: Encounter Books.

Robertson, G. (2002). *The Role of military in combating terrorism*. Paper presented at second Nato Russia-Conference, Moscow, Russia.

Sageman, M. (2014). The stagnation in terrorism research. *Terrorism and Political Violence*, *26*(4), 565–580. doi:10.1080/09546553.2014.895649

Said, E. (2001). The Clash of Ignorance. *Nation (New York, N.Y.)*, *4*(October). Available at http://www.thenation.com/article/clash-ignorance

Schmid, A. (2004). Frameworks for Conceptualizing Terrorism. *Terrorism and Political Violence*, *16*(2), 197–221. doi:10.1080/09546550490483134

Schwab, K. (2017). *The fourth industrial revolution*. New York: Crown Business.

Schweitzer, F., & Garcia, D. (2010). An agent-based model of collective emotions in online communities. *The European Physical Journal B*, *77*(4), 533–545. doi:10.1140/epjb/e2010-00292-1

Seib, P., & Janbek, D. M. (2010). *Global terrorism and new media: The post-Al Qaeda generation*. Abingdon, UK: Routledge.

Silke, A. (2001). The devil you know: Continuing problems with research on terrorism. *Terrorism and Political Violence*, *13*(4), 1–14. doi:10.1080/09546550109609697

Simon, J. D. (2013). *Lone wolf terrorism: understanding the growing threat*. Amherst, NY: Prometheus Books.

Skoll, G. (2011). *Social Theory of Fear*. New York: Palgrave Macmillan.

Skoll, G. R. (2016). *Globalization of American Fear Culture: the empire in the Twenty-First Century*. New York: Palgrave-Macmillan. doi:10.1007/978-1-137-57034-5

Skoll, G. R., & Korstanje, M. E. (2013). Constructing an American fear culture from red scares to terrorism. *International Journal of Human Rights and Constitutional Studies*, *1*(4), 341–364. doi:10.1504/IJHRCS.2013.057302

Smaw, E. (2008). From Chaos to Contrarianism: Hobbes, Pojman, and the Case of World Government. *Essays in Philosophy.*, *9*(2), 4–18.

Sontag, S. (2002). Seamos Realistas. In El Mundo Después del 11 de Septiembre de 2001. Barcelona, Editorial Península.

Stampnitzky, L. (2011). Disciplining an unruly field: Terrorism experts and theories of scientific/intellectual production. *Qualitative Sociology*, *34*(1), 1–19. doi:10.100711133-010-9187-4

Stampnitzky, L. (2013). *Disciplining Terror: how experts invented terrorism*. Cambridge, UK: Cambridge University Press. doi:10.1017/CBO9781139208161

Sunstein, C. (2005). *Laws of Fear: beyond the precautionary Principle*. Cambridge, UK: Cambridge University Press. doi:10.1017/CBO9780511790850

Talor-Gooby, P. (2004). *The Impact of New Social Risks on Welfare States*. Available at http://citeseerx.ist.psu.edu/viewdoc/download?doi=10.1.1.511.2369&rep=rep1&type=pdf

Timmermann, F. (2014). *El gran terror. Miedo, emoción y discurso. Chile, 1973-1980*. Santiago de Chile: Copygraph.

Vargas Llosa, M. (2002). La Lucha Final. In El Mundo Después del 11 de Septiembre de 2001. Barcelona: Editorial Península.

Virilio, P. (2010). *The University of Disaster*. Cambridge, UK: Polity Press.

Von Solms, R., & Van Niekerk, J. (2013). From information security to cyber security. *Computers & Security, 38*, 97-102.

Webster, F. (2002). *Theories of the Information Society*. Cambridge, UK: Routledge. doi:10.4324/9780203426265

Weisberg, J. (2005). *The Bush Tragedy*. New York: Random House.

Winner, L. (2013). Propaganda and dissociation from the truth. In *Jacques Ellul and the Technological society in the 21ˢᵗ century* (pp. 99–113). Heidelberg, Germany: Springer. doi:10.1007/978-94-007-6658-7_8

Wolin, R. (2010). The idea of cosmopolitanism: From Kant to the Iraq war and beyond. *Ethics & Global Politics, 3*(2), 143–153. doi:10.3402/egp.v3i2.5213

Young, J. K., & Findley, M. G. (2011). Promise and pitfalls of terrorism research. *International Studies Review, 13*(3), 411–431. doi:10.1111/j.1468-2486.2011.01015.x

ADDITIONAL READING

Altheide, D. (2009). Moral Panic: From sociological concept to public discourse. *Crime, Media, Culture, 5*(1), 79–99. doi:10.1177/1741659008102063

Arendt, H. (2013). *The Human Condition*. Chicago: University of Chicago Press.

Armitage, J. (2011). *Virilio now. Current perspectives in Virilio Studies*. Cambridge: Polity Press.

Asal, V. H., Rethemeyer, R. K., Anderson, I., Stein, A., Rizzo, J., & Rozea, M. (2009). The softest of targets: A study on terrorist target selection. *Journal of Applied Security Research, 4*(3), 258–278. doi:10.1080/19361610902929990

Bauman, Z. (2000). *Globalization: The human consequences*. New York: Columbia University Press.

Bauman, Z. (2006). *Liquid Fear*. Cambridge: Polity Press.

Bauman, Z. (2007). *Consuming Life*. Cambridge: Polity Press.

Becker, P. (2011). Whose Risks? Gender and the Ranking of Hazards. *Disaster Prevention and Management, 20*(4), 423–433. doi:10.1108/09653561111161743

Bernstein, R. J. (2013). *The abuse of evil: The corruption of politics and religion since 9/11*. New York: John Wiley & Sons.

Bianchi, R. (2007). Tourism and The Globalization of Fear: Analyzing the politics of risk and (in) security in global travel. *Tourism and Hospitality Research, 7*(1), 64–74. doi:10.1057/palgrave.thr.6050028

Enders, W., & Hoover, G. A. (2012). The nonlinear relationship between terrorism and poverty. *The American Economic Review, 102*(3), 267–272. doi:10.1257/aer.102.3.267

Enders, W., & Sandler, T. (2011). *The political economy of terrorism*. Cambridge: Cambridge University Press. doi:10.1017/CBO9780511791451

Hofstadter, R. (1992). *Social Darwinism in American Thoughts*. Boston: Beacon Press.

Ignatieff, M. (2001). *Human Rights. As Politics and Idolatry* (pp. 3–53). New Jersey: Princeton University Press.

Ignatieff, M. (2013). *The lesser evil: Political ethics in an age of terror*. Princeton: Princeton University Press.

Kagan, S., & Hahn, J. (2011). Creative cities and (un) sustainability: From creative class to sustainable creative cities. *Culture and Local Governance, 3*(1), 11–27. doi:10.18192/clg-cgl.v3i1.182

Kaplan, C. (2006). Mobility and war: The cosmic view of US 'air power'. *Environment & Planning A, 38*(2), 395–407. doi:10.1068/a37281

Korstanje, M. E., & Clayton, A. (2012). Tourism and terrorism: Conflicts and commonalities. *Worldwide Hospitality and Tourism Themes, 4*(1), 8–25. doi:10.1108/17554211211198552

Korstanje, M. E., & George, B. (2015). Dark Tourism: Revisiting Some Philosophical Issues. *Ereview of Tourism Research, 12*(1-2), 127–136.

Korstanje, M. E., & Ivanov, S. (2012). Tourism as a Form of New Psychological Resilience: The Inception of Dark Tourism. *Cultur: Revista de Cultura e Turismo, 6*(4), 56–71.

Korstanje, M. E., & Olsen, D. H. (2011). The discourse of risk in horror movies post 9/11: Hospitality and hostility in perspective. *International Journal of Tourism Anthropology, 1*(3-4), 304–317. doi:10.1504/IJTA.2011.043712

Morris, J. (2010). The Justification of Torture-Horror: Retribution and Sadism in Saw, Hostel, and the Devil's Rejects. In T. Fahy (Ed.), *The Philosophy of Horror Movies* (pp. 42–56). Lexington: The University Press of Kentucky.

Moskalenko, S., & McCauley, C. (2009). Measuring political mobilization: The distinction between activism and radicalism. *Terrorism and Political Violence, 21*(2), 239–260. doi:10.1080/09546550902765508

Moten, A. R. (2010). Understanding terrorism: Contested concept, conflicting perspectives and shattering consequences. *Intellectual Discourse, 18*(1), 1–17.

Pedahzur, Perliger, A., & Weinberg, L. (2003). Altruism and Fatalism: The Characteristics of Palestinian Suicide Terrorists. *Deviant Behavior, 24*(4), 405–423. doi:10.1080/713840227

Scribano, A. (2014). A look at some acts of violence and silenced repressions: Evictions in Argentina. *Research on Humanities and Social Sciences., 4*(5), 68–79.

Scribano, A., De Sena, A., & Cena, R. (2015). Social Policies and Emotions in Latinamerica: A theoretical approach to their Analysis [Budapest]. *Corvinus Journal of Sociology and Social Policy*, 6(2), 3–19. doi:10.14267/cjssp.2015.02.01

Scribano, A., Lisdero, P., & Bloch, B. (2014). "Sensibilités en conflit: Travail, protestation et expressivité dans une expérience de récupération d'entreprise en Argentine. Teme 2/2014 Časopis za društvene nauke. niš april - jun 2014. udk: 1+3 ISSN 0353-7919

Scribano, A., Vergara, G., Lisdero, P. Y., & Quattrini, D. (2015). Labor, Emotions and Social Structuration in Argentina. *The International Journal of Social Sciences and Humanities Invention*, 2(11), 1679–1688.

KEY TERMS DEFINITIONS

Adiaforization: This term was coined by Bauman and Lyon to symbolize the banality of instrumentality, which today uses technologies regardless the costs. Authors use the word to describe the lack of responsibilities of army forces in operating drones and military machines achieving their goals.

Democracy: It signals to a form of government based on republicanism, the division of branches, and the elections as the supreme signs of individual liberty.

Fourth Industrial Revolution: It consists in the industrial change that placed technology not only as the centerpiece of the productive system, but also fused the physical bodies with the virtual technology.

Radicalization: Process through which terrorism emerges. Per the studies and early published works, the terrorist minds are subject to different facet of radicalization.

Terrorism: A type of illegal violence that vulnerates innocent to impose its own agenda before the government. Unlike crime which follows individual goals, terrorism exploits the others innocent to press a third part.

Chapter 17
Cybersecurity Risks and Automated Maritime Container Terminals in the Age of 4IR

Peter Beaumont
University of London Royal Holloway, UK

ABSTRACT

This chapter presents a case study of automated maritime container terminals (CTs). It has the aim of demonstrating that the risks derived from the use of technology associated with the Fourth Industrial Revolution (4IR) are both real and dangerous. The work explains the critical function of CTs in the global supply chain and outlines the economic and social consequences that could result if their operations were to be disrupted. The motivations of a range of threat-actors are presented, and it is established that there are feasible scenarios in which any one of the major threat-actor categories may wish to cause disruption at CTs. The vulnerabilities of yard cranes are investigated, and it is concluded that there are likely to be exploitable vulnerabilities in the industrial control system (ICS) networks used on these cranes. The chapter argues that many CT operations are likely to be exposed to significant cyber-based risks and that this exposure will increase with the roll-out of further 4IR technologies unless appropriate control measures are implemented.

INTRODUCTION

Automated Maritime Container Terminals (CTs) have employed several of the technologies that are central to the concept of the Fourth Industrial Revolution (4IR) (Schwab, 2016) for some time. They fuse multiple data streams, they rely on advanced cyber-physical systems to handle freight and they use centralized planning tools to coordinate activity. The most recent developments at CTs in Malaysia and Singapore also include the use of Artificial Intelligence (AI) to allow selection of suspect containers for detailed security checks (Economist Intelligence Unit, 2015). The diversity and high degree of interconnectedness of Information Communications Technology (ICT) at CTs means that they present an informative case study for researchers aiming to investigate information security in the nascent stages of 4IR.

DOI: 10.4018/978-1-5225-4763-1.ch017

World Maritime News reports that approximately 30 CTs globally are classed as being automated (World Maritime News, 2016). This is a small proportion of the total number of roughly

2 000. However, the terminals that are automated tend to be large operations and play pivotal roles in the global CT network. Examples include Hong Kong International Terminal 6, Xiamen Yuanhai CT in China, and several of the terminals at the port of Rotterdam. The number of automated terminals continues to grow as terminal operators upgrade manual operations to streamline and compete with their rivals (Technavio, 2017).

The role of CTs is to enable the transition of freight from sea-borne to over-land modes of transport as goods move from their point of production to the point of consumption. All containerized freight moved by sea will be handled by at least 2 CTs in the course of its transit. The quantity of goods moved by sea is staggering and it was estimated that it amounted to 9.6 billion tonnes in 2013 (The Baltic Exchange, 2016). These figures saw a 200% increase in the two decades preceding 2014 (United Nations Conference on Trade and Development, 2014). The driver of this sustained increase has been the increasingly interconnected nature of the global economy and global economic development.

From these descriptions, it should be clear that disruption to one or more large CTs could quickly impact global supply chains and lead to economic losses for freight companies, CT operators and all of the companies that rely on dependable freight services as part of their business model. National and supra-national institutions have recognized that supply chain disruption poses a systemic risk to global trade and growth (Centre for the Protection of National Infrastructure, 2015; World Economic Forum/Accenture, 2013) and have called for improvements in resilience where possible. Ensuring resilience at CTs involves, among other things, controlling the cyber-risks that are introduced via networked technologies (Kramek, 2013).

This chapter will explore the nature of the cyber-risks to which CTs are exposed and conclude that the risks are indeed real and dangerous. This exploration takes the form of answering the following questions:

1. 'Why' do CTs present particularly attractive targets to would-be attackers?
2. 'How' could an attack be conducted against a CT and what impact would it have?

The chapter includes seven major sections. The first section provides the introduction while the second, entitled 'Container Terminal Operations', outlines the processes and technology employed by CTs. The third section, 'Container Terminals and Cybersecurity' explains that many CT operators have been slow to acknowledge and respond to the threats associated with their networked systems and that, consequently, many commentators consider CTs to be 'soft' targets (Port Strategy, 2013). The fourth section, 'Cyberbased Threats to CTs' provides a taxonomy of threat actors and explains their likely motivations and capabilities. The section 'Vulnerabilities of Container Terminal Operational Technology' uses the example of CT yard cranes to explain how vulnerabilities could be exploited to cause disruption. The chapter ends with recommendations and a conclusion.

CONTAINER TERMINAL OPERATIONS

Container terminal operations are ostensibly simple. They provide a service whereby containers are receipted, processed through a temporary storage area and are then delivered to a third party. However, the process is complicated by the additional requirements to process containers in the shortest possible time, with the highest degree of accuracy, in compliance with customs regulations and with the minimum use of resources (Lallo-Ruiz, 2017). Management of these 'complications' is achieved electronically and it is in this realm that the most significant changes have occurred in CT operations over recent years.

The ICT Revolution in Container Terminal Operations

Embedding ICT and automation within CT management and operational processes have had a positive effect on customer satisfaction and port competitiveness for those terminals which have embraced the technology (Lee, Tongzon & Yonghee, 2015). This technology includes the use of bespoke management tools to improve equipment utilization factors and to streamline administrative processes (Saanen, 2014), and the use of Industrial Control Systems (ICS) to reduce the cycle times of cranes and trucks. The result has been to increase container throughput and reduce waiting times for customers.

Where adopted, ICT has resulted in a revolution in CT operations, and, as is the nature of revolutions, new systems have been implemented in a very short time frame. It has been acknowledged in the maritime sector that security has commonly been overlooked in the rush to automate (ENISA, 2011). CT operators have been accused of introducing new technologies which have increased cyberattack surfaces while failing to implement adequate control measures to mitigate the associated risks.

The Automated Container Terminal

Figure 1 illustrates a simplified model of an automated CT and shows how a container moves through the three major sections of the terminal as it is being processed. These sections are seaside, stacking area and landside. Movement through the terminal for imported cargo involves transit from its arrival state as cargo stowed on a vessel, to its departure state as cargo loaded on wheels or rails. Typically, the transition from arrival to departure involves temporary storage on a container stacking yard. The reverse of this process is used for exports. The CT system comprises a number of discrete, yet integrated, processes where the output of one process feeds the input of the next. The individual processes can be thought of as sub-systems. Seaside sub-systems include the quay-side cranes and seaside land transport; stacking area sub-systems include the yard cranes, and landside sub-systems include landside transport and gates. Together these sub-systems form a System of Systems (SofS) - which is an apt description for a modern CT.

In an automated CT, the physical handling of containers is done by semi-automated Quay Cranes, Automated Guided Vehicles (AGVs) and fully automated Yard Cranes. Collectively this equipment is referred to as Container Handling Equipment (CHE). Automated CHE rely on onboard ICS to control operation and on ICT to carry instructions and updates to and from the Terminal Operating System (TOS) that manages them. Monitoring of the location of containers and CHE is achieved using Optical Character Recognition (OCR) systems, Radio Frequency Identification devices (RFID) and Global Positioning System (GPS), all of which rely on ICT for operation and information sharing.

The sub-systems are managed and integrated by a TOS. The TOS is a suite of applications that maintains databases of all container locations and is networked to all mobile hosts and data collection devices such that it can control the flow of containers through the CT in the most efficient manner.

A TOS is a complex piece of software that is at the center of the CT system. It plans, sequences and directs each container move in a manner designed to: optimize the use of space, minimize service time for vessels, minimize holding times for containers and to minimize waiting times for the trucks and trains

Figure 1. Loading and unloading process in a model CT

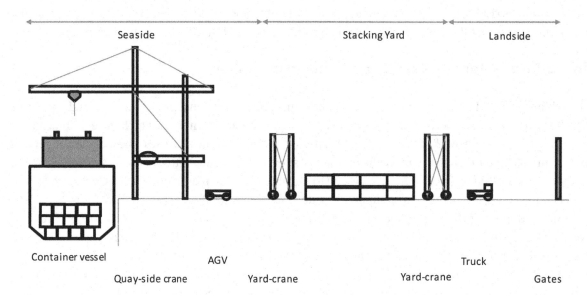

that move the containers to the hinterland (Choi, 2003). TOSs are generally based on Commercial off the Shelf (COTS) products that are then tailored to meet the specific needs of the CTs in which they are installed; they are modular packages with each module designed to undertake a specific task (Faouzi, Mabrouki & Semma, 2013). These tasks include but are not restricted to bi-directional exchange of business data with third parties, sharing a common operating picture with third parties, yard planning, berth scheduling, sub-system management and data archiving. Given the range of functionality of the TOS and its degree of integration with all CT subsystems, it is evident that dependable service from the TOS is critical to the operation of a CT. It is the brains behind the operation.

The manner in which a TOS operates reflects many of the key characteristics of 4IR as described by Schwab (2016). A TOS fuses multiple data streams, it embeds robotics, artificial intelligence and autonomous vehicles in the process it controls, and it significantly reduces the frictions that are often experienced at organizational interfaces. In this respect, TOSs can be viewed as a harbinger of the benefits promised by 4IR, albeit on a localized scale. They can also provide an early insight into the risks associated with 4IR.

The preceding paragraphs have described a CT system and its processes that are reliant on ICT for management, communication and control. Such is the complexity of the CT process, and the degree of optimization required for a modern CT to remain competitive, that the reliance of CT operations on ICT is near absolute. There is very limited scope to fall back to a manual modus operandi in the event of ICT failure. Kramek (2013) uses the analogy of ICT providing the undergird necessary for the global flow of maritime commerce. Using this analogy it should be evident that if the undergird fails the system collapses.

Structural Vulnerabilities at Container Terminals

There are two characteristics of CTs that commonly lead to structural vulnerabilities. These characteristics cause vulnerabilities and limitations to CT operations in their own right, and they also act to amplify vulnerabilities introduced from other sources, such as cyber. The first characteristic is the tendency for container handling to be concentrated at a relatively small number of ports; the second is the tendency for individual CTs to operate from restricted real-estate.

The tendency for CT operations to be concentrated at a relatively small number of sites is driven by the requirement for CTs to handle ever bigger container vessels. The size of these vessels means that there is a limited number of terminals which have the draught, quay length and handling capacity to service them (The LoadStar, 2016) and this has led to the rise of the mega-port. The mega-ports are those ports with terminals that are capable of servicing the largest vessels. They act as gateways for containers to come ashore and also as hubs for containers to be trans-shipped as part of a 'hub and spoke' shipping model. Rotterdam is a prime example of a mega-port; this port alone handled 9% of the total tonnage of the EU's seaborne freight in 2013 (Port of Rotterdam, 2015) and several of its terminals are among the most automated in the world. The mega-ports have a high degree of network centrality concerning the global freight network and, as a result, an effective attack on a single mega-port could lead to a significant regional economic impact (Coulter, 2002).

The second, and often unavoidable, vulnerability of CTs is that they operate on severely restricted real estate. This is especially true of European ports where the success of the ports has, over centuries, led to the growth of the cities which surround them. The ports are now constrained by the developments which they border (ESPO, 2010). A lack of real estate results in an imperative to maintain container throughput and ensure that containers enter and leave a CT with minimal dwell time (the duration for which containers are stored in the CT's container yard). Failure to maintain throughput results in container storage yards becoming saturated and the CT system becoming blocked. There is very little margin for error in modern CTs as their highly-optimized systems attempt to make the best use of all available space, hence they have limited capacity to absorb the impacts of any system disturbances.

Section 2 has described 'what' CTs are, how ICT is embedded in all of the sub-systems of modern automated CTs, and how the dependence on this technology is near absolute. Furthermore, it has been explained that the degree of network centrality of the largest ports, and their operation on restricted real estate means that there is very little redundancy in CT systems. Therefore, relatively small disturbances could lead to significant consequences.

CONTAINER TERMINALS AND CYBERSECURITY

The requirement for secure CTs is well understood, but security has generally been thought of in terms of physical security. The predominant physical security paradigm has been based on the principles of preventing unauthorzized access onto CT sites and the illicit movement of weapons (Kramek, 2013). This paradigm was reinforced by the terrorist attacks of 9/11 and the perceived threat of terrorist spectaculars involving Weapons of Mass Destruction (WMD) shipped in containers (ENEA, 2017). The focus on physical security is evidenced by the spending profile of the US Port Security Grant Program (PSGP). The US government has made over $2.6 billion of federal money available for security enhancements at US ports under the PSGP since 2002. Of the $2.6 billion invested up to 2013, less than 1% had been committed to projects relating to cybersecurity (Kramek, 2013).

It is ironic to note that efforts to improve physical security, which has often involved the installation of security technology such as automated access and egress points, RFID, and networked sensors and Closed-Circuit Television Cameras (CCTV) systems, may in itself have introduced new cyber vulnerabilities. These new networked systems can have the effect of increasing the attack-surface of a CT's IT network if they are installed without due regard to cybersecurity (ENISA, 2011).

Private research has ranked the 18 major industry sectors in the US in terms of a cybersecurity rating (Security Scorecard, 2016). This research ranks the transportation sector, of which CTs are a part, as 10th out of 18 sectors, placing it in the bottom half of the rankings list. As the transportation sector is highly coupled, with several companies all contributing to the movement of individual pieces of freight, there is a high degree of access to shared data systems and applications. This results in companies often having high degrees of exposure to third party information security risks which are very difficult to control (CPNI, 2015).

Potential Consequences of Cyber-Attacks Against CTs

The potential consequences of cyberattacks against a large CT vary significantly and depend on the objective and scale of the attack. They range from the social impact of the increased incidence of smuggling facilitated by cyber-means (BBC, 2013), to the economic consequences of a full terminal closure.

The economic consequences of disruption at a CT for any length of time could be catastrophic. In the short term (measured in hours), it would result in economic impact not only to the CTs but to those companies who rely on 'Just-In-Time' inventories that are supplied via shipping lines. In the medium term (measured in days to weeks), it could lead to food and fuel security issues.

The consequences of labor strikes in 2012 in the Port of Los Angeles-Long Beach provide an informative case study. The economic impact of the strike was estimated at $1 billion per day (White, 2012). This figure represents the value of the cargo diverted to other ports, missing revenue for truckers and other businesses, and forfeited worker pay.

In 2014, the National Association of Manufacturers and the National Retail Federation commissioned a report that predicted impacts of disruption to West Coast ports; the report forecast that widespread disruption at multiple ports and over a 5-day period could lead to a reduction in national GDP of $9.6 billion.

Quality of service impacts at the Maher Terminal in New York in 2013 provides another example of the results of disruptions to CTs. Although the disruptions at Maher were not caused by a malicious actor, they do provide an insight into the consequences of software faults in CT operating systems. The port's operations were severely disrupted for several weeks as it transitioned to a new TOS. During this transition, the TOS was incorrectly configured and was failing to sequence activity to make the best use of resources. The result was a sub-optimal process that was unable to meet customer demand. These disruptions led to 4 to 6-hour delays for trucks waiting to collect containers and caused knock-on effects in local supply chains (Mann, 2013). Faults, such as configuration errors, could conceivably be induced by a malicious actor attacking a CT's network infrastructure and operating software.

The huge financial implications associated with disruptions to large ports suggest that CTs could present a highly attractive target to malicious actors who are intent on committing acts of economic sabotage or extortion.

Section 3 has provided a number of explanations as to why cybersecurity at ports is often considered to be poor and hence why CTs have been described as 'soft' targets (Port Strategy, 2013). This characteristic is incompatible with CT's critical role as part of the global supply chain. The combination of CTs' critical yet vulnerable nature helps to explain '*why*' CTs may present attractive targets to malicious actors.

CYBER-BASED THREATS TO CONTAINER TERMINALS

Understanding the potential sources of threat – the threat actors – is a vital element of any risk management system and much work has been done to develop taxonomies to assist in this process. The UK Government employs a taxonomy which describes four major categories of threat actor considered to pose a threat to the UK's interests (HM Cabinet Office, 2011). These categories are criminals, state actors, terrorists and hacktivists. These categories provide the reference threats that the UK's national cybersecurity strategy is designed to secure against. This strategy includes measures to protect Critical National Infrastructure (CNI), including transport nodes such as CTs.

Here, we build on the UK government's taxonomy to describe potential threat actors and their motivations in the context of attacks against CTs. Table 1 outlines the characteristics and suggested motivations of the four core threat actor categories and adds a fifth – the insider threat.

Criminals

Analysis conducted by the global communications company Verizon, claims that the financial motive is by far the predominant motive for threat-actors engaged in cyber-attacks against organizations. Criminals intent on generating profit were responsible for over 75% of all detected malicious cyber-activity in 2015 (Verizon, 2016). Accordingly, a victim is considerably more likely to fall prey to a criminal than any other cyber-based threat actor category. Criminals can profit from cyber-attacks at CTs through techniques such as extortion (for example, use of ransomware), data theft (for example, financial or commercially sensitive data), and concealing smuggling.

Using cyber-attacks against CTs to facilitate smuggling is a known tactic of criminal gangs. The British Broadcasting Corporation (BBC) has reported on how criminals successfully penetrated the IT system at Antwerp port and used this access to conceal a drug smuggling operation; this operation was believed to have been active for up to 2 years from 2011 (BBC, 2013). Once inside the network, the

Table 1. Threat-actors' characteristics, capabilities and motivations

Threat Actor	Characteristics	Suggested Motivations for Conducting Cyber Attacks CT
Criminals	Modest technical abilities, predominantly motivated by financial gain	Smuggling, extortion
States	High levels of technical ability, motivated by intelligence gathering, military advantage	Tracking movement of goods of interest (military hardware and components), conducting reconnaissance in preparation for cyber-attacks as part of military campaigns, stealing data to assist domestic industry and commerce
Terrorists	Low to modest technical abilities (yet increasing).	Inflicting damage to routine pattern of life and/or inciting fear
Hacktivists	High levels of technical ability (often crowdsourced). May provide their services to terrorists and state-actors if their aims align	Making political statements about trade and globalization.
Insiders	High levels of access to systems and physical infrastructure. May act independently or assist other categories of threat-actor.	To cause damage to a company in response to a personal grievance or to work for financial gain on behalf of one of the other threat actor categories.

gang was able to access and manipulate records relating to containers to facilitate smuggling. Access to the network at Antwerp was initially achieved by social engineering and the inadvertent downloading of malware by staff. After the malware was discovered, the criminals changed tactics and used unsecured Ethernet connections within the port compound as an alternative point of entry.

Ransomware offers another potentially profitable and low-risk strategy for criminals. The impact of a criminal successfully encrypting operational data stored on a TOS, or on ICS components, could be crippling to a CT, particularly in the event that backup data Recovery Point Objectives (RPO) and Recovery Time Objectives (RTO) are found to be excessive. The loss of data relating to container location, ownership and onward shipping instructions would cause significant disruption at a CT in a very short space of time (Office of Cyber and Infrastructure Analysis, 2016). Formby et al. (2017) have suggested that Programmable Logic Controllers (PLCs) could also be vulnerable to ransomware attacks and demonstrated how skilled attackers could breach PLC defences, modify PLC code, and then demand a ransom in return for removal of the malicious code. In situations where the cost of paying the ransom will be less than the costs incurred through disruption to operations, there is a good chance that the operator will simply pay the ransom. PLCs are used extensively in CHE at CTs.

Recent data shows that criminal use of ransomware is increasing and that there is a growing trend for the criminals to target corporate organizations rather than individual consumers (McAfee Labs, 2016; Symantec, 2016). As such, the nature of the ransomware threat is transforming rapidly; it is evolving into a technique that is targeted against specific organizations, in the manner of an Advanced Persisaent Threat (APT). Given the lack of resilience in many CT operations, ransomware poses a particularly insidious threat.

State Actors

The motivations for state actors to breach cybersecurity at a CT could range from collecting data to gain commercial or military intelligence, through to disrupting CT operations as part of a military strategy, that is, as an act of war. The discovery of Stuxnet – a form of APT that is reputed to have been developed by state-level actors – with its express purpose of sabotaging Iranian nuclear enrichment facilities, was a watershed moment in cybersecurity. The discovery led to the assertion that the era of cyberwarfare had dawned (Weinberger, 2011).

Although Stuxnet was targeted at a particular facility, it was immediately clear that the sophistication of the malware, and a state's willingness to use it, had much broader implications for all CNI sectors. If malware can be: weaponized, hidden for extended periods, and cause significant disruption to highly regulated processes such as nuclear enrichment, it is reasonable to assert that the same techniques could be used against CT infrastructure. If APTs were to be designed specifically for use against CTs they could be engineered to achieve effects ranging from long-term, low-level background disruption (to cause lack of confidence in a service while remaining undetected), all the way to total disruption possibly requiring a reversion to manual techniques.

Analysis conducted by Verizon shows that the incidence of cyber-espionage, which includes national strategic and commercial espionage, constituted approximately 20% of detected cyber breaches against organizations in 2015 and was the second most common breach motivation in that reporting year. State-level espionage is not restricted to state-on-state activity. It is widely reported that targeted commercial espionage has been conducted by state-actors who then pass the intelligence to domestic companies to provide them with a competitive advantage (PwC, 2015; Everett, 2013). The discovery of the "Zombie

Zero" malware in 2014 suggested state-level involvement in schemes to steal commercially sensitive data (TrapX Security, 2014). This malware was embedded within barcode readers that were procured by Western transportation companies from a Chinese supplier. The data that was infiltrated by this malware related not only to the bar-codes that the devices were reading but also to financial data that was retrieved from victims' servers as part of a second stage of the attack.

The detection of cyber-reconnaissance activity, or industrial espionage against networks, is a key indicator of the potential for targeted cyber-attacks against that network in the future. This progression from reconnaissance to attack is explained as part of the cyber kill chain concept (Hutchins, Cloppert & Amin, 2011). The potential for future targeted attacks is a real threat to CTs and this is documented in the 2014 data breach report from Verizon (Verizon, 2014) which noted that 5% of all identified cyber-espionage incidents in that reporting year were directed against transportation companies and that the use of sophisticated techniques suggested state-actor involvement (direct or sponsored). The implication is that it is imperative for companies who discover that they have been subject to electronic espionage to harden their security quickly to avoid more damaging attacks at a later date.

Terrorists

The most likely motivations for terrorists to breach security at a CT would be to disrupt CT operations to cause economic damage, disrupt normal patterns of life or to smuggle weapons or components thereof. All three of these objectives have been proven feasible in recent years as demonstrated by the economic impact of the disruption caused by the Long Beach strike (White, 2012) and the potential for concealing smuggling activity as in the case of the Antwerp drug smuggling ring (BBC, 2013).

In the modern era of terrorism, where disrupting the normal pattern of life is a highly-prized aim, CTs present a particularly attractive target (Federal Bureau of Investigation, 2012). Preventing the normal operation of a CT would have an immediate economic impact and could be achieved with relatively unsophisticated attacks against IT infrastructure. Techniques may include the use of jammers to inter-rupt wide area WIFI networks or Denial of Service (DoS) attacks against a CT's network. These types of attacks are likely to be within the technical ability of many terrorist organizations.

Hacktivists

Hacktivists could provide state actors or terrorist organizations, with whom they share a common ideol-ogy or objective, with the means of achieving economic disruption or weapons smuggling. The technical competence of the best hacktivists means that it is feasible that APTs could be developed 'to order' with the explicit purpose of attacking CTs.

The Insider Threat

The insider threat is present in all security contexts and refers to an individual who has '*approved access, privilege, or knowledge of information systems, information services and missions*' (Maybury, Chase & Cheikes, 2005). The insider threat is particularly difficult to counter as insiders are, by definition, trusted entities operating within the boundaries of many of an IT network's defenses. The insider threat is particularly relevant to the CT environment as, due to the physical size of the sites, several hundred individuals will have authorized access either as permanent members of staff or as visitors (such as drivers with a requirement to visit the site to collect or deposit containers). The distinction between permanent staff and visitors can be made with the use of the terms 'insiders' and 'near-insiders'. Both insiders and, to a lesser degree, near-insiders have sufficient access to network infrastructure to present a threat to operations.

The insider and near insider threat at CTs could be exploited by any of the other four threat-actor categories which may be able to bribe or threaten insiders to undertake criminal activity on their behalf. The threat of insiders in the CT environment means that CT operators are unable to rely on gateway protection at the edges of their network and the results of risk assessments are likely to show that defence is required in depth, possibly down to the level of individual hosts.

Section 4 has identified '*who*' may be motivated to conduct cyber-attacks against CT infrastructure and feasible motivations for each threat-actor category have been described.

VULNERABILITIES OF CONTAINER TERMINAL OPERATIONAL TECHNOLOGY

The exact natures of vulnerabilities at CTs are site-specific and depend upon the hardware, software and network architectures that are employed. The information presented in this section is neither site-specific nor comprehensive and does not claim to present actual vulnerabilities that have been discovered at CTs. Rather, it aims to illustrate a sample of vulnerabilities that are reasonable to assert may be present at many CTs, and that could be discovered and exploited by malicious actors. In so doing it is hoped that the case is made that attacks pose a real risk unless adequate control measures are taken. To achieve this aim Section 5 will examine vulnerabilities that may be present in the onboard control networks of yard-cranes and the communication channels that serve them.

Industrial Control System Security

In recent years, the context of ICS has changed and so too have the vulnerabilities. The major context shift has been the increasing number of ICS devices deployed on networks equipped with gateways to conventional IT networks. This architecture enables the easy exchange of operational data between the industrial and enterprise networks of an organization. However, it also provides the possibility of threat-actors constructing multi-stage attacks from external networks all the way down to ICS field devices. The multi-stage nature of these attacks describes a sequence of attacks that penetrate successive layers of network defenses before finally accessing the target ICS networks and hosts.

The demand for efficient data exchange between ICS and enterprise networks has meant that ICS technology is increasingly making use of IP and Ethernet. In so doing, business has been able to reduce infrastructure costs, increase data availability and utilize standard ICT protocols. However, the use of Ethernet in ICS networks has not been matched by the development of ICS specific security controls (CPNI, 2011) and this has contributed to an increase in the number of known vulnerabilities relevant to ICS networks (Knapp & Langill, 2015).

The vendor community's failure to secure the new Ethernet communication channels on which their hardware relies was, until relatively recently, largely a result of them not foreseeing a requirement to do so. Before 2010, ICS specific vulnerabilities were relatively rare. However, today's threat environment is radically different. Data collected as part of the Open Source Vulnerability Database (OSVDB) shows how there was an explosion of vulnerability disclosures from 2010, with the annual number of disclosures jumping from less than 50 in 2010, to approximately 175 in 2011 and nearly 250 in 2012 (Knapp & Langill, 2015). 2011 was the year after the discovery of the Stuxnet virus which led to the increased profile of ICS security amongst the general public, the research community and most importantly, potential attackers.

It would seem that the ICS vendor and user communities enjoyed a honeymoon period before 2010. Consequently, security, if addressed at all, was an afterthought rather than being considered as critical functionality. Much of the ICS hardware installed before 2010 and for a period after that is likely to have been installed with inadequate security measures and a lack of capacity to allow the retrofitting of such measures. Given that the life expectancy of many ICS systems is measured in decades (Macaulay & Singer, 2012) there is likely to be a significant number of vulnerable components that remain in service for some years to come.

Yard Cranes: An Illustration of Potential ICS Vulnerabilities in CTs

The dependable operation of yard cranes relies on onboard ICS networks and control software. The compromise of either of these elements could negatively impact the crane's operation, which in turn could lead to a disruption in the process of stacking containers on the storage yard. Therefore, the sabotage of a crane's, or worse, a whole fleet of cranes', networks or software could seriously degrade the entire CT process.

Under normal operating conditions the use of automated cranes will improve the throughput, efficiency and safety at a CT when compared to a manual operation. However, it is also the case that automated CHE can be significantly less resilient to faults than their manual counterparts. This is because human operators are often able to compensate to a greater degree for deficiencies in machinery that are fully autonomous systems (Keskinen, Annala & Miedema, 2017). A recent industry publication highlights the greater potential for malfunctioning automatic CHE to disrupt CT operations and notes the requirement to safeguard their operation through pre-emptive maintenance regimes (Keskinen, Annala & Miedema, 2017). The same argument can logically be extended to the requirement for CTs to provide security for CHE ICS to safeguard networks and software.

The following sub-paragraphs discuss generic vulnerabilities in different elements of a yard crane's ICS architecture; an illustration of a typical ICS topology for such a crane can be found in Figure 2. It is important to note that the exploitation of all of these vulnerabilities requires that an attacker has already gained access to the industrial control network. It can be assumed that access to this network at a CT will be controlled and that the task of acquiring unauthorized access would be a non-trivial task. However, it is the case that a determined attacker may be able to achieve such access by conducting the early stages of a staged attack, or by physically accessing a network jack within the network.

Yard Cranes: Vulnerabilities in Hardware, Firmware and Access Control

As can be seen from Figure 2, a yard-crane's control system consists of several discrete elements of hardware, networked via a range of protocols. Any element of this hardware may suffer from one, or several, of the vulnerabilities listed below and it may be possible for malicious actors to access them remotely.

1. **Poor Implementation of Access Control Mechanisms:** Unauthorised access to ICS functionality can sometimes be gained as a result of poor implementation of access controls. This manifests

as passwords being stored and transmitted in the clear, 'pass the hash' vulnerabilities, or weak hashing (ICS-CERT, 2013). All of these weaknesses provide an attacker with the opportunity to authenticate to controllers, thereby accessing their parameters and logic.

2. **Passwords:** Weak or null passwords are passwords which are commonly known or easily guessed. The problems of weak or null passwords are well known across IT. However, they remain a particular problem in ICS systems (Sarkar, Sarkar & Ghosh, 2015). The practice of selecting weak or null passwords makes it easy for technicians to remember them but it also makes it easy for adversaries to guess passwords and gain unauthorised access, either remotely or locally.

Once an attacker has established communications and access to an ICS field device or controller it is possible to attack it in one of two ways:

1. **Abusing Functionality:** Once access has been gained to a field device, abusing the legitimate functionality the device is a relatively simple task. It requires only that the attacker has a basic knowledge of crane operation and of the parameter numbers and ranges used to control the plant. Much of this information is available from open sources. Techniques such as this were used in the 2015 attack against the Ukrainian power grid when hackers were able to gain remote access to power control systems and change the system state at will (Sullivan & Kamensky, 2017). In the case of a yard crane, an attack could take the form of disabling a motor, limiting the range of motion, or manipulating the outputs of the proximity sensors that are used for collision avoidance. Relatively subtle changes to a crane's operating parameters such as limiting ranges of movement would introduce faults that are difficult to find but would cause significant disruptions to a CT's operations until they were rectified.

2. **Modifying Firmware:** Modification of firmware is possible on any field-device which accepts unsigned firmware updates. This vulnerability is described in detail at (Schuett, Butts & Dunlap, 2014) about Programmable Logic Controllers (PLCs) manufactured by Allen Bradley. Modification of firmware is a particularly powerful means of attack as it provides the attacker with a persistent presence and allows firmware or Operating Systems (OS) to be programmed to execute malicious commands at a time of the attackers choosing. Modification of firmware also provides an attacker with the ability to mask any changes made to control parameters as part of an attack, thereby making stealthy attacks possible. This can be achieved by changing firmware source code such that control panels display the values that the attacker wants the operator to believe rather than the actual values. Stealth techniques such as this were used in the Stuxnet attack (Chen, 2011). In the case of a yard crane, this could involve an attacker altering the load cell readings which are incorporated into cranes as safety systems to provide overload protection.

The security vulnerabilities associated with PLCs and the potential for their direct exploitation are numerous and well reported. The Kaspersky Lab report entitled 'Industrial Control System Vulnerability Statistics' (Kaspersky Labs, 2016) provides a good overview of the numbers and natures. Several papers have discussed vulnerabilities within well-known product lines, including Beresford (2011); Schuett, Butts & Dunlap (2014).

Yard Cranes: Vulnerabilities in Software

Software vulnerabilities in ICS are similar to those in General Purpose (GP) software; they are dominated by coding errors that result in vulnerabilities to buffer overflows and lack of bounds checking for values entered by users to the system via user interfaces. It is likely that ICS software in the form of firmware, OS and applications, suffer from a higher incidence of coding errors than GP software from larger software houses. This is due to the fact that ICS specific software is produced in relatively low volumes and is often tailored for individual use cases. Software of this nature has tended to be produced outside of a comprehensive quality control process and for this reason suffers from higher error rates (Department for Homeland Security, 2011).

In 2011, the US Department of Homeland Security (DHS) identified that 47% of all disclosed vulnerabilities related to improper input validation meaning that in 2011, this method represented the single biggest vulnerability category in ICS software (Department for Homeland Security, 2011). The complexity and diversity of software employed at CTs have been identified as a particular vulnerability and calls have been made for increased efforts to evaluate and harden CT specific software packages (Heymann, Miller, Alghazzawi & Incertis, 2016; Hutchins, Cloppert & Amin, 2011). Successful software exploitations can result in attackers gaining root access to ICS elements and gaining the same levels of control that have been described in the section relating to hardware and firmware vulnerabilities. If a vulnerability is present the only means of preventing its exploitation is through physical and logical access control to Human Machine Interfaces (HMIs) and workstations and regular software patching regimes.

Yard Cranes: Vulnerabilities in Networks

Networks provide the means by which attackers can gain access to the firmware, software, and control signals that will allow them to degrade the performance of the yard crane. Data transmission on networks is governed by protocols which describe how data is passed between applications throughout the ICS hierarchy. Different protocols operate at different levels of the enterprise network (Williams, 1994) and at different layers of the Open Systems Interconnection (OSI) stack. ICS networks frequently employ special purpose fieldbus protocols at the process and local control levels as they have been specifically designed and engineered to deliver the required characteristics of low latency and determinism. Security was not a consideration at the time many of the fieldbus protocols were developed and consequently, they are a common source of vulnerability in ICS networks. ICS-CERT data from 2011 identified that at that time, 73% of disclosed ICS vulnerabilities originated at the supervisory control and local control levels (Department of Homeland Security, 2011), these are the levels at which ICS specific fieldbus protocols are employed. Two examples of network vulnerabilities at these levels include:

1. **Profinet Related Vulnerabilities:** The communication channels at the local control level of a crane ICS network will run on a fieldbus protocol such as Profinet. Profinet provides fieldbus functionality with the benefits of Ethernet compatibility and is used by major equipment vendors in the ICS network of cranes, as illustrated in Figure 2. Profinet is susceptible to Man in the Middle (MitM) attacks as a result of port stealing. Port stealing allows a MitM to poison the internal routing tables in switches and redirect traffic between a Profinet network controller and an Input/Output (IO) device via an attacker. As an intermediary in all controller/device communications, the attacker is

then in a position to modify frames and manipulate data on the channel (Paul, Schuster & Konig, 2013).

2. **Plain-Text Communications:** The real-time requirements of ICS networks mean that it is often not possible to encrypt the links at supervisory and local control levels, as, to do so would introduce message latency that would violate the real-time requirements. In other cases, encryption on ICS networks is not employed simply because there is no perceived need to do so. Consequently, it is possible to initiate attacks at these levels simply by intercepting and re-playing data that can be collected by network sniffing (Knapp & Langill, 2015), or even by capturing legitimate user credentials by sniffing plaintext usernames and passwords (Department for Homeland Security, 2011).

The vulnerabilities described above are by no means exhaustive; they merely provide examples of the vectors attackers may choose to disrupt a CT. All of the vulnerabilities listed are well known and described in detail in open source documentation. As such, one would expect that responsible CT operators would have taken measures to safeguard against them. However, the critical safety nature of ICS networks, including those used on cranes, means that patching software to protect against known vulnerabilities is difficult to manage. This difficulty is due to the fear that patches may introduce unexpected physical behavior that compromises safety. It is also the case that the process of patching can result in downtime to equipment that CT operators are unwilling to accept. The result is that archaic vulnerabilities can remain a threat for considerable lengths of time after their disclosure (Wang, Li, P De Aguiar, Menasche & Shafiq, 2017).

SOLUTIONS AND RECOMMENDATIONS

The age of 4IR will result in the number of devices hosted on a CTs network, and the degree of interaction between them, continuing to grow. This will result in an increasingly large and complex attack-surface. Consequently, CT operators must make all reasonable efforts to ensure that their networks are appropriately-secured if they are to reduce their exposure to cyber-risks. The term appropriately-secured makes for a convenient buzz-word and is easy to write into security documentation and book chapters, however, it is much more difficult to achieve in practice. The following two recommendations could help CT operators to work toward achieving appropriate-security.

The first recommendation is that CT operators, large and small, invest in the management structures and processes that are necessary to implement an effective Information Security Management System (ISMS). An ISMS involves a continual process of risk assessment, risk treatment and evaluation and is designed to manage an organisation's exposure to cyber risks. Documents such as ISO 27001 (ISO/IEC, 2013) provide a general purpose ISMS framework that could be employed in a port environment and the International Electrotechnical Commission (IEC) and the National Institute of Standards and Technology (NIST) have both published guides and standards specifically related to cybersecurity of Industrial Control Systems (IEC, 2012) (NIST, 2015). In the age of 4IR, the delivery of a well-resourced ISMS will reduce exposure to cyber-risk and should be considered as a core function of a CT operator.

The second recommendation is that groups of port authorities, trade organizations, and governmental bodies should seek to work collaboratively to reduce cyber-risks across the whole ports sector. Working collaboratively can be achieved through the formation of communities of interest and strategic public/private partnerships. The ISMS that are so crucial to maintaining appropriate security is based on risk assessments, and these risk assessments depend heavily on a thorough understanding of the threat environment. However, even for large port authorities, understanding the threat can be a time consuming, expensive and difficult task. Communities of interest can make this task easier by sharing raw data and threat analysis. The collaboration of this nature helps to coordinate and stimulate functional networks (Dunn-Cavelty & Suter, 2009) thereby reducing costs and spreading best practice. The Maritime and Port Security ISAO was formed in the USA in May 2016 to assist in this process and could provide a model for other nations or regions to follow. In the UK, the government the Institute of Engineering and Technology (IET) and a number of UK port authorities have recently collaborated to publish a code of practice for cybersecurity at ports (IET, 2016). The purpose of which is to improve standards across the ports sector.

FUTURE RESEARCH DIRECTIONS

It is widely accepted that no network can be perfectly secured and that security breaches are an inevitability. Given this context, research into increasing the resilience of CT IT networks in the face of cyber-attacks would make a useful contribution to the current body of knowledge. Research that offers insights into 'fall-back' operating modes that would allow CTs to maintain container throughput, even in the face of a sustained cyber-attack, would be particularly valuable.

CONCLUSION

This chapter has explored the issue of the security of ICS networks at CTs. This has been done as part of the more general thesis that cyber-based risks are both real and dangerous and are likely to become increasingly so as a result of technological developments associated with the Fourth Industrial Revolution.

It was found that a combination of factors – including the rapid pace of automation and a culture that has traditionally focused on physical security – have resulted in cybersecurity at CTs often being characterized as weak. It was also made clear that the impacts of a successful cyber-attack against either the enterprise or ICS networks of a CT are likely to be very significant in terms of economic and social costs. Consequently, CTs present attractive targets to attackers. Possible motivations for adversaries launching cyber-attacks against CTs were explored and feasible motivations were developed for each of five categories of threat actor. These motivations ranged from the profit motive for criminals to the national strategic objectives of foreign state actors.

The chapter investigated a sample of the means by which attackers could gain access to a yard-cranes ICS to cause disruption. It was determined that vulnerabilities are likely to exist within networks and that these vulnerabilities are often difficult to patch and mitigate. Consequently, unless a concerted effort is made to address the problem, the ICT networks of key plant and equipment at CTs could remain vulnerable for some time to come. The combination of critical facilities, well-motivated and resourced threat actors and ICS networks that have proven difficult to secure leads to the assertion that the threats to CTs are both real and dangerous.

The chapter responds to this assertion by making two key recommendations; the first is that CT operators should ensure that they have an ISMS in place to remediate the existing security deficiencies and to proactively respond to evolving cyber-risks. The second is that CT operators should work together collaboratively, and with other public and private organizations, to spread best practice and share information. These recommendations should contribute to the aim of raising standards of cyber risk management in CTs.

REFERENCES

BBC. (2013). *Police warning after drug traffickers' cyber-attack.* Retrieved Jan 23, 2016, from http://www.bbc.co.uk/news/world-europe-24539417

Beresford, D. (2011). *Exploiting Siemens Simatic S7 PLCs.* Retrieved Jun 21, 2017, from media.blackhat: https://media.blackhat.com/bh-us-11/Beresford/BH_US11_Beresford_S7_PLCs_WP.pdf

Centre for the Protection of National Infrastructure. (2015). *Mitigating Security Risk in the National Infrastructure Supply Chain.* Retrieved Jun 01, 2017, from cpni.gov.uk: https://www.cpni.gov.uk/system/files/documents/8b/d4/Mitigating%20Security%20Risk%20in%20Supply%20Chain.pdf

Chen, T. M., & Abu-Nimeh, S. (2011). Lessons from Stuxnet. *Computer*, *44*(4), 91–93. doi:10.1109/MC.2011.115

Choi, H. R., Kim, H. S., Park, B. J., Park, N.-K., & Lee, S. W. (2003). An ERP approach for container terminal operating systems. *Maritime Policy & Management*, *30*(3), 197–210. doi:10.1080/0308883032000089549

Coulter, D. Y. (2002). *Globalization and Maritime Power - Globalization of Maritime Commerce: The Rise of Hub Ports* (S. J. Tangredi, Ed.). Washington, DC: National Defense University.

CPNI. (2011). *Securing The Move To Ip-Based Scada/Plc Networks.* Retrieved Jun 21, 2017, from www.ncsc.gov.uk: https://www.ncsc.gov.uk/content/files/protected_files/document_files/The%20Move%20to%20IP%20Based%20SCADA%20Networks%20151111.pdf

CPNI. (2015). *Security for Industrial Control Systems - Manage Third Party Risks.* Retrieved Jun 06, 2017, from www.ncsc.gov.uk: https://www.ncsc.gov.uk/content/files/protected_files/guidance_files/SICS%20-%20Manage%20Third%20Party%20Risks%20Final%20v1.0.pdf

Department for Homeland Security. (2011). *Common Cyber Security Vulnerabilities in Industrial Control Systems.* Department for Homeland Security, Control Systems Security Program. DHS.

Dunn-Cavelty, M., & Suter, M. (2009). Public–Private Partnerships are no silver bullet: An expanded governance model for Critical Infrastructure Protection. *International Journal of Critical Infrastructure Protection*, *2*(4), 179–187. doi:10.1016/j.ijcip.2009.08.006

Economist Intelligence Unit. (2015). *A turning point: The potential role of ICT innovations in ports and logistics.* Retrieved Jul 4, 2016, from DPWorld.com: http://web.dpworld.com/wp-content/uploads/2015/11/ICT-innovations-DP-World_Eng.pdf

ENEA. (2017). *CBRN Risks in Maritime and Land Containers Transport* (G. G. Cartocci, Ed.). ENEA.

ENISA. (2011). *Analysis Of Cyber Security Aspects In The Maritime Sector*. Retrieved Jun 12, 2016, from https://www.enisa.europa.eu/.../cyber-security-aspects-in-the-maritime-sector.../fullRe

ESPO. (2010). *Code of Practice on Societal Integration of Ports*. Retrieved Jun 15, 2016, from https://www.espo.be/media/espopublications/ESPOCodeofPracticeonSocietalIntegrationofPorts2010.pdf

Everett, B. (2013). Optically transparant: the rise of industrial espionage and state sponsored hacking. *Computer Fraud and Security,* (10), 13-16.

Faouzi, A., Mabrouki, C., & Semma, A. (2013). Modeling a repository of modules for ports terminals. *International Journal of Computer Science Issues*, *10*(1), 766–773.

Federal Bureau of Investigation. (2012). *The Cyber Threat Part 1: On the Front Lines with Shawn Henry*. Retrieved Jun 13, 2016, from https://www.fbi.gov/news/stories/the-cyber-threat

Formby, D., Durbah, S., & Beyah, R. (2017). *Out of Control: Ransomware and Industrial Control Systems*. Retrieved May 12, 2017, from www.cap.gatech.edu/plcransomware.pdf

Heymann, E., Miller, B. E., Alghazzawi, M. J., & Incertis, D. (2016). *Addressing the cyber security of maritime shipping*. Retrieved May 24, 2017, from ftp://ftp.cs.wisc.edu/paradyn/papers/ETC_2016_Heymann_Miller.pdf

HM Cabinet Office. (2011). *The UK Cyber Security Strategy - Protecting and Promotoing the UK in a Digital World. UK Government, Cabinet Office*. London: UK Government.

Hutchins, E. M., Cloppert, M. J., & Amin, R. M. (2011). *Intelligence-Driven Computer Network Defense Informed by Analysis of Adversary Campaigns and Intrusion Kill Chains*. Retrieved Jun 2017, 1, from https://www.lockheedmartin.com/content/dam/lockheed/data/corporate/documents/LM-White-Paper-Intel-Driven-Defense.pdf

ICS-CERT. (2013). *Targeted Cyber Intrusion Detection and Mitigation Strategies (Update B)*. Retrieved May 30, 2017, from ICS _CERT: https://ics-cert.us-cert.gov/tips/ICS-TIP-12-146-01B

IEC. (2012). *IECTS 62443-1-1. International Electrotechnical Commission*. IEC.

IET. (2016). *Ports and port systems: cybersecurity code of practice. Institute of Engineering and Technology and UK Department for Transport*. IET.

ISO/IEC. (2013). *ISO/IEC 27001:2013 - Information Security - Security Techniques - Information Security Management Systems*. International Organisation for Standardisation. ISO.

Kaspersky Labs. (2016). *Industrial Control System Vulnerability Statistics*. Retrieved July 2, 2016, from https://kasperskycontenthub.com/securelist/files/2016/07/KL_REPORT_ICS_Statistic_vulnerabilities.pdf

Keskinen, A., Annala, I., & Miedema, P. (2017). *Maintenance of automated terminals*. Retrieved Jun 01, 2017, from Kalmarglobal. com: https://www.kalmarglobal.com/globalassets/services/kalmar-care/kalmar-maintenance-of-automated-terminals.pdf

Knapp, E. D., & Langill, J. T. (2015). Industrial Network Security - Chapter 3 Industrial Cyber Security History and Trends. Elsevier.

Kramek, J. (2013). *The Critical Infrastructure Gap: US Port Facilities and Cyber Vulnerabilities.* Retrieved May 27, 2016, from https://www.brookings.edu/research/the-critical-infrastructure-gap-u-s-port-facilities-and-cyber-vulnerabilities/

Lallo-Ruiz, E. (2017). Intelligent Management of Seaside Logistic Operations at Maritime Container Terminals. *4OR - A Quarterly Journal of Operations Research, 15*(2), 217-218.

Lee, S. Y., Tongzon, J. L., & Yonghee, K. (2015). Port e-transformation, customer satisfaction and competitiveness. *Maritime Policy & Management, 43*(5), 630–643. doi:10.1080/03088839.2015.1105394

Macaulay, T., & Singer, B. (2012). *Cybersecurity for Industrial Control Systems: SCADA, DCS, PLC, HMI and SIS.* Auerbach Publications.

Mann, T. (2013). Computer Problems Leaves Goods Stranded at New York Port. *The Wall Street Journal.*

Maybury, M., Chase, P., & Cheikes, B. (2005). *Analysis and Detection of Malicious Insiders.* Retrieved Jun 01, 2017, from https://www.mitre.org/publications/technical-papers/analysis-and-detection-of-malicious-insiders

McAfee Labs. (2016). *McAfee Labs Threats Report 2016.* Retrieved May 12, 2017, from https://www.mcafee.com/uk/resources/reports/rp-quarterly-threats-sep-2016.pdf

NIST. (2015). *NIST SP 800-82 Revision 2 - Guide to Industrial Control Security.* National Institute of Standards and Technology. NIST.

Office of Cyber and Infrastructure Analysis. (2016). *Consequences to Seaport Operations from Malicious Cyber Activity.* Retrieved Jun 31, 2017, from info.publicintelligence.net: https://info.publicintelligence.net/DHS-SeaportCyberAttacks.pdf

Paul, A., Schuster, F., & Konig, H. (2013). Towards the Protection of Industrial Control Systems – Conclusions of a Vulnerability Analysis of Profinet IO. In *Proceedings of the 10th international conference on Detection of Intrusions and Malware, and Vulnerability Assessment.* Berlin: Springer. 10.1007/978-3-642-39235-1_10

Port of Rotterdam. (2015). *Eurostat: Rotterdam 9% of EU maritime freight.* Retrieved Feb 24, 2016, from Port of Rotterdam.com: https://www.portofrotterdam.com/en/news-and-press-releases/eurostat-rotterdam-9-of-eu-maritime-freight-1

Port Strategy. (2013). *A Soft Target.* Retrieved May 24, 2017, from Port Strategy: http://www.portstrategy.com/news101/port-operations/safety-and-security/A-soft-target

PwC. (2015). *Corporate Espionage: Responding to the threat.* Retrieved August 4, 2016, from PwC.co.uk: http://www.pwc.co.uk/services/forensic-services/insights/corporate-espionage-responding-to-the-threat.html

Saanen, Y. A. (2014). *Optimisation for Operational Excellence.* Port Technology.

Sarkar, S., Sarkar, K., & Ghosh, S. (2015). Cyber Security Password Policy for Industrial Control Networks. In *2015 1st International Conference on Next Generation Computing Technologies (NGCT)* (pp. 408-413). NGCT.

Schuett, C., Butts, J., & Dunlap, S. (2014). An Evaluation of Modification Attacks on Programmable Logic Controllers. *International Journal of Critical Infrastructure Protection, 7*(1), 7. doi:10.1016/j. ijcip.2014.01.004

Schwab, K. (2016). *The fourth industrial revolution what it means and how to respond.* Retrieved May 24, 2017, from webforum: https://www.weforum.org/agenda/2016/01

Security Scorecard. (2016). *2016 Financial Industry Cybersecurity Report.* Retrieved Jun 02, 2017, from https://cdn2.hubspot.net/hubfs/533449/SecurityScorecard_2016_Financial_Report.pdf

Siemens. (2015). Retrieved Jun 14, 2016, from Drive and Control Components for Cranes: http://w3app. siemens.com/mcms/infocenter/dokumentencenter/mc/documentsu20catalogs/cr1-2015-en.pdf

Sullivan, J. E., & Kamensky, D. (2017). How cyber-attacks in the Ukraine show the vulnerability of the US power grid. *The Electricity Journal, 30*(3), 30–35. doi:10.1016/j.tej.2017.02.006

Symantec. (2016). *An ISTR Special Report: Ransomware and Business 2016.* Retrieved May 12, 2017, from https://www.symantec.com/content/en/us/enterprise/media/security_response/whitepapers/ ISTR2016_Ransomware_and_Businesses.pdf

Technavio. (2017). *Global Automated Container Terminal Market 2017-2021.* Retrieved May 24, 2017, from Technavio: https://www.technavio.com/report/global-automation-global-automated-container-terminal-market-2017-2021

The Baltic Exchange. (2016). *The Shipping Markets.* Retrieved August 3, 2016, from The Baltic Exchange: http://www.balticexchange.com/about-us/shipping-markets/

The LoadStar. (2016). *Mega-sized container vessels present mega-sized challenges to ports and shippers.* Retrieved August 2016, 4, from The Load Star: http://theloadstar.co.uk/mega-sized-container-vessels-present-mega-sized-challenges-ports-shippers/

Trap X Security. (2014). *TrapX discovers 'Zombie Zero' Advanced Persistent Threat.* Retrieved Jun 31, 2017, from TrapX.com: https://trapx.com/trapx-discovers-zombie-zero-advanced-persistent-malware/

United Nations Conference on Trade and Development. (2014). *Review of Maritime Transport 2014* (p. 3). Geneva: United Nations.

Verizon. (2014). *2014 Data Breach Investigations Report.* Retrieved Jun 6, 2016, from http://www. verizonenterprise.com/resources/reports/rp_Verizon-DBIR-2014_en_xg.pdf

Verizon. (2016). *2016 Data Breach Investigations Report.* Retrieved Jun 1, 2017, from http://www. verizonenterprise.com/resources/reports/rp_dbir-2016-executive-summary_xg_en.pdf

Wang, B., Li, X. P., De Aguiar, L., Menasche, D. S., & Shafiq, Z. (2017). Characterising and Modelling Patching Practices of Industrial Control Systems. *Proc. ACM Meas. Anal. Comput. Syst, 1*(1), 1-23.

Weinberger, S. (2011). Is this the start of Cyberwarfare. *Nature, 474*(7350), 142–145. doi:10.1038/474142a PMID:21654779

White, R. (2012). Port Labor Talks Shift into High Gear, but Strike Continues. *Los Angeles Times.* Retrieved from http://articles.latimes.com/2012/dec/01/business/la-fi-mo-ports-strike-continues-20121201

Williams, T. J. (1994). The Perdue enterprise reference architecture. *Computers in Industry, 24*(2), 141–158. doi:10.1016/0166-3615(94)90017-5

World Economic Forum/Accenture. (2013). *Building Resilience in Supply Chains.* World Economic Forum. Geneva: WEF.

World Maritime News. (2016). *Port Automation: Smart, Smarter, Smartest! World Maritime News.* Retrieved May 24, 2017, from World Maritime News: http://worldmaritimenews.com/archives/187691/port-automation-smart-smarter-smartest/

Chapter 18
Cyber Security Education in the Fourth Industrial Revolution:
The Case of South Africa

Paul Kariuki
University of KwaZulu Natal, South Africa

ABSTRACT

It is critical that cyber education curriculum considers the growing cyber technologies and which aspects of these technologies need to be aligned with the fourth industrial revolution. This chapter seeks to present a comprehensive analysis of the current level of cyber security education in South Africa. It will also track the current trends of cyber security education in the country as well as examining any challenges being experienced including any knowledge gaps. In the end, the chapter proposes recommendations for consideration in strengthening cybersecurity education in the country in to achieve advanced cyber security responses, capable of mitigating any cyber security threats. Offering quality cyber security education is important in preparing the next generation cyber security practitioners, who are highly competent and capable of developing innovative solutions in response to the growing global demand of cyber technologies. The chapter ends by proposing specific strategies that can guide towards this ideal in the context of the fourth industrial revolution.

INTRODUCTION

Individual and national security has been a priority since time immemorial. Evidence shows that information technology has played a positive and negative role in this regard. While the development of technology linked to the internet and other means of communication has ushered in a new way of life and transformed all economic sectors, it also provides a space for cyber and related crimes.

Growing use of the internet and related communication tools has raised the need to respond effectively to pervasive threats within state governance institutions, the transformation of goods, and security of borders and critical infrastructure. Research and policies are required to ensure that cyber-crime does not adversely affect citizens' development and well-being. There is growing demand for cyber security experts

DOI: 10.4018/978-1-5225-4763-1.ch018

to provide education on the unforeseen events that unfold due to information technology facilities around the world. Expert skills (Morgan, 2016) are required to ensure that devices are secure, prevent intruders from taking control of intellectual property, and alleviate and neutralise hacking, malware, viruses, etc.

However, globally, there is a dearth of experts in this field (Evans & Reeder, 2010). This calls for cyber security education curricula to be strengthened. While state institutions and businesses have made much progress in counter-balancing the threats and real effects of terrorists and cyber criminals, many challenges remain.

This chapter consists of four sections. The first examines trends and challenges relating to the cyber security curriculum. Section two highlights mitigation strategies that could be adopted to fight cyber-crime as well as their consequences for society. Section three addresses the policy implications for the government, educational institutions and cyber security professionals. Finally, section four focuses on the common responsibility of improving cyber education technologies in the fourth industrial revolution. The chapter ends with a conclusion.

THE CYBER SECURITY CURRICULUM IN SOUTH AFRICA: CURRENT TRENDS AND CHALLENGES

Cyber security education has gained traction in recent decades in South Africa. According to Dlamini (2012:5), it has been geared towards rebuilding the skills of practicing cyber security experts whilst at the same time increasing general awareness of such issues. Table 1 lists recent cyber security awareness initiatives in the country.

Thus, cyber security education in South Africa is geared towards raising awareness at all levels of society, focusing on diverse aspects.

Cyber security has been recognised as a national security issue in South Africa and the policy frame-work dates back to 2009. Grobler, van Vuuren, and Leenen (2012, p. 2) note that the 2011 draft policy framework set the stage for the launch of a Computer Security Incident Response Team (CSRIT) and the sector Computer Security Emergency Response Team (CSERT) by the end of 2012. The government has acknowledged the importance of cyber security and has invested in cyber security programmes and education (Conklin, Cline, & Roosa, 2014).

The literature notes the need for accreditation of institutions that offer cyber security education. This occurs in the United States (US), it is employed to ensure consistent quality. However, the most important aspect of accreditation is regulating the types of programmes offered to students. The common standard in the US is the IS 2010 Curriculum standard programme (Topi et al., 2010).

The IS 2010 curriculum covers different undergraduate programmes and offers the following seven modules: (1) IS 2010: Foundations of Information Systems; (2) IS 2010: Data and Information Management; (3) IS 2010 Enterprise Architecture; (4) IS 2010 IS Project Management; (5) IS 2010: IT Infrastructure; (6) IS 2010: Systems Analysis and Design; and (7) IS 2010 IS: Strategy, Management, and Acquisition (Conklin et al., 2014). In terms of supervision, the modules should be e-instinctive, student-friendly and methodically organised to facilitate knowledge acquisition.

Research suggests that students should be initiated on the use of codes in Information Technology. Some universities have expanded teaching of the theory and practice of secure coding to cover subjects such as Programming Secure Systems (Johnstone, 2013, p. 287).

Table 1. Cyber Security Awareness Initiatives in South Africa

Initiative	Goals/Objectives	Targeted Audience	Topics Discussed
Centre for Science and Industrial Research (CSIR)	To educate current and future users of computers on safe and secure online habits To increase awareness and understanding of the dangers of the Internet To provide individuals with the necessary knowledge to make the right decisions in Internet-related situations	Secondary schools, Further Education and Training colleges Technical university students Non-technical university students Community centres support staff Educators/teachers	Physical security, malware and countermeasures, surfing the Net, social aspects of cyber security
UP ICSAPumaScope	Falls under an existing project called PumaScope, and is the main focus of UP's cyber security awareness initiatives	Rural schools (children and adults), churches, orphanages	Topics vary as it is a community-based project
UNMM (ISM)	To educate users about information security, more specifically, to educate users on their individual roles in the effectiveness of one type of control, namely, operational controls.	General company end-users, entrepreneurs (public or private sectors), children, parents, tertiary students and senior citizens	Passwords management, information security principles and terminology, social engineering, phishing, desktop security, patch management, updating anti-virus software and backup procedures, email security.
University of South Africa (UNISA)	To contribute to the creation of a cyber-awareness culture.	Children	Cyber security concepts
University of Fort Hare (UFH)	To improve performance in the areas in which an organisation has identified performance deficiencies. To test students' personal information security competency level because a user can be aware of an issue but not necessarily act on that knowledge.	University students (1st and 3rd year)	Passwords management, information security principles and terminology, social engineering, phishing, desktop security, patch management, updating anti-virus software and backup procedures, email security
South African Bank (SABRIC	To deliver measurable value to clients through a team of energetic specialists who consistently provide high quality support services and products. To contribute to the reduction of bank related crime through effective public-private-partnerships.	South African Bank (SABRIC partners), employees	Commercial fraud, online scams, device scams, online safety practice
ISG Africa	To drive awareness and education around information security risk and governance.	Organisations and society	Cyber threats and information security
South African Centre for Information Security (SACIS)	To develop and promote a management and governance drive to implement effective information security programmes.	All organisations	Cyber-crime

The knowledge acquired in information systems programmes is useful in different domains including government structures and the private sector. It enhances security within countries and across borders. In today's world, nations need to work together to share security intelligence and address developmental issues. Globalisation calls for the pursuit of common security goals and strategic governance. This highlights the need to develop a cohort of well-trained cyber security professionals to address the cyber threats emanating from terrorism (Vogel, 2016, p. 32).

While some might define security as specific bodily threat or harm from others or external individuals or group(s), government structures and other stakeholders have adopted a broader definition when it comes to cyber security. It is important to differentiate between cyber security as a government monitoring system that controls the security of the state by means of infrastructure and other strategies. The field of cyber security includes disgruntled workers, trade spying, unintentional user errors that compromise infrastructure and information, and equipment failure as well as the actions of extremists and natural tragedies (Lee, 2015, p. 2). It is estimated that cyber-crime costs Australia approximately $15 billion per annum (Australian Crime Commission, 2015).

Vogel (2016, p. 32) notes that the September 11, 2001 terrorist attacks shifted security trends in the US and highlighted the need for counterterrorism efforts to supplement those of national security and law enforcement agencies. These attacks, that caused the deaths of thousands of people in the most protected country of the world, shifted leaders' mind-set on security. Counterterrorism should, therefore, be taken seriously in all structures. In the US, hackers took control of government and private systems. The FBI has noted that the number of economic cyber espionage cases has increased sharply, comprising companies such as DuPont, Lockheed Martin and Valspar (Federal Bureau of Investigation, 2015).

Cyber security has also become a particular concern of the armed forces. In most developed nations, cyber-crime has become a new way to destabilise governments and its structures. During the launch of the US Cyber Command in 2010, the US Deputy Defense Secretary stated that, cyberspace was considered as important a military domain as the land, sea, air and space. Former Director of the FBI, Robert Mueller noted that cyber risks to national security were more dangerous and more feared than the risk of terrorism (Office of the Inspector General, 2015). James Clapper, US Director of National Intelligence attested in congress in 2016: "The consequences of innovation and increased reliance on information technology in the next few years on both our society's way of life in general and how we in the intelligence community specifically perform our mission will probably be far greater in scope and impact than ever" (Clapper, 2016).

The Cyber Education Curriculum and Its Response to the Changing Nature of Cyber Security

While precautionary measures should be stepped up as cyber-crimes become more prevalent and varied, tertiary institutions that offer cyber security education programmes need to consider this issue from a variety of perspectives. Most accredited programmes in the US focus on the theoretical dimension rather than practical or training opportunities. As a consequence, students struggle to apply the material they cover in their four-year degree (Conklin et al., 2014).

However, some tertiary institutions have adopted curricula that are more comprehensive. The School of Computer and Security Science in Western Australia runs respected computer and network security programmes. Johnstone (2013, p. 288) notes that, the modules cover aspects such as, "major elements of secure programming such as buffer overflows, format string attacks, race conditions and cross-site scripting as well as code obfuscation." This places graduates in a better position to contribute to national security and the development of security infrastructure. Given the complexity of this domain, institutions should develop comprehensive curricula that cover all aspects of cyber security (Ma & Nickerson, 2006) and mix theory and practice. Students need to be equipped to apply the knowledge they gain in different sectors.

While computer (or information) practices have long been part of such curricula, "cyber security must be included within the framework of programme information incorporating technical aspects that are fundamentally related to computer science and engineering (Bishop, 2000:5)". The best undergraduate education would enable students to acquire all-encompassing skills that they are able to apply in the work place (Bishop, 2000, p. 6). Learning should not be based on a single situation or system and what has been learnt should not remain abstract but be able to be applied in different situations or systems.

Finally, on-going technological innovation means that new methods are constantly required to promote cyber security. Given the changing nature of this field, Conklin et al. (2014) suggest that networking concepts programme includes: Overview of Networking (OSI Model), Network Media, Network architectures (LANs, WANs), Network Devices (Routers, Switches, VPNs, Firewalls), Network Services, Network Protocols (TCP/IP, HTTP, DNS, SMTP), Network Topologies, Overview of Network Security Issues etc.

Gaps in Cyber Security Education Delivery and Mitigation Strategies

Information security in the public and private sectors can be compromised due to the fact that infrastructure is fragile and easy to breach. While organisations have installed security systems to protect their infrastructure, cyber criminals around the world are also adopting more sophisticated methods. It is, therefore, crucial to develop new strategies to fill the gap in human resources (institutions, students and professionals/specialists in cyber security) to increase their capacity to prevent fraud and crime. Cyber security education programmes should provide comprehensive hands-on training to ensure that the knowledge acquired is supported by practical skills.

The Role of Curriculum in Cyber Professional Development

Information security is a study domain that needs to comply with certain requirements. At tertiary level, the development and teaching of the cyber security curriculum is mainly based on courses that incorporate cyber security. Such programmes are taught worldwide, including at Purdue University in the US and the Birmingham University as well as commercial teaching institutions.

Such courses should equip students with tools to fight illegal software (Johnstone 2013, p. 287) such as secure coding. This requires that they are able to identify a system's strengths as well as its shortcomings.

Graduates of such programmes could be employed as IT experts or university academics and secure positions in national intelligence and the armed forces (Vogel, 2016, p. 32). As noted previously, cyber security is very much concerned with issues of national security (Morgan, 2016).

Gaps in Cyber Education

Identified gaps relate to the level of skills that graduates demonstrate to counter and control attacks from different sources. While the curriculum might be standard as required by accreditation requirements, successful application of the skills acquired depends on numerous factors. Experts believe that the lack of practical skills has significant consequences for security (Francis & Ginsberg, 2016) in the public and private sectors (Morgan, 2016).

The mushrooming of illegal online activities has revealed important limitations of information security programmes. Interpol (2016) highlights, that, cyber-crimes like fraud, exploitation of children by online services and scam payments require daily monitoring at the international level. There is thus growing demand for cyber security professionals.

The US Commission on Cyber Security noted that, "there is neither a broad cadre of cyber experts nor an established cyber career field to build upon, particularly within the Federal government" (Evans and Reeder, 2010). It added that there was need to increase cyber education and build a certification system that promotes partnerships between private corporations and education institutions.

The US government Accountability Office stated that 22% of posts in the Department of Homeland Security's National Protection and Programme Directorate's Office of Cybersecurity and Communications were vacant (US Government Accountability Office, 2013). A special Parliamentary Select Committee in the United Kingdom's House of Lords reported that almost two million cyber security experts were required in the United States of America alone (Morgan, 2016).

Responding to Gaps in Cyber Education

The shortage of cyber security and cyber-crime specialists is exacerbated by the low salaries offered in this field. One of the ways to fill the gap would be to encourage young people to enter the field and to provide them with adequate education and training (Vogel, 2016, p. 32).

The skills required are not limited to ensuring that systems are secure and maintained, but also to strategise and manage security domains and conduct computer forensics (Evans & Reeder, 2010).

Research suggests that the problem lies in the lack of posts as well as the ability to fill such posts (ISACA, 2015).While some point to the shortage of skilled personnel, others raise the issue of quality, believing that the focus should be on highly skilled or "red teaming specialists". This view was put forward in a 2008 CSIS report (Evans & Reeder, 2010, p. 2).

Furthermore, solutions should be based on sound evidence based on government and other organisation's experience of seeking suitable cyber security experts. It is also important to consider the capacity of those that educate such professionals.

It is predicted that the current shortage of cyber security professionals will grow in the future. The Global Information Security Workforce Study's survey of 14 000 information security personnel suggested that by 2020 the global shortfall would stand at 1.5 million (ISACA, 2015). CEO of Symantec security software, Michael Brown predicted that demand was likely to reach six million by 2019, with an anticipated deficit of 1.5 million (Morgan, 2016).

Fourie et al. (2014) propose short and long-term strategies to address this gap. On the one hand, they suggest involving people from IT backgrounds in short courses, and accreditation for those who would like to pursue a qualification. Longer term strategies could include partnerships between industry, universities and government to offer further skills training and follow-up to ensure that such skills are put into practice.

Security concerns affect everyone. Working together, government, academic institutions, non-governmental organisations, private companies, churches etc. can reach common understanding and launch coordinated efforts to address security threats to society.

Sound partnership with the private sector are important to guarantee that skills acquired are put to good use (Fourie et al., 2014). Education programmes at secondary school and tertiary level are required to improve the cyber security abilities of future personnel. Raytheon (2014) noted that, while good progress has been made at university level, 64% of high school learners in the US did not have access to computer science courses that would enable them to secure cyber security jobs.

POLICY IMPLICATIONS IN THE AGE OF INFORMATION TRANSFORMATION

Statistics show that the more developed and dependent on technology a country is, the more likely it is to become the target of criminals.

Policy Implications for Governments

The growth of the internet and computer use around the world has created many job opportunities, which is an advantage from the government perspective. Furthermore, information infrastructure has created trade and business opportunities. However, the high rate of cyber-crime has undermined such advantages (Longe & Chiemeke, 2008). Countries have responded by developing bilateral economic or security ties in order to prevent the loss of funds due to such crime. For example, the US, one of most powerful countries in the world, is believed to be the most vulnerable to cyber-crimes attacks due to its developed technology infrastructure.

Sectors like engineering, transport and electricity rely on information systems. Ten, Manimaran, and Liu (2010, p. 853) contend that recurrent security incidents weaken the entire system in terms of reliability and safety. In the past decade, the US has devoted considerable resources to address such threats (Shia, 2015, p. 825).

Academic analysts and policy specialists concur that, today, it is possible for extremists to launch cyber-attacks from close by or from a distance. This means that countries need to work together and share information to counter this threat.

Governments have developed various policies to fight illegal activities based on information technology. In Nigeria, these include the "Advance Fee Fraud Act of 2006, the Money Laundering Act of 2004 section 12(1) (c) - (d), the Economic and Financial Crime Commission Act of 2005 and the Evidence Act of 1948" (Olayemi, 2014, p. 120). The Nigerian government has the power to control the activities of structures like cyber cafes and take legal action against perpetrators of cyber-crime. South Africa was rated as the country with the third highest level of cyber-crime in 2011. While the Cybersecurity draft Policy was formulated in 2012, no holistic approach has been adopted to implement it.

The US adopted the Counterfeit Access Device and Computer Fraud and Abuse Act of 1984, the Electronic Communications Privacy Act (ECPA) of 1986, the Computer Security Act of 1987 and so forth (Fischer, 2013, pp. 52-61). These are said to be the foundation of cyber security legislation. Several other Acts have since been passed and cross-border cooperation has been expanded. For example, former US President Barack Obama and former UK Prime Minister David Cameron issued a joint statement on the need to strengthen cyber security intelligence including training (Obama, 2015). Further laws were enacted in the aftermath of Snowden's disclosure of thousands of confidential US government surveillance programmes. This led Congress to adopt the Cybersecurity Enhancement Act of 2014, the

Cybersecurity Protection Act of 2014 and the Cybersecurity Workforce Assessment Act. The country has adopted more than 50 pies of legislation in response to cyber security issues.

Policy Implications for Educational Institutions

Rowe, Lunt, and Ekstrom (2011, p. 8) point to the need for an all-encompassing approach centred on technical aspects of cyber education. They add that education providers should be affiliated to a body such as the Software Engineering Body of Knowledge (SWEBOK). This would capacitate cyber security professionals with the requisite knowledge and skills.

While information technology has enhanced national defence and manufacturing capacity, it should also be used to its full benefit in education. Universities offer research and skills training to assist organisations to deal with cyber security matters (Adebayo, 2012, p. 18). Except for Massachusetts that allows individuals to disclose cyber security breaches, the other US states have adopted Security Breach Notification Laws that allow private, governmental and educational institutions to notify an individual or business of their wrong doing. This enables such institutions to collaborate to monitor prospective threats to corporations or government property.

For example, in the US, the Integrated Postsecondary Education Data System (IPEDS) enables the US National Center for Education Statistics (NCES) to gather statistics from all principal providers of postsecondary education (Liu, Huang, & Lucas, 2016, p. 13). This assists the authorities to control and understand the dynamics of the issues faced by these institutions. Schools and universities are easy targets of criminals because they are able to recruit and train potential terrorists using the IT systems that students use on a daily basis. Regular collection of cyber security data is likely to counter such activities within educational institutions.

Policy Implications for Cyber Security Professionals/Practitioners

Professionals or specialists in cyber security provide key information that is beneficial to all. It is important to note that some individuals have used their skills to compromise the security of the very institutions they are supposed to serve. Examples include fraudulent online credit transactions and illegal transfer of funds including the movement of illegal drugs and arms trafficking, mainly in the Middle East and South Asia. Recent attacks in Africa, Europe and America are possibly the work of secret networks of extremists connected to firms with huge information technology hubs.

Bauer and Van Eeten (2009, p. 229) note that, most governments have focused on raising awareness through campaigns, improved international cooperation with law enforcement agencies, information sharing and the collection of security data.

However, from the perspective of law enforcement, some schools of thought posit that a certain level of tolerance of insecurity needs to be accepted (Bauer & Van Eeten, 2009, p. 229). This would render the eradication of cyber-crime well-nigh impossible.

It is immoral that, on the one hand, governments and corporations encourage cooperation between nations, while some countries hack one another by attacking networks and infrastructure, installing doorways and logic bombs (Borah, 2015, p. 31). Indeed, some suggest that, today, attacks have shifted from being physical to technological (Nicholson, Webber, Dyer, Patel, & Janicke, 2012, p. 431).

CYBER SECURITY EDUCATION IN THE FOURTH INDUSTRIAL REVOLUTION

Mathas (2013) notes, that, the first industrial revolution refers to the "industrial revolution in 1784 or the first mechanical loom". It was the era of production using mechanical facilities based on water and steam. The second is "the second industrial revolution" (the first assembly line Cincinnati slaughter houses, 1870)" that introduced the division of labour and mass production using electricity. This was followed by the "third industrial revolution (First programmable logic controller (PLC) Modicon 084, 1969)". Electronic and IT systems were introduced during this period. "The fourth industrial revolution" ushered in cyber-physical systems (Pil-Sung, 2016).

Steering Cyber Education in the Era of the Fourth Industrial Revolution

Progressive changes across the industrial revolutions have changed the lives of communities, with human capacity operating at different levels.

Among the innovations that ICT-led industrial technologies have achieved are "cars without drivers, lighter and tougher materials, robotics, 3D printing and biotechnology" (Chung & Kim, 2016, p. 1311). Most importantly, these technologies have the capacity to communicate among themselves and with human beings, offering opportunities to share information online.

However, the fourth industrial revolution has also had negative consequences that will increase inequality in society. Nonetheless, it is perceived as an opportunity to improve people's lives. The Industrie 4.0 Working Group (2013) states that the technological, economic and social impacts of the fourth industrial revolution have significant development implications. In Germany, this industrial revolution is referred to as Industry 4.0.

Different individuals and organisations will play different roles in steering cyber education in this new era. Trautman's (2015, p. 351) analysis of cyber security issues in the US identified consumers, investors, law enforcement agencies, business corporations and state structures. Tertiary institutions also play an important role in advancing technology. Government has funded institutions in some countries. In Australia, $22 million was invested in 2016 to enhance leaders' capacity in cyber security (Caelli & Liu, 2017).

Aligning Cyber Education With the Fourth Industrial Revolution

While the digital world is positively transforming many public and private institutions, it also has negative effects. Demirkan, Spohrer, and Welser (2016) note, that, the purpose of digital transformation is to improve production and enhance "decision making, connectivity, and innovation".

Education plays a primary role in the development and transformation of different assets in this new era. Cyber education should thus, scrutinise both the positive and negative aspects of the rapid development of information technology to alleviate the risks it poses. Besides the loss of jobs as a result of the introduction of technology, software faults can cause immense damage. The following examples suffice:

- Therac 25 is a Canadian machine that measures dosages of radiation to kill cancer cells. Due to a software error, patients were administered 100 times the dose they were supposed to receive. Many were injured and five lost their lives.

- The Toyota Company recalled more than 8 million vehicles around the world in 2009 due to an electronic Throttle Control System killing 89 people.

While these errors were later corrected, the loss of life can never be compensated for, exposing manufacturers to legal action.

The following principles should inform cyber education in the era of the fourth industrial revolution:

- Developing security measures to protect individuals, industries, corporations, government and other structures. McMillan (2007) states that the state has a key role to play in regulating the software and hardware employed in the country's security systems;
- Partnerships with the public sector: no single stakeholder is solely responsible for cyber security. The problem is that most governments are reluctant to involve other stakeholders given the importance of this critical infrastructure. There is thus a lack of cooperation between the state and the organisations that respond to cyber-crimes (Choo, 2011).
- Academic exchanges between universities on subjects related to cyber security research;
- Collaboration among university departments to strengthen course content to capture cyber security issues from a transdisciplinary perspective;
- Funding to support research and publications that contribute to new knowledge production on cyber education across different contexts.

CONCLUSION

Technological advancement is a positive phenomenon that promotes integration across regions and sectors and makes a significant contribution to the well-being of the global community. However, given growing cyber threats, citizen awareness is crucial. A multi-stakeholder approach is recommended where the public and private sectors and civil society are actively involved in designing a curriculum that provides comprehensive knowledge on cyber threats, cyber ethics, cyber safety and cyber security.

Connected to the above point, the national cyber education system should be upgraded to increase the number of educators and graduates with high level skills. There is a need to continually enlarge the supply of well-trained cyber practitioners that remain abreast with technology. Thus, cyber education and training should go hand in hand, to ensure that acquisition of knowledge and understanding is matched by acquisition of skills with a provable level of competence. Whilst education focuses more on preparing people for the future, training prepares them for the here and now. In order to produce a critical mass of highly professional cyber practitioners, cyber education scholarship should be advanced, especially in respect of:

1. Research and development to ensure that countries remain competitive;
2. A human resource strategy for the cyber community (cyber security practitioners, cyber educators and researchers, to name but a few) to provide guidance on how to attract and retain them, and their expertise in government and in other professional cyberspaces;
3. Public-private-partnerships for cyber education research and related issues such as cyber security, cyber safety and cyber ethics.

Education remains at the centre of a cyber-conscious society like South Africa. It is imperative that the cyber professional community, including cyber security educators, researchers, administrators and system developers stay informed so they can prepare themselves for new challenges as they embrace opportunities presented by the fourth industrial revolution. Curriculum development and cyber policies need to be aligned so they respond to this new era in a comprehensive manner. Increased funding is also required for cyber education. However, cyber education programmes should be designed in such a way that they promote immediate behavioural change whilst not violating citizens' privacy, independence and free expression.

REFERENCES

Adebayo, A. O. (2012). A foundation for breach data analysis. *Journal of Information Engineering and Applications*, *2*(4), 17–23.

Australian Crime Commission. (2015). *National Organised Crime Response Plan 2015-18*. Author.

Bauer, J. M., & van Eeten, M. J. G. (2009). Cybersecurity: Stakeholder incentives, externalities, and policy options. *Telecommunications Policy*, *33*(10), 706–719. doi:10.1016/j.telpol.2009.09.001

Bishop, M. (2000). Education in information security. *IEEE Concurrency*, *8*(4), 4–8. doi:10.1109/4434.895087

Borah, C. K. (2015). *Cyber war: the next threat to national security and what to do about it? by Richard A. Clarke and Robert K. Knake*. Taylor & Francis.

Caelli & Liu. (2017). *Cybersecurity education at formal university level: An Australian perspective*. Academic Press.

Choo, K.-K. R. (2011). Cyber threat landscape faced by financial and insurance industry. *Trends and Issues in Crime and Criminal Justice*, (408): 1.

Chung, M., & Kim, J. (2016). The Internet Information and Technology Research Directions based on the Fourth Industrial Revolution. *TIIS*, *10*(3), 1311–1320.

Clapper, J. R. (2016). *Statement for the Record Worldwide Threat Assessment of the US Intelligence Community Senate Select Committee on Intelligence*. Retrieved from http://www. intelligence. senate. gov/130312/clapper. pdf

Conklin, W. A., Cline, R. E., & Roosa, T. (2014). *Re-engineering cybersecurity education in the US: an analysis of the critical factors*. Paper presented at the System Sciences (HICSS), 2014 47th Hawaii International Conference on Cyber Security. 10.1109/HICSS.2014.254

Demirkan, H., Spohrer, J. C., & Welser, J. J. (2016). Digital Innovation and Strategic Transformation. *IT Professional*, *18*(6), 14–18. doi:10.1109/MITP.2016.115

Evans, K., & Reeder, F. (2010). *A Human Capital Crisis in Cybersecurity: Technical Proficiency Matters*. CSIS.

Faris, R., & Jones, R. (2014). *Platforms and policy, in internet monitor 2014: reflections on the digital world*. SAGE.

Federal Bureau of Investigation. (2015). *Economic Espionage - FBI Launches Nationwide Awareness Campaign*. Retrieved from https://www.fbi.gov/news/stories/2015/july/economicespionage/economic-espionage

Fischer, E. A. (2013). *Federal laws relating to cybersecurity: Overview and discussion of proposed revisions*. Academic Press.

Fourie, Pang, Kingston, Hettema, Watters, & Sarrafzadeh. (2014). *The global cyber security workforce: an ongoing human capital crisis*. SAGE.

Francis & Ginsberg. (2016). *The Federal Cybersecurity Workforce: Background and Congressional Oversight Issues for the Departments of Defense and Homeland Security*. Academic Press.

Geers, K. (2010). The challenge of cyber attack deterrence. *Computer Law & Security Review*, *26*(3), 298–303. doi:10.1016/j.clsr.2010.03.003

Grobler, M., van Vuuren, J. J., & Leenen, L. (2012). *Implementation of a cyber security policy in South Africa: Reflection on progress and the way forward*. Paper presented at the IFIP International Conference on Human Choice and Computers. 10.1007/978-3-642-33332-3_20

Industrie 4.0 Working Group. (2013). *Securing the Future of German Manufacturing Industry—Recommendations for Implementing the Strategic Initiative*. Acatech.

Interpol. (2016). *Coordinating Efforts to Better Combat Cybercrime Focus of INTERPOL Working Group*. Retrieved from http://www.interpol.int/News-and-media/News/2016/N2016-040

ISACA. (2015). *State of Cybersecurity: Implications for 2015 - An ISACA and RSA Conference*. Retrieved from http://www.isaca.org/cyber/Documents/State-of-Cybersecurity_Res_Eng_0415.pdf

Johnstone, M. N. (2013). Embedding Secure Programming in the Curriculum: Some Lessons Learned. *IACSIT International Journal of Engineering and Technology*, *5*(2), 287–290. doi:10.7763/IJET.2013.V5.560

Lee, N. (2015). *Cyber attacks, prevention, and countermeasures. In Counterterrorism and Cybersecurity* (pp. 249–286). Springer.

Liu, C.-W., Huang, P., & Lucas, H. C. (2016). *IT Governance, Security Outsourcing, and Cybersecurity Breaches: Evidence from US Higher Education*. SAGE.

Longe, O. B., & Chiemeke, S. C. (2008). *Cyber Crime And Criminality in Nigeria: What Roles are Internet Access Points Playing?* Academic Press.

Ma, J., & Nickerson, J. V. (2006). Hands-on, simulated, and remote laboratories: A comparative literature review. *ACM Computing Surveys*, *38*(3), 7.

Mathas, C. (2013). *Industry 4.0 is closer than you think, EDN's Hot Technologies*. Academic Press.

McMillan, R. (2007). *NSA helped Microsoft make vista secure*. CSO.

Morgan, S. (2016). One Million Cybersecurity Job Openings in 2016. *Forbes*.

Nicholson, A., Webber, S., Dyer, S., Patel, T., & Janicke, H. (2012). SCADA security in the light of Cyber-Warfare. *Computers & Security*, *31*(4), 418–436. doi:10.1016/j.cose.2012.02.009

Obama, B. (2015). *Remarks by the president at the NAACP conference*. The White House.

Office of the Inspector General. (2015). *Audit of the Federal Bureau of Investigation's Implementation of its Next Generation Cyber Initiative*. Author.

Olayemi, O. J. (2014). A socio-technological analysis of cybercrime and cyber security in Nigeria. *International Journal of Sociology and Anthropology*, *6*(3), 116–125. doi:10.5897/IJSA2013.0510

Pil-Sung, J. (2016). Davos Forum: Our strategy for the upcoming fourth industrial revolution. *Science and Technology Policy, 26*(2), 12-15.

Raytheon. (2014). *Preparing Millennials to Lead in Cyberspace*. Retrieved from www.consumeraction. org/recommended/articles/preparing_millennials_to_lead_in_cyberspace

Rowe, D. C., Lunt, B. M., & Ekstrom, J. J. (2011). *The role of cyber-security in information technology education*. Paper presented at the 2011 Conference on Information Technology Education. 10.1145/2047594.2047628

Shia, B. (2015). National Cybersecurity Strategy of the US and its Constructive Implications for China. *Sociology*, *5*(11), 825–831.

Ten, C.-W., Manimaran, G., & Liu, C.-C. (2010). Cybersecurity for critical infrastructures: Attack and defense modeling. *IEEE Transactions on Systems, Man, and Cybernetics. Part A, Systems and Humans*, *40*(4), 853–865. doi:10.1109/TSMCA.2010.2048028

Topi, Valacich, Wright, Kaiser, Nunamaker, & Jr, Sipior, & de Vreede. (2010). IS 2010: Curriculum guidelines for undergraduate degree programs in information systems. *Communications of the Association for Information Systems*, *26*(1), 18.

Trautman, L. J. (2015). Cybersecurity: What About US Policy? *Salus Journal*, *4*(1), 40.

Vogel, R. (2016). Closing the cybersecurity skills gap. *Salus Journal*, *4*(2), 32.

KEY TERMS AND DEFINITIONS

Curriculum: The content that informs a specific academic program.

Cyber Education: Knowledge related to information communication technologies and everything related to cyber space.

Cyber Security: The process and practice of securing all the networks that constitute cyberspace from all forms of illegal intrusion, maintaining confidentiality of information and ensuring that systems are protected from such incidences and that when illegal intrusion occurs, information can be retrieved and future intrusion prevented.

Cybercrime: Illegal intrusions that involve the use of information communication technologies.

Cyberspace: A non-physical space made up of computers, their systems, programs, and software and users such as programmers, data analysts, and computer technicians, to name but a few.

Education: Knowledge about a particular field of study.

Information Communication Technologies (ICT): Any communication device including computers, television, radio, mobile phones, satellite systems, networks, hardware, and software components.

Chapter 19
Mobile Device Brand Loyalty of Youth:
Perceived Value vs. Cybersecurity Choices

Thea Van der Westhuizen
University of KwaZulu Natal, South Africa

Thakur Singh
University of KwaZulu Natal, South Africa

ABSTRACT

Cybersecurity and security mechanisms of mobile device play an important part in product development, but are not often a top priority when customers select their favorite brand. A key factor that has been ignored as a result of the rapid pace of the market is that of youth brand loyalty. Brand loyalty remains one of the key factors in global markets that determine core consumers and security concerns feature became less important. This chapter aims to ascertain the key factors of brand loyalty and measure what consumers base their decision on whilst selecting a brand. The chapter will look at social value, emotional value, functional value, involvement, and perceived value of the consumer to the brand. Based on quantitative results, a conclusion will be drawn on what the key factors of brand loyalty are. Recommendations will be made on how mobile brand companies can use these KSFs when developing new products in order to procure more loyal consumers, as well as to increase awareness of the importance of the security features of the device when making a choice to purchase a brand.

INTRODUCTION

Mobile device brand loyalty is an important factor in decisions made by young people in choosing between perceived value received and cybersecurity (Peters, 2017). This chapter gives an account of a study that sought to evaluate pertinent factors relating to brand loyalty among young people in regard to the mobile industry and related issues of cybersecurity aspects.

DOI: 10.4018/978-1-5225-4763-1.ch019

With the advent of the fourth industrial revolution, developmental focus is on integration of physical and cyber systems (Bloem et al., 2014). This has had a ripple effect on the mobile industry, with the demise of many mobile brands. The study described here focused on young consumers, since they are major consumers and will continue to be the in years to come. There are also a number of implications for education of young people to encourage responsible use of mobile devices and responsible choices in selecting a brand to purchase (Xing & Marwala, 2017).

This chapter explores five research objectives in regard to brand loyalty and cybersecurity: 1) to determine the extent to which students are involved with a mobile device and how this leads to brand loyalty; 2) to establish the influence of perceived value on students' brand loyalty; 3) to explore the extent to which functional value engenders brand loyalty among young people; 4) to determine the influence of emotional value on young people's brand loyalty, and 5) to establish the influence of social value on young people's brand loyalty.

The study adds to the body of knowledge in that it considers issues that have hitherto tended to be overlooked, focusing in particular on the relative significance of brand loyalty issues versus cybersecurity options on young consumers' perceptions. It seems evident from the research that cybersecurity matters are of secondary importance in choice of mobile brand by young consumers and its recommended that mobile companies launch stronger campaigns to create awareness on the necessity of cybersecurity.

LITERATURE REVIEW

Young People and Brand Loyalty

Korpella (2015) and Xing and Marwala (2017) suggest that young people need training to raise their level of awareness about the key element of cybersecurity in the fourth industrial revolution. Bada and Sasse (2014) and Bloem, et al. (2014) found on the other hand that awareness-raising campaigns about cybersecurity mostly failed to change the security behaviour of consumers.

Giddens and Hofmann (2010) point out that brand loyalty is an endemic issue in today's markets. Consumers today have become much more knowledgeable about what they purchase. They now look at perceived value, functional value, emotional value, social value, brand trust, customer satisfaction, commitment, product price and quality, brand image, functionality and desirability, and they base their choice of device on these influencing factors – all of which influence consumer mindset and consumer loyalty to a specific brand that best fits the consumer's needs. In the mobile industry more specifically, major technological advances in recent decades have made it a rigorous and difficult market to compete in (Gerpott, Rams & Schindler, 2001; Kim & Yoon, 2004; Seo, Ranganathan & Babad, 2008).

Bada and Sasse (2014) identify several reasons why cybersecurity awareness campaigns conducted by mobile brands might fail:

1. Solutions are not aligned to business risks
2. Neither progress nor value are measured
3. Incorrect assumptions are made about people and their motivations
4. Unrealistic expectations are set
5. The correct skills are not deployed
6. Awareness is just background noise

Functionality plays a major role in brand loyalty among present-day young consumers as a consequence of advances in technology that differentiate mobile companies from one another. Blackberry, for example, attracted millions of purchasers with their easy-to-use BBM instant messaging network which connected people internationally. But its popularity waned when lack of strategic planning left Blackberry unable to sustain itself in the face of consumer demand once Android bought major shares and the app became available on Android devices. Formerly loyal consumers were thus lost to Blackberry's major competitors Samsung, Apple and Nokia. Brand loyalty factors are plainly very important in the mobile industry and hence to need to analyse the extent to which they apply in relation to the youth market (PRLOG, 2009). In relation to brand loyalty decisions versus cybersecurity choices there are various issues that influence selection of a device by young consumers.

Fourth industrial revolution advances in mobile technology have resulted in mobile brand companies neglecting brand loyalty and thus losing consumers to competitors (Kelan & Lehnert, 2009). Mobile brand companies need to give more attention to consumer satisfaction in order to procure more loyal consumers. In doing so they will thereby build a base of core consumers who are loyal to the brand, enabling the company to grow its market share and extend its longevity in the market. The importance of brand loyalty has been recognised in the marketing literature but relatively little research attention has been paid to brand loyalty among young people, especially in relation to mobile technology. The current study sought to ascertain why young consumers are not loyal to a specific mobile brand (Li et al., 2010). The reason may be that with fierce industry competition mobile brands are continually looking to produce a succession of device models each better than its predecessor to stay ahead of competitors. Another reason could be affordability, and with young consumers not necessarily purchasing the device themselves, choice of device may depend on affordability for parents rather than directly for the young consumer. Quality is also a major factor in determining loyalty to a mobile device. These are important issues to consider in determining how firmly brand loyalty in the mobile industry is established among young people.

Aaker's brand loyalty framework (Figure 1) shows how mobile companies differentiate between the different types of users that purchase brands in the mobile industry.

Figure 1. Adapted from Aaker, 2013

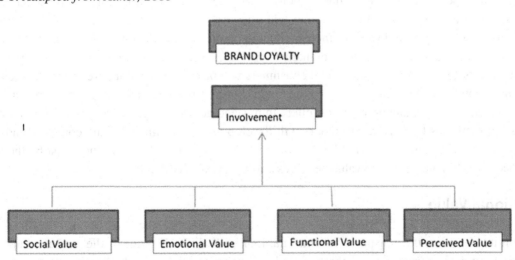

Data from questionnaire responses in this study were categorized according to a five-point scale: committed customer; consumer who likes the brand and considers it a friend; satisfied buyer willing to incur switching costs; satisfied consumer with no reason to change; and price-sensitive consumer with no loyalty.

Focal points in relation to the influence of brand loyalty were: 1) brand involvement with a mobile device; 2) perceived value; 3) functional value; 4) emotional value; and 5) social value influences.

Brand Involvement With a Mobile Device

A significant factor in mobile device brand loyalty among young people is their degree of involvement with the device (Keller, 2001), meaning that they are familiar with the functionality of the device and all its features and applications such as battery life, the camera, and the applications and services it has to offer. Familiarity with these considerations will determine whether they feel the device best fits their needs and desires (Keller, 2001) and in the longer term it develops the consumer's outlook on the brand. In Aaker's brand equity model (2013), once the consumer has become aware of the brand and the perceived quality is high, the consumer will then purchase the brand and will experience it through direct involvement. Brand functionality is just as important as consumer outlook towards the brand, because if the product is not appropriately functional then consumers' involvement will lead to dissatisfaction and they will not want to purchase it in the future. Therefore, it is very important for mobile brand companies to take all aspects of functionality into consideration.

Perceived Value

Perceived value is what the consumer perceives as the value or worth of a product: the higher the perceived value, the more likely it is that consumers will pay for the product, making it a crucial marketing factor (Aaker, 2012, p.85), and in this regard Bata and Sasse (2014) warn against "security fatigue", where impatience with security procedures lead consumers to perceive them as an obstacle. Consumers base their decision partly on the desirability of the product; it is therefore imperative for mobile device companies to convince the consumer that their brand is the best. Mobile brand companies need to ensure that consumers perceive them as unique, having the best technology, caring for the consumer, having style and being able to provide the consumer with the best product on the market. Failure to do so is likely to reduce the perceived value of their product in comparison with competitors. The advantage of high perceived value is that consumers are likely to pay, whatever the cost (Aaker 2012, p.85). The major disadvantage of low perceived value is that consumers will be sceptical about purchasing the brand and reluctant to commit and develop loyalty to the brand. Equally, however, false hope in a product should not be created. If a company promises excellent things and develops high perceived value among consumers but then fails to deliver, consumers will develop a negative image of the company and never purchase again. Consumers must not be duped; the perceived value of the product must be the actual value because ultimately the true value becomes known (Aaker 2012, p.85).

Functional Value

Through involvement, the consumer becomes familiar with all the features of the product. Functional value is of critical importance as it is this that enables a consumer to know whether they prefer one brand over another. Functional value enables consumers to decide whether the device meets their needs. If a consumer is not satisfied with the functionality and quality of the device there is a chance that they will not purchase the brand (Bruks, Zeithmal & Naylar, 2000). Generally, today's technology savvy young consumers prefer high-performance mobile devices that offer the widest range of functions and applications. Mobile brand companies therefore need to carry out the necessary research and development to maintain their product's functional value at an optimum level. If companies fail to do this, there will be a serious lag in their operations and they will quickly fall behind competitors due to the pace of change in the market in the technological sector. The advantage for companies that constantly do research and improve their products is that consumers will always be interested in their products and there is every chance that they will purchase the brand again (Bruks et al., 2000).

Emotional Value

Emotional value is when consumers develop a relationship between themselves and the brand, based on the quality and services of the product, to the point where they become attached to the product (Bruks, et al., 2000). Millions of consumers choose their mobile brand based on emotional value. They may overlook the monetary value of a product and prefer to develop a personal relationship with the brand based on memorable and quality user experience. Mobile device companies must make this experience possible, as brand loyalty is created when emotional value is established for the consumer. Generally, emotional-value consumers are ones who are familiar with technology (Bruks et al., 2000). Therefore if the brand of choice provides the customer with an experience that pleases them through functionality, they will slowly become loyal to the brand. However, once a relationship and bond has been built with the consumer it is important to be consistent and maintain this bond as it will lead to constant increase in the consumer market. Mobile brand companies need to ensure that they manage these clients well in order to maintain and build market share (Bruks et al., 2000).

Social Value Influences

Social value is when consumers base their purchase decision on the social status the product will potentially afford them (Youl & John, 2010). According to Bada and Sasse (2014), young consumers tend to conform to social norms and peer pressure plays a powerful role in creating awareness on cybersecurity issues. Social value also comes into play when the consumer considers monetary value in deciding which brand to purchase (Brakus, Schmitt & Zarantonello, 2009). Consumers generally look at the current trends in the world and in the market and follow suit just to fit in with social norms (Youl & John, 2010). If a company's brand is the current trend leader then consumers will generally follow suit and purchase its products for themselves. But if the brand is not a major brand in the market and is perceived to be of lower value or lower quality, then consumers will not want to purchase the brand, leading to reduced sales and profit margins with negative consequences for the company (Youl & John, 2010). Mobile brand companies need to research and develop their products extensively in order to manipulate their social value and shape consumer mindsets so that consumers purchase their mobile brands based on these principles and at the same time influence cybersecurity risk awareness in relation to the device (Brakus, et al. 2009).

The literature as noted above indicates that in the fourth industrial revolution there is a disconnect between brand loyalty and security considerations when purchasers choose a mobile brand. Further, it seems that (a) perceived value, (b) functional value, (c) emotional value and (d) social value influence young consumers' perceptions when selecting a mobile brand. These aspects will be further explored through empirical investigation.

RESEARCH METHODOLOGY

Research Approach

A descriptive quantitative methodology was adopted in the study, with data collected through closed-ended questionnaires completed by study respondents and analysed using descriptive statistics (Ghauri & Cateora, 2010). The questionnaire collected basic demographic data and the subsequent closed-ended questions included a five-point Likert scale.

The study used a descriptive research design that enabled the researcher to build a construct of brand loyalty that would get to the crux of the phenomenon (Baxter & Jack, 2008:544-559).

The research was undertaken at the University of KwaZulu-Natal in Durban, South Africa. The target population for the study was the total population of 488 first-year Management, IT and Governance students. A sample size of 217 was determined using the sampling table of Krejcie and Morgan (1970).

The information gathered from the respondents was entered into SPSS 17 according to the sequential sections on the questionnaire. Demographic information was collated and presented as pie charts and the data was calculated and presented in percentages (Fisher, 2007). The subsequent closed-ended questions were tabulated on a bar graph for easy comparison.

A Cronbach's Alpha test was conducted to ensure reliability, and validity was maintained in terms of the questionnaire and the study as a whole.

RESULTS AND DISCUSSION

Response Rate and Biographical Information

Questionnaires were given out after an academic event for which attendance by all students was compulsory, resulting in a 100% response rate. Respondents were one-third male and two-thirds female, and the majority were in the 17 to 19 year age range. All respondents owned a mobile device, and 20% owned two or more mobile devices.

Results from the study (in rounded percentages) and their significance are presented below in relation to the five question categories in the questionnaire.

Analysis and Interpretation

Research Question One: To what extent does involvement with a device lead to a student's brand loyalty?

Scaled responses were requested for the following related statements: (i) The brand I use allows me to learn new things and new techniques; (ii) The brand I use has sufficient cybersecurity features; (iii) The brand I use allows me to have a secure experience and (iv) The brand I use matches the person I am as a whole.

The first three statements received majority positive responses (agree or strongly agree) of 67%, 71% and 68% respectively. This indicates that respondents enjoyed a positive relationship with their brand of choice and were actively involved in understanding and using the product. This also shows that mobile brand companies are satisfying customers with features and functionality. Number of respondents undecided was fairly constant: 18%, 18% and 20% respectively. Negative responses (disagree or strongly disagree) were just 14%, 11% and 10% respectively. This means that mobile brand companies cannot be complacent, as the technological sector is a rapidly developing market space. Constant research and development will ensure that consumers are always learning new things and techniques through the brand and will heighten consumer loyalty.

The fourth statement was fairly evenly split: 38% agreed or strongly agreed, 31% disagreed and 30% were undecided. This suggests that respondents did not identify themselves through the brand. Generally, loyalty comes from the consumer connecting with the brand and feeling it matches their personality. Mobile brand companies need to ensure that they develop a better relationship between brand and consumer in order to bring the two closer together.

Research Question Two: What is the influence of perceived value on a student's brand loyalty?

Scaled responses were requested for the following related statements: (i) The brand I use has superior quality; (ii) The brand I use has a history of producing superior quality products; (iii) The brand I use produces durable products; and (iv) The brand I use resembles more than just a product for me.

Positive responses for all of these statements were 58.5%, 68.6%, 58% and 42% respectively. Negative response minorities were 15%, 17% and 15%, and 27.7% respectively. This suggests that perceived value plays a major role in brand loyalty. The positive responses suggest that the respondents were sufficiently familiar with their brand to perceive it to be of superior quality, having a history of producing superior products, and producing durable products.

The fourth statement did elicit positive responses but to a lesser extent. Although almost half (48%) agreed or strongly agreed that the brand "resembled more than just a product", at 29.5%, this statement elicited the highest number of undecided responses. This perhaps suggests that respondents had not thought about their brand in this way or that the brand did not yet meet all expectations and needs. This last statement also elicited the highest percentage of disagree or strongly disagree responses. For a consumer to be loyal there needs to be a strong relationship between the consumer and the brand, and a 57% majority of disagreeing or undecided respondents casts doubt on whether this was the case. And if consumers do not have a strong connection with the brand they might not hesitate to switch brands. Mobile brand companies therefore need to ensure they build relationships to increase perceived value of their products and thereby strengthen brand loyalty. To draw in customers, the undecided group should be specifically targeted in brand companies' marketing strategies.

Research Question Three: To what extent does functional value lead to young people's brand loyalty?

Scaled responses were requested for the following related statements: (i) The brand I use is worth the price tag it comes with; (ii) I would recommend the brand I use as a secure choice; (iii) The brand

I use has superior hardware functionalities; and (iv) The brand I use has superior and secure software functionalities.

Majority positive responses for all of these statements were 68.6%, 60%, 55.7% and 63% respectively. This indicates that functional value is a very important factor in brand loyalty, slightly more so than perceived value. It suggests that consumers know about and understand the functional value of their brands, and functionality is very important in terms of meeting needs. It also suggests that consumers are "tech savvy", which means that brand companies cannot be complacent about continuously developing functionality and need to be aware of consumer needs and expectations in order to win customers for the brand. It is interesting that a 68.6% majority of respondents agreed that the brand was worth the price tag, showing that they believed in value for money and were willing to pay for quality.

Minority negative responses were 12.4%, 16%, 15.6% and 15% respectively, and undecideds were 18.4%, 23%, 28% and 21%. The chief undecided response of 28% was for the statement about hardware functionality rather than software functionality (only 21% disagreed) which suggests that perhaps these respondents were not fully apprised of the functionality of their brand – also reflected perhaps in the 23% who were undecided about recommending the brand. It is clear that mobile brand companies need to promote the functionality of their brand and educate consumers in order to capture a greater share of the market and improve loyalty to the brand.

Research Question Four: What is the influence of emotional value on young people's brand loyalty?

A collation of all questions on the questionnaire was used to establish what the influence was of emotional value on respondents' brand loyalty.

Overall, a large percentage of respondents indicated having developed an emotional attachment to their brand due to various aspects of their involvement. Superior quality was one of the main factors giving rise to emotional value in the brand from the relationship that was built.

Responses to one of the statements connected with brand switching – "I would hesitate to brand switch due to the fear that my peers would judge me on my choice" – showed that respondents had developed an emotional bond with their brand since other people's opinions about their brand did not matter. They remained loyal to their brand because their needs were being satisfied and they had a strong emotional bond with the brand.

Research Question Five: What is the influence of social value on young people's brand loyalty?

To answer this research question, respondents were given a series of statements under the headings (a) social value, (b) brand switching and (c) brand loyalty.

Scaled responses were requested for the following related statements: (i) I am judged by others with the mobile device I have; (ii) The brand I use is well known and expensive; (iii) The brand I use is hip and has style; and (iv) The brand I use is the number one brand on the market.

The responses indicated that the social value of a brand is an important influence on brand loyalty and awareness of cybersecurity aspects has little influence on brand selection.

Social Value

In terms of social value, a 63% majority of respondents agreed or strongly agreed that their brand was well known in the market, was expensive, and was hip and had style, which indicates commitment to the brand, customer satisfaction, and thus loyalty to the brand. The positive percentages were high, showing the degree to which social value was important. Less than 20% of respondents gave negative responses (18% and 16.5% respectively) on the two statements regarding the brand being well known and expensive and being hip. However, there was a 56% majority negative response on the statement about being judged by others according to the brand owned, indicating that brand was not a factor in relation to the way consumers feel they are judged socially. On this point, 21% were undecided and 22% gave positive responses. This may suggest lack of relationship with the brand or that other factors were more important in purchasing decisions and brand loyalty. Identifying socially with a brand might need to be a focus for company research and development in order to ensure brand loyalty.

There were 41% positive responses on the statement that the brand was number one on the market, and this may reflect overall satisfaction across the range of functionality, cost, durability, visibility in the market, value for money and style. It is not clear why there were 30% negative responses on this point but it could be due to a lack of understanding of the features of a brand, dissatisfaction with certain aspects, or ignorance. The questionnaire did not collect reasons for this. Again, as with the other factors in questions 1 to 4, approximately one in four or five of respondents were undecided: 21%, 21.6%, 27.6% and 27.6% respectively.

Brand Switching

To provide answers about brand switching, the relevant literature was reviewed and scaled responses were requested for the following related statements: (i) I would hesitate to brand switch due to the fear that my peers would judge me on my choice; (ii) I would hesitate to brand switch due to the fear that I may lose important files if I do switch; (iii) I would hesitate to brand switch as I do not have the time to research a new brand thoroughly, and (iv) I would hesitate to brand switch as it would take time to learn new functionalities and features of a new brand.

Brand switching happens all the time in the mobile brand market since there are a number of brands to choose from, most of which offer the same or very similar features and services. It occurs for a variety of reasons, all having some relation to the factors already mentioned and all being linked in one way or another to brand loyalty.

A large majority, 71%, disagreed or strongly disagreed that peer judgment would affect their decision to switch brands. Only 14% agreed or strongly agreed and 13.8% were undecided.

This majority response indicates that brand choice is highly personalised and peer judgment is not important. It also supports the responses on social value, where a majority rejected the notion that they were judged according to the brand they own and indicated that other factors were more important. This is good news for mobile companies if the majority of consumers make decisions about their mobile brand on their own, and with good marketing and product development it will be easier to persuade individuals rather than groups to opt for a brand.

In relation to the other three statements about factors that might discourage brand switching, 47% agreed that losing files was an issue and 35% disagreed; 36% agreed that there was no time to research new brands and 44% disagreed; 27% agreed there was not enough time to research new functionality and 51% disagreed. This indicates that despite comfort with technology, file loss was an issue for respondents and stability in this area is something brand companies need to work on. There was, respectively, 44% and 51% disagreement that swopping brands would be affected either by time to research new brands or by functionality. This indicates that respondents were proactive in choice of brand, 'did their homework' ahead of purchase and were comfortable with technology. It means that brand companies cannot presume to retain customers or be dishonest, relying on existing loyalty, as consumers are becoming far more knowledgeable and take brand differences seriously. Consumers now have information at their fingertips and can research other brands in minutes; if they are satisfied with what another brand has to offer, they could possibly switch brands with little hesitation. Again, those who are undecided must be particularly targeted by brand companies to make sure that consumers are informed, involved and have correct and sufficient information to make choices.

Brand Loyalty

To provide answers about brand loyalty, the relevant literature was reviewed and Scaled responses were requested for the following related statements: (i) I would change to another brand if I had a chance; (ii) I would stay with my brand even if there is another brand with the same functionality and features; (iii) I express brand loyalty with my current brand; and (iv) My brand remains the first choice over any other brand.

Between 19% and 26% were undecided on the four brand loyalty statements. Positive responses were 54% on staying with the current brand if an equivalent was available and on expressing their loyalty with the current brand and 47% on the current brand remaining their first choice. This indicates that brand loyalty was high, presupposing satisfaction with all or most aspects of the current brand and a commitment by respondents to their brand. This is also supported by responses on the first statement, where only 34% agreed or strongly agreed that they would change brands if they could, as opposed to 43% who disagreed.

Because technology constantly advances, there are many brands competing on very similar grounds and offering similar, if not identical features; this makes it doubly important to maintain brand loyalty for survival in the mobile brand industry. However, the percentages of undecided consumers mean work for the industry in enticing new customers and retaining existing ones. Whole product development is important but equally so are service and relationship with customers.

CONCLUSION AND RECCOMMENDATIONS

Conclusion: Brand Loyalty Conquering Cybersecurity Choices

According to Holt (2004, p.95) "brand loyalty is the consumer's willingness to stay with a brand when competitors come knocking with offerings that would be considered equally attractive had not the consumer and brand shared a history." Kabiraj and Shanmugan (2011, p. 286) state that "brand loyalty is the consumer's conscious or unconscious decision, expressed through intention or behaviour, to repurchase a brand continually". Lam, Ahearne, Hu and Schillewaert (2010, p.131) describe brand loyalty as "a deeply held commitment to re-buy or re-patronise a preferred product/service consistently in the future, causing a repetitive same brand or same brand-set purchasing, despite situational influences and marketing efforts having the potential to cause switching behaviour." It is important for mobile companies to develop brand loyalty strategies for their consumers as this is the key factor in future profitability for companies. With loyal consumers there would be a core demand that would always be there if managed correctly. However, if it is not managed well and there is no brand loyalty, the company would quickly see a negative financial impact.

Brand image is a critical factor that leads to brand loyalty. "It is important for mobile companies to understand that there is a need to create a strong brand image in order to gain brand loyalty" (Lazarevic, 2011). This is where social value and emotional value is created for the consumer and mobile companies need to achieve a balance between meeting the consumer's needs and staying within the company core cultures to make a profit. Brand image is very important among young people today as it has become a status symbol and class issue: you make a better impression putting out your iPhone for others to see rather than a black and white Motorola.

Level of involvement with the mobile device among young consumers will determine brand loyalty. It's through involvement that consumers familiarise themselves with the functionality of the device and learn how to manage its touchscreen, its functionalities, its battery life, its camera, and its apps and services. And it's also through this involvement that they will decide whether the device best fits their needs and desires. Perceived value, functional value, emotional value and social value will also determine whether the mobile device best fits the consumer's needs and desires. There needs to be a "tick in every box" to ensure that brand loyalty among young people is created for a mobile company. This also requires establishment of brand trust between the consumer and the company, which will be attained through customer satisfaction and commitment. In combination, these factors will create brand loyalty which will lead to repeated purchase because there is a good relationship between the consumer and the product and brand they have invested in (Lam et al., 2010).

Perceived brand quality, switching costs, and brand experience will also play a major role in the consumer mindset in regard to continued brand loyalty (Jamal & Anastasiadou, 2009). If a consumer is loyal to a brand in the mobile industry but then has a change of mindset where they feel the brand that they are with does not meet their demands and they wish to opt out of the brand and choose another, this would not be a major problem for them. Competition is so intense in the mobile industry that with leading competitors in the market such as Samsung, iPhone, Blackberry and Nokia (joined now by Huawei) pricing of devices is very similar and switching costs are very affordable. This makes perceived brand quality all the more important.

Brand experience is significant in the mobile industry because consumers are less likely to buy a product that is new in the market if its name is not established, even if the product is of a high standard (Jamal & Anastasiadou, 2009). A good brand image first needs to be built so that loyal customers can begin to be acquired (Jamal & Anastasiadou, 2009).

What the study has shown is the leading significance of brand loyalty in the mobile industry. Rapid technological advances in the mobile industry require rapid market responses to accommodate new releases, new designs, and new competitors fighting for market share. The study aimed to provide insight into the basis on which young people make their decisions when purchasing a brand and what factors they see as relevant for them as consumers potentially becoming loyal to a specific brand. Generally the respondents were loyal to their brand to varying degrees, and all the factors that affect brand loyalty played a role in their preferences.

There are many factors that may lead to brand loyalty and mobile brand companies need to take these factors into consideration when producing a new product or offering a service to clientele they already have, as it is of critical importance to retain existing loyal clientele. The major factors at play here are involvement, perceived value, functional value, emotional value, social value, brand trust, customer satisfaction, commitment, repeated purchase and brand switching, as scrutinised in the literature review and as investigated by means of a questionnaire, with the responses then collated and analysed. In developing products and services that will create consumer loyalty, mobile brand companies need to make sure that consumer needs are met. Through repeated purchases the customer then becomes committed and loyal to the brand.

The Aaker model of brand equity shows that brand awareness, perceived quality, brand association and brand loyalty all lead to brand equity. In developing their products mobile brand companies can use this model along with social value, emotional value, functional value and involvement factors to ensure their consumers' needs are satisfied. This will enable mobile brand companies to procure more consumers who are loyal to the brand, and will encourage consumers to become loyal to a specific brand instead of constantly brand switching.

The participant responses show that although to some extent these objectives are being achieved, they do not come close enough to the targets mobile brand companies set for themselves. Further, the need for stronger cybersecurity awareness campaigns is highlighted, since the data indicated that security choices currently have little influence when young consumers select a brand to purchase.

RECOMMENDATIONS

The study as a whole significantly adds to the body of knowledge about brand loyalty among young people in relation to the mobile industry, as relevant questions have been tabled and then answered through the responses received. The study was however limited to a particular location and group of participants and data was collected from closed-ended questions only.

For added support in brand choice, cybersecurity awareness campaigns should take place along the following lines (Bada and Sasse, 2014):

1. Increased communication through all platforms such as social media and blogs on cybersecurity processes and procedures;
2. Training on secure usage of mobile device;
3. Security awareness events and programs;
4. Behavioural testing and teachable moments;
5. Teaching of new skills when mobile update or upgrade becomes available.

The following recommendations are made for future research:

1. Conduct an equivalent study across multiple campuses of UKZN or multiple universities to expand the body of data so that more general conclusions can be drawn about brand loyalty for this group of consumers, since this study focused solely on students attending one campus of UKZN.

2. Undertake the same research over time to establish changes over time in brand loyalty and factors affecting brand loyalty.
3. Undertake similar research to explore reasons why the respondents answered the way they did so as to provide richer data about attitudes and behaviours.

CONCLUSION

In the account given of this study, this chapter has outlined the research questions and objectives, its methodology, the study population, and the ultimate findings of the study as a whole. The significance of the study has accordingly been conveyed, and the research as a whole adds to the body of knowledge on brand loyalty of mobile devices in the fourth industrial revolution and, in particular, to empirical research in the South African context. As confirmed in the literature (Peters, 2017; Xing & Marwala, 2017) it is important to educate young consumers on responsible choice of mobile devices responsibly and careful consideration of the security options the device has to offer. The study can be used by mobile brand companies in order to learn about the consumer mindset and the factors on which consumers base their decisions when purchasing a mobile brand. What is important is that it also provides evidence for mobile brand companies on how and what they need to address to ensure they get more loyal consumers, which is basically by making sure that they meet consumer expectations and needs. It shows that there is a sizeable percentage of customers – those who indicated being undecided – who need to be targeted to increase their knowledge of and relationship with a brand in order to achieve brand loyalty. In relation to the research questions, all factors relating to brand loyalty were identified as having an influence, to a greater or lesser degree on brand loyalty. Recommendations for future research have been proposed to add to the richness of the data already collected.

ACKNOWLEDGMENT

The financial assistance of the National Research Foundation (NRF) towards this research is hereby acknowledged. Opinions expressed and conclusions arrived at, are those of the author and are not necessarily to be attributed to the NRF.

REFERENCES

Aaker, D. (2012). *Building strong brands*. New York: Simon and Schuster.

Aaker, D. A., & Biel, A. (2013). *Brand Equity & Advertising: Advertising's Role in Building Strong Brands*. Hoboken, NJ: Taylor and Francis.

Bada, M., & Sasse, A. (2014). *Cyber Security Awareness Campaigns: Why do they fail to change behaviour?* Oxford, UK: Global Cyber Security Capacity Centre, University of Oxford.

Baxter, P., & Jack, S. (2008). Qualitative case study methodologies: Study design and implementation for novice researchers. *Qualitative Report, 13*(1), 544–559.

Bloem, J., Van Doorn, M., Duivestein, S., Excoffier, D., Maas, R., & Van Ommeren, E. (2014). *The Fourth Industrial Revolution*. Things Tighten.

Brakus, J., Schmitt, B., & Zarantonello, L. (2009). Brand experience: What is it? How is it measured? Does it affect loyalty? *Journal of Marketing, 73*(3), 52–68. doi:10.1509/jmkg.73.3.52

Bruks, M., Zeithmal, V., & Naylar, G. (2000). Price and brand name as indicators of quality dimensions for consumer durable. *Journal of the Academy of Marketing Science, 28*(3), 359–374. doi:10.1177/0092070300283005

Fisher, C. (2007). *Researching and writing a dissertation: A guidebook for business students* (2nd ed.). Harlow: Pearson Education Limited.

Gerpott, T. J., Rams, W., & Schindler, A. (2001). Customer retention, loyalty, and satisfaction in the German mobile cellular telecommunication market. *Telecommunications Policy, 25*(4), 249–269. doi:10.1016/S0308-5961(00)00097-5

Ghauri, P. N., & Cateora, P. (2010). *International Marketing* (3rd ed.). Maidenhead, UK: McGraw- Hill Education.

Giddens, N., & Hofmann, A. (2010). *Brand loyalty*. AG Decision Maker.

Holt, D. (2004). *How brands become icons. The principles of cultural branding*. Boston: Harvard Business School Press.

Jamal, A., & Anastasiadou, K. (2009). Investigating the effects of service quality dimensions and expertise on loyalty. *European Journal of Marketing, 43*(3/4), 398–420. doi:10.1108/03090560910935497

Kabiraj, S., & Shanmugan, J. (2011). Development of a conceptual framework for brand loyalty: A Euro-Mediterranean perspective. *Journal of Brand Management, 18*(4), 285–299. doi:10.1057/bm.2010.42

Kelan, E., & Lehnert, M. (2009). *The millennial generation: generation y and the opportunities for a globalised, networked educational system*. Retrieved from https://www.academia.edu/4335172/The_millennial_generation_generation_y_and_the_opportunities_for_a_globalised_networked_educational_system

Keller, K. L. (2001). *Building Customer – based brand equity: a blueprint for creating strong brands* (Working paper 01-107). Cambridge, MA: Marketing Science Institution.

Kim, H. S., & Yoon, C. H. (2004). Determinants of subscriber churn and customer loyalty in the Korean Mobile telephony market. *Telecommunications Policy, 28*(9-10), 751–765. doi:10.1016/j.telpol.2004.05.013

Korpella, K. (2015). Improving Cyber Security Awareness and Training Programs with Data Analytics. *Information Security Journal: A Global Perspective, 24*, 72-77. Retrieved from http://www.tandfonline.com/doi/abs/10.1080/19393555.2015.1051676

Krejcie, R. V., & Morgan, D. W. (1970). Determining sample size for research activities. *Educational and Psychological Measurement, 30*(3), 607–610. doi:10.1177/001316447003000308

Lam, S. K., Ahearne, M., Hu, Y., & Schillewaert, N. (2010). Resistance to brand switching when a radically new brand is introduced: A social identity theory perspective. *Journal of Marketing, 74*(6), 128–146. doi:10.1509/jmkg.74.6.128

Lazarevic, V. (2011). Encouraging brand loyalty in fickle generation Y consumers. *Young Consumers*, *13*(1), 45–61. doi:10.1108/17473611211203939

Li, X., Ortiz, P. J., Browne, J., Franklin, D., Oliver, J. Y., Geyer, R., & Chong, F. T. (2010, September). Smartphone evolution and reuse: Establishing a more sustainable model. In *Parallel Processing Workshops (ICPPW), 2010 39th International Conference on* (pp. 476-484). IEEE.

Peters, M. A. (2017). *Technological unemployment: Educating for the fourth industrial revolution*. London: Taylor & Francis.

PRLOG. (2009). *Global Smartphone market and industry chain report*. Retrieved: 23 October 2015. http://www.prlog.org/10192174-global-smart-phone-market-industry-chain- report-20082009.html

Seo, D., Ranganathan, C., & Babad, Y. (2008). Two-level model of customer retention in the US mobile telecommunications service market. *Telecommunications Policy*, *32*(3-4), 751–765. doi:10.1016/j.telpol.2007.09.004

Xing, B., & Marwala, T. (2017). *Implications of the Fourth Industrial Age on Higher Education*. arXiv preprint arXiv:1703.09643.

Youl, H., & John, J. (2010). Role of customer orientation in an integrative model of brand loyalty in services. *Service Industries Journal*, *30*(7), 1025–1046. doi:10.1080/02642060802311252

Chapter 20

Mobile Security in Low-Income Households' Businesses:
A Measure of Financial Inclusion

Bibi Zaheenah Chummun
University of KwaZulu-Natal, South Africa

ABSTRACT

A wide range of technologies impinges on all disciplines including financial services in this era of the Fourth Industrial Revolution. The deployment and security of mobile phones have considerably increased financial services access such as mobile money to the low-income households in developing African markets recently. The financial services that were once randomly accessible to those financially excluded have now become a potential pathway to enhance financial inclusion in allowing the low-income households to transact through mobile financial services in a more speedy, reliable, and secure manner. However, many security challenges remain to be addressed to promote a more inclusive mobile financial system. This chapter focuses on mobile devices security landscape and unprecedented security breaches by cyber criminals and how those threats can be mitigated in a view to promote financial inclusion in the mobile financial services sector of emerging African markets in the midst of the Fourth Industrial Revolution.

INTRODUCTION

In the era of the Fourth Industrial Revolution where potential of billions of the population are connected by mobile telephony with access to mobile financial services are countless. The concept of mobile financial services is one of the most prominent mobile application in this era of industry 4.0, having no historical precedent to the low-income households in the emerging niche markets with regard to its storage capacity, multifunction applications, processing power, dictionary to knowledge and back-up secure system. Ouma, Odongo and Were (2017) showed in their previous work that the adoption of mobile phones to provide financial services to the low-income people who were financially unserved/unbanked and excluded by the main financial services stream continue to rise in developing countries. The sophistication in technology more specifically mobile phones have revolutionized the sector of financial services and introduced new ways of serving the poor to promote financial inclusion.

DOI: 10.4018/978-1-5225-4763-1.ch020

The mobile financial services have proven to be relatively reliable, affordable and accessible to the extent that many low-income earners are expanding their financial platforms to add other types of financial services such as mobile banking/payment and mobile micro insurance (Demirgüc-Kunt, Klapper, Dorothe, & Van Oudheusden, 2014). The scattered use of mobile technology has opened new markets across developing markets and has induced financial services to reach low-income earners in out-of-reach places where banking services are lacking. However, one of the area that has been of concern to most of low-income earners has been the aspect of security threats being the main reason for not adopting mobile financial services. Although the increased growth and deployment of mobile devices security have arouse interest to reduce infrastructural gaps, operational cost and bring profitability to providers, the security component has been listed to be still a huge grey area of concern for the low-income households to promote an all-fledged financially inclusive system, (Hughes & Lonie, 2007; Holmes, 2011; Dermish, Kneiding, Leishman, & Mas, 2010; 2012).

Although financial inclusion is still exploratory and in its infancy stage in most emerging economies around the world, it has become a bedrock of development policy to the extent that it has been classified as the United Nations main aim among its 2020 priorities. This emanates from the observation that an enhanced financial inclusion is important in mitigating extreme poverty, increased shared prosperity and is one of the recipes for economic growth and welfare (World Bank, 2014; International Monetary Fund, 2014; Demirgüç-Kunt, Beck & Honohan, 2008).

In comparison to the developed countries in the world where the population have access to formal financial services, in developing countries sustainable financial access are still lacking to the low-income households although quite a number of unserved population has now obtained access to financial services (Ismail & Masinge, 2011). According to Huet (2017), 2.5 billion low-income people earning less than 10 dollars per day lack access to basic financial services. Furthermore, the low-income people who are more vulnerable to financial risks by using cash and informal mechanisms makes the process more costly and risky.

The advances in information and communication technology (ICT) in the midst of the Fourth Industrial Revolution has generated an increase in the use and access to mobile phones in those emerging economies. The spreading velocity of mobile devices technology has resulted in a surge of previously unbanked, underbanked, uninsured, underinsured low-income earners to have more access to financial services in a more secure way and can be now brought into the mainstream of a more inclusive secure financial system, out of which more women have access to securely mobile money transactions. Although women are more likely than men to be less financially mobile when carrying financial transactions, the percentage of women from 2011 to 2014, in emerging countries with registered accounts have increased by thirteen percent as per a study made by the World Bank on Global Financial Inclusion (Global Findex) database (West, Villasenor & Lewis, 2016).

The secure practices in mobile financial services offer opportunities to provide financial services at relatively low-cost improving financial inclusion through achieving productivity gains across the emerging markets. Mobile financial services such as mobile banking, m-payment and mobile micro insurance that are currently revolutionizing the developing countries, enable the low-income households to financially transact digitally and have potential to grow despite some security barriers hampering the progress especially now that the Fourth Industrial Revolution has started to flow. Although the Government and other stakeholders in the financial services industry have made much concerted efforts counter-balancing the potential threats and the presence of cybercriminals, there are still many challenges making the field of mobile security, an indispensable part of cyber security, widely vulnerable by threat actors. This chapter is predicated on the thrust that while mobile security system can improve financial inclusion to some extent, largely security fears and security breaches facing the low-income households in performing financial transactions such as mobile banking/payments and mobile micro insurance can also negatively affect the level of financial inclusion.

This chapter has been divided into six main sections: The first section is mainly geared towards the importance of mobile security in the mobile financial business of the low-income people as a measure to promote financial inclusion in the African countries. The second section focuses on the types of security breaches involving mobile money under mobile financial services. The third section discusses the current scale of the problem of mobile security breaches facing low-income households. The fourth section provides suggestions as to how the security threats can be mitigated. Section five provides some cyber security recommendations focusing on how mobile security can promote financial access and inclusion to low-income people in the Fourth Industrial Revolution. Section six provides future research directions. A conclusion is found at the end of this chapter.

BACKGROUND

Importance of Mobile Security to Low-Income Households in Mobile Financial Services

Mobile computing conflates numerous inventions that are used into a single platform. While all these technologies advances mobile computing, people tend to use mobile devices everywhere at least where the mobile telephony infrastructure allows (Canbek, Sagiroglu, & Baykal, 2015). This has even been substantiated at the World Economic Forum in 2017 debating an important topic related to the rising use of mobile technology that continues to connect billions of low-income households (Schwab, 2017). While developed countries have been shifting digitally to undertake financial transactions through smart mobile phones, developing countries have also been using their mobile telephony by partnering with more Mobile Network Operators(MNOs) to conduct mobile financial services according to some authors among others (Etim, 2012; Holmes, 2011). According to Jenkins (2008), Ehrbeck & Tarazi (2011); Porteous, & Rotman (2012), mobile money consisting of mobile banking and payment is one of the prominent application of mobile tools to undertake financial transactions other than communication and has mostly been used by low-income households lately.

Recent studies have shown that in developing countries globally men are more likely to dominate the scene making more use of mobile-based financial services in developing countries compared to female gender (Fanta & Mutsonziwa, 2016).This is also relevant across Africa. Women represent an important source of economic development and opportunity to advance financial inclusion (Fanta, Mutsonziwa, Goosen, Emanuel & Kettles, 2016). However, financial exclusion prevented many women to bring their input and productivity in the economy and from enhancing their lives and those of their dependents. The majority of Kenyan smallholders' farmers are women. Women in Kenya are 40% less likely to have a mobile money account (GSMA, 2014). This is both a loss to women and to the providers; women are missing those benefits and the mobile financial services providers have yet to market those unserved women as subscribers. According to a survey made by GSMA in 2014, women have been more likely to be passive money receivers rather than senders involving mobile money. Women also claimed that transaction fees on mobile money services have been high and being an obstacle to frequent use of small frequent transactions. They claimed that they have been most involved through informal means to obtain informal income and to use cash for transactions rather than using the mobile money services. In today's increasingly interconnected emerging breakthroughs in this era of industry 4.0, almost 66% of the global women population are still financially excluded. It is an economic and social imperative that that they get access to financial services (Fanta & Mutsonziwa, 2016).

The diverse capabilities of mobile platforms such as mobile financial services where mobile money is one of the most important applications obviously present many opportunities to low-income users (Mas & Radcliffe, 2010; 2011). One of its prominent capabilities is mobile security which an indispensable part of cybersecurity in general. According to a study made by Javelin Strategy and Research (2009), mobile security also known wireless security relates to the implementation of security controls pertaining to the inherent security within mobile. In case of this process not being undertaken, the mobile is either less secure or not secure at all compared to other platforms. As Gustavo de Los Reyes, director for AT&T Security R&D mentioned, *the phones are being used frequently for sensitive transactions like mobile banking, mobile payments, and transmitting confidential business data, making them attractive targets if not protected.*

In this era of industry 4.0, as mobile devices thrive the way to undertake mobile financial services, there has been a rise in the number of financial institutions facing cyber criminals attacks (Manzoor, 2014). While the mobile tools makers focused on applications of mobile financial services and communication, security aspects have remained an afterthought (Leavitt, 2011). Many users download mobile applications without taking into account security aspects, which tend to open doors for hackers to attack the devices.

According to a study made by GSMA intelligence on "the Mobile Economy Africa 2016", smartphones usage in Africa has doubled in two years reaching more than half a billion people million, most of them are low-income households using smartphones for mobile financial services other than communication (GSMA, 2016). Accordingly, the financial losses and personal information have been immense to low-income subscribers drowning the poor back into poverty and leaving them to be financially included due to lack of security features embedded in the applications (Leavitt, 2011). Moreover, reputational damage have affected providers of mobile financial services. Although providers of financial services have made concerted efforts to provide outstanding customer service and advanced technology, the need for appropriate security features installed in phones continue to escalate.

Mobile security seems to be a worrisome component. The number and types of mobile threats have hiked recently including malware, skimming, Distributed Denial of Service (DDoS), phishing and exploitations of Near Field communication (NFC) among others, and will be discussed later in this chapter.

Mobile financial services organizations operate on large scale of confidential information. It is not a surprise that financial services institutions are in the crosshairs for cyber-attacks. Nowadays financial services organizations are operating under a constant state of attack, leaving security teams challenged in their ability to collect, disseminate and interpret malicious events and unprecedented security risks in this era of Fourth Industrial Revolution. Therefore to promote financial inclusion, as the teams strive to manage complexity of threats, it has become imperative that financial services organizations proactively be constantly on their alert to implement appropriate innovative security controls on the mobile devices to preserve information as well as to counteract any other threats cropping.

A Snapshot of Mobile Money as a Measure of Financial Inclusion: The Case of African Developing Countries

Mobile financial services have been classified as the most important thriving mobile application in the emerging African countries and mobile money has become its general platform of accommodation (Donovan, 2012). According to Alleman & Rappoport (2010), mobile money can be pertained to a series of activities related to mobile financial services available to customers through mobile telephony. The concept of mobile money is two-fold: mobile banking (m-banking) and mobile payment (m-payment) (Ally, 2014). The mobile banking services include savings, credit, bill payments, balance checks, long distance remittances cash withdrawal, funds transfer, airtime purchase and cash and cheque deposit (Donner & Tellez, 2008; Jenkins, 2008; Kasseeah & Tandrayen-Ragoobur, 2012;). Mobile payment transformative models, enable the unserved to access financial products offered by network operators and non-banking settings.

In 2007, a decade back when Safaricom, a mobile money services provider in Kenya introduced M-PESA, it was difficult to improvise the positive effect of mobile money on low-income earners lives. In 2016, there were approximately three hundred million people across ninety-three countries who sub-scribed to a mobile money service and around two billion people are expected to be connected by 2020 (Giusti, 2016). Therefore, what could have led to a hike in digital financial services was the connectivity through mobile phone technology. Although mobile money telephony has connected large number of low-income people there are many who are still not accommodated by the financial mainstream (Ismail & Masinge, 2011). The huge un-served gap represents a niche to be exploited by players and network operators (Lee, Levendis, & Gutierrez, 2012; Infosys, 2009). Further, in this era of industry 4.0, mobile money improves productivity and mitigate operating costs due to many other digital platforms being created. This is substantiated by the growth in the number of Mobile Network Operators (MNOs) and mobile devices penetration which has led to reduction in the infrastructural barriers of developing countries (Oluwatayo, 2013; De Sousa, 2010).

The proliferation of mobile money have introduced a hike in financial transactions that can spread financial services access to the financially excluded through mobile phones. Connecting on a large scale can only improve the welfare of every human being. For instance, the use of M-PESA commonly used in Kenya only brought down the transaction costs and improved their welfare (Suri & Jack, 2011). Following riot at the time of election held in Kenya some few years back, the only way for the Kenyans to access cash was through M-PESA (Morawczynski, 2009). M-PESA has been also used even in no war times when the low-income Kenyans have been able to perform financial transactions (Stuart & Cohen, 2011). In addition to M-PESA being an important mobile money system to the users, it can also be a considerable source of revenue to the providers of mobile money if they reach required volumes although the costs are included. A vivid instance is that in 2011, Safaricom reached $90 million that has benefitted cash agents in Kenya due to the receipt of fees. Gradually, more low-income households are also using mobile financial services. The disruption of the traditional financial services such as going physically to the bank have a pathway and potential unlock to inclusive financing (Giusti, 2016).

Another recent important wave of the Mobile Financial Services facing Industry 4.0 in emerging markets is related to mobile micro insurance. Before mobile micro insurance (MMI) can be explained, it is important to define micro insurance as "insurance that is accessed by the low-income households offered by a wide range of different providers and performed with generally accepted insurance practices" (National Treasury of South Africa, 2011). Therefore, mobile micro insurance can be broadly defined as any product/service of micro insurance that utilized the mobile technology to enhance the insurance value chain and include design of the cover, premium rates, marketing, underwriting and claims. The mobile platform that is mobile money can be applied as a tool to both the insured and the provider to bring down the transactions costs of micro insurance product/service. The opportunity to revolutionize financial services for mass emerging markets in developing countries so that everyone is insured at the touch of a mobile device recently has been felt through micro insurance and mobile micro insurance. Although relatively low-cost life insurance with associated low sums-assured has been around for many years in Africa, penetration rates for these micro insurance products remain low, especially outside of South Africa. As number of policyholders increase at subsequently low premium, the transactions become highly disruptive to traditional providers of risk protection in this new mass emerging market segment. The micro insurance market has little certainty for commercial players in terms of its profitability component (Chummun & Bisschoff, 2013).

Although being a non-lucrative market, the number of mobile micro insurance products have been growing since 2012. Mobile phone account for 71 out of the 84 products according to survey made by CGAP (Tellez & Zetterli, 2014). The concept of mobile money at low-cost can encourage more low-income users to subscribe to micro insurance. The low-income earners in remote places using affordable mobile channels offers the potential for providers to communicate with them and can contribute to financial inclusion. Using mobile phone in an efficient way in insurance mitigates costs, speeds up issuing of policies and payment of valid claims (Prashad, Saunders & Dalal, 2013).

Although approximately 90% of low-income people living on less than 2 dollars per day do not use advance financial services other than receiving and sending payments, the deployment of Mobile Micro insurance (MMI) is growing at a rapid pace. According to Tellez & Zetterli (2014), there has been a remarkable increase of two-thirds more MMI products since 2006 to 2013. However, some disruptions have occurred in this low-income market due to new customer needs and expectations of new distribution channels as well as difficulty to reach the low-income households in remote places (Smit, Denoon-Steevens, & Esser, 2017). Many micro insurance providers find it difficult to reach scale and make profits in this low-income niche market, it opens opportunities to cover more previously financially excluded people.

Nowadays micro insurance are poised to expand to other offerings. In a time when societal changes, technological developments and empowered customers are changing the nature of the insurance business, established insurers need to determine the recent technological advance for innovation. Within industry 4.0, one of the technological emerging breakthroughs has been the recent launch of InsurTech, which relates to the phenomenon of start-ups that are innovating using technology to fundamentally enhance the existing insurance business model and security of MMI (Kumbla, 2016). One of the most important challenges noted so far has been the lack of data/information (information assymetries) on low-income consumers that can compromise security aspects. Within the Fourth Industrial Revolution, big data that relates to large amount of dataset explores the opportunities for small policies in the micro insurance space and provides new information that can be utilized to counteract this disruption. Further, it allows providers to counteract information while processing claims and avoid fraud in micro insurance (Kumbla, 2016).

The proliferation of technology within industry 4.0 is generating a concept called "ephemeralisation", a word by the highly regarded American architect who defines ephemeralisation as the ability to produce more output with little input. By the same token mobile money has the urgent need to innovate in terms of security aspects due to a rise in breaches within the Fourth Industrial Revolution today so that every low-income household is financially included by the omnipresence of the effective use of mobile telephony spreading like wildfire in the emerging economies.

SECURITY BREACHES INVOLVING M-BANKING AND M-PAYMENT IN AFRICA

In the midst of industry 4.0, where digitization is increasingly being used in the financial services sector, mobile money lying at the core of banking has not been set free from cyber criminals attempts. The rise in the transfer from the conventional way to mobile money transfer has probed into vulnerabilities with regard to security (Symantec, 2016). These have been mobile insecurity and untested applications that tend to expose financial/personal information to cyber criminals. These exposures can easily lead to security issues such security breaches and threats for the industry.

One of the biggest security breaches is related to the risk of fraud. The use of unstructured supplementary service data (USSD) being a communication technology for transactions has been used for mobile financial services firms such as mobile banking/payment and insurance. The interception of mobile banking data by fraudsters can happen while it is being transferred. The encrypted mobile data on servers in developing countries compared to the unencrypted mobile data while transferred on servers makes it lenient to breach in developing countries while performing mobile money transactions (Macharia, 2011). Another noted identified weakness by Kenya Safaricom M-PESA a major provider of mobile money in Sub Sahara Africa is related to when low-income households have registered their information and a two-mode authentication is needed to match the user phone number and the account where their money lies. Fraudsters have constantly been on the lookout to breach this process. One of the reasons cited by the Kenya Bankers Association (KBA) Chief Executive, has been that fraudsters and hackers are closely connected with employees working on the system giving rise to identity theft (phishing) (Olaka, 2017). The cyber criminals are quick to connect with bank employees online to forge identity asking to change customers' personal details and contact phone numbers (Olaka, 2017). As employees believe to be dealing with the main account users, the change of details can easily allow the intermediary in the attack (fraudster) to move money across using the new phone details.

The loss of a mobile phone does not only imply losing contact details, history of messages and phone calls, it also mean losing and jeopardize financial information recorded on the mobile tool if stolen. Fraudsters could make use of this information to get hold of the user's bank account details or mobile money transactions. An attacker could also rob, expose publicly by selling any information extracted from the device. Although at a later stage if the user luckily retrieves the mobile tool, spam emails/messages may flood the device leading to future identity theft attacks.

Over the years, mobile banking/payment/remittances and insurance have been the centre of attraction of cyber criminals. (Choo 2011b; Martini & Choo 2013; Quick & Choo, 2013c). Malware experts have invaded mobile tools and the number of communication network attacks have increased in this regard (McAfee, 2013). For instance, a "trojaned" application could prevent mobile money activities to proceed on a mobile device such as moving funds on a mobile money platform. Alternatively, the application could illegally track all the purchases and movement of funds made by the target user, potentially giving the threat actor information about the users' strategies and physical location. Mobile malware can attack any data such as account details recorded on mobile tools (McAfee, 2013)

Cyber-attacks are not only fraud-related in the banking sector but also in the insurance sector (Bhasin, 2007; Arachchilage & Love, 2014; Lagazio, Sherif, & Cushman, 2014). According to Agostinho and Cherry (2016), claim fraud has been classified as a major attack in the field of micro insurance. Most of these fraudulent acts happen because of limited resources and expensive process to trace fraud-related claims by micro insurance providers (Agostinho & Cherry, 2016). Cyber attackers eye for mobile systems and use many techniques that would distract systems using worms, Trojans and viruses (Arachchilage & Love, 2014). The robbery of passwords known as skimming can include any malicious act relating to a mobile payment of a micro insurance policy lump sum or any malicious act relating to mobile banking such as withdrawing money from the main account in mobile money transactions. Malware, also called malicious systems include spam emails, spyware which is constant monitoring of software, are all malicious acts or attacks. The act of rendering mobile data not available to its intended users is evidence of a DDoS attack (Distributed Denial of-Service) in mobile money (Arachchilage & Love, 2014, p. 304). Further, identity theft through voice channel known as vishing and smishing also known as SMS phishing attacks are often conducted in mobile banking and payments (Stokkel & Smulders, 2013; Bhasin, 2007). Their losses and impact have been huge to all stakeholders (Choo, 2011a). Recently, mobile banking has faced many cyber financial crimes and account from robbing money to manipulation and deactivation of the mobile payment systems and banking mobile applications. These unprecedented cybercrimes are expected to continue at least in the near future if no address and measures to counteract them are urgently undertaken.

THE SCALE OF MOBILE SECURITY BREACHES

Implications of Mobile Money Security Breaches in Africa

Cybercrimes continue to escalate worldwide and have been ranked as the second most reported economic crime on the planet compared to fourth position in 2015 affecting many organizations badly (PriceWaterhouseCoopers, 2016, p.13). Since this chapter is mainly focused on mobile money for low-income households in Africa, its remarkable growth in developing countries especially Africa has compromised cyber security and privacy of information as major concerns that have led to application's abuse. According to Reaves, Scaife, Bates, Traynor and Butler (2015), a considerable number of applications has failed recently by digital financial services and has threatened to derail trust in mobile banking and hinder endeavor for financial inclusion.

Fraud has continued to invade the system of mobile money in Africa (Serianu Africa Cybersecurity Report, 2016). Fifteen countries in Africa out of twenty have mobile money services which have accommodated several platforms; banking, insurance and payments. As per the report, some mobile money applications do not have encryption of data as security controls. In the African continent, security breaches in mobile money are on the rise (Croock, 2016). Surprisingly two thirds of respondents surveyed during 2015/2016 have experienced a security breach and almost 10% of surveyed respondents claimed their organisation has suffered more than 10 security breaches, while almost half mentioned that they have encountered between one and five security breaches (Croock, 2016). According to Gemalto's Breach Level Index (2016), in South Africa alone, data breaches have increased by 15% in the first half of 2016. Africa's two largest economies, South Africa and Nigeria, have lost approximately $5130m annually to cyber criminals like hackers, fraudsters and those malicious intent on digital sabotage.

The problem appears to be getting more acute year by year. In 2016, East Africa has faced 37% more cyberattacks than in 2015 (Croock, 2016). Further, (BYOD) "Bring Your Own Device", can bring countless security breaches to many organizations and in Africa, where many employees own multiple devices, the risks are even greater. In South Africa, where staff members tend to bring more than one mobile device demands appropriate authentication security controls. The use of mobile data being costly in some African countries has been a demotivating factor in updating security applications on their mobile devices. Older device operating systems are less secure and users have jeopardized their information by not updating secure mobile applications. Wi-Fi fraud is simple and easy to manipulate, so too are the man-in-the-middle attacks (fraudster) against older applications where security features are not promising. In some African countries, as there has been no rule to make it mandatory for organizations to report these types of fraud or data breaches, it is hard to quantify the number of attacks.

As the adoption of financial technology thrives through, mobile money providers have become the centre of cybercrime attacks. According to Serianu's Cybersecurity Report (2016), the countries in Africa offering mobile money have inevitably lost $2 billion in cybercrimes in 2016. Security breaches have flooded the environment of cyberspace to the extent that in East Africa, $171 million was lost by Kenya mobile money providers followed by Tanzania ones which suffered a loss of $85 million and a loss of $35 million by Uganda providers in 2016. More than one-third of mobile money providers that suffered security breaches in 2016 reported a twenty percent substantial loss in their customers' portfolio and income. During the first quarter of 2017, Safaricom's M-PESA being the largest and oldest mobile money provider in Africa reported that the process of hacking has forged their way into M-PESA's platform before being tracked by the organization by risk management unit (Serianu Cybersecurity Report, 2016)

Privacy protection of mobile money users has been limited, inadequate and has proven to be vulnerable to the users. The Financial Action Task Force (FATF) requirements for user's transparency poses a potential problem for users. FATF recommendation number 10 states that any institution must undertake Customer Due Diligence (CDD) implying the submission of an identity document and monitoring user records of transactions. Requirement number 11 of the FATF requires that institutions maintain records of the users for five consecutive years. These requirements obviously probe concerns to the users regarding their data/information being in custody of institutions and are susceptible to leakage of information to other stakeholders. For instance, countries such as Tanzania, Uganda, Burundi and Rwanda have no laws and regulations that clearly stipulate who is eligible to mobile money and when, how and under what circumstances the access to mobile money can be obtained. This scenario is more likely to compromise users' trust and limit mobile money adoption in developing countries, thus does not assist to promote financial inclusion.

Thorough privacy and security measures are prerequisites to extend digital financial services to the low-income and unserved. For a user who has been used to a structured transparent financial system, being all of a sudden a victim to a security hiccups may permanently cause distrust in that particular person to use mobile financial services. Similarly, a subscriber with no existing structured financial experience who suddenly faces a security failure can outright dissuade that user from the financial systems as a whole. In the light of these reasons, security of mobile devices (information security and cyber security) and inherent privacy (information preservation) are critical when using mobile financial services.

Another security issue is the lack of regulatory and supervisory framework to regulate mobile network platforms in some African countries such as Uganda and Burundi. The Central Bank of Kenya is not eager to regulate the mobile money deposits, as the central bank perceives that the emerging industry of mobile money could stagnate innovation and development of the sector.

The consequences of cybercrime can be tremendous though hard to quantify and can be classified under three main areas (Anderson et al., 2013).

- Direct losses include fraud and loss of customers and trust;
- Indirect losses include loss of goodwill and theft of intellectual property and
- Defense costs (direct defense) relates to monetary costs related to security initiatives, training and awareness campaigns

The costs of cybercrime seem to have tremendous consequences for the financial institutions and leave the low-income households to feel that that they are financially excluded as customer trust, airtight security as well as digital privacy and well-being that customers expect have been derailed. (Raghavan & Parthiban, 2014; Anderson et al., 2013). Those large defense costs are key initiatives to induce strategic management of financial institutions to implement better security measures.

SOME SUGGESTIONS AS TO HOW THREATS CAN BE MITIGATED IN M-BANKING AND M-PAYMENT

Before providing mitigation suggestions to threats, it is important to highlight whether mobile security should be classified under information security or cyber security. In the author's opinion, mobile security should consist of both information and cyber security. Since the information on the mobile device is prone to threats hence information security, in an attempt to provide integrity, confidentiality and availability prevails. In the sense that mobile security relates to the security of information (financial data, personal data related to mobile money transactions), hence information preservation should be maintained. "Cybersecurity mostly deals with protection of cyber space against any sort of security risks that can be related or might not be related to provide information confidentiality, integrity, and availability".

In general, mobile banking requires security to support wireless transactions on multiple levels:

- The mobile device itself, the security of the particular banking application that may be run from the device;
- Securing of the data stored on the mobile phone, securing or encrypting the data transmitted over the air;
- Authentication of the customer is needed to guarantee that a legitimate and authorized customer is performing the transaction; authentication of the device guarantees that the transaction is occurring over an authorized mobile device; and
- Finally, authentication of the financial institution given to the customer helps avoid phishing scams and other attacks.

With security as a key driver of consumer acceptance and growth of the channel, it must be given top priority in product and marketing budgets for mobile financial services. Fortunately, for both financial institutions and consumers, the mobile channel can increase banking security if it is deployed correctly. Users are able to track their financial information in real-time from practically anywhere in the world. Frequent self-monitoring of accounts is an effective way for consumers to detect fraudulent transactions and activities. Text-message alerts allow users to receive regular updates on account activity, adding another level of security. The text message alerts sent to the mobile handsets is an effective way to fight fraud.

Over the years, one of the attributes of smart phones has been the improved security features embedded in their applications. Since managing finances is a personal and sensitive issue, the predominance of mobile money seems to be working well for the low-income people. Having access to own information relating to own banking records from mobile devices has now become a secure trend as banks have moved to mobile banking mainly due to an increase in security from the banking institution.

For some consumers, security consistently remains one of the biggest obstacles to mobile adoption, although usage of the channel seems to allay some of these fears. Nonetheless, almost half of mobile bankers cite security as their main concern (Javelin Strategy & Research, 2009). Although, one of the important disruptions facing industry 4.0 is the possibility to hack emerging breakthrough system, mobile money system is of no exception. Banks are maximizing their security levels and protocols for instance, some have locked down their applications of mobile money and made it compulsory that mobile money subscriber must consult physically a banking institution before being eligible to use the application that deploys mobile money. An obvious example would be Google Wallet that requires the user to insert a preset programmed four-digit security code or PIN when using the application of mobile money. Another example set by Apple Pay is that the subscriber should apply their finger to the screen to make payments hence generating an automatic receipt, implying that an incorrect fingerprint will not allow the system to accept the payment made and no receipt will be issued. Smartphones whether iPhone or Android allow the user to shut down the application/service remotely. Even if the smartphone is lost, the user can access the mobile wallet remotely and disconnect it. Although the security features of the mobile money application allows the third party in custody of the smartphone to access the features, the application will outright reject the transaction to be processed.

Mobile or wireless security relates to when the mobile channel must contend with smishing, vishing, phishing, malware, and man-in-the-middle attacks as explained earlier Despite these threats, if secured properly, the mobile channel is one of the safest. The security landscape is still favorable to mobile devices in some developing countries. In some other developing African countries, mobile financial services are still at a preliminary stage. There is no full customer adoption and mobile banking services are not fully in operation. For instance, some of the countries such as Rwanda and Burundi do not have a proper system infrastructure to move money across instead physical cash movement is still being used. This immature market is less attractive to criminals. Another mitigating factor is the diversity of operating systems, for instance, the diversity of mobile handsets and platforms makes it harder for criminals to write malware.

As FinTech that is "Financial Technology" thrives in some countries, some financial firms seek to liaise/team up with firms offering such technology. The use of block chain technology also known as distributed ledger offers opportunities to secure structured chained transactions in a systematic spreadsheet that are slowly constructed by new insertions of cells being pulled along together in parallel with the running of the software (Mori, 2016). Contrary to the system of a main controlling server owned by a single unit, block chain allows the user to be continuously connected and secured even if the users are removed. It supports an ineradicable record, which resists manipulation by any hacker (Mori, 2016). Block chain does not need a clearinghouse and its capacity to securely record valuable information on distributed ledgers could attract many businesses.

Further, the security in transmission of quantum computing communication provides a sense of cohesion, as there is a permanent quantum firewall to secure the device against any attack at all levels (Lo & Preskill, 2007). Quantum computing offers the users the opportunities to filter, control their data, oversee the conveying of information and also allows them to take calculated decisions of whether to accept or refuse access to other parties. Many financial firms have been advised to swap to quantum computing, as it consists of ease of use, appropriate controls of security, advanced authentication and has proven to be user-friendly in terms of use (Amellal, Meslouhi, Hassouni, & Bazi, 2015).

RECOMMENDATIONS: SOME CYBER SECURITY SOLUTIONS

The Role of Mobile Security in the Fourth Industrial Revolution in Promoting Financial Access to Low-Income People

The Fourth Industrial Revolution has started to flow and mobile security expectations are accordingly growing. There is an urgent need for organizations to find the equilibrium to spur innovation while providing an excellent customer service and security as well as privacy protection. The use and security of mobile phones have considerably increased financial services access to the low-income households in developing markets over the last decade, however the number of unprecedented risks have risen too. The question that arises relates as to how mobile security can promote more financial access to low-income people. Some few recommendations are provided in this regard:

Advanced Security Applications

The starting point is to have smart phones that are equipped with appropriate advanced embedded security applications and capabilities. Subsequently, the low-income households could have easier and fearless access to mobile money, mobile banking, and mobile micro insurance services applications through their phones. It would be easier for Mobile Network Operators and other parties such as intermediaries to reach the low-income people in remote places where Near Field Communication (NFC) is available. The technology behind digital payment is the mobile application and NFC allows for communication using magnetic field induction of Radio Frequency Identification (RFID) of the devices. This will set the scene to creating more opportunities to implement more of these technologies where they do not exist and to use graphical interfaces with users having a low literacy level. Further, the access will give rise to more freely communication in a quicker way due to the increase in the frequency of transactions and financial access is more likely to improve.

Proactive Preparation for Cyberattacks

It is important to proactively prepare for attacks to counteract resilient hackers. Attacks are increasingly becoming sophisticated. To stand ahead of cybercriminal games, security practices must go beyond keeping pace with the constantly evolving threat landscape on mobile devices. Doing so will demand constant attention and ongoing investments to prevent, protect, detect and respond to security risks. It is vital that financial services organizations invest in personnel, processes and technology to understand and monitor the various threat actors who may be motivated to disrupt core business functions on mobile devices.

Partnerships

An attack on one institution providing mobile money may signal an attack on the industry at large. By building partnerships, sharing attack information and collaborating with industry stakeholders, financial firms can further enhance their cyber resilience to security threats in the cyber space. According to the (World Economic Forum, 2016, p.61), collaboration and partnership create a more solid trustworthy environment where expertise and capabilities can be shared to counteract cybercrime management.

Data Records

To counteract information assymetries of low-income people in developing countries, there is an urgent need to record low-income households' biometric data. According to Gelb & Decker (2011), the Center for Global Development estimates that approximately more than a billion of people in developing countries will record their biometric data in the near future. There should be a rigorous biometric system that offers an identity document system, a solid iris scans for all the fingerprints and a picture for every citizen of the respective country. These processes of identification are generally equipped with appropriate security initiatives. Further, providers should make use of big data to gain access to data and information on consumers.

Regulatory Issues

Since many countries especially in Africa do not have a supervisory/regulatory framework that oversees the transactions pertaining to mobile financial services, it is imperative that these countries introduce their regulations in this sector to ensure security of transactions for both the providers and the users. The Anti-Money Laundering and the Combating of Financial transactions requires that Customer Due Diligence and Know-Your-Customer processes are performed on each and every transaction under the financial services body to promote security of mobile financial transactions.

Training and Development

In an attempt to generate inclusion in the mobile money sector, it is important that intermediaries are developed and trained appropriately and will be more poised to financially educate the low-income households on the benefits and security of related mobile-based financial services. Since women contribute a lot to the welfare of a country, therefore appropriate training on financial technology should be provided so that they can be financially included to perform mobile money transactions. Regulation should bear into account that customary laws do not take over statutory measures such as giving women equal rights to men with regard to property ownership. Since women in emerging countries tend not to be fully versed with financial terms, the policymakers should take calculated steps to adequately train those women who are showing low level of financial literacy and on security levels on their phone so that they can be equally financially included.

Cyber Liability Insurance and Key Signature Infrastructure (KSI)

As cyberattacks can lead to major financial losses of a business, the need to have adequate cyber liability insurance that covers cyber security incidents in recovering successfully from a cyberattack like claims fraud which is the main threat in micro insurance could be a wise move of a firm's cyber risk management strategy. Further Key Signature Infrastructure (KSI) can be thought of as a "lie detector for data", a simple process of signing a piece of data by software whether it is a policy, claim, reinsurance transaction, PDF document, email or analytical data. In the insurance industry as long-term storage of data is regulated and catastrophe/historical claims data grows the need for technologies, KSI can verify the authenticity of data as a key measure to process valid claims.

FUTURE RESEARCH DIRECTIONS

The Fourth Industrial Revolution is increasingly introducing drastic changes on the expectations of consumers and on the various ways institutions and people relate. New behavioral patterns and tastes are giving rise to the introduction of new technology such as digital that are opening doors to cater for new needs slowly but surely disrupting the existing ways of doing business by enhancing velocity, quality, security and value. These new business platforms are considerably indulging in other emerging breakthroughs such as financial services, a major part of them. Industry 4.0 is rapidly changing the behavioral ways of consumers having access to financial services. The proliferation of the new technology-driven platform in financial services "FinTech" and "InsurTech" are significantly gaining a lot of attention and causing important imbalances but are moving in a more organized setting in the sector.

The rising digitization and the ability to connect implies that cybercrimes are more likely to be rising as well. Block chain will pose security threats and so is quantum computing. Therefore, financial institutions must reconsider their investment opportunities to counteract cyber threats. As the velocity of digital innovation flows full swing, institutions need to rethink security strategies of where to emphasize and what digital technology to deploy to be able to survive in this most fierce competitive world as digital is obviously the future. Further the absence of regulatory framework in many developing countries of the African continent make it stringent to perform mobile money transactions, as there are no regulations favouring such services. Mobile money supporters have mentioned Central Bank of Kenya as one of the driving force for M-PESA success unlike other countries like Uganda, Burundi and other African countries where lack of regulation may also damage trust in mobile money to low-income households, thus financial access can be compromised. Crucial to the success of these systems is genuine co-operation between the technology that can accommodate the security of mobile money and policy regulations. Tools to help developers create secure codes, a clearing house to certify that applications provide a baseline of protection and laws to better protect users against fraud are necessary, as is keeping the cost of operation low. Therefore, those mentioned aspects still leave room for future stage of research.

CONCLUSION

The chapter provides a snapshot of the mobile devices security as a measure of financial inclusion for the low-income households in developing markets, especially in Africa. In an era of the Fourth Industrial Revolution, where security risks are emerging in the mobile financial services, more specifically mobile money affecting mostly the low-income households and hampering financial inclusion, advanced security measures to mitigate those threats and breaches, if not to erase them have never been felt as present. The disruptions happening in the industry are immense and will continue at least for the near future as mentioned earlier in the chapter. Several security breaches and threats have been taken into account in this context. The chapter has also given evidence of the current scale of security breaches facing the low-income households when undertaking mobile financial services transactions comprising of mobile banking, payment and micro insurance in Africa and how those threats can be reduced. Finally, the author gives some insightful recommendations relating as to what must be done to deepen mobile security to spur financial innovation and inspire confidence in the low-income households while undertaking mobile money transactions in this era of Fourth Industrial Revolution with an attempt of promoting financial access.

REFERENCES

Agostinho, P. J. F., & Cherry, C. J. (2016). The significance of claims fraud in microinsurance and a statistical method to channel limited fraud identification resources. *South African Actuarial Journal*, *16*(1), 143–181. doi:10.4314aaj.v16i1.6

Alleman, J., & Rappoport, P. (2010). Mobile Money: Implications for Emerging Markets. *Communications & Stratégies*, *79*(3).

Ally, A. (2014). The prospects and legal challenges posed by M-Payments and M-banking Services in Tanzania. *Open University Law Journal*, *5*(1), 49–57.

Amellal, H., Meslouhi, A., Hassouni, Y., & Bazi, M. (2015). A quantum optical firewall based on simple quantum devices. *Quantum Information Process Journal*, *14*(7), 2617–2633. doi:10.100711128-015-1002-4

Anderson, R., Barton, C., Böhme, R., Clayton, R., Levi, M., Moore, T., . . . Van Eeten, M. (2013), Measuring the Cost of Cybercrime. In The Economics of Information Security and Privacy (pp. 265-300). Berlin: Springer.

Arachchilage, N. A. G., & Love, S. (2014). Security awareness of computer users: A phishing threat avoidance perspective. *Computers in Human Behavior*, *38*, 304–312. doi:10.1016/j.chb.2014.05.046

Bhasin, M. (2007). Mitigating cyber threats to banking industry. *The Chartered Accountant*, *55*(10), 1618–1624.

Bold, C., Porteous, D., & Rotman, S. (2012). *Social cash transfers and financial inclusion: Evidence from four countries*. Consultative Group for Assisting the Poor (CGAP).

Canbek, G., Sagiroglu, S., & Baykal, N. (2015). New Comprehensive Taxonomies on Mobile security and Malware Analysis. International. *Journal of Information Security Science*, *5*(4), 106–138.

Choo, K. R. (2011a). The Cyber Threat Landscape: Challenges and Future Research Directions. *Computers & Security*, *30*(8), 719–731. doi:10.1016/j.cose.2011.08.004

Choo, K. R. (2011b). Cyber threats Landscape Faced by Financial and Insurance Industry. *Trends and Issues in Crime and Criminal Justice, 408*, 1–6.

Chummun, B. Z., & Bisschoff, C. A. (2013). Measuring the Business success of Microinsurance in South Africa. *KRE Journal of Social Sciences, 35*(2), 71–79. doi:10.1080/09718923.2013.11893148

Croock, G. (2016). *An Africa Perspective: Cyber Threats, Security and Data Protection.* Retrieved April 11, 2017, from https://www.bdo.co.za/en-za/insights/2016/cyber/an-africa-perspective-cyber-threats-security-and-data-protection

De Sousa, S. (2010). The role of payment systems in reaching the unbanked. *Journal of Payment Strategy & Systems, 4*(2).

Demirguc-Kunt, A., Beck, T., & Honohan, P. (2008). *Finance for All? Policies and Pitfalls in Expanding Access. World Bank Policy Research Report.* Washington, DC: World Bank.

Demirguc-Kunt, A., Klapper, L., Dorothe, S., & Van Oudheusden, P. (2014). *The Global Findex Database 2014: Measuring Financial Inclusion around the World: World Bank Policy Research Working Paper, 7255.* Washington, DC: World Bank.

Dermish, A., Kneiding, C., Leishman, P., & Mas, I. (2012). Branchless and Mobile Banking Solutions for the Poor: A Survey of Literature. *Innovations, 6*(4), 81–98. doi:10.1162/INOV_a_00103

Donner, J., & Tellez, C. A. (2008). Mobile banking and economic development: Linking adoption, impact, and use. *Asian Journal of Communication, 18*(4), 318–332. doi:10.1080/01292980802344190

Donovan, K. (2012). Mobile Money for Financial Inclusion. *International Journal of Communication, 6*, 61–93.

Ehrbeck, T., & Tarazi, M. (2011). *Putting the Bankingnin Branchless Banking: The Case for Interest-Bearing and Insured E-Money Savings Accounts.* The Mobile Financial Services Development Report, 37–42. Washington, DC: World Economic Forum.

Etim, A. S. (2012). The emerging market of Sub-Saharan Africa and technology adoption: Features of users' desire in mobile phones. *International Journal of ICT Research and Development in Africa, 3*(1), 14–16. doi:10.4018/jictrda.2012010102

Fanta, A. B., & Mutsonziwa, K. (2016). *Gender and financial inclusion Analysis of financial inclusion of women in the SADC region, Policy research paper No. 01/2016.* FinMark Trust.

Fanta, A. B., Mutsonziwa, K., Goosen, R., Emanuel, M., & Kettles, N. (2016). *The Role of Mobile Money in Financial Inclusion in the SADC region: Evidence using FinScope Surveys.* Prepared by FinMark Trust December 2016 Policy research paper No. 03/2016. Retrieved April 17, 2017, from http://www.finmark.org.za/wp-content/uploads/2016/12/mobile-money-and-financial-inclusion-in-sadc-1.pdf

Gelb, A., & Decker, C. (2011). *Cash at Your Fingertips: Biometric Technology for Transfers in Developing and Resource-Rich Countries.* Working paper 253, Center for Global Development, Washington, DC.

Gemalto Breach Level Index. (2016). *Data breaches in South Africa.* Retrieved April 03, 2017, from http://www6.gemalto.com/breach-level-index-report-full-2016-press-release

Giusti, J. (2016). *The future of digital finance lies in our mobile phones*. World Economic Forum. Retrieved May 23, 2017, from https://www.weforum.org/agenda/2016/01/the-future-of-digital-finance-lies-in-our-mobile-phones/

Global System for Mobile Association (GSMA). (2014). *The State of Mobile Money Usage – How many people use mobile money globally?* Retrieved, April 02, 2017, from http://www.gsma.com/mobilefordevelopment/

Global System for Mobile Association (GSMA). (2015). *The Mobile Economy 2015*. Retrieved May 17, 2017, from https://www.gsma.com/mobileeconomy/global/2015/

Global System for Mobile Association (GSMA). (2016). *The Mobile Economy Africa 2016*. Retrieved April 17, 2017, from https://www.gsmaintelligence.com/research/?file=3bc21ea879a5b217b64d62fa2 4c55bdf&download

Holmes, G. (2011). Card and mobile payment opportunities: A framework to consider potential winners and losers and a snapshot of the future payments landscape in Africa. *Journal of Payments Strategy and Systems*, *5*(2), 134–142.

Huet, J. M. (2017). *Will banks and telcos converge as money goes mobile*. Retrieved May 23, 2017, from https://www.bearingpoint.com/en-nl/about-us/news-and-media/press-releases/will-banks-and-telcos-converge-as-money-goes-mobile/

Hughes, N., & Lonie, S. (2007). M-PESA: Mobile money for the "Unbanked" and turning cellphones into 24-Hour tellers in Kenya. *Innovations*, *2*(2), 63–81. doi:10.1162/itgg.2007.2.1-2.63

International Monetary Fund. (2014). *Regional Economic Outlook: Sub-Saharan Africa*. International Monetary Fund.

Ismail, T., & Masinge, K. (2011). *Mobile banking: Innovation for the Poor* (Published Masters dissertation). University of Pretoria, South Africa.

Javelin Strategy & Research. (2009). *The State of Mobile Security in Banking and Financial Transactions Report*. Syniverse Technologies.

Jenkins, B. (2008). *Developing Mobile Money Ecosystems*. Washington, DC: International Finance (IFC) and the Havard Kennedy School. Retrieved from http://www.hks.harvard.edu/m-rcbg/CSRI/publications/report_30_MOBILEMONEY.pdf

Kasseeah, H., & Tandrayen-Ragoobur, V. (2012). Mobile Money in an Emerging Small Island Economy. *ARPN Journal of Science and Technology, 2*(5).

Kumbla, S. (2016). *The Big Data Effect on the Insurance Industry*. Retrieved April 07, 2017, from http://www.cuelogic.com/blog/big-data-effect-on-the-insurance-industry/

Lagazio, M., Sherif, N., & Cushman, M. (2014). A multi-level approach to understanding the impact of cybercrime on the financial sector. *Computers & Security*, *1*(1), 32.

Leavitt, N. (2011). *Mobile Security: Finally a Serious Problem*. Leavitt Communication Technologies.

Lee, S. H., Levendis, J., & Gutierrez, L. (2012). Telecommunications and economic growth: An empirical analysis of sub-Saharan Africa. *Applied Economics, 44*(4), 461–469. doi:10.1080/00036846.2010.508730

Lo, H.L., & Preskill, J. (2007). Security of quantum key distribution using weak coherent states with non-random phases. *Quant. Inf. Comp., 7*(58).

Macharia, K. (2011). *Fraudsters eye mobile money*. Retrieved April 23, 2017, from http://www.itweb. co.za/index.php?option=com_content&view=article&id=41727

Manzoor, A. (2014). Protecting Customers Online: Response from Banks. *International Journal of Science and Applied Information Technology, 3*(1), 1–7.

Martini, B., & Choo, K. R. (2013). Cloud Storage Forensics: Own Cloud as a Case Study. *Digital Investigation, 10*(4), 287–299. doi:10.1016/j.diin.2013.08.005

Mas, I. (2010). Savings for the Poor: Banking on Mobile Phones. *World Economy, 11*(4).

Mas, I. (2012). Transforming Access to Finance in Developing Countries through Mobile Phones: Creating an Enabling Policy, Framework. *Banking & Finance Law Review, 27*(2), 285–298.

Mas, I., & Radcliffe, D. (2010). *Mobile Payments Go Viral: M-PESA in Kenya*. Retrieved March 26, 2017 from Washington: http://ssrn.com/abstract=1593388

Mas, I., & Radcliffe, D. (2011). Scaling Mobile Money. *Journal of Payment Strategy & Systems, 5*(3), 298–315.

McAfee. (2013). *Mobile Security: McAfee Consumer Trends Report*. Retrieved April 25, 2017, from, http://www.mcafee.com/us/resources/reports/rpmobile- security-consumer-trends.pdf

Morawczynski, O. (2009). Exploring the usage and impact of "transformational" mobile financial services: The case of M-PESA in Kenya. *Journal of Eastern African Studies: the Journal of the British Institute in Eastern Africa, 3*(3), 509–525. doi:10.1080/17531050903273768

Mori, T. (2016). Financial technology: Blockchain and Securities Settlement. *Journal of Securities Operations & Custody, 8*(3).

National Treasury of South Africa. (2011). *The South African Microinsurance Regulatory Framework*. Retrieved April 13, 2017, from microinsurance@treasury.gov.za

Nordin, K., & Bowman, N. (2016). *Big data for small policies*. Retrieved April 19, 2017, from http:// www.i2ifacility.org/updates/blogs/2

Olaka, H. (2017). *Bank fraudsters focus on customer identity theft: Kenya Bankers Association*. Retrieved April 21, 2017, from https://www.capitalfm.co.ke/business/2017/05/bank-fraudsters-focus-customer-identity-theft-kba/

Oluwatayo, I. (2013). Banking the unbanked in rural Southwest Nigeria: Showcasing mobile phones as mobile banks among farming household. *Journal of Financial Services Marketing, 18*(1), 65–73. doi:10.1057/fsm.2013.2

Ouma, S., Odongo, M., & Were, M. (2017). Mobile financial services and financial inclusion: Is it a boon for savings mobilization? *Review of Development Finance, 7*(1), 29–35. doi:10.1016/j.rdf.2017.01.001

Prashad, P., Saunders, D., & Dalal, A. (2013). Mobile Phones and Microinsurance. Geneva: Microinsurance paper no.26, Geneva, International Labour Organization (ILO).

PriceWaterhouseCoopers. (2016). *Cyber Security.* Retrieved April 17, 2017, from https://www.pwc.com/gx/en/economic-crime-survey/pdf/GlobalEconomyCrimeSurvey 2016.pdf

Quick, D., & Choo, K. R. (2013c). Dropbox Analysis: Data Remnants on User Machines. *Digital Investigation, 10*(1), 3–18. doi:10.1016/j.diin.2013.02.003

Raghavan, A. R., & Parthiban, L. (2014). The effect of cybercrime on a Bank's finances. *International Journal of Current Research and Academic Review, 2*(2), 173–178.

Reaves, B., Scaife, N., Bates, A., Traynor, P., & Butler, K. R. B. (2015). *Mobile Problems: Analysis of Branchless Banking Application in the Developing World.* USENIX Security.

Report, S. C. (2016). *Africa Cyber security Report 2016.* Retrieved April 15, 2017, from http://www.serianu.com/downloads/AfricaCyberSecurityReport2016.pdf

Schwab, K. (2017). *The Fourth Industrial Revolution.* World Economic Forum (WEF), Davos.

Smit, H., Denoon-Steevens, C., & Esser, A. (2017). *The role of InsurTech in microinsurance: How is InsurTech addressing five challenges in microinsurance? Focus Notes. Centre for Financial Regulation and Inclusion.* CENFRI.

Stokkel, M., & Smulders, A. (2013). Cybersecurity: hoe wordt het behapbaar? *Keynotes,* 42 – 26.

Stuart, G., & Cohen, M. (2011). *Cash-In, Cash-Out: The Role of M-PESA in the Lives of Low-Income People.* Financial Services Assessment.

Suri, T., & Jack, B. (2011). *Risk Sharing and Transaction Costs: Evidence from Kenya's Mobile Money Revolution.* Working paper. Massachusetts Institute of Technology and Georgetown University. Retrieved April 19, 2017, from Washington: http://www.mit.edu/~tavneet/Jack_Suri.pdf

Symantec. (2016). *Cyber resilience.* Retrieved April 23, 2017, from https://www.symantec.com/page.jsp?id=cyber-resilience

Technologies, I. (2009). *Accessing the Unbanked: Branchless Banking in Africa, Delivering a secure and cost-effective solution to gain new customers.* iVeri White Paper.

Tellez, C., & Zetterli, P. (2014). *The Emerging Global Landscape of Mobile Microinsurance, CGAP.* Washington, DC: World Bank.

West, D. M., Villasenor, J., & Lewis, R. (2016). *Bridging the financial gender gap.* Retrieved April 16, 2017, from https://www.brookings.edu/blog/techtank/2016/04/01/bridging-the-financial-inclusion-gender-gap/

World Bank. (2014). *Global Economic Prospects: Coping with Policy Normalization in High-Income Countries*. Retrieved May 21, 2017, from Washington: http://documents.worldbank.org/curated/en/152891468168580041/Global-economic-prospects-January-2014-coping-with-policy-normalization-in-high-income-countries

World Economic Forum. (2016). *The Global Risks Report 2016*. Retrieved March, 15, 2017, from Switzerland: http://www3.weforum.org/docs/Media/TheGlobalRisksReport2016.pdf

KEY TERMS AND DEFINITIONS

Big Data: Large complex data sets that can be analyzed on a computer to inform patterns, trends, and associations, especially relating to human behavior and interactions.

Cyber Security: Measures that an institution uses to protect its information and data systems.

Financial Inclusion: The provision of financial services to the financial excluded at an affordable cost.

Fintech: Technology that converge financial services and digitization.

InsurTech: Insurance technology that deals with the inherent challenges of low-income cover.

Low-Income People: Any person who earns less than USD10 per day.

Microinsurance: Any low-income cover accessed by and for the low-income people.

Mobile Financial Services: The ability to deliver access to finance through phone devices.

Mobile Microinsurance: Any low-income insurance that leverages the use of mobile phones.

Mobile Money: The composition of mobile banking and mobile-payment.

Mobile Security: The protection of phones from threats and security breaches.

Mobile Security Threats: Attacks derived from online fraud such as phishing, pharming, malware, carding, or suspicious mobile applications.

Compilation of References

A Survey on Centralised and Distributed Clustering Routing Algorithms for WSNs. (2015). In *IEEE 81st Vehicular Technology Conference*. Glasgow, UK: IEEE. doi:10.1109/VTCSpring.2015.7145650

Aaker, D. (2012). *Building strong brands*. New York: Simon and Schuster.

Aaker, D. A., & Biel, A. (2013). *Brand Equity & Advertising: Advertising's Role in Building Strong Brands*. Hoboken, NJ: Taylor and Francis.

Abebe, D. (2016). Cyberwar, international politics, and institutional design. *The University of Chicago Law Review. University of Chicago. Law School*, *83*(1), 1–22.

Abraham, S., & Chengalur-Smith, I. (2010). An overview of social engineering malware: Trends, tactics, and implications. *Technology in Society*, *32*(3), 183–196. doi:10.1016/j.techsoc.2010.07.001

Abrams, M., & Weiss, J. (2008, July 23). *Malicious Control System Cyber Security Attack Case Study - Maroochy Water Services, Australia*. National Institute of Standards and Technology. Retrieved 30 December 2010 from http://csrc.nist.gov/groups/SMA/fisma/ics/documents/Maroochy-Water-Services-Case-Study_report.pdf

Access_Partnership. (2017). *Delivering the fourth industrial revolution: The role of government*. Retrieved from Washington, DC: Author.

Achcar, G. (2015). *Clash of Barbarisms: The Making of the New World Disorder*. Abingdon, UK: Routledge.

Adebayo, A. O. (2012). A foundation for breach data analysis. *Journal of Information Engineering and Applications*, *2*(4), 17–23.

Adeniran, & Adetayo, O. (2016). Impacts of the fourth industrial revolution on the transportation in the development nations. *International Educational Scientific Research Journal*, 56-60.

Advisory ICSA-15-125-01B: Hospira LifeCare PCA Infusion System Vulnerabilities (Update B) . (2015, June 10). Industrial Control Systems Cyber Emergency Response Team (ICS-CERT). Retrieved from: https://ics-cert.us-cert.gov/advisories/ICSA-15-125-01B

African National Congress. (2017). *5th National Policy Conference*. Johannesburg: African National Congress.

African News Agency. (2015). New cybersecurity hub to protect SA. *Independent Media*. Retrieved from http://www.iol.co.za/news/politics/new-cybersecurity-hub-to-protect-sa-1.1938479

Agostinho, P. J. F., & Cherry, C. J. (2016). The significance of claims fraud in microinsurance and a statistical method to channel limited fraud identification resources. *South African Actuarial Journal*, *16*(1), 143–181. doi:10.4314aaj.v16i1.6

Ahmad, A., Maynard, S., & Park, S. (2014). Information security strategies: Towards an organizational multi-strategy perspective. *Journal of Intelligent Manufacturing*, 25(2), 357–370. doi:10.100710845-012-0683-0

Ahmed, M. S., Al-Shaer, E., Taibah, M., & Khan, L. (2011). Objective risk evaluation for automated security management. *Journal of Network and Systems Management*, 19(3), 343–366. doi:10.100710922-010-9177-6

Ahnf, J. (2011). Cyberemotions – Collective Emotions in Cyberspace. *Procedia Computer Science*. DOI: 10.1016/j.procs.2011.09.076

AIDS trojan disk. (n.d.). Retrieved from the Virus Information wiki: http://virus.wikia.com/wiki/AIDS_trojan_disk

Ajam, K. (2015). Cybersecurity Hub launched at CSIR. *Independent Media*. Retrieved from http://www.iol.co.za/saturday-star/cybersecurity-hub-launched-at-csir-1938670

Al-Ahmad, W., & Mohammad, B. (2012). Can A Single Security Framework Address Information Security Risks Adequately? *International Journal of Digital Information and Wireless Communications*, 2(3), 222–230.

Al-Ahmad, W., & Mohammad, B. (2013). Addressing information security risks by adopting standards. *International Journal of Information Security Science*, 2(2), 28–43.

Alberts, D. S., & Hayes, R. E. (2003). *Power to the Edge: Command and Control in the Information Age*. CCRP. Retrieved 18 June 2017 from http://www.dodccrp.org/files/Alberts_Power.pdf

Alcorta, L. (2017). *Manufacturing the Future: the 4th Industrial Revolution and the 2030 Development Agenda*. Retrieved from http://unctad.org/meetings/es/Presentation/cstd2016_p23_Alcorta_en.pdf

Alexandrou, A. (2016). *A security risk perception model for the adoption of mobile devices in the healthcare industry*. Pace University.

Alfreds, D. (2012). *Hackers hit SA web users*. Retrieved from http://www.news24.com/SciTech/News/Hackers-hit-SA-web-users-20120702

Alfreds, D. (2013). *News 24. BYOD security threats to SA firms*. Retrieved April 2, 2016, from http://www.news24.com

Alhomidi, M., & Reed, M. (2013). Risk assessment and analysis through population-based attack graph modelling. In *Internet Security (WorldCIS), 2013 World Congress on* (pp. 19–24). Academic Press. 10.1109/WorldCIS.2013.6751011

Alhumrani, S. A., & Kar, J. (2016). Cryptographic Protocols for Secure Cloud Computing. *International Journal of Security and Its Applications*, 10(2), 301–310. doi:10.14257/ijsia.2016.10.2.27

Alleman, J., & Rappoport, P. (2010). Mobile Money: Implications for Emerging Markets. *Communications & Stratégies*, 79(3).

Allen, M. (2006). *Social engineering: A means to violate a computer system*. SANS Institute, InfoSec Reading Room. Retrieved from: http://www.sans.org/reading-room/whitepapers/engineering/social-engineering-means-

Allen, P. D., & Demehak, C. C. (2003, March – April). The Palestinian –Israeli cyberwar. *Military Review*, 52–59.

Allison, P. R. (2016, July 15). What does a bomb disposal robot actually do? *BBC*. Retrieved 7 June 2017 from http://www.bbc.com/future/story/20160714-what-does-a-bomb-disposal-robot-actually-do

Ally, A. (2014). The prospects and legal challenges posed by M-Payments and M-banking Services in Tanzania. *Open University Law Journal*, 5(1), 49–57.

Alotaibi, K. H. (2015). Threat in Cloud- Denial of Service (DoS) and Distributed Denial of Service (DDoS) Attack, and Security Measures. *Journal of Emerging Trends in Computing and Information Sciences*, 6(5), 241–244.

Altheide, D. (2006). *Terrorist and the Politics of Fear*. Oxford, UK: Altamira Press.

Altheide, D. (2009). Moral Panic, from sociological concept to public discourse. *Crime, Media, Culture, 5*(1), 79–99. doi:10.1177/1741659008102063

Altheide, D. (2017). *The Politics of Terrorism*. New York: Rowman and Littlefield.

Amellal, H., Meslouhi, A., Hassouni, Y., & Bazi, M. (2015). A quantum optical firewall based on simple quantum devices. *Quantum Information Process Journal, 14*(7), 2617–2633. doi:10.100711128-015-1002-4

Amer & Hamilton. (2010). Intrusion detection systems (IDS) taxonomy-a short review. *Defense Cyber Security, 13*(2).

Anderson, R., Barton, C., Böhme, R., Clayton, R., Levi, M., Moore, T., . . . Van Eeten, M. (2013), Measuring the Cost of Cybercrime. In The Economics of Information Security and Privacy (pp. 265-300). Berlin: Springer.

Andre, J. (2017). *What is the Difference between a SOC and a CSIRT?* Retrieved from https://blog.komand.com/difference-between-a-soc-and-a-csirt

Anitha, A., Girish, P., & Savera, K. (2016). Cyber defense using artificial intelligence. *International Journal of Pharmacy and Technology*, 25352-25357.

Anshul. (2017, June 14). This $5 Device Can Hack Password-Protected Computers In Just 30 Seconds. *Hacking-News & Tutorials*. Retrieved 13 June 2017 from http://hackingnewstutorials.com/this-5-device-can-hack-password/

Antonio, B., & Forti, S. (2017). QoS-aware Deployment of IoT Applications Through the Fog. *IEEE Internet of Things Journal.* doi:10.1109/JIOT.2017.2701408

Apostu, A., Puican, F., Ularu, G., Suciu, G., & Todoran, G. (2014). New Classes of Applications in the Cloud. Evaluating Advantages and Disadvantages of Cloud Computing for Telemetry Applications. *Database System Journal, 5*(1), 3–14.

Applegate, S. D. (2009). Social Engineering: Hacking the Wetware! *Information Security Journal: A Global Perspective, 18*(1), 40-46.

AppliedTrust. (2008). *Every company needs to have a security program*. Retrieved from https://www.appliedtrust.com/resources/security/every-company-needs-to-have-a-security-program

AppliedTrust. (2008). *Every company needs to have a security program*. Retrieved from https://www.appliedtrust.com/sites/default/files/assets/resources/every-company-needs-a-security-program.pdf

Arachchilage, N. A. G., & Love, S. (2014). Security awareness of computer users: A phishing threat avoidance perspective. *Computers in Human Behavior, 38*, 304–312. doi:10.1016/j.chb.2014.05.046

Arif, M., & Shakeel, H. (2015). Virtualization Security: Analysis and Open Challenges. *International Journal of Hybrid Information Technology, 8*(2), 237–246. doi:10.14257/ijhit.2015.8.2.22

Arkian, H. R., Diyanat, A., & Pourkhalili, A. (2017). MIST: Fog-based data analytics scheme with cost-efficient resource provisioning for IoT crowdsensing applications. *Journal of Network and Computer Applications, 82*, 152–165. doi:10.1016/j.jnca.2017.01.012

Årnes, A., Sallhammar, K., Haslum, K., Brekne, T., Moe, M. E. G., & Knapskog, S. J. (2005). Real-time risk assessment with network sensors and intrusion detection systems. In *International Conference on Computational and Information Science* (pp. 388–397). Academic Press.

Årnes, A., Valeur, F., Vigna, G., & Kemmerer, R. (2006). Using Hidden Markov Models to Evaluate the Risks of Intrusions. *Recent Advances in Intrusion Detection*, 145–164. doi:10.1007/11856214_8

Arquilla, J., & Ronfeldt, D. (1993, Spring). Cyberwar Is Coming! *Comparative Strategy, 12*(2), 141–165. doi:10.1080/01495939308402915

Aruba Network. (2013). *Conquering today's bring your own device challenges: A framework for successful BYOD initiatives.* Aruba White Paper.

Ashford, W. (2012). *UK to expand cyber info-sharing hub after initial success.* Retrieved from ComputerWeekly.com website: http://www.computerweekly.com/news/2240149725/UK-to-expand-cyber-info-sharing-hub-after-initial-success-says-minister

Ashford, W. (2015, April 10). French TV5Monde network cyber-attack the latest in destructive trend in system intrusions. *Computer Weekly.* Retrieved 15 June 2017 from http://www.computerweekly.com/news/4500244107/French-TV5Monde-network-cyber-attack-the-latest-in-destructive-trend-in-system-intrusions

Ashford, W. (2017). *Human-machine teaming key to cyber defence, says Intel Security.* Retrieved from http://www.computerweekly.com/ehandbook/Focus-Securing-for-the-future

Ashktorab, V., & Taghizadeh, S. R. (2012). Security Threats and Countermeasures in Cloud Computing. *International Journal of Application or Innovation in Engineering & Management, 1*(2), 234–245.

Astani, M., Ready, K., & Tessema, M. (2013). BYOD Issues and strategies in organizations. *Issues in Information Systems, 14*(2).

Auditor, G. S. A. (2015). *About Us.* Retrieved January 29, 2015, from http://www.agsa.co.za/Home.aspx

Auditor, G. S. A. (2013). *PFMA 2012-2013 Consolidated General Report.* Pretoria: Auditor General South Africa.

Auditor, G. S. A. (2014). *PFMA 2013-2014 Consolidated General Report.* Pretoria: Auditor General South Africa.

Auditor, G. S. A. (2017). *Consolidated general report on the national and provincial audit outcomes 2015-16.* Pretoria: Auditor General South Africa.

Augé, M. (2002). *Diario de Guerra: el mundo después del 11 de Septiembre.* Barcelona: Gedisa.

Aula, P. (2010). Social media, reputation risk and ambient publicity management. *Strategy and Leadership, 38*(6), 43–49. doi:10.1108/10878571011088069

Australian Crime Commission. (2015). *National Organised Crime Response Plan 2015-18.* Author.

Australian Signals Directorate. (2015). *Australian Government Information Security Manual.* Australian Signals Directorate. Retrieved from http://www.asd.gov.au/publications/Information_Security_Manual_2015_Exec_Companion.pdf

Awan, M. S. K., Burnap, P., & Rana, O. (2016). Identifying cyber risk hotspots: A framework for measuring temporal variance in computer network risk. *Computers & Security, 57,* 31–46. doi:10.1016/j.cose.2015.11.003

Backe, A., & Lindén, H. (2015). *Cloud computing security: A systematic review.* Uppsala University.

Bada, M., & Sasse, A. (2014). *Cyber Security Awareness Campaigns: Why do they fail to change behaviour?* Oxford, UK: Global Cyber Security Capacity Centre, University of Oxford.

Bailey, T., Kaplan, J., & Rezek, C. (2014). *Why senior leaders are the front line against cyberattacks.* Retrieved from http://www.mckinsey.com/insights/business_technology/why_senior_leaders_are_the_front_line_against_cyberattacks

Bakshi, A., & Yogesh, B. (2010). Securing cloud from DDOS Attacks using Intrusion Detection System in virtual machine. *ICCSN '10 Proceedings of the 2010 Second International Conference on Communication Software and Networks,* 260-264.

Balachandran, A., Voelker, G. M., & Bahl, P. (2005). Wireless hotspots: Current challenges and future directions. *Mobile Networks and Applications, 10*(3), 265–274. doi:10.100711036-005-6421-5

Baldassari, P., & Roux, J. (2017). Industry 4.0: Preparing for the Future of Work. *People & Strategy, 40*(3), 20–23.

Barlette & Fomin. (2010). The Adoption of Information Security Management Standards. *Information Resources Management: Concepts, Methodologies, Tools and Applications: Concepts, Methodologies, Tools and Applications*, 69.

Bar-Magen, N. J. (2013). *XMPP Distributed Topology as a Potential Solution for Fog Computing*. MESH 2013 The Sixth International Conference on Advances in Mesh Networks.

Barro, R. (1991). Economic Growth in a cross section countries. *The Quarterly Journal of Economics, 106*(2), 407–443. doi:10.2307/2937943

Barth, B. (2017). *Pro-ISIS hacker group defaces state, local government websites*. Retrieved from https://www.scmagazine.com/pro-isis-hacker-group-defaces-state-local-government-websites/article/671041/

Bartholomew, D. (2009). *Cloud rains opportunities for software developers*. Retrieved from http://career-resources.dice.com/articles/content/entry/cloud_rains_opportunities_for_software

Bates, J. (1990, January). Trojan Horse: AIDS Information Introductory Diskette Version 2.0. *Virus Bulletin*, 3-6.

Bathon, J. (2013, Nov. 5). How little data breaches cause big problems for schools. *Legal Issues in IT*, 1 – 5.

Baudrillard, J. (2006). Virtuality and Events: the hell of power. *Baudrillard Studies, 3*(2). Available at http://www.ubishops.ca/BaudrillardStudies/

Baudrillard, J. (1995a). *The systems of the objects*. Siglo XXI.

Baudrillard, J. (1995b). *The Gulf War Did Not Take Place*. Sydney: Power Publications.

Bauer, J. M., & van Eeten, M. J. G. (2009). Cybersecurity: Stakeholder incentives, externalities, and policy options. *Telecommunications Policy, 33*(10), 706–719. doi:10.1016/j.telpol.2009.09.001

Bauman, Z., & Lyon, D. (2013). *Liquid surveillance: A conversation*. New York: John Wiley & Sons.

Baxter, P., & Jack, S. (2008). Qualitative case study methodologies: Study design and implementation for novice researchers. *Qualitative Report, 13*(1), 544–559.

BBC. (2013). *Police warning after drug traffickers' cyber-attack*. Retrieved Jan 23, 2016, from http://www.bbc.co.uk/news/world-europe-24539417

Beaver, K. (2015). *The Importance of a Security Culture Across the Organization*. Retrieved from https://securityintelligence.com/the-importance-of-a-security-culture-across-the-organization/

Behavior change communication. (2017, July 17). In *Wikipedia*. Retrieved from https://en.wikipedia.org/wiki/Behavior_change_communication#cite_note-:0-5

Behnia, A., Rashid, R. A., & Chaudhry, J. A. (2012). A survey of information security risk analysis methods. *SmartCR, 2*(1), 79–94.

Bejarano, J. A. (1983). Campesinado, luchas agrarias e historia social: Notas para un balance historiográfico. *Anuario Colombiano de Historia Social y de la Cultura*, (11): 251–304.

Bello, A., Armarego, J., & Murray, D. (2015). Bring your own device organizational information security and privacy. *Journal of Engineering and Applied Sciences (Asian Research Publishing Network), 10*(3), 1279–1287.

Bellovin, S. M. (2013, May/June). Military cybersomethings. *IEEE Security and Privacy, 11*(3), 88. doi:10.1109/MSP.2013.63

Bendovschi, A. (2015). Cyber-Attacks – Trends, Patterns and Security Countermeasures. *Procedia Economics and Finance, 28*, 24–31. doi:10.1016/S2212-5671(15)01077-1

Bendrath, R. (2001). The cyberwar debate: Perception and politics in the U.S. critical infrastructure protection. *Information & Security, 7*, 80–103.

Benini, M., & Sicari, S. (2008). Risk assessment in practice: A real case study. *Computer Communications, 31*(15), 3691–3699. doi:10.1016/j.comcom.2008.07.001

Beresford, D. (2011). *Exploiting Siemens Simatic S7 PLCs*. Retrieved Jun 21, 2017, from media.blackhat: https://media.blackhat.com/bh-us-11/Beresford/BH_US11_Beresford_S7_PLCs_WP.pdf

Berger, S. (2015, 13 August). Mexico Drug Trafficking: Drone Carries 28 Pounds of Heroin across Border to US. *International Business Times*. Retrieved 6 June 2017 from http://www.ibtimes.com/mexico-drug-trafficking-drone-carries-28-pounds-heroin-across-border-us-2051941

Bernstein, D., Ebrahim, W., & Cibane, S. (2015). *SA's cybersecurity bill raises big concerns*. Retrieved from http://www.techcentral.co.za/sas-cybersecurity-bill-raises-big-concerns/60695/

Besser, L., Sturmer, J., & Sveen, B. (2016). *Government computer networks breached in cyber attacks as experts warn of espionage threat*. Retrieved from http://www.abc.net.au/news/2016-08-29/chinese-hackers-behind-defence-austrade-security-breaches/7790166

Bezuidenhout, M., Mouton, F., & Venter, H. S. (2010). Social engineering attack detection model: SEADM. In Information Security for South Africa (ISSA), (pp. 1-8). IEEE.

Bhadauria, R., & Sanyal, S. (2012). Survey on Security Issues in Cloud Computing and Associated Mitigation Techniques. *International Journal of Computers and Applications, 47*(18), 47–66. doi:10.5120/7292-0578

Bhasin, M. (2007). Mitigating cyber threats to banking industry. *The Chartered Accountant, 55*(10), 1618–1624.

Bigger, J. (2015). *5 Benefits of Cloud Computing for the Financial Services Industry*. Retrieved from https://blog.marconet.com/blog/5-benefits-of-cloud-computing-for-the-financial-services-industry

Bilal, M., & Sankar, G. (2011). Trust & Security issues in Mobile banking and its effect on Customers. *School of Computing. Blekinge Institute of Technology, SE-371*, 79.

Bishop, M. (2000). Education in information security. *IEEE Concurrency, 8*(4), 4–8. doi:10.1109/4434.895087

Bishop, M. (2003). *Computer Security – Art and Science*. Boston, MA: Pearson Education.

Bishop, M., Bhumiratana, B., Crawford, R., & Levitt, K. (2004). How to sanitize data. *Proceedings of the 13th IEEE International Workshops on Enabling Technologies: Infrastructure for Collaborative Enterprises.*

Bisson, D. (2017, April 19). The Hajime IoT worm fights the Mirai botnet for control of your devices. *Graham Cluley*. Retrieved 20 April 2017 from https://www.grahamcluley.com/hajime-iot-worm-fights-mirai-botnet-control-devices/

Blank, R. M., & Gallagher, P. D. (2012). *Guide for Conducting Risk Assessments*. NIST Special Publication.

Bloem, J., Doorn, M., Duivestein, S., Excoffier, D., Maas, R., & Ommeren, E. (2014). *The Fourth Industrial Revolution: Things to tighten the link between IT and OT*. Retrieved from Online: https://www.fr.sogeti.com/globalassets/global/downloads/reports/vint-research-3-the-fourth-industrial-revolution

Bloem, J., Van Doorn, M., Duivestein, S., Excoffier, D., Maas, R., & Van Ommeren, E. (2014). *The Fourth Industrial Revolution*. Things Tighten.

Blom, K. (2017). *FinTech - new opportunities (and risks)*. Retrieved from http://www.itweb.co.za/index.php?option=com_content&view=article&id=162426

Blunden, B. (2010). Manufactured consent and cyberwar. In *Proceedings of Lockdown 2010*. University of Wisconsin-Madison. Retrieved from http://www.belowgotham.com/LD-2010-WP.pdf

BMC. (2017). *ITIL Information Security Management*. Retrieved from http://www.bmcsoftware.co.za/guides/itil-information-security-management.html

Boddington, R. (2015, March 17). *The Challenges of digital forensics*. Retrieved 22 June 2017from https://phys.org/news/2015-03-digital-forensics.html

Bodenheimer, D. Z. (2012). Cyberwarfare in the Stuxnet age: Can cannonball law keep pace with the digital battlefield? *The SciTech Lawyer, 8*(3), 1–4.

Bogatin, D. (2006). *Google CEO's new paradigm: Cloud computing and advertising go hand-in-hand*. Retrieved from http://www.zdnet.com/blog/micro-markets/google-ceos-new-paradigmcloud-computing-and-advertising-go-hand-inhand/369

Bold, C., Porteous, D., & Rotman, S. (2012). *Social cash transfers and financial inclusion: Evidence from four countries*. Consultative Group for Assisting the Poor (CGAP).

Bollo, J. (2017). *Mobile Forensics Must Keep Up with the Times*. Retrieved 22 June 2017 from https://www.forensicmag.com/article/2017/06/mobile-forensics-must-keep-times

Bolton, D. (2015, December 6). Terrorists could use Drones to Attack Planes and Spread Propaganda. *The Independent*. Retrieved 7 May 2017 from http://www.independent.co.uk/life-style/gadgets-and-tech/news/drone-terrorist-attack-isis-propaganda-colin-smith-a6762411.html

Booysen, J. (2015). *Cybercrime cost SA R5bn in 2014*. Retrieved from IOL Business website: http://www.iol.co.za/business/news/cybercrime-cost-sa-r5bn-in-2014-1.1810007

Booysen, J. (2017, May 19). Most vulnerable remain at risk of cyber-attack. *Business Report*, p. 4.

Borah, C. K. (2015). *Cyber war: the next threat to national security and what to do about it? by Richard A. Clarke and Robert K. Knake*. Taylor & Francis.

Botzakis, S. (2013). Reviewed works: Six word memoirs. *Journal of Adolescent & Adult Literacy, 57*(2), 162 – 163.

Bowden, M. (2011). *Worm: The First Digital World War*. New York: Atlantic Monthly Press.

Bowen, B. M., Salem, M. B., Hershkop, S., Keromytis, A. D., & Stolfo, S. (2009). Designing host and network sensors to mitigate the insider threat. *IEEE Security and Privacy, 7*(6), 22–29. doi:10.1109/MSP.2009.109

Bowen, T., Segal, M., Shanbhag, T., & Uppuluri, P. (2000). Building survivable systems: an integrated approach based on intrusion detection and damage containment. *Proceedings of the DARPA Information Survivability Conference and Exposition*, 84-99.

Bowne, M. (2015, August 18). IOT VS. IIOT. *Profinet.com*. Retrieved 13 June 2017 from http://us.profinet.com/iot-vs-iiot/

Boyer, S., Dain, O., & Cunningham, R. (2005). Stellar: A fusion system for scenario construction and security risk assessment. In *Information Assurance, 2005. Proceedings. Third IEEE International Workshop on* (pp. 105–116). IEEE. 10.1109/IWIA.2005.16

Boyles, Smith, & Madden. (2012). Privacy and data management on mobile devices. *Pew Internet & American Life Project, 4.*

Brakus, J., Schmitt, B., & Zarantonello, L. (2009). Brand experience: What is it? How is it measured? Does it affect loyalty? *Journal of Marketing, 73*(3), 52–68. doi:10.1509/jmkg.73.3.52

Brand, K., & Boonen, H. (2007). *IT Governance based on CobiT® 4.1-A Management Guide.* Van Haren.

Brazzoli, M. S. (2007). Future Prospects of Information Warfare and Particularly Psychological Operations. In L. le Roux (Ed.), South African Army Vision 2020 (pp. 217-232). Pretoria: Institute for Security Studies.

Brewer, R. (2016). Ransomware attacks: Detection. Prevention and cure. *Network Security, 2016*(9), 5–9. doi:10.1016/S1353-4858(16)30086-1

British Broadcasting Corporation. (2017). *Rebooting industry for the digital age.* Retrieved from http://www.bbc.com/future/bespoke/specials/connected-world/industry-4-0.html

Broderick, J. S. (2006). ISMS, security standards and security regulations. *Information Security Technical Report, 11*(1), 26–31. doi:10.1016/j.istr.2005.12.001

Brodin, M. (2016). *BYOD vs. CYOD: What is the difference?* Paper presented at the 9th IADIS International Conference Information Systems 2016.

Bronk, C. (2013). Between War & Peace: Considering the Statecraft of Cyberspace. In J. Krüger, B. Nickolay, & S. Gaycken (Eds.), *The Secure Information Society.* London: Springer. doi:10.1007/978-1-4471-4763-3_1

Brook, C. (2017, May 4). Many Commercial Drones 'Insecure by Design'. *ThreatPost.* Retrieved 8 May 2017 from https://threatpost.com/many-commercial-drones-insecure-by-design/125420/

Broomhead, S. (2013). *Gartner says BYOD is disruptive.* Retrieved February 23, 2016, from http://www.ehna.acfee.org/read/art-54e605c41el4a

Brose, R. (2015). Cyberwar, netwar, and the future of cyberdefense. *Proceedings of the 2015 7th International Conference on Cyber Conflict: Architectures in Cyberspace.* Retrieved from https://www.youtube.com/watch?v=0vWG62o_XaA&ab_channel=CareersatBurlington

Broughton, A., Higgins, T., Hicks, B., & Cox, A. (2009). Workplaces and social networking-The implications for employment relations. Institute for Employment Studies, Brighton.

Brown, A. (2011). *The Grey Line: Modern Corporate Espionage and Counterintelligence.* Amur Strategic Research Group.

Bruks, M., Zeithmal, V., & Naylar, G. (2000). Price and brand name as indicators of quality dimensions for consumer durable. *Journal of the Academy of Marketing Science, 28*(3), 359–374. doi:10.1177/0092070300283005

Bryce, H. (2017, May 18). *The Internet of Things Will Be Even More Vulnerable to Cyber Attacks.* London: Chatham House. Retrieved 13 June 2017 from https://www.chathamhouse.org/expert/comment/internet-things-will-be-even-more-vulnerable-cyber-attacks

Buecker, A., Borrett, M., Lorenz, C., & Powers, C. (2010). *Introducing the ibm security framework and ibm security blueprint to realize business-driven security.* International Technical Support Organization.

Bulgurcu, B., Cavusoglu, H., & Benbasat, I. (2010). Information security policy compliance: An empirical study of rationality-based beliefs and information security awareness. *Management Information Systems Quarterly, 34*(3), 523–548. doi:10.2307/25750690

Bullée, J. H., Montoya, L., Pieters, W., Junger, M., & Hartel, P. H. (2015). The persuasion and security awareness experiment: Reducing the success of social engineering attacks. *Journal of Experimental Criminology, 11*(1), 97–115. doi:10.100711292-014-9222-7

Buller, D. B., & Burgoon, J. K. (1996). Interpersonal deception theory. *Communication Theory, 6*(3), 203–242. doi:10.1111/j.1468-2885.1996.tb00127.x

Burgess, M. (2017, January 23). This ridiculous drone gun can shoot down UAVs from 2km away. *Wired*. Retrieved 6 June 2017 from http://www.wired.co.uk/article/droneshield-dronegun-shoot-drone-uav-sky

Business Continuity Institute. (2017). *BCI Cyber Resilience Report*. Berkshire, UK: Author.

BusinessDictionary. (2017). *Definition of system*. Retrieved from http://www.businessdictionary.com/definition/information-system.html

Buyya, R., Caheiros, R. N., & Son, J. (n.d.). *Software-Defined Cloud Computing: Architectural Elements and Open Challenges*. Department of Computing and Information Systems, The University of Melbourne, Australia. Retrieved from http://www.cloudbus.org/papers/SDCC-Keynote2014.pdf

Caelli & Liu. (2017). *Cybersecurity education at formal university level: An Australian perspective*. Academic Press.

Calder, A., & Watkins, S. G. (2010). *Information Security Risk Management for ISO27001/ISO27002*. Retrieved from https://books.google.com/books?hl=es&lr=&id=8Ffa1dOFgO4C&pgis=1

Campbell, A. (2010). *These issues need to be resolved before Cloud computing becomes ubiquitous*. Retrieved from https://www.openforum.com/articles/these-issues-need-to-be-resolvedbefore-cloud-computing-becomesubiquitous-1

Campbell, T. (2016). Information Security Implementation. In *Practical Information Security Management* (pp. 63–70). Springer. doi:10.1007/978-1-4842-1685-9_5

Canbek, G., Sagiroglu, S., & Baykal, N. (2015). New Comprehensive Taxonomies on Mobile security and Malware Analysis. International. *Journal of Information Security Science, 5*(4), 106–138.

Caralli, R. A., Stevens, J. F., Young, L. R., & Wilson, W. R. (2007). *Introducing octave allegro: Improving the information security risk assessment process*. Academic Press.

Casner, S. (2017). *Careful: A User's Guide to our Injury-Prone Minds*. New York: Riverhead Books.

CAT. (2017). *CAT® S60 Smartphone*. Retrieved 14 June 2017 from http://www.catphones.com/en-gb/phones/s60-smartphone

Cautionary tale. (2017, May 31). In *Wikipedia*. Retrieved from https://en.wikipedia.org/wiki/Cautionary_tale

Cavelty, M. D. (2010). The reality and future of cyberwar. *CSS Analysis in Security Policy*. Retrieved from https://pdfs.semanticscholar.org/bbba/7d388cb67e0d2b2ca7d7b2ed60ca2de65b1c.pdf

Cavelty, M. D. (2010). Cyberwar concept, status quo, and limitations. *CSS Analysis in Security Policy, 71*, 1–3.

Centre for the Protection of National Infrastructure, & National Technical Authority for Information Assurance. (2015). *Security Incident Management*. Retrieved from https://www.ncsc.gov.uk/content/files/guidance_files/Security%20Incident%20Management%20%28Good%20Practice%20Guide%2024%29_1.2_0.pdf

Centre for the Protection of National Infrastructure. (2015). *Mitigating Security Risk in the National Infrastructure Supply Chain*. Retrieved Jun 01, 2017, from cpni.gov.uk: https://www.cpni.gov.uk/system/files/documents/8b/d4/Mitigating%20Security%20Risk%20in%20Supply%20Chain.pdf

Centrify. (2013). *TOP 3 Reasons to Give Insiders a Unified Identity*. Retrieved from http://www.centrify.com/downloads/public/centrify-top-three-reasons-to-give-insiders-a-unified-identity.pdf

Chambers, D. (2013). *Social Media and Personal Relationships: Online Intimacies and Networked Friendship*. New York: Palgrave Macmillan. doi:10.1057/9781137314444

Chanda, R. A. J. I. B., & Zaorski, S. T. E. V. E. (2013). Social media usage in the financial services industry: Toward a business-driven compliance approach. *Journal of Taxation and Regulation of Financial Institutions*, 26(5), 5–20.

Chandra, J. V., Challa, N., & Hussain, M. A. (2014). Data and Information Storage Security from Advanced Persistent Attack in Cloud Computing. *International Journal of Applied Engineering Research*, 9(2), 7755–7768.

Chappell, D. (2011). *The Benefits and Risks of Cloud Platforms - A Guide for Business Leaders*. Retrieved from http://www.storm.ie/PublishingImages/Documents/Azure%20for%20Business%20Leaders.pdf

Chen, G. (2010). Research on network security real-time risk assessment model. In *Electronics and Information Engineering (ICEIE), 2010 International Conference On* (Vol. 2, pp. V2--548). ICEIE. 10.1109/ICEIE.2010.5559746

Chen, P. (2016, July 12). Why security in the Internet of Things is different from cybersecurity. *EDN-Europe*. Retrieved 12 July 2016 from http://www.edn-europe.com/blog/why-security-internet-things-different-cybersecurity

Chen, Y., Jensen, C. D., Gray, E., Cahill, V., & Seigneur, J.-M. (2003). *A general risk assessment of security in pervasive computing*. Retrieved from Https://www. Cs. Tcd. Ie/publications/techreports/reports, 3

Chen, C.-M., Chen, Y.-H., Lin, Y.-H., & Sun, H.-M. (2014). Eliminating rouge femtocells based on distance bounding protocol and geographic information. *Expert Systems with Applications*, 41(2), 426–433. doi:10.1016/j.eswa.2013.07.068

Cheng, W., Xu, X., Jia, Y., & Zou, P. (2008). Network Dynamic Risk Assessment Based on the Threat Stream Analysis. In *The Ninth International Conference on Web-Age Information Management* (pp. 532–538). IEEE. 10.1109/WAIM.2008.65

Chen, P., Desmet, L., & Huygens, C. (2014). Lecture Notes in Computer Science: Vol. 8735. *A Study on Advanced Persistent Threats*. Berlin: Springer.

Chen, T. M., & Abu-Nimeh, S. (2011). Lessons from Stuxnet. *Computer*, 44(4), 91–93. doi:10.1109/MC.2011.115

Cheok, A. D., Levy, D., & Karunanayaka, K. (2016). Lovotics: Love and sex with robots. In G.N. Yannakakis (Ed.), Emotion in Games. Springer.

Cherdantseva, Y., Burnap, P., Blyth, A., Eden, P., Jones, K., Soulsby, H., & Stoddart, K. (2016). A review of cyber security risk assessment methods for SCADA systems. *Computers & Security*, 56, 1–27. doi:10.1016/j.cose.2015.09.009

Chih-Han, Y. (2010). *Bilogically-Inspired Control for Self-Adaptive Multiagent Systems* (PhD Thesis). Harvard University.

Chitrey, A., Singh, D., & Singh, V. (2012). A Comprehensive Study of Social Engineering Based Attacks in India to Develop a Conceptual Model. *International Journal of Information and Network Security*, 1(2), 45–53.

Chmiel A, Sienkiewicz J, Thelwall M, Paltoglou G, Buckley K, et al. (2011). Collective Emotions Online and Their Influence on Community Life. *PLoS ONE, 6*(7). doi:10.1371/journal.pone.0022207

Choi, H. R., Kim, H. S., Park, B. J., Park, N.-K., & Lee, S. W. (2003). An ERP approach for container terminal operating systems. *Maritime Policy & Management*, 30(3), 197–210. doi:10.1080/0308883032000089549

Chołda, P., & Jaglarz, P. (2016). Optimization/simulation-based risk mitigation in resilient green communication networks. *Journal of Network and Computer Applications*, 59, 134–157. doi:10.1016/j.jnca.2015.07.009

Chonka, A. X. Y., Zhou, W., & Bonti, A. (2011). Cloud security defence to protect cloud computing against HTTP-DoS and XML-DoS attacks. Elsevier.

Choo, K. R. (2011a). The Cyber Threat Landscape: Challenges and Future Research Directions. *Computers & Security*, *30*(8), 719–731. doi:10.1016/j.cose.2011.08.004

Choo, K. R. (2011b). Cyber threats Landscape Faced by Financial and Insurance Industry. *Trends and Issues in Crime and Criminal Justice*, *408*, 1–6.

Choo, K.-K. R. (2011). Cyber threat landscape faced by financial and insurance industry. *Trends and Issues in Crime and Criminal Justice*, (408): 1.

Chou, T. (2013). Security threats on cloud computing vulnerabilities. *International Journal of Computer Science & Information Technology*, *5*(3), 79–88. doi:10.5121/ijcsit.2013.5306

Christina, A. A. (2015). Proactive Measures on Account Hijacking in Cloud Computing Network. *Asian Journal of Computer Science and Technology*, *4*(2), 31–34.

Chummun, B. Z., & Bisschoff, C. A. (2013). Measuring the Business success of Microinsurance in South Africa. *KRE Journal of Social Sciences*, *35*(2), 71–79. doi:10.1080/09718923.2013.11893148

Chung, M., & Kim, J. (2016). The Internet Information and Technology Research Directions based on the Fourth Industrial Revolution. *TIIS*, *10*(3), 1311–1320.

Chung, M., & Kim, J. (2016). The Internet Information and Technology Research Directions based on the Fourth Industrial Revolution. *Transactions on Internet and Information Systems (Seoul)*, *3*(10), 1311–1320.

Cimbala, S.J. (2011). Nuclear crisis management and 'cyberwar.' *Strategic Studies Quarterly*, 117 – 131.

Cimpanu, C. (2016). *Anonymous hacks and leaks South African Dept of Water Affairs data*. Retrieved from https://www.databreaches.net/anonymous-hacks-and-leaks-south-african-dept-of-water-affairs-data/

Cimpanu, C. (2017, February 14). University DDoSed by Its Own IoT Devices. *Bleeping Computer*. Retrieved 20 February 2017 from https://www.bleepingcomputer.com/news/security/university-ddosed-by-its-own-iot-devices/

Cisco RFP-2013-078. (n.d.). *Fog Computing, Ecosystem, Architecture, and Applications*. Cisco.

Cisco. (2013). *BYOD Smart Solution*. Retrieved 7 January, 2015, from http://www.cisco.com/web/solutions/trends/byod_smart_solutions/index.html

Clamp, C. (2017). *King III vs King IV What you really need to know*. Retrieved June 22, 2017, Johannesburg: https://www.grantthornton.co.za/globalassets/1.-member-firms/south-africa/pdfs/kingiv_feb17.pdf

Clapper, J. R. (2016). *Statement for the Record Worldwide Threat Assessment of the US Intelligence Community Senate Select Committee on Intelligence*. Retrieved from http://www. intelligence. senate. gov/130312/clapper. pdf

Clark, P. G. (2013). *Firewall policy diagram: Novel data structures and algorithms for modeling, analysis, and comprehension of network firewalls*. Academic Press.

Clark, D. D. (2011). Protecting the Internet as a public commons. *Bulletin - American Academy of Arts and Sciences. American Academy of Arts and Sciences*, *64*(2), 62–63.

Clarke, R. Y. (2013, October). Smart Cities and the Internet of Everything: The Foundation for Delivering Next-Generation Citizen Services. *IDC Government Insights*. Retrieved 7 June 2017 from http://119.15.167.84:8080/share/proxy/alfresco-noauth/api/internal/shared/node/q9Ij_C2XQhS0ElSMm-jJnA/content/GI243955.pdf

Clarke, R. A., & Knake, R. K. (2010). *Cyber War: The Next Threat to National Security and What to Do about It*. New York: HarperCollins Publishers.

Claycomb, W. R., & Nicoll, A. (2012). *Insider threats to cloud computing: Directions for new research challenges*. Paper presented at the Computer Software and Applications Conference (COMPSAC), 2012 IEEE 36th Annual. 10.1109/COMPSAC.2012.113

Clinch, J. (2009, May). ITIL v3 and information security. *Clinch Consulting White Paper*, 1–40.

Cloud Endure. (2017). *Five Experts Predict Cloud Computing Trends for 2017*. Retrieved from https://www.cloudendure.com/blog/5-cloud-experts-predict-cloud-computing-trends-2017/

Cloud Security Alliance. (n.d.). *Cloud Controls Matrix Version 3.0.1*. Retrieved from https://cloudsecurityalliance.org/group/cloud-controls-matrix/#_overview

Coburn, D. (2007, May 30). Land Warrior System: Inside the Pentagon's New High-Tech Gear. *Popular Mechanics*. Retrieved 18 June 2017 from http://www.popularmechanics.com/military/a1591/4215725/

Cohen, N. (2017, Oct. 13). Silicon Valley is not your Friend. Sunday Review. *The New York Times*. Retrieved from https://nyti.ms/2kLUnZP

Cole, J. (2017). *Why Cyber Resilience is the UK's first line of Defence*. Retrieved from https://www.publictechnology.net/articles/opinion/why-cyber-resilience-uks-first-line-defence

Cole, H., & Griffiths, M. D. (2007). Social interactions in massively multiplayer online role-playing games. *Cyberpsychology & Behavior*, *10*(4), 575–583. doi:10.1089/cpb.2007.9988 PMID:17711367

Coleman, G. (2016). *How Africa can lead the way in the Fourth Industrial Revolution*. Retrieved from https://www.weforum.org/agenda/2016/05/how-africa-can-lead-the-way-in-the-fourth-industrial-revolution/

Colwill, C. (2009). Human factors in information security: The insider threat–Who can you trust these days? *Information Security Technical Report*, *14*(4), 186–196. doi:10.1016/j.istr.2010.04.004

Company85 Briefing. (2012). *BYOD and the security implications of consumerization*. Retrieved May 5, 2016, from http://safebridge.pt/Whitepapers/BYOD/Company85%20BYOD%20and%20the%20security%20implications%20of%20consumerisation.pdf

Computer Sciences Corporation. (2014). *Is Your Organisation Prepared to Respond to a Cyber-Attack*. Retrieved from http://www.csc.com/cybersecurity/offerings/107161/103293-cybersecurity_incident_response

Computer-mediated communication. (2017, Sept. 18). In *Wikipedia*. Retrieved from https://en.wikipedia.org/wiki/Computer-mediated_communication

Confidence trick. (2017, Sept. 13). In *Wikipedia*. Retrieved from https://en.wikipedia.org/wiki/Confidence_trick

Conklin, W. A., Cline, R. E., & Roosa, T. (2014). *Re-engineering cybersecurity education in the US: an analysis of the critical factors*. Paper presented at the System Sciences (HICSS), 2014 47th Hawaii International Conference on Cyber Security. 10.1109/HICSS.2014.254

Connolly, W. (1993). *The Terms of Political Discourse*. Princeton, NJ: Princeton University Press.

Constantin, L. (2017, Sept. 21). Researchers link CCleaner hack to cyberespionage group. *Motherboard*. Retrieved from https://motherboard.vice.com/en_us/article/7xkxba/researchers-link-ccleaner-hack-to-cyberespionage-group

Constantine, L. (2017, January 3). Ransomware on smart TVs is here and removing it can be a pain. *PC World*. Retrieved from: https://www.pcworld.com/article/3154226/security/ransomware-on-smart-tvs-is-here-and-removing-it-can-be-a-pain.html

Contos, B. (2015). *Cyber Security Culture is A Collective Effort*. Retrieved from http://www.csoonline.com/article/2977014/security-awareness/cyber-security-culture-is-a-collective-effort.html

Copeland, R., & Crespi, N. (2012). *Analyzing consumerization-Should enterprise business context determine session policy?* Paper presented at the Intelligence in Next Generation Networks (ICIN), 2012 16th International Conference on. 10.1109/ICIN.2012.6376024

Corey, R. (2009). *Fear, the history of Political Ideas*. Fondo de Cultura Económica.

Corporation, E. M. C. (2014). *ECM as a Service in Government*. Retrieved from http://www.emc.com/collateral/white-papers/h12586-ecm-as-a-service.pdf

Coulter, D. Y. (2002). *Globalization and Maritime Power - Globalization of Maritime Commerce: The Rise of Hub Ports* (S. J. Tangredi, Ed.). Washington, DC: National Defense University.

Coulter, G. (2012). *Jean Baudrillard: from the ocean to the desert or the poetics of radicality*. Intertheory Press.

Council Payment Card Industry. (2010). *PCI DSS 2.0*. PCI Council Publication/United States.

Coyne, E. M. (2016). Huawei Exec: SDN's Become a Completely Meaningless Term. *Light Reading*. Retrieved from http://www.lightreading.com/carrier-sdn/sdn-architectures/huawei-exec-sdns-become-a-completely-meaningless-term/d/d-id/726364

CPNI. (2011). *Securing The Move To Ip-Based Scada/Plc Networks*. Retrieved Jun 21, 2017, from www.ncsc.gov.uk: https://www.ncsc.gov.uk/content/files/protected_files/document_files/The%20Move%20to%20IP%20Based%20SCADA%20Networks%2020151111.pdf

CPNI. (2015). *Security for Industrial Control Systems - Manage Third Party Risks*. Retrieved Jun 06, 2017, from www.ncsc.gov.uk: https://www.ncsc.gov.uk/content/files/protected_files/guidance_files/SICS%20-%20Manage%20Third%20Party%20Risks%20Final%20v1.0.pdf

Craft, A. J. (2007). Sin in cyber-eden: Understanding the metaphysics and morals of virtual worlds. *Ethics and Information Technology*, *9*(3), 205–217. doi:10.100710676-007-9144-4

Crawford, K. (2017). *Cybercrimes and Cybersecurity Bill to be tabled in Parliament*. Retrieved from https://www.fanews.co.za/article/legal-affairs/10/general/1120/cybercrimes-and-cybersecurity-bill-to-be-tabled-in-parliament/21678

Crespo, F. L., Amutio-Gómez, M. A., Candau, J., & Mañas, J. A. (2006). Methodology for Information Systems Risk Analysis and Management (MAGERIT version 2). In Book II-Catalogue of Elements. Madrid: Ministerio de Administraciones Públicas.

Crittenden, P. M. (1990, Fall). Internal representational models of attachment relationships. *Infant Mental Health Journal*, *11*(3), 259–277. doi:10.1002/1097-0355(199023)11:3<259::AID-IMHJ2280110308>3.0.CO;2-J

Cronin, B., & Crawford, H. (1999). Information Warfare: Its Application in Military and Civilian Contexts. *The Information Society*, *15*(4), 257–263. doi:10.1080/019722499128420

Croock, G. (2016). *An Africa Perspective: Cyber Threats, Security and Data Protection*. Retrieved April 11, 2017, from https://www.bdo.co.za/en-za/insights/2016/cyber/an-africa-perspective-cyber-threats-security-and-data-protection

CSA. (2012). *SecaaS Implementation Guidance, Category 8: Encryption*. CSA.

CSA. (2016). *The Treacherous 12: Cloud Computing Top Threats in 2016*. CSA.

CSA. (2017). *Security Guidance - For Critical Areas in Cloud Computing v4.0*. CSA.

Cummings, J. N., Butler, B., & Kraut, R. (2002, July). The quality of online social relationships. *Communications of the ACM, 7*(45), 103–108. doi:10.1145/514236.514242

Cwele, S. (2014). *Minister Cwele Budget Vote Speech 2014*. Retrieved from http://www.dtps.gov.za/mediaroom/minister-s-speeches-mr-yunus-carrim/348-minister-cwele-budget-vote-speech-2014.html

CweleS. (2015). *Launch of Cybersecurity Hub*. Retrieved from http://www.gov.za/speeches/minister-siyabonga-cwele-launch-cybersecurity-hub-30-oct-2015-0000

Cyber Resilience. (2016). *Safeguarding the Digital Organization*. Retrieved from https://www.cybrary.it/channelcontent/cyber-resilience-safeguarding-digital-organization-white-paper/

Cyber Security Coalition. (2015). *Cyber Security Incident Management Guide*. Retrieved from Belgium: https://www.cybersecuritycoalition.be/content/uploads/cybersecurity-incident-management-guide-EN.pdf

Cyber Security Understanding the Cyber World. (2017, Mar. 8). The Sage Group.

Cyber Warfare. (2017). RAND Corporation. Retrieved from https://www.rand.org/topics/cyber-warfare.html

CyberEdge Group. (2014). *Cyberthreat Defense Report*. Retrieved from USA: http://www.brightcloud.com/pdf/CyberEdge-2014-CDR.pdf

Cybersecurity Agency of Singapore. (2016). *Singapore's Cybersecurity Strategy*. Singapore: Author.

Cybersecurity Vulnerabilities Identified in St. Jude Medical's Implantable Cardiac Devices and Merlin@homeTransmitter: FDA Safety Communication. (2017, January 9). Retrieved from: http://www.fda.gov/MedicalDevices/Safety/AlertsandNotices/ucm535843.htm

cybersecurity. (2016, Nov.). Retrieved from http://whatis.techtarget.com/definition/cybersecurity

Dantu, R., Kolan, P., & Cangussu, J. (2009). Network risk management using attacker profiling. *Security and Communication Networks, 2*(1), 83–96. doi:10.1002ec.58

Darktrace. (2016). *Darktrace Discoveries: Global Threat Case Studies 2016*. Accessed 14 June 2017 from http://www.informationweek.com/whitepaper/cybersecurity/security/darktrace-discoveries-global-threat-case-studies-2016/383043

Darwish, M. (2017, Nov. 3). Did Russia make this ship disappear? *Cable News Network (CNN)*. Retrieved from http://money.cnn.com/2017/11/03/technology/gps-spoofing-russia/index.html

Dasgupta, D., Roy, A., & Nag, A. (2016). Toward the design of adaptive selection strategies for multi-factor authentication. *Computers & Security, 63*, 85-116.

Dassah, M. (2014). Role of Technology in the functioning of the State. In C. Thorhnill, G. Van Dijk, & I. Ile (Eds.), *Public Administration and Management in South Africa: A Developmental Perspective* (pp. 338–372). Cape Town: Oxford University Press.

Davis, N. (2016). *What is the fourth industrial revolution?* Retrieved from https://www.weforum.org/agenda/2016/01/what-is-the-fourth-industrial-revolution/

Davis, N., & Larsen, A. M. E. (2018). *5 ways the Fourth Industrial Revolution transformed 2017 (and 5 ways it did not)*. Retrieved from https://www.weforum.org/agenda/2018/01/5-ways-the-fourth-industrial-revolution-transformed-2017-and-5-ways-it-did-not de Gusmão, A. P. H., Silva, L. C., Silva, M. M., Poleto, T., & Costa, A. P. C. S. (2016). Information security risk analysis model using fuzzy decision theory. *International Journal of Information Management*, *36*(1), 25–34. doi:10.1016/j.ijinfomgt.2015.09.003

De Haes, S., Van Grembergen, W., & Debreceny, R. S. (2013). COBIT 5 and Enterprise Governance of Information Technology: Building Blocks and Research Opportunities. *Journal of Information Systems*, *27*(1), 307–324. doi:10.2308/isys-50422

De Sousa, S. (2010). The role of payment systems in reaching the unbanked. *Journal of Payment Strategy & Systems*, *4*(2).

Deka, R. K., Kalita, K. P., Bhattacharya, D. K., & Kalita, J. K. (2015). Network defense: Approaches, methods and techniques. *Journal of Network and Computer Applications*, *57*, 71–84. doi:10.1016/j.jnca.2015.07.011

Dekker, M., Livery, D., & Lakka, M. (2013). *Cloud security incident reporting*. Academic Press.

Deloitte. (2017). *Industry 4.0 Is Africa ready for digital transformation*. Johannesburg: Author.

Deltek Solutions. (2014). *Guide to Data Security*. Retrieved from http://www.informationweek.com/whitepaper/Security/Attacks-Breaches/guide-to-data-security-wp1412021175?articleID=200000757&download=true&popup=true&_=1415718908717&thankyou=true

Demirguc-Kunt, A., Klapper, L., Dorothe, S., & Van Oudheusden, P. (2014). *The Global Findex Database 2014: Measuring Financial Inclusion around the World: World Bank Policy Research Working Paper, 7255*. Washington, DC: World Bank.

Demirguc-Kunt, A., Beck, T., & Honohan, P. (2008). *Finance for All? Policies and Pitfalls in Expanding Access. World Bank Policy Research Report*. Washington, DC: World Bank.

Demirkan, H., Spohrer, J. C., & Welser, J. J. (2016). Digital Innovation and Strategic Transformation. *IT Professional*, *18*(6), 14–18. doi:10.1109/MITP.2016.115

Denning, D. E., & Strawser, B. J. (2014). Active cyber defense: Applying air defense to the cyber domain. In *Cyber Analogies*. Calhoun: The National Postgraduate School (NPS) Institutional Archive. Retrieved Sept. 19, 2017, from http://hdl.handle.net/10945/40037

Department for Homeland Security. (2011). *Common Cyber Security Vulnerabilities in Industrial Control Systems*. Department for Homeland Security, Control Systems Security Program. DHS.

Department of Communication. (2002). *Electronic Communications and Transactions Act 2002 (23708)*. Pretoria: Author.

Department of Communications. (2013). *Protection of Personal Information Act 2013 (4)*. Pretoria: Author.

Department of Homeland Security. (2014). *Law Enforcement Cyber Incident Reporting*. Author.

Department of Homeland Security. (2017). *What is Security and Resilience?* Retrieved from https://www.dhs.gov/what-security-and-resilience

Department of Justice and Constitutional Development. (2015). *Justice publishes draft Cybercrimes and Cybersecurity Bill for public* [Press release]. Retrieved from http://www.gov.za/speeches/justice-publishes-cybercrimes-and-cybersecurity-bill-public-comments-28-aug-2015-0000

Department of Justice and Constitutional Development. (2017). *Cybercrimes and Cybersecurity Bill*. Pretoria: Author.

Department of Public Service and Administration. (2003). *The Machinery of Government*. Pretoria: Department of Public Service and Administration, Retrieved from http://www.dpsa.gov.za/dpsa2g/documents/lkm/mog.pdf

Department of Public Service and Administration. (2017). *Information and Communication Technology Security Guideline*. Pretoria: Author.

Department of Telecommunications & Postal Services. (2016a). *Incident Management Process*. Retrieved from https://www.cybersecurityhub.gov.za/incident-management-process

Department of Telecommunications & Postal Services. (2016b). *The National Cybersecurity Hub*. Retrieved from https://www.cybersecurityhub.gov.za/

Dermish, A., Kneiding, C., Leishman, P., & Mas, I. (2012). Branchless and Mobile Banking Solutions for the Poor: A Survey of Literature. *Innovations, 6*(4), 81–98. doi:10.1162/INOV_a_00103

Destructive KillDisk malware encrypts Linux machines, ESET researchers discover. (2017, January 5). Retrieved from: https://www.eset.com/us/about/newsroom/press-releases/destructive-killdisk-malware-encrypts-linux-machines-eset-reseachers-discover/

Device, Y. O. (n.d.). Retrieved March 10, 2015, from http://www.bringyourownit.com/2012/06/25/byod-bring-your-own-device/

Diaz, D. (2017, Sept. 13). Cruz blames 'staffing issue' for porn video 'liked' on his Twitter account. *CNN Politics*. Retrieved from http://www.cnn.com/2017/09/12/politics/ted-cruz-twitter/index.html

Dillon, R. L., & Carlson, K. (2017). *Seeking advice from experts: A cautionary tale*. IEEE.

Dillow, C. (2016, February 12). This Counter-Drone System Will Safely Hijack and Capture Rogue Drones. *Fortune*. Retrieved 19 February 2016 from http://fortune.com/2016/02/12/falcon-shield-counter-drone-system/

Dimensional Research. (2013). *The impact of mobile devices on information security: A survey of professionals*. Retrieved 30 December, 2014, from http://www.dimensionalresearch.com

Dimensional_Research. (2013). *The impact of mobile devices on information security: A survey of professionals*. Retrieved 30 December, 2014, from http://www.dimensionalresearch.com

Dinicu, A. (2014). Cyber threats to national security, specific features and actors involved. *Buletin Stiintific, 2*(38), 109–113.

Disterer, G., & Kleiner, C. (2013). *BYOD Bring Your Own Device*. Retrieved 19 December, 2014, from http://www.dx.doi.org/10.1016/j.protcy

Dlamini, M. T., Eloff, J. H., & Eloff, M. M. (2009). Information security: The moving target. *Computers & Security, 28*(3), 189–198. doi:10.1016/j.cose.2008.11.007

Dlamini, Z., & Modise, M. (2012). Cyber Security Awareness in South Africa: A Synergy Approach. *7th International Conference on Information Warfare and Security: ICIW 2012*.

Dobrygowski, D. (2017). *Why being a responsible leader means cyber resilient*. Retrieved from https://www.weforum.org/agenda/2017/01/why-being-a-responsible-leader-means-being-cyber-resilient/

Dobson, I., & Hietala, J. (2011). *Risk Management: The Open Group Guide*. Van Haren Pub.

Döge, J. (2010). Cyber warfare: Challenges for the applicability of the traditional laws of war regime. *Archiv des Völkerrechts, 48*(4), 486–501. doi:10.1628/000389210794439416

Dongmei, Z., Changguang, W., & Jianfeng, M. (2007). A risk assessment method of the wireless network security. *Journal of Electronics (China), 24*(3), 428–432. doi:10.100711767-006-0247-6

Donner, J., & Tellez, C. A. (2008). Mobile banking and economic development: Linking adoption, impact, and use. *Asian Journal of Communication, 18*(4), 318–332. doi:10.1080/01292980802344190

Donovan, K. (2012). Mobile Money for Financial Inclusion. *International Journal of Communication, 6*, 61–93.

Dooley, R. (2017). *Cyber security at the heart of the Fourth Industrial Revolution.* Retrieved 09 October 2017, from https://instrumentsignpost.wordpress.com/2017/02/08/cybersecurity-at-the-heart-of-the-fourth-industrial-revolution-schneiderelec-pauto-industrie40/

Dooley, R. (2017, June 15). Cyber security at the heart of the Fourth Industrial Revolution. *UK Construction Online.* Retrieved 15 June 2017 from https://www.ukconstructionmedia.co.uk/features/cyber-security-industrial-revolution/

Dover, R. (2016, Summer-Fall). Regulation by revelation: The opportunities and challenges of information control in an intelligence era. *SAIS Review (Paul H. Nitze School of Advanced International Studies), 36*(2), 103–111.

Doyle, K. (2017). *SA lacks cyber security skills.* Retrieved from http://www.itweb.co.za/index.php?option=com_content&view=article&id=160813

Dridex botnet spreading Locky Ransomware. (2016, March 10). Retrieved from: http://www.securityweek.com/dridex-botnet-spreading-locky-ransomware-javascript-attachments

Druckrey, T. (1996). *Electronic Culture: technology and visual representation.* New York: Aperture.

Du & Zhang. (2006). *Risks and Risk Control of Wi-Fi Network Systems.* Academic Press.

du Plessis, W. (2014). Software-Defined Radio (SDR) as a Mechanism for Exploring Cyber-Electronic Warfare (EW) Collaboration. *6th Workshop on ICT uses in Warfare and the Safeguarding of Peace, Proceedings of the 2014 Information Security for South Africa Conference.* Retrieved 14 June 2017 from http://icsa.cs.up.ac.za/issa/2014/Proceedings/Workshop/15_Final_Document.pdf

Dua, I. V. (2013). Data Security in Cloud Oriented Application Using SSL/TLS Protocol. *International Journal of Application or Innovation in Engineering & Management, 2*(12), 79–85.

Duncan, J. (2015). *Inside SA's cyber-insecurity problem.* Retrieved from https://mg.co.za/article/2015-10-15-inside-sas-cyber-insecurity-problem

Dunlap, C.J. (2011). Perspectives for cyber strategists on law for cyberwar. *Strategic Studies Quarterly,* 81 – 99.

Dunn, J. E. (2009). *Spammers break Hotmail's CAPTCHA yet again.* Retrieved from NetworkWorld website: http://www.networkworld.com/article/2262871/lan-wan/spammers-break-hotmail-s-captcha-yet-again.html

Dunn, J. E. (2013, October 16). Hackers planted remote devices to smuggle drugs through Antwerp port, Europol reveals. *Techworld.* Retrieved from http://news.techworld.com/security/3474018/hackers-planted-remote-devices-to-smuggle-drugs-through-antwerp-port-europol-reveals/

Dunn-Cavelty, M., & Suter, M. (2009). Public–Private Partnerships are no silver bullet: An expanded governance model for Critical Infrastructure Protection. *International Journal of Critical Infrastructure Protection, 2*(4), 179–187. doi:10.1016/j.ijcip.2009.08.006

Dunnett, R. (2012). *Information Security, Mobile Security and Internet of Things.* BYOD- Bring.

Dunnewold, M. (2000). Why am I here? Six-word stories about the first month of law school. *Journal of Legal Education, 59*(4), 653–656. Retrieved from https://jle.aals.org/cgi/viewcontent.cgi?referer=https://www.google.com/&httpsredir=1&article=1285&context=home

Dwight, J. S., Boler, M., & Sears, P. (2006). Reconstructing the Fables: Women on the Educational Cyberfrontier. In J. Weiss, . . . (Eds.), The International Handbook of Virtual Learning Environments: 1467 – 1494. Academic Press.

Dwyer, C., Hiltz, S. R., & Passerini, K. (2007). Trust and privacy concern within social networking sites: A comparison of Facebook and MySpace. *Proceedings of the Thirteenth Americas Conference on Information Systems.*

Dynes, S., Goetz, E., & Freeman, M. (2007). Cyber security: Are economic incentives adequate? *International Conference on Critical Infrastructure Protection*, 15 – 27. https://link.springer.com/chapter/10.1007/978-0-387-75462-8_2

Economist Intelligence Unit. (2015). *A turning point: The potential role of ICT innovations in ports and logistics.* Retrieved Jul 4, 2016, from DPWorld.com: http://web.dpworld.com/wp-content/uploads/2015/11/ICT-innovations-DP-World_Eng.pdf

ECS-CSIRT. (2012). *CSIRT Newsletter.* Pretoria: State Security Agency.

Edwards, S., & Profetis, I. (2016, October 16). Hajime: Analysis of a decentralized internet worm for IoT devices. *Rapidity Networks*. Retrieved 20 April 2017 from https://security.rapiditynetworks.com/publications/2016-10-16/hajime.pdf

Eggers, W. D. (2016). Government's cyber challenge: Protecting sensitive data for the public good. *Deloitte Review*, *19*, 138–155.

Ehimen & Bola. (2010, January). Cybercrime in Nigeria. *Business Intelligence Journal*, 93-98.

Ehrbeck, T., & Tarazi, M. (2011). *Putting the Bankingnin Branchless Banking: The Case for Interest-Bearing and Insured E-Money Savings Accounts.* The Mobile Financial Services Development Report, 37–42. Washington, DC: World Economic Forum.

Ehrenfeld, J. M. (2017). WannaCry, Cybersecurity and Health Information Technology: A Time to Act. *Journal of Medical Systems*, *41*(7), 104. doi:10.100710916-017-0752-1 PMID:28540616

Eid, M. (Ed.). (2015). *Exchanging Terrorism Oxygen for Media Airwaves: The Age of Terroredia: The Age of Terroredia.* Hershey, PA: IGI Global.

Elf, M. (2011, Feb. 12). Robert Plutchik's Wheel of Emotions (1980). In *Wikipedia*. Retrieved from https://commons.wikimedia.org/wiki/File:Plutchik-wheel.svg

Elliott, R. J., Aggoun, L., & Moore, J. B. (2008). *Hidden Markov models: estimation and control* (Vol. 29). Springer Science & Business Media.

Ellison, N. B., Steinfield, C., & Lampe, C. (2007, July). The benefits of Facebook 'friends:' Social capital and college students' use of online social network sites. *Journal of Computer-Mediated Communication*, *12*(4), 1143–1168. doi:10.1111/j.1083-6101.2007.00367.x

Ellul, J. (1964). *The Technological society*. New York: Vintage books.

Ellul, J. (1965). *Propaganda*. New York: Knopf.

Elwess, T. (2015). *Bring your own device* (Doctoral dissertation). Utica College.

Enck, W., Gilbert, P., Han, S., Tendulkar, V., Chun, B.-G., Cox, L. P., ... Sheth, A. N. (2014). TaintDroid: An information-flow tracking system for realtime privacy monitoring on smartphones. *ACM Transactions on Computer Systems*, *32*(2), 5. doi:10.1145/2619091

ENEA. (2017). *CBRN Risks in Maritime and Land Containers Transport* (G. G. Cartocci, Ed.). ENEA.

eNews Channel Africa. (2016). *Hackers shut down SABC websites*. Retrieved from www.enca.com/south-africa/hackers-shut-down-sabc-websites

eNews Channel Africa. (2017a). *New Wave of cyber attacks spreads from Russia across the globe*. Retrieved from http://www.enca.com/technology/new-wave-of-cyber-attacks-spreads-from-russia-across-globe

eNews Channel Africa. (2017b). *Sweden rattled by massive confidential data leak*. Retrieved from http://www.enca.com/technology/sweden-rattled-by-massive-confidential-data-leak

ENISA. (2011). *Analysis Of Cyber Security Aspects In The Maritime Sector*. Retrieved Jun 12, 2016, from https://www.enisa.europa.eu/.../cyber-security-aspects-in-the-maritime-sector.../fullRe

Ensey, C. (2017, January 4). *Ransomware Has Evolved, And Its Name Is Doxware*. Retrieved from: https://www.darkreading.com/attacks-breaches/ransomware-has-evolved-and-its-name-is-doxware/a/d-id/1327767

Enzenberger, H. (1996). Constituents of a theory of media. In T. Druckrey (Ed.), *Electronic culture: technology and visual representation* (pp. 62–85). New York: Aperture.

Erebus Linux Ransomware: Impact to Servers and Countermeasures. (2017, June 15). Retrieved from: https://www.trendmicro.com/vinfo/us/security/news/cyber-attacks/erebus-linux-ransomware-impact-to-servers-and-countermeasures

Ernest Hemingway – Baby Shoes. (2008). *Snopes*. Retrieved from https://www.snopes.com/language/literary/-babyshoes.asp

Ernst & Young. (2014). *Cyber threat intelligence - how to get ahead of cybercrime*. Author.

Ernst and Young. (2015). *Cybersecurity and the Internet of Things*. Retrieved from http://www.ey.com/Publication/vwLUAssets/EY-cybersecurity-and-the-internet-of-things/$FILE/EY-cybersecurity-and-the-internet-of-things.pdf

ESET. (2016, October). En Route with Sednit, Part 3: A Mysterious Downloader. *We Live Security*. Retrieved 12 June 2017 from https://www.welivesecurity.com/wp-content/uploads/2016/10/eset-sednit-part3.pdf

Eshel, D. (2007). Defeating IEDs. *Journal of Electronic Defense, 30*(12), 38–42.

Espen, B. E., & Anja, K. (2015). *The dark side of the Fourth Industrial Revolution – and how to avoid it*. Retrieved from World Economic Forum: https://www.weforum.org/agenda/2015/11/the-dark-side-of-the-digital-revolution-and-how-to-avoid-it/

ESPO. (2010). *Code of Practice on Societal Integration of Ports*. Retrieved Jun 15, 2016, from https://www.espo.be/media/espopublications/ESPOCodeofPracticeonSocietalIntegrationofPorts2010.pdf

Etim, A. S. (2012). The emerging market of Sub-Saharan Africa and technology adoption: Features of users' desire in mobile phones. *International Journal of ICT Research and Development in Africa, 3*(1), 14–16. doi:10.4018/jictrda.2012010102

Eun, Y.-S., & Abmann, J. S. (2016). Cyberwar: Taking stock of security and warfare in the digital age. *International Studies Perspectives, 17*, 343–360.

European Cybersecurity Forum. (2016). *CYBERSEC 2016 Recommendations*. Retrieved from Krakow: https://azor.app.box.com/v/CYBERSEC2016Recommendations

European Union Agency for Network and Information Security. (2011). *Measurement Frameworks and Metrics for Resilient Networks and Services. Challenges and Recommendations*. Retrieved from https://www.enisa.europa.eu/publications/metrics-tech-report/at_download/fullReport

Evans, B. (2015). *The Importance of Building an Information Security Strategic Plan*. Retrieved from https://security-intelligence.com/the-importance-of-building-an-information-security-strategic-plan/

Evans, K., & Reeder, F. (2010). *A Human Capital Crisis in Cybersecurity: Technical Proficiency Matters.* CSIS.

Everett, B. (2013). Optically transparant: the rise of industrial espionage and state sponsored hacking. *Computer Fraud and Security,* (10), 13-16.

Evripidis, R. (2008). *Lawful Interception and Countermeasures: In the era of Internet Telephony.* Academic Press.

Experts, I. D. (2014). *The CISO's Secret Weapon for Reducing Enterprise Risk.* Retrieved from http://forms. madisonlogic.com/FormConfirmation.aspx?pub=18&pgr=259&src=2318&cmp=13434&ast=41617&frm=446& pd=3147146-19-7-57-336-0

Fanta, A. B., Mutsonziwa, K., Goosen, R., Emanuel, M., & Kettles, N. (2016). *The Role of Mobile Money in Financial Inclusion in the SADC region: Evidence using FinScope Surveys.* Prepared by FinMark Trust December 2016 Policy research paper No. 03/2016. Retrieved April 17, 2017, from http://www.finmark.org.za/wp-content/uploads/2016/12/ mobile-money-and-financial-inclusion-in-sadc-1.pdf

Fanta, A. B., & Mutsonziwa, K. (2016). *Gender and financial inclusion Analysis of financial inclusion of women in the SADC region, Policy research paper No. 01/2016.* FinMark Trust.

Faouzi, A., Mabrouki, C., & Semma, A. (2013). Modeling a repository of modules for ports terminals. *International Journal of Computer Science Issues, 10*(1), 766–773.

Faris, R., & Jones, R. (2014). *Platforms and policy, in internet monitor 2014: reflections on the digital world.* SAGE.

Farwell, J. P. (2014). The media strategy of ISIS. *Survival, 56*(6), 49–55. doi:10.1080/00396338.2014.985436

Federal Bureau of Investigation. (2012). *The Cyber Threat Part 1: On the Front Lines with Shawn Henry.* Retrieved Jun 13, 2016, from https://www.fbi.gov/news/stories/the-cyber-threat

Federal Bureau of Investigation. (2013). *Internet Crime Report.* Author.

Federal Bureau of Investigation. (2015). *Economic Espionage - FBI Launches Nationwide Awareness Campaign.* Retrieved from https://www.fbi.gov/news/stories/2015/july/economicespionage/economic-espionage

Feil, J. A. (2012). Cyberwar and unmanned aerial vehicles: Using new technologies, from espionage to action. *Case Western Reserve Journal of International Law, 45,* 513–544.

Feldman, A. (1991). *Formation of Violence: the narrative of the body and the political terror in Northern Ireland.* Chicago: University of Chicago Press. doi:10.7208/chicago/9780226240800.001.0001

Felt, A. P., Finifter, M., Chin, E., Hanna, S., & Wagner, D. (2011). A survey of mobile malware in the wild. *Proceedings of the 1st ACM workshop on Security and privacy in smartphones and mobile devices.* 10.1145/2046614.2046618

Fernando, S. (2014). *Internal Control of Secure Information and Communication Practices through Detection of User Behavioural Patterns.* Niigata, Japan: Nagaoka University of Technology.

Fifield, J. (2016, July 1). How drones raised privacy concerns across cyberspace. *Stateline.* Retrieved 6 June 2017 from http://www.pbs.org/newshour/rundown/how-drones-raised-privacy-concerns-across-cyberspace/

Fin24. (2017). *Alert: Massive cyber attack hits several companies.* Retrieved from http://www.fin24.com/Tech/News/ alert-massive-cyber-attack-hits-several-companies-20170627

Finnigan, J. (2017). *Cybercrimes and Cybersecurity Bill introduced in Parliament.* Retrieved from http://www.wylie. co.za/articles/cybercrimes-and-cybersecurity-bill-introduced-in-parliament/

Fischer, E. A. (2013). *Federal laws relating to cybersecurity: Overview and discussion of proposed revisions.* Academic Press.

Fisher, C. (2007). *Researching and writing a dissertation: A guidebook for business students* (2nd ed.). Harlow: Pearson Education Limited.

Fisher, D. (2013, December 3). How to Skyjack a Drone in an Hour for Less Than $400. *ThreatPost.* Retrieved 5 December 2013 from http://threatpost.com/how-to-skyjack-drones-in-an-hour-for-less-than-400/103086

Fitzpatrick, D., & Griffin, D. (2016, April 15). Cyber-extortion losses skyrocket, warns FBI. *CNN Tech.* Retrieved from: http://money.cnn.com/2016/04/15/technology/ransomware-cyber-security/

Flinders, K. (2016). *UK government re-announces £1.9bn cybersecurity spend.* Retrieved from http://www.computerweekly.com/news/450402098/UK-government-re-announces-19bn-cybersecurity-spend

Flores, W. R., Holm, H., Svensson, G., & Ericsson, G. (2013). Using Phishing Experiments and Scenario-based Surveys to Understand Security Behaviours in Practice. *Proceedings of the European Information Security Multi-Conference.*

Flowers, A., & Zeadally, S. (2014). Cyberwar: The what, when, why, and how. *IEEE Technology and Society Magazine,* 14–21.

Foley, K. (2011). Maintaining a proactive and sustainable security program while hosting and processing personally identifiable information. *Information Systems Security Association Journal, 9*(5), 25–32.

Formby, D., Durbah, S., & Beyah, R. (2017). *Out of Control: Ransomware and Industrial Control Systems.* Retrieved May 12, 2017, from www.cap.gatech.edu/plcransomware.pdf

Fortinet. (2017, February 9). *Understanding the IoT Explosion and its Impact on Enterprise Security.* Retrieved 13 August 2016 from https://www.fortinet.com/demand/gated/WP-Understanding-The-IoT-Explosion-And-Its-Impact-On-Enterprise-Security.html

Fourie, Pang, Kingston, Hettema, Watters, & Sarrafzadeh. (2014). *The global cyber security workforce: an ongoing human capital crisis.* SAGE.

Fourth Industrial Revolution. (2017). In *Wikipedia.* Retrieved from https://en.wikipedia.org/wiki/-Fourth_Industrial_Revolution

Francis & Ginsberg. (2016). *The Federal Cybersecurity Workforce: Background and Congressional Oversight Issues for the Departments of Defense and Homeland Security.* Academic Press.

Francis, R. (2017, May 25). How to conduct an IoT pen test. *Network World.* Retrieved 15 June 2017 from http://www.networkworld.com/article/3198495/internet-of-things/how-to-conduct-an-iot-pen-test.html

Freedman, A. (2015). Managing personal device use in the workplace: How to avoid data security issues and to dig yourself out of your failed BYOD policy. *Suffolk J. Trial & App. Adv., 20,* 284–361.

Friedman, J., & Hoffman, D. V. (2008). Protecting data on mobile devices: A taxonomy of security threats to mobile computing and review of applicable defenses. *Information, Knowledge, Systems Management, 7*(1-2), 159–180.

Frigault, M., & Wang, L. (2008). *Measuring network security using bayesian network-based attack graphs.* IEEE. doi:10.1109/COMPSAC.2008.88

Fripp, C. (2014). *South Africa is second most targeted for Phishing Attacks.* Retrieved from IT News Africa website: http://www.itnewsafrica.com/2014/04/south-africa-is-second-most-targeted-for-phishing-attacks/

Fripp, C. (2015). *Why the draft cybercrimes bill should concern South Africans.* Retrieved from http://www.htxt.co.za/2015/09/14/why-the-draft-cybercrimes-bill-should-concern-south-africans/

Fu, C., Ye, J., Zhang, L., Zhang, Y., & LanSheng, H. (2010). A Dynamic Risk Assessment Framework Using Principle Component Analysis with Projection Pursuit in Ad Hoc Networks. *Ubiquitous Intelligence & Computing and 7th International Conference on Autonomic & Trusted Computing (UIC/ATC), 2010 7th International Conference on,* 154–159. doi:10.1109/UIC-ATC.2010.42

Fu, S., & Zhou, H. (2011). The information security risk assessment based on AHP and fuzzy comprehensive evaluation. In *2011 IEEE 3rd International Conference on Communication Software and Networks* (pp. 124–128). IEEE. 10.1109/ICCSN.2011.6014018

Fukuyama, F. (1989). The End of History. *National Interest, 16*(Summer), 4–18.

Fuller, G. E. (2010). *A world without Islam.* New York: Little Brown.

Funk, G., Zarzhitsky, D., & Carrol, T. (n.d.). *Security and Privacy Challenges for the Internet of Things.* Retrieved from cybersecurity.pnnl.gov/documents/security_and_privacy.pdf

Gagnon, B., & Mickahail, A. (2014). *Building top-notch information security teams.* Retrieved from http://fcw.com/articles/2014/10/31/building-top-notch-information-security-teams.aspx

Galvin, J. (2013, May 24). How to escape a submerged car. *Popular Mechanics.* Retrieved Sept. 24, 2017, from http://www.popularmechanics.com/adventure/outdoors/tips/a11919/how-to-escape-a-submerged-car-15510924/

Ganapathy, S., Yogesh, P., & Kannan, A. (2012). Intelligent Agent-Based Intrusion Detection System Using Enhanced Multiclass SVM. *Computational Intelligence and Neuroscience, 2012,* 1–10. doi:10.1155/2012/850259 PMID:23056036

Gao, F., Sun, J., & We, Z. (2003). The prediction role of hidden Markov model in intrusion detection. *CCECE 2003 - Canadian Conference on Electrical and Computer Engineering. Toward a Caring and Humane Technology (Cat. No.03CH37436), 2,* 893–896. doi:10.1109/CCECE.2003.1226038

Garba, Armarego, Murray, & Kenworthy. (2015). Review of the information security and privacy challenges in Bring Your Own Device (BYOD) environments. *Journal of Information Privacy and Security, 11*(1), 38-54.

Gartner. (2012). *Creating a Bring Your Own Device (BYOD) Policy.* Retrieved April 4, 2016, from https://www.gartner.com/doc/1983515/creating-bring-device-byod-policy

Gartzke, E. (2013). The myth of cyberwar: Bringing war in cyberspace back down to earth. *International Security, 38*(2), 41–73. doi:10.1162/ISEC_a_00136

Garvey, P. R. (2008). *Analytical methods for risk management: A systems engineering perspective.* CRC Press. doi:10.1201/9781420011395

Geer, D. (2014). *The Internet of Things: Top Five Threats to IoT Devices.* Retrieved from http://www.csoonline.com/article/2134265/network-security/the-internet-of-things--top-five-threats-to-iot-devices.html?page=2

Geers, K. (2010). The challenge of cyber attack deterrence. *Computer Law & Security Review, 26*(3), 298–303. doi:10.1016/j.clsr.2010.03.003

Gehling, B., & Stankard, D. (2005). eCommerce security. In *Proceedings of the 2nd annual conference on Information security curriculum development - InfoSecCD '05* (p. 32). New York: ACM Press. 10.1145/1107622.1107631

Gelb, A., & Decker, C. (2011). *Cash at Your Fingertips: Biometric Technology for Transfers in Developing and Resource-Rich Countries.* Working paper 253, Center for Global Development, Washington, DC.

Gemalto Breach Level Index. (2016). *Data breaches in South Africa.* Retrieved April 03, 2017, from http://www6.gemalto.com/breach-level-index-report-full-2016-press-release

Gemalto. (2017). *Breach Level Index Report 2016.* US: Author.

Gerpott, T. J., Rams, W., & Schindler, A. (2001). Customer retention, loyalty, and satisfaction in the German mobile cellular telecommunication market. *Telecommunications Policy, 25*(4), 249–269. doi:10.1016/S0308-5961(00)00097-5

Gharibi, W. (2012). *Some Recommended Protection Technologies for Cyber Crime Based on Social Engineering Techniques--Phishing.* arXiv preprint arXiv:1201.0949

Ghauri, P. N., & Cateora, P. (2010). *International Marketing* (3rd ed.). Maidenhead, UK: McGraw- Hill Education.

Ghosh, M. (2014, August 4). *Computer Ransomware Leads a Man to Kill Himself & Son.* Retrieved from: http://trak.in/tags/business/2014/03/14/computer-ransomware-threat/

Giddens, N., & Hofmann, A. (2010). *Brand loyalty.* AG Decision Maker.

Giess, M. (2015, June 18). How to fit a Raspberry Pi with mobile M2M connectivity. *EMnify.* Retrieved 15 June 2017 from https://www.emnify.com/2015/06/18/how-to-fit-a-raspberry-pi-with-mobile-connectivity/

Gilbert, E., & Karahalios, K. (2009). Predicting tie strength with social media. *Proceedings of the SIGCHI Conference on Human Factors in Computing Systems*, 211 – 220. Retrieved from https://dl.acm.org/citation.cfm?id=1518736

Giles, J. (2016). *King IV Code and IT Governance.* Retrieved from https://www.michalsons.com/blog/king-iv-code-and-it-governance/18691

Gill, S., & Bokhari, B. (2016). *Technology and Sourcing Alert.* Retrieved from https://www.cliffedekkerhofmeyr.com/export/sites/cdh/en/news/publications/2016/Technology/downloads/Technology-and-Sourcing-Alert-11-May-2016.pdf

Gill, S., & Bokhari, B. (2016). *Technology and Sourcing Alert.* Retrieved from Johannesburg https://www.cliffedekker-hofmeyr.com/export/sites/cdh/en/news/publications/2016/Technology/downloads/Technology-and-Sourcing-Alert-11-May-2016.pdf

Giroux, H. (2016). *Beyond the Spectacle of Terrorism. Global Uncertainty and the challenges of a new media.* Abingdon, UK: Routledge.

Giusti, J. (2016). *The future of digital finance lies in our mobile phones.* World Economic Forum. Retrieved May 23, 2017, from https://www.weforum.org/agenda/2016/01/the-future-of-digital-finance-lies-in-our-mobile-phones/

Global Forum on Cyber Expertise. (2016). *Outcomes High-Level Meeting Cyber Security.* Retrieved from file:///C:/Users/patrick/Downloads/OutcomeReport+FINAL%20(1).pdf

Global System for Mobile Association (GSMA). (2014). *The State of Mobile Money Usage – How many people use mobile money globally?* Retrieved, April 02, 2017, from http://www.gsma.com/mobilefordevelopment/

Global System for Mobile Association (GSMA). (2015). *The Mobile Economy 2015.* Retrieved May 17, 2017, from https://www.gsma.com/mobileeconomy/global/2015/

Global System for Mobile Association (GSMA). (2016). *The Mobile Economy Africa 2016.* Retrieved April 17, 2017, from https://www.gsmaintelligence.com/research/?file=3bc21ea879a5b217b64d62fa24c55bdf&download

Goche, M., & Gouveia, W. (2014). *Why Cyber Security Is Not Enough: You Need Cyber Resilience.* Retrieved from US: https://www.forbes.com/sites/sungardas/2014/01/15/why-cybersecurity-is-not-enough-you-need-cyber-resilience/#5c4f237c1bc4

Golde, N., Redon, K., & Borgaonkar, R. (2012). *Weaponizing Femtocells: The Effect of Rogue Devices on Mobile Telecommunications.* Paper presented at the NDSS.

Goldman, E. O., & Arquilla, J. (2014, Feb. 28). *Cyber Analogies.* Calhoun: The National Postgraduate School (NPS) Institutional Archive. Retrieved Sept. 19, 2017, from http://hdl.handle.net/10945/40037

Goldman, H., McQuaid, R., & Picciotto, J. (2011). Cyber resilience for mission assurance. In *Technologies for Homeland Security (HST), 2011 IEEE International Conference on* (pp. 236-241). IEEE. 10.1109/THS.2011.6107877

González, Tapiador, Estévez, & Garnacho. (2008). *Content authentication and access control in pure peer-to-peer networks.* Universidad Carlos Iii De Madrid.

Gonzalez, J. J., & Sawicka, A. (2002). A framework for human factors in information security. *Proceedings of 2002 World Scientific and Engineering Academic Society International Conference on Information Security.*

Gonzalez, N., Miers, C., Redigolo, F., Simplicio, M., Carvalho, T., Näslund, M., & Pourzandi, M. (2012). A quantitative analysis of current security concerns and solutions for cloud computing. *Journal of Cloud Computing: Advances. Systems and Applications, 1*(11), 1–18.

Gorodetski, V. I. (2012). Self-organization and multiagent systems: I. Models of multiagent self-organization. *Journal of Computer and Systems Sciences International, 51*(2), 256–281. doi:10.1134/S106423071201008X

Gottfried, J., & Shearer, E. (2016, May 26). *News use across social media platforms 2016.* Pew Research Center. Received Sept. 22, 2017, from http://www.journalism.org/2016/05/26/news-use-across-social-media-platforms-2016/

Gourley, S. R. (2013, June 25). The Rise of the Soldier System. *Defense Media Network.* Retrieved 18 June 2017 from http://www.defensemedianetwork.com/stories/the-rise-of-the-soldier-system/

Government Accountability Office. (2017, May). *Internet of Things: Status and implications of an increasingly connected world.* Report to Congressional Requesters, Technology Assessment GAO-17-75.

Govloop. (2014). *Your Cybersecurity Crash Course.* Retrieved from http://img.en25.com/Web/GovDeliveryInc/%7B85bade5e-e97f-49d4-8c74-3aacea547259%7D_Your-Cybersecurity-Crash-Course2.pdf?elq=~~eloqua.type--emailfield.syntax--re cipientid~~&elqCampaignId=~~eloqua.type--campaign.campaignid--0.fieldname--id~~

Grabosky, P., & Walkley, S. (2007). Computer Crime and White-Collar Crime. In H. N. Pontell & G. Geis (Eds.), *International Handbook of White-Collar and Corporate Crime.* Boston, MA: Springer. doi:10.1007/978-0-387-34111-8_17

Granger, S. (2001). Social engineering fundamentals, part I: hacker tactics. *Security Focus.* Retrieved from: http://www.symantec.com/connect/articles/social-engineering-fundamentals-part-i-hacker-tactics

Granneman, J. (2013). IT security frameworks and standards: Choosing the right one. *TechTarget Network.* Available: http://searchsecuri ty. tech target. comlti p/IT-securi ty frameworks-and-standards-Choosing-the-right-one

Granneman, J. (2014). *Basing incident response management on NIST SP 800-61.* Retrieved from http://searchsecurity. techtarget.com/tip/Basing-incident-response-management-on-NIST-SP-800-61

Granovetter, M. S. (1973, May). The strength of weak ties. *American Journal of Sociology, 78*(6), 1360 – 1380. Retrieved from http://www.journals.uchicago.edu/doi/pdfplus/10.1086/225469

Gray, A. (2015). A new generation of cyber risks: Is NZ ready for what's coming? *NZ Business+Management*, 8-12.

Gray, C. S. (2007). *The Implications of Preemptive and Preventive war Doctrines: Reconsideration.* Department of the Army, Department of Defense, US Government. Available at http://www.strategicstudiesinstitute.army.mil/Pubs/display. cfm?pubid=789

Greenberg, A. (2013, Oct. 2). End of the Silk Road: FBI says it's busted the Web's biggest anonymous drug black market. *Forbes*. Retrieved from https://www.forbes.com/sites/andygreenberg/2013/10/02/end-of-the-silk-road-fbi-busts-the-webs-biggest-anonymous-drug-black-market/#4039e6275b4f

Greenberg, A. (2017, Sept. 6). Hackers gain direct access to U.S. power grid controls. *Wired Magazine*. Retrieved from https://www.wired.com/story/hackers-gain-switch-flipping-access-to-us-power-systems/

Greenberg, A., Feng, L., & Chin, C. (2017). The hotel room hacker. *Wired Magazine*. Retrieved Sept. 18, 2017, from https://www.wired.com/2017/08/the-hotel-hacker/

Greene, F. (2015). Cybersecurity Detective Controls Monitoring to Identify and Respond to Threats. *ISACA*, *5*, 51–53.

Grieco, A. (2017). *Demanding a Plan for Cyber Resilience in the IoT*. Retrieved from https://blogs.cisco.com/security/demanding-a-plan-for-cyber-resilience-in-the-iot

Grimes, R. A. (2010). How to thwart employee cybercrime. *Insider Threat Deep Drive – Combating the Enemy Within, InfoWorld – Special Report*, 2-7. Retrieved August 5, 2012, from http://resources.idgenterprise.com/original/AST-0001528_insiderthreat_2_v1.pdf

Grobler, M., & Dlamini, Z. (2012). Global Cyber Trends: A South African Reality. *IST-Africa 2012 Conference Proceedings*.

Grobler, M., van Vuuren, J. J., & Leenen, L. (2012). *Implementation of a cyber security policy in South Africa: Reflection on progress and the way forward*. Paper presented at the IFIP International Conference on Human Choice and Computers. 10.1007/978-3-642-33332-3_20

Grobler, M., vanVuuren, J. J., & Jannie, Z. (2013). Preparing South Africa for Cyber Crime and Cyber Defense. *Systemics, Cybernetics and Informatics*, 32-41.

Grobler, M., Van Vuuren, J. J., & Zaaiman, J. (2013). Preparing South Africa for Cyber Crime and Cyber Defense. *Sytematics. Cybernetics and Informatics*, *11*(7), 32–41.

Grzonka, D., Jakobik, A., Kolodziej, J., & Pllana, S. (2017). *Using a multi-agent system and artificial intelligence for monitoring and improving the cloud performance and security. In Future Generation Computer Systems*. Elsevier.

Guidance Software. (2013). *Incident Response: Six Steps for Managing Cyber Breaches*. Author.

Gui-Hong, L., Hua, Z., & Gui-Zhi, L. (2010). *Building a Secure Web Server Based on OpenSSL and Apache*. Paper presented at the 2010 International Conference on E-Business and E-Government. 10.1109/ICEE.2010.334

Guinard, D., Trifa, V., & Mattern, F. (2011). *From the Internet of Things to the Web of Things: Resource Oriented Architecture and Best Practices*. Springer.

Gulati, R. (2003). *The Threat of Social Engineering and your defense against it*. SANS Institute, InfoSec Reading Room. Retrieved from: http://www.sans.org/reading-room/whitepapers/engineering/threat-social-engineering-defense-1232

Gunjan, K., Tiwari, R. K., & Sahoo, G. (2013). Towards Securing APIs in Cloud Computing. *International Journal of Computer Engineering & Applications*, *2*(2), 27-34.

Ha, T. (2017). *Ensuring Information Security in 4th Industrial Revolution*. Retrieved from https://www.vietnambreakingnews.com/2017/04/ensuring-information-security-in-4th-industrial-revolution/

Hackett, R. (2016, February 2). Drones Stand No Chance Against Trained Assassin Eagles. *Fortune*. Retrieved 6 June 2017 from http://fortune.com/2016/02/02/drone-eagle-take-down-video/

Hai-Jew, S. (2009). Exploring the immersive parasocial: Is it you or the thought of you? *MERLOT Journal of Online Learning and Teaching, 5*(3), 550 – 561. Retrieved from http://jolt.merlot.org/vol5no3/hai-jew_0909.pdf

Hak5. (n.d.). Hakshop. *Hakshop.com.org*. Retrieved 15 June 2017 from https://hakshop.com/

Haleplidis, E., Pentikousis, K., & Denazis, S. (2015). *Software-defined Networking (SDN): Layers and Architecture Terminology*. RFC 7426, IETF. Retrieved from https://www.rfc-editor.org/info/rfc7426

Hallsworth, S., & Lea, J. (2011). Reconstructing Leviathan: Emerging contours of the security state. *Theoretical Criminology, 15*(2), 141–157. doi:10.1177/1362480610383451

Haraoka, N. (2017, March). Cybersecurity: A Challenge to Business in the Era of the Fourth Industrial Revolution. *Japan Spotlight,* 1-45.

Harduth, N., & Sampson, L. (2017). *A Review of the King IV Report on Corporate Governance*. Retrieved from http://www.werksmans.com/assets/pdf/061741%20WERKSMANS%20king%20iv%20booklet.pdf

Harris, J., Ives, B., & Junglas, I. (2012). IT Consumerization: When Gadgets Turn Into Enterprise IT Tools. *MIS Quarterly Executive, 11*(3).

Harris, S., & Maymi, F. (2016). *CISSP All-in-One Exam Guide* (7th ed.). New York, NY: McGraw-Hill Education.

Haslum, K., & Årnes, A. (2006). Multisensor real-time risk assessment using continuous-time hidden markov models. In *International Conference on Computational and Information Science* (pp. 694–703). Academic Press. 10.1109/ICCIAS.2006.295318

Haslum, K., Abraham, A., & Knapskog, S. (2008). Fuzzy online risk assessment for distributed intrusion prediction and prevention systems. *Proceedings - UKSim 10th International Conference on Computer Modelling and Simulation, EUROSIM/UKSim2008,* 216–223. 10.1109/UKSIM.2008.30

Haslum, K., Moe, M. E. G., & Knapskog, S. J. (2008). Real-time intrusion prevention and security analysis of networks using HMMs. *2008 33rd IEEE Conference on Local Computer Networks (LCN),* 927–934. doi:10.1109/LCN.2008.4664305

Haslum, K., Abraham, A., & Knapskog, S. (2007). DIPS: A Framework for Distributed Intrusion Prediction and Prevention Using Hidden Markov Models and Online Fuzzy Risk Assessment. In *Third International Symposium on Information Assurance and Security* (pp. 183–190). IEEE. 10.1109/IAS.2007.67

Hathaway, M. E. (2016, Summer-Fall). Toward a closer digital alliance. *SAIS Review (Paul H. Nitze School of Advanced International Studies), 36*(2), 57–67.

Hatwar, V.S., & Chavan, H.K. (2015). Cloud Computing Security Aspects, Vulnerabilities and Countermeasures. *International Journal of Computer Applications, 119*(17), 46-53.

Hatwar, S. V., & Chavan, R. K. (2015). Cloud Computing Security Aspects, Vulnerabilities and Countermeasures. *International Journal of Computers and Applications, 119*(17), 46–53. doi:10.5120/21163-4218

Havlin, S., Kenett, D. Y., Ben-Jacob, E., Bunde, A., Cohen, R., Hermann, H., ... Solomon, S. (2012). Challenges in network science: Applications to infrastructures, climate, social systems, and economics. *The European Physical Journal. Special Topics, 214*(1), 273–293. doi:10.1140/epjst/e2012-01695-x

Hayden, M. V. (2016). *Playing to the Edge: American Intelligence in the Age of Terror*. New York: Penguin Press.

Hedin, Y., & Moradian, E. (2015). Security in Multi-Agent Systems. *Procedia Computer Science, 60,* 1604–1612. doi:10.1016/j.procs.2015.08.270

Hegarty, R. C., Lamb, D. J., & Attwood, A. (2014). Digital Evidence Challenges in the Internet of Things. *Proceedings of the Tenth International Network Conference*, 163-172.

Hegazy, I. M., Al-Arif, T., Fayed, Z. T., & Faheem, H. M. (2003). A multi-agent based system for intrusion detection. *IEEE Potentials*, *22*(4), 28–31. doi:10.1109/MP.2003.1238690

Henning, C. (2015, March 3). IOT is not IIOT. *Profinet.com*. Retrieved 13 June 2017 from http://us.profinet.com/iiot-is-not-iot/ ,

Herath, T., & Rao, H. R. (2009). Protection motivation and deterrence: A framework for security policy compliance in organisations. *European Journal of Information Systems*, *18*(2), 106–125. doi:10.1057/ejis.2009.6

Herrmann, M. (2009). Security Strategy: From Soup to Nuts. *Information Security Journal: A Global Perspective*, *18*(1), 26-32.

Herzog, S. (2011). Revisiting the Estonian Cyber. *Journal of Strategic Security*, 49-60.

Hewlett Packard Enterprise, FireEye, & Companies, M. M. (2016). Cyber resiliency in the Fourth Industrial Revolution. Author.

Hewlett-Packard Enterprise. (2014). *Cyber risk report 2013*. Hewlett-Packard Enterprise.

Heymann, E., Miller, B. E., Alghazzawi, M. J., & Incertis, D. (2016). *Addressing the cyber security of maritime shipping*. Retrieved May 24, 2017, from ftp://ftp.cs.wisc.edu/paradyn/papers/ETC_2016_Heymann_Miller.pdf

Higgins, K. J. (2015, June 10). Hospital Medical Devices Used as Weapons in Cyberattacks. *Dark Reading*. Retrieved 10 June 2015 from http://www.darkreading.com/vulnerabilities---threats/hospital-medical-devices-used-as-weapons-in-cyberattacks/d/d-id/1320751

Hilbert, M. (2012). How much information is there in the "information society"? *Significance*, *9*(4), 8–12. doi:10.1111/j.1740-9713.2012.00584.x

Hinson, G. (2008). Social engineering techniques, risks, and controls. *EDPAC: The EDP Audit, Control, and Security Newsletter*, *37*(4-5), 32–46. doi:10.1080/07366980801907540

History of the World Wide Web. (2017). In *Wikipedia*. Retrieved from https://en.wikipedia.org/wiki/History_of_the_-World_Wide_Web

HM Cabinet Office. (2011). *The UK Cyber Security Strategy - Protecting and Promotoing the UK in a Digital World. UK Government, Cabinet Office*. London: UK Government.

Hoffman, P. A. (2015). *National Critical Infrastructure Security and Resilience Month: Improving the Security and Resilience of the Nation's Grid*. Retrieved from https://energy.gov/articles/national-critical-infrastructure-security-and-resilience-month-improving-security-and

Hogan, B. Li, N., & Dutton, W.H. (2011, Feb. 14). *A global shift in the social relationships of networked individuals: Meeting and dating online comes of age*. Me, My Spouse and the Internet Project. Oxford Internet Institute, University of Oxford.

Holden, S. (1996). Theater Review: Hemingway, two years before the end. *The New York Times*. Retrieved from http://www.nytimes.com/1996/05/06/theater/theater-review-hemingway-two-years-before-the-end.html

Holeton, R. (1998). *Composing Cyberspace: Identity, Community, and Knowledge in the Electronic Age*. Boston: Mc-Graw Hill.

Holgado, P., Perez, M. G., Perez, G. M., & Villagra, V. A. (n.d.). Evolving from a static toward a proactive and dynamic risk-based defense strategy. Jornadas Nacionales de Investigacion en Ciberseguridad (JNIC 2015).

Hollis, D.M. (2011). Cyberwar case study: Georgia 2008. *Small Wars Journal,* 1 – 10.

Holloway, J., & Paláez, E. (2002). La guerra de todos los estados contra toda la gente. In *Guerra Infinita: hegemonía y terror mundial* (pp. 159–166). Buenos Aires: CLACSO.

Holmes, G. (2011). Card and mobile payment opportunities: A framework to consider potential winners and losers and a snapshot of the future payments landscape in Africa. *Journal of Payments Strategy and Systems, 5*(2), 134–142.

Holt, D. (2004). *How brands become icons. The principles of cultural branding.* Boston: Harvard Business School Press.

Holtfreter, R. E., & Harrington, A. (2014). Towards a Model for Data Breaches: An Universal Problem for the Public. *International Journal of Public Information Systems, 10*(1).

Holtzhausen, N. (2016). Ethical public information services. In E. Draai (Ed.), *A practical introduction to Public Management* (pp. 91–115). Cape Town: Oxford University Press.

Hong, J. (2012). The state of phishing attacks. *Communications of the ACM, 55*(1), 74–81. doi:10.1145/2063176.2063197

Hooper, E. (2008). Intelligent Techniques for Effective Network Protocol Security Monitoring, Measurement and Prediction. *Internal Journal of Security and its Applications,* 1-10.

Horton, D., & Wohl, R. R. (1956). Mass communication and para-social interaction: Observations on intimacy at a distance. *Psychiatry, 19*(3), 215–229. doi:10.1080/00332747.1956.11023049 PMID:13359569

How It Works. SmartThings. (2015). Retrieved from http://www.smartthings.com/how-it-works

Howie, L. (2012). *Witnesses to terror: Understanding the meanings and consequences of terrorism.* Basingstoke, UK: Pallagrave-Macmillan.

Howie, L. (2009). A Role for Business in the War on Terror. *Disaster Prevention and Management, 18*(2), 100–107. doi:10.1108/09653560910953180

Howie, L. (2011a). *Terror on the Screen: Witnesses and the Re-animation of 9/11 as Image-event, Popular Culture.* Washington, DC: New Academia Publishing, LLC.

Howie, L. (2011b). They were created by Man and they have a plan: Subjective and objective violence in BattleStar Galactica and the war on terror. *International Journal of Zizek Studies, 5*(2), 1–23.

Hu, Z.-H., Ding, Y.-S., & Huang, J.-W. (2008). Knowledge-based framework for real-time risk assessment of information security inspired by danger model. In *Intelligent Information Technology Application Workshops, 2008. IITAW'08. International Symposium on* (pp. 1053–1056). Academic Press.

Hubeschle, A. (2011). *The Dark Side of the Internet: Cybercrime.* Retrieved from http://www.issafrica.org/iss-today/the-dark-side-of-the-internet-cybercrime

Hudson, B. (2014). *Advanced Persistent Threats: Detection, Protection and Prevention.* Retrieved from http://resources.idgenterprise.com/original/AST-0112935_sophos-advanced-persistent-threats-detection-protectionprevention.pdf

Huet, J. M. (2017). *Will banks and telcos converge as money goes mobile.* Retrieved May 23, 2017, from https://www.bearingpoint.com/en-nl/about-us/news-and-media/press-releases/will-banks-and-telcos-converge-as-money-goes-mobile/

Hughes, D., & Colarik, A. (2017). The hierarchy of cyber war definitions. In G. A. Wang & ... (Eds.), *PAISI 2017. 15 – 33.* doi:10.1007/978-3-319-57463-9_2

Hughes, N., & Lonie, S. (2007). M-PESA: Mobile money for the "Unbanked" and turning cellphones into 24-Hour tellers in Kenya. *Innovations*, *2*(2), 63–81. doi:10.1162/itgg.2007.2.1-2.63

Hume, T., & Greene, R. A. (2016, April 18). Investigations launched after suspected drone strikes passenger jet in London. *CNN*. Retrieved 6 June 2017 from http://edition.cnn.com/2016/04/17/europe/london-heathrow-drone-strikes-plane/index.html

Hungtinton, S. P. (1997). *The Clash of Civilizations: Remaking of World Order*. New York: Touchstone Book.

Huntington, S. P. (2000). The Clash of Civilizations? In Culture and Politics (pp. 99-118). Palgrave Macmillan US.

Huntington, S. P. (1993). *The Third Wave. Democratization in the Late Twentieth Century*. Oklahoma University Press.

Huntley, W. L. (2016). Strategic implications of offense and defense in cyberwar. *2016 49th Hawaii International Conference on System Sciences*, 5588 – 5595. 10.1109/HICSS.2016.691

Hutchins, E. M., Cloppert, M. J., & Amin, R. M. (2011). *Intelligence-Driven Computer Network Defense Informed by Analysis of Adversary Campaigns and Intrusion Kill Chains*. Retrieved Jun 2017, 1, from https://www.lockheedmartin.com/content/dam/lockheed/data/corporate/documents/LM-White-Paper-Intel-Driven-Defense.pdf

Hutchinson, W., & Warren, M. (2001). *Information Warfare: Corporate Attacks and Defence in a Digital World*. Oxford, UK: Butterworth Heinemann.

IBM. (2014). *Building a security incident response plan that works*. Retrieved from USA: http://www-01.ibm.com/common/ssi/cgi-bin/ssialias?infotype=PM&subtype=XB&htmlfid=SEE03005USEN&attachment=SEE03005USEN.PDF#loaded

ICS-CERT. (2013). *Targeted Cyber Intrusion Detection and Mitigation Strategies (Update B)*. Retrieved May 30, 2017, from ICS _CERT: https://ics-cert.us-cert.gov/tips/ICS-TIP-12-146-01B

ICSPA. (2012). *Government needs to address cybersecurity at top level*. Retrieved from https://www.icspa.org/media/icspa-news/icspa-news-publications/p/6/article/government-needs-to-address-cybersecurity-at-top-level-23/abp/7/

Idris, N. B., & Shanmugam, B. (2005). Artificial Intelligence Techniques Applied to Intrusion Detection. *INDICON 2005 Annual IEEE Conference*, 52-55.

IEC. (2012). *IECTS 62443-1-1. International Electrotechnical Commission*. IEC.

IET. (2016). *Ports and port systems: cybersecurity code of practice. Institute of Engineering and Technology and UK Department for Transport*. IET.

Igor, K. (2010). Agent-based modelling and simulation of network cyber-attacks and cooperative mechanisms. *Discrete Event Simulations*, 1-25.

Igor, K. (2005). Agent-Based Modeling and Simulation of Cyber-Warfare between Malefactors and Security Agents in Internet. *Proceedings of 19th European Simulation Multiconference on Simulation in wider Europe*, 1-25.

Igor, K. (2007). Multi-agent Modelling and Simulation of Cyber-Attacks and Cyber-Defense for Homeland Security. *IEEE International Workshop on Intelligent Data Acquisition and Advanced Computing Systems: Technology and Applications*, 614-619.

Igor, K., & Alexander, U. (2005). Agent-based simulation of DDOS attacks and defence mechanisms. *Journal of Computers*, 1–10.

Industrie 4.0 Working Group. (2013). *Securing the Future of German Manufacturing Industry—Recommendations for Implementing the Strategic Initiative.* Acatech.

Insider, U. A. V. (2013). *What is the difference between a Drone, a UAV and a UAS?* Retrieved 5 June 2017 from http://www.uavinsider.com/what-is-the-difference-between-a-drone-a-uav-and-a-uas/

Institute of Directors South Africa. (2016). *KING IV.* Johannesburg: Author.

International Business Machines. (n.d.). *Cyber Resilience in the Age of IoT: Ask Bruce.* Retrieved from https://www.resilientsystems.com/cyber-resilience-knowledge-center/cyber-resilience-age-iot-ask-bruce/

International Data Group. (2016). *State of Resilience.* Retrieved from http://resources.idgenterprise.com/original/AST-0175041_2016-State-of-Resilience-Report.pdf

International Monetary Fund. (2014). *Regional Economic Outlook: Sub-Saharan Africa.* International Monetary Fund.

International Organization for Standardization. (2017). *ISO/IEC 27000 family - Information security management systems.* Retrieved from https://www.iso.org/isoiec-27001-information-security.html

Internet of Things Council. (n.d.). *The Internet of Things.* Retrieved from http://www.theinternetofthings.eu/what-is-the-internet-of-things

Internet relationship. (2017, Sept. 1). In *Wikipedia.* Retrieved from https://en.wikipedia.org/wiki/Internet_relationship

Internet Security Threat Report . (2017, April). Symantec Corporation. Retrieved from: https://www.symantec.com/content/dam/symantec/docs/reports/istr-22-2017-en.pdf

Interpol. (2016). *Coordinating Efforts to Better Combat Cybercrime Focus of INTERPOL Working Group.* Retrieved from http://www.interpol.int/News-and-media/News/2016/N2016-040

Invernizzi, L., McRoberts, K., & Bursztein, E. (2017). *Tracking desktop ransomware payments* [Google Slides]. Presented at the Black Hat USA 2017 Conference. Retrieved from: https://www.elie.net/talk/tracking-desktop-ransomware-payments-end-to-end

Ionita, D., Hartel, P. H., Pieters, W., & Wieringa, R. J. (2013). *Current established risk assessment methodologies and tools.* Technical Report TR-CTIT-14-04, Centre for Telematics and Information Technology, University of Twente, Enschede. Retrieved from http://eprints.eemcs.utwente.nl/24541/01/%5Btech_report%5D_D_Ionita_-_Current_Established_Risk_Assessment_Methodologies_and_Tools.pdf

ISACA. (2011). *COBIT 4.1.* Retrieved 24 May, 2016, from www.isaca.org

ISACA. (2013). *CISM Review Manual 2013.* .

ISACA. (2015). *State of Cybersecurity: Implications for 2015 - An ISACA and RSA Conference.* Retrieved from http://www.isaca.org/cyber/Documents/State-of-Cybersecurity_Res_Eng_0415.pdf

Ismail, T., & Masinge, K. (2011). *Mobile banking: Innovation for the Poor* (Published Masters dissertation). University of Pretoria, South Africa.

ISO. (2005). *Information technology–Security techniques–Information security management systems–Requirements.* ISO.

ISO/IEC 270001. (2005). *Information technology – Security techniques – Information security management systems – Requirements.* Geneva, Switzerland: ISO.

ISO/IEC. (2013). *ISO/IEC 27001:2013 - Information Security - Security Techniques - Information Security Management Systems.* International Organisation for Standardisation. ISO.

Israeli Homeland Security. (2013, August 7). *$80 million yacht hijacked by students spoofing GPS signals*. Retrieved from http://i-hls.com/2013/08/80-million-yacht-hijacked-by-students-spoofing-gps-signals/

Israeli Homeland Security. (2017a). *Unmanned Surface Drones Supply Naval Electronic Jamming*. Retrieved 13 April 2017 from http://i-hls.com/archives/75887

Israeli Homeland Security. (2017b, April 12). *Drone-Based EW System Will Hijack Phones*. Retrieved 20 April 2017 from http://i-hls.com/archives/76008

IST-Africa. (2011). Conference & Exhibition in Botswana. Gaborone: Author.

IT News Africa. (2017). *2016 Breach Level Index Shows 86% Rise in Data Breaches*. Retrieved from http://www.itnews-africa.com/2017/03/2016-breach-level-index-shows-86-rise-in-data-breaches/

IT-Online. (2016). *Kenya cyber attacks growing in sophistication*. Retrieved from http://it-online.co.za/2016/12/07/kenya-cyber-attacks-growing-in-sophistication/

Ivanov, A., Emm, D., Sinitsyn, F., & Pontiroli, S. (2016, December). Story of the year: The Ransomware revolution. *Kaspersky Security Bulletin 2016*. Retrieved from: https://securelist.com/kaspersky-security-bulletin-2016-story-of-the-year/76757/

Ivanov, A., Mamedov, O., & Sinitsyn, F. (2017, October 24). *Bad Rabbit ransomware*. Retrieved from: https://securelist.com/bad-rabbit-ransomware/82851/

Ixia. (2014). *Cyber Range: Improving Network Defense and Security Readiness*. Retrieved from http://info.ixiacom.com/rs/ixiacom/images/915-6729-01-Cyber-Range.pdf

Jackson, S., & Ferris, T. (2012). *Resilience Principles for Engineered Systems*. Wiley. DOI 10.1002ys.21228

Jackson, K. (1990). *Electronic computer conferencing and the AIDS disk. In Virus Bulletin* (p. 7). Oxon, UK: Virus Bulletin Ltd.

Jamal, A., & Anastasiadou, K. (2009). Investigating the effects of service quality dimensions and expertise on loyalty. *European Journal of Marketing*, *43*(3/4), 398–420. doi:10.1108/03090560910935497

James, D., & Philip, M. (2012). *A novel anti phishing framework based on visual cryptography*. Paper presented at the Power, Signals, Controls and Computation (EPSCICON), 2012 International Conference on. 10.1109/EPSCICON.2012.6175228

Janczewski, L. J., & Fu, L. (2010). Social engineering-based attacks: Model and new zealand perspective. *Computer Science and Information Technology (IMCSIT), Proceedings of the 2010 International Multiconference on Computer Science and Information Technology*, 847-853.

Jansson, K. (2011). *A model for cultivating resistance to social engineering attacks* (Doctoral dissertation). Retrieved from: http://dspace.nmmu.ac.za:8080/xmlui/handle/10948/1588

Javelin Strategy & Research. (2009). *The State of Mobile Security in Banking and Financial Transactions Report*. Syniverse Technologies.

Jeffery, J. (2017). *Media briefing on Cybercrimes and Cybersecurity Bill*. Retrieved from http://www.gov.za/speeches/cybercrimes-and-cybersecurity-bill-19-jan-2017-0000%20

Jenik, A. (2009). Cyberwar in Estonia and the Middle East. *Network Security*, 4–6.

Jenkins, B. (2008). *Developing Mobile Money Ecosystems*. Washington, DC: International Finance (IFC) and the Havard Kennedy School. Retrieved from http://www.hks.harvard.edu/m-rcbg/CSRI/publications/report_30_MOBILEMONEY.pdf

Jin, S. (2017). *IoT Devices Forensic Research*. Retrieved 22 June 2017 from https://www.troopers.de/downloads/troopers17/TR17_What_happened_to_your_home.pdf

Johnson, K. (2016, November 28). Ransomware Attacks the Cloud! *Posted to the cloud Cybersecurity blog*. Retrieved from: https://spinbackup.com/blog/ransomware-attacks-cloud/

Johnston, A. C., Warkentin, M., McBride, M., & Carter, L. (2016). Dispositional and situational factors: Influences on information security policy violations. *European Journal of Information Systems*, *25*(3), 231–251. doi:10.1057/ejis.2015.15

Johnstone, M. N. (2013). Embedding Secure Programming in the Curriculum: Some Lessons Learned. *IACSIT International Journal of Engineering and Technology*, *5*(2), 287–290. doi:10.7763/IJET.2013.V5.560

Joint Chiefs of Staff (2016, February 15). *Joint Publication 1-02: Department of Defense Dictionary of Military and Associated Terms*. US Department of Defense.

Jones, G. (2014). *South Africa neglects alarming effect of cybercrime*. Retrieved from http://www.bdlive.co.za/business/2014/01/14/south-africa-neglects-alarming-effect-of-cybercrime

Jones, S. (2017, January 6). Drone crashes into Boeing 737 jet plane coming into land at Mozambique airport. *The Mirror*. Retrieved 6 June 2017 from http://www.mirror.co.uk/news/world-news/drone-crashes-boeing-737-jet-9574073

Jones, G. R., & George, J. M. (2009). *Contemporary Management* (6th ed.). McGraw-Hill/Irwin.

Jose, G. J. A., & Sajeev, C. (2011). Implementation of Data Security in Cloud Computing. *International Journal of P2P Network Trends and Technology*, 18-22.

Jump, S. (2015). *Keeping your Organisation Safe wherever you are*. Paper presented at the National Science and Technology, South Africa: National Science and Technology Forum.

Juniper Network. (2011). *Mobile Device Security- Emerging threats, Essentials Strategies*. Retrieved 29 December, 2015, from www.google.co.uk/url?sa=t&rct=j&q=&esrc=s&source=web&cd=1&ved=0ahUKEwj60-6g5oDKAhWMWBoKHWjtASwQFggyMAA&url=http%3A%2F%2Fwww.bytes.co.uk%2Fdownload_file%2Fview%2F943%2F537%2F&usg=AFQjCNGVmC_t7GmVQqdw36AgYtv9orttwg

Jurišin, P., & Ivanička, K. (2010). Social engineering as a threat to it security in times of economic crisis. *6th International Scientific Conference, Vilnius, Lithuania. Business and management*, 836-841. 10.3846/bm.2010.111

Kabiraj, S., & Shanmugan, J. (2011). Development of a conceptual framework for brand loyalty: A Euro-Mediterranean perspective. *Journal of Brand Management*, *18*(4), 285–299. doi:10.1057/bm.2010.42

Kagan, R. (2004). *Of Paradise and Power: America and Europe in the new World Order*. New York: Vintage books.

Kahate, A. (2013). *Cryptography and network security*. Tata McGraw-Hill Education.

Kahneman, D., & Tversky, A. (1979). Prospect theory: An analysis of decision under risk. *Economoetrica*, *47*(2), 263–291. doi:10.2307/1914185

Kahn, J. (2017, May 03). Cyber extortion on the rise: Government organisations targeted. *Network*, 8.

Kaiser, R. (2015). The birth of cyberwar. *Political Geography*, *46*, 11–20. doi:10.1016/j.polgeo.2014.10.001

Kallberg, J. & Thuraisingham, B. (2013, May/June). State actors' offensive cyberoperations: The disruptive power of systematic cyberattacks. IT Pro. *IEEE Computer Society*, 32 – 35.

Kallberg, J., Thuraisingham, B., & Lakomaa, E. (2013). Societal Cyberwar Theory applied: The disruptive power of state actor aggression for public sector information security. *2013 European Intelligence and Security Informatics Conference (EISIC)*, 212 – 215. 10.1109/EISIC.2013.47

Kamara, S., & Lauter, K. (2010). *Cryptographic Cloud Storage.* Paper presented at the Financial Cryptography and Data Security, Tenerife, Canary Islands, Spain. 10.1007/978-3-642-14992-4_13

Kaminski, M. E. (2016, May 17). Enough With the "Sunbathing Teenager" Gambit. *Slate.* Retrieved 6 June 2017 from http://www.slate.com/articles/technology/future_tense/2016/05/drone_privacy_is_about_much_more_than_sunbathing_teenage_daughters.html

Kan, M. (2016, October 26). DDoS attack on Dyn came from 100,000 infected devices. *Computer World.* Retrieved 31 October 2016 from http://www.computerworld.com/article/3135434/security/ddos-attack-on-dyn-came-from-100000-infected-devices.html

Kandias, M., Virvilis, N., & Gritzalis, D. (2011). *The insider threat in cloud computing.* Paper presented at the International Workshop on Critical Information Infrastructures Security.

Kane, G. (n.d.). *The internet of things: An argument for cyber resilience.* Retrieved from https://www.zurich.com/_/media/dbe/corporate/knowledge/docs/zna-iot-an-argument-for-cyber-resilience.pdf

Kaplan, F. (2016). Inside 'Eligible Receiver': The NSA's disturbingly successful hack of the American military. *Slate.* Retrieved from http://www.slate.com/articles/technology/future_tense/2016/03/inside_the_nsa_s_-shockingly_successful_simulated_hack_of_the_u_s_military.html

Kaplan, S., & Garrick, B. J. (1981). On the quantitative definition of risk. *Risk Analysis, 1*(1), 11–27. doi:10.1111/j.1539-6924.1981.tb01350.x PMID:11798118

Karen, T. (2015). *Device Debacles – Lost, Stolen, and Neglected Data Risks.* Retrieved from https://www.allclearid.com/blog/device-debacles-lost-stolen-and-neglected-data-risks

Karim, K. H., & Eid, M. (2012). Clash of ignorance. Global Media Journal—Canadian Edition, 5(1), 7-27.

Karnwal, T., Sivakumar, T., & Aghila, G. (2012). *A Comber Approach to Protect Cloud Computing against XML DDoS and HTTP DDoS attack.* Paper presented at the 2012 IEEE Students' Conference on Electrical, Electronics and Computer Science, Bhopal, India.

Kaspersky Labs. (2016). *Industrial Control System Vulnerability Statistics.* Retrieved July 2, 2016, from https://kasperskycontenthub.com/securelist/files/2016/07/KL_REPORT_ICS_Statistic_vulnerabilities.pdf

Kasseeah, H., & Tandrayen-Ragoobur, V. (2012). Mobile Money in an Emerging Small Island Economy. *ARPN Journal of Science and Technology, 2*(5).

Kathleen, R. (2015). *Lack of cybersecurity awareness linked to CIOs.* Retrieved from www.searchsecurity.techtarget.com/opinion/Lack-of-cybersecurity-awareness-linked-to-CIOs

Kaufman, L. M. (2006). Data security in the world of cloud computing. *IEEE Security and Privacy*, 61–64.

Kazim, M., & Zhu, S. Y. (2015). A survey on top security threats in cloud computing. *(IJACSA). International Journal of Advanced Computer Science and Applications, 6*(3), 109–113. doi:10.14569/IJACSA.2015.060316

Kee, J. (2008). Social engineering: Manipulating the source. *GCIA Gold Certification*, 1-33. Retrieved from http://www.giac.org/paper/gcia/2968/social-engineering-manipulating-source/115738

Kelan, E., & Lehnert, M. (2009). *The millennial generation: generation y and the opportunities for a globalised, networked educational system*. Retrieved from https://www.academia.edu/4335172/The_millennial_generation_generation_y_and_the_opportunities_for_a_globalised_networked_educational_system

Keller, K. L. (2001). *Building Customer – based brand equity: a blueprint for creating strong brands* (Working paper 01-107). Cambridge, MA: Marketing Science Institution.

Kellner, D. (2003). Jean Baudrillard. In The Blackwell companion to major contemporary social theorists. Oxford, UK: Blackwell Publishing.

Kelly, H. (2012, Aug. 3). 83 million Facebook accounts are fakes and dupes. *CNN*. Retrieved from http://www.cnn.com/2012/08/02/tech/social-media/facebook-fake-accounts/index.html

Kelson, R., Paganini, P., Gittins, B., & Pace, D. (2012). The 'cyber war' era began long ago. *Security Affairs*. Retrieved from http://securityaffairs.co/wordpress/6776/security/the-cyber-war-era-began-long-ago.html

Kenny, L. (2017, April 12). IoT: The Internet of Trouble. *Security Intelligence*. Retrieved 7 June 2017 from https://securityintelligence.com/iot-the-internet-of-trouble/

Keohane, N., & Zeckhauser, R. (2003). The ecology of Terror defense. *Journal of Risk and Uncertainty, 26*(2-3), 201–229. doi:10.1023/A:1024167124083

Kepel, G. (2002). Los Hechos del 11 de Septiembre de 2001. In El Mundo Después del 11 de Septiembre de 2001. Barcelona: Editorial Península.

KeRanger: First Ransomware to Target Mac Users Found in BitTorrent Client. (2016, March 7). Retrieved from: https://www.trendmicro.com/vinfo/us/security/news/cybercrime-and-digital-threats/keranger-ransomware-target-mac-users-bittorrent-client/

Keskinen, A., Annala, I., & Miedema, P. (2017). *Maintenance of automated terminals*. Retrieved Jun 01, 2017, from Kalmarglobal.com: https://www.kalmarglobal.com/globalassets/services/kalmar-care/kalmar-maintenance-of-automated-terminals.pdf

Kganyago, L. (2016). *Collaboration for building cyber resilience* [Press release]. Retrieved from http://www.bis.org/review/r160825b.pdf

Khalil, I. M., Khreishah, A., & Azeem, M. (2014). Cloud Computing Security: A Survey. *Computers, 3*(4), 1–35. doi:10.3390/computers3010001

Khan, A. R. (2012). Access control in cloud computing environment. *Journal of Engineering and Applied Sciences (Asian Research Publishing Network), 7*(5), 613–615.

Kim, D., & Solomon, M. G. (2016). *Fundamentals of Information Systems Security* (3rd ed.). Burlington, MA: Jones & Bartlett Learning.

Kim, H. S., & Yoon, C. H. (2004). Determinants of subscriber churn and customer loyalty in the Korean Mobile telephony market. *Telecommunications Policy, 28*(9-10), 751–765. doi:10.1016/j.telpol.2004.05.013

Kim, Y. J., Kolesnikov, V., & Thottan, M. (2012). Resilient end-to-end message protection for large-scale cyber-physical system communications. *2012 IEEE Third International Conference on Smart Grid Communications (SmartGridComm)*, 193-198. 10.1109/SmartGridComm.2012.6485982

Kirk, J. (2009, January 19). Virus attacks Ministry of Defence. *CIO.co.uk*. Retrieved from http://www.cio.co.uk/news/3460/virus-attacks-ministry-of-defence/

Kirkpatrick, D. (2014). *Can Government Get a Better Grip on Tech?* Retrieved from Techonomy website: http://techonomy.com/2014/11/can-government-get-better-grip-tech/

Klimburg, A. (2017). *The Darkening Web: The War for Cyberspace*. New York: Penguin Press.

Klosowski, T. (2015, October 29). How to build a portable hacking station with a Raspberry Pi and Kali Linux. *Lifehacker.com*. Retrieved 19 June 2017 from http://lifehacker.com/how-to-build-a-portable-hacking-station-with-a-raspberr-1739297918

Knapp, E. D., & Langill, J. T. (2015). Industrial Network Security - Chapter 3 Industrial Cyber Security History and Trends. Elsevier.

Knorn, S., Chen, Z., & Middleton, R. H. (2016). Overview: Collective Control of Multi agent Systems. *Proceedings of the IEEE Transactions on Control of Network Systems*, 334-347.

Kolkowska, E., & Dhillon, G. (2013). Organisational power and information security rule compliance. *Computers & Security*, *33*(0), 3–11. doi:10.1016/j.cose.2012.07.001

Koppel, E. J. (2015). *Lights Out: A cyberattack, a nation unprepared, surviving the aftermath*. New York: Crown Publishers.

Korpella, K. (2015). Improving Cyber Security Awareness and Training Programs with Data Analytics. *Information Security Journal: A Global Perspective, 24*, 72-77. Retrieved from http://www.tandfonline.com/doi/abs/10.1080/19393555.2015.1051676

Korstanje, M. E. (2015b). *The Anthropology of dark Tourism, exploring the contradictions of Capitalism*. Centre for Ethnicity and Racism Studies, CERS. School of Sociology and Social Policy, University of Leeds UK. Working Paper #22.

Korstanje, M. E. (2013a). Preemption and Terrorism. When the Future Governs. *Cultura, 10*(1), 167–184. doi:10.5840/cultura20131019

Korstanje, M. E. (2013b). Del Patrimonio al Terrorismo. Regular el Turismo en una Época de Incertidumbre. *Rosa Dos Ventos, 5*(4), 655–658.

Korstanje, M. E. (2015a). *A Difficult World: examining the roots of capitalism*. New York: Nova Science Publishers.

Korstanje, M. E. (2016a). *The rise of Thana Capitalism and Tourism*. Abingdon, UK: Routledge.

Korstanje, M. E. (2016b). *Threat Mitigation and Detection of Cyber Warfare and Terrorism Activities*. Hershey, PA: IGI Global.

Kortjan, N., & Von Solms, R. (2014). A conceptual framework for cyber-security awareness and education in SA. *South African Computer Journal, 52*, 29–41. doi:10.18489acj.v52i0.201

Kotoky, A. (2017). *Cyberattack reaches Asia as new targets hit by ransomware*. Retrieved from http://www.fin24.com/Tech/News/cyberattack-reaches-asia-as-new-targets-hit-by-ransomware-20170628

Kovacs, E. (2014, June 6). Default password exposes digital highway signs to hacker attacks. *Security Week*. Retrieved from http://www.securityweek.com/default-password-exposes-digital-highway-signs-hacker-attacks

Kozlowski, A. (2015). *The 'cyber weapons gap.' The assessment of China's cyber warfare capabilities and its consequences for potential conflict over Taiwan*. University of Lodz Repository

KPMG International. (2016). *Cybersecurity for the fourth industrial revolution*. Author.

Kramek, J. (2013). *The Critical Infrastructure Gap: US Port Facilities and Cyber Vulnerabilities*. Retrieved May 27, 2016, from https://www.brookings.edu/research/the-critical-infrastructure-gap-u-s-port-facilities-and-cyber-vulnerabilities/

Kramer, A. D. I., & Guillory, J. E., & Hancock, J. T. (2014). Experimental evidence of massive-scale emotional contagion through social networks. *Proceedings of the National Academy of Sciences of the United States of America*, (24): 17. PMID:24889601

Krebbs, B. (2016). *Hacked Cameras, DVRs Powered Today's Massive Internet Outage*. Retrieved from https://krebsonsecurity.com/2016/10/hacked-cameras-dvrs-powered-todays-massive-internet-outage/

Krebs, B. (2014). *Spam Nation: The Inside Story of Organized Cybercrime—from Global Epidemic to your Front Door*. Naperville: Sourcebooks, Inc.

Krehel, O., & Bloom, E. (2016). *Data breach readiness*. Retrieved from http://www.securitysa.com/8655a

Krejcie, R. V., & Morgan, D. W. (1970). Determining sample size for research activities. *Educational and Psychological Measurement*, *30*(3), 607–610. doi:10.1177/001316447003000308

Kristol, W., & Kagan, R. (1996). Toward a Neo-Reaganite Foreign Policy. *Foreign Affairs*.

Kritzinger, E., & Von Solms, S.H. (2012). A Framework for Cyber Security in Africa. *Journal of Information Assurance & Cybersecurity*. DOI:10.5171/2012.322399

Krombholz, K., Hobel, H., Huber, M., & Weippl, E. (2015). Advanced Social Engineering Attacks. SBA Research, Favoritenstrae 16, AT-1040 Vienna, Austria.

Kudelski, A. (2016). *The dark side of the Fourth Industrial Revolution*. Retrieved from https://www.weforum.org/agenda/2016/01/the-dark-side-of-the-fourth-industrial-revolution/

Kumar, A. (2016). *As India Gears Up for Cybersecurity Challenges, Threats Are Multiplying*. Retrieved from https://securityintelligence.com/as-india-gears-up-for-cybersecurity-challenges-threats-are-multiplying/

Kumar, J. S., & Patel, D. R. (2014). A Survey on Internet of Things: Security and Privacy Issues. *International Journal of Computers and Applications*, *90*(11), 20–26. doi:10.5120/15764-4454

Kumar, S. V. K., & Padmapriya, S. (2014). A Survey on Cloud Computing Security Threats and Vulnerabilities. *International Journal of Innovative Research in Electrical, Electronics, Instrumentation and Control Engineering*, *2*(1), 622–625.

Kumbla, S. (2016). *The Big Data Effect on the Insurance Industry*. Retrieved April 07, 2017, from http://www.cuelogic.com/blog/big-data-effect-on-the-insurance-industry/

Kunkel, M. (2008a). EA/SIGINT Payloads for UAVs. *Journal of Electronic Defense*, *31*(6), 32–40.

Kurosu, M. (2013). Human-Computer Interaction: Towards Intelligent and Implicit Interaction. In *15th International Conference, HCI International 2013 Proceedings* (Vol. 8008). Springer.

Kushner, D. (2013, February 26). The Real Story of Stuxnet. *IEEE Spectrum*. Retrieved 12 June 2017 from http://spectrum.ieee.org/telecom/security/the-real-story-of-stuxnet

Kushner, D. (2016, Feb. 1). Scammers and spammers: Inside online dating's sex bot con job. *Rolling Stone*. Retrieved from http://www.rollingstone.com/culture/features/scammers-and-spammers-inside-online-datings-sex-bot-con-job-20160201

Kvedar, D., Nettis, M., & Fulton, S. P. (2010). The use of formal social engineering techniques to identify weaknesses during a computer vulnerability competition. *Journal of Computing Sciences in Colleges*, *26*(2), 80–87.

Kyobe, M., Matengu, S., Walter, P., & Shongwe, M. (2012). Factors inhibiting recognition and reporting of losses from cyber-attacks: The case of government departments in the Western Cape province of South Africa. In *Proceedings of the European Conference on Information Management and Evaluation*. Academic Conferences Ltd.

Lacey, D. (2009). *Managing the Human Factor in Information Security: How to win over staff and influence business*. West Sussex, England: Wiley.

Ladakis, E., Koromilas, L., Vasiliadis, G., Polychronakis, M., & Ioannidis, S. (2013). You can type, but you can't hide: A stealthy GPU-based keylogger. *Proceedings of the 6th European Workshop on System Security (EuroSec)*.

Lagazio, M., Sherif, N., & Cushman, M. (2014). A multi-level approach to understanding the impact of cybercrime on the financial sector. *Computers & Security*, *1*(1), 32.

Lallo-Ruiz, E. (2017). Intelligent Management of Seaside Logistic Operations at Maritime Container Terminals. *4OR - A Quarterly Journal of Operations Research*, *15*(2), 217-218.

Lam, S. K., Ahearne, M., Hu, Y., & Schillewaert, N. (2010). Resistance to brand switching when a radically new brand is introduced: A social identity theory perspective. *Journal of Marketing*, *74*(6), 128–146. doi:10.1509/jmkg.74.6.128

Langley, S. (2017). *What is your Understanding of Cyberterrorism?* Retrieved from https://tcsfs.org/2017/01/12what-is-your-understanding-of-cyber-terrorism/

Larson, K. (2016, October 4). Drones open new cyber-physical attack vector. *Control Global*. Retrieved 17 October 2016 from http://www.controlglobal.com/articles/2016/drones-open-new-cyber-physical-attack-vector/

Lawson, S. (2016, Dec. 7). Does 2016 mark the end of Cyber Pearl Harbor hysteria? Tech. *Forbes Magazine*. Retrieved from https://www.forbes.com/sites/seanlawson/2016/12/07/does-2016-mark-the-end-of-cyber-pearl-harbor-hysteria/#346ddd3d22c2

Lazarevic, V. (2011). Encouraging brand loyalty in fickle generation Y consumers. *Young Consumers*, *13*(1), 45–61. doi:10.1108/17473611211203939

Leavitt, N. (2011). *Mobile Security: Finally a Serious Problem*. Leavitt Communication Technologies.

Leavitt, N. (2013). Today's mobile security requires a new approach. *Computer*, *46*(11), 16–19. doi:10.1109/MC.2013.400

Lebek, Degirmenci, & Breitner. (2013). *Investigating the Influence of Security, Privacy, and Legal Concerns on Employees' Intention to Use BYOD Mobile Devices*. Academic Press.

Lee, E. A. (2008). Cyber Physical Systems: Design Challenges. *2008 11th IEEE International Symposium on Object and Component-Oriented Real-Time Distributed Computing (ISORC)*, 363–369. doi:10.1109/ISORC.2008.25

Lee, M. (2014). *IT security is not an optional extra*. Retrieved from ZDNet website: http://www.zdnet.com/it-security-is-not-an-optional-extra-7000025991/

Lee, N. (2015). *Cyber attacks, prevention, and countermeasures. In Counterterrorism and Cybersecurity* (pp. 249–286). Springer.

Lee, S. H., Levendis, J., & Gutierrez, L. (2012). Telecommunications and economic growth: An empirical analysis of sub-Saharan Africa. *Applied Economics*, *44*(4), 461–469. doi:10.1080/00036846.2010.508730

Lee, S. Y., Tongzon, J. L., & Yonghee, K. (2015). Port e-transformation, customer satisfaction and competitiveness. *Maritime Policy & Management*, *43*(5), 630–643. doi:10.1080/03088839.2015.1105394

Levine, T. R. (2014). Truth-Default Theory (TDT): A theory of human deception and deception detection. *Journal of Language and Social Psychology*, *33*(4), 378–392. doi:10.1177/0261927X14535916

Lewis, J. A. (2011, September). Oct.) Cyberwar thresholds and effects. *IEEE Security and Privacy*, *9*(5), 23–29. doi:10.1109/MSP.2011.25

Leyden, J. (2008, January 11). Polish teen derails tram after hacking train network. *The Register*. Retrieved from http://www.theregister.co.uk/2008/01/11/tram_hack/

Li, X., Ortiz, P. J., Browne, J., Franklin, D., Oliver, J. Y., Geyer, R., & Chong, F. T. (2010, September). Smartphone evolution and reuse: Establishing a more sustainable model. In *Parallel Processing Workshops (ICPPW), 2010 39th International Conference on* (pp. 476-484). IEEE.

Li, X.-Y., Shi, Y., Guo, Y., & Ma, W. (2011). *Multi-Tenancy Based Access Control in Cloud*. Paper presented at the Computational Intelligence and Software Engineering (CiSE).

Liao, N., Li, F., & Song, Y. (2010). Research on real-time network security risk assessment and forecast. In *Intelligent Computation Technology and Automation (ICICTA), 2010 International Conference on* (Vol. 3, pp. 84–87). Academic Press. 10.1109/ICICTA.2010.273

Libicki, M.C. (2011). Cyberwar as a confidence game. *Strategic Studies Quarterly, 132 – 146.*

Libicki, M. C. (2009). *Cyberdeterrence and cyberwar. Project Airforce*. RAND Corporation.

Libicki, M. C. (2013). Brandishing cyberattack in a nuclear confrontation. In *Brandishing Cyberattack Capabilities*. RAND Corporation.

Li, J. H., & Levy, R. (2010). Using Bayesian networks for cyber security analysis. *2010 IEEE/IFIP International Conference on Dependable Systems & Networks (DSN)*, 211–220. doi:1109/DSN.2010.5544924

Lim, M. (2005). Islamic radicalism and anti-Americanism in Indonesia: The role of the Internet. *Policy Studies*, (18).

Lindemann, L. (2015). *Towards Abuse Detection and Prevention in IaaS Cloud Computing*. Paper presented at the Availability, Reliability and Security (ARES), 10th International Conference on. 10.1109/ARES.2015.72

List of cognitive biases. (2017, Oct. 2). In *Wikipedia*. Retrieved from https://en.wikipedia.org/wiki/List_of_cognitive_biases

Liu, F., Chen, Y., Dai, K., Wang, Z., & Cai, Z. (2005). *Research on Risk Probability Estimating Using Fuzzy Clustering for Dynamic Security*. Academic Press.

Liu, A., Martin, C., Hetherington, T., & Matzner, S. (2005). A comparison of system call feature representations for insider threat detection. In *Proceedings of the 2005 IEEE Workshop on Information Assurance*. West Point, NY: United States Military Academy. 10.1109/IAW.2005.1495972

Liu, C.-W., Huang, P., & Lucas, H. C. (2016). *IT Governance, Security Outsourcing, and Cybersecurity Breaches: Evidence from US Higher Education*. SAGE.

Liu, Y., Sun, Y., Ryoo, J., Rizvi, S., & Vasilakos, A. V. (2015). A Survey of Security and Privacy Challenges in Cloud Computing: Solutions and Future Directions. *Journal of Computing Science and Engineering: JCSE, 9*(3), 119–133. doi:10.5626/JCSE.2015.9.3.119

Livadas, C., Walsh, R., Lapsley, D., & Strayer, W. T. (2006). Using Machine Learning Technliques to Identify Botnet Traffic. *Proceedings of the 31st IEEE Conference on Local Computer Networks*, 967-974.

Li, W., & Guo, Z. (2009). Hidden Markov Model Based Real Time Network Security Quantification Method. *2009 International Conference on Networks Security, Wireless Communications and Trusted Computing*, 94–100. 10.1109/NSWCTC.2009.375

Li, X., Hess, T. J., & Valacich, J. S. (2008). Why do we trust new technology? A study of initial trust formation with organizational information systems. *The Journal of Strategic Information Systems, 17*(1), 39–71. doi:10.1016/j.jsis.2008.01.001

Li, Z., Jin, D., & Hannon, C. (2016). Assessing and mitigating cybersecurity risks of traffic light systems in smart cities. *IET Cyber-Physical Systems: Theory & Applications*, *1*(1), 60–69.

Lo, H.L., & Preskill, J. (2007). Security of quantum key distribution using weak coherent states with non-random phases. *Quant. Inf. Comp., 7*(58).

Lomas, N. (2015, February 10). Samsung Edits Orwellian Clause Out Of TV Privacy Policy. *Tech Crunch*. Retrieved 12 June 2017 from https://techcrunch.com/2015/02/10/smarttv-privacy/

Longe, O. B., & Chiemeke, S. C. (2008). *Cyber Crime And Criminality in Nigeria: What Roles are Internet Access Points Playing?* Academic Press.

López, D., Pastor, O., & Villalba, L. J. G. (2013). Dynamic risk assessment in information systems: State-of-the-art. *Proceedings of the 6th International Conference on Information Technology*, 8–10. Retrieved from http://sce.zuj.edu.jo/icit13/images/Camera Ready/Sorftware Engineering/772.pdf

Lowman, S. (2016). *WEF 2016: 4th Industrial Revolution. 5mn jobs, women in the firing line.* Retrieved from http://www.biznews.com/wef/davos-2016/2016/01/18/wef-2016-4th-industrial-revolution-5mn-jobs-women-in-the-firing-line/

Loy, D. (2007). CyberBabel? *Ethics and Information Technology*, *9*(4), 251–258. doi:10.100710676-007-9146-2

Lua, R., & Yow, K. (2011). Mitigating DDoS attacks with transparent and intelligent fast-flux swarm network. *IEEE Network*, *25*(4), 28–33. doi:10.1109/MNET.2011.5958005

Lucas, E. (2015). *Cyberphobia: Identity, Trust, Security and the Internet.* New York: Bloomsbury.

Lye, D. (2017). *The Fourth Industrial Revolution and Challenges for Government.* Retrieved from http://www.gereports.com/fourth-industrial-revolution-challenges-government/

Lynch, D. M. (2006). Securing against insider attacks. *Information Security and Risk Management*, 39-47. Retrieved August 5, 2012, from http://www.csb.uncw.edu/people/ivancevichd/classes/MSA%20516/Supplemental%20Readings/Supplemental%20Reading%20for%20Wed,%2011-5/Insider%20Attacks.pdf

Lyon, D. (2010). Liquid surveillance: The contribution of Zygmunt Bauman to surveillance studies. *International Political Sociology*, *4*(4), 325–338. doi:10.1111/j.1749-5687.2010.00109.x

Lyons, J. (2013). *How can Governments be motivated to collaborate internationally to mitigate cybercrime effectively?* Retrieved from https://www.icspa.org/uploads/media/John_Lyons_Chief_Executive_ICSPA_GES_Kiel_2013_Challenge.pdf

Lyra, M., & Simoes, J. (2015). Checking the Maturity of Security Policies for Information and Communication. *ISACA*, *2*, 48–53.

Ma, J., Li, Z., & Zhang, H. (2009). A fusion model for network threat identification and risk assessment. In Artificial Intelligence and Computational Intelligence, 2009. AICI'09. International Conference on (Vol. 1, pp. 314–318). Academic Press. doi:10.1109/AICI.2009.487

MacAskill, E., & Syal, R. (2017). *Cyber-attack on UK parliament: Russia is suspected culprit.* Retrieved from https://www.theguardian.com/politics/2017/jun/25/cyber-attack-on-uk-parliament-russia-is-suspected-culprit

Macaulay, T., & Singer, B. (2012). *Cybersecurity for Industrial Control Systems: SCADA, DCS, PLC, HMI and SIS.* Auerbach Publications.

Macharia, K. (2011). *Fraudsters eye mobile money.* Retrieved April 23, 2017, from http://www.itweb.co.za/index.php?option=com_content&view=article&id=41727

Macias, F., & Thomas, G. (2011). *Cloud Computing Advantages in the Public Sector.* Retrieved from http://www.cisco.com/c/dam/en_us/solutions/industries/docs/c11-687784_cloud_omputing_wp.pdf

Maclntosh, J. P., Reid, J., & Tyler, L. R. (2011). *Cyber Doctrine: Towards A Coherent Evolutionary Framework for Learning Resilience.* Institute for Security and Resilience Studies, UCL. Retrieved from https://www.ucl.ac.uk/isrs/publications/CyberDoctrine

Madzima, K., Dube, E.L., & Mashwama, P.M. (2013). *ICT Education in Swaziland Secondary Schools: Opportunities and Challenges.* Academic Press.

Maggi, F., Quarta, D., Pogliani, M., & Polino, M. (2017, May 3). *Rogue Robots: Testing the limits of an industrial robot's security.* A TrendLabs Research Paper. Retrieved from: https://www.trendmicro.com/vinfo/us/security/news/internet-of-things/rogue-robots-testing-industrial-robot-security

Mahajan, H., & Giri, N. (2014). Threats to Cloud Computing Security. *International Journal of Application or Innovation in Engineering & Management.*

Mahlobo, D. (2017, March 27). Time to protect confidentiality of information. *Business Report,* p. 14.

Mahlobo, D. (2017). *State Security Agency Budget Vote 2017/18.* Pretoria: State Security Agency.

Ma, J., & Nickerson, J. V. (2006). Hands-on, simulated, and remote laboratories: A comparative literature review. *ACM Computing Surveys, 38*(3), 7.

MalwareHunterTeam. (2016, December 12). *Someone is continuously working on a new ransomware in the past days.* Retrieved from https://twitter.com/malwrhunterteam/status/808280549802418181

MalwareHunterTeam. (2016, December 7). *Next ransomware on the table: Popcorn Time.* Retrieved from https://twitter.com/malwrhunterteam/status/806595092177965058

Mann, T. (2013). Computer Problems Leaves Goods Stranded at New York Port. *The Wall Street Journal.*

Manske, K. (2000). An introduction to social engineering. *Information Systems Security, 9*(5), 1-7.

Manzoor, A. (2014). Protecting Customers Online: Response from Banks. *International Journal of Science and Applied Information Technology, 3*(1), 1–7.

Marcella, A. J., & Terwilliger, B. A. (2017). *Rise of the Drones: Is Your Enterprise Prepared?* Rolling Meadows, IL: ISACA.

Marenko, B. (2010). Contagious Affectivity. The Management of Emotions in Late Capitalist Design. *"Negotiating Futures – Design Fiction". Proceedings from the 6th Swiss Design Network Conference,* 134-149.

Mark, O. (2014). *Bring your own internet of things.* Retrieved 01 January, 2015, from http://www.bringyourowninternetofthingscomingtobusinessin2015/

Mark, T., & Jethro, M. (2017, May 14). *CNN tech.* Retrieved from CNN Money Website: http://money.cnn.com/2017/05/14/technology/ransomware-attack-threat-escalating/

Market Share Statistics for Internet Technologies. (2017). *Net Market Share.* Retrieved from: https://www.netmarketshare.com/

Marsan, D. C. (2015). IAB Releases Guidelines for Internet-of-Things Developers. *IETF Journal, 11*(1), 6-8. Retrieved from https://www.internetsociety.org/sites/default/files/Journal_11.1.pdf

Martell, L. (2010). *The sociology of globalization.* Cambridge, UK: Polity Press.

Martin, W. (2016, February 17). *Security: are we overlooking the most critical aspect of the fourth industrial revolution?* Retrieved from Memeburn: https://memeburn.com/2016/02/security-are-we-overlooking-the-most-critical-aspect-of-the-fourth-industrial-revolution/

Martini, B., & Choo, K. R. (2013). Cloud Storage Forensics: Own Cloud as a Case Study. *Digital Investigation, 10*(4), 287–299. doi:10.1016/j.diin.2013.08.005

Mas, I., & Radcliffe, D. (2010). *Mobile Payments Go Viral: M-PESA in Kenya*. Retrieved March 26, 2017 from Washington: http://ssrn.com/abstract=1593388

Mas, I. (2010). Savings for the Poor: Banking on Mobile Phones. *World Economy, 11*(4).

Mas, I. (2012). Transforming Access to Finance in Developing Countries through Mobile Phones: Creating an Enabling Policy, Framework. *Banking & Finance Law Review, 27*(2), 285–298.

Mas, I., & Radcliffe, D. (2011). Scaling Mobile Money. *Journal of Payment Strategy & Systems, 5*(3), 298–315.

Masters, G. (2017). *Loss from cybercrime exceeded $1.3B in 2016*. Retrieved from https://www.scmagazine.com/loss-from-cybercrime-exceeded-13b-in-2016-fbi-report/article/671047/

Mataracioglu, T., & Ozkan, S. (2011). *User Awareness Measurement through Social Engineering*. Academic Press.

Mathas, C. (2013). *Industry 4.0 is closer than you think, EDN's Hot Technologies*. Academic Press.

Mathew, S., Upadhyaya, S., Ha, D., & Ngo, H. Q. (2008). *Insider abuse comprehension through capability acquisition graphs*. Paper presented at the Information Fusion, 2008 11th International Conference on.

Matinde, V. (2015). *The rise of BYOD and corporate data threats*. Academic Press.

Matloob, G., & Siddiqui, F. (2017). Data at rest and it's security solutions-A survey. *International Journal of Advanced Research in Computer Science, 8*(5), 1491–1493.

Matsubara, M. (2016). *Cybersecurity is Not a Cost - Leverage the Fourth Revolution for Economic Growth*. Retrieved from https://researchcenter.paloanetworks.com/2016/06/cso-cybersecurity-is-not-a-cost-leverage-the-fourth-industrial-revolution-for-economic-growth/

Mawhinney, M. (2017, April 4). Islamic State using hobby drones with deadly effect. *Sky News*. Retrieved 7 May 2017 from http://news.sky.com/story/islamic-state-using-hobby-drones-with-deadly-effect-10823505

Maybury, M., Chase, P., & Cheikes, B. (2005). *Analysis and Detection of Malicious Insiders*. Retrieved Jun 01, 2017, from https://www.mitre.org/publications/technical-papers/analysis-and-detection-of-malicious-insiders

Mazur, M. A., Burns, R. J., & Emmers-Sommer, T. M. (2000). Perceptions of relational interdependence in online relationships: The effects of communication apprehension and introversion. *Communication Research Reports, 17*(4), 397–406. doi:10.1080/08824090009388788

McAfee Labs. (2016). *McAfee Labs Threats Report 2016*. Retrieved May 12, 2017, from https://www.mcafee.com/uk/resources/reports/rp-quarterly-threats-sep-2016.pdf

McAfee. (2013). *Mobile Security: McAfee Consumer Trends Report*. Retrieved April 25, 2017, from, http://www.mcafee.com/us/resources/reports/rpmobile- security-consumer-trends.pdf

McCarthy, I. P., Collard, M., & Johnson, M. (2017). Adaptive organizational resilience: An evolutionary perspective. *Current Opinion in Environmental Sustainability, 28*, 33–40. doi:10.1016/j.cosust.2017.07.005

McCauley, C., & Moskalenko, S. (2008). Mechanisms of political radicalization: Pathways toward terrorism. *Terrorism and Political Violence*, *20*(3), 415–433. doi:10.1080/09546550802073367

McCoy, A. W. (2017). *In the Shadows of the American Century: The Rise and Decline of US Global Power*. Chicago, IL: Haymarket Books.

McKelvey, F., Tiessen, M., & Simcoe, L. (2015). A consensual hallucination no more? The Internet as simulation machine. *European Journal of Cultural Studies*, *18*(4-5), 577–594. doi:10.1177/1367549415584856

McKinley, D. (2003). *The State of Access to Information in South Africa*. Retrieved from http://www.ritecodev.co.za/csvrorig/docs/trc/stateofaccess.pdf

McMillan, R. (2007). *NSA helped Microsoft make vista secure*. CSO.

Meads, D. (2017). *Here's how Africa can take advantage of 4th Industrial Revolution*. Retrieved from http://ewn.co.za/2017/05/02/here-s-how-africa-can-take-advantage-of-the-fourth-industrial-revolution#

Mendel, J. M. (1995). Fuzzy logic systems for engineering: A tutorial. *Proceedings of the IEEE*, *83*(3), 345–377. doi:10.1109/5.364485

Mercer, C. (2017). *What is a DDoS attack? What happens during a DDoS attack*. Retrieved from http://www.techworld.com/security/how-does-ddos-attack-work-3659197/

Merkle, E. R., & Richardson, R. A. (2000, April). Digital dating and virtual relating: Conceptualizing computer mediated romantic relationships. *Family Relations*, *49*(2), 187–192. doi:10.1111/j.1741-3729.2000.00187.x

Merriam-Webster. (2017). *Definition of resilience*. Retrieved from https://www.merriam-webster.com/dictionary/resilience

Mesch, G. S., & Talmud, I. (2007). Similarity and the quality of online and offline social relationships among adolescents in Israel. *Journal of Research on Adolescence*, *17*(2), 455–466. doi:10.1111/j.1532-7795.2007.00529.x

Mesch, G., & Talmud, I. (2006). The quality of online and offline relationships: The role of multiplexity and duration of social relationships. *The Information Society*, *22*(3), 1–25. doi:10.1080/01972240600677805

Mettler, K. (2016, June 6). Somebody keeps hacking these Dallas road signs with messages about Donald Trump, Bernie Sanders and Harambe the gorilla. *Washington Post*. Retrieved 15 June 2017 from https://www.washingtonpost.com/news/morning-mix/wp/2016/06/06/somebody-keeps-hacking-these-dallas-road-signs-with-messages-about-donald-trump-bernie-sanders-and-harambe-the-gorilla/

Michalopoulos, D., Mavridis, I., & Jankovic, M. (2014). GARS: Real-time system for identification, assessment and control of cyber grooming attacks. *Computers & Security*, *42*, 177–190. doi:10.1016/j.cose.2013.12.004

Michalsons. (2017). *Cybersecurity Bill - Overview of the Cyber Bill*. Retrieved from https://www.michalsons.com/blog/cybercrimes-and-cybersecurity-bill-the-cac-bill/16344

Microsoft. (2011). *Microsoft Security Intelligence Report* (Vol. 11). Microsoft Corporation.

Miller, Voas, & Hurlburt. (2012). BYOD: Security and privacy considerations. *IT Professional, 14*(5), 0053-0055.

Miller, M. (2015). *New York State Cyber Incident Reporting Procedures*. New York: New York State.

Mills, R. F., Grimaila, M. R., Peterson, G. L., & Butts, J. W. (2011). A scenario-based approach to mitigating the insider threat. *Information Systems Security Association Journal*, *9*(5), 12–19.

Mitcham, C. (1997). Thinking Ethics in Technology. Golden, Division of liberal arts and international Studies. Colorado School of Mines.

Mitnick, K. D., & Simon, W. L. (2001). *The art of deception: Controlling the human element of security*. Indianapolis: Wiley.

Moavenzadeh, J. (2015). *The 4th Industrial Revolution: Reshaping the Future of Production*. Paper presented at the DHL Global Engineering & Manufacturing Summit, Amsterdam.

Moavenzadeh, J. (2016). *The fourth industrial revolution: Reshaping the future of production*. Retrieved 20 November, 2017, from www.eiseverywhere.com/file_uploads/fe238270f05e2dbf187e2a60cbcdd68e_2_Keynote_John_Moavenzadeh_World

Modi, C., Patel, D., Borisaniya, B., Patel, A., & Rajarajan, M. (2013). A Survey on Security Issues and Solutions at Different Layers of Cloud Computing. *The Journal of Supercomputing, 63*(2), 561–592. doi:10.100711227-012-0831-5

Moir, R. (2003). *Defining Malware: FAQ*. Retrieved from: https://technet.microsoft.com/en-us/library/dd632948.aspx

Mokati, N. (2016). *Panic hits as Anonymous hack SA sites*. Retrieved from http://www.iol.co.za/news/politics/panic-hits-as-anonymous-hack-sa-sites-1984103

Monk, T., Van Niekerk, J., & von Solms, R. (2009). Concealing the Medicine: Information Security Education through Game Play. ISSA, 467-478.

Montresor, F. (2016). *The 7 technologies changing your world*. Retrieved from https://www.weforum.org/agenda/2016/01/a-brief-guide-to-the-technologies-changing-world/

Moorad, Z. (2011). *Local business 'underinsured against hacking'*. Retrieved from http://mg.co.za/article/2011-06-21-local-business-underinsured-against-hacking

Moore, J. (2014). *Business Intelligence takes to Cloud for small businesses*. Retrieved from https://www.cio.com/article/2375744/business-intelligence/business-intelligence-takes-to-cloud-for-small-businesses.html

Moore, A. W., & Zuev, D. (2005). Internet traffic classification using bayesian analysis techniques. *Proceedings of the 2005 ACM SIGMETRICS international conference*, 50-60. 10.1145/1064212.1064220

Morawczynski, O. (2009). Exploring the usage and impact of "transformational" mobile financial services: The case of M-PESA in Kenya. *Journal of Eastern African Studies: the Journal of the British Institute in Eastern Africa, 3*(3), 509–525. doi:10.1080/17531050903273768

Morgan, S. (2016). One Million Cybersecurity Job Openings in 2016. *Forbes*.

Morgan, S. (2016, Jan. 17). Cyber crime costs projected to reach $2 trillion by 2019. *Forbes Magazine*. Retrieved from https://www.forbes.com/sites/stevemorgan/2016/01/17/cyber-crime-costs-projected-to-reach-2-trillion-by-2019/#95c83ba3a913

Mori, T. (2016). Financial technology: Blockchain and Securities Settlement. *Journal of Securities Operations & Custody, 8*(3).

Morrison, J. (2017, March 29). *2017: The Year of Ransomware. Posted to plixer cyber-attack blog*. Retrieved from: https://www.plixer.com/blog/cyber-attack-2/ransomware-attacks-2017/

Motivation and emotion / Book/ 2014 / Plutchik's wheel of emotions. (2017, Sept. 23). In *Wikiversity*. Retrieved from https://en.wikiversity.org/wiki/Motivation_and_emotion/Book/2014/Plutchik%27s_wheel_of_emotions#Plutchik.27s_wheel_of_emotions

Motti, V. G., & Caine, K. (2015). Users' Privacy Concerns about Wearables: impact of form factor, sensors and type of data collected. *19th International Conference Financial Cryptography and Data Security 2015*. Retrieved 12 June 2017 from http://fc15.ifca.ai/preproceedings/wearable/paper_2.pdf

MS-ISAC. (2013). *Cyber Security Getting Started: A Non Technical Guide*. Retrieved from http://msisac.cisecurity.org/resources/guides

Muggah, R., Diniz, G., & Glenny, M. (2014). *Brazil doubles down on cybersecurity*. Retrieved from https://www.opendemocracy.net/robert-muggah-gustavo-diniz-misha-glenny/brazil-doubles-down-on-cybersecurity

Mulligan, P., & Gordon, S. R. (2002). The impact of information technology on customer and supplier relationships in the financial services. *International Journal of Service Industry Management, 13*(1), 29–46. doi:10.1108/09564230210421146

Mungo, P., & Clough, B. (1992). *Approaching zero: The extraordinary underworld of hackers, phreakers, virus writers, and keyboard criminals*. New York, NY: Random House.

Munir, A. M. (2014). An Integrated Approach to Enterprise Risk. *ISACA Journal*, 1-10.

Musa, S. (n.d.). *Smart City Roadmap*. Retrieved from http://www.academia.edu/21181336/Smart_City_Roadmap

Musa, F. A., & Sani, S. M. (2016). Security Threats and Countermeasures In Cloud Computing. *International Research Journal of Electronics & Computer Engineering, 2*(4), 22–27.

Mussomeli, A., Gish, D., & Laaper, S. (2017). *The rise of the digital supply network Industry 4.0 enables the digital transformation of supply chains*. Deloitte University Press. Retrieved 11 October 2017, from https://dupress.deloitte.com/content/dupress/dup-us-en/focus/industry-4-0/digital-transformation-in-supply-chain.html

Myburgh, F., & De Costa, A. (2017). *The key differences between King III and King IV*. Retrieved from http://www.polity.org.za/article/the-key-differences-between-king-iii-and-king-iv-2017-01-11

Nacos, B. (2016). *Mass-mediated terrorism: Mainstream and digital media in terrorism and counterterrorism*. New York: Rowman & Littlefield.

Nadeem, A., & Howarth, M. P. (2013). A survey of manet intrusion detection & prevention approaches for network layer attacks. *IEEE Communications Surveys and Tutorials, 15*(4), 2027–2045. doi:10.1109/SURV.2013.030713.00201

Nadine, W., & Hadas, K. (2017). Artificial Intelligence in Cybersecurity. *Cyber, Intelligence, and Security*, 103-119.

Nagpal, B., Kumar, M., & Vij, S. (2016). Internet of Things: Effective Security View through Artificial Intelligence. *International Journal of Science Technology & Engineering*, 1-10.

Nagurney, A. & Shukla, S. (2016, Dec.) Multifirm models of cybersecurity investment competition vs. cooperation and network vulnerability. *European Journal of Operational Research, 260*(2017), 588 – 600.

Naidoo, S. (2016). *SA losing billions each year to cyber-crime*. Retrieved from http://www.sabc.co.za/news/a/d2825f-804c7c4a338a38db3b0fa74342/SA-losing-billions-each-year-to-cyber-crime-20160421

Nair, Y. (2017, May 17). Cybercrimes a threat to SA, warns minister. *The Mercury*, p. 6.

Naisbitt, J. (1993). *Global Paradox: The Bigger the World Economy, the More Powerful Its Smallest Players*. New York: William Morrow & Co., Inc.

Nakashima, E. (2017). U.S. declares North Korea carried out massive WannaCry cyberattack. National Security. *The Washington Post*. Retrieved from https://www.washingtonpost.com/world/national-security/us-set-to-declare-north-korea-carried-out-massive-wannacry-cyber-attack/2017/12/18/509deb1c-e446-11e7-a65d-1ac0fd7f097e_story.html?utm_term=.0d8c6361a841

Narwane, S. V., & Vaikol, S. L. (2012). *Intrusion Detection System in Cloud Computing Environment*. Paper presented at the International Conference on Advances in Communication and Computing Technologies (ICACACT).

Nate, L. (2016). *Data Security Experts Reveal The #1 Information Security Issue Most Companies Face with Cloud Computing & Storage*. Retrieved from https://digitalguardian.com/blog/27-data-security-experts-reveal-1-information-security-issue-most-companies-face-cloud

National Cryptologic Centre. (2017). *National Security Framework Cyber-Incident Management*. Retrieved from Spain: https://www.ccn-cert.cni.es/pdf/2025-ccn-stic-817-national-security-framework-cyber-incident-management/file.html

National Institute of Standards and Technology. (2012). *Computer Security Incident Handling Guide*. Author.

National Institute of Standards and Technology. (2014). *Framework for Improving Critical Infrastructure Cybersecurity*. Retrieved from http://www.nist.gov/cyberframework/upload/cybersecurity-framework-021214.pdf

National Institute of Standards and Technology. (2017). *The National Initiative for Cybersecurity Education (NICE) National Initiative for Cybersecurity Education*. Retrieved from http://csrc.nist.gov/nice/about/index.html

National Institute of Standards and Technology. (n.d.). *Cybersecurity Framework Draft Version 1.1*. Retrieved from https://www.nist.gov/cyberframework/draft-version-11

National Institute of Standards and Technology. (n.d.). *Special Publication 800-160: Systems Security Engineering*. Retrieved from http: http://www.nist.gov

National Protection and Programs Directorate - Office of Cyber and Infrastructure Analysis. (2015). (n.d.). The future of smart cities: Cyber-physical infrastructure risk, U.S. *Department of Homeland Security New Solutions on the Horizon*.

National Security Telecommunications Advisory Committee. (n.d.). *STAC, NSTAC Report to the President on the Internet of Things*. Retrieved from https%3A%2F%2Fwww.dhs.gov%2Fsites%2Fdefault%2Ffiles%2Fpublications%2FIoT%2520 Final%2520Draft%2520Report%252011-2014.pdf

National Treasury of South Africa. (2011). *The South African Microinsurance Regulatory Framework*. Retrieved April 13, 2017, from microinsurance@treasury.gov.za

Ndabeni-Abrahams, S. (2017). *4th Industrial Revolution and the continued pursuit of inclusive economic growth through ICTs: Investing in the Youth*. Cape Town: Department of Telecommunications & Postal Services. Retrieved from https://www.dtps.gov.za/index.php?option=com_content&view=article&id=710:address-by-ms-stella-ndabeni-abrahams,-the-deputy-minister-of-telecommunications-postal-services-parliament,-cape-town&catid=10:deputy-minister-s-speeches&Itemid=137

Needham & Lampson. (2008). *Network Attack and Defense*. White Paper.

Netskope Cloud Report. (2016, September). Retrieved from: http://go.netskope.com/rs/665-KFP-612/images/september-2016-worldwide-cloud-report.pdf

Neudert, L.-M. N. (2017). *Computational propaganda in Germany: A cautionary tale*. Working Paper No. 2017.7. University of Oxford. Computational Propaganda Research Project. Retrieved from http://comprop.oii.ox.ac.uk/2017/06/19/computational-propaganda-in-germany-a-cautionary-tale/

Newberg, M. (2017, Mar. 10). As many as 48 million Twitter accounts aren't people, says study. *CNBC*. Retrieved from https://www.cnbc.com/2017/03/10/nearly-48-million-twitter-accounts-could-be-bots-says-study.html

Newman, L. H. (2017, April 4). That Dallas siren hack wasn't novel- it was just really loud. *Wired*. Retrieved 17 June 2017 from https://www.wired.com/2017/04/dallas-siren-hack-wasnt-novel-just-really-loud/

Newman, L. H. (2017, May 28). How to spring clean your digital clutter to protect yourself. *Wired Magazine*. Retrieved Sept. 18, 2017, from https://www.wired.com/2017/05/spring-clean-digital-clutter-protect/

Ngoqo, B., & Flowerday, S. V. (2015). Information Security Behaviour Profiling Framework (ISBPF) for student mobile phone users. *Computers & Security, 53*, 132–142. doi:10.1016/j.cose.2015.05.011

Ngubeni, T. (2014). *Govt working on 'cyber security hub'*. Retrieved from http://www.itweb.co.za/index.php?option=com_content&view=article&id=136238:Govt-working-on-cybersecurity-hub-&catid=234

Nguyen, Tian, Cho, Kwak, Parab, Kim, Yuseung, . . . Zhang. (2013). *UnLocIn: Unauthorized location inference on smartphones without being caught*. Paper presented at the Privacy and Security in Mobile Systems (PRISMS), 2013 International Conference on.

Nian, L., Sunjun, L., Rui, L., & Yong, L. (2009). A Network Intrusion Detection Model Based on Immune Multi-Agent. *International Journal of Communications, Network and System Sciences*, 569-574.

Nicholson, A., Webber, S., Dyer, S., Patel, T., & Janicke, H. (2012). SCADA security in the light of Cyber-Warfare. *Computers & Security, 31*(4), 418–436. doi:10.1016/j.cose.2012.02.009

Nicos, K. (2013). What makes cities intelligent? In *Smart Cities: Governing, Modelling and Analyzing the Transition* (p. 77). Taylor and Francis.

Niesen, T., Houy, C., Fettke, P., & Loos, P. (2016). *Towards an integrative big data analysis framework for data-driven risk management in industry 4.0*. Paper presented at the System Sciences (HICSS), 2016 49th Hawaii International Conference on.

Ning, P., Jajodia, S., & Wang, X. S. (2003). *Intrusion Detection in Distributed Systems – An Abstraction-Based Approach*. Norwell, MA: Kluwer Academic Publishers.

NIST. (2012). *NIST Special Publication 800-30, Revision 1, "Guide for Conducting Risk Assessments"*. Retrieved 8 June, 2016, from www.nist.org

NIST. (2015). *NIST SP 800-82 Revision 2 - Guide to Industrial Control Security*. National Institute of Standards and Technology. NIST.

Nohlberg, M. (2008). *Securing information assets: understanding, measuring and protecting against social engineering attacks* (Doctoral dissertation).

Nordin, K., & Bowman, N. (2016). *Big data for small policies*. Retrieved April 19, 2017, from http://www.i2ifacility.org/updates/blogs/2

Nyamsuren, E., & Choi, H. J. (2007). Preventing social engineering in ubiquitous environment. Future Generation Communication and Networking, 2, 573-577. doi:10.1109/FGCN.2007.185

Nye, J. S. Jr. (2016/2017, Winter). Deterrence and dissuasion in cyberspace. *International Security, 41*(3), 44–71. doi:10.1162/ISEC_a_00266

O'Gorman, G., & MacDonald, G. (2012). *Ransomware: A growing menace*. Symantec Security Response. Retrieved from: http://www.symantec.com/content/en/us/enterprise/media/security_response/whitepapers/ransomware-a-growing-menace.pdf

Obama, B. (2015). *Remarks by the president at the NAACP conference*. The White House.

Observe, I. T. (2014). *Your Critical Missing Security Vantage Point*. Author.

Office of Cyber and Infrastructure Analysis. (2016). *Consequences to Seaport Operations from Malicious Cyber Activity*. Retrieved Jun 31, 2017, from info.publicintelligence.net: https://info.publicintelligence.net/DHS-SeaportCyberAttacks.pdf

Office of the Inspector General. (2015). *Audit of the Federal Bureau of Investigation's Implementation of its Next Generation Cyber Initiative*. Author.

Ogundeji, O. (2016, November 4). Mirai malware aims DDoS attacks on Liberia. *ITWeb Africa*. Retrieved 10 February 2017 from http://www.itwebafrica.com/security/808-liberia/237027-mirai-malware-aims-ddos-attacks-on-liberia

Oh, H. J., Ozkaya, E., & LaRose, R. (2014). How does online social networking enhance life satisfaction? The relationships among online supportive interaction, affect, perceived social support, sense of community, and life satisfaction. *Computers in Human Behavior*, *30*, 69–78. doi:10.1016/j.chb.2013.07.053

Olaka, H. (2017). *Bank fraudsters focus on customer identity theft: Kenya Bankers Association*. Retrieved April 21, 2017, from https://www.capitalfm.co.ke/business/2017/05/bank-fraudsters-focus-customer-identity-theft-kba/

Olasanmi, O. O. (2010). Computer crimes and counter measures in the Nigerian banking sector. *Journal of Internet Banking and Commerce*, *15*(1), 1.

Olayemi, O. J. (2014). A socio-technological analysis of cybercrime and cyber security in Nigeria. *International Journal of Sociology and Anthropology*, *6*(3), 116–125. doi:10.5897/IJSA2013.0510

Olenick, D. (2016, June 13). *FLocker ransomware now targeting Smart TVs*. Retrieved from: https://www.scmagazine.com/flocker-ransomware-now-targeting-smart-tvs/article/529419/

Oliver Wyman. (2017). *Cyber risk in Asia-Pacific*. Retrieved from http://www.oliverwyman.com/content/dam/oliver-wyman/v2/publications/2017/may/Cyber_Risk_In_Asia-Pacific_The_Case_For_Greater_Transparency.pdf

Oliver Wyman. (2017). *Cyber-risk in Asia-Pacific*. Retrieved from http://www.oliverwyman.com/content/dam/oliver-wyman/v2/publications/2017/may/Cyber_Risk_In_Asia-Pacific_The_Case_For_Greater_Transparency.pdf

Olstik, J. (2014). *The Internet of Things: A CISO and Network Security Perspective*. Enterprise Strategy Group. Retrieved from http://www.cisco.com/c/dam/en_us/solutions/industries/docs/energy/network-security-perspective.pdf

Oltsik, J. (2013). *The Big Data Security Analytics Era Is Here*. Retrieved from http://southafrica.emc.com/collateral/analyst-reports/security-analytics-esg-ar.pdf?isPublic=false

Oluwatayo, I. (2013). Banking the unbanked in rural Southwest Nigeria: Showcasing mobile phones as mobile banks among farming household. *Journal of Financial Services Marketing*, *18*(1), 65–73. doi:10.1057/fsm.2013.2

Oosterloo, B. (2008). *Managing social engineering risk: making social engineering transparent*. Retrieved from: http://essay.utwente.nl/59233/1/scriptie_B_Oosterloo.pdf

OpenFog. (2017). *OpenFog Reference Architecture for Fog Computing*. Produced by the OpenFog Consortium Architecture Working Group. Retrieved from https://www.openfogconsortium.org

Oredo, J. O., & Njihia, J. (2014). Challenges of Cloud computing in business: Towards new organizational competencies. *International Journal of Business and Social Science*, *5*(3), 150–160.

Organization of American States, & Symantec. (2014). *Latin American + Caribbean Cybersecurity Trends*. Retrieved from https://www.thegfce.com/initiatives/c/cybersecurity-initiative-in-oas-member-states

Orgill, G. L., Romney, G. W., Bailey, M. G., & Orgill, P. M. (2004). The urgency for effective user privacy-education to counter social engineering attacks on secure computer systems. *Proceedings of the 5th conference on Information technology education*, 177-181. 10.1145/1029533.1029577

Osborne, C. (2017, January 20), *Satan RaaS starts trading in the Dark Web*. Retrieved from: http://www.zdnet.com/article/satan-ransomware-as-a-service-starts-trading-in-the-dark-web/

Osterman Research. (2012). *The Byod (Bring Your Own Device) Trend- Putting IT in control of BYOD*. Retrieved May 13, 2017, from http://www.hyperoffice.com/byod-whitepaper/

Oteafy, S. M. A., & Hassanein, H. S. (2017). Resilient IoT Architectures Over Dynamic Sensor Networks with Adaptive Components. *IEEE Internet of Things Journal*, 4(2), 474–483. doi:10.1109/JIOT.2016.2621998

Ouma, S., Odongo, M., & Were, M. (2017). Mobile financial services and financial inclusion: Is it a boon for savings mobilization? *Review of Development Finance*, 7(1), 29–35. doi:10.1016/j.rdf.2017.01.001

Oxford Dictionaries. (2017). *Definition of cyberattack*. Retrieved from https://en.oxforddictionaries.com/definition/cyberattack

Palacios, M. (2003). *Entre la legitimidad y la violencia: Colombia 1875-1994*. Bogotá: Editorial Norma.

Palo Alto Networks. (2017). *What is a Denial of Service Attack DoS?* Retrieved from https://www.paloaltonetworks.com/cyberpedia/what-is-a-denial-of-service-attack-dos

Parvizi, R., Oghbaei, F., & Khayami, S. R. (2013). *Using COBIT and ITIL frameworks to establish the alignment of business and IT organizations as one of the critical success factors in ERP implementation*. Paper presented at the Information and Knowledge Technology (IKT), 2013 5th Conference on. 10.1109/IKT.2013.6620078

Pathak, P. K. (2015). Integrated Intrusion Detection System in Cloud Computing Environment. *International Journal of Innovations & Advancement in Computer Science*, 4, 206–210.

Patidar, P., & Bhardwaj, A. (2011). Network Security through SSL in Cloud Computing Environment. *International Journal of Computer Science and Information Technologies*, 2(6), 2800–2803.

Patrick, H. (2016). *Security Information Flow in the Public Sector: KZN Health & Education* (Unpublished doctoral dissertation). School of Management Information Technology & Governance, South Africa.

Patrick, H. (2016). *Security Information Flow in the Public Sector: KZN Health & Education* (Unpublished doctoral dissertation). University of KwaZulu-Natal.

Patterson, D. (2017). Cyberweapons are now in play: From US sabotage of a North Korean missile test to hacked emergency sirens in Dallas. *Tech Republic*. Retrieved 17 June 2017 from http://www.techrepublic.com/article/cyberweapons-are-now-in-play-from-us-sabotage-of-a-north-korean-missile-test-to-hacked-emergency/

Paul, A., Schuster, F., & Konig, H. (2013). Towards the Protection of Industrial Control Systems – Conclusions of a Vulnerability Analysis of Profinet IO. In *Proceedings of the 10th international conference on Detection of Intrusions and Malware, and Vulnerability Assessment*. Berlin: Springer. 10.1007/978-3-642-39235-1_10

Pavkovic, N., & Perkov, L. (2011). Social Engineering Toolkit—A systematic approach to social engineering. *MIPRO, 2011 Proceedings of the 34th International Convention*, 1485-1489.

Peltier, T.R (2006). Social Engineering: Concepts and Solutions. *Information Systems Security, 15*(5), 13-21.

Peltier, T. R. (2002). *Information Security Policies, Procedures and Standards: Guidelines for Effective Information Security Management*. Boca Raton, FL: Auerback Publications.

Pennebaker, J. W., Booth, R. J., Boyd, R. L., & Francis, M. E. (2015). *Linguistic Inquiry and Word Count: LIWC2015 Operator's Manual*. Austin, TX: Pennebaker Conglomerates. Retrieved from www.LIWC.nethttps://s3-us-west-2.amazonaws.com/downloads.liwc.net/LIWC2015_OperatorManual.pdf

Pereira, N., Elvitigala, V., Athukorala, M., Fernando, P., Ehelepola, D., Sameera, K., & Dhammearatchi, D. (2016). Secure User Data in Cloud Computing through Prevention of Service Traffic Hijacking and Using Encryption Algorithms. *International Journal of Scientific and Research Publications*, *6*(4), 350–355.

Perlroth, N., Wines, M., & Rosenberg, M. (2017, Sept. 1). Russian election hacking efforts, wider than previously known, draw little scrutiny. *The New York Times*. Retrieved from https://www.nytimes.com/2017/09/01/us/politics/russia-election-hacking.html

Perry Johnson Registrars. (2017). *What is an Information Security Management System?* Retrieved from http://www.pjr.com/standards/iso-27001/information-security-management-system

Peters, M. A. (2017). *Technological unemployment: Educating for the fourth industrial revolution*. London: Taylor & Francis.

Petrowisch, J. (2017). *The benefits of cloud computing in the manufacturing industry*. Retrieved from http://www.tech-pageone.co.uk/industries-uk-en/benefits-cloud-computing-manufacturing-industry/

Petterson, D. (2016). *Critical Infrastructure Protection Bill under fire*. Retrieved from http://www.infrastructurene.ws/2016/07/06/critical-infrastructure-protection-bill-under-fire/

Petty, R.E., & Cacioppo, J.T. (1986). The elaboration likelihood model of persuasion. In *Communication and persuasion*. Springer.

Petya (malware). (n.d.). Retrieved from Wikipedia wiki: https://en.wikipedia.org/wiki/Petya_(malware)

Pfleeger, S. L., & Caputo, D. D. (2012). Leveraging behavioral science to mitigate cyber security risk. *Computers & Security*, *31*(4), 597–611. doi:10.1016/j.cose.2011.12.010

Phillips, C., & Swiler, L. P. (1998). A graph-based system for network-vulnerability analysis. In *Proceedings of the 1998 workshop on New security paradigms* (pp. 71–79). Academic Press. 10.1145/310889.310919

Phillips, D. E. (2008). Terrorism and Security in the Caribbean Before and After 9/11. *Conflict Management, Peace Economics and Development.*, *7*, 97–138. doi:10.1016/S1572-8323(08)07007-0

Piazza, J. A. (2011). Poverty, minority economic discrimination, and domestic terrorism. *Journal of Peace Research*, *48*(3), 339–353. doi:10.1177/0022343310397404

Pieters, W. (2011). The (Social) Construction of Information Security, *The Information Society*. *International Journal (Toronto, Ont.)*, *27*(5), 326–335.

Piggin, R. (2016). *Is Europe ready to defend critical infrastructure?* Retrieved from http://www.atkinsglobal.com/en-gb/angles/all-angles/is-europe-ready-to-defend-critical-infrastructure

Piggin, R. (2016). *Risk in the Fourth Industrial Revolution*. Academic Press.

Pillay, K. (2017). *Cybercrime and Cybersecurity Bill*. Retrieved from http://www.polity.org.za/article/cybercrime-and-cybersecurity-bill-2017-04-06

Pillay, Nham, Tan, Diaki, Senanayake, & Deshpande. (2013). *Does BYOD increase risks or drive benefits?* Academic Press.

Pil-Sung, J. (2016). Davos Forum: Our strategy for the upcoming fourth industrial revolution. *Science and Technology Policy, 26*(2), 12-15.

Pleasance, C. (2015, January 22). *Autistic A-level student, 17, hanged himself after being sent a fake police email claiming he was being investigated for having indecent images and demanding £100.* Retrieved from: http://www.dailymail.co.uk/news/article-2921979/Autistic-level-student-17-hanged-sent-fake-police-email-claiming-investigated-having-indecent-images.html

Poelker, C. (2014). *The foundation of clouds: Intelligent abstraction.* Academic Press.

Pojman, L. (2006). *Terrorism, Human Rights and the case for World Government.* Lanham: Rowman and Littlefield.

Pollins, B. M. (1989). Does trade still follow the flag? *The American Political Science Review, 83*(2), 465–480. doi:10.2307/1962400

Pomerleau, M. (2017, April 7). Drones 'a critical component' for Marine electronic warfare tactics. *C4ISR Net.* Retrieved 13 April 2017 from http://www.c4isrnet.com/articles/drones-a-critical-component-for-marines-electronic-warfare-tactics

Ponemon Institute. (2016). *The Cyber Resilient Organisation in the United Kingdom: Learning to Thrive against Threats.* Author.

Ponemon Institute. (2016). *The Second Annual Study on the Cyber Resilience Organization.* Retrieved from http://info.resilientsystems.com/hubfs/IBM_Resilient_Branded_Content/White_Papers/2016

Ponemon Institute. (2017). *Cost of Data Breach Study.* Author.

Poolsappasit, N., Dewri, R., & Ray, I. (2012). Dynamic security risk management using bayesian attack graphs. *IEEE Transactions on Dependable and Secure Computing, 9*(1), 61–74. doi:10.1109/TDSC.2011.34

Poovendran, R. (2010). Cyber-physical systems: Close encounters between two parallel worlds. *Proceedings of the IEEE, 98*(8), 1363–1366. doi:10.1109/JPROC.2010.2050377

Popp, J. (1989). *Part of AIDS DOS trojan horse payload* [Image: PNG]. Retrieved from Wikipedia wiki: https://commons.wikimedia.org/wiki/File:AIDS_DOS_Trojan.png

Port of Rotterdam. (2015). *Eurostat: Rotterdam 9% of EU maritime freight.* Retrieved Feb 24, 2016, from Port of Rotterdam.com: https://www.portofrotterdam.com/en/news-and-press-releases/eurostat-rotterdam-9-of-eu-maritime-freight-1

Port Strategy. (2013). *A Soft Target.* Retrieved May 24, 2017, from Port Strategy: http://www.portstrategy.com/news101/port-operations/safety-and-security/A-soft-target

Potiron, K., El Fallah, S., & Taillibert, P. (2013). *From Fault Classification to Fault Tolerance for Multi-agent systems.* Springer-Verlag. doi:10.1007/978-1-4471-5046-6

Prashad, P., Saunders, D., & Dalal, A. (2013). Mobile Phones and Microinsurance. Geneva: Microinsurance paper no.26, Geneva, International Labour Organization (ILO).

Pratt Jr. & Jones. (2013). Mobile device management in the DoD enterprise network. *Practice, 44*(3), 179-196.

Prelert. (2015). *Anomaly Detective for IT Security.* Author.

PricewaterhouseCoopers LLP. (2012). *Eye of the Storm: Key findings from 2012 Global State of Information Security Survey.* Retrieved May 13, 2017, from: http://www.pwc.se/sv_SE/se/riskhantering/assets/2012-global-state-ofinformation-security-survey.pdf

PricewaterhouseCoopers. (2013). *Future of Government.* Author.

PriceWaterhouseCoopers. (2016). *Cyber Security.* Retrieved April 17, 2017, from https://www.pwc.com/gx/en/economic-crime-survey/pdf/GlobalEconomyCrimeSurvey 2016.pdf

Prisecaru, P. (2016). Challenges of the Fourth Industrial Revolution. *Knowledge Horizons - Economics*, 57-62.

Prisecaru, P. (2016). Challenges of the Fourth Industrial Revolution. *Knowledge Horizons - Economics, 8*(1), 57-62.

PRLOG. (2009). *Global Smartphone market and industry chain report*. Retrieved: 23 October 2015. http://www.prlog.org/10192174-global-smart-phone-market-industry-chain- report-20082009.html

Putnam, R. (2000). *Bowling Alone: Collapse and Revival of American Community*. New York: Simon & Schuster. doi:10.1145/358916.361990

PwC. (2015). *Corporate Espionage: Responding to the threat*. Retrieved August 4, 2016, from PwC.co.uk: http://www.pwc.co.uk/services/forensic-services/insights/corporate-espionage-responding-to-the-threat.html

Qasaymeh, K. (2015). *The Effectiveness of South Africa's Legislative Framework Governing Cybersecurity in Nuclear Facilities*. Paper presented at the National Science and Technology Forum, Gauteng, South Africa.

Qi, W., Liu, X., Zhang, J., & Yuan, W. (2010). *Dynamic Assessment and VaR-Based Quantification of Information Security Risk. In 2010 2nd International Conference on E-business and Information System Security* (pp. 1–4). IEEE; doi:10.1109/EBISS.2010.5473537.

Quarterly Threat Summary: Q4 2016 & Year in Review . (2016, December). Proofpoint Report. Retrieved from: https://www.proofpoint.com/sites/default/files/proofpoint_q4_threat_report-final-cm.pdf

Quick, D., & Choo, K. R. (2013c). Dropbox Analysis: Data Remnants on User Machines. *Digital Investigation, 10*(1), 3–18. doi:10.1016/j.diin.2013.02.003

Racuciu, C., & Eftimie, S. (2015). Security threats and risks in Cloud computing. *Mircea cel Batran. Naval Academy Scientific Bulletin, 18*, 105–108.

Raghavan, A. R., & Parthiban, L. (2014). The effect of cybercrime on a Bank's finances. *International Journal of Current Research and Academic Review, 2*(2), 173–178.

Rainys, R. (2006). Network and Information Security. Assessments and Incidents Handling. *Electronics and Electrical Engineering, 6*(70), 69–74.

Raman, K. (2008). Ask and You Will receive. *Mcafee Security Journal,* 9-12.

Ramluckan, T., Ally, S. E., & van Niekerk, B. (2017). Twitter Use in Student Protests: The Case of South Africa's #FeesMustFall Campaign. In M. Korstanje (Ed.), *Threat Mitigation and Detection of Cyber Warfare and Terrorism Activities* (pp. 220–253). Hershey, PA: IGI Global. doi:10.4018/978-1-5225-1938-6.ch010

Ramluckan, T., & Van Niekerk, B. (2009). The Terrorism/Mass Media Symbiosiys. *Journal of Informatfion Warfare, 8*(2), 1–12.

Randell, R. (2006). *Virtualization Security and Best Practices*. Retrieved from http://www.cpd.iit.edu/netsecure08/ROBERT_RANDELL.pdf

Ransomware. (n.d.). Retrieved from Wikipedia wiki: https://en.wikipedia.org/wiki/Ransomware

Raoa, R. V., & Selvamanib, K. (2015). Data Security Challenges and Its Solutions in Cloud Computing. *Procedia Computer Science, 48*, 204–209. doi:10.1016/j.procs.2015.04.171

Rao, C., Leelaran, M., & Kumar, Y. R. (2013). Cloud: Computing Services And Deployment Models. *International Journal Of Engineering And Computer Science, 2*(12), 3389–3392.

Rashid, A. (2002). Los Hechos del 11 de Septiembre de 2001. In El Mundo Después del 11 de Septiembre de 2001. Barcelona: Editorial Península.

Rashid, F. Y. (2016). *The dirty dozen: 12 cloud security threats*. Retrieved from http://www.infoworld.com/article/3041078/security/the-dirtydozen-12-cloud-security-threats.html

Raspberry Pi Foundation. (n.d.). *Raspbian*. Retrieved 15 June 2017 from https://www.raspberrypi.org/downloads/raspbian/

Raytheon. (2014). *Preparing Millennials to Lead in Cyberspace*. Retrieved from www.consumeraction.org/recommended/articles/preparing_millennials_to_lead_in_cyberspace

Reagan, J. (2015, June 4). 5 Anti-Drone Solutions That Could Change the Game. *dronelife*. Retrieved 6 June 2017 from http://dronelife.com/2015/06/04/5-anti-drone-solutions-that-could-change-the-game/

Reaves, B., Scaife, N., Bates, A., Traynor, P., & Butler, K. R. B. (2015). *Mobile Problems: Analysis of Branchless Banking Application in the Developing World*. USENIX Security.

Reeves, J. (2017). *Citizen Spies: The Long Rise of America's Surveillance Society*. New York: New York University Press.

Rehman, M. H., Liew, C. S., Wah, T. Y., Shuja, J., & Daghighi, B. (2015). Mining Personal Data Using Smartphones and Wearable Devices: A Survey. *Sensors (Basel)*, *15*(1), 4430–4469. doi:10.3390150204430 PMID:25688592

Reich, R. B. (2005). *Reason: why liberals will win the battle for America*. New York: Vintage Books.

Remembering Pearl Harbor. A Pearl Harbor Fact Sheet. (n.d.). National WWII Museum. U.S. Census Bureau. Retrieved Sept. 24, 2017, from https://www.census.gov/history/pdf/pearl-harbor-fact-sheet-1.pdf

Rene, W., Tyler Lewis, R. H., & Carton, R. (2017, March 21). *Managing risk in an age of connected production*. Retrieved from Deloite University Press: https://dupress.deloitte.com/dup-us-en/focus/industry-4-0/cybersecurity-managing-risk-in-age-of-connected-production.html

Report, S. C. (2016). *Africa Cyber security Report 2016*. Retrieved April 15, 2017, from http://www.serianu.com/downloads/AfricaCyberSecurityReport2016.pdf

Republic of South Africa. (1996). *Constitution of the Republic of South Africa of 1996*. Pretoria: Government Printer.

Republic of South Africa. (2002). *Electronic Communications and Transactions Act No 25 of 2002*. Pretoria: Government Printer.

Republic of South Africa. (2002). *Promotion of Access to Information Act No 2 of 2002*. Pretoria: Government Printer.

Republic of South Africa. (2002). *Regulation of Interception of Communications and Provision of Communication-related Information Act No 70 of 2002*. Pretoria: Government Printer.

Republic of South Africa. (2015). National Cybersecurity Policy Framework for South Africa. No 39475. Government Gazette, 4 December 2015. Pretoria: Government Printer.

Revel, J. F. (2003). *Anti-americanism*. San Francisco: Encounter Books.

Reynolds, M. (2016, March 4). Anti-drone net launcher can down quadcopters from 100 metres. *Wired*. Retrieved 6 June 2017 from http://www.wired.co.uk/article/anti-drone-net-launcher-downs-quadcopters

Rezvani, M., Ignjatovic, A., Bertino, E., & Jha, S. (2014). Provenance-aware security risk analysis for hosts and network flows. In Network Operations and Management Symposium (NOMS), 2014 IEEE (pp. 1–8). IEEE. doi:10.1109/NOMS.2014.6838250

Rid, T. (2013). Cyberwar and peace: Hacking can reduce real-world violence. *Foreign Affairs, 92*(6), 77–87.

Rid, T. (2016). *Rise of the Machines: A Cybernetic History*. New York: W.W. Norton & Company.

Right2Know. (2016). *R2K briefing: the draft Critical Infrastructure Protection Bill*. Retrieved from http://www.r2k.org.za/2016/06/14/briefing-draft-critical-infrastructure-protection-bill/

Ristenpart, T., Tromer, E., Shacham, H., & Savage, S. (2009). Hey, you, get off of my cloud: exploring information leakage in third-party compute clouds. *Proceedings of the 16th ACM conference on Computer and communications security*. 10.1145/1653662.1653687

Ritchie, H. (2016, December 30). The biggest fake news stories of 2016. *CNBC*. Retrieved 17 June 2017 from http://CNBC.Com /2016/12/30/read-all-about-it-the-biggest-fake-news-stories-of-2016

Roberts, P. (2011, October 12). Air Force struggled for weeks with malware in drone fighter systems. *ThreatPost*. Retrieved from http://threatpost.com/en_us/blogs/report-air-force-struggled-weeks-malware-drone-fighter-systems-101211

Robertson, G. (2002). *The Role of military in combating terrorism*. Paper presented at second Nato Russia-Conference, Moscow, Russia.

Robin Sage. (2016, Dec. 16). In *Wikipedia*. Retrieved from https://en.wikipedia.org/wiki/Robin_Sage

Robinson, S. (2013). Software-defined Storage: The reality beneath the hype. *Computer Weekly*.

Roger, R., Apeh, E., & Richardson, C. J. (2016). Resilience of the Internet of Things (IoT) from an Information Assurance (IA) Perspective. *10th International Conference on Software, Knowledge, Information Management & Applications (SKIMA)*. 10.1109/SKIMA.2016.7916206

Romer, H. (2014). Best practices for BYOD security. *Computer Fraud & Security, 2014*(1), 13–15. doi:10.1016/S1361-3723(14)70007-7

Roncero-Menendez, S. (2014). In six words, these writers tell you an entire story. *Huffington Post*.

Ronen, E., O'Flynn, C., Shamir, A., & Weingarten, A. (2017). *IoT Goes Nuclear: Creating a ZigBee Chain Reaction*. Retrieved 5 June 2017 from http://iotworm.eyalro.net/iotworm.pdf

Rose, C. (2013). BYOD: An examination of bring your own device in business. *The Review of Business Information Systems (Online), 17*(2), 65. doi:10.19030/rbis.v17i2.7846

Rosenzweig, P. (2012). Making good cybersecurity law and policy: How can we get tasty sausage? *I/S: A Journal of Law and Policy for the Information Society*, 388 – 407.

Ross, R. S. (2011). Guide for conducting risk assessments. *NIST Special Publication*, 800-830.

Ross. (2014). Cyber Recovery Preparation. *Journal of ISACA, 3*, 3-5.

Rossmiller, S. (2011, Apr. 21). Stalking terrorists online. International Spy Museum. *Spycast*. Retrieved from https://www.spymuseum.org/multimedia/spycast/episode/stalking-terrorists-online/

Ross, S. (2013). Barbarians at the Ramparts. *ISACA, 3*, 4–5.

Ross, S. (2015). Frameworkers of the World, Unite 2. *ISACA, 3*, 4–6.

Rotenberg, M. (2015). EPIC: The first twenty years. In *Privacy in the Modern Age: The Search for Solutions* (pp. 1–18). New York: The New Press.

Roughan, M., Sen, S., Spatscheck, O., & Duffield, N. (2004). Class-of-service mapping for qos: a statistical signature-based approach to ip traffic classification. *Proceedings of the 4th ACM SIGCOMM conference on Internet measurement*, 135-148. 10.1145/1028788.1028805

Rouse, M. (2013). *Definition: software-defined storage*. Tech Target.

Rowe, B., Reeves, D., Wood, D., & Braun, F. (2010). *Estimating the market for Internet service provider-based cyber security solutions*. Retrieved June 15, 2017, from: https://www.ihssnc.org/portals/0/2010%20IHSS%20Research%20Summit_Rowe.pdf

Rowe, D. C., Lunt, B. M., & Ekstrom, J. J. (2011). *The role of cyber-security in information technology education*. Paper presented at the 2011 Conference on Information Technology Education. 10.1145/2047594.2047628

RSA. (2012). *Getting ahead of advanced threats: Achieving Intelligence-Driven Information Security*. Retrieved from http://www.emc.com/collateral/industry-overview/ciso-rpt-2.pdf

Rubin, A. J. (2015, December 30). Cellphone Contacts in Paris Attacks Suggest Foreign Coordination. *The New York Times*. Retrieved 19 June 2017 from https://www.nytimes.com/2015/12/31/world/europe/cellphone-contacts-in-paris-attacks-suggest-foreign-coordination.html

Rutkowski, L., & Cpalka, K. (2003). Flexible neuro-fuzzy systems. *IEEE Transactions on Neural Networks*, *14*(3), 554–574. doi:10.1109/TNN.2003.811698 PubMed

Rwakenya, E. (2017). *Kenya set to pass cyber-crime bill as east Africa seeks legal harmony*. Retrieved from https://www.scmagazineuk.com/kenya-set-to-pass-cyber-crime-bill-as-east-africa-seeks-legal-harmony/article/652047/

Ryan, T. (2011, Oct. 9). Identity, espionage, and social media. *Spycast. International Spy Museum*. Retrieved from https://www.spymuseum.org/multimedia/spycast/episode/identity-espionage-and-social-media/

Saanen, Y. A. (2014). *Optimisation for Operational Excellence*. Port Technology.

Sabett, R. V. (2011). Have you seen the latest and greatest "security game changer"? *Journal of Information Systems Security Association*, *9*(5), 5.

Sadeghi, A.-R., Wachsmann, C., & Waidner, M. (2015). Security and privacy challenges in industrial internet of things. In *Proceedings of the 52nd Annual Design Automation Conference on - DAC '15* (pp. 1–6). New York: ACM Press. 10.1145/2744769.2747942

Sageman, M. (2014). The stagnation in terrorism research. *Terrorism and Political Violence*, *26*(4), 565–580. doi:10.1080/09546553.2014.895649

Said, E. (2001). The Clash of Ignorance. *Nation (New York, N.Y.)*, *4*(October). Available at http://www.thenation.com/article/clash-ignorance

Saint-Marc, E. (2014). *7 benefits of cloud from an enterprise architect point of view*. Retrieved from IBM Cloud Computing News website: https://www.ibm.com/blogs/cloud-computing/2014/03/seven-benefits-of-cloud-from-an-enterprise-architect-point-of-view/

Salama, U. (2017, March 22). *Smart Forensics for the Internet of Things (IoT)*. Retrieved 22 June 2017 from https://securityintelligence.com/smart-forensics-for-the-internet-of-things-iot/

Sandouka, H., Cullen, A. J., & Mann, I. (2009). Social Engineering Detection using Neural Networks. *CyberWorlds, 2009. CW'09. International Conference on CyberWorlds*, 273-278. 10.1109/CW.2009.59

Sarah. (2017, August 15). *Ransomware payment methods. Posted to Emsisoft blog*. Retrieved from: https://blog.emsisoft.com/2017/08/15/ransomware-payment-methods/

Sarkar, S., Sarkar, K., & Ghosh, S. (2015). Cyber Security Password Policy for Industrial Control Networks. In *2015 1st International Conference on Next Generation Computing Technologies (NGCT)* (pp. 408-413). NGCT.

Savage, K., Coogan, P., & Lau, H. (2015). *The evolution of ransomware*. Symantec Security Response. Retrieved from: www.symantec.com/content/en/us/enterprise/media/security_response/whitepapers/the-evolution-of-ransomware.pdf

Saxena, H. (2016, February 14). *CTB-Locker Ransomware hijacks the entire BACP website*. Retrieved from: http://news.thewindowsclub.com/ctb-locker-ransomware-website-82130/

Scarlett, L. (2016). *Energy Evolves as Fourth Industrial Revolution Looks to Nature*. Retrieved from https://www.livescience.com/53555-energy-and-technology-will-drive-fourth-industrial-revolution.html

Scheidell, M. (2009). *Intrusion detection system*. Google Patents.

Schell, R. R. (2016, November). Privacy and Security: Cyber Defense Triad for where Security Matters. *Communications of the ACM, 59*(11), 20–23. doi:10.1145/3000606

Schlag, C. (2013). The New Privacy Battle: How the Expanding Use of Drones Continues to Erode Our Concept of Privacy and Privacy Rights. *Journal of Technology Law & Policy, 13*. Retrieved 6 June 2017 from http://tlp.law.pitt.edu

Schmid, A. (2004). Frameworks for Conceptualizing Terrorism. *Terrorism and Political Violence, 16*(2), 197–221. doi:10.1080/09546550490483134

Schneier, B. (2000, Oct. 15). Semantic Attacks: The Third Wave of Network Attacks. *Crypto-Gram. Schneier on Security*. Retrieved from https://www.schneier.com/crypto-gram/archives/2000/1015.html#1

Schneier, B. (2008). *The psychology of security*. Retrieved August 5, 2012, from http://www.schneier.com/essay-155.html

Schneier, B. (n.d.). *Click Here to Kill Everyone*. Retrieved from http://nymag.com/selectall/2017/01/the-internet-of-things-dangerous-future-bruce-schneier.html

Schneier, B. (n.d.). *The internet era of fun and games is over*. Retrieved from https://www.dailydot.com/layer8/bruce-schneier-internet-of-things/

Schneier, B. (2012). *Liars and Outliers: Enabling the Trust that Society Needs to Thrive*. Indianapolis, IN: John Wiley & Sons, Inc.

Schneier, B. (2015). *Data and Goliath: The Hidden Battles to Collect your Data and Control your World*. New York: W.W. Norton & Company.

Schneier, B. (2015). Fear and convenience. In *Privacy in the Modern Age: The Search for Solutions* (pp. 200–203). New York: The New Press.

Schuett, C., Butts, J., & Dunlap, S. (2014). An Evaluation of Modification Attacks on Programmable Logic Controllers. *International Journal of Critical Infrastructure Protection, 7*(1), 7. doi:10.1016/j.ijcip.2014.01.004

Schwab, K. (2015). *The Fourth Industrial Revolution: What It Means and How to Respond*. Retrieved from http://www.vassp.org.au/webpages/Documents2016/PDevents/The%20Fourth%20Industrial%20Revolution%20by%20Klaus%20Schwab.pdf

Schwab, K. (2015, December 2). The Fourth Industrial Revolution: what it means, how to respond. *Foreign Affairs*. Retrieved 2 June 2017 from https://www.foreignaffairs.com/articles/2015-12-12/fourth-industrial-revolution

Schwab, K. (2016). Navigating the fourth industrial revolution. *BIZNEWS*. Retrieved from http//www.biznews.com/wef/davos-2016/01/20/Klaus-schwab-navigating-the-fourth-industrial-revolution/

Schwab, K. (2016). *The fourth industrial revolution what it means and how to respond*. Retrieved May 24, 2017, from webforum: https://www.weforum.org/agenda/2016/01

Schwab, K. (2016). *The Fourth Industrial Revolution*. Geneva: World Economic Forum.

Schwab, K. (2016). *The Fourth Industrial Revolution: what it means, how to respond*. Retrieved from https://www.weforum.org/agenda/2016/01/the-fourth-industrial-revolution-what-it-means-and-how-to-respond/

Schwab, K. (2016, Jan. 14). *The Fourth Industrial Revolution: What it means, how to respond*. World Economic Forum.

Schwab, K. (2016, Jan. 14). *The Fourth Industrial Revolution: What it means, how to respond*. World Economic Forum. Retrieved from https://www.weforum.org/agenda/2016/01/the-fourth-industrial-revolution-what-it-means-and-how-to-respond

Schwab, K. (2016a). *Four leadership principles for the Fourth Industrial Revolution*. Retrieved from https://www.weforum.org/agenda/2016/10/four-leadership-principles-for-the-fourth-industrial-revolution/

Schwab, K. (2016b). *The Fourth Industrial Revolution: what it means, how to respond*. Retrieved from https://www.weforum.org/agenda/2016/01/the-fourth-industrial-revolution-what-it-means-and-how-to-respond/

Schwab, K. (2017). *The Fourth Industrial Revolution*. World Economic Forum (WEF), Davos.

Schwab, K. (2017). *The fourth industrial revolution*. New York: Crown Business.

Schweitzer, F., & Garcia, D. (2010). An agent-based model of collective emotions in online communities. *The European Physical Journal B*, *77*(4), 533–545. doi:10.1140/epjb/e2010-00292-1

Schweitzer, J. A. (1996). *Protecting Business Information*. Newton, MA: Butterworth-Heinemann.

Security Agency. (2016). *Computer Security Incident Response Team (CSIRT)*. Retrieved from http://www.ssa.gov.za/CSIRT.aspx

Security Breach. (2015) In *BusinessDictionary online*. Retrieved from http://www.businessdictionary.com/definition/security-breach.html

Security Scorecard. (2016). *2016 Financial Industry Cybersecurity Report*. Retrieved Jun 02, 2017, from https://cdn2.hubspot.net/hubfs/533449/SecurityScorecard_2016_Financial_Report.pdf

Segal, A. (2017, July 31). The hacking wars are going to get much worse. *The New York Times*. Retrieved Sept. 18, 2017, from https://nyti.ms/2ub9j36

Seib, P., & Janbek, D. M. (2010). *Global terrorism and new media: The post-Al Qaeda generation*. Abingdon, UK: Routledge.

Sen, S., Spatscheck, O., & Wang, D. (2004). Accurate, scalable innetwork identification of p2p traffic using application signatures. *Proceedings of the 13th international conference on World Wide Web*, 512-521.

Senanayake, T., & Fernando, S. (2017). Information Security Education: Watching your steps in cyberspace. *Proceedings of the International Science and Technology Conference 2017*.

Seneta, E. (1981). *Non-negative Matrices and Markov Chains*. Springer Verlag. doi:10.1007/0-387-32792-4

Seo, D., Ranganathan, C., & Babad, Y. (2008). Two-level model of customer retention in the US mobile telecommunications service market. *Telecommunications Policy*, *32*(3-4), 751–765. doi:10.1016/j.telpol.2007.09.004

Servin, A., & Kudenko, D. (2008). Multi-Agent Reinforcement Learning for Intrusion Detection: A Case Study and Evaluation. *Proceedings of the German Conference on Multiagent System Technologies*, 159-170. 10.1007/978-3-540-87805-6_15

Shachtman, N. (2008, March 4). Isreali Drones Jamming Phones in Gaza? *Wired*. Retrieved 12 August 2009 from http://www.wired.com/dangerroom/2008/03/israel-drones-j/

Shachtman, N. (2009a, October 30). The Army's New Land Warrior Gear: Why Soldiers Don't Like It. *Popular Mechanics*. Retrieved 18 June 2017 http://www.popularmechanics.com/military/a1590/4215715/

Shachtman, N. (2009b, December 17). Insurgents Intercept Drone Video in King-Size Security Breach (Updated, with Video). *Wired*. Retrieved 18 December 2009 from http://www.wired.com/dangerroom/2009/12/insurgents-intercept-drone-video-in-king-sized-security-breach/

Shachtman, N. (2009c, December 21). Report: Drone Feeds Gave Insurgents 'Early Warning' (Updated). *Wired*. Retrieved 22 December 2009 from http://www.wired.com/dangerroom/2009/12/drone-feds-gave-insurgents-early-warning-report/

Shachtman, N. (2011, October 8). Computer virus hits US Predator and Reaper drone fleet. *ARS Technica*. Retrieved from http://arstechnica.com/business/news/2011/10/exclusive-computer-virus-hits-drone-fleet

Shafahi, M., Kempers, L., & Afsarmanesh, H. (2016). Phishing through social bots on Twitter. *Proceedings of the 2016 IEEE International Conference on Big Data (Big Data)*, 3703 – 3712.

Shaikh, F. B., & Haider, S. (2011). *Security Threats in Cloud Computing*. Paper presented at the 6th International Conference on Internet Technology and Secured Transactions, Abu Dhabi, UAE.

Shameli-Sendi, A., Ezzati-jivan, N., Jabbarifar, M., & Dagenais, M. (2012). Intrusion Response Systems : Survey and Taxonomy. *International Journal of Computer Science and Network Security*, *12*(1), 1–14. Retrieved from http://paper.ijcsns.org/07_book/201201/20120101.pdf

Shazmeen & Prasad. (2012). A Practical Approach for Secure Internet Banking based on Cryptography. *International Journal of Scientific and Research Publications, 2*(12), 1-6.

Shedden, P., Scheepers, R., Smith, W., & Ahmad, A. (2011). Incorporating a knowledge perspective into security risk assessments. *Vine*, *41*(2), 152–166. doi:10.1108/03055721111134790

Sheldon, R. M. (2017, Oct. 20). Ancient Espionage: The Greeks and the Great Game. *Spycast. International Spy Museum*. Retrieved from https://www.youtube.com/watch?v=uVFJYCayeEs&ab_channel=IntlSpyMuseum

Sheldon, P. (2009). "I'll poke you. You'll poke me!" Self-disclosure, social attraction, predictability and trust as important predictors of Facebook relationships. *Cyberpsychology (Brno)*, *3*(2), 1. Retrieved from https://cyberpsychology.eu/article/view/4225/3267

Shia, B. (2015). National Cybersecurity Strategy of the US and its Constructive Implications for China. *Sociology*, *5*(11), 825–831.

Shoemaker, D., & Conklin, W. A. (2011). *Cybersecurity: The Essential Body Of Knowledge*. Cengage Learning. Retrieved from https://books.google.com/books?id=TUUKAAAAQBAJ&pgis=1

Siemens. (2015). Retrieved Jun 14, 2016, from Drive and Control Components for Cranes: http://w3app.siemens.com/mcms/infocenter/dokumentencenter/mc/documentsu20catalogs/cr1-2015-en.pdf

Sikula, N. R., Mancillas, J. W., Linkov, I., & McDonagh, J. A. (2015). Risk management is not enough: A conceptual model for resilience and adaptation-based vulnerability assessments. *Environment Systems & Decisions, 35*(2), 219–228. doi:10.100710669-015-9552-7

Silke, A. (2001). The devil you know: Continuing problems with research on terrorism. *Terrorism and Political Violence, 13*(4), 1–14. doi:10.1080/09546550109609697

Simmons, L. (2015, October 14). What is the difference between the Internet of Everything and The Internet of Things. *Cloud Rail Blog*. Retrieved 7 June 2017 from https://blog.cloudrail.com/internet-of-everything-vs-internet-of-things/

Simon, J. D. (2013). *Lone wolf terrorism: understanding the growing threat*. Amherst, NY: Prometheus Books.

Singer, P. W., & Friedman, A. (2014). *Cybersecurity and Cyberwar: What Everyone Needs to Know*. Oxford, UK: Oxford University Press.

Six Word Stories. (2013). Retrieved from http://www.sixwordstories.net/category/subject/funny/

Skoll, G. (2011). *Social Theory of Fear*. New York: Palgrave Macmillan.

Skoll, G. R. (2016). *Globalization of American Fear Culture: the empire in the Twenty-First Century*. New York: Palgrave-Macmillan. doi:10.1007/978-1-137-57034-5

Skoll, G. R., & Korstanje, M. E. (2013). Constructing an American fear culture from red scares to terrorism. *International Journal of Human Rights and Constitutional Studies, 1*(4), 341–364. doi:10.1504/IJHRCS.2013.057302

Smaw, E. (2008). From Chaos to Contrarianism: Hobbes, Pojman, and the Case of World Government. *Essays in Philosophy., 9*(2), 4–18.

Smit, H., Denoon-Steevens, C., & Esser, A. (2017). *The role of InsurTech in microinsurance: How is InsurTech addressing five challenges in microinsurance? Focus Notes. Centre for Financial Regulation and Inclusion*. CENFRI.

Snow, J. (2016, June 29). *Ransomware on mobile devices: knock-knock-block*. Posted to Kaspersky Lab Daily. Retrieved from: https://www.kaspersky.com/blog/mobile-ransomware-2016/12491/

Software-Defined Networking Architecture Overview. (n.d.). Retrieved from https://www.opennetworking.org/images/stories/downloads/sdn-resources/technical-reports/SDN-architecture-overview-1.0.pdf

Software-Defined Networking. (n.d.). *Definition*. Retrieved from https://www.opennetworking.org/sdn-resources/sdn-definition

Sommer, P., & Brown, I. (2011). Reducing Systemic Cybersecurity Risk (IFP/WKP/FGS(2011)3). OECD.

Sontag, S. (2002). Seamos Realistas. In El Mundo Después del 11 de Septiembre de 2001. Barcelona, Editorial Península.

Spam Laws. (2017). *Good Computer Viruses: The Future?* Retrieved 12 June 2017 from http://www.spamlaws.com/good-computer-viruses.html

Sree. (2008). Exploring a novel approach for providing software security using soft computing systems. *International Journal of Security and Its Applications, 2*, 51-58.

Srinivasan, R. (2007). *Protecting anti-virus software under viral attacks*. Citeseer.

Sritapan, V., Stewart, W., Zhu, J., & Rohm, C. Jr. (2014). Developing a Metrics Framework for the Federal Government in Computer Security Incident Response. *Communications of the IIMA, 11*(3), 5.

Stair, R. M., & Reynolds, G. W. (2016). *Principles of information systems* (12th ed.). Boston: Cengage Learning.

Stampnitzky, L. (2011). Disciplining an unruly field: Terrorism experts and theories of scientific/intellectual production. *Qualitative Sociology, 34*(1), 1–19. doi:10.100711133-010-9187-4

Stampnitzky, L. (2013). *Disciplining Terror: how experts invented terrorism*. Cambridge, UK: Cambridge University Press. doi:10.1017/CBO9781139208161

Stancioiu, A. (2017). The fourth industrial revolution "industry 4.0". *Fiability & Durability/Fiabilitate si Durabilitate,* (1).

Starr, M. (2014, January 19). Fridge caught sending spam emails in botnet attack. *CNET*. Accessed 10 March 2015 from http://www.cnet.com/news/fridge-caught-sending-spam-emails-in-botnet-attack/

State of the Cloud. (2017). *Right Scale Report*. Retrieved from: https://www.rightscale.com/lp/state-of-the-cloud

State Security Agency. (1996). *Minimum Information Security Standards*. Pretoria: Author.

State Security Agency. (2010). *The Protection of Information Bill Pretoria*. Department of Communication.

State Security Agency. (2015). *The National Cybersecurity Policy Framework (NCPF)*. Pretoria: Author.

State, B. (2014, Feb. 12.) *Flings or lifetimes? The duration of Facebook relationships*. Retrieved from https://www.facebook.com/notes/facebook-data-science/flings-or-lifetimes-the-duration-of-facebook-relationships/10152060513428859/

Sterbenz, P. G., & Kulkarni, P. (2013). *22nd International Conference on Computer Communication and Networks (ICCN)*. Doi: : 2013.661412510.1109/ICCCN

Stevens-Adams, S., Carbajal, A., Silva, A., Nauer, K., Anderson, B., Reed, T., & Forsythe, C. (2013). Enhanced training for cyber situational awareness. In D.D. Schmorrow & C.M. Fidopiastis (Eds.), AC/HCII 2013, LNAI 8027 (pp. 90 – 99). Spriger. doi:10.1007/978-3-642-39454-6_10

Stewart, J. (2014). *Rethinking cyber security in an interconnected world*. Retrieved from http://www.scmagazine.com/rethinking-cybersecurity-in-an-interconnected-world/article/358555/

Stohl, M. (2014). Dr. Strangeweb: Or how they stopped worrying and learned to love cyber war. Ch. 5. In Cyberterrorism (pp. 85 – 102). New York: Springer.

Stojmenovic, I., & Sheng, W. (2014). The fog computing paradigm: Scenarios and security issues. In *Computer Science and Information Systems (FedCSIS), 2014 Federated Conference on*. IEEE 10.15439/2014F503

Stokkel, M., & Smulders, A. (2013). Cybersecurity: hoe wordt het behapbaar? *Keynotes*, 42 – 26.

Stoll, C. (1989). *The Cuckoo's Egg: Tracking a Spy through the Maze of Computer Espionage*. New York: Doubleday, Random House.

Storage Networking Industry Associates. (2014). *Technical Whitepaper: Software Defined Storage*. Author.

Storm, D. (2017). Hackers can exploit smartwatches, fitness trackers to steal your ATM PIN. *Computer World IDG*. Retrieved from http://www.computerworld.com/article/3092407/security/hackers-can-exploit-smartwatches-fitness-trackers-to-steal-your-atm-pin.html

Stouffer, K., Falco, J., & Scarfone, K. (2008). NIST SP 800-115: Technical Guide to Information Security Testing and Assessment. National Institute of Standards and Technology.

StrategyPage.com. (2008, December 3). *Israeli Telephone Commandos Strike Again*. Retrieved April 7, 2010, from StrategyPage.com: http://www.strategypage.com/htmw/htiw/20081203.aspx

StrategyPage.com. (2009, January 2). *Gaza Cell Phones Targeted*. Retrieved July 27, 2009, from StrategyPage.com: http://www.strategypage.com/htmw/htiw/articles/20090102.aspx

Stuart, G., & Cohen, M. (2011). *Cash-In, Cash-Out: The Role of M-PESA in the Lives of Low-Income People*. Financial Services Assessment.

Such, J. M., Criado, N., Vercouter, L., & Rehak, M. (2016). Intelligent Cybersecurity Agents. *IEEE Intelligent Systems*, *31*(5), 2–7. doi:10.1109/MIS.2016.79

Suler, J. (2004). The online disinhibition effect. *Cyberpsychology & Behavior*, *7*(3), 321–326. doi:10.1089/1094931041291295 PMID:15257832

Sullivan, D. (2014). *Protecting cloud networks against DDoS and DoS attacks* Retrieved from http://searchcloudcomputing.techtarget.com/answer/Protecting-cloud-networks-against-DDoS-and-DoS-attacks

Sullivan, J. E., & Kamensky, D. (2017). How cyber-attacks in the Ukraine show the vulnerability of the US power grid. *The Electricity Journal*, *30*(3), 30–35. doi:10.1016/j.tej.2017.02.006

Sun Tzu. (5th century B.C.). *The Art of War* (L. Giles, Trans.). Retrieved from http://classics.mit.edu/Tzu/artwar.html

Sun, S., Yan, C., & Feng, J. (2012). Analysis of Influence for Social Engineering in Information Security Grade Test. *Computer Science and Electronics Engineering (ICCSEE), 2012 International Conference on Computer Science and Electronics Engineering*, *2*, 282-284. 10.1109/ICCSEE.2012.163

Sundar, R. (n.d.). *Android.Lockdroid.E*. Symantec Security Response. Retrieved from: https://www.symantec.com/security_response/writeup.jsp?docid=2014-103005-2209-99&tabid=2

Sunstein, C. (2005). *Laws of Fear: beyond the precautionary Principle*. Cambridge, UK: Cambridge University Press. doi:10.1017/CBO9780511790850

Suri, T., & Jack, B. (2011). *Risk Sharing and Transaction Costs: Evidence from Kenya's Mobile Money Revolution*. Working paper. Massachusetts Institute of Technology and Georgetown University. Retrieved April 19, 2017, from Washington: http://www.mit.edu/~tavneet/Jack_Suri.pdf

Sutcliffe, H. (2017). *The 4th Industrial Revolution or the 1st Empowerment Revolution?* Retrieved from http://societyinside.com/4th-industrial-revolution-or-1st-empowerment-revolution

Sutcliffee, H. R. (2017). *The 4th Industrial Revolution or the 1st Empowerment Revolution*. Retrieved from http://societyinside.com/4th-industrial-revolution-or-1st-empowerment-revolution

Sutton, D. (2016). *Cybersecurity at the heart of the Fourth Industrial Revolution*. Retrieved from http://www.smartbuildingsmagazine.com/features/cybersecurity-at-the-heart-of-the-fourth-industrial-revolution

Swanbeck, S. (2015, June 22). Coast Guard Commandant Addresses Cybersecurity Vulnerabilities on Offshore Oil Rigs. *CSIS-Tech.org*. Retrieved from http://www.csis-tech.org/blog/2015/6/22/coastguard-commandant-addresses-cybersecurity-vulnerabilities-in-offshore-oil-rigs

Symantec. (2014a). *The Cyber Resilience Blueprint: A New Perspective on Security*. Author.

Symantec. (2014b). *A Manifesto for Cyber Resilience*. Author.

Symantec. (2016). *An ISTR Special Report: Ransomware and Business 2016*. Retrieved May 12, 2017, from https://www.symantec.com/content/en/us/enterprise/media/security_response/whitepapers/ISTR2016_Ransomware_and_Businesses.pdf

Symantec. (2016). *Cyber resilience.* Retrieved April 23, 2017, from https://www.symantec.com/page.jsp?id=cyber-resilience

Tabak, D., & Levis, A. H. (1985). Petri net representation of decision models. *IEEE Transactions on Systems, Man, and Cybernetics. SMC, 15*(6), 812–818. doi:10.1109/TSMC.1985.6313468

Taddei, S., & Contena, B. (2013). Privacy, trust and control: Which relationships with online self-disclosure? *Computers in Human Behavior, 29*(3), 821–826. doi:10.1016/j.chb.2012.11.022

Talor-Gooby, P. (2004). *The Impact of New Social Risks on Welfare States.* Available at http://citeseerx.ist.psu.edu/viewdoc/download?doi=10.1.1.511.2369&rep=rep1&type=pdf

Tamarkin, E. (2014). *South Africa must pay attention to cybercrime.* Retrieved from http://www.issafrica.org/crimehub/news/south-africa-must-pay-more-attention-to-cybercrime

Tambotoh & Latuperissa. (2014). *The Application for Measuring the Maturity Level of Information Technology Governance on Indonesian Government Agencies Using COBIT 4.1 Framework.* Intelligent Information Management.

Techcentral. (2016). *Hacktivists breach Armscor website.* Retrieved from https://techcentral.co.za/hacktivists-breach-armscor-website/66835/

TechFinancials. (2016). *Data breaches cost South Africa R28,6 million.* Retrieved from https://techfinancials.co.za/2016/07/26/data-breaches-cost-south-africa-r286-million/

Technavio. (2017). *Global Automated Container Terminal Market 2017-2021.* Retrieved May 24, 2017, from Technavio: https://www.technavio.com/report/global-automation-global-automated-container-terminal-market-2017-2021

Technologies, I. (2009). *Accessing the Unbanked: Branchless Banking in Africa, Delivering a secure and cost-effective solution to gain new customers.* iVeri White Paper.

TechTarget. (2015). *NIST definition.* Retrieved from http://searchsoftwarequality.techtarget.com/definition/NIST

Tellez, C., & Zetterli, P. (2014). *The Emerging Global Landscape of Mobile Microinsurance, CGAP.* Washington, DC: World Bank.

Ten, C.-W., Manimaran, G., & Liu, C.-C. (2010). Cybersecurity for critical infrastructures: Attack and defense modeling. *IEEE Transactions on Systems, Man, and Cybernetics. Part A, Systems and Humans, 40*(4), 853–865. doi:10.1109/TSMCA.2010.2048028

Tengimfene, N. (2013). *Media Statement on Progress made by the Justice, Crime Preventation & Security Cluster in the Fight Against Corruption.* Pretoria: Government Communications and Information System.

Teravainen, T. (2016). *Information security (infosec).* Retrieved from http://searchsecurity.techtarget.com/definition/information-security-infosec

Tetri, P., & Vuorinen, J. (2013). Dissecting social engineering. *Behaviour & Information Technology,* 1–10.

Thawte. (2014). *Top 10 Website Security Security Myths Revealed.* Author.

The anatomy of a ransomware attack. (2016). Exabeam Threat Research Report. Retrieved from: https://www.exabeam.com/library/anatomy-ransomware-attack/

The Baltic Exchange. (2016). *The Shipping Markets.* Retrieved August 3, 2016, from The Baltic Exchange: http://www.balticexchange.com/about-us/shipping-markets/

The Huffington Post. (2017). *Department of Basic Education Website Hacked*. Retrieved from http://www.huffingtonpost.co.za/2017/06/29/department-of-basic-education-website-hacked_a_23007370/?utm_hp_ref=za-news

The Internet Society. (2015). *The Internet of things: An overview*. Retrieved from https://www.internetsociety.org/sites/default/files/ISOC-IoT-Overview-20151014_0.pdf

The LoadStar. (2016). *Mega-sized container vessels present mega-sized challenges to ports and shippers*. Retrieved August 2016, 4, from The Load Star: http://theloadstar.co.uk/mega-sized-container-vessels-present-mega-sized-challenges-ports-shippers/

The reign of ransomware . (2016). TrendLabs 2016 1H Security Roundup. Retrieved from: www.trendmicro.com/cloud-content/us/pdfs/security-intelligence/reports/rpt-the-reign-of-ransomware.pdf

The Scottish Government. (2015). *Safe, Secure and Properous: A Cyber Resilience Strategy for Scotland*. Author.

The Virus Encyclopedia. (n.d.). *Nematode*. Retrieved 12 June 2017 from http://virus.wikidot.com/nematode

Thomas, G. (2017). *Industrial Revolution and the potential challenges and opportunities for Wales*. Retrieved from https://assemblyinbrief.wordpress.com/2017/03/31/march-of-the-robots-the-fourth-industrial-revolution-and-the-potential-challenges-and-opportunities-for-wales/

Thompson, C. (2011, Apr. 24). Innocent man accused of child pornography after neighbor pirates his wifi. *HuffPost Tech*, 1 – 4.

Thompson, K. (2015). *The Best Guides for Information Security Management*. Retrieved from http://www.crypt.gen.nz/papers/infosec_guides.html

Thompson, S. T. (2006). Helping the hacker? Library information, security, and social engineering. *Information Technology and Libraries*, 25(4), 222–225. doi:10.6017/ital.v25i4.3355

Thompson, S. T. C. (2004). Policies to Protect Information Systems. *Library & Archival Security*, 19(1), 1, 3–14. doi:10.1300/J114v19n01_02

Thornburgh, T. (2004). Social engineering: the dark art. *Proceedings of the 1st annual conference on Information security curriculum development*, 133-135. 10.1145/1059524.1059554

Threat model. (2017, Aug. 28). In *Wikipedia*. Retrieved from https://en.wikipedia.org/wiki/Threat_model

Tien, J. M. (2012). The next industrial revolution: Integrated services and goods. *Journal of Systems Science and Systems Engineering*, 21(3), 257–296. doi:10.100711518-012-5194-1

Timmermann, F. (2014). *El gran terror. Miedo, emoción y discurso. Chile, 1973-1980*. Santiago de Chile: Copygraph.

Tinnel, L. S., Saydjari, O. S., & Farrell, D. (2002). Cyberwar strategy and tactics: An analysis of cyber goals, strategies, tactics, and techniques. *Proceedings of the 2002 IEEE Workshop on Information Assurance*, 228 – 234.

Topi, Valacich, Wright, Kaiser, Nunamaker, & Jr, Sipior, & de Vreede. (2010). IS 2010: Curriculum guidelines for undergraduate degree programs in information systems. *Communications of the Association for Information Systems*, 26(1), 18.

TraceSecurity. (2012). *Five Critical Components for a Strategic and Risk-Based Information Security Program for SMBs*. Author.

Trap X Security. (2014). *TrapX discovers 'Zombie Zero' Advanced Persistent Threat*. Retrieved Jun 31, 2017, from TrapX.com: https://trapx.com/trapx-discovers-zombie-zero-advanced-persistent-malware/

Trautman, L. J. (2015). Cybersecurity: What About US Policy? *Salus Journal*, 4(1), 40.

Trendle, G. (2002). Cyberwar. *The World Today*, *58*(4), 7–8.

Trepal, H., Haberstroh, S., Duffey, T., & Evans, M. (2007). Considerations and strategies for teaching online counseling skills: Establishing relationships in cyberspace. *Counselor Education and Supervision*, *46*(4), 266–278. doi:10.1002/j.1556-6978.2007.tb00031.x

Tripwire. (2014). *Russia Announces Development of Cyber Military Unit*. Retrieved from Portland: https://www.tripwire.com/state-of-security/latest-security-news/russia-announces-development-cyberwar-military-unit/

Tsai, Y. H., Lin, C.-P., Chiu, C.-K., & Joe, S.-W. (2010). Learning cyber trust using a triadic functioning analysis: A qualitative approach. *Quality & Quantity Journal*, *44*(6), 1165–1174. doi:10.100711135-009-9273-4

Tu & Yuan. (2015). *Coping with BYOD Security Threat: From Management Perspective*. Academic Press.

Twinomurinzi, H., & Mawela, T. (2014). Employee perceptions of BYOD in South Africa: Employers are turning a blind eye? *Proceedings of the Southern African Institute for Computer Scientist and Information Technologists Annual Conference 2014 on SAICSIT 2014 Empowered by Technology*. 10.1145/2664591.2664607

Twitchell, D. P. (2006). Social engineering in information assurance curricula. *Proceedings of the 3rd annual conference on Information security curriculum development*, 191-193. 10.1145/1231047.1231062

Tworek, H. (2017, May 9). Microsoft is right: We need a digital Geneva Convention. *Wired Magazine*. Retrieved from https://www.wired.com/2017/05/microsoft-right-need-digital-geneva-convention/

Tyugu, E. (2011). Artificial Intelligence in Cyber Defense. *Proceedings of the 3rd International Conference on Cyber Conflict*, 1-11.

U.S. Department of Homeland Security. (2013). *NIPP 2013: Partnering for Critical Infrastructure Security and Resilience*. Retrieved from https://www.dhs.gov/sites/default/files/publications/NIPP-Fact-Sheet-508.pdf

U.S. Department of Homeland Security. (n.d.). *Cybersecurity & Privacy*. Retrieved from https://www.dhs.gov/sites/default/files/publications/privacy_cyber_0.pdf

UK Construction Online. (2017). *Scottish government outlines new digital strategy*. Retrieved from https://www.ukconstructionmedia.co.uk/news/scotland-outline-new-digital-strategy/

Umar. (2015). Financial Regulations and the Nigeria's Banking Sector. *Journal of Research in Business and Management*, *3*(11),05-13.

Understanding Denial-of-Service Attacks. (2013). *United States Computer Emergency Readiness Team*. Retrieved from https://www.us-cert.gov/ncas/tips/ST04-015

Underwood, H., & Findlay, B. (2004). Internet relationships and their impact on primary relationships. *Behaviour Change*, *21*(2), 127–140. doi:10.1375/bech.21.2.127.55422

United Nations Conference on Trade and Development. (2014). *Review of Maritime Transport 2014* (p. 3). Geneva: United Nations.

United States Computer Emergency Readiness Team. (2017). *Assessments: Cyber Resilience Review (CRR)*. Retrieved from https://www.us-cert.gov/ccubedvp/assessments

US-CERT. (2015). *US-CERT Federal Incident Notification Guidelines*. Author.

Uz, Ali. (2014). *The Effectiveness of Remote Wipe as a Valid Defense for Enterprises Implementing a BYOD Policy*. Academic Press.

Vaid, S., & Holme, G. (2016). *Fourth industrial revolution poses new security challenges.* Retrieved from http://www.channelwise.co.za/fourth-industrial-revolution-poses-new-security-challenges/

Vamshi, A. (2016, September 27). *Cloud Malware Fan-out with Virlock Ransomware.* Posted to Cloud Security Blog – Netskope. Retrieved from: https://www.netskope.com/blog/cloud-malware-fan-virlock-ransomware/

Van Jaarsveldt, L. C. (2010). Information technology skills for the South African Public Service. *Administratio Publica, 18*(4), 174–192.

van Niekerk, B. (2011). *Vulnerability Assessment of Modern ICT Infrastructures from an Information Warfare Perspective* (Doctoral Thesis). Durban, South Africa: University of KwaZulu-Natal.

van Niekerk, B. (2015). Convergence of functional areas in information operations. *South African Journal of Information Management, 17*(1). doi:10.4102ajim.v17i1.605

van Niekerk, B. (2017). Analysis of Cyber-Attacks against the Transportation Sector. In M. Korstanje (Ed.), *Threat Mitigation and Detection of Cyber Warfare and Terrorism Activities* (pp. 68–91). Hershey, PA: IGI Global. doi:10.4018/978-1-5225-1938-6.ch004

Van Zyl. (2016). *Controversial cybersecurity bill gets Cabinet approval.* Retrieved from http://www.fin24.com/Tech/News/controversial-cybersecurity-bill-gets-cabinet-approval-20161212

Vance, A., Siponen, M., & Pahnila, S. (2012). Motivating IS security compliance: Insights from habit and protection motivation theory. *Information & Management, 49*(3), 190–198. doi:10.1016/j.im.2012.04.002

Vargas Llosa, M. (2002). La Lucha Final. In El Mundo Después del 11 de Septiembre de 2001. Barcelona: Editorial Península.

Varsha, M., & Patil, P. (2015). A Survey on Authentication and Access Control for Cloud Computing using RBDAC Mechanism. *International Journal of Innovative Research in Computer and Communication Engineering, 3*(12), 12125–12129.

Vaughn-Nichols, S. (2017, May 3). The Internet of messy things. *Computer World.* Retrieved 8 May 2017 from http://www.computerworld.com/article/3193941/internet-of-things/the-internet-of-messy-things.html

Veix, J. (2017, February 3). Hackers Hijack Radio Stations to Play YG's Anti-Trump Anthem 'FDT'. *Newsweek.* Retrieved 19 June 2017 from http://www.newsweek.com/hackers-hijack-radio-stations-play-ygs-anti-trump-anthem-fdt-552003

Venkatraman, A. (2013). *Software-defined datacenters demystified.* TechTarget.

Venktess, K. (2017). *SA ICT spend to exceed R287m.* Retrieved from http://www.fin24.com/Budget/sa-ict-spend-to-exceed-r287m-20170222

Ventre, D. (2011). *Cyberware and information warfare.* London: Wiley. doi:10.1002/9781118603482

Ventre, D. (2016). *Information Warfare* (2nd ed.). London, UK: Wiley. doi:10.1002/9781119004721

Verizon. (2014). *2014 Data Breach Investigations Report.* Retrieved Jun 6, 2016, from http://www.verizonenterprise.com/resources/reports/rp_Verizon-DBIR-2014_en_xg.pdf

Verizon. (2016). *2016 Data Breach Investigations Report.* Retrieved Jun 1, 2017, from http://www.verizonenterprise.com/resources/reports/rp_dbir-2016-executive-summary_xg_en.pdf

Verizon. (2017). *2017 Data Breach Investigations Report* (10th ed.). Author.

Vertical Market. (n.d.). Retrieved from http://www.investorwords.com/5242/vertical_market.html

Vidalis, S., & Kazmi, Z. (2007). Security through deception. *Information Systems Security*, *16*(1), 34–41. doi:10.1080/10658980601051458

Vignesh, U., & Asha, S. (2015). Modifying security policies towards BYOD. *Procedia Computer Science*, *50*, 511–516. doi:10.1016/j.procs.2015.04.023

Virilio, P. (2010). *The University of Disaster*. Cambridge, UK: Polity Press.

Vishwanath, A., Herath, T., Chen, R., Wang, J., & Rao, H. R. (2011). Why do people get phished? Testing individual differences in phishing vulnerability within an integrated, information processing model. *Decision Support Systems*, *51*(3), 576–586. doi:10.1016/j.dss.2011.03.002

Viva Sarah Press. (2015, April 5). Cyber terrorism triggers psychological and physical stress. *ISREAL 21c*. Retrieved 17 June 2017 from https://www.israel21c.org/cyber-terrorism-exposure-triggers-psychological-and-physical-stress/

Vogel, R. (2016). Closing the cybersecurity skills gap. *Salus Journal*, *4*(2), 32.

Volftrub, A. B., & Polikarpov, A. K. (2007). Methods of multifactor damage risk management in automated information systems. *Automatic Documentation and Mathematical Linguistics*, *41*(1), 46–52. doi:10.3103/S0005105507010074

Volonino, L., & Anzaldua, R. (2008). *Computer Forensics for Dummies*. Indianapolis, IN: Wiley Publishing.

Von Solms, B. (2015). What South Africa is doing to make a dent in cybercrime. *The Conversation*. Retrieved 8 December 2015, from The Conversation Africa, Inc http://theconversation.com/what-south-africa-is-doing-to-make-a-dent-in-cyber-crime-49470?utm_medium=email&utm_campaign=Latest+from+The+Conversation+for+Novemb er+4+2015+-+3749&utm_content=Latest+from+The+Conversation+for+November+4+2015+-+3749+CID_57502 8a66d3378263b9e824989e78ed8&utm_source=campaign_monitor_africa&utm_term=What%20South%20Africa%20 is%20doing%20to%20make%20a%20dent%20in%20cyber%20crime

Von Solms, R., & Van Niekerk, J. (2013). From information security to cyber security. *Computers & Security, 38*, 97-102.

Von Solms, S. H. (2005). Information Security Governance - Compliance management vs operational management. *Computers & Security*, *24*(6), 443–447. doi:10.1016/j.cose.2005.07.003

Vroom, C., & von Solms, R. (2003). Information security: Auditing the behaviour of the employee. *IFIP TC11 18th International Conference on Information Security (SEC2003)*.

Vulnerability CVE-2017-0144. (2017). *Common Vulnerabilities and Exposures*. Retrieved from: https://www.cve.mitre. org/cgi-bin/cvename.cgi?name=CVE-2017-0144

Wada, F., & Odulaja, G.O. (2012). *Electronic Banking and Cyber Crime In Nigeria-A Theoretical Policy Perspective on Causation*. Academic Press.

Wainaina, E. (2016). *Kenya Government to boost Cybersecurity efforts with Kshs. 13 Billion Investment*. Retrieved from http://www.techweez.com/2016/01/28/cybersecurity-in-kenya/

Walker, D. (2014, June 25). 'Havex' malware strikes industrial sector via watering hole attacks. *SC Magazine*. Retrieved 27 July 2014 from http://www.scmagazine.com/havex-malware-strikes-industrial-sector-via-watering-hole-attacks/ article/357875/

Walters, R. (2017). US Federal Cyber Breaches in 2012 Analysis. *Eurasiareview*. Retrieved December 2017 from http:// www.eurasiareview.com/08012018-us-federal-cyber-breaches-in-2017-analysis/

Walther, J. B. (1996). Computer-mediated communication: Impersonal, interpersonal, and hyperpersonal interaction. *Communication Research*, *23*(1), 3–43. doi:10.1177/009365096023001001

Waltz, E. (1998). *Information Warfare: Principles and Operations*. Boston: Artech House.

Wang, Y., Wei, J., & Vangury, K. (2014). *Bring your own device security issues and challenges*. Paper presented at the Consumer Communications and Networking Conference (CCNC), 2014 IEEE 11th. 10.1109/CCNC.2014.6866552

Wang, B., Li, X. P., De Aguiar, L., Menasche, D. S., & Shafiq, Z. (2017). Characterising and Modelling Patching Practices of Industrial Control Systems. *Proc. ACM Meas. Anal. Comput. Syst, 1*(1), 1-23.

WannaCry ransomware attack. (2017). In *Wikipedia*. Retrieved from https://en.wikipedia.org/wiki/WannaCry-_ransomware_attack

WannaCry ransomware attack. (n.d.). Retrieved from Wikipedia wiki: https://en.wikipedia.org/wiki/WannaCry_ransomware_attack

Wan, Z., Liu, J., & Deng, R. H. (2012). HASBE: A hierarchical attribute-based solution for flexible and scalable access control in cloud computing. *IEEE Transactions on Information Forensics and Security, 7*(2), 743–754. doi:10.1109/TIFS.2011.2172209

Ward, C. C., & Tracey, T. J. G. (2004). Relation of shyness with aspects of online relationship involvement. *Journal of Social and Personal Relationships, 21*(5), 611–623. doi:10.1177/0265407504045890

Waslo, R., Lewis, T., Hajj, R., & Carton, R. (2017). *Industry 4.0 and cybersecurity: Managing risk in an age of connected production*. Deloitte University Press. Retrieved 11 October 2017, from: https://dupress.deloitte.com/dup-us-en/focus/industry-4-0/cybersecurity-managing-risk-in-age-of-connected-production.html

Watering hole attack. (2017). Retrieved from http://searchsecurity.techtarget.com/definition/watering-hole-attack

Webster, F. (2002). *Theories of the Information Society*. Cambridge, UK: Routledge. doi:10.4324/9780203426265

Weinberger, S. (2011). Is this the start of Cyberwarfare. *Nature, 474*(7350), 142–145. doi:10.1038/474142a PMID:21654779

Weisberg, J. (2005). *The Bush Tragedy*. New York: Random House.

Weiss, D. (2017, May 2). *Victimized by ransomware, law firm sues insurer for $700K in lost billings*. Retrieved from: http://www.abajournal.com/news/article/victimized_by_ransomware_law_firm_sues_insurer_for_700k_in_lost_billings

Wellman, B., & Gulia, M. (1997/1999). Net surfers don't ride alone: Virtual communities as communities. In M. A. Smith & P. Kollock (Eds.), *Communities in cyberspace* (pp. 167–194). London: Routledge.

West, D. M., Villasenor, J., & Lewis, R. (2016). *Bridging the financial gender gap*. Retrieved April 16, 2017, from https://www.brookings.edu/blog/techtank/2016/04/01/bridging-the-financial-inclusion-gender-gap/

West-Brown, M. J., Stikvoort, D., Kossakowski, K., Killcrece, G., Ruefle, R., & Zajicek, M. (2003). *Handbook for Computer Security Incident Response Teams (CSIRTs)*. Carnegie Mellon Software Engineering Institute. doi:10.21236/ADA413778

West, R. (2008). The psychology of security. *Communications of the ACM, 51*(4), 34–41. doi:10.1145/1330311.1330320

White, R. (2012). Port Labor Talks Shift into High Gear, but Strike Continues. *Los Angeles Times*. Retrieved from http://articles.latimes.com/2012/dec/01/business/la-fi-mo-ports-strike-continues-20121201

Whitman, M., & Mattord, H. (2011). *Roadmap to Information Security For IT and Infosec Managers*. Course Technology, Cengage Learning.

Whitty, M. T. (2002). Liar, liar! An examination of how open, supportive and honest people are in chat rooms. *Computers in Human Behavior, 18*(4), 343–352. doi:10.1016/S0747-5632(01)00059-0

Whitty, M. T. (2005). The realness of cybercheating: Men's and women's representations of unfaithful Internet relationships. *Social Science Computer Review, 23*(1), 57–67. doi:10.1177/0894439304271536

Whitty, M. T. (2008). Liberating or debilitating? An examination of romantic relationships, sexual relationships and friendships on the Net. *Computers in Human Behavior, 24*(5), 1837–1850. doi:10.1016/j.chb.2008.02.009

Whitty, M., & Gavin, J. (2001). Age/sex/location: Uncovering the social cues in the development of online relationships. *Cyberpsychology & Behavior, 4*(5), 623–630. doi:10.1089/109493101753235223 PMID:11725656

Why Ransomware Works: The Psychology and Methods Used to Distribute, Infect and Extort. (2016, June 16). Retrieved from: https://www.trendmicro.com/vinfo/us/security/news/cybercrime-and-digital-threats/why-ransomware-works-psychology-and-methods-to-distribute-infect-and-extort

Wilder, U. M. (2017). Why Spy Now? The Psychology of Espionage and Leaking in the Digital Age. *Studies in Intelligence, 61*(2), 1 – 36. Retrieved from https://www.cia.gov/library/center-for-the-study-of-intelligence/csi-publications/csi-studies/studies/vol-61-no-2/pdfs/why-spy-why-leak.pdf

Wilkin, C. L., & Chenhall, R. H. (2010). A Review of IT Governance: A Taxonomy to Inform Accounting Information Systems. *Journal of Information Systems, 24*(2), 107–146. doi:10.2308/jis.2010.24.2.107

Williams, B. R. (2011). Do it differently. *Journal of Information Systems Security Association, 9*(5), 6.

Williams, T. J. (1994). The Perdue enterprise reference architecture. *Computers in Industry, 24*(2), 141–158. doi:10.1016/0166-3615(94)90017-5

Wilson & Hash. (2003). Building an information technology security awareness and training program. *NIST Special Publication, 800*(50), 1-39.

Wilson, L. (1994). Cyberwar, God and television: Interview with Paul Virilio. *Ctheory.net*. Retrieved from https://journals.uvic.ca/index.php/ctheory/article/view/14355

Wind River. (2015). *Security in the Internet of Things: Lessons from the Past for the Connected Future*. Retrieved from http://www.windriver.com/whitepapers/security-in-the-internet-of-things/wr_security-in-the-internet-of-things.pdf

Winkler, V. (2011). *Securing the Cloud*. Elsevier Inc.

Winner, L. (2013). Propaganda and dissociation from the truth. In *Jacques Ellul and the Technological society in the 21st century* (pp. 99–113). Heidelberg, Germany: Springer. doi:10.1007/978-94-007-6658-7_8

Wirtz, J. J. (2014, Feb. 28). The cyber Pearl Harbor. In *Cyber Analogies*. Calhoun: The National Postgraduate School (NPS) Institutional Archive. Retrieved Sept. 19, 2017, from http://hdl.handle.net/10945/40037

With big data comes big responsibility. (2014, Nov.) Harvard Business Review Staff. *Harvard Business Review*. Retrieved from https://hbr.org/2014/11/with-big-data-comes-big-responsibility

Wolak, J., Mitchell, K. J., & Finkelhor, D. (2002, Fall). Close online relationships in a national sample of adolescents. *Adolescence. Roslyn Heights, 37*(147), 441–455. PMID:12458686

Wolak, J., Mitchell, K. J., & Finkelhor, D. (2003). Escaping or connecting? Characteristics of youth who form close online relationships. *Journal of Adolescence, 26*(1), 105–119. doi:10.1016/S0140-1971(02)00114-8 PMID:12550824

Wolfpack. (2013). *The South African Cyber Threat 2012/3 Barometer*. Author.

Wolin, R. (2010). The idea of cosmopolitanism: From Kant to the Iraq war and beyond. *Ethics & Global Politics, 3*(2), 143–153. doi:10.3402/egp.v3i2.5213

Woolf, N. (2016, October 26). DDoS attack that disrupted internet was largest of its kind in history, experts say. *The Guardian*. Retrieved 9 June 2016 from https://www.theguardian.com/technology/2016/oct/26/ddos-attack-dyn-mirai-botnet

Workman, M. (2007). Gaining access with social engineering: An empirical study of the threat. *Information Systems Security*, *16*(6), 315–331. doi:10.1080/10658980701788165

Workman, M. (2008). A test of interventions for security threats from social engineering. *Information Management & Computer Security*, *16*(5), 463–483. doi:10.1108/09685220810920549

Workman, M. (2008). Wisecrackers: A theory-grounded investigation of phishing and pretext social engineering threats to information security. *Journal of the American Society for Information Science and Technology*, *59*(4), 662–674. doi:10.1002/asi.20779

World Bank. (2014). *Global Economic Prospects: Coping with Policy Normalization in High-Income Countries*. Retrieved May 21, 2017, from Washington: http://documents.worldbank.org/curated/en/152891468168580041/Global-economic-prospects-January-2014-coping-with-policy-normalization-in-high-income-countries

World Economic Forum Report. (2016). *The Global Risks Report 2016*. Author.

World Economic Forum. (2012). *Global Risk Report, Davos, Switzerland*. Retrieved from http://www3.weforum.org/docs/WEF_GlobalRisks_Report_2012.pdf

World Economic Forum. (2015). *Advancing Cyber Resilience: Project Scoping Workshop*. Retrieved from http://www3.weforum.org/docs/IP/2015/ICT/19Nov_CyberResilience_PreRead.pdf

World Economic Forum. (2016). *The Global Risks Report 2016*. Retrieved March, 15, 2017, from Switzerland: http://www3.weforum.org/docs/Media/TheGlobalRisksReport2016.pdf

World Economic Forum. (2017). *Advancing Cyber Resilience*. Geneva: Author.

World Economic Forum. (2017). *Navigating the Fourth Industrial Revolution*. Retrieved from https://www.weforum.org/agenda/2017/08/fourth-industrial-revolution-990fcaa6-9298-471d-a45e-e6ed9238dde9/

World Economic Forum. (2018). *Fourth Industrial Revolution Book Calls for Urgent Upgrade to the Way We Govern Technology*. Retrieved from https://www.weforum.org/press/2018/01/fourth-industrial-revolution-book-calls-for-urgent-upgrade-to-the-way-we-govern-technology

World Economic Forum/Accenture. (2013). *Building Resilience in Supply Chains*. World Economic Forum. Geneva: WEF.

World Maritime News. (2016). *Port Automation: Smart, Smarter, Smartest! World Maritime News*. Retrieved May 24, 2017, from World Maritime News: http://worldmaritimenews.com/archives/187691/port-automation-smart-smarter-smartest/

Wright, G. A., & Schaetzel, T. N. (2015). *Cyber Security: Designing and Maintaining Resilience*. Retrieved from http://www.globalsciencecollaboration.org/public/site/PDFS/cyber/Cyber%20Security%20white%20paper%20final.pdf

Wright, F. A. (2012). 2014). The short story just got shorter: Hemingway, narrative, and the six-word urban legend. *Journal of Popular Culture*, *47*(2), 327–340.

Wrona, K., & Hallingstad, G. (2010). Real-time automated risk assessment in protected core networking. *Telecommunication Systems*, *45*(January), 205–214. doi:10.100711235-009-9242-1

Wu, J., Ping, L., Ge, X., Wang, Y., & Fu, J. (2010). *Cloud Storage as the Infrastructure of Cloud Computing*. Paper presented at the 2010 International Conference on Intelligent Computing and Cognitive Informatics. 10.1109/ICICCI.2010.119

Wu, X. (2009). *SIP on an Overlay Network*. Academic Press.

Wu, T., & Zhao, G. (2014). A novel risk assessment model for privacy security in Internet of Things. *Wuhan University Journal of Natural Sciences, 19*(5), 398–404. doi:10.100711859-014-1031-3

Wyld, B. (2004, July 17). The Fear Factor. *The Age.* Retrieved 31 July 2009 from http://www.theage.com.au/articles/2004/07/16/1089694549469.html

Xiao-Feng, X., & Jiming, L. (2009). Multiagent Optimization System for Solving the Traveling Salesman Problem (TSP). *IEEE Transactions on Systems, Man, and Cybernetics. Part B, Cybernetics, 39*(2), 489–502. doi:10.1109/TSMCB.2008.2006910 PMID:19095545

Xie, B. (2008, September). The mutual shaping of online and offline social relationships. *IR Information Research, 13*(3), 1–18.

Xing, B., & Marwala, T. (2017). *Implications of the Fourth Industrial Age on Higher Education.* arXiv preprint arXiv:1703.09643.

Xu, R., Saïdi, H., & Anderson, R. J. (2012). *Aurasium: practical policy enforcement for android applications.* Paper presented at the USENIX Security Symposium.

Yadav, P., & Sujata. (2013). Security Issues in Cloud Computing Solution of DDOS and Introducing Two-Tier CAPTCHA. [*International Journal on Cloud Computing: Services and Architecture, 3*(3), 25–40.

Yamaguchi, L., & Watanabe, R. (2000). Interactive self-self-reflection based multiagent reinforcement learning for coordination. *The Third Asia-Pacific Conference on Simulated Evolution And Learning,* 2885-2890. 10.1109/IECON.2000.972456

Yazar, Z. (2002). *A qualitative risk analysis and management tool--CRAMM.* SANS InfoSec Reading Room White Paper.

Youl, H., & John, J. (2010). Role of customer orientation in an integrative model of brand loyalty in services. *Service Industries Journal, 30*(7), 1025–1046. doi:10.1080/02642060802311252

Young, A., & Yung, M. (1996). Cryptovirology: Extortion based security threats and countermeasures. In *Proceedings of the IEEE Symposium on Security and Privacy.* Oakland, CA: IEEE. 10.1109/SECPRI.1996.502676

Young, J. K., & Findley, M. G. (2011). Promise and pitfalls of terrorism research. *International Studies Review, 13*(3), 411–431. doi:10.1111/j.1468-2486.2011.01015.x

Young, K. S., Cooper, A., Griffiths-Shelley, E., O'Mara, J., & Buchanan, J. (2000). Cybersex and infidelity online: Implications for evaluate and treatment. *Sexual Addiction & Compulsivity, 7*(10), 59–74. doi:10.1080/10720160008400207

Yu-Ting, D., Hai-Peng, Q., & Xi-Long, T. (2014). Real-time risk assessment based on hidden Markov model and security configuration. In *2014 International Conference on Information Science, Electronics and Electrical Engineering* (Vol. 3, pp. 1600–1603). IEEE. 10.1109/InfoSEEE.2014.6946191

Zahadat, N., Blessner, P., Blackburn, T., & Olson, B. A. (2015). BYOD security engineering: A framework and its analysis. *Computers & Security, 55,* 81–99. doi:10.1016/j.cose.2015.06.011

Zaidi, K. (2016). *Finding the Right Balance in Cyber Security Operations.* Retrieved from https://www.cybrary.it/0p3n/finding-right-balance-cybersecurity-operations/

Zamora, W. (2016, October 19). *The global impact of ransomware.* Posted to Malwarebytes Labs blog. Retrieved from: https://blog.malwarebytes.com/101/2016/10/the-global-impact-of-ransomware/

Zawoad, S., & Hasan, R. (2015). FAIoT: Towards Building a Forensics Aware Eco System for the Internet of Things. *2015 IEEE International Conference on Services Computing (SCC),* 279-284. 10.1109/SCC.2015.46

Zetter, K. (2015, May 15). Feds say that banned researcher commandeered plane. *Wired*. Retrieved from http://www.wired.com/2015/05/feds-say-banned-researcher-commandeered-plane/

Zhang, Y., Jiang, S., Cui, Y., Zhang, B., & Xia, H. (2010). A qualitative and quantitative risk assessment method in software security. In *2010 3rd International Conference on Advanced Computer Theory and Engineering(ICACTE)* (Vol. 1, pp. V1-534-V1-539). IEEE. doi:10.1109/ICACTE.2010.5578960

Zhao, S., Grasmuck, S., & Martin, J. (2008). Identity construction on Facebook: Digital empowerment in anchored relationships. *Computers in Human Behavior*, *24*(5), 1816–1836. doi:10.1016/j.chb.2008.02.012

Zheng, M., & Jain, R. (2011). *Virtualization security in data centers and clouds*. Retrieved from http://www.cse.wustl.edu/~jain/cse571-11/ftp/virtual.pdf

Zhiwei, Y., & Zhongyuan, J. (2012). A survey on the evolution of risk evaluation for information systems security. *Energy Procedia*, *17*, 1288–1294. doi:10.1016/j.egypro.2012.02.240

Zhou, B., Arabo, A., Drew, O., Llewellyn-Jones, D., Merabti, M., Shi, Q., Yau, A. K. L. (2010). *Data flow security analysis for system of systems in public security incident*. Academic Press.

Zhou, L., & Chen, S. (2012). A survey of research on smart grid security. In *Network Computing and Information Security* (pp. 395–405). Springer. doi:10.1007/978-3-642-35211-9_52

About the Contributors

Ziska Fields (PhD) is an Associate Professor and Academic Leader at the University of KwaZulu-Natal, South Africa. Her research interests focus on creativity, innovation, entrepreneurship, human resources, Information technology, education and sustainable and responsible management. She developed two theoretical models to measure creativity in South Africa, focusing on the youth and tertiary education specifically. She has published in various internationally recognized journals and various book chapters. She is the editor of two books titled 'Incorporating Business Models and Strategies into Social Entrepreneurship' and 'Collective Creativity for Responsible and Sustainable Business Practice'. She is a member of the South African Institute of Management (SAIM), the Ethics Institute of South Africa (Ethics SA), and the Institute of People Management (IPM).

* * *

Stephen Akandwanaho is a researcher and lecturer at University of KwaZulu-Natal, Department of Information Systems and Technology. He has taught various IT courses including Programming. Stephen's areas of research interest include Information Security, Artificial Intelligence, Optimization, Hyper-heuristics & Cyber-security.

* * *

Peter Beaumont completed his BEng in Mechanical Engineering at Southampton University in 1998. He then worked as a military engineer in the British Army until 2015. On retirement from the Army he completed the MSc in Information Security at Royal Holloway, University of London and graduated with a distinction. He is currently studying for a PhD in cyber security at Royal Holloway where he is undertaking research into the security of Cyber Physical Systems.

* * *

John G. Chaka holds a B.Sc. in Computer Science from the University of Abuja and an M.Sc. in the same field from Abubakar Tafawa Balewa University, Bauchi all in Nigeria. He is currently a PhD candidate in the discipline of Information Systems and Technology, University of Kwazulu-Natal, South Africa. With about 18 years of experience lecturing in the department of Computer Science Education, Federal College of Education, Pankshin in Nigeria, Chaka's research endeavorscenters mostly on improving teaching and learning using computer technology. He is currently researching on improving teaching and learning in Colleges of Education using mobile learning on the Nigerian perspective. Chaka has about 16 Journal publications in circulation and five chapters in various books.

Rajashree Chaurasia received her B.Tech. (I.T.) and M.Tech. (I.T.) degrees from Guru Gobind Singh Indraprastha University, Delhi, India, in 2009 and 2014, respectively. She is a gold medalist in both, B.Tech. as well as in M.Tech. and UGC NET qualified. She was with Infosys Technologies Ltd. from 2009 to 2011 and thereafter taught at Guru Tegh Bahadur Institute of Technology for a year. She is currently serving as a Lecturer in the Department of Computer Engineering, at Guru Nanak Dev Institute of Technology, Delhi (a Government of NCT of Delhi institution), since 2012. She is an active researcher in the fields of Computer Security, Computer Graphics and Computational Biology.

Bibi Zaheenah Chummun is a Senior Lecturer at the University of KwaZulu-Natal (UKZN) Graduate School of Business and Leadership (GSB&L) based on Westville Campus in Durban - South Africa. Dr. Chummun has published several papers in the field of microinsurance and financial inclusion. She is supervising Masters and PhD students in the field of management and financial inclusion. She is a Chartered Insurer from the Chartered Insurance Institute in UK. She obtained her MBA from Nelson Mandela Metropolitan University (NMMU- South Africa) in 2010 and her PhD is from North West University (NWU-South Africa). Dr. Chummun is originally from the island of Mauritius.

José María de Fuentes is visiting lecturer at the Computer Security Lab of the Carlos III University in Madrid. His research interests are framed in cybersecurity and privacy, with emphasis on the internet of things and other resource-constrained, decentralized environments. He is currently involved in different projects related to risk management (CIBERDINE project), security in IoT (SPINY project) and in fog computing (SMOG-DEV project). He has published numerous articles in journals with impact factor and international conferences. In addition, he participates in the program committee of various conferences and is editor of the Wireless Networks journal.

Ncamiso Nkululeko Jahalenkhosi Dlamini holds a Master of Commerce (M.Com) degree in Information Systems and Technology. He has developed interest in securing BYOD environment after completing his masters research on exploring the implications of BYOD environment in Swaziland Banking sector. Thus, for his masters degree he carried out a study focusing on employees' awareness of the security implications emanating from Bring Your Own Device (BYOD). He is currently pursuing PhD in Informations Systems & Technology at the University of KwaZulu-Natal, South Africa.

Suchinthi Fernando is a researcher, lecturer, and software engineer, and is currently affiliated with Rutgers University, NJ, as faculty of the School of Communication & Information. She obtained her Doctor of Engineering degree in Information Science and Control Engineering, and her Master of Engineering degree in Management and Information Systems Engineering from Nagaoka University of Technology, Japan. She graduated with First Class Honors from University of Moratuwa, Sri Lanka with her Bachelor of Science in Information Technology. Her ongoing scholarship is on information security management. Suchinthi teaches many different graduate and undergraduate courses pertaining to computer and information science ranging from software engineering, internetworking, information security management, database design and management, to IT quality assurance, social aspects of IT, etc.

Harry J. Foxwell, Ph.D., is an Associate Professor in the Department of Information Sciences and Technology. Dr. Foxwell is a graduate of George Mason University, and taught at Mason for several years as an Adjunct before joining IS&T as a full-time Instructional Faculty member. He previously worked as a Principal System Engineer for the Oracle Corporation and for Sun Microsystems, specializing in Cloud Computing infrastructure and Operating Systems. Dr. Foxwell earned his Ph.D. in Information Technology at George Mason University, an M.S. in Applied Statistics from Villanova University, and a B.A. in Mathematics from Franklin and Marshall College. He is also a Vietnam War veteran, having served in the U.S. Army's First Infantry Division as a Platoon Sergeant.

Lorena González-Manzano is assistant professor working in the Computer Security Lab at the University Carlos III of Madrid, Spain. She is Computer Scientist Engineer and Ph.D. in Computer Science by the University Carlos III of Madrid. Her Ph.D. focuses on security and privacy in social networks. She is currently focused on Internet of Things and cloud computing security, as well as, on cybersecurity. She has published several papers in national and international conferences and journals and she is also involved in national R+D projects.

Irene Govender (PhD) is Assoc. Prof in Information systems and Technology at the University of KwaZulu-Natal (UKZN) where she has taught a range of modules including Research methodology, Advanced Systems Design, Networking and Security for information systems and more recently Personal and Mobile information Systems. Her research interests are interdisciplinary involving computer programming, educational technologies, teacher education in computing, and ICT4D. She has published widely in scholarly journals, attended and delivered conference papers internationally.

Shalin Hai-Jew works as an instructional designer at Kansas State University (K-State). She has taught at the university and college levels for many years (including four years in the People's Republic of China) and was tenured at Shoreline Community College but left tenure to pursue instructional design work. She has Bachelor's degrees in English and psychology, a Master's degree in English / Creative Writing from the University of Washington (Hugh Paradise Scholar), and an Ed.D in Educational Leadership with a focus on public administration from Seattle University (where she was a Morford Scholar). She reviews for several publishers. She has authored and edited a number of books. She is currently working on an edited text on open learning and an authored text on the harnessing of online learning data. Hai-Jew was born in Huntsville, Alabama, in the U.S.

Thokozani Ian Nzimakwe is a senior lecturer in the School of Management, IT and Governance at the University of KwaZulu-Natal, South Africa. His research interests include governance, electronic governance and ICT applications in public sector settings.

Paul Kariuki is the Programmes Manager of the Democracy Development programme. He has been involved in development sector for the past 14 years, ten of which in senior leadership positions within the civil society sector. He holds a Masters Degree in Development Studies and several postgraduate qualifications in the areas of human rights, NPO Leadership and Management, as well as Monitoring and Evaluation. He recently completed his doctoral degree at the University of KwaZulu Natal, specializing in the area of monitoring and evaluation in South African local government. He has written and published on the topics of Local Economic Development, HIV/AIDS, Water and Sanitation as well as

Monitoring and Evaluation. He is passionate about program and project monitoring and evaluation in the Public and NPO sectors as well as impact evaluations. He presently serves as a board member of the KwaZulu-Natal Civil Society Organizations Coalition (KZNCSOC), South African Monitoring and Evaluation Association (SAMEA) and Greater Durban YMCA.

Maximiliano E. Korstanje is editor in chief of International Journal of Safety and Security in Tourism (UP Argentina) and International Journal of Cyber Warfare and Terrorism (IGI-GlobalUS). With more than 1200 published works, and 40 books, Korstanje was awarded as Outstanding Reviewer 2012. International Journal of Disaster Resilience in the Built Environment. University of Salford, UK, Outstanding Reviewer 2013. Journal of Place Management and Development. Institute of Place, Manchester Metropolitan University, UK and Reviewer Certificate of Acknowledgement 2014. International Journal of Contemporary Hospitality Management (IJCHM), University of Central Florida, US. Now he co-edits almost 10 specialized journals in such themes as human rights, mobility, tourism and terrorism. Korstanje is subject to biographical records for Marquis Who`s Who in the World since 2009. He had nominated to 5 honorary doctorates for his contribution in the study of the effects of terrorism in tourism. In 2015 he was awarded as Visiting Research Fellow at School of Sociology and Social Policy, University of Leeds, UK and Visiting Professor at University of La Habana Cuba 2016.

Jhaharha Lackram studied a BCom undergraduate degree majoring in Information Systems and Technology and Marketing. She then subsequently completed a postgraduate BCom Honours degree (Cum Laude) in Information Systems and Technology. Since then she has ventured into corporate and started her career in consulting at Accenture in 2014, where she is currently a digital strategist having worked on projects within the spheres of management consulting, technology consulting, and growth and strategy. Her educational and professional background has allowed her to see how business and IT intersect. She believes that technology is the bedrock of everything in today's world and using this, she help clients enhance their digital enterprise transformations by harnessing technology as a key underpinning enabler. Her research interests include artificial intelligence, information security, social technology and online activism.

Mudaray Marimuthu is a lecturer in the School of Management, Information Technology and Governance at the University of KwaZulu-Natal. He currently lectures Systems Analysis and Design, Databases, Programming and Software Engineering. His research interests are in e-Commerce, Information Systems Adoption and Software Development Methodologies.

Omid Mirzaei is a Ph.D. candidate in the Computer Security Lab (COSEC) at the Department of Computer Science and Engineering of Universidad Carlos III de Madrid. Omid's main area of research is computer security. However, Omid is particularly interested in reverse engineering, malware analysis, and the study of protocols for secure communication using artificial intelligence tools and techniques. In addition, Omid is eager to tackle security issues from a multi-objective perspective, i.e. trying to deal with such problems by consuming the least possible amount of in hand resources. Currently, Omid is working on security analysis, malware analysis and risk management with a special focus on smartphone devices. Omid is currently involved in different security projects, including CIBERDINE and SMOG-DEV and have published various top journal and conference papers.

Lizzy Oluwatoyin Ofusori is a researcher with specific interest in Information system and technology. She teaches at the University of KwaZulu-Natal, Durban South Africa. She has also conducted an extensive research on security frameworks in the Nigerian banking sector. She holds a Master's Degree in information technology from National Open University of Nigeria. She is presently pursuing her doctoral degree at the University of KwaZulu-Natal, specializing in the area of information system and technology.

Indira Padayachee is a Senior Lecturer in Information Systems & Technology at the University of KwaZulu-Natal, where she has taught a number of subjects including Systems Analysis and Design, Database Design and Management, Software Engineering and Human Computer Interaction. Prior to that she was employed at the Durban University of Technology at the rank of Associate Director in the Department of Computer Studies. Indira has a PhD in Information Systems obtained from the University of South Africa. She has published articles in Alternation, the South African Computer Journal and the Journal of Contemporary Management. In addition, she has presented research papers in various peer-reviewed conferences, namely SACLA, the Annual Conference on World Wide Web Applications and SAICSIT. Her research interests include eLearning, smart education, information security, human-computer interaction and information technology adoption.

Harold Patrick is a Forensic Investigation Specialist at the University of KwaZulu-Natal, South Africa. His research interests include Information Security, Information Security Incident Management, Information Security Collaboration, Information Security Information Flow, Cybercrime and Forensics. He received his MCom and PhD in Information Technology from the University of KwaZulu-Natal, South Africa. He is a Certified Fraud Examiner. He is a committee member of the Association of Certified Fraud Examiners (South Africa) Cyber Forum.

Barend Pretorius holds a Masters in Information Systems as well as a Bachelor's of Science (Honours) in Mathematical Statistics. He is currently studying towards a PhD focusing on the cyber-security and governance of Industrial Internet of Things. He is a Certified Information Security Manager (CISM) through ISACA. He joined a large State Owned Company in 2014 as a Senior Information Security Analyst and is currently an Information Security Officer at one of its divisions. Prior to that he was a Manager at one of the Big 4 audit firms where gained more than eight years' experience in information technology, information security, governance, risk, compliance and data analytics. He has recently published an international journal on cyber-security for Industrial Control Systems / SCADA and presented at local and international conferences.

Trishana Ramluckan has been an academic and researcher in the I.T field for the past 12 years. She holds a Doctor of Administration degree focussing on social media in crisis communication and disaster management at the School of Management, Information Systems & Technology and Public Governance, University of KwaZulu-Natal. In 2006, she graduated with an MA from the University of KwaZulu-Natal, South Africa, and has a BA majoring in Politics, Legal Studies and Classics. She is a member of the IFIP working group on ICT Uses in Peace and War and serves as an academic advocate for ISACA.

Adrian Scribano is Director of the Centre for Sociological Research and Studies (CIES estudiosocio-logicos.org) and an Principal Researcher at the National Council for Scientific and Technical Research of Argentina. He is also the Director of the Latinamerican Journal of Studies on Bodies, Emotions and Society and Study Group on Sociology of Emotions and Bodies, in the Gino Germani Research Institute, Faculty of Social Sciences, University of Buenos Aires. He also serves as Coordinator of the 26 Working Group on Bodies and Emotions of the Latin American Association of Sociology (ALAS) and as Vice-President of the Thematic Group 08 Society and Emotions of the International Sociological Association (ISA). His latest books are "Normalization, Enjoyment and Bodies/Emotions. Argentine Sensibilities" 2017 Nova Science Publishers, USA forthcoming, "La sociología de las emociones en Carlos Marx" Editorial A Contracorriente, Raleigh, NC EEUU, (2016), Investigación social basada en la Creatividad/ Expresividad. ESEditora: Buenos Aires (2016) and ¡Disfrútalo! Una aproximación a la economía política de la moral desde el consumo. Elaleph.com Bs As. Edit. 2015. With countless publications in reviewed journals, his main research areas are sociology of body/emotions, social research based on creativity and expressiveness, social theory (critical realism) and collective action.

Prabhakar Rontala Subramaniam is currently associated with Discipline of Information Systems & Technology, University of KwaZulu-Natal, South Africa. He has 25 years of work experience in both industry and academic fields. He has presented and published many research articles in peer-reviewed international conferences and journals. He is a member in IEEE Computer Society. His current research interests are in the area of MANETs, VANETs, Software Engineering, Security, Big Data and Soft Computing Techniques.

Marcus Tanque is a highly-regarded technology strategist and an author with proven skills in business/ data analytics, corporate security/engineering strategies, policies. He also has vested skills in artificial intelligence, cyber security practices, governance, enterprise infrastructure & management and diverse IT consulting practices. Dr. Tanque has a repertoire of technical competencies in assorted consultative functions for the government, public and private sectors. His natural entrepreneurial flair coupled with unparalleled contributions to academic, federal, and industry customers is of significance. Dr. Tanque has been supporting mission-critical business and technology projects: IT engineering, program/project management, systems security, machine learning, cyber security operations, artificial intelligence, big data analytics, information & communications technology as well as cloud-based solutions. Dr. Tanque holds a Ph.D. in Information Technology with a dual specialization in Information Assurance and Security; Masters in Information Systems Engineering.

Thea Van der Westhuizen is a multi-award-winning academic professional, acting as Deputy Convener for Department of Higher Education and Training to develop academic entrepreneurship in South-Africa (www.theavander.com). Founder of SHAPE (Shifting Hope, Activating Potential Entrepreneurship) which was awarded as Best Youth Development Organisation in KZN (www.shapentrepreneurs.com). She acts as International Director of Paddle for the Planet: Official flagship project of the International Olympics Committee (www.paddlefortheplanet.org). Dr van der Westhuizen has over 15 years of international work experience in the corporate and academic sectors. High profile collaborations with Ambassadors, Municipality Managers, Sheikhs as well as CEOs of multi-national companies all forms part of her portfolio.

Brett van Niekerk graduated with his PhD in 2012 from the University of KwaZulu-Natal, and has completed two years of postdoctoral research into information operations, information warfare, and critical infrastructure protection. Currently he works as a Senior Information Security Analyst at a large state owned enterprise, and is an Honorary Research Fellow at the University of KwaZulu-Natal. He is CISM certified and holds a BSc and a MSc in electronic engineering. His research includes 20 journal articles, 6 book chapters, over 30 conference papers and presentations, and successful supervision of postgraduates in the field. He has served on the ISACA South Africa Chapter Board as co-Editor-in-Chief for the International Journal of Cyber Warfare and Terrorism (IJCWT), and as secretary of the IFIP WG 9.10 on ICT in Peace and War, and has contributed to ISO/IEC standards on information security.

Index

W

Y

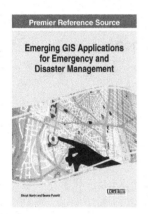
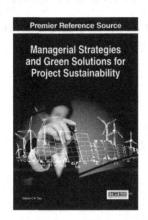

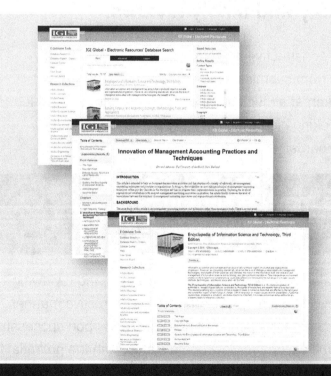

Printed in the United States
By Bookmasters